Coin World
Almanac

Publisher: John Amos

Editor: Beth Deisher

Coordinating Editors: P. Bradley Reed, William T. Gibbs

Staff Contributors: Pat Boerger, Dorothy Cernyar, Sharie Francis, Rusty Geiger, Richard Giedroyc, Jay Guren, Jane Hutchins, Robert M. Lacewell, Michele Orzano, Marilyn Van Allen, Jenni St. Myers, Keith M. Zaner

Cover Design: Elyse Strongin

Distributed in the United States by Ballantine Books, a division of Random House, Inc., and in Canada by Random House of Canada, Ltd.

THE COIN WORLD ALMANAC
Copyright © 1987 by Amos Press Inc.
Library of Congress Catalog Card Number 75-649406
Pharos Books ISBN (Hardcover) 0-88687-324-x
Pharos Books ISBN (Paperback) 0-88687-325-8
Ballantine Books ISBN (Hardcover) 0-345-34976-8
Ballantine Books ISBN (Paperback) 0-345-34974-1

Printed in the United States of America

World Almanac
An Imprint of Pharos Books
A Scripps Howard Company
New York, NY 10166

Foreword

This fifth edition of *Coin World Almanac* brings to the fingertips of beginning collectors, advanced numismatists and researchers alike a vast storehouse of facts and figures chronicling the many decisions and events which shaped the lives of previous generations as well as our own. Three years of numismatic happenings and change have been sorted and updated to add to the core of knowledge published in our four previous editions.

Two new chapters have been added to the fifth edition of *Coin World Almanac*: Chapter 14, about the ever-growing field of bullion coins, and Chapter 15, about the controversial subject of grading. Both new chapters reflect the changing emphasis of numismatics.

For those who are reading a *Coin World Almanac* for the first time, the following pages represent a concept developed and designed when our staff became frustrated in the early 1970s at the lack of a compact source of numismatic information. We realized a one-volume reference would fill a great need, not only for us, but for the informed hobbyist and those who deal with monetary affairs.

Whether you have need for a single definition or general background on various aspects of coinage, unfolding in the pages which follow are the essential facts which form the permanent record of numismatics. In one sense they represent a compilation of the working knowledge that many active in the hobby possess. But nowhere else is such information available in such a concise and affordable form.

We have taken great care in this edition to consolidate and present the information in a logical and readable format. Drawing upon many sources, we have painstakingly brought uniformity of style to the diverse elements which make up our great hobby.

We wish to express our thanks to those who have assisted us in the preparation of this new edition — collectors who have made comments, suggestions and criticisms and various officials within government agencies who have cooperated by expediently providing information which is a part of the public record.

It is with pride that we at *Coin World* present this latest edition of *Coin World Almanac* and share the knowledge that we have compiled. We do so in a spirit of collector friendship and advancement of knowledge in the hobby.

THE EDITORS

Contents

Review of Numismatics 1984-1987

1

A major trend in numismatics from 1984 to 1987 is that governments — especially the United States — are taking a more active role in the production and sales of numismatic items.

Since the 1984 edition of the *Coin World Almanac* was published, the United States Mint has completed both the Los Angeles Olympic commemorative coin program and the Statue of Liberty/Ellis Island coin program, and has begun work on a commemorative program for the Bicentennial of the United States Constitution. The Constitution commemoratives were scheduled to be struck beginning in July 1987, with no coins to be struck later than June 1988.

During the fall of 1986, the United States Mint launched sales of gold and silver bullion coins for investors and Proof versions for collectors. All this while resuming production and sales of Uncirculated Mint sets in 1984 after a two-year lapse, and offering Proof sets at Treasury sales outlets to broaden their distribution.

Internationally, the Krugerrand gold bullion coin became a victim of South Africa's racially-segregating apartheid system, as the United States and many other nations in protest banned the importation of the once-king bullion coin.

Many countries were quick to fill the gap left in the bullion coin market. Canada with its Maple Leaf gained the top of the market, at least until the United States' American Eagles debuted in late 1986. Australia also joined the bullion coin fray with its Nuggets, and Great Britain has served notice that its Britannia bullion coin would be available in late 1987.

Readers of previous editions of the *Coin World Almanac* will notice a change of format in this edition. The review in the current edition is presented chronologically from 1984 through May 1987 in an effort to make the review easier to follow. Previous editions presented the years in reverse chronological order. Dates referred to are *Coin World* issue dates.

News happenings, 1984

Date refers to *Coin World* issue in which the news item was published.

January

JANUARY 4

Donald C. Evans, executive director of the Industry Council for Tangible Assets, says the Reagan administration is continuing to study an IRS regulation requiring brokers to report bullion purchases.

American Numismatic Society is offering 10 grants-in-aid for its 32nd Seminar in Numismatics to be held June 12 to Aug. 11.

Graduate fellowships are being offered for the 1984-85 academic year.

Stack's will hold a four-session, 1,798-lot auction of the Amon G. Carter Family Collection in New York City. Among the lots will be the "finest known" 1794 silver dollar.

JANUARY 11

As many as 100,000 1983-S Proof sets went on sale at Treasury outlets Nov. 17 in a surprise Mint experiment to broaden distribution of the traditionally mail-order-only sets. In addition to the first direct sales at Treasury retail facilities in 20 years, the Mint will sell the 1983-S Proof sets at coin shows in 1984, and will accept orders for the sets in 1984, another departure from the past.

The Mint also expands marketing of Olympic commemorative coinage.

JANUARY 18

A major victory for the nation's coin dealers and collectors came Dec. 30 when the IRS proposed amendments to existing rules that would, in effect, remove reporting requirements for numismatic coin transactions.

Collector and dealer concern over the declining bullion market and pending anti-industry legislation in Washington depressed the mood of the 29th Annual Florida United Numismatists Convention in Tampa.

JANUARY 25

American Numismatic Society awards its Archer M. Huntington Medal award for numismatic scholarship to Herbert A. Cahn of Basel, Switzerland.

Italian sculptor Guido Veroi received the ANS's prestigious J. Sanford Saltus Medal award for lifetime achievement in medallic art.

The new North American director of the Israeli Government Coins and Medals Corp., Menachem Weiss, believes that fresh marketing approaches and new issues that appeal to both serious collectors and the general public are vital to rejuvenate American interest in Israel numismatics.

February

FEBRUARY 1

Bidders paid $5 million for the first 800 lots in the four-session Amon G. Carter Jr. Family Collection sale conducted in New York by Stack's, with 998 lots and two sessions to go. A 1794 silver dollar realized $240,000, an 1804 silver dollar brought $180,000, and an 1885 Trade dollar was sold for $100,000.

A December conference devoted to U.S. half and large cents with the nation's leading specialists participating will be sponsored by the American Numismatic Society at its New York headquarters.

FEBRUARY 8

ANA President Q. David Bowers names Nancy Green, ANA librarian, chairwoman of National Coin Week 1984. Theme of this year's event is "Numismatics: A Foundation for Friendship."

A final total of $7,874,665 was realized for the 1,798 lots in the Amon G. Carter Jr. Family Collection auction held in New York by Stack's Jan. 18-21.

Director of the Mint Donna Pope announced Jan. 25 the official renaming of the Bureau of the Mint to the United States Mint.

FEBRUARY 15

Sweeping changes for the Bureau of Engraving and Printing and the United States Mint, including some consolidation of the two agencies, are recommended in a Grace Commission survey of cost control for the federal government commissioned by the Reagan Administration.

For the first time in history, the nation's minting facilities produced in excess of one billion business-strike coins of each denomination except the half dollar in one year.

The 1984-W $10 gold eagle is available. At least one official distributor reports brisk sales of the Olympic commemorative coin.

FEBRUARY 22

The American Numismatic Association will sponsor a week-long numismatic festival in New England, featuring tours of Augustus Saint-Gaudens' studios, historic Old Sturbridge Village and the American Antiquarian Society headquarters. The festival is limited to 40 participants.

Director of the Mint Donna Pope announces a change in Treasury policy permitting collectors to purchase the Proof Olympic gold eagle separately.

A stronger bust of Lincoln is a noticeable improvement on the obverse of the 1984 cents.

FEBRUARY 29

A bill designating April 15-21 as National Coin Week in the United States was introduced Feb. 9 by Rep. Frank Annunzio, D-Ill.

Legislation for United States Mint production of commemorative coins in 1986 to honor anniversaries of the Boy Scouts of America and the Girl Scouts USA has been introduced by Rep. William E. Dannemyer, R-Calif.

The 150th anniversary of Toronto's city charter is the subject of the 1984 commemorative Canadian silver dollar.

Postmaster General William F. Bolger presents the first check from the USPS for sales of the Olympic commemorative coins, amounting to $151,737.50, to Katherine Davalos Ortega, Treasurer of the United States.

March

MARCH 7 ·

Collectors and dealers will be permitted unlimited orders for 1984-S Proof sets when the United States Mint begins accepting orders in early March, although the Mint reserves the right to cut orders if volume warrants.

The Province of Manitoba has filed a civil suit against five parties in connection with the 1982 theft and sale of 568 1925 United States Fort Vancouver commemorative half dollars from the Provincial Archives in Winnipeg.

MARCH 14

American Numismatic Association governors advocate both a coin and a stamp to commemorate the 100th anniversary of the ANA in 1991, 1986 production of coins commemorating Scouting and the sesquicentennial of the historic battle of the Alamo, and considered a Statue of Liberty commemorative coin. In another resolution, the board proposed a Mint study of design changes on United States coins.

The Industry Council for Tangible Assets names Donald Evans Jr. president and chief operational officer; discusses a code of ethics and a cooperative lobby effort with the newly formed American Council for Tangible Assets.

MARCH 21

Elizabeth Jones, Chief Sculptor-Engraver of the United States, is the 1984 recipient of the Daughters of the American Revolution medal of honor.

A previously unverified type of paper money error — a $1 reverse image offset onto the otherwise normally-printed Series 1981 $5 Federal Reserve note — has been authenticated by officials at the Bureau of Engraving and Printing.

MARCH 28

Two representatives of the Industry Council for Tangible Assets will appear before the Commissioner of Internal Revenue to dispute an IRS ruling requiring "brokers" to report transactions of commodities from individuals to retail dealers.

A federal judge in California has dismissed a $3 million suit against prominent West German coin dealer Achim Becker, citing the court's lack of personal jurisdiction in the case which deals with sales of United States Olympic commemorative coins overseas.

"Expertly artificially toned" cast counterfeits of 1793 half cents, Chain cents and Wreath cents are appearing on the East Coast.

Whether questionable precious metals operations represent a "growth industry" in the United States was to be the topic of discussion in hearings before the Senate Permanent Subcommittee on Investigations.

April

APRIL 4

Sen. Warren Rudman, R-N.H., says he will recommend formation of an ad hoc task force to examine questionable precious metals operations, and suggests that legislation giving the proper federal agencies greater powers might be considered. The recommendations come as a result of hearings before the Senate Permanent Subcommittee on Investigations.

Ancient and foreign coinage from the collections of the Johns Hopkins University, Baltimore, including holdings of the famed Garrett family, will go on the auction block in Beverly Hills. The sale will be conducted by Numismatic Fine Arts, Beverly Hills, and Bank Leu A.G., Zurich, Switzerland.

APRIL 11

Josten's, a U.S. private minter, and the Sarajevo, Yugoslavia, Mint will jointly strike two of three bronze "Friendship" medals authorized by the Los Angeles Olympic Organizing Committee and the Yugoslavia Olympic Committee. A third medal will be produced by Josten's exclusively in the United States.

APRIL 18

A special *Coin World* issue marks the 45th Anniversary Convention of the Central States Numismatic Society in Milwaukee.

The United States Mint sets up a one-day hotline in honor of National Coin Week and National Consumer Week, through which Director of the Mint Donna Pope and Deputy Director of the Mint Eugene Essner will be available to speak directly to the general public.

APRIL 25

A bill calling for United States Mint appropriations for fiscal years 1985 and 1986 has been introduced in the House of Representatives at the request of Treasury Department officials. The bill requests $47,758,000 for fiscal 1985 and "such sums as may be necessary" for 1986.

In ceremonies at the U.S. Capitol, Fred Schwengel, president of the U.S. Capitol Historical Society, presents specimens of the society's 1984 commemorative medal, marking Maryland's 350th anniversary, to members of the Maryland congressional delegation.

Canadian paper money collectors will be looking for a new signature variety on the seven circulating denominations of current, multi-colored notes of that country's central bank following the retirement of Senior Deputy Governor R. William Lawson. Lawson is to be succeeded by John W. Crow.

Thomas K. DeLorey, senior authenticator

of the American Numismatic Association Certification Service, has submitted his resignation effective April 30.

May

MAY 2

Harry W. Bass Jr. will step down from the American Numismatic Society presidency to an ANS council seat. Bass will be succeeded by Harry W. Fowler, first vice president.

The United States Supreme Court reversed a Second Circuit Court of Appeals decision and held 8-1 that the Warsaw Convention of 1929 governing flights and valuation of cargo should be upheld literally, and the official price of gold — $42.22 an ounce — and not its market price should prevail. The controversy stems from a lost shipment of gold and other items from the Franklin Mint to the United Kingdom.

Olympic coins will be sold at a booth inside the Los Angeles Memorial Coliseum during the Summer Games by PandaAmerica Numismatics, officially recognized by the Treasury Department.

MAY 9

Coin World marks the centennial of the birth of Harry S Truman with a special issue.

Uncirculated (Mint) coin set order forms will be in the mail in September, says Mint Director Donna Pope.

Production of 1-cent coins at the nation's Mint during March dropped below the billion-piece level for the first time since July 1981.

MAY 16

Rep. Fortney H. Stark, D-Calif., backs down on introducing an amendment to eliminate capital gains treatment for collectibles.

A virtually-complete set of Morgan and Peace silver dollars collected by silver dollar specialist Wayne Miller is sold to dealer David Hall for a reported sum in excess of $1 million.

The $17 million numismatic portfolio managed by the Asset Lending Division of West Coast Bank of Los Angeles is "safe and sound" despite the fact that California banking officials declared the bank insolvent.

The re-establishment of formal diplomatic relations between the U.S. and the Vatican brings Vatican numismatics to the forefront.

MAY 23

Revelations concerning the management of the Mint's fund to purchase metals for coinage plus the current status of the Olympic coinage program took center stage during a Mint appropriations authorization hearing before the House Banking Subcommittee on Consumer Affairs and Coinage and its chairman, Rep. Frank Annunzio, D-Ill.

U.S. Mint Director Donna Pope has called what hobby experts say is a 1983 Doubled Die cent a probable striking error and not a doubled die, even though no Mint personnel had seen a specimen of the coin when the statement was made.

The House Armed Services Committee has recommended passage of a bill which would authorize the sale of 10 million troy ounces of silver from the national defense stockpile. The bill leaves open the possibility of minting coins from the silver.

MAY 30

Eliminating capital gains tax treatment for such collectibles as coins may be a "bargaining chip" when House and Senate Conference Committee members meet to discuss differing versions of a tax bill.

The 1982 United States George Washington commemorative half dollar was the winner of "Coin of the Year" honors in a competition sponsored by Krause Publications.

Mint technicians in Washington and Philadelphia have examined a specimen of what coin collectors have accepted as a 1983 Doubled Die cent, but Mint experts say they are not ready to publicly state formal conclusions.

The House passed and sent to the Senate the United States Mint's 1985 budget request.

June

JUNE 6

Coin World recalls the Invasion of Normandy 40 years later with an examination of coins, medals and scrip related to D-day in a special issue.

The Treasury Department will offer the Proof 1984 Olympic gold eagle with Mint marks from the Philadelphia Mint, the Denver Mint and the San Francisco Assay Office in addition to the West Point Mint mark, and sets Jan. 18, 1985, as the cut-off date for ordering the commemorative coins.

Officials of the U.S. Mint confirm the existence of a 1983 reverse Doubled Die cent examined by Mint technicians.

Treasury Secretary Donald Regan presented President Reagan with the first strike 1984-W Olympic gold eagle in a Rose Garden ceremony. Reagan then transfered the first U.S. gold coin struck in 50 years to F. Donald Miller, executive director of the United States Olympic Committee.

JUNE 13

Two separate measures now being acted upon in Congress could pave the way for

Americans to buy newly-minted Morgan silver dollars this year.

As a quality control measure, the S Mint mark used for Proof coinage will be placed on the master die beginning in 1985.

The Federation Internationale de la Medaille will hold its 21st Congress in Colorado Springs, Colo., in 1987.

A concentration of 1983 reverse Doubled Die cents in the Lewistown, Pa., area has focused national media attention there.

JUNE 20

The U.S. Treasury has "agreed in principle" to terminate its contract with J. Aron & Co. as the prime distributor of U.S. Mint-produced American Arts Gold Medallions.

The Senate has accepted an amendment to the Defense Authorization Act which calls for 10 million ounces of stockpile silver to be minted into coins.

A three-week International Medallic Art Workshop and a medallic exhibition are scheduled to open July 16 at Pennsylvania State University, University Park, Pa.

The IRS issues a reminder that South African Krugerrands, Canadian Maple Leafs and Mexican 1-ounce gold coins purchased by "brokers" since Jan. 1, 1984, and $1,000 bags of silver coins purchased since July 1, 1983, must be reported.

JUNE 27

The 20 member nations of the XIII World Mint Masters' Conference are experiencing an unprecedented decline in demand for coin production, representatives of the Mints report.

Harvey Stack of New York coin firm Stack's reports overwhelming reponse to the auction of the Floyd T. Starr collection of U.S. large cents and half cents.

Ancient traditions are being kept alive in both medallic sculpture and amateur athletics with the gold, silver and bronze medals to be awarded at the 1984 Summer Olympic Games.

July

JULY 4

A Senate-House conference committee is expected to battle on the Defense Authorization Act, which would authorize the minting of coins from 10 million troy ounces of defense stockpile silver.

Salomon Brothers eighth annual survey of returns on tangible assets reveals that over the last 10 years the compounded annual rate of return of rare coins ranks first among 15 categories.

Battelle Memorial Institute, Columbus, Ohio, is conducting tests on experimental

multi-colored paper money designed to foil amateur counterfeiting by color copier.

JULY 11

In the capital gains section of a tax bill passed by Congress and sent to the President, the holding period has been temporarily reduced to six months and coins were not eliminated from capital gains treatment.

The United States Mint is continuing with plans to strike the 1984 American Arts Gold Medallions, even in the absence of a distribution contract.

Chester Martin of Chattanooga, Tenn., is the winner of the Food and Agriculture Organization of the United Nations annual medal design competition.

JULY 18

Slightly expanded 1982 and 1983 United States Mint reports were released in July, two years after a greatly abbreviated 1981 report signified lessened importance placed by the Mint on the annual reports.

Error doubled die expert John A. Wexler identifies two Uncirculated 1984-D Olympic silver dollars as varieties of Class 5 doubled die obverse coins.

JULY 25

Coin World presents a special souvenir issue in two sections celebrating the 93rd Anniversary ANA Convention in Detroit and the 1984 Los Angeles Olympic Games.

The U.S. Mint transfers 114 items — Olympic coins, American Arts Gold Medallions and bronze and pewter national medals — to the National Numismatic Collections at the Smithsonian Institution.

The Supreme Court rules that photographs of paper money can still be regulated by the Treasury Department.

Approximately 90 apparently-stolen Venezuelan coins valued at about $500,000 are confiscated from the Royale Auction Corp. gallery in New York by the FBI.

August

AUGUST 1

Harry W. Fowler, first vice president of the American Numismatic Society, is named president pro tem, to succeed Harry W. Bass Jr. as president of ANS.

President Reagan signs into law a tax bill which reduces the holding period for capital gains tax treatment from one year to six months, effective until 1988.

AUGUST 8

Representatives Frank Annunzio, D-Ill., and Ron Paul, R-Texas, have proposed a new law which would prohibit the Secretary of the

Treasury from adopting new designs for paper money or coins, unless the design is authorized by law. New coins would also have to be approved by the Commission of Fine Arts.

Pedigreed coins dominate each session of Auction '84, by a consortium of Superior, Paramount, Stack's and Rarcoa in Dearborn, Mich.

AUGUST 15

Seven thousand plus collectors and dealers attend the 93rd Anniversary Convention of the American Numismatic Association July 28-Aug. 1 in Detroit.

In a business session, ANA Certification Service Director Kenneth Bressett states that turnaround time for grading and authentication of coins submitted to ANACS can be reduced to two weeks by the end of 1984.

Clifford Mishler, publisher of *Numismatic News* and co-author with Chester L. Krause of the *Standard Catalog of World Coins*, receives the ANA's prestigious Farran Zerbe Award.

AUGUST 22

For the first time since 1981, Uncirculated sets of United States coins will be offered for sale through the United States Mint. Cost is $7, down from $11 previously.

The Secret Service is investigating the disappearance of an undisclosed amount of paper money from the Bureau of Engraving and Printing.

The doubling found on numerous 1984 Olympic silver dollars has been positively identified as an unusual form of strike doubling and is not the result of doubled dies, reports a battery of experts from the United States Mint and the numismatic community.

Eva B. Adams, William F. Fivaz and David R. Cervin named ANA Medal of Merit winners.

AUGUST 29

Despite committee criticism, Sen. Robert Dole, R-Kan., author of legislation establishing reporting rules, has stated for the public record that he supports the Internal Revenue Service's interpretation of broker reporting regulations.

A comprehensive new addition to the literature of the United States' earliest copper coinage, *Walter Breen's Encyclopedia of United States Half Cents, 1793-1857*, has been released by the American Institute of Numismatic Research of Southgate, Calif.

United States Treasury officials expect to reach their goal of selling $65 million worth of Olympic commemorative coins after huge sales during the 16 days of the Olympic Games.

September

SEPTEMBER 5

At the Republican national convention in Dallas, U.S. Treasurer Katherine Ortega was keynote speaker, and Director of the Mint Donna Pope was termed a "potential future star of the Republican Party."

A history of the Morgan dollar by R.W. Julian begins in a *Coin World* series.

Sen. Sam Nunn, D-Ga., publicly expresses doubt that a measure calling for the minting of coins from defense stockpile silver would be approved.

SEPTEMBER 12

The Mexican government re-enters the silver bullion market with a 1982 dated 1-ounce .999 fine Libertad, replacing the .925 silver Onza.

The American Numismatic Society will sponsor a Collector-Dealer Round Table, a numismatic education Festival and an interim board meeting in Washington, D.C., Oct. 15-16.

Popular collector items related to the 1984 Los Angeles Summer Olympic Games are the pins of official sponsors.

SEPTEMBER 19

The Royal Canadian Mint unveils Canada's 1984 gold $100 coin marking the 450th anniversary of Jacques Cartier's voyage of discovery to Canada.

Rep. Frank Annunzio, D-Ill., will retain his chairmanship of the House Subcommittee on Consumer Affairs and Coinage with his election this month as chairman of the Committee on House Administration.

SEPTEMBER 26

Multimillionaire Dr. Jerry H. Buss, once known as the "mystery collector," plans to sell his entire numismatic collection, including an 1804 silver dollar, 1913 Liberty Head nickel, and an 1894-S Barber dime.

The Israel Government Coins and Medals Corp. has temporarily halted sales within the United States of its official Israeli government medal commemorating the 1984 Summer Games in Los Angeles, because the United States Olympic Committee claims IGCMC was not properly authorized to market the medals.

Sandra Roth replaces Menachem Weiss as North American Director of IGCMC.

A gold medal honoring the late Hubert H. Humphrey was presented Sept. 11 to his widow, Muriel Humphrey Brown, five years after the medal was authorized.

October

OCTOBER 3

It appears a bill will be introduced in the next Congress seeking to issue commemorative coins honoring the Statue of Liberty on its 100th anniversary.

Rep. Robert T. Matsui, D-Calif., has introduced a bill which would allow investment in coins, precious metals, stamps and art in self-directed retirement accounts.

Mint Director Donna Pope has announced that 1984 Uncirculated coin sets, priced at $7 and the first such sets since 1981, are now available from the United States Mint.

The General Services Administration is to auction rolling mill equipment from the Philadelphia Mint. The equipment was formerly used to produce metal strip for clad coinage, now produced for the Mint by private firms.

OCTOBER 10

The amendment authorizing the minting of coins from defense stockpile silver was deleted from the Defense Authorization Act before the Act's passage by Congress.

The United States will begin selling 1984 American Arts Gold Medallions at the end of October. The Mint will try telemarketing the 1-ounce medallion featuring actress Helen Hayes and the half-ounce featuring novelist John Steinbeck.

The American Numismatic Society in New York is offering from its vaults two of its medals produced early in this century.

OCTOBER 17

A U.S. Senate and House conference committee has dropped a bill provision which would prohibit the importation of Krugerrands and Soviet Union gold coins.

A bill was introduced in the final days of the 98th Congress to continue the U.S. gold medallion program, but modify it to make the issues legal tender $20 one-ounce coins showing the Statue of Liberty and a family of eagles.

The London numismatic firm of Spink & Son and the fine arts auction firm of Christie's in New York will sell portions of the renowned Norweb collection of coins and numismatic items.

OCTOBER 24

The presidential campaign of 1984 has spawned a gold mine of political buttons and other paraphernalia, described in a series by Roger Fischer, editor of *The Keynoter*, a publication of American Political Items Collectors.

An automatic stitcher and trimmer will improve the look of *Coin World* and will speed its delivery.

"The Emperor Huang Shi Qin Collection" of five Proof quality gold and silver coins commemorate China's first emperor as part of the celebration of the 35th anniversary of the current government.

OCTOBER 31

In Washington, D.C., 35 American Numismatic Association members discussed "the problem" of ANA Certification Service grading.

Ranges of pastel colors in the blank areas on either side of vignettes on the faces of Federal Reserve notes could be a reality within 18 months, says Bureau of Engraving and Printing Director Robert J. Leuver.

Coin collectors will be served by the most modern order processing system available with the installation of a new United States Mint computer network in 1985, Francis B. "Barry" Frere, Assistant Mint Director for Marketing, told participants in the American Numismatic Association's Washington Mini-Festival Oct. 15.

Coin World's International section celebrates Halloween by tracing "coins of Dracula."

November

NOVEMBER 7

The fifth annual National Silver Dollar convention will bring four days of intensive numismatic activity to St. Louis' Monsanto Hall at the Cervantes Convention Center Nov. 8-11.

An accelerated advertising campaign for U.S. Olympic coins is well under way, said Treasury Department spokesmen.

The fourth edition of the *Coin World Almanac*, the one-volume reference considered a "must" for collectors and researchers alike, is available.

NOVEMBER 14

The Bureau of Engraving and Printing is expected to recommend to the Treasury Department that the current BEP facility be replaced by a new Washington, D.C., facility or that a West Coast satellite plant be built, or both.

Two views of the Statue of Liberty will appear on a spider press plate proof to be released by the Bureau of Engraving and Printing at the Nov. 15-18 American Stamp Dealers Association show in New York City.

Ann Marie Aldrich joins the staff of *Coin World* as marketing-promotion director.

NOVEMBER 21

The Comprehensive Crime Control Act, signed into law Oct. 12, is described by federal officials as a "dandy new weapon" to stop mail fraud such as advertisements misrepresenting the value of coins for sale.

A reader reports large and small Mint marks on 1984-S Proof Kennedy half dollars.

The pioneer gold coin collection of 170 coins and additional related pieces owned by the Kagin family has been placed on the market to be sold by private treaty.

NOVEMBER 28

The United States Mint will commission a study of coinage needs through 1990, with an extended look through 2000 for "basic planning."

Over the past 24 years, coin collectors have contributed $257,583,000 to the general fund of the Treasury Department through the purchase of Proof sets, Mint sets and other coins made especially for collectors by the U.S. Mint.

Britain drops £1 note effective Dec. 31. The note is being replaced by a £1 pale-yellow coin, which was introduced into circulation April 21, 1983.

A Mint State 64 grade and a price guide for Morgan and Peace dollars using MS-64 and MS-64 prooflike columns has been adopted by the dealer-dominated board of directors of the National Silver Dollar Roundtable.

December

DECEMBER 5

Research by Henry A. Merton, author of *The Big Silver Melt*, points to a vast overhaul of numismatic values for late-issue silver coins.

Mexico's new silver bullion coin, the Libertad, is selling beyond expectations, with the 1983 version released Nov. 1 and a new method of pricing due to be introduced with the release of the 1985 coins.

The American Numismatic Society is holding a competition to choose a design for a medal to commemorate the centennial of the Statue of Liberty.

The British £1 coin is meeting stiff resistance since the Nov. 12 announcement that after the end of the year the production of the £1 bank note will cease permanently.

DECEMBER 12

Coin World salutes 25 years of statehood for Alaska and Hawaii with feature articles about the money of the youngest states in America.

Secretary of the Treasury Donald T. Regan releases his proposal for a new income tax structure; coin industry lobbyist Donald Evans Jr. believes it would have little effect on the coin collector.

Witnesses testifying before the U.S. Senate Permanent Subcommittee on Investigation say fraudulent sales of rare coins are growing in South Florida, but bogus sales of precious metals are not quite as widespread as in the past.

Five weeks into the United States Mint's telemarketing of the U.S. Gold medallions series, Mint officials are seeing a "planned, smooth" rise in sales.

DECEMBER 19

Copper was the topic of an intensive three-day American Numismatic Society conference Nov. 30-Dec. 12 in New York City.

A committee appointed by the American Numismatic Association makes a ten-point list of recommendations on "buyer-seller relationships."

The New York International Numismatic Convention attracts more than 1,800 registrants and 113 coin dealers from 14 countries Nov. 30-Dec. 2.

Coin World's holiday thoughts are expressed for 1984 on the cover, wishing for all "Peace on Earth" and in a more personal form as staff members share their thoughts on numismatic gifts.

DECEMBER 26

Rumored improprieties and exploitation involving the American Numismatic Association's Grading Service in Colorado Springs were confirmed in an unofficial report submitted to ANA President Q. David Bowers by ANA Governor Bob Medlar Dec. 8.

Coin World has learned that Paramount International Coin Corp. has been awarded the worldwide exclusive distribution rights for the sale of Mexican Proof silver and gold coins for the World Cup Games in 1986.

Articles by Alan Stahl and John P. Burnham recount the history of the Col. William Bliss gold medal presented to the American Numismatic Society in New York in memory of the late Benjamin Stack.

1984 OBITUARIES

Issue date

February 29

   Roland C. Atwood, pioneer vecturist.

March 28

   Mrs. Rae V. Biester, first woman Superintendent of the Philadelphia Mint.

   Dr. Busso Peus, German numismatist.

April 11

   Mrs. R. Henry Norweb, *grande dame* of numismatics.

   Dr. Dexter C. Seymour Jr., U.S. pioneer gold coinage authority.

June 27

   Jonas K. Karys, former Director of the Lithuanian State Mint.

Issue date
August 29
    Rudolph Gjurovich, California's "King of
    Coins."

September 19
    Joseph A. Lowande, ration specialist.

Issue date
November 21
    Benjamin Stack, senior partner in the New
    York Stack's Rare Coins.
    Louise Horan Graham, first and only
    woman president of the Canadian Num-
    ismatic Association.

News happenings, 1985

Date refers to *Coin World* issue in which the news item was published.

January

JANUARY 2

A special *Coin World* issue previews the
Florida United Numismatists convention
Jan. 3-6 in Orlando.

Special Correspondent David L. Ganz analyzes proposed changes in capital gains taxes
and their effects on the numismatic hobby.

The Franklin Mint is reported sold by
Warner Communications to American Protection Industries.

Treasury officials hope to end collector
skepticism about cut-off of Olympic coin
sales when 25 obverse dies will be defaced in
a "symbolic ceremony" Jan. 3 in Washington.

JANUARY 9

The long neglected site of the famed Bechtler Mint near Rutherford, N.C., appears on
the verge of a preservation effort with the appropriation of $5,000 by the North Carolina
legislature.

A collection of Bechtler coins has been giv-
en to Isothermal Community College in
Spindale, N.C., on an indefinite loan by an
anonymous donor.

A major gap in numismatic research has
been filled with the publication of *Early
United States Dimes: 1796-1837,* compiled by
a quintet of researchers.

Estimated sales and mintage figures for
Olympic commemorative coins through
Nov. 30 were released by Treasury Depart-
ment officials Christmas week.

Canadian authorities are studying possible
confiscation of a 1969 25-cent piece struck
over a gold 1906 Prussian 20-mark coin that
sold in a July London auction.

JANUARY 16

Legislation authorizing the minting and
sale of coins to commemorate the centennial
of the Statue of Liberty was introduced Jan. 3
by Chairman Frank Annunzio, D-Ill., of the
House Consumer Affairs and Coinage Subcommittee.

Annunzio also reintroduced the Currency
Design Act calling for congressional approval
prior to any change in the design of U.S.
money.

Treasurer Katherine D. Ortega Jan. 3 sym-
bolically defaced dies used to mint Olympic
commemorative coins.

Sen. William Proxmire, D-Wis., introduced a bill Jan. 3 that would ban the importation of South African Krugerrands or other
gold coins offered by that government to protest South Africa's racially-segregating Apartheid policy.

JANUARY 23

The American Numismatic Association
Board of Governors, after meeting behind
closed doors for nearly five hours Jan. 3 in
Orlando, Fla., voted to reinstate ANA Certi-
fication Service grader/authenticator David
Jones to his position effective Jan. 7.

Treasury Secretary Donald T. Regan and
White House Chief of Staff James A. Baker
III will switch jobs, President Reagan said
Jan. 8 in a surprise announcement.

Numismatics has been incorporated as an
important art form in the "Treasures of
Islam" exhibition organized by the Musee
d'Art et d'Historie of the City of Geneva,
Switzerland. The exhibition will be held at
the Musee Rath, Place Neuve in Geneva June
25-Oct. 27.

The Florida United Numismatists convention in Orlando was well-attended and activity on the bourse floor and at the auction was
strong.

JANUARY 30

The American Numismatic Society in New
York awards its 1984 Archer M. Huntington
Medal to Professor Peter Berghaus; the J.
Sanford Saltus Medal goes to Marcel Jovine.

New government checks incorporating
more than a dozen anti-counterfeiting security features are scheduled to enter distribution
channels in February in the East.

Canada plans 10 silver $20 coins and one

$100 gold coin to commemorate the 1988 Winter Olympics in Calgary.

Director of the Mint Donna Pope announced Jan. 17 that she had directed the melting operation of all silver Olympic coins remaining in inventory to begin Jan. 31.

February

FEBRUARY 6

Coin World reviews recently-discovered correspondence revealing the early history of the Idler specimen 1804 dollar.

For the first time the Archaeological Institute of America presented its gold medal for distinguished archaeological achievement to a numismatist — Margaret Thompson, American Numismatic Society chief curator emeritus.

Nancy W. Green, general chairwoman of the American Numismatic Association's National Coin Week 1985, said the theme will be "Numismatics: Open the Door with Books."

FEBRUARY 13

Two famous numismatists and a Hollywood actress are new owners of three great American coin rarities from the Dr. Jerry Buss collection of United States coins sold Jan. 28-30 by Superior Galleries, Beverly Hills, Calif.

The House Committee on Banking, Finance and Urban Affairs' Consumer Affairs and Coinage Subcommittee is expected to hold hearings Feb. 20 on the proposed Statue of Liberty/Ellis Island Commemorative Coin Act, H.R. 47.

The U.S. Senate voted 95-0 Jan. 29 to confirm James A. Baker III as Secretary of the Treasury, clearing the way for Donald T. Regan to assume Baker's former position as White House chief of staff.

Uncirculated Susan B. Anthony dollars of 1979 and 1980 are being offered to collectors and the public in a new collector-oriented program initiated by the United States Mint Feb. 1.

FEBRUARY 20

A special *Coin World* issue previews the American Numismatic Association's Midwinter Convention in San Antonio.

ANA Executive Vice President Edward C. Rochette establishes specific policies regarding conflict of interest and employee conduct effective Jan. 21.

Congressional committees will hold a joint hearing on the Statue of Liberty/Ellis Island commemorative coin proposal Feb. 20.

The 1984-S Proof silver dollar appears destined to be the most purchased U.S. Olympic coin, Treasury Department figures indicate.

Coins being released by the Netherlands and the Isle of Man are modern versions of coins not minted for centuries.

FEBRUARY 27

Iowa Rep. Jim Leach introduced legislation Feb. 7 which seeks to extend the American Arts Gold Medallion program another 10 years.

The American Arts Gold Medallion program will offer an additional ordering period after its Jan. 31 closing date, due to jammed phone lines in its closing days.

Fifty of the 200 United States Federation Internationale de la Medaille medals struck will be made available to the public beginning March 1.

Coin World's International Section features coins of India, saluting the year-long celebration in the United States of the Festival of India.

March

MARCH 6

Statue of Liberty/Ellis Island commemorative coin legislation amended to include an Uncirculated version of the gold $5 appears headed for quick congressional approval after a joint hearing Feb. 20.

The American Numismatic Association Board of Governors announced in the opening minutes of its public session Feb. 20 in San Antonio, Texas, implementation of major policy changes for the ANA Certification Service and the selection of Richard Montgomery as assistant director for the service.

There are growing signs that the Krugerrand may be feeling the impact of constant political protests against the South African government, reports Ed Reiter.

The United States Mint has released a solicitation seeking private bidders to produce planchets for coins of all denominations except the 1-cent piece, which are already being produced outside the Mint.

MARCH 13

A Mint solicitation for privately-produced planchets for the Denver Mint draws strong criticism from Rep. Frank Annunzio, D-Ill., chairman of the House Subcommittee on Consumer Affairs and Coinage.

Rep. Philip M. Crane, R-Ill., warns the board of the Industry Council for Tangible Assets not to rest easy on tangible asset legislation.

The centennial of Canada's national park system is the theme of the 1985 Canadian silver dollar and $100 gold commemoratives, released in March.

In an unprecedented move, the American Numismatic Association's Board of Governors has voted an outright grant of $5,000 to numismatic researcher Fred Reed to assist with the commercial publication of the first of seven volumes which Reed envisions as "A Numismatist's Perspective of the Civil War."

MARCH 20

Statue of Liberty/Ellis Island commemorative coin legislation passes the House March 5 by voice vote; Rep. Frank Annunzio, chairman of Coinage subcommittee, says all three coins will bear representations of the statue.

Mint officials get a leg up on Statue of Liberty commemorative coinage by working on preliminary designs and selecting minting facilities prior to the legislation's passage.

The Mint asks Congress for fiscal year 1986 budget of $47 million for salaries and expenses.

Coin World reviews Elvira Clain-Stefanelli's new *Numismatic Bibliography,* published 20 years after her *Select Numismatic Bibliography.*

Margo Russell retires Feb. 28 from 23 years as *Coin World* editor; Beth Deisher takes over the helm.

MARCH 27

The only privately held specimen of the 1911 Canadian pattern silver dollar, Canada's version of the 1804 U.S. silver dollar, has been purchased by a Montreal firm for an undisclosed sum.

Efforts under way in the United States Congress to impose sanctions — including a ban on the importation of Krugerrands — against South Africa in protest of its apartheid policy are illegal under an international trade agreement, South African government officials insist.

The United States Mint begins accepting orders for 1985-S Proof sets at $11 each.

April

APRIL 3

Statue of Liberty/Ellis Island commemorative coinage legislation, which passed the House March 5 and seemed headed toward quick authorization, appears to have hit a snag in the Senate and the delay threatens to upset an already tight timetable for 1986 sales.

Twenty ancient coins, including six of the 12 Caesars, were reported stolen from the Numismatic Fine Arts auction-lot viewing tables at the Chicago International Coin Fair March 19.

Ohio Gov. Richard F. Celeste's March 15 closing of state-insured savings and loans fuels record gold price increases and unprecedented bullion sales for many coin dealers.

APRIL 10

Secretary of the Treasury James A. Baker III has approved the second phase of research by the Bureau of Engraving and Printing into obtaining a second paper money printing plant.

U.S. Gold & Silver Investments Inc., a Portland, Ore., precious metals firm, has filed a multi-million dollar claim against the United States Mint for alleged infringement in the use of "U.S. Gold" as a marketing name for the American Arts Gold Medallions.

Coin World special correspondents David L. Ganz and Ed Reiter report about two New York auctions that point to a significant upturn in the numismatic market.

APRIL 17

Coin World, which pioneered reporting coin value trends in its first issue 25 years ago, this week introduces graphs depicting percentage movement, enabling coin collectors to follow in a glance the entire market as well as individual series.

As part of its silver anniversary observance, *Coin World* presents in a special pull-out section a historical overview of the founding of the weekly coin publication, and spotlights significant contributions and innovations which have been brought to readers over the years.

APRIL 24

The upcoming Central States Numismatic Society convention spawns a special *Coin World* issue, including a feature article by Anthony Swiatek reviewing the history of the Norse-American medals of 1925, and a history of Minnesota vectures by Dick Grinolds.

Industry Council for Tangible Assets President Donald C. Evans Jr. resigns after two years with the lobby group; ICTA names Howard Segermark executive director.

In continuing the process of revamping federally-printed instruments, the Treasury Department has redesigned Series EE savings bonds.

Two of the strongest influences in American numismatics, the United States Mint and the American Numismatic Association, have planned activities to celebrate National Coin Week April 21-27.

May

MAY 1

The 450th anniversary of continuous operation of the Mexico City Mint, in conjunction with the Sociedad Numismatica de Mexico convention in Mexico City, is the focus of a *Coin World* special edition.

President Ronald Reagan presented congressional gold medals to Danny Thomas and

Elie Wiesel in White House ceremonies April 16 and 19, respectively.

The Canadian House of Commons on April 15 authorized the Royal Canadian Mint to issue a series of commemorative coins for the 1988 Winter Olympic Games in Calgary, Alberta.

MAY 8

Saying Congress is in a "buy American" mood, Rep. Frank Annunzio, D-Ill., chairman of the House Subcommittee on Consumer Affairs and Coinage, imposed a restriction in the United States Mint's Fiscal Year 1986 budget authorization request that the Mint obtain materials and services from domestic sources, unless there is no domestic alternative or costs are unreasonable.

Legislation calling for three denominations of commemorative coins to raise funds to support restoration efforts on the Statue of Liberty and Ellis Island immigration center remains stalled in the Senate because some senators see the bill as a possible vehicle upon which to attach their own coinage proposals.

The United States Capitol Historical Society's eighth medal features "Women of the American Revolutionary Era," a break with the traditional male subjects featured on past medals.

President Ronald Reagan presented the first National Medal of Arts to seven internationally-known artists and five longtime patrons during a White House luncheon April 23.

MAY 15

In keeping a tradition of observing National Coin Week, the United States Mint offered collectors the opportunity to speak directly with Mint Director Donna Pope or Deputy Director Eugene Essner via a special telephone hotline April 24.

The United States Mint, in withdrawing a solicitation for coin planchets that attracted several foreign bidders, has said "Uncle" (Sam, that is) to Rep. Frank Annunzio's insistence that it "buy American."

Series 1985 $1 Federal Reserve notes may enter circulation about June 22, according to a Bureau of Engraving and Printing preliminary schedule, with production having begun April 24.

MAY 22

Legislation seeking three coins to commemorate the Statue of Liberty's centennial in 1986 has passed the Senate Banking Committee and is expected to see action on the Senate floor the week of May 13.

Despite persistent rumor to the contrary,

the United States Mint will not attempt to recirculate the Susan B. Anthony dollar.

Pursuit of numismatic knowledge and the role education is expected to play in attracting and retaining collectors appeared to be foremost in the minds of coin collectors during the American Israel Numismatic Association's 13th Annual Greater New York Numismatic Convention May 2-5 at the Omni Park Central Hotel in New York City.

Legislation backed by 153 co-sponsors calling for sanctions against South Africa, including a ban on the importation of Krugerrands, passed the House Foreign Affairs Committee May 2 by a vote of 29-6.

May 29

As the Senate on May 16 readied to act on legislation authorizing three coins to commemorate the Statue of Liberty's centennial in 1986, the bill hit yet another roadblock.

A $1 admission fee and modification of "rather restrictive" rules concerning bourse assistants are among the seven recommendations to be reported to the American Numismatic Association membership and board by a three-man bourse committee.

A new camera system will allow the American Numismatic Association Certification Service to return coins to owners within nine days as compared to 50 days four years ago.

June

JUNE 5

The United States Postal Inspection Service in Los Angeles is conducting an investigation into allegations of mail and wire fraud involving Panda America Numismatics, a joint venture between PandaAmerica Corp. and Numismatics Ltd. to sell U.S. Olympic coins.

Effective with the July 3 issue, *Coin World* is instituting a policy of minimum standards for grading terms used to describe Uncirculated coins advertised within its pages. Advertising Manager Thomas Ehler said the new policy is designed to help buyer and seller communicate.

The Mexican government is eyeing reducing the size of its 1-peso coin and possibly other denominations.

JUNE 12

Troubles continue for the United States Mint over a solicitation for bids to supply 5-cent, 10-cent, quarter dollar and half dollar coinage blanks for the Denver Mint. Arrow-Head Metals Ltd., Toronto, Canada, on May 15 filed suit against the United States in U.S. Claims Court, Washington, D.C., claiming the Mint's cancellation of the tender is unfair and illegal.

A commemorative medal celebrating the colonization of Maryland on its obverse, and honoring the state's colorful naval tradition on the reverse, will mark the American Numismatic Association's 94th Anniversary Convention Aug. 20-25 at the Baltimore Convention Center.

JUNE 19

Legislation passed the House of Representatives June 5 that if signed into law would impose immediate sanctions against the South African government, including a ban on the importation of Krugerrands.

A commemorative medal to honor Martin Luther King Jr. will be distributed to an estimated 49 million American schoolchildren to commemorate the first federal holiday to honor a black American.

Legislation authorizing three coins to commemorate the Statue of Liberty centennial in 1986 may be moved to the Senate floor beginning June 10 if supporters can dislodge holds put on by several senators.

JUNE 26

Rare coins continue to outpace inflation and nearly all other tangible properties, according to the ninth annual Salomon Brothers survey of financial assets released in New York June 6.

The 94th Anniversary Convention of the American Numismatic Association Aug. 20-25 in Baltimore will be staged in the center of the nation's numismatic heartland and promises to be "a show for the collector" as none ever have been before, with a schedule of tours which will assure the enrichment of every member's numismatic experience.

July

JULY 3

The Department of the Treasury June 18 requested two basic exceptions to the provisions of the proposed Currency Design Act, which would require congressional approval of any design changes in U.S. coin and paper money, in testimony before the House Banking Subcommittee on Consumer Affairs and Coinage.

The Senate June 21 passed the Statue of Liberty commemorative coin bill with an amendment calling for a 1-ounce silver bullion coin to follow the Statue program.

A standing committee of the House of Commons in Canada's Parliament June 14 presented to the Canadian cabinet an eight-point recommendation to phase out the $1 note in favor of a lightweight coin.

Copper-plated iron medals, struck from metal taken from the Statue of Liberty and Ellis Island National Monument, are being offered to help raise funds for the restoration project to celebrate the Statue's centennial.

JULY 10

Congress passes the Statue of Liberty/Ellis Island commemorative coin bill, with an amendment calling for a silver bullion coin.

Cory Gillilland reports on the XXth Federation Internationale de la Medaille Congress in Stockholm, Sweden.

Officials of the American Numismatic Association Certification Service have temporarily turned off the ANA's new camera system for producing ANACS certificates and are having new optics ground to improve the certificate's coin images.

Marlboro, Mass., collector Herbert P. Hicks reports receiving a Series 1985 $5 Federal Reserve note in change June 26 in Neeham, N.Y.

JULY 17

Coin World salutes the Diamond Anniversary of the Boy Scouts of America with a special issue.

Whitman Publishing releases the 1986 *A Guide Book of United States Coins.*

Some bullion dealers are reporting that the Canadian Maple Leaf is overtaking the South African Krugerrand in the bullion coin market.

JULY 24

Investors are a step closer to an American gold bullion coin as the Senate passes its version of the anti-apartheid act containing a bullion coin amendment.

President Ronald Reagan July 9 signed Public Law 99-61, the Statue of Liberty/Ellis Island Commemorative Coin/Liberty Coin Act, providing for the minting of three commemorative coins and a silver bullion coin.

The American Numismatic Association Board of Governors names Ruthann Brettell executive director and Rick Montgomery director of its Certification Service.

JULY 31

As many as 35 lawmakers are expected to be named to the joint congressional conference committee which will decide the specifics of the gold coin amendment that could provide Americans with an alternative to the Krugerrand as early as 1986.

The United States Mint accepts orders for the 10-coin 1985 Uncirculated sets at $7 per set.

The House of Representatives July 15 passed and sent to the Senate the Currency Design Act and a resolution to mint gold medals honoring George and Ira Gershwin.

August

AUGUST 7

During a three-hour visit with *Coin World* staff in Sidney, Ohio, July 25, United States Treasurer Katherine Davalos Ortega appeared enthusiastic and confident that the Statue of Liberty commemorative coin program will move quicker and smoother than the recently completed Olympic coin program.

Reports from the Canadian Numismatic Association convention indicate that Canada's 1988 Calgary Winter Olympic commemoratives will be priced at $28 in U.S. funds.

Although the American Numismatic Association's election officially closed July 20, the auditing firm will be watching for ballots returned with July 21-22 postmarks, due to a delay in mailing about 2,000 ballots.

AUGUST 14

House members Aug. 1 approved by a 380-48 vote the anti-apartheid bill which includes an amendment calling for four gold bullion coins, but the Senate failed to act on the conference report before Congress left for the August recess.

Saying new sales figures do not accurately describe the state of the total Krugerrand market, South African officials are no longer releasing worldwide sales figures for the gold bullion coin.

Coin World introduces a numismatic trivia game, featuring nearly 2,600 questions and answers covering all aspects of the hobby.

Auction '85 participants bid more than $8 million for the 2,000 lots in the four-session sale July 26-27 in Chicago.

AUGUST 21

Coin World salutes Baltimore, host city for the 94th Anniversary Convention of the American Numismatic Association, with a special issue.

Mint list customers will be offered a discount on Statue of Liberty commemorative coins from Nov. 1 to Dec. 31 that tentatively amounts to getting a free half dollar and silver dollar when the coins are purchased in a set with the half eagle, at the price of the gold coin.

The Department of the Treasury plans an ambitious 18-month Statue of Liberty/Ellis Island commemorative coin domestic program that officials project will result in sales of 9 million coins and surcharges totaling $53 million.

AUGUST 28

A special issue marks the 40th anniversary of the Japanese surrender which ended World War II. *Coin World* traces coinage and collectibles of the Pacific Theater.

Coin World presents an update of coinage law codified in United States Code Title 31, and examines how a bullion coinage amendment included in anti-apartheid legislation would change Title 31 statutes.

Upholding 35 of 36 complaints of false representation, Administrative Law Judge William Duvall ruled Aug. 12 that U.S Coin Reserve and Verret Enterprises Inc. of Beaumont, Texas, must desist from its advertising of silver dollars and Kennedy half dollars because the advertising was found to be misleading.

September

SEPTEMBER 4

Former American Numismatic Association president and current Treasurer Adna G. Wilde Jr. received the ANA's highest honor, the Farran Zerbe Memorial Award, at the Aug. 24 ANA convention banquet in Baltimore.

The board of governors of the American Numismatic Association approved a 1986 revised, balanced budget of $3,426,600, predicated on dues increases, $1.4 million generated from its Certification Service and anticipated income of $340,000 from ANA-sanctioned auctions.

Rep. Frank Annunzio, D-Ill., Cheryl and Robert Maisch and J. Roy Pennell Jr. receive ANA Medals of Merit.

SEPTEMBER 11

The United States Mint plans Oct. 18 first-strike ceremonies for Statue of Liberty/Ellis Island commemorative coins; Treasury awards Grey Advertising of New York its domestic marketing/advertising contract.

Proof sets produced by the Mint of Mexico and issued by the Bank of Mexico surfaced on the American coin market just two days after three top monetary officials representing the American government at a press conference in Baltimore proclaimed the 1986 World Championship of Soccer series to be the "first-ever" Proof coins of Mexico.

Coin World continues coverage of the American Numismatic Association's 94th Anniversary Convention, with a special focus on an ANA salute to former *Coin World* Editor Margo Russell.

SEPTEMBER 18

Low-mintage Proof sets of Mexican coins which surfaced on the American coin market in late August are the Bank of Mexico's way of testing the feasibility of a full-fledged Proof set program in the future, but they are not the first Proof coins of Mexico, says Mexico's

Mint Director Napoleon Gomez Urrutia.

Leaders of the American Medallic Sculpture Association unveiled during an Aug. 23 meeting in Baltimore a draft bill which seeks establishment of a national medallic sculpture advisory committee, which would set rules for conducting competitions to select designs for congressionally authorized medals.

The American Numismatic Association has launched a new program under which it will make or commission videotape recordings of major people, places and events.

American Numismatic Association Certification Service authenticators July 23 issued a recall for 20 certificates authenticating unplated zinc cents after they determined some of the coins may have been altered prior to authentication with a post-striking plating of silver or zinc.

SEPTEMBER 25

An American alternative to the South African Krugerrand may become a reality in light of President Ronald Reagan's Sept. 9 executive order for economic sanctions against the government of South Africa and a request for a Department of the Treasury report on the feasibility of minting U.S. gold coins.

The Senate may soon consider a new bill calling for the minting of U.S. gold coins introduced late Sept. 12 by Sen. J. James Exon, D-Neb.

Director of the United States Mint Donna Pope reports a "very favorable" reception by potential Statue of Liberty commemorative coin distributors from eight European nations.

October

OCTOBER 2

The numismatic world will be looking at the Oct. 2-6 Long Beach Numismatic and Philatelic fall exposition, hoping that the enthusiasm and momentum of the American Numismatic Association convention in August will carry over.

The Royal Canadian Mint launches the 1988 Olympic commemorative coin program in Calgary, Alberta, Canada Sept. 16.

Numismatic-related legislation in the 99th Congress focused heavily on Krugerrand import bans, new U.S. gold coins and the Statue of Liberty commemoratives, reveals *Coin World's* "Legislative Update."

OCTOBER 9

Rep. Frank Annunzio, D-Ill., Sept. 23 introduced a bill that calls for the minting of gold and silver coins to commemorate the bicentennial of the United States Constitution in 1987.

American Numismatic Association Executive Director Ruthann Brettell names Pete Carrigan membership director and Deborah Muehleisen communications coordinator.

Paper money collector David Klein of Fairfield, Conn., reports finding a Series 1985 $1 Federal Reserve note with erroneously placed back check number 129.

In a quiet ceremony Sept. 24 in Washington, D.C., Vice President George Bush was presented with his copy of the official 1985 inaugural medal.

OCTOBER 16

President Reagan Oct. 1 signed an executive order banning importation of the South African Krugerrand effective Oct. 11.

U.S. congressional representatives and international monetary experts will discuss in November the possibility of returning to a gold standard when they meet at the Congressional Summit on Exchange Rates and the Dollar Nov. 12-13.

A 28-coin Olympic coin program for the 1988 Summer Games in Seoul, South Korea, has been unveiled by the Seoul Olympic Organizing Committee.

OCTOBER 23

A Senate bill authorizing four U.S. gold bullion coins was polled out of the Senate Banking Committee Oct. 9 after it was combined with a bill calling for three congressional gold medals.

"Aditi: The Monies of India," the first exhibition built completely in-house by the Smithsonian Institution's Numismatic Division, will open Oct. 24 at the National Museum of American History in Washington, D.C., as part of the "Festival of India" celebration.

At least one 1985-S Proof set containing a 1984-S dime has been discovered by a collector, William Rizzo of Missouri.

A federal judge ruled Sept. 19 that the United States Mint was justified in not awarding a blanking contract to ArrowHead Metals Ltd. of Toronto, Ontario.

OCTOBER 30

Simultaneous first-strike ceremonies in West Point and San Francisco kick off production of Proof Statue of Liberty/Ellis Island commemorative coins, offer the public its first look at the designs for the three coins.

The *Annual Report of the Director of the Mint* for fiscal year 1984 is now available.

Excellent counterfeit 1917-S Walking Liberty, Obverse Mint mark half dollars have been received by the International Numismatic Society Authentication Bureau in recent weeks, Director Charles Hoskins reports.

The first of three numismatic celebrations of the Festival of India opened Oct. 12 in New York at the headquarters and museum of the American Numismatic Society.

November

NOVEMBER 6

A survey of numismatists who attended Oct. 18 Statue of Liberty/Ellis Island striking ceremonies reveals overall support for the three coin designs.

The entire 49-member British Commonwealth may join Austria, the United States and other countries and ban the importation of the South African Krugerrand into their individual countries.

Collector buying was strong at Stack's Oct. 22-23 50th anniversary auction.

NOVEMBER 13

The Sixth National Silver Dollar Convention Nov. 13-17 in St. Louis will offer 400 bourse tables, an investment forum featuring nine silver dollar specialists, exhibits and other information for silver dollar collector/investors. *Coin World* picks up the theme with an issue devoted to silver dollars.

Dwight H. Stuckey retraces events leading up to a "mini-melting" of 40 million Morgan dollars in 1919 and 1920.

NOVEMBER 20

Legislation drafted by Department of Treasury officials would, if passed, give the Treasury Secretary authority to adopt distinctive counterfeit deterrents for use on U.S. paper money, provide stiff criminal penalties for unauthorized possession of currency paper and supercede congressional efforts to have changes in U.S. paper money subject to final approval by Congress.

The second annual "Coinage of the Americas Conference" of the American Numismatic Society opened to 42 registered paper money aficionados Oct. 31 at the Society's headquarters in New York.

Collectors and dealers were active at the Nov. 4-6 five-session Abe Kosoff estate auction conducted by Auctions by Bowers and Merena Inc., paying prices that reached market levels and more.

Chart shows Statue of Liberty/Ellis Island commemorative coin purchase options, with pre-issue discount prices and regular issue prices.

NOVEMBER 27

The United States Senate Nov. 14 passed and sent to the House legislation authorizing American gold bullion coins.

Final issuance by the Internal Revenue Service of regulations designed to govern purchases by dealers of some numismatic items are slated to go into effect by Dec. 31.

The Wayne Miller collection of Morgan and Peace silver dollars, widely regarded as the finest ever assembled, will be offered at auction by Superior early in 1986 in the Hoagy Carmichael collection sale.

December

DECEMBER 4

Passage of gold bullion coin legislation by the House of Representatives has been blocked at the request of the Department of the Treasury so as to provide an opportunity to amend the bill to conform with Treasury recommendations.

The "strong possibility" that the Bureau of Engraving and Printing may obtain a new Washington, D.C., area printing facility before it puts a Western satellite plant into operation was among the subjects of discussion by BEP personnel during the International Paper Money Convention in Cherry Hill, N.J., Nov. 14-17.

Bidding at the 1985 National Silver Dollar Sale in St. Louis gave indications to dealers that the silver dollar market is weakening after years of domination of the coin market.

DECEMBER 11

Collectors purchase nearly 1 million Susan B. Anthony dollars in two months through United States Mint catalog offerings of six-coin sets and bags of 100.

Rep. William Dannemeyer, R-Calif., introduces the Gold Standard Act of 1985, making eagle gold coins the standard unit of currency in the United States, and with other provisions effectively returning the United States to a gold standard.

Israel's high inflation is causing consternation among collectors, as commemorative denominations can't keep pace with circulating currency denominations.

One aspiring young journalist will be given the opportunity to experience the work-a-day world of numismatic publications during the summer of 1986 as the first participant in the Margo Russell Journalism Internship Program sponsored by *Coin World.*

The Internal Revenue Service revises its schedule for issuing reporting regulations, extending the date to the end of 1986.

DECEMBER 18

Coin World focuses on the numismatics of comets, as Comet Halley makes its 76-year return approach in Earth's skies.

American gold coin supporters inched closer to their goal when the House of Representatives passed gold bullion coin legislation on Dec. 2 already approved by the Senate.

The United States Mint has selected European distributors for Statue of Liberty commemorative coins, and officials express hope that the distributors may evolve into permanent outlets for the Mint's products.

DECEMBER 25

Production of the Uncirculated 1986-D Immigrant copper-nickel half dollar at the Denver Mint got under way Dec. 6 with a small first-strike ceremony.

"Final" sales figures for Los Angeles Olympics commemorative coins shows the big sellers to be Proof 1983-S and 1984-S silver dollars, while the major rarities are Philadelphia and Denver Mint varieties of Proof gold eagles.

1985 OBITUARIES

Issue date

January 23

Samuel R. Milbank, former president of the American Numismatic Society and honorary president for life.

March 20

Phyllis Duncan Ellis, president of the Numismatic Association of Southern California.

Issue date

June 26

Joseph L. Lepczyk, numismatic auctioneer and coin dealer.

October 23

John W. Snyder, former Secretary of the Treasury.

November 13

Virginia Culver, 38th president of the American Numismatic Association and first woman elected to the ANA post.

News happenings, 1986

Date refers to *Coin World* issue in which the news item was published.

January

JANUARY 1

President Reagan signed legislation Dec. 17 authorizing the minting of four different sizes of gold bullion coins, but there was a hint that the law may undergo changes by the Treasury Department sometime in the near future to bring the coins more in line, with Treasury officials' requirements.

American Numismatic Association negotiators on Dec. 20 persuaded Salt Lake City officials to vote a special provision allowing the ANA's Midwinter convention bourse and public auction to operate under a considerably less stringent reporting law than is normally enforced in the city.

David L. Ganz, American Numismatic Association governor, said he will submit a proposal to eliminate numerical grading from the association's grading certificates during the ANA Board of Governors meeting at the ANA Midwinter convention in early 1986.

JANUARY 8

The 25th anniversary of the inauguration of John F. Kennedy is the impetus for a 25th anniversary medal by Gilroy Roberts, sculptor who designed the obverse of the Kennedy half dollar.

Final sales figures by purchase option are released by the United States Mint for the Olympic commemorative coin program; top-selling option is the 1984-S Proof silver dollar.

JANUARY 15

In response to interest by the United States Congress, Mint Director Donna Pope and Treasurer Katherine D. Ortega made available "a limited number" of Statue of Liberty commemorative Proof coins to members of Congress before the Christmas holiday; meanwhile, delivery begins to pre-issue orderers.

Astute collectors will notice subtle changes in regular circulating coinage in 1986, as United States Mint officials say new dies will result in better images on coinage.

JANUARY 22

More than 430,000 pre-issue orders for Statue of Liberty commemorative coins have poured into the United States Treasury; $12.9 million in surcharges turned over to the Statue of Liberty/Ellis Island Foundation.

The Florida United Numismatists' 31st anniversary convention Jan. 2-5 in Tampa proved to be a numismatic name-dropper's paradise as U.S. Treasurer Katherine D. Ortega and other dignitaries visited.

A new computerized coin trading network, Teletrade, described by its founder as the numismatic equivalent of the New York

Stock Exchange, will begin operation Jan. 22.

United States Mint Director Donna Pope announced during the Jan. 2-5 Florida United Numismatists convention in Tampa, Fla., that 1986-S Proof sets will be available for sale in early March; Prestige Proof sets will also be offered.

Calendar year 1985 coinage production figures show United States Mint output down some 3 billion coins from 1984.

JANUARY 29

Coin World conducts a poll seeking readers' opinions of the American Numismatic Association Certification Service.

Swiss numismatist Leo Mildenberg wins American Numismatic Society's Archer M. Huntington Medal award; Florida medalist Edward R. Grove receives J. Sanford Saltus Medal award.

About 3,000 coins, 3,000 books and 600 paintings taken by the Nazis from Jews during the German occupation of Austria during World War II will be returned to their owners or auctioned, according to a law unanimously approved by the Austrian parliament Dec. 13.

February

FEBRUARY 5

The United States Mint and U.S. Treasury marketing plans for the Statue of Liberty commemorative coins must shift gears and place more emphasis on the two-coin silver dollar/half dollar set now that the $5 gold coin is a virtual sell-out, officials in both offices say.

At least one of Canada's 1988 Speed Skating silver $20 coins in its Calgary Winter Olympic Games series left the Hull Mint without the innovative bilingual edge lettering normally added to the coin after striking; a Texas collector found the coin.

The city of Omaha, Neb., which had planned to house the $7 million Byron Reed coin collection in the city's prestigious Joslyn Art Museum, has received a bid by Omaha's Western Heritage Museum to provide a permanent home for the collection.

The United States Mint will be affected by the Gramm-Rudman-Hollings Deficit Reduction Act, but officials have not determined to what extent; cent production at the West Point Bullion Depository has been suspended due to decreased demand.

FEBRUARY 12

The Wayne Miller pedigree on 160 Morgan and Peace silver dollars led a collector-dominated crowd to drive prices for even lesser quality dollars to new heights out of what one dealer said was frustration over not winning

the "nicer coins" in Superior Galleries' Jan. 27-28 auction in Beverly Hills, Calif.

The first 1986 coin reported to *Coin World* is a 1986-D Lincoln cent struck 75 percent off center; Michigan readers Mark Longas and Ken Potter found the coin while searching through a batch of the newly struck cents.

"Coin Collecting — Family Fun" is the theme for National Coin Week April 20-26.

The American Numismatic Association Board of Governors has voted not to enter into a contract with Mayflower Coin and Stamp Co. Inc. of Boston to conduct the auction at the 1987 annual convention in Atlanta; ANA legal counsel George Hatie said the alternate, Auctions by Bowers and Merena Inc., Wolfeboro, N.H., would conduct the auction.

FEBRUARY 19

The Eighth American Numismatic Association Midwinter convention in Salt Lake City Feb. 20-22 is the subject of a special *Coin World* issue focusing on the numismatic and syngraphic history of the Mormon church.

The Proof Statue of Liberty gold $5 coin outsold its Uncirculated counterpart 4-to-1 on the way to an early sell-out of the gold coins issued in a series commemorating the centennial of the Statue of Liberty.

The House Feb. 6 approved legislation introduced by Rep. Mickey Leland, D-Texas, calling on President Reagan to award the Presidential Medal of Freedom posthumously to the seven astronauts killed in the Jan. 28 explosion of the space shuttle *Challenger*.

FEBRUARY 26

A check for $24 million — about 80 percent of that amount contributed by customers on the United States Mint's mailing list — was presented to the Statue of Liberty/Ellis Island Foundation at a Feb. 10 ceremony in the Cash Room of the United States Treasury in Washington, D.C.

Findings of an informal, non-random polling of *Coin World* readers finds the 1,626 respondents split over adjectival or numerical grading, while American Numismatic Association Certification Service users generally agree with ANACS graders.

A federal district court judge ruled in favor of a Minnesota man in a recently settled breach of contract lawsuit involving the resale of Morgan and Peace dollars to a Minnesota firm. According to court documents, the firm had guaranteed to repurchase the coins at the same grade at which it sold them but later tried to purchase at lower grades, claiming grading standards had changed. The judge ruled ANA grading standards had not changed.

March

MARCH 5

The American Numismatic Association Board of Governors issued a public statement Feb. 20 acknowledging for the first time that the ANA Certification Service has in recent times graded coins more conservatively than in the past and that the same coin which was graded Mint State 65 in 1981 would likely receive a grade today of MS-63 or lower if regraded.

Complaints from consumers who have purchased rare coins and who are "unhappy for one reason or another" are definitely being scrutinized by the Federal Trade Commission, confirms the director of the FTC's regional office in Boston, Phoebe Morse.

Coin club forums, a dealer bourse and an auction will highlight the 11th annual Chicago International Coin Fair, taking place March 7-9 at the Hyatt Regency Hotel in Chicago.

MARCH 12

Salt Lake City residents, many eager to experience and see first-hand "America's most prestigious coin show," swarmed the Salt Palace Convention Center Feb. 22, becoming a significant factor in establishing an all-time attendance record for American Numismatic Association Midwinter conventions.

A strong attendance by the non-collecting public at the ANA's Midwinter convention in Salt Lake City Feb. 20-22 spurred sales at the United States Mint's booth to $91,000.

United States Mint Director Donna Pope predicted 2.2 million ounces of gold bullion coins and 4 million ounces of silver bullion coins will be sold during the first full year of production. Pope made her prediction before the House Appropriations Subcommittee on Treasury, Postal Services and General Government Feb. 27 during presentation of her fiscal year 1987 budget request of $47.8 million.

MARCH 19

The addition of anti-counterfeiting devices to United States paper money has been approved by President Ronald Reagan and Treasury Secretary James A. Baker III, a spokesman at the Bureau of Engraving and Printing says.

A *Coin World* reader survey determines demographics, collecting habits of subscribers.

Robert Morris Lacewell, a senior at the University of Texas at San Antonio, has been selected as the first participant in *Coin World's* Margo Russell Journalism Internship program.

MARCH 26

The United States Mint launched its international sales program for the Statue of Liberty commemorative coin program March 11 in the Liberty Room of the chancellery of the Embassy of France in Washington with a gift of two coins bearing likenesses of France's gift of a century ago.

An offering of Proof sets to United States Mint mailing list customers was put in the mails March 10, and for the first time customers may use credit cards to order the sets; the offering includes 1986 Prestige Proof sets.

Designs for U.S. gold and silver bullion coins are in the hands of Secretary of the Treasury James A. Baker III and key legislators who introduced legislation calling for the coins want a say in the design selection process.

April

APRIL 2

A special Central States convention issue features obsolete bank notes of Kansas and Missouri.

Federal Reserve notes with inscribed security threads and microprinting around the portrait will begin circulating in 15-18 months, Treasury officials confirmed March 18.

The United States Mint and Walt Disney World's Epcot Center team up to survey the public about coins and coin use.

APRIL 9

Richard G. Doty is named curator of Western Hemisphere numismatics for the National Numismatic Collections at the Smithsonian Institution's National Museum of American History in Washington, D.C.

A reduced-size, 26.5 millimeter, 11-sided, yellow-gold colored Canadian dollar planned to replace the $1 note in circulation will be introduced in January 1987, Canadian officials report.

The United States Capitol Historical Society's 1986 medal has been approved as an official medal of the Commission on the Bicentennial of the United States Constitution.

APRIL 16

A special issue of *Coin World*, "The Faces of Liberty," traces the history of the Statue of Liberty, the United States commemorative coins and other Statue-related collectibles.

Despite the fact that no Statue of Liberty $5 gold coins were available to international distributors through the U.S. Mint's bulk distributor program, the three-coin sets containing the half eagle are hot sellers in Europe.

American Numismatic Association legal

counsel George Hatie issued a statement April 3 specifying that "the announcement in the March 1986 issue of *The Numismatist* of the suspension of Anthony Swiatek for failure to comply with an ANA directive regarding a complaint is incorrect."

APRIL 23

Reliable sources in Washington, D.C., indicate that the Augustus Saint-Gaudens double eagle design of Liberty — used on double eagles from 1907 until 1933 — is likely to grace the obverse of the new gold bullion coins and Adolph A. Weinman's Walking Liberty obverse design and eagle reverse — used on half dollars from 1916 until 1947 — are the odds-on favorites for the new silver bullion coins.

The Industry Council for Tangible Assets, the Washington-based lobbying organization for numismatic coin dealers, bullion, gemstone, antique and other tangible-related industries, is banking on pledges of some $25,000 to alleviate a temporary "emergency financial crunch" so its lobbying activities can continue uninterrupted.

The American Numismatic Association is experimenting with an in-depth grading analysis form for coins submitted for re-examination but officials say this does not represent a policy change in regards to the way the ANA grading service grades coins.

APRIL 30

A Minnesota lower court judge on April 7 turned down a request for a new trial and said his original ruling that American Numismatic Association grading standards have not changed will stand, despite a statement by the ANA Board of Governors that ANA standards have changed.

Some 77,000 schools throughout the United States have been mailed a teaching packet about United States coins — specifically the Statue of Liberty/Ellis Island commemorative coins. The kit is the cornerstone of a Treasury Department goal of increasing interest in coins and coin collecting among the United States' young people.

May

MAY 7

A legislative effort to allow Americans to acquire American gold bullion coins for individually-directed retirement accounts is currently under way in the Senate.

According to figures included in solicitations for bids for supplying silver and gold planchets for United States bullion coins, the United States Mint expects to mint about 1.3 million ounces of gold and 4 million ounces of silver per year into the coins.

The American Numismatic Association releases a preliminary schedule for its 95th Anniversary Convention in Milwaukee Aug. 6-10.

MAY 14

Bronze duplicates of the Vietnam Veterans national medal are available from the United States Mint in two sizes, a 1.5-inch diameter, low relief version and a 3-inch, high relief version.

An April 29 141-lot numismatic auction is conducted at the Anaheim Hilton in Anaheim, Calif., for investors under the umbrella of RUFFCO, a new investment enterprise headed by Howard Ruff.

Investment newsletter guru and best-selling author Howard Ruff thinks that rare coins are positioned for a dramatic increase in value.

MAY 21

Gold Statue of Liberty coins from the United States and France are two of the hottest properties on the current market, with the sold-out Uncirculated U.S. coin bringing four times issue price and the U.S. allocation of the French Proof version nearing depletion.

Rep. William Dannemeyer, R-Calif., introduced legislation May 6 to repeal the $10 denomination in the gold bullion coin law signed by President Reagan in December.

A copyrighted two-part series appearing in the *San Francisco Examiner* points to breaches of security at the San Francisco Assay Office.

MAY 28

A special *Coin World* issue marks the celebration of 1,100 years of continuous operation of the British Royal Mint.

Steve R. Mead has been appointed as the Associate Director of Marketing for the U.S. Mint in a reorganization of the Mint marketing team. He will oversee marketing for the soon-to-be-released gold and silver bullion coins and all other domestic and international marketing for the U.S. Mint.

Congressional sources viewing sketches of the new U.S. bullion coins indicate by description that thin is in and art is out for the gold coin.

June

JUNE 4

The American Numismatic Association Certification Service risks losing its position as the most prominent of the grading services unless it begins using the Mint State 64 grade on its grading certificates, say six dealer consultants.

Dr. Alan M. Stahl, curator of medieval

coins and medals at the American Numismatic Society and president of the American Medallic Sculpture Association, has been appointed United States delegate to the Federation Internationale de la Medaille and chairman of the steering committee of FIDEM '87; Cory Gillilland, associate curator for the Division of Numismatics in the Museum of American History at the Smithsonian Institution, will serve as associate delegate to FIDEM, the post formerly held by Stahl.

JUNE 11
The U.S. Treasury may face strong resistance June 12 when it goes before the federal Commission of Fine Arts to seek design approval for its new gold and silver bullion coins.

South Dakota may soon join California and Texas as a producer of bullion pieces. The appeal of royalties being deposited in the state's treasury and the chance to commemorate historically significant events in the state has enhanced the idea of state-issued bullion pieces.

On May 20, just five days before nearly 5 million Americans joined hands across the country in an effort to fight hunger and homelessness, President Reagan signed legislation honoring Harry Chapin with a congressional medal, who fought a different fight for the hungry people of the world.

JUNE 18
U.S. Mint Director Donna Pope has been renominated by President Reagan for a second five-year term as Mint Director.
In a *Coin World* interview, Rep. Frank Annunzio, D-Ill., chairman of the House Banking Subcommittee on Consumer Affairs and Coinage, says he would like to slow the pace of new commemorative coinage issues.

Statue of Liberty commemorative coin sales have topped the 5 million coin mark, raising about $38 million of Treasury's initial goal of $40 million in surcharges for the Statue of Liberty/Ellis Island Foundation.

JUNE 25
The federal Commission of Fine Arts approved the designs of the new U.S. gold and silver bullion coins at its monthly meeting June 12 in Washington, D.C. — but only after a lengthy public hearing during which some members voiced concern about U.S. coin designs in general and the bullion coin designs in particular.

The Smithsonian Institution, particularly the Numismatic Division, is hard-pressed to meet Gramm-Rudman budget cut require-

ments and still maintain meaningful operations of the museum.

A class action suit has been filed in U.S. District Court in Savannah, Ga., against the United States Mint, the Department of the Treasury and their respective chief officers by a Georgia couple who contend their credit card order for Statue of Liberty/Ellis Island commemorative coins, and possibly the orders of 13,000 others, were wrongly rejected.

July

JULY 2
Thefts at the Long Beach (Calif.) Numismatic and Philatelic Exposition and at the Convention of International Numismatics in early June in the Los Angeles area are apparently only the tip of the iceberg of an organized group that is suspected in the theft of coins and jewelry from dealers around the country, according to the Los Angeles Police Department and a June 19 statement issued by the American Numismatic Association in Colorado Springs, Colo.

The United States Mint is warning collectors that a recently advertised Statue of Liberty gold and silver Proof set does not contain the Statue of Liberty gold half eagle coin struck by the U.S. Mint, nor is the set packaged by or in any way connected with the U.S. Mint or the U.S. government.

Australia will join the parade of countries issuing internationally marketed gold bullion coins when it begins selling four different sized "Nugget" coins Sept. 1.

The U.S. Mint is requiring potential marketing-advertising firms to submit a trade name or logo to promote the soon-to-be-released U.S. gold and silver bullion coins.

JULY 9
A Senate provision in the massive tax overhaul package would allow American gold and silver bullion coins to be invested in Individual Retirement Accounts, but whether those accounts will retain their full tax deductible status is still under consideration by Congress.

The Department of the Treasury officially announced June 26 the designs for the American gold and silver bullion coins will feature modified versions of traditional U.S. coin designs, a new design for the silver coin reverse and a new design for the reverse of the gold bullion coins "symbolizing the unity and family traditions of America."

The publishers of the 1987 edition of *A Guide Book of United States Coins* raised the price to $6.95, but for the extra dollar collectors get 16 more pages, a revamped commemorative coin section and the opportunity to purchase a silver medal commemorating the 40th edition of the familiar "Red Book."

JULY 16

The American Numismatic Association Board of Governors June 28-29 voted the most sweeping changes to its official grading standards for United States coins since the ANA Certification Service began just over seven years ago to grade coins for a fee and issue grade certificates. Effective immediately, ANA grading standards recognize 11 levels of Mint State from MS-60 through MS-70 in addition to the circulated grade of About Uncirculated 58.

Few are looking forward to seeing the first-strike specimens of the United States' new gold bullion coinage more than Dallas sculptor Miley Busiek, who created the reverse design which will grace all four coins.

JULY 23

The unification and solidification of the various U.S. coin grading systems will be the agenda Aug. 7 when representatives of the American Numismatic Association Certification Service and other grading services meet in a closed-door workshop at the ANA convention in Milwaukee.

For the first time in its history, the American Numismatic Association's official convention medal will honor living numismatists.

New COPE Pak machinery is helping increase productivity at the Bureau of Engraving and Printing.

JULY 30

Sixteen specialists in "America's Silver Coinage, 1794-1891," will discuss their specialties Nov. 1-2 at the American Numismatic Society's 1986 Coinage of the Americas Conference in New York City.

The rarely given Mint State 70 grade classification was awarded by the American Numismatic Association Certification Service to an Uncirculated 1986-W Statue of Liberty gold half eagle that the ANACS staff considered perfect.

Collectors, dealers and investors got their first instructions in grading under the American Numismatic Association's new 11-level Mint State grading system during the July 7-12 ANA Summer Seminar.

August

AUGUST 6

The American Numismatic Association's 95th Anniversary Convention in Milwaukee Aug. 6-10 is the focus of a special *Coin World* issue featuring research by Fred L. Reed III regarding Sands' Ale encased postage.

Heavy sales of Statue of Liberty two-coin sets results in a packaging shortage; final sales figures for the George Washington commemorative half dollar show that more than 7 million coins were sold.

AUGUST 13

Coin and precious metals dealers who want to become authorized purchasers of the new United States gold bullion coins directly from the U.S. Mint must have experience as a "marketmaker," a tangible net worth in excess of $50 million and liquid assets of $10 million, according to criteria released by the Mint July 28.

The Senate Banking, Housing and Urban Affairs Committee July 29 approved U.S. Mint Director Donna Pope's renomination to another five-year term.

Congress is expected to quickly consider legislation setting standards, a specific design and criteria for recipients nominated to receive a national gold medal awarded by Congress.

Quality was the key to high prices with strong floor bidding evident at Auction '86 in Chicago July 25-26, although rarity, not condition, resulted in a $230,000 winning bid for the unique 1870-S Seated Liberty half dime.

AUGUST 20

The Board of Governors of the American Numismatic Association voted Aug. 4 to create a task force "for the purpose of designing a comprehensive program for the self regulation of the coin industry."

Charles H. Wolfe was named recipient of the Farran Zerbe Memorial Award at the 95th Anniversary Convention of the American Numismatic Association in Milwaukee.

Pre-issue demand for the United States gold coins has been far greater than anticipated, causing U.S. Mint officials to delay sales until Oct. 20 in order to strike sufficient quantities.

The U.S. Senate Aug. 2 confirmed Donna Pope to continue in her second five-year term as Director of the United States Mint.

AUGUST 27

Despite a record deluge of 6.84 inches of rain opening day and competition from the Wisconsin State Fair, the American Numismatic Association's 95th Anniversary Convention in Milwaukee Aug. 6-10 drew 9,500 participants.

Five prominent hobbyists, two of whom are deceased, were inducted Aug. 9 into the American Numismatic Association's Hall of Fame.

An international organization of allied grading services working toward common goals took its first steps during the American

Numismatic Association convention in Milwaukee, following two meetings of representatives of more than a dozen grading services.

September

SEPTEMBER 3

America will have its first gold bullion coin when it is officially struck during ceremonies Sept. 8 at the West Point Bullion Depository by Secretary of the Treasury James A. Baker III; Oct. 29 is tentatively set as date for ceremonies launching the silver bullion coin.

Representatives from at least 39 countries are expected to attend the first world Mintmasters' conference ever held outside of Europe.

In 10 months the Statue of Liberty commemorative coin program has raised more than $60 million for the Statue of Liberty/Ellis Island Foundation.

SEPTEMBER 10

The chairman of the House Banking Subcommittee on Consumer Affairs and Coinage, Rep. Frank Annunzio, D-Ill., has criticized the U.S. Mint's requirements for bulk purchases of U.S. gold and silver bullion coins, saying the requirements violate the Gold Bullion Coin Act and the Small Business Act.

The United States Mint's gold bullion coin bulk purchase requirements leave out many dealers who have participated in and supported the Mint's other programs such as the George Washington commemorative half dollar, the Los Angeles Olympic coins and the Statue of Liberty/Ellis Island commemorative coins.

Grey Advertising of New York, the company that handles publicity and marketing efforts for the Statue of Liberty/Ellis Island commemorative coin program, has been awarded a one-year contract to market and publicize the five U.S. gold and silver bullion coins.

SEPTEMBER 17

When the American Eagle bullion coins enter the marketplace in October the United States Mint is hoping the response to the U.S. gold and silver bullion coins is as strong as the name implies; Mint officials say they are committed to following the marketing path of the other successful bullion coins available.

The opportunity for other collectors to experience the thrill of adding to their collections is the reason Robinson S. Brown Jr. is willing to part company with his nearly complete U.S. large cent collection.

The importation ban against the South African gold Krugerrand and economic sanctions have been extended by President Ronald Reagan.

SEPTEMBER 24

Senior Treasury officials launched the United States' entry into the gold bullion coin market Sept. 8 with a strong "buy American" campaign in brief speeches before pushing the buttons on the HME coining press at the West Point Bullion Depository for the ceremonial first strikes of the new American Eagle 1-ounce gold bullion coin.

Volume I of a special supplement, "How to Order Foreign Coins," is a bonus for all *Coin World* readers.

Maurice Lafontaine, 48, who has devoted his career to government service, is the new Mintmaster and president of the Royal Canadian Mint, replacing James V. Corkery who has been named chairman of the board of directors of the Crown corporation which operates the RCM.

October

OCTOBER 1

The importance of accurate and timely reporting of coinage production information, how collectors perceive coinage issues, gold and silver in coinage, and the marketing of Olympic coins were topics presented during the final working session Sept. 17 of the XIV Mint Directors' Conference in Ottawa, Canada.

Directors of 22 national Mints ended three days of meetings in Ottawa, Canada, Sept. 17 by voting to cross the Atlantic for a second time and selected the United States as host country for their next world gathering in May of 1988.

The U.S. District Court for the District of Massachusetts in Boston granted a temporary restraining order and froze the assets of Rare Coin Galleries of America, a Boston rare coins firm, its Fort Lauderdale, Fla., subsidiary and principal officers of both companies in response to a suit filed Sept. 16 by the Federal Trade Commission.

OCTOBER 8

The legislative push is on to garner 218 cosponsors for legislation authorizing commemorative coins marking the 200th anniversary of the United States Constitution in 1987.

Coin collectors succeeded in opening a new chapter in numismatic history Sept 20 by bringing together for the first time three Chief Sculptor-Engravers of the United States — Gilroy Roberts, Frank Gasparro and Elizabeth Jones.

Two new sculptor-engravers — Chester Martin and James Licaretz — began duties at the United States Mint in Philadelphia in August and September, to bring the engraving department back to full complement following recent retirements.

OCTOBER 15
The 200th anniversary of the U.S. Constitution is well on its way to being commemorated with two new gold and silver coins. But it took some last minute tinkering before the measure got to the House floor without the standard hearing by the House Banking Subcommittee on Consumer Affairs and Coinage.

Mint Director Donna Pope responds to criticisms of the American Eagle bullion coin distribution plan made by Rep. Frank Annunzio, D-Ill.

The 1-ounce American Eagle gold bullion coin debuts in *Coin World's* Gold, Platinum, Silver Prices chart.

OCTOBER 22
The United States Mint has approved more than 30 different bulk distributors worldwide for the American Eagle gold and silver bullion coins.

Investors wanting to place the new American Eagle gold and silver bullion coins into Individual Retirement Accounts will have to let a trustee or a third party take physical possession of the coins.

Rarity won out over condition as a winning bid of $22,000 claimed a 1795 Liberty Cap cent in Good 6 condition at the auction of the Robinson S. Brown collection of large cents, conducted by Superior Galleries Sept. 30-Oct. 1 in West Hollywood, Calif.

OCTOBER 29
The 200th anniversary of the drafting of the U.S. Constitution will be marked with commemorative coins if legislation approved by Congress is signed by President Reagan.

Beginning Oct. 20 rare coins are prime time in investment news; that's when David Lisot, an independent producer, was to return to Financial News Network to broadcast live, daily reports of news from the numismatic world.

November
NOVEMBER 5
The United States Mint sold all of the 845,500 gold bullion coins — 558,000 ounces — it had on hand less than 48 hours after sales began Oct. 20.

The Proof 1-ounce American Eagle gold coin will sell for $550 and the Proof American Eagle silver dollar will sell for $21 during the one-month sales period ending Dec. 1, Mint officials said the week of Oct. 19.

NOVEMBER 12
The 1-ounce, $1 silver American Eagle bullion coin had its moment in the spotlight during ceremonial first strikes at the United States Assay Office in San Francisco Oct. 29.

The American Eagle gold bullion coin soared as 134,000 ounces were sold within a matter of hours after the U.S. Mint opened its bullion coin sales Oct. 27.

President Ronald Reagan signed into law Oct. 29 legislation authorizing gold and silver commemorative coinage marking the 200th anniversary of the drafting of the U.S. Constitution.

NOVEMBER 19
The 1-ounce American Eagle gold bullion coin may be king of the new coins but the fractional denominations — particularly the tenth-ounce — are the power behind the throne.

United States Mint officials are advising anyone who receives the Mint's order for the Proof versions of the American Eagle gold and silver bullion coins to use that form, although the Mint will honor orders sent in letter form.

Despite the fact that it was held at the end of the week in which the Mets won the World Series, the Statue of Liberty was rededicated on its 100th birthday, Halloween was celebrated and some 20,000 runners came to town to be part of the New York City marathon, the third annual Coinage of the Americas Conference drew a strong showing of ardent early U.S. silver coinage devotees.

NOVEMBER 26
The U.S. Mint is actively pursuing a number of strategies designed to make sure that the 1986 Uncirculated American Eagle gold bullion coins, especially the fractional pieces, do not ultimately become numismatic coins.

With sales approaching the 1-million-ounce level in the first four weeks, American Eagle gold bullion coins are a formidable competitor for the Canadian Maple Leaf, but Canada is not about to relinquish its claim to No. 1, says Jack Julien, head of Canada's bullion program.

December
DECEMBER 3
United States Mint officials have expanded production capabilities for the American Eagle silver bullion coins to include the Denver Mint in an effort to head off an anticipated sell-out.

In light of the unprecedented popularity of the American Eagle gold bullion coins, the United States Mint has set several production goals to meet by the end of 1986: 1.4 million

1-ounce coins; 550,000 half-ounce coins; 600,000 quarter-ounce coins; and 650,000 tenth-ounce coins.

Battelle Memorial Institute has been commissioned by Amos Press Inc., parent firm of *Coin World*, to determine the feasibility and practicality of using equipment to objectively grade collectible and investment quality coins.

DECEMBER 10

No Kennedy half dollars will be struck for circulation in 1987, U.S. Mint Deputy Director Eugene Essner confirmed Nov. 28; the copper-nickel coins will be struck strictly for collectors and sold only in 1987 Proof and Uncirculated sets.

After seven years of searching, the Bureau of Engraving and Printing has chosen Fort Worth, Texas, as the location for its Western paper currency production facility.

Sales of the American Eagle silver bullion coins their first day surpassed by weight the first six weeks of sales for the gold bullion coins.

DECEMBER 17

The United States Mint as of Dec. 3 has received orders for 216,127 Proof 1986-W American Eagle gold bullion coins, and 624,743 Proof American Eagle silver dollars.

The Mint mark for the Proof 1986-S American Eagle silver bullion dollar will appear on the reverse, a departure from United States Mint practice since 1968.

Declarations of intent have been made by current members of the American Numismatic Association Board of Governors regarding their candidacy for positions open in the 1987 ANA elections.

DECEMBER 24

U.S. Mint officials have decided to sell Proof versions of the 1987 American Eagle gold and silver bullion coins, as sales of the 1986 Proofs exceeded the $187 million total with more orders still coming in.

The financial health of the American Numismatic Association — both immediate and long-range — dominated considerations of the ANA Board of Governors at its meeting Dec. 6-7 in Colorado Springs, Colo.

The American Numismatic Association Certification Service will offer a new dateless color photograph grading certificate and two discount programs in early 1987 as part of an aggressive marketing package designed to lure back some of its former customers and attract new ones.

DECEMBER 31

The American Numismatic Society in New York names William L. Bischoff as its Assistant Curator of Modern Coins and Currency, to fill the vacancy left when Richard Doty took a position with the Smithsonian Institution.

The United States Mint may buy gold that is not necessarily newly mined or domestic in an effort to pay back the gold it used from national reserves to start up the American Eagle bullion coin program.

Sales of the Proof versions of the American Eagle gold and bullion coins top $200 million, with orders still coming in.

OBITUARIES

Issue date

June 25

Jesse F. Cornish, chairman of the Industry Council for Tangible Assets and vice president of Investment Rarities Inc. of Minneapolis.

News happenings, 1987
Date refers to *Coin World* issue in which the news item was published.

JANUARY 7

The American Numismatic Society will kick off a $4 million fund-raising campaign Jan. 8 to combat a financial situation that ANS officials say threatens its resources and the society's ability to reach out and affect the world at large.

Surcharges generated by sales of the 1986 Statue of Liberty coins surpassed the surcharges raised by the former surcharge record holder, the Olympic coin program, during the week of Dec. 19, in half the time and with less

than half the number of coin varieties available.

The dramatic story of the adoption of the U.S. Constitution is captured on the 1987 Bicentennial of the Constitution medal by Marcel Jovine commissioned by the United States Capitol Historical Society.

JANUARY 14

The United States Mint will not produce business strike versions of 1986-dated American Eagle gold and silver coins in 1987, having met year-end production targets.

1986 in the rare coin market appears to be the year of retracement as values of rare coins tended to move lower from the highs posted in 1985, according to *Coin World* Index charts.

The Royal Canadian Mint's 1987 commemorative silver dollar will honor the exploration of Canada's Cumberland Sound and Davis Strait by British explorer John Davis.

JANUARY 21

The American Numismatic Society bestowed its two most prestigious honors, recognizing excellence in medallic design and numismatic scholarship, to Finnish medalist Kauko Rasanen and Belgian scholar Paul Naster at its 128th annual meeting Jan. 28 at ANS headquarters in New York City.

The mysterious disappearance of a pair of master dies for Canada's new smaller Voyageur aureate-nickel dollar has forced the Canadian Parliament to approve a new reverse design depicting a common loon, selected from a Royal Canadian Mint bank of coinage designs obtained in past design competitions.

The potential damage from the manipulation of the numismatic market has long been cited as a reason for keeping secret the list of coins used in compiling the influential Salomon Brothers Inc. report of the annual price performance of rare coins; however, a version of the list was published in *The Investor's Guide to United States Coins* by Neil S. Berman with Hans M.F. Schulman.

JANUARY 28

A-Mark Precious Metals Inc. will likely be granted an American Eagle gold coin distributorship because of an out-of-court settlement in the company's lawsuit against the United States Mint over its rejection as a gold bullion coin distributor.

The American Numismatic Society launched its $4 million development campaign Jan. 8 with an announcement that more than 50 percent of the goal has been received in the form of pledges.

The first issue of *World Coins* debuts, a magazine-style feature-oriented monthly supplement focusing on numismatics of the world.

FEBRUARY 4

The U.S. Mint Office of Marketing is in place, headed by recently appointed Associate Director for Marketing Daniel P. Cahill.

On Feb. 25, New York entrepreneur Bernard Rome will hold his first televised rare coin auction, establishing the format for regularly scheduled monthly auctions thereafter.

FEBRUARY 11

The 125th anniversary year of the Bureau of Engraving and Printing was ushered in Jan. 29 with a formal ceremony attended by high-ranking officials from the department of the Treasury, the United States Postal Service and the Federal Reserve System.

"Currency Worth Noting" is the theme of the April 19-25 National Coin Week 1987, in recognition of the 125th anniversary of the Bureau of Engraving and Printing.

FEBRUARY 18

The United States Treasury Department is inviting a limited number of American artists to submit designs for two U.S. coins to be issued in 1987 which will commemorate the Bicentennial of the drafting of the U.S. Constitution.

The United States Mint offered the American Eagle gold bullion coins two days in a row during the third week of sales in 1987, taking orders for a total of 241,000 gold coins.

The education of the public and working with the media regarding fraudulent advertising were the subjects of a hearing Feb. 5 before the Commodities Futures Trading Commission in Washington, D.C.

FEBRUARY 25

Four hundred years of North Carolina are commemorated in *Coin World's* special issue marking the American Numismatic Association's Midwinter convention in Charlotte.

United States Mint officials expect to have designs for the 1987 Constitution coins in hand by the first of March and be ready by mid-June to begin striking the commemorative gold and silver coins.

American Numismatic Association President Florence Schook has named ANA Governor David L. Ganz to head a six-member task force charged with developing "a comprehensive program for the self regulation of the coin industry by the participants in the industry."

The Dec. 1 postmark was not the final determining factor in the final cut-off of orders for the Proof 1986 American Eagle bullion coins, according to a five-page reply from the U.S. Mint to Rep. Frank Annunzio, D-Ill.

MARCH 4

Approximately 6,500 coins making up the American portion of the Norweb collection, one of the most important numismatic collections ever gathered in the United States, will be offered at public auction in a series of three sales beginning in October in New York City.

Coin World takes an inside look at the operations of the Professional Coin Grading Service.

A court-ordered special counsel has closed the doors of New England Rare Coin Galleries in Boston and fired all but a dozen employees as the result of a court order to liquidate the assets of the rare coin firm.

MARCH 11

The American Numismatic Association Board of Governors Feb. 26 approved a change in the way the ANA Certification Service grades coins to make the service more marketable in the face of declining revenues.

Heritage Numismatic Auctions Inc. has been selected to auction nearly $1 million worth of coins and currency confiscated three years ago by the federal Deposit Insurance Corporation as the result of a California bank failure.

The ANA, the largest coin collector organization in the United States, has formally declared advocacy for changing all designs on the five circulating denominations of United States coins — the cent, 5-cent piece, dime, quarter dollar and half dollar.

MARCH 18

Self-regulation of the rare coin industry appears to be the prime focus of efforts to seek a blueprint for good business conduct individually launched by at least two of the most active organizations in numismatics, the ANA and ICTA.

Steve Ivy, co-chairman of the board of Heritage Capital Corp., Dallas, presents a plan for self-regulation of the numismatic industry.

Diane Wolf, member of the Commission of Fine Arts, makes seeking new designs for U.S. coinage her "full-time crusade."

MARCH 25

Great Britain will enter the gold bullion coin market in 1987 with the release of the Britannia, a legal tender coin containing an ounce of fine gold, to be followed by three smaller pieces.

United States Mint and Treasury officials attempted to reassure Congress that the American Eagle gold bullion coin program will not be pulled out of the U.S. Bullion Depository at West Point.

Budget reductions for the fiscal year ending 1988 have resulted in a reorganization at American Numismatic Association headquarters and a staff reduction resulting in the lay-off of several ANA staff members in the past 30 days, according to ANA Executive Director Ruthann Brettell.

APRIL 1

A nine-question survey sent by the House Banking Subcommittee on Consumer Affairs and Coinage to 25 eligible distributors of the American Eagle gold bullion coins has created feelings of uncertainty among some distributors which could change the initial highflying course of the coins into a fatal plummet.

A 1787 Brasher doubloon, purchased for $430,000 in 1979 by Chicago dealer Walter Perschke, is now on a cross-country tour as a numismatic window dressing for the most important documents in democracy — the Magna Carta, the Declaration of Independence, the Articles of Confederation and the Bill of Rights.

APRIL 8

From 1976 to 1986 the United States Mint deposited $224,064,000 into the general fund of the Treasury from the sale of numismatic items. More than half of that figure, $167,339,000, was raised between fiscal years 1982-1986.

In response to heavy demand for intermediate grading of commemorative gold coinage, commemorative half dollars and U.S. gold coinage of the period 1807-1908, the American Numismatic Association Certification Service now has the necessary representative coins to add the Mint State 62 and MS-64 intermediate grades to all six gold denominations and MS-64 for all commemoratives, both silver and gold.

Excessive delays in processing orders for its products have caused the Bureau of Engraving and Printing to adopt a series of changes to its order-fulfillment system.

APRIL 15

A bold eagle and a representation of one of the most revered documents in United States history, the Constitution, will be featured on the obverses of the 1987 Bicentennial of the Constitution commemorative coins.

For the first time in marketing commemorative coins, the United States Mint is considering limiting the number of coins it will make available in its pre-issue discount, direct mail offering to customers on its mailing list.

APRIL 22

The American Numismatic Association 1988 Midwinter Convention will be held in Little Rock, Ark., as planned, after city and state officials granted the ANA certain exemptions to several restrictive regulations concerning dealer purchases of numismatic items.

"Roads to Liberty: Magna Carta to the Constitution," a traveling exhibit sponsored by the Commission on the Bicentennial of the U.S. Constitution, the U.S. Constitution Council of the Thirteen Original States Inc. and American Express Co., began its six-month journey March 11 in Washington, D.C.

APRIL 29

The American Numismatic Association's 11-point Mint State grading system has been standardized in written form for the first time, in the third edition of the *Official ANA Grading Standards for United States Coins,* just off the printing presses.

The Walt Disney Co. will start circulating its own paper money soon.

Allegations that the United States Mint has sold millions of underweight American Eagle gold bullion fractional coins has been strongly refuted by Mint Director Donna Pope.

MAY 6

In an effort to take a leadership role in the self-regulation of the coin and precious metals industry, the Industry Council for Tangible Assets is proposing a national certification program.

Like the legendary phoenix which rises from its own ashes, the silver price levitated from $5.55 per troy ounce March 13 to $8.90 when the market closed April 23.

A U.S. District Court has decided order forms issued by the United States Mint for the Statue of Liberty/Ellis Island commemorative coins were solicitations of offers, not contracts as alleged in a lawsuit filed by a Georgia couple against the Mint.

MAY 13

The U.S. Mint is adamant that the American Eagle bullion coins will not be offered to the public like numismatic coins, U.S. Mint Director Donna Pope told members of the Gold Institute April 22.

With an April 25 ground-breaking ceremony the Bureau of Engraving and Printing has moved one step closer to the realization of a Western currency-production facility in Fort Worth, Texas.

If a U.S. District Court judge approves a settlement submitted by the Federal Trade Commission and the principal officers of Rare Coin Galleries of America Inc., a Massachusetts rare coin firm, and its two subsidi-

aries, those principal officers will be permanently prohibited from selling rare coins to the public and from grading rare coins for sale to the public.

MAY 20

Coin World sponsors a petition drive to provide the American public with an opportunity to call upon government officials in both the executive and legislative branches to bring about issuance of new designs for all circulating coins in the United States.

Canada begins striking its new small-sized aureate-nickel dollar coin with loon reverse at ceremonies at the Royal Canadian Mint's Winnipeg facility May 7.

MAY 27

Rep. John P. Hiler, R-Ind., ranking minority member of the House Banking Subcommittee on Consumer Affairs and Coinage, does not expect Congress to make any changes in the distribution plan of the American Eagle bullion coins.

What appears to be a plague of production errors has some collectors and dealers criticizing the newly-published third edition of the *Official A.N.A. Grading Standards for United States Coins,* while American Numismatic Association officials, in conceding there are problems, say they are trying to determine just to what extent.

1987 OBITUARIES

Issue date
January 14
Dr. J. Hewitt Judd, 87, author of *United States Pattern, Experimental and Trial Pieces.*

March 25
Clement F. Bailey, 66, numismatic journalist.

April 8
Esther Lasure Gaver, 62, former president of Collectors Research.

April 29
Lee F. Hewitt, founder of *Numismatic Scrapbook* magazine.

May 6
Virgil Hancock, 84, past president and four-term governor of the American Numismatic Association.

Numismatics and Washington

2

Senate

Phone numbers
(All numbers Area Code 202)

Information, Capitol Switchboard (office telephone and room numbers)........... 224-3121
Senate Locator Office (individual's phone number)............................ 224-3207
Bill Clerk (for bill status try Office of Legislation first) 224-2120
Cloakroom — Democratic (tape of floor action and scheduling information) 224-8541
Cloakroom — Democratic (Assistant Secretary for the Majority) 224-4691
Cloakroom — Republican (tape of floor action and scheduling information)........ 224-8601
Cloakroom — Republican (Assistant Secretary for the Minority) 224-6391
Daily Digest (chamber action, committee meetings as in back of *Record*) 224-2658
Enrolling Clerk (whether bill has been signed, sent to the White House)............ 224-6250
Executive Clerk (status of treaties and nominations)......................... 224-4341
Legislative Information (bill status — first place to call) 224-2971
National Association of Manufacturers (tape of legislative activity) 626-3900
Periodical Press Gallery... 224-0265
Radio-Television Gallery 224-6421
Secretary of the Senate (calendars, membership rosters, etc.).................... 224-2115
Senate Document Room (copies of bills, reports, public laws, calendars, etc.)....... 224-7860
Senate Librarian (legislative history, general reference)......................... 224-7106
Senate Press Gallery.. 224-0241
U.S. Chamber of Commerce (tape of legislative news, positions, etc.)............. 872-1313

Senate office buildings
(All Zip Codes 20510)

Senate Dirksen Office Building, Constitution Ave. between 1st St. and 2nd St., NE
Senate Hart Office Building, 2nd St. and Constitution Ave., NE
Senate Russell Office Building, Constitution Ave., between Delaware Ave. and 1st St., NE
Carroll Arms Hotel (offices), 301 1st St., NE
Capitol Hill Apartments Annex (offices), 128 C St., NE
Immigration and Naturalization Building, 119 D St., NE
Plaza Hotel (offices), 331 1st St., NE
Senate Courts (offices), 120 C St., NE

Forms of address

Address	Salutation	Complimentary close
The Honorable...... Senate ...... Office Building Washington, D.C. 20510	Dear Senator.......	Sincerely yours,

House of Representatives

Phone numbers
(All numbers Area Code 202)

Information, Capitol Switchboard (office telephone and room numbers)........... 224-3121
Personnel Locator in the House Finance Office (individual's phone number)....... 225-6515
Bill Clerk (for bill status try Office of Legislation first) 225-4470
Cloakroom — Democratic (updated tape of current House floor action) 225-7400
Cloakroom — Democratic (legislative program, upcoming floor schedule on tape) .. 225-1600
Cloakroom — Democratic (manager) 225-7330
Cloakroom — Democratic (messages only)...................................... 225-0466
Cloakroom — Republican (updated tape of current House floor action)........... 225-7430
Cloakroom — Republican (legislative program, upcoming floor schedule on tape)... 225-2020
Cloakroom — Republican (manager)... 225-7350
Daily Digest (chamber action, committee meetings as in back of *Record*) 225-2868
Enrolling Clerk (Whether bill has been signed, sent to the White House) 225-5848
House Document Room (copies of bills, reports, public laws, calendars, etc.)....... 225-3456
House Librarian (legislative history) 225-0462
House Press Gallery.. 225-3945
National Association of Manufacturers (tape of legislative activity) 626-3900
Office of Legislative Information (bill status - first place to call) 225-1772
Periodical Press Gallery.. 225-2941
Radio-Television Gallery 225-5214
U.S. Chamber of Commerce (tape of legislative news, positions, etc.).............. 872-1313

House office buildings
(All Zip Codes 20515 except HHS)

Cannon House Office Building, Independence Ave. between C St. and 1st St., SE
Longworth House Office Building, Independence Ave. between C St. and South Capitol St., SE
Rayburn House Office Building, Independence Ave. between South Capitol St. and 1st St., SE
Annex 1, 300 New Jersey Ave., SE
Annex 2, 2nd St. and D St., SW
Health and Human Services Bldg. (HHS), 330 Independence Ave., SW, Washington, D.C. 20201

Forms of address

Address	Salutation	Complimentary close
The Honorable...... ..... House Office Building Washington, D.C. 20515	Dear Rep........	Sincerely yours,

Effective letters to Washington

Because senators and representatives rely in large part on the opinions of their constituents for direction in voting on legislation, it is important to make your voice heard in Congress.

There are several ways to inform your elected representatives. One way is to visit personally, but in session he is likely to have a tight schedule, and it is difficult for most people to travel to Washington, D.C. You can also place a telephone call, and the information numbers for both House and Senate are included in this chapter for that reason, but it can be extremely difficult to catch him free in his office in session. Personal visits and phone calls are possible when the congressman is home during recess, but then issues are not timely.

The most effective voice you can have in Congress, therefore, is by way of a well-written personal letter. Some letters are more effective than others in influencing your senator or representative's vote, however. Following are some tips on how to write an effective letter to your elected representatives to maximize your influence on his voting.

• Know your congressman's full name and spell it correctly. Guessed-at or incorrect spelling sends a signal that you are not well-informed and your letter will carry little weight. Proper forms of address are included for both the House and Senate.

• Identify yourself at the head of the letter by name, mailing address, and phone number if you wish. This will help your congressman if he should want to communicate with you on the issue in the future.

• Use plain stationery or personal letterhead. Use business or organization letterhead only if you officially represent its opinion.

• Be concise. Keep the letter to one typed, double-spaced page if possible. Don't hesitate to go longer than that if necessary, but the shorter the letter, the more likely your congressman will pay close attention to it.

• If you can't type the letter, use clear handwriting on ruled paper and double-space it. Use ball-point pens rather than felt tips or pencils, as these tend to smudge. Neatness counts.

• Identify the measure or bill by number when possible. Also include the name of the bill and be specific as to its content or subject. A letter concerning a measure the congressman cannot identify is useless.

• State your position or opinion clearly and at the beginning of the letter. Don't waste time with personal chit-chat; get to the point. Stating your case first will get the congressman's attention and help him classify your vote as for or against the measure.

• Having gotten to the point, stay there. If you have comments on more than one issue, separate letters will be more effective. By no means include impertinent facts or opinions on non-related matters. If you want to comment on coin legislation, don't bring up aid to foreign countries.

• Include any reasons why you hold a certain stance on an issue. Knowing why you think the way you do is as important to the congressman as knowing what side of the issue you are on. Again, keep to the issue at hand. Include a brief statement on how an issue would affect the congressman's constituency. He listens to voters in his home district.

• Be polite and sincere. Anger, sarcasm and flattery will subtract from the weight your voice carries.

• Finally, sign your name in your own handwriting, and follow that with your city and state. Use your voice in Congress to your best advantage.

Senate Committee on Banking, Housing and Urban Affairs

Bills introduced to the Senate concerning coinage and other numismatic subjects are referred to the Senate Committee on Banking, Housing and Urban Affairs.

Consisting of 18 Senators, the committee is referred all proposed legislation, messages, petitions, memorials and other matters related to the following subjects:

1) Banks, banking and financial institutions. 2) Control of prices of commodities, rents and services. 3) Deposit insurance. 4) Economic stabilization and defense production. 5) Export and foreign trade promotion. 6) Export controls. 7) Federal monetary policy, including Federal Reserve System. 8) Financial aid to commerce and industry. 9) Issuance and redemption of notes. 10) Money and credit, including currency and coinage. 11) Nursing home construction. 12) Public and private housing (including veterans' housing). 13) Renegotiation of government contracts. 14) Urban development and urban mass transit.

Chairman..... Sen. William Proxmire, D-Wis.
Ranking minority member..... Sen. Jake Garn, R-Utah

534 Senate Dirksen Office Building . . . . (202) 224-7391
Staff Director..... Kenneth McLean . . . . (202) 224-7391
Minority Staff Director..... M. Danny Wall . . . . (202) 224-1575

House Committee on Banking, Finance and Urban Affairs

Bills introduced to the House concerning coinage and other numismatic subjects are referred to the House Committee on Banking, Finance and Urban Affairs, specifically to the Subcommittee on Consumer Affairs and Coinage.

The 51-member committee's scope includes: 1) Banks and banking, including deposit insurance and federal monetary policy. 2) Money and credit, including currency and the issuance of notes and redemption thereof; gold and silver, including the coinage thereof; valuation and revaluation of the dollar. 3) Urban development. 4) Public and private housing. 5) Economic stabilization, defense production, renegotiation, and control of the price of commodities, rents and services. 6) International finance. 7) Financial aid to commerce and industry (other than transportation). 8) International financial and monetary organizations.

The Chairman and Ranking Minority Member are ex officio members of all subcommittees.

Chairman..... Rep. Fernand J. St Germain, D-R.I.
Ranking minority member..... Rep. Chalmers P. Wylie, R-Ohio

Majority Staff
2129 Rayburn House Office Building.....................................(202) 225-4247
Clerk and Staff Director..... Dr. Paul Nelson ....(202) 225-7057

Minority Staff
B-301C Rayburn House Office Building ....(202) 225-7502
Staff Director..... Robert Ruddy.......................................(202) 225-7502

Subcommittee on Consumer Affairs and Coinage

Chairman..... Rep. Frank Annunzio, D-Ill.
Ranking minority member..... Rep. John P. Hiler, R-Ind.

Staff Director..... Curtis Prins...........................212 Annex 1   (202) 226-3280

Source: Congressional Staff Directory

Federal Bureau of Investigation

Ninth St. and Pennsylvania Ave. NW, Washington, D.C. 20535; Phone (202) 324-3444

The Federal Bureau of Investigation (FBI) is a division of the Department of Justice, headed by the Attorney General. Robert M. Gates was nominated Feb. 2, 1987, to replace William H. Webster as FBI Director after Webster was nominated as CIA Director.

The FBI is charged with investigating all violations of federal laws with the exception of those which have been assigned by legislative enactment or otherwise to some other federal agency.

The FBI's jurisdiction includes a wide range of responsibilities in the criminal, civil, and security fields. Among these are major numismatic thefts, extortion, bank robbery, and interstate transportation of stolen property. Cooperative services of the FBI for other duly authorized law enforcement agencies include fingerprint identification, laboratory services, police training and the National Crime Information Center.

Field Divisions — Federal Bureau of Investigation

Division	Address	Office Phone
Albany, N.Y. 12207	502 U.S. Post Office and Courthouse.......	(518) 465-7551
Albuquerque, N. Mex. 87102 ..	301 Grand Ave. NE	(505) 247-1555
Alexandria, Va. 22314	300 N. Lee St.	(703) 683-2680
Anchorage, Alaska 99513......	701 C. St...........................	(907) 276-4441
Atlanta, Ga. 30303	275 Peachtree St. NE	(404) 521-3900
Baltimore, Md. 21207	7142 Ambassador Rd.	(301) 265-8080
Birmingham, Ala. 35203	Room 1400, 2121 Building	(205) 252-7705
Boston, Mass. 02203..........	John F. Kennedy Federal Office Bldg.......	(617) 742-5533
Buffalo, N.Y. 14202	111 W. Huron St.	(716) 856-7800

Division	Address	Office Phone
Butte, Mont. 59701	U.S. Courthouse and Federal Bldg.	(406) 782-2304
Charlotte, N.C. 28202	6010 Kenley Lane.	(704) 529-1030
Chicago, Ill. 60604	Everett McKinley Dirksen Federal Office Bldg.	(312) 431-1333
Cincinnati, Ohio 45202	550 Main St.	(513) 421-4310
Cleveland, Ohio 44199	1240 E. 9th St.	(216) 522-1400
Columbia, S.C. 29201	1529 Hampton St.	(803) 254-3011
Dallas, Tex. 75202	1801 N. Lamar	(214) 741-1851
Denver, Colo. 80202	Federal Office Bldg.	(303) 629-7171
Detroit, Mich. 48226	Patrick V. McNamara Federal Office Bldg.	(313) 965-2323
El Paso, Tex. 79901	202 U.S. Courthouse Bldg.	(915) 533-7451
Honolulu, Hawaii 96850	Kalanianaole Federal Office Bldg.	(808) 521-1411
Houston, Tex. 77002	515 Rusk Ave.	(713) 224-1511
Indianapolis, Ind. 46204	575 N. Pennsylvania St.	(317) 639-3301
Jackson, Miss. 39201	100 W. Capitol St.	(601) 948-5000
Jacksonville, Fla. 32211	7820 Arlington Expressway	(904) 721-1211
Kansas City, Mo. 64106	300 U.S. Courthouse Bldg.	(816) 221-6100
Knoxville, Tenn. 37919	1111 Northshore Dr.	(615) 588-8571
Las Vegas, Nev. 89101	Room 219, Federal Office Bldg., Las Vegas Blvd.	(702) 385-1281
Little Rock, Ark. 72201	215 U.S. Post Office Bldg.	(501) 372-7211
Los Angeles, Calif. 90024	11000 Wilshire Blvd.	(213) 477-6565
Louisville, Ky. 40202	600 Federal Pl.	(502) 583-3941
Memphis, Tenn. 38103	167 N. Main St.	(901) 525-7373
Miami, Fla. 33137	3801 Biscayne Blvd.	(305) 573-3333
Milwaukee, Wis. 53202	517 E. Wisconsin Ave.	(414) 276-4684
Minneapolis, Minn. 55401	392 Federal Bldg.	(612) 339-7861
Mobile, Ala. 36602	U.S. Courthouse, 113 St. Joseph St.	(205) 438-3674
Newark, N.J. 07101	Gateway 1, Market St.	(201) 622-5613
New Haven, Conn. 06510	150 Court St.	(203) 777-6311
New Orleans, La. 70113	701 Loyola Ave.	(504) 522-4671
New York, N.Y. 10278	26 Federal Plaza	(212) 553-2700
Norfolk, Va. 23510	200 Granby Mall	(804) 623-3111
Oklahoma City, Okla. 73118	50 Penn Pl.	(405) 842-7471
Omaha, Nebr. 68102	215 N. 17th St.	(402) 348-1210
Philadelphia, Pa. 19106	600 Arch St.	(215) 829-2700
Phoenix, Ariz. 85004	2721 N. Central Ave.	(602) 279-5511
Pittsburgh, Pa. 15222	1000 Liberty Ave.	(412) 471-2000
Portland, Ore. 97201	Crown Plaza Bldg., 500 SW First Ave.	(503) 224-4181
Quantico, Va. 22135	FBI Academy.	(703) 640-6131
Richmond, Va. 23220	200 W. Grace St.	(804) 644-2631
Sacramento, Calif. 95825	2800 Cottage Way.	(916) 481-9110
St. Louis, Mo. 63103	1520 Market St.	(314) 241-5357
Salt Lake City, Utah 84138	125 S. State St.	(801) 355-7521
San Antonio, Tex. 78206	615 E. Houston	(512) 225-6741
San Diego, Calif. 92188	880 Front St.	(619) 231-1122
San Francisco, Calif. 94102	450 Golden Gate Ave.	(415) 553-7400
San Juan, P.R. 00918	Room 526, U.S. Courthouse and Federal Office Bldg., Hato Rey, P.R.	(780) 754-6000
Savannah, Ga. 31405	5401 Paulsen St.	(912) 354-9911
Seattle, Wash. 98174	Room 710, 915 Second Ave., Federal Office Bldg.	(206) 622-0460
Springfield, Ill. 62702	535 W. Jefferson St.	(217) 522-9675
Tampa, Fla. 33602	Room 610, 500 Zack St., Federal Office Bldg.	(813) 228-7661
Washington, D.C. 20401	1900 Half St. SW.	(202) 324-3000

Source: U.S. Federal Directory

Federal Trade Commission

Pennsylvania Ave. at 6th St. NW, Washington, D.C. 20580. Phone (202) 523-3711

Chairman . . . . Daniel Oliver
Commissioner . . . . Terry Calvani
Commissioner . . . . Mary Azcuenaga
Commissioner . . . . Patricia P. Bailey
Commissioner . . . . Andrew Strenio
Secretary . . . . Emily H Rock
General Counsel . . . . Robert Paul
Executive Director . . . . Winston Moore
Director, Office of Public Affairs . . . . Richard McGowan
Bureau of Consumer Protection (Hobby Protection Act
  enforcement) Director . . . . William MacLeod

The Federal Trade Commission was organized as an independent administrative agency in 1951, pursuant to the Federal Trade Commission Act of 1914.

The basic objective of the Commission is the maintenance of strongly competitive enterprise as the keystone of the American economic system. Although the duties of the Commission are many and varied under law, the foundation of public policy underlying all these duties is essentially the same: to prevent the free enterprise system from being stifled, substantially lessened or fettered by monopoly or restraints on trade, or corrupted by unfair or deceptive trade practices.

In brief, the Commission is charged with keeping competition both free and fair. Part of the FTC's responsibility is the enforcement of the Hobby Protection Act (See Chapter 3 for details).

This basic purpose finds its primary expression in the Federal Trade Commission Act, cited above, and the Clayton Act, both passed in 1914 and both successively amended in the years that have followed. The Federal Trade Commission Act lays down a general prohibition against the use in commerce of "unfair methods of competition" and "unfair or deceptive acts or practices." The Clayton Act outlaws specific practices recognized as instruments of monopoly.

As an administrative agency, acting quasi-judicially and quasi-legislatively, the Commission was established to deal with trade practices on a continuing and corrective basis. It has no authority to punish; its function is to prevent, through cease-and-desist orders and other means, those practices condemned by the law of federal trade regulation; however, court-ordered civil penalties up to $10,000 may be obtained for each violation of a commission order.

Sources of information

PUBLICATIONS

A copy of the "Federal Trade Commission — List of Publications," which lists publications of interest to the general public, is available free upon application to the Division of Legal and Public Records, Federal Trade Commission, Washington, D.C. 20580.

CONSUMER PROTECTION, RESTRAINT OF TRADE INFORMATION, AND COMPLAINTS

For information about consumer protection, restraint of trade questions, or to register a complaint, should contact the nearest Federal Trade Commission office.

FEDERAL TRADE COMMISSION REGIONAL OFFICES
Telephone and Address Listings

ATLANTA, 1718 Peachtree St. NW., Atlanta, Ga. 30367. Phone (404) 881-4836. Serves Alabama, Florida, Georgia, Mississippi, North Carolina, South Carolina, Tennessee, Virginia.

BOSTON, 150 Causeway St., Boston, Mass. 02114. Phone (617) 223-6621. Serves Connecticut, Maine, Massachusetts, New Hampshire, Rhode Island, Vermont.

CHICAGO, 55 E. Monroe St., Chicago, Ill. 60603. Phone (312) 353-4423. Serves Illinois, Indiana, Iowa, Kentucky, Minnesota, Missouri, Wisconsin.

CLEVELAND, 118 St. Clair Ave., Cleveland, Ohio 44144. Phone (216) 522-4207. Serves Michigan, western New York, Ohio, Pennsylvania, West Virginia, Delaware, Maryland.

DALLAS, 8303 Elmbrook Dr., Dallas, Texas 75247. Phone (214) 767-7050. Serves Arkansas, Louisiana, New Mexico, Oklahoma, Texas.

DENVER, 1405 Curtis St., Denver, Colo. 80202. Phone (303) 844-2271. Serves Colorado, Kansas, Montana, Nebraska, North Dakota, South Dakota, Utah, Wyoming.
LOS ANGELES, 11000 Wilshire Blvd., Los Angeles, Calif. 90024. Phone (213) 209-7575. Serves Arizona, southern California.
NEW YORK, 26 Federal Plaza, New York, N.Y. 10007. Phone (212) 264-1207. Serves New Jersey, eastern New York.
SAN FRANCISCO, 450 Golden Gate Ave., San Francisco, Calif. 94102. Phone (415) 556-1270. Serves northern California, Hawaii, Nevada.

SEATTLE, 915 Second Ave., Seattle, Wash. 98174. Phone (206) 442-4655. Serves Alaska, Idaho, Oregon, Washington.

HONOLULU Field Station, 300 Ala Moana Blvd., Honolulu, Hawaii 96850. Phone (808) 546-5685.

For further information, contact the Director, Office of Public Affairs, Federal Trade Commission, Pennsylvania Avenue at Sixth Street NW., Washington, D.C. 20580. Phone (202) 523-3830.

General Services Administration
General Services Bldg., 18th and F streets NW, Washington, D.C. 20405
Phone (202) 566-1231

Administrator of General Services............................... Terence C. Golden
18th and F streets NW, Washington, D.C. 20405, Phone (202) 566-1212
Acting Archivist of the United States............................. Dr. Frank G. Burke
Acting Deputy Archivist of the United States..................... Claudine K. Weiher

The General Services Administration (GSA) establishes policy and provides an economical and efficient system for the management of the government's property and records, including construction and operation of buildings, procurement and distribution of supplies, utilization and disposal of property, transportation, traffic, and communications management, stockpiling of strategic materials, and the management of the government-wide resources program.

Numismatically, the GSA is best known for its sales of precious metals. Beginning in April 1968, and continuing through November 1970, the GSA sold silver on the market of varying fineness and amounts.

The same law authorizing the Eisenhower dollar, signed Dec. 31, 1970, authorized the GSA to sell the 2.9 million silver dollars in the vaults of the Treasury. The Carson City specimens went on sale on a bid basis beginning Oct. 31, 1972, and continued through Oct. 31, 1973. In 1980, the GSA administered a sale of nearly 1 million Carson City silver dollars. On Oct. 14, 1981, the GSA began weekly sales of 1.25 million troy ounces of silver from the National Defense Strategic and Critical Materials Stockpile in the form of 1,000-ounce bars, with expected total disposal of 46.5 million ounces (see SILVER CHRONOLOGY, Chapter 13).

In early 1984, Congress attempted several times to pass legislation authorizing the use of stockpile silver for future coinage but was unsuccessful. What followed was a series of bills that mandated the use of stockpile silver in such coins as the George Washington commemorative, issued in 1982 and the silver dollar coin issued to mark the 1984 Olympic Games in Los Angeles.

Then in 1986, the Ellis Island silver dollar was issued to mark the 100th anniversary of the Statue of Liberty. Authorizing legislation allowed for 10 million of the coins to be issued. Included in that legislation was authorization for a 1-ounce silver bullion dollar coin to be issued later that year.

Both coins were mandated to use stockpile silver but while the Ellis Island coin was released for a limited time the bullion coin, later named the American Eagle, has an unlimited mintage. As of April 1987, 5.3 million Uncirculated silver bullion coins had been issued and 1.4 million Proof silver bullion coins were struck. The open-ended program could provide an even larger decrease in the stockpile.

In mid-1987, the Mint released a silver Bicentennial of the Constitution coin, also mandated to use stockpile silver. Congress authorized 10 million of the commemorative coins to be struck.

GSA consists of operating services and supporting staff offices, with functions carried out at three levels of organization: the central office, regional offices, and field activities. Operations are administered largely by the regional and field offices.

The General Services Administration was established by Section 101 of the Federal Property and Administrative Services Act of 1949, effective July 1, 1949. The act consolidated and transferred to the agency a variety of real and personal property and related functions formerly assigned to various agencies. Subsequent laws and executive orders assigned other related functions and programs.

National Archives and Records Service

The Declaration of Independence, the Constitution, and the Bill of Rights, as well as other exhibits depicting the history of the nation, are on display for visitors to the National Archives Building.

Functions and activities

ARCHIVAL PROGRAM

The National Archives and Records Service (NARS), performs a variety of functions relating to the preservation, use, and disposition of the records of the U.S. Government. In the National Archives Building and regional branches, NARS preserves and makes available for further government use and for private research the nation's records of enduring value, both textual and audiovisual.

Among its other activities are the administration of a regional network of storage-type facilities for non-archival records, operation of the Presidential library system and a government records management program, and publication of legislative, regulatory, and other widely used materials.

In addition to furnishing information about the nature and extent of the records in the custody of the Archivist and the conditions under which they may be used, NARS also supplies data from the records themselves. Persons who come to the National Archives Building and the Archives branches in the regional records centers to use the records are assisted in every way possible. Insofar as personnel are available, guides, inventories, lists, and indexes are prepared and they are made available. A trained reference staff is ready to aid researchers in finding and using the material desired. NARS is equipped to provide photographs, photostats, or microfilm copies of documents to investigators.

RECORDS MANAGEMENT

NARS maintains liaison with federal agencies to improve the management and the quality of records created by the government; to facilitate prompt and orderly disposition of inactive records; and to improve the usefulness of those that may be offered to the Archivist for preservation.

Upon request, advice and technical assistance is given on organizing records management programs and establishing schedules and procedures for the retirement of records no longer needed currently. Evaluations of the record creation, maintenance, and disposition practices of federal agencies are made and agencies may request guidance and assistance in their paperwork problems.

FEDERAL RECORDS CENTERS

Federal Records Centers are maintained to store and service noncurrent records of federal agencies and historically valuable regional records of the National Archives of the United States. Federal Records Centers also provide reimbursable microfilming service for federal agencies.

PUBLISHING LAWS AND PRESIDENTIAL DOCUMENTS

Federal legislation consists of both the acts of Congress and "regulations" which government agencies have issued under authority delegated by the Congress. Acts of Congress are published immediately upon issuance in slip law form and are cumulated and published for each session of Congress in the "United States Statutes at Large."

All current Presidential proclamations and Executive orders and regulations of government agencies having general applicability and legal effect are published in the *Federal Register* which appears five times a week. At least annually, all regulations in force are published in codified form in the Code of Federal Regulations.

Presidential speeches, news conferences, messages, and other materials made public by the White House are published currently in the "Weekly Compilation of Presidential Documents" and annually in the "Public Papers of the Presidents." Further information on federal agencies is provided in the annual United States Government Manual.

PRESIDENTIAL LIBRARIES

The libraries preserve, describe, and render reference service on Presidential papers and collections, prepare documentary and descriptive publications and exhibit historic documents and museum items.

For general information on Presidential libraries, contact: Dr. James E. O'Neill, Assistant Archivist for Presidential Libraries, Room 104, 7th and Pennsylvania Ave., NW, Washington, D.C. 20408

Herbert Hoover Library, Parkside Drive, Box 488, West Branch, Ia. 52358. Phone (319) 643-5301. Director: Robert S. Wood.

Franklin D. Roosevelt Library, 259 Albany Post Road, Hyde Park, N.Y. 12538. Phone (914) 229-8835. Director: Dr. William R. Emerson.

Harry S. Truman Library, Independence, Mo. 64050. Phone (816) 833-1400. Director: Dr. Benedict K. Zorbrist.

Dwight D. Eisenhower Library, Abilene, Kan. 67410. Phone (913) 263-4751. Director: Dr. John E. Wickman.

John F. Kennedy Library, Columbia Point, Boston, Mass. 02125. Phone (617) 929-4500. Acting Director: John Stewart.

Lyndon Baines Johnson Library, 2313 Red River St., Austin, Tex. 78705. Phone (512) 482-5137. Director: Harry J. Middleton.

Gerald R. Ford Library, 1000 Beal Avenue, Ann Arbor, Mich. 48109. Phone (313) 668-2218. Director: Dr. Don W. Wilson.

Gerald R. Ford Museum, 303 Pearl St., NW, Grand Rapids, Mich. 49504. Phone (616) 456-2675.

Nixon Presidential Materials Staff, Office of Presidential Libraries, National Archives, Washington D.C. 20408. Phone (703) 756-6498. Deputy Director: James J. Hastings.

Jimmy Carter Library, One Copenhill Ave., Atlanta, Ga. 30307. Phone (404) 331-3942. Director: Dr. Donald B. Schewe.

Sources of information

Inquiries for information on the following subjects should be directed to the specified office, General Services Administration, Washington, D.C. 20405.

READING ROOMS

Facilities for inspecting and copying documents are available at the Business Service Centers.

Archives and other historical material for research purposes are available at the National Archives Building, 7th Street and Pennsylvania Avenue NW, Washington, D.C.; at the Presidential Libraries; and the national and regional Federal Records Centers. Requests for additional information should be directed to the Central Information Division (NNC), mailing address: General Services Administration (NNC), Washington, D.C. 20408. Phone (201) 523-3141.

FILMS

The National Audiovisual Center has motion pictures, film strips, slide sets, and video and audio tapes available to schools, educational, civic, and community groups on a sale, rental, or free distribution basis, depending on the particular film. The subject matter includes vocational training, educational, documentary, and military films, made for and by government agencies. Requests for additional information should be directed to the National Audiovisual Center, Washington, D.C. 20409. Phone (301) 763-1860.

PUBLICATIONS

The National Archives has many publications of interest to the public. For a list, request the "General Information Leaflet No. 3, Publications of the National Archives and Records Service" from the Publications Sales Branch (NEPS), General Services Administration (NEPS), Washington, D.C. 20408.

For further information concerning the General Services Administration, contact the Director of Information, General Services Administration, Washington, D.C. 20405. Phone (202) 566-1231.

Government Printing Office

N. Capitol and H streets NW, Washington, D.C. 20401, Phone (202) 783-3238

Public Printer . . . . Ralph Kennickel

The Government Printing Office (GPO) began operations in accordance with Congressional Joint Resolution 25 of June 23, 1860. The activities of the Government Printing Office are outlined and defined in the Act of Oct. 22, 1968, as amended.

The congressional Joint Committee on Printing acts as the board of directors of the Government Printing Office. The Public Printer is required by law to be a practical printer versed in the art of bookbinding and is appointed by the President with the advice and consent of the Senate.

The Government Printing Office executes

orders for printing and binding placed by Congress and the departments and establishments of the federal government. It furnishes blank paper, inks, and similar supplies to all governmental activities on order. It prepares catalogs and distributes and sells government publications.

The Annual Report of the Director of the Mint, and other Mint and Treasury Department publications are available from the GPO.

GPO invites bids from commercial suppliers on a wide variety of printing and binding services, awards and administers contracts, and maintains liaison between ordering agencies and contractors.

Printing and binding processes used are electronic photocomposition; linotype, monotype and hand composition; letterpress printing and photopolymer platemaking; offset photography, stripping, platemaking, and press; and manual and machine bookbinding.

GPO sells through mail orders and government bookstores nearly 20,000 different publications which originated in various government agencies, and administers the depository library program through which selected government publications are made available in libraries throughout the country.

Sources of information

CONTRACTS

Printing and binding enterprises should direct inquiries to the Manager, Printing Procurement Department, Government Printing Office, Washington, D.C. 20401, or contact the GPO Regional Printing Procurement Office in the following cities: Atlanta, Boston, Chicago, Columbus, Dallas, Denver, Hampton, Va., Los Angeles, New York, Philadelphia, St. Louis, San Francisco, Seattle, or Washington, D.C.

Suppliers of paper and kindred products; printing and binding equipment, related parts, and supplies; purchasers of scrap, or surplus printing and binding equipment, waste, and salvage materials; and freight carriers should contact the Director of Materials Management, Government Printing Office, Washington, D.C. 20401.

A booklet, "How to Do Business with the Government Printing Office, A Guide for Contractors" is available on request from any of the offices above.

EMPLOYMENT

Office of Personnel Management registers are used in filling administrative, technical and clerical positions. College recruitment is directed toward filling positions in printing management and general administration. Inquiries should be directed to Government Printing Office, Chief, Employment Branch, Washington, D.C. 20401. Phone (202) 275-2476.

PUBLICATIONS

Orders and inquiries concerning publications for sale by the Government Printing Office should be directed to the Assistant Public Printer (Superintendent of Documents), Government Printing Office, Washington, D.C. 20402. Phone (202) 783-3238.

The "GPO Sales Publications Reference File (PRF)" provides author, title and subject access to government publications available for sale through the Superintendent of Documents. Issued in bimonthly microfiche editions, it is available as a subscription from the Superintendent of Documents.

The "Monthly Catalog of U.S. Government Publications" is the most comprehensive listing of government publications issued by federal departments and agencies. It is available as a subscription from the Superintendent of Documents.

Remittance for all publications ordered from the Superintendent of Documents must be received in advance of shipment by check or money order payable to the Superintendent of Documents. Orders may also be charged to MasterCard or VISA accounts.

A list of depository libraries is available from the Assistant Public Printer (Superintendent of Documents).

Popular government publications may be purchased at the GPO bookstores listed below.

Washington, D.C.:
Main Bookstore, 710 N. Capitol St.
Commerce Department, 4th & E Sts. NW
HHS, 330 Independence Ave. SW
Retail Sales Branch, 8660 Cherry Lane, Laurel, Md.
Pentagon Building, Main Concourse
State Department, 21st & C Sts. NW
Atlanta, Ga.:
Room 100, Federal Bldg., Box 56445, 275 Peachtree St. NE, 30343. Phone (404) 221-6947
Birmingham, Ala.:
9220-B Parkway East, 35206. Phone (205) 254-1056
Boston, Mass.:
Room G25, John F. Kennedy Federal Bldg., Sudbury Street, 02203. Phone (617) 223-6071
Chicago, Ill.:
Room 1365, Everett McKinley Dirksen Building, 219 S. Dearborn St., 60604. Phone (312) 353-5133
Cleveland, Ohio:
Federal Office Bldg., 1240 E. Ninth St., 44199. Phone (216) 522-4922
Columbus, Ohio:
Room 207, Federal Office Bldg., 200 N. High St., 43215. Phone (614) 469-6956
Dallas, Tex.:
Room IC50, Federal Bldg.-U.S. Courthouse, 1100 Commerce St., 75242. Phone (214) 767-0076

Denver, Colo.:
Room 117, Federal Bldg., 1961 Stout St., 80294. Phone (303) 844-3964

Detroit, Mich.:
Patrick V. McNamara Federal Bldg., 477 Michigan Ave., 48226. Phone (313) 226-7816

Houston, Texas:
9319 Gulf Freeway, 77017. Phone (713) 229-3515

Jacksonville, Fla.:
Room 158, Federal Bldg., 400 W. Bay St., 32202. Phone (904) 791-3801

Kansas City, Mo.:
Room 120, Bannister Mall, 5600 E. Bannister Road, 64137. Phone (816) 765-2256

Los Angeles, Calif.:
ARCO Plaza, C Level, 505 S. Flower St., 90071. Phone (213) 688-5841

Milwaukee Wis.:
Room 190, Federal Bldg., 517 E. Wisconsin Ave., 53202. Phone (414) 291-1304

New York, N.Y.:
Room 110, Federal Building, 26 Federal Plaza, 10278. Phone (212) 264-3825

Philadelphia, Pa.:
Room 1214, Federal Office Bldg., 600 Arch St., 19106. Phone (215) 597-0677

Pittsburgh, Pa.:
Room 118, Federal Office Bldg., 1000 Liberty Ave., 15222. Phone (412) 644-2721

Pueblo, Colo.:
720 N. Main St., 81003. Phone (303) 544-3142

San Francisco, Calif.:
Room 1023, Federal Office Bldg., 450 Golden Gate Ave., 94102. Phone (415) 556-0643

For further information, contact the Customer Service Manager, Government Printing Office, North Capitol & H Sts. NW, Washington, D.C. 20401. Phone (202) 275-3238.

Numismatics and the Law

3

Edited by David L. Ganz

David L. Ganz, a special correspondent and columnist for COIN WORLD since 1974, is an attorney admitted to practice in New York, New Jersey and Washington, D.C. He has developed a specialty in coinage law and its subsidiary aspects. He is in private practice as managing partner of Ganz, Hollinger & Towe, P.C., 1394 Third Avenue, New York, New York 10021.

Ganz has served as legislative counsel since 1978 to the American Numismatic Association. Since 1985, Ganz has served as an elected governor of the ANA. He has been general counsel to the Professional Numismatists Guild Inc. since 1981. The research assistance of Timothy Garrett, a doctor of law candidate at St. John's University Law School, and clerk for Ganz, Hollinger & Towe, Professional Corporation, is acknowledged with thanks. The assistance of Barbara Parrotto, executive assistant at Ganz & Sivin, P.A., in the preparation of this manuscript is deeply appreciated.

INTRODUCTION

Numismatics and the law is a fairly broad field. When the first edition of *Coin World Almanac* was published in 1975, this chapter largely consisted of a listing of recent numismatic laws and bills, statutory authority for coinage, the advisory policies of the Treasury Department, and a listing of the contents of title 18 of the Criminal Code (counterfeiting) Title 31 (governing coinage and gold) and a listing of laws authorizing medals.

Changes in the following edition, published in 1976, reflected a major change in the way government dealt with collectors, because it involved a change in coin designs for the Bicentennial of U.S. Independence and also took into account the regulatory effect of the Hobby Protection Act.

Starting with the third edition, published in 1977, the number of features began to crop up with my editorship of this chapter. Many new laws were passed, of course, and by the time that the 1984 *Almanac* was published, there was considerable information concerning the amendment to all of Title 31 (now enacted as positive law) and increased government regulation in the coin field.

The year 1987 is an equally exciting field for numismatics and the law. First, Congress has enacted a number of bills that have an intense impact on the coin field. Second, regulatory agency activity has been heightened in ways that will affect all collectors, investors and dealers. Third, the need for information in the field is still scanty, except for publications like the *Coin World Almanac*.

Potential users of the chapter concerning numismatics and the law should be aware that certain legal shorthands are utilized, just as they are by the U.S. Mint itself, which for many years has utilized the phrase "do." to stand for ditto in its annual reports. Abbreviations will be explained the first time that they are used in order to avoid confusion. A more complete explanation can be found in various legal style publications available in most public libraries.

It is impossible, within the scope of a chapter, to cover everything that ought to be found in "Numismatics and the Law." It would be ideal to be able to list, for example, every bill introduced in Congress in the last 25 years that relates to coins. The problem is that in each Congress, more than 25,000 bills are introduced in the House of Representatives alone. Perhaps as many as 200-300 relate to coins, medals, gold, silver or other assorted topics in which researchers might have an interest in. The Senate has a comparable number.

By contrast, perhaps a half dozen to a dozen bills each year that have a direct impact on the coinage field go on to hearings or some type of staff report. These have been noted and annotated because of their important historical use. So have the hearings themselves, which provide a serial or chronicle of what has transpired in the field of coinage law over the decades.

All of the material contained in this chapter is designed for desk top analysis, and a quick answer. It is not designed for in-depth analysis. For the first time, however, this chapter does list bibliographic sources, where appropriate, so that interested researchers can locate more definitive and additional information. Most of the resources referred to are available in larger public libraries, at colleges or universities with federal depositories for government documents or in larger law libraries.

United States Code, Title 31

The coinage laws of the United States, for many years, were uncodified. The Coinage Act of 1873 was the first attempt to codify existing law, and in many instances (for example, the elimination of the 2-cent piece, and the demonetization of the Trade dollar) changed existing law extensively. The Revised Statutes of 1874-1878 actually constituted the first serious revision of the minting and coinage laws, and for a century that followed, these were the official versions that were referred to. Elsewhere, a correlation table notes what became of the various sections of the revised statute as pertains to contemporary numismatics. Interestingly enough, some of the sections in the revised statute, and indeed in the laws of today, actually date back to the United States' founding when, for example, Congress first debated the designs that ought to be on the coinage of the United States.

Back in March 1792, the House of Representatives debated the possible use of the portrait of the president appearing on the coinage "with an inscription which shall express the initial or first letter of his Christian or first name, and his surname at length, and the year of coinage; and upon the reverse . . . the figure or representation of an eagle with the inscription "United States of America. . . ." [3 Annals of Congress 1348 (1792).] What emerged as Sec. 10 of the original Mint Act was an "impression emblematic of liberty with an inscription of the word Liberty and the year of coinage." On the reverse, of course, precious metal coinage was required to bear the figure of an eagle in addition to an imprimatur of national origin.

This ultimately became Sec. 18 of the Coinage Act of 1873, Sec. 3517 of the revised statutes, and later, in uncodified form, was known as 31 USC 324.

The relevance of this section, in 1987, can be seen in modest calls that have been made for changing and revamping the designs that appear on U.S. coinage, governed by this section, now know as 31 USC 5112(b)(1) and another section which permits the Secretary of the Treasury to change the design or die of a coin only once every 25 years. This came from the Coinage Act of Sept. 26, 1890, not found in the Revised Statutes, and later located in 31USC 276 [today 31 USC 5112(d)(2)].

These are the very sections that will have to be considered by the Secretary of the Treasury, or if he declines to exercise his mandate, by Congress, in making any design alterations.

Starting in the 97th session of Congress, a proposal was advanced to revise, codify and enact without substant to change certain general and permanent laws relative to money and finance as Title 31 of the United States Code. The bill, H.R. 6128, in its final form, and H.R. 4774 in its earlier version, was reported on as H.R. Rep. No. 97-651, and ultimately became Public Law 97-258, approved by President Reagan Sept. 13, 1982.

Section 4(a) of Public Law 97-258, 96 Stat. 1067, provided that "sections 1-3 of this Act [encompassing all of the money and finance and coinage laws] restate, without substant of change, laws enacted before April 16, 1982, that were replaced by those sections. Those sections may not be construed as making a substant of change in the laws replaced. Laws enacted after April 16, 1982, that are inconsistent with this Act supersede this Act to the extent of the inconsistency." To the extent that there are any outstanding order, rules or regulations that precede the codification in terms of time, Sec. 4(c) of the Act provides that they shall remain "in effect under the corresponding provision enacted by this Act until repealed, amended, or superseded."

Unlike earlier versions of the United States Code, Title 31 in now considered to be positive law. That means that each section, as stated, is the law itself, rather than an interpretation of it.

United States Code, Title 31

Following are some important excerpts from U.S. Code, Title 31, "Money and Finance," as applicable to numismatics. Sections not dealing with numismatics have been omitted.

Sec. 301. Department of the Treasury

(a) The Department of the Treasury is an executive department of the United States government at the seat of the government.

(b) The head of the department is the Secretary of the Treasury. The Secretary is appointed by the president, by and with the advice and consent of the Senate.. . .

. . .(c) The department shall have a seal.

Sec. 302. Treasury of the United States

The United States government has a Treasury of the United States. The Treasury is in the Department of the Treasury.

Sec. 303. Bureau of Engraving and Printing

(a) The Bureau of Engraving and Printing is a bureau in the Department of the Treasury.

(b) The head of the Bureau is the Director of the Bureau of Engraving and Printing appointed by the Secretary of the Treasury. The Director —

(1) shall carry out duties and powers prescribed by the Secretary; and

(2) reports directly to the Secretary.

Sec. 304. Bureau of the Mint

(a) The Bureau of the Mint is a bureau in the Department of the Treasury.

(b)(1) The head of the Bureau is the Director of the Mint. The Director is appointed by the president, by and with the advice and consent of the Senate. The term of the Director is five years. The president may remove the Director from office. On removal, the president shall send a message to the Senate giving the reasons for removal.

(2) The Director shall carry out duties and powers prescribed by the Secretary of the Treasury.

Sec. 307. Office of the Comptroller of the Currency

The Office of the Comptroller of the Currency, established under Section 324 of the Revised Statues (12 U.S.C. 1), is an office in the Department of the Treasury.

Sec. 308. United States Customs Service

The United States Customs Service, established under Section 1 of the Act of March 3, 1927 (19 U.S.C. 2071), is a service in the Department of the Treasury.

Sec. 309. Continuing in office

When the term of an office of the Department of the Treasury ends, the officer may continue to serve until a successor is appointed and qualified.

Administrative

Sec. 321. General authority of the Secretary

(a) The Secretary of the Treasury shall —

— issue warrants for money drawn on the Treasury consistent with appropriations;

— mint coins, engrave and print currency and security documents, and refine and assay bullion, and may strike medals;. . .

b) The Secretary may —

(1) prescribe regulations to carry out the duties and powers of the Secretary;

(2) delegate duties and powers of the Secretary to another officer or employee of the Department of the Treasury; . . .

Sec. 331. Reports

— The Secretary of the Treasury shall submit to Congress each year an annual report.

— The Secretary shall report to either House of Congress in person or in writing, as required, on matters referred to the Secretary by that House of Congress.

Sec. 3301. General duties of the Secretary of the Treasury

(a) The Secretary of the Treasury shall —

(1) receive and keep public money;

(2) take receipts for money paid out by the Secretary;

(3) give receipts for money deposited in the Treasury;

(4) endorse warrants for receipts for money deposited in the Treasury;

(5) submit the accounts of the Secretary to the Comptroller General every three months, or more often if required by the Comptroller General; and

(6) submit to inspection at any time by the Comptroller General of money in the possession of the Secretary.

Sec. 3327. General authority to issue checks and other drafts

The Secretary of the Treasury may issue a check or other draft on public money in the Treasury to pay an obligation of the United States government. When the Secretary decides it is convenient to a public creditor and in the public interest, the Secretary may designate a depositary to issue a check or other draft on public money held by the depositary to pay an obligation of the government. As directed by the Secretary, each depositary shall report to the Secretary on public money paid and received by the depositary.

Monetary system

Sec. 5101. Decimal system

United States money is expressed in dollars, dimes or tenths, cents or hundredths, and mills or thousandths. A dime is a tenth of a dollar, a cent is a hundredth of a dollar, and a mill is a thousandth of a dollar.

Sec. 5102. Standard weight

The standard troy pound of the National Bureau of Standards of the Department of Commerce shall be the standard used to ensure that the weight of the United States coins conforms to specifications in Section 5112 of this title.

Sec. 5103. Legal tender

United States coins and currency (including Federal reserve notes and circulating notes of Federal reserve banks and national banks) are legal tender for all debts, public charges, taxes, and dues. Foreign gold or silver coins are not legal tender for debts.

General Authority

Sec. 5111. Minting and issuing coins, medals, and numismatic items

(a) The Secretary of the Treasury—

(1) shall mint and issue coins described in Section 5112 of this title in amounts the Secretary decides are necessary to meet the needs of the United States;

(2) may prepare national medal dies and strike national and other medals if it does not interfere with regular minting operations but may not prepare private medal dies;

(3) may prepare and distribute numismatic items; and

(4) may mint coins for a foreign country if the minting does not interfere with regular minting operations, and shall prescribe a charge for minting the foreign coins equal to the cost of the minting (including labor, materials, and the use of machinery).

(b) The Department of the Treasury has a coinage metal fund and a coinage profit fund. The Secretary may use the coinage metal fund to buy metal to mint coins. The Secretary shall credit the coinage profit fund with the amount by which the nominal value of the coins minted from the metal exceeds the cost of the metal. The Secretary shall charge the coinage profit fund with waste incurred in minting coins and the cost of distributing the coins. The Secretary shall deposit in the Treasury as miscellaneous receipts excess amounts in the coinage profit fund.

(c) The Secretary may make contracts on conditions the Secretary decides are appropriate and in the public interest to acquire equipment, manufacturing facilities, patent rights, technical knowledge and assistance,

and materials necessary to produce rapidly an adequate supply of coins referred to in Section 5112(a)(1)—(4) of this title.

(d)(1) The Secretary may prohibit or limit the exportation, melting, or treatment of United States coins when the Secretary decides the prohibition or limitation is necessary to protect the coinage of the United States.

(2) A person knowingly violating an order or license issued or regulation prescribed under paragraph (1) of this subsection, shall be fined not more than $10,000, imprisoned not more than five years, or both.

(3) Coins exported, melted, or treated in violation of an order or license issued or regulation prescribed, and metal resulting from the melting or treatment, shall be forfeited to the United States government. . . .

Sec. 5112. Denominations, specifications, and design of coins

(1) a dollar coin that is 1.043 inches in diameter and weighs 8.1 grams.

(2) a half dollar coin that is 1.205 inches in diameter and weighs 11.34 grams.

(3) a quarter dollar coin is 0.955 inch in diameter and weighs 5.67 grams.

(4) a dime that is 0.705 inch in diameter and weighs 2.268 grams.

(5) a 5-cent coin that is 0.835 inch in diameter and weighs 5 grams.

(6) except as provided under subsection (c) of this section, a 1-cent coin that is 0.75 inch in diameter and weighs 3.11 grams.

(7) A fifty dollar gold coin that is 32.7 millimeters in diameter, weighs 33.931 grams, and contains one troy ounce of fine gold.

(8) A twenty-five dollar gold coin that is 27.0 millimeters in diameter, weighs 16.9666 grams, and contains one-half troy ounce of fine gold.

(9) A ten dollar gold coin that is 22.0 millimeters in diameter, weighs 8.483 grams, and contains one-fourth troy ounce of fine gold.

(10) A five dollar gold coin that is 16.5 millimeters in diameter, weighs 3.393 grams, and contains one-tenth troy ounce of fine gold.

(b) The dollar, half dollar, quarter dollar, and dime coins are clad coins with three layers of metal. The two identical outer layers are an alloy of 75 percent copper and 25 percent nickel. The inner layer is copper. The outer layers are metallurgically bonded to the inner layer and weight at least 30 percent of the weight of the coin. The 5-cent coin is an alloy of 75 percent copper and 25 percent nickel. In minting 5-cent coins, the Secretary shall use bars that vary not more than 2.5 percent from the percent of nickel required. Except as provided under subsection (c) of this section, the 1-cent coin is an alloy of 95 percent copper and 5 percent zinc. The specifications for alloys are by weight.

(c) The Secretary may prescribe the weight and the composition of copper and zinc in the alloy of the 1-cent coin that the Secretary decides are appropriate when the Secretary decides that a different weight and alloy of copper and zinc are necessary to ensure an adequate supply of 1-cent coins to meet the needs of the United States.

(d)(1) United States coins have the inscription IN GOD WE TRUST. The obverse side of each coin has the inscription LIBERTY. The reverse side of each coin has the inscriptions UNITED STATES OF AMERICA and E PLURIBUS UNUM and a designation of the value of the coin. The design on the reverse side of the dollar, half dollar, and quarter dollar is an eagle. The eagle on the reverse side of the dollar is the symbolic eagle of Apollo 11 landing on the moon. The obverse side of the dollar has the likeness of Susan B. Anthony. The coins have an inscription of the year of minting or issuance. However, to prevent or alleviate a shortage of a denomination, the Secretary may inscribe coins of the denomination with the year that was last inscribed on coins of the denomination.

(2) The Secretary shall prepare the devices, models, hubs, and dies for coins, emblems, devices, inscriptions, and designs authorized under this chapter. The Secretary may adopt and prepare new designs or models of emblems or devices that are authorized in the same way as when new coins or devices are authorized. The Secretary may change the design or die of a coin only once within 25 years of the first adoption of the design, model, hub, or die for that coin. The Secretary may procure services under Section 3109 of Title 5 in carrying out this paragraph.

(e) Notwithstanding any other provision of law, the Secretary shall mint and issue, in quantities sufficient to meet public demand, coins which:

(1) are 40.6 millimeters in diameter and weigh 31.103 grams;

(2) contain .999 fine silver;

(3) have a design —

(A) symbolic of Liberty on the obverse side; and

(B) of an eagle on the reverse side;

(4) have inscriptions of the year of minting or issuance, and the words "Liberty", "In God We Trust", "United States of America",

"1 Oz. Fine Silver", "E Pluribus Unum", and "One Dollar"; and

(5) have reeded edges.

(f) The Secretary shall sell the coins minted under subsection (e) to the public at a price equal to the market value of the bullion at the time of sale, plus the cost of minting, marketing, and distributing such coins (including labor, materials, dies, use of machinery, and overhead expenses).

(g) For purposes of section 5132(a)(1) of this title, all coins minted under subsection (e) of this section shall be considered to be numismatic items.

(h) The coins issued under this title shall be legal tender as provided in section 5103 of title 31, United States Code.

(i) (1) Notwithstanding section 5111(a)(1) of this title, the Secretary shall mint and issue the gold coins described in paragraphs (7), (8), (9), and (10) of subsection (a) of this section, in quantities sufficient to meet public demand, and such gold coins shall —

(A) have a design determined by the Secretary, except that the fifty dollar gold coin shall have —

(i) on the obverse side, a design symbolic of Liberty; and

(ii) on the reverse side, a design representing a family of eagles, with the male carrying an olive branch and flying above a nest containing a female eagle and hatchlings;

(B) have inscriptions of the denomination, the weight of the fine gold content, the year of minting of issuance, and the words "Liberty", "In God We Trust", "United States of America", and "E Pluribus Unum"; and

(C) have reeded edges.

(2) (A) The Secretary shall sell the coins minted under this subsection to the public at a price equal to the market value of the bullion at the time of sale, plus the cost of minting, marketing, and distributing such coins (including labor, materials, dies, use of machinery, and promotional and overhead expenses).

(B) The Secretary shall make bulk sales of the coins minted under this subsection at a reasonable discount.

(3) For purposes of section 5132(a)(1) of this title, all coins minted under this subsection shall be considered to be numismatic items.

Sec. 5113. Tolerances and testing of coins

(a) The Secretary of the Treasury may prescribe reasonable manufacturing tolerances for specifications in Section 5112 of this title (except for specifications that are limits) for the dollar, half dollar, quarter dollar, and dime coins. The weights of the 5-cent coin may vary not more than 0.194 gram. The weight of the 1-cent coin may vary not more than 0.13 gram.

(b) The Secretary shall keep a record of the kind, number, and weight of each group of coins minted and test a number of the coins separately to determine if the coins conform to the weight specified in Section 5112(a) of this title. If the coins tested do not conform, the Secretary—

(1) shall weigh each coin of the group separately and deface the coins that do not conform and cast them into bars for reminting; or

(2) may remelt the group of coins.

Sec. 5114. Engraving and printing currency and security documents

(a) The Secretary of the Treasury shall engrave and print United States currency and bonds of the United States government and currency and bonds of United States territories and possessions from intaglio plates on plate printing presses the Secretary selects. However, other security documents and checks may be printed by any process the Secretary selects. Engraving and printing shall be carried out within the Department of the Treasury if the Secretary decides the engraving and printing can be carried out as cheaply, perfectly, and safety as outside the department.

(b) United States currency has the inscription "In God We Trust" in a place the Secretary decides is appropriate. Only the portrait of a deceased individual may appear on United States currency and securities. The name of the individual shall be inscribed below the portrait.

(c) The Secretary may make a contract for a period of not more than four years to manufacture distinctive paper for United States currency and securities. To promote competition among manufacturers of the distinctive paper, the Secretary may split the award for the manufacture of the paper between the two bidders with the lowest prices a pound. When the Secretary decides that is necessary to operate more than one mill to manufacture distinctive paper, the Secretary may—

(1) employ individuals temporarily at rates of pay equivalent to the rates of pay of regular employees; and

(2) charge the pay of the temporary employees to the appropriation available for manufacturing distinctive paper.

Sec. 5115. United States currency notes

(a) The Secretary of the Treasury may issue United States currency notes. The notes—

(1) are payable to bearer; and

(2) shall be in a form and in denominations of at least $1 that the Secretary prescribes.

Sec. 5116. Buying and selling gold and silver

(a)(1) With the approval of the president, the Secretary of the Treasury may—

(A) buy and sell gold in the way, in amounts, at rates, and on conditions the Secretary considers most advantageous to the public interest; and

(B) buy the gold with any direct obligations of the United States government or United States coins and currency authorized by law, or with amounts in the Treasury not otherwise appropriated.

(2) Amounts received from the purchase of gold are an asset of the general fund of the Treasury. Amounts received from the sale of gold shall be deposited in the general fund of the Treasury.

(3) The Secretary shall acquire gold for the coins issued under section 5112(i) of this title by purchase of gold mined from natural deposits in the United States, or in a territory or possession of the United States, within one year after the month in which the ore from which it is derived was mined. The Secretary shall pay not more than the average world price for the gold. In the absence of available supplies of such gold at the average world price, the Secretary may use gold from reserves held by the United States to mint the coins issued under section 5112(i) of this title. The Secretary shall issue such regulations as may be necessary to carry out this paragraph.

(b)(1) The Secretary may buy silver mined from natural deposits in the United States, or in a territory or possession of the United States, that is brought to a United States mint or assay office within one year after the month in which the ore from which it is derived was mined. The Secretary may use the coinage metal fund under section 5111(b) of this title to buy silver under this subsection.

(2) The Secretary may sell or use Government silver to mint coins, except silver transferred to stockpiles established under the Strategic and Critical Materials Stock Piling Act (50 U.S.C. 98 et seq.). The Secretary shall obtain the silver for the coins authorized under section 5112(e) of this title by purchase from stockpiles established under the Strategic and Critical Materials Stock Piling Act (50 U.S.C. 98 et seq.). The Secretary shall sell silver under conditions the Secretary considers appropriate for at least $1.292929292 a fine troy ounce.

Sec. 5117. Transferring gold and gold certificates

(A) All right, title, and interest, and every claim of the Board of Governors of the Federal Reserve System, a Federal Reserve Bank, and a Federal Reserve agent, in and to gold is transferred to and vests in the United States government to be held in the Treasury. Payment for the transferred gold is made by crediting equivalent amounts in dollars in accounts established in the Treasury under the 15th paragraph of Section 16 of the Federal Reserve Act (12 U.S.C. 467). Gold not in the possession of the government shall be held in custody for the government and delivered on the order of the Secretary of the Treasury. The Board of Governors, Federal Reserve Banks, and Federal Reserve agents shall give instructions and take action necessary to ensure that the gold is so held and delivered.

(b) The Secretary shall issue gold certificates against gold transferred under subsection (a) of this section. The Secretary may issue gold certificates against other gold held in the Treasury. The Secretary may prescribe the form and denominations of the certificates. The amount of outstanding certificates may be not more than the value (for the purpose of issuing those certificates, of 42 and two-ninths dollars a fine troy ounce) of the gold held against gold certificates. The Secretary shall hold gold in the Treasury equal to the required dollar amount as security for gold certificates issued after January 29, 1934.

(c) With the approval of the president, the Secretary may prescribe regulations the Secretary considers necessary to carry out this section.

Sec. 5118. Gold clauses and consent to sue

(a) In this section—

(1) "gold clause" means a provision in or related to an obligation alleging to give the obligee a right to require payment in—

(A) gold;

(B) a particular United States coin or currency; or

(C) United States money measured in gold or a particular United States coin or currency.

(2) "public debt obligation" means a domestic obligation issued or guaranteed by the United States government to repay money or interest.

(b) The United States Government may not pay out any gold coin. A person lawfully holding United States coins and currency may present the coins and currency to the Secretary of the Treasury for exchange (dollar for dollar) for other United States coins and currency (other than gold and silver coins) that may be lawfully held. The Secretary shall make the exchange under regulations prescribed by the Secretary.

(c)(1) The government withdraws its consent given to anyone to assert against the government, its agencies, or its officers, employees, or agents, a claim—

(A) on a gold clause public debt obligation or interest on the obligation;

(B) for United States coins or currency; or

(C) arising out of the surrender, requisition, seizure, or acquisition of United States coins or currency, gold, or silver involving the effect or validity of a change in the metallic content of the dollar or in a regulation about the value of money.

(2) Paragraph (1) of this subsection does not apply to a proceeding in which no claim is made for payment or credit in an amount greater than the face or nominal value in dollars of public debt obligations or United States coins or currency involved in the proceeding.

(3) Except when consent is not withdrawn under this subsection, an amount appropriated for payment on public debt obligations and for United States coins and currency may be expended only dollar for dollar.

(d)(1) In this subsection, "obligation" means any obligation (except United States currency) payable in United States money.

(2) An obligation issued containing a gold clause or governed by a gold clause is discharged on payment (dollar for dollar) in United States coin or currency that is legal tender at the time of payment. This paragraph does not apply to an obligation issued after October 27, 1977.

Sec. 5119. Redemption and cancellation of currency

(a) Except to the extent authorized in regulations the Secretary of the Treasury prescribes with the approval of the president, the Secretary may not redeem United States currency (including Federal Reserve notes and circulating notes of Federal Reserve Banks and national banks) in gold. However, the Secretary shall redeem gold certificates owned by the Federal Reserve Banks at times and in amounts the Secretary decides are necessary to maintain the equal purchasing power of each kind of United States currency. When redemption in gold is authorized, the redemption may be made only in gold bullion bearing the stamp of a United States Mint or assay office in an amount equal at the time of redemption to the currency presented for redemption.

(b)(1) Except as provided in subsection

(c)(1) of this section, the following are public debts bearing no interest:

(A) gold certificates issued before January 30, 1934.

(B) silver certificates.

(C) notes issued under the Act of July 14, 1890 (ch. 708, 26 Stat. 289).

(D) Federal Reserve notes for which payment was made under Section 4 of the Old Series Currency Adjustment Act.

(E) United States currency notes, including those issued under Section 1 of the Act of February 25, 1862 (ch. 33, 12 Stat. 345), the Act of July 11, 1862 (ch. 142, 12 Stat. 532), the resolution of January 17, 1863 (P.R. 9; 12 Stat. 822), Section 2 of the Act of March 3, 1863 (ch. 73, 12 Stat. 710), or Section 5115 of this title.

(2) The Secretary shall redeem from the general fund of the Treasury and cancel and destroy currency referred to in paragraph (1) of this subsection when the currency is presented to the Secretary.

(c)(1) The Secretary may determine the amount of the following United States currency that will not be presented for redemption because the currency has been destroyed or irretrievably lost:

(A) circulating notes of Federal Reserve Banks and national banks issued before July 1, 1929, for which the United States government has assumed liability.

(B) outstanding currency referred to in subsection (b)(1) of this section.

(2) When the Secretary makes a determination under this subsection, the Secretary shall reduce the amount of that currency outstanding by the amount the Secretary determines will not be redeemed and credit the appropriate receipt account.

(d) To provide a historical collection of United States currency, the Secretary may withhold from cancellation and destruction and transfer to a special account one piece of each design, issue, or series of each denomination of each kind of currency (including circulating notes of Federal Reserve Banks and national banks) after redemption. The Secretary may make appropriate entries in Treasury accounts because of the transfers.

Sec. 5120. Obsolete, mutilated, and worn coins and currency

(a)(1) The Secretary of the Treasury shall melt obsolete and worn United States coins withdrawn from circulation. The Secretary may use the metal from melting the coins for reminting or may sell the metal. The Secretary shall account for the following in the coinage metal fund under Section 5111(b) of this title:

(A) obsolete and worn coins and the metal from melting the coins.

(B) proceeds from the sale of the metal.

(C) losses incurred in the sale of the metal.

(D) losses incurred because of the difference between the face value of the coins melted and the coins minted from the metal.

(2) The Secretary shall reimburse the coinage metal fund for losses under paragraph (1)(C) and (D) of this subsection out of amounts in the coinage profit fund under Section 5111(b) of this title.

(b) The Secretary shall—

(1) cancel and destroy (by a secure process) obsolete, mutilated, and worn United States currency withrawn from circulation; and

(2) dispose of the residue of the currency and notes.

(c) The Comptroller General shall audit the cancellation and destruction of United States currency and the accounting of the cancellation and destruction. Records the Comptroller General considers necessary to make an effective audit easier shall be made available to the Comptroller General.

Sec. 5121. Refining, assaying, and valuation of bullion

(a) The Secretary of the Treasury shall—

(1) melt and refine bullion;

(2) as required, assay coins, metal, and bullion;

(3) cast gold and silver bullion deposits into bars; and

(4) cast alloys into bars for minting coins.

(b) A person owning gold or silver bullion may deposit the bullion with the Secretary to be cast into fine, standard fineness, or unrefined bars weighing at least 5 troy ounces. When practicable, the Secretary shall weigh the bullion in front of the depositor. The Secretary shall give the depositor a receipt for the bullion stating the description and weight of the bullion. When the Secretary has to melt the bullion or remove base metals before the value of the bullion can be determined, the weight is the weight after the melting or removal of the metals. The Secretary may refuse a deposit of gold bullion if the deposit is less than $100 in value or the bullion is so base that it is unsuitable for the operations of the Bureau of the Mint.

(c) When the gold and silver are combined in bullion that is deposited and either the gold or silver is so little that it cannot be separated economically, the Secretary may not pay the depositor for the gold or silver that cannot be separated.

(d)(1) Under conditions prescribed by the Secretary, a person may exchange unrefined bullion for fine bars when—

(A) gold and silver are combined in the bullion in proportions that cannot be economically refined; or

(B) necessary supplies of acids cannot be procured at reasonable rates.

(2) The charge for refining in an exchange under this subsection may be not more than the charge imposed in an exchange of unrefined bullion for refined bullion.

(3) The Secretary shall prepare bars for payment of deposits. The Secretary shall stamp each bar with a designation of the weight and fineness of the bar and a symbol the Secretary considers suitable to prevent fraudulent imitation of the bar.

Sec. 5122. Payment to depositors

(a) The Secretary of the Treasury shall determine the fineness, weight, and value of each deposit and bar under Section 5121 of this title. The value and the amount of charges under subsection (b) of this section shall be based on the fineness and weight of the bullion. The Secretary shall give the depositor a statement of the charges and the net amount of the deposit to be paid in money or bars of the same species of bullion as that deposited.

(b) The Secretary shall impose a charge equal to the average cost of material, labor, waste, and use of machinery of a United States Mint or assay office for—

(1) melting and refining bullion;

(2) using copper as an alloy when bullion deposited is above standard;

(3) separating gold and silver combined in the bullion; and

(4) preparing bars.

(c) The Secretary shall pay to the depositor or to a person designated by the depositor money or bars equivalent to the bullion deposited as soon as practicable after the value of the deposit is determined. If demanded, the Secretary shall pay depositors in the order in which the bullion is deposited with the Secretary. However, when there is an unavoidable delay in determining the value of a deposit, the Secretary shall pay depositors in the denominations requested by the depositors. After the depositor is paid, the bullion is the property of the United States government.

(d) To allow the Secretary to pay depositors with as little delay as possible, the Secretary shall keep in the Mints and assay offices, when possible, money and bullion the Secretary decides are convenient and necessary.

Sec. 5131. Organization

(a) The Bureau of the Mint has—

(1) a United States Mint at Philadelphia, Penn.

(2) a United States Mint at Denver, Colo.

(3) a United States assay office at New York, N.Y.

(4) a United States assay office at San Francisco, Calif.

(b) The Secretary of the Treasury shall carry out duties and powers relating to refining and assaying bullion, minting coins, striking medals, and numismatic items at the Mints and assay offices, except that only bars may be made at the assay offices. However, until the Secretary decides that the Mints are adequate for minting and striking an ample supply of coins and medals, the Secretary may use any facility of the Bureau to Mint coins and strike medals and to store coins and medals.

(c) Each Mint and the assay office at New York have a superintendent and an assayer appointed by the president, by and with the advice and consent of the Senate. The Mint at Philadelphia has an engraver appointed by the president, by and with the advice and consent of the Senate.

(d) Laws on Mints, officers and employees of Mints, and punishment of offenses related to Mints and minting coins apply to assay offices, as applicable.

(e) The Secretary shall operate, maintain, and have custody of, the Mint at Philadelphia. However, the administrator of General Services shall make repairs and improvements to the Mint.

Section 5132, Administrative

(a) (1) Except as provided in this chapter, the Secretary of the Treasury shall deposit in the Treasury as miscellaneous receipts amounts the Secretary received from the operations of the Bureau of the Mint. However, amounts from numismatic items shall be reimbursed to the current appropriation used to pay the cost of preparing and selling the items. The Secretary shall annually sell to the public, directly and by mail, sets of uncirculated and proof coins minted under paragraphs (1) through (6) of section 5112(a) of this title, and shall solicit such sales through the use of the customer list of the Bureau of the Mint. The Secretary may not use amounts the Secretary receives from profits on minting coins or from charges on gold or silver bullion under section 5122 of this title to pay officers and employees.

(2) Not more than $50,165,000 may be appropriated to the Secretary for the fiscal year

ending September 30, 1983, to pay costs of the mints and assay offices.

(b) To the extent the Secretary decides is necessary, the Secretary may use amounts received from depositors for refining bullion and the proceeds from the sale of byproducts (including spent acids from surplus bullion recovered in refining processes) to pay the costs of refining the bullion (including labor, material, waste and loss on the sale of sweeps). The Secretary may not use amounts appropriated for the mints and assay offices to pay those costs.

(c) The Secretary shall make an annual report at the end of each fiscal year on the operation of the Bureau.

Section 5133. Settlement of accounts

(a) The Secretary of the Treasury shall —
(1) charge the superintendent of each mint and the assay office at New York and the officer in charge of the assay office at San Francisco with the amount in weight of standard metal of bullion the superintendent or officer receives from the Secretary;

(2) credit each superintendent and the officer with the amount in weight of coins. clippings, and other bullion the superintendent or officer returns to the Secretary; and

(3) charge separately to each superintendent and the officer, who shall account for, copper to be used in the alloy of gold and silver bullion.

(b) At least once a year, the Secretary shall settle the accounts of the superintendents and the officer in charge. At settlement, each superintendent and the officer shall return to the Secretary coins, clippings, and other bullion in their possession with a statement of bullion received and returned since the last settlement (including bullion returned for settlement). The Secretary shall —

(1) audit the accounts and statements of each superintendent and the officer;

(2) allow each superintendent the waste of precious metals, within limitations prescribed by the Secretary, that the Secretary decides is necessary for refining and minting; and

(3) allow the officer the waste, within the limitations prescribed for refining, that the Secretary decides is necessary in casting fine gold and silver bars, except that the waste allowance may not apply to deposit operations.

(c) After settlement, the Secretary shall compare the amount of gold and silver bullion and coins on hand with the total liabilities of the mints and assay offices. The Secretary also shall make a statement of the ordinary expense account.

(d) The Secretary shall procure for each mint and assay office a series of standard weights corresponding to the standard troy pound of the National Bureau of Standards of the Department of Commerce. The series shall include a one pound weight and multiples and subdivisions of one pound from .01 grain to 25 pounds. At least once a year, the Secretary shall test the weights normally used in transactions at the mint and assay offices against the Standard Weights.

Section 5141. Operation of the Bureau of Engraving and Printing

(a) The Secretary of the Treasury shall prepare and submit to the President an annual business-type budget for the Bureau of Engraving and Printing.***

Section 5142. Bureau of Engraving and Printing Fund

(a) The Department of the Treasury has a Bureau of Engraving and Printing Fund. Amounts —

(1) in the Fund are available to operate the Bureau of Engraving and Printing;
(2) in the Fund remain available until expended; and
(3) may be appropriated to the Fund.

(b) The Fund consists of —

(1) property and physical assets (except building and land) acquired by the Bureau;
(2) all amounts received by the Bureau;

Section 5144. Providing impressions of portraits and vignettes

The Secretary of the Treasury may provide impressions from an engraved portrait or vignette in the possession of the Bureau of Engraving and Printing. An impression shall be provided —

(1) at the request of —
　(A) a member of Congress;
　(B) a head of an agency;
　(C) an art association; or
　(D) a library; and
(2) for a charge and under conditions the Secretary decides are necessary to protect the public interest.

As a convenience to readers and researchers, below is a parallel reference table for sections of Title 31 of the U.S. Code showing prior sections and where they are presently located in the revised section. Those using the prior edition of the *Coin World Almanac* can consult this table as a means of ascertaining the current status of a particular section. For example, the old section enumerating the various Mints (31 USC 261) is now found in Section 5131.

BUREAU OF ENGRAVING AND PRINTING

Old section	Precise	New section
171	Powers of BEP Director; reports	303
174	Impressions of portraits	5144
175	Portraits of deceased members	5155
177	Intaglio printing requirements	5114

UNITED STATES MINT

Old section	Precise	New section
251	Establishment of Mint with Director	304, 5131
253	Powers of Director; reports	5132
261	Mints (P, D, S)	5131
263	Officers of Mints	5131
266	Appointment of assistants at Mint	(Note 1)
267	Duties of coiner; refiner; Superintendent	(Note 2)
272	Duties of Superintendent	5111
273	Superintendent's duties regarding bullion and coin	5122, 5132
274	Superintendent's duties regarding melting and refining	5121
275	Superintendent's duties as to coining	5111
276	Duties of Engraver	5112
277	Duties of Assayer	5121
278	Business of Assay Office at New York	5131
279	Assay Office at New York	5131
281	Duties at New York Assay Office	5131
283	Duties at San Francisco Assay Office	5131, 5133
287	Mint legally on par with Assay Offices	5131
291	Construction of Buildings	(Note 3)
292	Operations of buildings; maintenance	5131
293	Additional item regarding buildings	(Note 4)
294	Appropriation for new Mint	(Note 5)
301-304	Provisions for Joint Commission on the Coinage	(Note 6)
311	Policy of U.S. as to bimetallism	(Note 7)
312	International Monetary Conference	(Note 8)
313	International Bimetallism	(Note 9)
314	Standard Unit of Value	(Note 10)
315b	Halt to gold coinage	5118
317	Minor coins (cent) weight and alloy	5112
317c	Melting of old coins	5120
317d-e1	Melting of silver dollars; expenses	(Note 11)
317f	Regulations to carry out meltings	321
321	Standard for silver coins	5112
322	Prohibition against issue of non-standard coins	5111
324	Inscription on coins	5112
324a	IN GOD WE TRUST on coins	5114
324b-324c	Eisenhower dollars authorized	5112
324d-324e	Bicentennial coinage issues	(Note 12)
324f	Use of various Mint facilities to coin	5131
324g; 324i	Bicentennial coin issues	(Note 12)
324h	Numismatic items production authorized	5111
325	Gold and silver bars	5121
326	Exchange of gold coins for gold bars	(Note 13)
327	Deposit of gold bullion with Mint	5121
328	Silver bullion deposit with Mint	5121
329	Weighing bullion; receipts	5121
330	Assay of bullion	5121
331	Report on quality of assay of bullion	5122

Old section	Precise	New section
332	Charges for converting bullion to coin	5122
334	Verification of Superintendent by assayer	5122
335	Bullion purchase for silver coinage	5116
337	Silver coinage exchange for currency	(Note 14)
338	Exchange of silver coin by Treasurer	(Note 15)
339	Free transportation of silver coin	(Note 16)
340	Profit fund for minor coin purchases	5111
341	Redemption of minor coins	(Note 17)
342	Cleaning of minor coins; reissuance	5111
343	Transfer of bullion for ingots	5121
344	Assay of ingots	5121
345	Delivery of ingots for coinage	5111
346	Deviation of standard of ingots for coinage	5112
347	Stamping of bars deposited	5121
349	Deviations allowed; silver coins	(Note 18)
350	Deviations allowed; minor coins	5113
351	Delivery of trial pieces to Superintendent	5113
352	Sealing and transmitting of trial pieces	(Note 19)
353	Disposal of clippings; records of weight and composition	5111
354	Yearly settlement of account	5133
355	Allowance of wastage from coins	5133
356	Balance sheet from Superintendent to Director	5133
357	Delivery of bars or coins to depositor	5122
358	Payment to depositors in coin or money	5122
359	Payment for bullion in coin certificate	(Note 20)
360	Exchange of unparted bullion for fine bars	5121
361	Refining and parting bullion	5131, 5132
362	Exchange of unparted bullion for bars	5121
363	Assay Commission	(Note 21)
364	Standard for troy pound	5102
365	Standard for weights at Mint	5133
367	Coinage for foreign countries	5111
368	National Mint medals	5111
369	Reimbursables to Mint for production	5132
370	Redemption for gold coins	(Note 22)
371	Establishment of decimal system	5101
372	Conversion of currency	5151
373	Recoinage of foreign coin	(Note 23)
374	Spanish and Mexican coin legal tender	(Note 24)
375	Transmittal of Spanish and Mexican coins for recoinage	(Note 25)
376a	Commemorative coins; no reissues	(Note 26)
391(a)	Clad coinage authorization	5111
391(b)-(d)	Clad coin specifications	5112
392	Legal tender for U.S. coins	5103
393(a)	Contract authority for clad technology	5111
393(b)	Elimination of procurement requirements	(Note 27)
394	Silver purchase at $1.25 an ounce	5116
395	Melting and export of coins prohibited	5116
396	Forfeiture of coins melted; exported	5111
397	Authority for Secretary to issue rules	321
398	Definitions regarding clad coinage	5112, 5113

U.S. CURRENCY

Old section	Precise	New section
401	U.S. notes	5115
402	Limitation of U.S. notes in circulation	5115
403	Issue of $1, $2 and $5 U.S. notes	(Note 28)
404	Cancellation of legal tender notes prohibited	5119
405	Silver certificates	(Note 29)
405a-1	Use of silver for coinage or sale	5116

Old section	Precise	New section
405a-2	Destroyed silver certificates	5119
405a-3	Redemption of silver certificates	5119
406	Denomination of silver certificates	(Note 30)
407	Redemption of fractional currency	(Note 31)
408a	Redemption of currency with gold ended	5119, 5119
408b	Conversion of gold weight to Treasury dollars explained	(Note 32)
409	Parity of dollar	(Note 33)
410	Treasury notes as national bank reserve	(Note 34)
411	Cancellation of Treasury notes	(Note 35)
413	Portraits of living people on currency	5114
414	Names inscribed under portraits	5114
415	Work on engraving at Treasury	5114
416	Equipment at Treasury for currency manufacture	5114
417	Expense of issuing notes	(Note 36)
418	Distinctive paper for currency	5114
418a	Multiple paper suppliers	5114
419	Additional employees for paper mills	5114
420	Replacing mutilated notes	5119
421	Destruction of notes	5120
422	Maceration of notes	5120
423	Laundering of paper money	(Note 37)
424	Counterfeit notes to be marked	5153
425	Taxation of national bank notes	5154
426	Taxation of national banks	5154
427	Treasury Secretary rules and regulations	321
428	Gold certificates for bullion	(Note 38)
429	Gold coin deposits - gold certificates	(Note 39)
430	Depositaries for receipt of bullion	(Note 40)
440	Short title: Gold Reserve Act of 1934	(Note 41)
441	Title to Federal Reserve gold to U.S.	5117
443	Regulations for forfeiture	(Note 42)
444	Definitions in Gold Reserve Act	5119
449	Par Value Modification	(Note 43)
451-455	Legal tender provision for gold certificates; U.S. notes; Treasury notes; interest bearing notes.	(Note 44)
456	No foreign coins a legal tender	5103
457-460	Legal tender status of minor, subsidiary and other coins	(Note 45)
463	"Gold clause" contracts	5118

Notes

The following relate to various sections of the old Title 31 which has since been superseded by the codification. Some of the material comes from House Report 97-651 (1982); others are from sources which explain the demise of laws. Where the phrase "Repealed 9/13/82" appears, it means that it was one of the sections of the law that was expressly repealed by the new Title 31 codification. In other instances, there was no repeal per se but it is clear that the section has no corollary provision in the codification.

1. Repealed 9/13/82 as unnecessary because of the authority of the Treasury Secretary under Section 3101 of Title 5 of the U.S. Code (5 USC 3101).
2. Repealed 9/13/82, as superseded by Section 321 of Title 31 (transferring functions to Treasury Secretary).
3. Repealed 9/13/82 because the Philadelphia Mint (for which this section authorizes the construction) has been completed since 1969.
4. Repealed 9/13/82 because the Philadelphia Mint (which this section authorizes the construction of) has been completed since 1969.

5. Repealed 9/13/82 because appropriations for the Philadelphia Mint were extended to build it.
6. Repealed 9/13/82 as obsolete. Joint Commission on the Coinage expired 1/4/75 under provisions of the Federal Advisory Committee Act (five years of non-use).
7. Repealed 9/13/82 as superseded. The House report notes "the monetary system of the United States is no longer based on gold and silver."
8. Repealed 9/13/82 as obsolete.
9. Repealed 9/13/82 as obsolete; see note 7.
10. Repealed 9/13/82; initially superseded by Par Value Modification Act (Pub. L. 92-268), which

directed Treasury Secretary to seek new par value of dollar. That was repealed in turn by Bretton Woods Agreement Act (Pub. L. 94-564).

11. Repealed 9/13/82, as superseded by Section 321 of Title 31 (transferring functions to Treasury Secretary); also obsolete (Treasury Secretary has powers under Section 5118 to melt uncurrent or worn coins).

12. Repealed 9/13/82 as executed since Bicentennial coin designs were created and issued.

13. Repealed 9/13/82 as obsolete (the House report notes that gold coinage was discontinued in 1934; the provision would have no effect even with current gold commemorative production).

14. Repealed 9/13/82 as superseded by 31 USC 5116 providing for exchange of all coin of U.S. for other coin and currency that may be legally acquired.

15. Repealed 9/13/82 as superseded by 31 USC 5116 providing for exchange of all coin of U.S. for other coin and currency that may be legally acquired.

16. Repealed 9/13/82 as obsolete (the House report notes that silver coinage was discontinued and is not now produced for circulation (except for Proof and Uncirculated issues); the provision would have no effect even with current gold commemorative production).

17. Repealed 9/13/82 as unnecessary and superseded. Section 5111(b) of the revised title provides for charging costs against the coinage profit fund.

18. Repealed 9/13/82 as superseded by Treasury Secretary authority in Section 5112(d) to set standards for Mint to coin.

19. Obsolete by virtue of elimination of Assay Commission by Pub. L. 96-209 (3/14/80).

20. Repealed 9/13/82, as obsolete and superseded.

21. Obsolete by virtue of elimination of Assay Commission by Pub. L. 96-209 (3/14/80).

22. Repealed 9/13/82 as superseded by Section 5118 (prohibiting redemption of gold except with approval and by regulations approved by Treasury Secretary).

23. Repealed 9/13/82 as obsolete (the House report notes that gold coinage was discontinued in 1934 and that there are currently no circulating silver or gold coins (as of 1982); the provision would have effect even with current gold com-

memorative production but are now repealed.

24. Repealed 9/13/82 as obsolete (Mexican coins to be recoined; see note to 23).

25. See note to 24.

26. Repealed 9/13/82 as executed.

27. Repealed 9/13/82 as obsolete. Procurement for clad coinage technology expired 7//70.

28. Repealed 9/13/82 as obsolete (since 31 USC 406 is omitted [29 below]).

29. Repealed 9/13/82 as superseded by Section 5116.

30. Repealed 9/13/82 as superseded; see Act of June 4, 1963, eliminating this.

31. Repealed 9/13/82 as obsolete.

32. Repealed 9/13/82 as superseded; Par Value Modification Act and Bretton Woods Agreements Act supersede. See 10 above.

33. Repealed 9/13/82 as obsolete.

34. Repealed 9/13/82 as superseded. Allowed Treasury notes to be counted as part of lawful reserves (12 USC 145); now 31 USC 5103 makes all currency legal tender.

35. Repealed 9/13/82 as obsolete (House report states standard silver dollars are no longer struck).

36. Repealed 9/13/82 as superseded; BEP revolving fund is used pursuant to 31 USC 5142.

37. Repealed 9/13/82 as superseded; BEP does not launder currency though under 31 USC 3101 Treasury Secretary still retains authority to hire employees to do so.

38. Repealed 9/13/82 as obsolete; Section 5117 of revised title authorizes gold certificates to be kept as a public debt item.

39. Repealed 9/13/82 as obsolete; Section 5117 of revised title authorizes gold certificates to be kept as a public debt item.

40. Repealed 9/13/82, as superseded by Section 321 of Title 31 (transferring functions to Treasury Secretary).

41. Repealed 9/13/82; obsolete. No longer are short titles required because of the restatement.

42. Previously repealed.

43. Repealed 9/13/82 as superseded. See Par Value Modification Act and Bretton Woods Agreements Act (Note 10 above).

44. Repealed 9/13/82; superseded by 31 USC 5103.

45. Repealed 9/13/82; superseded by 31 USC 5103.

Other legal and legislative issues

Banning of the Krugerrand

The South African Krugerrand was the world's best selling gold bullion coin until anti-apartheid movements in the mid-1980s took some of the glitter off the coin. Some 40 million pieces have been produced, and nearly half of them were imported into the United States. Difficulties with the racial apartheid policies of South Africa caused political con-

sternation, and the Krugerrand became an important symbol that opponents of apartheid sought to ban, in order to use an economic weapon against the South African government.

As Congress moved towards a legislative ban on the Krugerrand, which some claimed might be illegal under the Articles of Agreement of the International Monetary Fund which govern foreign exchange, including legal tender pieces such as the Krugerrand, or under the General Agreement on Tariffs and Trade (GATT), which prohibits any discriminatory tariff, President Reagan took the matter out of the hands of Congress by issuing Executive Order 12535 on Oct. 1, 1985 (50 Fed. Reg. 40325), which effectively banned future importation of the coin.

The text of the regulation is as follows:

"By the authority vested in me as President by the Constitution and laws of the United States of America, including the International Emergency Economic Powers Act (50 U.S.C. 1701 et seq.) in order to take steps additional to those set forth in Executive Order No. 12532 of Sept. 9, 1985, to deal with the unusual and extraordinary threat to the foreign policy and economy of the United States referred to in that Order, and in view of the continuing nature of that emergency, the recommendations made by the United Nations Security Council in Resolution No. 569 of July 26, 1985, and the completion of consultations by the Secretary of State and the United States Trade Representative directed by Section 5(a) of Executive Order No. 12532, it is hereby ordered that the importation into the United States of South African Krugerrands is prohibited effective 12:01 a.m. Eastern Daylight Time Oct. 11, 1985. The Secretary of the Treasury is authorized to promulgate such rules and regulations as may be necessary to carry out this prohibition.

/s/ Ronald Reagan THE WHITE HOUSE, Oct. 1, 1985"

Regulations covering this are found in Volume 31 of the Code of Federal Regulations commencing at Sec. 545.101 et seq. Only the pertinent portions of these regulations dealing with Krugerrands are listed; the act governs all transactions with South Africa:

Sec. 545.201 Prohibition on the importation of Krugerrands.

Except as authorized under this part, the importation into the United States of South African Krugerrands is prohibited.

Sec. 545.204 Evasions.

Any transaction for the purpose of, or which has the effect of, evading any of the prohibitions in this part is prohibited.

Sec. 545.301 Krugerrands.

The term "Krugerrands" includes Krugerrands of all denominations and sizes, and Krugerrands that have been modified, as by addition of a clasp or loop, into items that can be worn as jewelry.

Sec. 545.403 Krugerrand jewelry.

Section 545.201 prohibits the importation into the United States of Krugerrands that

have been modified, as by the addition of a clasp or loop, into items that can be worn as jewelry. For example, importation of a necklace consisting of a Krugerrand mounted on a chain would be prohibited. Section 545.201 does not prohibit the reimportation into the United States of Krugerrand jewelry which was originally imported into the United States prior to October 11, 1985.

Sec. 545.701 Penalties.

(a) A civil penalty of not to exceed $10,000 may be imposed on any person who violates any license, order, or regulation issued under this title. (b)Whoever willfully violates any license, order, or regulation issued under this title shall, upon conviction, be fined not more than $50,000, or, if a natural person, may be imprisoned for not more than ten years, or both. . . .

Sec. 545.801 Licensing.

(b) Transactions prohibited under subpart B [including Krugerrand importation] may be effected only under specific license. (1) The specific licensing activities of the Office of Foreign Assets Control are performed by its Washington Office and by the Foreign Assets Control Division of the Federal Reserve Bank of New York. (2) Applications for specific licenses. Applications for specific licenses to engage in any transaction prohibited under this part are to be filed in duplicate with the Federal Reserve Bank of New York, Foreign Assets Control Division, 33 Liberty Street, New York, NY 10045. . . .

Collectibles in retirement accounts

Utilizing a collection of numismatic material for long-term investment is a significant economic and emotional issue to many individuals. Use of numismatic acumen to help plan a "rare coin retirement" still remains a widely used method that many people use.

Until passage of the Economic Recovery Act of 1981, self-directed pension plans and individual retirement accounts (IRAs) were permitted to purchase coins as part of retirement planning.

The reason that this made economic sense was that coins, in the long run, have a good track record of substantially increasing in value. From the Salomon Brothers survey of a selected portfolio of collectibles to nearly every other objective view of the marketplace, coins are a significant tangible asset from which an individual can reap substantial financial rewards.

Section 314-b of the Economic Recovery Act of 1981 (now section 408(m) of the Internal Revenue Code), placed severe restrictions on the ability of using coins in this vehicle. Persons who placed coins in an individual retirement account, or in the self-directed retirement plans such as a Keogh Plan were considered having made a "distribution"; this meant that income tax would have to be paid, and, additionally, that the plans could not further be used for a five-year period of time. In effect, there was an economic bar.

It should be noted that the original section, and the present law, do not prohibit a trustee of a pension plan who believes that it is prudent to invest in rare coins to do so. The "prudent person" rule applies. For details concerning this little-explored aspect, one should consult with his own accountant or legal counsel.

While in general collectors are no longer able to place most coins in an individual retirement account, Congress did make a modification of the law to give a specific allowance to coins produced under the Gold Bullion Coin Act of 1985 (Public Law 99-185), and the Liberty Coin Act (Pub. L. 99-61, Title II).

This exception applies only to U.S. 1-ounce, half-ounce, quarter-ounce and tenth-ounce American Eagle gold bullion coins, and the new American Eagle 1-ounce silver coin, each of which was first produced by the Treasury Department in October 1986. A number of banks and some dealers have created individual retirement account programs involving these pieces. One may use existing funds in an IRA account to purchase them (a "rollover"), or may place 1986 or 1987 contributions, and subsequent years as well if eligible.

Section 408(m) Investment in collectibles treated as distributions

(1) In general. The acquisition by an individual retirement account or by an individually-directed account under a plan described in section 401(a) [26 USC Sec. 401(a)] of any collectible shall be treated (for purposes of this section and section 402 [26 USC Sec. 402]) as a distribution from such account in an amount equal to the cost to such account of such collectible.

(2) Collectible defined. For purposes of this subsection, the term "collectible" means—

(A) any work of art,

(B) any rug or antique,

(C) any metal or gem,

(D) any stamp or coin,

(E) any alcoholic beverage, or

(F) any other tangible personal property specified by the Secretary for purposes of this subsection.

On Jan. 23, 1984, some three years after passage of the original legislation, the Treasury Department issued a proposed regulation Sec. 1.408-1 governing investment in collectibles. The regulation does not reflect amendments made to the Internal Revenue Code to allow, for example, gold American Eagles and silver American Eagles to be placed in an IRA.

The regulation appears below:

Sec. 1.408-1 Investment in collectibles.

(a) In general. The acquisition by an individual retirement account or by an individually-directed account under a plan described in Section (401(a) of any collectible shall be treated (for purposes of Section 402 and 408) as a distribution from such account in an amount equal to the cost to such account of such collectible.

(b) **Collectible defined.** For purposes of this section, the term "collectible" means—

(1) Any work or art,

(2) Any rug or antique,

(3) Any metal or gem,

(4) Any stamp or coin,

(5) Any alcoholic beverage,

(6) Any musical instrument,

(7) Any historical objects (documents, clothes, etc.), or

(8) Any other tangible personal property which the Commissioner determines is a "collectible" for purposes of this section.

(c) **Individually-directed account.** For purposes of this section, the term "individually-directed account" means an account under a plan that provides for individual accounts and that has the effect of permitting a plan participant to invest or control the manner in which the account will be invested.

(d) **Acquisition.** For purposes of this section, the term acquisition includes purchase, exchange, contribution, or any method by which an individual retirement account or individually-directed account may directly or indirectly acquire a collectible.

(e) **Cost.** For purposes of this section, cost means fair market value.

(f) **Premature withdrawal penalty.** The 10 percent described in Sections 72(m)(5) and 408(f)(1) shall apply in the case of a deemed distribution from an individual retirement account described in paragraph (a) of this section.

(g) **Amounts subsequently distributed.** When a collectible is actually distributed from an individual retirement account or an individually-directed account, any amounts included in gross income because of this section shall not be included in gross income at the term when the collectible is actually distributed.

(h) Effective date. This section applies to property acquired after December 31, 1981, in taxable years ending after such date.

The IRS issued a notice offering guidance with respect to certain provisions of the Economic Recovery Tax Act of 1981 on qualified retirement plans, Keogh plans, individual retirement accounts and simplified employee pensions. Some, in part, relate to collectibles, and an extract appears below in the form issued by IRS in Notice 82-13, 1982-1 Cumulative Bulletin 360. III. Miscellaneous

A. Investments in Collectibles

1. For taxable years ending after December 31, 1981, the acquisition of a "collectible" by an individually-directed account under a plan described in section 401(a), or by an individual described in section 401(a), or by an individual retirement account (whether or not individually-directed), is treated as a distribution from the plan or account.

2. Questions and Answers

III-1. Q. What is a collectible?

A. The term "collectible" includes: (a) any work of art; (b) any rug or antique; (c) any metal or gem; (d) any stamp or coin; (e) any alcoholic beverage; or (f) any other tangible personal property that may be specified by the Secretary of the Treasury for this purpose.

III-2. Q. What is an individually-directed account?

A. The term "individually-directed account" means in account under a qualified plan that provides for individual accounts and that has the effect of permitting a participant or beneficiary to direct the manner in which his or her account will be invested.

III-3. Q. What is the effect of the new requirement on collectibles that were acquired on or before December 31, 1981?

A. Since the new provision is not applicable to collectibles that were acquired on or before December 31, 1981, the retention of a collectible acquired prior to January 1, 1982, by an IRA or an individually-directed account is not treated as a distribution.

III-4. Q. If an owner-employee who has not attained age 59½ directs the investment in a "collectible" by his or her individual-directed account, is the owner-employee liable for the penalties on premature distributions?

A. Yes. An investment in a collectible by an individually-directed account is treated as a distribution from the plan and is subject to the premature distribution penalty if the participant is not age 59½ or disabled. A similar conclusion would apply in the case of an IRA.

III-5. Q. Is the acquisition of a collectible by a plan treated as a distribution to the plan participant if the participant has the authority to direct that assets in the participant's account will be invested in collectibles but has no authority to direct that a specific investment be acquired?

A. Yes. An account is "individually directed" for purposes of this provision even if the participant's control over the assets in the participant's account is limited to the authority to determine that such assets will be used to acquire a class of collectibles even if it does not permit the participant to identify specific investments within that class.

"Brokers" and reporting sales

Just as section 314-b of the Economic Recovery Act of 1981 had a profound impact on the manner in which collectibles could be utilized in pension accounts, a little-noted provision contained in the Tax Equity and Fiscal Responsibility Act (TEFRA) passed by Congress has affected the privacy of investors and collectors, and also on the manner in which they can buy and sell coins.

The substances of the provision added a new section to the Internal Revenue Code (Section 6045) and required that regulations be written to encompass brokerage transactions, and the prices paid by brokers for tendered commodities. While there is substantial dispute about the position taken by the Internal Revenue Service in the regulations (the Industry Council for Tangible Assets and its counsel believe that the IRS is mistaken in its position that all coin and bullion sales are intended to be, and are covered — a view shared by the Senate Appropriations Committee, but not the Senate Finance Committee) it does seem clear that there is an intent with respect to certain commodities — such as 33-ounce gold contracts, 1,000-ounce silver bars, and some silver coins — there is a requirement that a dealer buying such commodities must issue a "1099" tax form to the seller (Senate Report 98-562).

The IRS issued one set of regulations, but as a result of the embroiling dispute, withdrew them and planned to substitute a new set. A final version had still not been released by April 1987.

This is clearly a case where there is a genuine, factual dispute that may not be resolved in the absence of litigation; however, the IRS points out that the fact that there is a dispute in some quarters does not obviate the alleged requirement that the filing take place.

The best bet in a case like this is that one should consult with his accountant, tax professional, or attorney for a formalized opinion based upon available facts as to whether or not the pertinent provisions apply to you.

It is useful to remember that the text of the regulation is very specific as to who it perceived as covered; only sales by individuals must be reported. Sales by corporations, even if owned by a single shareholder, are not reportable.

Public Law 99-514 amended section 6045(b) of the Internal Revenue Code [the text below is for returns due after Dec. 31, 1986] in order to make clear that the requirement to supply a copy of the information return to the taxpayer is triggered where there is an obligation to file (instead of the actual filing of) an information return with the IRS.

For convenience, the text of Internal Revenue Code Section 6045 and Treasury Regulation 1.6045-1, accompany this section.

Text of 6045 and Reg. follow:

Sec. 6045. Returns of brokers.

(a) General rule. Every person doing business as a broker shall, when required by the Secretary, make a return, in accordance with such regulations as the Secretary may prescribe, showing the name and address of each customer, with such details regarding gross proceeds and such other information as the Secretary may by forms or regulations require with respect to such business.

(b) Statements To Be Furnished To Customers. Every person required to make a return under subsection (a) shall furnish to each customer whose name is required to be set forth in such return a written statement showing-

(1) the name and address of the person required to make such return, and

(2) the information required to be shown on such return with respect to such customer. The written statement required under the preceding sentence shall be furnished to the customer on or before January 31 of the year following the calendar year for which the return under subsection (a) was required to be made.

(c) Definitions. For purposes of this section—

(1) *Broker.* The term "broker" includes—

(A) a dealer,

(B) a barter exchange, and

(C) any other person who (for a consideration) regularly acts as a middleman with respect to property or services.

(2) *Customer.* The term "customer" means any person for whom the broker has transacted any business.

(3) *Barter exchange.* The term "barter exchange" means any organization of members providing property or services who jointly contract to trade or barter such property or services.

(4) *Person.* The term "person" includes any governmental unit and any agency or instrumentality thereof.***

Sec. 1.6045-1 (Proposed Treasury Regulation, published 11/15/82.) Returns of information of brokers and barter exchanges.

(a) Meaning of terms. The following definitions apply for purposes of this section:

(1) the term "brokerage transaction" means—

(i) A transfer of property;

(ii) A redemption of securities;

(iii) A retirement of indebtedness; or

(iv) A closing transaction.

(2) The term "broker" means a person who, in the ordinary course of a trade or business, stands ready to effect brokerage transactions in securities, commodities or forward contracts for others.

(3) The term "customer" means, with respect to a broker, a person for whom a sale is executed by the broker acting as—

(i) An agent in such sale for such person; or

(ii) A principal in such sale.

(4) The term "security" means—

(i) A share of stock in a corporation (foreign or domestic);

(ii) An interest in a trust;

(iii) An interest in a partnership;

(iv) A debt obligation;

(v) An interest in or right to purchase any of the foregoing . . .

(vi) An interest in a security described in paragraph (a)(4)(i) or (iv) . . .

(6) The term "commodity" means—

(i) Any type of personal property or an interest therein (other than securities as defined in paragraph (a)(4) of this section) the trading of regulated futures contracts in which has been approved by the Commodity Futures Trading Commission;

(ii) Lead, palm oil, rapeseed, tea, tin, or an interest in any of the foregoing; or

(iii) Any other personal property or an interest therein that is of a type the Secretary determines is to be treated as a "commodity" under this section, from and after the date specified in a notice of such determination published in the Federal Register.

Proposed revision

(5)(i) Except as otherwise provided in paragraph (a)(5)(ii) of this section, the term "commodity" means—

(A) Any form or quality of personal property that is deliverable (whether or not subject to price adjustment for form or quality) in satisfaction of a regulated futures contract that has been approved for trading by the Commodity Futures Trading Commission (whether or not the regulated futures contract is actually traded);

(B) Any form or quality of lead, palm oil, rapeseed, tea, or tin;

(C) Any form or quality of personal property that the Secretary determines is to be treated as a "commodity" under this section, from and after the date specified in a rule-related notice of such determination published in the *Federal Register*;

(D) Any form or quality of personal property a form or quality of which is described in paragraph (a)(5)(i) (A) of this section; or

(E) Any interest in personal property that is described in paragraph (a)(t)(i)(A), (B), (C), or (D) of this section.

(ii) The term "commodity" does not include—

(A) A security as defined in paragraph (a)(3) of this section;

(B) A regulated futures contract as defined in paragraph (A)(6) of this section;

(C) A forward contract as defined in paragraph (a)(7) of this section;

(D) A form of tangible personal property, or an interest therein, gross proceeds from the sale of which exceed by more than 15 percent the value on the date of sale of the underlying personal property determined, at the election of the broker, by either exact valuation or approximate valuation (as defined in paragraph (a)(5)(ii) of this section); or

(E) A form of quality of tangible personal property or an interest therein if no single type of tangible personal property described in paragraph (a)(t)(i) of this section comprises at least 30 percent of the weight or volume of the underlying personal property and the gross proceeds from the sale of such property are less than three thousand dollars ($3,000).

(iii) For purposes of paragraph (a)(5)(ii)(D) of this section—

(A) The term "exact valuation" means to determine the value of the underlying personal property —

(1) By separately determining the value of each type of tangible personal property described in paragraph (a)(5)(i) of this section of which the underlying personal property is composed at the price at which each such type of tangible personal property is bought and sold in the ordinary course of the buyer's business, or a similarly situated business if such price cannot be determined for the buyer's business; and

(2) Aggregating all such separately determined values; and

(B) The term "approximate valuation" means to determine the value of the underlying personal property—

(1) Solely with reference to its weight or volume;

(2) As if such weight or volume were composed entirely of a single type of tangible personal property described in paragraph (a)(5)(i) of this section identical in kind and quality to the most valuable type of tangible personal property described in paragraph

(a)(5)(i) of this section that comprises at least 30 percent of such weight or described in paragraph (a)(5)(i) of this section comprises at least 30 percent of such weight or volume, the most valuable type of tangible personal property described in paragraph (a)(5)(i) of this section that comprises any portion of the underlying personal property);

(3) At the price at which the tangible personal property treated as composing the entire weight or volume is bought and sold in the ordinary course of the buyer's business, or a similarly situated business if such price cannot be determined for the buyer's business.

(iv) For purposes of paragraph (a)(5)(ii)(E) and (iii) of this section, "type of tangible personal property" means any tangible personal property described in paragraph (a)(5)(i)(A), (B), or (C) of this section and any other tangible personal property that cannot be commercially reduced into two or more elements.

(7) The term "regulated futures contract" means a regulated futures contract within the meaning of section 1256(b).

(8) The term "forward contract" means—

(i) A regulated futures contract;

(ii) A contract that requires delivery of a commodity; or

(iii) A contract that requires delivery of personal property or an interest therein that is of a type the Secretary determines is to be treated as a "forward contract" under this section, from and after the date specified in a notice of such determination published in the Federal Register.

(9) . . .

(10) The term "sale" means all dispositions of securities, commodities and forward contracts for cash, and includes redemptions of securities, retirements of indebtedness, closing transactions . . .

(11) The term "effect" means, with respect to a sale, to act as—

(i) An agent in such sale for a party thereto; or

(ii) A principal in such sale.

Acting as an agent or principal with respect to the grant or purchase of an opinion, the entry into a contract that requires delivery of personal property or an interest therein, or the entry into a short sale, is not of itself effecting a sale. A broker that has on its books a forward contract under which delivery is made effects such delivery.

(b) Examples. The following examples illustrate the definitions in paragraph (a) of this section:

Example (1). The following persons generally are brokers within the meaning of paragraph (a)(2) of this section:

(i) A mutual fund or an underwriter of the

mutual fund that stands ready to redeem shares in such a mutual fund.

(ii) A borrower that regularly issues and retires its own short-term or demand notes.

(iii) A clearing organization.

Example (2). The following persons are not brokers within the meaning of paragraph (a)(2) of this section in the absence of additional facts that indicate the person is a broker:

(i) A stock transfer agent for a corporation, which agent daily records transfers of stock in transactions to which such corporation and the agent are not parties and which agent receives an amount of compensation for its activies with respect to such transfers that indicates the agent is only providing recordkeeping.

(ii) A person, such as a stock exchange, that merely provides facilities in which others effect brokerage transactions and that does not clear such transactions.

(iii) An escrow agent or nominee if such agency is not pursuant to the ordinary course of a trade or business.

(iv) An escrow agent who is not otherwise a broker and who effects no brokerage transactions other than such transactions as are incidental to the purpose of the escrow (such as sales to collect on collateral).

(v) A corporation that issues and retires long-term debt on an irregular basis.

Example (3). A, B, and C belong to a carpool in which they commute to and from work. Every third day, each member of the carpool provides transportation for the other two members. Because the carpool arrangement provides solely for the informal exchange of similar services on a noncommercial basis, it is not a barter exchange within the meaning of paragraph (a)(5) of this section . . .

Example (9). If the gross proceeds from the sale of a gold coin (such as a Krugerrand, Maple Leaf, 50-peso coin, or 100-crown coin) do not exceed by more than 15 percent the bullion value of the gold in the coin, the coin is a commodity under paragraph (a)(5)(i)(D) of this section and is not excluded by paragraph (a)(5)(ii)(D) of this section.

Example (10). U.S. silver dimes, quarters, and half dollars minted before 1965 are personal property deliverable in satisfaction of a regulated futures contract approved by the Commodity Futures Trading Commission. The coins are a commodity under paragraph (a)(5)(i)(A) of this section. If, however, the gross proceeds from the sale of an individual coin exceed by more than 15 percent the bullion value of the silver in the coin, the coin is not a commodity under paragraph (a)(5)(ii)(D) of this section. If the gross proceeds from the sale of coins as a unit do not exceed by more than 15 percent the bullion value of the silver in the entire unit, all the coins in the unit are a commodity under paragraph (a)(5)(i)(A) of this section notwithstanding the possibility that the gross proceeds from the sale of one or more individual coins in the unit might exceed by more than 15 percent the bullion value of the silver in such individual coins.

Example (11). If the gross proceeds from the sale of a U.S. silver dollar minted before 1970 do not exceed by more than 15 percent the bullion value of the silver in the coin, the coin is a commodity under paragraph (a)(5)(i)(D) of this section and not excluded by paragraph (a)(5)(ii)(D) of this section.

Example (12). Customer E sells to jewelry store S, a broker, a gold necklace. The gross proceeds from the sale of the necklace do not exceed by more than 15 percent of the value of the gold as bullion. Consequently, the gold necklace is a commodity under paragraph (a)(5)(i)(D) of this section and not excluded under paragraph (a)(5)(ii)(D) of this section.

Example (13). Customer F sells to jewelry store T, a broker, a diamond ring. The diamond ring (composed of a gold band and gem) weighs 0.5 troy ounces. The gold in the ring comprises more than 30 percent of the total weight of the ring, and the gross proceeds from the sale of the diamond ring exceed by more than 15 percent the value of 0.5 troy ounces of gold as bullion. Consequently, the diamond ring is not a commodity under paragraph (a)(5)(i)(D) of this section because of its exclusion under paragraph (a)(5)(ii)(D) of this section.

Example (14). Customer G sells to smelter U, a broker, a gold and silver goblet. More than 30 percent of the weight or volume of the goblet is gold. Assume that the broker chooses to use the "approximate valuation" method described in paragraph (a)(5)(iii)(B) of this section and that the goblet weighs 10 troy ounces. If the gross proceeds from the sale of the goblet do not exceed by more than 15 percent the value of 10 troy ounces of gold as bullion, the goblet is a commodity under paragraph (a)(5)(i)(D) of this section and not excluded under paragraph (a)(5)(ii)(D) of this section.

Example (15). V, a jeweler, generally purchases inventory (that is a commodity under paragraph (a)(5) of this section) from wholesalers and purchases inventory from the general public only when sufficient inventory cannot be secured from wholesalers. V does not accept offers for sale, but seeks out sellers when inventory is needed. Since V does not stand ready to effect sales to be made by others, V is not a broker.

Example (16). W, a coin dealer, regularly advertises that it will buy gold items for bullion value. Since W stands ready to effect sales to be made by others, W is a broker.

Example (17). X, a coin dealer, regularly buys gold items when they are offered for sale and this is known to sellers of such items. Since X stands ready to effect sales to be made by others, X is a broker whether or not it advertises.

(c) Reporting by brokers — (1) Requirement of reporting. Any broker shall, except as otherwise provided, report in the manner prescribed in this section.

(2) Sales required to be reported. Except as provided in paragraphs (c)(3) and (g) of this section, a broker shall return of information with respect to each sale of securities, commodities, or forward contracts that the broker effects for a person who is a customer of the broker in such sale.

(3) Exceptions—(i) Sales for exempt recipients. No return of information is required with respect to a sale effected for a customer who is an exempt recipient described in section 3452(c)(2)(A) through (I) and (K)(i) and (ii) (relating to exemptions from withholding) [by U.S. and foreign corporations — editor's note] as determined under Section 35.3452(c)-1 insofar as it relates to persons described in section 3452(c)(2)(A) through (1) and (K)(i) and (ii) . . .

(vii) Foreign currency. No return of information is required with respect to a sale of foreign currency unless —

(A) Such sale is pursuant to a regulated futures contract or forward contract that requires or permits delivery of foreign currency; or

(B) Such foreign currency is a form or quality of or interest in gold or silver (not) described in paragraph (a)(5)(ii)(D) of this section . . .

(d)(2) Transactional reporting. As to each sale with respect to which a broker is required to make a return of information under this section, the broker shall show on Form 1099 the name, address, and taxpayer identification number of the customer for whom the sale was effected, the property sold, the Committee on Uniform Security Identification Procedures number of the security sold (if known), the gross proceeds of the sale, the date on which the sale occurred, and such other information as may be required by Form 1099, in the form, manner, and number of copies required by Form 1099 . . .

(4) Sale date—(i) In general. Except as otherwise provided . . . a sale is considered to occur for purposes of this section on the date the customer becomes entitled to the gross proceeds therefrom . . .

(k) Use of magnetic media—(1) In general. Except as otherwise provided by paragraph (k)(2) of this section, a broker who effects sales for 250 or more customers during a calendar year or a barter exchange who has 250 or more members or clients during a calendar year, in lieu of filing Forms 1099 for such year, shall submit returns of information required by this section on magnetic media authorized by the Commissioner and shall follow the appropriate revenue procedures for such magnetic media filing in lieu of following Form 1099.

(2) Exceptions. (i) The Commissioner may authorize the submission of returns of information on other media if undue hardship is shown on an application filed with the appropriate Internal Revenue Service Center.

(ii) In the case of a person who is a broker or barter exchange on July 1, 1983, an application to file returns of information on Form 1099 must be filed on or before (INSERT 30 DAYS AFTER PUBLICATION OF THIS DOCUMENT IN THE FEDERAL REGISTER). In the case of a person who becomes a broker or barter exchange after July 1, 1983, such application must be filed by the later of (INSERT 30 DAYS AFTER PUBLICATION OF THIS DOCUMENT IN THE FEDERAL REGISTER) or the end of the second month following the month in which such person becomes a broker or barter exchange.

(3) When permitted. Any broker or barter exchange required to submit a return of information under this section not required to do so on magnetic media may make such returns on magnetic media upon consent thereto from the Commissioner under Sec. 1.9101-1.

(l) Reporting on options transactions. (Reserved.)

(m) Reporting on bond discounts. (Reserved.)

(n) Additional reporting by stock transfer agents. (Reserved.)

(o) Effective date. This section applies to calendar year 1983 and all succeeding calendar years, and, as to 1983, only to transactions occurring on or after July 1, 1983.

Mint Regulations

Regulations are a key way in which the government operates. Below appears the current regulations of the manner in which the Mint operates, and performs a number of its functions. In years past, Treasury regulations contained in Title 31 of the Code of Federal Regulations included the Office of Domestic Gold and Silver Operations, now defunct. Part 56 of the Code of Federal Regulations is its vestige. Part 90 relates to the table of charges and regulations for processing bullion. Part 91 relates to the Mint. A subsequent part relating to the Bureau of Engraving and Printing is with substant of matters only; the on-sight regulation is virtually identical to that of the Bureau of the Mint, except for the change in name.

PART 56 Domestic gold and silver operations sale of silver

Sec. 56.1 Conditions upon which silver will be sold.

The General Services Administration, as agent for the Treasury Department, will conduct periodic sales of silver as agreed upon between GSA and the Treasury Department. Sales will be under competitive bidding procedures established by agreement between GSA the Treasury Department. Details of the bidding and selling procedures are obtainable by telephone or by writing to General Services Administration, Property Management and Disposal Service, Industry Materials Division, Metals Project, Washington, D.C. 20405.

Sec. 56.2 Sales price.

Sales of silver will be at prices offered through the competitive bidding procedures referred to in Sec. 56.1, and accepted by the GSA.

Note: Subject to the provisions of Pub. Law 90-29, approved June 24, 1967, silver certificates will continue to be exchangeable for silver on demand until June 24, 1968, as specified in the first paragraph of the notice appearing at 29 FR 3819, March 27, 1964.

PART 90 (1976) Table of Charges and Regulations of the Mints and Assay Offices of the United States for Processing Silver and Assaying Bullion Metals, and Ores.[1]

Source: 35 Fed. Reg. 19177 (12/18/70). The information below is for historical purposes only and is no longer in effect. It nonetheless is useful to note the standards of the Mint.

Sec. 90.1 Application and general regulations.

(a) *Scope.* This part prescribes policies, regulations, and charges of the U.S. Mints and Assay Offices governing the acceptance and treatment of silver deposited for purchase, under provisions of the Newly Mined Domestic Silver Regulations of 1965, the regulations of the Office of Domestic Gold and Silver Operations (Parts 81 and 93 of this chapter, respectively) and Title 31 of the United States Code.

(b) *Assaying, melting, parting and refining and other related services.* The charges for the various operations on bullion deposited, for the preparation of bullion deposited, for the preparation of bars, and for the assay of sam-

ples of bullion and ores are fixed from time to time by the Director of the Mint, with the concurrence of the Secretary of the Treasury, so as to equal but not exceed in their judgment the actual average costs. The U.S. Mints and Assay Offices shall impose appropriate charges for services performed under this regulations.

(c) *Metals not returned to depositors.* Metals other than silver contained in bullion accepted will not be returned to the depositor, nor will credit or payment be given for them.

Sec. 90.2 Silver bullion which may be accepted.

The U.S. Mints and Assay Offices will accept for purchase, silver which meets the requisites set forth in Parts 81 and 93 of this chapter, and the general regulations in this part.

Sec. 90.3. Requisites for acceptable bullion as to fineness.

(a) Silver governed by the regulations in Parts 81 and 93 of this chapter must contain at least 600 parts of silver in 1,000 to be eligible for deposit under the regulation in this part.

(b) In addition to this requisite as to fineness, deposits in this category must also be accompanied by duly executed affidavits as evidence that such silver is eligible. Forms for this purpose are prescribed in Part 93 of this chapter.

Sec. 90.4 Return or rejection of silver deposited.

(a) *Unsatisfactory silver bullion.* Any silver bullion that fails to meet the necessary requisites set forth in parts 81 and 93 of this chapter, and this part, or that is unsuitable for Mint operations, shall not be accepted, but shall be returned according to provisions of paragraph (b) of this section.

(b) *Return of bullion.* Subject to payment in cash to the government for charges incurred, bullion may be returned to the depositor at any time before settlement is made or payment is tendered therefore, and thereafter at the option of the Superintendent of the Mint or the officer in charge of the Assay Office handling the bullion.

Sec. 90.5 Charges for treating and processing silver.

(a) *Melting charges.* A melting charge of $5 shall be imposed for the first 1,000 gross troy ounces of each deposit of bullion. An additional melting charge of 50 cents shall be imposed for each additional 100 gross troy ounces or fraction thereof. These rates shall be applied to the aftermelting gross weight of the deposit.

(b) *Excess melting loss charge.* When there is a melting loss in excess of 15 percent of the before-melting weight of a deposit of bullion, an additional melting charge of $3 shall be imposed for the first 100 gross troy ounces. An additional melting charge of $1 shall be imposed in this case for each additional 100 gross troy ounces or fraction thereof. These additional rates shall be applied to the before melting gross weight of the deposit.

(c) *Abnormal treatment charges.* At the discretion of the Superintendent of the Mint or the officer in charge of the Assay Office, deposits of bullion which require abnormal treatment shall be subjected to additional charges equal to the extra cost, including remelting and retreatment if necessary. When charges for abnormal treatment are assessed, a charge will not be made for an excess melting loss.

(d) *Parting and refining charge (rate per gross troy ounce to the nearest hundredth) — Silver Bullion.*

Silver content:	Charge (cents)
600 to 850 thousandths	12
850½ to 995¾ thousandths	6

Sec. 90.6 Charges for special assays and assays of ores and fine gold certification.

(A) *Bullion Special Assays.* Gold or silver bullion samples for special assay will be accepted at the U.S. Assay Office in N.Y. and at the U.S. Mint in Denver. Charges will be in accordance with the following table of charges.

Charges per assay

	Gold or silver bullion (under 800 base metal)	Plated or filled goods and white gold
Gold	$11	$12
Silver	11	12
Gold and silver (same sample)	19	23
Additional charge when the sample contains any of the platinum group metals	5	5

(B) *Assay of ores.* Assays of ore samples will be made at the U.S. Mint in Denver. The charge for each metal determined will be:

	Charge
Gold	$5
Silver	5
Gold and silver (same sample)	8
Lead	8
Zinc	8
Copper	7

Sec. 90.7 Transactions not subject to various treating and processing charges.

(a) *Deposits exempt from melting charges.*

(1) Uncurrent U.S. Coin.

(2) Silver bullion of at least .999 thousandths fineness when a satisfactory assay can be obtained without melting.

(b) *Deposits exempt from parting and refining charges.* Deposits of domestic mutilated or uncurrent silver coin received in accordance with Part 100 of this chapter, are not subject to charges for parting and refining, except as provided in Sec. 90.5

Sec. 90.8 Settlement for transactions conducted.

(A) *Advance settlement.* When the approximate fineness of bullion containing 5,000 or more ounces of silver may be readily determined, settlement of 90 percent of the value may be made at the discretion of the Superintendent or officer in charge. If the fineness is closely determined by assay, and the bullion is awaiting remelting and reassay for exact determination, settlement of 98 percent of the value may be made. Other advances may be authorized by the Secretary of the Treasury. In any case of an advance the depositor may give a written guarantee that the value of the deposit is at least equal to the amount advanced.

(b) *Statement of charges.* The detailed memorandum of the weight of bullion after melting, the report of the Assayer as to fineness, the value of the bullion deposited and the amount of the charges shall be given to the depositor.

(c) *Payment for silver bullion deposits.* Payment for silver bullion is made, in so far as practicable, in the order in which the deposits are received, by check drawn in favor of the depositor or to such other person as he may designate. In no case is a check in payment of a deposit drawn in favor of any officer or employee of the institution where the deposit is made, and in no case may any person employed in the institution act as agent for the depositor. Checks may be sent by ordinary mail at the risk of the payee or by registered mail at his request and expense.

Footnote:

[1]Coinage Mints are located at Philadelphia, Pa., and Denver, Colo.; U.S. Assay Offices are located at New York, N.Y. [Editor's note: closed December 1982], and San Francisco, Calif. Deposits are not accepted in Washington, D.C.

Part 91 — Regulations governing conduct in

or on the Bureau of the Mint buildings and grounds

Sec.
91.1 Authority.
91.2 Applicability.
91.3 Recording presence.
91.4 Preservation of property.
91.5 Compliance with signs and directions.
91.6 Nuisances.
91.7 Gambling.
91.8 Alcoholic beverages, narcotics, hallucinogenic and dangerous drugs.
Sec.
91.9 Soliciting, vending, debt collection, and distribution of handbills.
91.10 Photographs.
91.11 Dogs and other animals.
91.12 Vehicular and pedestrian traffic.
91.13 Weapons and explosives.
91.14 Penalties and other law.

Authorized by 31 USC Sec. 301 by delegation of the Administrator of General Services, 35 Federal Register 14426, and Treasury Department No. 177-25 (Revision No. 2), 38 Federal Register 21947. The source of this is 34 Federal Register 503, Jan. 14, 1969, unless otherwise noted.

In the case of Sec. 91.1 and 91.2, as well as the section concerning hallucinogens and drugs, the source is Federal Register of September 11, 1973, 38 Federal Register 24897.

Sec. 91.1 Authority.

The regulations in this part governing conduct in and on the Bureau of the Mint buildings and grounds located as follows: U.S. Mint, Colfax, and Delaware Streets, Denver, Colo.; U.S. Bullion Depository, Fort Knox, Ky.; U.S. Assay Office, 32 Old Slip New York, N.Y.; U.S. Mint, 5th and Arch Streets, Philadelphia, Penn.; U.S. Assay Office, 155 Hermann Street, and the Old U.S. Mint Building, 88 Fifth Street, San Francisco, Calif.; and U.S. Bullion Depository, West Point, New York; are promulgated pursuant to the authority vested in the Secretary of the Treasury . . .

Sec. 91.2 Applicability.

The regulations in this part apply to the buildings and grounds of the Bureau of the Mint located as follows: U.S. Mint, Colfax and Delaware Streets, Denver, Colo.; U.S. Bullion Depository, Fort Knox, Ky.; U.S. Assay Office, 32 Old Slip, New York, New York; U.S. Mint, Fifth and Arch Streets, Philadelphia, Penn.; U.S. Assay Office, 155 Hermann Street, and the Old U.S. Mint Building, 88 Fifth Street, San Francisco, Calif.; and U.S. Bullion Depository, West Point, N.Y.; and to all persons entering in or

on such property. Unless otherwise stated herein, the Bureau of the Mint buildings and grounds shall be referred to in these regulations as the "property".

Sec. 91.3 Recording presence.

Except as otherwise ordered, the property shall be closed to the public during other than normal working hours. The property shall also be closed to the public when, in the opinion of the senior supervising official of any Bureau of the Mint establishment covered by these regulations, or his delegate, an emergency situation exists, and at such other times as may be necessary for the orderly conduct of the Government's business. Admission to the property during periods when such property is closed to the public will be limited to authorized individuals who will be required to sign the register and/or display identification documents when requested by the guard.

Sec. 91.4 Preservation of property.

It shall be unlawful for any person without proper authority to wilfully destroy, damage, deface, or remove property or any part thereof or any furnishings therein.

Sec. 91.5 Compliance with signs and directions.

Persons in and on the property shall comply with the instructions of uniformed Bureau of the Mint guards (U.S. Special Policemen), other authorized officials, and official signs of a prohibitory or directory nature.

Sec. 91.6 Nuisances.

The use of loud, abusive, or profane language, unwarranted loitering, unauthorized assembly, the creation of any hazard to persons or things, improper disposal of rubbish, spitting, prurient prying, the commission of any obscene or indecent act, or any other disorderly conduct on the property is prohibited. The throwing of any articles of any kind in, upon, or from the property and climbing upon any part thereof, is prohibited. The entry, without specific permission, upon any part of the property to which the public does not customarily have access, is prohibited.

Sec. 91.7 Gambling.

(a) Participating in games for money or other property, the operation of gambling devices, the conduct of a lottery or pool, the selling or purchasing of numbers tickets, or any other gambling in or on the property, is prohibited.

(b) Possession in or on the property of any numbers slip or ticket, record, notation, receipt, or other writing of a type ordinarily used in any illegal form of gambling such as a tip sheet or dream book, unless explained to the satisfaction of the head of the bureau or his delegate, shall be prima facie evidence that there is participation in an illegal form of gambling in or on such property.

Sec. 91.8 Alcoholic beverages, narcotics, hallucinogenic and dangerous drugs.

Entering or being on the property, or operating a motor vehicle thereon by a person under the influence of alcoholic beverages, narcotics, hallucinogenic or dangerous drugs is prohibited. The use of any narcotic, hallucinogenic or dangerous drug in or on the property is prohibited. The use of alcoholic beverages in or on the property is prohibited except on occasions and on property upon which the Director of the Mint has for appropriate official uses granted an exemption permit in writing.

Sec. 91.9 Soliciting, vending, debt collection, and distribution of handbills.

The unauthorized soliciting of alms and contributions, the commercial soliciting and vending of all kinds, the display or distribution of commercial advertising, or the collecting of private debts, in or on the property, is prohibited. This rule does not apply to Bureau of the Mint concessions or notices posted by authorized employees on the bulletin boards. Distribution of material such as pamphlets, handbills, and flyers is prohibited without prior approval from the Director of the Mint, or the delegate of the Director.

Sec. 91.10 Photographs.

The taking of photographs on the property is prohibited, without the written permission of the Director of the Mint.

Sec. 91.11 Dogs and other animals.

Dogs and other animals, except seeing-eye dogs, shall not be brought upon the property for other than official purposes.

Sec. 91.12 Vehicular and pedestrian traffic.

(a) Drivers of all vehicles in or on the property shall drive in a careful and safe manner at all times and shall comply with the signals and directions of guards and all posted traffic signs.

(b) The blocking of entrances, driveways, walks, loading platforms, or fire hydrants in or on the property is prohibited.

(c) Parking in or on the property is not allowed without a permit or specific authority. Parking without authority, parking in authorized locations or in locations reserved for other persons or continuously in excess of eight hours without permission, or contrary to the direction of a uniformed Bureau of the Mint guard, or of posted signs, is prohibited.

(d) This paragraph may be supplemented from time to time with the approval of the Director of the Mint, or the delegate of the

Director, by the issuance and posting of such specific traffic directives as may be required and when so issued and posted such directives shall have the same force and effect as if made a part hereof.

Sec. 91.13 Weapons and explosives.

No person while on the property shall carry firearms, other dangerous or deadly weapons, or explosives, either openly or concealed, except for official purposes.

Sec. 91.14 Penalties and other law.

Whoever shall be found guilty of violating any of the regulations in this part while on the property is subject to a fine of not more than $50, or imprisonment of not more than 30 days or both (see 40 U.S.C. 318c. Nothing contained in the regulations in this part shall be construed to abrogate any other Federal laws or regulations or those of any state or municipality applicable to the property referred to in Sec. 91.2 and governed by the regulations in this part.

Part 92 — Bureau of the Mint operations and procedures
Sec.
92.1 Manufacture of medals.
92.2 Sale of "list" medals.
92.3 Manufacture and sale of "Proof" coins.
92.4 Uncirculated Mint Sets.
92.5 Procedure governing availability of Bureau of the Mint records.
92.6 Appeal
Authority: U.S.C. 301.
Source: 47 FR 56353, Dec. 16, 1982, unless otherwise noted.

Sec. 92.1 Manufacture of medals.

With the approval of the Director of the Mint, dies for medals of a national character designated by Congress may be executed at the Philadelphia Mint, and struck in such field office of the Mints and Assay Offices as the Director shall designate.

Sec. 92.2 Sale of "list" medals.

Medals on the regular Mint list, when available, are sold to the public at a charge sufficient to cover their cost, and to include mailing cost when mailed. Copies of the list of medals available for sale and their selling prices may be obtained from the Director of the Mint, Washington, D.C.

Sec. 92.3 Manufacture and sale of "proof" coins.

"Proof" coins, i.e., coins prepared from blanks specially polished and struck, are made as authorized by the Director of the Mint and are sold at a price sufficient to cover their face value plus the additional expense of their manufacture and sale. Their manufacture and issuance are contingent upon the

---

demands of regular operations. Information concerning availability and price may be obtained from the Director of the Mint, Treasury Department, Washington, D.C. 20220.

Sec. 92.4 Uncirculated Mint Sets.

Uncirculated Mint Sets, i.e., specially packaged coin sets containing one coin of each denomination struck at the Mints at Philadelphia and Denver, and the Assay Office at San Francisco, will be made as authorized by the Director of the Mint and will be sold at a price sufficient to cover their face value plus the additional expense of their processing and sale. Their manufacture and issuance are contingent upon demands of regular operations. Information concerning availability and price may be obtained from the Director of the Mint, Treasury Department, Washington, D.C. 20220.

Sec. 92.5 Procedure governing availability of Bureau of the Mint records.

(a) Regulations of the Office of the Secretary adopted. The regulations on the Disclosure of Records of the Office of the Secretary and other bureaus and offices of the Department issued under 5 U.S.C. 301 and 552 and published as Part 1 of this title, 32 FR No. 127, July 1, 1967, except for Sec. 1.7 of this title entitled "Appeal," shall govern the availability of Bureau of the Mint records.

(b) Determination of availability. The Director of the Mint delegates authority to the following Mint officials to determine, in accordance with Part 1 of this title, which of the records or information requested is available, subject to the appeal provided in Sec. 92.6: The Deputy Director of the Mint, Division Heads in the Office of the Director, and the Superintendent or Officer in Charge of the field office where the record is located.

(c) Requests for identifiable records. A written request for an identifiable record shall be addressed to the Director of the Mint, Washington, D.C. 20220. A request presented in person shall be made in the public reading room of the Treasury Department, 15th Street and Pennsylvania Avenue, NW, Washington, D.C., or in such other office designated by the Director of the Mint.

Sec. 92.6 Appeal

Any person denied access to records requested under Sec. 92.5 may file an appeal to the Director of the Mint within 30 days after notification of such denial. The appeal shall provide the name and address of the appellant, the identification of the record denied, and the date of the original request and its denial.

31 CFR Part 94 (1976)

Information concerning regulations prohibiting the exportation of 1-cent pieces, as well as their melting, has expired. It is reprinted for historical significance, since it is possible that higher metal prices for this or other coins may create a situation wherein it could be utilized again.

It is interesting to note in the course of this that there have been criminal prosecutions, and convictions, for violation of this section. The penalties, as stated, are quite substantial.

Sec. 94.1 Prohibition.

Except as specifically authorized by the Secretary of the Treasury (or any person, agency, or instrumentality designated by him) or as provided in this part, no 1-cent coin of the United States may be melted, treated, or exported from the United States or any place subject to the jurisdiction thereof. This prohibition shall not apply to any department or agency of the United States.

Sec. 94.2 Exceptions.

The prohibition contained in Sec. 94.1 against exporting 1-cent coin of the United States shall not apply to the following:

(a) Exports of 1-cent coins having an aggregate face amount value not exceeding $5 in any one shipment, to be legitimately used as coins or for numismatic purposes. This paragraph does not authorize export for the purpose of the sale or resale of coins for melting or treating by any person;

(b) 1-cent coin of the United States having an aggregate face amount value not exceeding $1 carried in the personal effects of any individual departing from a place subject to the jurisdiction of the United States.

Sec. 94.3 Definitions.

(a) "Person" means an individual, partnership, association, corporation, or other organization.

(b) "Treat" means to melt, smelt, refine, or otherwise treat by heating or by a chemical or electrical process.

Sec. 94.4 Penalties.

(a) Any person who melts, treats or exports 1-cent coin of the United States in violation of Sec. 94.1 shall be subject to the penalties provided in section 105 of the Coinage Act of 1965, which provides:

(1) Whenever in the judgment of the Secretary such action is necessary to protect the coinage of the United States, he is authorized under such rules and regulations as he may prescribe to prohibit, curtail, or regulate the exportation, melting, or treating of any coin of the United States.

(2) Whoever knowingly violates any order,

rule, regulation, or license issued pursuant to paragraph (a) of this section shall be fined not more than $10,000, or imprisoned not more than five years, or both.

(b) Any coins exported, melted, or treated (or any metal resulting from such melting or treating) in violation of any provision of this part or of the provisions of any authorization, license, ruling, regulation, order, direction, or instruction issued by or pursuant to the direction or authorization of the Secretary of the Treasury pursuant to this part shall be forfeited to the United States as provided in section 106 of the Coinage Act of 1965.

(c) Attention is also directed to 18 U.S.C. 1001 which provides:

Whoever, in any matter within the jurisdiction of any department or agency of the United States knowingly and willfully falsifies, conceals or covers up by any trick, scheme, or device a material fact, or makes any false, fictitious or fraudulent statements or representations, or makes or uses any false writing or document knowing the same to contain any false, fictitious, or fraudulent statement or entry, shall be fined not more than $10,000 or imprisoned not more than five years, or both.

Part 100—Exchange of paper currency and coin
Sec. 100.2 Scope of regulations; transactions effected through Federal Reserve Banks and branches; distribution of coin and currencies.
Subpart A — In general
100.3 Lawfully held coins and currencies in general.
100.4 Gold coin and gold certificates in general.
Subpart B — Exchange of mutilated paper currency
100.5 Mutilated paper currency.
100.6 Destroyed paper currency.
100.7 Treasury's liability.
100.8 Packaging of mutilated currency.
100.9 Where mutilated currency should be transmitted.
Subpart C — Exchange of coin
100.10 Exchange of uncurrent coins.
100.11 Exchange of bent and partial coins.
100.12 Exchange of fused and mixed coins.
100.13 Criminal penalties.
Subpart D — Other information
100.16 Exchange of paper and coin to be handled through Federal Reserve Banks and branches.
100.17 Location of Federal Reserve Banks and branches.
100.18 Counterfeit notes to be marked; "redemption" of notes wrongfully so marked.

100.19 Disposition of counterfeit notes and coins.
Authority: Sec. 1, 49 Stat. 938; 31 U.S.C. 773a.
Source: 47 FR 32044, July 23, 1982, unless otherwise noted.

100.2 Scope of regulations; transactions effected through Federal Reserve Banks and branches; distribution of coin and currencies.
The regulations in this part govern the exchange of the coin and paper currency of the United States (including national bank notes and Federal Reserve Bank notes and Federal Reserve Bank notes in process of retirement and Federal Reserve notes). Under authorization in the act approved May 29, 1920, 41 Stat. 655 (31 U.S.C. 476), the Secretary of the Treasury transferred to the Federal Reserve Banks and branches the duties and functions performed by the former Assistant Treasurers of the United States in connection with the exchange of paper currency and coin of the United States. Except for the duties in this respect to be performed by the Treasurer of the United States and the director of the Mint, as may be indicated from time to time by the Secretary of the Treasury, exchanges of the paper currency and coin of the United States and the distribution and replacement thereof will, so far as practicable, be effected through the Federal Reserve Banks and branches. The Federal Reserve Banks and branches are authorized to distribute available supplies of coin and currency to depository institutions, as that term is defined in Section 103 of the Monetary Control Act of 1980 (Pub. L. 96-221). As authorized by Section 107 of the Act, transportation of coin and currency and coin wrapping services will be provided according to a schedule of fees established by the Board of Governors of the Federal Reserve system. Inquiries by depository institutions regarding distribution and related services should be addressed to the Federal Reserve Bank of the district where the institution is located.

Subpart A — In general
Sec. 100.3 Lawfully held coin and currencies in general.
The official agencies of the Department of the Treasury will continue to exchange lawfully held coins and currencies of the United States, dollar for dollar, for other coins and currencies which may be lawfully acquired and are legal tender for public and private debts. Paper currency of the United States which has been falsely altered and coins altered to render them for use as other denominations will not be redeemed since such cur-

rency and coins are subject to forfeiture under title 18, United States Code, section 492. Persons receiving such currency and coins should notify immediately the nearest local office of the U.S. Secret Service of the Department of the Treasury, and hold the same pending advice from the Service.

Sec. 100.4 Gold coin and gold certifictes in general.

Gold coins, and gold certificates of the type issued before Jan. 30, 1934, are exchangeable, as provided in this part, into other currency or coin which may be lawfully issued.

Subpart B — Exchange of mutilated paper currency

Sec. 100.5 Mutilated paper currency.

(a) Lawfully held paper currency of the United States which has been mutilated will be exchanged at face amount if clearly more than one-half of the original whole note remains. Fragments of such mutilated currency which are not clearly more than one-half of the original whole note will be exchanged at face value only if the Commissioner, Bureau of Government Financial Operations, Department of the Treasury, is satisfied that the missing portions have been totally destroyed. The Commissioner's judgment shall be based on such evidence of total destruction as is necessary and shall be final.

Definitions

(1) Mutilated currency is currency which has been damaged to the extent that (i) one-half or less of the original note remains or (ii) its condition is such that its value is questionable and the currency must be forwarded to the Treasury Department for examination by trained experts before any exchange is made.

(2) Unfit currency is currency which is unfit for further circulation because of its physical condition such as torn, dirty, limp, worn or defaced. Unfit currency should not be forwarded to the Treasury, but may be exchanged at commercial banks.

Sec. 100.6 Destroyed paper currency.

(a) Payment will be made to lawful holders of mutilated currency at full value when:

(1) Clearly more than 50 percent of a note identifiable as United States currency is present; or

(2) Fifty percent or less of a note identifiable as United States currency is present and the method of mutilation and supporting evidence demonstrate to the satisfaction of the Treasury that the missing portions have been totally destroyed.

(b) No payments will be made when:

(1) Fragments and remnants presented are not identifiable as United States currency; or

(2) Fragments and remnants presented which represent 50 percent or less of a note are identifiable as United States currency but the method of destruction and supporting evidence do not satisfy the Treasury that the missing portion has been totally destroyed.

(c) All cases will be handled under proper procedures to safeguard the funds and interests of the claimant. In some cases, the amount repaid will be less than the amount claimed. In other cases, the amount repaid may be greater. The amount paid will be determined by an examination made by trained mutilated currency examiners and governed by the above criteria.

(d) The Commissioner of the Bureau of Government Financial Operations shall have final authority with respect to settlements for mutilated currency claims.

Sec. 100.8 Packaging of mutilated currency.

Mutilated currency examiners are normally able to determine the value of mutilated currency when it has been carefully packed and boxed as described below:

(a) Regardless of the condition of the currency, do not disturb the fragments more than is absolutely necessary.

(b) If the currency is brittle or inclined to fall apart, pack it carefully in cotton and box it as found, without disturbing the fragments, if possible.

(c) If the money was in a purse, box, or other container when mutilated, it should be left therein, if possible, in order to prevent further deterioration of the fragments or from their being lost.

(d) If it is absolutely necessary to remove the fragments from the container, send the container with the currency and any other contents found, except as noted in (h) below.

(e) If the money was flat when mutilated, do not roll or fold.

(f) If the money was in a roll when mutilated, do not attempt to unroll or straighten.

(g) If coin or any other metal is mixed with the currency, remove carefully. Do not send coin or other metal in the same package with mutilated paper currency, as the metal will break up the currency. Coin should be forwarded as provided in Section 100.12 (c) and (d).

(h) Any fused or melted coin should be sent to: Superintendent, United States Mint, P.O. Box 400, Philadelphia, Pa. 19105.

Sec. 100.9 Where mutilated currency should be transmitted.

Mutilated currency shipments must be addressed as follows: Department of the Treasury, Bureau of Government Financial Operations, Room 132, Treasury Annex No. 1, DCS/BEPA, Washington, D.C. 20226.

Subpart C — Exchange of Coin
Sec. 100.10 Exchange of uncurrent coins.

(a) *Definition.* Uncurrent coins are whole U.S. coins which are merely worn or reduced in weight by natural abrasion yet are readily and clearly recognizable as to genuineness and denomination and which are machine countable.

(b) *Redemption basis.* Uncurrent coins will be redeemed at face value.

(c) *Criteria for acceptance.* Uncurrent coins, forwarded for redemption at face value, must be shipped at the expense and risk of the owner. Shipments of subsidiary or minor coins for redemption at face value should be sorted by denomination into packages in sums of multiples of $20. Not more than $1,000 in any silver or clad coin, $200 in 5-cent pieces, or $50 in 1-cent pieces should be shipped in one bag or package.

(d) *Redemption sites.* Uncurrent coins will be redeemed only at the Federal Reserve banks and branches listed in Sec. 100.17.

Sec. 100.11 Exchange of bent and partial coins.

(a) Definitions.

(1) Bent coins are U.S. coins which are bent or deformed so as to preclude normal machine counting but which are readily and clearly identifiable as to genuineness and denomination.

(2) Partial coins are U.S. coins which are not whole; partial coins must be readily and clearly identifiable as to genuineness and denomination.

(b) *Redemption basis.* Bent and partial coins shall be redeemed on the basis of their weight and denomination category rates, (which is the weight equivalent of face value) provided such coins are presented separately by denomination category in lots of at least one pound for each category. Bent and partial coins not presented separately by denomination category will be redeemed as mixed coins. Denomination categories and rates are 1. Cents, @ $1.4585 per pound 2. 5-cent pieces, @ $4.5359 per pound 3. Dimes, Quarters, Halves, and Eisenhower Dollars @ $20.00 per pound and 4. Anthony Dollars @ $56.00 per pound. Copper plated zinc cents shall be redeemed at the face value equivalent of copper 1-cent coins.

(c) *Redemption Site.* Bent and partial coins will be redeemed only at the United States Mint, P.O. Box 400, Philadelphia, Pa. 19105. Coins are shipped at sender's risk and expense.

Sec. 100.12 Exchange of fused and mixed coins.

(a) Definitions.

(1) Fused coins are U.S. coins which are melted to the extent that they are bonded together and the majority of which are readily and clearly identifiable as U.S. coins.

(2) Mixed coins are U.S. coins of several alloy categories which are presented together, but are readily and clearly identifiable as U.S. coins.

(b) Redemption basis.

(1) Fused and mixed coins shall be redeemed at the lesser of:

(i) The inventory value of the copper and nickel as priced in the Philadelphia Mint, Coinage Metal Account at the end of the preceding calendar quarter or;

(ii) $1.5327 per pound of contained copper, which is the face value equivalent of a pound of copper in the copper 1-cent coin plus $18.1442 per pound of contained nickel which is the face value equivalent of a pound of nickel in the 5-cent coin.

(2) The redemption rate (discussed in subparagraph (1) (a)) will take effect on the 15th day of each new calendar quarter.

(c) Criteria for acceptance.

(1) A minimum of two pounds of fused and mixed coins is required for redemption.

(2) Fused and mixed coins containing lead, solder, or other substance which will render them unsuitable for coinage metal will not be accepted.

(d) Redemption site. Fused and mixed coins will be redeemed only at the United States Mint, P.O. Box 400, Philadelphia, Pa. 19105. Coins are shipped at sender's risk and expense.

Sec. 100.13 Criminal penalties.

Criminal penalties connected with the defacement or mutilation of U.S. coins are provided in the United States Code, Title 18, Section 331.

Subpart D — Other information
Sec. 100.16 Exchange of paper and coin to be handled through Federal Reserve banks and branches.

Other than as provided in this document all transactions including the exchange of paper currency and coin shall be handled through the Federal Reserve banks and branches.

Sec. 100.17 Location of Federal Reserve banks and branches.

Federal Reserve Bank and address
Boston — 600 Atlantic Avenue, Boston, Mass. 02106

New York — 33 Liberty Street (Federal Reserve P.O. Station), New York, N.Y. 10045

Buffalo Branch — 160 Delaware Avenue (P.O. Box 961), Buffalo, N.Y. 14240

Philadelphia — 100 North Sixth Street (P.O. Box 66), Philadelphia, Pa. 19105

Cleveland — 1455 East Sixth Street (P.O. Box 6387), Cleveland, Ohio 44101

Cincinnati Branch — 150 East Fourth Street (P.O. Box 999), Cincinnati, Ohio 45201

Pittsburgh Branch — 717 Grant Street (P.O. Box 867), Pittsburgh, Pa. 15230

Richmond — 701 East Byrd Avenue (P.O. Box 27622), Richmond, Va. 23261

Baltimore Branch — 114-120 East Lexington Street (P.O. Box 1378), Baltimore, Md. 21203

Charlotte Branch — 401 South Tryon Street (P.O. Box 30248), Charlotte, N.C. 28230

Atlanta — 104 Marietta Street, NW., Atlanta, Ga. 30303

Birmingham Branch — 1801 Fifth Avenue, North (P.O. Box 10447), Birmingham, Ala. 35202

Jacksonville Branch — 515 Julia Street Jacksonville, Fla. 32231

Miami Branch — 9100 NW., 36th Street (P.O. Box 520847), Miami, Fla. 33152

Nashville Branch — 301 Eighth Avenue, North, Nashville, Tenn. 37203

New Orleans Branch — 525 St. Charles Avenue (P.O. Box 61630), New Orleans, La. 70161

Chicago — 230 South LaSalle Street (P.O. Box 834), Chicago, Ill. 50590

Detroit Branch — 160 Fort Street, West (P.O. Box 1059), Detroit, Mich. 48231

St. Louis — 411 Locust Street (P.O. Box 442), St. Louis, Mo. 63166

Little Rock Branch — 325 West Capitol Avenue (P.O. Box 1261), Little Rock, Ark. 72203

Louisville Branch — 410 South Fifth Street (P.O. Box 32710), Louisville, Ky. 40232

Memphis Branch — 200 North Main Street (P.O. Box 407), Memphis, Tenn. 38101

Minneapolis — 250 Marquette Avenue, Minneapolis, Minn. 55480

Helena Branch — 400 North Park Avenue, Helena, Mont. 59601

Kansas City — 925 Grand Avenue (Federal Reserve Station), Kansas City, Mo. 64198

Denver Branch — 1020 16th Street (P.O. Box 5228, Terminal Annex), Denver, Colo. 80217

Oklahoma City Branch — 226 Northwest Third Street (P.O. Box 25129), Oklahoma City, Okla. 73125

Omaha Branch — 102 South Seventeenth Street, Omaha, Neb. 68102

Dallas — 400 South Akard Street (Station K), Dallas, Texas 75222

El Paso Branch — 301 East Main Street (P.O. Box 100), El Paso, Texas 79999

Houston Branch — 1701 San Jacinto Street (P.O. Box 2578), Houston, Texas 77001

San Antonio Branch — 126 East Nueva Street (P.O. Box 1471), San Antonio, Texas 78295

San Francisco — 400 Sansome Street (P.O. Box 7702), San Francisco, Calif. 94120

Los Angeles Branch — 409 West Olympic Boulevard (P.O. Box 2077), Los Angeles Calif. 90051

Portland Branch — 915 SW Stark Street (P.O. Box 3436), Portland, Ore. 97208

Salt Lake City Branch — 120 South State Street (P.O. Box 30780), Salt Lake City, Utah 84125

Seattle Branch — 1015 Second Avenue (P.O. Box 3567), Seattle, Wash. 98124

Sec. 100.18 Counterfeit notes to be marked; "redemption" of notes wrongfully so marked.

The act of June 30, 1876 (19 Stat. 4; 31 U.S.C. 424), provides that all U.S. Officers charged with the receipt or disbursement of public moneys, and all officers of national banks, shall stamp or write in plain letters the word "counterfeit," "altered," or "worthless" upon all fraudulent notes issued in the form of, and intended to circulate as money, which shall be presented at their places of business; and if such officers shall wrongfully stamp any genuine note of the United States, or of the national bank, they shall, upon presentation, "redeem" such notes at the face amount thereof.

Sec. 100.19 Disposition of counterfeit notes and coins.

All counterfeit notes and coin found in remittances are canceled and delivered to the U.S. Secret Service of the Department of the Treasury or to the nearest local office of that service, a receipt for the same being forwarded to the sender. Communications with respect thereto should be addressed to the Director, U.S. Secret Service, Department of the Treasury, Washington, D.C. 20223.

Sec. 100.20 Disposition of counterfeit notes and coins.

All counterfeit notes and coins found in remittance are canceled and delivered to the U.S. Secret Service of the Treasury Department or to the nearest local office of that Service, a receipt for the same being forwarded to the sender. Communications with respect thereto should be addressed to the Director,

U.S Secret Service, Treasury Department, Washington, D.C. 20226.

Part 101 — Mitigation of Forfeiture of Counterfeit Gold Coins
Authority: 18 U.S.C. 492.

Sec. 101.1 Purpose and scope
The purpose of this part is to establish a policy whereby certain purchasers or holders of gold coins who have forfeited them to the United States because they were counterfeit may, in the discretion of the Secretary of the Treasury, recover the gold bullion from the coins. This part sets forth the procedures to be followed in implementing this policy.

Sec. 101.2 Petition for mitigation.
(a) *Who may file.* Any person may petition the Secretary of the Treasury for return of the gold bullion of counterfeit gold coins forfeited to the United States if:

(1) The petitioner innocently purchased or received the coins and held them without the knowledge that they were counterfeit, and,

(2) The petitioner voluntarily submitted the coin to the Treasury Department for a determination of whether they were legitimate or counterfeit; and,

(3) The coins were determined to be counterfeit and were seized by the Treasury Department and forfeited to the United States.

(b) *To whom addressed.* Petitions for mitigation of the forfeiture of counterfeit gold coins should be addressed to the Assistant Secretary, Enforcement, Operations, Tariff Affairs, Department of Treasury, 15th and Pennsylvania Avenue, N.W., Washington, D.C. 20220.

(c) *Form.* The petition need not be in any particular form, but must be under oath, and set forth at least the following:

(1) The full name and address of the petitioner;

(2) A description of the coin or coins involved;

(3) The name and address of the person from whom the coins were received or purchased by the petitioner;

(4) The date and place where they were voluntarily submitted for examination;

(5) Any other circumstances relied upon by the petitioner to justify the mitigation;

(6) A statement that the petitioner purchased or received and held the coins without the knowledge that they were counterfeit.

Sec. 101.3 Petitions reviewed by Assistant Secretary, Enforcement, Operations, Tariff Affairs.
(a) The Assistant Secretary will receive and review all petitions for mitigation of the forfeiture of counterfeit gold coins. He shall conduct such further investigation, and may request such further information from the petitioner as he deems necessary. Petitions will be approved if the Assistant Secretary determines that:

(1) The gold coins have not been previously disposed of by normal procedures;

(2) The petitioner was an innocent purchaser or holder of the gold coins and is not under investigation in connection with the coins at the time of submission or thereafter;

(3) The coins are not needed and will not be needed in the future in any investigation or as evidence in legal proceedings; and

(4) Mitigation of the forfeiture is in the best interest of the government.

Sec. 101.4 Extraction of gold bullion from the counterfeit coins.
If the petition is approved, the Assistant Secretary shall then forward the gold coins to the Bureau of the Mint where if economically feasible, the gold bullion will be extracted from the counterfeit coins. The Bureau of the Mint will then return the bullion to the Assistant Secretary.

Sec. 101.5 Payment of smelting costs.
The petitioner shall be required to pay all reasonable costs incurred in extracting the bullion from the counterfeit coins, as shall be determined by the Assistant Secretary. Payment must be made prior to the return of the gold bullion to the petitioner.

Sec. 101.6 Return of the bullion.
After receiving the gold bullion from the Bureau of the Mint, the Assistant Secretary shall notify the petitioner that his petition has been approved and that payment of the smelting costs in an amount set forth in such notice must be made prior to the return of the bullion.

Sec. 101.7 Exceptions.
The provisions of this part shall not apply where the cost of smelting the gold coins exceeds the value of the gold bullion to be returned.

Sec. 101.8 Discretion of the Secretary.
The Secretary of the Treasury retains complete discretion to deny any claim of any petitioner when the Secretary believes it is not in the best interest of the government to return the bullion to the petitioner or when the Secretary is not convinced that the petitioner was an innocent purchaser or holder without knowledge that the gold coins were counterfeit.

(FR Doc. 77-566 Filed 1-5-77;)

31 CFR Part 601 — Distinctive Paper For United States Currency and Other Securities.
Source: Department Circular 394, Feb. 1,

1928, unless otherwise noted. Redesignated at 39 FR 17839, May 21, 1974.

Sec. 601.1 Notice to the public.

Notice is hereby given that the Secretary of the Treasury, by authority of law, has adopted a new distinctive paper for use in printing United States currency and other securities.

Sec. 601.2 Description of paper.

The paper is cream-white bank-note paper which closely resembles in general appearance the paper now in use, and which must conform to specifications prescribed by the Secretary of the Treasury, in which currency paper and bond paper may be differentiated. The distinctive feature, identical for all paper used for the production of paper currency and public debt issues of the United States, shall consist of small segments of fiber, either natural or synthetic, colored red and blue, incorporated in the body of the paper while in process of manufacture and evenly distributed throughout.

Sec. 601.3 Use of paper.

The new distinctive paper shall be used for printing currency of the reduced size, including United States notes, gold certificates, silver certificates, Federal Reserve notes, and national bank notes. The use of the present distinctive paper adopted on July 30, 1891, the distinctive feature of which consists of localized red and blue silk fiber incorporated in the body of the paper while in the process of manufacture so placed as to form perpendicular stripes, will be continued for any printing of currency of the present size hereafter required.

Sec. 601.4 Use of paper; interest-bearing securities of the United States.

After the issue of the reduced size currency, the new distinctive paper shall thereafter be used for the printing of interest-bearing securities of the United States, and for any other printing where the use of distinctive paper is indicated: *Provided, however,* That any then existing stocks of blank paper containing the present distinctive feature may be utilized.

Sec. 601.5 Penalty for unauthorized control or possession.

The Secretary of the Treasury hereby gives notice that the new distinctive paper, together with any other distinctive paper, heretofore adopted for the printing of paper currency or other obligations or securities of the United States is and will be subject to the provisions of section 474 of Public Law 722, 80th Congress, which provides, in part as follows:

Whoever has or retains in his control or possession, after a distinctive paper has been adopted by the Secretary of the Treasury for the obligations and other securities of the United States, any similar paper adapted to the making of any such obligation or other security, except under the authority of the Secretary of the Treasury or some other proper officer of the United States, shall be fined not more than $5,000, or imprisoned not more than 15 years, or both.

Sec. 601.6 Modifications of Department Circular No. 121.

The provisions of Department Circular No. 121, dated July 30, 1891, are modified accordingly.[1]

Footnote:

[1]Department Circular No. 121, July 30, 1891, provided for a new distinctive paper for all obligations except checks and drafts, the distinctive feature of which consisted of localized red and blue silk fiber incorporated in the body of the paper while in process of manufacture so placed as to form perpendicular stripes on either side of the center portrait or vignette.

Department of the Treasury Use of Metal Tokens

On Sept. 2, 1983, the Mint notified the public that it was proposing to change its policy that opposed the use of metal tokens provided that certain criteria was met. 48 Federal Register 40054. Public comment was invited and, for the most part, comments were received that were aimed at preventing the unlawful use of tokens in vending machines and other coin operated devices. On June 21, 1984, the Mint published revised token restrictions which generally adopted the increased restrictions, but invited additional comments. 49 Fed. Reg. 25556. Those proposed revisions are found on Pages 128 and 129 of the fourth edition of the *Coin World Almanac.* Effective July 15, 1985, final regulations were issued by the Mint. The policy reflected is intended as advice and guidance for token manufacturers and users as well as the general public. It represents the views of the Treasury Department concerning measures which should minimize the possibility of violating the counterfeiting provisions of Title 18 of the United States Code. It does not prescribe mandatory specifications concerning the size, composition or any other requirements of the metal token. These matters, however, may be the subject of state or local regulation. What it does state is that the Treasury Department does not object to tokens which meet the restrictions set forth in the notice. It should be noted that prosecution of violations of the counterfeiting statutes is vested in the Justice Department which assesses each claimed violation based upon the facts presented.

Restrictions on the diameter of metal tokens is the most essential means of minimizing the possibility that tokens will be unlawfully used to slug vending and other gaming machines, according to the Treasury Department. 50 Fed. Reg. 28680 (July 15, 1985). The Treasury Department determine that restrictions on minimum weight and thickness on tokens are not necessary in view of the restrictions imposed on token diameters.

Below follow the conditions for departmental approval:

Conditions for Department Approval

The Department does not oppose the production or use of tokens which meet the following conditions:

1: Tokens should be clearly identified with the name and location of the establishment from which they originate on at least one side. Alternatively, tokens should contain an identifying mark or logo which clearly indicates the identity of the manufacturer.

2. Tokens should not be within the following diameter ranges (inches):

0.680-0.775
0.810-0.860
0.910-0.980
1.018-1.068
1.180-1.230
1.475-1.525

3. Tokens shall not be manufactured from a three-layered material consisting of a copper-nickel alloy clad on both sides of a pure core, nor from a copper-based material except if the total of zinc, nickel, aluminum, magnesium and other alloying materials is a least 20 percent of the token's weight. In addition, tokens shall not be manufactured from material which possesses sufficient magnetic properties so as to be accepted by a coin mechanism.

4. Establishments using these tokens shall prominently and conspicuously post signs on their premises notifying patrons that federal law prohibits the use of such tokens outside the premises for any monetary purpose whatever.

5. The issuing establishment shall not accept tokens as payment for any goods or services offered by such establishment with the execption of the specific use for which the tokens were designed.

6. The design on the token shall not resemble any current or past foreign or U.S. coinage.

The Department of Treasury believes that the observance of these restrictions will minimize the possibility of a violation of the counterfeiting statutes. The prosecution of violations of these statutes is vested with the Department of Justice which must evaluate any claimed violation on the particular facts presented.

Katherine D. Ortega, Treasurer of the United States.

Cash Transactions

Internal Revenue Code Sec. 6050I acts as a supplement to a prior existing record-keeping transaction for financial institutions found in 31 CFR Part 103.

Essentially, Sec. 6050-I provides that any person engaged in a trade or business who receives $10,000 or more in cash in one transaction or two or more related transactions is required to file a return with the Secretary of the Treasury.

Below follows the text of the law, after which the regulations (with examples involving auction firms, and coin dealers) may be found. Following that is 31 CFR Part 103 which relates to financial institutions (coin dealers were found not to be financial institutions, informally, a number of years ago — but they are covered under 6050I). It should be noted that penalties for failure to report a transaction are quite severe. For example, assume a transaction involving $10,001 takes place. Assume that, innocently, and without any type of improper intent, a report is not properly filed. Internal Revenue Service takes the position that this is the same as failure to withhold income for an employee. This leaves the employer (or in this case, the recipient) liable for a penalty of 25 percent. It also leaves the person liable for an additional penalty of 5 percent per month (up to a total of 25 percent), plus statutory interest. Thus, on a relatively modest transaction, a draconian penalty comes into play.

For further details, consult with your lawyer, or your certified public accountant.

The version appearing below includes the latest set of amendments, including Public Law 99-514, applying to returns due after Dec. 31, 1986 (i.e., in calendar year 1987 and beyond). As is also true under Sec. 6045, the bill clarifies the provisions relating to furnishing a written statement to the taxpayer of the number of substantive information reporting provisions. The obligation will be triggered, under the new provision, when there is an obligation to file (instead of the actual filing) of the return. To see the Committee Reports on this underlying provision, created by Public Law 98-369, see 1984-3 Cumulative Bulletin at 241. Text of Internal Revenue Law Sec. 6050-I. Returns relating to cash received in trade or business.

(a) Cash receipts of more than $10,000. Any person —

(1) who is engaged in a trade or business, and

(2) who, in the course of such trade or business, receives more than $10,000 in cash in 1 transaction (or 2 or more related transactions), shall make the return described in subsection (b) with respect to such transaction (or related transactions) at such time as the Secretary may by regulations prescribe.

(b) Form and manner of returns. A return is described in this subsection if such return —

(1) is in such form as the Secretary may prescribe,

(2) contains

(A) the name, address, and [taxpayer identification number] of the person from whom the cash was received,

(B) the amount of cash received,

(C) the date and nature of the transaction, and

(D) such other information as the Secretary may prescribe.

(c) Exceptions.

(1) Cash received by financial institutions. Subsection (a) shall not apply to —

(A) cash received in a transaction reported under title 31, United States Code [31 USCS Sec. 101 et seq.], if the Secretary determines that reporting under this section would duplicate the reporting to the Treasury under title 31, United States Code [31 USCS Sec. 101 et seq.], or

(B) cash received by any financial institution (as defined in subparagraphs (A), (B), (C), (D), (E), (F), (G), (J), (K), (R), and (S) of section 5312(a)(2) of title 31, United States Code [31 USCS Sec. 5312(a)(2)(A)-(G), (J), (K), (R), (S)].

(2) Transactions occurring outside the United States. Except to the extent provided in regulations prescribed by the Secretary, subsection (a) shall not apply to any transaction if the entire transaction occurs outside the United States.

(d) Cash includes foreign currency. For purposes of this section, the term "cash" includes foreign currency.

(e) Statements to be furnished to persons with respect to whom information is required. —

Every person required to make a return under subsection (a) shall furnish to each person whose name is required to be set forth in such return a written statement showing —

(1) the name and address of the person required to make such return, and

(2) the aggregate amount of cash described in subsection (a) received by the person required to make such return. The written statement required under the preceding sentence shall be furnished to the person on or before January 31 of the year following the calendar year for which the return under subsection (a) was required to be made.

Regulations Sec. 1.6050 I-1. Returns relating to cash in excess of $10,000 received in a trade or business. —

(a) Reporting requirement —

(1) In general. Any person (as defined in section 7701(a)(1)) who, in the course of a trade or business in which such person is engaged, receives cash in excess of $10,000 in 1 transaction (or 2 or more related transactions) shall, except as otherwise provided, make a return of information with respect to thereceipt of cash.

(2) Cash received for the account of another. Cash in excess of $10,000 received by a person for the account of another must be reported under this section. Thus, for example, a person who collected delinquent accounts receivable for an automobile dealer must report with respect to the receipt of cash in excess of $10,000 from the collection of a particular account even though the proceeds of the collection are credited to the account of the automobile dealer (i.e., where the rights to the proceeds from the account are retained by the automobile dealer and the collection is made on a fee-for-service basis).

(3) Cash received by agents — (i) General rule. Except as provided in paragraph (a)(3)(ii) of this section, a person who in the course of a trade or business acts as an agent (or in some other similar capacity) and receives cash in excess of $10,000 from a principal must report the receipt of cash under this section.

(ii) Exception. An agent who receives cash from a principal and uses all of the cash within 15 days in a cash transaction (the "second cash transaction") which is reportable under section 6050I or section 5312 of Title 31 of the United States Code and the regulations thereunder (31 CFR Part 103), and who discloses the name, address, and taxpayer identification number of the principal to the recipient in the second cash transaction need not report the initial receipt of cash under this section. An agent will be deemed to have met the disclosure requirements of this paragraph (a)(3)(ii) if the agent discloses only the

[d]ay after the date the cash is received. If [pers]on elects to report as one payment sev[eral] independently reportable payments [receiv]ed within a 15-day period (as described [in par]agraph (b)(1) of this section), the report [must] be filed with the Internal Revenue Ser[vice] [b]y the 15th day after the date the initial [paym]ent is received.

[ ] Form of reporting. A report required by [parag]raph (a) of this section must be made on [Form] 8300. A return of information made in [comp]liance with this paragraph must contain [the n]ame, address, and taxpayer identifica[tion n]umber of the person from whom the [cash] was received; the name, address, and [taxpa]yer identification number of the person [on w]hose behalf the transaction was conduct[ed i]f the recipient knows or has reason to [know] that the person from whom the cash [was r]eceived conducted the transaction as an [agen]t for another person); the amount of cash [recei]ved; the date and nature of the transac[tion] and any other information required by [Form] 8300. Form 8300 can be obtained from [the] Internal Revenue Service Forms Distri[buti]on Center.

[(e]) Manner of reporting — (i) Where to file. [A p]erson making a return of information un[der] this section must file Form 8300 by mail[ing] it to the address shown in the instructions [to t]he form.

[(i]i) Verification. A person making a return [of i]nformation under this section must verify [the] identity of the person from whom the re[por]table cash is received. Verification of the [ide]ntity of a person who purports to be an [alie]n must be made by examination of such [per]son's passport, alien identification card, or [oth]er official document evidencing nationali[ty o]r residence. Verification of the identity of [any] other person may be made by examina[tio]n of a document normally acceptable as a [me]ans of identification when cashing or ac[cep]ting checks (for example, a driver's license [or a] credit card). In addition, a return will be [con]sidered incomplete if the person required [to] make a return knows (or has reason to [kno]w) that an agent is conducting the trans[act]ion for a principal, and the return does not [ide]ntify both the principal and the agent.

[(i]ii) Retention of returns. A person re[qui]red to make an information return under [thi]s section must keep a copy of each return [fil]ed for five years from the date of filing.

[(]f) Requirement of furnishing statements [ ](1) In general. Any person required to [m]ake an information return under this sec[tio]n must furnish a single, annual, written [sta]tement to each person whose name is set

forth in a return ("identified person") filed with the Internal Revenue Service.

(2) Form of statement. The statement required by the preceding paragraph need not follow any particular format, but it must contain the following information:

(i) The name and address of the person making the return;

(ii) The aggregate amount of reportable cash received by the person who made the information return required by this section during the calendar year in all cash transactions relating to the identified person; and

(iii) A legend stating that the information contained in the statement is being reported to the Internal Revenue Service.

(3) When statement is to be furnished. Statements required under this paragraph (f) must be furnished to an identified person on or before January 31 of the year following the calendar year in which the cash is received.

Part 103

The following are the financial record-keeping and reporting requirements of currency and foreign transactions, which mostly apply to banks. However the underlying regulations, here, form the basis for the reporting requirements under 6050I.

Part 103 — Financial record-keeping and reporting of currency and foreign transaction.

Authority: Sec. 21, Federal Deposit Insurance Act, Pub. L. 91- 508, Title I, 84 State. 1114, 1116 (12 USC 1829b, 1951, 1959); and the Currency and Foreign Transactions Reporting Act, Pub. L. No. 91-508, Title II, 84 Stat. 1118, as amended (31 USC 5311-23). Source: 37FR 6912, Apr. 5, 1972, unless otherwise noted.

Section 103.21 Determination by the Secretary.

The Secretary hereby determines that the reports required by this subpart have a high degree of usefulness in criminal, tax, or regulatory investigations or proceedings.

Section 103.22 Reports of currency transaction.

(a)(1) Each financial institution other than a casino shall file a report of each deposit, withdrawal, exchange of currency or other payment or transfer, by, through, or to such financial institution, which involves a transaction in currency of more than $10,000.

Section 103.23 Reports of transportation of currency or monetary instruments.

(a) Each person who physically transports, mails, or ships, or causes to be physically transported, mailed, or shipped, or attempts to physically transport, mail or ship, or attempts to cause to be physically transported, name of the principal and the agent knows that the recipient has the principal's address and taxpayer identification number. . . .

(b) Multiple payments. The receipt of cash deposits or cash installment payments (or other similar payments or prepayments) relating to a single transaction (or two or more related transactions) are reported under this section in different manners depending on the dollar amounts of the initial and subsequent payments. Reporting of multiple payments is effected as follows:

(1) Initial and subsequent payments in excess of $10,000. If the initial payment exceeds $10,000 and any subsequent payment exceeds $10,000, the recipient must report each payment that exceeds $10,000. These payments must be reported separately (or if the payments are made less than 15 days apart, the recipient may (if it so elects) make a single report with respect to such payments).

(2) Initial payment only in excess of $10,000. If the initial payment exceeds $10,000 but no subsequent payment exceeds $10,000, the recipient must report with respect to the initial $10,000 payment (within 15 days of receipt of the initial payment), but need not report with respect to any subsequent payment.

(3) Initial payment of $10,000 or less. If the initial payment does not exceed $10,000, the recipient must aggregate the initial payment and subsequent payments made within one year of the initial payment until such aggregate amount exceeds $10,000, and report with respect to the aggregate amount within 15 days after receipt of the payment that causes the aggregate amount to exceed $10,000. Any subsequent payment which by itself exceeds $10,000 must be separately reported.

(c) Meaning of terms. The following definitions apply for purposes of this section —

(1) The term "cash" means the coin and currency of the United States or of any other country, which circulate in and are customarily used and accepted as money in the country in which issued. Cash includes United States notes and Federal Reserve notes, but does not include bank checks, travelers checks, bank drafts, wire transfers or other negotiable or monetary instruments not customarily accepted as money.

(2) The term "trade or business" has the same meaning as under section 162 of the Internal Revenue Code of 1954.

(3)(i) The term "transaction" means the underlying event precipitating the payer's transfer of cash to the recipient. . . .

(ii) The term "related t[...] any transaction conducte[...] (or its agent) and a recipie[...] hour period. Additionally[...] ducted between a payer ([...] cash recipient during a pe[...] 24 hours are related if the[...] has reason to know that e[...] one of a series of connected[...]

(iii) The following exam[...] definition of paragraphs (c)[...]

Example (1). A person[...] ment with a gold dealer to[...] in gold bullion. The $36,0[...] sents a single transaction[...] (c)(3)(i) of this section and[...] quirements of this section c[...] by recasting the single sales[...] separate $9,000 sales transac[...]

Example (4). K, an indi[...] one day auction and purcha[...] items, at a cost of $9,240 a[...] spectively (tax and buyer's[...] ed). Because the transacti[...] transactions as defined in pa[...] of this section, the auction h[...] to report the aggregate a[...] received from the related sa[...] even though the auction hous[...] rately on its books for each[...] presents the purchaser with s[...] each item purchased.

Example (5). F, a coin deale[...] $9,000 worth of gold coins t[...] on three successive days. U[...] (c)(3)(ii) of this section the thr[...] actions are related transactio[...] $27,000 if F knows, or has re[...] that each transaction is one of[...] nected transactions.

(4)(i) The term "recipient" [...] son receiving the cash. Except[...] paragraph (c)(4)(ii) of this secti[...] division, branch, department,[...] or office ("branch") (regardless[...] cation) comprising a portion[...] trade or business shall for pur[...] section be deemed a separate rec[...]

(ii) A branch that receives ca[...] will not be deemed a separate r[...] branch (or a central unit linking[...] with other branches) would in[...] course of business have reason[...] identity of payers making cash[...] other branches of such person. . .[...]

(e) Time, manner, and form of[...] (1) Time of reporting. The repo[...] by paragraph (a) of this section n[...] with the Internal Revenue Ser[...]

mailed or shipped, currency or other monetary instruments in an aggregate amount exceeding $10,000 on any one occasion from the United States to any place outside the United States, or into the United States from any place outside the United States, shall make a report thereof. A person is deemed to have caused such transportation, mailing or shipping when he aids, abets, counsels, commands, procures, or requests it to be done by a financial institution or any other person.

(b) Each person who receives in the U.S. currency or other monetary instruments in an aggregate amount exceeding $5,000 on any one occasion which have been transported, mailed, or shipped to such person from any place outside the United States with respect to which a report has not been filed under paragraph (a) of this section, whether or not required to be filed thereunder, shall make a report thereof, stating the amount, the date of receipt, the form of monetary instruments, and the person from whom received.

Section 103.26 Filing of reports.

(a) A report required to be filed by paragraph (a)(1) or (a)(2) of Sec. 103.22 shall be filed within 15 days following the day on which the transaction occurred. The reports shall be filed with the Commissioner of Internal Revenue on forms to be prescribed by the Secretary. All information called for in such forms shall be furnished. A copy of each report shall be retained by the financial institution for a period of five years from the date of the report.

Section 103.41 Dollars as including foreign currency.

Wherever in this part an amount is stated in dollars, it shall be deemed to mean also the equivalent amount in any foreign currency.

Section 103.47 Civil penalty.

(a) For any willful violation of any requirement of this part, the Secretary may assess upon any domestic financial institution, and upon any partner, director, officer of employee thereof who willfully participates in the violation, a civil penalty not exceeding $10,000.

(b) For any failure to file a report required under Sec. 103.23 or for filing such a report containing any material omission or misstatement, the Secretary may assess a civil penalty up to the amount of the currency or monetary instruments transported, mailed or shipped, less any amount forfeited under Sec. 103.48.

Section 103.48 Forfeiture of currency or monetary instruments.

Any currency or other monetary instruments which are in the process of any transportation with respect to which a report is required under Sec. 103.23 are subject to seizure and forfeiture to the United States if such report has not been filed as required. . . .

Part 406 - Seizure and Forfeiture of Gold for Violations of Gold Reserve Act of 1934 and Gold Regulations

Sec. 406.1 Secret Service officers authorized to make seizures of gold.

406.2 Custody of seized gold valued not in excess of $2,500.

406.3 Forfeiture of gold valued not in excess of $2,500.

406.4 Duties of customs officers.

406.5 Forfeiture of gold valued in excess of $2,500.

Authority: R.S. 161, as amended, sec. 4, 48 Stat. 340; 5 USC 301, 31 USC 443. Source: 33 FR 4258, March 7, 1968, unless otherwise noted.

Sec. 406.1 Secret Service officers authorized to make seizures of gold.

All agents of the U.S. Secret Service, in addition to officers of the customs, are hereby authorized and designated to seize any gold which may be subject to forfeiture for violations of the Gold Reserve Act of 1934 (31 USC 440-445) and the Gold Regulations.

Sec. 406.2 Custody of seized gold valued not in excess of $2,500.

Any gold, the value of which does not exceed $2,500, seized by officers of the Secret Service pursuant to the Gold Reserve Act of 1934 and the Gold Regulations, if not needed as evidence or for further investigation by the Secret Service, shall be placed forthwith by the seizing officer in the custody of the district director of customs for the customs district in which such seizure is made. Such gold shall be accompanied by a report from the Secret Service showing the basis of the seizure and a citation to each of the statutes and sections of the Gold Regulations violated.

Sec. 406.3 Forfeiture of gold valued not in excess of $2,500.

The district director of customs receiving custody of gold seized by the Secret Service, shall, if no petition is filed for the remission of mitigation of the forfeiture incurred, institute summary forfeiture proceedings in the judicial district in which such seizure is made under the appropriate provisions of the law and Customs Regulations applicable to the forfeiture of merchandise imported contrary to law.

Sec. 406.4 Duties of customs officers.

The appropriate officials of the Bureau of

Customs are hereby authorized and designated as the officers who shall perform such administrative duties in connection with the summary forfeiture of gold seized by the Secret Service, the sale or other disposition of such gold, and the remission of mitigation of the forfeiture of such gold, as may be necessary of proper by virtue of the provisions of the Gold Reserve Act of 1934 and the Gold Regulations, and by virtue of the provisions of the customs laws which the said Gold Reserve Act makes applicable in connection with the seizures and forfeitures incurred or alleged to have been incurred under the said act and regulations. In the performance of said administrative duties the appropriate officials of the Bureau of Customs shall be governed by the procedures established by the Customs Regulations insofar as such procedures are applicable and not inconsistent with the provisions of the Gold Reserve Act of 1934 and the Gold Regulations.

Sec. 406.5 Forfeiture of gold valued in excess of $2,500.

When the value of the gold seized by the Secret Service exceeds $2,500, the seizing officer shall furnish a report, approved by the principal local officer, to the U.S. attorney, and shall include in such report a statement of all the facts and circumstances of the case, together with the names of the witnesses and a citation to each of the statutes and sections of the Gold Regulations believed to have been violated and on which reliance may be had for forfeiture.

Executive orders

The Executive Order is a prerogative of the president which, when constitutionally permitted, has the full force of law. For example, the president has the authority to proclaim "National Coin Week," either of his own volition (as President Nixon did in 1974) or at the request of Congress (as President Reagan did in 1983). Below follows a brief listing of the use of Executive Orders in the coin field from the Harding administration (March 4, 1921) to the present.

The use has been sparing, and foreign financial transaction in foreign exchange, credit, coin and currency restrictions with respect to occupied countries during World War II have been omitted.

The largest single use relates to gold and silver, and is simply presented for historic interest. The abbreviations used in the Congressional Information Service Index to Presidential Executive Orders and Proclamations includes: PR, for Presidential Proclamation, and EO, for Executive Order. No designation means it was an administrative order.

The fact that the annual Assay Commission has its membership designated by an Executive Order in 1926 does not mean that it was subsequently followed. Subsequent years, typically, had their recipient's name listed in the official Presidential Documents.

Annual Assay Commission, 1926-
  Membership designation
  1926-08-9
Coin Week, Natl, proclamation
  1974-PR-4286; 1983-PR-5027
Commission of Fine Arts functions expansion
  1921-EO-3524

Emergency preparedness, economic functions assignment to Treas. Dept. Sec.
  1969-EO-11490
Gold Coin, bullion, and currency transactions, restrictions estab.
  1933-EO-6260
Holding abroad by persons subject to U.S. jurisdiction, prohibition with exception for licensed coin collectors
  1962-EO-11037
Revision
  1934-EO-6556; 1960-EO-10896; 1961-EO-10905
Revocation
  1974-EO-11825
Gold dollar weight, established
  1934-PR-2072
Silver and silver coins importation and transportation regulations revision
  1935-24-1
Silver coinage suspension until Dec. 31, 1937, previously extracted silver minting authorization
  1937-24-1
Silver coinage suspension until Dec. 31, 1938, previously extracted silver minting authorization
  1938-24-2
Silver mined from U.S. natural deposits, coinage mints receipt and addition to U.S. monetary stocks regs extension
  1938-PR-2317
Regulations implementation
  1933-PR-2067
Regulations partial revocation
  1938-PR-2282
Regulations revision
  1934-PR-2092; 1935-PR-2124; 1935-PR-2125

Regulations revision and extension
1937-PR-2268; 1939-PR-2342
Silver purchase for U.S. mints, delivery requirement and procedure established
1934-EO-6814
Revision
1934-EO-6895-A

Revocation
1938-EO-7877

Silver withdrawal from monetary use, suspension of free silver sales and use in
coinage
1961-21-20

Gold ownership

It is 55 years, now, since Americans were prohibited from private gold ownership. The right was not restored until Dec. 31, 1974.

It is easy, with a dozen years of retrospect, and hindsight, to reflect on how ridiculous it seems that Americans were prohibited from owning gold. What follows now are extracts from the Order of the Acting Secretary of the Treasury, Henry Morgenthau Jr., requiring the delivery of gold coin bullion and gold cer-tificates to the Treasurer of the United States, followed by Executive Order 6260, relating to the hoarding, export and earmarking of gold coin, bullion, or currency, issued by President Franklin Delano Roosevelt Aug. 28, 1933. Those form the substant of basis for gold pro-hibition regulations.

Gold coin turn-in order of the Secretary of the Treasury

Requiring the Delivery of Gold Coin, Gold Bullion, and Gold Certificates to the Treasur-er of the United States

WHEREAS Section 11 of the Federal Re-serve Act of December 23, 1913, as amended . . . provides . . .

"Whenever in the judgment of the Secre-tary of the Treasury such action is necessary to protect the currency system of the United States, the Secretary of the Treasury, in his discretion, may require any or all individuals, partnerships, association and corporations to pay and deliver to the Treasurer of the Unit-ed States any or all gold coin, gold bullion, and gold certificates owned by such individu-als, partnerships, associations and corpora-tions. Upon receipt of such gold coin, gold bullion or gold certificates, the Secretary of the Treasury shall pay therefor an equivalent amount of any other form of coin or currency coined or issued under the laws of the United States. . . .

WHEREAS in my judgment such action is necessary to protect the currency system of the United States;

NOW, THEREFORE, I, HENRY MOR-GENTHAU, JR., ACTING SECRETARY of the TREASURY, do hereby require every person subject to the jurisdiction of the Unit-ed States forthwith to pay and deliver to the Treasurer of the United States all gold coin, gold bullion, and gold certificates situated in the United States, owned by such person, ex-cept as follows:

A. Gold bullion owned by a person now holding such gold under a license heretofore granted by or under authority of the Secretary of the Treasury, pursuant to the Executive Order of August 23, 1933, Relating to the Hoarding, Export, and Earmarking of Gold Coin, Bullion, or Currency and to Transac-tions in Foreign Exchange;

B. Gold coin having a recognized special value to collectors or rare and unusual coin (but not including quarter eagles, otherwise known as $2.50 pieces);

C. Unmelted scrap gold and gold sweepings in an amount not exceeding in the aggregate $100 belonging to any one person; . . .

D. Gold coin, gold bullion, and gold certifi-cates owned by a Federal reserve bank or the Reconstruction Finance Corporation; and

E. Gold bullion and foreign gold coin now situated in the Philippine Islands, American Samoa, Guam, Hawaii, Panama Canal Zone, Puerto Rico, or the Virgin Islands of the United States, owned by a person not domi-ciled or doing business in the continental United States.

Section 2. Delivery. The gold coin, gold bullion, and gold certificates herein required to be paid and delivered to the Treasurer of the United States shall be delivered by plac-ing the same forthwith in the custody of a Federal reserve bank or branch or a bank member of the Federal Reserve System for the account of the United States. . . .

Section 3. Payment and Reimbursement of Costs. Upon receipt of the confirmation signed and delivered as required under Sec-tion 2, the Secretary of the Treasury will pay for the gold coin, gold bullion, and gold certi-ficates placed in custody for the account of the United States in accordance with Section 2, and equivalent amount of any form of coin or currency coined or issued under the laws of the United States designated by the Secre-tary of the Treasury. . . .

Section 4. Definitions. As used in this Order, the term "person" means any individual, partnership, association, or corporation; the term "United States" means the United States and any place subject to the jurisdiction thereof; the term "continental United States" means the States of the United States, the District of Columbia, and the Territory of Alaska; the term "gold coin" means any coin containing gold, including foreign gold coin; and the term "gold bullion" means any gold which has been put through a process of smelting or refining that is in such form that its value depends upon the gold content and not upon the form, but does not include gold coin or metals containing less than five troy ounces of fine gold per short ton.

Section 5. Any individual, partnership, association, or corporation failing to comply with any requirement hereof or of any rules or regulations issued by the Secretary of the Treasury hereunder shall be subject to the penalty provided in Section 11(n) of the Federal Reserve Act, as amended.

This order may be modified or revoked at any time.

H. Morgenthau, Jr., Acting Secretary of the Treasury.

APPROVED: Franklin D. Roosevelt

THE WHITE HOUSE

December 28, 1933

Executive Order [No. 6260]
August 28, 1933

Relating to the Hoarding, Export, and Earmarking of Gold Coin, Bullion, or Currency and to Transactions in Foreign Exchange:

By virtue of the authority vested in me by section 5(b) of the act of October 6, 1917, as amended by section 2 of the act of March 9, 1933, entitled "An act to provide relief in the existing national emergency in banking and for other purposes," I, FRANKLIN D. ROOSEVELT, PRESIDENT of the UNITED STATES OF AMERICA, do declare that a period of national emergency exists, and by virtue of said authority and of all other authority vested in me, do hereby prescribe the following provisions for the investigation and regulation of the hoarding, earmarking, and export of gold coin, gold bullion, and gold certificates by any person within the United States or any place subject to the jurisdiction thereof; and for the investigation and regulation of transactions in foreign exchange and transfers of credit and the export and withdrawal of currency from the United States or any place subject to the jurisdiction thereof by any person within the United States or any place subject to the jurisdiction thereof. . . .

Section 3. Returns. Within 15 days from the date of this order every person in possession of and every person owning gold coin, gold bullion, or gold certificates shall make under oath and file as hereinafter provided a return to the Secretary of the Treasury containing true and complete information relative thereto, including the name and address of the person making the return; the kind and amount of such coin, bullion, or certificates held and the location thereof; if held for another, the capacity in which held and the person for whom held, together with the post-office address of such person; and the nature of the transaction requiring the holding of such coin, bullion, or certificates and a statement explaining why such transaction cannot be carried out by the use of currency other than gold certificates; provided that no returns are required to be filed with respect to —

(a) Gold coin, gold bullion, and gold certificates in an amount not exceeding in the aggregate $100 belonging to any one person; (b) Gold coin having a recognized special value to collectors of rare and unusual coin; (c) Gold coin, gold bullion, and gold certificates acquired or held under a license heretofore granted by or under authority of the Secretary of the Treasury; and (d) Gold coin, gold bullion, and gold certificates owned by Federal-Reserve banks. . . .

Section 4. Acquisition of gold coin and gold bullion. No person other than a Federal Reserve bank shall after the date of this order acquire in the United States any gold coin, gold bullion, or gold certificates except under license therefor issued pursuant to this Executive order. . . .

The Secretary of the Treasury, subject to such further regulations as he may prescribe, shall issue licenses authorizing the acquisition of —

(a) Gold coin or gold bullion which the Secretary is satisfied is required for a necessary and lawful transaction for which currency other than gold certificates cannot be used, by an applicant who establishes that since March 9, 1933, he has surrendered an equal amount of gold coin, gold bullion, or gold certificates to a banking institution in the continental United States or to the Treasurer of the United States; (b) Gold coin or gold bullion which the Secretary is satisfied is required by an applicant who holds a license to export such an amount of gold coin or gold bullion issued under subdivisions (c) or (d) of section 66 hereof, and (c) Gold bullion which the Secretary, or such agency as he may designate, is satisfied is required for legitimate and customary use in industry, profession, or art by an applicant regularly engaged in such industry, profession, or art, or in the business of furnishing gold therefor. Licenses issued pursuant to this section shall authorize the holder to acquire gold coin and gold bullion only from the sources specified by the Secretary of the Treasury in regulations issued hereunder.

Section 5. Holding of gold coin, gold bullion, and gold certificates. After 30 days from the date of this order no person shall hold in his possession or retain any interest, legal or equitable in any gold coin, gold bullion, or gold certificates situated in the United States. . . .

Section 9. The Secretary of the Treasury is hereby authorized and empowered to issue such regulations as he may deem necessary to carry out the purposes of this order. Such regulations may provide for the detention in the United States of any gold coin, gold bullion, or gold certificates sought to be transported beyond the limits of the continental United States, pending an investigation to determine if such coin, bullion, or certificates are held or

are to be acquired in violation of the provisions of this Executive order. Licenses and permits granted in accordance with the provisions of this order and the regulations prescribed hereunder, may be issued through such officers or agencies as the Secretary may designate.

Section 10. Whoever willfully violates any provision of this Executive order or of any license, order, rule, or regulation issued or prescribed hereunder, shall, upon conviction, be fined not more than $10,000, or, if a natural person, may be imprisoned for not more than 10 years, or both; and any officer, director, or agent of any corporation who knowingly participates in such violation may be punished by a like fine, imprisonment, or both.

Section 11. The Executive orders of April 5, 1933, forbidding the hoarding of gold coin, gold bullion, and gold certificates, and April 20, 1933, relating to foreign exchange and the earmarking and export of gold coin or bullion or currency, respectively, are hereby revoked. . . .

FRANKLIN D. ROOSEVELT.
THE WHITE HOUSE,
August 28, 1933.

United States Code, Title 18

Title 18 of the United States Code governs "crimes and criminal procedure," and several sections relate to currency mutilation, debasement of coinage, counterfeiting and other criminal offenses. What follows are extracts of Title 18. Title 18 has been enacted as positive law. This means that unlike many other sections of the United States Code, which merely evidence what the law is, Title 18 is itself the law of the land. The same is applicable to Title 31.

One recent development is worth noting. The Supreme Court recently had occasion to analyze Sec. 504, concerning illustrations utilizing numismatic themes. See the notation (footnote) following Sec. 504 for an analysis of this.

The title has been clarified for use by the layman and to make it easily readable. Sections not dealing with numismatics have been omitted.

Presidential seal

A section of Title 18 not outlined below gives the president authority to change regulations governing the seals of the president and vice president.

On May 28, 1976, President Ford, by authority of this section of the Title, amended subsection (b) of section 1 of Executive Order No. 11649 to read that the presidential and vice presidential seals may be used "in encyclopedias, dictionaries, books, journals, pamphlets, periodicals, or magazines incident to a description or history of seals, coats of arms, heraldry or the Presidency or Vice Presidency."

Chapter 17 — coins and currency

Sec. 331. Mutilation, diminution, and falsification of coins

Whoever fraudulently alters, defaces, mutilates, impairs, diminishes, falsifies, scales, or lightens any of the coins coined at the Mints of the United States, or any foreign coins which are by law made current or are in actual use or circulation as money within the United States; or

Whoever fraudulently possesses, passes, utters, publishes, or sells, or attempts to pass, utter, publish, or sell, or brings into the United States, any such coin, knowing the same to be altered, defaced, mutilated, impaired, diminished, falsified, scaled, or lightened—

Shall be fined not more than $2,000 or imprisoned not more than five years, or both.

Sec. 332. Debasement of coins; alteration of official scales, or embezzlement of metals

If any of the gold or silver coins struck or coined at any of the Mints of the United States shall be debased, or made worse as to the proportion of fine gold or fine silver therein contained, or shall be of less weight or value than the same ought to be, pursuant to law, or if any of the scales or weights used at any of the Mints or assay offices of the United States shall be defaced, altered, increased, or diminished through the fault or connivance of any officer or person employed at the said Mints or assay offices, with a fraudulent intent; or if any such officer or person shall embezzle any of the metals at any time committed to his charge for the purpose of being coined, or any of the coins struck or coined at the said Mints, or any medals, coins, or other moneys of said Mints or assay offices at any time committed to his charge, or of which he may have assumed the charge, every such officer or person who commits any of the said offenses shall be fined not more than $10,000 or imprisoned not more than 10 years, or both.

Sec. 333. Mutilation of national bank obligations

Whoever mutilates, cuts, defaces, disfigures, or perforates, or unites or cements together, or does any other thing to any bank bill, draft, note, or other evidence of debt issued by any national banking association, or Federal Reserve bank, or the Federal Reserve System, with intent to render such bank bill, draft, note, or other evidence of debt unfit to be reissued, shall be fined not more than $100 or imprisoned not more than six months, or both.

Sec. 334. Issuance of Federal Reserve or national bank notes

Whoever, being a Federal Reserve Agent, or an agent or employee of such Federal Reserve Agent, or of the Board of Governors of the Federal Reserve System, issues or puts in circulation any Federal Reserve notes, without complying with or in violation of the provisions of law regulating the issuance and circulation of such Federal Reserve notes; or

Whoever, being an officer acting under the provisions of Chapter 2 of Title 12, countersigns or delivers to any national banking association, or to any other company or person, any circulating notes contemplated by that chapter except in strict accordance with its provisions,

Shall be fined not more than $5,000 or imprisoned not more than five years, or both.

Sec. 335. Circulation of obligations of expired corporations

Whoever, being a director, officer, or agent of a corporation created by Act of Congress, the charter of which has expired, or trustee thereof, or an agent of such trustee, or a person having in his possession or under his control the property of such corporation for the purpose of paying or redeeming its notes and obligations, knowingly issues, reissues, or utters as money, or in any other way knowingly puts in circulation any bill, note, check, draft, or other security purporting to have been made by any such corporation, or by any officer thereof, or purporting to have been made under authority derived therefrom, shall be fined not more than $10,000 or imprisoned not more than five years, or both.

Sec. 336. Issuance of circulating obligations of less than $1

Whoever makes, issues, circulates, or pays out any note, check, memorandum, token, or other obligation for a less sum than $1, intended to circulate as money or to be received or used in lieu of lawful money of the United States, shall be fined not more than $500 or imprisoned not more than six months, or both.

Sec. 337. Coins as security for loans

Whoever lends or borrows money or credit upon the security of such coins of the United States as the Secretary of the Treasury may from time to time designate by proclamation published in the Federal Register, during any period designated in such a proclamation, shall be fined not more than $10,000 or imprisoned not more than one year, or both.

Chapter 25 — counterfeiting and forgery

Sec. 471. Obligations or securities of United States

Whoever, with intent to defraud, falsely makes, forges, counterfeits, or alters any obligation or other security of the United States, shall be fined not more than $5,000 or imprisoned not more than 15 years, or both.

Sec. 472. Uttering counterfeit obligations or securities

Whoever, with intent to defraud, passes, utters, publishes, or sells, or attempts to pass, utter, publish, or sell, or with like intent brings into the United States or keeps in possession or conceals any falsely made, forged, counterfeited, or altered obligation or other security of the United States, shall be fined not more than $5,000 or imprisoned not more than 15 years, or both.

Sec. 473. Dealing in counterfeit obligations or securities

Whoever buys, sells, exchanges, transfers, receives, or delivers any false, forged, counterfeited, or altered obligation or other security of the United States, with the intent that the same be passed, published, or used as true and genuine, shall be fined not more than $5,000 or imprisoned not more than 10 years, or both.

Sec. 474. Plates or stones for counterfeiting obligations or securities

Whoever, having control, custody, or possession of any plate, stone, or other thing, or any part thereof, from which has been printed, or which may be prepared by direction of the Secretary of the Treasury for the purpose of printing, any obligation or other security of the United States, uses such plate, stone, or other thing, or any part thereof, or knowingly suffers the same to be used for the purpose of printing any such or similar obligation or other security, or any part thereof, except as may be printed for the use of the United States by order of the proper officer thereof; or

Whoever makes or executes any plate, stone, or other thing in the likeness of any plate designated for the printing of such obligation or other security; or

Whoever sells any such plate, stone, or other thing, or brings into the United States any such plate, stone, or other thing, except under the direction of the Secretary of the Treasury or other proper officer, or with any other intent, in either case, than that such plate, stone, or other thing be used for the printing of the obligations or other securities of the United States; or

Whoever has in his control, custody, or possession any plate, stone, or other thing in any manner made after or in the similitude of any plate, stone, or other thing, from which any such obligation or other security has been printed, with intent to use such plate, stone, or other thing, or to suffer the same to be used in forging or counterfeiting any such obligation or other security, or any part thereof; or

Whoever has in his possession or custody, except under authority from the Secretary of the Treasury or other proper officer, any obligation or other security made or executed, in whole or in part, after the similitude of any obligation or other security issued under the authority of the United States, with intent to sell or otherwise use the same; or

Whoever prints, photographs, or in any other manner makes or executes any engraving, photograph, print, or impression in the likeness of any such obligation or other security, or any part thereof, or sells any such engraving, photograph, print, or impression, except to the United States, or brings into the United States, any such engraving, photograph, print, or impression, except by direction of some proper officer of the United States; or

Whoever has or retains in his control or possession, after a distinctive paper has been adopted by the Secretary of the Treasury or some other proper officer of the United States,

Shall be fined not more than $5,000 or imprisoned not more than 15 years, or both.

Sec. 475. Imitating obligations or securities; advertisements

Whoever designs, engraves, prints, makes, or executes, or utters, issues, distributes, circulates, or uses any business or professional card, notice, placard, circular, handbill, or advertisement in the likeness or similitude of any obligation or security of the United States issued under or authorized by any Act of Congress or writes, prints, or otherwise impresses upon or attaches to any such instrument, obligation, or security, or any coin of the United States, any business or professional card, notice, or advertisement, or any notice or advertisement whatever, shall be fined not more than $500.

Sec. 476. Taking impressions of tools used for obligations or securities

Whoever, without authority from the United States, takes, procures, or makes an impression, stamp, or imprint of, from or by the use of any tool, implement, instrument, or thing used or fitted or intended to be used in printing, stamping, or impressing, or in making other tools, implements, instruments, or things to be used or fitted or intended to be used in printing, stamping, or impressing any obligation or other security of the United States, shall be fined not more than $5,000 or imprisoned not more than 10 years, or both.

Sec. 477. Possessing or selling impressions of tools used for obligations or securities

Whoever, with intent to defraud, possesses, keeps, safeguards, or controls, without authority from the United States, any imprint, stamp, or impression, taken or made upon any substance or material whatsoever, of any tool, implement, instrument or thing, used, fitted or intended to be used, for any of the purposes mentioned in Section 476 of this title; or

Whoever, with intent to defraud, sells, gives, or delivers any such imprint, stamp, or impression to any other person shall be fined not more than $5,000 or imprisoned not more than 10 years, or both.

Sec. 478. Foreign obligations or securities

Whoever, within the United States, with intent to defraud, falsely makes, alters, forges, or counterfeits any bond, certificate, obligation, or other security of any foreign government, purporting to be or in imitation of any such security issued under the authority of such foreign government, or any Treasury note, bill, or promise to pay, lawfully issued by such foreign government and intended to circulate as money, shall be fined not more than $5,000 or imprisoned not more than five years, or both.

Sec. 479. Uttering counterfeit foreign obligations or securities

Whoever, within the United States, knowingly and with intent to defraud, utters, passes, or puts off, in payment or negotiation, any false, forged, or counterfeited bond, certificate, obligation, security, Treasury note, bill, or promise to pay, mentioned in Section 478 of this title, whether or not the same was made, altered, forged, or counterfeited within the United States, shall be fined not more than $3,000 or imprisoned not more than three years, or both.

Sec. 480. Possessing counterfeit foreign obligations or securities

Whoever, within the United States, knowingly and with intent to defraud, possesses or delivers any false, forged, or counterfeit bond, certificate, obligation, security, Treasury note, bill, promise to pay, bank note, or bill issued by a bank or corporation of any foreign country, shall be fined not more than $1,000 or imprisoned not more than one year, or both.

Sec. 481. Plates or stones for counterfeiting foreign obligations or securities

Whoever, within the United States except by lawful authority, controls, holds, or possesses any plate, stone, or other thing, or any part thereof, from which has been printed or may be printed any counterfeit note, bond, obligation, or other security, in whole or in part, or any foreign government, bank, or corporation, or uses such plate, stone, or other thing, or knowingly permits or suffers the same to be used in counterfeiting such foreign obligations, or any part thereof; or

Whoever, except by lawful authority, makes or engraves any plate, stone, or other thing in the likeness or similitude of any plate, stone, or other thing designated for the printing of the genuine issues of the obliga-

tions of any foreign government, bank, or corporation; or

Whoever, except by lawful authority, prints, photographs, or makes, executes, or sells any engraving, photograph, print, or impression in the likeness of any genuine note, bond, obligation, or other security, or any part thereof, of any foreign government, bank, or corporation; or

Whoever brings into the United States any counterfeit plate, stone, or other thing, engraving, photograph, print, or other impressions of the notes, bonds, obligations, or other securities of any foreign government, bank, or corporation shall be fined not more than $5,000 or imprisoned not more than five years, or both.

Sec. 482. Foreign bank notes

Whoever, within the United States, with intent to defraud, falsely makes, alters, forges, or counterfeits any bank note or bill issued by a bank or corporation of any foreign country, and intended by the law or usage of such foreign country to circulate as money, such bank or corporation being authorized by the laws of such country, shall be fined not more than $2,000 or imprisoned not more than two years, or both.

Sec. 483. Uttering counterfeit foreign bank notes

Whoever, within the United States, utters, passes, puts off, or tenders in payment, with intent to defraud, any such false, forged, altered, or counterfeited bank note or bill, mentioned in Section 482 of this title, knowing the same to be so false, forged, altered, and counterfeited, whether or not the same was made, forged, altered, or counterfeited within the United States, shall be fined not more than $1,000 or imprisoned not more than one year, or both.

Sec. 484. Connecting parts of different notes

Whoever so places or connects together different parts of two or more notes, bills, or other genuine instruments issued under the authority of the United States, or by any foreign government, or corporation, as to produce one instrument, with intent to defraud, shall be guilty of forgery in the same manner as if the parts to put together were falsely made or forged, and shall be fined not more than $1,000 or imprisoned not more than five years, or both.

Sec. 485. Coins or bars

Whoever falsely makes, forges, or counterfeits any coin or bar in resemblance or similitude of any coin of a denomination higher than 5 cents or any gold or silver bar coined or stamped at any Mint or assay office of the United States, or in resemblance or similitude of any foreign gold or silver coin current in the United States or in actual use and circulation as money within the United States; or

Whoever passes, utters, publishes, sells, possesses, or brings into the United States any false, forged, or counterfeit coin or bar, knowing the same to be false, forged, or counterfeit, with intent to defraud any body politic or corporate, or any person, or attempts the commission of any offense described in this paragraph, shall be fined not more than $5,000 or imprisoned not more than 15 years, or both.

Sec. 486. Uttering coins of gold, silver or other metal

Whoever, except as authorized by law, makes or utters or passes, or attempts to utter or pass, any coins of gold or silver or other metal, or alloys of metals, intended for use as current money, whether in the resemblance of coins of the United States or of foreign countries, or of original design, shall be fined not more than $3,000 or imprisoned not more than five years, or both.

Sec. 487. Making or possessing counterfeit dies for coins

Whoever, without lawful authority, makes any die, hub, or mold, or any part thereof, either of steel or plaster, or any other substance, in likeness or similitude, as to the design or the inscription thereon, of any die, hub, or mold designated for the coining or making of any of the genuine gold, silver, nickel, bronze, copper, or other coins coined at the Mints of the United States; or

Whoever, without lawful authority, possesses any such die, hub, or mold, or any part thereof, or permits the same to be used for or in aid of the counterfeiting of any such coins of the United States, shall be fined not more than $5,000 or imprisoned not more than 15 years, or both.

Sec. 488. Making or possessing counterfeit dies for foreign coins

Whoever, within the United States, without lawful authority, makes any die, hub, or mold, or any part thereof, either of steel or of plaster, or of any other substance, in the likeness or similitude, as to the design or the inscription thereon, of any die, hub, or mold designated for the coining of the genuine coin of any foreign government; or

Whoever, without lawful authority, possesses any such die, hub, or mold, or any part thereof, or conceals, or knowingly suffers the same to be used for the counterfeiting of any foreign coin, shall be fined not more than

$5,000 or imprisoned not more than five years, or both.

Sec. 489. Making or possessing likeness of coins

Whoever, within the United States, makes or brings therein from any foreign country, or possesses with intent to sell, give away, or in any other manner uses the same, except under authority of the Secretary of the Treasury or other proper officer of the United States, any token, disk, or device in the likeness or similitude as to design, color, or the inscription thereon of any of the coins of the United States or of any foreign country issued as money, either under the authority of the United States or under the authority of any foreign government shall be fined not more than $100.

Sec. 490. Minor coins

Whoever falsely makes, forges, or counterfeits any coin in the resemblance or similitude of any of the one-cent and 5-cent coins minted at the Mints of the United States; or

Whoever passes, utters, publishes, or sells, or brings into the United States, or possesses any such false, forged, or counterfeited coin, with intent to defraud any person, shall be fined not more than $1,000 or imprisoned not more than three years, or both.

Sec. 491. Tokens or paper used as money

(a) Whoever, being 18 years of age or over, not lawfully authorized, makes, issues, or passes any coin, card, token, or device in metal, or its compounds, intended to be used as money, or whoever, being 18 years of age or over, with intent to defraud, makes, utters, inserts, or uses any card, token, slug, disk, device, paper, or other thing similar in size and shape to any of the lawful coins or other currency of the United States or any coin or other currency not legal tender in the United States, to procure anything of value, or the use or enjoyment of any property or service from any automatic merchandise vending machine, postage-stamp machine, turnstile, fare box, coinbox telephone, parking meter or other lawful receptacle, depository, or contrivance designed to receive or to be operated by lawful coins or other currency of the United States, shall be fined not more than $1,000, or imprisoned not more than one year, or both.

(b) Whoever manufactures, sells, offers, or advertises for sale, or exposes or keeps with intent to furnish or sell any token, slug, disk, device, paper, or other thing similar in size and shape to any of the lawful coins or other currency of the United States, or any token, disk, paper, or other device issued or authorized in connection with rationing or food and fiber distribution by any agency of the United States, with knowledge or reason to believe that such tokens, slugs, disks, devices, papers, or other things are intended to be used unlawfully or fraudulently to procure anything of value, or the use or enjoyment of any property or service from any automatic merchandise vending machine, postage-stamp machine, turnstile, fare box, coinbox telephone, parking meter, or other lawful receptacle, depository, or contrivance designed to receive or to be operated by lawful coins or other currency of the United States shall be fined not more than $1,000 or imprisoned not more than one year, or both.

Nothing contained in this section shall create immunity from criminal prosecution under the laws of any state, Commonwealth of Puerto Rico, territory, possession, or the District of Columbia.

(c) "Knowledge or reason to believe," within the meaning of paragraph (b) of this section, may be shown by proof that any law enforcement officer has, prior to the commission of the offense with which the defendant is charged, informed the defendant that tokens, slugs, disks, or other devices of the kind manufactured, sold, offered, or advertised for sale by him or exposed or kept with intent to furnish or sell, are being used unlawfully or fraudulently to operate certain specified automatic merchandise vending machines, postage-stamp machines, turnstiles, fare boxes, coin-box telephones, parking meters, or other receptacles, depositories, or contrivances, designed to receive or to be operated by lawful coins of the United States.

Sec. 492. Forfeiture of counterfeit paraphernalia

All counterfeits of any coins or obligations or other securities of the United States or of any foreign government, or any articles, devices, and other things made, possessed, or used in violation of this chapter or of this title, or any material or apparatus used or fitted or intended to be used, in the making of such counterfeits, articles, devices or things, found in the possession of any person without authority from the Secretary of the Treasury or other proper officer, shall be forfeited to the United States.

Whoever, having the custody or control of any such counterfeits, material, apparatus, articles, devices, or other things, fails or refuses to surrender possession thereof upon request by any authorized agent of the Treasury Department, or other proper officer, shall be

fined not more than $100 or imprisoned not more than one year, or both.

Whenever, except as hereinafter in this section provided, any person interested in any article, device, or other thing, or material or apparatus seized under this section files with the Secretary of the Treasury, before the disposition thereof, a petition for the remission or mitigation of such forfeiture, the Secretary of the Treasury, if he finds that such forfeiture was incurred without willful negligence or without any intention on the part of the petitioner to violate the law, or finds the existence of such mitigating circumstances as to justify the remission or the mitigation of such forfeiture, may remit or mitigate the same upon such terms and conditions as he deems reasonable and just.

If the seizure involves offenses other than offenses against the coinage, currency, obligations or securities of the United States or any foreign government, the petition for the remission or mitigation of forfeiture shall be referred to the Attorney General, who may remit or mitigate the forfeiture upon such terms as he deems reasonable and just.

Sec. 504. Printing and filming of United States and foreign obligations and securities*

Notwithstanding any other provision of this chapter, the following are permitted:

(1) the printing, publishing, or importation, or the making or importation of the necessary plates for such printing or publishing, of illustrations of —

(A) postage stamps of the United States,

(B) revenue stamps of the United States,

(C) any other obligation or other security of the United States, and

(D) postage stamps, revenue stamps, notes, bonds, and any other obligation or other security of any foreign government, bank, or corporation, for philatelic, numismatic, educational, historical, or newsworthy purposes in articles, books, journals, newspapers, or albums (but not for advertising purposes, except illustrations of stamps and paper money in philatelic or numismatic advertising of legitimate numismatists and dealers in stamps or publishers of or dealers in philatelic or numismatic articles, books, journals, newspapers, or albums). Illustrations permitted by the foregoing provisions of this section shall be made in accordance with the following conditions —

(i) all illustrations shall be in black and white, except that illustrations of postage stamps issued by the United States or by any foreign government, and stamps issued under the Migratory Hunting Stamp Act of 1934 may be in color;

(ii) all illustrations (including illustrations of uncanceled postage stamps in color) shall be of a size less than three-fourths or more than one and one-half, in linear dimension, of each part of any matter so illustrated which is covered by subparagraph (A), (B), (C), or (D) of this paragraph, except that black and white illustrations of postage and revenue stamps issued by the United States or by any foreign government and colored illustrations of canceled postage stamps issued by the United States may be in the exact linear dimension in which the stamps were issued; and

(iii) the negatives and plates used in making the illustrations shall be destroyed after their final use in accordance with this section.

(2) the making or importation, but not for advertising purposes except philatelic advertising, of motion-picture films, microfilms, or slides, for projection upon a screen or for use in telecasting, of postage and revenue stamps and other obligations and securities of the United States, and postage and revenue stamps, notes, bonds, and other obligations or securities of any foreign government, bank, or corporation. No prints or other reproductions shall be made from such films or slides, except for the purposes of paragraph (1), without the permission of the Secretary of the Treasury.

For the purposes of this section the term "postage stamp" includes postage meter stamps.

* The Supreme Court of the United States offered a definitive interpretation of the meaning of this section of the law in Regan v. Time Inc., 468 US 641 (1984). The court held that subsection D, which purports to regulate the use in a newsworthy article, or for a newsworthy purpose, was unconstitutional. Despite the declaration, no change was made in the law or regulation.

Key American coinage laws, resolutions

Following is a list of key coinage laws and resolutions acted on by Congress from the Joint Resolution which authorized creation of a Mint in March 1791, through the present day. The list is incomplete in that it does not include every enacted bill pertaining to coinage, but insofar as today's laws are derived from historical precedent, the listings may be of use to collectors and researchers.

To further assist in this, a brief annotation offering explanation of the general tenor of the legislation follows each law. The manner that the law is listed is as follows: The date of passage (either approved by the president, or date a veto was overridden by the Senate and House), followed by the chapter in the session laws or, if after 1959, the Public Law number. This is then followed by a number signifying in which volume of the *Statutes at Large* the complete text of the law is found.

In addition to containing public laws and resolutions acted on by Congress, some key executive orders and proclamations are also listed inasmuch as they relate to the coinage field.

Following the date of passage of an Act, reference is made to the *Statutes at Large* (Stat.) in which the law appears. The number preceding "Stat." is the volume; the number following is the page.

The abbreviation "ch." stands for the chapter of the session law in which the act passed.

Where a resolution or proclamation or other relevant citation is appropriate, it is likewise noted.

In 1983 Title 31 of the United States Code (which contained many of these older laws) was revised and cleansed of obsolete statutes, while those remaining were codified into more contemporary language. The precise text of each of these laws that resulted appears elsewhere under the heading "United States Code, Title 31." The codified Title 31, rather than the original text of the law, is now enacted as positive law (though there remains a provision calling for the original to prevail in case of doubt). The laws referred to below, the dates of passage, and prior citations appear as a matter of historical record.

It is useful to remember that the legal effect of government on numismatics is not limited to laws. In 1974, for example, President Nixon proclaimed "National Coin Week," Presidential Proclamation No. 4286 (April 19, 1974), page 14,183 (*Federal Register*), just as President Reagan did a decade later (Proclamation No. 5027, 48 Fed. Reg. 9837). The "Hobby Protection Act," passed by Congress, became effective with the passage of regulations by the Federal Trade Commission (16

CFR part 304). The information following is a short list of those legislative pieces which are of recurring usefulness.

J. Res. No. 3, March 3, 1791, 1 Stat. 225
Joint Resolution to authorize a Mint for the United States.

April 2, 1792, ch. 16, 1 Stat. 246.
Original Mint Act.

May 8, 1792, ch. 39, 1 Stat. 283.
Authorization for purchase of copper for cents and half cents.

Jan. 14, 1793, ch. 2, 1 Stat. 299.
Changes weight of copper cent and half cent.

Feb. 9, 1793, ch. 5, 1 Stat. 300.
Legal status of foreign coins in U.S.

March 3, 1795, ch. 47, 1 Stat. 439.
Permits president to reduce weight of copper coinage and allows seigniorage.

Feb. 1, 1798, ch. 11, 1 Stat. 539.
Legal status of foreign coins in U.S.

May 14, 1800, ch. 70, 2 Stat. 86.
Extension of Mint location at Philadelphia for two years.

March 3, 1801, ch. 21, 2 Stat. 111.
Further extension of Mint location at Philadelphia.

April 10, 1806, ch. 22, 2 Stat. 374.
Legal status of foreign coins in U.S.

March 3, 1819, ch. 97, 3 Stat. 525.
Continues in force legal tender values of foreign coin in U.S.

May 19, 1828, ch. 67, 4 Stat. 277.
Continuation of Mint at Philadelphia until otherwise provided by law.

June 28, 1834, ch. 96, 4 Stat. 700.
Reduces weight of foreign gold coins (revaluation of the dollar).

March 3, 1835, ch. 39, 4 Stat. 774.
Authorizes establishment of branch Mints.

Jan. 18, 1837, ch. 3, 5 Stat. 136.
Coinage Act of 1837, codification repealing all prior inconsistent laws.

April 22, 1864, ch. 64, 13 Stat. 54.
Two-cent piece created.

Feb. 12, 1873, ch. 131, 17 Stat. 424.
Coinage Act of 1873 (codification).

Jan. 29, 1874, ch. 19, 18 Stat. 6, 31 U.S.C. Sec. 5111(a)(4).
Permits U.S. Mint to strike coins for foreign governments.

June 20, 1874, ch. 320, 18 Stat. 97.
Re-establishes New Orleans as a branch Mint.

Jan. 14, 1875, ch. 15, 18 Stat. 296.
Resumption of specie payment authorized.

March 3, 1875, ch. 143, 18 Stat. 478.
Creation of 20-cent piece.

April 17, 1876, ch. 63, 19 Stat. 33.
Use of silver coin to redeem fractional currency permitted.

Feb. 28, 1878, ch. 20, 20 Stat. 25.
Bland-Allison Act.

May 2, 1878, ch. 79, 20 Stat. 47
Prohibits further coining of 20-cent piece.

June 9, 1879, ch. 12, 21 Stat. 8, now part of 31 U.S.C. Sec. 5103.
Limits legal tender status of silver coins.

March 3, 1887, ch. 396. 24 Stat. 634.
Trade dollar eliminated.

July 14, 1890, ch. 708, 26 Stat. 289.
Silver purchase act, discontinuance of dollar coinage.

Sept. 26, 1890, ch. 944, 26 Stat. 484, 31 U.S.C. Sec. 5112.
Prohibits design changes more often than once in 25 years.

Sept. 26, 1890, ch. 945, 26 Stat. 485.
Discontinues $3 and $1 gold coins, nickel 3-cent piece.

Nov. 1, 1893, ch. 8, 28 Stat. 4 (formerly 31 USC 311)
Bimetallism.

June 4, 1897, ch. 2, 30 Stat. 27.
Recoinage of uncurrent gold and silver coin authorized by appropriation.

March 14, 1900, ch. 41, 31 Stat. 45.
Gold Standard Act of 1900.

Aug. 23, 1912, ch. 350, 37 Stat. 384.
Redefines duties of superintendents of the Mints and New York Assay Office.

Aug. 28, 1933, EO 6260.
Recall of all gold coins.

Jan. 30, 1934, ch. 6, 48 Stat. 337.
Gold Reserve Act of 1934, effectively ending gold coinage.

Dec. 18, 1942, ch. 767, 56 Stat. 1064.
War Powers Act of 1942 (authorizes compositional change in cent and creation of a 3-cent piece).

Sept. 5, 1962, Pub. L. 87-643, 76 Stat. 440.
Compositional change eliminating tin.

Aug. 20, 1963, Pub. L. 88-102, 77 Stat. 129.
Permits appropriations for new Philadelphia Mint; subsequently, Denver Mint.

Dec. 30, 1963, Pub. L. 88-256, 77 Stat. 843.
Authorizes Kennedy half dollar.

Sept. 3, 1964, Pub. L. 88-580, 78 Stat. 908, repealed by Pub. L. 89-81, Title II Sec. 204(b).
Authorizes "date freeze" on coinage.

July 23, 1965, Pub. L. 89-81, 79 Stat. 254, 31 U.S.C.
Coinage Act of 1965; clad coinage composition; Joint Commission on the Coinage.

Dec. 31, 1970, Pub. L. 91-607, Title II, 84 Stat. 1769.

One Bank Holding Company Act of 1970, creation of Eisenhower dollar, elimination of silver in half dollar.

Feb. 15, 1972, Pub. L. 92-228, 86 Stat. 37.

Bicentennial medallic commemoration authorized.

Oct. 18, 1973, Pub. L. 93-127, 87 Stat. 456, 31 U.S.C.

Bicentennial coinage legislation (creates new reverse for quarter, half dollar and dollar, authorizes dual-date obverse, and silver-clad collector coins)

Nov. 29, 1973, Pub. L. 93-167, 87 Stat. 686, 15 U.S.C. Sec. 2101 et seq.

Hobby Protection Act.

Dec. 11, 1973, Pub. L. 93-179, 87 Stat. 704.

Bicentennial medal program curtailed.

Oct. 11, 1974, Pub. L. 93-441.

Authorizes compositional change in 1-cent coin under certain prescribed circumstances, by either lowering the copper content or alternatively permitting a new composition other than copper-zinc.

Dec. 26, 1974, Pub. L. 93-541.

Amends Bicentennial legislation to permit simultaneous production of Bicentennial coinage and other dates during calendar year 1975 and gives Mint additional time to produce the whole 45 million silver-clad commemorative collector issues.

Oct. 10, 1978, Pub. L. 95-447, 92 Stat. 1072.

Approved Susan B. Anthony dollar.

Nov. 10, 1978, Pub. L. 95-630, 92 Stat. 3679.

American Arts Gold Medallion Act.

March 14, 1980, Pub. L. 96-209. Title II, 94 Stat. 98.

Abolition of Assay Commission.

Dec. 23, 1981, Pub. L. 97-104, 95 Stat. 1491 (formerly 31 U.S.C. 399).

George Washington commemorative coin authorized.

July 22, 1982, Pub. L. 97-220, 96 Stat. 222.

Olympic commemorative coin legislation.

Sept. 13, 1982, Pub. L. 97-258, 96 Stat. 877.

Revision of Title 31, U.S. Code (codification).

Nov. 14, 1983, Pub. L. 98-151, 97 Stat. 979.

Section 123 directs annual sale of Uncirculated and Proof sets.

July 9, 1985, Pub. L. 99-61, Title 1, 99 Stat. 113 (31 USC Sec. 5112 note).

Statue of Liberty-Ellis Island Commemorative Coin Act.

July 9, 1985, Pub. L. 99-61, Title 2, 99 Stat. 113 (31 USC Sec. 5112)

Liberty Coin Act-Silver Dollar Liberty Coin

Pub. L. 99-185

Gold Bullion Coin Act of 1985

Dec. 17, 1985, Pub. L. 99-188, 99 Stat. 1177 (31 USC Sec. 5112)

Gold Bullion Coin Act of 1985 and Silver Bullion Coin.

Oct. 29, 1986, Pub. L. 99-582, 100 Stat. 3315 (31 USC Sec. 5112 note)

Bicentennial of Constitution commemorative coins.

Laws authorizing medals, 1874-1970

Issuance of national Mint medals is governed by section 3551 of the Revised Statutes, and codified in section 368 of Title 31 of the U.S. Code. Regular production of medals began under Treasury Department authority in 1856, according to the *Annual Report of the Director of the Mint for 1873*, and when the nation's coinage legislation was codified in that same year, a clause was written into the law to permit continuance of the practice provided that the dies for the medals were of national character, produced at the Philadelphia Mint, executed by the chief engraver, and used without interference with the regular coinage operations.

The legislative origins of national Mint medals can be traced to Sec. 52 of the Coinage Act of 1873; prior to the enactment of this general coinage statute, national Mint medals had been struck under departmental authority only (HR Executive Document No. 42, 43rd Congress, 1st Session 471 (1873)).

Aside from the medals on the Mint list, national medals must be authorized by Act of Congress, which may either be by Public Law, or Joint or Concurrent Resolution of the two houses. Whenever a foreign sovereign or state wishes to award a national medal of its own device to an American official, a private law must be passed by Congress approving it.

This is because Article I, section 9, clause 8 of the U.S. Constitution prohibits any person holding office of the United States from receiving "any present, Emolument, Office or Title." These private laws are not included in this digest of laws authorizing production of medals.

Laws enacted by Congress are cited either by their volume and page number in the *Statutes at Large,* or by the law number in each session of Congress, which is consecutive from year to year.

Since 1959, the first two digits of each public law number indicate which Congress passed the law, while the digits following the dash indicate the number of the law enacted. Thus, Public Law 95-8 would be the eighth law enacted by the 95th Congress (the Marian Anderson medal).

Thus, Public Law 89-382 would be the 382nd law enacted by the 89th Congress (the San Antonio Medal). As indicated above, all of the medallic commemorations since 1971 are included in the section above listing numismatic actions and laws by Congress since 1965. The reason for the break is that commencing in 1971, new standards for national medals were imposed by the Subcommittee on Consumer Affairs of the House Banking Committee, and the result is more in keeping with the section on legislative developments than on pure commemoration *per se.*

Following is a list of laws authorizing medals, from 1874 to 1970.

1874-1900

Public Law No. 71 (Extract), approved June 20, 1874. Lifesaving medals of the first and second class.

Public Law No. 109 (Extract) 45th Congress, approved June 18, 1878. Secretary of the Treasury is hereby authorized to bestow the life-saving medal of the second class on certain people.

Public Law No. 67 (Extract) 47th Congress, approved May 4, 1882. Authorizing the gold and silver life-saving medal.

Public Law No. 217 (Extract) 47th Congress, approved August 7, 1882. To replace life-saving medals which have been stolen from parties upon whom they have been bestowed.

Public Res. No. 51, 54th Congress, approved May 2, 1896. Relative to the Medal of Honor authorized by the Acts of July 12, 1862, and March 3, 1863.

Act of Aug. 5, 1892, ch. 381 sec. 3, 27 Stat. 389. Authorizing striking of 50,000 bronze medals for the Columbian Exposition.

Public Res. No. 27, 55th Congress, approved May 4, 1898. Relative to the Medal of Honor authorized by the Acts of December 21, 1861, and July 16, 1862.

Public Res. No. 38, 55th Congress, approved June 3, 1898. Authorizing the secretary of the Navy to present a sword of honor to Commodore George Dewey, and to cause to be struck bronze medals commemorating the Battle of Manila Bay, and to distribute such medals to the officers and men of the ships of the Asiatic Squadron of the United States.

1901-1920

Public Res. No. 17, 56th Congress, approved March 3, 1901. Authorizing the secretary of the Navy to cause bronze medals to be struck and distributed to certain officers and men who participated in the war with Spain.

Public Law No. 155, 56th Congress, approved March 3, 1901. An Act for the reward of enlisted men of the Navy or Marine Corps.

Public Law No. 192, 57th Congress, approved June 28, 1902. Directing the Secretary of the Treasury to bestow medals upon 1st Lt. David H. Jarvis, 2nd Lt. Ellsworth P. Bertholf, and Samuel J. Call, surgeon, all of the Revenue-Cutter Service.

Public Res. No. 23, 58th Congress, approved April 15, 1904. Authorizing issuance of duplicate medals where the originals have been lost or destroyed through no fault of the beneficiary.

Act of April 13, 1904, ch. 1253, sec. 6, 33 Stat. 178. Authorizing medals to be struck for the Lewis and Clark centennial exposition.

Public Law No. 149 (Extract) 58th Congress, approved April 23, 1904. The furnishing of a national trophy and medals and other prizes to be provided annually under regulations prescribed by the secretary of War.

Public Law No. 264, 58th Congress, approved April 28, 1904. Making appropriations for national trophy and medals for rifle contests.

Public Law No. 360, 59th Congress, approved June 29, 1906. An Act providing medals for certain persons.

Public Res. No. 8, 59th Congress, approved January 27, 1907. Authorizing the secretary of War to award the Congressional Medal of Honor to Roe Reisinger.

Public Res. No. 17, 59th Congress, approved February 27, 1907. Relating to the holders of the Medals of Honor.

Public Res. No. 42, 62nd Congress, approved July 6, 1912. Conveying the thanks of Congress to Capt. Arthur Henry Rostron and his officers and crew of the steamship *Carpathia* of the Cunard Line for the rescuing of 704 lives from the wreck of the steamship *Titanic* in the North Atlantic Ocean.

Public Law No. 271 (extract) 63rd Congress, approved March 3, 1915. Preparing a Medal of Honor to be awarded to any officer of the Navy, Marine Corps, or Coast Guard who shall have distinguished himself in battle or displayed extraordinary heroism in the line of his profession.

Public Law No. 56, 64th Congress, approved April 27, 1916. Establishing the Army and Navy Medal of Honor Roll.

Public Law No. 85 (extract) 64th Congress, approved June 3, 1916. Investigation concerning Medals of Honor.

Public Law No. 193 (extract) 65th Congress, approved July 9, 1918. The furnishing of a National trophy and medals for rifle contests.

Public Law No. 253, 65th Congress, approved February 4, 1919. To provide for the award of Medals of Honor, Distinguished Service Medals, and Navy Crosses.

Public Law No. 125, 66th Congress, approved January 24, 1920. Appropriations for Medal of Honor, Distinguished Service Crosses, and Distinguished Service Medals.

Public Law No. 215 (extract) 66th Congress, approved June 5, 1920. To present to the city of Verdun, France, a suitable memorial medal or tablet.

1921-1929

Public Law No. 388, 66th Congress, approved March 4, 1921. Authorizing bestowal upon the unknown, unidentified British soldier buried in Westminster Abbey and unknown, unidentified French soldier buried in the Arc de Triomphe of the Congressional Medal of Honor.

Public Law No. 67, 67th Congress, approved August 24, 1921. Authorizing bestowal upon the unknown, unidentified American to be buried in the Memorial Amphitheater of the National Cemetery at Arlington, Va., the Congressional Medal of Honor and the Distinguished Service Cross.

Public Res. No. 23, 67th Congress, approved October 12, 1921. For the bestowal of the Congressional Medal of Honor upon an unknown, unidentified Italian soldier buried in the National Monument to Victor Emanuel II, in Rome, Italy.

Public Law No. 190, 67th Congress, approved April 7, 1922. To extend the limitations of time upon the issuance of Medals of Honor, Distinguished Service Crosses, and Distinguished Service Medals to persons who served in the Army of the United States during the World War.

Public Law No. 438, 67th Congress, approved February 24, 1923. To prohibit the unauthorized wearing, manufacture, or sale of medals and badges awarded by the War Department.

Public Law No. 470, 68th Congress, approved February 25, 1925. To recognize and reward the accomplishment of the world flyers.

Public Law No. 524, 68th Congress, approved March 2, 1925. To authorize the Secretary of the Treasury to prepare a medal with appropriate emblems and inscriptions commemorative of the Norse-American Centennial.

Public Law No. 466 (extract) 69th Congress, approved July 2, 1926. Authorizing the president to present, but not in the name of Congress, a medal to be known as The Soldiers Medal.

Public Law No. 538, 69th Congress, approved January 5, 1927. Providing for the promotion of Lt. Commander Richard E. Byrd, United States Navy, retired, and awarding to him a Congressional Medal of Honor.

Public Law No. 539, 69th Congress, approved January 5, 1927. Providing for the promotion of Floyd Bennett, aviation pilot United States Navy, and awarding to him a Congressional Medal of Honor.

Public Law No. 1, 70th Congress, approved December 14, 1927. Authorizing the president of the United States to present in the name of Congress a Medal of Honor to Col. Charles A. Lindbergh.

Public Law No. 288, 70th Congress, approved April 21, 1928. To amend the Act of February 24, 1923, an act to prohibit the unauthorized wearing, manufacture, or sale of medals and badges by the War Department.

Public Law No. 341, 70th Congress, approved May 2, 1928. To authorize the president to present the Distinguished Flying Cross to Col. Francesco de Pinedo, Dieudonne Costes, Joseph LeBrix, Ehrenfried, Gunther von Huenefeld, James C. FitzMaurice and Hermann Koehl.

Public Res. No. 39, 70th Congress, approved May 4, 1928. To provide for the coinage of a medal in commemoration of the achievements of Col. Charles A. Lindbergh.

Public Law No. 369, 70th Congress, approved May 12, 1928. To provide for the gratuitous issue of service medals and similar devices.

Public Law No. 515 (extract) 70th Congress, approved May 26, 1928. That all recommendations for decorations by the United States of America shall be considered before the proper board.

Public Law No. 557, 70th Congress, approved May 28, 1928. An Act to amend the Defense Act.

Public Res. No. 66, 70th Congress, approved May 29, 1928. To provide for the striking of a medal commemorative of the achievements of Thomas A. Edison.

Private Law No. 287, 70th Congress, approved May 29, 1928. Awarding a gold medal to Lincoln Ellsworth.

Public Law No. 1024, 70th Congress, approved March 4, 1929. To provide for the recognition for meritorious service by members of the police and fire departments of the District of Columbia.

1930-1935

Public Res. No. 75, 71st Congress, approved May 23, 1930. Authorizing the presentation of medals to the officers and men of the Byrd Antarctic expedition.

Public Law No. 324, 71st Congress, approved June 9, 1930. An Act waiving the limiting period of two years in Executive Order Numbered 4576 to enable the board of awards of the Navy Department to consider recommendations of the award of the Distinguished Flying Cross to members of the Alaskan Aerial Survey Expedition.

Public Law No. 661, 71st Congress, approved February 14, 1931. An Act for the award of The Air-mail Flyer's Medal of Honor.

Public Law No. 694, 71st Congress, approved Feb. 20, 1931. Authorizing the manufacturing of a medal in commemoration of the 150th anniversary of the surrender of Lord Cornwallis at Yorktown, Va., and of the establishment of the independence of the United States.

Public Res. No. 31, 72rd Congress, approved July 2, 1932. Authorizing the president of the United States to present the Distinguished Flying Cross to Amelia Earhart Putnam.

Private Law No. 237, 72rd Congress, approved March 1, 1933. Authorizing the president to make a posthumous award of a distinguished-flying cross to Glenn H. Curtiss, deceased, and to present the same to Lua Curtiss, mother of the said Glenn H. Curtiss, deceased.

Public Law No. 114, 73rd Congress, approved March 5, 1934. An act to award the Distinguished Service Cross to former holders of the certificate of merit.

Public Law No. 223, 73rd Congress, approved May 14, 1934. Act to amend the Act authorizing the issuance of the Spanish War Service Medal.

Private Law No. 2, 73rd Congress, approved June 18, 1934. Authorizing the president of the United States to present the Dis-

tinguished Flying Cross to Emory B. Bronte.

Private Law No. 8, 74th Congress, approved March 21, 1935. Authorizing the president of the United States to present in the name of Congress a medal of honor to Major General Adolphus Washington Greely.

Public Law No. 31, 74th Congress, approved April 10, 1935. Authorizing the president to present Distinguished Flying Crosses to Air Marshal Italo Balbo and General Aldo Pellegrini, of the Royal Italian Air Force.

Public Law No. 43, 74th Congress, approved April 25, 1935. Authorizing personnel of the naval service to whom a commemorative or special medal has been awarded to wear in lieu thereof a miniature facsimile of such medal and a ribbon symbolic of the award.

Public Law No. 61, 74th Congress, approved May 15, 1935. To give proper recognition to the distinguished services of Colonel William L. Keller.

Public Law No. 398, 74th Congress, approved August 29, 1935. To authorize the transfer of a certain military reservation to the Department of the Interior.

1936-1940

Public Law No. 523, 74th Congress, approved April 17, 1936. Authorizing the president to present the Distinguished Service Medal to Commander Percy Todd, British Navy, and the Navy Cross to Lt. Commander Charles A. DeW. Kitcat, British Navy.

Public Res. No. 103, 74th Congress, approved June 4, 1936. Authorizing the president of the United States to award posthumously a Distinguished Service Medal to Major General Clarence Ransom Edwards.

Private Res. No. 5, 74th Congress, approved June 20, 1936. Authorizing the president to present the Navy Cross to J. Harold Arnold.

Private Law No. 727, 74th Congress, approved June 29, 1936. Authorizing the president to present a gold medal to George M. Cohan.

Public Res. No. 98, 74th Congress, approved June 30, 1936. Authorizing the presentation of silver medals to the personnel of the second Byrd Antarctic expedition.

Private Law No. 165, 75th Congress, approved June 18, 1937. Awarding a Navy Cross to John W. Thomason and Robert Slover.

Private Law No. 329, 75th Congress, approved August 23, 1937. To authorize the award of a decoration for distinguished service to Acors Rathbun Thompson.

Public Law No. 581, 75th Congress, approved June 7, 1938. Authorizing the president to present the Distinguished Service Medal to Rear Admiral Reginal Vesey Holt, British Navy, and to Capt. George Eric Maxia O'Donnell, British Navy, and the Navy Cross to Vice Admiral Lewis Gonne Eyre Crabbe, British Navy, and to Lt. Commander Harry Douglas Barlow, British Navy.

Private Res. No. 2, 76th Congress, approved July 15, 1939. Providing for consideration of a recommendation for decoration of Sergeant Fred W. Stockham, deceased.

Private Law No. 115, 76th Congress, approved July 28, 1939. Authorizing the president to present a Distinguished Service Medal to Rear Admiral Harry Ervin Yarnell, United States Navy.

Private Law No. 214, 76th Congress, approved Aug. 7, 1939. To provide for the presentation of a medal to Howard Hughes in recognition of his achievements in advancing the science of aviation.

Private Law No. 235, 76th Congress, approved Aug. 10, 1939. To provide for the presentation of a medal to Reverend Francis X. Quinn in recognition of his valor in saving the lives of two of his fellow citizens.

Private Res. No. 5, 76th Congress, approved April 30, 1940. To authorize the president to present the Distinguished Flying Cross to Frank W. Seifert and Lt. V. Hine, deceased.

Public Law No. 507, 76th Congress, approved May 13, 1940. To authorize the striking of an appropriate medal in commemoration of the 300th anniversary of the establishment of Greenwich, Conn., as a town.

Private Law No. 378, 76th Congress, approved June 15, 1940. Authorizing the president to present the Navy Cross to Capt. Frank N. Roberts, United States Army.

1941-1945

Private Law No. 128, 77th Congress, approved July 22, 1941. Authorizing the Secretary of the Navy Expeditionary Medal to certain Army and civilian personnel.

Public Law No. 322, 77th Congress, approved Nov. 21, 1941. Authorizing the procurement and issue of an Army of Occupation of Germany Medal for each person who served in Germany or Austria-Hungary during the period of occupation.

Public Law No. 524, 77th Congress, approved April 11, 1942. To provide decorations for outstanding conduct or service by persons serving in the American Merchant Marine.

Public Law No. 671, 77th Congress, approved July 20, 1942. To authorize officers and enlisted men of the Armed Forces of the United States to accept decorations, orders, medals and emblems tendered them by governments of cobelligerent nations or other American republics and to create the decorations to be known as the "Legion of Merit" and the "Medal for Merit."

Public Law No. 702, 77th Congress, approved Aug. 7, 1942. To amend the Act approved February 4, 1919, so as to change the conditions for the award of medals.

Public Law No. 805, 77th Congress, approved Dec. 15, 1942. To amend the Act of Jan. 24, 1920, so as to authorize the award of a silver star to certain persons serving with the Army of the United States.

Public Law No. 811, 77th Congress, approved Dec. 17, 1942. To authorize the president to confer decorations and medals upon units of, or persons serving with, the military forces of cobelligerent nations.

Public Law No. 52, 78th Congress, approved May 10, 1943. To provide for the issuance of devices in recognition of the services of merchant sailors.

Private Law No. 106, 78th Congress, approved Oct. 23, 1943. Authorizing the president to present, in the name of Congress, a Distinguished Service Cross to George F. Thompson.

Private Law No. 166, 78th Congress, approved Jan. 28, 1944. To provide for the presentation of silver medals to certain members of the Peary Polar Expedition of 1908-1909.

Private Law No. 203, 78th Congress, approved Feb. 22, 1944. Authorizing the president to present, in the name of Congress, a Distinguished Service Medal to Lt. General Thomas Holcomb, United States Marine Corps.

Private Law No. 260, 78th Congress, approved April 3, 1944. Authorizing the president to present, in the name of Congress, a Distinguished Service Medal to Admiral Chester W. Nimitz, United States Navy.

Private Law No. 1, 79th Congress, approved Feb. 28, 1945. To authorize Lewis Hobart Kenney, Charles Garner, Charles Clement Goodman and Henry Charles Robinson to accept decorations and orders tendered them by the government of the United States.

Public Law No. 112, 79th Congress, approved July 2, 1945. To authorize an award of merit for uncompensated personnel of the Selective Service System.

Public Law No. 114, 79th Congress, approved July 2, 1945. To provide for the issuance of the Mexican Border Service Medal to certain members of the Reserve forces of the Army on active duty in 1916 and 1917.

Public Law No. 135, 79th Congress, approved July 6, 1946. Providing for a medal for service in the Armed Forces during the present war.

Public Law No. 169, 79th Congress, approved July 31, 1945. To amend the Act of May 10, 1943.

Public Law No. 185, 79th Congress, approved Sept. 24, 1945. To provide for the presentation of medals to members of the United States Antarctic Expedition of 1939-1941.

1946-1950

Private Law No. 438, 79th Congress, approved March 22, 1946. Providing for the striking and presentation to General Marshall and Fleet Admiral King of appropriate gold medals in the name of the people of the United States.

Public Law No. 444, 79th Congress, approved June 26, 1946. To modify the time limitations governing the award of certain military and naval decorations for acts performed during the present war.

Public Law No. 631, 79th Congress, approved Aug. 7, 1946. To amend the Act to provide for the issuance of devices in recognition of the services of merchant sailors.

Private Law No. 831, 79th Congress, approved Aug. 7, 1946. Authorizing the president of the United States to award a special medal to General of the Armies of the United States John J. Pershing.

Public Law No. 698, 79th Congress, approved Aug. 8, 1946. Providing for a medal for service in the merchant marine during the present war.

Private Law No. 884, 79th Congress, approved Aug. 8, 1946. Authorizing the president of the United States to award posthumously in the name of Congress a Medal of Honor to William Mitchell.

Public Law No. 58, 80th Congress, approved May 15, 1947. To amend the Act of July 20, 1942.

Private Law No. 35, 80th Congress, approved June 30, 1947. Authorizing the presentation of the Distinguished Flying Cross to Rear Admiral Charles E. Rosendahl, United States Navy.

Public Law 314, 80th Congress, approved Aug. 1, 1947. To amend section 1 of the Act of July 20, 1942.

Public Law No. 438, 80th Congress, approved March 9, 1948. To authorize the president to award a Medal of Honor to the Un-

known American who lost his life while serving overseas in the Armed Forces of the United States during the World War II.

Private Law No. 8, 81st Congress, approved March 24, 1949. To authorize certain personnel and former personnel of the Naval Establishment to accept certain gifts and a foreign decoration tendered by foreign governments.

Public Law No. 178, 81st Congress, approved July 20, 1949. To establish the Medal of Humane Action for award to persons serving in or with the Armed Forces of the United States participating in the current military effort to supply necessities of life to the people of Berlin, Germany.

Public Law No. 221, 81st Congress approved Aug. 12, 1949. To provide for the coinage of a medal in recognition of the distinguished services of Vice President Alben W. Barkley.

Public Law No. 501, 81st Congress, approved May 3, 1950. To extend the time limits for the award of certain decorations.

Public Law No. 503, 81st Congress, approved May 5, 1950. To authorize the acceptance of foreign decorations for participation in the Berlin airlift.

Public Law No. 638, 81st Congress, approved Aug. 3, 1950. Authorizing the Dept. of Justice of the United States to recognize and to award to outstanding courageous young Americans a medal for heroism known as the Young American Medal for Bravery.

Public Law No. 661, 81st Congress, approved Aug. 4, 1950. To amend title 18, United States Code, section 705, to protect the badge, medal, emblem and other insignia of auxiliaries to veterans organizations.

1951-1955

Public Law No. 117, 82rd Congress, approved Aug. 17, 1951. To protect the Girl Scouts of the United States of America in the use of emblems and badges, descriptive or designating marks, and words or phrases heretofore adopted and to clarify existing law relating thereto.

Private Law No. 504, 82rd Congress, approved March 31, 1952. To provide for the presentation of the Merchant Marine Distinguished Service Medal to Henrik Kurt Carlsen, master, steamship *Flying Enterprise*.

Private Law No. 536, 83rd Congress, approved July 16, 1954. Authorizing the president to present a gold medal to Irving Berlin.

Public Law No. 259, 84th Congress, approved Aug. 9, 1955. To authorize the issuance of commemorative medals to certain societies of which Benjamin Franklin was a member, founder, or sponsor in observance of the 250th anniversary of his birth.

Public Law No. 338, 84th Congress, approved Aug. 9, 1955. To provide for the striking of medals in commemoration of the 120th anniversary of the signing of the Texas Declaration of Independence and the Battle of the Alamo, Goliad, and San Jacinto in the year 1836.

1956-1960

Public Law No. 727, 84th Congress, approved July 18, 1956. To provide for the striking of medals in commemoration of the 100th anniversary of the birth of the late Justice Louis Dembitz Brandeis.

Public Law No. 730, 84th Congress, approved July 18, 1956. To provide for a medal to be struck and presented to each surviving veteran of the U.S. Civil War.

Public Law No. 759, 84th Congress, approved July 24, 1956. To authorize medals and decorations for outstanding and meritorious conduct and service in the United States Merchant Marine.

Public Law No. 917, 84th Congress, approved Aug. 2, 1956. To extend the time limit within which awards of certain military and naval decorations may be made.

Private Law No. 14, 85th Congress, approved May 16, 1957. To waive the limitation on the time within which a medal of honor may be awarded to Commander Hugh Barr Miller Jr., United States Navy.

Public Law No. 85-50, Congress approved June 13, 1957. To amend the Medals of Honor Act to authorize awards for acts of heroism involving any motor vehicle.

Public Law No. 85-251, approved Aug. 31, 1957. To authorize the president to award the Medal of Honor to the unknown American who lost his life while serving overseas in the Armed Forces of the United States during the Korean conflict.

Public Law No. 85-826, approved Aug. 28, 1958. To authorize the chairman of the Joint Committee on Atomic Energy to confer a medal on Rear Admiral Hyman George Rickover, United States Navy.

Public Law No. 85-879, approved Sept. 2, 1958. To amend the Act of Feb. 28, 1929, to include therein the name of Roger P. Ames.

Public Law No. 86-29, approved May 20, 1959. To provide for the striking of medals in commemoration of the 100th anniversary of the first significant discovery of silver in the United States, June 1859.

Public Law No. 86-65, approved June 23, 1959. To provide for the striking of medals in commemoration of the 100th anniversary of

the settlement of the state of Colorado and in commemoration of the establishment of the United States Air Force Academy.

Public Law No. 86-184, approved Aug. 24, 1959. To provide for the striking of medals in commemoration of the 100th anniversary of the admission of West Virginia into the Union as a state.

Public Law No. 86-277, approved Sept. 16, 1959. To authorize the issuance of a gold medal in honor of the late Professor Robert H. Goddard.

Public Law No. 86-393, approved March 18, 1960. To provide for the striking of medals in commemoration of the 100th anniversary of the statehood of Kansas.

Public Law No. 86-394, approved March 18, 1960. To provide for the striking of medals in commemoration of the 100th anniversary of the founding of the Pony Express.

Public Law No. 86-582, approved July 5, 1960. To amend title 10, United States Code, to authorize the award of certain medals within two years after a determination by the Secretary concerned that because of loss or inadvertence the recommendation was not processed.

Public Law No. 86-593, approved July 6, 1960. To amend Title 10, United States Code, with respect to certain medals.

Public Law No. 86-600, approved July 7, 1960. To provide for the presentation of a medal to persons who have served as members of a United States expedition to Antarctica.

Public Law No. 86-656, approved July 14, 1960. To authorize the award posthumously of appropriate medals to Chaplain George L. Fox, Chaplain Alexander D. Goode, Chaplain Clark V. Polling and Chaplain John P. Washington.

Public Law No. 86-696, approved Sept. 2, 1960. To provide for the striking of medals in commemoration of the 100th anniversary of the founding of Idaho as a territory.

Public Law No. 86-697, approved Sept. 2, 1960. To provide for the striking of a medal in commemoration of Century 21 Exposition to be held in Seattle, Wash.

Public Law No. 86-747, approved Sept. 13, 1960. Authorizing the president of the United States to present a gold medal to Robert Frost, a New England poet.

1961-1965

Public Law No. 87-21, approved April 24, 1961. To provide for the striking of medals in commemoration of the 250th anniversary of the founding of Mobile, Ala.

Public Law No. 87-42, approved May 27,

1961. To authorize the president to award posthumously a medal to Dr. Thomas Anthony Dooley II.

Public Law No. 87-478, approved June 8, 1962. Authorizing the issuance of a gold medal to entertainer Bob Hope.

Public Law No. 87-702, approved Sept. 26, 1962. To provide for the coinage of a medal in recognition of the distinguished services of Sam Rayburn, Speaker of the House of Representatives.

Public Law No. 87-711, approved Sept. 27, 1962. To amend Public Law No. 184, 86th Congress, an Act to provide for the striking of medals in commemoration of the 100th anniversary of the admission of West Virginia into the Union as a state.

Public Law No. 87-760, approved Oct. 9, 1962. Authorizing the issuance of a gold medal to General of the Army Douglas MacArthur.

Public Law No. 88-77, approved July 25, 1963. To amend titles 10, 14, and 38, United States Code, with respect to the award of certain medals and the Medal of Honor Roll.

Public Law No. 88-107, approved Aug. 27, 1963. To authorize the presentation of an Air Force Medal of Recognition to Major General Benjamin D. Foulois, retired.

Public Law No. 88-143, approved Oct. 16, 1963. To furnish to the Padre Junipero Serra 250th Anniversary Association medals in commemoration of the 250th anniversary of his birth.

Public Law No. 88-147, approved Oct. 16, 1963. To provide for the striking of medals in commemoration of the 100th anniversary of the admission of Nevada to statehood.

Public Law No. 88-184, approved Nov. 20, 1963. To provide for the striking of medals in commemoration of the 150th anniversary of the statehood of Indiana.

Public Law No. 88-185, approved Nov. 20, 1963. To provide for the striking of medals in commemoration of the 50th anniversary of the founding of the first union health center in the United States by the International Ladies Garment Workers Union.

Public Law No. 88-262, approved Jan. 31, 1964. To provide for the striking of three different medals in commemoration of the Federal Hall National Memorial, Castle Clinton National Monument and Statue of Liberty National Monument American Museum of Immigration in New York, N.Y.

Public Law No. 88-270, approved Feb. 11, 1964. To provide for the striking of medals in commemoration of the 200th anniversary of the founding of St. Louis.

Public Law No. 88-651, approved Oct. 13, 1964. To amend section 560 of title 38, United States Code, to permit the payment of special pension to holders of the Congressional Medal of Honor awarded such medal for actions not involving conflict with an enemy.

1966-1970

Public Law No. 89-382, approved March 31, 1966. To provide for the striking of medals in commemoration of the 250th anniversary of the founding of San Antonio.

Public Law No. 89-393, approved April 14, 1966. To provide for the striking of medals in commemoration of the 100th anniversary of the purchase of Alaska by the United States from Russia.

Public Law No. 89-400, approved April 16, 1966. To furnish to the Scranton Association Inc. medals in commemoration of the 100th anniversary of the founding of the city of Scranton, Pa.

Public Law No. 89-401, approved April 16, 1966. To provide for the striking of medals in commemoration of the 75th anniversary of the founding of the American Numismatic Association.

Public Law No. 89-402, approved June 24, 1966. To provide for the striking of medals in commemoration of the 100th anniversary of the founding of the United States Secret Service.

Public Law 89-469, approved June 24, 1966. Authorizes U.S. Secret Service medal.

Public Law No. 89-527, approved August 5, 1966. To provide for the striking of medals to commemorate the 1,000th anniversary of the founding of Poland.

Public Law No. 89-529, approved August 11, 1966. To authorize the award of trophies for the recognition of special accomplishments related to the Armed Forces.

Public Law No. 89-534, approved August 11, 1966. To provide gold star lapel buttons for the next of kin of members of the Armed Forces who lost or lose their lives in war or as a result of Cold War incidents.

Public Law No. 89-676, approved October 15, 1966. To provide for the striking of a medal in commemoration of the designation of Ellis Island as a part of the Statue of Liberty National Monument in New York, N.Y.

Public Law No. 89-679, approved October 15, 1966. To provide for the striking of medals in commemoration of the 50th anniversary of the Federal Land Bank system in the United States.

Public Law No. 89-783, approved November 6, 1966. To provide for the striking of medals in commemoration of the United

States Naval Construction Battalions (SEABEES) 25th anniversary and the United States Navy Civil Engineers Corps (CEC) 100th anniversary.

Public Law No. 90-124, approved November 4, 1967. To provide for the striking of medals in commemoration of the 200th anniversary of the founding of San Diego.

Public Law No. 90-125, approved November 4, 1967. To provide for the striking of medals in commemoration of the 300th anniversary of the explorations of Father Jacques Marquette in what is now the United States.

Public Law No. 90-127, approved November 4, 1967. To provide for the striking of medals in commemoration of the 50th anniversary of the founding of the American Legion.

Public Law No. 90-128, approved November 4, 1967. To provide for the striking of medals in commemoration of the 150th anniversary of the founding of the state of Mississippi.

Public Law No. 90-303, approved May 10, 1968. To provide for the striking of medals in commemoration of the 100th anniversary of the completion of the first transcontinental railroad.

Public Law No. 90-316, approved May 24, 1968. To provide for the issuance of a gold medal to the widow of Walt Disney and for the issuance of bronze medals to the California Institute of the Arts in recognition of the distinguished public service and the outstanding contributions of Walt Disney to the United States and to the world.

Public Law No. 90-528, approved September 28, 1968. To provide for the striking of medals in commemoration of the 200th anniversary of the founding of Dartmouth College.

Public Law No. 90-600, approved October 17, 1968. To provide for the striking of medals in commemoration of the 150th anniversary of the founding of the city of Memphis.

Public Law No. 91-12, approved May 7, 1969. To provide for the striking of medals in honor of the dedication of the Winston Churchill Memorial and Library at Westminster College, Fulton, Mo.

Public Law No. 91-13, approved May 15, 1969. To strike a medal commemorating the founding of the American Fisheries Society.

Public Law No. 91-16, approved May 28, 1969. To strike a medal in commemoration of the 300th anniversary of the founding of South Carolina.

Public Law No. 91-18, approved May 28, 1969. To strike a medal in commemoration of the 150th anniversary of the founding of the city of Wichita.

Public Law No. 91-29, approved June 17, 1969. To strike a medal in commemoration of the 150th anniversary of the state of Alabama.

Public Law No. 91-48, approved July 22, 1969. To strike a medal in commemoration of the U.S. Diplomatic Courier Service.

Public Law 91-244, approved May 9, 1970. To strike a medal in commemoration of the many contributions to the founding and early development of the state of Texas and the city of San Antonio by Jose Antonio Navarro.

Public Law 91-254, approved May 14, 1970. To strike a medal in commemoration of the completion of the carvings on Stone Mountain, Ga., depicting heroes of the Confederacy.

Public Law 91-381, approved August 17, 1970. To strike a medal in commemoration of the 100th anniversary of the founding of Ohio Northern University.

Recent numismatic bills

Numerous numismatically related pieces of legislation have been introduced in the House and the Senate. From 1963, onward, the vast majority of these related to the proposed issuance of national medals by the United States Mint. National Mint medals emerged as a major alternative to commemorative coins nearly half a century ago. Following 1963 hearings by the subcommittee on Consumer Affairs (which then had jurisdiction over coinage matters), it became clear that the Mint would continue to oppose commemorative coinage issues, but would accept national medals as an alternative.

The present requirements for national medal status are multifold; dies for the medals must be of national character (not further defined), they must be produced at the Philadelphia Mint, may be executed by the Chief Sculptor-Engraver provided the work does not interfere with regular coinage, and no private medal dies may be prepared at the Mint or any machinery used for that purpose. Despite these requirements, Congress has always had the power to alter them, which it did in 1973 by allowing the San Francisco Assay Office to strike a national Mint medal commemorating the Centennial of the San Francisco Cable Car. Likewise, the Centennial of Colorado Statehood was authorized to be struck as a national medal at the Denver Mint.

Under current standards, a national Mint medal will not be considered in the absence of 218 co-sponsors, one vote more than a simple majority of the membership of the House of Representatives. This is purely a procedural decision on the part of the chairman, and staff, of the House Subcommittee on Consumer Affairs and Coinage of the House Banking Committee.

More recently, in addition to national medals, there have been commemorative coin bills which have been fully considered and enacted. It seems probable, in light of the profits being made from this venture, that many more commemorative coin bills are likely in the future.

What follows is a brief description of the legislative history of bills introduced over the past 15 years in the House and Senate that relate to coin collectors in several ways: legislation affecting the Mint, the Bureau of Engraving and Printing, and the Department of the Treasury (other than ordinary annual appropriations), together with proposals for commemorative coinages, national medals, alteration of coin designs or compositions, and topics that are of general concern to collectors such as counterfeits, metal stockpiles, and sale of government numismatic properties. National and other medals authorized by Congress up to 1971 are categorized separately in the section "Public laws authorizing medals."

Congress meets for a two-year period commencing in early January in odd-numbered years. (Elections take place in even-numbered years, with presidential elections every other term, such as 1988). Each meeting of Congress is divided into two sessions (usually one for each year, though in earlier times a "lame duck" third session was known to take place). During each two-year period, more than 20,000 bills are introduced in the House, with 435 members, and a slightly lesser number in the Senate, with 100 members (two per state). Few bills are actually enacted into law.

Typically, when a coin-related bill is introduced in the House, it is referred to the House Committee on Banking, Finance and Urban Affairs, and then to a subcommittee, usually the Subcommittee on Consumer Affairs and Coinage.

Historically, the parent committee was known as the House Committee on Banking, Housing and Urban Affairs (under the chairmanship of Rep. Fernand St. Germain, D-R.I., and earlier Rep. Henry Reuss, D-Wis.); before that it was the House Committee on Banking and Currency (whose chairman was Rep. Wright Patman, D-Texas, from 1963-74).

Numismatic matters were handled first by a numbered subcommittee (later named the Subcommittee on Consumer Affairs), chaired by Rep. Leonor K. Sullivan, D-Mo., whose key aide was Charles B. ("Chuck") Holstein, until 1974. In 1975, the name of the committee handling these matters became the Subcommittee on Historic Preservation and Coinage, chaired by Rep. Robert G. Stephens Jr., D-Ga., whose staff director, Jackson O'Neal Lamb, also served the successor, Rep. Walter E. Fauntroy, D-D.C., in the following Congress. Starting in 1979, Rep. Frank Annunzio, D-Ill., has headed the Subcommittee on Consumer Affairs and Coinage with Curtis Prins as staff director.

In the Senate, Sen. William Proxmire, D-Wis., was the chairman of the Senate Committee on Banking, Finance and Urban Affairs, with Marian Mayer as his chief of staff for numismatics until Republicans gained control of the Senate in 1980. Earlier, an ad hoc subcommittee on Minting and Coinage, chaired by Sen. William Hathaway, D-Maine, handled coinage legislation that came up with the assistance of Edward Sokol. Then, in 1981, Sen. Jake Garn, R-Utah, became committee chairman and Linda Zemke became the key staff person in charge of numismatic matters. In 1987, the Democrats regained control of the Senate. Proxmire became chairman; Garn assumed the role of ranking minority member. A major staff shakeup took place.

While the popular perception remains that members of Congress handle most matters including the drafting of legislation and the follow-up that brings it to a vote, and, if successful, the law books, the more knowledgeable are well aware that it is the staff aide who closely governs the position taken by a political leader. Typically, it is the aide (and not the lawmaker) who prepares the draft of a bill, writes the introductory remarks reprinted in the *Congressional Record* that are made when the bill is introduced, records questions that are to be asked (and answered) at hearings, and often advances the theory behind a particular piece of legislation.

Thus, Marian Mayer of the Proxmire staff was singularly responsible for advancing the idea of utilizing the Susan B. Anthony portrait on the new smaller-sized dollar as a concept to advance women's rights, and Curtis Prins of the Annunzio office pushed hard for the contemporary Olympic commemorative coin program that contemplated the first gold coin in half a century.

In the listing that follows, two distinct approaches have been utilized. The first notes bills of interest that have become law since 1965 and gives their legislative history. (This includes all of the medal bills since 1971.) The second is partially duplicative (since it lists bills introduced that are of numismatic concern, but were not enacted into law).

Since the passage of the Bland-Allison Act of 1878 (which created the Morgan dollar) over the veto of President Hayes, no numismatic-related bill has been passed over the veto of an incumbent president. (Some commemorative coin bills were vetoed between 1928 and 1960; all were sustained by Congress.) Hence, no mention is made of the chief executive who signed the bill into law.

Some bills are introduced annually by members of Congress with no action taken whatsoever (except to refer the matter to committee, where it uniformly dies), and while these are noted for historical accuracy, no mention is made of the pertinent committee unless it is other than the Senate or House Banking Committee.

With one exception all appropriations and authorizations are ignored in the chronology. The exception is a bill that refers to authorization and appropriations, and which was added to the U.S. Code as 31 USC 5132(a) (1) in November 1983 requiring Uncirculated (Mint) sets to be produced by the Mint.

Also left out for reasons of space are the intricacies of how various measures became law, itself a fascinating story. In the 20 years that this writer has examined and reviewed Congress, several numismatic measures have

become law after intricate battles of major newsworthiness. Still others have become reality for political usefulness of the sponsor, or the advancement of the nation as a whole.

A good introduction to one of the bills, in about 100 printed pages in length, affords an understanding as to why each cannot be so annotated. It is found in "Tribute to 200 Years of Freedom: The Story of How the U.S. Got Its Bicentennial Coinage," which appeared in the American Numismatic Association's monthly journal, *The Numismatist,* from March to June of 1975. On more recent legislation, the index to the *Wall Street Journal* (and that publication itself) for the year 1982 will afford interesting coverage from a different perspective of the move to create Olympic commemorative coinage.

Finally, the texts of several laws that are deemed of continuing significance to serious collectors are provided for easy reference and use. All are available in the *Statutes at Large,* which can be found in many public libraries, nearly all law libraries as well as federal government document centers around the country.

For those interested in serious research on how a particular coin bill became law, there are several starting points. First, there are indices to the committee hearings held on Capitol Hill, and the texts of the hearings themselves. Next are speeches and comments found in the *Congressional Record,* and, earlier (prior to 1873) *The Congressional Globe* as well as the *Annals of Congress,* a virtual register of debates constituting a privately published summary. There may be presidential messages and other documents (usually referred to on the engrossed copy of the bill found in the *Statues at Large,* together with the dates of House and Senate passage) and unofficial documents available in the national archives. Each forms a part of a history of contemporary American coinage law.

Recent bills

Below, grouped by categories, are bills that have been introduced and considered by Congress since 1981. Most fall into the status of those bills referred to in the introduction — legislative proposals that were never enacted and that never even were considered in the hearing process. They are noted for historical accuracy only. When a bill went further (i.e., hearings were held) it is noted. Where no committee is cited, it is the House Banking Committee (Subcommittee on Consumer Affairs and Coinage) or the Senate Banking Committee (full committee) that held the hearings. Those bills which were enacted into law have their fuller history printed elsewhere and are cited to public law number.

George Washington commemorative coinage

All are for 90 percent silver half dollar unless otherwise noted.

3/16/81 H.R. 5424 (Barnard).
4/7/81 H.R. 3133 (Annunzio and Barnard).
5/7/81 H.R. 348A (Annunzio and Barnard). See Pub. L. 97-104.
5/18/81 S. 1228 (McClure).
11/6/81 S. 1822 (McClure and Symms). - 90 percent silver $10 coin.

Olympic commemorative coinage.

5/20/81 S. 1230 (Cranston). See Pub. L. 97-220 (Original 29 coin proposal).
6/11/81 H.R. 3879 (Annunzio). Single dollar coin.
6/17/81 H.R. 3958 (Patterson). Same as S. 1230.
3/23/82 H.R. 5933 (Patterson). 17 coin bill plus additional resold medallions (bulk sales).
4/1/82 H.R. 6058 (St Germain). 17 coin program. Hearing 4/6/82.
4/5/82 H.R. 6069 (Annunzio). One coin proposal. Hearing 4/6/82.
4/26/82 H.R. 6158 (Annunzio). Became Pub. L. 97-220.

Paper currency

1/5/81 H.R. 391 (Paul). Eliminates paper money as legal tender; sold coins to be authorized.
1/13/81 H.R. 831 (Crane). Return to gold standard; paper currency redeemable into gold.
1/16/81 H.R. 875 (Jacobs). Georgia N. Clark portrait on $50 bill.
3/5/81 H.R. 2345 (Bellenson). To prevent printing of $100 bills.
5/20/81 H.R. 3656 (Starke). Braille use on currency requirement.
7/27/81 H.R. 4275 (McClory). To allow color reproduction of U.S. currency and its use in advertising (Judiciary Committee); Hearings 7/27/81. Note: Supreme Court Decision (Time v Regan, 1984). comes from this in part.
9/30/81 H.R. 4628 (St Germain and Annunzio). Allows BEP to use non-intaglio (offset). printing for $1 bill reverse.
10/14/81 S. 1736 (Garn). Offset printing for $1 bill.
10/1/82 H.R. 7283 (Schulze). Demonetize $100 bill.
2/15/83 H.R. 1453 (Jacobs). Clark portrait, 1/16/81.
2/17/83 H.R. 1548 (Schulze). Demonetize $100 bill (10/1/82).
4/20/83 H.R. 2666 (Starke). Change currency for visually handicapped.
4/21/83 S. 1120 (Garn). Offset currency $1 reverse. 10/14/81; 9/30/81; Hearings 6/22/83. Hearings before House 7/24/84.

9/13/83 H. Con. Res. 163 (Panetta). Recommends development of currency for visually impaired.
10/27/83 H.R. 4238 (Minish). Offset $1 bill reverse. See 9/30/81; 10/14/81; (Hearings, Senate, 6/22/83).

Taxation

The Economic Recovery Act of 1981 contained a clause, Section 314-b (now Section 408(m). of the Internal Revenue Code). which effectively prohibited self-directed pension plans, and individual retirement accounts, from investing in coins. Several bills have attempted to amend this.

9/9/81 H.R. 4418 (Archer). To repeal Sec. 314-b (Ways and Means).
9/9/81 H.R. 4439 (Paul). To repeal Sec. 314-b (Ways and Means).
9/18/81 S. 1645 (Moynihan). To repeal Section 314-b. Hearings before Senate Finance Committee Subcommittee on Savings, Pensions and Investment Policy, 12/4/81 (#97-63).

It is also useful to note that as part of several revenue bills since that time, amendments and riders have been offered in various conferences and committees to remove the capital gains status of collectibles in general and coins in particular. Such attempts have not been successful.

Bullion coins

Bullion coin proposals have been introduced regularly in Congress since 1974 when Americans regained their right to own gold. The American Arts Gold Medallion Act, passed as Public Law 95-630 in 1978, was the first way that Congress dealt with the issue. The Gold Bullion Coin Act of 1985 authorized creation of four different denominations of gold bullion coins, later called the American Eagles. Title II of the Statue of Liberty/Ellis Island commemorative coin legislation authorized a silver bullion dollar coin.

Elsewhere, the text of the banning of the Krugerrand by executive order appears. Bullion refers to coinage primarily produced for its metal content rather than normal circulation or as a commemorative. Some may have legal tender status. Regulation 6045 under the Internal Revenue Code offers some additional definitions of bullion, as do some Treasury (IRS) revenue rulings.

4/2/81 H.R. 3008 (Solarz). Bans Krugerrand importation. See Executive Order 12535, October 1, 1985 (obviates further congressional action).

6/4/81 H.R. 3789 (Daniel Crane). New gold coinage proposed: 1 troy oz.; 1 oz.; 10 gram; 5 gram (JFK; Lincoln; Jefferson; Adam Smith).

10/5/81 S. 1704 (Symms, McClure, Helms, Goldwater). 4 gold coins: 1 troy oz., 1 oz., 10 grams, 5 grams.

11/6/81 S. 1823 (McClure and Symms). Part requires silver bullion coin production for silver disposal. Armed Services Committee.

3/1/82 H.R. 1944 (Hansen). 3/20, 3/8, 3/4, 1½ oz. gold coins (Jefferson, Hamilton, Madison, Benjamin Franklin).

4/1/82 H.R. 6054 (Paul). American Eagle Gold Coin Act of 1982. 1/10, 1/4, 1/2 and 1 oz. gold coins. Hearings 9/28/82. S. 2330. (Schmitt). (Same as H.R. 6054).

5/27/82 S. 2598 (McClure, Symms). 1 troy ounce Liberty silver dollar; New Morgan dollar.

6/22/82 H.R. 6649 (same as 5/27/82).

1/3/83 H.R. 138 (Hansen). One million troy ounces of gold coins.

1/6/83 H.R. 510 (Philip Crane). Authorize gold bullion sales of reserves.

1/25/83 H.R. 840 (McDonald). Annual audit of gold reserves.

1/25/83 H.R. 878 (Paul). Monetary Freedom Act (repeals right to use emergency powers to seize gold).

1/26/83 S. 42 (Helms). American Eagle Gold Coin Act of 1983. Hearings 4/15/83.

1/27/83 S. 269 (McClure). Silver one ounce coins. Hearing 4/15/83.

2/24/83 H.R. 1662 (Paul). American eagle gold coin act.

2/24/83 H.R. 1663 (Paul). Additional sponsors to gold coin act.

2/25/83 H.R. (Solarz). Prohibits South African Krugerrand importation. Hearings 3/2/83 H.R. 1814 (Paul). Tax income on coins based on face value (Ways and Means).

6/8/83 (Financial Institution Subcommittee). Placed as a rider into Export Administration Act (no action by 8/84).

10/26/83 H.R. 4226 (Paul). Bullion-based monetary standard.

Susan B. Anthony dollar legislative history

Following is a complete legislative history of the Susan B. Anthony dollar.

5/12/75 Contract for study of coinage awarded by U.S. Mint to Research Triangle Institute.

9/15/76 RTI recommends small-sized dollar in completed study as Frank Gasparro works on experimental Liberty design.

12/31/76 Treasury Secretary William Simon's "State of the Coinage" report recommends 26.5mm diameter dollar coin.

4/7/77 Treasury Secretary Blumenthal concurs with Simon recommendation.

4/17/78 Carter administration's recommendation to Congress.

5/1/78 H.R. 12444 introduced by Rep. Walter E. Fauntroy for adminstration.

5/3/78 S. 3036 introduced by Sen. William Proxmire for administration (same as H.R. 12444).

5/15/78 H.R. 12728 introduced by Reps. Mary Rose Oakar and Patricia Schroeder calling for Susan B. Anthony portrait.

5/17/78 Hearings on H.R. 12444 before Subcomm. on Historic Preservation and Coinage.

5/22/78 H.R. 12819 introduced by Rep. William Frenzel, for Susan B. Anthony portrait.

5/25/78 H.R. 12872 introduced by Rep. James A.S. Leach for Anthony and Harriet Tubman portrait.

5/31/78 Rep. Mary Rose Oakar introduced H.R. 12904 for Anthony coin (same as HR 12819) with multiple co-sponsors.

June, 1978 Frank Gasparro, chief engraver, starts Anthony design.

6/14/78 H.R. 13134 introduced by Rep. Oakar in house (same as prior Susan B. Anthony bills, but with additional co-sponsors).

7/11/78 H.R. 13415 introduced by Rep. Oakar, same as prior bills with additional co-sponsors.

7/17/78 S. 3036 hearings before Senate Banking Committee.

7/18/78 H.R. 13520 introduced by Rep. Oakar. Same as prior bills with additional consponsors.

7/20/78 H.R. 13558 introduced by Rep. Oakar. Additional consponsors.

7/21/78 H.R. 13570 introduced by Rep. Oakar. Additional co-sponsors.

7/25/78: H.R. 12728 from House subcommittee to full Banking committee.

8/16/78 S. 3036 passed by voice vote.

9/7/78 S. 3036 referred to House Banking Committee.

9/18/78 H.R. 12728 approved by House Banking unit 38 to 1.

9/18/78 House Banking unit recommends passage (Rept. 95-1576).

5/16/78 House passages H.R. 12728 by 368 to 38 vote; vacates and passes S. 3036; Fine Arts Commission approves Gasparro design.

9/29/78 S. 3036 delivered to the president.

10/10/78 Public Law 95-447 signed.

George Washington commemorative coinage legislative history

The first commemorative coin issue since 1954 marked the 250th anniversary of the birth of George Washington. Struck in 90 percent silver, with a maximum mintage of 10 million pieces, and offered for sale by the Mint in 1982 and 1983, the coin's issuance was remarkably uncontroversial — despite the prior opposition of the Treasury Department over a half century to any commemorative issues, a policy which successfully ended all commemorative coin issues in 1954.

At the hearings before the House coinage subcommittee, the Treasury Department came out in favor of the issue, making it a foregone conclusion that the coins would be isssued.

3/16/81 H.R. 2524 introduced by Rep. Barnard.

4/7/81 H.R. 3133 introduced by Rep. Annunzio and Barnard.

5/7/81 H.R. 3483 introduced by Rep. Annunzio and Barnard with Treasury modifications (10 million maximum mintage) use of earmarked silver from Ike dollar program; hearings before House coinage subcommittee.

5/18/81 S. 1228 introduced by Sen. McClure (similar to H.R. 3483).

5/19/81 H.R. 3483 Passes House on voice vote (unanimous) (H. Rept. 97-3484).

11/20/81 H.R. 3493 reported by Senate Banking Committee to full Senate (Sen. Rept. 97-277).

12/9/81 Senate approved by unanimous consent.

12/13/81 Signed into Public Law 97-104 by President Reagan.

11/6/83 S. 1822 introduced by Sens. McClure and Symms (90 percent silver $10 coin). No further action.

Olympic commemorative coinage legislative history

In modern times, the Olympic commemorative coinage program initiated 1983-84 constitutes the most ambitious American commemorative coinage program ever conceived. A total of 50 million silver coins and 2 million gold coins were authorized.

Final sales of the Olympic coinage confirmed that this was the most impressive showing to that time: 573,364 gold coins were sold, and 4,472,110 silver dollars were sold. Total surcharges exceeded $73.3 million; total sales were in excess of $308 million.

It is no secret that the Olympic program was also one of the most controversial in modern times, with private interests competing with the U.S. Mint for the right to market the program that initially began as a 29-coin program and eventually was enacted as a three-coin issue (two silver dollars, one gold coin) that, with Mint marks and Proof and Uncirculated versions, became a 13-coin issue.

Some of the controversy spilled over into the daily press as well as the hobby journals. *The Wall Street Journal* index will list fully those articles concerning the

Olympic program that were covered there, including at least one Page One story that offers analysis of the behind-the-scenes machinations.

5/20/81 S. 1230 introduced in Senate by Cranston. Original proposal calling for 29 coins.

6/11/81 H.R. 6069 introduced by Rep. Annunzio. Single $1 coin.

6/17/81. H.R. 3958 introduced in House by Rep. Patterson. Parallels S. 1230.

9/23/81 Rep. Annunzio attacks S. 1230 & H.R. 3958 in *Congressional Record.*

10/15/81 Senate Banking Committee meets and marks up S. 1230 in modified form (25 coins).

10/30/81 Senate Report 97-264 issued on S. 1230.

12/9/81 S. 1230 passes Senate unanimously (Rept. 97-264).

3/23/82 H.R. 5933 introduced. Calls for one copper-nickel $1 coin; 12 silver coins; four gold coins. (17 coins).

3/29/82 Senate passes H.R. 5708 (17-coin proposal).

4/1/82 H.R. 6058 introduced by Rep. St Germain (same as Senate bill, with private marketer).

4/5/82 H.R. 6069 introduced by Rep. Annunzio (one coin proposal).

4/6/82 Hearings before House coinage subcommittee.

4/21/82 Hearings before House coinage subcommittee.

4/26/82 H.R. 6158 introduced by Rep. Annunzio (three coin bill); *Wall Street Journal* article appears.

4/29/82 Hearings before House coinage subcommittee.

5/11/82 Hearings before House coinage subcommittee.

5/12/82 Hearings before House coinage subcommittee.

5/13/82 House Coinage subcommittee reports bill to full committee; H.R. 6058 substituted for S. 1230. (Replaced by H.R. 6158, Annunzio version).

5/13/82 House Banking Committee substitutes St Germain bill for Annunzio version by 32 to 7 vote.

5/20/82 H. Res. 470 is considered for debate on Olympic coin proposals. House votes down St Germain bill 302-84 and approves Annunzio version, H.R. 6158. (Rept. 97-554).

6/10/82 Senate Hearing on S. 1230 as amended.

7/1/82 Senate concurs with House amendments.

7/22/82 President Reagan signed Public Law 97-220 into law.

Statue of Liberty-Ellis Island commemorative coinage and Liberty Coin Act of 1985 legislative history

The 100th anniversary of the dedication of the Statue of Liberty was celebrated in 1986 with three U.S. commemorative coins: a gold $5 half eagle honoring the Statue of Liberty, a silver dollar honoring the Ellis Island immigration facility and a copper-nickel half dollar commemorating the accomplishments of immigrants to the United States. All three coins were offered in Proof and Uncirculated versions.

By the time sales had ended Dec. 31, 1986, sales of the Statue of Liberty commemorative coins had raised a record $82.3 million in surcharges (with not all sales reported as of press time).

1/3/85 H.R. 47 introduced in House by Rep. Annunzio.

1/3/85 H.R. 47 referred to House Banking Committee.

2/20/85 Hearings held before House Banking Subcommittee on Consumer Affairs and Coinage.

3/5/85 H.R. 47 discharged by House Banking Committee, with amendments adopted by voice vote.

3/6/85 Referred to the Senate Banking Committee.

3/6/85 Reported without amendments by the Senate Banking Committee.

6/21/85 Passed by the Senate, voice vote, with amendments authorizing a silver bullion dollar.

6/24/85 House agreed to the Senate amendment.

7/2/85 Sent to the president.

7/9/85 Signed into Public Law 99-61 by President Reagan.

Gold Bullion Coin Act of 1985
legislative history

As noted earlier, numerous bills calling for one or more gold bullion coins were introduced in Congress after Americans regained the right to own gold coins in December 1974. None were successful until 1985, when the Gold Bullion Coin Act of 1985 passed through both houses of Congress and was signed into law by President Reagan.

The act authorized four gold coins: a $50 coin containing 1 ounce of .999 fine gold; a $25 half-ounce coin; a $10 quarter-ounce coin; and a $5 tenth-ounce coin.

The reverse design for the 1-ounce coin was specified by the legislation to ensure use of a design by Dallas sculptor Miley Busiek, showing a family of American eagles. The design was used on the reverses of all four designs.

9/12/85 S. 1639 introduced in Seante by Sen. J. James Exon.
11/13/85 S. 1639 reported with amendments.
11/14/85 Passed by the Senate.
11/20/85 Rejected by the House by unanimous consent.
12/2/85 Passed in House under suspension.
12/5/85 Sent to the president.
12/17/85 Signed into Public Law 99-185 by President Reagan.

Constitution Bicentennial
commemorative coin
legislative history

The 200th anniversary of the framing of the United States Constitution in 1987 is latest national event to be commemorated by U.S. coinage. Two coins were authorized: a gold $5 half eagle and a silver dollar. A provision in the legislation calling for national medals was dropped before a vote in the full House.

After the legislation became law, Treasury officials announced a limited competition for the designs, and designs by two non-Mint employees were selected.

9/23/85 H.R. 3415 introduced in House by Rep. Annunzio.
9/23/85 Referred to House Banking Committee.
10/1/85 House Banking Committee discharged H.R. 3415, and voted on amendments.
10/10/85 H.R. 3415 passed by the House.
10/16/85 Passed by Senate, voice vote.
10/16/85 Senate amendments adopted in House by voice vote.
10/29/85 Signed into Public Law 99-582 by President Reagan.

National Coin Week

National Coin Week has been sponsored by the American Numismatic Association since Julius Guttag conceived it in 1924. It was proclaimed nationally by President Nixon (Proc. No. 4286) in 1974, on its 50th anniversary. In 1983, President Reagan declared National Coin Week acting pursuant to the request of Public Law 97-239, asking that the president proclaim April 17-24, 1983, as National Coin Week. Below is the National Coin Week Proclamation as it appeared in the *Federal Register* on March 8, 1983.

Proclamations
National Coin Week 1983
(No. 5027, 48 Fed. Reg. 9837)
National Coin Week, 1983.
By the president of the United States of America,
A Proclamation.
Since the beginning of history, coins have played an important role in the story of civilization. They reflect the economic development of their country of origin, as well as the scientific advancement and artistic values of

the people who produce and use them. Today, millions of Americans collect coins for both pleasure and profit. To help foster the public's interest in coin collecting, the United States Mint annually offers Proof sets of the current year's coinage. In 1982, the United States Mint struck a commemorative silver half dollar, marking the 250th anniversary of the birth of George Washington. In 1983-1984, the first commemorative Olympic coinage ever issued by our country will be introduced in gold and silver. Recognizing that coin collecting has educational and cultural value, promotes greater understanding of our history and heritage, and is enjoyed by millions of Americans, the Congress, pursuant to House Joint Resolution 516 (Public Law 97-239), has authorized and requested the president to issue a proclamation designating the week beginning April 17, 1983, as "National Coin Week." NOW, THEREFORE, I, RONALD REAGAN, president of the United States of American, do hereby proclaim the week beginning April 17, 1983, as "National Coin Week" and call upon the people of the United States to observe this week with appropriate ceremonies and activities. IN WITNESS WHEREOF, I have hereunto set my hand this 7th day of March, in the year of our Lord nineteen hundred and eighty-three, and of the Independence of the United States of America the two hundred and seventh.

Ronald Reagan

Freedom of Information Act

Collectors can avail themselves of privileges under the Freedom of Information Act, Public Law 93-502, passed by the 93rd Congress (H. R. 12471 Nov. 21, 1974, over a presidential veto.)

Known as 5 U.S.C. 552, the act requires agencies to maintain and make available for public inspection and copying, current indexes providing identifying information for the public as to any matter issued, adopted or promulgated after July 4, 1967, and required to be made available or published. There are certain exceptions.

The agency involved will answer inquiries as to the availability of records under the Freedom of Information Act.

The Freedom of Information Act (FOIA) is a boon to researchers and scholars, as well as collectors. Material that has yet to reach the National Archives is accessible under the FOIA. All administrative agencies of the government are liable (except for certain specific exceptions) to comply, and must furnish the information requested. There may be charges for the information requested, designed to reflect its actual cost, and (usually) it must be requested with specificity. A number of detailed books on the FOIA are available in many libraries. It is worth noting that some state governments have similar acts.

Each agency is required to separately state and publish in the Federal Register the procedures it will follow. It is required to make a determination within 10 days of receipt (Saturdays, Sundays and public holidays excepted) whether or not they will reply, and, if an appeal is taken, determine that within 20 days. If an agency improperly withholds documents, it is possible for attorney's fees and other litigation costs to be assessed against the government.

There are several types of documents which are specifically exempt from disclosure. First, those pertaining to national defense or foreign policy; second, those relating solely to internal personnel rules and practices; third, those exempted from disclosure by statute; fourth, trade secrets and commercial and financial nature obtained in a confidential or privileged manner; fifth, inter-agency or intra-agency memorandums which would not be available in litigation against the agency; sixth, personnel and medical files which would create an unwarranted invasion of personal privacy; seventh, investigatory records compiled for law enforcement purposes; eighth, regulatory reports concerning financial institutions; ninth, geological or geophysical information including maps concerning wells.

Below appears significant and relevant extracts from the Freedom of Information Act regulations of the Department of the Treasury, which covers the Bureau of the Mint, the Bureau of Engraving and Printing, the Customs Service, and a number of other agencies.

Sec. 1.1 Purpose and scope of regulations.

The regulations in this subpart are issued to implement the public information provisions of section 552 of Title 5, United States Code, as amended. These regulations apply to all constituent units of the Department of the Treasury. . . .

The constituent units of the Department of the Treasury for the purposes of this part are:

(a) The Office of the Secretary of the Treasury, which includes the offices of:

(1) The Secretary, including immediate staff;

(2) The Deputy Secretary, including immediate staff;

(3) The Under Secretary for Monetary Affairs, including immediate staff;

(4) The Under Secretary, including immediate staff;

(5) The General Counsel and also the Legal Division, . . .

Sec. 1.2 Information made available.

(a) General. Section 552 of Title 5 of the United States Code provides for access to information and records developed or maintained by Federal agencies. Generally, such section divides agency information into three major categories and provides methods by which each category is to be made available to the public. The three major categories, for which the disclosure requirements of the constituent units of the Department of the Treasury are set forth in this subpart, are as follows:

(1) Information required to be published in the Federal Register (see Sec. 1.3 below);

(2) Information required to be made available for public inspection and copying or, in the alternative, to be published and offered for sale (see Sec. 1.4 below); and

(3) Information required to be made available to any member of the public upon specific request (see Sec. 1.5 below). The provisions of section 552 are intended to assure the right of the public to information. Section 552 is not authority to withhold information from Congress.

(b) Subject only to the exemptions set forth in Sec. 1.2(c) the public generally or any member thereof shall be afforded access to information or records in the possession of any constituent unit of the Department of the Treasury. Such access shall be governed by the regulations in this subpart A and any regulations of a constituent unit implementing or supplementing them.

(c) Exemptions — (1) In general. Under 5 U.S.C. 552(b), the disclosure requirements of section 552(a) do not apply to certain matters which are: [a list of statutory criteria follows]. . .

(3) Segregable portions of records. Any reasonably segregable portion of a record shall be provided to any person, after deletion of the portions which are exempt under 5 U.S.C. 552(b) (see paragraph (c)(1) of this sec-

tion). The term "reasonably segregable portion" as used in this paragraph means any portion of the record which is not exempt from disclosure by 5 U.S.C. 552 (b) and which after deletion of the exempt material still conveys meaningful and nonmisleading information. . . .

Sec. 1.4 Public inspection and copying.

(a) In general. Subject to the application of the exemptions described in Sec. 1.2(c) each constituent unit of the Department of the Treasury is hereby required in conformance with 5 U.S.C. 552(a)(2), to make available for public inspection and copying or, in the alternative, to promptly publish and offer for sale the following information with respect to such constituent unit:

(1) Final opinions, including concurring and dissenting opinions, and orders, if such opinions and orders are made in the adjudication of cases;

(2) Those statements of policy and interpretations which have been adopted by the constituent unit but are not published in the *Federal Register*; and

(3) Its administrative staff manuals and instructions to staff that affect a member of the public.

(b) Indexes. Each constituent unit of the Department of the Treasury is hereby also required, in conformance with 5 U.S.C. 552(a)(2), to maintain and make available for public inspection and copying current indexes identifying any matter described in paragraphs (a)(1) through (3) of this section which is issued, adopted, or promulgated after July 4, 1967, and which is required to be made available for public inspection or published. In addition, each constituent unit shall promptly publish, quarterly or more frequently, and distribute (by sale of otherwise) copies of each index or supplements thereto unless the head of such unit (or his delegate) determines by order published in the Federal Register that the publication would be unnecessary and impracticable, in which case the constituent unit shall nonetheless provide copies of such index on request at a cost not to exceed the direct cost of duplication. . . .

(3) Public reading rooms. Each constituent unit of the Department of the Treasury shall make available for inspection and copying, in a reading room or otherwise, the matters described in paragraphs (a) (1) through (3) of this section which are required by such paragraph (a) to be made available for public inspection or published in the current indexes such matters. Facilities shall be provided whereby a person may inspect the material

and obtain copies of that which is shelved. Fees shall not be charged for access to materials, but fees are to be charged in accordance with Sec. 1.6 for copies of material provided to the person. (See the appendices to this subpart for the location of established reading rooms of constituent units of the Department of the Treasury.)

Sec. 1.5 Specific requests for other records.

(a) In general. Except with respect to the records made available . . . above, but subject to the application of the exemptions . . . each constituent unit of the Department of the Treasury, shall, in conformance with 5 U.S.C. 552 (a) (3), upon any request, which is for reasonably described records and conforms in every respect with the rules and procedures of this Subpart A, . . . make the requested records promptly available to any person. . . .

(c) Form of request. In order to be subject to the provisions of this section, a request for records shall:

(1) Be made in writing and signed by the person making the request,

(2) State that it is made pursuant to the Freedom of Information Act, 5 U.S.C. 552 or these regulations,

(3) Be addressed to the office or officer of the constituent unit to which the subject matter of the request is of paramount concern, unless the requester is unable to ascertain the appropriate unit, in which event, the request shall be addressed as specified in Appendix A hereto for the Office of the Secretary (See the appendices to this subpart for the office or officer to which requests shall be addressed for each constituent unit),

(4) Reasonably describe the records in accordance with paragraph (d) of this section,

(5) Set forth the address where the person making the request desires to be notified of the determination as to whether the request will be granted,

(6) State whether the requester wishes to inspect the records or desires to have a copy made and furnished without first inspecting them, and

(7) State the firm agreement of the requester to pay the fees for search and duplication ultimately determined in accordance with Sec. 1.6 hereof, or request that such fees be reduced or waived and state the justification for such request (see Sec. 1.6(d) below). Where the initial request, rather than stating a firm agreement to pay the fees ultimately determined in accordance with Sec. 1.6, places an upper limit on the amount the requester agrees to pay, which upper limit is deemed likely to be lower than the fees esti-

mated to ultimately be due, or where the requester asks for an estimate of the fees to be charged, the requester shall be promptly advised of the estimate of fees due and asked to agree to pay such amount. . . .

(g) Initial determination (1) In general. Initial determinations as to whether to grant requests for records will be made by the officers designated in the appendices to this part. Those determinations will be made and notification thereof mailed within 10 days (excepting Saturdays, Sundays, and legal public holidays) after the date of receipt of the request, . . .

(3) Denial of request. If it is determined that the request for records should be denied (whether in whole or in part or subject to conditions or exceptions), the person making the request will be so notified by mail. . . .

(h) Administrative appeal. At any time within 35 days after the date of the notification described in paragraph (g) of this section or the date of the letter transmitting the last records released, whichever is later, the requester may submit an administrative appeal to the official specified in the appropriate appendix to this subpart whose title and address should also have been included in the initial determination to deny access to the records. The appeal shall:

(1) Be made in writing and signed by the requester,

(2) Be addressed to and mailed or hand delivered, within 35 days of the date of the initial determination, to the office or officer specified in the appropriate appendix to this subpart and also in the initial determination. (See the appendices to this subpart for the address to which appeals made by mail should be addressed.),

(3) Reasonably describe, in accordance with paragraph (d) of this section, the records requested from the denial of access to which an appeal is being taken,

(4) Specify the date of the initial request and date of the letter denying the initial request, and

(5) Petition such official to grant the request for records and state any arguments in support thereof. . . .

Sec. 1.6 Fees for services.

(a) In general. (1) This fee schedule is applicable uniformly to all constituent units of the Department of the Treasury and supersedes fees schedules heretofore published by any constituent unit of the Department. . . .

(e) Avoidance of unexpected fees. In order to protect the requester from unexpected fees, all requests for records shall state the agreement of the requester to pay the fees determined in accordance with paragraph (g) of this section or state the amount which the requester has set as an acceptable upper limit he is willing to pay to cover the costs of processing the request. When the fees for processing the request are estimated by the constituent unit of the Department of the Treasury to exceed that limit, or when the requester has failed to state a limit and the costs are estimated to exceed $50 and the relevant constituent unit has not then determined to waive or reduce the fees, a notice shall be sent to the requester. This notice shall:

(1) Inform the requester of the estimated costs;

(2) Extend an offer to the requester to confer with personnel of the relevant constituent unit of the Department of the Treasury in an attempt to reformulate the request in a manner which will reduce the fees and still meet the needs of the requester; and

(3) Inform the requester that the running of the time period, within which the relevant constituent unit of the Department of the Treasury is obliged to make a determination on the request, has been tolled pending a reformulation of the request or the receipt of advance payment or an agreement from the requester to bear the estimated costs.

(f) Form of payment

(1) Payment shall be made by check or money order payable to the order of the Treasury of the United States or that relevant constituent unit of the Department of the Treasury.

(2) When the estimated costs exceed $50, the requester may be required to enter into a contract for the payment of actual costs determined in accordance with paragraph (g) of this section, which contract may provide for prepayment of the estimated costs in whole or in part.

(3) The Department of the Treasury reserves the right to request prepayment before releasing documents. If fees for previous requests have not been paid, documents will not be released without prepayment.

(g) Amounts to be charged for specified services. The fees for services performed by the relevant constituent unit fo the Department of the Treasury shall be imposed and collected as set forth in this paragraph. . . .

(1) Copying records. (i) $.15 per copy of each page, up to 8½" X by 14", made by photocopy or similar method.

(ii) Photographs, films, and other materials-actual cost of reproduction.

(iii) Records may be released to a private contractor for copying and the requester will be charged the actual cost of duplication charged by the private contractor.

(2) Search services. (i) Searches other than for computerized records — $10.00 for each hour or fraction thereof for time spent by each clerical, professional, and supervisor in finding the records and information within the scope of the request, and for transportation of personnel and records necessary to the search at actual cost.

(ii) Searches for computerized records — Actual direct cost of the search. The fee for computer printouts will be actual cost. . . .

Appendix A-Office of the Secretary

1. In general. This appendix applies to the Office of the Secretary as defined in 31 CFR 1.1(a). It identifies the location of the public reading room at which Office of the Secretary documents are available for public inspection and copying, the officers designated to make the initial and appellate determinations with respect to requests, the officer designated to receive service of process and the addresses for delivery of requests, appeals and service of process.

2. Public reading room. The public reading room for the Office of the Secretary is maintained at the following location: Library, Room 5030, Main Treasury Building, 1500 Pennsylvania Avenue NW, Washington, D.C. 20220.

3. Requests for records. Initial determinations under 31 CFR 1.5 (g) as to whether to grant requests for records for the Office of the Secretary will be made by the head of the organizational unit having immediate custody of the records. . . .

Appendix H-Bureau of the Mint

1. In General. This appendix applies to the Bureau of the Mint. It identifies the location of the public reading room at which documents of the Bureau of the Mint are available for public inspection and copying, the titles of officers designated to make the initial and appellate determinations with respect to requests, the officer designation to receive service of process and the addresses for delivery of requests, appeals and service of process.

2. Public reading rooms. No room has been set aside for this purpose. The Bureau of the Mint will provide a room on an ad hoc basis when necessary.

3. Requests for records. Initial determinations under 31 CFR 1.5 (g) as to whether to grant requests for records of the Bureau of the Mint will be made by the Assistant Director for Public Services, Bureau of the Mint. Re-

quests made by mail should be addressed to: Chief, Information Systems and Documentation Branch, Bureau of the Mint, Department of the Treasury, Room 912, Warner Building Washington, D.C. 20220.

Requests may be delivered personally to Information Systems and Documentation Branch of the Bureau of the Mint, Room 912, Warner Building located at 501 13th Street NW, Washington, D.C.

4. Administrative appeal of initial determination to deny records. Appellate determinations under 31 CFR 1.5(h) with respect to records of the Bureau of the Mint will be made by the Director of the Mint. Appeals made by mail should be addressed to: Director of the Mint, Department of the Treasury, Washington, D.C. 20220.

Requests may be delivered personally to the office of the Director of the Mint in Room 2064, Main Treasury Building, 1500 Pennsylvania Avenue NW, Washington, D.C.

5. Delivery of process. Service of process will be received by the Director of the Mint and shall be delivered to such officer at the following location: Director of the Mint, Judiciary Square Building, 633 Third Street NW, Washington, D.C. 20220.

Similar regulations are applicable for the Bureau of Engraving and Printing (also no public reading room) and other agencies.

Copyright Law Revisions

The "new" copyright law is now a dozen years old. Information pertaining to the law and regulations may be obtained from the Copyright Office, Library of Congress, Crystal Mall Annex, Arlington, Va. 20559. Any necessary forms to copyright materials may be obtained from that office.

Chronological listing of coin laws since 1965

The following are coin-related laws that have passed Congress since 1965 which may be of interest to collectors. (Medal legislation increases commencing in 1971 because some of the significant Bicentennial and other medals, precursors to debate over the future of national medals, and ultimately, a return to commemorative coinage, became more numerous then. Prior medal issues are listed separately.) The citations given show the public law number and page reference to the *Statutes at Large* (Stat.), which is available in many libraries. Where codification in the United States Code has taken place, it is also noted. When the U.S. Code was revised in 1982, some provisions were deleted as obsolete (the most obvious of which related to Bicentennial coin issues, last produced in 1976). The listings are necessarily duplicative at least in part of the section listing "significant" laws. Appended as a footnote is a listing of hearings and legislative developments of potential interest to researchers, identified by the number preceding each law.

1. **Pub. L. 89-81, July 23, 1965, 79 Stat. 254**
Authorized clad coinage; silver-clad half dollars.
2. **Pub. L. 90-29, Sec. 5, June 24, 1967, 81 Stat. 77**
Restores Mint marks to coinage.
3. **Pub. L. 91-607, Title II, Dec. 31, 1970, 84 Stat. 1768**
Authorizes Eisenhower dollar; ends silver in half dollar; directs transfer of Carson City silver dollars to General Services Administration.
4. **Pub. L. 92-228, Feb. 15, 1972, 86 Stat. 37**
Authorizes Bicentennial medal production by Mint for American Revolution Bicentennial Commission.
5. **Pub. L. 92-266, March 30, 1972, 86 Stat. 116**
Medals for Transpo '72.
6. **Pub. L. 92-268, March 31, 1972, 86 Stat. 116**
Set value of gold at $38 an ounce.

7. **Pub. L. 92-384, Aug. 14, 1972, 86 Stat. 539**
Medal for 175th anniversary of frigate *Constitution*.
8. **Pub. L. 92-463, Oct. 6, 1972, 86 Stat. 770**
Federal Advisory Committee Act of 1972; effectively abolished Assay Commission as of Jan. 4, 1975. See Pub. L. 96-209 below.
9. **Pub. L. 93-33, May 14, 1973, 87 Stat. 71**
Roberto Clemente national medal.
10. **Pub. L. 93-110, Sept. 21, 1973, 87 Stat. 352**
Set gold value at $42.22 an ounce. Legalizes private gold ownership when Treasury Secretary determines it to be in national interest (see Pub. L. 93-373).
11. **Pub. L. 93-114, Oct. 1, 1973, 87 Stat. 417**
San Francisco cable car national medal.
12. **Pub. L. 93-132, Oct. 19, 1973, 87 Stat. 461**
Jim Thorpe national medal.

13. **Pub. L. 93-127, Oct. 18, 1973, 87 Stat. 455**
Creates America's Bicentennial coinage.
14. **Pub. L. 93-167, Nov. 29, 1973, 87 Stat. 686**
Hobby Protection Act (text and regulations appear elsewhere in this section).
Debate: House (H. Rept. 93-159) 5/16/73
Senate: (S. Rept. 93-345) 7/31 - 8/1-2; 11/16/82
15. **Pub. L. 93-177, Dec. 11, 1973, 87 Stat. 704**
Repeals portion of Pub. L. 92-228.
16. **Pub. L. 93-179, Dec. 11, 1973, 87 Stat. 697**
American Revolution Bicentennial Administration created as successor to Bicentennial Commission.
17. **Pub. L. 93-221, Dec. 23, 1973, 87 Stat. 913**
International Environmental Exposition national medal.
18. **Pub. L. 93-227, Dec. 29, 1973, 87 Stat. 944**
National medal for Colorado statehood centennial.
19. **Pub. L. 93-309, June 8, 1974, 88 Stat. 234**
National medal for J. Edgar Hoover, FBI director.
20. **Pub. L. 93-373, Aug. 14, 1974, 88 Stat. 445**
Legalizes private gold ownership Dec. 31, 1974.
21. **Pub. L. 93-441, Oct. 11, 1974, 88 Stat. 1262**
Authorizes transfer of 10 percent of Ike dollar sales to Eisenhower College; authorizes date changes for Bicentennial coins; allows compositional change in cent to zinc-copper until 1977.
22. **Pub. L. 93-541, Dec. 26, 1974, 88 Stat. 1739**
Amends Bicentennial coinage legislation to allow for simultaneous striking of Bicentennial and regular-dated (1974) coins.
23. **Pub. L. 93-554, Dec. 17, 1974, 88 Stat. 1771**
Releases funds to Eisenhower College from Pub. L. 93-441.
24. **Pub. L. 93-617, Jan. 2, 1975, 88 Stat. 1978**
Jim Thorpe national medal; San Francisco cable car national medal (adds time to produce).
25. **Pub. L. 94-117, Oct. 17, 1975, 89 Stat. 602**
Medallic commemoration of Army and Navy bicentennial.
26. **Pub. L. 94-179, Oct. 17, 1975, 89 Stat. 1029**
Medal for Gen. "Chuck" Yeager.
27. **Pub. L. 94-257, April 1, 1976, 90 Stat. 302**
Commemorates bicentennial of John Carroll (of Maryland) signing Declaration of Independence.
28. **Pub. L. 94-564, Oct. 19, 1976, 90 Stat. 2661**
Bretton Woods Agreements Act regarding value of gold/dollar.
29. **Pub. L. 95-9, March 8, 1977, 91 Stat. 18**
Gold medal for Marian Anderson.
30. **Pub. L. 95-229, Feb. 14, 1979, 92 Stat. 26**
Capitol Historical Society medal legislation.
31. **Pub. L. 95-438, Oct. 10, 1978, 92 Stat. 1068**
Gold medal for Gen. Ira C. Eaker
32. **Pub. L. 95-447, Oct. 10, 1978, 92 Stat. 1072**
Authorizes Susan B. Anthony dollar design.
33. **Pub. L. 95-560, Nov. 1, 1978, 92 Stat. 2142**
Gold medal for Robert F. Kennedy.
34. **Pub. L. 95-630, Nov. 10, 1978, 92 Stat. 3679**
American Arts Gold Medallion Act.
35. **Pub. L. 96-2, March 7, 1979, 93 Stat. 4**
Carson City silver dollar sale (final disposal).
36. **Pub. L. 96-15, May 26, 1979, 93 Stat. 32**
John Wayne gold medal.
37. **Pub. L. 96-20, June 13, 1979, 93 Stat. 45**
Ben Abruzzo, Maxie Anderson, Larry Newman (transatlantic balloon trip) gold medal.
38. **Pub. L. 96-21, June 13, 1979, 93 Stat. 46**
Hubert H. Humphrey gold medal.
39. **Pub. L. 96-138, Dec. 12, 1979, 93 Stat. 1063**
National medal for U.S. Red Cross.
40. **Pub. L. 96-201, March 6, 1980, 94 Stat. 79**
National medal for Canadian ambassador Kenneth Taylor (Iranian hostage situation).
41. **Pub. L. 96-209, March 14, 1980, 94 Stat. 98**
Abolishes position of Assay Commissioner.
42. **Pub. L. 96-211, March 17, 1980, 94 Stat. 101**
Gold medal for Simon Wiesenthal.
43. **Pub. L. 96-306, July 8, 1980, 94 Stat. 937**
Gold plated medals to U.S. Olympic team because of nonparticipation in Olympic Games (U.S. boycott of Moscow Games).

44. **Pub. L. 97-104, Dec. 23, 1981, 95 Stat. 1491**
George Washington commemorative half dollar.
45. **Pub. L. 97-158, March 22, 1982, 96 Stat. 18**
Gold medal to Her Majesty Queen Beatrix (Netherlands) in commemoration of 200 years of friendship with the Netherlands.
46. **Pub. L. 97-201, June 23, 1982, 96 Stat. 126**
Gold medal for Adm. Hyman G. Rickover.
47. **Pub. L. 97-220, July 22, 1982, 96 Stat. 222**
Olympic coin legislation.
48. **Pub. L. 97-239, Aug. 20, 1982, 96 Stat. 271**
National Coin Week request proposal.
49. **Pub. L. 97-246, Aug. 26, 1982, 96 Stat. 315**
Gold medals for Fred Waring, Joe Louis, Louis L'Amour.
50. **Pub. L. 97-258, Sept. 13, 1982, 96 Stat. 877**
Codifies Title 31 of the United States Code into positive law (repealing all inconsistent laws).
51. **Pub. L. 98-94, Sept. 24, 1983, 97 Stat. 614**
Contains a section providing for striking of bronze medal honoring missing Vietnam veterans.
52. **Pub. L. 98-136, Oct. 24, 1983, 97 Stat. 863**
Medal for Louisiana World Exposition.
53. **Pub. L. 98-151, Nov. 14, 1983, 97 Stat. 979**
Directs Treasury Secretary to produce Mint (Uncirculated coin) sets.
54. **Pub. L. 98-159, Nov. 18, 1983, 97 Stat. 992**
Gold medal for Rep. Leo Ryan (murdered in Jonestown, Guyana).
55. **Pub. L. 98-172, Nov. 29, 1983, 97 Stat. 1119**
Gold medal for Danny Thomas.
56. **Pub. L. 98-278, May 5, 1984, 98 Stat. 173**
Gold medals for Harry S Truman, Lady Bird Johnson, Elie Wiesel.
57. **Pub. L. 98-285, May 17, 1984, 98 Stat. 186**
Gold medal for Roy Wilkins.
58. **Pub. L. 98-306, May 31, 1984, 98 Stat. 223**
National Medal of the Arts.
59. **Pub. L. 98-566, Oct. 30, 1984, 98 Stat. 2923**
Vietnam Veterans National Medal Act.

60. **Pub. L. 98-599, Oct. 30, 1984, 98 Stat. 3144**
Missing in Action Medal Act.
61. **Pub. L. 99-61, Title I, July 9, 1985, 99 Stat. 113**
Statue of Liberty commemorative coin.
62. **Pub. L. 99-61, Title II, July 9, 1985, 99 Stat. 115**
Liberty Coin Act (silver bullion coin).
63. **Pub. L. 99-86, Aug. 9, 1985, 99 Stat. 288**
George & Ira Gershwin medal.
64. **Pub. L. 99-185, Dec. 17, 1985, 99 Stat. 1177 (31 USC Sec. 5712)**
Gold Bullion Coin Act of 1985.
65. **Pub. L. 99-295, May 12, 1986, 100 Stat. 427**
Young Astronaut Program Medal Act.
66. **Pub. L. 99-298, May 13, 1986, 100 Stat. 432**
Natan (Anatoly) Sharansky Gold Medal.
67. **Pub. L. 99-311, May 20, 1986, 100 Stat. 464**
Harry Chapin Gold Medal.
68. **Pub. L. 99-418, Sept. 23, 1986, 100 Stat. 952**
Aaron Copland Medal Act.
69. **Pub. L. 99-514, Oct. 11, 1986, Sec. 1144, (26 USC 40)8(m))**
Tax Reform Act of 1986 (Bullion coins with IRAs).
70. **Pub. L. 99- 582, Oct. 29, 1986, 100 Stat. 3315**
Bicentennial of Constitution commemorative coin.

Notes to laws (1965-1984)
Each footnote refers to the number preceding the law above and is intended to give the legislative history of the various statutes, including hearing dates, pertinent reports, and the like.

1. The Coinage Act of 1965, Hearings on Coin Shortage, House Subcom. of Comm. on Government Operations, 6/30/64; 7/1-2/64
On silver dollars: Appropriations Committee, 5/24/65
Hearing on H.R. 8746 (Banking Comm) 6/4-7 and 8/65
Hearing on S. 2671 (4/1-2/64)
Sixth Rept. of Comm. on Gov't Operations (Rept. 194) 3/22/65
House debate: 7/13-14/65 (H. Rept. #509); Senate debate: 6/23-24; 7/15/65 (Sen. Rept. #317)
2. Mint mark restoration. Hearings (S. 1008) Senate Financial Institutions Subcomm. 3/67
3. Eisenhower dollar (Hearing on Coinage Act of 1969, H.R. 13252), 10/1 and 3/69; "CC" dollars: Hearing on H.R. 13150, 7/26-28/66
4. Bicentennial medals. Hearing on H.R. 7987, 6/29/71

10. Private gold ownership, Hearing (S. 929) 2/27/73; Hearing (S. 359, 395, 413, 741), 5/1-2/73

11. San Francisco Cable Car medal, Hearing on H.R. 2353 and 7358, 5/2-3/73

12. Jim Thorpe medal, Hearing on H.R. 5760, 5/2-3/73

13. Bicentennial coinage, Hearing on H.R. 5244, 5/2-3/73
Hearing on S. 422 and others, 6/6/73
Debate: (H. Rept. 93-391) 9/12; 10/4/73; (S. Rept. 93-144) 7/11; 10/4/73; Conference Rept. (H. Rept. 93-521)

14. Hearing (H.R. 4678) before Comm. on Interstate and Foreign Commerce, 2/28/73 (Serial 93-3)

17. Environmental Expo medal, Hearing on H.R. 5760, 5/2-3/73

18. Colorado statehood medal, hearing on H.R. 4738, 5/2-3/73

19. J. Edgar Hoover medal, Hearing on H.R. 1817, 5/2-3/73

21. Eisenhower college receipts, Hearing on H.R. 1020 and 7322, 5/2-3/73; 1 cent composition change: Hearing on H.R. 11841 3/27/74; Hearing on "The Proposed Change in the Penny" (House Serial #97-4) 3/31/81

22. No hearings. Debate: (S. Rept. 93-1303) 12/11/74; House (12/13/74

26. Yeager medal. Hearing on H.R. 8051 and others, 9/23/75

27. Charles Carroll medal. Hearing on H.R. 3427, 9/23/75

30. Capitol Historical Society medals. Hearing on H.J. Res. 386, 6/29/77; Senate hearing on H.J. Res. 386, 11/28/77

31. Eaker medal, hearing (numerous bills) 4/26/78

32. Susan B. Anthony dollar. Hearings (S. 3036) 7/17/78;
Hearings (H.R. 12444), 5/17 and 31/78
House Oversight hearings Serial 96-30, 9/25-26/79
Debate: House (H. Rept. 95-1576) 9/26/78; Senate (S. Rept.95-1576) 8/22/78. Presidential statement in *Weekly Compilation of Presidential Documents*, 10/10/78.

33. Robert F. Kennedy medal, hearing (numerous bills) 4/26/78

34. American Arts Gold Medallion Act. Hearings (S. 2843) 8/25/78

35. Carson City Silver Dollars (H.R. 9937), Hearings 4/3/78
Also see Hearing (Serial 96-67) 8/19/80 and follow-up: Committee Print 96-23 (12/80) reporting on sale.

36. John Wayne Medal. Hearings (H.R. 3767) 5/21/79. Senate Rept. 96-110. Debate: Senate 5/3/79; House 5/23/79

37. Balloonists medal, see Senate Rept. 96-108. Debate: Senate 5/3 and 6/5/79; House 6/4/79

38. Hubert Humphrey medal. See Senate Rept. 96-109

44. George Washington Commemorative Coin, (H.R. 3133) 5/7/81

45. Queen Beatrix medal (H.J. Res. 348) 2/26/82

46. Adm. Rickover medal (H.R. 5432) 3/9/82

47. Olympic coinage. Hearings, S. 1230 (7/14/81); (House) 4/6, 21 and 29/82; 5/11-12/82; Oversight hearings on Olympic coin designs: House serial #97-98, 12/1/82; Hearings (S. 1230) 6/10/82
Senate debate: 12/9/81 (Rept. 97-264); House debate: 5/20/82 (Rept. 97-554)

48. National Coin Week. No hearings held. President did proclaim as requested (3/7/83).

49. Fred Waring, Joe Louis, Louis L'Amour medals (H.R. 4647) 7/22/81

51. Defense Authorization Act (contains bronze medals for Missing In Action). Numerous hearings on bill (not related to numismatics).

52. Louisiana Expo medals (H.R. 3321) 9/20/83

53. Mint set annual production. See Senate rept. 98-131 (5/18/83)

56. Harry S Truman; Lady Bird Johnson; Elie Wiesel medals. Hearings on H.R. 3614 and H.J. Res. 394 (3/6/84) Serial No. 98-74

57. Roy Wilkins medal. Hearing on H.R. 3240 (3/6/84) Serial No. 98-74

58. National Medal of the Arts, Pub. L. 98-306, 98 Stat. 223, 5/31/84

59. Vietnam Veterans National Medal Act, Pub. L. 98-566, 98 Stat. 2923, 10/30/84

60. Missing in Action Medal Act, Pub. L. 98-599, 98 Stat. 3144, 10/30/84

61. Statue of Liberty commemorative coins, Pub. L. 99-61, Title I, 99 Stat. 113, 7/9/85

62. Liberty Coin Act (silver bullion coin), Pub. L. 99-61, Title II, 99 Stat. 115, 7/9/85

63. George and Ira Gershwin, Pub. L. 99-86, 99 Stat. 288, 8/9/85

64. Gold Bullion Coin Act of 1985, Pub. L. 99-185, 99 Stat. 1177 (31 USC Sec. 5712), 12/17/85

65. Young Astronaut Program Medal Act, Pub. L. 99-295, 100 Stat. 427, 5/12/86

66. Natan (Anatoly) Scharansky gold medal, Pub. L. 99-298, 100 Stat. 432, 5/13/86

67. Harry Chapin gold medal, Pub. L. 99-311, 100 Stat. 464, 5/20/86

68. Aaron Copland Medal Act, Pub. L. 99-418, 100 Stat. 952. 9/23/86

69. Tax Reform Act of 1986 (bullion coins with IRAs), Pub. L. 99-514, Sec. 1144, (26 USC 408(m)), 10/11/86

70. Bicentennial of Constitution commemorative coins, Pub. L. 99-582, 100 Stat. 3315, 10/29/86

Extracts of texts of laws

Following are the edited texts of major numismatic laws passed since 1955. To the extent that numismatic portions are included as separate sections, or as titles to laws which do not relate to the subject matter of *Coin World Almanac,* they have been omitted. Other sections have been edited for convenience. A complete version may be found in *The Statues at Large,* available in most public libraries, as well as in government document centers at universities and law schools. Some of the legislative reports may conveniently be found in *U.S. Code Congressional & Administrative News,* a legal publication also found in many libraries.

All laws begin with the identical language: "Be it enacted by the Senate and House of Representatives of the United States of American in Congress assembled," after which the text of the law appears.

Sometimes, the legislation has what is call a "short title," meaning an official version or abbreviation. For example, for coins produced to honor the 200th anniversary of the American Constitution, the short title is called the "Bicentennial of the Constitution Coins Act," which might be the official version, but inevitably will be parochialized into the Constitution Bicentennial Coin Act, or something similar.

Constitution Bicentennial

Public Law 99-582, 99th Congress, approved Oct. 29, 1986.

SHORT TITLE

Section 1. This Act may be cited as the "Bicentennial of the Constitution Coins Act".

Definitions Sec. 2. For purposes of this Act-

(1) the term "Commission" means the Commission on the Bicentennial of the United States Constitution; and

(2) the term "Secretary" means the Secretary of the Treasury.

Title I-Bicentennial of the United States Constitution Commemorative Coins

COIN SPECIFICATIONS

Sec. 101. (a)(1) The Secretary shall issue not more than 1,000,000 five dollar coins which shall weigh 8.359 grams, have a diameter of 0.850 inches, and shall contain 90 percent gold and 10 percent alloy.

(2) The design of such five dollar coins shall be emblematic of the bicentennial of the United States Constitution. On each such five dollar coin there shall be a designation of the value of the coin, an inscription of the year "1987", and inscriptions of the words "Liberty", "In God We Trust", "United States of America", and "E Pluribus Unum".

(b)(1) The Secretary shall issue not more than 10,000,000 one dollar coins which shall weigh 26.73 grams, have a diameter of 1.500 inches, and shall contain 90 percent silver and 10 percent copper.

(2) The design of such dollar coins shall be emblematic of the bicentennial of the United States Constitution. On each such dollar coin there shall be a designation of the value of the coin, an inscription of the year "1987", and inscriptions of the words "Liberty", "In God We Trust", "United States of America", and "E Pluribus Unum".

(c) The coins issued under this title shall be legal tender as provided in section 5103 of title 31, United States Code.

(d) For purposes of section 5132(a)(1) of title 31, United States Code, all coins minted under this title shall be considered to be numismatic items.

SOURCES OF BULLION

Sec. 102. (a) The Secretary shall obtain gold for the coins minted under this title pursuant to the authority of the Secretary under existing law.

(b) The Secretary shall obtain silver for the coins minted under this title only from stockpiles established under the Strategic and Critical Minerals Stock Piling Act (50 USC 98 et seq.).

DESIGN OF THE COIN

Sec. 103. The design for each coin authorized by this title shall be selected by the Secretary after consultation with the Commission and the Commission of Fine Arts.

SALE OF THE COINS

Sec. 104. (a) Notwithstanding any other provision of law, the coins issued under this title shall be sold by the Secretary at a price equal to the face value, plus the cost of designing and issuing such coins (including labor, materials, dies, use of machinery, and overhead expenses).

(b) The Secretary shall make bulk sales at a reasonable discount to reflect the lower cost of such sales.

(c) The Secretary shall accept prepaid orders for the coins prior to the issuance of such coins. Sales under this subsection shall be at a reasonable discount to reflect the benefit of prepayment.

(d) All sales shall include a surcharge of $35 per coin for the five dollar coins and $7 per coin for the one dollar coins.

ISSUANCE OF COINS

Sec. 105. (a) The gold coins authorized under this title shall be issued in uncirculated and proof qualitites and shall be struck at the United States Bullion Depository at West Point.

(b) The silver coins authorized under this title may be issued in uncirculated and proof qualities, except that not more than one facility of the United States Mint may be used to strike each such quality.

(c) The Secretary may issue the coins minted under this title beginning January 1, 1987.

(d) No coins shall be minted under this title after June 30, 1988.

FINANCIAL ASSURANCES

Sec. 106. (a) The Secretary shall take all actions necessary to ensure that the issuance of the coins authorized by this title shall result in no net cost to the United States Government.

(b) No coin shall be issued under this title unless the Secretary has received —

(1) full payment therefor;

(2) security satisfactory to the Secretary to indemnify the United States for full payment; or

(3) a guarantee of full payment satisfactory to the Secretary from a depository institution whose deposits are insured by the Federal Deposit Insurance Corporation, the Federal Savings and Loan Insurance Corporation, or the National Credit Union Administration Board.

NATIONAL DEBT REDUCTION

Sec. 107. An amount equal to the amount of all surcharges which are received by the Secretary from the sale of coins issued under this title shall be deposited in the general fund of the Treasury and shall be used for the sole purpose of reducing the national debt.

PROCUREMENT OF GOODS AND SERVICES

Sec. 108. No provision of law governing procurement or public contracts shall be applicable to the procurement of goods or services necessary for carrying out the provisions of this title. Nothing in this section shall relieve any person entering into a contract under the authority of this title from complying with any law relating to equal employment opportunity.

Gold Bullion Coins

Public Law 99-185, 99th Congress, approved December 17, 1985.

SHORT TITLE

Section 1. This Act may be cited as the "Gold Bullion Coin Act of 1985".

MINTING GOLD BULLION COINS

Sec. 2. (a) Section 5112(a) of title 31, United States Code, is amended by adding at the end thereof the following new paragraphs:

"(7) A fifty dollar gold coin that is 32.7 millimeters in diameter, weighs 33.931 grams, and contains one troy ounce of five gold.

"(8) A twenty-five dollar gold coin that is 27.0 millimeters in diameter, weighs 16.966 grams, and contains one-half troy ounce of fine gold.

"(9) A ten dollar gold coin that is 22.0 millimeters in diameter, weighs 8.483 grams, and contains one-fourth troy ounce of fine gold.

"(10) A five dollar gold coin that is 16.5 millimeters in diameter, weighs 3.393 grams, and contains one-tenth troy ounce of fine gold."

(b) Section 5112 of title 31, United States Code, is amended by adding at the end thereof the following new subsection:

"(i)(1) Notwithstanding section 5111(a)(1) of this title, the Secretary shall mint and issue the gold coins described in paragraphs (7) (8), (9), and (10) of subsection (a) of this section, in quantities sufficient to meet public demand, and such gold coins shall —

"(A) have a design determined by the Secretary, except that the fifty dollar gold coin shall have —

"(i) on the obverse side, a design symbolic of Liberty; and

"(ii) on the reverse side, a design representing a family of eagles, with the male carrying an olive branch and flying above a nest containing a female eagle and hatchlings;

"(B) have inscriptions of the denomination, the weight of the fine gold content, the year of minting or issuance, and the words 'Liberty', 'In God We Trust', 'United States of America', and 'E Pluribus Unum'; and

"(C) have reeded edges.

"(2)(A) The Secretary shall sell the coins minted under this subsection to the public at a price equal to the market value of the bullion at the time of sale, plus the cost of minting, marketing, and distributing such coins (including labor, materials, dies, use of machinery, and promotional and overhead expenses).

"(B) The Secretary shall make bulk sales of the coins minted under this subsection at a reasonable discount.

"(3) For purposes of section 5132(a)(1) of this title, all coins minted under this subsection shall be considered to be numismatic items."

(c) Section 5116(a) of title 31, United States Code, is amended by adding at the end thereof the following:

"(3) The Secretary shall acquire gold for the coins issued under section 5112(i) of this title by purchase of gold mined from natural deposits in the United States, or in a territory or possession of the United States, within one year after the month in which the ore from which it is derived was mined. The Secretary shall pay not more than the average world price for the gold. In the absence of available supplies of such gold at the average world price, the Secretary may use gold from reserves held by the United States to mint the coins issued under section 5112(i) of this title. The Secretary shall issue such regulations as may be necessary to carry out this paragraph."

(d) Section 5118(b) of title 31, United States Code, is amended —

(1) in the first sentence, by striking out "or deliver"; and

(2) in the second sentence, by inserting "(other than gold and silver coins)" before "that may be lawfully held".

(e) The third sentence of section 5132(a)(1) of title 31, United States Code, is amended by striking out "minted under section 5112(a) of this title" and inserting in lieu thereof "minted under paragraphs (1) through (6) of section 5112(a) of this title".

(f) Notwithstanding any other provision of law, an amount equal to the amount by which the proceeds from the sale of the coins issued under section 5112(i) of title 31, United States Code, exceed the sum of —

(1) the cost of minting, marketing, and distributing such coins, and

(2) the value of gold certificates (not exceeding forty-two and two-ninths dollars a fine troy ounce) retired from the use of gold contained in such coins, shall be deposited in the general fund of the Treasury and shall be used for the sole purpose of reducing the national debt.

(g) The Secretary shall take all action necessary to ensure that the issuance of the coins minted under section 5112(i) of title 31, United States Code, shall result in no net cost to the United States Government.

EFFECTIVE DATE

Sec. 3. This Act shall take effect on October 1, 1985, except that no coins may be issued or sold under section 5112(i) of title 31, United States Code, before October 1, 1986.

Public Law 99-514 (approved October 22, 1986) authorizes these coins to be placed in an individual retirement account under Sec. 408(m) of the Internal Revenue Code.

The same applies to the silver issues of the Statue of Liberty-Ellis Island coin program.

Statue of Liberty-Ellis Island Commemorative Coins

Public Law 99-61, 99th Congress, approved July 9, 1985.

SHORT TITLE

Sec. 101. This Act may be cited as the "Statue of Liberty-Ellis Island Commemorative Coin Act".

COIN SPECIFICATIONS

Sec. 102. (a)(1) The Secretary of the Treasury (hereafter in this title referred to as the "Secretary") shall issue not more than 500,000 five dollar coins which shall weigh 8.359 grams, have a diameter of 0.850 inches, and shall contain 90 percent gold and 10 percent alloy.

(2) The design of such five dollar coins shall be emblematic of the centennial of the Statue of Liberty. On each such five dollar coin there shall be a designation of the value of the coin, an inscription of the year "1986", and inscriptions of the words "Liberty", "In God We Trust", "United States of America", and "E Pluribus Unum".

(b)(1) The Secretary shall issue not more than ten million one dollar coins which shall weigh 26.73 grams, have a diameter of 1.500 inches, and shall contain 90 percent silver and 10 percent copper.

(2) The design of such dollar coins shall be emblematic of the use of Ellis Island as a gateway for immigrants to America. On each such dollar coin there shall be a designation of the value of the coin, an inscription of the year "1986", and inscriptions of the words "Liberty", "In God We Trust", "United States of America', and "E Pluribus Unum".

(c)(1) The Secetary shall issue not more than twenty-five million half dollar coins which shall weigh 11.34 grams, have a diameter of 1.205 inches, and shall be minted to the specifications for half dollar coins contained in section 5112(b) of title 31, United States Code.

(2) The design of such half dollar coins shall be emblematic of the contributions of immigrants to America. On each such half dollar coin there shall be a designation of the value of the coin, an inscription of the year "1986", and inscriptions of the words "Liberty", "In God We Trust", "United States of America", and "E Pluribus Unum".

(d) The coins issued under this title shall be legal tender as provided in section 5103 of title 31, United States Code.

SOURCES OF BULLION
Sec. 103. (a) The Secretary shall obtain silver for the coins minted under this title only from stockpiles established under the Strategic and Critical Materials Stock Piling Act (50 USC 98 et seq.).

DESIGN OF THE COINS
Sec. 104. The design for each coin authorized by this title shall be selected by the Secretary after consultation with the Chairman of the Statue of Liberty-Ellis Island Foundation, Inc. and the Chairman of the Commission of Fine Arts.

SALE OF THE COINS
Sec. 105. (a) Notwithstanding any other provision of law, the coins issued under this title shall be sold by the Secretary at a price equal to the face value, plus the cost of designing and issuing such coins (including labor, materials, dies, use of machinery, and overhead expenses).

(b) The Secretary shall make bulk sales at a reasonable discount to reflect the lower costs of such sales.

(c) The Secretary shall accept prepaid orders for the coins prior to the issuance of such coins. Sales under this subsection shall be at a reasonable discount to reflect the benefit of prepayment.

(d) All sales shall include a surcharge of $35 per coin for the five dollar coins, $7 per coin for the one dollar coins, and $2 per coin for the half dollar coins.

ISSUANCE OF THE COINS
Sec. 106. (a) The gold coins authorized by this title shall be issued in uncirculated and proof qualities and shall be struck at no more than one facility of the United States Mint.

(b) The one dollar and half dollar coins authorized under this title may be issued in uncirculated and proof qualitites, except that not more than one facility of the United States Mint may be used to strike any particular combination of denomination and quality.

(c) Notwithstanding any other provision of law, the Secretary may issue the coins minted under this title beginning October 1, 1985.

(d) No coins shall be minted under this title after December 31, 1986.

GENERAL WAIVER OF PROCUREMENT REGULATIONS
Sec. 107. No provision of law governing procurement or public contracts shall be applicable to the procurement of goods or services necessary for carrying out the provi-

sions of this title. Nothing in this section shall relieve any person entering into a contract under the authority of this title from complying with any law relating to equal employment opportunity.

DISTRIBUTION OF SURCHARGE
Sec. 108. All surcharges which are received by the Secretary from the sale of coins issued under this title shall be promptly paid by the Secretary to the Statue of Liberty-Ellis Island Foundation, Inc. (hereinafter in this title referred to as the "Foundation"). Such amounts shall be used to restore and renovate the Statue of Liberty and the facilities used for immigration at Ellis Island and to establish an endowment in an amount deemed sufficient by the Foundation, in consultation with the Secretary of the Interior, to ensure the continued upkeep and maintenance of these monuments.

AUDITS
Sec. 109. The Comptroller General shall have the right to examine such books, records, documents, and other data of the Foundation as may be related to the expenditure of amounts paid, and the management and expenditures of the endowment established, under section 108.

COINAGE PROFIT FUND
Sec. 110. Notwithstanding any other provision of law —
(1) all amounts received from the sale of coins issued under this title shall be deposited in the coinage profit fund;
(2) the Secretary shall pay the amounts authorized under this title from the coinage profit fund; and
(3) the Secretary shall charge the coinage profit fund with all expenditures under this title

FINANCIAL ASSURANCES
Sec. 111. (a) The Secretary shall take all actions necessary to ensure that the issuance of the coins authorized by this title shall result in no net cost to the United States Government.

(b) No coin shall be issued under this title unless the Secretary has received —
(1) full payment therefor;
(2) security satisfactory to the Secretary to indemnify the United States for full payment; or
(3) a guarantee of full payment satisfactory to the Secretary from a depository institution whose deposits are insured by the Federal Deposit Insurance Corporation, the Federal Savings and Loan Insurance Corporation, or the National Credit Union Administration Board.

Title II-Liberty Coins
SHORT TITLE
Sec. 201. This title may be cited as the "Liberty Coin Act".

MINTING OF SILVER COINS
Sec. 202. Section 5112 of title 31, United States Code, is amended to striking out subsections (e) and (f) and inserting in lieu thereof the following new subsections:

"(e) Notwithstanding any other provision of law, the Secretary shall mint and issue, in quantities sufficient to meet public demand, coins which —

"(1) are 40.6 millimeters in diameter and weigh 31.103 grams;

"(2) contain .999 fine silver;

"(3) have a design —

"(A) symbolic of Liberty on the obverse side; and

"(B) of an eagle on the reverse side;

"(4) have inscriptions of the year of minting or issuance, and the words 'Liberty', 'In God We Trust', 'United States of America', '1 Oz. Fine Silver', 'E Pluribus Unum', and 'One Dollar'; and

"(5) have reeded edges.

"(f) The Secretary shall sell the coins minted under subsection (e) to the public at a price equal to the market value of the bullion at the time of sale, plus the cost of minting, marketing, and distributing such coins (including labor, materials, dies, use of machinery, and overhead expenses).

"(g) For purposes of section 5132(a)(1) of this title, all coins minted under subsection (e) of this section shall be considered to be numismatic items.

"(h) The coins issued under this title shall be legal tender as provided in section 5103 of title 31, United States Code."

PURCHASE OF SILVER
Sec. 203. Section 5116(b) of title 31, United States Code, is amended-

(1) in the first sentence of paragraph (1), by striking out "The Secretary shall" and inserting in lieu thereof "The Secretary may";

(2) by striking out the second sentence of paragraph (1); and

(3) by inserting after the first sentence of paragraph (2) the following new sentence: "The Secretary shall obtain the silver for the coins authorized under section 5112(e) of this title by purchase from stockpiles established under the Strategic and Critical Materials Stock Piling Act (50 USC 98 et seq.)."

CONFORMING AMENDMENT
Sec. 204. The third sentence of section 5132(a)(1) of title 31, United States Code, is amended by inserting "minted under section 5112(a) of this title" after "proof coins".

EFFECTIVE DATE
Sec. 205. This title shall take effect on October 1, 1985, except that no coins may be issued or sold under subsection (e) of section 5112 of title 31, United States Code, before September 1, 1986, or before the date on which all coins minted under title I of this Act have been sold, whichever is earlier.

Olympic Coins
Public Law 97-220, 97th Congress, approved July 22, 1982.

SHORT TITLE
Section 1. This Act may be cited as the "Olympic Commemorative Coin Act".

COIN SPECIFICATIONS
Sec. 2. (a)(1) Notwithstanding any other provision of law, the Secretary of the Treasury (hereinafter in this Act referred to as the "Secretary") shall issue not more than 50 million $1 coins which shall weigh 26.73 grams, have a diameter of 1.50 inches, and shall contain 90 per centum silver and 10 per centum copper.

(2) The Secretary shall determine the design of such $1 coins. Such design shall be emblematic of the 1984 Summer Olympic Games which are to be held in Los Angeles, Calif. On each such $1 coin there shall be a designation of the value of the coin, an inscription of the year of issue, and inscriptions of the words LIBERTY, IN GOD WE TRUST, UNITED STATES OF AMERICA, and E PLURIBUS UNUM.

(3) The coins shall be issued in two separate designs, one in 1983 and one in 1984.

(b)(1) Notwithstanding any other provision of law, the Secretary shall issue not more than two million $10 coins which shall weigh 16.718 grams, have a diameter of 1.06 inches, and shall contain 90 per centum gold and 10 per centum copper.

(2) The Secretary shall determine the design of such $10 coin. Such design shall be emblematic of the 1984 Summer Olympic Games which are to be held in Los Angeles, Calif. On each such $10 coin there shall be a designation of the value of the coin, an inscription of the year 1984, and inscriptions of the words LIBERTY, IN GOD WE TRUST, UNITED STATES OF AMERICA, and E PLURIBUS UNUM.

(c) The coins issued under this section shall be issued in Uncirculated and Proof qualities.

(d) All coins issued under this section shall be legal tender as provided in Section 102 of the Coinage Act of 1965.

(e)(1) The Secretary shall obtain gold for

the coins minted under this Act pursuant to the authority of the Secretary under existing law.

(2) The Secretary shall obtain silver for the coins minted under this Act from stocks of silver held by the Secretary of the Treasury or from any other federally owned stocks of silver.

SALES WITHIN THE UNITED STATES

Sec. 3. (a) Notwithstanding any other provision of the law, the coins issued under this Act shall be sold within the United States (including United States military and diplomatic establishments outside the United States) by the Secretary under such regulations as he may prescribe and at a price equal to face value, plus the cost of issuing such coins (including labor, materials, dies, use of machinery, and overhead expenses).

(b) The Secretary shall make bulk sales at a reasonable discount to reflect the lower costs of such sales.

(c) The Secretary shall accept prepaid orders for the coins prior to the issuance of such coins. Sales under this subsection shall be at a reasonable discount to reflect the benefit of prepayment.

(d) All sales shall include a surcharge, established by the Secretary, of not less than $10 per coin for $1 coins and not less than $50 per coin for $10 coins.

INTERNATIONAL SALES

Sec. 4. (a) The Secretary shall assign the rights to market the coins outside the United States (excluding United States military and diplomatic establishments outside the United States) to a marketing organization selected under Section 5.

(b) The marketing organization assigned the rights under this section shall pay a price determined under Sections 3 (b) and (d).

SELECTION OF INTERNATIONAL MARKETERS

Sec. 5. (a) As soon as possible after the effective date of this Act, a committee consisting of the Sectretary of the Treasury, the executive director of the United States Olympic Committee, and the president of the Los Angeles Olympic Organizing Committee, shall solicit, in accordance with procedures specified by the Secretary of the Treasury, proposals from marketing organizations to carry out a marketing agreement. Such procedures shall include the publication of evaluation criteria that will serve as a basis for selecting one or more marketing organizations. Such criteria shall include —

(1) the financial resources and coin marketing experience of the marketing organization;

(2) the estimated proceeds from the sale or other disposition of the coins; and

(3) the commitment of the marketing organization to purchase a certain minimum number of such coins or to pay the surcharge on such coins; and

(4) the terms and conditions for the marketing of the coins, including —

(A) proper and equitable distribution of the coins, and

(B) accurate and otherwise appropriate advertising materials to be used in promoting the coins.

(b) Within 45 days after the effective date of this Act, the committee shall consider all proposals received from marketing organizations under subsection (a) and select by majority vote one or more marketing organizations which offer the terms for marketing of the coins most favorable in accordance with the published evaluation criteria. Any marketing organization selected shall be acceptable to the Secretary of the Treasury.

DISTRIBUTION OF PROCEEDS

Sec. 6. (a) Fifty per centum of the amount of all surcharges which are received by the Secretary from the sale of coins issued under this Act shall be promptly paid by the Secretary to the United States Olympic Committee. Such amounts shall be used to train United States Olympic athletes, to support local or community amateur athletic programs, and to erect facilities for the training of such athletes.

(b) Fifty per centum of the amount of all surcharges which are received by the Secretary from the sale of coins under this Act shall be promptly paid by the Secretary of the Los Angeles Olympic Organization Committee. Such amounts shall be used to stage and promote the 1984 Los Angeles Olympic games.

(c) Amounts received by the Secretary from advance sale of coins to be issued under this Act shall be paid to the United States Olympic Committee and the Los Angeles Olympic Organization Committee under subsections (a) and (b), provided that any amounts paid to the Committees shall not exceed an amount equivalent to the surcharges received by the Secretary from the advance sale of coins.

(d)(1) On March 31, 1985, the Los Angeles Olympic Organization Committee shall remit to the United States Olympic Committee all amounts remaining from the disposition of the coins under this Act. In no event may such amount be less than that portion of the unobligated funds of the committee on that date represented by the ratio of the total amount of income received by the committee from the disposition of the coins minted under this Act to the total amount of income received by the committee from all sources.

(2) After March 31, 1985, all amounts received by the committee from the disposition of coins minted under this Act shall be remitted within 10 days to the United States Olympic Committee.

(3) All amounts received by the United States Olympic Committee under this subsection shall be used solely for the purposes described in subsection (a).

IMPLEMENTATION AGREEMENT

Sec. 7. (a) The Secretary of the Treasury shall enter into an agreement with the marketing organization selected under Section 5 which shall provide for the implementation of that section and which shall include an agreement on —

(1) the price and schedule of payments for the coins;

(2) the schedule and other provisions for the delivery of the coins; and

(3) the proportions of Proof and Uncirculated coins.

(b) The agreement between the Secretary of the Treasury and the committee shall ensure that the issuance of coins under this section shall result in no net cost to the United States government.

(c) The agreement between the Secretary of the Treasury and the marketing organization shall direct that the marketing organization shall not use any words, perform any act, or make any statement, written or oral, which would imply or indicate, or tend to imply or indicate, that any portion of the coins' sale price to the public constitutes a tax-deductible contribution.

(d) To the extent possible, the agreement between the Secretary of the Treasury and the marketing organization shall be concluded within 60 days of the date of the selection of the marketing organization.

(e) The Secretary may terminate the implementation agreement and cease minting and the delivery of the coins issued under this section if the Secretary of the Treasury finds that such termination is in the best interests of the United States. Reasons for such termination may include actions which are inconsistent with the terms of the implementation agreement or advertising materials that are inappropriate for advertising the sale of United States coinage or otherwise not in keeping with the dignity of the United States coinage.

(f) If the Secretary of the Treasury exercises his authority under subsection (e), the amount of any proceeds guaranteed to the Los Angeles Olympic Organization Committee and the United States Olympic Committee by a marketing organization under a marketing agreement shall not be reduced.

COINAGE PROFIT FUND

Sec. 8. Notwithstanding any other provision of law —

(1) all amounts received from the sale of coins issued under this Act shall be deposited in the coinage profit fund;

(2) the Secretary shall pay the amounts authorized under Section 6 from the coinage profit fund; and

(3) the Secretary shall charge the coinage profit fund with all expenditures under this Act.

AUDITS

Sec. 9. The Comptroller General of the United States shall have the right to examine such books, records, documents, and other data of the United States Olympic Committee and the Los Angeles Olympic Organization Committee as may be related to the expenditure of amounts paid under Section 6.

FINANCIAL ASSURANCES

Sec. 10. (a) The Secretary shall take all actions necessary to ensure that the issuance of the coins authorized by this Act shall result in no net cost to the United States Government.

(b) No coin shall be issued under this Act unless the Secretary has received full payment therefor.

(c) The Secretary shall certify, in reports required to be filed under Section 11 of this Act, that he is in compliance with this section.

REPORTS TO CONGRESS

Sec. 11. Not later than 45 days after the last day of each calendar quarter, the Secretary shall transmit a report to the Congress regarding the activities carried out under this Act during such calender quarter. No such report shall be required with respect to any calendar quarter beginning after December 31, 1985.

George Washington commemorative coin

Public Law 97-104, 97th Congress, approved Dec. 23, 1981.

In the Fourth Edition of *Coin World Almanac*, the George Washington commemorative coin legislation was reprinted in the text, starting on Page 78, in 31 USC Sec. 5112(f)(1)-(4). It does not appear in that same location in this edition because the compilers and codifiers of the law determined that no purpose would be served. The reason for this is Sec. 3 of the law which stated that coins produced under the section could not be minted after December 31, 1983. Hence, the section has been eliminated. Since this is the first commemorative coin produced since 1954, it is of historic importance, and the text of the law is here reprinted in its entirety.

Sec. (1) Notwithstanding this section and sections 5111(a)(1) of this title, the Secretary shall mint and issue, in quantities the Secretary decides are necessary to meet public demand (but not more than 10,000,000), half dollar coins that —

(A) are 30.61 millimeters in diameter and weigh 12.5 grams;

(B) are an alloy of 90 percent silver and 10 percent copper;

(C) have a design on each side of the coin, decided by the Secretary, symbolizing the 250th anniversary of the birth of George Washington; and

(D) have a designation of the value of the coin and an inscription of the year "1982" and the words "Liberty", "In God We Trust", "United States of America", and "E Pluribus Unum".

Sec. (2) The Secretary shall sell the coins minted under this subsection to the public at a price equal to the cost of minting and distributing the coins (including labor, materials, dies, use of machinery, promotion, and overhead expenses) plus a surcharge of not more than 20 percent of the cost. The Secretary shall deposit an amount equal to the surcharge received under this paragraph in the Treasury to be used only to reduce the national debt.

Sec. (3) The Secretary may not mint coins under this subsection after December 31, 1983.

Sec. (4) Amounts necessary to carry out this subsection may be appropriated.

Typical gold medal bill

An act to provide for the awarding of a special gold medal to Aaron Copland. . . .

Section 1. Findings and Statement of Policy.

(a) findings. The Congress finds that —

(1) Aaron Copland has contributed to American music as a composer, a pianist, a lecturer, an author, and an organizer of various musical societies;

(2) Aaron Copland has composed patriotic musical works, such as "Lincoln Portrait", which was composed during World War II as a patriotic tribute to the United States and distributed worldwide;

(3) Aaron Copland has enjoyed great popularity and critical acclaim as evidenced by his

receiving many awards, including a Guggenheim Fellowship, a Pulitzer Prize, an Academy Award, and the Presidential Medal of Freedom; and

(4) Aaron Copland is referred to as the "dean" of American musical composition as the result of his contributions to American music.

(b) State of Policy. The incomparable contributions of Aaron Copland to American musical composition should be recognized by awarding him a special congressional gold medal.

Sec. 2. Authorization to Present Gold Medal.

The President is authorized to present on behalf of the Congress 1 gold medal of appropriate design to Aaron Copland.

Sec. 3. Production of Gold Medals and Production and Sale of Bronze Medals.

(a) Production of Gold Medal. The Secretary of the Treasury shall coin 1 gold medal and shall deliver the medal to the President for presentation under section 2. The gold medal shall contain suitable emblems, devices, and inscriptions to be determined by the Secretary.

(b) Production and Sale of Bronze Duplicate Medals. The Secretary of the Treasury may coin and sell bronze medals which are duplicates of the gold medal coined pursuant to subsection (a) under such regulations as the Secretary may prescribe, at a price sufficient to cover the cost of the gold medal and such duplicates, including the cost of labor, materials, dies, use of machinery, and overhead.

Sec. 4. Authorization of Appropriations.

There are authorized to be appropriated for any fiscal year beginning on or after October 1, 1986, not to exceed $20,000 to carry out the purposes of this Act.

Sec. 5. Effect on Other Law.

The Medals provided for in this Act are national medals for the purpose of section 5111 of title 31, United States Code.

American Arts Gold Medallions

Public Law 95-630, 95th Congress, approved Nov. 11, 1978.

TITLE IV — AMERICAN ARTS GOLD MEDALLIONS

Sec. 401. This title may be cited as the "American Arts Gold Medallion Act".

Sec. 402. The Secretary of the Treasury (hereinafter referred to as the "Secretary") shall, during each of the first five calendar years beginning after the date of enactment of this title, strike and sell to the general public, as provided by this title, gold medallions (hereinafter referred to as "medallions") containing, in the aggregate, not less than one million troy ounces of fine gold, and commemorating outstanding individuals in the American arts.

Sec. 403. (a) Medallions struck under authority of this title shall be minted in two sizes containing, respectively, one troy ounce and one-half troy ounce of fine gold. During the first year in which such medallions are struck, at least 500,000 troy ounces of fine gold shall be struck in each size of medallions authorized by this subsection. In succeeding years, the proportion of gold devoted to each size of medallions shall be determined by the Secretary on the basis of expected demand.

(b) Medallions struck under authority of this title shall be of such fineness that, of 1,000 parts by weight, 900 shall be of fine gold and 100 of alloy. Medallions shall not be struck from ingots which deviate from the standard of this subsection by more than one part per thousand.

(c) Medallions struck under the authority of this title shall bear such designs and inscriptions as the Secretary may approve subject to the following —

(1) during the first calendar year beginning after the date of enactment of this title, one ounce medallions shall be struck with a picture of Grant Wood on the obverse side and one-half ounce medallions shall be struck with a picture of Marian Anderson on the obverse side;

(2) during the second calendar year beginning after the date of enactment of this title, one ounce medallions shall be struck with a picture of Mark Twain on the obverse side and one-half ounce medallions shall be struck with a picture of Willa Cather on the obverse side;

(3) during the third calendar year beginning after the date of enactment of this title, one ounce medallions shall be struck with a picture of Louis Armstrong on the obverse side and one-half ounce medallions shall be struck with a picture of Frank Lloyd Wright on the obverse side;

(4) during the fourth calendar year beginning after the date of enactment of this title, one ounce medallions shall be struck with a picture of Robert Frost on the obverse side and one-half ounce medallions shall be struck with a picture of Alexander Calder on the obverse side; and

(5) during the fifth calendar year beginning after the date of enactment of this title, one ounce medallions shall be struck with a picture of Helen Hayes on the obverse side and one-half ounce medallions shall be struck with a picture of John Steinbeck on the obverse side.

The reverse side of each medallion shall be of different design, shall be representative of the artistic achievements of the individual on the obverse side, and shall include the inscription AMERICAN ARTS COMMEMORATIVE SERIES.

Sec. 404. Dies for use in striking the medallions authorized by this title may be executed by the engraver, and the medallions struck by the Superintendent of coining department of the Mint at Philadelphia, under such regulations as the Superintendent, with the approval of the Director of the Mint, may prescribe. In order to carry out this title, the Secretary may enter into contracts: *Provided,* That suitable precautions are maintained to secure against counterfeiting and against unauthorized issuance of medallions struck under authority of this title.

Sec. 405. For purposes of Section 485 of Title 18 of the United States Code, a coin of a denomination of higher than 5 cents shall be deemed to include any medallion struck under the authority of this title.

Sec. 406. (a) Medallions struck under the authority of this title shall be sold to the general public at a competitive price equal to the free market value of the gold contained therein plus the cost of manufacture, including labor, materials, dies, use of machinery, and overhead expenses including marketing costs. In order to carry out the purposes of this section, the Secretary shall enter into such arrangements with the administrator of General Services (hereinafter referred to as the "administrator") as may be appropriate.

(b) The administrator shall make such arrangements for the sale of medallions as will encourage broad public participation and will not preclude purchases of single pieces.

(c) The administrator may, after consultation with the Secretary, issue rules and regulations to carry out this section.

Sec. 407. This title shall take effect on October 1, 1979.

Gold ownership

Public Law 93-373, 93rd Congress, S. 2665, approved Aug. 14, 1974.

An Act To permit United States citizens to purchase, hold, sell, or otherwise deal with gold in the United States or abroad.

Sec. 2. Subsections 3 (b) and (c) of Public Law 93-110 (87 Stat. 352) are repealed and in lieu thereof add the following:

"(b) No provision of any law in effect on the date of enactment of this Act, and no rule, regulation, or order in effect on the date subsections (a) and (b) become effective may be construed to prohibit any person from purchasing, holding, selling, or otherwise dealing with gold in the United States or abroad.

"(c) The provisions of subsections (a) and (b) of this section shall take effect . . . on December 31, 1974...

Legislative history

House Reports: No. 93-749 accompanying H.R. 11354 (Committee on Banking and Currency) and No. 93-1142 accompanying H.R. 15465 (Committee on Banking and Currency).

Senate Report No. 93-834 (Committee on Foreign Relations).

Congressional Record, Vol. 120 (1974): May 22, 29, considered and passed Senate. July 2, considered and passed House, amended, in lieu of H.R. 15465. July 25, Senate concurred in House amendments. July 30, Senate vitiated action of July 25; concurred in House amendments with an amendment. July 31, House concurred in Senate amendment.

Hobby Protection Act

Public Law 93-167, (15 U.S.C. 2101) 93rd Congress, H.R. 5777, November 29, 1973.

An Act To require that reproductions and imitations of coins and political items be marked as copies with the date of manufacture.

This Act may be cited as the "Hobby Protection Act."

MARKING REQUIREMENTS

Sec. 2. (a) Political Items. — The manufacture in the United States, or the importation into the United States, for introduction into or distribution in commerce of any imitation political item which is not plainly and permanently marked with the calendar year in which such item was manufactured, is unlawful and is an unfair or deceptive act or practice in commerce under the Federal Trade Commission Act.

(b) Coins and Other Numismatic Items. — The manufacture in the United States, or the importation into the United States, for introduction into or distribution in commerce of any imitation numismatic item which is not plainly and permanently marked COPY, is unlawful and is an unfair or deceptive act or practice in commerce under the Federal Trade Commission Act.

(c) Rules and Regulations. — The Federal Trade Commission shall prescribe rules for determining the manner and form in which

items described in subsection (a) or (b) shall be permanently marked.

(d) Exemption. — Subsections (a) and (b), and regulations under subsection (c), shall not apply to any common carrier or contract carrier or freight forwarder with respect to an imitation political item or imitation numismatic item received, shipped, delivered, or handled by it for shipment in the ordinary course of its business.

PRIVATE ENFORCEMENT

Sec. 3. If any person violates section 2 (a) or (b) or a rule under section 2 (c), any interested person may commence a civil action for injunctive relief restraining such violation, and for damages, in any United States district court for a district in which the defendant resides or has an agent. In any such action, the court may award the costs of the suit, including reasonable attorneys' fees.

ENFORCEMENT BY
FEDERAL TRADE COMMISSION

Sec. 4. (a) Except as provided in section 3, this Act shall be enforced by the Federal Trade Commission under the Federal Trade Commission Act.

(b) The Commission shall prevent any person from violating the provisions of this Act in the same manner, by the same means, and with the same jurisdiction, powers, and duties as though all applicable terms and provisions of the Federal Trade Commission Act were incorporated into and made a part of this Act; and any such person violating the provisions of this Act shall be subject to the penalties and entitled to the privileges and immunities provided in said Federal Trade Commission Act, in the same manner, by the same means, and with the same jurisdiction, powers, and duties as though the applicable terms and provisions of the said Federal Trade Commission Act were incorporated into and made a part of this Act.

IMPORTS

Sec. 5. Any item imported into the United States in violation of section 2 (a) or (b) or regulations under section 2 (c) shall be subject to seizure and forfeiture under the customs laws.

APPLICATION OF OTHER LAW

Sec. 6. The provisions of this Act are in addition to, and not in substitution for or limitation of, the provisions of any other law of the United States or of the law of any state.

DEFINITIONS

Sec. 7. For purposes of this Act:
(1) The term "original political item" means any political button, poster, literature,

sticker, or any advertisement produced for use in any political cause.

(2) The term "imitation political item" means an item which purports to be, but in fact is not, an original political item, or which is a reproduction, copy, or counterfeit of an original political item.

(3) The term "original numismatic item" means any thing which has been a part of coinage or issue which has been used in exchange or has been used to commemorate a person or event. Such term includes coins, tokens, paper money, and commemorative medals.

(4) The term "imitation numismatic item" means an item which purports to be, but in fact is not, an original numismatic item or which is a reproduction, copy, or counterfeit of an original numismatic item.

(5) The term "commerce" has the same meaning as such term has under the Federal Trade Commission Act.

(6) The term "Commission" means the Federal Trade Commission.

(7) The term "United States" means the states, the District of Columbia, and the Commonwealth of Puerto Rico.

EFFECTIVE DATE

Sec. 8. This Act shall apply only to imitation political items and imitation numismatic items manufactured after the date of enactment of this Act.

Approved November 29, 1973.

Legislative history

House Report No. 93-159 (Committee on Interstate and Foreign Commerce).

Senate Report No. 93-345 accompanying S. 1880 (Committee on Commerce).

Congressional Record, Vol. 119 (1973): May 16, considered and passed House. July 31, Aug. 1, 2, considered and passed Senate, amended in lieu of S. 1880. Nov. 16, Senate receded from its amendments.

Rules and regulations

The following is an excerpt from the *Federal Register*, Vol. 40, No. 26, Feb. 6, 1975. Written by Charles A. Tobin, secretary, Federal Trade Commission, it includes comments on the Hobby Protection Act, and the new law as it appears in the U.S. Code.

On July 19, 1974 (39 FR 26429) a notice of proposed regulations to be promulgated under the Hobby Protection Act, 15 U.S.C. 2101, et seq., was published in the *Federal Register*. Promulgation of these proposals would regulate the manner and form of permanently marking imitation political and imitation numismatic items. The proposals af-

forded all interested persons the opportunity to submit data, and express views or comments.

The Commission received 67 comments from federal and local officials, private citizens and industry representatives. Fifty-four of the comments objected to the proposal in Sec. 304.1(d) that the term "imitation numismatic item" not include any re-issue or restrike of any original numismatic item by the United States Mint. [T]he specific language in the Act and its legislative history exempts the United States Mint from the marking requirements of the Act. . .

It was suggested that the Commission make it clear that the regulations do not permit the otherwise unlawful reproduction of genuine currency simply because it is marked with the word COPY. This suggestion prompted new Sec. 304.4 which incorporates section 6 of the Hobby Protection Act and provides, in effect, that the regulations are in addition to and not in substitution for or limitation of the existing statutes and regulations prohibiting the reproduction of genuine currency.

It has been brought to the Commission's attention that marking requirements for imitation political and imitation numismatic items should be amended to require that the calendar year or the word COPY, as appropriate, be marked only on either the obverse or reverse surface of the items. Such a requirement would prevent any attempt to subvert the purpose of the regulations by marking the edge of the items, which would be inconsistent with the requirement that the items be conspicuously marked. The Commission considers this proposed change to be justified to avoid circumvention of the Act's requirements, and therefore has incorporated it in Secs. 304.5 and 304.6.

Following are the regulations promulgated by the Federal Trade Commission under the Hobby Protection Act. The materials are found in 16 CFR 304.1 et seq. (1987).
Section

304.1 Terms defined.
304.2 General requirement.
304.3 Applicability.
304.4 Application of other laws and regulations.
304.5 Marking requirements for imitation political items.
304.6 Marking requirements for imitation numismatic items.
Authority: 15 U.S.C. 2101 et seq.

Sec. 304.1. Terms defined.
(a) "Act" means the Hobby Protection Act

(approved November 29, 1973; Pub. L. 93–167, 87 Stat. 686, [15 U.S.C. 2101, et seq.]).

(b) "Commerce" has the same meaning as such term has under the Federal Trade Commission Act.

(c) "Commission" means the Federal Trade Commission.

(d) "Imitation numismatic item" means an item which purports to be, but in fact is not, an original numismatic item or which is a reproduction, copy, or counterfeit of an original numismatic item. Such term includes an original numismatic item which has been altered or modified in such a manner that it could reasonably purport to be an original numismatic item other than the one which was altered or modified. The term shall not include any re-issue or re-strike of any original numismatic item by the United States or any foreign government.

(e) "Imitation political item" means an item which purports to be, but in fact is not, an original political item, or which is a reproduction, copy or counterfeit of an original item.

(f) "Original numismatic item" means anything which has been a part of a coinage of issue which has been used in exchange or has been used to commemorate a person, object, place, or event. Such term includes coins, tokens, paper money, and commemorative medals.

(g) "Original political item" means any political button, poster, literature, sticker, or any advertisement produced for use in any political cause.

(h) "Person" means any individual, group, association, partnership, or any other business entity.

(i) "Regulations" means any or all regulations prescribed by the Federal Trade Commission pursuant to the Act.

(j) "United States" means the states, the District of Columbia, and the commonwealth of Puerto Rico.

Sec. 304.2. General requirement.

Imitation political or numismatic items subject to the Act shall be marked in conformity with the requirements of the Act and the regulations promulgated thereunder. Any violation of these regulations shall constitute a violation of the Act and of the Federal Trade Commission Act.

Sec. 304.3. Applicability.

Any person engaged in the manufacturing, or importation into the United States for introduction into or distribution in commerce, of imitation political or imitation numismatic items shall be subject to the requirements

of the Act and the regulations promulgated thereunder.

Sec. 304.4. Application of other law or regulation.

The provision of these regulations are in addition to, and not in substitution for or limitation of, the provisions of any other law or regulation of the United States (including the existing statutes and regulations prohibiting the reproduction of genuine currency) or of the law or regulation of any state.

Sec. 304.5. Marking requirements for imitation political items.

(Requires imitation political items to be marked).

(a) An imitation political item which is manufactured in the United States, or imported into the United States for introduction into or distribution in commerce, shall be plainly and permanently marked with the calendar year in which such item was manufactured.

(b) The calendar year shall be marked upon the item legibly, conspicuously and nondeceptively, and in accordance with the further requirements of these regulations.

(1) The calendar year shall appear in Arabic numerals, shall be based upon the Gregorian calendar and shall consist of four digits.

(2) The calendar year shall be marked on either the obverse or the reverse surface of the item. It shall not be marked on the edge of the item.

(3) An imitation political item of incusable material shall be incused with the calendar year in sans-serif numerals. Each numeral shall have a vertical dimension of not less than two millimeters (2.0mm) and a minimum depth of three-tenths of one millimeter (0.3mm) or one-half (½) the thickness of the reproduction, whichever is the lesser. The minimum total horizontal dimension for the four numerals composing the calendar year shall be six millimeters (6.0 mm).

(4) An imitation political button, poster, literature, sticker, or advertisement composed of nonincusible material shall be imprinted with the calendar year in sans-serif numerals. Each numeral shall have a vertical dimension of not less than two millimeters (2.0mm). The minimum total horizontal dimension of the four numerals composing the calendar year shall be six millimeters (6.0mm).

Sec. 304.6. Marking requirements for imitation numismatic items.

(a) An imitation numismatic item which is manufactured in the United States, or imported into the United States for introduction into or distribution in commerce, shall be plainly and permanently marked COPY.

(b) The word COPY shall be marked upon the item legibly, conspicuously, and nondeceptively, and in accordance with the further requirements of these regulations.

(1) The word COPY shall appear in capital letters, in the English language.

(2) The word COPY shall be marked on either the obverse or the reverse surface of the item. It shall not be marked on the edge of the item.

(3) An imitation numismatic item of incusable material shall be incused with the word COPY in sans-serif letters having a vertical dimension of not less than two millimeters (2.0mm) and a minimum depth of three-tenths of one millimeter (0.3mm) or to one-half (½) the thickness of the reproduction, whichever is lesser. The minimum total horizontal dimension of the word COPY shall be six millimeters (6.0mm).

(4) An imitation numismatic item composed in nonincusable material shall be imprinted with the word COPY in sans-serif letters having a vertical dimension of not less than two millimeters (2.0mm). The minimum total horizontal dimension of the word COPY shall be six millimeters (6.0mm).

In May 1983, The Federal Trade Commission made proposals to alter the Hobby Protection Act's regulations to take miniature coin and medal issues into account. The proposed changes called for allowing the word COPY to appear in the size previously proposed except on coins smaller than a diameter of 6.0mm. There, it would have been at least the diameter of the reproduction.

Two areas would have been amended: Sec. 304.1(k) would have been added to read as follows:

(k) "Diameter" of a reproduction means the length of the longest possible straight line connecting two points on the perimeter of the reproduction.

In addition, a new section would have been added on marking requirements as Sec. 304.6(b) (3)-(4):

(3) An imitation numismatic item of incusable material shall be incused with the word COPY in sans-serif letters having a vertical dimension of not less than two millimeters (2.0mm) or not less than one-sixth of the diameter of the reproduction, and a minimum depth of three-tenths of one millimeter (0.3mm) or to one-half (½) the thickness of the reproduction, whichever is the lesser. The minimum total horizontal dimension of the word COPY shall be six millimeters (6.0mm)

or not less than one-half of the diameter of the reproduction.

(4) An imitation numismatic item composed of nonincusable material shall be imprinted with the word COPY in sans-serif letters having a vertical dimension of not less than two millimeters (2.0mm) or not less than one-sixth of the diameter of the reproduction. The minimum total horizontal dimension of the word COPY shall be six millimeters (6.0mm) or not less than one-half of the diameter of the reproduction.

As of May 1987, no action had been taken by the FTC to implement the proposed changes.

Bicentennial coinage

Public Law 93-127, (formerly 31 U.S.C. 324d-324g) 93rd Congress, S. 1141, approved Oct. 18, 1973.

An Act To provide a new coinage design and date emblematic of the Bicentennial of the American Revolution for dollars, half dollars, and quarter dollars, to authorize the issuance of special silver coins commemorating the Bicentennial of the American Revolution, and for other purposes.

Be it enacted by the Senate and House of Representatives of the United States of America in Congress assembled, That the reverse side of all dollar, half-dollar, and quarter-dollar coins minted for issuance on or after July 4, 1975, and until such time as the Secretary of the Treasury may determine, shall bear a design determined by the Secretary to be emblematic of the Bicentennial of the American Revolution.

Sec. 2. All dollar, half-dollar, and quarter-dollar coins minted for issuance between July 4, 1975, and January 1, 1977, shall bear "1776-1976" in lieu of the date of coinage; and all dollar, half-dollar, and quarter-dollar coins minted thereafter until such time as the Secretary of the Treasury may determine shall bear a date emblematic of the Bicentennial in addition to the date of coinage.

Sec. 3. Until the Secretary of the Treasury determines that the Mints of the United States are adequate for the production of ample supplies of coins and medals, any facility of the Bureau of the Mint may be used for the manufacture and storage of medals and coins.

Sec. 4. Notwithstanding any other provision of law with respect to the design of coins, the Secretary shall mint prior to July 4, 1975, for issuance on and after such date, 45 million silver-clad alloy coins authorized under section 101(a) of the Coinage Act of 1965, (31 U.S.C. 391a) commemorating the Bicentennial of the American Revolution, of such design, in such denomination, and containing such quantities of such other metals as he determines appropriate. In addition, the Secretary shall coin and issue not more than an additional 15 million such coins, if he determines such coins are needed to meet public demand. Coins minted under this section may only be distributed by the Secretary as Proof or Uncirculated coins at such prices as he may determine. The Secretary is authorized, by regulation, to limit the number of silver coins minted under this section which any one person may purchase. Coins minted under this section shall be treated as pieces subject to the 150 million piece limitation contained in section 101(d) of the Coinage Act of 1965, and shall be subject to such limitation. Receipts from the sale of coins under this section shall be covered into the Treasury as miscellaneous receipts.

Sec. 5. In connection with the operations of the Bureau of the Mint, the Secretary of the Treasury is authorized to manufacture and distribute numismatic items. Proceeds from the sale of numismatic items shall be reimbursed to the current appropriation for the cost of manufacturing and handling of such items.

Legislative history

House Reports: No. 93-391 accompanying H.R. 8789 (Committee on Banking and Currency) and No. 93-521 (Committee of Conference).

Senate Report No. 93-244.

Congressional Record, Vol. 119 (1973): July 11, considered and passed Senate. Sept. 12, considered and passed House, amended, in lieu of H.R. 8789. Oct. 4, House and Senate agreed to conference report.

Bank Holding Company Act amendments

Public Law 91-607 (31 U.S.C. 391), 91st Congress, H.R. 6778, approved Dec. 31, 1970.

TITLE II — PROVISIONS RELATING TO COINAGE

Sec. 201. Section 101 of the Coinage Act of 1965 (31 U.S.C. 391) is amended to read as follows:

"Sec. 101. (a). The Secretary may mint and issue coins of the denominations set forth in subsection (c) in such quantities as he determines to be necessary to meet national needs.

"(b). Any coin minted under authority of subsection (a) shall be a clad coin. The cladding shall be an alloy of 75 per centum copper and 25 per centum nickel, and shall weigh not less than 30 per centum of the weight of the whole coin. The core shall be copper.

"(c). (1) The dollar shall be 1.500 inches in diameter and weigh 22.68 grams.

"(2) The half dollar shall be 1.205 inches in diameter and weigh 11.34 grams.

"(3) The quarter dollar shall be 0.955 inch in diameter and weigh 5.67 grams.

"(4) The dime shall be 0.705 inch in diameter and weigh 2.268 grams.

"(d). Notwithstanding the foregoing, the Secretary is authorized to mint and issue not more than 150 million $1 pieces which shall have —

"(1) a diameter of 1.500 inches;

"(2) a cladding of an alloy of 800 parts of silver and 200 parts of copper; and

"(3) a core of an alloy of silver and copper such that the whole coin weighs 24.592 grams and contains 9.837 grams of silver and 14.755 grams of copper."

Sec. 202. For the purposes of this title, the Administrator of General Services shall transfer to the Secretary of the Treasury 25.5 million fine troy ounces of silver now held in the national stockpile established pursuant to the Strategic and Critical Materials Stock Piling Act (50 U.S.C. 98-98h) which is excess to strategic needs. Such transfer shall be made at the value of $1.292929292 for each fine troy ounce of silver so transferred. Such silver shall be used exclusively to coin $1 pieces authorized in section 101(d) of the Coinage Act of 1965, as amended by this Act.

Sec. 203. The dollars initially minted under authority of section 101 of the Coinage Act of 1965 shall bear the likeness of the late President of the United States Dwight David Eisenhower, and on the other side thereof a design which is emblematic of the symbolic eagle of Apollo 11 landing on the moon.

Sec. 204. Half dollars, as authorized under section 101(a)(1) of the Coinage Act of 1965, as in effect prior to the enactment of this Act may, in the discretion of the Secretary of the Treasury, continue to be minted until January 1, 1971.

Sec. 205. (a) The Secretary of the Treasury is authorized to transfer, as an accountable advance and at their face value, the approximately three million silver dollars now held in the Treasury to the administrator of General Services. The administrator is authorized to offer these coins to the public in the manner recommended by the Joint Commission on the Coinage at its meeting on May 12, 1969. The administrator shall repay the accountable advance in the amount of that face value out of the proceeds of and at the time of the public sale of the silver dollars. Any proceeds received as a result of the public sale in excess of the face value of these coins shall be covered into the Treasury as miscellaneous receipts.

(b) There are authorized to be appropriated, to remain available until expended, such amounts as may be necessary to carry out the purposes of this section.

Sec. 206. The last sentence of section 3517 of the Revised Statutes, as amended (31 U.S.C. 324), is amended by striking the following: "except that coins produced under authority of sections 101(a) (1), 101(a) (2), and 101(a) (3) of the Coinage Act of 1965 shall not be dated earlier than 1965".

Sec. 207. Section 4 of the Act of June 24, 1967 (Public Law 90-29; 31 U.S.C. 405a-1 note), is amended by adding at the end thereof the following new sentence: "Out of the proceeds of and at the time of any sale of silver transferred pursuant to this Act, the Treasury Department shall be paid $1.292929292 for each fine troy ounce."

Sec. 208. Section 3513 of the Revised Statutes (31 U.S.C. 316) and the first section of the Act of February 28, 1878 (20 Stat. 25; 31 U.S.C. 316,458) are repealed.

Sec. 209. Coins produced under the authority of section 101(d) of the Coinage Act of 1965, as amended by this Act, shall bear such date as the Secretary of the Treasury determines.

Approved December 31, 1970.

Silver certificates

Public Law 90-29, 90th Congress, S. 1352, approved June 24, 1967.

An Act To authorize adjustments in the amount of outstanding silver certificates, and for other purposes.

Be it enacted by the Senate and House of Representatives of the United States of America in Congress assembled, that the Secretary of the Treasury is authorized to determine from time to time the amount of silver certificates (not exceeding $200,000,000 in aggregate face value), issued after June 30, 1929, which in his judgment have been destroyed or irretrievably lost, or are held in collections, and will never be presented for redemption. In the case of each determination he shall credit the appropriate receipt account with an equivalent amount, and shall reduce accordingly the amount of silver certificates outstanding on the books of the Treasury.

Sec. 2. Silver certificates shall be exchangeable for silver bullion for one year following the enactment of this Act. Thereafter they shall no longer be redeemable in silver but shall be redeemable from any moneys in the general fund of the Treasury not otherwise appropriated.

Sec. 3. Effective upon the expiration of one year after the date of enactment of this Act, section 2 of the Act of June 4, 1963, as amended (31 U.S.C. 405a-1), is amended to read as follows:

"Sec. 2. The Secretary of the Treasury is authorized to use for coinage, or to sell on such terms and conditions as he may deem appropriate, any silver of the United States (other than silver transferred to the stockpiles established pursuant to the Strategic and Critical Materials Stock Piling Act) at a price not less than the monetary value of $1.292929292 per fine troy ounce."

Sec. 4. From and after the date of enactment of this Act, and until transferred to the stockpiles established pursuant to the Strategic and Critical Materials Stock Piling Act in accordance with this Act, the Secretary of the Treasury shall hold as a reserve for purposes of the common defense not less than 165 million fine troy ounces of silver. Upon the expiration of one year after the date of enactment of this Act, the Secretary of the Treasury shall transfer not less than 165 million fine troy ounces of silver to the stockpiles established pursuant to the Strategic and Critical Materials Stock Piling Act. For the purposes of that Act, the silver shall be deemed to have been transferred pursuant to that Act.

Sec. 5. The last sentence of section 3517 of the Revised Statutes (31 U.S.C. 324) is repealed.

Legislative history

House Report No. 261 accompanying H.R. 7476 (Committee on Banking and Currency).

Senate Report No. 232 (Committee on Banking and Currency).

Congressional Record, Vol. 113 (1967): June 1: Considered in Senate. June 5: Considered and passed Senate. June 12: Considered and passed House, in lieu of H.R. 7476.

Coinage Act of 1965

Public Law 89-81, 89th Congress, S. 2080, approved July 23, 1965.

An Act To provide for the coinage of the United States.

Be it enacted by the Senate and House of Representatives of the United States of America in Congress assembled, That this Act may be cited as the "Coinage Act of 1965".

TITLE I — AUTHORIZATION OF ADDITIONAL COINAGE

Sec. 101. (a) The Secretary may coin and issue pursuant to this section half dollars or 50-cent pieces, quarter dollars or 25-cent pieces, and dimes or 10-cent pieces in such quantities as he may determine to be necessary to meet the needs of the public. Any coin minted under authority of this section shall be a clad coin the weight of whose cladding is not less than 30 per centum of the weight of the entire coin, and which meets the following additional specifications:

(1) The half dollar shall have —

(A) a diameter of 1.205 inches;

(B) a cladding of an alloy of 800 parts of silver and 200 parts of copper; and

(C) a core of an alloy of silver and copper such that the whole coin weighs 11.5 grams and contains 4.6 grams of silver and 6.9 grams of copper.

(2) The quarter dollar shall have —

(A) a diameter of 0.955 inch;

(B) a cladding of an alloy of 75 per centum copper and 25 per centum nickel; and

(C) a core of copper such that the weight of the whole coin is 5.67 grams.

(3) The dime shall have —

(A) a diameter of 0.705 inch;

(B) a cladding of an alloy of 75 per centum copper and 25 per centum nickel; and

(C) a core of copper such that the weight of the whole coin is 2.268 grams.

(b) Half dollars, quarter dollars, and dimes may be minted from 900 fine coin silver only until such date as the Secretary of the Treasury determines that adequate supplies of the coins authorized by this Act are available, and in no event later than five years after the date of enactment of this Act.

(c) No standard silver dollars may be minted during the five-year period which begins on the date of enactment of this Act.

Sec. 102. All coins and currencies of the United States (including Federal Reserve notes and circulating notes of Federal Reserve banks and national banking associations), regardless of when coined or issued, shall be legal tender for all debts, public and private, public charges, taxes, duties, and dues.

Sec. 103. (a) In order to acquire equipment, manufacturing facilities, patents, patent rights, technical knowledge and assistance, metallic strip, and other materials necessary to produce rapidly an adequate supply of the coins authorized by Section 101 of this Act, the Secretary may enter into contracts upon such terms and conditions as he may deem appropriate and in the public interest.

(b) During such period as he may deem necessary, but in no event later than five

years after the date of enactment of this Act, the Secretary may exercise the authority conferred by subsection (a) of this section without regard to any other provisions of law governing procurement or public contracts.

Sec. 104. The Secretary shall purchase at a price of $1.29 per fine troy ounce any silver mined after the date of enactment of this Act from natural deposits in the United States or any place subject to the jurisdiction thereof and tendered to a United States Mint or assay office within one year after the month in which the ore from which it is derived was mined.

Sec. 105. (a) Whenever in the judgment of the Secretary such action is necessary to protect the coinage of the United States, he is authorized under such rules and regulations as he may prescribe to prohibit, curtail, or regulate the exportation, melting, or treating of any coin of the United States.

(b) Whoever knowingly violates any order, rule, regulation, or license issued pursuant to subsection (a) of this section shall be fined not more than $10,000, or imprisoned not more than five years, or both.

Sec. 106. (a) There shall be forfeited to the United States any coins exported, melted, or treated in violation of any order, rule, regulation, or license issued under Section 105(a), and any metal resulting from such melting or treating.

(b) The powers of the Secretary and his delegates, and the judicial and other remedies available to the United States, for the enforcement of forfeitures of property subject to forfeiture pursuant to subsection (a) of this section shall be the same as those provided in part II of subchapter C of Chapter 75 of the Internal Revenue Code of 1954 for the enforcement of forfeitures of property subject to forfeiture under any provision of such Code.

Sec. 107. The Secretary may issue such rules and regulations as he may deem necessary to carry out the provisions of this Act.

Sec. 108. For the purposes of this title —

(1) The term "Secretary" means the Secretary of the Treasury.

(2) The term "clad coin" means a coin composed of three layers of metal, the two outer layers being of identical composition and metallurgically bonded to an inner layer.

(3) The term "cladding" means the outer layers of a clad coin.

(4) The term "core" means the inner layer of a clad coin.

(5) A specification given otherwise than as a limit shall be maintained within such

reasonable manufacturing tolerances as the Secretary may specify.

(6) Specifications given for an alloy are by weight.

TITLE II — AMENDMENTS TO EXISTING LAW

Sec. 201. The first sentence of Section 3558 of the Revised Statutes (31 U.S.C. 283) is amended to read: "The business of the United States assay office in San Francisco shall be in all respects similar to that of the assay office of New York except that until the Secretary of the Treasury determines that the Mints of the United States are adequate for the production of ample supplies of coins, its facilities may be used for the production of coins."

Sec. 202. Section 4 of the Act of August 20, 1963 (Public Law 88-102; 31 U.S.C. 294), is amended by changing "$30,000,000" to read "$45,000,000".

Sec. 203. (a) Section 3 of the Act of December 18, 1942 (56 Stat. 1065; 31 U.S.C. 317c), is amended by striking "minor" each place it appears.

(b) Section 9 of the Act of March 14, 1900 (31 Stat. 48; 31 U.S.C. 320), is repealed.

Sec. 204. (a) Section 3517 of the Revised Statutes (31 U.S.C. 324) is amended to read:

"Sec. 3517. Upon one side of all coins of the United States there shall be an impression emblematic of liberty, with an inscription of the word 'Liberty', and upon the reverse side shall be the figure or representation of an eagle, with the inscriptions 'United States of America' and 'E Pluribus Unum' and a designation of the value of the coin; but on the dime, 5-, and 1-cent piece, the figure of the eagle shall be omitted. The motto 'In God we trust' shall be inscribed on all coins. Any coins minted after the enactment of the Coinage Act of 1965 from 900 fine coin silver shall be inscribed with the year 1964. All other coins shall be inscribed with the year of the coinage or issuance unless the Secretary of the Treasury, in order to prevent or alleviate a shortage of coins of any denomination, directs that coins of that denomination continue to be inscribed with the last preceding year inscribed on coins of that denomination, except that coins produced under authority of Sections 101(a) (1), 101(a) (2), and 101(a) (3) of the Coinage Act of 1965 shall not be dated earlier than 1965. No Mint mark may be inscribed on any coins during the five-year period beginning on the date of enactment of the Coinage Act of 1965, except that coins struck at the Denver Mint as authorized by

law prior to such date may continue to be inscribed with that Mint mark."

(b) The Act of September 3, 1964 (Public Law 88-580; 31 U.S.C. 324 note), is repealed.

Sec. 205. The first sentence of Section 3526 of the Revised Statutes (31 U.S.C. 335) is amended to read: "In order to procure bullion for coinage or to carry out the purposes of Section 104 of the Coinage Act of 1965, the Secretary of the Treasury may purchase silver bullion with the bullion fund."

Sec. 206. (a) Section 3528 of the Revised Statutes (31 U.S.C. 340) is amended to read:

"Sec. 3528. The Secretary of the Treasury may use the coinage metal fund for the purchase of metal for coinage. The gain arising from the coinage of metals purchased out of such fund into coin of a nominal value exceeding the cost of such metals shall be credited to the coinage profit fund. The coinage profit fund shall be charged with the wastage incurred in such coinage, with the cost of distributing such coins, and with such sums as shall from time to time be transferred therefrom to the general fund of the Treasury."

(b) The effect of the amendment made by subsection (a) of this section shall be to redesignate the minor coinage metal fund established under Section 3528 of the Revised Statutes as the coinage metal fund, and not to authorize the creation of a new fund.

Sec. 207. The second sentence of Section 3542 of the Revised Statutes (31 U.S.C. 355) is amended by changing ", in the case of the superintendent of melting and refining department, one-thousandth of the whole amount of gold, and one and one-half thousandths of the whole amount of silver delivered to him since the last annual settlement, and in the case of the superintendent of coining department, one-thousandth of the whole amount of silver, and one-half thousandth of the whole amount of gold that has been delivered to him by the superintendent" to read "such limitations as the Secretary shall establish".

Sec. 208. Section 3550 of the Revised Statutes (31 U.S.C. 366) is repealed.

Sec. 209. The second sentence of Section 2 of the Act of June 4, 1963 (Public Law 88-36; 31 U.S.C. 405a-1), is amended to read: "The Secretary of the Treasury is authorized to use for coinage, or to sell on such terms and conditions as he may deem appropriate, at a price not less than the monetary value of $1.292929292 per fine troy ounce, any silver of the United States in excess of that required to be held as reserves against outstanding silver certificates."

Sec. 210. The last sentence of Section 43(b) (1) of the Act of May 12, 1933 (Public Law 10, 73d Congress; 31 U.S.C. 462), is repealed.

Sec. 211. (a) Section 485 of Title 18 of the United States Code is amended to read: (see reprinted statute section).

Sec. 212. (a) Chapter 17 of Title 18 of the United States Code is amended by adding at the end:

"**Sec. 337. Coins as security for loans.**

"Whoever lends or borrows money or credit upon the security of such coins of the United States as the Secretary of the Treasury may from time to time designate by proclamation published in the Federal Register, during any period designated in such a proclamation, shall be fined not more than $10,000 or imprisoned not more than one year, or both."

(b) The table of sections at the beginning of such chapter is amended by adding at the end:

"337. Coins as security for loans."

(c) The amendments made by this section shall apply only with respect to loans made, renewed, or increased on or after the 31st day after the date of enactment of this Act.

TITLE III — JOINT COMMISSION ON THE COINAGE

Sec. 301. The president is hereby authorized to establish a Joint Commission on the Coinage to be composed of the Secretary of the Treasury as chairman; the Secretary of Commerce; the Director of the Bureau of the Budget; the Director of the Mint; the chairman and ranking minority member of the Senate Banking and Currency Committee, and four members of the Senate, not members of such committee, to be appointed by the president of the Senate; the chairman and ranking minority member of the House Banking and Currency Committee, and four members of the House of Representatives, not members of such committee, to be appointed by the Speaker; and eight public members to be appointed by the president, none of whom shall be associated or identified with or representative of any industry, group, business, or association directly interested as such in the composition, characteristics, or production of the coinage of the United States.

Sec. 302. No public official or member of Congress serving as a member of the Joint Commission shall continue to serve as such after he has ceased to hold the office by virtue of which he became a member of the Joint

Commission. Any vacancy on the Joint Commission shall be filled by the choosing of a successor member in the same manner as his predecessor.

Sec. 303. The Joint Commission shall study the progress made in the implementation of the coinage program established by this Act, and shall review from time to time such matters as the needs of the economy for coins, the standards for the coinage, technological developments in metallurgy and coinselector devices, the availability of various metals, renewed minting of the silver dollar, the time when and circumstances under which the United States should cease to maintain the price of silver, and other considerations relevant to the maintenance of an adequate and stable coinage system. It shall, from time to time, give its advice and recommendations with respect to these matters to the president, the Secretary of the Treasury, and the Congress.

Sec. 304. There are authorized to be appropriated to remain available until expended, such amounts as may be necessary to carry out the purposes of this title.

Legislative history

House Report No. 509 accompanying H.R. 8926 (Committee on Banking and Currency).

Senate Report No. 317 (Committee on Banking and Currency).

Congressional Record, Vol. 111 (1965): June 23: Considered in Senate. June 24: Considered and passed Senate. July 13: H.R. 8926 considered in House. July 14: Considered and passed House, amended, in lieu of H.R. 8926. July 15: Senate concurred in House amendments.

(Commission phased out Jan. 5, 1975).

1964 date freeze

Public Law 88-580, 88th Congress, S. 2950, approved Sept. 3, 1964.

An Act To authorize the Mint to inscribe the figure 1964 on all coins minted until adequate supplies of coins are available.

Be it enacted by the Senate and House of Representatives of the United States of America in Congress assembled, That, notwithstanding section 3517 of the Revised Statutes (31 U.S.C. 324), all coins minted from the date of enactment of this Act until July 1 or January 1, whichever date first occurs after the date on which the Secretary of the Treasury determines that adequate supplies of coins are available, shall be inscribed with the figure "1964" in lieu of the year of the coinage.

Sec. 2. The requirement of section 3550 of the Revised Statutes (31 U.S.C. 366) that the obverse working dies at each Mint shall be destroyed at the end of each calendar year shall not be applicable during the period provided for in section 1 of this Act.

Legislative history

House Report No. 1644 accompanying H.R. 11893 (Committee on Banking and Currency).

Senate Report No. 1237 (Committee on Banking and Currency).

Congressional Record, Vol. 110 (1964): July 24: Considered and passed Senate. Aug. 20: Considered and passed House, amended, in lieu of H.R. 11893. Aug. 21: Senate agreed to House amendments.

Kennedy half dollar

Public Law 88-256, 88th Congress, H.R. 9413, approved Dec. 30, 1963.

An Act To provide for the coinage of 50-cent pieces bearing the likeness of John Fitzgerald Kennedy.

Be it enacted by the Senate and House of Representatives of the United States of America in Congress assembled, that in lieu of the coinage of the 50-cent piece known as the Franklin half dollar, there shall be coined a silver 50-cent piece which shall bear on one side the likeness of the late president of the United States John Fitzgerald Kennedy, and on the other side an appropriate design to be prescribed by the Secretary of the Treasury.

Legislative history

House Report No. 1038 (Committee on Banking and Currency).
Congressional Record, Vol. 109 (1963): Dec. 17: Considered and passed House. Dec. 18: Considered and passed Senate.

Tin eliminated from 1-cent piece

Public Law 87-643, 87th Congress, H.R. 11310, approved Sept. 5, 1962.

An Act To amend section 3515 of the Revised Statutes to eliminate tin in the alloy of the 1-cent piece.

Be it enacted by the Senate and House of Representatives of the United States of America in Congress assembled, That the third sentence of section 3515 of the Revised Statutes, as amended (31 U.S.C. 317) is amended to read as follows: "The alloy of the 1-cent piece shall be 95 per centum of copper and 5 per centum of zinc."

Sec. 2. The first and second sentences of section 3552 of the Revised Statutes, as amended (31 U.S.C. 369), are amended by striking out "medals and proof coins" and inserting "medals, proof coins, and uncirculated coins" in lieu thereof.

"In God We Trust"

Public Law 84-140, 84th Congress, H.R. 619, July 11, 1955.

An Act To provide that all United States currency shall bear the inscription IN GOD WE TRUST.

Be it enacted by the Senate and House of Representatives of the United States of America in Congress assembled, that at such time as new dies for the printing of currency are adopted in connection with the current program of the Treasury Department to increase the capacity of presses utilized by the Bureau of Engraving and Printing, the dies shall bear, at such place or places thereon as the Secretary of the Treasury may determine to be appropriate, the inscription IN GOD WE TRUST, and thereafter this inscription shall appear on all United States currency and coins.

Authority for coinage

Following is a listing of the enabling legislation for U.S. coinage. Included also are the standard weights and finenesses, and the total number of pieces coined (for gold, through 1933; for silver, through 1964). Data for composite coinage begins in 1965; like minor coinage, it is current through the end of 1986.

Gold coinage[1]

Denomination	Authorizing act	Standard weight (Grains)	Standard fineness (Thousandths)	Total coined (Pieces)	(Face value)
$50 commemorative, Panama-Pacific International Exposition:					
Octagonal	Jan. 16, 1915	1,290	900	1,509	$75,450
Round	do.	1,290	900	1,510	75,500
Double eagle ($20)	March 3, 1849	516	900		
Do	Feb. 12, 1873	516	900	174,105,606	3,482,112,120

Authority for coinage

Gold coinage[1]

Denomination	Authorizing act	Standard weight (Grains)	Standard fineness (Thousandths)	Total coined (Pieces)	Total coined (Face value)
Eagle ($10)	April 2, 1792	270	916.67		
Do	June 28, 1834	258	899.225	57,683,485	576,834,850
Do	Jan. 18, 1837	258	900		
Do[2]	Feb. 12, 1873	258	900		
Do[2]	July 22, 1982	258	900	800,000	8,000,000
Half eagle ($5)	April 2, 1792	135	916.67		
Do	June 28, 1834	129	899.225	78,911,869	394,559,345
Do	Jan. 18, 1837	129	900		
Do	Feb. 12, 1873	129	900		
Do	July 9, 1985	8.359[5]	900		
Quarter eagle ($2.50)[4]	April 2, 1792	67.5	916.67		
Do[3]	June 28, 1834	64.5	899.225	20,216,590	50,541,475
Do[3]	Jan. 18, 1837	64.5	900		
Do[3]	Feb. 12, 1873	64.5	900		
Quarter eagle ($2.50) commemorative:					
Panama-Pacific International Exposition	Jan. 16, 1915	64.5	900	10,017	25,042.50
Sesquicentennial Exhibition	Mar. 3, 1925	64.5	900	200,226	500,565.00
	Feb. 21, 1853				
$3[4]	Feb. 12, 1873	77.4	900	539,792	1,619,376.00
	Mar. 3, 1849				
$1[4]	Feb. 12, 1873	25.8	900	19,499,337	19,499,337.00
$1, commemorative:					
Louisiana Purchase Exposition	June 28, 1902	25.8	900	250,258	250,258.00
Lewis and Clark Exposition	Apr. 13, 1904	25.8	900	60,069	60,069.00
Panama-Pacific International Exposition	Jan. 16, 1915	25.8	900	25,034	25,034.00
McKinley memorial	Feb. 23, 1916	25.8	900	30,040	30,040.00
Grant memorial	Feb. 2, 1922	25.8	900	10,016	10,016.00
Total gold				351,545,358	4,526,218,477.50

[1] Sec. 5 of the Gold Reserve Act of Jan. 30, 1934, provides in part as follows:
"No gold shall hereafter be coined, and no gold coin shall hereafter be paid out or delivered by the United States ... All gold coin of the United States shall be withdrawn from circulation, and, together with all other gold owned by the United States, shall be formed into bars of such weights and degrees of fineness as the Secretary of the Treasury may direct."

[2] From 1934 until September 1983, no gold coins were struck for circulation by the United States Mint. As part of the commemorative coinage program of the XXIII Olympiad, a gold eagle or $10 gold piece was authorized specifically by Congress. Pieces were struck, and Mint marks appropriately placed to reflect the striking facilities, at Philadelphia (P), Denver (D), San Francisco (S) and a new site, West Point (W). Authority to strike coins at West Point derives from the ability of the Secretary of the Treasury to designate any facility of the U.S. Mint for that purpose reflected in the 1982 coinage legislation revision, 31 U.S.C. 5131(b). No more than 2 million gold eagles were authorized (each of traditional weight and measure). The Statue of Liberty program followed with a $5 gold piece, the Bicentennial of the Constitution followed with its own gold coin, making it clear that these were the wave of the future. In accordance with current practice, legislation calls for the weight to be expressed in grams rather than grains. The numbers are easily convertible. (1 grain equals 0.0648 gram, 480 grains equals 31.1035 grams 1 troy ounce)

[3] Discontinued by act of Apr. 11, 1930.

[4] Discontinued by act of Sept. 26, 1890.

[5] Weight specified in grams, not grains.

With respect to all gold coins issued in 1933 and prior, it is useful to note that tens of thousands of them were melted by the Mint during the recall of 1933-34. Evidence in Mint records suggests that as much as one third of all double eagles ever coined were melted into bullion bars, as were comparable numbers of other denominations. The same became true of silver coins half a century later. Mintage figures attached do not reflect these melts since no dates were ever kept and only denominational totals were noted by weight, not actual number.

Silver coinage

Denomination	Authorizing act	Standard weight (Grains)	Standard fineness (Thousandths)	Total coined to Dec. 31, 1986 (Pieces)	(Face Value)
Dollar[1][2]	April 2, 1792	416	892.4		
Do.[1][2]	Jan. 18, 1837	412.5	900		
Do.[2]	Feb. 28, 1878	412.5	900	855,611,127 [2]	$855,611,127.00
Do.[2]	July 14, 1890	412.5	900		
Do.[2]	March 3, 1891	412.5	900		
Do.[2]	April 23, 1918	412.5	900		
Do.[2] (Olympic)	July 22, 1982	412.5	900	10,506,570	10,506,570
Do.[2] (Statue of Liberty)	July 9, 1985	26.73[12]	900		
Do.[2] (Constitution)	Oct. 29, 1986	26.73[12]	900		
Trade dollar[3][4]	Feb. 12, 1873	420	900	35,965,924	35,965,924.00
Dollar, commemorative: Lafayette	Mar. 3, 1899	412.5	900	50,026	50,026.00
Half dollar (homogeneous alloy)	Apr. 2, 1792	208	892.4		
Do.	Jan. 18, 1837	206.25	900	1,740,669,234	870,334,617.00
Do.	Feb. 21, 1853	192	900		
Do.	Feb. 12, 1873	[5] 192.9	900		
Half dollar, commemorative:					
Columbian Exposition	Aug. 5, 1892	192.9	900	5,002,105	2,501,052.50
Panama-Pacific International Exposition	Jan. 16, 1915	192.9	900	60,030	30,015.00
Illinois Centennial	June 1, 1918	192.9	900	100,058	50,029.00
Maine Centennial	May 10, 1920	192.9	900	50,028	25,014.00
Landing of Pilgrims, Tercentennial	May 12, 1920	192.9	900	300,165	150,082.00
Alabama Centennial	May 10, 1920	192.9	900	70,044	35,022.00
Missouri Centennial	Mar. 4, 1921	192.9	900	50,028	25,014.00
Grant	Feb. 2, 1922	192.9	900	100,061	50,030.50
Monroe Doctrine Centennial	Jan. 24, 1923	192.9	900	274,077	137,038.50
Huguenot-Walloon	Feb. 26, 1923	192.9	900	142,080	71,040.00
Stone Mountain	Mar. 17, 1924	192.9	900	2,314,709	1,157,354.50
Battle Lexington-Concord	Jan. 14, 1925	192.9	900	162,099	81,049.50
California Diamond Jubilee	Feb. 24, 1925	192.9	900	150,200	75,100.00
Fort Vancouver	do.	192.9	900	50,028	25,014.00
Sesquicentennial Exhibition	Mar. 3, 1925	192.9	900	1,000,528	500,264.00
Battle of Bennington	Feb. 24, 1925	192.9	900	40,034	20,017.00
Oregon Trail	May 17, 1926	192.9	900	264,419	132,209.50
Hawaiian Discovery	Mar. 7, 1928	192.9	900	10,008	5,004.00
Texas Centennial	June 15, 1933	192.9	900	304,193	152,096.50
Daniel Boone Bicentennial	May 26, 1934	192.9	900	108,603	54,301.50
Maryland Tercentennial	May 9, 1934	192.9	900	25,015	12,507.50
Arkansas Centennial	May 14, 1934	192.9	900	120,166	60,083.00
Connecticut Tercentennial	June 21, 1934	192.9	900	25,018	12,509.00
City of Hudson, N.Y.	May 2, 1935	192.9	900	10,008	5,004.00
Providence, R.I., Tercentennial	do.	192.9	900	50,034	25,017.00
California-Pacific Exposition	May 3, 1935	192.9	900	430,224	215,112.00
Old Spanish Trail	June 5, 1935	192.9	900	10,008	5,004.00
Columbia, S.C., Sesquicentennial	Mar. 18, 1936	192.9	900	25,023	12,511.50
Cincinnati, Ohio, 50th anniversary as music center	Mar. 31, 1936	192.9	900	15,016	7,508.00
Long Island, N.Y., Tercentennial	Apr. 13, 1936	192.9	900	100,053	50,026.50
Great Lakes Exposition — Cleveland, Ohio, Centennial	May 5, 1936	192.9	900	50,030	25,015.00
New Rochelle, N.Y., 250th anniversary	do.	192.9	900	25,015	12,507.50
Bridgeport, Conn., Centennial	May 15, 1936	192.9	900	25,015	12,507.50
Wisconsin Centennial	do.	192.9	900	25,015	12,507.50
Swedes' landing in Delaware, Tercentennial	do.	192.9	900	25,015	12,507.50

Silver coinage

Denomination	Authorizing act	Standard weight (Grains)	Standard fineness (Thousandths)	Total coined to Dec. 31, 1986 (Pieces)	(Face Value)
Lynchburg, Va., Sesquicentennial	May 28, 1936	192.9	900	20,013	10,006.50
Albany, N.Y., 250th anniversary ..	June 16, 1936	192.9	900	25,013	12,506.50
Elgin, Ill., Centennial	do.	192.9	900	25,015	12,507.50
Battle of Gettysburg, 75th anniversary	do.	192.9	900	50,028	25,014.00
Roanoke Island, N.C., 350th anniversary	June 24, 1936	192.9	900	50,030	25,015.00
San Francisco-Oakland Bay Bridge	June 26, 1936	192.9	900	100,055	50,027.50
York County, Maine, Tercentennial	do.	192.9	900	25,015	12,507.50
Battle of Antietam, 75th anniversary	June 24, 1937	192.9	900	50,028	25,014.00
Norfolk, Va., Tercentennial of land grant and Bicentennial of city	June 28, 1937	192.9	900	25,013	12,506.50
Iowa Centennial	Aug. 7, 1946	192.9	900	100,057	50,028.50
Booker T. Washington	do.	192.9	900	3,167,205	1,583,602.50
Booker T. Washington — George Washington Carver	Sept. 21, 1951 amending act of Aug. 7, 1946	192.9	900	2,422,392	1,211,196.00
George Washington[11]	Dec. 23, 1981	192.9	900		
Quarter dollar.....................	Apr. 2, 1792	104	892.4		
Do............................	Jan. 18, 1837	103.125	900	4,444,428,069	1,111,107,017.25
Do............................	Feb. 21, 1853	96	900		
Do............................	Feb. 12, 1873	6 96.45	900		
Quarter dollar, commemorative: Columbian Exposition	Mar. 3, 1893	96.45	900	40,023	10,005.75
20 cents [7]	Mar. 3, 1875	8 77.16	900	1,355,000	271,000.00
Dime	Apr. 2, 1792	41.6	892.4		
Do............................	Jan. 18, 1837	41.25	900	9,887,550,205	988,755,020.50
Do............................	Feb. 21, 1853	38.4	900		
Do............................	Feb. 12, 1873	9 38.58	900		
Half dime [10]	Apr. 2, 1792	20.8	892.4		
Do. [10]	Jan. 18, 1837	20.825	900	97,604,388	4,880,219.40
Do. [10]	Feb. 21, 1853	19.2	900		
3 cents [10].........................	Mar. 3, 1851	12.375	750		
Do. [10]	Mar. 3, 1853	11.52	900	42,736,240	1,282,087.20
Total silver				**17,123,584,252**	**3,877,054,052.10**

[1] Dollar of 1792 discontinued by act of Jan. 18, 1837; dollar of 1837 discontinued by act of Feb. 12, 1873.

[2] Silver-dollar coinage:

Act Apr. 2, 1792:		
From 1792 to 1805...	$ 1,439,517	
During 1836	1,000	
		$ 1,440,517
Act Jan. 18, 1837: From 1839 to Feb. 12, 1873		6,590,721
Act Feb. 28, 1878 (Bland-Allison Act)		378,166,793
Act July 14, 1890 (Sherman Act), to date of repeal of purchasing clause thereof		
Oct. 31, 1893...	$ 36,087,285	
Act Nov. 1, 1893, to June 12, 1898	42,139,872	
Act June 13, 1898, war revenue bill.....................................	108,800,188	
		187,027,345
Act Mar. 3, 1887 and 1891, trade-dollar conversion		5,078,472
Act Apr. 23, 1918, Pittman Act replacement (represents equivalent number of dollars converted into bullion — 259,121,554 for export to India and 11,111,168 for domestic subsidiary coin):		
Old design, since Feb. 21, 1921	$ 86,730,000	
Peace dollar, since Dec. 21, 1921	183,502,722	
		270,232,722

Authority for coinage

Act May 12, 1933 (sec. 43), Executive proclamation, Dec. 21, 1933.	7,021,528
Act June 19, 1934 (sec. 7), Executive proclamation, Aug. 9, 1934	53,029
Total	855,611,127

[3] Coinage limited to export demand by joint resolution July 22, 1876. Redeemed $7,689,036 at face amount under act Mar. 3, 1887, converted into 5,078,472 standard dollars and $2,889,011 subsidiary silver coin.
[4] Discontinued by act of Mar. 3, 1887.
[5] 12½ grams, or 192.9 grains.
[6] 6¼ grams, or 96.45 grains.
[7] Discontinued by act of May 2, 1878.
[8] 5 grams, or 77.16 grains.
[9] 2½ grams, or 38.58 grains.
[10] Discontinued by act of Feb. 12, 1873.
[11] George Washington commemorative half dollar authorized Dec. 23, 1981, was authorized to be struck in 1982 and 1983 with the 1982 date to commemorate the 250th anniversary of Washington's birth.
[12] Weight given in grams, not grains.

Composite coinage

Denomination	Authorizing act	Standard Weight and composition	Total pieces coined
Dollar	Dec. 30, 1970	22.68 grams clad composition[1]	384,498,701
Numismatic	Dec. 30, 1970	24.59 grams silver-clad[2]	14,784,064
Dollar (Bicentennial)	Oct. 18, 1973		220,565,274
Dollar (Anthony)	Oct. 10, 1978		
Half dollar	July 23, 1965	11.50 grams silver-clad[3]	844,273,423
	Dec. 30, 1970	11.34 grams clad composition[1]	1,381,767,824
Bicentennial	Oct. 18, 1973	11.5 grams silver-clad[4]	521,873,243
Statue of Liberty	July 9, 1985	11.34 grams clad composition[1]	
Quarter	July 23, 1965	5.67 grams clad composition[1]	8,010,526,612
Bicentennial	Oct. 18, 1973	5.75 grams silver-clad[4]	1,425,990,155
Dime	July 23, 1965	2.268 grams clad composition[1]	11,039,144,438

[1] Clad composition consists of an outer cladding of 75 percent copper and 25 percent nickel bonded to a core of pure copper.
[2] The One Bank Holding Company Act of 1970 authorized the striking of silver-clad Eisenhower dollars, consisting of outer cladding of 800 parts silver, 200 parts copper, bonded to a core of approximately 209 parts silver, 791 parts copper. It also authorized striking of clad composition half dollars.
[3] The Coinage Act of 1965 authorized striking of 40 percent half dollars of the same silver-clad composition as described in (2).
[4] Bicentennial coinage was authorized for production as ordinary clad composition coinage (per number one), and as special numismatic coins struck in silver-clad composition (per number 2).

Minor coinage[1]

Denomination	Authorizing act	Standard weight (Grains)	Standard composition (Percent)	Total coined
5 cents	May 16, 1866	77.16	75 copper, 25 nickel	
Do.	Feb. 12, 1873	77.16	do.	15,384,163,214
Do.	(²)	77.16	56 copper, 35 silver, 9 manganese	869,923,700
3 cents[3]	Mar. 3, 1865	30	75 copper, 25 nickel	
Do.[3]	Feb. 12, 1873	30	do.	31,378,316
2 cents[4]	Apr. 22, 1864	96	95 copper, 5 tin and zinc	45,601,000

Denomination	Authorizing act	Standard weight (Grains)	Standard composition (Percent)	Total coined
1 cent..........	Apr. 2, 1792	264	100 copper	
Do............	Jan. 14, 1793	208	do.........................	156,288,744
Do............	Jan. 26, 1796	168	do.........................	
Do. [6]..........	Jan. 18, 1837	168	do.........................	
Do. [7]..........	Feb. 21, 1857	72	88 copper, 12 nickel	200,772,000
Do............	Apr. 22, 1864	48	Bronze and copper-zinc, with	
Do............	Feb. 12, 1873	48	95 copper and 5 zinc and	115,220,965,665
Do............	([8])	48	tin or 5 zinc. [8] [9]	
Do............	([9])	48		
Do............	Dec. 23, 1942[10]	41.5	Steel covered with zinc coat-	
Do............	May 15, 1943[10]	42.5	ing not to exceed .001 inch	1,093,838,670
Do............	Oct. 11, 1974	2.5[12]	pure copper plated to zinc planchet	
Half cent	Apr. 2, 1792	132	100 copper	
Do............	Jan. 14, 1793	104	do.........................	
Do............	Jan. 25, 1796[5]	84	do.........................	7,981,822
Do. [6]..........	Jan. 18, 1837	84	do	

[1] Minor coinage by law was confined to the Mint at Philadelphia until the act of Apr. 24, 1906. Minor coins were first manufactured at Philadelphia in 1793, at San Francisco in 1908, and at Denver in 1911.

[2] Coined under provisions of act of Mar. 27, 1942, as amended by act of Dec. 28, 1945. Coinage extended from Oct. 1, 1942 until expiration of authority Dec. 31, 1945.

[3] Discontinued by act of Sept. 26, 1890.

[4] Discontinued by act of Feb. 12, 1873.

[5] Proclamation of the President in conformity with act of Mar. 3, 1795.

[6] Discontinued by act of Feb. 21, 1857.

[7] Discontinued by act of Apr. 22, 1864.

[8] Alloy of 95 percent copper and 5 percent zinc coined 1944-46 by order of Secretary of the Treasury of Dec. 16, 1943, pursuant to act of Dec. 18, 1942.

[9] Tin was eliminated from the bronze alloy by act of Sept. 5, 1962.

[10] Order of Secretary of the Treasury pursuant to act of Dec. 18, 1942.

[11] In October 1974, Congress authorized the Secretary of the Treasury, whenever the situation was warranted in order to preserve and protect the issuance of United States coinage, to alter the composition of the cent. Originally, it was thought that this would become an aluminum cent. What ultimately emerged was nothing, until 1982, when the Secretary made a determination that the coinage supply was critical, meaning that the price of copper would soon exceed the face value of the coin. The composition was then changed to a 99.2 percent zinc, 0.8 percent copper planchet plated with pure copper, for a total content of 97.5 percent zince, 2.5 percent copper. It may be changed again at any time without approval of Congress.

[12] Weight specified in grams, not grains.

Source: United States Mint

Government Marketing of Commemorative Coins

One of the most interesting aspects in recent times has been the marketing by the government of commemorative coins. The Treasury has managed to go to non-traditional sources, including the banking community. One of the reasons that the banking community has been a non-traditional source has been that fact that, at least among bank examiners, acquisition of coins for purposes of disposition to the public was frowned upon. A 1981 directive prohibited national banks from buying or selling coins except in very narrow circumstances. Banking circular 58

(revised) supplement 1, dated Dec. 28, 1983, concerned the sale of commemorative coins. Its contents appear below.

To: Chief Executive Officer of All National Banks, Deputy Comptrollers/Regional Administrators, and Examining Personnel. Purpose: This banking circular provides general guidelines for national banks which are considering purchasing and reselling or acting as agent in the sale of commemorative coins minted by the Bureau of the Mint for the U.S. Department of the Treasury. Policy BC - 58 (REV) dated 11-3-81 states that national banks are prohibited from buying or selling coins the value of which is not based on metallic content. The Circular makes it clear that banks may not speculate by purchasing coins, such as rare coins, the value of which is based upon such factors as rarity, age, condition, a mistake in the minting or other intangible factors. Commemorative coins are minted by the Bureau of the Mint for the U.S. Department of the Treasury. The coins commemorate events such as George Washington's birthday, the Olympic Games and other events of national importance. The fixed price of such coins is based upon the cost of the metal, production, distribution and, in the case of the Olympic coins, a surcharge earmarked for contribution to the U.S. Olympic Committee. National banks may take such commemorative coins on a consignment basis and act as selling agent for the Department of the Treasury. National banks may also choose to purchase an inventory of commemorative coins for resale to their customers. Prudence and care should be exercised by Boards of Directors in formulating policies and procedures when purchasing commemorative coins. Dollar limits on coin inventories should be consistent with safe and sound banking practices. Accounting Commemorative coins purchased by a national bank should be recorded as "Other Assets". The bank's books should reflect the lower of cost or market value with adjustments made monthly. This is consistent with the accounting treatment stated in BC-58 (Rev). Originating Office, Chief National Bank Examiner's Office, Commercial Examinations Division (202) 447-1165.

Sales tax and numismatic items

Perhaps no more emotional issue has recently surfaced among collectors than the right of various states to impose sales tax on coin and bullion purchases. There are several states, of course, that have no sales tax at all (Alaska, Delaware, Montana, New Hampshire and Oregon), and others who have (by statute or regulation or court fight) altered the use of sales tax collection on numismatic sales.

Sometimes the dispute centers around precious metal coinage such as the South African Krugerrand, the Canadian Maple Leaf, and other coins bought as much for their bullion value as a brick of gold would be. (In most states, even with sales taxes, commodities such as gold and silver are not taxed on acquisition.)

Purchases of what is frequently termed "monetized" bullion are permitted in several other states: California, Connecticut, Idaho, Illinois, Louisiana, North Dakota, Rhode Island, Texas and Utah. There, if the minimum is met (frequently $1,000), no sales tax is collectible.

There are a number of states, like New Jersey, which do not tax the sales of gold and silver in the stores thereof (Statute, Title 54, Sec. 32B-8.32).

In some other locales, for example Florida, sales of Krugerrands are not subject to sales tax because they have been judicially declared to be coin of the realm — the same as a Kennedy half dollar sold for 50 cents.

When collectors buy by mail from a dealer in another state, whether or not that state has sales tax or not, there is no obligation for the selling merchant to collect the tax and remit it to the state where the buyer resides. The purchaser is, however, under an obligation to pay what is called a "compensating use tax" on the purchase. Until recently, as New York State officials once acknowledged, the compensating use tax had been on the books for more than a dozen years and there were no forms available, anywhere in the state, to allow someone to do so except in the case of the purchase of an automobile.

That, however, is in the process of changing. States in the Great Lakes region recently signed an agreement to collect use taxes by out-of-state purchasers. The individual states began notifying merchants in early 1987 that they would be required to collect use taxes in addition to sales taxes.

Because sales taxes are usually considered to be "trust" funds, and subject a collector to personal liability, it is suggested that questions regarding them be referred to competent tax counsel.

Regulations by governmental agencies

In order for various laws and procedures to be effected and have public impact, governmental agencies must frequently write rules and regulations to explain the impact, and state how a particular course of action or conduct is to be carried out. As a means of internal government, comparable rules are required within each government agency or bureau.

Rules written by each of the governmental

agencies must first be published in the *Federal Register,* a daily government publication. When the tentative plans are approved, they are annually compiled into a many volumed set known as the *Code of Federal Regulations,* usually abbreviated CFR. In the CFR are all the necessary requirements for operating entities such as the United States Mint and the Bureau of Engraving and Printing, as well as actions that the U.S. Customs Service can take against attempted importation of counterfeit coins.

Often, it is the governmental interpretation of a statute in the CFR that is the dominant factor in enforcement, rather than the law itself. This is true, for example, in the case of the Hobby Protection Act, whose regulations promulgated by the Federal Trade Commission are the keystone of its effectiveness.

Below are reprinted in edited form selected sections from the CFR that pertain to numismatics. The volume of the CFR that the material appears in precedes the Code, while the section follows it. The year of publication of the volume appears in parentheses following this. Thus, 16 CFR sec. 304.1(d) would refer to Volume 16 of the Code of Federal Regulations at Section 304.1 (d), which was printed by the government in 1977.

United States Customs Service
Counterfeit Coins, Obligations and Other Securities; Illustrations or Reproduction of Coins or Stamps
19 CFR Sec. 12.48 Importation prohibited; exception to prohibition of importation; procedure.

(a) In accordance with Chapter 25, Title 18, United States Code, any token, disk, or device in the likeness or similitude of any coin of the United States or of a foreign country; counterfeits of coins in circulation in the United States; counterfeited, forged, or altered obligations or other securities of the United States[31] or of any foreign government; or plates, dies, or other apparatus which may be used in making any of the foregoing, when brought into the United States, shall be seized, and delivered to the nearest representative of the United States Secret Service, together with a report of the facts, for appropriate disposition.

(b) In accordance with Section 504 of Title 18, United States Code, the printing, publishing, or importation or the making or importation of the necessary plates for such printing or publishing for philatelic, numismatic, educational, historical, or newsworthy purposes in articles, books, journals, newspapers, or albums (but not for advertising purposes, except illustrations of stamps and paper money in philatelic or numismatic advertising of legitimate numismatists and dealers in stamps or publishers of or dealers in philatelic or numismatic articles, books, journals, newspapers, or albums) of black and white illustrations of canceled and uncanceled United States postage stamps shall be permitted.

(c) The importation (but not for advertising purposes except philatelic advertising) of motion-picture films, microfilms, or slides, for projection upon a screen or for use in telecasting, of postage and revenue stamps and other obligations and securities of the United States and postage and revenue stamps, notes, bonds, and other obligations or securities of any foreign government, bank or corporation shall be permitted.

(d) Printed matter of the character described in Section 504, Title 18, United States Code[32], containing reproductions of postage or revenue stamps, executed in accordance with any exception stated in Section 504, or colored reproductions of canceled foreign postage stamps may be admitted to entry. Printed matter containing illustrations or reproductions not executed in accordance with such exceptions shall be treated as prohibited importations. If no application for exportation or assent to forfeiture and destruction is received by the district director within 30 days from the date of notification to the importer that the articles are prohibited, the articles shall be reported to the United States attorney for forfeiture.

It should be noted that the Supreme Court has declared the plenary statutory section under which this has been enacted, unconstitutional. The regulation, likewise, should follow. No change, however, has been made.

Footnotes
[31]"The term 'obligation or other security of the United States' includes all bonds, certificates of indebtedness, national bank currency, Federal Reserve notes, Federal Reserve Bank notes, coupons, United States notes, Treasury notes, gold certificates, silver certificates, fractional notes, certificates of deposits, bills, checks, or drafts for money, drawn by or upon authorized officers of the United States, stamps and other representatives of value, of whatever denomination, issued under any act of Congress, and canceled United States stamps." (18 U.S.C. 8.)

[32]Notwithstanding any other provision of this chapter, the following are permitted:
(1) The printing, publishing, or importation, or the making or importation of the nec-

essary plates for such printing or publishing, or illustrations of:

(A) Postage stamps of the United States,

(B) Revenue stamps of the United States,

(C) Any other obligation or other security of the United States, and

(D) Postage stamps, revenue stamps, notes, bonds, and any other obligation or other security of any foreign government, bank, or corporation, for philatelic, numismatic, educational, historical, or newsworthy purposes in articles, books, journals, newspapers, or albums (but not for advertising purposes, except illustrations of stamps and paper money in philatelic or numismatic advertising of legitimate numismatists and dealers in stamps or publishers of or dealers in philatelic or numismatic articles, books, journals, newspapers, or albums). Illustrations permitted by the foregoing provisions of this section shall be made in accordance with the following conditions—

(i) All illustrations shall be in black and white, except that illustrations of postage stamps issued by the United States or by any foreign government may be in color;

(ii) All illustrations (including illustrations of uncanceled postage stamps in color) shall be of a size less than three-fourths or more than one and one-half, in linear dimension, of each part of any matter so illustrated which is covered by subparagraph (A), (B), (C), or (D) of this paragraph, except that black and white illustrations of postage and revenue stamps issued by the United States or by any foreign government and colored illustrations of canceled postage stamps issued in the United States may be in the exact linear dimension in which the stamps were issued; and

(iii) The negatives and plates used in making the illustrations shall be destroyed after their final use in accordance with this section.

(2) The making or importation, but not for advertising purposes except philatelic advertising, of motion-picture films, microfilms, or slides, for projection upon a screen or for use in telecasting, of postage and revenue stamps and other obligations and securities of the United States, and postage and revenue stamps, notes, bonds, and other obligations or securities of any foreign government, bank, or corporation. No prints or other reproductions shall be made from such films or slides, except for the purposes of paragraph (1), without the permission of the Secretary of the Treasury.

For the purposes of this section the term "postage stamp" includes "postage meter stamps." (18 U.S.C. 504).

Coins across borders

A U.S. Customs Service advisory, issued Oct. 13, 1976, in response to the American Numismatic Association inquiry concerning the transport of coins to Canada and back into the United States, suggests consultation with a Customs pamphlet, "Know Before You Go," which contains general information of interest to all U.S. residents who travel to a foreign country. Restraints on gold coins were lifted on Dec. 31, 1974.

Dealers may wish to take the coins they plan to carry to Canada to the Customs office nearest them, and register them on Customs Form 4455, certificate of registration. A copy of the form will be given to the dealers to present to U.S. Customs on their return from Canada. This will facilitate the identification of the coins on their return to the United States.

With regard to coins which dealers purchase in Canada, the Customs Service has ruled that metal coins issued or specifically authorized by the government whose coinage it is, including official restrikes or exact copies authorized by the government concerned, are classifiable under the provision for metal coins in item 653.22, Tariff Schedules of the United States (TSUS), and are free of duty.

The Customs Service has also had occasion to issue a ruling with respect to certain unofficial reproductions of various gold coins manufactured by a foreign private Mint. In brief, these unofficial reproductions are generally under the provision for articles of precious metal, of gold, including rolled gold, in item 656.10, TSUS, and dutiable at the rate of 20 percent ad valorem.

Also, these gold pieces would be subject to the marking requirements of the Hobby Protection Act as imitation numismatic items, and must be marked "Copy" if imported into the United States, pursuant to regulations issued by the Federal Trade Commission.

Finally, if the unofficial gold pieces were manufactured in a country other than the country of issuance as shown on the faces of the pieces, they would be required to be marked "Made in (name of country)" pursuant to 19 U.S.C. 1304 and Section 134.47 of the Customs Regulations.

All coins imported into the United States for non-monetary purposes (for example, for resale or numismatic purposes) are considered merchandise subject to Customs entry requirements, even though they are free of duty. Therefore, if the coins are part of a dealer's personal hand-carried baggage, they should be reported on the back side of Customs Declaration Form 6059-B as articles acquired while abroad. The District Director of the port of entry has the discretion to require a formal Customs entry to be made if he feels that the particular importation could be handled more properly by such an entry procedure.

In any event, the value which should be declared for the coins should be the actual numismatic value of the coins in the place where they were purchased. Ordinarily, this would mean that the importer would declare as value the price which he actually paid for the coins and this does of course include an equivalent valuation of foreign currency.

An individual collector who took his collection to Canada solely for viewing could return his collection to the United States free of duty, pursuant to item 813.10, Tariff Schedules of the United States, which exempts from duty personal and household effects taken abroad by a person who is a returning resident of the United States. For a dealer who is in the business of buying and selling these reproductions or commemorative medals, however, these items would not be considered his personal effects and, accordingly, this exemption would not be applicable.

A dealer could bring back his unofficial reproductions or medals free of duty as tools of trade or samples for taking orders under Section 10.68 of the Customs Regulations if he took the articles to Canada for the sole purpose of viewing and taking orders. Unless such merchandise is imported under carnet, the dealer must register it on Customs Form 4455 at the time of exportation and file an appropriate entry or declaration at the time of return.

If the dealer is taking such merchandise out for sale or if he sells some of the merchandise, he is liable for the duty on the returning items. If not all the medals or reproductions listed on CF 4455 are returned,

there will be a presumption that the missing medals were sold and the returning ones will be dutiable, unless the dealer can show Customs that the missing medals were not sold.

With regard to medals, Customs has held that they are classifiable as articles of metal depending on the metal they are composed of, under one of the items 656.10, 656.15, or 657.35 TSUS. Item 656.10 TSUS, applies to articles of gold (20 percent ad valorem), item 656.15 TSUS, applies to articles of silver (10.5 percent ad valorem), and item 657.35 TSUS applies to articles of bronze (0.6 cents/lb. plus 7.5 percent ad valorem). Some medals could, in fact be jewelry, if designed as objects of personal adornment, i.e., if the medal has a loop for attaching with a neck chain or ribbon.

For further information regarding procedures for taking rare coins into Canada and returning them, collectors and dealers can write to Customs and Excise, Connaught Building, Sussex Drive, Ottawa, Ontario, Canada KIA-OL5, for information and guidance.

For those importing and exporting coins, there are currency control requirements both in the exporting country and the importing country that must be taken into consideration. In the case of the United States, where items are still a legal tender they must be reported if on your person and in an amount exceeding $5,000. (No duty is charged, but the sum must be reported; not to do so is a serious violation of the law.) In the case of exporting countries, there is also the added requirement (particularly true in the case of ancient coins) that the national patrimony not be unduly disturbed in a manner violative of the UNESCO convention regulating removal of antiquities.

It is also useful to remember that reproductions of coins must also be in accordance with the marking requirements of the Hobby Protection Act to be eligible for importation into the United States.

The 1986 Tax Act made modest duty changes for some items. See Page 143.

Treasury, Secret Service advisory policies

Following is a guide to Treasury and Secret Service advisory policies frequently requested by *Coin World* readers. These policies are interpretations the Treasury has made of various parts of the U.S. Code dealing with numismatics.

Coin jewelry

Most coin jewelry, including cut-out coinage and engraved coinage, is legal, according to the present interpretation of Sec. 331, Title 18, United States Code, which prohibits fraudulent mutilation of coins.

Coin jewelry is not prohibited by this section in the absence of fraud and treating of the coins used to produce these novelties. Manufacture and sale of two-headed and two-tailed coins are also legal according to the Secret Service.

This opinion is advisory only, and is not binding upon the Department of Justice or any U.S. attorney, however, according to the Secret Service.

The official Treasury Department statement pertaining to coin jewelry is: "Section 331, Title 18, U.S. Code, prohibits the fraudulent alteration and mutilation of United States and foreign coins, but does not prohibit said defacement if done without fraudulent intent, or if the mutilated coins are not used fraudulently.

"The Bureau of the Mint feels that it is unfortunate that laws at this time do not specifically prohibit this undesirable and reprehensible practice.

"The Mint also has very strong feelings about disfigurement of United States coins or their use other than as a means of exchange. If the practice cannot otherwise be prevented, the Mint would strongly support legislation prohibiting this use of coins.

"Coins so withdrawn from circulation must be replaced and when practiced on a wholesale scale by many firms, an unnecessary cost and burden is imposed upon the Mint."

Coin replicas

Sec. 489, Title 18, United States Code, prohibits making, importing, possessing with intent to sell, give away or use in any manner, any token, disk or device in the likeness or similitude as to design, color or inscription of any of the coins of the United States, or of any foreign country.

This section is directed at devices which, although not strictly counterfeit coins, may be mistaken for genuine coins by unwary persons, because they approximate genuine coins in size, color, design and inscription.

However, items made to sell, give away or use in any manner, which are substantially larger and heavier than any coin of the United States, or any coin of a foreign country, and which do not bear any indication of value and therefore do not purport to be money, do not violate Sec. 489.

The policy of the Treasury regarding substantially enlarged replicas of coins is that any coin reproduction must be more than twice the size of a United States dollar coin, the largest United States coin. Consequently, all reproductions must be more than three inches in diameter. Thickness of the item is not material, according to the Treasury.

The manufacture of a raised impression of a coin is considered to be in violation of Sec. 489, if the impression is removable; approximately the size of a genuine coin; and is sufficiently in likeness of a genuine coin to be capable of being passed off as such.

Gold-plated coins

Since the gold regulations were amended April 19, 1971, it has been legal to obtain, hold, transport, import or export any gold-plated coins.

These restrictions were imposed to prevent the diversion of coins to decorative uses during the coin shortage of the 1960s. Since all coins are now in ample supply, such restrictions became unnecessary, according to the Treasury Department.

Paper money reproductions

According to Title 18, U.S. Code, Section 504, and other sections of the U.S. Code, printed illustrations of paper money, checks, bonds and other obligations and securities of the United States and foreign governments are permissible for numismatic, educational, historical and newsworthy purposes, and for numismatic or philatelic advertising but not for general advertising purposes.

Illustrations must be in black and white and must be less than three-fourths or more than one and one-half times the size of the genuine instrument. No individual facsimiles of such obligations are permitted, and no illustrations of paper money, checks or bonds may be in color.

Several years ago, Time Inc. challenged the regulations, and for a time succeeded in having them declared unconstitutional. In mid-1984, however, the U.S. Supreme Court, in a major decision interpreting the statute, declared that the regulations were valid insofar as they prohibited color reproduction of paper currency and required illustrations to be black and white, and of a particular size.

To meet these regulations, paper money art reproduction must be at least these measurements:

Fractional Currency

Actual size: sizes vary; smallest note is the 3-cent third issue note, measuring 39mm by 64mm; largest note in width is the 50-cent third issue, measuring 46mm by 133mm; deepest note is the Crawford 50-cent fifth issue note at 52mm by 108mm.

Unless exact note size is known so as to comply with legal requirements, illustrations should be at least 2¼x3¾ in. (58.5 x 96mm) or smaller than 1⅛ by 1⅞ in. (29.25 x 48mm).

Small Size Paper Money
(Including Federal Reserve notes, silver certificates, etc.)

Actual size: 6⅛ x 2⅝ in. or 156 x 67mm
Over 1½: 9¼ x 4 in. or 235 x 102mm
Under ¾: 4 19/32 x 1 31/32 in. or 117 x 50mm

Large Size Paper Money

Actual size: 7½ x 3⅛ in. or 191 x 79mm
Over 1½: 11¼ x 4¾ in. or 286 x 121mm
Under ¾: 5⅝ x 2 7/32 in. or 143 x 56mm

To be permissible, an illustration must be accompanied by numismatic, educational, historical or newsworthy information relating directly to the item that is illustrated, according to the Treasury.

Insofar as this purports to allow the government to examine newspapers for the "educational" content of their illustrations, the Supreme Court ruling declares that this is indeed unconstitutional. But the bulk of the requirement remains.

Motion-picture films, microfilms and slides of paper money, checks, bonds and other obligations and securities of the United States and foreign governments are permitted in black and white or in color for projection upon a screen or for use in telecasting. They may not be used for advertising purposes, except philatelic or numismatic advertising.

However, Treasury regulations permit the illustration of United States bonds in connection with a campaign to sell of such bonds.

The plates and negatives, including glossy prints, of any United States or foreign obligations produced for any of these purposes must be destroyed after their final use for the purpose for which they were made.

Notes issued by the various states are not obligations or securities of the United States, and it is probable that most of them do not resemble such obligations or securities.

In some cases, however, it has been found that certain features appearing on such notes, such as the numerals and lettering, bear a close resemblance to the corresponding features of genuine currency of the United States. In such cases, the reproduction of such features would constitute a technical violation of the U.S.Code.

Defacing paper money

Sec. 333 of Title 18 of the U.S. Code prohibits, among other things, mutilating, cutting, defacing, disfiguring, or perforating or uniting or cementing together any National Bank or Federal Reserve note with intent to render such currency unfit to be reissued.

Instances such as dollar bills embedded in jewelry, or portraits of popular persons superimposed on Federal Reserve notes as souvenirs do not usually constitute intent to render the currency unfit to be reissued, and so are not prohibited.

Stamp reproduction

Printed illustrations of canceled and uncanceled United States postage stamps are permissible for articles, books, journals, newspapers or albums for philatelic, educational, historical and newsworthy purposes.

Black and white illustrations may be of any size. Colored illustrations of canceled United States postage stamps may be of any size. However, illustrations in color of uncanceled United States postage stamps must be less than three-fourths or more than one and one-half times and size of the genuine stamp.

Printed illustrations of canceled foreign stamps in black and white or color are permissible in any size and for any purpose.

Black and white and color illustrations of uncanceled foreign postage stamps are permitted for philatelic, educational, historical and newsworthy purposes. Black and white illustrations may be of any size, but color illustrations must be more than one and one-half times the size of the genuine stamp, or less than three-fourths times its size.

Motion-picture films and slides of postage stamps are permissible in black and white or in color for projection upon a screen or for use in telecasting. They are not permissible for advertising purposes except for philatelic advertising.

Black and white illustrations of canceled and uncanceled United States and foreign postage stamps, as well as colored illustrations of canceled postage stamps are permissible in any size, for philatelic advertising. Uncanceled colored illustrations of United States and foreign postage stamps are permitted for philatelic advertising, but must meet the three-fourths or one and one-half size restrictions.

Canceled U.S. and foreign postage stamps must bear an official cancellation mark, i.e., the stamps must have been used for postage.

Regulations for printed illustrations of United States and foreign revenue stamps are the same as for postage stamps, except that colored illustrations of United States revenue stamps are not permitted.

Coin reproductions

Photographs or printed illustrations, motion-picture films or slides of United States and foreign coins may be used for any purpose including advertising.

With few exceptions, existing law generally prohibits the manufacture, sale or use of any token, disk or device in the likeness or similitude of any coins which are issued as money.

Scrip

Congress has enacted legislation to prevent scrip certificates from circulating as or in lieu of lawful money. Sec. 336 of Title 18 of the U.S. Code prohibits the making, issuing, circulating, or payment out of any obligation of less than a dollar "intended to circulate as money or to be received or used in lieu of lawful money of the United States."

After analyzing the statute and the cases interpreting it the Treasury has ruled that scrip redeemable only in merchandise and not in coin or currency, that is not negotiable and that is redeemable only at the particular store location where issued would not be in violation of the statute.

The Treasury is still examining the question of whether scrip that is redeemable at more than one store under single ownership or franchise would violate the statute.

Commission of Fine Arts

The Commission of Fine Arts was established by the Act of May 17, 1910. Since then it has frequently been called upon by Congress to make determinations with respect to coin designs. A portion of the enabling Act, now codified in Title 40 of the United States Code, follows:

40 US Code, Section 104. Commission of Fine Arts

A permanent Commission of Fine Arts is created to be composed of seven well-qualified judges of the fine arts, who shall be appointed by the president, and shall serve for a period of four years each, and until their successors are appointed and qualified. The president shall have authority to fill all vacancies. It shall be the duty of each commission to advise upon the location of statues, fountains and monuments in public squares, streets and parks in the District of Columbia, and upon the selection of models for statues, fountains and monuments erected under the authority of the United States and upon the selection of artists for the execution of the same. . . The commission shall also advise generally upon questions of art when required to do so by the president, or by any committee of either house of Congress. . .

Copyright law revision

Public Law 94-553 (S 22), an act for the general revision of Copyright Law, Title 17 of the United States Code, was signed into law October 19, 1976.

Inquires should go to: Copyright Office, Library of Congress, Crystal Mall Annex, Arlington, Va. 20559.

Tax Act Changes of 1986

One effect of the 1986 Tax Act was to add a customs duties surcharge to all imported items, including gold and silver coinage and medals. Its effect on collectors is minimal but it has had impact on pricing by sellers and importers.

The Treasury   4

History of the Treasury Department

Even before the signing of the Declaration of Independence, the Continental Congress provided by resolution on Feb. 17, 1776, "that a committee of five be appointed for superintending the Treasury." During the first session of the Constitutional Congress, a law "to establish the Treasury Department" was enacted on Sept. 2, 1789. This was only six months after the Constitution became the basic law of the land on March 4, 1789.

For several years Philadelphia was the temporary capital of the nation. When plans to move the seat of government to Washington were made, they included recommendations for a Treasury building. This building, located on the east side of the site of the present building, was completed in 1799 and occupied in 1800 by the 69 employees of Treasury, seven employees (total employment) of the State Department, and some personnel of the Navy Department.

This first building was partially destroyed by fire in 1801. Repaired, it continued to house Treasury personnel until 1814, when a fire set by the British as a spectacle for an invading army destroyed the building.

Following withdrawal of the British forces, prompt authority was granted for a new Treasury building. Once again the Treasury fell victim to a fire when the second structure and most of its contents were destroyed in the early morning of March 31, 1833. A searching investigation authorized by President Jackson led to the arrest of two brothers who were charged with setting the fire to destroy certain papers which would prove fraudulent conduct by persons engaged as Treasury agents. One brother was finally acquitted after four trials because of the statute of limita-

tions, while the other was sentenced to 10 years in prison.

Apparently the next three years left the department without a home of its own, but on July 4, 1836, Congress authorized the construction of a "fireproof building of such dimensions as may be required for the present and future accommodations" of the Treasury Department. Perhaps the building when completed in 1842 was an imposing structure at the time, but it fell far short of providing accommodations for the future. Having cost less than $700,000, the building, which is now only a part of the east wing, contained 150 rooms.

It was necessary in a few years to enlarge the building, and Congress in March of 1855 granted authority to extend the building. Construction of what is now the south wing was begun in July 1855 and completed in September 1861. The Civil War more or less interrupted further construction, but by 1864 the west wing had been carried up to the line of the present north facade.

The department continued to grow, and the government building housing the Department of State was removed from the north area of the site to make room for the north wing which was completed in 1869.

On its way up

Thus, after more than a third of a century, the Treasury building became the structure originally intended. But one of the results of its expansion was the violation of the original plan for the city — to leave unobstructed the view from the White House to the Capitol. The building as it is today is estimated to have cost approximately $8 million.

Because early planning had the entire official city facing the canal which at one time ran through downtown Washington where the mall is now located, the south entrances of both the White House and the Treasury building are the historical front entrances of the buildings. However, as the city grew, the north entrance of the White House became its front entrance; and many people think of the 15th Street entrance to the Treasury as its main entrance, perhaps because it is the easiest to enter since the other three have long flights of stone steps.

The stone used in the south, west and north wings was quarried on Dix Island, near Rockland, Maine, and transported in sailing vessels. The facades are adorned by monolithic columns of the Ionic order, each 36 feet tall, each costing $5,000 and weighing 30 tons. There are 34 of these pillars on the 15th Street side of the building, 30 of them forming a colonnade 341 feet long. This colonnade has for many years provided viewing space for inaugural parades and other state functions. There are 18 columns on the west side and 10 each on the north and south sides.

A statue of Alexander Hamilton, first Secretary of the Treasury, is located on the south patio of the building, while a statue of Albert Gallatin, fourth Secretary of the Treasury, who served as Secretary for the longest period of time, 1801 to 1814, is located on the north patio. The grounds of the building — rose gardens at the north and south ends, and grass, magnolia trees and other plants gracing the west side — add much to the beauty of the building.

The interior, although it has been altered many times, reminds one that this is an old building. The deeply worn stone steps leading to all floors show the many years they were used before elevators were installed. Until 1959, even the elevators were nearly collector's items, one having been installed in 1898. Since 1959, all elevators have been replaced by automatic, self-operating cars. There are still signs of the early heating devices in the form of fireplaces, some of which can still be used. The building was originally lighted by oil lamps, and the sanitary accommodations were just as primitive.

Offices for 10 percent

The Treasury building is used primarily for executive offices, the Secretary of the Treasury occupying a suite on the third floor. Despite its size, the building can today accommodate only about 10 percent of all Treasury personnel located in Washington, D.C. More than 20 other buildings house Treasury employees, and it is necessary to rent additional space to meet all needs.

In the basement there are 15 vaults ranging in size from 10-by-16-feet to 50-by-90-feet. Stored therein are currency, coins, bonds and securities. At one time most of the nation's gold and silver bullion was also stored in the vaults, but there are no longer any bulk quantities of bullion located in the Main Treasury building. The vaults are securely protected by combination and time locks and by an electrical protection system which alerts the captain of the guard, the U.S. Secret Service and local police headquarters to any attempt to tamper with the locks or otherwise violate the security of the system. Partially because of these vaults, the building is protected by the Treasury Security Force, supervised by the Secret Service. The basement also houses a pistol range used by the Secret Service and other enforcement personnel to maintain marksmanship. The rest of the basement area is used for maintenance equipment and personnel, store rooms, etc.

The large Cash Room at the north end of the building was often used for special occasions such as the March 4, 1869, inaugural ball for President Grant's first inauguration. However, it was used daily as a check cashing facility and operated well into the early 1970s. Treasury officials then determined the cost of clerical and security personnel could no longer be justified and the room was closed June 30, 1976.

After a brief period of renovation the room was reopened for special events such as the presentation by Treasury officials of a $24 million check to the Statue of Liberty/Ellis Island renovation fund.

In early 1987, the Cash Room was closed for a total floor-to-ceiling renovation. The project was expected to be completed in late summer or early fall of 1987. As part of the continuing renovation of the main Treasury building, the office of the Treasurer Katherine D. Ortega was moved to the second floor, just down the hall from the Cash Room. Her office was formerly used as a vault area years ago and a part of the wall of the vault was discovered during the renovation.

Among the many interesting architectural features of the main Treasury building are the unique stairways that appear somehow to be suspended in mid-air. Actually the steps are cut-worked granite and marble blocks cantilevered from structural walls, partially supported by the arch action of the steps.

The fifth floor, which was formerly the attic, was renovated for office space in 1910. It is also interesting to note that the name of the building was not made a permanent part of the structure until 1958, more than 100 years after the Treasury was built.

Treasury souvenirs

The Treasury no longer maintains an exhibit hall but information about the Treasury as well as the Mint and other Washington D.C. area attractions is available at the Washington Tourist Information Center, 1400 Pennsylvania Ave. NW, (202) 566-5221.

Top officials

In addition to the Secretary of the Treasury and his top staff, the Main Treasury Building houses the top officials of the Office of the Treasurer of the United States, and the Office of the Assistant Secretary for International Affairs. Other important activities of the department, such as the United States Mint, Internal Revenue Service, Engraving and Printing, Customs, the Savings Bonds Division, the U.S. Secret Service, Bureau of the Public Debt, Comptroller of the Currency, and the Bureau of Accounts, are housed in nearby buildings.

Among the activities which once were a part of the Treasury Department and are now parts of other organizations are the Postal Service, until 1829; the General Land Office (now the Interior Department); some of the activities which later were assigned to the Departments of Commerce and Labor in 1903; some of the major functions now assigned to the General Accounting Office; the Public Health Service of the Department of Health, Education, and Welfare; the Public Buildings Service (formerly the Supervising Architect) and the Federal Supply Service (formerly the Procurement Division) of the General Services Administration; the Bureau of the Budget; the United States Coast Guard (now a part of the Department of Transportation); and the Bureau of Narcotics (now the Bureau of Narcotics and Dangerous Drugs of the Department of Justice).

Location for history

In this building were developed the ideas for organizations such as the International Monetary Fund and the International Bank for Reconstruction and Development, and more recently the Inter-American Development Bank and the Asian Development Bank. Also in this building plans were made for the lend-lease program of World War II, and for expediting the building of the United States Air Corps as it was in World War II.

The Treasury Department building has been the locale of a number of interesting events, one of the earliest involving President Jackson who, during the laying of the cornerstone, placed therein a satin-lined case containing a golden lock of the hair of the infant daughter of his confidential adviser and secretary, who was Mrs. Jackson's nephew. This girl, Mary Emily Donelson, was later employed in the Treasury. Today the location of that cornerstone is inaccessible because of the extension of the outer limits of the building.

President Andrew Johnson used one of the Treasury offices on the present third floor as his office immediately following the assassination of President Lincoln, to allow Mrs. Lincoln to move from the White House unhurried. A picture of a Cabinet meeting held in that room testifies to this unusual arrangement.

During World War II a tunnel connected the White House to the Treasury. There was in the basement a furnished shelter area for the President of the United States in case he was unable to avoid enemy attack any other way. During this period the basement of the Treasury would also have served as a refuge for the entire Cabinet, had that been necessary.

As recently as the early 1940s, some of the offices contained important historical documents — the Louisiana Purchase, one of George Washington's travel account books, files containing notes from President Lincoln. These have been turned over to the National Archives and other organizations for preservation.

The First Baptist Church of Washington, D.C., held its first meeting in the building, and in recent years has held commemorative meetings on the south steps. These steps were used during World War II for massive bond rallies in which entertainment celebrities participated to sell war bonds to finance the nation's war effort. They have also been used for inaugurating community chest and other drives.

To help preserve the Treasury building itself, an organization called the Treasury Historical Association was formed Dec. 13, 1973.

Although the Treasury Historical Association was chartered as an "in-house" organization, with memberships open to present and former Treasury employees, members of the public interested in the maintenance and preservation of this important Federal landmark are invited to join the association also.

Treasury Historical Association chairman

is Dr. Charles E. Walker. Applications for membership should be mailed to: Treasury Historical Association, 1500 Pennsylvania Ave. N.W., Washington, D.C. 20220.

Membership categories include:

General, $10, and supporting, $50. These members shall receive a membership card, publications issued by the association periodically, and are eligible for historic tours and to attend quarterly and annual meetings. All members have voting rights.

Patron, $100; members will be listed in the annual report of the association and will receive an engraved certificate.

Sustaining, $250; members will be listed in the annual report of the association and will receive an engraved certificate.

Life sponsor, $500; members will receive membership for life, will be listed in the annual report as those making a regular contribution to the activities of the association, and will receive an engraved certificate.

Life donor, $1,000 or more; members will receive membership for life, will be listed in the annual report as those making a regular contribution to the activities of the association, and will receive an engraved certificate. The names of life donors will be inscribed on a plaque on display in the Treasury Building.

Time capsule

Early in 1976 as part of the Treasury Department's celebration of the Bicentennial, Secretary of the Treasury William E. Simon approved the establishment of a Time Capsule to be dedicated in a ceremony on Sept. 8, 1976, and to be opened by the Secretary of the Treasury in the tricentennial year. The capsule will serve as a symbol to Americans living in the 21st century of 20th century Americans' faith in the nation's future.

Treasury officials were asked to prepare messages to be read by their counterparts in 2076 for inclusion in the capsule. These messages addressed the key issues facing each office or bureau so that future generations of Americans may have a clearer perspective on the times in which we are living. A message from President Gerald R. Ford is included in the contents of the capsule, along with various Bicentennial medals, a $2 bill signed by U.S. Treasurer Francine I. Neff and Secretary Simon, and other contemporary memorabilia. The container itself remained unsealed until the end of the year so that other mementos of the Bicentennial celebration could be included.

The capsule, which measures 40 inches in height, 36 inches at the base, and 30 inches at the top, was designed by the Department's Graphics Branch and was to stand on display in the Main Treasury Building for 100 years. Its four sides are made of reinforced concrete three inches thick. The Treasury seal and the numerals "2076" will be displayed on one side of the container. An airtight inner chamber preserves the contents of the capsule.

"America's greatest resource is the vibrant heritage of a free people. May we have the wisdom and the vision to nourish this birthright forever."   *— William E. Simon*

These words, inscribed on the capsule's dedication plaque, form the keystone of Secretary Simon's message to his counterpart in 2076 and serve as a message of hope and confidence to Americans celebrating the 300th anniversary of the United States.

Secretaries of the Treasury, 1789-1987

President	Secretaries	Term of Service
Washington	Alexander Hamilton, New York	Sept. 11, 1789 - Jan. 31, 1795
	Oliver Wolcott, Connecticut	Feb. 3, 1795 - Mar. 3, 1797
Adams, John	Oliver Wolcott, Connecticut	Mar. 4, 1797 - Dec. 31, 1800
	Samuel Dexter, Massachusetts	Jan. 1, 1801 - Mar. 3, 1801
Jefferson	Samuel Dexter, Massachusetts	Mar. 4, 1801 - May 13, 1801
	Albert Gallatin, Pennsylvania	May 14, 1801 - Mar. 3, 1809
Madison	Albert Gallatin, Pennsylvania	Mar. 4, 1809 - Feb. 8, 1814
	George W. Campbell, Tennessee	Feb. 9, 1814 - Oct. 5, 1814
	Alexander J. Dallas, Pennsylvania	Oct. 6, 1814 - Oct. 21, 1816
	William H. Crawford, Georgia	Oct. 22, 1816 - Mar. 3, 1817
Monroe	William H. Crawford, Georgia	Mar. 4, 1817 - Mar. 6, 1825
Adams, J.Q.	Richard Rush, Pennsylvania	Mar. 7, 1825 - Mar. 5, 1829
Jackson	Samuel D. Ingham, Pennsylvania	Mar. 6, 1829 - June 20, 1831
	Louis McLane, Delaware	Aug. 8, 1831 - May 28, 1833
	William J. Duane, Pennsylvania	May 29, 1833 - Sept. 22, 1833

President	Secretaries	Term of Service
	Roger B. Taney, Maryland	Sept. 23, 1833 - June 25, 1834
	Levi Woodbury, New Hampshire	July 1, 1834 - Mar. 3, 1837
Van Buren	Levi Woodbury, New Hampshire	Mar. 4, 1837 - Mar. 3, 1841
Harrison, W.H.	Thomas Ewing, Ohio	Mar. 6, 1841 - Apr. 4, 1841
Tyler	Thomas Ewing, Ohio	Apr. 5, 1841 - Sept. 11, 1841
	Walter Forward, Pennsylvania	Sept. 13, 1841 - Mar. 1, 1843
	John C. Spencer, New York	Mar. 8, 1843 - May 2, 1844
	George M. Bibb, Kentucky	July 4, 1844 - Mar. 4, 1845
Polk	George M. Bibb, Kentucky	Mar. 5, 1845 - Mar. 7, 1845
	Robert J. Walker, Mississippi	Mar. 8, 1845 - Mar. 5, 1849
Taylor	Wm. M. Meredith, Pennsylvania	Mar. 8, 1849 - July 9, 1850
Fillmore	Wm. M. Meredith, Pennsylvania	July 10, 1850 - July 22, 1850
	Thomas Corwin, Ohio	July 23, 1850 - Mar. 6, 1853
Pierce	James Guthrie, Kentucky	Mar. 7, 1853 - Mar. 6, 1857
Buchanan	Howell Cobb, Georgia	Mar. 7, 1857 - Dec. 8, 1860
	Philip F. Thomas, Maryland	Dec. 12, 1860 - Jan. 14, 1861
	John A. Dix, New York	Jan. 15, 1861 - Mar. 6, 1861
Lincoln	Salmon P. Chase, Ohio	Mar. 7, 1861 - June 30, 1864
	Wm. P. Fessenden, Maine	July 5, 1864 - Mar. 3, 1865
	Hugh McCulloch, Indiana	Mar. 9, 1865 - Apr. 15, 1865
Johnson, A.	Hugh McCulloch, Indiana	Apr. 16, 1865 - Mar. 3, 1869
Grant	Geo. S. Boutwell, Massachusetts	Mar. 12, 1869 - Mar. 16, 1873
	Wm. A. Richardson, Massachusetts	Mar. 17, 1873 - June 3, 1874
	Benjamin H. Bristow, Kentucky	June 4, 1874 - June 20, 1876
	Lot M. Morrill, Maine	June 7, 1876 - Mar. 3, 1877
Hayes	Lot M. Morrill, Maine	Mar. 4, 1877 - Mar. 9, 1877
	John Sherman, Ohio	Mar. 10, 1877 - Mar. 3, 1881
Garfield	William Windom, Minnesota	Mar. 8, 1881 - Sept. 19, 1881
Arthur	William Windom, Minnesota	Sept. 20, 1881 - Nov. 13, 1881
	Charles J. Folger, New York	Nov. 14, 1881 - Sept. 4, 1884
	Walter Q. Gresham, Indiana	Sept. 25, 1884 - Oct. 30, 1884
	Hugh McCulloch, Indiana	Oct. 31, 1884 - Mar. 3, 1885
Cleveland	Hugh McCulloch, Indiana	Mar. 4, 1885 - Mar. 7, 1885
	Daniel Manning, New York	Mar. 8, 1885 - Mar. 31, 1887
	Charles S. Fairchild, New York	Apr. 1, 1887 - Mar. 3, 1889
Harrison, B.	Charles S. Fairchild, New York	Mar. 4, 1889 - Mar. 6, 1889
	William Windom, Minnesota	Mar. 7, 1889 - Jan. 29, 1891
	Charles Foster, Ohio	Feb. 25, 1891 - Mar. 3, 1893
Cleveland	Charles Foster, Ohio	Mar. 4, 1893 - Mar. 6, 1893
	John G. Carlisle, Kentucky	Mar. 7, 1893 - Mar. 3, 1897
McKinley	John G. Carlisle, Kentucky	Mar. 4, 1897 - Mar. 5, 1897
	Lyman J. Gage, Illinois	Mar. 6, 1897 - Sept. 14, 1901
Roosevelt, T.	Lyman J. Gage, Illinois	Sept. 15, 1901 - Jan. 31, 1902
	L.M. Shaw, Iowa	Feb. 1, 1902 - Mar. 3, 1907
	G.B. Cortelyou, New York	Mar. 4, 1907 - Mar. 7, 1909
Taft	Franklin MacVeagh, Illinois	Mar. 8, 1909 - Mar. 5, 1913
Wilson	W.G. McAdoo, New York	Mar. 6, 1913 - Dec. 15, 1918
	Carter Glass, Virginia	Dec. 16, 1918 - Feb. 1, 1920
	David F. Houston, Missouri	Feb. 2, 1920 - Mar. 3, 1921
Harding	Andrew W. Mellon, Pennsylvania	Mar. 4, 1921 - Aug. 2, 1923
Coolidge	Andrew W. Mellon, Pennsylvania	Aug. 3, 1923 - Mar. 3, 1929
Hoover	Andrew W. Mellon, Pennsylvania	Mar. 4, 1929 - Feb. 12, 1932
	Ogden L. Mills, New York	Feb. 13, 1932 - Mar. 4, 1933
Roosevelt, F.D.	William H. Woodin, New York	Mar. 5, 1933 - Dec. 31, 1933
	Henry Morgenthau, Jr., New York	Jan. 1, 1934 - Apr. 12, 1945
Truman	Henry Morgenthau, Jr., New York	Apr. 13, 1945 - July 22, 1945
	Fred M. Vinson, Kentucky	July 23, 1945 - June 23, 1946
	John W. Snyder, Missouri	June 25, 1946 - Jan. 20, 1953

President	Secretaries	Term of Service
Eisenhower	George M. Humphrey, Ohio	Jan. 21, 1953 - July 29, 1957
	Robert B. Anderson, Connecticut	July 29, 1957 - Jan. 20, 1961
Kennedy	Douglas Dillon, New Jersey	Jan. 21, 1961 - Nov. 22, 1963
Johnson, L.B.	Douglas Dillon, New Jersey	Nov. 23, 1963 - Apr. 1, 1965
	Henry H. Fowler, Virginia	Apr. 1, 1965 - Dec. 20, 1968
	Joseph W. Barr, Indiana	Dec. 21, 1968 - Jan. 20, 1969
Nixon	David M. Kennedy, Utah	Jan. 22, 1969 - Feb. 10, 1971
	John B. Connally, Texas	Feb. 11, 1971 - June 12, 1972
	George P. Shultz, Illinois	June 12, 1971 - May 7, 1974
	William E. Simon, New Jersey	May 8, 1974 - Aug. 9, 1974
Ford	William E. Simon, New Jersey	Aug. 10, 1974 - Jan. 20, 1977
Carter	W. Michael Blumenthal, Michigan	Jan. 23, 1977 - Aug. 4, 1979
	G. William Miller, Rhode Island	Aug. 7, 1979 - Jan. 20, 1981
Reagan	Donald T. Regan, Massachusetts	Jan. 22, 1981 - Feb. 2, 1985
	James A. Baker III, Texas	Feb. 3, 1985 -

Treasurers of the United States, 1775-1987

Treasurer	Term
Michael Hillegas, Pennsylvania	July 29, 1775 - Sept. 11, 1789
Samuel Meredith, Pennsylvania	Sept. 11, 1789 - Oct. 31, 1801
Thomas T. Tucker, South Carolina	Dec. 1, 1801 - May 2, 1828
William Clark, Pennsylvania	June 4, 1828 - May 31, 1829
John Campbell, Virginia	May 26, 1829 - July 20, 1839
William Selden, Virginia	July 22, 1839 - Nov. 23, 1850
John Sloan, Ohio	Nov. 27, 1850 - April 6, 1852
Samuel Casey, Kentucky	April 4, 1853 - Dec. 22, 1859
William C. Price, Missouri	Feb. 28, 1860 - Mar. 21, 1861
F.E. Spinner, New York	Mar. 16, 1861 - June 30, 1875
John C. New, Indiana	June 30, 1875 - July 1, 1876
A.U. Wyman, Wisconsin	July 1, 1876 - June 30, 1877
James Gilfillan, Connecticut	July 1, 1877 - Mar. 31, 1883
A.U. Wyman, Wisconsin	April 1, 1883 - April 30, 1885
Conrad N. Jordan, New York	May 1, 1885 - May 23, 1887
James W. Hyatt, Connecticut	May 24, 1887 - May 10, 1889
J.N. Huston, Indiana	May 11, 1889 - April 24, 1891
Enos H. Nebecker, Indiana	April 25, 1891 - May 31, 1893
D.N. Morgan, Connecticut	June 1, 1893 - June 30, 1897
Ellis H. Roberts, New York	July 1, 1897 - June 30, 1905
Charles H. Treat, New York	July 1, 1905 - Oct. 30, 1909
Lee McClung, Tennessee	Nov. 1, 1909 - Nov. 21, 1912
Carmi A. Thompson, Ohio	Nov. 22, 1912 - Mar. 31, 1913
John Burke, North Dakota	April 1, 1913 - Jan. 5, 1921
Frank White, North Dakota	May 2, 1921 - May 1, 1928
H.T. Tate, Tennessee	May 31, 1928 - Jan. 17, 1929
W.O. Woods, Kansas	Jan. 18, 1929 - May 31, 1933
W.A. Julian, Ohio	June 1, 1933 - May 29, 1949
Georgia Neese Clark, Kansas	June 21, 1949 - Jan. 27, 1953
Ivy Baker Priest, Utah	Jan. 28, 1953 - Jan. 29, 1961
Elizabeth Rudel Smith, California	Jan. 30, 1961 - April 13, 1962
Kathryn O'Hay Granahan, Pennsylvania	Jan. 3, 1963 - Nov. 20, 1966
Dorothy Andrews Elston Kabis, Delaware	May 8, 1969 - July 3, 1971
Romana Acosta Banuelos, California	Dec. 17, 1971 - Feb. 15, 1974
Francine Irving Neff, New Mexico	June 21, 1974 - Jan. 19, 1977
Azie Taylor Morton, Texas	Sept. 12, 1977 - Jan. 20, 1981
Angela Buchanan, Maryland	Jan. 21, 1981 - July 1, 1983
Katherine Davalos Ortega, New Mexico	Sept. 23, 1983 -

Department of the Treasury seal

The seal of the Treasury Department is older than the United States government. The Continental Congress in 1778 appointed a committee of finance, or board of treasury, and John Witherspoon, Gouverneur Morris and Richard Henry Lee were authorized to design a treasury seal. The earliest example of the seal is found on papers dated 1782. When the U.S. government was established in 1789, the Continental seal was continued in use.

In 1849 the Treasury needed to replace its badly worn seal and ordered Edward Stabler to make a facsimile. Apparently Stabler carried out his orders with reservations, for his seal showed differences from the original; but they are so minute that a casual observer would not notice them.

The seal of the Department of the Treasury is overprinted on the face of each note printed in the U.S.

On Jan. 29, 1968, a revision of the official seal was approved. The new seal has an inscription, in English, reading "The Department of the Treasury." This inscription replaces the earlier Latin legend "Thesaur. Amer. Septent. Sigil.," an abbreviation said to represent "Thesauri Americae Septentrionalis Sigillum," translated as "The Seal of the Treasury of North America." The new seal bears the date 1789, recording the year of the department's creation.

The arms on the seal depict balance scales, representing the scales of justice; a key, the emblem of official authority; and a chevron with 13 stars for the original states. The revised design of the seal appears on $100 United States notes, beginning with Series 1966, and on Federal Reserve notes, beginning with Series 1969.

On United States notes, the Treasury seal, along with the serial numbers, is overprinted in red; on Federal Reserve notes, these features are overprinted in green.

Treasury officials

15th Street and Pennsylvania Avenue NW, Washington, D.C. 20220. Phone (202) 566-2000

Secretary of the Treasury — James A. Baker III.

Deputy Secretary of the Treasury — VACANT (M. Peter McPherson was nominated by President Reagan April 6, 1987, for this position. No Senate confirmation as of May 1, 1987.)

Undersecretary for Finance — George D. Gould.

General Counsel — Robert M. Kimmitt.

Fiscal Assistant Secretary — Gerald Murphy.

Treasurer of the United States — Katherine D. Ortega.

Assistant Secretary (Management) — John F.W. Rogers.

Assistant Secretary (Domestic Finance) — Charles O. Sethness.

Assistant Secretary (Economic Policy) — Michael R. Darby.

Assistant Secretary (Enforcement) — Francis A. Keating II.

Assistant Secretary (International Affairs) — David C. Mulford.

Assistant Secretary (Legislative Affairs) — J. Michael Hudson.

Assistant Secretary (Public Affairs and Public Liason) — Margaret Tutwiler.

Assistant Secretary (Tax Policy) — J. Roger Mentz.

Deputy Assistant Secretary (Tax Policy) — C. Eugene Steuerle.

Executive Secretary — Robert B. Zoellick.

Special Assistant to the Secretary (National Security) — Douglas P. Mulholland.

Director, Bureau of Alcohol, Tobacco and Firearms — Stephen E. Higgins.

Comptroller of the Currency — Robert L. Clarke.

Commissioner, U.S. Customs Service — William von Raab.

Director, Bureau of Engraving and Printing — Robert J. Leuver.

Director, Federal Law Enforcement Training Center — Charles F. Rinkevich.

Commissioner, Financial Management Service — William E. Douglas.

Commissioner, Internal Revenue Service — Lawrence B. Gibbs.

Director, United States Mint — Donna Pope.

Commissioner, Bureau of the Public Debt — Richard L. Gregg.

Director, U.S. Savings Bonds Division — Katherine D. Ortega.

Director, U.S. Secret Service — John R. Simpson.

Inspector General — Michael R. Hill.

James A. Baker III

James A. Baker III became the 67th Secretary of the Treasury on Feb. 3, 1985.

Prior to this, Secretary Baker had been appointed by President Reagan as chief of staff to the president, a position which he occupied from January 1981 through January 1985. Former Secretary of the Treasury Donald T. Regan proposed the two men switch jobs, which Baker agreed to do. While at the White House, Baker was a member of the National Security Council and remains a member as Secretary of the Treasury. He is also chairman of the President's Economic Policy Council.

In 1980, Secretary Baker served as senior adviser to the Ronald Reagan/George Bush general election campaign. From January 1979 to May 1980 he was the chairman of Vice President Bush's campaign for the 1980 Republican presidential nomination.

Secretary Baker was the Republican Party's nominee for attorney general of the state of Texas in 1978. He is a native of Houston and practiced law there with the firm of Andrews & Kurth from 1957 to 1975.

In August 1975, Secretary Baker was appointed by President Ford to be the under secretary of Commerce. Secretary Baker joined President Ford's presidential campaign in May 1976 as deputy chairman for Delegate Operations and in August became national chairman of the President Ford Committee.

Baker graduated from Princeton University in 1952. After two years of active duty as a lieutenant in the United States Marine Corps, he entered the University of Texas School of Law at Austin. He received his doctorate in law with honors in 1957.

A member of the American, Texas and Houston Bar Associations, the American Judicature Society and the Phi Delta Phi honorary legal fraternity, Baker also serves on the board of trustees of the Woodrow Wilson International Center for Scholars at the Smithsonian Institution. He has served on the governing bodies of the Texas Children's Hosptial and the M.D. Anderson Hospital and Tumor Institute.

Baker has been the recipient of the Jefferson Award for distinguished public service from the American Institute for Public Service, an award for Distinguished Public Service from the John F. Kennedy School of Government at Harvard and the Woodrow Wilson Award for distinguished achievement in the nation's service from Princeton University. Secretary Baker was selected in 1986 as a Distinguished Alumnus of the University of Texas. He has received numerous honorary degrees.

Baker was born April 28, 1930. He and his wife, the former Susan Garrett, reside in Washington, D.C. They have eight children.

Katherine Davalos Ortega

Katherine Davalos Ortega was sworn in Oct. 3, 1983, to replace Angela M. Buchanan, who resigned as Treasurer of the United States effective July 1, 1983. Ortega is the second woman of Hispanic ancestry to hold the post.

As Treasurer, Ortega oversees the Bureau of Engraving and Printing, the U.S. Mint, and the U.S. Savings Bond Division. Ortega is national director of the U.S. Savings Bond Division and serves as a member of Treasury Secretary Baker's senior staff.

Prior to being appointed Treasurer, Ortega was one of the commissioners of the Copyright Royalty Tribunal, a position she took in 1982. She has served as a member of the Presidential Advisory Committee on Small and Minority Business Ownership.

An active role in local Republican politics

and her work on the campaign of Sen. Pete V. Domenici, R-N.M., eventually earned Ortega the senator's recommendation for the Treasurer's seat.

Before joining the Reagan administration, Ortega was a veteran adminstrator in the banking and savings and loan industries. She became the first woman bank president in California when she was elected president of the Santa Ana State Bank in 1975.

As a consultant in a family concern from 1977 to 1982, Ortega helped to found and build the Otero Savings and Loan Association in Alamogordo, N.M.

From 1972-1975, she was a vice president and cashier of the Pan-American National Bank in Los Angeles. Ortega, who is a certified public accountant, was also tax supervisor for the Los Angeles-based Peat, Marwick,

Mitchell & Co. from 1969-1972.

She was the 1977 recipient of the Outstanding Alumni Award from Eastern New Mexico University in Portales, where she received her bachelor's degree in business and economics in 1957.

In addition, she has been a winner of the California Business Women's Achievement Award and the Danas de Commercio Outstanding Woman of the Year Award in Los Angeles.

Ortega, a bilingual native of New Mexico, has traveled throughout Europe, Asia and Central and South America.

Function of the Treasury Department

The Department of the Treasury performs four basic functions: formulating and recommending financial, tax and fiscal policies; serving as a financial agent for the U.S. government; law enforcement; and manufacturing coins and currency.

Office of the Secretary

As a major policy adviser to the President, the Secretary has primary responsibility for formulating and recommending domestic and international financial, economic and tax policy; participating in the formulation of broad fiscal policies that have general significance for the economy; and managing the public debt. The Secretary also oversees the activities of the department in carrying out its major law enforcement responsibility; in serving as the financial agent for the U.S. government; and in manufacturing coins, currency and other products for customer agencies.

Office of the Comptroller of the Currency

The Office of the Comptroller of the Currency was created by act of Congress approved Feb. 25, 1863, as an integral part of the national banking system.

The Comptroller, as the administrator of national banks, is responsible for the execution of laws relating to national banks and promulgates rules and regulations governing the operations of approximately 4,550 national and District of Columbia banks. Approval of the Comptroller is required for the organization of new national banks, conversion of state-chartered banks into national banks, consolidations or mergers of banks where the surviving institution is a national bank, and the establishment of branches by national banks.

The Office of the Comptroller exercises general supervision over the operations of national banks, including trust activities and overseas operations. Each bank is examined periodically through a nationwide staff of approximately 2,100 bank examiners under the immediate supervision of six deputy comptrollers and six regional administrators. These examinations operate in the public interest by assisting the Comptroller in appraising the financial condition of the banks, the soundness of their operations, the quality of their management, and their compliance with laws, rules and regulations.

For further information, contact the Communications Division, Office of the Comptroller of the Currency, Department of the Treasury, 490 L'Enfant Plaza East SW, Washington, D.C. 20219. Phone (202) 447-1810.

U.S. Customs Service

1301 Constitution Ave. NW
Washington, D.C. 20229
Phone, (202) 566-8195

The U.S. Customs Service was created by the act of March 3, 1927. Authority for the collection of customs revenue was established by the second, third, and fifth acts of the first Congress in 1789.

Customs engages in activities for the collection and protection of the revenue; the prevention of fraud and smuggling; and the processing and regulation of people, carriers, cargo and mail into and out of the United States; and performs a variety of functions for other government agencies in safeguarding agriculture, business, health, security and related consumer interests.

Customs is active in suppressing the traffic in illegal narcotics (in conjunction with the Drug Enforcement Administration and in cooperation with foreign governments); in enforcing munitions control in cargo theft prevention; in enforcing regulations affecting articles in international trade where parallel regulations control domestic articles (such as copyright, trademark, and patent restrictions regulated domestically by the Patent Office or the Copyright Office; and special marking provisions for wool, fur and textile products, controlled domestically by the Federal Trade Commission); and in enforcing regulations related to dumping.

The Bureau of Customs enforces certain environmental protection programs for other agencies, such as enforcing the prohibition on discharge of refuse and oil into or upon coastal navigable waters of the United States (for the U.S. Coast Guard) as outlined in the Oil Pollution Act; enforcing laws and regulations regarding wild animals and birds of the endangered species and those injurious to community health, plant and animal life, as well as other agriculture and plant quarantine regulations concerning animal, poultry, animal byproducts; and insuring that imported vehicles and equipment conform to safety and emission standards required under the National Traffic and Motor Vehicle Safety Act of 1966 and the Clean Air Act.

Headquarters for the Customs Service is located in Washington, D.C., under the supervision of the Commissioner of Customs who is appointed by the Secretary of the Treasury. The Service is decentralized and most of its personnel are stationed throughout the country and overseas, where its operational functions are performed.

The 50 states, plus the Virgin Islands and Puerto Rico, are divided into seven Customs Regions. Contained within these regions are 46 subordinate district offices under which there are approximately 300 ports of entry.

For further information, contact the Public Affairs Office, U.S. Customs Service, Department of the Treasury, 1301 Constitution Avenue NW, Washington, D.C. 20229. Phone, (202) 566-5286.

United States Mint
633 Third St. NW, Washington, D.C. 20220
Phone, (202) 376-0560

The Mint of the United States was established by act of Congress April 2, 1792. The Bureau of the Mint was established by act of Congress February 12, 1873. Mint Director Donna Pope changed the name of the agency to the U.S. Mint on Jan. 25, 1984.

The functions of the Mint are the production of coins, both domestic and foreign; the manufacture and sale of medals of a national character; the manufacture and sale of Proof and Uncirculated coin sets and other numismatic items; and the custody, processing and movement of bullion. The Mint disburses gold and silver for authorized purposes; directs the distribution of coins from the Mints to the Federal Reserve Banks and branches; and compiles and analyzes general data of worldwide scope relative to gold, silver and coins.

For further information, contact the United States Mint, Department of the Treasury, 633 Third St. NW, Washington, D.C. 20220. Phone, (202) 376-0560.

(See Chapter 5 for more information.)

United States Secret Service
1800 G Street NW, Washington, D.C. 20223
Phone, (202) 535-5708

The responsibilities and jurisdiction of the United States Secret Service are prescribed by law in Title 18, United States Code, Section 3056.

Subject to the direction of the Secretary of the Treasury, the United States Secret Service is authorized to protect the person of the president of the United States, the members of his immediate family, the president-elect, the vice president or other officer next in the order of succession to the Office of President, the immediate family of the vice president, the vice president-elect, major presidential and vice presidential candidates, former presidents and their wives during his lifetime, widows of former presidents until their death or remarriage, and minor children of a former president until they reach age 16, and visiting heads of a foreign state or foreign government.

The Secret Service is also authorized to detect and arrest any person committing any offense against the laws of the United States relating to coins, currency, and other obligations, and securities of the United States and of foreign governments; detect and arrest any person violating any of the provisions of sections 508, 509, and 871 of Title 18 of the United States Code; execute warrants issued under the authority of the United States; carry firearms; and perform such other functions and duties as are authorized by law.

The Director of the Secret Service is charged with the supervision of the Executive Protective Service and the Treasury Security Force.

For further information, contact any District Office or Office of Public Affairs, United States Secret Service, Department of the Treasury, 1800 G Street NW, Washington, D.C. 20223. Phone, (202) 535-5708.

Bureau of Engraving and Printing
14th and C streets SW
Washington, D.C. 20228
Phone (202) 447-0193

The Bureau operates on basic authorities conferred by the acts of July 11, 1862, March 3, 1877, June 4, 1897, and additional authorities contained in past appropriations made to the Bureau for work to be undertaken, which are still in force. A working capital fund of $3,250,000 was established in accordance with the provisions of Section 2 of the Act of Aug. 4, 1950, which placed the Bureau on a completely reimbursable basis. The Bureau is headed by a Director who is appointed by the Secretary of the Treasury.

The Bureau of Engraving and Printing designs, engraves and prints all major items of financial character issued by the U.S. government. It produces paper currency; Treasury bonds, bills, notes, and certificates; postage, revenue and certain customs stamps. All Bureau operations are conducted in Washington, D.C., although a second printing plant is planned for Fort Worth, Texas.

For further information, contact the Public Affairs Section, Bureau of Engraving and Printing, Department of the Treasury, Room 602-11A, 14th and C streets SW, Washington, D.C. 20228. Phone (202) 447-0193. **(See Chapter 8 for more information.)**

Fiscal Services

The Fiscal Service of the Treasury Department was created by Reorganization Plan III, effective June 30, 1940 (5 U.S.C. Appendix).

BUREAU OF GOVERNMENT FINANCIAL OPERATIONS

The Bureau of Government Financial Operations has responsibility for a variety of fiscal activities of a government-wide scope.

CENTRAL ACCOUNTING AND REPORTING

The Bureau maintains a system of central accounting and reporting, disclosing the monetary assets and liabilities of the United States Treasury and providing for the integration of Treasury cash and funding operations with the financial operations of disbursing and collecting officers and of Federal program agencies. Periodic reports are prepared to show budget results, other financial operations, and the financial status of the government.

CENTRAL DISBURSING AND CHECK CLAIMS

Disbursing service is provided for most civilian agencies of the government, including the issuance of monthly payments to beneficiaries under major federal benefit programs and the issuance of U.S. Savings Bonds under the Federal Payroll Savings Plan. Through the Department of State, foreign disbursing service is provided for agencies other than the Department of Defense. The Bureau adjudicates and settles claims against the United States on Treasury checks that are lost in the mails, or which bear forged endorsements, and issues new checks to authorized payees.

FEDERAL TAX DEPOSITS

The Bureau provides technical support, including the issuance of federal tax deposit forms, for the system of tax payments by business organizations through authorized commercial banks and the Federal Reserve System.

CASH MANAGEMENT

The Bureau supervises the government-wide letter-of-credit system for financing federal grant-in-aid programs; monitors all cash held outside the Treasury, including foreign currency balances resulting from federal programs; and supervises the government's depository system.

MUTILATED CURRENCY

The Bureau handles claims from the public for the redemption of partially destroyed U.S. currency, determines its value and authorizes payment to claimants.

SURETY BONDING

The Bureau administers functions relating to the qualification of surety companies as acceptable sureties on bonds running in favor of the United States, including the examination of financial statements and the determination of underwriting limitations for such companies.

MISCELLANEOUS FINANCIAL ACTIVITIES

The Bureau makes payment to holders of claims awards under international claims programs, judgments rendered by certain United States courts and private relief acts passed by the Congress; supervises the liquidation of terminated agencies; bills and collects amounts due from foreign governments under lend-lease, surplus property agreements and other Treasury loans; and audits the procedures of Federal Reserve Banks in verifying and destroying U.S. currency which is unfit for circulation.

For further information, contact the Comptroller's Office, Bureau of Government Financial Operations, Department of the Treasury, 490 L'Enfant Plaza East SW, Washington, D.C. 20219.

Office of the Treasurer

The Office of the Treasurer of the United States was originally created by the act of Sept. 2, 1789, for the purpose of receiving, holding and paying out the public moneys for the federal government. However, most of the responsibilities of the office were transferred to the Bureau of Government Financial Operations with its creation Feb. 1, 1974.

The Treasurer is responsible for reviewing and endorsing U.S. currency and represents the Secretary of the Treasury and Undersecretary for Monetary Affairs as a major spokesman in communicating and coordinating departmental programs and policies.

During the Reagan administration, the office of Treasurer was upgraded to include the responsibilities of direct oversight of the United States Mint, the Bureau of Engraving and Printing and the United States Savings Bond program, and serving on the Treasury Secretary's senior staff.

As National Director of the U.S. Savings Bond Division, the Treasurer supervises a bureau-level organization of the Department of the Treasury whose primary mission is to promote the sale of U.S. savings bonds. Among other duties, the Treasurer consults with the Secretary and Undersecretary on the role of the savings bonds program in Treasury's debt management policies.

For further information, contact the Office of the Treasurer, Department of the Treasury, 15th St. and Pennsylvania Ave. NW, Washington, D.C. 20220. Phone (202) 566-2843.

Sources of information
OFFICE OF THE SECRETARY

GENERAL

For general information about the Treasury Department, including copies of news releases and texts of speeches by Treasury officials, write to the Office of the Assistant Secretary (Public Affairs), Room 3430, Office of the Secretary, Treasury Department, Washington, D.C. 20220.

For further information concerning the Office of the Secretary or Treasury-wide activities, contact the Public Affairs Office, Department of the Treasury, 15th St. and Pennsylvania Ave. NW, Washington, D.C. 20220. Phone (202) 566-2041.

CONTRACTS

Write to Director, Office of Procurement, Room 1450, Main Treasury Bldg., Washington, D.C. 20220.

SMALL AND DISADVANTAGED BUSINESS ACTIVITIES

Write to Director, Office of Small and Disadvantaged Business Utilization, Room 1320, Main Treasury Bldg., Washington, D.C. 20220.

READING ROOM

Treasury Library, Room 5030, Main Treasury Building, 15th St. and Pennsylvania Ave. NW., Washington, D.C. 20220.

THE ENVIRONMENT

Environmental statements prepared by the Treasury Department are available for review in the Departmental Library.

TAX LEGISLATION

Write to Assistant Secretary (Tax Policy), Office of the Secretary, Treasury Department, Washington, D.C. 20220.

TELEPHONE DIRECTORY

The Treasury Department telephone directory is available for sale by the Superintendent of Documents, Government Printing Office, Washington, D.C. 20402.

OFFICE OF THE COMPTROLLER OF THE CURRENCY

CONTRACTS

Contact the procurement officer at 490 L'Enfant Plaza East SW., Washington, D.C. 20219.

EMPLOYMENT

Civil Service registers, including mid-level and senior-level examinations, are used. A college recruitment program is conducted for positions of assistant national bank examiner and assistant national trust examiner. Additional recruiting is performed for the position of financial intern, which involves a program of cooperative work and college study. Descriptive literature and information are available from the Director of Human Resources, 490 L'Enfant Plaza East SW, Washington, D.C. 20219.

U.S. CUSTOMS SERVICE

Address inquiries on the following subjects to the specified office, U.S. Customs Service, 1301 Constitution Avenue NW, Washington, D.C. 20229.

READING ROOM

Located at the headquarters library and in each of the seven regional offices.

CONTRACTS

Write to the Director, Logistics Management Division in Washington, D.C.

INFORMATION

Contact the nearest district director's office for information regarding customs regulations and procedures for all persons entering the United States and the entry and clearance of imported merchandise.

FORMS

Available from any district director's office. (There is a nominal charge for large quantities of certain forms.)

PUBLICATIONS

The U.S. Customs Service issues publications of interest to the general, importing, and traveling public obtainable from any of the district directors' offices, or by writing to the

Public Affairs Office in Washington, D.C. Single copies of many of these publications are available at no charge to the public.

EMPLOYMENT

The U.S Customs Service recruits by competitive examination, primarily through the Professional and Administrative Career Examination (PACE), given throughout the United States by the Office of Personnel Management, the Treasury Enforcement Agent (TEA) examination and the Customs Patrol Officer/Border Patrol Agent Examination.

Employment inquiries may be addressed to any of the seven regional commissioners, or to the Director, Personnel Management Division in Washington, D.C.

SPEAKERS

Speakers are available for private organizations or community groups throughout the country. Contact any local customs officer or the Public Affairs Office in Washington, D.C.

BUREAU OF ENGRAVING AND PRINTING

Address inquiries on the following subjects to the specified office, Bureau of Engraving and Printing, Fourteenth and C streets SW, Washington, D.C. 20228.

READING ROOM

Contact the Bureau Disclosure Officer, Bureau of Engraving and Printing Annex.

CONTRACTS

Contact the Manager, Procurement Division.

SMALL BUSINESS ACTIVITY

Contact the Manager, Procurement Division.

EMPLOYMENT

The Bureau uses the following civil service registers: Worker-Trainee, Apprentice Printing Crafts, Apprentice Mechanical Trades, Professional and Administrative Career Examination, Examination for Mid-Level Positions and Journeyman Printing Crafts. Contact the Head, Personnel Staffing Branch, Office of Industrial Relations.

SPEAKERS

Direct requests to the Deputy Director. Speakers are available in the Washington area. Availability of speakers outside the Washington area is based upon the individual merits of the request.

TOURS

Self-guided tour facilities are available for the public to view the printing and processing of securities at no charge. The visitors gallery is open each day, Monday through Friday (except legal holidays) from 8 a.m. to 2 p.m. in the Main Bureau Building.

PRODUCT SALES

The Bureau offers for sale engraved portraits of the presidents, vignettes of public buildings and a selection of engraved and lithographed prints of historical themes. This material is sold through mail order and over the counter in the Visitors Center located in the lobby of the main building. The sales area business hours are from 9 a.m. to 2 p.m. weekdays. Contact the Office of Planning and Policy Development Division for listing of available items and purchase order forms.

UNITED STATES MINT

PUBLICATIONS

The *Annual Report of the Director of the Mint, Domestic and Foreign Coinage Manufactured by the Mints of the United States 1793-1980, The World's Monetary Stocks of Gold, Silver and Coins, Medals of the United States Mint* and *Medals of the United States*, an illustrated catalog, are available from the United States Mint, Washington, D.C., and the Superintendent of Documents, Government Printing Office, Washington, D.C. 20402. A current price list of medals is available free of charge from the United States Mint, Washington, D.C. 20220.

CONTRACTS AND EMPLOYMENT

Inquiries should be directed to the facility head of the appropriate field office, or to the Director of the Mint.

SPEAKERS

Requests should be directed to the Director of the Mint, 633 Third St. NW, Washington, D.C. 20220.

NUMISMATIC

The Mint maintains public exhibit and sales areas at the Philadelphia and Denver Mints, the Old San Francisco Mint and at the Washington Tourist Information Center, 1400 Pennsylvania Ave., N.W. Order forms for Proof sets, medals and other numismatic items may be obtained by writing to the United States Mint, Customer Service, 10001 Aerospace Road, Lanham, Md. 20706.

UNITED STATES SAVINGS BONDS DIVISION

SAVINGS BONDS

Savings Bonds are continuously on sale at more than 30,000 issuing agencies and their branches in virtually every locality in the United States. Information about bonds may be provided by such issuing agents.

Free informational materials are available from District Savings Bonds Offices and from the Office of Public Affairs, U.S. Savings Bonds Division, Department of the Treasury, Washington, D.C. 20226.

Source: Congressional Staff Directory

U.S. Currency and Coin Outstanding and in Circulation

[Source: Financial Management Service]

AMOUNTS OUTSTANDING AND IN CIRCULATION

Mar. 31, 1987

	Total currency and coin	Currency				Coin[2]		
		Total	Federal Reserve notes	U.S. notes	Currency no longer issued	Total	Dollars[3]	Fractional coin
Amounts outstanding	$254,583,760,942	$237,459,710,044	$236,867,132,471	$322,539,016	$270,038,557	$17,124,050,898	$2,024,703,898	$15,099,347,000
Less amounts held by:								
The Treasury	536,075,931	37,217,841	6,476,133	30,506,639	235,069	498,858,090	348,781,980	150,076,110
The Federal Reserve banks	46,265,577,331	45,697,041,041	45,697,023,740	—	17,301	568,536,290	129,092,105	439,444,185
Amounts in circulation	207,782,107,680	191,725,451,162	191,163,632,598	292,032,377	269,786,187	16,056,656,518	1,546,829,813	14,509,826,705

CURRENCY IN CIRCULATION BY DENOMINATION

Mar. 31, 1987

Denomination	Total	Federal Reserve notes	U.S. notes	Currency no longer issued
$1	$3,861,978,135	$3,709,378,949	$143,481	$152,455,705
$2	732,424,020	599,513,064	132,897,966	12,990
$5	5,042,310,335	4,892,261,175	112,176,410	37,872,750
$10	11,062,944,800	11,038,128,930	5,950	24,809,920
$20	55,521,996,220	55,501,795,280	3,380	20,197,560
$50	25,139,097,450	25,127,480,200	—	11,617,250
$100	90,030,098,600	89,961,016,500	46,805,000	22,277,000
$500	152,508,000	152,318,500	—	189,500
$1,000	176,833,000	176,625,000	—	208,000
$5,000	1,800,000	1,755,000	—	45,000
$10,000	3,460,000	3,360,000	—	100,000
Fractional parts	487	—	—	487
Partial notes	115	—	90	25
Total currency	191,725,451,162	191,163,632,598	292,032,377	269,786,187

COMPARATIVE TOTALS OF MONEY IN CIRCULATION—SELECTED DATES

Date	Amount (in millions)	Per capita[4]
Mar. 31, 1987	$207,782.1	$855.00
Feb. 28, 1987	205,950.2	847.89
Mar. 31, 1986	193,193.9	802.61
June 30, 1985	185,890.8	778.38
June 30, 1980	127,097.2	558.28
June 30, 1975	81,196.4	380.08
June 30, 1970	54,351.0	265.39
June 30, 1965	39,719.8	204.14
June 30, 1960	32,064.6	177.47
June 30, 1955	30,229.3	182.90
June 30, 1950	27,156.3	179.03

[1] Issued on and after July 1, 1929.
[2] Excludes coin sold to collectors at premium prices.
[3] Includes $481,781,898 in standard silver dollars.
[4] Based on Bureau of the Census estimates of population.
[5] Represents value of certain partial denominations not presented for redemption.

Source: Treasury Bulletin, June 1987

The Mint

5

United States Mint

The Act of April 2, 1792, provided for gold, silver and copper coinage, and also created the first United States Mint in the city of Philadelphia, which was then the nation's capital. President Washington placed the operation under the supervision of the secretary of state where it remained until 1799, when the Mint became an independent agency reporting directly to the president. Subsequent legislation set up branch Mints, Assay Offices, and fixed public depository functions upon such establishments. The Coinage Act of 1873 put all Mint and Assay Office activities under the newly-organized Bureau of the Mint in the Department of the Treasury.

The Director of the Mint is appointed by the president, with the advice and consent of the Senate. The Director is responsible for coinage production and the distribution of coins to and among the Federal Reserve Banks and Branches, which in turn release them, as required, to commercial banks.

In addition, the Mint maintains physical custody of Treasury stocks of gold and silver and moves, places into storage and releases these metals from custody for such purposes as authorized. It also manufactures coinage dies.

On a reimbursable basis, the Mint manufactures and sells medals of a national character, manufactures coinage for foreign governments, produces Proof and Uncirculated coin sets for sale to collectors, and strikes commemorative coinage for sale to the public.

The Director administers the Philadelphia and Denver Mints, the Assay Office at San Francisco, and two depositories for the storage of precious metals, one at Fort Knox, Ky., for gold bullion and the other at West Point, N.Y., for silver and gold bullion. Cents when demand requires, gold commemorative coins and the gold American Eagle bullion coins are struck at West Point, also. The Assay Office at San Francisco is the site of the striking of coins, Proof coins and the silver American Eagle bullion coin.

The Mint also maintains the restored Old San Francisco Mint, which houses the Mint Museum. Mint service activities are administered by the Director of the Mint and staff from Mint headquarters in Washington, D.C.

A customer service center is located in suburban Washington, D.C., in Lanham, Md.

The United States Mint Director makes annual reports to the Secretary of the Treasury concerning Mint operations for the fiscal year. The report includes estimates of domestic and foreign production of gold and silver, as well as monetary statistics pertaining to the United States and most of the countries of the world.

The main offices of the Mint are located in Washington, D.C., in the Judiciary Square Building. The Mint moved its offices from the Warner Building in 1985. The Mint and its Washington officials, named later in this chapter, may be contacted by writing:

United States Mint, Department of the Treasury, 633 Third St. NW, Washington, D.C. 20220.

Questions concerning the purchase of collector coins sold by the Mint should be directed to U.S. Mint Customer Service, 10001 Aerospace Road, Lanham, Md. 20706; telephone (301) 436-7400.

For general information, address the request to Office of Public Services.

Mint officials

Office of the Director
Director — Donna Pope
Special Assistant to the Director and Press Secretary — Michael J. Brown
Deputy Director — Eugene H. Essner
Counsel to the Mint — Kenneth B. Gubin
Security Officer — William F. Daddio
Equal Employment Opportunity Officer — Harold Davidson

Office of Marketing
Associate Director for Marketing — Daniel P. Cahill
Assistant Director for Marketing — Kevin M. Cullinane
Assistant Director for Sales Operations — Francis B. Frere

Office of Operations
Associate Director — Andrew Cosgarea Jr.
Chief, Federal Reserve Liaison — Francis R. DeLeo
Assistant Director (Technology) — George E. Hunter
Assistant Director (Production) — John J. Papa

Office of Policy and Management
Associate Director — Dennis H. Fischer
Assistant Director (Management Services) — Judith L. Wagner
Assistant Director (Budget and Finance) — Joseph M. Wagner
Assistant Director (Procurement) — Glenn H. Carter
Assistant Director (ADP Management) — Robert Jenkins
Assistant Director (Personnel) — Ben Benitez

Mint field institutions
United States Mint
Fifth St. at Independence Mall
Philadelphia, Pa. 19106
Anthony J. Murray Jr., Superintendent

United States Mint
Colfax and Delaware Streets
Denver, Colo. 80204
Nora Hussey, Superintendent

United States Assay Office
155 Hermann St.
San Francisco, Calif. 94102
Thomas Miller, Officer in Charge

United States Bullion Depository
Fort Knox, Ky. 40121
James Curtis, Officer in Charge

United States Bullion Depository
West Point, N.Y. 10996
Clifford M. Barber, Superintendent

Old Mint
88 Fifth St.
San Francisco, Calif. 94103
Thomas H. Miller, Officer in Charge

Customer Service Center
10001 Aerospace Road
Lanham, Md. 20706

Mint Director's report
The latest Annual Report of the Director of the Mint, giving complete Mint statistics and a report of Mint activities for fiscal year which ended Sept. 30, 1985, 46 pages, is available from the Superintendent of Documents, U.S. Government Printing Office, Washington, D.C. 20402.

Beginning with fiscal year 1981, the Mint has released greatly abbreviated reports from those issued prior to 1981.

Present Mint institutions

Philadelphia Mint
The Act passed on April 2, 1792, established the United States Mint. As a result, a plot of ground was purchased in Philadelphia, located on the east side of Seventh Street, below Arch Street. This was the first public building to be erected by the government of the fledgling United States. For 40 years the federal government continued to use the building on Seventh Street as the national Mint.

Guards are essential to the Mint's elaborate security system. In the past, as now, security precautions were very important. In 1793, the sum of $3 was paid for a watchdog to protect the Mint. The first dog, named Nero, was a savage one which accompanied the watchman on his hourly rounds. The watchman, armed with a dirk and pistol, in making his rounds would ring a bell at regular intervals in order that the populace of Philadelphia might know that the Mint was still safe.

Food for the dog was considered an essential expense of the Mint, the same as hay and other food was considered essential for the horses which provided power for operating the Mint machinery in those days.

On the Fourth of July, 1829, construction began for a new Mint on the northwest corner of Chestnut and Juniper streets, at a cost of $291,000. For more than 70 years this building was used as the Philadelphia Mint.

The third Mint building on Spring Garden Street between 16th and 17th streets, built in 1900, covered a ground area of 58,000 square feet. The exterior of the building was of Maine granite and faced a street on each of the four sides. The main entrance was on Spring Garden Street.

The front portion of the building rose three stories above the basement and terraces. The rear portion was one story lower than the front, but owing to the slope of the ground the basement was almost entirely above ground, which gave three clear stories to this portion also.

The lobby, reached by the Spring Garden Street entrance, was finished with strongly-veined Italian marble walls and vaulted mosaic ceilings. The panels were formed by mosaics illustrating the ancient methods and processes of coinage. These mosaics formed one of the most beautiful and expressive features in the building. The ceilings were covered with a solid mosaic of gold — each unit being a piece of glass backed with gold.

These beautiful mosaics make a link between the third Philadelphia Mint and its replacement, dedicated Aug. 14, 1969. The third Mint served the nation for more than 65 years, but the growth of the country made demands which could no longer be handled by the then-outmoded facilities.

After the completion of the fourth Philadelphia Mint, the mosaics were painstakingly removed and re-installed in the new facility. There they are a prime attraction for the Mint's thousands of visitors.

Groundbreaking ceremonies held Sept. 17, 1965, launched construction of the fourth Philadelphia Mint, nearly three times the size of the Spring Garden Street plant. On Aug. 14, 1969, another milestone in Mint history was marked by the official opening of an impressive modern building with a pink granite facade and bronze-tinted glass, covering more than five acres of ground, approximately three city blocks. The main entrance plaza and lobby, facing Fifth Street at Independence Mall, overlooks the original site.

Offices, production divisions and public areas occupy more than 500,000 square feet of space and are planned to afford the maximum in efficiency of operation and comfortable working conditions.

The new Mint was designed for an annual production capability of 2 billion coins on a five-day, 40-hour week, or a total capacity of about 8 billion coins per year on a 24-hour day, seven-day week basis. Facilities originally included melting, casting, rolling and annealing facilities, plus cladding lines to produce clad strip for composite coins, in addition to the coining areas. However, the Mint began shutting cladding operations down during fiscal year 1982, and officially shut down the facilities in fiscal 1983, relying instead totally on private sector strip producers.

The entire operation can be viewed from a glass-enclosed elevated gallery designed to accommodate 2,500 visitors an hour.

The numismatic room on the mezzanine ordinarily contains Mint relics, historic coins and medals.

A sales counter is maintained where Mint medals, coin sets and certain Mint publications may be purchased.

Denver Mint

Gold was first discovered in 1858 in what is now the state of Colorado, on the Platte River, near the city of Denver. For some years mining in Colorado was chiefly from placer claims, which were deposits formed by water currents in river beds. Lode gold was found, however, near present Central City, Colo., on May 6, 1859, and other discoveries followed.

When the California Gold Rush of '49 lost its impetus with the declining production of mines in California, miners turned their attention to Denver City where, within a few years, a small village of cottonwood log cabins began to emerge. This town became an "outfitting" point for miners. Recognizing a need for a circulating medium, much as necessity is the mother of invention, several firms in Colorado organized themselves as private Mints. They melted "raw" gold in the form of dust and nuggets, all of which contained an appreciable amount of silver, and formed it into what are now known as Pikes Peak coins. These were much like some of the gold coins struck privately in California some years previously.

Congress, in January 1862, received a proposal from the Treasury Department that a branch Mint be established at Denver, Colo., for gold coinage. As indicative of the need, they were informed that in the two preceding years the private Mint of Clark, Gruber and Co. had turned out gold coins to the extent of $120,000. The government bought the Clark-Gruber plant in the fall of 1862, for the sum of $25,000.

In the early days of Denver, when Indian raids were anticipated, the Mint building was used as a place of refuge for women and children, it being the town's most substantial structure. "The hostility of the Indian tribes along the routes . . ." was one of the reasons given by the Director of the Mint for the Denver plant not being able to assume its position as a branch Mint.

Not to achieve its destiny as a Mint until some years later, the Denver plant opened its doors in September 1863 as an Assay Office. Its activities were restricted to melting and stamping bullion brought in by miners without refining. Under the regulations which were prescribed, the plant was to accomplish this task "within a day or an hour" after it was received. The bars were to be stamped as to the "fineness" (amount of gold and silver contained) and weight. Also stamped on the bars was a device bearing the American eagle and around it the words "U.S. Branch Mint, Denver."

By 1867 the miners had exhausted, to a large extent, the rich beds of placer gold appearing in the streams, and the Assay Office at Denver had little business while miners turned their attention to "lode" mining, uncovering underground veins of ores having a high percentage of gold and silver. It was found, however, that to crush and pulverize these ores and to extract the precious metals required complicated apparatus and skilled labor, as well as rail transportation, all of which were lacking to a large extent.

Heartbroken as they were to see the Union Pacific Railroad pass them to the north, a group of Colorado citizens banded together. Through their enterprise a rail line was built in 1870 which connected Denver with Cheyenne, Wyo., tying them in with the economic life of the nation, from coast to coast.

In the late 19th century Colorado felt the effect of an acceleration in silver mining because of government purchasing programs. When they were terminated, the abrupt reduction in silver output was offset by the rise of the great gold camp at Cripple Creek, Colo.

The Clark-Gruber plant which the government had used continuously began to deteriorate and in 1877 was reported as being so dilapidated as to be considered unsafe.

Hopes for a branch Mint status were again kindled when on Feb. 20, 1895, Congress provided for the establishment of a Mint at Denver for the coinage of gold and silver. A $500,000 appropriation provided that until it could become a Mint in accordance with law it would have to operate as an Assay Office.

On April 22, 1896, a site was purchased at a cost of about $60,000. In the meantime, the deposit activity at the Denver Mint stepped up considerably. The sources of the deposits were principally the mines of Arizona, New Mexico, Colorado and Utah. In 1895 the aggregate value of gold and silver deposited annually was in excess of $5.6 million.

Plans for the new Mint developed slowly, but surely. Moving day took place on Sept. 1, 1904, when the Mint transferred its operations from the historic Clark-Gruber building at 16th and Market streets to the handsome Renaissance structure at West Colfax and Evans streets.

Coinage organization was effected by the naming of officials for the superintendency and various departments on Oct. 15, 1904. Earlier it had been the practice for Denver to send its bullion deposits to Philadelphia for parting and refining. Bullion shipments to Philadelphia ceased Dec. 31, 1904.

The new structure, viewed from the street, provided two stories above ground. Actually it had five floors. It was 175 feet long and 100 feet wide.

The stone facing of the building is Colorado granite, up to and including the water table. The Arkins granite between the water table and the cornice was procured in Maine. Tennessee marble forms the window trimmings, and the marble used in the interior finish was obtained in Vermont.

The decorations of the main corridor on the first floor, the mezzanine floor, and the second floor were completed in 1909 under the direction of John Gibson, a member of an old Philadelphia firm. This firm also furnished the three mural paintings in the area above the cornice inside the main vestibule. They are the work of an Italian named Vincent Adriente who worked under the supervision of the celebrated mural artist Edwin Howland Blashfield, of New York City. The paintings are purely symbolic and typify Commerce, Mining and Manufacturing.

The Great Seal of the United States, in the form of a large metal casting, was placed in the center of the vestibule floor. In the summer of 1961 this seal had worn so smooth it was considered unsafe and was replaced by a mosaic replica.

The new Mint was equipped with all the

latest methods and machinery, the coinage apparatus having been built at Philadelphia where a large part of the machinery used by the Mints was made.

In its first year of operation the coining room turned out gold coin valued at $23.8 million, and subsidiary coin, halves, quarters and dimes, amounting to $3.2 million.

By Act of Congress, the Mint has had authority since 1874 to strike coins for friendly foreign governments. In 1906 the Denver Mint started its first production of foreign coinage — 4.8 million 5-peso gold pieces for the government of Mexico.

The Mint Act of 1873, which codified all existing Mint laws, had restricted the manufacture of 5-cent pieces and cents to the Mint at Philadelphia. At the time that act was passed few if any of these coins were in use in the West, although by legislation in 1906 Congress gave recognition to the fact that they were then in circulation all over the country. The Secretary of the Treasury was then authorized to direct the coinage of 5-cent pieces and cents at any of the Mints. Minor coinage started at the Denver Mint in 1911, the production of cents that year amounting to 12.6 million pieces.

It had always been the practice in the United States to conduct refineries in connection with coinage operations, thus enabling the facilities to receive crude bullion. The installation of a refinery at the Denver Mint in 1906 was itself as momentous as its commencement of coinage. In its first six months of operations the new Denver refinery turned out refined gold and silver valued at $32 million. Operating through the years, it contributed substantially to the total output of refined gold and silver of the Mint.

In 1937 an addition was made to the Denver Mint, covering an area of approximately 6,000 square feet and consisting of a basement and two stories. The old building was remodeled and 10 coining presses, with back-up equipment, were installed.

In October 1945, ground was broken for a three-story addition, 161 feet long by 96 feet wide. The cost of this addition was more than $1.5 million. The new wing was built to house modérn "brass mill" melting and rolling equipment. The rolling system and equipment, designed by one of the foremost rolling mill engineering firms in the nation, was engineered to process a bronze coinage ingot weighing 420 pounds.

Out of consideration for an interested public, a visitor's balcony was constructed in each of the first two floors, suspended under

the 24-f[...] may lo[...] tions.

As c[...] and in[...] began[...] new D[...] cilitie[...] man[...] facil[...]

A[...] confe[...] allocate $1.5 mi[...] new Denver Mint. The Bur[...] went shopping for land.

Two sites were chosen, the South Platte River basin and the Clayton Trust property in the Park Hill section of Denver. The first site was abandoned when the Burlington Northern Railroad stuck to its plans to install mainline tracks adjacent to the area.

Brooks announced on July 16, 1974, the new Mint would be built on the Park Hill site. Construction was set to begin in the fall of 1975 or early 1976 with a completion date around 1980.

The new Mint was to be designed to produce 10.7 billion coins annually and possibly up to 16 billion.

A House bill to provide funds for the new Denver Mint was introduced March 26, 1975. It passed the House Sept. 19, 1975, and went to the Senate Public Works Committee Sept. 22, 1975.

In an unusual procedure, Assistant Secretary of the Treasury David Macdonald and Frank H. MacDonald, Deputy Director of the Mint, testified at an executive session of the Public Works Committee. Witnesses are not normally called into an executive session.

If passed, the bill would have authorized an increase of $60 million in the amount of money that could be appropriated to the Treasury Department for the construction of Mint facilities. The bill would have raised the total authorized by Congress since 1963 for Mint construction to $105 million.

On Feb. 27, 1976, Mint and Treasury officials testified in support of the Denver Mint legislation before the Senate Banking, Housing and Urban Affairs committee.

At one point, Mint officials considered the purchase of an empty . tire manufacturing plant in Littleton, Colo., as a potential site for the Denver Mint. However, the plant was sold in March 1976 to a tire firm.

Rep. William Armstrong, R-Colo., said moving the Mint to suburban Littleton would save the Bureau of the Mint about $20 mil-

lion. Rep. Pat Schro[...] the Littleton move[...] use of the present[...] and expansion o[...] At this poi[...] Wis., chair[...] mittee, di[...] examin[...] ties to[...]

...der, D-Colo., opposed ...advocated the continued ...Mint downtown in Denver, ...f the Philadelphia Mint.

...t, Sen. William Proxmire, D-...an of the Senate Banking com-...rected a General Accounting Office ...tion of all Bureau of the Mint facili-...determine total-picture needs.

...he GAO came out against the construc-...on of a new branch Mint in Denver, prima-...ily because of the 1-cent coin's then-dubious future in the U.S. coinage lineup.

The GAO report criticized Treasury Department estimates of future coinage demands. The proposed phase-out of the cent, which accounts for more than 70 percent of the production of the nation's Mints, diminishes the need for construction of a new coinage facility at this time, the GAO report said.

The report proposed several alternatives, including upgrading current production capacity and modifying production strategies to meet the short-term needs.

The report concluded with the recommendation that the Treasury Secretary require the Bureau of the Mint to make a comprehensive study of the various options for increasing production within its present facilities.

On March 7 during budgetary hearings before the House Appropriations Subcommittee, Acting Mint Director Frank H. MacDonald told representatives the Bureau management was "totally in disagreement with" the GAO report regarding the Denver Mint.

He characterized the report as being full of things that "seem like cheap shots like how we can put coinage presses in the restrooms."

Mint officials abandoned their plans for a new Denver Mint in the Nixon administration and sold the Park Hill site to an Alaskan firm six years later on Jan. 19, 1984, for $3,351,356.05.

Expansion of the present Denver facility was approved, and construction began in late May 1984. Mint Director Donna Pope reported that the expansion would be done in two phases. Phase one would comprise construction of an expanded south dock for all material deliveries and coin shipments, roadway approaches and departures from the south dock, and a two-story building addition on the west side to provide for storage and processing of coinage materials on the ground floor, and secured storage in the basement for coins. The second phase included the relocation and installation of production equipment, support facilities for increased coin production and utilities systems. The con-

struction was expected to be completed by mid-1987, according to a presentation made by Pope during a House Appropriations Committee hearing March 5, 1987, where she outlined her fiscal year 1988 budget request.

San Francisco Mint and Assay Office

The discovery of gold at Coloma (Sutter's Mill) by John Marshall, in 1848, was the world-echoing event which contributed to the recommendation by President Millard Fillmore in 1850 that a branch Mint be established in California. Gold being mined in the hills had grown from a trickle to a deluge too heavy for facilities at the distant Philadelphia Mint to handle and much time was consumed in transporting the precious metal on its hazardous journey. The coinage situation in the West was in a chaotic state. Many different kinds circulated — French louis d'ors, Dutch guilders, Indian rupees, Mexican reales, English shillings, as well as American pieces — but even so, there was a scarcity; and gold dust, while acceptable, was not a convenient medium of exchange. To remedy the difficulty, private Mints sprang up which converted the gold into coins, but this was not the solution to the problem.

The United States Mint at San Francisco, Calif., was authorized by the Act of Congress approved July 3, 1852, and the coins produced there gradually replaced the miscellaneous assortment in circulation. The Mint commenced receiving deposits on April 3, 1854. Supply of materials retarded and diminished the coinage operations during that year. However, $4,084,207, all in gold pieces, was coined between April and December 1854.

Operations were conducted in a small building on Commercial Street, just 60 feet square. The Director remarked: "It is almost impossible to conceive how so much work can be well done, and so much business transacted safely, in so small a space. The entrance to the business office is up a steep pair of stairs and through a dark hall rendered unwholesome by the fumes of acids, and uncomfortable by the noise of machinery and the heat of the engine. The apartments of the different officers and the desks of the clerks are cramped and inconvenient, and the vaults depend for their safety chiefly upon the presence of well-tried watchmen."

About 10 years later, the suggestion was made that there be purchased "a suitable site upon which should be speedily erected a mint building creditable to the Government, and commensurate with the wants of the great mineral districts of the Pacific Coast." It was not until 1872-73, however, that the building was completed and the work of fitting up the necessary machinery, fixtures and apparatus was begun. The new Mint at Fifth and Mission was occupied in the summer of 1874, and was one of the best-appointed Mints in the world.

The work of the San Francisco Mint was interrupted by the great earthquake of April 18, 1906. The structure and its contents were saved from the fire by intelligent and courageous work on the part of the superintendent and employees, but as the fuel used for its melting, annealing and assaying operations was city gas, the destruction of the gas works made a discontinuance of operations necessary. Moreover, the Mint, by reason of the destruction of the subtreasury and all of the banks of the city, became the only financial institution able to do business in the city and the agency through which all remittances to and from the city, and disbursements within the city were made. The Mint became the depository and treasury for the relief fund, and its superintendent, Frank A. Leach, had many new and very important responsibilities suddenly thrust upon him, all of which were borne with fidelity and ability.

The steadily increasing coinage demands of the nation following the Depression made mandatory the enlargement of minting facilities, and in the summer of 1937, San Francisco personnel made another move, this time into an imposing three-story marble edifice some distance from the principal business district where the 1874 building was located. The approximately 33,000 square feet of space in the 1937 structure housed the most modern facilities of the day and new equipment to replace worn and obsolete machinery.

The newest San Francisco Mint went into operation in 1937, striking U.S. coins of all denominations, plus coins for the Philippine Islands in 1944 and 1945, as World War II came to a close. In most years, the San Francisco mintages of U.S. coins lagged behind those of Philadelphia and Denver, although for some denominations, San Francisco totals were slightly higher than Denver mintages during a few years.

Meanwhile, in the decade following the end of World War II, the Philadelphia and Denver Mints were being improved. It was the belief that these expanded facilities would be adequate to meet the nation's coin demand for some time to come. Therefore, in March 1955, coinage operations at San Francisco

were discontinued. The equipment was removed and most of the building was remodeled for occupancy by other agencies of the government. Only a small area was retained by the Mint for the conduct of assay functions, including receipts of gold and silver deposits.

A profound change in the classification of the 1937 Mint structure came in the mid-1960s when it once again became an operating minting facility. During the fall of 1963, it became apparent that a coin shortage was building up, and by July 1964, emergency measures had been adopted to relieve the situation. One of these measures was the utilization of space in the 1937 San Francisco Mint building (called the San Francisco Assay Office since approval of a law July 11, 1962). The Treasury reacquired and once again adapted the space to the making of coins. However, despite its rebirth as a minting facility, the Bureau of the Mint continued to call the 1937 facility an Assay Office.

With the additional equipment secured from the Department of Defense, San Francisco began producing 1-cent and 5-cent coin blanks and took on annealing and upsetting operations also, thus lessening the load at the Denver Mint and allowing it more leeway for the other manufacturing functions. The finished blanks were then shipped to Denver for the final stamping process. This enabled the making of many more coins at Denver than would ordinarily have been possible.

Reactivation of coining operations at San Francisco was authorized by the Coinage Act of 1965, approved by President Johnson July 23, and on Sept. 1 the presses began turning out the first coins struck there since coinage was discontinued 10 years before.

In 1968, the San Francisco Assay Office assumed production of all Proof coinage; not until 1983 and 1984 with the Olympic coinage program were U.S. Proof coins intended for public purchase struck at another Mint facility. From 1968 to 1974, only some of the business-strike coinage bore the San Francisco Mint mark. Since 1974, only the Anthony dollars of 1979-1981 struck in San Francisco have borne the S Mint mark, except for Proof coinage.

The Assay Office was also the site in 1986 for the striking of the Statue of Liberty/Ellis Island Commemorative Proof Immigrant half dollar and the Proof Ellis Island dollar coins as well as the Uncirculated and Proof versions of the silver American Eagle bullion coin.

In late 1985, during Mint Appropriation

hearings before the House Banking Subcommittee on Consumer Affairs and Coinage, Mint officials hoped to get approval to change the status of the Assay Office to a Mint. But the appropriations bill was never voted out of the subcommittee and that change in status died along with the bill.

Old San Francisco Mint

After it was abandoned by the Mint in 1937, the 1874 Mint building, which came to be lovingly known as the "Granite Lady," spent decades in limbo, serving various government organizations. In 1968, however, the federal government vacated the nearly century-old building and declared it surplus to government needs.

Various groups fought over the empty and deteriorating building, some wanting to demolish it, and others wanting to restore and preserve it. In the spring of 1972, President Nixon intervened to save the 1874 Mint structure at Fifth and Mission streets from its then uncertain fate. He announced the transfer of the building from the General Services Administration to the Department of the Treasury's Bureau of the Mint for restoration and continued use by the government and the enjoyment of the public.

A year later, in April 1973, the Mint's Special Coins and Medals and Computer employees were able to move their operations into the rooms in the rear of the building, newly renovated and equipped to speed the processing of mail orders received from the public for the special coins and medals produced by the Mint.

On June 16, 1973, the Old San Francisco Mint was officially re-opened as a public museum and working Mint facility under Mint Director Mary Brooks. The museum rooms are authentically restored to their original 1874 appearance and are open to the public. Exhibits of historical and educational significance will continue to be developed for display.

Produced as a Bicentennial project by the Bureau of the Mint was a film titled "The Granite Lady," which tells the story of the Old San Francisco Mint. With Mercedes McCambridge as narrator, the film features two child actors and some of the 200 Mint employees in contemporary costumes.

Following a preview on National Educational Television, the award-winning film is screened daily for visitors to the Mint.

On Nov. 7, 1976, a VIP reception hosted by Mint Director Mary Brooks celebrated the completion of the restoration of the Old San Francisco Mint. Brooks told the several hundred reception guests that the sale of the millions of U.S. coins and national medals financed the $4.5 million restoration of the century-old edifice.

Jan. 28, 1977, was another "red letter" day in the illustrious history of the Old Mint. Ceremonies at the Mint that day were held to commemorate official recognition of the Fifth and Mission streets' structure as "California Registered Historical Landmark No. 875."

A plaque unveiled that day is inscribed with the following thumbnail sketch of the role played by the Old Mint in the growth of San Francisco from a tiny mission to a great metropolis:

> "The Old Mint (1869), San Francisco's second, is California's only such Greek Revival structure. Due to unsurpassed productivity, it became a subtreasury in 1874. Intact after the 1906 disaster, it served as a clearing house-bank, thus aiding in the city's reconstruction. Closed in 1937: Restored 1972-76 by Mint Director Mary Brooks."

Although the Old San Francisco Mint, its current official designation, continues to serve the United States Mint, some of its duties have been transferred to other facilities. Among the changes were the transfer of the Mint Data Center and consolidation of the Old San Francisco Mint with the San Francisco Assay Office.

Fort Knox Gold Bullion Depository

A large amount of the monetary gold stocks of the United States is stored in the vault of the Fort Knox Bullion Depository. The balance of the government's holdings is stored at the Denver Mint and the West Point Bullion Depository, with only small quantities stored at the Philadelphia Mint and the San Francisco Assay Office.

The Depository was completed in December 1936 at a cost of $560,000. It is located approximately 30 miles southwest of Louisville, Ky., on a site which formerly was a part of the Fort Knox military reservation. The first gold was moved to the Depository by railroad in January 1937. That series of shipments was completed in June 1937.

The two-story basement and attic building is constructed of granite, steel and concrete; exterior dimensions measure 105 by 121 feet. Its height is 42 feet above the first floor level.

Construction was under supervision of the Procurement Division of the Treasury Department, now the Public Buildings Administration of the General Services Administration. Upon completion, the Depository was placed under the jurisdiction of the Director of the Mint.

Within the building is a two-level steel and concrete vault, divided into compartments. The vault door weighs more than 20 tons. No one person is entrusted with the combination. Various members of the Depository staff must separately dial combinations known only to them. The vault casing is constructed of steel plates, steel I-beams and steel cylinders laced with hoop bands and encased in concrete. The vault roof is of similar construction and is independent of the depository roof.

Between the corridor encircling the vault and the outer wall of the building is space utilized for offices, storerooms and the like.

The outer wall of the depository is of granite, lined with concrete. Included in the materials used in construction were 16,500 cubic feet of granite, 4,200 cubic yards of concrete, 750 tons of reinforcing steel and 670 tons of structural steel.

Over the marble entrance at the front of the building is the inscription "United States Depository" with the seal of the Treasury Department in gold. Offices of the Officer in Charge and the Captain of the Guard open upon the entrance lobby. At the rear of the building is another entrance for the reception of bullion and supplies.

At each corner of the structure, on the outside, but connected with it, are four guard boxes. Sentry boxes, similar to the guard boxes at the corners of the Depository, are located at the entrance gate. A driveway encircles the building and a steel fence marks the boundaries of the site.

The building is equipped with the latest and most modern protective devices. The nearby Army Post gives additional protection. The Depository is equipped with its own emergency power plant, water system and other facilities. In the basement is a pistol range for the guards.

The gold in the Depository is in the form of standard Mint bars of almost pure gold, or coin gold bars resulting from the melting of gold coins. These bars are slightly smaller than an ordinary building brick. The approximate dimensions are 7 x 3⅝ x 1¾ inches. The fine gold bars contain approximately 400 troy ounces of gold. The avoirdupois weight is about 27½ pounds. They are stored without wrappings in the vault compartments. When they are handled, great care is exercised to avoid abrasion of the soft metal.

While all of the physical gold stock is stored in the various institutions of the United States Mint, it is not, as sometimes supposed, "kept out of circulation." Most of it is made part of the money stream through the medium of gold certificates or gold certificate credits, which are issued only to the Federal Reserve Banks. The Federal Reserve Banks may obtain gold by redemption of the certificates when necessary for the settlement of international balances.

The guard force, under the supervision of the Officer in Charge, is made up of men selected from various government agencies, or recruited from Civil Service Registers.

Ordinarily, no visitors are allowed inside the Fort Knox Depository. Franklin D. Roosevelt visited there in 1943, the one and only time a gold vault was opened for inspection for anyone other than authorized personnel until Sept. 23, 1974.

On that date, a seven-man congressional inspection team and nearly 100 reporters toured the Depository for the first public check of the nation's gold hoard.

Rep. Philip M. Crane, R-Ill., started things off when he discussed a rumor with Treasury Secretary William Simon in mid-1974 that gold was missing from the vault.

To dispel any doubts that the gold was really there, Mint Director Mary Brooks conducted the Fort Knox inspection. A special audit followed the tour, conducted by the General Accounting Office and the Treasury. Provision has since been made by Congress for continuing audits by the Bureau of the Mint.

Secretary of the Treasury W. Michael Blumenthal paid his first visit to the Depository in July 1977, accompanied by Undersecretary of the Treasury Bette B. Anderson. This was the first visit to Fort Knox by a Secretary of the Treasury since John W. Snyder paid a call in 1947.

Director of the Mint Donna Pope paid a visit to the Depository in the summer of 1981. In June of 1985, James M. Curtis was appointed Officer in Charge of the Depository, replacing Eugene Kimbler as acting officer in charge. Curtis, formerly a Staff Inspector with the New York Police Department, retired from the NYPD after 23 years of service to take the Mint position.

West Point
Bullion Depository

Formerly the West Point Silver Bullion Depository, in New York, the Depository serves as a fourth "Mint" of the United States, in addition to its status as the main storehouse of the nation's silver and the holder of one-quarter of the nation's gold supply.

The depository was completed at a cost of about $500,000 and occupied in 1938. It is a rectangular, windowless, one-story concrete building, 170 x 256 feet, situated on a four-acre tract of land formerly a part of the West Point Military Reservation. The building is within 500 feet of the Storm King Highway, near West Point's "Old North Gate."

Offices and guard rooms are on the first floor and mezzanine, at the front of the building, with entrance through a vestibule. Light and air for this section are obtained through skylights. The remainder of the structure is under a solid composition roof. A vertical-lift steel door in the center of the front affords passage for bullion trucks. With this door closed, complete isolation is provided for loading operations. To the rear of the loading platform are rolling steel doors and checking rooms through which the storage vault is reached. A series of vault compartments is guarded by a master vault door and an emergency door. The master vault door is equipped with a time lock, and is of drill-proof and flame-proof metal.

A nine-foot steel fence surrounds the building, with a steel gate controlled by guards that regulates the entrance and departure of persons and vehicles. The outside walls are of reinforced concrete. An inside corridor connects the four turrets or watchtowers at the corners, where sentries may observe the terrain in all directions. The depository's outside walls may be placed under floodlight.

Gold from the New York Assay Office began to arrive at the Depository Nov. 8, 1981, with the last shipment from the NYAO arriving Aug. 12, 1982. During that time, 25 convoys using 133 tractor-trailers transferred 193,782 gold bars weighing from 5 ounces to 125 pounds each. The total gross weight

transferred was about 2,318 tons. Law enforcement officials cooperating in the move included U.S. Secret Service special agents, New York and New Jersey state police, and local law enforcement agencies. The U.S. Army assisted in security on arrival at the Depository.

To help the Bureau of the Mint absorb the increased coinage demands beginning with the Bicentennial coins, first struck in 1975, the Depository is now being used for coinage purposes. Permission to use the Depository facilities to coin money was granted in the law providing for the Bicentennial coinage, signed Oct. 18, 1973. The section reads:

"Until the Secretary of the Treasury determines that the Mints of the United States are adequate for the production of ample supplies of coins and medals, any facility of the Bureau of the Mint may be used for the manufacture and storage of medals and coins."

Mint Director Mary Brooks announced in mid-1974 that some of the older Mint presses were being installed at West Point to produce coins and medals.

Twenty dual coin presses, some retired from the Philadelphia Mint, were installed. Ten began operations in November 1974, and the others began operations in early 1975.

Following the end of the Bicentennial program, the West Point facility continued to produce cents on its coin presses. In late 1976, it began test striking quarters. In 1975 and again in May 1977 it also produced bronze 1-centesimo coins for Panama.

At first, no West Point-struck coins bore Mint marks. That changed on Sept. 13, 1983, when the ceremonial first 1984 Olympic $10 gold eagles were struck, each bearing a W Mint mark. The Proof and Uncirculated versions of the Statue of Liberty gold half eagles, which were struck at West Point in 1986, also bear a W Mint mark.

All of the American Arts Gold Medallions were also struck at West Point as were several denominations of the Statue of Liberty/Ellis Island commemorative coins and the four denominations of the American Eagle gold bullion coins.

Former Mint institutions

Charlotte, North Carolina

The discovery of gold in the southern Appalachian Mountains and the unearthing of large quantities of the precious metal presented a major problem for prospectors in that

then-inaccessible region of the nation, in the 1820s.

Miners, once they had recovered the gold, were faced with a long trip to the Philadelphia Mint to have their finds smelted and struck into gold coins. The infant industry soon sought relief from Washington, D.C.

When the demands for a local Mint were not met by the federal government, a German immigrant named Christian Bechtler established a private Mint at Rutherfordton, N.C., in 1831. Seeing a potentially large supply of gold being diverted away from government control inspired Congress to authorize the Charlotte Mint in 1835.

The building and equipment were budgeted at $50,000, but the costs overran this figure and the opponents of a branch Mint tried to use this to stop the construction. The Mint opened on July 27, 1837, for the assaying and processing of gold, but no coins were struck until the following year.

Like the Dahlonega Mint in Georgia, the Charlotte facility struck only gold coins. Its production was limited to half eagles, quarter eagles and dollars, with a more even distribution of the three than at Dahlonega.

Production was halted for a year and a half, until 1846, after a fire damaged the building on the night of July 27, 1844. The fire has been attributed to a burglar who was either careless or malicious.

The branch Mints were considered by the Philadelphia Mint to be poor stepsisters, and they consequently received the worst equipment. Worn-out presses received repairs when they should have received a decent burial, and rusted reverse dies unfit for duty in Philadelphia were Mint-marked and shipped south. One redeeming feature of this practice is that it is hard to convincingly alter a Philadelphia coin to one from a scarcer Mint, because the resulting fake will be literally too good to be true.

During the 1850s production at the Charlotte Mint became increasingly irregular, as the local gold supplies dried up and were not replaced by California bullion. Half eagles were the only denomination consistently struck during this decade.

Throughout the entire period of Federal control the Charlotte Mint struck a total of $5,059,188 worth of gold coin. This compares with $4,084,773 worth of gold coin struck in San Francisco in 1854 alone, and $18,008,300 struck there the following year.

The Mint struck 5,992 half eagles in 1861 before it was seized by the Confederate forces on April 20, and 887 pieces afterward. A quantity of bullion remained uncoined, either because of technical difficulties or because the bullion value of the gold was greater than the face value of the coins that could have been made from it.

It is a tribute to the dedication of bureaucrats everywhere that somebody in the then Confederate Mint in October 1861 sent to Philadelphia 12 half eagles that had been struck under the Federal government in early 1861 and had been set aside for assay purposes. Millions of dollars' worth of Federal property had been seized by the Confederacy, and yet somebody was more concerned with the integrity of the Charlotte Mint than the Confederate Treasury.

Throughout the remainder of the Civil War the building was used for office space by the Confederate armed forces. After the war it was occupied for a while by officials of the Union army, and eventually it was restored to the status of an Assay Office.

In 1935, one century after the authorization of the Mint, it was decided to tear the building down to make room for a new post office building. A local citizens' group purchased the materials and reconstructed the building on a new site, where it now serves as an art museum.

Dahlonega, Georgia

The Dahlonega Mint was opened in 1838 to accommodate the gold miners of northern Georgia, and to help the Charlotte Mint compete with the private Bechtler Mint doing business in North Carolina.

The area of northern Georgia had been a part of the Cherokee nation, but it was obtained in 1830 in exchange for lands in Oklahoma. The name of the town is taken from the Indian word Tah-lon-e-ka, which means "yellow metal."

Gold had been known in small quantities in this area for many years by the Indians and the white men, but the first large strike did not occur until the 1820s. The exact year is uncertain, but there are many colorful tales describing the first major find.

The most popular story is that a running deer kicked up a nugget which was spotted by the pursuing hunter. History does not record the name of the hunter or the fate of the deer.

Throughout its existence the Dahlonega Mint struck gold coins exclusively. The most common denomination produced was the half eagle, with only token coinages of quarter eagles and dollars.

In 1854, the Mint produced its only issue of $3 pieces. Presumably this denomination was less popular in the South than it was in the North, as the New Orleans Mint also struck in it just this first year, and the Charlotte Mint never did. Only 1,120 pieces were struck at Dahlonega.

Although all Dahlonega gold coins bear the name of the United States of America, this legend did not always apply. In 1861 the Confederate States of America confiscated all Federal property within its boundaries, including the three branch Mints in the South. The Dahlonega Mint was placed under the management of the governor of Georgia.

Unlike the New Orleans Mint, there was little bullion on hand at the Dahlonega and Charlotte Mints at the commencement of hostilities. The Dahlonega Mint is thought to have contained $13,345 worth of uncoined gold when it was seized on April 8, 1861, but the official records were never recovered after the Civil War.

The small quantity of 1861-D dollars in existence must have been struck under either Confederate or Georgian authority, as the U.S. Mint Report lists no dollars for this date and Mint. It is thought that a number of half eagles may also have been produced, and poorly struck pieces are often attributed to this alleged striking. As the Mint did produce half eagles under Federal auspices in this year, and as it had never been known for its fine workmanship, it is impossible to state with certainty who produced any particular piece.

The small amount of bullion remaining on hand was not struck into coins for a number of reasons, mainly because of technical problems and the lack of die-making facilities. Late in the war the Mint served as a temporary repository for the Confederate Treasury, before the city was overrun.

The Dahlonega and Charlotte Mints were considered by many to have been redundant ever since the opening of the San Francisco Mint, and there were proposals to close them even before the Civil War. The Dahlonega Mint never reopened after the war, and its building was donated to the state of Georgia for educational purposes.

The structure was reopened as the main building of North Georgia College in 1873, but it was destroyed by fire in 1878. Price Memorial Hall was built on its foundation the following year and occupied in 1880. It stands today as the administration building for the college, and houses a complete set of Dahlonega Mint gold coins, assembled by H.A. Alexander, an Atlanta lawyer.

The "golden heritage" of the area is attested to by a large plaque, erected in connection with "Project Golden Steeple," through which Price Memorial Hall's steeple was leafed with native gold donated for the purpose.

Carson City, Nevada

The bill to establish a branch Mint in Nevada was passed on March 3, 1863. It was urged in the Senate that the heavy tax of transportation cost upon producers in Nevada, the wonderful increase of gold and silver bullion and the necessity of keeping it in the United States through coinage, were to be considered sufficient inducements for Congress to order the establishment of a Mint.

Hugh McCulloch, U.S. Secretary of the Treasury, on Dec. 27, 1865, authorized a committee of three Nevada citizens to select and approve a location for a Mint in Carson City. The committee included Abe Curry (founder of Carson City), F. Rice and John Mills. Curry facilitated the work of the commissioners by donating an entire city block as the Mint site.

On July 18, 1866, the three commissioners received authority to proceed with the construction of the Mint. On Sept. 18, 1866, the cornerstone was dedicated and laid by the Grand Masonic Lodge of Nevada.

The Director's Report for 1866 carried the following item: ". . . This building is in rapid process of erection. It is of good size, sixty by ninety feet, of two stories, built of a good quality of sandstone, and is exceedingly well arranged. It is located upon a large and handsome lot of ground, entirely disconnected from other buildings. . . .

"As the mines of Nevada are almost entirely silver, and as the exportation of silver is almost wholly in bars, there being very little demand for silver coin, it will be inexpedient to introduce machinery for coinage into this institution at present. . . ."

All of 1868 and most of 1869 were spent installing machinery and fixtures and it was not until December of 1869 that the fitting of the branch Mint at Carson City for business as a Mint was completed. On Jan. 8, 1870, it was opened for the receipt of bullion.

On Nov. 6, 1885, it was directed that the Mint be closed, except for the receipt of bullion for "parting and refining" and local purchases of silver for the standard dollar coinage. The Mint remained closed to the receipt of deposits until Oct. 1, 1886. Under the usual provision for the Mint at Carson City in the legislative appropriation act for the year, it was reopened for deposits as an Assay Office, with an acid refinery.

The coinage department of the Mint was reopened July 1, 1889, but owing to the dilapidated condition in which the building and machinery were found, after four years of idleness, repairs and betterments of the building and overhauling and repairing of the machinery were necessary. Consequently, coinage of gold and silver was not commenced until Oct. 1, 1889.

Coinage operations continued until 1893 when, by direction of the Secretary of the Treasury, they were suspended, effective June 1, and the force employed in the coiner's department dispensed with.

Upon suspension of coinage operations, the presses and other machinery used in the coining department were painted and leaded under the supervision of Charles Colburn, the retiring coiner, to prevent corrosion.

From July 1 to Nov. 14, 1898, the Mint was open to the receipt of gold and silver deposits. Following this came the order of the Secretary of the Treasury reducing the Mint to an Assay Office, to take effect July 1, 1899, as authorized by an Act of Congress approved Feb. 24, 1899.

A steadily decreasing volume of work resulted in the final closing of the Carson City Mint. No appropriation having been provided for its maintenance, operations ceased June 30, 1933. The property then passed out of the custody of the Mint Service but remained under government control until legislation approved May 22, 1939, authorized the sale of the property. It is now owned by the state of Nevada and a museum is operated on the premises.

Contained in the museum is the original Carson City dollar press. The old press was used to strike the official Nevada 1976 Bicentennial medals.

The state Bicentennial commission paid approximately $29,000 to get the press into operation once again. It was built originally in the Virginia and Truckee Railroad shops in Carson City.

The press is to be continued for automated use as a revenue source.

The museum, in addition to housing the Carson City dollar press, also possesses the original 1876 Nevada U.S. Centennial medal die. This was used to strike the state Bicentennial medal.

New Orleans, Louisiana

The Act of Congress approved March 3, 1835, established a branch Mint at New Orleans, and for that purpose the mayor and city council offered to deed to the United States government a portion of ground bounded by Esplanade, Barracks Street and Bayou Road, which was surrounded by a moat, and formerly known as old Fort St. Charles.

"On the 19th of June 1835 the municipal authorities of the city of New Orleans conveyed to the United States, . . . a certain piece . . . of land situated in the City of New Orleans, known as 'Jackson Square,' immediately fronting the river Mississippi, for the express purpose of erecting thereon a branch of the Mint of the United States . . ."

By this liberal and patriotic act, the United States became possessed of one of the most valuable squares of ground in the city, without any cost to the government. The value of this donation has been estimated at a little less than $500,000.

In consideration for deeding this ground it was agreed that a building should be erected thereon for minting purposes, and should it happen in the future that this Mint cease to operate, the title of the property would revert back to the city.

The Mint building was erected under the supervision of William Strickland, the architect who drew the plans. The cornerstone of the original building, an edifice 280 feet long and three stories high, was laid in September 1835. Due to sickness and other delays, the work was not completed until 1838; operations commenced March 8, 1838. It is presumed since legislation authorizing Mints at Charlotte, N.C., and Dahlonega, Ga., for the coinage of gold was passed at the same time, that the New Orleans Mint was meant to handle, along with the other two, the influx of metal from recently opened mines in the Southern region. The first coinage consisted of dimes, in the sum of $40,242.00; this was the total coinage for 1838.

The Mint suspended operations in 1839, from July 1 until Nov. 30, because of an outbreak of yellow fever, which is said to have been one of the worst scourges the city has ever known.

At the beginning, the machinery used for minting purposes was run by hand, and it was not until 1845 that the first steam boiler and steam press were used in New Orleans. Coinage operations continued until Jan. 31, 1861, when the Mint was taken over by the state of Louisiana and all operations were carried on by it with the same officers who functioned under the United States. On March 31, it was again taken over, this time by the Confederate States of America, in whose custody it continued until it was closed on May 31 of that year. According to old records, there was in the vaults at that time more than $200,000 in bullion, which was coined by the Confederate forces, and a good portion of the machinery was later taken from the Mint by the

Confederates and transferred to various gun factories in the state.

Acting under orders of Secretary of the Treasury Salmon P. Chase, Dr. M.F. Bonzano, Melter and Refiner at New Orleans, returned to that city from the North, whence he had gone during the war, and took possession of the Mint and its property following recapture of the city May 1, 1862.

During the war much of the machinery had been damaged and otherwise rendered ineffective by disuse and other causes incident to the war. Extensive repairs, besides additional machinery, were required before coinage operations could be resumed. In 1874, John Jay Knox, then Deputy Comptroller of the Currency, said that it was not probable that coinage would ever again be necessary in New Orleans and that the Mint at Philadelphia had sufficient capacity for all coinage requirements. However, after a period of inactivity, the New Orleans Mint reopened its doors Oct. 23, 1876, as an Assay Office.

Because the provisions of the original land grant were not being followed, and no coins were being manufactured, the United States marshal, a Mr. Packard, proposed on July 28, 1876, that the Mint be seized for the state of Louisiana, on the grounds that it was not being used as a Mint. No action was taken, however, for the Mint continued in the capacity of an Assay Office until 1879, when coinage operations were resumed.

In connection with the reopening of the New Orleans Mint, the Annual Report of the Director of the Mint for 1878 contains the following:

"The Act of Congress making appropriation for the Mint at New Orleans provided that no expenditure of money should be made for that Mint until the city should release all title and claim and all conditions of forfeiture to the lands or premises upon which the Mint is located, and negotiations looking to that effect were entered into with the city authorities, which resulted in the square of ground being deeded in fee-simple to the government."

In the early days, the officers were housed in the Mint, and an old record book contains an entry to the effect that "Dr. Bonzano moved his residence from the Mint to his plantation ..." In 1884, all persons still maintaining living quarters in the building were informed by the Director that they must move out by Aug. 1 of that year.

Coinage operations continued uninterrupted from 1879 to 1909, at which time they were discontinued because it was felt that facilities at the more modern Denver and San Francisco Mints were adequate to handle the demand. From 1909 to 1919, the building was used exclusively as an Assay Office. The Veterans Bureau was granted permission to occupy a portion of the space, remaining for one year, during 1919. Beginning in 1922, the Veterans Bureau Dispensary was housed in the Mint and continued there for a number of years. The building was vacated June 30, 1931, and the Assay Office activities transferred to space in the customhouse, where operations were continued until June 30, 1942, when they ceased for good.

In 1966, the federal government presented the Mint building to Louisiana with the understanding that the state would provide face-lifting funds and renovation work would be completed in 10 years.

The Louisiana legislature faced a deadline in 1976 on the proposed appropriation of $3.5 million to the state's museum board for the restoration of the New Orleans Mint.

In 1976, the state was given four more years of grace by the federal government in which to renovate the Old Mint.

Meanwhile, in April 1976 a numismatic exhibit sponsored by the Orleans Token and Medal Society was installed in the Old Mint which was opened to the public on an extended basis by the New Orleans Bicentennial Commission.

A set of "O" Mint coins represented the first of several exhibits planned by OTAMS on both concurrent and alternating bases.

State plans to renovate the New Orleans Mint, however, came to a temporary halt on May 27, 1976, because of a Louisiana state supreme court ruling that tidelands revenues received from the federal government could not be used at this time. The Louisiana state museum board had counted on this funding to develop the Mint restoration.

Exactly one year later on May 27, 1977, Gov. Edwin W. Edwards of Louisiana told state legislators he agreed to support amendments to bond bills to provide the full $3.5 million necessary to restore the Old Mint in New Orleans.

Plans for the restoration called for leasing part of the space in the Mint for private business, such as curio shops and restaurants, developing an area for media presentations for tourists, plus creating an auditorium and museum library on the third floor of the building.

The capital outlay bill, which included funds for the Mint restoration, was signed into law July 14 by Gov. Edwards. The bill was divided into cash and bond portions and included other construction projects besides the Mint restoration.

The restoration process began in 1977, with the majority of the work being done in 1979. The interior and exterior of the building were restored to their mid-1850s appearance, and a new roof was erected.

The third floor of the Mint houses the Louisiana Historical Center, including the museum's 40,000-volume library concerning the history of Louisiana. Also on the third floor is the Amistad Research Center, a 2-million volume library about minorities in the United States.

Former Assay Offices

U.S. Assay Office, St. Louis, Mo., authorized by the Act of Feb. 1, 1881; opened July 1, 1881; closed June 30, 1911.

U.S. Assay Office, Helena, Mont., author-

ized by the Act of May 12, 1874; commenced operations Jan. 15, 1877; closed June 30, 1933.

U.S. Assay Office, Salt Lake City, Utah, authorized by the Act of May 30, 1908; opened Feb. 1, 1909; closed June 30, 1933.

U.S. Assay Office, Deadwood, S.D., established by the Acts of June 11, 1896, and Feb. 19, 1897; opened April 20, 1898; closed June 30, 1927.

U.S. Assay Office, Boise, Idaho, established by the Act of Feb. 19, 1869, first deposits received in March of 1872; closed June 30, 1933.

U.S. Assay Office, Seattle, Wash., authorized by the Act of May 21, 1898; closed March 31, 1955.

U.S. Assay Office, New York, N.Y., authorized by Act of March 3, 1853; commenced operation Oct. 10, 1854; closed Dec. 30, 1982.

Source: United States Mint

Directors of the U.S. Mint, 1792-1987

The Director of the Mint is appointed by the President of the United States, by and with the advice and consent of the Senate. The length of the term of office was not fixed by law from 1792 to 1873. The Act of February 12, 1873, fixed the term of the Director at five years. However, there is no restriction on the reappointment of Directors.

Director	Term of service
David Rittenhouse, Pennsylvania	April 1792-June 1795
Henry William de Saussure, South Carolina	July 1795-October 1795
Elias Boudinot, New Jersey	October 1795-July 1805
Robert Patterson, Pennsylvania	January 1806-July 1824
Samuel Moore, Pennsylvania	July 1824-July 1835
Robert Maskell Patterson, Pennsylvania	July 1835-July 1851
George N. Eckert, Pennsylvania	July 1851-April 1853
Thomas M. Pettit, Pennsylvania	April 1853-May 1853
James Ross Snowden, Pennsylvania	June 1853-April 1861
James Pollock, Pennsylvania	May 1861-September 1866
William Millward, Pennsylania	October 1866-April 1867
Henry Richard Linderman, Pennsylvania	April 1867-April 1869
James Pollock, Pennsylvania	May 1869-March 1873
Henry Richard Linderman, Pennsylvania	April 1873-December 1878
Horatio C. Burchard, Illinois	February 1879-June 1885
James P. Kimball, Pennsylvania	July 1885-October 1889
Edward O. Leech, District of Columbia	October 1889-May 1893
Robert E. Preston, District of Columbia	November 1893-Feb. 1898
George E. Roberts, Iowa	February 1898-July 1907
Frank A. Leach, California	September 1907-Nov. 1909
A. Piatt Andrew, Massachusetts	November 1909-June 1910
George E. Roberts, Iowa	July 1910-November 1914
Robert W. Woolley, Virginia	March 1915-July 1916
F.J.H. von Engelken, Florida	September 1916-Feb. 1917
Raymond T. Baker, Nevada	March 1917-March 1922
F.E. Scobey, Ohio	March 1922-September 1923
Robert J. Grant, Colorado	November 1923-May 1933

Director	Term of service
Nellie Tayloe Ross, Wyoming	May 1933-April 1953
William H. Brett, Ohio	July 1954-January 1961
Eva Adams, Nevada	October 1961-August 1969
Mary Brooks, Idaho	September 1969-February 1977
Stella Hackel Sims, Vermont	November 1977-April 1981
Donna Pope, Ohio	July 1981-present

Mint Superintendents

It was 80 years from the time David Rittenhouse took over as first director of the U.S. Mint until future directors were given an "assistant" via the office of the superintendent.

The Coinage Act of 1873 put all Mint and assay office activities under the newly-organized Bureau of the Mint in the Department of the Treasury and the director's headquarters were moved to the Treasury Building in Washington, D.C. The top officer at Philadelphia was thereafter designated as superintendent.

Philadelphia

Superintendents, their term of service, and the name of the Mint director(s) at the time of their service, include:

Superintendent	Mint Director(s)	Term
James Pollock	Henry R. Linderman	1873-1879
Col. A. Loudon Snowden	Horatio C. Burchard	1879-1885
Daniel M. Fox	James P. Kimball	1885-1889
Col. O.C. Bosbyshell	Edward O. Leech, Robert E. Preston	1889-1894
Dr. Eugene Townsend	Robert E. Preston	1894-1895
Maj. Herman Kretz	Robert E. Preston	1895-1898
Henry Boyer	George E. Roberts	1898-1902
John H. Landis	George E. Roberts, Frank A. Leach	1902-1914
	A. Piatt Andrews, George E. Roberts	
Adam M. Joyce	R.W. Wooley, F.J.H. von Engelken,	1914-1921
	Raymond T. Baker	
Freas Styer	Raymond Baker, F.E. Scobey,	1921-1934
	R.S. Grant, Nellie T. Ross	
A. Raymond Raff	Nellie Tayloe Ross	1934-1935
Edward H. Dressel	Nellie Tayloe Ross	1935-1953
Rae V. Biester	William H. Brett	1953-1961
Michael H. Sura	Eva Adams	1961-1969
Nicholas G. Theodore	Eva Adams, Mary Brooks, Stella Hackel	1969-1977
Shallie M. Bey Jr.	Stella Hackel Sims	1978-1981
Anthony H. Murray Jr.	Donna Pope	1981-date

New Orleans

Superintendent	Term
David Bradford	1837-1839
Joseph M. Kennedy	Oct. 18, 1839-Sept. 1850
Robert M. McAlpine	1850-May 13, 1853
Charles Bienvenu	1853-Dec. 31, 1857
Logan McNight	Jan. 1, 1858-May 8, 1858
John H. Alpuente (acting)	May 8, 1858-May 25, 1858
Howard Millspaugh (acting)	May 25, 1858-July 9, 1858
William A. Elmore	July 9, 1858-Jan. 30, 1861*
M.F. Bonzano (Assayer in Charge)	1874-1875
M.F. Bonzano (Custodian)	1875-1876
M.F. Bonzano (Assayer in Charge and Superintendent)	1876-1877
M.F. Bonzano (Assayer in Charge)	1877-1878

Superintendent	Term
Michael Hahn	1878-Dec. 28, 1878
Henry S. Foote	Dec. 28, 1878-May 19, 1880
Martin V. Davis	June 11, 1880-1882
A.W. Smyth	Aug. 15, 1882-June 24, 1885
Gabriel Montegut	June 24, 1885-1893
Overton Cade	1893-1898
Charles W. Boothby	1898-99(?)-1902
Hugh S. Sithon	1902-1911
William M. Lynch	1911-1914
Leonard Magruder	1914-1932
Cecil Grey	1932-1933
Hugh T. Rippeto	1933-1941
Charles M. Miller	April 21, 1941-June 30, 1942

The New Orleans Mint closed June 30, 1942.

*The State of Lousiana took possession of the Mint Jan. 31, 1861, and carried on all the operations with the same officers as under the U.S. until March 31. The Confederate States of America took possession April 1 and continued with the same officers and men. Operations were suspended May 14, 1861, and the facility was closed May 31, 1861. An Assay Office was established by an Act of the Confederate Congress approved Jan. 27, 1862. The facility reverted to federal control following the recapture of the city May 1, 1862, and M.F. Bonzano, under orders of Secretary of the Treasury Salmon P. Chase, dated May 16, 1862, returned to New Orleans and took possession of the Mint and its property.

San Francisco

Superintendent	Term
L. A. Birdsall	June 30, 1853-June 29, 1855
P.G. Lott	June 30, 1855-June 29, 1857
C.H. Hempstead	June 30, 1857-June 29,1861
R.J. Stevens	June 30, 1861-June 29, 1863
R.B. Swain	June 30, 1863-July 31, 1869
A.H. La Grange	Aug. 1, 1869-Dec. 31, 1877
H.L. Dodge	Jan. 1, 1878-June 30, 1882
E.F. Burton	July 1, 1882-July 31, 1885
I. Lawton	Aug. 1, 1885-July 31, 1889
W.H. Diamond	Aug. 1, 1889-July 31, 1893
J. Daggett	Aug. 1, 1893-July 31, 1897
F.A. Leach	Aug. 1, 1897-Sept. 18, 1907
E. Sweeney	Sept. 19, 1907-Aug. 17, 1912
F.A. Leach	Aug. 23, 1912-Aug. 15, 1913
T. W. Shanahan	Aug. 16, 1913-June 30, 1921
M. J. Kelly	July 1, 1921-June 30, 1933
P. J. Haggerty	July 1, 1933-Dec. 31, 1944
N. H. Callaghan	June 1, 1945-Nov. 4, 1947
G. B. Gillin	July 1, 1948-Nov. 30, 1951
J. P. McEnery	June 1, 1952-Nov. 5, 1952
R. P. Buell	July 1, 1953-June 30, 1955
A. C. Carmichael	July 1, 1955-July 31, 1958

OFFICER IN CHARGE, U.S. ASSAY OFFICE

J. R. Carr	Aug. 1, 1958-Oct. 1968
John F. Brekle	Oct. 1968-June 30, 1972
Bland T. Brockenborough	Aug. 20, 1972-Nov. 15, 1980
Thomas H. Miller	Nov. 30, 1980-present

Denver

Superintendent	Term
Frank M. Downer	Oct. 15, 1904-Aug. 29, 1913
Thomas Annear	Aug. 29, 1913-July 1, 1921
Robert J. Grant	July 1, 1921-Nov. 12, 1923
Frank E. Shepard	Nov. 25, 1923-June 30, 1933
Mark A. Skinner	June 16, 1933-Dec. 1, 1942
Moses E. Smith	April 1, 1943-April 5, 1952
Gladys P. Morelock	Aug. 1, 1952-Feb. 8, 1953
Alma K. Schneider	Feb. 9, 1953-May 18, 1961
Fern V. Miller	May 19, 1961-July 31, 1967
Marian N. Rossmiller	Aug. 1, 1967-March 20, 1969
Betty Higby	March 21, 1969-March 18, 1978
Evelyn Davidson	March 20, 1978-Aug. 14, 1981
Nora Hussey	Aug. 9, 1981-present

Charlotte

Superintendent	Term
John Hill Wheeler	Jan. 19, 1837 - July 1841
Burgess Sidney Gaither	July 1841-1844
Greene Washington Caldwell	1844-1846
William Julius Alexander	1846-1849
James Walker Osborne	1849-1853
Greene Washington Caldwell	1853-April 20, 1861*

OFFICER IN CHARGE, U.S. ASSAY OFFICE

Isaac W. Jones	1867-1869
Calvin Josiah Cowles	1869-1885
Robert P. Waring	1885-1889
Stuart Warren Cramer	1889-1893
W.E. Ardrey	1893-1897
W.S. Clanton	1897-1903
D. Kirby Pope	1903-1908
William S. Pearson	1908-1911
Frank Parker Drane	1911-1913

The Charlotte Assay Office was closed June 30, 1913.

*On April 20, 1861, the Charlotte Mint was seized by Confederate forces, who continued coining operations until May 20, 1861. The Mint was officially closed May 31, 1861. An Assay Office was authorized by an Act of the Confederate Congress approved Aug. 24, 1861, and Dr. J.H. Gibbon received appointment as Assayer. In May 1862, the facility was turned over to the Confederate Navy Department. Following the war, it was reopened as a U. S. Assay Office March 19, 1867.

Carson City

Superintendent	Term
Abraham Curry	Jan. 1870-Sept. 1870
H.F. Rice	Sept. 1870-May 1873
Frank D. Hetrich	May 1873-Aug. 1875
James Crawford	Sept. 1875-March 8, 1885
Theodore R. Hofer	(temporary superintendent)
William Garrard	March 18, 1885-June 30, 1889
Samuel Coleman Wright	July 1, 1889-Aug. 1, 1892
Theodore R. Hofer	Aug. 6, 1892-May 20, 1894
Jewett W. Adams	May 20, 1894-Sept. 1898
Roswell K. Colcord	Sept. 1898-July 1, 1899

The Carson City Mint became an Assay Office effective July 1, 1899.

Dahlonega

Superintendent	Term
Joseph J. Singleton	Jan., 1837-April, 1841
Paul Rossignol	April, 1841-May, 1843
James F. Cooper	May, 1843-Sept., 1849
Anderson W. Redding	Sept., 1849-June, 1853
Julius M. Patton	June, 1853-Sept., 1860
George Kellogg	Oct. 1860-?

Coiner	
David H. Mason	March, 1837-Aug., 1848
John D. Field, Jr.	Sept., 1848-Nov., 1849
Robert H. Moore	Nov., 1849-May, 1853
John D. Field, Jr.	May, 1853-?

Assayer	
Joseph W. Farnum	Feb., 1837-May, 1843
Isaac L. Todd	May, 1843-Dec. 1850
M.F. Stephenson	Dec., 1850-May, 1853
Isaac L. Todd	May, 1853-?

The Dahlonega Mint was seized by Confederate forces April 8, 1861; continued in operation until May 14, 1861; and officially closed May 31, 1861. An Act of the Confederate Congress, approved Aug. 24, 1861, authorized the opening of an Assay Office and Lewis W. Quillian was appointed Assayer.

Chief engravers

President George Washington, as fitting for the first president of the United States, had the honor in August 1793 of appointing the man who was to become the first Engraver of the United States Mint — Joseph Wright.

Although Wright (1756-1793), a native of Bordentown, N.J., and a portrait painter, never lived to see his appointment become official, *Coin World* and many numismatic scholars count him as the first Engraver because he was the first to serve in that capacity. However, because his appontment was never official, the Mint considers his successor the first Engraver, or as the title is known today, Chief Sculptor-Engraver.

Wright was first appointed as a draughtsman and later became the first designer and die-sinker at the newly-formed Mint. He made the dies of a medal honoring George Washington, the bust on the obverse of which was considered to be the best medallic profile likeness of Washington. Wright also made the medal honoring Maj. Henry Lee which was authorized by Congress Sept. 24, 1779. The medal was for the Battle of Paulus Hook.

Wright is also believed to have designed the Liberty Cap cent struck on the thick cent planchets between 1793-95, and to have engraved the 1793 Liberty Cap cent.

However, before Wright's official appointment as engraver of the Mint could take place, he died of yellow fever in September 1793. On Nov. 6, 1793, Thomas Jefferson reportedly wrote a letter suggesting that David Rittenhouse, the first Director of the U.S. Mint, recommend an engraver to replace Wright.

Robert Scot

At the time of Wright's death, Henry Voight (also spelled Voigt), acting Chief Coiner and Superintendent, filled in for a few months before a replacement was found. He continued to make the dies used by the Mint until the appointment of Robert Scot. Voight held the office of Chief Coiner until his death in February 1814. Voight is credited with the nation's first coins and the production of the Washington half dismes and silver-center cents of 1792.

According to the Mint's records, it is believed that Rittenhouse recommended Scot to be the first official Chief Engraver. On Nov. 23, 1793, Scot received a letter from Jefferson advising him of his appointment and enclosing his commission signed by Washington.

There is very little known of Scot, except

that he was sometimes confused with the Scottish bank note engraver of the same name. What is known comes from Foster Wild Rice's book, *Antecedents of the American Bank Note Company of 1858,* which states Scot, born in England, came to Philadelphia about 1783 and engraved for Dodson's edition of *Ree's Encyclopedia* from 1794 to 1803.

The length of Scot's term as Chief Engraver varies depending on which source is checked. In Frank Stewart's book, *First United States Mint,* Scot reportedly served until Nov. 1, 1823, and Leonard Forrer, in his *Biographical Dictionary of Medalists,* says Scot served until January 1824. However, it is believed that Scot died in November 1823.

William Kneass

The third man to become Chief Engraver, William Kneass (1781-1840), was appointed to the position Jan. 28, 1824, with a salary of $2,000 a year. Little is known about Kneass's early life or training, except he was born in Lancaster, Pa. He became famous as an engraver in Philadelphia in 1815 with studios located on Fourth Street near Chestnut. His studio was well known as a rendezvous for many prominent Philadephians. Most researchers say a friend, Adam Eckfeldt, the Chief Coiner at that time, was most responsible for his appointment. Kneass had been chiefly a plate engraver for book-work before his appointment as Chief Engraver.

During his term as Chief Engraver there were some notable changes in coinage, as in 1834 and 1838 for gold, and 1836, 1838 and 1840 for silver, although some of this work was done by Christian Gobrecht, an Assistant Engraver at the Mint. He is also credited with a pattern half dollar dated 1838.

Christian Gobrecht

Kneass died in office Aug. 27, 1840. His successor was his assistant, Christian Gobrecht, who, although he was Chief Engraver for only three years and eight months, left behind many mementos of his work. Gobrecht designed pattern coins and regular-issue coins. He is probably best known for his designing of the famous silver dollars of 1836, 1838 and 1839, generally called Gobrecht dollars, although his work in medallic art is also famous.

Gobrecht was born in Hanover, Pa., in 1785 and exhibited mechanical ability and a talent for drawing and design at an early age, according to a December 1911 article in *The Numismatist.* He began his working years as an apprentice to a clockmaker. After spending several years in the trade he turned to engraving.

Gobrecht began small, cutting headlines for newspapers and punches for type founders. He later became a writer and seal engraver. In 1811, Gobrecht moved to Philadelphia where he continued to supply portrait plates for publishers while becoming established as an engraver and diesinker for medals.

In 1816 he began working for Murray, Draper, Fairman and Co., bank note engravers. Within 10 years he had furnished designs and models of dies to the U.S. Mint in Philadelphia. Among his better known dies and medals at this time were the Franklin Institute medal of 1825 based on a design by Thomas Sully; a portrait medal of Charles Wilson Peale; a portrait medal of Charles Carroll of Carrollton; the seal of St. Peter's Church, Philadelphia; and award medals for the New England Society for the Promotion of Manufactures and the Massachusetts Charitable Merchants Association and the Seal of Pennsylvania Hospital.

In 1836, Gobrecht was appointed draughtsman and diesinker to the U.S. Mint and Kneass' assistant. After Kneass' death, Gobrecht held the position of Chief Engraver until his death July 23, 1844. Coins he designed include the famous dollars of 1836, 1838 and 1839 and several varieties of half dollars of that period. His obverse design of one of the dollars, with stars around a seated figure of Liberty, was retained as the regular device in 1840 (although a new reverse was selected) and was used on the dollar until 1873 when the denomination was abandoned briefly.

When the first 1836 silver dollars were struck, Gobrecht's name appeared in the field between the base and the date. Because he received much criticism for doing this, his name was removed, but later in the year it was added on the base by the order of Mint Director Robert Patterson.

Gobrecht's obverse design was continued on the half dollar, quarter dollar, dime and half dime. The first three designs being used until 1892, when the new Barber designs were adopted. Gobrecht also produced six varieties of large cents.

James Barton Longacre

James Barton Longacre succeeded Gobrecht as Chief Engraver Sept. 6, 1844. He was born in Delaware County, Pa., in 1794 and as a young man he was an apprentice in a bookstore in Philadephia. He later studied under George Murray of Philadelpiha who taught him engraving. While serving his apprenticeship, Longacre did some high-class plate work before he became free of his apprenticeship in 1834. His earliest known work is in the *S.F. Bradford Encyclopedia.*

There are no records of Longacre ever sering as an Assistant Engraver at the U.S. Mint. He was hired specifically as the Chief Engraver. Among the coins designed by Longacre are the Flying Eagle cent, Indian Head cent, the 2-cent coin, both 3-cent coins, Shield 5-cent coin, all three gold dollars, the $3 gold coin and the Coronet double eagle. In 1867, Longacre completely remodeled the coinage of the Republic of Chile.

Two of Longacre's coins were known to have caused some controversy, the Coronet double eagle and the Flying Eagle cent, but the criticism was minor and ignored by Longacre. But when the design and execution of the designs were criticized, he reportedly became upset, according to various Mint scholars' research.

Although Longacre spent 25 years as Chief Engraver, he only designed two medals, the reverse of the medal awarded to Capt. Ingraham, the obverse of which was done by P.F. Cross, one of his assistants. Longacre also designed the 1860 Assay Commission medal.

In 1928 Longacre's work was represented in the exhibition of the 100 notable American engravers held in the New York Public Library. Longacre's hiring of William Barber in 1865 as an Assistant Engraver paved the way for the first of two Barbers to occupy the position of Chief Engraver. But that did not come until after Longacre's death Jan. 1, 1879.

William Barber

William Barber (1807-1879) was appointed Chief Engraver shortly after James B. Longacre's death and served in that post until his death Aug. 31, 1879. Although he is one of the most well-known Mint Engravers who did much original work on pattern coins, he only designed two coins for circulation — the 20-cent coin and the Trade dollar.

Barber produced more than 40 public and private medals. Among his most famous works are medals honoring David Rittenhouse, Jean Louis Rodolphe Agassiz and Cyrus Field. Other medal works include medals of James Pollock, Joseph Pancoast, Dr. Henry Linderman, the Centennial medals of 1876 and the Valley Forge medal of 1877.

He also designed several Assay Commission medals, the most famous of which was his 1868 piece showing Liberty using her torch to destroy the implements of the recent Civil War. His Assay Commission medal of 1876 commemorates the 100th anniversary of America's Independence with a bust of Washington on the reverse.

Two of Barber's assistants at the time would later become Chief Engravers — Charles E. Barber and George T. Morgan. His son, Charles was appointed to the position in 1880 upon the death of his father.

Charles E. Barber

Charles E. Barber (1840-1917) served as an assistant for 10 years before being appointed to the top engraver post. Among his designs, known as the Liberty Head or Barber design, were the half dollar which was struck from 1892 until 1915; the quarter struck from 1892 until 1916; and the dime obverse struck from 1892 until 1916. He also designed the Liberty Head 5-cent coin struck from 1883 until 1913. He also designed the 1915-S Panama-Pacific Exposition gold $2.50 piece.

Charles Barber is also credited with the Flowing Hair Stella $4 pattern obverse, as well as the obverse of the Columbian Exposition half dollar with a bust of Columbus, issued in 1892 and 1893 (the reverse was done by George Morgan).

In 1905, the U.S. government sent him to study the Mints of Europe and as the result of his travels the medal department of the U.S. Mint improved, according to historical records. His work is visible in all the principal medals executed after 1869. His best work is seen in the medals of Presidents Garfield and Arthur; Indian Peace, Army and Marksmanship medals; and the Great Seal of the United States.

Other medals include the *Metis* shipwreck and John Horn medals; a medal for the International Medical Congress at Washington in 1887; the International Exhibition, Chicago, 1893; and President Cleveland medals. Reports conflict on whether Charles or his father did the Assay Commission medal of 1879, honoring H.R. Linderman, a Director of the Mint and Joseph Henry, the first director of the Smithsonian Institution.

Charles Barber continued his service until his death Feb. 18, 1917. At that time, his assistant, George T. Morgan, was appointed to the position.

George T. Morgan

George T. Morgan (1845-1925) was 31 years old when he was appointed as an Assistant Engraver and worked at the Mint until his death 48 years later. Little is known about his early life except he was born in Birmingham, England, and attended the Birmingham Art School before he won a national scholarship to the South Kensington Art School. He studied at South Kensington for two years and later studied under Wyon of the Royal Mint in London for four years.

Probably his most famous work while employed by the U.S. Mint was the Morgan dollar (called the "Bland" dollar when it was first struck) of 1878 to 1904 and 1921.

The Morgan dollar was the first U.S. coin to bear an engraver's initial (large M) on the obverse and reverse. The dollar was authorized by the Bland-Allison Act of Feb. 28, 1878, which provided for a minimum monthly silver coinage of 2 million and established this coin weighing 412.5 grains troy as legal tender.

The name Bland dollar is taken from the name of Rep. Richard Bland of Missouri, one of the authors of the act responsible for the minting of the Morgan dollar.

In addition to his well-known dollar, Morgan designed the reverse of the 1892 Columbian Exposition half dollar, the obverse of the 1918 Lincoln-Illinois Centennial half dollar, the reverse of the 1916 and 1917 McKinley Memorial gold dollar and collaborated with Charles Barber to design the 1915-S Panama-Pacific Exposition quarter eagle. He also designed the obverse of the Coiled Hair Stella patterns.

He was also known for his portraits of the Mint's presidential series of medals. He designed presidential medals honoring Rutherford B. Hayes, Woodrow Wilson and Warren G. Harding. Collaborating with Charles Barber, he designed medals depicting Abraham Lincoln, Martin Van Buren, James Garfield, Chester Arthur, Benjamin Harrison, William McKinley, Theodore Roosevelt and William Taft. His portraits of Presidents Hayes, Cleveland and Harrison appeared on the obverse of the Assay Commission medals of 1880, 1886 and 1893.

In addition to his work at the U.S. Mint, Morgan also designed a medal of David Roberts for the Art Union Co. of London; Thomas Carlyle on his 80th birthday; Railway Exhibition at Chicago in 1883 (in conjunction with Barber); and Henry Bessemer, 1879 (a specimen in gold was presented to King Edward VII in 1906).

Morgan also designed medals honoring Secretaries of the Treasury Alexander Hamilton, Daniel Manning, George Cortelyou, Franklin MacVeagh, William McAdoo and Carter Glass. Medals done by Morgan and Barber honoring Treasury Secretaries include

William Windom, John G. Carlisle, Lyman J. Gage and Leslie Shaw. He also designed four Directors of the Mint medals and collaborated with Barber to design four others.

Morgan was also a life member of the Philadelphia Academy of the Fine Arts and a member of the famous Philadelphia Sketch Club.

John Ray Sinnock

When George T. Morgan died in 1925, John R. Sinnock was appointed Chief Engraver by President Calvin Coolidge. Sinnock had served as Assistant Engraver and medalist in 1917 before he resigned two years later.

Sinnock, born in Raton, N.M., in 1888 attended the Pennsylvania Museum Art School in Philadelphia. There he won the A.W. Mifflin scholarship for advanced study and traveled in Europe.

When he returned from Europe, he served as an instructor at the Pennsylvania Museum Art School for eight years and also taught art classes at Western Reserve University in Cleveland.

His appointment as Assistant Engraver came when he was 29 but it would be eight years before he would assume the Chief Engraver's duties. He worked at that job until his death May 14, 1947, at the age of 59 after an illness of several months' duration.

In his 22 years as Chief Engraver, Sinnock left behind many works including his best known, the redesigned Purple Heart in 1931. But probably the best known of his coin designs, and the only one still being minted today, is the Roosevelt dime, placed into circulation in 1946.

According to an interview with Sinnock shortly after the release of the coin, he said the obverse portrait of Roosevelt is a composite of two studies, sculptured in relief, which he made from life in 1933-1934. He also consulted photographs of Roosevelt taken shortly before his death.

One of the best known stories that circulated about the dime was the mild uproar created because of the designer's initials, "JS," at the trunk of Roosevelt's neck. Some of the public mistook the initials for those of Joseph Stalin, the Soviet Union's leader.

Sinnock was also the designer of the Franklin half dollar, which didn't appear in circulation until after his death. The Franklin half was struck from 1948 until 1963. Sinnock's initials, JRS, appear under Franklin's shoulder.

In 1926 Sinnock designed two commemorative coins for the Philadelphia Sesquicentennial celebration — the gold quarter eagle and silver half dollar. The half dollar is known as the Sesquicentennial of American Independence commemorative half; the dies were in very low relief. The $2.50 gold piece and commemorative half dollar were to help raise funds for financing the International Fair held in Philadelphia in 1926.

Sinnock also designed the reverse of the 1918 Lincoln-Illinois Centennial half dollar, while he was an assistant at the Mint. The obverse was done by George T. Morgan, who was then Chief Engraver. Sinnock also designed the Cuban 1-peso coin of 1934, the 1 lempira for Honduras in 1931 and a $1 pattern piece for China in 1929 which was never adopted by the Chinese. A medal design by Sinnock, "Vanguard of the Nation," was purchased by the French government.

Among the most notable and nationally award-winning medals Sinnock designed were the special congressional gold medals honoring Thomas A. Edison; the Yangtze medal for Naval and Marine Corps personnel serving in 1926-1927 and in the Shanghai-Yangtze area in 1930-32; and the Ellsworth-Admundsen-Nobile medal commemorating the flight over the North Pole of the dirigible *Norge* in 1929.

Sinnock designed four medals for the Mint's presidential series including those depicting Calvin Coolidge in 1926; Herbert Hoover in 1929; Franklin D. Roosevelt in 1935; and the obverse of the Harry S Truman medal in 1945. He also designed Secretaries of the Treasury medals for Andrew Mellon in 1931; Ogden L. Mills in 1932; William Woodin in 1933; Henry Morgenthau Jr. in 1938; Fred Vinson; and John W. Snyder.

Sinnock also designed medals for two under secretaries of the Treasury and four assistant secretaries of the Treasury. Sinnock designed two medals honoring Directors of the Mint, Robert J. Grant in 1931 and the obverse of the Nellie Tayloe Ross medal in 1933.

Sinnock is also credited with a special congressional silver medal to honor members of the party with Adm. Perry in his 1909 expedition to the North Pole, and the 1945 Navy Department medal. He also designed Assay Commission medals in 1926, 1927, the obverse of 1928, 1929, 1930, 1931, 1932, 1933, 1934, 1935, 1937 and 1938.

He was a member of the National Sculpture Society, the Philadelphia Sketch Club, the American Federation of Arts, the Philadelphia Art Alliance and American Artists Professional League and an honorary member of the Philadelphia Water Color Club.

Gilroy Roberts

Gilroy Roberts was appointed as Chief Engraver July 22, 1948, but he was no stranger to the U.S. Mint. By the time he received the appointment he had worked both at the Philadelphia Mint and the Bureau of Engraving and Printing in Washington, D.C.

Roberts, who was born in Philadelphia March 5, 1905, was appointed by President Harry S Truman to head the Mint's engraving division in 1948. Roberts, whose father originally wanted him to be a musician, took his inherited artistic talents into medallic art.

He grew up in an artistic world. His father was a sculptor and Roberts' earliest sculpturing experience was with modeling clay, then wood carving and stone sculpturing. In 1934 and 1935, Roberts attended evening art classes at Frankfort High in Philadelphia, where he studied under Paul Remy. In his spare time, he modeled and carved small sculptures for commission and for exhibit in national exhibitions.

In 1936, Roberts took and passed a competitive Civil Service examination for the position of Assistant Sculptor-Engraver at the U.S. Mint. He was hired June 3, 1936, as Sinnock's understudy and continued in that job until Jan. 6, 1938, when he became an Engraver in the Bureau of Engraving and Printing in Washington.

While serving at the BEP, Roberts became proficient in the art of note and stamp engraving. He did the portraits on a number of official revenue stamps and postage stamps, including the 3-cent Ralph Waldo Emerson stamp and the 3-cent Charles W. Elliot stamp, the 1-cent Stephen Collins Foster stamp and the 1-cent Eli Whitney stamp in the Famous American series.

During his time in Washington, Roberts studied under Eugene Weis and Heinz Warneke at the Corcoran Art School from 1939 until 1943. He returned to the Mint May 1, 1944, as an assistant to Sinnock, where he continued the study of bas-relief with Sinnock.

Roberts' best known work is the obverse of the John F. Kennedy half dollar. Upon completion of the half dollar, Roberts placed his stylized initials, GR, on the truncated bust of the coin. When the coin was released, rumors flew around that the initials were really a hammer and sickle marking the spot where the late president was shot.

The Treasury Department continuously denied the rumor and eventually issued a press release, which included an enlargement of the coin showing Roberts' initials, not a hammer and sickle.

Other coins designed by Roberts include the Denmark 5 kroner in 1944; El Salvador, 50 and 25 centavos, obverse in 1953; Cuba, 1 peso, obverse in 1953; 50-, 25-, 5- and 1-centavo coins in 1953; Haiti, 10- and 5-centime coins, obverse in 1958; and the Liberian $1, 50-, 25-, 10-, 5- and 1-cent obverses in 1959.

United States Mint list medals: presidential series, Harry S Truman reverse; portraits of Dwight D. Eisenhower, first and second terms; John F. Kennedy; and Lyndon B. Johnson. Secretary of the Treasury series: portraits of G.M. Humphrey and Douglas Dillon. Director of the Mint series: portraits of William H. Brett and Eva Adams.

Roberts also designed several congressional medals including: Irving Berlin, 1954; Dr. Jonas Salk, 1955; Sir Winston Churchill, obverse, 1955; a medal of Ulysses S. Grant and Robert E. Lee honoring the surviving veterans of the Civil War, 1956; and Adm. Hyman George Rickover, reverse, 1958. Other medals include: annual Assay Commission series of many years, both obverse and reverse; Perry Navy, reverse, 1945; Director of the Mint marksman, 1948; Department of the Interior award, obverse, 1948; Atomic Energy Commission medals: Enrico Fermi, 1956; Ernest Orlando Lawrence, 1960; Citation medal, 1960.

Some of his private commissions include: American Numismatic Society medal of Louis C. West; Medallic Art Co. of New York, medals of William T. Louth, Julius Lauth, Frances Trees; Helen Keller Foundation portrait of Helen Keller; Drexel Institute medal of founder Anthony Drexel; memorial tablet of Charles T. Bach; Patriots Memorial, Valley Forge, Pa.; a series of state seals; Institute for Advanced Study, Princeton, N.J. medal of Albert Einstein; Metropolitan Life Insurance Co. portrait of F.W. Eckers; Scripps Howard Newspaper Alliance medal of Ernie Pyle.

Also included in Roberts' portfolio: a portrait of Bobby Jones for the American Golf Association; Life Golf Tournament portrait of Ben Hogan; Yeshiva University, New York City, portrait of Albert Einstein; Radio Corporation of America medal of Gen. David Sarnoff; Woods Hole Oceanographic Institute portrait of Henry Bigelow; American Medical Association portrait of Dr. Hektoen; Montana Centennial Medal of three governors of Montana, Babcock, Toole and Edgerton; National Commemorative Society, "In God We Trust" medal and others.

His exhibitions have included the Pennsyl-

vania Academy of Fine Arts, Philadelphia in 1930, 1934, 1945, 1946; Corcoran Gallery of Art, Washington, D.C.; National Sculpture Society in New York; Paris, France and Italy, 1961; The Hague, Netherlands, 1963.

He has also lectured about U.S. coins at the American Numismatic Society in New York in 1961 and the Exchange Club in Philadelphia in 1962. Among his awards are the National Sculpture Society Bas-Relief exhibition, 1951, honorable mention. International exhibition coins and medals in Madrid, Spain, 1951, gold medal and citation.

Roberts resigned his position as Chief Engraver at the age of 59 Oct. 8, 1964, when he became the first Chief Engraver in the history of the Mint who did not die in office. He had served as Chief Engraver for 16 years and had spent a total of 28 years working for the government, 26 years at the Mint and two years at the BEP.

Roberts resigned from the Mint under the advice of his physician, but he did not resign from the world of minting, however. He accepted a position as chairman of the board of General Numismatics Corp., forerunner of the Franklin Mint. He later became chairman of the board emeritus and a director of the Franklin Mint.

In this capacity, Roberts was given the opportunity to travel and he personally "shopped" for the intricate machinery being installed in the Franklin Mint. His travels took him to the Orient, among other places.

Roberts is married to the former Lillian Pancoast and they have one son. When he is not designing medals or sculpture, he is interested in astronomy, telescope making and boating. In 1960, Roberts presented a lecture about Maksutov telescopes at the Astronomical League Convention at Haverford College at Haverford, Pa.

Roberts also designed dozens of medals including the following for commemorative societies while he was with the Franklin Mint: Abba Eban, Martin Luther King, Malcom X, Mahalia Jackson, Geoffrey Chaucer, Miraculous medal, Cardinal Spellman, Saint Peter, Abraham, Eisenhower, Three Astronauts, First Step on the Moon, Joan of Arc and Sarah Bernhardt.

He also designed special medallic greeting cards from 1965-1968 as well as the Robert F. Kennedy Memorial medal and the Richard Nixon and Spiro Agnew Inauguration medal in 1973. Other medallic series include the U.S. president's series for the White House Historical Association, the Franklin Mint's "Roberts' Birds" series of 50 silver medals,

Pandora's Box, baby announcement medals for boys and girls, 12 signs of the Zodiac (also made into jewelry). Also, he designed the Franklin Mint's Bicentennial medals with portraits of 30 great Americans 1976, a John F. Kennedy Inaugural 25th Anniversary medal in 1986 and the Encyclopaedia Britannica Award in 1986 struck by Medallic Art Co.

Large plaques designed by Roberts include: Benjamin Franklin, Franklin Mint official emblem; John F. Kennedy Memorial, wild geese, horses, 12 signs of the zodiac, self-portrait for Pennsylvania Association of Numismatists Award.

He also designed plates including a Liberty Tree etched in glass, Nixon and Agnew in silver and 12 signs of the Zodiac in silver as well as three-dimensional sculptures, a large sundial at the Franklin Mint museum, a Great American Eagle and four bird groups in pewter.

Frank Gasparro

Gilroy Roberts' successor, Frank Gasparro, was sworn in Feb. 23, 1965. He was born in Philadelphia Aug. 26, 1909, and showed his artistic talent at a young age. He attended classes at the Samuel Fleisher Art Memorial school in Philadephia while still in grade school. At the age of 15, he began taking private lessons from Guiseppe Donato, a former foreman to the sculptor Rodin. Donato took Gasparro under his wing and when Gasparro would visit Donato's studio, the master would show him the fine points of the art.

Gasparro continued to study under Donato until 1929, even after his graduation from South Philadelphia High School. He enrolled at the Pennsylvania Academy of Fine Arts in Philadelphia in 1928, where he studied under sculptors and medalists Charles Grafly, Walker Hancock and Albert Laessle until 1931.

Gasparro launched his professional career in 1932, at the age of 23, as a freelance sculptor working primarily in statuary art and commercial plaster models. He continued in that field until 1937 when he joined the staff of the Federal Art Administration, which was a part of the Works Progress Administration under the Roosevelt administration during the Great Depression.

Under the FAA, each artist was given a salary and allowed to work on any project; all the artists' work became the property of the government. He did sculptures at this time which were placed in wading pools in playgrounds in the Philadelphia area, where some can still be seen.

He returned to freelance sculpturing in 1941 and then became a junior engraver in 1942 at the U.S. Mint. On Feb. 11, 1965, Gasparro was appointed to the Chief Engraver's position by President Lyndon B. Johnson.

During his tenure, Gasparro supervised the production of some 30,000 dies a year for all U.S. coinage and medals produced at the Philadelphia Mint. His work at the Mint included portraiture, low and high relief medals and insignia designing. He is probably best known to coin collectors for his reverse of the Kennedy half dollar, 1964; his design and execution of the reverse of the Lincoln Memorial cent in 1959; his Eisenhower/Apollo 11 dollar introduced in 1971; and the Susan B. Anthony dollar.

He also designed the Philadelphia Medal of Honor in 1955. In 1964, he won the emblem contest sponsored by the Treasury Safety Council. Foreign coins also occupied his design capabilities including 1943 Guatemala Revenue 25 centavos, among others.

Gasparro also designed annual Assay Commission medals in 1949, 1950, 1951, 1952 and 1965. He also designed the Eisenhower reverse in 1954 and the Kennedy reverse for the presidential medals series of the Mint.

Other designs and models prepared by Gasparro at the U.S. Mint include: Federal Security Agency medal and Federal Security Agency Service Award emblem in 1951; Provost Marshal General badge, 1951; Coast Guard Commendation medal, 1952; White House Cap Device insignia, 1953; Secretary of the Treasury medal, 1953; Department of Commerce medal and emblem, 1952; Central Intelligence medal, 1953; Central Intelligence star, 1953; Central Intelligence Distinguished medal, 1955; Treasury department Secret Service Guard Cap and Breast Badge, 1954; U.S. Secretary of the Treasury, Robert B. Anderson; Dr. Thomas A. Dooley III congressional medal.

Also included among his works are: the 1-5/16 inch and the 2.25-inch Pony Express medals, 1960; U.S. Secretary of the Treasury medal George M. Humphrey and one for Douglas Dillon. Private commissions include the Stroud Jordan medal, 1953.

Exhibitions include: Victory medal of World War II in plaster, private collection, at the Pennsylvania Academy of the Fine Arts in 1950. His work has also been exhibited at the Philadelphia Museum of Arts. His medallion works and his sculptures in the round have also been placed on display. He has five medals on permanent exhibition at the Smithsonian Institution. His work has been shown in foreign exhibits at the Paris Mint, 1949-50 annual Assay Commission medals, 1949; International Medallic Exposition, 1951; and at the Rome International Medallic Exhibition he showed a 1953 Coast Guard Commendation medal and the reverse of the 1949 annual Assay Commission medal.

He has also been an instructor in sculpture at the Fleisher Art Memorial in Philadelphia and he was honored by the Italian government in 1973 with the decoration of Cavaliere Ufficiale.

In 1968 Gasparro was named the Outstanding Numismatic Sculptor of the Year by the American Numismatic Association and in 1969 he designed the medal for the ANA's convention. He is also credited with the Jimmy Carter medal in the Mint's presidential series as well as a congressional medal honoring Marian Anderson.

He is a member of the Society of Medalists, the French Society of the Medal and Pennsylvania Academy of the Fine Arts Fellowship board of directors.

Gasparro is married to the former Julia Johnston and he and his wife have a daughter. After his retirement as Chief Engraver Jan. 16, 1981, Gasparro continued his artistic work including a George Washington 250th anniversary commemorative medal in 1982 and President's Day Celebration medal in 1983 for Design-Pak Inc.

He also has designed a number of medals for Bowers and Merena Galleries including the Virgil Brand medal in 1983, the Salute to the Olympics medal in 1984, the President Ronald Reagan medal in 1984, the Walter Mondale medal in 1984, the Frank Gasparro medal in 1985, the Abraham Lincoln medal in 1986 and the Jefferson Davis medal in 1986.

Gasparro continued to work on additional medals, the following from Unicover Corp.: St. Francis di Assisi commemorative in 1981, Jacques Cartier in 1984, Rose Bowl in 1984, space shuttle-NASA in 1983, Babe Ruth in 1983, Migratory Bird Stamp medal in 1984, Brandenburg Gate-Berlin Anniversary in 1986, President Ronald Reagan in 1984 and Walter Mondale in 1984.

In 1986, Gasparro was the designer of the American Numismatic Association medal and then he did several medal series for Paramount International Coin Co. including an 11-medal series for the Statue of Liberty Centennial, 1985-1986, and an 11-medal series to commemorate the United States Constitution in 1987.

Elizabeth Jones

U.S. Mint Chief Engraver Elizabeth A.B. Jones has Italy to thank for many of the high points in her life. In part her appointment as Chief Engraver in 1981 can be traced back to her studies in Rome when she switched from oil painting to sculpture. That change lead her to medallic art and a wide range of artistic endeavors.

Before moving to Italy, Jones graduated from Vassar College with a bachelor's degree in the History of Art in 1957. She then studied at the Art Students League in New York City until 1962. She spent the next two years studying at the Scuolo dell'Arte della Medaglia inside the Italian Mint.

It was there, under the guidance of the Italian Mint's paper money engraver, Jones and other students learned how to engrave in steel. She also learned how to sculpture medals, medallic art and low relief.

While still a student, she was invited to exhibit her work in the Federation Internationale de la Medaille. Shortly thereafter, her services as a translator were called upon when fellow American U.S. Mint Director Eva Adams visited the Italian Mint.

"I really hadn't been noticed by Americans until then. She asked me right then and there if I would come back and work in Philadelphia," Jones said, recalling her first meeting with the woman who was to become a good friend. "I said I had only been here two or three years and I really want to stay. When Mr. Gasparro retired, she was on the phone to me in Washington, D.C., where I was visiting during the Christmas holidays, and told me to apply for the position."

Jones was nominated by President Ronald Reagan July 13, 1981, confirmed by the Senate Sept. 28 and sworn in Oct. 27. She is the first woman named Chief Sculptor-Engraver of the United States.

It was less than six months after her nomination was confirmed that she was faced with her first major project — designing the first U.S. commemorative coin issued since 1954 to honor the 250th anniversary of the birth of George Washington.

"As soon as I heard about the possibility of my doing the Washington half dollar coin, I decided instantaneously I was going to put him on a horse," she said. "He was such a famous horseman and general, often portrayed in paintings on his horse in battles, and he is also portrayed in innumerable outdoor equestrian monuments throughout the country."

In her mind, she envisioned a move away from the standard profile-type of design which Jones said is so prominent in all other medals, paintings and coins, to a younger-looking Washington astride a horse.

She had already decided on the image she wanted when, in the course of her research, she visited the portrait gallery of the Second Bank of the United States and came across an oval painting by Rembrandt Peale which depicts Washington astride a horse.

"I really was shocked. It was almost like a vision because that's just what I had in mind of doing," she said.

In order to carry out her design image, Jones said she often worked weekends but admits now she was nervous and she overdrew.

"When you work too long at something, you don't see it anymore," she said, recalling her first drawings for the Washington commemorative. That may have made it all the worse for her when, after turning the sketch over to U.S. Mint Director Donna Pope for her approval, Jones was invited to a function at the Union League Club in Philadelphia.

While there, inspiration arrived in the form of a floor-to-ceiling portrait by Thomas Sully of Washington on horseback.

"I was so inspired. I wanted to stop the original design and I asked Mrs. Pope, 'Please don't let it be published,' because I wanted to make changes but she said it was too late," Jones said. "I was sick. But I knew in my mind what I was going to do anyway with the coin. And as it turns out, the coin came out far better than the original design."

That's just a small part of the extensive research Jones does when looking for different versions of a subject's face or clothing.

It was a different kind of atmosphere when it came time to submit designs for the 1984 Los Angeles Olympic Games. Jones said when she and her staff of sculptor/engravers, which she affectionately refers to as "my guys," were approached to design the commemorative 1983 $1 silver Olympic coin. The initial designs were an attempt to move away from traditional themes.

"We did not do the discus thrower on purpose, because it had been done and re-done over and over again. But at a certain point, after [Treasury] Secretary [Donald] Regan had seen everything, he still wasn't satisfied and he said he wanted some drawings using the discus thrower," she recalled.

Jones and the other engravers submitted the discus thrower designs, which she said presented a challenge to provide a fresh, different and modern look to the "discobolus," so she employed the technique of a multiple image to convey motion. The design apparently caught the Treasury Secretary's eye.

But even then Regan was still not pleased, Jones recalled, because her design displayed only the Olympic rings, without the stars, for the sake of simplicity and clarity of design.

"He insisted that the stars be placed with the Olympic rings as he said it was the official logo of the Los Angeles Olympic Games," she said. "That was a terrible job because the stars had to be much bigger than they should have been because of the reduction process. To me it just fouled up the whole coin because it complicated and overloaded the design."

But that disappointment faded and two years later, Jones again felt the exhilaration of designing a successful and popular coin — the Statue of Liberty gold $5 commemorative coin. She said because the dimensions of the coin were so small, 21.59 millimeters, the design needed to be as simple and direct as possible.

"You simply have to have a bold concept when you do such a tiny coin," she said. "I didn't want to cut the Statue in half, I had seen that on some medals and I think that's a very graceless design on a small coin."

She saw the view she had in mind in a photograph used in a mail-order advertisement. Although part of Liberty's face was in the shadows, Jones used her knowledge of the structural elements of the face to reconstruct what she needed. That was just one of the times photographs, her own or someone else's, played a major part in the design process and her work in general.

"If you look at a group of different photographs of the Statue, from some angles her nose looks very Roman, in another photographs her forehead is very pronounced. She changes in many photographs, in some her face looks oval, some her chin is very square and her face is very full," Jones observed. "One photograph is never enough. When I did portraits of people, I would do the photographs myself. I would take four of five rolls of 36 frames each. I would take them from all angles, on different days and in different lights."

That interest in photography began years ago and her tastes run towards cityscapes and landscapes but she is also attracted to bold combinations of color. But that hobby, like the many different art forms she practiced before becoming Chief Engraver, have been set aside for now.

"Designing coins is much more difficult than designing medals. You have much more freedom in designing medals, in every aspect," she said. "I did seven different pieces for the Franklin Mint so I was used to working in low relief. But they did not have the criteria of incredible precision that we have because they would tell me it couldn't be higher than 'such and such.' Well, that was child's play compared to making a coin in the U.S. Mint. They didn't have the problem of making thousands of dies. I imagine they could afford to throw away the die after 800 strikes where we have to get 8,000 strikes or more for the 'penny,' for example. The design has to be compatible with long die life."

In addition to honing her administrative skills, the job has provided Jones with a variety of new challenges and opportunities to learn.

"This is such a unique experience here. It's been fascinating and I certainly enjoyed it immensely," she said. "I've learned so much, especially technically. You can't know everything before you get inside a Mint. It's very tough work inside here. We have very tough schedules, very tight deadlines. I just hope I've contributed something artistically to the U.S. Mint."

In addition to contributing to her professional success, Rome also holds special personal memories — she was married to Ludwig Glaeser there April 26, 1986.

As a tribute to her artistic successes, the Scuolo dell'Arte della Medaglia in Rome is planning a retrospective exhibition of her work in September 1987. It will be the first in a series of alumni restrospective exhibits planned by the school. Jones said U.S. Mint Director Donna Pope has written a preface for the exhibition catalog.

In addition, Jones has participated in numerous one-person shows and group exhibitions. Before her appointment as Chief Engraver, she completed several commemorative medals including those depicting Picasso and Wolfgang Amadeus Mozart for the Stefano Johnson Mint in Milano, Italy; Pablo Casals, International Numismatic Agency in New York City; the University of Pennsylvania Art Museum (Lucy Wharton Drexel Award — gold medal); the Johns Hopkins University; Creighton University; silver medal of Cardinal Spellman for the American Episcopate; Salute to Israel (25th anniversary); Gloria Steinem for the Food and Agricultural series of CERES medals honoring outstanding women of the world; the Holy Year Jubileum for the Medallic Art Co.; medal for Israel's 30th anniversary for the Judaic Heritage Society; annual prize medals for St. Stephen's School, Rome; Dubai Sheraton Hotel, United Arab Emirates, including the portrait of H.E. Sheikh Rashid; Pope Paul II, for Premier Giulio Andreotti — medal cast in solid gold as gift of Italian Government; Nobel Prize Laureates, Stockholm, 1979; anniversary medal, Judaic Heritage Society in 1980.

She was awarded an honorary diploma from the Academia Brasileiro das Belas Artes in Rio de Janeiro in 1967; the Outstanding Sculptor of the Year from the American Numismatic Association in 1972; and the Louis Bennett Award from the National Sculpture Society in 1978.

Her commissioned work for the Franklin Mint includes medallic portraits of Albert Schweitzer, Susan B. Anthony, Charles Dickens, Richard Wright, Walter Reed and Gen. Campbell. She has also completed dozens of commissioned oil paintings and several pieces of commissioned jewelry.

Jones is a member of both national and international numismatic and medallic associations including American Numismatic Association, American Medallic Sculpture Association, American Numismatic Society, Federation Internationale de la Medaille and the National Sculpture Society. Since 1981 she has been a member of the advisory committee of the National Museum of Women in the Arts in Washington, D.C., which was formally inaugurated in April 1987.

Services offered by the Mint

The United States Mint offers several collector's items and services to collectors and interested non-collectors. Among these are Proof sets, Uncirculated Mint sets, souvenir Mint sets, bronze duplicates of national medals and Mint tours. Since 1982, the Mint has offered a variety of commemorative coins and since 1986, gold and silver bullion coins (through wholesalers).

Annual offerings comprise Proof sets and sets of Uncirculated coinage (after the Mint did not produce Uncirculated sets in 1982 and 1983, Congress passed a law requiring yearly sales). National medals are struck when supplies run low to fill orders. Souvenir sets — each offering the coins of a single Mint — are offered as well.

Persons on the Mint's customer mailing list will receive order forms for all Mint products offered by mail as well as a catalog each fall. The catalog of Mint products was first issued in late 1985 and was such a success a second catalog was issued in 1986. To be placed on the Mint's mailing list, interested persons may write to United States Mint, Customer Services, 10001 Aerospace Road, Lanham, Md. 20706. The Mint's customer service telephone number is (301) 436-7400.

Some items, like the souvenir Mint sets, are offered at over-the-counter locations only, and not through the mail. The Mint also produces special souvenir sets of coins or medals for selected numismatic conventions, including the annual American Numismatic Association show; these, too, are not offered through the mail.

The Mint in 1983 experimented with sales of Proof sets at over-the-counter locations to attract more non-collectors to the hobby of coin collecting. Mint officials have continued to offer Proof sets at its over-the-counter outlets since then.

Mint tours

Philadelphia Mint, (215) 597-2529; Monday through Friday, 9 a.m. to 4:30 p.m. January, February and March. Monday through Saturday April and October, November and December. Monday through Sunday May through September.

San Francisco Old Mint, (415) 454-0788); Monday through Friday, 10 a.m. to 3 p.m.

Denver Mint, (303) 327-5588; Monday through Friday, 8:30 a.m. to 3 p.m. September through May and 8 a.m. to 3 p.m. May through September. Tours are available Wednesdays year-round from 9:30 a.m. to 3 p.m.

Admission is free. Hours are subject to change without notice. Call for information.

The San Francisco Assay Office, the Fort Knox Gold Bullion Depository, and the West Point facility are closed to the public.

Medals sold by the U.S. Mint

Following is a list of medals sold by the U.S. Mint. In 1984, the Mint held an inventory reduction sale, offering bargain prices for remaining stocks of certain medals. Money orders or checks should be sent to: United States Mint (Medals), P.O. Box 500, Philadelphia, Pa. 19105. For orders originating overseas, only checks drawn on American banks or international money orders will be accepted as payment.

The Mint reserves the right to reduce or cancel any order whether or not it has been acknowledged. The acceptance of orders is conditioned upon the Mint's ability to meet the demand. In the event of a reduction or cancellation by the Mint, appropriate refunds will be made. Orders are not subject to cancellation by the purchaser. All sales are final.

Items may not be returned for refund or exchange. However, any item found damaged when received will be exchanged if returned to the Mint within 15 days after receipt by the purchaser. Damaged medals will be exchanged only if plastic wrapping has not been opened.

Secretaries of the Treasury

Mail Order Price: $16.00
($15.00 over-the-counter*)
Mail Order Price for (1): $1.25
($1.00 over-the-counter*)

Medals	Size in Inches	Medals	Size in Inches
201 Alexander Hamilton	3	223 David M. Kennedy	3
211 Andrew W. Mellon	3	224 John B. Connally	3
216 John W. Snyder	3	225 George P. Shultz	3
217 George M. Humphrey	3	226 William E. Simon	3
218 Robert B. Anderson	3	227 W. Michael Blumenthal	3
219 Douglas Dillon	3	228 G. William Miller	3
220 Henry H. Fowler	3	229 Donald T. Regan	3
221 Albert Gallatin	3	230 Donald T. Regan	1-5/16 (1)
222 Joseph W. Barr	3	231 James A. Baker III	3

Presidents

Medal	Size 3" Mail order price: $16.00 $15.00 over-the-counter*	Size 1-5/16" Philadelphia (No Mint mark) Mail order price: $1.25 $1.00 over-the-counter*	Size 1-5/16" Denver ("D" Mint mark) Mail order price: $1.25 $1.00 over-the-counter*	Size 1-5/16" Gold washed With loop Mail order price: $5.50 ($4.75 over-the-counter*) Without loop Mail order price: $5.00 $4.25 over-the-counter*
George Washington	101	801	801D	801G
John Adams	102	802	802D	802G
Thomas Jefferson	103	803	803D	803G
James Madison	104	804	804D	804G
James Monroe	105	805	805D	805G
John Quincy Adams	106	806	806D	806G
Andrew Jackson	107	807	807D	807G
Martin Van Buren	108	808	808D	808G
William Henry Harrison	109	809	809D	809G
John Tyler	110	810	810D	810G
James K. Polk	111	811	811D	811G
Zachary Taylor	112	812	812D	812G
Millard Fillmore	113	813	813D	813G
Franklin Pierce	114	814	814D	814G
James Buchanan	115	815	815D	815G
Abraham Lincoln	116	816	816D	816G
Andrew Johnson	117	817	817D	817G
Ulysses S. Grant	118	818	818D	818G
Rutherford B. Hayes	119	819	819D	819G
James A. Garfield	120	820	820D	820G
Chester A. Arthur	121	821	821D	821G
Grover Cleveland	122	822	822D	822G
Benjamin Harrison	123	823	823D	823G
William McKinley	124	824	824D	824G
Theodore Roosevelt	125	825	825D	825G
William H. Taft	126	826	826D	826G
Woodrow Wilson	127	827	827D	827G
Warren G. Harding	128	828	828D	828G
Calvin Coolidge	129	829	829D	829G
Herbert Hoover	130	830	830D	830G
Franklin D. Roosevelt	131	831	831D	831G
Harry S Truman	132	832	832D	832G
Dwight D. Eisenhower (1st term)	133	833	833D	833G
Dwight D. Eisenhower (2nd term)	134			
John F. Kennedy	135	835	835D	835G
Lyndon B. Johnson (1st term)	136			
Lyndon B. Johnson (2nd term)	137	837	837D	837G
Richard M. Nixon (1st term)	138	838	838D	838G
Richard M. Nixon (2nd term)	139	839	839D	839G
Gerald R. Ford	140	840	840D	840G
Jimmy Carter	141	841	841D	841G
Ronald Reagan	142	842	842D	842G

Numismatic products

011 Plastic Easel for Small Medal. Over-the-counter, 10¢ each. Mail orders, first five, 15¢ each; each additional on same order, 11¢ each.

012 Plastic Easel for Large Medal. Over-the-counter, 15¢ each. Mail orders, first five, 25¢ each; each additional on same order, 16¢ each.

021 Presentation Case for Miniature (1-5/16 inch) medal Over-the-counter, $1.25 each. Mail orders, $1.35 each.

022 Presentation Case for Three Inch Size Medal. Over-the-counter, $2 each. Mail orders, $2.15 each.

023 Delux Presentation Case with Display Stand for Large Medals. Over-the-counter, $6 each. Mail orders, $7 each.

031 Single Plastic Display Case for Miniature (1-5/16 inch) Medal. Over-the-counter, 60¢ each. Mail orders, 70¢ each.

041 Presidential Display Board for Miniature Presidential Series (1-5/16 inch). Over-the-counter, $3.50 each. Mail orders, $4 each.

Official Mint medals and historic buildings

Medal		Over-the-Counter*	Mail Order	Size in Inches
701	Opening of New Mint at Philadelphia (August 14, 1969)	$1.00	1.25	1-5/16
703	Denver Mint	$1.00	1.25	1-5/16
704	San Francisco Assay Office	$1.00	1.25	1-5/16
705	First Coinage Medal (Struck twice)	$1.00	1.25	1-5/16
706	The White House	$1.00	1.25	1-5/16
707	Treasury Building	$15.00	16.00	3
708	U.S. Assay Office, New York	$1.00	1.25	1-5/16
709	U.S. Bullion Depository, West Point, New York	$1.00	1.25	1-5/16
710	U.S. Bullion Depository, Ft. Knox, Ky.	$1.00	1.25	1-5/16
713	Treasury Building	$1.00	1.25	1-5/16
750	New Orleans Mint, 1838-1931	$1.00	1.25	1½
751	Old San Francisco Mint, 1874-1937	$1.00	1.25	1½

Army

Mail Order Price: $16.00
($15.00 over-the-counter*)

Medal		Size in Inches
401	Gen. George Washington, "Washington before Boston".	2½
402	Gen. Horatio Gates, for battles of Bennington, Fort Stanwix, and Saratoga	2⅛
403	Gen. Daniel Morgan, for victory at Cowpens.	2 3/16
404	Lt. Col. John E. Howard, for battle of Cowpens.	1¾
405	Lt. Col. William Washington, for battle of Cowpens.	1¾
406	Lt. Col. Francois Louis Teisseidre De Fleury, for assault on Stony Point	1 9/16
407	Gen. Anthony Wayne, for victory at Stony Point.	2 1/16

Medals		Size in Inches
408	Gen. Nathaniel Greene, for battle of Eutaw Springs	2¼
409	Maj. Henry Lee for battle of Paulus Hook.	1 13/16
416	Maj. Gen. Alexander Macomb, for battle of Plattsburgh.	2½
417	Maj. Gen. Andrew Jackson, for battle of New Orleans	2½
423	Maj. Gen. Zachary Taylor, for battle of Buena Vista	3½
424	Maj. Gen. Winfield Scott, for battles of Mexican Campaign	3½
425	Maj. Gen. Ulysses Grant, for battles of Ft. Donelson, Vicksburg, and Chattanooga	3
429	200th Anniversary of the U.S. Army	3

Navy

Mail Order Price: $16.00
($15.00 over-the-counter*)
Mail Order Price for (1): $2.25
($2.00 over-the-counter*)

Medal		Size in Inches
501	Capt. John Paul Jones, for capture of the *Serapis*	2¼
502	Capt. Thomas Truxtun, for action against *La Vengeance*	2 3/16
503	Commodore Edward Preble, for attack on Tripoli.	2½
504	Capt. Issac Hull, for capture of *Guerriere*	2½
506	Capt. Stephen Decatur, for capture of *Macedonian*.	2½
507	Capt. William Bainbridge, for capture of *Java*.	2½

Medals		Size in Inches
510	Capt. Oliver Perry, for victory in battle of Lake Erie	2½
519	Capt. Charles Stewart, for capture of *Cyane* and *Levant*	2½
525	Rescue of passengers, officers, and men of steamship *San Francisco*	3⅛
533	Vice Adm. Hyman Rickover, for achievement in practical use of atomic energy	3
534	200th Anniversary of the U.S. Navy	3
535	200th Anniversary of the U.S. Marine Corps	3
536	Adm. Hyman Rickover, for service to the country. (1)	1½

Directors of the Mint

Mail Order Price: $16.00
($15.00 over-the-counter*)

Medal		Size in Inches	Medals		Size in Inches
301	David Rittenhouse	1¾	319	Eva Adams (2nd term)	3
316	Nellie Tayloe Ross	3	320	Mary Brooks	3
317	William H. Brett	3	321	Stella Hackel Sims	3
318	Eva Adams (1st term)	3	322	Donna Pope	3

National historic series

Medal		Over-the-Counter*	Mail Order	Size in Inches
635	U.S. Diplomatic (July 4, 1776)	15.00	16.00	2-13/16
636	Great Seal Centennial, 1782-1882	15.00	16.00	2-7/16
637	Joseph Francis for livesaving service	15.00	16.00	3
645	Charles A. Lindbergh	15.00	16.00	2¾
647	Mount Vernon	15.00	16.00	2
648	Benjamin Franklin	15.00	16.00	3
651	Vice-President Alben W. Barkley	15.00	16.00	3
652	Dr. Jonas E. Salk	15.00	16.00	3
653	Dr. Robert H. Goddard	15.00	16.00	2¾
654	Robert Frost	15.00	16.00	3
655	Dr. Thomas A. Dooley III	15.00	16.00	3
656	Sam Rayburn	15.00	16.00	3
657	U.S. Secret Service 100th Anniversary	15.00	16.00	2½
658	Diplomatic Courier, 1918-1968	15.00	16.00	3
661	J. Edgar Hoover	15.00	16.00	3
662	Brig. Gen. Charles Yeager	15.00	16.00	3
663	Marian Anderson	15.00	16.00	3
664	Lt. General Ira C. Eaker	15.00	16.00	3
665	Transatlantic Balloonists	2.00	2.25	1½
666	John Wayne	15.00	16.00	3
667	John Wayne	2.00	2.25	1-5/16
668	Robert F. Kennedy	15.00	16.00	3
669	Robert F. Kennedy	2.00	2.25	1-5/16
670	Hubert H. Humphrey	15.00	16.00	3
671	Simon Wiesenthal	15.00	16.00	3
672	Ambassador Kenneth Taylor	15.00	16.00	3
673	American Red Cross Centennial	2.00	2.25	1½
674	U.S./Netherlands Treaty Bicentennial	2.00	2.25	1½
675	Fred Waring	2.00	2.25	1½
676	Louis L'Amour	2.00	2.25	1½
678	POW-MIA	2.00	2.25	1-5/16
679	Congressman Leo Ryan	2.00	2.25	1½
680	Danny Thomas	2.00	2.25	1½
681	Harry S. Truman Centennial	2.00	2.25	1½
683	Elie Wiesel	2.00	2.25	1½
684	Roy Wilkins	2.00	2.25	1½
685	Vietnam Veterans National Medal	2.00	2.25	1½
686	Vietnam Veterans National Medal	15.00	16.00	3

Chief Justices of the United States

Mail Order Price: $16.00
($15.00 Over-the-counter*)

Medal		Size in Inches
901	John Jay	3
902	John Rutledge	3
914	Earl Warren	3
915	Warren E. Burger	3

*Over-the-counter prices apply only in the U.S. Mint public areas in the following locations: Philadelphia Mint, Denver Mint, Old San Francisco Mint and the Washington Tourist Information Center, 1400 Pennsylvania Ave., N.W, Washington, D.C.

Source: U.S. Mint

History of the United States presidential medal series

Many of the medals which are now included in the U.S. Mint's presidential series were made originally for presentation to American Indian chiefs and warriors. The Spanish, the French and the British had presented medals to the Indians, and the British especially had produced large and magnificent silver medals, each bearing the likeness of the reigning monarch on one side and his coat of arms on the other. The British medals were solid silver, impressed in clear relief, and were given to the Indian chiefs as marks of friendship and special recognition. They were highly prized by the Indians.

When the United States replaced the British in dealing with the Indians, the new government found that it was necessary to continue the practice of presenting medals if it hoped to have peaceful relations with the tribes and influence with the chiefs. The federal government, then, began the production of Indian peace medals, which became a settled and extremely important part of American Indian policy.

As early as 1787, Henry Knox, the secretary of war under the Articles of Confederation, urged Congress to comply with the request of the Indians for "medals, gorgets, wrist and arm bands with the arms of the United States impressed or engraved thereon." Congress was pressed for funds, but Knox noted that the Indians would turn in their British medals, which could be melted down to produce new ones. Thomas Jefferson, as secretary of state, outlined the policy behind the distribution of medals to the Indians; he spoke of it as "an ancient custom from time immemorial." The medals, he said, "are considered as complimentary things, as marks of friendship to those who come to see us, or who do us good offices, conciliatory of their good will toward us, and not designed to produce a contrary disposition towards others. They confer no power, and seem to have taken their origin in the European practice, of giving medals or other marks of friendship to the negotiators of treaties and other diplomatic characters, or visitors of distinction."

Firm hold

Whatever the origin, the practice took firm hold in the United States. Medals were given to Indian chiefs on important occasions, such as the signing of a treaty, a visit of important Indians to the national capital, or a tour of the Indian country by some federal official. Lewis and Clark, on their famous exploratory expedition to the Pacific Coast in 1804-06, carried along a large supply of medals, which they handed out with impressive ceremonies to important chiefs along the way. Indian agents on the frontier distributed the medals to their charges, in recognition of friendship and peace with the United States. These Indian agents or treaty negotiators used their own discretion in making the presentations, but they were guided by fixed norms. In 1829, in fact, Lewis Cass, governor of Michigan Territory, and William Clark, superintendent of Indian Affairs at St. Louis, drew up a series of regulations for the governing of the Indian Department, including rules for the presentation of medals. What these two experienced Indian agents set down in their proposed regulations represented the practice that they had observed on the frontier:

"In the distribution of medals and flags, the following rules will be observed:

"1. They will be given to influential persons only.

"2. The largest medals will be given to the principal village chiefs, those of the second size will be given to the principal war chiefs, and those of the third size to the less distinguished chiefs and warriors.

"3. They will be presented with proper formalities, and with an appropriate speech, so as to produce a proper impression upon the Indians.

"4. It is not intended that chiefs should be appointed by an officer of the department, but that they should confer these badges of authority upon such as are selected or recognized by the tribe, and as are worthy of them, in the manner heretofore practiced.

"5. Whenever a foreign medal is worn, it will be replaced by an American medal, if the Agent should consider the person entitled to a medal."

The Indians expected to receive medals, and it was impossible to conduct Indian affairs without the use of them. Thomas L. McKenney, head of the Office of Indian Affairs, in 1829 wrote to the secretary of war about the policy of distributing medals. "So important is its continuance esteemed to be," he said, "that without medals, any plan of operations among the Indians, be it what it may, is essentially enfeebled. This comes of the high value which the Indians set upon these tokens of Friendship. They are, besides this indication of the Government Friendship, badges of power to them, and trophies of renown. They will not consent to part from this ancient right, as they esteem it; and according to the value they set upon medals is the importance to the Government in having them to bestow."

The U.S. government took great pains to produce medals of real artistic merit for the Indians. This cultural concern is surprising in a young nation trying to establish itself in a troubled world. Yet the medals which were made in the early years of the nation's existence are collector's items, not only because of the history associated with them, but also because of their artistic value. And this was a conscious policy. About one of the medals, McKenney wrote: "I am certainly anxious that these medals should be as perfect in their resemblance of the original, as the artist can make them. They are intended, not for the Indians, only, but for posterity."

The medals given to the Indians were supposed to bear the likeness of the president currently in office, and the medals can be traced administration by administration.

Washington medals

The Washington medals were unique. The government presented a number of medals to Indian chiefs during Washington's term of office, but it did not mass-produce the medals — undoubtedly because it did not command the technical means to do so. Instead, each medal was a separate production, hand engraved on oval plates of silver, the large ones roughly 4 by 6 inches in size. On one side was engraved the figure of Washington with that of an Indian in the peaceful gesture of throwing away his tomahawk. On the reverse was an eagle bearing the crest of the United States on its breast, with an olive branch in its right talon, a sheaf of arrows in its left. The plate was bound with a silver band and provided with a loop at the top by which it could be hung around the neck of the chief. The most famous of these Washington Indian medals was the one presented to the Seneca chief, Red Jacket, in 1792. The medal of Washington in today's presidential series, however, was designed to match later Indian medals and was not made until early in the 20th century.

No medals for Indians were made while John Adams was president. Medals distributed to the chiefs during his term of office were the so-called Seasons medals, which had been produced in England during Washington's second administration. They showed scenes of a farmer sowing grain, women spinning and weaving, and domestic cattle, which were supposed to incite in the Indians a desire for white civilization. Later, a John Adams medal similar in design to other Indian peace medals was struck in order to make the presidential series complete.

The production of Indian peace medals began to be regularized during the administration of President Thomas Jefferson. The pattern for the medals was more or less established, although the methods of manufacture were still not quite set. Medals in three sizes were ordered — large (4 inches in diameter), medium (3 inches), and small (2 inches). The medals were struck from dies cut by a special engraver who worked directly in the steel of the die, cutting out the features that would appear in relief on the finished medal. On the obverse was a bust of Jefferson in profile, with a legend which read: TH. JEFFERSON PRESIDENT OF THE U.S. A.D. 1801. On the reverse were two hands clasped, one with a cuff showing three stripes and three buttons, the other wearing a bracelet engraved with spread eagle. A crossed peace pipe and tomahawk and the words PEACE AND FRIENDSHIP completed the design.

One feature of the Jefferson medals distinguished them from later medals. They were hollow shells rather than solid medals. Possibly because there was no press in the country at the time powerful enough to strike the medals from solid discs of silver, two thin plates were used. The obverse and reverse of the medals were struck separately, then fastened together with a silver band to form a hollow medal. It was a satisfactory expedient as far as the appearance of the medal was concerned, but the Indians compared them unfavorably with the heavy medals they were accustomed to receiving from the British. The Jefferson medal issued today by the Mint in the presidential series is a solid medal which follows the 3-inch design of the original medals.

New design

When James Madison succeeded Jefferson in 1809, new medals had to be designed and struck. The task of ordering the medals fell to John Mason, who held the office of superintendent of Indian Trade. He turned to a friend in Philadelphia, John Vaughan, to engage an artist and to oversee the production of the medals at the Mint. Mason insisted that the hollow medals be replaced by solid ones and the Mint undertook to strike such medals. The Madison medals, like the Jefferson ones, came in three sizes, although the diameters — 3, 2.5, and 2 inches — differed from those of the Jefferson medals. They were solid silver, and at the suggestion of Vaughan, the reverse had a slightly changed design.

Vaughan objected to having both the wrists encuffed as they appeared on the Jefferson medals. This, he said, did not indicate the diversity of the races who were joined in the handclasp of friendship. He had the artist leave one of the arms bare, and this new design was used repeatedly until completely new designs were substituted for the reverse of the medals in the 1850s and later. Mason asked that the lettering on both sides of the medal be "so arranged that a small hole may be made through the medal exactly over the head of the President (so as to suspend it erect when worn by the Chiefs) without interfering with the letters." But for some unaccountable reason this wise advice was never heeded.

When it was time to have medals struck for President James Monroe, both the man directing the work and the artist-engraver were new. Thomas L. McKenney had replaced John Mason as superintendent of Indian Trade, and Moritz Furst was engaged in place of John Reich, who had engraved the Madison medals. The general form of the medals, nevertheless, followed the set formula. Furst prepared satisfactory likenesses of Monroe on the three sizes of the medals, and the dies of the previous reverse were used again.

Furst was also engaged to make the medals of Presidents John Quincy Adams, Andrew Jackson and Martin Van Buren. These medals, like those that followed, were ordered by the head of the Indian Office (the commissioner of Indian Affairs, after that office was created in 1832), who was the official responsible for the distribution of the medals to the chiefs. It was the custom to order 100 of each of the three sizes, although from time to time not all the medals were given out during the administration they represented. Rather than give the Indian chiefs medals of a previous administration, with the portrait of a president who was no longer in office, medals left over at the end of a president's tenure were regularly melted down to help provide the silver needed for the new medals.

As the series of medals progressed, they began to be considered as "presidential medals," quite apart from their original purpose as Indian peace medals. Franklin Peale, who became Chief Coiner at the Mint in 1839, believed that the Mint should be the depository of dies of all national medals, and he urged that medals missing from the presidential series (for example, one for John Adams) be supplied. He was supported by Robert M. Patterson, Director of the Mint, who in 1841 suggested making a medal of President William Henry Harrison, whose term had been too short to permit making Indian medals bearing his portrait. Nothing came of the proposals at the time, however.

Technical advance

When it came time to prepare medals for President John Tyler, technical advances had taken some of the difficulties out of medal making. The invention in France of a "portrait lathe," a mechanical means of cutting dies, did away with the need for the special engraver. A medallion of the president could now be modeled in wax, with full possibilities for making corrections until a suitable likeness was obtained. From this, by use of an intermediate plaster cast, a casting in fine iron was made of the medallion. With the use of the steam-powered lathe, reduced facsimilies were turned out in steel, and the lettering was then stamped in.

The new machine at the Mint was used for making the dies of the President John Tyler Indian peace medal from a medallion modeled by Ferdinand Pettrich, the President James K. Polk medal from a model made by the artist John Gadsby Chapman, and the President Zachary Taylor medal from a medallion sculptured by Henry Kirke Brown. The portrait lathe was adjusted to make the various sizes of the dies from the same model, so that all three sizes of these medals are identical and do not show the variations that occurred in the earlier medals, when the dies were cut individually by hand.

The next medals were again made from dies cut by engravers, who signed contracts with the commissioner of Indian Affairs to engrave the dies and strike the medals for presentation to the Indians. The two young New York artists who were engaged were Salathiel Ellis and Joseph Willson. Ellis engraved the dies for the portraits of Presidents Millard Fillmore, Franklin Pierce, James Buchanan and Abraham Lincoln, while Willson made the reverses for the medals. The old peace and friendship design which had been used for so many years on the reverse of the medals was now laid aside, and scenes depicting the adoption of civilization were used instead. One such design was used on the reverse of the Fillmore and Pierce medals, another on the Buchanan and Lincoln Indian peace medals. For these medals only the large and medium size were made; the small size was discontinued.

Copies of the medals designed for presentation to the Indians from Jefferson to Buchanan are issued by the Mint in bronze as part of the presidential series, uniformly now in the 3-inch size, although in past times the smaller sizes as well were reproduced. With President Buchanan, however, the presidential series begins to diverge from the Indian peace medal series. The Buchanan medal uses the reverse from the Fillmore and Pierce medals, instead of the one designed for it by Willson, and the Lincoln medal in the Mint presidential series is an inaugural medal, not the one designed for presentation to the Indian chiefs.

Paquet designs

The Indian peace medal for President Andrew Johnson's administration was engraved by Anthony Paquet. He had begun to make the medal for presentation to Indians during Lincoln's second administration and changed the obverse to show the bust of Johnson after Lincoln's assassination. The reverse was a completely new design, one suggested by the commissioner of Indian Affairs to show the change from Indian culture to white civilization. This medal became part of the presidential series.

Although the presidential series for presidents following Andrew Johnson are not those made for the Indians, special peace medals continued to be produced for each administration up to and including that of President Benjamin Harrison. That for President Ulysses S. Grant was made by Paquet and was struck in only one size, 2.5 inches in diameter. Those for Presidents Rutherford B. Hayes, James A. Garfield, Chester A. Arthur and Grover Cleveland were oval medals measuring 3 by 2.25 inches and on the reverse showed an Indian and a white man in a rural scene. They were designed by the engravers in the Mint, Charles E. Barber and George T. Morgan. For Benjamin Harrison, both an oval and a round Indian peace medal were made. Only small numbers of these later medals were struck in silver, for the Indian tribes were no longer treated as sovereign nations, and the importance of the chiefs in dealings with the U.S. government had declined. Bronze copies of all these Indian medals are available in the Mint's miscellaneous series.

Many persons today who collect these medals do not realize that the medals are relics of U.S. policy toward Indians and that the early medals were designed and produced exclusively to provide suitable symbols of peace and friendship for the Indian chiefs. But in a sense, Thomas L. McKenney's prophecy has come true. These medals were indeed designed "not for the Indians only, but for posterity."

Source: U.S. Mint

Description of presidential medals

George Washington, 1789, Obv. GEORGE WASHINGTON PRESIDENT OF THE UNITED STATES. Nude bust to right; below, 1789. By DuVivier. Rev. PEACE : AND : FRIENDSHIP. Pipe of peace and tomahawk, in saltire, above two clasped hands.

John Adams, 1797. Obv. JOHN ADAMS PRESIDENT OF THE U.S. Bust to right; below, A.D. 1797. Rev. Similar to Washington medal.

Thomas Jefferson, 1801. Obv. TH. JEFFERSON PRESIDENT OF THE U.S., A.D. 1801. Bust to left. Rev. Similar to Washington medal. By Reich.

James Madison, 1809. Obv. JAMES MADISON PRESIDENT OF THE U.S., A.D. 1809. Bust to left. Rev. Similar to Washington medal. By Reich.

James Monroe, 1817. Obv. JAMES MONROE PRESIDENT OF THE U.S., A.D. 1817. Bust to right. Rev. Similar to Washington medal. By Furst.

John Quincy Adams, 1825. Obv. JOHN QUINCY ADAMS PRESIDENT OF THE UNITED STATES. Draped bust to right; below, 1825. Rev. Similar to Washington medal. By Furst.

Andrew Jackson, 1829. Obv. ANDREW JACKSON PRESIDENT OF THE UNITED STATES. Bust to right; below, 1829. Rev. Similar to Washington medal. By Furst.

Martin Van Buren, 1837. Obv. MARTIN VAN BUREN PRESIDENT OF THE UNITED STATES. Bust to right; below, A.D. 1837. Rev. Similar to Washington medal. By Furst.

William Henry Harrison, 1841. Obv. WILLIAM H. HARRISON. Facing bust. Rev. INAUGURATED : PRESIDENT : OF THE : UNITED STATES : MARCH 4, 1841. : DIED : APRIL 4, 1841, within a laurel wreath. By Morgan.

John Tyler, 1841. Obv. JOHN TYLER PRESIDENT OF THE UNITED STATES.

Draped bust to left; below, 1841. Rev. Similar to Washington medal.

James K. Polk, 1845. Obv. JAMES K. POLK PRESIDENT OF THE UNITED STATES. Draped bust to left; below, 1845. Rev. Similar to Washington medal.

Zachary Taylor, 1849. Obv. ZACHARY TAYLOR PRESIDENT OF THE UNITED STATES. Draped bust to left; below, 1849. Rev. Similar to Washington medal.

Millard Fillmore 1850. Obv. MILLARD FILLMORE PRESIDENT OF THE UNITED STATES. Nude bust to right; below, 1850; beneath truncation of bust, S. Ellis. Rev. A white man and an Indian, standing before a flag, in an agricultural scene; above, LABOR VIRTUE HONOR. By Ellis and Willson.

Franklin Pierce, 1853. Obv. FRANKLIN PIERCE, PRESIDENT OF THE UNITED STATES. Nude bust to left; below, 1853. Rev. Similar to Fillmore medal.

James Buchanan, 1857. Obv. JAMES BUCHANAN, PRESIDENT OF THE UNITED STATES. Bust to right; below, 1857. Rev. Similar to Fillmore medal. By Ellis and Willson.

Abraham Lincoln, 1862. Obv. ABRAHAM LINCOLN, PRESIDENT OF THE UNITED STATES. Bust to right; below, 1862. Rev. In center, scenes of white civilization, with Indian behind plow, church and other buildings in background. Top, around, Indian preparing to scalp second man; below, at left, quiver with arrows, and at right, long bow and peace pipe. Bust below, center.

Andrew Johnson, 1865. Obv. ANDREW JOHNSON PRESIDENT OF THE UNITED STATES. Nude bust to right; below, 1865; beneath bust, PAQUET F. Rev. A female figure, Columbia, in long chiton and flowing robe, grasping the hand of an Indian chief before a tomb surmounted with a bust of Washington; below, PAQUET.

Ulysses S. Grant, 1869. Obv. ULYSSES S. GRANT. Nude bust to right; beneath, W. & C. BARBER F. Rev. PRESIDENT OF THE UNITED STATES. Within a laurel wreath, INAUGURATED : FIRST TERM : MARCH 4. 1869 : —+— : SECOND TERM : MARCH 4. 1873; beneath, two small branches of oak, in saltire. W. & C. BARBER.

Rutherford B. Hayes, 1877. Obv. RUTHERFORD B. HAYES. Nude bust to left. Rev. Similar to Grant medal, but within the wreath reading INAUGURATED : MARCH 5 : 1877; outside wreath, PRESIDENT OF THE UNITED STATES. By Morgan.

James A. Garfield, 1881. Obv. JAMES A. GARFIELD. Nude bust to left. By C.E. Barber. Rev. Similar to Lincoln medal, but within the wreath reading INAUGURATED : PRESIDENT : OF THE : UNITED STATES : MARCH 4, 1881 : —+— : ASSASSINATED : JULY 2, 1881 : DIED : SEPT. 19, 1881. By Morgan.

Chester A. Arthur, 1881. Obv. CHESTER A. ARTHUR. Nude bust to right. Rev. Similar to Grant medal, but within the wreath reading INAUGURATED : SEPTEMBER 20 : 1881. By C.E. Barber.

Grover Cleveland, 1885 and 1893. Obv. GROVER CLEVELAND. Bust to right. Rev. Within a laurel wreath, INAUGURATED : PRESIDENT : OF THE : UNITED STATES : MARCH 4 : 1885. By C.E. Barber.

Benjamin Harrison, 1889. Obv. BENJAMIN HARRISON. Bust to left. Rev. Similar to Cleveland medal, but inside wreath, INAUGURATED : PRESIDENT : OF THE : UNITED STATES : MARCH 4 : 1889. By C.E. Barber.

William McKinley, 1901. Obv. WILLIAM McKINLEY. Bust to left. Rev. INAUGURATED : PRESIDENT OF THE : UNITED STATES : MARCH 4, 1897. : SECOND TERM : MARCH 4, 1901 : ASSASSINATED : SEPT. 6, 1901 : DIED SEPT. 14, 1901 : To left Columbia standing, weeping; below palm branch and oak wreath. By Barber & Morgan.

Theodore Roosevelt, 1901. Obv. THEODORE ROOSEVELT. Bust to left. Rev. INAUGURATED : PRESIDENT : OF THE : UNITED STATES : SEPT. 14, 1901 : SECOND TERM : MARCH 4, 1905. To left, Columbia standing, her right hand resting upon an altar, on which is a cinerary urn, in her extended left, a scroll; above NATIONAL CAPITOL. By Barber and Morgan.

William H. Taft, 1909. Obv. WILLIAM H. TAFT. Bust to right. Rev. INAUGURATED : PRESIDENT OF THE : UNITED STATES : MARCH 4, 1909. Sibyl seated in front of National Capitol. By Barber and Morgan.

Woodrow Wilson: Obv. Portrait bust to left; around border, left WOODROW; right WILSON. Rev. An eagle with wings spread standing on oak and laurel branches; in background the Capitol building in Washington; across lower field, INAUGURATED : PRESIDENT OF THE : UNITED STATES : MAR. 4 1913 : SECOND TERM : MAR. 5 1917. By George T. Morgan.

Warren G. Harding : Obv. Portrait bust to left; around left border, WARREN G.; around right border HARDING. Rev.

Female figure draped in mourning facing right, holding laurel branch; column on left; upper field, an eagle within a wreath; INAUGURATED : PRESIDENT OF THE : UNITED STATES : MAR. 4 1921; a horizontal band of leaves; below, DIED : AUG. 2 : 1923; at bottom a laurel wreath, flowers and palm branches; on exergue a patterned band. By George T. Morgan.

Calvin Coolidge: Obv. Portrait bust to right; around border, CALVIN COOLIDGE, PRESIDENT OF THE UNITED STATES. Rev. Seated draped female figure of Liberty, holding fasces, facing left; in left field INAUG : URATED and U.S. shield with eagle; upper right field, AUG. 3 1923 : AND : MAR. 4 1925; lower right field, a cornucopia; in exergue, 1928 around edge, a border of 48 leaves, one for each state in the Union. By John R. Sinnock.

Herbert Hoover: Obv. Portrait of President Hoover to right, above PRESIDENT OF THE UNITED STATES. In background MCMXXIX HERBERT HOOVER. Rev. Standing figure of Columbia facing front and holding a fasces in either arm; in background INAUGURATED MARCH 4 1929, ENGINEER SCHOLAR STATESMAN HUMANIST. By John R. Sinnock.

Franklin D. Roosevelt: Obv. Portrait of President Roosevelt facing right. Rev. A seated figure, draped, with head bowed, represents the sorrowing nation and all the human race. Her right hand is extended in the act of dropping a wreath upon waters upon which a ship symbolizing the spirit of the late president sails into the distant mists of the horizon, and in her left hand is the palm branch of mourning. The inscription at the top, FOR COUNTRY AND HUMANITY, is intended to indicate his labors for the benefit of the oppressed of all mankind. In the left field are the dates of inauguration; in the right background are rows of crosses signifying that he also was a war casualty. Below this is the date of death. In the lower left field is a stump of an olive tree from which new leaves are sprouting, representing the dawn of a new era of peace; in the exergue, IN MEMORIAM. By John R. Sinnock.

Harry S Truman: Obv. Portrait of President Truman to left; around border PRESIDENT OF THE UNITED STATES; in the background HARRY S TRUMAN. Rev. In center view of the White House; above, the seal of the president; below, inscription INAUGURATED APRIL 12 1945 JANUARY 20 1949. By Sinnock and Gilroy Roberts.

Dwight D. Eisenhower: Obv. Portrait of President Eisenhower to left; around border DWIGHT D. EISENHOWER. Rev. Standing draped female figure of Freedom, which stands on the Capitol dome; background to left, pioneers on the prairie schooner and oxen; to right, ploughman; above, 13 stars; around border INAUGURATED PRESIDENT JAN. 20, 1953; lower background, UNITED STATES OF AMERICA. By Gilroy Roberts and Frank Gasparro.

Dwight D. Eisenhower: Obv. Portrait of President Eisenhower to left; around border DWIGHT D. EISENHOWER. Rev. Center figure is reproduced from statue of Freedom above the Capitol dome; directly below, the shield of the United States, with 13 stars representing original 13 States. Upper left of center is the atomic symbol; the kneeling figure on the upper left represents Agriculture: the figure on the upper right, Industry; lower left, Science, Research; lower right, Commerce, Transportation. Above around border the inscription ATOMS FOR PEACE. Below is the inscription: INAUGURATED PRESIDENT OF THE UNITED STATES, SECOND TERM, JANUARY 20, 1957. By Gilroy Roberts and von Hebel.

John F. Kennedy: Obv. Portrait of President Kennedy to left: Around border JOHN F. KENNEDY. Rev. seal of the president of the United States, above INAUGURATED PRESIDENT; below a portion of President Kennedy's Inaugural Address, his name and the date JANUARY 20, 1961. On either side, a lighted torch denoting enlightenment. By Gilroy Roberts and Frank Gasparro.

Lyndon B. Johnson: Obv. Portrait of President Johnson to left: around border LYNDON B. JOHNSON. Rev. seal of the president of the United States, below NOVEMBER 22, 1963; encircling seal PRESIDENT OF THE UNITED STATES; below seal a portion of his address before the joint session of Congress on Nov. 27, 1963. By Gilroy Roberts and Frank Gasparro.

Richard M. Nixon: Obv. Portrait of President Nixon to right: above and around border PRESIDENT OF THE UNITED STATES; to left of bust RICHARD MILHOUS NIXON. Rev. seal of the president of the United States within a wreath of 50 stars; below the date of inauguration and a statement from his August 1968 speech accepting the nomination for president. By Frank Gasparro.

Richard M. Nixon second term medal: same Obv. Rev. seal of the president of the United States within a wreath of 50 stars; above PEACE; below date JANUARY 20,

1973, and an excerpt from a speech on world peace. By Frank Gasparro.

Gerald R. Ford: Obv. Portrait of President Ford to right: Above and around border GERALD R. FORD. Reverse dominated by the presidential seal, surrounded by the date of the Ford inauguration, AUGUST 9, 1974, and the legend, "I WILL BE PRESIDENT OF ALL THE PEOPLE." By Frank Gasparro and Matthew Peloso.

Jimmy Carter: Obv. Three-quarters bust of President Carter facing left. Above PRESIDENT OF THE UNITED STATES, at right JIMMY CARTER. Rev. Presidential seal; eagle with olive branch and arrows, surrounded by 50 stars. INAUGURATED : JANUARY 20, 1977 : "THE AMERICAN DREAM : ENDURES ... WE MUST : ONCE AGAIN HAVE FAITH : IN OUR COUNTRY ... : JIMMY CARTER. By Frank Gasparro.

Ronald Reagan: Obv. President Reagan facing right, E.A.B. JONES below. RONALD REAGAN above; PRESIDENT OF THE UNITED STATES below. Rev. View of Half Dome in Yosemite National Park. Above, 'LET US RENEW OUR FAITH AND OUR HOPE. WE HAVE EVERY RIGHT TO DREAM HEROIC DREAMS.' By Elizabeth Jones.

Source: U.S. Mint

Seigniorage

Seigniorage is the difference between the monetary value of coins and their cost, including the manufacturing expense. The seigniorage on coins, arising from the exercise of the government's monetary powers, differs from receipts coming from the public, since there is no corresponding payment on the part of another party. Therefore, seigniorage is excluded from receipts and treated, like borrowing, as a means of financing a budget deficit, or as a supplementary amount to be applied (to reduce debt or to increase the cash in the treasury) in the years of a budget surplus.

In a historical sense, seigniorage is a charge imposed by the agency that is legally entrusted with the power to produce coins for circulation as money. The term is borrowed from the French word "seigneurage," which literally means "the right of the lord."

Indeed, the delegation of the right (or privilege) to the sovereign is a tradition that can be traced back to Roman times. In the Middle Ages, the prerogative was exercised by the governing nobles of each state — the feudal lords and kings — and it was mainly the abuse of the prerogative that caused the most famous cases of currency debasements.

In fact, up to the reign of Charles VII, the seigniorage obtained by reducing the amount of gold or silver in coins or by raising the charge for manufacturing coins was considered an important source of revenue for the French crown. It was not until 1803 that France passed laws to limit the seigniorage charge that could be imposed by the state.

The question of seigniorage in the U.S. goes back to the first Secretary of the Treasury, Alexander Hamilton, whose views on seigniorage were generally unfavorable. Hamilton apparently preferred to have the metallic value of coins equal to their monetary value, as he believed counterfeiters would be induced to duplicate coins if the monetary value of coins exceeded the metallic value.

Thus, when Congress adopted Hamilton's coinage recommendations in 1792, the seigniorage charge was limited to one half of 1 percent of the value of bullion presented to the Mint for immediate coinage. If the person presenting bullion had to wait for delivery of the coins, there was to be no seigniorage charge at all. In practice, however, seigniorage did not actually disappear. Increased coin production after 1795 resulted in lower minting costs and the weight of some of the minor coins was reduced.

In 1800, the U.S. Mint showed a net profit of about $5,000 on coinage, and in the years that followed, a small margin of seigniorage was usually realized.

During fiscal years 1934-1964, total silver seigniorage in the U.S. amounted to $1,916.2 million. Of this total, $1,172.9 million originated from the revaluation of silver bullion behind silver certificates and $743.3 million was from the production of silver coins. The seigniorage from revaluation of silver bullion was the result of increases in the price of silver during 1934-1964 and a law in May 1933 that permitted the Treasury to hold silver in either bullion (bar) form or coins as reserve backing for the Treasury's silver certificates in circulation. Before May 1933, the law allowed only silver dollars as reserve backing for silver certificates.

The price of silver in the New York market increased from an average price of 45 cents per troy ounce in 1933 to $1.293 in 1964; as a result, the dollar value of silver bars was required as reserve for the same amount of certificates, with the difference representing the amount of seigniorage.

The nature and composition of seigniorage after fiscal year 1964 reflect the results of changes in the law regarding coinage, as well as increases in coin production. During fiscal years 1964-1967, the U.S. Treasury received a total of $1,665.1 million of seigniorage. Unlike the 1934-1964 period, nearly all the seigniorage in the latter period resulted from coin production, with a relatively small amount due to revaluation. The difference between the two periods largely reflects that in recent years the market price of silver has been as high as the monetary value of silver; consequently, no revaluation of seigniorage could be realized.

A huge jump in coin seigniorage occurred in fiscal year 1966, an increase of $530 million over fiscal year 1965. The major reason for the sharp increase reflects the enactment of the Coinage Act of 1965, which, by altering the metallic composition of half dollars, quarters and dimes, drastically reduced the cost of metals used in producing coins. The bulk ($546 million) of seigniorage was the result of coining clad quarters and clad dimes.

Coinage seigniorage is the difference between the cost of the metals that go into coin — alloy costs — and the monetary value of the coin. Not all seigniorage thus derived can be considered as net profit to the government, because in addition to the cost of the metal, coin manufacturing also involves the cost of production.

In 1966, for example, the cost to the government for producing 8.7 billion coins amounted to $11.1 million. This figure, however, does not include production and security costs, nor capital investment outlays for plants and equipment. All these costs are associated with coin production, and when taken into account, indicate that the seigniorage that goes into the general fund of the government does not represent net profit.

Seigniorage revenues, fiscal years 1984-1986

(Note: Recovery of Mint manufacturing expenses reduces the total for copper-nickel clad coinage by the amount indicated in the last column.)

Fiscal Year Facility	Minor coinage	Copper-nickel clad	Silver clad	Recovery of manufacturing expenses
1984				
Philadelphia	55,046,590.94	223,347,688.85	— — —	
San Francisco	97,924.96	2,834,915.61	15,419.98	
Denver	45,544,584.22	201,793,255.71	— — —	
West Point	11,051,134.82	— — —	— — —	
Total	111,740,234.94	386,616,087.17	15,419.98	498,371,742.09
1985				
Philadelphia	48,359,743.73	267,034,163.87	— — —	
San Francisco	84,956.67	2,394,823.15	5,285.33	
Denver	43,811,556.97	192,963,686.82	— — —	
West Point	4,639,026.88	— — —	— — —	
Total	96,895,284.25	419,016,970.39	5,285.33	43,375,703.45
1986				
Philadelphia	43,299,530.46	194,626,598.95	— — —	
San Francisco	59,623.01	2,077,929.73	6,669.96	
Denver	38,486,319.89	153,577,115.68	— — —	
West Point	1,087,085.29	— — —	— — —	
Total	82,932,558.65	309,506,445.96	6,669.96	40,775,198.40

Source: United States Mint

Domestic coinage executed during calendar 1986

Denomination	Philadelphia	Denver	West Point	Total value	Total pieces
DOLLARS - NON-SILVER	$0.00	$0.00	$0.00	$0.00	0
SUBSIDIARY					
Half dollars	$6,553,816.50	$7,683,072.50	$0.00	$14,236,889.00	28,473,778
Quarter dollars	$137,799,833.25	$126,074,665.00	$0.00	$263,874,498.25	1,055,497,993
Dimes	$68,264,969.30	$47,332,697.40	$0.00	$115,597,666.70	1,155,976,667
Total subsidiary	$212,618,619.05	$181,090,434.90	$0.00	$393,709,053.95	2,239,948,438
MINOR					
5-cent pieces	$26,844,174.65	$18,090,957.00	$0.00	$44,935,131.65	898,702,633
1-cent pieces	$44,909,954.93	$44,428,666.98	$4,000.00	$89,342,621.91	8,934,262,191
Total minor	$71,754,129.58	$62,519,623.98	$4,000.00	$134,277,753.56	9,832,964,824
Total domestic coinage	$284,372,748.63	$243,610,058.88	$4,000.00	$527,986,807.51	12,072,913,262

COINAGE EXECUTED FOR FOREIGN GOVERNMENTS .... Panama 2,200,000

Source: United States Mint, Office for Production

The Assay Commission

The Assay Commission was one of the oldest institutions in the annals of American history until public participation was eliminated during the Carter administration. The original provision for this body was made in the Act of April 2, 1792, Section 18, which established the Mint and provided for a national coinage.

The duty of the Commission was to test the weight and fineness of the coins reserved by the operating Mints during the preceding calendar year, in order to assure that they conformed to their respective legal standards. During each calendar year, coins were selected at random from each Mint's coinage and shipped quarterly to the Philadelphia Mint, where they were preserved for delivery with the selected Philadelphia coins, to the Commission when it met the following February.

If it appeared by such examination and test that these coins did not differ from the standard fineness and weight by a greater quantity than is allowed by law, the trial was considered and reported as satisfactory. If, however, any greater deviation from the legal standard or weight appeared, this fact was certified to the president of the United States; and if, on a view of the circumstances of the case, he so decided, the officers implicated in the error were thenceforward disqualified from holding their respective offices.

Those pyx coins not used for the assay test were returned to Mint stocks for circulation. They were not mutilated or marked in any manner to distinguish them from other coins.

The pieces upon which assay tests were made were returned to the Mint for melting.

The Assay Commission was established by the founding fathers to serve as an impartial check upon the nation's coinage, additional to that routinely performed by Mint employees.

The Commission met in one-day session at the Mint in Philadelphia, on the second Wednesday in February, as required by law.

There were three ex officio members of the Commission: A judge of the United States District Court for the Eastern District of Pennsylvania; the Comptroller of the Currency; and the Assayer of the United States Assay Office at New York. The membership always included a representative of the National Bureau of Standards. The weights used by the Commission were sent to the National Bureau of Standards to be calibrated before the Assay Commission meeting to assure that they conformed to the standard troy weight measure used in the Mints. The standards representative delivered them.

While there was no statutory limit to the number who could serve, both a ceiling on appropriated funds for expenses to cover the meeting, and that the membership must be divided into three small committees assigned to the task of counting, weighing and assaying coin samples, dictated the size. Owing to the smallness of the Commission, and the honor which attaches to service, it had been customary to make very few repeat appointments in the final years.

First authorized to serve on the commission in 1837, public members had been appointed by the president continuously at least since 1874, according to available records.

Although outgoing Director of the Mint Mary Brooks had submitted 117 names to the White House, a list from which about 25 members would by tradition have been named to the 1977 Assay Commission, the Carter administration declined to name any public members to the historic body. It is believed about 34 public members would have been nominated.

Thirty-one of the original 50 1977 Assay Commission medals produced were distributed to participants, key Treasury and Mint officials and staff and to the Smithsonian Institution Division of Numismatics and the Bureau of the Mint archives. The remaining 19 were melted.

However, following public outcry over distribution of the medals, the Mint struck pewter duplicates of the medal for sale to collectors. The only distinguishing marks on the original medals are the names of the persons receiving them engraved on the edges.

The failure of the Carter Administration to name public members to the 1977 Commission sent shock waves through the numismatic fraternity, which had a natural predilection for the mission of the Assay Commission and had enjoyed notable recognition among commissioners in years past.

Hobby representation on this select body was not of recent origin, however. Numismatists had a natural inclination towards the tradition and mission of the Assay Commission and had readily accepted appointment to the group as a signal honor, despite being obliged to pay their own expenses. The Mint expended $2,500 annually for the event.

Among the scores of hobby notables accepting this appointment early in this century were James E. Fraser, designer of the Indian Head 5-cent piece (1921), and former American Numismatic Association presidents Waldo C. Moore (1912), H.O. Granberg (1916 and 1917), J.M. Henderson (1911, 1916, 1920 and 1921) and Judson Brenner (1912, 1913, 1921, 1922, 1926 and 1928).

The last meeting of the statutory members of the Assay Commission came in 1980. No meetings were held during the Reagan administration and with the closing of the New York Assay Office, the statutory member's position has been eliminated.

U.S. Assay Commission medals

For more than a century, when a group of distinguished presidential appointees had assembled at the Philadelphia Mint in February to renew the annual "Trial of the Pyx" sitting as the U.S. Assay Commission, they had received a tangible memento of their service to their country in the form of a specially issued, limited edition medal.

These medals, representing the zenith of the die sinking art in America, are among the most cherished yet little known of the official medals of the United States.

Among the earliest federal institutions, the U.S. Assay Commission dated back to 1792 and was formalized under provisions of the same legislation which authorized the U.S. Mint itself. The traditional official assay ceremony to assure the correct standard of a nation's coins, however, dates back to England in the 13th century, when it was felt to be a necessary measure to discourage counterfeiting, debasement and to bolster public confidence in the coins of the realm.

Although largely a ceremonial body in the United States in recent years, and eliminated altogether in 1977, consideration of the traditional British "Trial of the Pyx" received a high priority in the mind of the nation's financial architect Alexander Hamilton, the first Secretary of the Treasury.

In 1791, in presenting to Congress his "inquiries and reflections" relative to the establishment of a Mint, he concluded that the "remedy for errors in the weight and alloy of the coins must necessarily form a part in the system of the Mint; and the manner of applying it will require to be regulated."

In his message he described the English system of preserving samples of the coinage in the pyx (box), for mass-assaying by a jury of the Company of Goldsmiths in the presence of the Lord Chancellor, the officers of the Treasury and others.

With the adoption of "Statute One," the Mint Act of April 2, 1792, Hamilton's conception became a reality. Government officers were specified as assay commissioners, directed to convene on the last Monday in July annually. It is believed the Assay Commission had met since with few exceptions until 1977.

The meeting date was changed and in 1801, when the capital was moved from Philadelphia to Washington, D.C., the February meeting was postponed. It is presumed that the condition of the roads in mid-winter made it impossible to travel with horses from Washington to Philadelphia.

Confidence undermined

When the meeting could not be held on the prescribed date, Director of the Mint Elias Boudinot wrote an indignant letter to President John Adams complaining that the public's confidence was being undermined and that the depositors were clamoring for the coins retained for examination.

In those days the Mint operated on a "custom" basis, taking in bullion from individuals and returning to them an appropriate weight of coins. Thus the specimens retained for the annual assaying really belonged to the customers of the Mint. Congress solved the problem by providing for a meeting in April of that year.

There is some evidence that an Assay Commission did not meet in 1817 to examine the prior year's silver and gold coinage because there was none. The reason was that on Jan. 11, 1816, a fire broke out in the millhouse, an old wooden shack in the Mint's backyard. The blaze spread to the adjoining building which contained the rolling and drawing apparatus necessary to make planchets for the specie issues, causing extensive damage which was not repaired until the following year.

The first authorization for the public to serve on the Assay Commission was provided by statute in 1837. Being henceforth almost entirely composed of impartial citizens, independent of the Mint, the commission reported to the president any deviations in coins beyond the legal limits.

The object of its meeting was to ensure the greatest care on the part of the coiners in conforming in all respects to legal weights and finenesses. The knowledge that any coin may be selected for this check has a psychological effect upon the officers of the Mints, it was reasoned, and this is of value in keeping coinage standards at the highest possible levels.

The random sample on which the commission conducted its tests included not less than one piece for each 100,000 pieces, or fractional part thereof, of subsidiary coins and dollars delivered, except that one piece for each 200,000 dimes delivered was taken.

Inasmuch as the Mints now produce billions of coins and since the pyx (box) contained many thousands of coins taken at random throughout the year from production, it is clear that the commission did not examine every single piece. Commissioners examined only such number as satisfies themselves as being representative of the whole.

Ceremonial medals

The ceremony was already two generations old in the United States before the first medal was struck for the occasion. The issue of 1860, which bears on obverse James B. Longacre's French head of Liberty facing right wearing a chaplet of oak leaves, as employed on his half dollar patterns of 1859, is believed to be the first such medal. Anthony Paquet's laurel wreath reverse encloses the simple legend, ANNUAL / ASSAY / 1860.

Receiving the historic medal were commission members John Cadwalader, U.S. District Judge for the Eastern District of Pennsylvania; government officials James C. Van Dyke and Joseph Baker; Dr. Barnard of Mississippi; Robert Bridges and Thomas C. Porter of Pennsylvania; Dr. Zenia Pitcher of Michigan; James M. Porter; and Asa Packer.

Struck in bronzed copper and silver, this 33-mm medal inaugurated a tradition the practice of which had been followed more or less consistently to 1977. The introduction of the assay medal also created a numismatic specialty fitting for the connoisseur.

Although an early cataloger of this series could not determine "by whose authority the Assay Medals were first issued in 1860, nor by whose suggestion these semi-official souvenirs were originated," it is probably no mere coincidence that they commenced during the period of fervent collector interest following the mid-19th century.

Flushed with the first large-scale outpouring of numismatic preoccupation in the United States, private citizens who had been granted representation on the annual commission a generation before could have lobbied successfully with friendly Mint officials for such a token of their participation. It is also known that Mint Director Snowden was an ardent proponent of the Mint's Medal Department and was actively seeking to improve the artistic quality of U.S. coinage. The additional vehicle provided by these medals became a splendid showcase for the Mint engravers' talents.

A long-standing numismatic tradition links the Mint's "First Steam Coinage" medal with such ceremonial presentations. Dated March

23, 1836 (an earlier version is dated Feb. 22), the radiated Liberty Cap medal commemorates the introduction of steam coinage presses into production at the Philadelphia facility. Restruck in both silver and copper, on thick and thin planchets for years (and currently still offered on the Mint's medal list), it is not inconceivable that such presentations were made, although documentation to this effect is slight.

The 1860 design was resurrected the following year and again in 1867. No medals are known for the intervening years and it is presumed that the wartime exigencies of the Civil War account for this omission.

Reflecting the tenor of their times as much as the caprice of the Mint's engravers, who were given wide latitude in executing the medal designs, the 1868 medal witnesses the desires of a war-torn nation to bind up the wounds so recently inflicted. The William Barber design portrays Columbia as Peace putting the torch to the implements of war.

Allegory predominates

Allegorical and historical allusions predominate on the assay medal designs through the nation's Centennial years. Barber's 1871 design portraying Archimedes, the originator of the humid assay, was reused on several subsequent assay medals. His 1870 allegory of Columbia, as Moneta or Science, holding the scales, was likewise redeployed, but perhaps his most noble effort was the medal for the 1876 meeting. Featuring founding father George Washington on the obverse, the medal's reverse proudly proclaims YEAR ONE HUNDRED OF AMERICAN INDEPENDENCE.

It is also during this period that we witness the growth of the regal personalization the nation's "Pater Patriae" forsook in his own lifetime. Not only is Washington commemorated, but Mint Director Pollock's name and title gratuitously adorn several issues, and the death of Smithsonian and Mint officers Torrey, Henry and Linderman are recalled.

Following the double funerary issue of 1879, the 1880 medal marks the fulfillment of the trend towards personal aggrandizement. Featuring the obverse bust of a prominent individual, usually the president but more frequently in recent years a Treasury Department official, this tradition is broken only infrequently down to the present era.

The medal of 1880 bears the bust of President Rutherford B. Hayes, on the recommendation of Chief Coiner Col. Oliver C. Bosbyshell. It is interesting to note that an early

collector of assay medals and friend of Bosbyshell welcomed this trend to contemporary portraiture as "the series becoming historic."

It is also interesting to note that while so-called patterns of earlier assay medals are known, the issue for 1880 compasses four such unadopted designs. Both Charles Barber, who had succeeded his father William as Chief Engraver, and George Morgan, who felt he should have gotten the choice job, prepared competing designs for the medal. As an exercise in Mint harmony the adopted design incorporated the skills of both talented engravers.

The issue of 1880 marks a departure in another regard. With the assay medals' obverses locked into a portrait bust format the exquisite allegorical and historical allusions of earlier years replace the rather drab assemblage of wreaths which had predominated on the reverses of many issues to that date.

The Barber-Morgan collaboration prevailed until the former's death and the succession of portrait-and-allegory medals commemorate each successive incumbent of the Oval Office with general regularity until the remarkable issue of 1901. Stylistically the portrait of President McKinley combined with a Mint workman is unexceptional; however, instead of a circular medallion, the assay medal presented to commissioners was in the form of a rectangular plaque.

New departure

"This is an entirely new departure for the Mint; nothing like it in shape has ever been produced by that branch of the Treasury Department," a contemporary exclaimed. He likened the general appearance of the 40-by-55-millimeter silver plaque to the "silver ore of 1625, the old plate money of Sweden, the bar money of other countries, and the Mexican wooden money before 1849."

At the time he also lauded the Mint's decision not to place the assay medals on its list of offerings generally available to collectors. Although 19th century evidence suggests strongly that certain issues were restruck for sale to favored individuals and the multiplicity of metal varieties known are obviously outside the scope of the ceremonial presentation, the Mint's official position has remained the same down to the present time with two notable exceptions explained later.

"To be of any value to the members of the Assay Commission, these medals ought not to be sold to the general public, and hence not so exposed," he commented. "Somehow or other, a few of them find their way into the hands of coin dealers every year, some months after their issue," he recorded.

The following year, the assay medal reverted to its pre-turn-of-the-century configuration, but in 1903 and continuing through 1909, the French medalists' oblong plaque prevailed with the bust of President Theodore Roosevelt, except in the latter year when Treasury Secretary George Cortelyou appeared.

The annual assay meeting of 1908 is numismatically far more important, however, than for the mere issue of Barber and Morgan's silver plaque to commission members. Due to the magnanimity of newly appointed Mint Director Frank A. Leach, a major and innovative U.S. coin design escaped virtual extinction in the Mint's melting pot.

Known to collectors today as Judd 1775, this scarce Saint-Gaudens $10 gold piece design, (distinguished by rolled rims and periods), remains collectible, albeit excessively rare today, because specimens of the proposed design were given the assay commissioners by Director Leach.

Struck before Leach assumed the directorship in 1907, these Indian Head eagles "were found impracticable and I ordered them to be re-melted," Leach later recalled. A few pieces had already "got out through the President and others connected with designing the coin and could not be recalled," he added.

"As the matter of re-melting the issue came up at or about the time of the meeting of the Assay Commission [February 1908] it occurred to me to present one to each of the Commission. . . . These and the pieces that were given out through the President number 42," he said.

It is highly likely the suggestion to present the Saint-Gaudens eagle to assay commission members was espoused by Rep. William A. Ashbrook from Johnstown, Ohio. A member of the House Committee on Coinage, Weights and Measures and quite familiar with the coin, Ashbrook not only chaired the 1908 assay meeting but was an avid collector and proponent of beneficial hobby measures.

Worthy representative

"American numismatists have a worthy and earnest representative in Congress in the person of [the] Honorable William A. Ashbrook," *The Numismatist* associate editor Edgar H. Adams enthused. Elected to the ANA board of governors later that very year, this "enthusiastic collector of U.S. coins and close student of numismatics and finance," was also prominent in the Ohio Numismatic Society and largely responsible for the federal

charter which the ANA secured in 1912. He was also to serve on the Assay Commission an additional dozen times, both in and out of Congress.

Another lucky recipient of the Assay Commission bonus was Thomas P. Burns, employed at the U.S. subtreasury in San Francisco. Never before or later chosen to the Assay Commission, Burns later sold his rare eagle to prominent numismatist Farran Zerbe.

An extremely elusive coin which seldom appears in the numismatic marketplace, a private sale of one of the extant examples netted $24,000 in 1974, and public sales by Superior Galleries in 1975 brought $19,000; by American Auction Association in 1973, $16,000; and in 1977, $65,000.

On its most recent trip to the auction block, a Proof 67 example brought $40,000 in the Paramount session of Auction '84.

The following year's medal, the George B. Cortelyou issue of 1909, may well be the most "common" issue of this series, because until the mid-1960s the U.S. Mint offered the medal with its Assay Commission commemorative reverse as the Cortelyou medal in its series honoring the Secretaries of the Treasury. After considerable prompting by numismatists, the Mint adopted its present obverse uniface version for sale to collectors.

As indicated, modern assay medals have continued the tradition of portrait busts; however, the engravers of this century have mostly turned from allegory to historical reflection with their medal designs. As a true showcase for their sculpturing and engraving talents, the issues successively of John Sinnock and Adam Pietz, Gilroy Roberts and Frank Gasparro, and the more recent Mint artists have captured an essential aesthetic which is unfortunately not translatable in the short word descriptions in the catalog appended herein.

It should be pointed out that these assay medals of more recent vintage are also among the less frequently encountered specimens in the series. Widely dispersed, most medals were reserved for members of the actual Assay Commission and are thereby highly cherished mementoes. Not usually parted with during one's lifetime, the most recent medals are often lacking in even the most advanced collections.

These 20th century medals are also not without their quasi-official attractions, since trial or specimen strikes of several issues have emerged. These include uniface obverse trial strikes of the 1914 medal, a purported mule of the 1918-1919 medals, a uniface bronze trial strike of the later issue, and a trial strike of the 1926-1929 obverse on a square chunk of steel. There is also contemporary evidence that grateful 1921 Assay Commissioners subscribed funds for striking an unprecedented gold specimen to be presented to outgoing President Wilson.

Felt gratitude

Included on that 1921 Assay Commission were two past ANA presidents, Judson Brenner and J.M. Henderson; sculptor James Earle Fraser, designer of the then current Indian Head 5-cent piece; and at least three prominent educators, James L. Howe of Washington and Lee University, Albert Levitt of George Washington University, and C.A. McLain of Harvard University. The present whereabouts of this gold specimen of the 1921 Assay Commission medal is unknown, if in fact it was struck, but apparently a number of commission members had good reason to feel gratitude to the departing president of the United States and former president of Princeton University.

In the 1978 edition of the *Coin World Almanac,* it was thought a "rare" 20th century numismatic item, the 1977 U.S. Assay Commission medal, would go down in the annals of the collecting fraternity as rarer still as the result of the Mint's decision to melt 19 of the 50 special medals struck for the 1977 abbreviated Assay Commission session.

After 31 of the medals were distributed to public officials, including many not serving in any capacity on the abbreviated Assay Commission, Mint officials decided to restrike the medals and offer them to the public. With a price tag of $20, the medals were first offered at the American Numismatic Association Midwinter convention, Feb. 15-19, 1978, in Colorado Springs, Colo. The medals are still available from the Mint for $25 (plus 75 cents for mail orders).

The original medals can be distinguished only by their engraved edge inscriptions, each bearing the name of the recipient.

Unappointed public representatives to 1977's annual but abbreviated renewal of the Assay Commission ceremony who thereby didn't receive the 1977 medal can take heart in one regard, however: members who were appointed and served at the 1954 session received a "thanks but no thanks" reception for their efforts. No official medal was issued for the occasion and commission members voted to purchase the Lincoln presidential medal from the Mint list as their unofficial souvenir.

In 1980, statutory members meeting in what became the last Assay Commission received the Jimmy Carter presidential medal inscribed on the edge with 1980 ANNUAL ASSAY COMMISSION.

The end result of the public furor growing out of 1977's mini-meeting should help to redefine this medal series for the growing number of collecting connoisseurs availing themselves of the choicest fruits of the Mint engravers' labor.

Among the most beautiful products of the U.S. Mint, the assay medals give virtually free rein to the imagination and skill of the die engraver. Unrestricted by the statutory, size and commercial constraints which inhibit the artistry attainable on the nation's commercial coinage, the Mint engravers' medals for this series reflect the greatest credit on their talents.

Although all but the 1977 medals may be termed rare, early collectors were quick to recognize the collecting virtues of the assay medal series. Struck primarily for presentation to individual commission members, fine collections of these medals have been prime desiderata of some of the nation's most avid collectors and pressures brought to bear by influential numismatists are known to have caused restrikes of certain 19th century issues.

Listing unavailable

Unfortunately for the collector of these medals (and the general collector with no particular aspirations in that direction, but maybe a miscellaneous piece acquired through the years), no definitive listing of this series had been available for study, comparison or other purposes prior to the trial listing of assay medals prepared for the 1977 edition of the *Coin World Almanac.*

Compiled from various sources, the revised trial listing appended herein substantially constitutes such a catalog of U.S. Assay Commission medals.

Apparently the first such attempt in this direction was taken by Edmund J. Cleveland in the July 1897 issue of *The American Journal of Numismatics.* Ostensibly based on the U.S. Mint's own collection of these pieces, but obviously supplemented by specimens residing elsewhere, Cleveland's listing and supplements through the turn of the century provide much basic data, particularly on the extremely rare 19th century strikes considered patterns and trial specimens.

The Mint assay medal holdings were further examined by its long-time curator, T.L.

Comparette as a portion of his *Catalogue of Coins, Tokens and Medals in the Numismatic Collection of the Mint of the U.S. at Philadelphia, Pa.*, published in three editions from 1912 to 1914. Descriptions of later issues from the Mint cabinet were supplied to *Coin World* by Mint Archivist Eleanora Hayden.

Further details have been culled from vintage auction catalogs, notably those of H. and S.H. Chapman and Thomas L. Elder, contemporaneous accounts in the periodical literature, price lists, and several 1970s sales with extensive offerings of assay medals.

A special thanks for assistance rendered accrues to numismatic scholar Robert W. Julian and veteran collector Maxwell E. Brail.

Julian's 1977 *Medals of the United States Mint: The First Century, 1792-1892* provided a detailed listing of the medals of 1860 through 1892. The latest listing is Francis Pessolano-Filos' *The Assay Medals and The Assay Commissioners: 1841-1977*; this latter work, however, suffers from errors.

Every effort has been expended to make this listing both accurate and comprehensive, but unfortunately much of the research was done "at arms' length" from the medals based on sources described. Readers knowing of specimens not listed below, or such other pertinent data as would improve this listing, are urged to contact *Coin World*.

A revised trial listing of U.S. Assay Commission medals

1860. OBV: MINT OF THE UNITED STATES above French head of Liberty facing right, wearing chaplet of oak leaves, LIBERTY on ribbon at truncation, PHILADELPHIA. below.
REV: ANNUAL/ASSAY/1860 within wreath of laurel.
Bronzed copper and silver. Proof. 33 mm. By Paquet and Longacre.

1861. OBV: similar to 1860.
REV: ANNUAL/ASSAY/1861 within wreath of laurel.
Bronzed copper. Proof. 33 mm. By Longacre.

1867. OBV: similar to 1860.
REV: ANNUAL/ASSAY/1867 within wreath of laurel.
Aluminum, bronzed copper, copper and silver.
Proof. Thick and thin planchets. 33 mm. By Longacre. (Note: trial impressions struck in nickel.)

1868. OBV: MINT OF THE/UNITED STATES separated by Columbia as Peace destroying the implements of war by fire, .PHILAD. below.
REV: ANNUAL/ASSAY/1868 within wreath of oak leaves and olive.
Aluminum, bronzed copper and copper. Proof. Thick and thin planchets. 33 mm. By W. Barber.

1869. OBV: Columbia (Moneta) seated facing left before liberty cap on pole, hand on U.S. shield.

REV: ANNUAL/ASSAY/1869 within wreath of oak leaves and olive; wreath joined at top by ribbon inscribed LET US HAVE PEACE.
Aluminum, bronzed copper, copper and silver. Proof. Thick and thin planchets. 33 mm. By W. Barber. (Note: two additional types are known, one with obv. of 1868 in aluminum and the other with obv. of 1869 surrounded by 13 stars. The latter type is known in Proof. Aluminum, bronze and silver; all of latter two have a die break from the fifth star to the rim.)

1870. OBV: Columbia (Moneta) as Science standing, holding scales and coiled snake, at her feet a lion guarding a treasure chest, below J. POLLOCK, DIRECTOR curved near edge.
REV: ANNUAL/ASSAY/1870 within wreath of oak and laurel.
Aluminum, bronzed copper and copper Proofs exist. A so-called silver Proof has also been described.
Thick and thin planchets. 33 mm. By W. Barber. (Note: so-called silver specimens are invariably plated. Die break progression evidence on the reverse shows the striking order to be bronze, then aluminum, and then the silver [plated] in that sequence.)

1871. OBV: Archimedes (originator of the humid assay) stands leaning to left against mantle.

REV: ANNUAL/ASSAY/1871 within a cartouche of cotton, corn leaves and scroll work.
Aluminum, bronzed copper, copper and silver. Silver-plated specimens are also known. Brilliant and Matte Proof. Thick and thin planchets. 33 mm. By W. Barber. (Note: a second obverse is known which is similar but has in the exergue J. POLLOCK/DIRECTOR. It was struck in Proof in bronzed copper and copper and in silver on a thin planchet and a trial piece struck in aluminum. Perspective modification on the obverse provides detail in right side of archway.)

1872. OBV: similar to 1870, but J. POLLOCK/DIRECTOR in straight line below.
REV: ANNUAL/ASSAY/1872 within wreath.
Bronzed copper, silver and white metal. Proof. Thick and thin planchets. 33 mm. By W. Barber.

1873. OBV: similar to 1871, with addition of J. POLLOCK/DIRECTOR below.
REV: Tomb within wreath of cypress, inscribed ECKFELDT, ANNUAL/ASSAY/1873 below.
Aluminum, bronzed copper, copper, silver and white metal. Proof. Thick and thin planchets. 33 mm. By W. Barber. (Note: evidence suggests the 1871 obverse was reused on this issue.)

1874. OBV: similar to 1871.
REV: ANNUAL/ASSAY/1874 below casket inscribed J. TORREY, /OB. MAR. 10, '73 on which rests an urn and heavy pall, within a wreath of bay. Bronzed copper, copper, silver and white metal. Proof. Thick and thin planchets. 33 mm. By W. Barber. (Note: Proof specimens exist with obverse of the 1871 pattern without J. POLLOCK/DIRECTOR in bronze, silver and white metal; specimens in bronze and silver Proof have also been described with the reverse of 1873, but this is probably in error.)

1875. OBV: similar to 1871.
REV: ANNUAL/ASSAY/1875 within olive wreath and below laurel spray. Bronzed copper and silver. Proof. 33 mm. By W. Barber.

1876. OBV: Nude bust of Washington facing right.
REV: YEAR ONE HUNDRED/.OF AMERICAN INDEPENDENCE. around circumference, 1776/ANNU-

AL /ASSAY/1876 within an oak wreath, surrounded by a circle. Aluminum, bronzed copper and silver. Proof. 33 mm. By W. Barber.

1877. OBV: similar to 1871.
REV: ANNUAL/ASSAY/1877 within wreath of oak and olive.
Bronzed copper and silver. Proof. 33 mm. By W. Barber.

1878. OBV: similar to 1876.
REV: ANNUAL/ASSAY/1878 within wreath of olive.
Bronzed copper and silver. Proof 33 mm. By W. Barber.

1879. OBV: H. R. LINDERMAN./NA 1825. OB 1879 around circumference, bust of Linderman facing right within dentilated circle, laurel spray to left and right.
REV: ANNUAL ASSAY 1879. / SCIENTIA VIRTUS VERITAS around circumference, Liberty (as Knowledge) with urn and wreath beneath cypress, tomb inscribed HENRY, NA/1795/OB/1879, JOSEPH HENRY below, within dentilated circle.
Bronzed copper, copper and silver. Proof. 38 mm. By W. Barber.

1880. OBV: THE MINT OF THE UNITED STATES/ . ANNUAL ASSAY 1880 . around bust of President Hayes facing left within circle.
REV: "EFFICACI DO MANUS SCIENTIAE" above female kneeling left lighting the lamp of science, PHILADELPHIA below.
Bronzed copper and silver. Proof. Thick and thin planchets. 33 mm. By Morgan and C. Barber. (Note: pattern strikes are known, one having a refiner and below IGNIS PROBABIT/OPUS on reverse by Morgan in bronzed copper, pewter and silver Proofs; a second having ANNUAL/ASSAY/1880 in ornate letters within wreath by Barber in bronzed copper and silver Proofs on thick and thin planchets. A third pattern with a reverse similar to that used in 1882 in bronze and a fourth type is also known having an obverse design similar to that of 1870 but with slightly differing details by W. Barber muled with C. Barber's pattern reverse (type II) in bronze Proof. Evidence suggests only three of these latter pieces were struck and presented to Mint officers A. L. Snowden, C. Barber and O. C. Bosbyshell.)

1881. OBV: similar to 1880, but dated 1881.
REV: A coining press, Liberty to left with a box of coins and Justice to right holding scales, NE QUID DETRIMENTI / RESPUBLICA / CAPIAT below.
Bronzed copper and silver. Brilliant and Matte Proof. 33 mm. By Morgan and C. Barber.

1882. OBV: THE MINT OF THE UNITED STATES/ANNUAL ASSAY 1882 around bust of President Garfield.
REV: LIBRA PROBAT OPUS above Juno Moneta kneeling and young boy standing facing right testing scales.
Bronzed copper and silver. Proof. 33 mm. By Morgan and C. Barber.

1883. OBV: THE MINT OF THE UNITED STATES/ANNUAL ASSAY 1883 around bust of President Arthur facing left, within beaded circle.
REV: similar to 1882.
Bronzed copper and silver. Proof. 33 mm. By Morgan and C. Barber.

1884. OBV: similar to 1883, but dated 1884.
REV: similar to 1882.
Bronzed copper and silver. Proof. 33 mm. By Morgan and C. Barber.

1885. OBV: similar to 1883, but dated 1885.
REV: similar to 1882.
Bronzed copper, silver and white metal. Proof. 33 mm. By Morgan and C. Barber. (Note: the reverse die of the previous year was reused.)

1886. OBV: The MINT OF THE UNITED STATES/ . ANNUAL ASSAY 1886 . around bust of President Cleveland facing right.
REV: JUSTITIAE LAMPAS / MONETAE ALLUCET above Justice holding blazing torch which divides legend, standing in front of Mint building.
Bronzed copper and silver. Proof. 33 mm. By Morgan and C. Barber.

1887. OBV: similar to 1886 but dated 1887.
REV: similar to 1886.
Bronzed copper, silver and silver plated bronze. Brilliant and Matte Proof. 33 mm. By Morgan and C. Barber.

1888. OBV: GROVER/CLEVELAND around bust of Cleveland facing right.
REV: MINT / OF THE / UNITED STATES / ASSAY / COMMISSION / 1888 within laurel and olive wreath.
Bronze and silver. Brilliant and Matte Proof. 78 mm. By C. Barber.

1889. OBV: similar to 1888.
REV: similar to 1888 but dated 1889.
Bronze and silver. Proof. 78 mm. By C. Barber.

1890. OBV: THE MINT OF THE UNITED STATES/ . ANNUAL ASSAY 1890 . around bust of President Benjamin Harrison facing left, BENJAMIN/HARRISON divided by head, all within beaded circle.
REV: similar to 1882, but palm branch in exergue, inscription larger, all within beaded circle.
Bronzed copper and silver. Brilliant and Matte Proof. Thick and thin planchets. 33 mm. By Morgan and C. Barber. (Note: This issue is of exceedingly high relief for a small-diameter medal. Specimens have been described with the reverse of 1891.)

1891. OBV: THE.MINT.OF.THE.UNITED.STATES/.ANNUAL.ASSAY.1891. around circumference, bust of Windom facing right, WILLIAM/WINDOM divided by head, within circle.
REV: SCIENTIA CORONAT OPUS above a workman examining metal in a crucible in a furnace.
Bronzed copper, copper and silver. Proof. 33 mm. By Morgan and C. Barber.

1892. OBV: BENJAMIN HARRISON, around bust of Harrison facing left.
REV: THE MINT OF THE UNITED STATES/ANNUAL ASSAY/1892, type of 1882.
Bronze and silver. Brilliant and Matte Proof. 33 mm. By Morgan and C. Barber.

1893. OBV: THE . MINT . OF . THE . UNITED . STATES/.ANNUAL.ASSAY.1893. around bust of President Harrison facing left within circle.
REV: FIDEM. REIPUBLICAE. UT. SERVEM above Justice seated right beside Great Seal, testing scales in front of Mint.
Aluminum, bronzed copper and silver. Matte Proof. 33 mm. By Morgan and C. Barber. (Note: die break evidence shows the specimen strikes were accomplished after the regular pieces were struck.)

1894. OBV: similar to 1886, but dated 1894.
REV: Female seated facing left holding a weight, before her a child standing holding a box of weights, REM ACU below.
Bronzed copper, copper, and silver.

Proof. Thick and thin planchets. 33 mm. By Morgan and C. Barber.

1895. OBV: GROVER/CLEVELAND around bust of Cleveland facing right, similar to 1888.
REV: MINT / OF THE / UNITED STATES / ASSAY / COMMISSION / 1895 within a laurel and olive wreath, similar to 1888 but different date.
Bronze and silver. Proof. Thick and thin planchets. 78 mm. By C. Barber.

1896. OBV: similar to 1895, but with larger bust of Cleveland.
REV: THE . MINT . OF . THE . UNITED . STATES . ANNUAL AS-SAY . 1896.
Female standing holding scales, at right a helmeted Pallas on a medallion over a branch.
Bronze and silver. Proof. 33 mm. By Morgan and C. Barber. (Note: in 1898 a silver Proof specimen of this issue was restruck at the Mint for presentation to Treasury Secretary Lyman J. Gage.)

1897. OBV: similar to 1896.
REV: similar to 1896, but dated 1897.
Bronze and silver. Proof. 33 mm. By Morgan and C. Barber.

1898. OBV: WILLIAM/McKINLEY divided by bust of McKinley facing left within beaded border.
REV: MINT OF THE UNITED / STATES ANNUAL ASSAY. Pallas in Corinthian helmet on fasces; to left female holding palm branch and scales; to right a workman; 1898 below.
Bronze, silver and white metal. Brilliant and Matte Proof. 33 mm. By Morgan and C. Barber.

1899. OBV: similar to 1898.
REV: UNITED STATES MINT/AN-NUAL ASSAY 1899 divided by bust of Pallas in Corinthian helmet above, scales on shield center, eagle below, all within an olive wreath.
Bronzed copper, silver and white metal. Matte Proof. 33 mm. By Morgan and C. Barber.

1900. OBV: similar to 1898.
REV: UNITED STATES MINT AN-NUAL ASSAY 1900, similar to 1893.
Bronze and silver. Matte Proof. 33 mm. By Morgan and C. Barber.

1901. OBV: WILLIAM. McKINLEY / PRESIDENT / OF THE / UNITED STATES around bust of McKinley facing left.

REV: Workman examining metal in furnace, MINT . OF . THE . UNITED . STATES . / ANNUAL . / ASSAY . 1901.below.
A plaque. Bronze and silver. Matte Proof. 40x55 mm. By Morgan and C. Barber. (Note: although the Mint report shows 40 specimens struck in silver only, bronze specimens were struck for the Mint cabinet, and additional Matte Proof bronze specimens also exist.)

1902. OBV: FIRST MEETING OF ASSAY COMMISSION IN THE/NEW MINT, Liberty with blazing torch facing three-quarters left in front of new Mint building.
REV: UNITED STATES MINT/AN-NUAL ASSAY 1902, similar to 1899.
Bronze and silver. Matte Proof. 33 mm. By Morgan. (Evidence exists that the 1899 reverse was redated for this issue.) (Note: in addition to two bronze Matte Proof specimens struck for the Mint cabinet, other bronze specimens also exist.)

1903. OBV: THEODORE ROOSEVELT / PRESIDENT / OF THE / UNITED STATES around bust of Roosevelt facing two-thirds left.
REV: similar to 1901, but dated 1903.
A plaque. Bronzed copper and silver. Matte Proof. 40 x 55 mm. By Morgan and C. Barber. (Note: a uniface bronze trial strike of the Roosevelt obverse, 1903-1908, exists.)

1904. OBV: THEODORE ROOSEVELT above . PRESIDENT . / . OF . THE . / . UNITED . STATES . below a bust of Roosevelt facing left.
REV: MINT/OF THE/UNITED STATES . / . ANNUAL . / . ASSAY / 1904, Treasury seal upper left corner surmounted by eagle, olive branch at bottom right.
A plaque. Silver and possibly bronze. Matte Proof. 40 x 55 mm. By Morgan and C. Barber. (Note: this issue is sometimes attributed to Augustus Saint-Gaudens.)

1905. OBV: similar to 1904.
REV: similar to 1904, but dated 1905.
A plaque. Bronze and silver. Matte Proof. 40 x 55 mm. By Morgan and C. Barber.

1906. OBV: Similar to 1903.
REV: Treasury seal surmounted by eagle within a scroll pattern, on which appears E PLURIBUS UNUM, MINT

. OF . THE . UNITED . STATES . /
ANNUAL ASSAY . 1906 . below.
A plaque. Silver. Matte Proof. 40 x 55
mm. By Morgan and C. Barber. (Note:
This issue was struck on a thicker
planchet than the preceding years.)

1907. OBV: similar to 1903.
REV: similar to 1906, but dated 1907.
A plaque. Silver. Matte Proof. 40 x 55
mm. By Morgan and C. Barber. (Note:
uniface die trials of both obverse and
reverse in bronze Matte Proof exist.)

1908. OBV: similar to 1903.
REV: similar to 1906, but dated 1908.
A plaque. Silver. Matte Proof. 40 x 55
mm. By Morgan and C. Barber. (Note:
in addition to the plaque, Proof specimens of the 1907 Saint-Gaudens Indian Head $10 gold piece With Rounded
Rims and Periods were presented to
members of the commission by Director of the Mint Frank A. Leach.)

1909. OBV: GEORGE . B. CORTELYOU /
SECRETARY . OF . / THE . TREAS-
URY . around bust of Cortelyou facing
right.
REV: Similar to 1904, but dated 1909.
A plaque. Bronze, yellow bronze and
silver. Matte Proof. Thick and thin
planchets. 40 x 55 mm. By Morgan
and C. Barber. (Note: This issue may
well be the most "common" of this series, because until the mid-1960s the
U.S. Mint offered this medal with its
Assay Commission commemorative
reverse as the Cortelyou medal in its
series honoring the Secretaries of the
Treasury. After considerable prompting by numismatists, the Mint adopted
its present obverse uniface version for
sale to collectors.)

1910. OBV: WILLIAM . H. TAFT . PRESI-
DENT / OF . THE . / UNITED .
STATES . around bust of Taft facing
right.
REV: MINT . OF . THE . UNITED .
STATES / . ANNUAL ASSAY .
around two genii seated holding a tab-
let between them surmounted by an
eagle, on tablet 1910, on ribbon below
E PLURIBUS UNUM.
Bronze, yellow bronze and silver.
Matte Proof. 45 mm. By C. Barber and
Morgan.

1911. OBV: similar to 1910.
REV: similar to 1910, but dated 1911.
Silver. Matte Proof. 45 mm. By C.
Barber and Morgan.

1912. OBV: similar to 1910.
REV: similar to 1910, but dated 1912.
Silver. Matte Proof. 45 mm. By C.
Barber and Morgan.

1913. OBV: similar to 1910.
REV: similar to 1910, but dated 1913.
Bronze and yellow bronze. Matte
Proof. 45 mm. By C. Barber and Mor-
gan.

1914. OBV: WOODROW / WILSON divided by bust of Wilson facing left.
REV: Radiated spread wing eagle facing left standing on a rounded tablet
from the four corners of which extend
spirals, 1914 on tablet, to left a semi-
circular band on which appears MINT
. OF . THE, to right another band on
which appears UNITED STATES,
scales below tablet, and on a third
band at bottom appears ANNUAL .
ASSAY, foliage fills in background.
Bronze and possibly yellow bronze. 45
mm. By C. Barber and Morgan. (Note:
Bronze and yellow bronze uniface trial
strikes of the obverse are known.)

1915. OBV:+ THESAURI . AMERICAE .
SEPTENTRIONALIS . SIGILLUM +
around Treasury seal within laurel
wreath.
REV: Similar to 1914, but with 1915 at
center.
Silver and Matte Proof yellow bronze.
44 mm.
By Morgan and C. Barber.

1916. OBV: Similar to 1915.
REV: similar to 1910, but dated 1916.
Silver. 45 mm. By Morgan and C.
Barber.

1917. OBV: Similar to reverse of 1910, ex-
cept dated 1917.
REV: Similar to obverse of 1915.
Bronze and silver. 50 mm.

1918. OBV: WILLIAM GIBBS McADOO
around bust of McAdoo facing left.
REV: MINT OF THE UNITED
STATES / ANNUAL ASSAY / 1918
around Liberty (Columbia) beholding
a large coining press operated by a
workman.
Bronze and yellow bronze. 50 mm.
Brilliant and Matte Proof.

1919. OBV: WOODROW / WILSON divided by bust of Wilson facing left.
REV: MINT OF THE UNITED
STATES / ANNUAL ASSAY / 1919
below in incuse letters around Mercury
in flowing cape, to left stylized medallion on which appears a dragon head.
Bronze and yellow bronze. 50 mm.

Brilliant and Matte Proof. By Sinnock.
(Note: pieces for this year have been
described with the obverse similar to
that of 1918. A uniface die trial of the
reverse in bronze Proof exists.)

1920. OBV: Portrait of President Wilson facing right.
REV: MINT OF THE UNITED
STATES / ANNUAL ASSAY around
circumference, Victory holding olive
branch and sword. PEACE left, VIC-
TORY right, 1920 below.
Bronze and yellow bronze. Brilliant
and Matte Proof. 50 mm. By Sinnock.

1921. OBV: similar to 1919.
REV: MINT / OF THE / UNITED
STATES / ANNUAL ASSAY / 1921,
to left Standing Liberty in flowing
cape; scales, olive branch and Treasury
seal to right.
Bronze. Brilliant and Matte Proof. 50
mm. By Sinnock and Morgan. (Note:
according to a contemporary account,
commission members subscribed
funds for striking of a gold specimen to
be presented to ex-President Wilson.)

1922. OBV: ANDREW W. / MELLON divided by bust of Mellon facing left.
REV: Eagle facing left holding olive
and oak branches, scales and Treasury
key, MINT OF THE UNITED
STATES ANNUAL ASSAY/1922.
Bronze and yellow bronze. Matte
Proof. 50 mm. By Morgan and Sinnock. (Note: A trial piece of the
obverse in yellow bronze Matte Proof
exists.)

1923. OBV: WARREN G. HARDING, bust
of President Harding.
REV: THESAURI AMERICAE SEP-
TENTRIONALIS SIGILLUM above,
MINT OF THE UNITED STATES
ANNUAL ASSAY 1923 in four lines
below, surrounding torch and balance.
Bronze. Proof. 50 mm. By Morgan.

1924. OBV: CALVIN / COOLIDGE divided
by bust of Coolidge facing right.
REV: MINT OF THE UNITED
STATES / ANNUAL ASSAY surrounding large eagle, head left, with
plaque and date 1924 across breast.
Bronze. Proof. 50 mm. By Morgan.

1925. OBV: CALVIN/COOLIDGE divided
by bust of Coolidge facing right, simi-
lar to 1924 but the modified portrait of
Coolidge is in lower relief.
REV: UNITED . STATES . MINT /
ANNUAL ASSAY and Treasury seal

above bold wingspread eagle in portico
of building, 1925 in exergue.
Bronze and yellow bronze. Matte
Proof.
50 mm. By Morgan and Sinnock.

1926. OBV: CALVIN . COOLIDGE . PRES-
IDENT . OF . THE . UNITED .
STATES around bust of Coolidge facing right.
REV: ANNUAL . ASSAY .
1926/MINT of the UNITED .
STATES divided by Treasury seal
above draped Seated Liberty facing
right weighing coins, PHILADEL-
PHIA in exergue.
Bronze and yellow bronze. Matte
Proof. 50 mm. By Sinnock. (Note: a
trial specimen of obverse type of 1926-
1929 exists struck on a 2.5-inch square
of hardened steel.)

1927. OBV: similar to 1926.
REV: MINT / OF THE / UNITED
STATES / ANNUAL / ASSAY to the
left of Mercury facing left holding cornucopia from which spills a bountiful
harvest, 1927 and Treasury seal to
right, NATIONAL PROSPERITY below.
Bronze. Matte Proof. 50 mm. By Sinnock.

1928. OBV: similar to 1926.
REV: UNITED . STATES . MINT
and Treasury seal above coining scene
from first Mint; at left coiner grasps
press counterweight; hand-operated
screw press on table at center; at right
assistant examines newly struck coins,
FIRST / COINAGE / PRESS / U.S. /
MINT to left and 1793 to right in
small incused letters, ANNUAL AS-
SAY / 1928 in exergue.
Bronze and yellow bronze. Matte
Proof. 50 mm. By Sinnock and Pietz.

1929. OBV: similar to 1926.
REV: MINT . OF . THE . UNITED .
STATES / . ANNUAL ASSAY 1929 .
around circumference, first U.S. Mint
building PHILADELPHIA within in-
scription THE FIRST MINT ERECT-
ED 1792 AND THE FIRST PUBLIC
BUILDING AUTHORIZED BY THE
CONGRESS OF THE UNITED
STATES.
Bronze and yellow bronze. Matte
Proof. 50 mm. By Sinnock and Pietz.

1930. OBV: . PRESIDENT OF THE UNIT-
ED STATES. above bust of Hoover
facing right, MCMXXIX left and
HERBERT/HOOVER right.

REV: similar to 1929 but dated 1930. Bronze and yellow bronze. Matte Proof. 50 mm. By Sinnock and Pietz. (Note: the date in Roman numerals on obverse refers to the inauguration date of President Hoover.)

1931. OBV: similar to 1930.
REV: MINT OF THE UNITED STATES / . PHILADELPHIA . PA . around edge, front view of Mint building, ANNUAL ASSAY / 1931 below. Bronze and yellow bronze. Matte Proof. 50 mm. By Sinnock and Pietz.

1932. OBV: MOUNT VERNON above panorama of Mount Vernon, George Washington bust in cameo facing right, 1732 left and 1932 right.
REV: similar to 1929 but dated 1932. Bronze and yellow bronze. Matte Proof. 50 mm. By Sinnock and Pietz.

1933. OBV: SECRETARY . OF . THE . TREASURY / . OGDEN . L. MILLS . around bust of Mills facing left.
REV: similar to 1931 but dated 1933. Bronze and yellow bronze. Matte Proof. 50 mm. By Sinnock and Pietz. (Note: evidence exists that the 1931 reverse was redated for this issue.)

1934. OBV: similar to the reverse of 1931 without inscription ANNUAL ASSAY and date.
REV: similar to 1929 but dated 1934. Bronze and yellow bronze. Matte proof. 50 mm. By Sinnock and Pietz.

1935. OBV: FRANKLIN DELANO ROOSEVELT PRESIDENT OF THE UNITED STATES around bust of Roosevelt facing right.
REV: MELTING - REFINING - COINING - ASSAYING - ENGRAVING around Seated Liberty with scales and Treasury seal behind, coining press and stack of gold, ANNUAL ASSAY / PHILADELPHIA / 1935 below. Bronze. 50 mm. By Sinnock.

1936. OBV: Franklin D. Roosevelt.
REV: George Washington. (Note: There was no special medal designed, but the stock Roosevelt presidential medal die was used for the obverse and a George Washington die for the reverse. The edge was engraved with ANNUAL ASSAY 1936.

1937. OBV: THOMAS JEFFERSON PRESIDENT OF THE UNITED STATES around bust of Jefferson facing right.
REV: U.S. MINT PHILADELPHIA above two coiners and massive coining press, ANNUAL ASSAY / 1937 below. Bronze. 57 mm. Proof. By Sinnock.

1938. OBV: . BENJAMIN . FRANKLIN . above Houdon bust of Franklin facing right, * 1706/1790 * below bust, laurels tied with bow at bottom third near edge.
REV: ANNUAL ASSAY / COMMISSION divided by Justice standing holding scales, corner view of Mint in background, 1938 left, UNITED . STATES . MINT / PHILADELPHIA below. Bronze. 57 mm. By Sinnock.

1939. OBV: HENRY MORGENTHAU, Secretary of the Treasury around bust of Morgenthau facing left.
REV: Mint worker pouring molten metal into ingots. Bronze. 57 mm. By Sinnock and Pietz.

1940. OBV: PRESIDENT of the UNITED STATES above bust of Roosevelt facing right, FRANKLIN / DELANO / ROOSEVELT below. Bronze. Proof. 50 mm. By Sinnock.

1941. OBV: MELTING . REFINING . COINING / ASSAYING . ENGRAVING divided by woman seated left weighing coins in scales and holding scroll in front of Treasury seal, stack of bars left, coining press right.
REV: * ANNUAL . ASSAY . COMMISSION . 1941 / UNITED . STATES . MINT . PHILA * surrounding workman pouring molten metal into ingot molds, within circle. Bronze. By Sinnock. (Note: Mint Director Nellie Tayloe Ross posed for the figure on the obverse.)

1942. OBV: ANNUAL ASSAY COMMISSION / **1942** around bust of Roosevelt facing right within circle.
REV: 150TH ANNIVERSARY UNITED STATES MINT / . 1792 . 1942 . around nude bust of Washington facing right within circle. Bronze. Proof. 57 mm. By Sinnock. (Note: the reverse is taken from the familiar Houdon bust of Washington.)

1943. OBV: ABRAHAM LINCOLN around bust of Lincoln facing right.
REV: Similar to 1922 medal, but ANNUAL ASSAY COMMISSION U.S. MINT, PHILA, PA. around, and 1943 below. Bronze. By Sinnock.

1944. OBV: DAVID RITTENHOUSE .
FIRST DIRECTOR UNITED
STATES MINT around bust of Ritten-
house facing left; 1792 to left, 1795 to
right. Scales below.
REV: . ANNUAL ASSAY COMMIS-
SION . UNITED STATES MINT .
PHILADELPHIA. around Independ-
ence Hall; INDEPENDENCE HALL /
1944 below.
Bronze and Matte Proof yellow
bronze. 50.1 mm. By Sinnock.

1945. OBV: Libertas Americana bust facing
left, liberty cap on pole in rear, AN-
NUAL ASSAY COMMISSION
above, 1945 below bust, UNITED
STATES MINT PHILADELPHIA below.
REV: Great Seal of the United States,
eagle holding ribbon in beak inscribed
E PLURIBUS UNUM, clouds and circle containing thirteen stars, THE
UNITED STATES / OF AMERICA in
two lines below.
Bronze. 67 mm. By Sinnock.

1946. OBV: Bust of George Washington in
military uniform. Below in three lines
LAURA GARDIN FRASER and
1732 / 1799.
REV: Scene of Mount Vernon between
trees, with MOUNT VERNON above;
below is UNITED STATES / ASSAY
COMMISSION 1946 / 154TH AN-
NUAL SESSION / AT PHILADEL-
PHIA / MINT.
Bronze and Matte Proof yellow
bronze. 50.25 mm. By L.G. Fraser.
Bronze. By Sinnock.

1947. OBV: Similar to 1941.
REV: UNITED STATES ASSAY
COMMISSION AT PHILADELPHIA
MINT/1947 around circumference,
155th ANNUAL SESSION within
wreath of palms.
Bronze. 50 mm.

1948. OBV: Bust of Harry S Truman, PRES-
IDENT OF THE UNITED STATES;
HARRY S. TRUMAN to right of bust.
REV: Mint building, PHILADEL-
PHIA 1792-1948 below; UNITED .
STATES . MINT . ANNUAL . AS-
SAY.

1949. OBV: UNITED STATES MINT
around three allegorical figures count-
ing, weighing and recording assay.
REV: *ANNUAL . ASSAY . COM-
MISSION* / TREASURY . DE-
PARTMENT around view of Treasury
Building, TREASURY BUILDING /

WASHINGTON, D.C. / 1949 below.
Bronze and Matte Proof yellow
bronze. 50.1 mm. By Roberts and
Gasparro.

1950. OBV: FIRST MEETING ASSAY
COMMISSION, figures of three men,
JEFFERSON/JAY/HAMILTON IN
SCRIP, 1792 below.
REV: ASSAY MEDAL YEAR 1950
above Independence Hall with three
trees each side, INDEPENDENCE
HALL on ribbon below, with Liberty
Bell at bottom.
Bronze and Matte Proof yellow
bronze. 51 mm. By Gasparro and En-
gelhardus von Hebel.

1951. OBV: UNITED . STATES . MINT
above, with striding eagle at left, facing
right. In right background is Treasury
Building; 1951 below. At bottom, AS-
SAY / COMMISSION.
REV: FIRST DIRECTOR OF THE
UNITED STATES MINT VIEWING
INITIAL COINAGE around scene of
David T. Rittenhouse reviewing coin-
age with two other men. Below scene is
PHILADELPHIA / 1792.
By Gasparro and von Hebel.

1952. OBV: Above, ANNUAL ASSAY, with
standing woman holding cornucopia,
flanked by a woman on left and man
on right; 1792 to left of figures, 1952 to
right. UNITED STATES MINT in
exergue.
REV: First Philadelphia Mint, with individual walking dog in front; YE .
OLD . MINT below. At bottom,
shield-shaped Treasury seal. Wave-
like border around.
By Roberts and Gasparro.

1953. OBV: UNITED STATES MINT
around; MERCURIUS / MONETAE /
CUSTOS to right of Mercury or
Hermes holding caduceus.
REV: ANNUAL / ASSAY / on either
side of figure holding cornucopia of
coins; surrounded by four smaller figures representing mining, melting,
pouring ingots and striking coinage.
1953 and scales below. Crossed shovel
and pickax above.
Bronze. 50 mm. By Roberts.

1954. No medal. (Note: members of the
Commission purchased the Lincoln
presidential medal from the Mint list.)

1955. OBV: DWIGHT D. EISENHOWER
around bust facing left.
REV: UNITED . STATES . MINT
around scene of screw-type coining

press; to left, FIRST COINING PRESS U.S. MINT in five lines, and at right, 1793. In exergue, ANNUAL ASSAY / 1955.
By Roberts and Adam Pietz.

1956. OBV: similar to 1955.
REV: Similar to 1953, but 1956 below.

1957. OBV: ALEXANDER HAMILTON above bust of Hamilton three-quarters facing; 1757 to left, 1804 to right.
REV: UNITED STATES MINT ANNUAL ASSAY around, with 1792 and 1957 on either side of Treasury seal.

1958. OBV: DWIGHT D. / EISENHOWER divided by bust of Eisenhower facing left.
REV: ATOMS FOR PEACE above U.S. shield surmounted by Freedom and atomic symbol, at left allegorical vignettes representing Agriculture and Science, at right Industry and Commerce, UNITED STATES / MINT / ANNUAL ASSAY / 1958.
Bronze. By Roberts and von Hebel.

1959. OBV: ABRAHAM LINCOLN divided by bust of Lincoln facing right.
REV: Above, 1792-1959, with UNITED STATES / MINT / ANNUAL ASSAY to right center. Palm and laurel branches with E PLURIBUS UNUM on ribbon. Small eagle on shield at lower right.
Silver.

1960. OBV: Similar to 1959.
REV: Similar to 1958, but for date.

1961. OBV: THOMAS JEFFERSON PRESIDENT OF THE UNITED STATES around three-quarters bust of Jefferson facing left.
REV: Similar to 1939, but dated 1961.
By Sinnock and Pietz.

1962. OBV: JOHN F. / KENNEDY divided by bust of Kennedy facing left.
REV: similar to the obverse of 1939, but dated 1962.
Bronze. By Gasparro and Sinnock.

1963. OBV: C. DOUGLAS DILLON around bust of Dillon facing right.
REV: ANNUAL . ASSAY . COMMISSION . / UNITED STATES MINT PHILADELPHIA around circumference, 1963 above modern assay scene of four individuals and Mint guard. Shield-shaped Treasury seal below.

1964. OBV: LYNDON B. / JOHNSON divided by bust of President Johnson facing left
REV: UNITED STATES MINT AT PHILADELPHIA above hand holding 1964 Kennedy half dollar in front of scales, flasks and other apparatus, ANNUAL ASSAY / COMMISSION / 1964 below.
By Roberts and Grove.

1965. OBV: . LYNDON B. JOHNSON . above bust of Johnson facing three-quarters left.
REV: . ANNUAL ASSAY . above scene of George Washington and other dignataries examining the first coinage based on the painting by Dinsmore, PHILADELPHIA . / 1792-1965 below.
Bronze. By Gasparro.

1966. OBV: . HENRY H. FOWLER . above bust of Fowler facing front.
REV: . ASSAY . / COMMISSION / . 1966. across set of scales in balance.
Bronze. By Gasparro and Fowler.

1967. OBV: Eva Adams facing, EVA ADAMS above, Nevada state seal and Treasury seal.
REV: FOURTH UNITED STATES MINT above New Mint building in Philadelphia; ASSAY COMMISSION / 1792-1967 / PHILADELPHIA, PENNA.
By Gasparro and Iacocca.

1968. OBV: SECRETARY OF THE TREASURY above bust of Gallatin facing three-quarters right, 1801/1814 at left, ALBERT GALLATIN at right.
REV: ANNUAL ASSAY/COMMISSION divided by first official troy pound weight and lesser weights, larger weight inscribed POUND TROY / 1824 beneath British crown and BATE LONDON, lesser weights below labeled GRAIN, GRAM and OUNCE, 1968 below between laurel and oak sprays.
Bronze. By Gasparro and Steever.

1969. OBV: PRESIDENT OF THE UNITED STATES above bust of Nixon facing right, RICHARD / MILHOUS / NIXON to left.
REV: New Mint building above UNITED STATES MINT . PHILA-

DELPHIA / ASSAY COMMISSION / 1969 in exergue.
Bronze. By Gasparro and Fowler.

1970. OBV: . DAVID M. KENNEDY . above bust of Kennedy facing front.
REV: UNITED STATES MINT above, 1792 left, 1970 right, ANNUAL ASSAY below, surrounding Treasury seal originally engraved by Morgan.
Bronze. By Gasparro.

1971. OBV: MARY BROOKS / DIRECTOR OF THE MINT around bust of Brooks facing three-quarters right.
REV: similar to 1965, but dated 1971.
Bronze. 57 mm. By Gasparro.

1972. OBV: . JOHN B. CONNALLY . around bust of Secretary of the Treasury Connally facing three-quarters left.
REV: UNITED STATES / TREASURY / DEPARTMENT above Main Treasury Building in Washington, D.C.; 1972 / ASSAY COMMISSION below.
Bronze. 57 mm. By Gasparro and Winter.

1973. OBV: . GEORGE P. SHULTZ . above bust of Shultz facing three-quarters left.
REV: ASSAY COMMISSION above view of Treasury Building, TREASURY BUILDING / WASHINGTON, D.C. / 1973 / NATIONAL HISTORIC LANDMARK below.
Bronze. 57 mm. By Gasparro and Winter.

1974. OBV: GEORGIO WASHINGTON SUPREMO DUCI EXERCITUUM ADSERTORI LIBERTATIS / COMITIA AMERICANA, ASSAY / COMMISSION / 1974 to right, surrounding nude bust of Washington facing right. (An adaptation of the "Washington Before Boston" medal obverse, signed DUVIVIER PARIS F. below bust.)
REV: Fifty stars around circumference, PEACE above adaptation of presidential seal, below which is the Northern Hemisphere with the inscription, WE STAND ON THE / THRESHOLD OF A NEW / ERA OF PEACE IN / THE WORLD ... / RICHARD M. NIXON.
Pewter and yellow bronze. 57 mm. By Fowler (from Duvivier) and Gasparro.
(Note: Commission members were

presented pewter specimens of the medal; notwithstanding that the Annual Report of the Director of the Mint for 1974 reports on Page 6 that "bronze" specimens were presented to 1974 Assay Commission members.)

1975. OBV: . GERALD R. FORD . above bust of Ford facing three-quarters right.
REV: similar to 1965 but dated 1975.
Bronze. 57 mm. By Gasparro.

1976. OBV: . ANNUAL ASSAY COMMISSION . bust of Simon, WILLIAM F. SIMON / SECRETARY OF THE / TREASURY left, MARY BROOKS / DIRECTOR / OF THE MINT right.
REV: INDEPENDENCE . BICENTENNIAL / 1776 . 1976 above, WASHINGTON CROSSING THE DELAWARE below, representation of the event after Emanuel Leutz's painting.
Oval. Pewter. By Gasparro.

1977. OBV: . ANNUAL ASSAY COMMISSION . above bust of Martha Washington facing right, 1977 left, MARTHA / WASHINGTON right.
REV: FIRST UNITED STATES MINT / 1792 above building flanked by trees, watchman and dog in foreground, PHILADELPHIA below.
Pewter. Oval. 63 by 76 mm. By Fowler and Peloso. (Note: the obverse is an adaptation of Edward Grove's 1965 experimental coinage design; both Grove's and Philip Fowler's initials appear incuse at truncation. The reverse is Matthew Peloso's rendition of the earlier Gasparro design. Only the latter's name appears.)

1980. OBV: PRESIDENT OF THE UNITED STATES above three-quarters facing left bust of Carter; JIMMY / CARTER to right of bust.
REV: Adaptation of presidential seal, dividing INAUGURATED JANUARY 20, 1977, . . THE AMERICAN DREAM ENDURES . . WE MUST ONCE AGAIN HAVE FAITH IN OUR COUNTRY . . . JIMMY CARTER.

(Note: No special medal struck, but Carter presidential medal used, with edge engraved 1980 ANNUAL ASSAY COMMISSION.

Donna Pope

Donna Pope was confirmed as Director of the Mint by the Senate July 13, 1981, and was sworn into office by Treasurer Angela Buchanan Sept. 10, 1981. She was reconfirmed for a second term Aug. 1, 1986.

An Ohio native, Pope was in her sixth term in the Ohio House of Representatives when nominated by President Reagan for the Mint post. As Director of the Mint, Pope is responsible for ensuring that the nation has an adequate supply of coins, manufacturing 16 billion to 18 billion coins a year; managing a large numismatic coin and medal program, which returned a profit of $366 million to the general fund for the two-year period of 1984-85; overseeing the six Mint field facilities and safeguarding the nation's gold bullion inventory.

Operations necessary for the conduct of business of the Mint are performed in Washington, D.C. Pope oversees operations of Mint facilities in Philadelphia and Denver, minting and bullion depositories in West Point, N.Y., and the bullion depository in Fort Knox, Ky. She is also responsible for coining operations at the San Francisco Assay Office, and the Old San Francisco Mint Museum.

Pope has managed numerous political campaigns and in 1980 served as co-chairman of the Reagan campaign in Ohio and as one of the two chairmen of the Ohio Republican delegation to the 1980 Republican Convention. She was the ranking Republican in Ohio's delegation to the 1984 GOP convention in Dallas. From 1968 to 1972 Pope was a supervisor at the Cuyahoga County (Ohio) Board of Elections.

She has served on the President's Task Force for Legal Equity for Women in Government and as vice chairman of Executive Women in Government.

While serving in the Ohio legislature, Pope was named one of the outstanding woman legislators in the nation by Rutgers University Institute of Politics, and was recognized as one of the 50 most influential women legislators by Mt. Vernon College, Washington, D.C., in 1978.

Pope and her husband, Raymond, of Parma, Ohio, are the parents of two grown daughters.

The Bureau of Engraving and Printing

6

The Bureau of Engraving and Printing

The Bureau of Engraving and Printing, which came into existence Aug. 29, 1862, is an indirect consequence of the Civil War, and primarily the result of the self-confidence, courage, ingenuity and patriotism of one man — Spencer Morton Clark. It also is the result of the foresight of Salmon P. Chase (President Lincoln's first Secretary of the Treasury), his confidence in Clark's ability, and his recognition of Clark's accomplishments.

President Lincoln called Congress into extra session on July 4, 1861, following the firing on Fort Sumter. At the time the nation was on the edge of bankruptcy and hardly in condition to finance a war. During the special session of Congress, Secretary Chase recommended that Congress set up a system of taxation and one of floating loans. His scheme for borrowing included the issuance of non-interest-bearing notes which would circulate as money.

Although there was some doubt that the government had the constitutional authority to issue paper money, Congress adopted Chase's plan in the Act of July 17, 1861, and as a result the first U.S. government-issued paper money came into being. The first notes, popularly known as "demand notes" because of certain provisions of their issuance, were produced by the American Bank Note Co. and the National Bank Note Co., both of New York, under contract with the government.

One of the provisions of the new law specified that the authorized securities should be signed by the First or Second Comptroller, or the Register of the Treasury, and counter-signed by such other officers of the Treasury as the Secretary of the Treasury cared to designate. It was soon evident that if the designated officers were to perform duties other than signing currency, the law would have to be revised.

Signatures

On Aug. 5, 19 days after enactment of the original law, President Lincoln signed a bill to change the signature requirements. Under the new law, the notes were to be signed by the Treasurer of the United States and the Register of the Treasury. The new legislation also provided that the Secretary could designate other personnel to sign the notes for these officers. A force of 70 clerks was assigned to sign these early notes — with their own names.

With such a variety of signatures on notes, security was poor. Spencer Clark, the chief clerk of the Bureau of Construction in the department, who at the time was acting engineer in charge of the Bureau, suggested to Secretary Chase that the notes be imprinted with the facsimile signatures of the required officers. Also, he suggested that the notes be imprinted with a copy of the Treasury seal as additional evidence of lawful issue.

The Secretary approved Clark's proposal and Congress approved the act on Feb. 25, 1862. Clark was then directed to procure the necessary machinery for the imprinting. A variation of the seal designed by Clark is still used on U.S. securities.

Clark described the original seal design as having for its interior a facsimile of the seal adopted by the Treasury Department for its documents on a ground of geometric lathe work, the exterior being composed of 34 similar points. "These points," Clark said, "were designed to be typical of the 34 states, and to simulate the appearance of the seals ordinarily affixed to public documents."

Clark was loyal to the government and gave no recognition to the rebellion then going on and included a point in his design for each of the 11 states then in secession. He further said of his seal: "It was difficult of execution, and it was believed that counterfeiters could not readily make a successful imitation of it. So far [1864] the belief has seemed well founded, for it has not, that I am aware of, been successfully imitated."

Clark told Secretary Chase that it would be both proper and economical to print the signatures by "a peculiar process and with peculiar ink." Two presses were secured for overprinting the signatures, an operation that began in March of 1862. Early records do not explain how long this practice continued.

Automation

Notes printed by the two New York bank note companies were delivered to the Treasury for final processing and issuing. The notes were printed in sheets of four subjects and in the beginning were trimmed and separated manually by the use of shears. Approximately 70 women were employed, at a salary of $50 per month, for the trimming and separating operations.

Because of the expense and tediousness of this method, Clark gained authority to construct two machines on a trial basis, one for trimming and one for separating. The trials of Clark's machines were reported to Secretary Chase as failures and Chase gave orders to have them removed. However, Clark asked the Secretary to personally check the machines, an inspection which revealed to Chase that actually the machines were quite effective. He rescinded his order to have them removed and directed Clark to submit plans for performing the work on machines operated by steam.

A steam engine and boilers were secured, along with necessary auxiliary equipment, and set up in the southwest room of the south wing of the basement in the main Treasury building. Presses for sealing, trimming and separating also were installed. On Aug. 29, 1862, Clark commenced with one male assistant and four female operators. Chase, in a diary entry dated Sept. 13, 1862, said: "Visited Mr. Clark's sealing and trimming machines for the ones and twos and found them a perfect success."

Secretary Chase was so pleased with Clark's machines that he asked him to investigate further possibilities relating to the printing of securities. Clark's investigations determined that the government was paying enormous prices to the bank note companies for printing notes. He told Secretary Chase that he could produce the work in the department for "a comparatively small outlay, at a great saving of cost in the issues."

Chase had introduced in Congress a proposal based on Clark's report, asking for authority to engrave and print notes at the Treasury in Washington. This authority was given by the Act of July 11, 1862, and in August, little more than a month after passage of the act, Clark reported to Chase that the first engraver (James Duthie) had been hired and was progressing satisfactorily. Date of the first printing in the department is in question. A congressional report of 1864 states that printing of some public moneys was begun in the autumn of 1862, but Clark reported to Secretary Chase on Dec. 13, 1862, "no printers are yet employed." One account says plate printing in the Treasury did not begin until January 1863.

Clark had great executive talent and was very careful in his selection of skilled artists and tradesmen for the department. He submitted a list of American engravers of known reputation. Two of those named, Joseph P. Ourdan and John F.E. Prud'homme, became full-time employees in the department. Other well-known engravers, working on a piece basis, included Charles Burt, Louis Delnoce, Alfred Sealey and Archibald McLees. Joseph James P. Ourdan, father of Joseph P. Ourdan, also came to work for the department. He had been instructed in the art of engraving by his son.

The Bureau's first engraver, James Duthie, was a skilled etcher, and served as Superintendent of Engraving until 1865. Another early craftsman was Elisha Hobart, trained as an engraver, but later a transferrer. Hobart is remembered for his engraving of Sargent's painting "Landing of the Pilgrims," on which he worked for two years.

Clark also hired George W. Casilear as an engraver, but soon afterward he was made Custodian of Dies and Rolls. Later, he became Superintendent of Engraving and served in that capacity, except during President Cleveland's first administration, until October 1893.

Still another early engraver was Henry Gugler, hired in January 1863. A native of Germany, Gugler had been in the United

States only about 10 months when hired by Clark. Gugler later founded the lithographic firm of H. Gugler and Son, Milwaukee, Wis., which is now the Gugler Lithographic Co.

Fractional currency

One of the first products produced by the Bureau was fractional currency, issued in place of coins during and for some 10 years after the Civil War. In all, there were five issues of postage and fractional currency. The second and third were printed at the department. The greater part of the fourth issue was produced by a private bank note firm but were sealed by the plate printers at the Bureau. There were three different 50-cent notes in the fourth issue and the faces of two of these were printed at the Bureau. Faces of the fifth issue were done at the Bureau and the work on the reverses was done by a private firm.

The third issue of 5-cent fractional currency bore a portrait of Clark and was the subject of much controversy (see Chap. 9, "Portraits on U.S. Paper Money"). The controversy reached Congress and resulted in the law that remains in effect today that the portrait of a living person shall not be used on a security of the U.S. (31 U.S.C. 413).

The first paper money produced at the Treasury establishment, other than fractional notes, were the compound interest notes of 1863 and 1864 and the 5 percent Treasury notes of 1863.

By 1864, the Bureau had grown to a point where it employed 237 men and 288 women. In November 1864, Clark reported equipment in use as 15 transfer machines, 72 hydraulic and 96 hand presses, 14 sealing presses, six ink mills and 22 numbering machines.

It is not known for certain when the title "Bureau of Engraving and Printing" began. Early records show such names for the Bureau as "Small Note Department," "Small Note Bureau," "Small Note Room," "Note Bureau," "National Note Bureau," and "First Division of the National Currency Bureau."

Formal recognition

The first reference on record of the use of the name "Bureau of Engraving and Printing" is found in a copy of an order of July 31, 1868, placed with John R. Hoole and Sons, New York City, for an ornamental strip with that wording, for use in printing a form needed by the Bureau. The first legislative recognition of the agency is found in the Act of March 3, 1869, which prohibited any work from being done "in the engraving and printing bureau for private parties."

Additional organizational recognition is found in the Act of July 11, 1896, which provides "That all business of the Bureau of Engraving and Printing shall be under the immediate control of the director of the Bureau, subject to the direction of the Secretary of the Treasury, and the director of said Bureau shall report to and be responsible directly to the Secretary of the Treasury."

The extent to which steam presses were being used in those early days of the Bureau is recounted in the Bureau's annual report for the fiscal year 1888, which reads: "The steam presses are now printing much more than one-third of the work at the Bureau, with a great economy of rooms, labor and expense. The cost of the printing done by them is less than $80,000. To print the same work by hand would cost $180,000."

The use of distinctively marked paper in printing paper money, limited by law to this single purpose, was early recognized as one of the prime deterrents to counterfeiting.

In 1862, Secretary Chase authorized Clark to make "investigations and experiments in reference to the manufacture of a distinctive paper in the [Treasury] building." Early suppliers of such distinctive paper were Stuart Gwynn of Boston, Mass.; J. M. Wilcox and Co., Philadelphia, Pa.; and the Crane Paper Co. of Dalton, Mass. Crane, the latest firm contracted with, still supplies the Bureau with distinctive paper, which will soon include an embedded plastic security thread.

Although Spencer Clark made a formal recommendation for separate facilities for the printing and processing of currency a scant three years after beginning operations, it was a good many years before the Bureau had its own building. Land for this purpose was purchased on June 26, 1878, from William W. Corcoran, Washington historical figure best known as the founder of the world-famous Corcoran Gallery of Art.

A contract for the excavation for the project was awarded the following month, and the structure, designed in Romanesque style by James G. Hill, Supervising Architect of the Treasury, was completed in record time at a cost of $300,000. It was ready for occupancy on July 1, 1880. The Bureau remained in this building until 1914 when the present Bureau headquarters was built. An annex to the Bureau was completed in 1938.

The Bureau today

The Bureau of Engraving and Printing is the world's largest securities manufacturing establishment. It employs 2,300 people and operates 24 hours a day. The Bureau designs, engraves, and prints United States paper currency; Treasury bonds and notes; United States postage, customs and revenue stamps; and miscellaneous engraved items for approximately 75 departments and independent agencies of the Federal government, and its insular possessions. White House invitations, commissions, diplomas, certificates, identification cards and liquor strip stamps are some of the approximately 800 miscellaneous products printed by the Bureau.

Operations of the century-old Bureau of Engraving and Printing are housed in two specially constructed buildings with a combined floor space of approximately 25 acres. The Bureau will add 288,000 square feet of additional floor space when the western currency-producing facility is completed near Fort Worth, Texas.

Ground was broken for the Fort Worth plant on April 25, 1987; the plant is to produce 25 percent of the annual U.S. currency supply and will serve the Kansas City, Dallas and San Francisco Federal Reserve banks.

On Aug. 4, 1950, Public Law 656 was passed by the 81st Congress, which authorized the working capital fund method of financing the operations of the Bureau, placing all operations on a completely reimbursable basis and providing for business-type accounting and budgeting procedures. The effective date of the law was July 1, 1951, and on that date the Bureau's accounting and budgeting procedures were operating fully under the new system.

The principal product of the Bureau is United States paper currency. A face value of more than $78 billion is printed annually, averaging approximately 25 million notes a day.

All of the currency notes printed are Federal Reserve notes, which are issued in denominations of $1, $2, $5, $10, $20, $50, and $100. They are primarily used to replace worn or mutilated currency taken out of circulation. The Bureau has printed $100 United States notes as recently as the early first Nixon administration (by Act of Congress dated May 3, 1878, the value of United States notes outstanding must be maintained at $346,681,016).

Federal Reserve notes and United States notes are the only classes that can now be printed; printing of Federal Reserve Bank notes, national bank notes, gold certificates, and most recently, silver certificates, has been discontinued. Some notes from each of these classes are still in public circulation.

The Department of the Treasury announced on July 14, 1969, that currency in denominations of $500, $1,000, $5,000, and $10,000 would no longer be produced because of the lack of demand.

The largest denomination of currency ever printed was the $100,000 gold certificate of 1934, which featured the portrait of President Wilson. This note was designed for official transactions only, and none of these notes ever circulated outside Federal Reserve Banks.

The $2 Federal Reserve note was issued on April 13, 1976, as the latest permanent addition to the denominations of United States currency.

Beginning in 1966, a collection of 306,275 of the BEP's "certified proofs," proofs which were produced for nearly every instrument printed by that agency, was transferred in 1984 to the Smithsonian Institution's Division of Numismatics.

The transfer began when the BEP ran out of room to store the proofs, which represent all the major note types of the United States, plus such other items as Cuban silver certificates and Philippine Treasury certificates, printed for former U.S. possessions, bonds, stocks, revenue items, checks and other instruments.

The proofs are inked impressions pulled from new printing plates and submitted to BEP officials for examination and approval.

How paper money is printed

To assure the best protection against counterfeiting, all United States paper money, as well as nearly all postage stamps and other evidences of a financial character issued by the United States government, are printed by the "line engraved," or intaglio process, from engraved plates.

Intaglio-printed documents are the most difficult to produce and to counterfeit. Other processes lack the fidelity of fine lines and the distinctive three-dimensional effect of raised line on paper inherent in intaglio printing. An outstanding element of protection is the portrait. The use of portraits in security designs takes full advantage of the characteristics of intaglio printing since even a slight alteration in breadth, spacing, or depth of line on the part of a counterfeiter will cause a perceptible facial change. The portraits used in the designs of securities are those of persons of historical importance. By law, no portrait of a living person may be used.

In the intaglio process, the individual features of a chosen design are hand-tooled by highly skilled engravers who engrave in varying depths into steel with delicate steel-cutting instruments called gravers. With infinite care, each feature, such as the portrait, the vignette, the numerals, the lettering, the script, and the scroll work is hand-engraved by a different master craftsman expertly trained in his own particular skill.

The Bureau prints all paper money by the intaglio process on high-speed sheet-fed Giori presses. Each press has four 32-note printing plates and is capable of printing 9,000 sheets per hour. Each sheet is forced, under extremely high pressure, into the fine engraved lines of a plate to pick up the ink. The backs of the notes are printed with green ink on one day, and the faces are printed with black ink at least 24 hours later.

The use of a specially formulated fast-drying non-offset ink, developed in the Bureau's laboratories, has eliminated the former time-consuming need for tissuing or interleaving between sheets. The inks and distinctive paper used by the Bureau in the manufacture of currency are produced under specifications designed to deter counterfeiting and to assure a high-quality product.

In June 1985, the Bureau began using a system called COPE Pak to streamline the printing, overprinting and cutting operations, as well as the parceling and shrink wrapping phases of the currency making process.

COPE Pak is an acronym for "currency overprinting, processing and packaging equipment." Before the acquisition of the COPE Pak equipment, the overprinting, note examining and packaging operations took place in three separate areas of the Bureau.

COPE Pak machines reduce the number of times employees must handle the money.

The printing process for the COPE Pak machinery begins in the same way as with the previously-used COPE machines.

Currency is still printed in 32-subject sheet form, first the back, then 24 or more hours later, the face. The sheets are then trimmed, split into two 16-subject sheets and examined by human inspectors in the mechanical examining process.

The 16-subject sheets are then delivered to the COPE Pak machines for overprinting, examining, counting and packaging. They are fed into the equipment in two 10,000-sheet stacks.

Blowers separate the sheets and suction feet pick up one sheet at a time. Grippers then pull the sheets along the feedboard into the printing cylinders. "Two-sheet detectors," actuated by the excessive thickness of the combined sheets, tell the system to shut down when more than one sheet is picked up by the suction heads.

At the printing cylinders the black Federal Reserve Bank seals and FRB letters, plus the green Treasury seals and serial numbers are applied to the face of the note.

Sheets are then collated into stacks of 100. When a stack of 100 sheets accumulates, it is cut lengthwise and widthwise and the stacks of individual notes are fed into a paper bander.

With the paper banding process, the similarity between COPE and COPE Pak ends.

With the COPE Pak system, after the notes have been banded, they pass into a note examining station, where an examiner randomly samples and inspects the stacks for quality and accountability purposes.

Once the notes are inspected, they travel to a rotating carousel with 32 compartments, corresponding to each plate position number on the 32-subject printing plates.

When 10 packages of 100 notes are collated in the carousel, they pass to another paper bander. From this bander 1,000-note packages are automatically sent on to counting stations where the contents are counted twice to ensure 100 percent accountability for all the notes processed.

Upon being counted, the packages get shrink-wrapped and labeled. A label placed on the end of the package identifies the package by denomination, bank and beginning and ending serial numbers.

Finally, the shrink-wrapped 1,000-note packages are collated in groups of four in a collating drum and delivered to another shrink-wrapping apparatus, making a finished "brick" of 4,000 notes, ready for shipment to the 12 Federal Reserve Banks.

COPE Pak combines into a single steamlined continuum the operations of overprinting (serial numbers, Treasury seals, Federal Reserve seals and bank numbers), inspection, counting, banding and shrink-wrapping, all with automatic mechanical transfer of work from station to station.

If a mechanical problem should occur in

the system, a malfunction indicator provides a digital readout, telling the operator which part is malfunctioning. More than 700 functions can be monitored by this device.

Despite the potential complications of combining operations, BEP officials say the COPE Pak machines can overprint more notes per shift than the COPE equipment, which only overprinted and banded the 100-note bundles.

The net increase in production of notes per shift by the COPE Pak equipment is approximately 10 percent. COPE Paks have been known to turn out as many as 41,500 notes in a nine-hour day.

Besides increased productivity and reduced costs, there has been improvement in the quality of the product itself, BEP officials say.

All currency is now counted four times, double overwrapped for greater protection, bar-coded to facilitate accountability and inventory control and is separable into four packages of 1,000 notes to admit easier breakdown and transfer of currency from Federal Reserve District Banks to other, smaller institutions.

COPE Pak machines are the result of a combined manufacturing effort by factories in several West German cities and one English factory. The headquarters of this combination is in Switzerland, where the U.S. government has a contract for the machines with DeLaRue Giori of Lausanne.

Koenig and Bauer of Wurzburg makes the numerota (the serial numbering system); Zeiser of Emmingen produces the numbering boxes and computer controls; Bielomatic of Nueffen is responsible for the processing lines; Herma of Stuttgart makes the labeling equipment; and Kalfass, also of Stuttgart, makes the overwrapping apparatus. The English company Vacuumatic, in Harwich, manufactures the counting equipment.

The parts are collected and assembled by Koenig and Bauer in its Wurzburg facility.

A further step in the direction of advancing the technological level of the BEP was taken when the Bureau awarded a $10.2 million contract to the Hamilton Tool Co. of Hamilton, Ohio, for the construction of a web-fed press for printing U.S. currency.

The press will be able to perform simultaneous intaglio face and back printing on the continuous roll of currency paper and adds the overprinting during a single pass through the machine.

The press was expected to take about four years to build.

In the event a finished note is found to be imperfect after it has been overprinted, it is replaced with a "star" note. In design, star notes are exactly like the notes they replace, but they carry an independent series of serial numbers. The star appears in place of the prefix letter before the serial number on United States notes and after the serial number in place of the suffix letter on Federal Reserve notes. The serial number of the imperfect note which was replaced is not used again in the same numbering sequence.

The life of a $1 note is about 18 months. Higher denominations remain in circulation longer since they are not used in transactions as frequently as the $1 note. The average $5 bill lasts two years; a $10 bill lasts three years; a $20 bill lasts five years; a $50 lasts nine years; and a $100 bill lasts about 23 years. The size of a currency note is approximately 2.61 inches x 6.14 inches and the thickness is .0043 inch. There are 233 new notes to an inch-high stack (not compressed) and 490 equal a pound. A million notes weigh approximately a ton and occupy approximately 42 cubic feet of space (with moderate pressure).

Distribution

After paper money is printed, the Bureau of Engraving and Printing ships the currency to the 12 Federal Reserve Banks and their 26 branches. These agencies, in turn, distribute the money to the commercial banking system throughout the country.

Member banks of the Federal Reserve System carry their reserve accounts with the Federal Reserve Bank of their district. When member banks need additional currency, they authorize the Federal Reserve Bank to charge their reserve account and ship the currency. The Federal Reserve Banks will ship such currency as is required. Usually, nonmember banks procure their currency through a correspondent member bank located in the same city with the Federal Reserve Bank, or by arrangement whereby the currency is shipped directly to the nonmember bank with the reserve account of the correspondent bank charged for the shipment.

To obtain Federal Reserve notes, a Federal Reserve Bank applies to the Federal Reserve agent, a representative of the board of governors of the Federal Reserve System, who is located at the reserve bank and who maintains a stock of unissued notes. In applying for notes, a Federal Reserve Bank must pledge with the agent the required collateral equal to the face value of the notes. This collateral must consist of the following assets, alone or in any combination: 1) gold certificates, 2) Special Drawing Right certificates, 3) United States government securities, and 4) "eligible paper" as described by statute.

United States government securities are acquired by the Federal Reserve Banks in open market operations. Eligible paper consists of short-term notes, drafts, bills of exchange, or acceptances discounted or purchased by the Reserve banks.

Exchange of mutilated paper currency

Lawfully held paper currency of the United States which has been mutilated will be exchanged at its face amount if clearly more than one-half of the original whole note remains.

Fragments of mutilated currency which are not clearly more than one-half of the original whole note will be exchanged at face value only if the Bureau of Government Financial Operations is satisfied that the missing portions have been totally destroyed. This judgment is based on such evidence of total destruction as is deemed necessary and is final.

No relief will be granted an account of paper currency of the United States which has been totally destroyed.

The public should address all correspondence regarding mutilated currency to the Department of the Treasury, Bureau of Engraving and Printing, OCS/BEPA, Room 344, P.O. Box 37048, Washington, D.C. 20013. Return receipt requested when sending mutilated currency; this address accepts only mutilated paper money and not coins.

Destruction of unfit currency

When paper currency becomes worn and no longer fit for general use, it is withdrawn from circulation, destroyed, and replaced by new notes. The worn out notes are destroyed by incineration or shredding at Federal Reserve banks and branches throughout the country, under procedures prescribed by the Department of the Treasury. The destruction process is not complete until the notes have been reduced to an unidentifiable residue so that no recovery of the notes and of the distinctive paper on which they are imprinted is possible. About 98 percent of the currency is shredded and 2 percent is incinerated.

Before they are destroyed, the currency is verified as to genuineness, kind, value, and number of pieces. One-dollar bills make up the bulk of the currency which is retired because of unfitness.

Silver certificates, United States notes and Federal Reserve notes in all denominations below $500 that are no longer fit for use are verified and destroyed at Federal Reserve Banks and branches throughout the country, under procedures prescribed by the Department of the Treasury.

Federal Reserve notes in denominations of $500 and above are canceled with distinctive perforations and cut in half lengthwise. The lower halves are shipped to the Department of the Treasury in Washington, D.C., where they are verified and destroyed. The upper halves are retained by the Federal Reserve Banks and destroyed after the banks are notified by the Treasury that the lower halves have been verified.

Souvenir cards

Beginning in 1969, the BEP has engraved and manufactured in honor of special events souvenir cards containing engraved reproductions of various United States paper currency issues. The cards measure 8.5 by 10.5 inches except the 1969 American Numismatic Association card, which measures 6 by 9 inches.

Following is a list of all BEP souvenir cards issued since 1969, a description of each card and how they were produced, and the number issued. A complete listing of philatelic souvenir cards is published in *Linn's World Stamp Almanac*, Fourth Edition.

Aug. 12-16, 1969, American Numismatic Association, 78th Anniversary Convention, Philadelphia, Pa.

The large American eagle on this card is a reproduction of the die designed and engraved by craftsmen of the Continental Bank Note Co. for use on various United States securities. This eagle was flanked by smaller

eagles which were reproduced from the engravings used on the $10 United States notes of Series 1869, 1875, 1878, 1880.

According to the legend on this ANA card, the large American eagle design notes were dubbed "jackass notes," the explanation being that "over the years many fanciful explanations have been proffered concerning the engraver's intent in executing the design. None has any real basis in fact.

"The resemblance of the eagle, in inverted position, to the lowly donkey's head is purely illusionary."

Quantity issued: 12,347.

Aug. 18-22, 1970, 79th Anniversary Convention of the American Numismatic Association, St. Louis, Mo.

Collage in original colors of portions of various securities from original dies used in their production by the Bureau to exemplify arts and skills of high-quality engraving and intaglio printed renditions.

Card designed by Leonard Buckley.

Card data: Vignette, die stamping; text and Department of the Treasury seal (within collage), flatbed typographic.

Quantity issued: 12,013.

Aug. 10-14, 1971, 80th Anniversary Convention of the American Numismatic Association, Washington, D.C.

Face of the $1 silver certificate, Series 1896, designed by Will H. Low, New York City artist, and printed from a plate prepared from original master die.

Card data: Vignette, rotary sheet-fed intaglio; text, flatbed typographic.

Quantity issued: 54,694.

Aug. 15-19, 1972, 81st Anniversary Convention of the American Numismatic Association, New Orleans, La.

Reproduction of face of $2 silver certificate, Series 1896, printed from plate specially produced from original master die. Design, "Science Presenting Steam and Electricity to Commerce and Manufacture," by Edwin H. Blashfield, 19th century allegorical painter. Engravers: George Smillie, G. Rose Jr., Robert Ponickau, Edward E. Myers, J. Hill, James Kennedy. (See ANA card, Aug. 10-14, 1971.)

Card data: Vignette, rotary sheet-fed intaglio; text, flatbed typographic.

Quantity issued: 69,078.

Aug. 23-27, 1973, 82nd Anniversary Convention of the American Numismatic Association, Boston, Mass.

Reproduction of face of $5 silver certificate, Series 1896, printed from a plate specially produced from original master die. Design, titled "America," was executed by Walter Shirlaw, illustrator and bank note engraver. Engravers: Vignette, G.F.C. Smillie; lettering and numerals: J. Kennedy, E.E. Myers, G.W. Rose Jr., W. Ponichau, R. Ponichau, D.M. Cooper, E. M. Hall, J.R. Hall, H.L. Charlton, S.B. Many. (See also, ANA

card, 1971, Aug. 10-14; ANA card, 1972, Aug. 15-19.)

Card data: Vignette, rotary sheet-fed intaglio; text, offset, surface.

Quantity issued: 49,530.

Aug. 13-17, 1974, 83rd Anniversary Convention of the American Numismatic Association, Bal Harbour, Fla.

Reproduction of proposed face of $10 silver certificate, Series 1897, "Educational" series. Titled "Agriculture and Forestry" the design never appeared on the $10 note. Designer, Walter Shirlaw; vignette engraved by Charles Schlecht after Shirlaw's design; letter and numeral engravers: Charles Schlecht, J. Kennedy, G.V. Rose Jr., J.R. Hill.

Card data: Vignette, rotary sheet-fed intaglio press; text; offset surface.

Quantity produced: 41,591.

1975, International Women's Year.

A brochure including a removable souvenir card, honoring the International Women's Year, depicting a portrait of Martha Washington on the Series 1886 $1 silver certificate. Also engravings from three postage stamps honoring women. $1 silver certificate, Series 1886: Designer, Thomas F. Morris; engravers, Charles Burt, Alfred Sealy, Thomas F. Morris. 5-cent Frances E. Willard postage stamp: Design from a photograph by Perry Pictures (No. 152) from Public Library, Washington, D.C.; portrait engraver, James R. Lowe; letter engravers, James T. Vail, William B. Wells; frame engraver, Carl T. Arlt. 10-cent Jane Addams postage stamp: Design from a photograph by Moffett, Chicago; portrait engraver, Carl T. Arlt; letter engraver, William B. Wells; frame engraver, James T. Vail. 3-cent 100 Years Progress of Women postage stamp: Designer, Victor McCloskey Jr.; portrait engraver, Carl T. Arlt; letter, numeral, and frame engraver, John S. Edmondson.

Card data: Vignette of currency, rotary sheet-fed intaglio; vignette of stamps, rotary sheet-fed intaglio; tint and text, offset surface.

Quantity issued: 28,022.

Aug. 19-24, 1975, 84th Anniversary Convention of American Numismatic Association, Los Angeles, Calif.

Reproduction of the back of the $1 silver certificate, Series 1896, which was designed and executed by Thomas F. Morris. Portrait of Martha Washington originally engraved in 1878 by Charles Burt. George Washington's portrait was engraved in 1867 by Alfred Sealy. Portrait engravers, J. Kennedy, W. Pontchon, Dr. S. Ronaldson, E.M. Hall; letter engravers, L.T. Ellis, R. Pontchon, George U. Rose Jr.

Card data: Vignette, rotary sheet-fed intaglio; text, offset surface.

Quantity issued: 45,593.

Aug. 24-29, 1976, 85th Anniversary Convention of American Numismatic Association, New York, N.Y.

Reproduction of the back of the $2 silver certificate, Series 1896, which was designed and executed by Thomas F. Morris.

Card data: Vignette, rotary sheet-fed intaglio; text, offset surface.

Quantity issued: 38,636.

Aug. 23-28, 1977, 86th Anniversary Convention of American Numismatic Association, Atlanta, Ga.

Reproduction of the face of $5 silver certificate, Series 1899. Only issue of U.S. paper money for which an Indian (Running Antelope of Sioux tribe) was selected as central figure. Portrait engraved by G.F.C. Smillie.

Card data: Vignette, rotary sheet-fed intaglio; text, offset surface.

Quantity issued: 57,806.

June 2-4, 1978, International Paper Money Show, Memphis Coin Club, Memphis, Tenn.

Reproduction of vignette on the back of the $10 national bank note, First Charter Period, titled "Discovery of the Mississippi by Hernando DeSoto, 1541." The model for the vignette is from a painting by W.H. Powell which now hangs in the Capitol Rotunda, Washington, D.C. Frederick Girsch engraved the vignette in 1869.

Card data: Vignette, rotary sheet-fed intaglio; text, offset surface.

Quantity issued: 28,004

Feb. 15-17, 1980, Midwinter Convention of American Numismatic Association, Albuquerque, N.M.

Reproduction of the back of $5 silver certificate, Series 1896, completing the Bureau's "educational note" souvenir card series. Portraits of U.S. Grant and Philip Sheridan flanking head of a goddess with outstretched wings. Thomas F. Morris created the design; Lorenzo Hatch engraved the portraits and G.F.C. Smillie engraved the head and wings.

Card data: Vignette, rotary sheet-fed intaglio; text, offset surface.

Quantity issued: 21,933.

June 6-8, 1980, International Paper Money Show, Memphis Coin Club, Memphis, Tenn.

Reproduction of the face of $10 United States note, Series 1901, commonly known as "bison note" or "buffalo note." Portraits of explorers Meriwether Lewis and William Clark flank a central vignette of a bison

named Pablo. The bison design by Ostrander Smith was based on a sketch by Charles R. Knight; Marcus W. Baldwin executed the engraving of the bison. G.F.C. Smillie engraved the two portraits.

Card data: Vignette, rotary sheet-fed intaglio; text, offset surface.

Quantity issued: 30,907.

June 19-21, 1981, International Paper Money Show, Memphis Coin Club, Memphis, Tenn.

Reproduction of face of $20 gold certificate, Series 1905, commonly known as the "technicolor note" for its elaborate color scheme. The portrait of George Washington was engraved by A. Sealey in June 1867, based on a portrait by Gilbert Stuart.

Card data: Vignette, rotary sheet-fed intaglio, with offset color overlay; text, offset surface.

Quantity issued: 21,794.

July 27-Aug. 2, 1981, 90th Anniversary Convention of American Numismatic Association, New Orleans, La.

Reproduction of back of $5 silver certificate, Series 1886, featuring engravings of five Morgan silver dollars, comprising four back engravings and one face, dated 1886. The design was engraved by Lorenzo J. Hatch.

Card data: Vignette, rotary sheet-fed intaglio; text, offset surface.

Quantity issued: 21,709.

June 18-20, 1982, International Paper Money Show, Memphis Coin Club, Memphis, Tenn.

Reproduction of back of $100 national bank note, Second Charter Period, Series 1882, of The First National Bank of Nashville, Tenn., with charter number 150. The notes are known as "Brown Backs" because of the back colors; the centrally located charter number is printed in green ink.

Card data: Engraving, combination of intaglio and offset printings; text, offset surface.

Quantity issued: 12,362.

Aug. 17-22, 1982, 91st Anniversary Convention of American Numismatic Association, Boston, Mass.

Reproduction of the Great Seal of the United States, during the bicentennial celebration year of the seal. The seal shown is the one appearing on the back of modern $1 Federal Reserve notes, and is backed by a red, white and blue ribbon.

Card data: Vignettes, rotary sheet-fed intaglio, with offset ribbon; text, offset surface.

Quantity issued: 11,445.

Jan. 5-8, 1983, 28th annual convention of Florida United Numismatists, Orlando, Fla.

Reproduction of back of $100 Treasury or coin note, Series 1890, commonly referred to as the "watermelon note" due to the resemblance of the large figure zeros in the denomination to the large summer fruit. The back design was engraved by W.A. Copenhaver, W.H. Dougal, G.U. Rose Jr. and J.A. Rueff.
Card data: Vignette, rotary sheet-fed intaglio; text, offset surface.
Quantity issued: 10,250.

Aug. 16-20, 1983, 92nd Anniversary Convention of American Numismatic Association, San Diego, Calif.

Reproduction of back of $20 Federal Reserve Bank note, Series 1915, depicting various forms of pre-World War I land, sea and air transportation. M.W. Baldwin engraved the vignette, "Land, Sea and Air."
Card data: Vignette, rotary sheet-fed intaglio; text, offset surface.
Quantity issued: 10,649.

Jan. 4-7, 1984, 29th annual convention of Florida United Numismatists, Tampa, Fla.

Reproduction of back of $10 United States note, Series 1880. Commonly known as "sawhorse note," due to crossed bars of central device.
Card data: Vignette, rotary sheet-fed intaglio; text, offset surface.
Quantity issued: 8,365.

June 15-17, 1984, International Paper Money Show, Memphis Coin Club, Memphis, Tenn.

Reproduction of face of $10,000 United States note, Series 1878. The note depicted is unknown in any collection. The portrait of Andrew Jackson was engraved by A. Sealey from a painting by Thomas Sully.
Card data: Vignette, combination of rotary sheet-fed intaglio and offset printings; text, offset surface.
Quantity issued: 17,489.

July 28-Aug. 1, 1984, 93rd Anniversary Convention of American Numismatic Association, Detroit, Mich.

Reproduction of face of $500 gold certificate, Series 1882. The portrait of Abraham Lincoln was engraved by Charles Burt.
Card data: Vignette, combination of rotary sheet-fed intaglio and offset printings; text, offset surface.
Quantity issued: 12,491.

Jan. 31-Feb. 3, 1985, Long Beach Numismatic and Philatelic Exposition, Long Beach, Calif.

Reproduction of the back of $20 gold certificate, Series 1865. Vignette also includes block of four 3-cent stamps from 1948, commemorating the discovery of gold in California.
Card data: Vignette, combination of rotary sheet-fed intaglio and offset printings; text, offset surface.
Quantity issued: 7,511.

April 19-21, 1985, International Coin Club of El Paso, Texas.

Reproduction of the back of $50 national bank note, Third Charter period, Series 1902, featuring the vignette "Mechanics and Navigation."
Card data: Vignette, rotary sheet-fed intaglio; text, offset surface.
Quantity issued: 7,808.

May 17-19, 1985, Pacific Northwest Numismatic Association convention, Seattle, Wash.

Reproduction of the back of $50 Federal Reserve note, Series 1914. Vignette depicts the symbolic figure of Panama positioned between two ships.
Card data: Vignette, rotary sheet-fed intaglio; text, offset surface.
Quantity issued: 6,864.

June 14-16, 1985, International Paper Money Show, Memphis, Tenn.

Reproduction of the back of $10,000 United States note, Series 1878. The issuance of United States notes was originally opposed by both the House of Representatives and the Senate, but they were eventually issued in 1862.
Card data: Vignette, rotary sheet-fed intaglio; text, offset surface.
Quantity issued: 8,745.

Aug. 20-25, 1985, 94th Anniversary Convention of the American Numismatic Association, Baltimore, Md.

Reproduction of the back of $500 gold certificate, Series 1882. Gold certificates were withdrawn from circulation in 1933.
Card data: Vignette, rotary sheet-fed intaglio; text, offset surface.
Quantity issued: 10,060.

Nov. 14-17, 1985, International Paper Money Convention, Cherry Hill, N.J.

Reproduction of the face of $10 national bank note, Second Charter period, Series 1882. The bill features two vignettes: the left vignette, "Franklin and Electricity 1752," was engraved by Alfred Jones and Louis Delnoce for the American Bank Note Co.; the right vignette depicts "America Seizing Lightning," created by artist Theodore A. Liebler and engraved by Charles K. Burt.
Card data: Vignette, combination rotary

sheet-fed intaglio and offset printings; text, offset surface.

Quantity issued: 7,926.

Jan. 2-5, 1986, 31st annual convention of the Florida United Numismatists, Tampa, Fla.

Reproduction of face of $100 Treasury note, Series 1890. The note features the portrait of David G. Farragut, the first admiral in the United States Navy.

Card data: Vignette, combination rotary sheet-fed intaglio and offset printings; text, offset surface.

Quantity issued: 8,140.

Feb. 19-23, 1986, Eighth Midwinter Convention of the American Numismatic Association, Salt Lake City, Utah.

Reproduction of the back of $10 United States note, Series 1901. Vignette depicts the allegorical figure of "Progress" in the form of a woman, positioned between two columns, forming an arch over her head.

Card data: Vignette, rotary sheet-fed intaglio; text, offset surface.

Quantity issued: 7,986.

June 20-22, 1986, International Paper Money Show, Memphis Coin Club, Memphis, Tenn.

Reproduction of back of $5 national bank note, Third Charter period, Series 1902. Vignette is called "Landing of the Pilgrims" and shows several families disembarking in the New World.

Card data: Vignette, rotary sheet-fed intaglio; text, offset surface.

Quantity issued: 8,693.

Aug. 6-10, 1986, 95th Anniversary Convention of the American Numismatic Association, Milwaukee, Wis.

Reproduction of the face of 5-cent Second Issue fractional currency note, bearing a portrait of George Washington engraved by James Duthie.

Card data: Vignette, rotary sheet-fed intaglio; text, offset surface.

Quantity issued: Not available at press time.

Oct. 2-5, 1986, Long Beach Numismatic and Philatelic Exposition, Long Beach, Calif.

Reproduction of face of $10 gold certificate, Series 1907 and block of four Western Mining Prospector stamps, Series 1898. Vignette is a portrait of Michael Hillegas, the first Treasurer of the United States.

Card data: Vignette, combination of rotary sheet-fed intaglio and offset printings; text, offset surface.

Quantity issues: Not available at press time.

Nov. 13-16, 1986, first National World Paper Money Convention, St. Louis, Mo.

Vignette features an offset-printed montage of U.S. fractional currency and an intaglio vignette of Samuel Dexter, Secretary of War and Treasury, 1800-02, under Thomas Jefferson.

Card data: Vignette, combination of rotary sheet-fed intaglio and offset printings; text offset surface.

Quantity issued: Not available at press time.

Dec. 11-14, 1986, Dallas Coin and Stamp Exposition, Dallas, Texas.

Reproduction of the back of $10,000 Federal Reserve note, Series 1918, with "The Embarkation of the Pilgrims" and a block of four 5-cent stamps commemorating the 300th anniversary of the landing of the Pilgrims.

Card data: Vignette, rotary sheet-fed intaglio; text, offset surface.

Quantity issued: Not available at press time.

Jan. 7-10, 1987, 32nd annual convention of the Florida United Numismatists, Lake Buena Vista, Fla.

Reproduction of the face of $1 United States note, Series 1874, with left vignette of Christopher Columbus designed by Joseph P. Ourdan; also on note is portrait of George Washington, engraved by Alfred Sealy, based on a painting by Gilbert Stuart.

Card data: Vignette, combination of rotary sheet-fed intaglio and offset printings; text, offset surface.

Quantity issued: Not available at press time.

Feb. 27-March 1, 1987, Ninth Midwinter Convention of the American Numismatic Association, Charlotte, N.C.

Vignette features the $500,000,000 coupon Treasury note, the largest fiduciary instrument ever printed by the BEP and issued by the U.S. government.

Card data: Vignette, combination of rotary sheet-fed intaglio and offset printings; text, offset surface.

Quantity issued: Not available.

1987, 125th anniversary of the Bureau of Engraving and Printing.

Multicolor intaglio vignette of the Bureau of Engraving and Printing building, surrounded by cherry trees in full bloom. The vignette is printed in green, blue, pink and red.

Card data: Vignette: rotary sheet-fed intaglio; text, offset surface.

Quantity issued: Not available.

Spider press plate prints

Beginning with the 1984 Florida United Numismatists Convention in Tampa, Fla., the Bureau began issuing plate prints produced on an operational 19th century spider press. The press was purchased by the Bureau between 1890 and 1904 for currency production, and was also used by the Flatbed Printing Division for specialized printing until the late 1930s or early 1940s. It features a single-plate hand roller and a long radial handle. The iron bed on which the plate is mounted moves between two steel rollers, the top covered with felt.

The Bureau began taking the spider press to numismatic conventions with the FUN '84 show, demonstrating its use by printing examples of plate prints. However, all plate prints sold at the conventions are produced before the convention since the paper is dampened before printing and takes several days to dry.

Jan. 4-7, 1984, 29th annual convention of Florida United Numismatists, Tampa, Fla.

Plate print of American eagle vignette based on an original watercolor by William A. Roach. Printed in brown ink on cream parchment.

Quantity issued: 1,846.

June 15-17, 1984, International Paper Money Show, Memphis Coin Club, Memphis, Tenn.

Plate print of American eagle vignette based on original watercolor by William A. Roach. Printed in deep blue ink on cream parchment.

Quantity issued: 1,378.

July 28-Aug. 1, 1984, 93rd Anniversary Convention of American Numismatic Association, Detroit, Mich.

Plate print of American eagle vignette based on an original watercolor by William A. Roach. Printed in blue ink on cream parchment.

Quantity issued: 1,231.

Nov. 21-24, 1985, American Stamp Dealers' Association national postage stamp show, New York, N.Y.

Plate print of Statue of Liberty vignette, some printed in green ink and some printed in brown, both on cream parchment.

Quantity issued: 1,824.

April 19-21, 1985, International Coin Club of El Paso show, El Paso, Texas.

Plate print of Statue of Liberty vignette, some printed in maroon ink and some printed in dark brown, both on cream parchment.

Quantity issued: 1,336.

Aug. 20-25, 1985, 94th Anniversary Convention of the American Numismatic Association, Baltimore, Md.

Plate print of Statue of Liberty vignette, some printed in green ink and some in blue, both on cream parchment.

Quantity issued: 2,126.

Nov. 14-17, 1985, International Paper Money Convention, Cherry Hill, N.J.

Plate print of Liberty Bell vignette. Printed in blue on cream parchment.

Quantity issued: 1,424.

May 22-June 1, 1986, Ameripex '86, Chicago, Ill.

Plate print of Liberty Bell vignette. Printed in green on cream parchment.

Quantity issued: 2,832.

Aug. 6-10, 1986, 95th Anniversary Convention of the American Numismatic Association, Milwaukee, Wis.

Plate print of Liberty Bell vignette. Printed in brown on cream parchment.

Quantity issued: 2,449.

Availability of cards

Souvenir cards of the Bureau of Engraving and Printing are available in unlimited quantity for 90 days after issue, unless stocks are depleted sooner. Plate proofs will be available for 30 days after issue. Mail orders accompanied by check or money order made payable to the Bureau of Engraving and Printing should be addressed to [souvenir card/plate proof name], Bureau of Engraving and Printing, 14th and C streets, SW, Washington, D.C. 20228.

Engraved and lithographed printings

Bureau products, unless otherwise indicated, are black-ink engravings produced from intaglio plates in a manner similar to currency and postage stamp reproductions.

Following is a list of portraits, building vignettes, government seals, and miscellaneous printings available from BEP.

Small presidential portraits

Paper six by eight inches, image approximately two by two and a half inches.

1. Washington	11. Polk	21. Arthur	31. F.D. Roosevelt
2. J. Adams	12. Taylor	22. Cleveland	32. Truman
3. Jefferson	13. Fillmore	23. B. Harrison	33. Eisenhower
4. Madison	14. Pierce	24. McKinley	34. Kennedy
5. Monroe	15. Buchanan	25. T. Roosevelt	35. L. Johnson
6. J.Q. Adams	16. Lincoln	26. Taft	36. Nixon
7. Jackson	17. A. Johnson	27. Wilson	37. Ford
8. Van Buren	18. Grant	28. Harding	38. Carter
9. W.H. Harrison	19. Hayes	29. Coolidge	39. Reagan
10. Tyler	20. Garfield	30. Hoover	

Portraits of chief justices

Paper six by eight inches, image approximately two by two and a half inches.

100. John Jay	104. Roger Taney	108. E.D. White	111. Harlan Stone
101. John Rutledge	105. Salmon Chase	109. W.H. Taft	112. Fred Vinson
102. Oliver Ellsworth	106. Morrison Waite	110. Charles E. Hughes	113. Earl Warren
103. John Marshall	107. Melville Fuller		

Large presidential portraits

Paper nine by 12 inches, image approximately four by five inches.

200. Washington	205. T. Roosevelt	210. Hoover	215. L. Johnson
201. Jefferson	206. Taft	211. F.D. Roosevelt	216. Nixon
202. Lincoln	207. Wilson	212. Truman	217. Ford
203. Grant	208. Harding	213. Eisenhower	218. Carter
204. McKinley	209. Coolidge	214. Kennedy	219. Reagan

Vignettes of buildings

Paper six by eight inches, image approximately two by four and a quarter inches.

300. Bureau of Engraving and Printing	308. Wakefield
301. Capitol: East View	309. Washington City Post Office
302. Capitol: Southeast View	310. White House: Northeast View
303. Lincoln Memorial	311. White House: South View
304. Monticello	312. White House: Southeast View
305. Mount Vernon	313. Independence Hall
306. Supreme Court	314. Washington Monument
307. Treasury Department	315. Jefferson Memorial

Government seals

Lithographed in color, 5⅜ inches in diameter. Item 400 is on 7½-inch paper; Item 402 is on 8- by 10-inch paper.
400. Obverse of Great Seal of U.S.

402. Department of the Treasury Seal.

Miscellaneous documents

410. Gettysburg Address, paper size 10 by 13 inches.

Sheets of U.S. paper money

The Bureau offers uncut sheets and partial sheets of U.S. $1 and $2 Federal Reserve notes in two series: 1976 $2 FRNs and 1985 $1 FRNs. The sheets are available in three sizes: full 32-note sheets ($1 only), half sheets of 16 notes each and four-note partial sheets.

Prices for over-the-counter sales are $7.50 for $1 four-note sheets and $12 for four $2 notes; $21.50 for 16-note $1 half sheets and $38.50 for 16-note $2 half sheets; and $40.50 for 32-note $1 sheets.

Mail orders are priced at $10.25 for four-note $1 sheets and $14.75 for $2 four-note sheets; $28 for 16-note $1 half sheets and $45 for $2 half sheets; and $47 for 32-note $1 sheets.

Money orders, bank-type cashier's checks and certified checks only are accepted for mail orders; no personal checks will be accepted. Orders should be sent to Bureau of Engraving and Printing, Uncut Currency/Souvenir Card Sales Program, 14th and C streets, S.W., Washington, D.C. 20228.

Customs regulations and prohibitive mailing costs prevent the Bureau from accepting orders for sheets of currency from customers outside the United States.

BEP officials

14th and C streets SW, Washington, D.C. 20228, Phone (202) 447-0193

Director	Robert J. Leuver
Deputy Director	Peter H. Daly
Assistant Director (Administration)	L. Paul Blackmer Jr.
Assistant Director (Operations)	Joseph M. DeBose Jr.
Assistant Director (Research and Engineering)	Milton J. Seidel

Bureau Directors

Director	Term
Spencer Morton Clark	Aug. 22, 1862 - Nov. 17, 1868
George B. McCartee	March 18, 1869 - Feb. 19, 1876
Henry C. Jewell	Feb. 21, 1876 - April 30, 1877
Edward McPherson	May 1, 1877 - Sept. 30, 1878
O.H. Irish	Oct. 1, 1878 - Jan. 27, 1883
Truman N. Burrill	March 30, 1883 - May 31, 1885
Edward O. Graves	June 1, 1885 - June 30, 1889
William M. Meredith	July 1, 1889 - June 30, 1893
Claude M. Johnson	July 1, 1893 - May 10, 1900
William M. Meredith	Nov. 23, 1900 - June 30, 1906
Thomas J. Sullivan	July 1, 1906 - May 4, 1908
Joseph E. Ralph	May 11, 1908 - Oct. 31, 1917
James L. Wilmeth	Dec. 10, 1917 - March 31, 1922
Louis A. Hill	April 1, 1922 - Feb. 14, 1924
Wallace W. Kirby	June 16, 1924 - Dec. 15, 1924
Alvin W. Hall	Dec. 22, 1924 - Dec. 15, 1954
Henry J. Holtzclaw	Dec. 16, 1954 - Oct. 8, 1967
James A. Conlon	Oct. 9, 1967 - July 1, 1977
Seymour Berry	June 30, 1978 - April 6, 1979
Harry R. Clements	July 15, 1979 - Jan. 3, 1983
Robert J. Leuver	Feb. 22, 1983 - present

Robert J. Leuver

Robert J. Leuver was appointed the nation's 21st Director of the Bureau of Engraving and Printing on Feb. 22, 1983, to replace resigned BEP Director Harry Clements. Leuver had served as Acting Director since Jan. 1, 1983.

Leuver joined the BEP in April 1979. Before his appointment to the top BEP post, he served as Deputy Director and as Assistant Director (Administration). Prior to joining the Bureau, Leuver worked five years in the Office of the Secretary of the Treasury as

Chief of the Treasury Employee Data and Payroll Division, and as program manager for Management Information Systems. He also served two years with ACTION, the parent organization of the Peace Corps, as chief of the Planning Division and as chief of the Management Analysis Staff.

In the private sector, Leuver was executive vice president of Claretians Inc. for four years and a financial officer for 14 years.

A native of Chicago, Leuver is married to the former Hilda Ortiz; they have one child, a daughter named Mary Ellen. Leuver graduat-ed from Loyola University at Los Angeles with majors in philosophy and English, and has a masters degree in sacred theology from Catholic University of America, Washington, D.C.

On Dec. 8, 1986, Leuver was awarded the Distinguished Presidential Rank Award for his outstanding service to the government. He has also succeeded in establishing a site near Fort Worth, Texas, for a currency producing facility to serve the Federal Reserve banks of Dallas, Kansas City and San Francisco.

Tours of the Bureau of Engraving and Printing

The Bureau of Engraving and Printing is charged with the responsibility for the production of major items of a financial character issued by the United States, the two most prominent of which are the government's paper money and postage stamps. A tour facility is available for the public to view the various operations in the manufacture of currency notes.

Location: The Bureau is located in Washington, D.C., at 14th and C streets S.W., just south of the Washington Monument and in the vicinity of the Smithsonian complex.

Tour admission and hours: The tour facility is open Monday through Friday (except legal holidays), 9 a.m. to 2 p.m. Admission is free and the tour takes approximately 25 minutes.

24-hour information: Current information can be obtained by dialing (202) 447-9709.

At the end of the tour, visitors can browse in the newly-remodeled Visitors' Center, which is situated at the 15th Street entrance to the Bureau.

The Visitors' Center offers exhibits aimed at all audiences, from small children to the handicapped to senior citizens and includes items of interest to both numismatists and philatelists.

At the center, visitors can use interactive exhibits which test their knowledge of the placement of special features on U.S. paper money or practice examining for defective currency. They may try their hand at distinguishing between real and counterfeit currency or they may test their knowledge with a paper money trivia game.

BEP products such as sheets of uncut currency and bags of shredded money are also obtainable at the center.

The Bureau is included on the Tourmobile "Washington Mall" Tour. Service operates continually during the day among 11 of Washington's landmarks. There is a Tourmobile stop across the street from the Bureau on 15th Street.

The Federal Reserve 7

History of the Federal Reserve System

A National Monetary Conference, appointed by Congress in 1908, sought to remedy money crises involving banks in the United States. Senator Nelson W. Aldrich was chairman.

A recognized depression had occurred in 1907, similar to previous crises in 1837, 1857, 1871 and 1894. The National Monetary Conference was to seek a solution to mitigating or eliminating these recurring dips in the economy.

The result of their efforts was reflected in the Federal Reserve Act, signed Dec. 23, 1913, by President Woodrow Wilson. The basic purpose of the new organization was "to give the country an elastic currency, to provide facilities for discounting commercial paper and to improve supervision of banking."

Founders of the Federal Reserve System believed that the amount of currency and credit would be balanced if issued against real bills, that is, short-term, self-liquidating paper based on commercial, industrial and agricultural transactions. Excessive changes in the domestic price level, they believed, could also be held in check if rules of the international gold standard were faithfully observed (see Chapter 13).

The founders also believed that if the money and credit system were based on real bills and gold, it would work more or less automatically; there would be no need to "manage" money. Finally, policies could be adapted closely to local conditions, and control by either politicians or Wall Street could be avoided if power were decentralized by regions.

The first decade

As the new Federal Reserve System felt its way, the act was amended from time to time primarily in the interest of greater operating efficiency: procedure for electing directors simplified, larger denomination Federal Reserve notes provided, trust powers of national banks broadened, etc.

Amendments were also passed to strengthen the financial structure of the Federal Reserve Banks. Member bank reserves were concentrated in the Federal Reserve Banks, gold was mobilized and provision was made to build up the surplus of Federal Reserve Banks. Some of these measures and the experience gained from a few years of operations enabled the Federal Reserve System to undertake successfully its job of helping to finance World War I.

After the war came inflation and sharp recession. Farmers were particularly hard hit, and changes in the act give a hint of the repercussions on the Federal Reserve System. The number of appointed members of the Federal Reserve Board was increased from five to six, and agricultural interests were given representation on the board. Not long after, the act was amended further to facilitate agricultural financing.

Although action was taken to strengthen the Federal Reserve System generally during the first decade, no major new tool of credit control was added. In 1920, it is true, the Federal Reserve Banks were given authority to impose graduated discount rates on banks which borrowed excessively, but this provision was repealed in 1923. As early as 1916 the board recommended that it be given power to raise reserve requirements in emergencies; this authority was not obtained until 17 years later.

Two early changes which, at first glance, seem only technical, really marked a departure from the strict real-bills principle. In 1916, Federal Reserve Banks were authorized to make direct advances to member banks on their promissory notes secured by government securities or eligible paper. The change was made primarily in the interest of operating efficiency, but it actually broke the direct link, so important to founders of the Federal Reserve System, between self-liquidating transactions and the flow of credit.

The next year the relation between real bills and Federal Reserve notes was officially changed. The original act provided that notes must be collateraled by an equivalent amount of eligible paper. Whenever a Federal Reserve Bank had to issue notes it would get them from the Federal Reserve Agent, depositing eligible paper as collateral. In practice, however, the bank could then cancel its liability for the notes by depositing gold with the Federal Reserve Agent and taking back the eligible paper. The close relationship between real bills and Federal Reserve notes was actually broken because, in essence, notes were collateraled by gold in addition to eligible paper. In 1917, an amendment to the act turned practice into law by permitting the use of gold as collateral for notes.

The "new era"

After the first decade came a period of legislative quiet — the age of "new era" complacency. Confidence in monetary policy as a solution to the economic troubles of the country rose to an all-time peak.

For several years after its organization, the Federal Reserve Board included in its annual reports a section describing legislation passed during the year and another section detailing legislation which it recommended for action. Proposed legislation in one year was likely to be reported as actual legislation the next. Congress acted promptly on most of these recommendations during the early years of the Federal Reserve System, particularly during World War I.

In the 1920s the situation was quite different. The section on proposed legislation did not appear in the annual reports for a number of years. No amendments were proposed or enacted for the years 1924-26 and only minor changes were made in most other years. Only one of the proposed changes was enacted in 1928, none in 1929.

The board's list of recommended legislation in 1929 included items like these: permit officers of mutual savings banks to be Class B or C directors of Federal Reserve Banks, clarify the section of the act which describes procedures for counting ballots in elections of Federal Reserve Bank directors, make it a federal offense to rob a Federal Reserve Bank or member bank, etc.

All this time, pressures were building up within the economy which were to show that the '20s were not so calm as this legislative status quo might suggest.

Depression and emergency

The early '30s were as hectic as the '20s were placid. Within five years the act was amended 23 times, and most of the action was confined to two years — 1933 and 1935.

Business activity was already well on its way downward in 1930. During that year a few minor changes were made in the act along lines recommended in the Board's annual report for the year before. No amendments were made in 1931.

It was not until 1932 that the act was changed materially. In that year and the one following, the Depression hit the banking system hard. Banks were caught by three developments: (1) panicky withdrawals of currency, (2) conversion of deposits and currency into gold, and (3) declining values on which bank assets were based. The result was a severe liquidity crisis in 1932 and a banking crisis in 1933.

In this atmosphere of emergency, reluctant permission was given to temporary deviations from some of the principles on which the original act was based. The Glass-Steagall Act, passed early in 1932, reduced further the relationship between real bills and Federal Reserve notes. Collateral requirements, first altered in 1917, were relaxed once again, this time because they stood in the way of an easy-money policy. The Federal Reserve wanted to meet the public's demand for liquidity and also to buy more government securities to help stimulate the economy. But the Federal Reserve System was hamstrung by collateral requirements. Federal Reserve Banks were required to hold 100 percent collateral, in the form of eligible paper and gold, against their notes. They also had to hold gold reserves equal to 40 percent of their note liabilities and 35 percent of their deposit liabilities. Any gold used as collateral against notes could also be used as reserve against notes, but not as reserve against deposits. With the amount of commercial paper shrinking with commerce, and gold disappearing into private hoards, there just was not enough to permit the necessary expansion of the money supply.

In order to break this logjam, Congress authorized Federal Reserve Banks to use government securities, in addition to eligible paper and gold, as collateral for Federal Reserve notes. The grant of authority was temporary, but after a number of extensions, it was finally made permanent in 1945.

The year 1932 also saw a further break in the link between real bills and credit. The public was seeking greater liquidity and safety by drawing out currency and converting to gold; the banks, in turn, sought liquidity by calling loans and selling assets on an already depressed market. A vicious spiral developed, feeding upon itself and making banks weaker and weaker. Banks could not get enough funds from Federal Reserve Banks to break out of this spiral because they did not have enough eligible paper to discount.

So the Glass-Steagall Act provided that Federal Reserve Banks could make loans to member banks on notes "secured to the satisfaction of such Federal Reserve Banks." But these loans were to be made only "in exceptional and exigent circumstances," the discount rate was to be at least 1 percent higher than the regular rate, and the authority was granted only for about a year. The real-bills principle was dying, but it was dying hard. After two extensions, a significant break with the real-bills principle came with the Banking Act of 1935 which removed most of the conditions, reduced the interest rate differential to 0.5 percent, and made this provision a permanent part of the act.

1933 crisis

The year 1933 was even more hectic. On March 9, five days after the new administration took office and in the midst of the banking holiday, the Emergency Banking Act of 1933 passed through the complete legislative process in a single day. E. A. Goldenweiser relates that a draft of the law was prepared by the General Counsel of the Federal Reserve Board in one night. Among its many provisions, the Emergency Banking Act amended the Federal Reserve Act in several respects. In an effort to make currency more readily available, Congress broadened the powers of the Federal Reserve Banks to issue Federal Reserve bank notes. In order to facilitate access to Federal Reserve Bank credit, it liberalized the 1932 provision authorizing loans to member banks on paper previously considered ineligible, and gave the Federal Reserve Banks power to make advances to individuals, partnerships and corporations on notes secured by government obligations.

Shortly after this, Congress passed the so-called Thomas Inflation Amendment. This law contained several measures affecting the Federal Reserve — especially provision for direct purchases of government securities from the Treasury — but actually amended the Federal Reserve Act, as such, in only one major respect. Curiously, this particular provision was anti-inflationary, not inflationary; it provided that the Federal Reserve Board could change reserve requirements if "an emergency existed by reason of credit expansion."

Up to this point, action was essentially of an emergency nature. The Banking Act of 1933, however, (passed, incidentally, just about when the depression hit bottom) undertook to get at some of the basic causes of the situation.

In the first place, it struck at speculative excesses to which banks had contributed. Banks were required to divorce themselves from security affiliates and to correct certain other undesirable practices which had developed during the 1920s. Behind some of these measures was increasing doubt about the real-bills principle as a means of channeling credit into "productive" uses. Thus one provision required the Reserve Banks to keep informed as to the uses which banks were making of Federal Reserve credit so as to avoid "undue use . . . for the speculative carrying of or trading in securities, real estate or commodities, or for any other purposes inconsistent with the maintenance of sound credit conditions."

Meanwhile the idea of regional autonomy was also being reassessed. Ten years earlier Federal Reserve Banks had discovered that their open-market operations, undertaken initially to bolster earnings, had noticeable effects on the money market. So in order to coordinate their activities, they set up an informal committee. The Banking Act of 1933 gave statutory basis to this committee and authorized the Federal Reserve Board to prescribe regulations for its conduct. No member of the board was a member of the committee, however, and any Reserve Bank could still decline to go along with the committee's policies.

In the case of dealings with foreign central banks, the change was more abrupt. Most of the negotiations on foreign matters had been carried on by the Federal Reserve Bank of

New York, which handled the financial operations involved. The Banking Act of 1933 changed that by providing that "no officer or other representative of any Federal Reserve Bank shall conduct negotiations of any kind with the officers or representatives of any foreign bank or banker without first obtaining the permission of the Federal Reserve Board."

Among the many provisions of the Banking Act designed to strengthen the banking system perhaps the most outstanding was deposit insurance. Although this measure related only indirectly to the Federal Reserve, Congress included it in the Federal Reserve Act. It remained there after a major revision in 1935 and was not removed until 1950 when it became the subject of a separate law.

In 1934 the government called in all gold (see Chapter 13). Actually, most of the rules of the gold standard as a guide for monetary policy had not been honored for years, but no indication of this can be seen in the Federal Reserve Act. Even in 1934 about the only hint that something had happened was the substitution of the words "gold certificates" for the word "gold" wherever it occurred. If we were to judge by the act alone, gold would seem to occupy today essentially the same position it did in 1913.

During the same year, however, two other developments reflected a widening concept of the Federal Reserve System's responsibilities. One was the grant of authority for Federal Reserve Banks to make working capital loans to existing industrial and commercial businesses unable to get credit through usual channels. This marked a further departure from the traditional idea that the Federal Reserve Banks should be simply bankers' banks. The other development had nothing to do with the Federal Reserve Act itself, but because it introduced a new principle of credit control it deserves special mention. It was a provision of the Securities Exchange Act which authorized the Federal Reserve Board to prescribe margins for stock purchases and sales. This was the first of the selective credit regulations and the permanent tool of policy.

Major revision

By 1935, business was on its way up again. Compared with 1933, unemployment was down by two million and industrial production was up 25 percent. All the time the economy was recovering from depression, ideas were fermenting. The result was the most comprehensive reappraisal and revision of the Federal Reserve Act in all its history. The Banking Act of 1935 contained many

important provisions which need not be discussed in detail; it clarified many sections of the act and generally strengthened the banking system. As had been mentioned, it marked a significant break with the real-bills doctrine. It also marked a further departure from the principle of regional decentralization. The organization of the Federal Reserve System as we know it dates from 1935.

The Federal Reserve Board became the Board of Governors of the Federal Reserve System. Congress provided terms of four years for the chairmanship and vice-chairmanship (both officials being eligible for reappointment), lengthened terms of board members from 12 to 14 years, and removed the Secretary of the Treasury and the Comptroller of the Currency (who had been serving as ex-officio members) from the board.

The internal structure of the Federal Reserve Banks was reorganized. Executive responsibilities, which had been divided between the chairman of the board of directors and non-statutory governor, were consolidated in the newly created position of president, and the chairmanship became a non-salaried position. The president and first vice president were to be appointed by the board of directors for five-year terms, subject to approval of the Board of Governors.

The makeup of the Federal Open Market Committee was changed even more drastically. The Banking Act of 1933 had set up a committee of 12 men, one from each Federal Reserve Bank. The Banking Act of 1935 reduced representation of the Federal Reserve Banks to five men and included all seven members of the Board of Governors.

Changes in powers went in the same direction as changes in organization. Decisions of the Open Market Committee were made binding on all Federal Reserve Banks. The Board of Governors was given power to change reserve requirements, within limits, without the necessity of declaring an emergency or securing approval of the President. Federal Reserve Banks were required to establish their discount rates every 14 days, or more often if deemed necessary by the board; this meant that the rate would come up for formal review and determination more frequently.

After 1935

The repairs of the early 1930s put the Federal Reserve Act in good working order. It has, in fact, weathered war and inflation, prosperity and recession without another major overhaul. But this is not to say that Federal Reserve operations have been standing still. For the most part, the Federal Reserve System has been able to adapt and up-date its techniques within the existing framework of the Act.

The recession of 1937-1938 passed with no noticeable repercussions on the act. Then came Munich, Poland, Dunkirk and Pearl Harbor. Congress made several changes to facilitate war financing. It gave the Federal Reserve power to buy limited amounts of securities direct from the Treasury and exempted war-loan accounts from reserve requirements, a temporary war-time measure. To ease reserve positions, Congress reduced the gold certificate backing required against Federal Reserve notes and deposits to 25 percent. Without changing the act, the President gave the Federal Reserve selective controls over consumer credit. The purpose was to fight inflation and help divert resources to military production. This executive order expired in 1947.

After the war the Federal Reserve continued the war-time policy of supporting the government securities market. The Board of Governors, concerned with the inability of the Federal Reserve System to restrain inflation and support securities prices at the same time, suggested additional powers — either new kinds of reserve requirements or an across-the-board increase in ordinary reserve requirements. Congress granted the board authority to raise requirements above regular limits in 1948. The provision was temporary, however, and expired about a year later.

When fighting broke out in Korea, the Federal Reserve System was given selective controls over consumer and real estate credit. As in World War II, selective controls were instituted by executive order without changing the act. The board requested controls on a permanent, stand-by basis but Congress did not comply.

In 1951 the Federal Reserve again sharpened its tools without legislative action. It negotiated an accord with the Treasury which ended the bond support program. This left the Federal Reserve System free to pursue a vigorous, contra-cyclical policy with its existing monetary instruments.

Legislative changes in the act since 1953, as in the preceding 18 years, have been relatively minor. More effective regulation of bank holding companies was added and certain sections regarding real estate loans by national banks were changed. In 1954 Federal Reserve Banks were permitted to pay out notes of other Reserve Banks, thus eliminating another vestige of the old idea of regional au-

tonomy. In 1958 authority for Reserve Banks to make commercial and industrial loans under Section 13b of the Federal Reserve Act was terminated by the Small Business Investment Act, effective August 21, 1959. And in 1959 Congress passed legislation affecting reserve requirements. Vault cash may be counted as legal reserves; the central reserve city classification has terminated; and the board was given broader authority in reclassifying banks for reserve purposes.

In the year 1958, a new problem emerged to confront the Federal Reserve System, one that had lain dormant for many years. That problem was a persistent deficit in the United States balance of payments. The United States was spending more abroad for imports, investments, military and economic aid than it received for exports of goods and services and for other transactions. One result was a substantial outflow of gold.

The Federal Reserve System reacted to this new problem on several fronts, mostly within the framework of the existing Act. In 1961, the so-called "bills only" policy of the Federal Open Market Committee was discontinued. Under "bills only," Federal Reserve System purchases and sales of securities had been confined primarily to short maturities, but the Open Market Committee now authorized operations throughout the maturity structure. The Committee hoped thereby "to encourage bank credit and monetary expansion while avoiding direct downward pressures on short-term interest rates and thus moderate outflows of short-term capital attracted by higher interest rates abroad."

In 1962, the Federal Open Market Committee authorized open market transactions in foreign currencies to "moderate and offset short-term pressures on the dollar in the foreign exchange markets." One technique devised by the Federal Reserve System to gain foreign funds to implement these transactions was the "swaps" arrangements first negotiated in August 1962 with several foreign central banks and with the Bank for International Settlements. In essence, the "swaps" provide us with reciprocal "lines of credit" which may be drawn upon when foreign currencies are needed to provide temporary relief from international flows of funds which might affect adversely U.S. balance-of-payments and gold position.

Congress also, for balance-of-payments reasons, amended the Federal Reserve Act in 1962 "to exempt for three years deposits of foreign governments and certain foreign institutions from regulation by the Board of

Governors as to rates of interest that member banks may pay on time deposits."

Finally, in a 1963 measure unrelated to the balance of payments, the Federal Reserve Act was amended to authorize Federal Reserve System issuance of $1 and $2 Federal Reserve notes. This legislation was aimed at eliminating Treasury silver certificates of those denominations and thus making "monetary silver available for coinage."

Since 1963, several changes have been made in the way the international and domestic money system operates (see Chapter 13). In 1965, Congress passed legislation to repeal the remaining requirement for 25 percent gold backing of commercial banks' deposits at Federal Reserve banks, freeing about $5 billion of the country's gold stock for additional sale to dollar-holding foreign governments and for future growth of the domestic money supply.

That same year the Coinage Act of 1965 was passed, eliminating silver in United States coins. Despite these measures, the gold and silver draining out of Treasury coffers continued at a steady, debilitating rate.

In 1967, then, President Johnson signed a bill authorizing the eventual end of the redemption of silver certificates with silver bullion, setting a June 24, 1968, deadline for their redemption. Reserve requirements for Federal Reserve notes, United States notes and Treasury notes of 1890 were removed by Congress in March 1968.

(For more information on Federal Reserve notes, see Chapter 8.)

Congress from time to time has introduced legislation to curb the power of the Federal Reserve System. The latest of these attempts was a bill, strongly opposed by the Federal Reserve System, recommended by the House Banking and Currency committee in October 1973, calling for an outside audit of the Federal Reserve System every three years. So far the idea has not been enacted into law.

In 1974, the System joined with the Treasury in putting into effect regulations prohibiting the export, melting or treating of the 1-cent piece to help offset the cent shortage.

With the International Banking Act of 1978, the Federal Reserve Board gained the authority to impose reserve requirements and interest rate ceilings on branches and agencies of foreign banks in the United States. The act also gave the board the authority to grant loans to foreign banks in the United States and to limit interstate banking activities.

Under the Depository Institutions Deregulation and Monetary Control Act of 1980, Federal Reserve Banks receive and hold on deposit the reserve or clearing account deposits of depository institutions. In addition, the act requires the Fed to open its discount window to any nonmember depository institution that maintains transaction accounts or nonpersonal time deposits, on the same basis as to banks that are members of the Federal Reserve System.

The Federal Reserve adopted a new operating procedure Oct. 6, 1979, that changed the emphasis from tight control on interest rates to better short-run control of the money supply (i.e., to lower inflation) at the expense of short-term volatility in interest rates. The money supply is now controlled by adjustments to the federal funds rate, which influences banks to buy or sell assets, thus changing the money supply. If the federal funds rate is higher than rates for other assets, banks tend to sell more assets and place the funds into the federal funds market, decreasing the money supply. Conversely, a lower federal funds rate causes an increase in the money supply — inflation.

The strength wielded by the Federal Reserve, and its chairman, plus its relative freedom to control the money supply and interest rates without congressional curbs, has given it considerable power over the economy.

Function of the Federal Reserve System

The Federal Reserve System as it operates today consists of the Board of Governors in Washington; the 12 Federal Reserve Banks, their 25 branches and other facilities situated throughout the United States; the Federal Open Market Committee; the Federal Advisory Council; the Consumer Advisory Council; the Thrift Institutions Advisory Council; and the member commercial banks, which include all national banks in the United States and any state-chartered banks that have voluntarily joined the Federal Reserve System. Some of these functions are outlined below.

Board of Governors

Broad supervisory powers are vested in the Board of Governors, which has its offices in Washington. The board is composed of seven members appointed by the President by and with the advice and consent of the Senate. The chairman of the Board of Governors is by executive order a member of the National Advisory Council on International Monetary and Financial Policies.

The board determines general monetary, credit and operating policies for the Federal Reserve System as a whole and formulates the rules and regulations necessary to carry out the purposes of the Federal Reserve Act. The board's principal duties consist of exerting an influence over credit conditions and supervising the Federal Reserve Banks and member banks.

POWER TO INFLUENCE CREDIT CONDITIONS

The Board is given the power, within statutory limitations, to fix the requirements concerning reserves to be maintained by member banks against deposits and the power to determine the maximum rate of interest that may be paid by member banks on their time and savings deposits. Another important instrument of credit control is found in open market operations. The members of the Board of Governors are also members of the Federal Open Market Committee. The Board of Governors reviews and determines the discount rates charged by the Federal Reserve Banks on their discounts and advances. For the purpose of preventing excessive use of credit for the purchase or carrying of securities, the board is authorized to regulate the amount of credit that may be initially extended and subsequently maintained on any security (with certain exceptions).

Pursuant to the provisions of the Defense Production Act of 1950 and Executive Order 10480 of Aug. 14, 1953, the board prescribes regulations under which the Federal Reserve Banks act as fiscal agents of certain government departments and agencies in guaranteeing loans made by banks and other private financing institutions to finance contracts for the procurement of materials or services which the guaranteeing agencies consider necessary for the national defense.

SUPERVISION OF FEDERAL RESERVE BANKS

The board is authorized to make examinations of the Federal Reserve Banks, to require statements and reports from such banks, to supervise the issue and retirement of Federal Reserve notes, to require the establishment or discontinuance of branches of Federal Reserve Banks, and to exercise supervision over all relationships and transactions of those banks with foreign banks. The Board of Governors reviews and follows the examination and supervisory activities of the Federal Reserve Banks with a view to furthering coordination of policies and practices.

SUPERVISION OF MEMBER BANKS

The board has jurisdiction over the admission of state banks and trust companies to membership in the Federal Reserve System, the termination of membership of such banks, the establishment of branches by such banks, and the approval of bank mergers and consolidations where the resulting institution will be a state member bank. It receives copies of condition reports submitted by them to the Federal Reserve Banks. It has power to examine all member banks and the affiliates of member banks and to require condition reports from them. It has authority to require periodic and other public disclosure of information with respect to an equity security of a member state bank that is held by 500 or more persons.

It establishes minimum standards with respect to installation, maintenance and operation of security devices and procedures by member state banks. It has authority to issue cease and desist orders in connection with violations of law or unsafe or unsound banking practices by member state banks and to remove directors or officers of such banks in certain circumstances, and it may, in its discretion, suspend member banks from the use of the credit facilities of the Federal Reserve System for making undue use of bank credit for speculative purposes or for any other purpose inconsistent with the maintenance of sound credit conditions.

The board may grant authority to member banks to establish branches in foreign countries or dependencies or insular possessions of the United States, to invest in the stocks of banks or corporations engaged in international or foreign banking, or to invest in foreign banks. It also charters, regulates, and supervises certain corporations that engage in foreign or international banking and financial activities.

The board is authorized to issue general regulations permitting interlocking relationships in certain circumstances between member banks and organizations dealing in securities or between member banks and other banks.

OTHER FUNCTIONS

Under the Bank Holding Company Act of 1956 the board is required to pass upon certain acquisitions of bank stock or assets by bank holding companies and to make determinations relating to engagement in nonbanking activities and to the acquisition and retention of nonbank stock by bank holding companies. Under the Change in Bank Control Act of 1978, the board is required to review other bank acquisitions. Under the Truth in Lending Act, the board is required to prescribe regulations to assure a meaningful disclosure by lenders of credit terms so that consumers will be able to compare more readily the various credit terms available and avoid the uninformed use of credit, and with respect to issuance of credit cards and liabilities for their unauthorized use.

Under the International Banking Act of 1978, the board has the authority to impose reserve requirements and interest rate ceilings on branches and agencies of foreign banks in the United States, to grant loans to them, to provide them access to Federal Reserve services, and to limit their interstate banking activities. The board also is the rule-making authority for the Equal Credit Opportunity Act, the Home Mortgage Disclosure Act, the Fair Credit Billing Act, and certain provisions of the Federal Trade Commission Act as they apply to banks.

EXPENSES

To meet its expenses and pay the salaries of its members and its employees, the board makes semiannual assessments upon the Federal Reserve Banks in proportion to their capital stock and surplus.

CURRENCY ISSUE

An important function of the Federal Reserve System is to ensure that the economy has enough currency and coin to meet the public's demand. Currency and coin are put into or retired from circulation by the Federal Reserve Banks, which use depository institutions as the channel of distribution. The Federal Reserve Banks issue Federal Reserve notes, which constitute the bulk of money in circulation. These notes are obligations of the United States and are a prior lien upon the assets of the issuing Federal Reserve Bank. They are issued against a pledge by the Reserve Bank with the Federal Reserve agent of collateral security consisting of gold certificates, paper discounted or purchased by the bank, and direct obligations of the United States.

OTHER POWERS

The Federal Reserve Banks are empowered to act as clearinghouses and as collecting agents for depository institutions in the collection of checks and other instruments. They are also authorized to act as depositories and fiscal agents of the United States and to excercise other banking functions specified in the Federal Reserve Act. They perform a number of important functions in connection with the issue and redemption of United States government securities.

Sources of information

READING ROOM

A reading room where persons may inspect records that are available to the public is located in Room B-1122 at the board's headquarters, 20th and C streets NW., Washington, D.C. Information regarding the availability of records may be obtained by calling 202-452-3684.

FILMS

The board has available for public use a variety of 16mm sound films relating to money, credit and the Federal Reserve, and a filmstrip for consumers explaining the basic provisions of the Truth in Lending Act. For further information call 202-452-3244.

PUBLICATIONS

Among publications issued by the board are *The Federal Reserve System — Purposes and Functions,* and these short pamphlets suitable for classroom use: "What Truth in Lending Means to You," "U.S. Currency," "If You Borrow To Buy Stock," "Fair Credit Billing," "Alice in Debitland," "If You Use A Credit Card," "Consumer Handbook," "Consumer Handbook on Adjustable Rate Mortgages," "Consumer Handbook to Credit Protection Laws," "Federal Reserve Glossary," "Guide to Federal Reserve Regulations," "How to File A Consumer Credit Complaint," "Instructional Materials of the Federal Reserve System," and several pamphlets describing the Equal Credit Opportunity Act. Multiple copies of these pamphlets are available free of charge. Information regarding publications may be obtained by writing Publication Services, Mail Stop 138, Board of Governors of the Federal Reserve System, Washington, D.C. 20551. Phone 202-452-3244.

EMPLOYMENT

Inquiries regarding employment should be addressed to Director, Division of Personnel, Board of Governors of the Federal Reserve System, Washington, D.C. 20551.

PROCUREMENT

Firms desiring to do business with the board should address their inquiries to Director, Division of Support Services, at the above address.

For further information, contact the Office of Public Affairs, Board of Governors, Federal Reserve System, Washington, D.C. 20551. Phone, 202-452-3204 or 452-3215.

Source: U.S. Government Manual

Federal Reserve Bank Branches and Offices

Bank Branch or Facility	Chairman Deputy Chairman	President First Vice President	Vice President in Charge of Branch
Boston*........	Joseph A. Baute	Frank E. Morris	
	George N. Hatsopoulos	Robert W. Eisenmenger	
New York*.....	John R. Opel	E. Gerald Corrigan	
	Virginia A. Dwyer	Thomas M. Timlen	
Buffalo	Mary Ann Lambertsen		John T. Keane
Philadelphia* ..	Nevius M. Curtis	Edward G. Boehne	
	George E. Bartol III	William H. Stone Jr.	
Cleveland*.....	Charles W. Parry	Vacancy	
	E. Mandell de Windt	William H. Hendricks	
Cincinnati	Owen B. Butler		Charles A. Cerino
Pittsburgh.....	James E. Haas		Harold J. Swart
Richmond*.....	Leroy T. Canoles Jr.	Robert P. Black	
	Robert A. Georgine	Jimmie R. Monhollon	
Baltimore.....	Gloria L. Johnson		Robert D. McTeer Jr.
Charlotte	Wallace J. Jorgenson		Albert D. Tinkelenberg
(Culpepper Communications and Records Center)			John G. Stoides
Atlanta*.......	Bradley Currey Jr.	Robert P. Forrestal	
	Larry L. Prince	Jack Guynn	Delmar Harrison
Birmingham...	Margaret E.M. Tolbert		Fred R. Herr
Jacksonville...	Andrew A. Robinson		James D. Hawkins
Miami........	Robert D. Apelgren		Patrick K. Barron
Nashville	C. Warren Neel		Jeffrey J. Wells
New Orleans ..	Caroline K. Theus		Henry H. Bourgaux
Chicago*	Robert J. Day	Silas Keehn	
	Marcus Alexis	Daniel M. Doyle	
Detroit	Robert E. Brewer		Roby L. Sloan
St. Louis.......	W.L. Hadley Griffin	Thomas C. Melzer	
	Robert L. Virgil Jr.	Joseph P. Garbarini	
Little Rock....	James R. Rodgers		John F. Breen
Louisville.....	Raymond M. Burse		James E. Conrad
Memphis	Katherine H. Smythe		Paul I. Black Jr.
Minneapolis....	John B. Davis Jr.	Gary H. Stern	
	Michael W. Wright	Thomas E. Gainor	
Helena	Warren H. Ross		Robert F. McNellis
Kansas City	Irvine O. Hockaday Jr.	Roger Guffey	
	Robert G. Lueder	Henry R. Czerwinski	
Denver	James E. Nielson		Enis Alldredge Jr.
Oklahoma City	Patience S. Latting		William G. Evans
Omaha	Kenneth L. Morrison		Robert D. Hamilton
Dallas.........	Bobby R. Inman	Robert H. Boykin	Tony J. Salvaggio
	Hugh G. Robinson	William H. Wallace	Sammie C. Clay
El Paso	Mary Carmen Saucedo		J.Z. Rowe
Houston......	Walter M. Mischer Jr.		Thomas H. Robertson
San Antonio...	Robert F. McDermott		
San Francisco ..	Fred W. Andrew	Robert T. Parry	
	Robert F. Erburu	Carl E. Powell	
Los Angeles ...	Richard C. Seaver		Thomas C. Warren
Portland......	Paul E. Bragdon		Angelo S. Carella
Salt Lake City .	Don M. Wheeler		E. Ronald Liggett
Seattle........	John W. Ellis		Gerald R. Kelly

* Additional offices of these banks are located at Lewiston, Maine 04240; Windsor Locks, Conn. 06096; Cranford, N.J. 07016; Jericho, N.Y. 11753; Utica at Oriskany, N.Y. 13424; Columbus, Ohio 43216; Columbia, S.C. 29210; Charleston, W.V. 25311; Des Moines, Iowa 50306; Indianapolis, Ind. 46204; and Milwaukee, Wis. 53202.

Source: Federal Reserve Bulletin

Board of Governors

Chairman. . . . . Alan Greenspan*
Vice Chairman . . . . Manuel H. Johnson
Member. . . . . Martha R. Seger
Member. . . . . Wayne D. Angell
Member. . . . . H. Robert Heller
Member. . . . . Vacant
Member. . . . . Vacant

* Nominated in June by President Ronald Reagan to replace Paul A. Volcker, who was to resign in August 1987 at the end of his second four-year term. As of June 13, Greenspan had not been confirmed by the Senate.

U.S. Paper Money   8

Pre-federal paper money
When paper money was issued in America, it became the first authorized paper money to be issued by a government in the western world.

American paper money was produced in a number of different phases before the Bureau of Engraving and Printing effectively took over sole production in 1862.

Colonial Currency
The Massachusetts Bay Colony financed a military expedition to Canada in 1690 by issuing bills of credit. Other military campaigns were financed by other colonies in a similar way.

Revolutionary War State Issues
The states also issued money during the American Revolution to cover their governmental and military expenditures.

Some of these notes carried messages freighted with propaganda, like the Maryland issue of July 25, 1775, which depicted George III trampling on the Magna Carta while setting fire to an American city, and American Liberty trampling on slavery while backed by a large army.

Continental Currency
Beginning in the middle of 1775, the Continental Congress issued paper money with which to purchase war supplies from foreign countries. The Congress asked the states to redeem the currency, but most states were preoccupied with the need to support their own military activities; consequently, taxes were neglected.

The English forbade the circulation of the money in areas they occupied and attempted to undermine public confidence in it in other areas, often counterfeiting the money.

By 1780, economic circumstances had combined to reduce Continental Currency to one-fortieth of its original face value and the Continental Congress ceased printing it.

1812 interest-bearing notes
When the war of 1812 began, the U.S. government once again found itself being forced to borrow money. In 1812, Congress began issuing Treasury Notes to cover short-term loans.

Five series of these notes were authorized for issue during the war, between 1812 and 1815, in denominations ranging from $3 to $1,000.

The notes were not legal tender, but were receivable for all public dues and payable to public creditors. All notes under $100 were payable to the bearer on demand. The $5 notes did not bear interest.

Obsolete notes
Between 1800 and 1865, during periods when the need for a medium of exchange exceeded the amounts of available specie, numerous banks and companies began printing their own paper currency. Although states were Constitutionally forbidden to issue their own money, a large number of state-chartered banks circumvented this problem by issuing bank notes as private entities, which were not expressly restrained by the Constitution.

Although commonly called "broken-bank notes," not all banks which issued this currency failed. Some of the issuers successfully liquidated and others converted into national banks.

The tremendous demand for currency created by the Civil War eventually exceeded the production capacities of the private banking system and the governments of both the north and south began to print national currency. The end of currency production in the private sector was hastened by steep taxes levied by the federal government on private emissions.

Before the private banking era was over, bank notes had been produced by such diverse concerns as railroads, insurance companies, mining companies and pharmacies.

United States large-sized paper money catalog

Early federal issues

In 1862 the United States government issued its first legal tender paper money although government obligations were issued periodically between 1812 and 1861 in the form of interest-bearing Treasury notes. These bore interest at 5 or 6 percent and were payable after two years.

The demand notes were authorized by Congressional Acts of July 17 and Aug. 5, 1861. They were soon nicknamed "greenbacks," a term that became so popular it was passed on through the years and is heard even today, most often when paper money specialists, or syngraphists, get together.

The demand notes bear the signatures of various employees of the Treasury Department who signed their own names, as well as the words "For The" for the Register of the Treasury and Treasurer of the United States. Demand notes do not carry the Treasury Seal nor the actual names of the Register and Treasurer, and are unique in that respect.

With this beginning, the United States soon settled down and began production of paper money as it is known today, that is, with series year, signatures of the Treasury officials, and so on.

Notes issued until 1928 were large-sized notes, commonly called "horse blankets," sometimes known as "saddle blankets."

Interest-bearing Treasury notes

The constitutionality of the Treasury notes issued between 1812 and 1861 was an ever-present topic in Congress. Most interest-bearing notes bore interest at 5 or 6 percent and were payable after two years. A few 60-day notes, in denominations of $50 through $5,000, were issued. With few exceptions all of the 121,000-plus notes that were issued have been redeemed and are unavailable to collectors.

Demand notes of 1861

Demand notes of 1861, authorized by the July 17 and Aug. 5, 1861, Acts of Congress, were issued in three denominations: $5, $10 and $20. Each note bears the first authorization date, July 17, and also the date of issue, Aug. 10. These notes were not originally legal tender but were later specified as such. The major portion of the face designs are identical to the legal tender notes of the same denominations.

The demand notes were made payable, on demand, by the Assistant Treasurer of the United States at Boston, New York, Philadelphia, St. Louis and Cincinnati. The $5 note features a portrait of Alexander Hamilton at right and a statue of Columbia at left. Lincoln is portrayed at left on the $10 note with a woman representing Art at right. The $20 note features Liberty.

Legal tender notes

Legal tender notes consisted of five issues. The first issue of March 10, 1862, was produced in $5, $10, $20, $50, $100, $500 and $1,000 denominations. Issue two was confined to $1 and $2 notes, although the face design does indicate that a $3 denomination was planned, but not released. The third issue, dated March 10, 1863, was printed in the same denominations as the first issue, but changes were made in the back design.

The fourth issue consisted of series 1869, 1875, 1878, 1880, 1907, 1917 and 1923, with all except the 1869 notes carrying the designation "United States note." The 1869 series was designated as "Treasury note." Also, with the 1869 series, the U.S. introduced paper with silk threads as a deterrent to counterfeiting.

Denominations in the fourth issue are as follows:

1869 series, $1, $2, $5, $10, $20, $50, $100, $500, and $1,000.

1874 series, $1, $2, $50, and $500.

1875 series, $1, $2, $5, $10, $20, $50, $100, and $500.

1878 series, $1, $2, $5, $10, $20, $50, $100, $500, $1,000, $5,000 and $10,000.

1880 series, $1, $2, $5, $10, $20, $50, $100, $500 and $1,000.

1907 series, $5.

1917 series, $1, and $2.

1923 series, $1, and $10.

The fifth issue was limited to the $10 denomination.

Face designs on the first and third issues are:

$5, Alexander Hamilton on lower right, with Washington Capitol statue of Columbia on left side.

$10, Vignette of Lincoln, upper right, allegorical female representing Art, on left.

$20, Liberty with shield and sword.

$50, Alexander Hamilton. Different pose than on $5 note.

$100, American eagle. This was the first note to feature the American eagle.

$500, Albert Gallatin, Secretary of the Treasury 1801-1813.

$1,000, Robert Morris, a signer of the Declaration of Independence, and Superintendent of Finance 1781-1784.

Face designs on second issue:

$1, Vignette of Salmon P. Chase, Secretary of the Treasury, 1861-1864.

$2, Capitol building and Thomas Jefferson.

The obligation on the first, second and third issues states "United States will pay the Bearer ... Dollars at the Treasury of New York."

Back designs of the first, second and third issues are:

First and third issues, denominations $5 to $1,000, feature lathe-work design with two types of inscriptions, commonly called obligations.

Type one states: "This note is Legal Tender for all debts public and private, except on duties on Imports and Interest on Public Debt, and is exchangeable for U.S. Six percent Twenty Years Bonds, redeemable at the pleasure of the U. States after Five Years."

Type two states: "This note is a Legal Tender for all debts public and private, except duties on Imports and Interest on the Public Debt, and is receivable in payment for all Loans made to the United States."

The type two inscription (obligation) appears in the center of lathe-work design on the $1 and $2 notes of the second issue.

Face designs on the fourth issue are:

$1, 1869 to 1917, head of Washington facing left, and Columbus sighting land.

$1, 1923, head of Washington facing right.

$2, Capitol building and vignette of Thomas Jefferson.

$5, "Pioneer Family" and bust of Andrew Jackson.

$10, 1869 to 1880, Daniel Webster, and presentation of Indian Princess, representing introduction of Old World to the New. Popular name of this note is "Jackass Note," so-called because the eagle on face design, when note is inverted, appears to be a jackass.

$10, 1923, Andrew Jackson.

$20, Alexander Hamilton and figure of Victory with shield and sword.

$50, 1869, Henry Clay, and female holding statue of Mercury.

$50, 1874 to 1880, Benjamin Franklin, with figure of Liberty.

$100, Abraham Lincoln, with allegorical figure of Architecture.

$500, 1869, John Quincy Adams.

$500, 1874 to 1880, Major General Joseph K. Mansfield.

$1,000, Dewitt Clinton, governor of New York.

$5,000, James Madison.

$10,000, Andrew Jackson.

The major portion of the face designs in the fourth issue remained the same. The obligation states "United States will pay the Bearer ... Dollars." The words "At the Treasury in New York" which appeared on the first three issues were removed and the single word "Washington" substituted on the 1869 series, and "Washington, D.C." on later issues. Stars following serial numbers on the 1869 series do not indicate replacement notes.

Back designs of the fourth issue differ from previous issues in that the words "and is receivable in payment for all Loans made to the United States" have been removed from the Type Two clause. Throughout the fourth issue, except on Series 1923 $1 and $10 notes, the warning against counterfeiting, which first appeared on the 1869 series, is used.

Series 1923 $1 has plain back, unlike the ornate lathe-work of earlier issues.

Series 1923 $10 notes have lathe-work design.

Face design of the fifth issue, consisting of a $10 note, features a bison in center, with portraits of Lewis and Clark on sides.

Back design of the fifth issue shows Columbus standing between two pillars and two scrolls which carry the inscription found on the fourth issue.

Compound interest Treasury notes

The Congressional Acts of March 3, 1863, and June 30, 1864, authorized $10, $20, $50, $100, $500 and $1,000 compound interest Treasury notes. They bear the following inscription: "Three years after date the United States will pay the bearer ... dollars with interest at the rate of six percent compounded semi-annually" on the face. The back has "By Act of Congress, this note is legal tender for ... dollars but bears interest at six percent only at maturity as follows [table of interest]. This sum ... will be paid the holder for principal and interest at maturity of note three years from date."

These notes were issued to raise money to finance the Civil War.

Interest-bearing notes

The interest-bearing notes were the successors to the Treasury notes which were issued between 1812 and 1861 and were issued for the same purpose as the compound interest Treasury notes, to raise money to finance the Civil War.

One- and two-year notes bearing interest at 5 percent were authorized by the Act of March 3, 1863. Three-year notes bearing 7.3 percent interest were authorized by the Acts of July 17, 1861, June 30, 1864, and March 3, 1865, and were issued at three different times. These three-year notes had five attached coupons which were detached and redeemed at six-month intervals.

The one-year notes were issued in denominations of $10 to $5,000, the two-year notes in denominations of $50 to $1,000 and the three-year notes ranged from $50 to $5,000. All are extremely rare due to immediate redemption on the expiration date.

Currency certificates of deposit

The Secretary of the Treasury was authorized to issue currency certificates of deposit by the Act of June 8, 1872. Denominations of the notes were $5,000 and $10,000. The $5,000 notes were payable on demand in U.S. notes at the place of deposit and were also accepted in settlement of clearinghouse balances at the locations where deposits were made. The $10,000 notes were receivable on deposit without interest from national banking houses but were not to be included in the legal reserves.

Authorization of these large denomination certificates was repealed March 14, 1900.

Silver certificates

The large-sized silver certificates were authorized by Acts of Congress dated Feb. 28, 1878, and Aug. 4, 1886. There were five issues from series 1878 to series 1923.

The first issue, Series 1878 and 1880, consisted of $10, $20, $50, $100, $500 and $1,000 denominations. The front side states that "There have been deposited with the Treasurer of the United States at Washington, D.C. payable at his office to the bearer on demand ... Silver Dollars." "Certificate of Deposit" is inscribed on the notes. All certificates of the 1878 series and one of the notes in the 1880 series are countersigned by Assistant Treasurers of the United States at New York and bear the signatures of G.W. Scofield and James Gilfillan.

Face designs of the first issue feature the following:

$10, Robert Morris, signer of the Declaration of Independence, and U.S. senator.

$20, Stephen Decatur, naval commander.

$50, Edward Everett, governor of Massachusetts, U.S. senator and secretary of state under President Fillmore.

$100, James Monroe, fifth president.

$500, Charles Sumner, U.S. senator and leader in the abolition of slavery.

$1,000, William L. Marcy, governor of New York, secretary of war under President Polk and secretary of state under President Pierce.

The Treasury seal on countersigned certificates of 1878 has the key in red seal pointing to the right instead of to the left. This error was corrected on the 1880 series.

The face design of Series 1878-1880 silver certificates has the word SILVER in large letters appearing on black scroll work. The inscription says "This Certificate is Receivable for Customs, Taxes, and all Public Dues and When So Received May be Reissued."

The second issue of silver certificates consists of Series 1886, 1891 and 1908. The 1886 series was printed in denominations of $1, $2, $5, $10 and $20. The 1891 series included these, but added denominations of $50, $100 and $1,000. Only the $10 note was issued in Series 1908. On the front of Series 1886, 1891 and 1908 appears the wording "This certifies that there have been deposited in the Treasury of the United States ... Silver Dollars payable to the Bearer on Demand."

Face designs of the second issue are:

$1, Series 1886 and 1891, Martha Washington.

$2, Series 1886, General Winfield Scott Hancock.

$2, Series 1891, William Windom, twice Secretary of the Treasury.

$5, Series 1886 and 1891, Ulysses S. Grant.

$10, Series 1886 and 1908, Thomas A. Hendricks, U.S. vice president.

$20, Series 1886 and 1891, Daniel Manning, Secretary of the Treasury.

$50, Series 1891, Edward Everett.

$100, Series 1891, James Monroe.

$1,000, Series 1891, William L. Marcy.

Back design of the 1886 series features green overall lathe-work. Large numbers denoting the denomination also are used. The certification is identical to that on the 1878 and 1880 series. The back design of the $5 note is unique, featuring five silver dollars with the obverse of one dated 1886.

The back design of Series 1891 and 1908 features a more open lathe-work presentation. Large numbers, and on some denominations, Roman numerals, indicate the denomination. The certification remains the same as on previous series.

The third issue of silver certificates, Series 1896, is one of the most popular and deemed by collectors as the most beautiful series ever produced by the United States. Titled the "Educational Series," the notes were designed or redesigned by Thomas F. Morris, designer and chief of the Engraving Division of the Bureau of Engraving and Printing from Nov. 1, 1893, to June 30, 1897. Other designers of this famed series were Will H. Low, $1; Edwin H. Blashfield, $2; and Walter Shirlaw, $5. Known engravers of the series were Charles Schlecht and George F.C. Smillie.

Claude M. Johnson, who was chief of the Bureau, is credited with advocating the printing of more artistic and representative designs in paper money, and the original plan was to have educational designs on all silver certificate denominations from $1 to $1,000 but only the $1, $2 and $5 were released. The $10 was designed but never released, and records do not indicate that higher denominations were ever designed.

The fronts of these educational notes are as follows:

$1, History Instructing Youth, with the background featuring the Washington Monument and the Capitol building. The U.S. Constitution is shown in an open book, and the names of 23 great Americans are featured in the border design.

$2, Steam and Electricity, represented by two youthful figures being presented to Commerce and Manufacture, represented by two mature female figures. Another mature female figure, Science, is making the presentation.

$5, Electricity, represented by a winged female, is depicted as a controlling factor in world history.

The obligation to redeem the notes in silver dollars is carried on the front of all three notes.

The backs of the Educational notes feature portraits of George and Martha Washington on the $1; inventors Samuel Morse and Robert Fulton on the $2; and Gens. Ulysses Grant and Philip Sheridan on the $5.

The fourth issue, Series 1899, was released in three denominations, $1, $2 and $5. The front design of the $1 features the American eagle with portraits of Lincoln and Grant. The $2 note portrays Washington between figures representing Mechanics and Agriculture, and the $5 note features Ta-to-ka-in-yna-ka, Running Antelope, a Sioux Indian.

There is an interesting story behind the printing of the $5 note. Running Antelope was a member of the Oncpapa or Hunkpapa Sioux tribe. The portrait used on the note came from a photograph taken in 1872 for the Bureau of Ethnology; however, Running Antelope wore a headdress with three feathers which projected too high for a good image on the note. To correct the problem, an employee of the Bureau of Engraving and Printing posed wearing a warbonnet belonging to another tribe, and the headdress was cut out and superimposed on the photograph of Running Antelope; George F.C. Smillie engraved the design in November of 1899. The headdress, ironically, belonged to the Pawnee tribe, rivals of the tribe of Running Antelope.

Back designs for the fourth issue were modified from those of earlier issues. The denomination is indicated by large numerals, with the Roman numeral "V" in the center design of the $5 note. The notes carry the same inscription on the backs as do earlier issues.

The fifth issue of silver certificates, Series 1923, consists of two denominations, $1 and $5. Washington is portrayed on the $1 and Lincoln on the $5. On the latter note, Lincoln is shown in the center of a circular design and as a result this note is sometimes called the "porthole" note.

Certification on the fifth issue is the same as on previous issues. However, the inscription, previously part of the back design, was

moved to the front at left of the seal. The
back of the $1 note in the fifth issue features
the words "United States of America" prominently in the center. The $5 note shows the
front of the Great Seal of the United States
and the words "United States of America."

Refunding certificates

The U.S. government authorized refunding
certificates, on Feb. 26, 1879, to reduce the
circulation of the "fiat" greenbacks when specie payments were resumed. The more notes
that were converted to non-legal tender obligations, the less cold, hard, cash that the
Treasury had to pay out on its paper obligations. The face design of the notes, issued in
$10 denomination only, bears the portrait of
Benjamin Franklin (most probably based on
the painting by James Barton Longacre).

The 4 percent annual interest was to accumulate indefinitely. However, by 1907 the
$10 note was worth $21.30 so Congress
passed a law that allowed the government to
stop payment on July 1 of that year.

Treasury or coin notes

The Legal Tender Act of July 14, 1890, authorized Series 1890 and 1891 coin notes in
denominations of $1 to $1,000. The Treasury
Department used these notes to purchase silver bullion. It was left to the Secretary of the
Treasury to decide if gold or silver would be
paid out when the notes were redeemed. The
redemption of the notes almost bankrupted
the Treasury by 1893 and caused a major
panic.

National bank notes

The national bank notes were authorized
by the National Currency Act of Feb. 25,
1863, and National Banking Act of June 3,
1864, and were issued by chartered banks
from 1863 to 1928.

During the Civil War coins of gold and silver were hoarded and practically disappeared
from circulation. The unsecured legal tender
notes commonly known as "greenbacks"
were not popular and not readily accepted by
skeptical persons having no confidence in the
government's promise to pay.

Although Secretary of the Treasury Chase
recommended a national bank currency secured by government bonds in his financial
report of December 1861, the National Currency Act was not passed until February
1863. Spencer M. Clark, Chief of Construction of the Treasury Department, as early as
April 1862 conceived the plan to have the
national banks issue their own currency. The
plan was endorsed by then Secretary of the
Treasury Salmon P. Chase, who directed

Clark to invite artists and engravers to submit proposals and designs.

Clark had previously suggested that historic pictures be used as back designs for the
"greenbacks" of 1862 claiming that these designs offered greater protection against counterfeiting. His proposed designs were not
adopted for the legal tender notes, but were
adopted for the national bank notes issued
under Secretary of the Treasury W.P. Fessenden. Clark suggested that these designs cover
the entire back of the notes, but while the
designs were adopted the size of each was reduced to allow space for denomination and
legends.

National banks qualifying under terms of
the Act were granted 20-year charters which
were renewable for 20-year periods. Banks so
chartered were permitted to issue national
bank notes not to exceed 90 percent of the
total of the U.S. government bonds deposited
with the Treasurer of the United States.

Early issues will be found with the imprints
of the American, Continental and National
Bank Note Companies. These companies
supplied the paper and delivered the printed
notes to the Treasury. The Treasury number
and Treasury seal were then imprinted by the
Bureau.

The *History of the Bureau of Engraving
and Printing* supplies this information: "National bank notes were printed exclusively by
private contractors until September 1875.
Thereafter this type of currency was partially
printed by the Bureau of Engraving and
Printing. Beginning in October 1877, the Bureau executed all work in connection with the
printing of national currency."

Some notes will be found bearing the imprint of one of the three bank note companies
in the design, and in very small type in the
margin of the note, the notation: "Printed at
the Bureau of Engraving and Printing."

The dates appearing on national bank
notes do not always indicate the date the
charter was granted, nor the date the notes
were issued. Nor do these dates denote the
term of office of the Treasury officials whose
signatures appear on the notes. Plates with
the names of the U.S. Treasurer and Register
of the Treasury were frequently used after the
officials left office. The date appearing on the
note is usually later than the granting of the
charter. Some banks organized late in the
First Charter period continued to issue Series
1875 notes until February 1902.

At the close of 1928, 13,269 banks had
been chartered but many did not issue bank
notes. Notes issued by banks in small com-

munities were usually scarcer than those of large city banks. This thinking has at times been upset when a small-town bank released a stock of notes held in their reserve funds.

In addition to the engraved signatures of the two Treasury officials, national bank notes have the signatures of two bank officers, usually the president and cashier. Early issues did not carry the plate number on face or back.

The First Charter notes of $1 and $2 denominations were usually printed in sheets of three $1 notes and one $2 note. Check letters on notes so printed are A, B, and C, on the $1 notes and A on the $2 note. Known exceptions to "three ones and a two" are:

The Westchester County National Bank, Peekskill, N.Y., Charter #1422; The Merchants National Bank, Bangor, Maine, Charter #1437; The City National Bank, Manchester, N.H., Charter #1530. The above three banks were supplied with sheets of two $1 notes, check letters A and B, and two $2 notes, check letters A and B.

The other known exception is the First National Bank of Philadelphia, with sheets of four $1 and sheets of four $2 notes.

The word "National" appears in the title of all chartered banks with the exception of The Bank of North America, Philadelphia, Pa., which was allowed to retain the title it used as a state bank.

To assist in sorting notes presented for redemption, a large letter was printed with the charter numbers on national bank notes for a period of about 25 years, approximately 1901-1925. These regional letters indicated the geographical area or region in which the issuing bank was located, and may be found on Second and Third Charter notes. Six letters were used as follows: E - Eastern Region, M - Middle States Region, N - New England Region, P - Pacific Region (including Alaska and Hawaii), S - Southern Region and W - Western Region.

Bank charter numbers were overprinted on Series 1875 and all later series, and may also be found on some notes of the Original Series. The exact position varies on the face of the notes. These numbers on the first issue are in red with the exception of a very few banks which were supplied with notes bearing black charter numbers.

Known "Black Charters" are the $5 notes of the following banks: Merchants National Bank, Minneapolis, Minn., charter 1830; First National Bank, Central City, Colorado Territory, charter 2129; First National Bank, Red Oak, Iowa, charter 2130; National Bank, Green Lane, Pa., charter 2131; Kellogg National Bank, Green Bay, Wis., charter 2132; First National Bank, Boyertown, Pa., charter 2137; National Bank, Rochester, N.H., charter 2138; and The National Bank, Pontiac, Ill., charter 2141.

The first charter period covered the years 1862-1882.

The first issue of national bank notes is known as the "Original Series." This was followed by Series 1875. These two series comprise the issue of First Charter notes, and were issued in denominations of $1 to $1,000. Very few banks issued First Charter notes in denominations higher than $100.

The obligation of the issuing bank to pay appears on the face of the notes and reads: "This note is secured by Bonds of the United States, deposited with the United States Treasurer at Washington. The ... [Bank] ... will pay the Bearer on Demand ... Dollars."

Face designs of the First Charter notes are as follows:

$1, "Concordia." Two maidens clasping hands before an altar of earlier times, which bears the coat of arms of the United States. The design represents the new Union brought about with the aid of Heaven, and the eventual return to peace. Vignette designed by T. A. Liebler, and engraved by Charles Burt.

$2, "America Seated" depicted by a maiden unfurling the American flag. The bank serial number is at upper right, and the Treasury number is at lower left in a vertical position.

This design is best known as the "Lazy 2" because of the large numeral "2" which reclines on its side and carries the certification that bonds have been deposited with the Treasurer of the United States in Washington. The design is very popular. Similar large numeral designs were previously used on obsolete currency.

$5, "Columbus Sighting Land" showing the discoverer with some of his crew on the deck of the caravel. The scene at lower right depicts Columbus introducing America, represented by an Indian princess, to the Old World, Africa, Asia and Europe. Continental Bank Note Co. designer Fenton produced the design for engraving by Charles Burt.

$10, "Franklin and the Lightning" is the historical scene at left, representing Benjamin Franklin's experimentation with electrical energy and his assistant seated near him with a Leyden jar placed nearby. The year is marked by the figures "1752" in the corner. Eagle in flight bearing Liberty is shown at right, symbolizing "America Grasping the Lightning." Engraving by Alfred Jones.

$20, "Battle of Lexington 1775" depicted by Colonists in action and nurses attending the wounded. At right a symbolic design of "Loyalty," a procession for the defense and preservation of the Union, is led by Columbia with flag. The design is by Felix O.C. Darley.

$50, "Washington Crossing the Delaware" before his victorious battle at Princeton is the vignette at left. "A Prayer for Victory" is depicted at right. Engraved by Alfred Jones.

$100, Powell's painting "The Battle of Lake Erie" was the inspiration for the vignette at left, which shows Commodore Perry leaving his burning ship *The Lawrence*. At right, Columbia is seated with a fasces, a bundle of rods with a projecting ax handle. Inscribed are the words "The Union" and to the right "Maintain It." Engraved by Louis Delnoce.

$500, *Civilization* appears on the left. At right is a nautical scene titled "Arrival of the *Sirius*, 1838."

$1,000, General Scott entering Mexico City, is shown at left. At right the Capitol Building, Washington, D.C. The painting is by John Trumbull. The engraving by Alfred Jones. This note is believed to be nonexistent.

Tableau scenes are illustrated on the back designs of the notes of the First Charter period. The original murals decorated the rotunda of the Capitol Building in Washington and were the work of early American artists.

The coat of arms of the state of issue appears in the oval at left, with the exception of notes issued by banks in Arizona, New Mexico, Oklahoma and the state of Washington, on which the American eagle is shown in oval at right. A rather lengthy inscription qualifying the acceptance of the note, and the warning against counterfeiting "punishable by $1000 fine, or fifteen years' imprisonment at hard labor, or both" is also part of the back design.

The border designs are green with center illustrations in black on the reverses:

$1, "Landing of the Pilgrims" in center of back design depicts one of the memorable events in United States history. It is framed by the legend. Engraved by Charles Burt.

$2, Sir Walter Raleigh, with a long-stemmed smoking pipe, demonstrates the use of tobacco brought from America. Engraved by Louis Delnoce.

$5, "The Landing of Columbus" from the well-known mural by John Vanderlyn.

$10, "DeSoto Discovering the Mississippi 1541." The mural by W.H. Powell shows a group of natives, soldiers and monks. A crucifix is being erected on the spot. Engraved by Girsch.

$20, "The Baptism of Pocahontas" at Jamestown, Va. The scene shows Pocahontas kneeling, with John Smith and spectators, some of whom express interest and surprise. The painting is by John G. Chapman.

$50, "Embarkation of the Pilgrims," a reproduction of Robert W. Wier's mural, which depicts the Pilgrims before departing for America, kneeling to ask the Divine blessing. Engraved by W.W., Rice.

$100, "The Signing of the Declaration of Independence" July 4, 1776. One of John Trumbull's masterpieces, showing Washington, Jefferson, Franklin and a dignified group assembled for the acceptance and signing of the historic document. Engraved by Girsch.

$500, "The Surrender of Burgoyne." Another mural by artist John Trumbull vividly portraying the surrender of the general to General Gates of the American Army, at Saratoga, N.Y., Oct. 17, 1777. Engraved by Girsch.

$1,000, "Washington Resigning His Commission" Dec. 23, 1783, at Annapolis, Md. John Trumbull's mural shows the commander-in-chief presenting his resignation to the Congress. Engraved by Girsch and Delnoce.

The Second Charter Period spans Series 1882 Brown Backs; Series 1882-1908; and Series 1882 with denomination spelled out on back of note.

First Issue: Series 1882. The well-known and very popular Brown Backs.

Second Issue: Series 1882-1908 emergency issue. Whereas banks had previously been required to deposit United States government bonds with the Treasurer, by Act of Congress, May 30, 1908, they were permitted to deposit other types of securities, thus enabling the banks to place a larger number of notes into circulation.

Third Issue: Series 1882. Denomination spelled out on back. Scarcest of the three series of 1882 nationals. Not all banks issued this series.

Face designs of the first, second and third issues are as follows:

The face designs of the three Second Charter issues are the same as the First Charter issues, with the exception of the $5 notes. The bank obligation to pay is also the same.

The face design of the $5 denomination of all three issues of 1882 is distinctly different from the higher denominations of this series, or the $5 First Charter notes. A portrait of

James A. Garfield, 20th president, is in oval at left, possibly used to immortalize the statesman following his assassination in 1881, the same year in which he assumed office. The design is by Geo. W. Casilear, engraved by Alonzo C. Hatch.

Back Designs of the first issue — 1882 Brown Backs — are as follows:

"Brown Backs" is the well-known description of the First Series of Second Charter notes. The state seals are in ovals at left in the back design, as on the First Charter notes, and the American eagle is again shown in oval at right.

The striking change in the "Brown Backs" is in the center design, which prominently features the Bank Charter Number in large numerals against a green background, surrounded by brown lathe-work design.

The legend appears in the top margin and the rather lengthy counterfeiting warning, extends across bottom of back design.

Green Back designs of the second issue, 1882-1908 series are as follows:

The back design of the Emergency Series, 1882-1908, shows various persons and designs in the small oval at left, instead of the state seals as used on the Brown Backs and First Charter notes. Various subjects are shown in the oval at right. Featured are the following:

$5, Washington at left; Capitol Building, Washington, D.C., at right.

$10, William P. Fessenden at left; right, Mechanics represented by seated workmen.

$20, American eagle, two different poses, left and right ovals.

$50, eagle with shield, left and right.

$100, eagle with flag at left, and with shield at right.

Green Back designs of the third issue, "Denomination Back," are as follows:

The center designs spell out in large letters the denomination of the notes. Vignettes in small ovals at left and right, remain the same as the Second Issue, also legend at top and the counterfeiting warning at bottom.

The Third Charter period started in 1902. The First Issue was Series 1902, Red Seals and Numbers.

Notes of this issue are scarce, having been issued by comparatively few of all chartered banks. Red Seals were printed with only three signature combinations of Treasury officials.

Second Issue: 1902-1908, blue seals, Emergency Series. Dates on back.

Authorized under Act of May 30, 1908, as were the Series 1882-1908 Second Charter notes. First issued in 1908 and with two ex-

ceptions discontinued in 1916. Fifty dollar and $100 denominations were issued through 1925.

Third Issue: 1902 Blue Seals. No dates on back.

First issued in 1916 and most common of the three issues of Third Charter notes. There were 15 signature combinations, the scarcest being the Jones-Woods signatures. Edward E. Jones assumed the office of Register, and Walter O. Woods the office of Treasurer in 1929, the same year in which large-sized notes were discontinued.

Face designs of the Third Charter notes are as follows:

The Treasury seal is at right on all denominations in the three issues. Prominent statesmen are featured in oval, at left.

$5, Benjamin Harrison, 23rd president of the United States.

$10, William McKinley, 25th president, assassinated in Buffalo, 1901.

$20, Hugh McCulloch, Secretary of Treasury, 1865-1869 and 1884-1885.

$5, John Sherman, Secretary of the Treasury 1877-1881; Secretary of State 1897-1898.

$100, John J. Knox, Comptroller of Currency 1872-1884, later, president of the National Bank of the Republic, New York City.

Ostrander Smith designed all of the above. The $20 note was engraved by Charles Burt, all others by Geo. F.C. Smillie.

Back designs of the Third Charter notes are as follows:

Back designs of the three issues of Third Charter notes feature:

$5, Landing of the Pilgrims.

$10, Female figure, with ships in background.

$20, Columbia and Capitol at Washington.

$50, Allegorical scene. Train and female figure at right. Railroad worker reclining at left.

$100, American eagle on shield, with two male figures.

The back design of all denominations bear a rather lengthy inscription: "This note is receivable at par in all parts of the United States in payment of all taxes and excises and all other dues to the United States except duties on imports and also for all salaries and other debts and demands owing by the United States to individuals, corporations and associations within the United States except interest on public debt."

Gold certificates

Acts of March 3, 1863, July 12, 1882, March 14, 1900, and Dec. 24, 1919, authorized the issuance of gold certificates.

First, Second and Third Issues may be considered to be non-collectible, having been used principally in transactions between banks. Some of these issues were uniface. In the First Issue, denominations ranged from $20 to $10,000, in later issues $100 to $10,000. The $20 and $100 certificates of these issues are extremely rare. The higher denominations have not been discovered. Dates of issue were filled in with pen and ink on these three issues.

Fourth Issue of Series 1882 is as follows:

$20 to $10,000 denomination. As with the first three issues, denominations higher than $100 are extremely rare, practically unknown.

The obligation to pay in gold is on the face of the note. It reads: "This certifies that there have been deposited in the Treasury of the United States . . . Dollars in Gold Coin, payable to the Bearer on Demand." This issue is indicated as "Department Series" on the face of the certificates.

Face designs of Series 1882 are as follows:

$20, James A. Garfield, 20th president. Assassinated six months after his inauguration in 1881. Portrait at right.

$50, Silas Wright, U.S. senator 1833-1844; New York governor 1845-1846. Portrait at left.

$100, Thomas H. Benton, U.S. senator for more than 30 years, left.

$500, Abraham Lincoln, portrait at left.

$1,000, Alexander Hamilton, at right.

$5,000, James Madison, at left.

$10,000, Andrew Jackson, at left.

Some notes of the 1882 series, bearing Bruce-Gilfillan signatures and a brown seal, were countersigned by Thomas C. Acton, Assistant Treasurer, and were payable in New York. Notes so countersigned are rare.

Back designs of Series 1882 are as follows:

The American eagle in various poses is featured on the back design of all denominations of this series. There is no legend or inscription. Large Roman numerals "C" "D" and "M" in the back design, indicate the $100, $500 and $1,000 denominations. "United States" without "of America" is used on all back designs of this series.

Fifth Issue of Series 1888 is as follows:

Two denominations only: $5,000 James Madison, portrait at left. Back design: "5000" and eagle. $10,000 Andrew Jackson, portrait at left, Back design: "10000" and eagle with flag.

Sixth Issue of Series 1900 is as follows:

$10,000 only. Andrew Jackson, as on Series 1888. Back design same as 1888.

Seventh Issue of Series 1905, 1906 and 1907 is as follows:

$10, Series 1907. Michael Hillegas, center, U.S. Treasurer 1775-1789. Large "X" Roman equivalent of "10" at left.

$20, Series 1905, George Washington. The blending of gold, red, black and white, has caused this note to be known as the "technicolor" note.

$20, Series 1906, George Washington. Gold and black design with Roman numeral "XX."

The back design of gold for this series, carries no inscription, simply the designation "Gold Certificate," the denomination and the seal.

Eighth Issue of Series 1907 is as follows:

$1,000, Alexander Hamilton. One denomination.

Ninth Issue of Series 1913 is as follows:

$50, Series 1913. Portrait of Grant. Issued with two signature combinations, both of which were offered in the Grinnell sale, in 1945. Series 1913 and Series 1922, were the only two issues of the $50 denomination.

Last Issue of Series 1922 is as follows:

$10 to $1,000 denominations. All bear signature combination Speelman-White.

A legend was added to the face of the notes: "This certificate is a Legal Tender in the amount thereof, in payment of all debts and dues public and private. Acts of March 14, 1900, as amended, and December 24, 1919."

$10, Michael Hillegas, first U.S. Treasurer.

$20, George Washington

$50, Ulysses Grant

$100, Thomas H. Benton

$500, Abraham Lincoln

$1,000, Alexander Hamilton

The back designs in gold feature the seal, the denomination and the words "United States of America." There is no legend or inscription.

National gold bank notes

The national gold bank notes are gold-tinted and are extremely rare. Ten national gold banks were authorized by Congress to assuage the burden of handling the gold produced by the California Gold Rush. Nine of the banks were in California and one was in Boston. It is generally believed that the Kidder National Gold Bank of Boston did not circulate gold notes, though proof impressions do exist.

Authorized denominations were $5 to $5,000, redeemable in gold. Since the gold banks were also national banks, it was necessary for them to deposit U.S. bonds as security with the U.S. Treasurer. The obligation on these notes is similar to the national bank notes except that the gold bank notes were payable in gold coin.

Federal Reserve Bank notes

The large-sized Federal Reserve Bank notes were authorized by the Federal Reserve Acts of Dec. 23, 1913, and April 23, 1918. They were issued in two series in denominations of $1 to $50 and are often confused with national bank notes because they have the inscription "National Currency" across the top. They have blue seals and blue serial numbers.

The first issue, Series 1913, consisted only of $5, $10 and $20 notes issued by the Federal Reserve Banks of Atlanta, Chicago, Kansas City, Dallas and San Francisco. Only $5 notes were issued by the San Francisco Federal Reserve Bank.

The obligation to pay the bearer is similar to that on the first charter national bank notes, differing only slightly in wording but not in meaning.

The second issue, Series 1918, consisted of $1, $2, $5, $10, $20 and $50 notes issued by all 12 Federal Reserve Banks (though all banks did not necessarily issue all denominations).

The obligation to pay the bearer differs completely from the first issue, reading "Secured by United States Bonds or Certificates of Indebtedness or one-year gold notes."

Although Federal Reserve Bank notes are a rather recent issue, all are quite scarce. Treasury Department records show that only slightly more than $2 million is outstanding from a total issue of nearly $762 million.

Federal Reserve notes Series 1914 and 1918

Federal Reserve Act, Dec. 23, 1913.
Series 1914, Red Seals, $5 to $100, scarce. Signatures: John Burke, Treasurer of the United States; Wm. G. McAdoo, Secretary of the Treasury.
Series 1914, Blue Seals, $5 to $100.
Series 1918, Blue Seals, $500 to $10,000.
Blue Seal signatures: John Burke-Wm. G. McAdoo; John Burke-Carter Glass; John Burke-D.F. Houston; Frank White-A.W. Mellon.

There are three types of notes with White-Mellon signatures. Type one: District numeral and letter, rather large, lower left and upper right. Most common of the three types. Type two: Smaller numerals and letters of the vari-

ous districts. Type three: Larger numerals and letters, slightly to the left and higher. Seals closer to center of note. Scarcest of the three types.

Unlike the Federal Reserve Bank notes, the obligation to pay is by the United States and reads: "The United States of America will pay the Bearer on Demand ... Dollars."

Face designs of Series 1914 are as follows:

Portraits of presidents featured on Federal Reserve Bank notes, are repeated on Federal Reserve notes on denominations $5 to $50, but are shown in center oval of the face design. Seal with numeral and letter of issuing bank is at left, and seal of the Treasury is at right. $100 Series 1914, Portrait of Benjamin Franklin, American statesman.

Face designs of Series 1918 all with Blue Seals are as follows:
$500, John Marshall, secretary of state and Chief Justice of the United States.
$1,000, Alexander Hamilton, first Secretary of the Treasury.
$5,000, James Madison, fourth president of the United States.
$10,000, Salmon P. Chase, Secretary of Treasury under Lincoln.

Back Designs of Series 1914 and 1918, Red and Blue seals are as follows:
Series 1914, $5 to $50 same as back design of the Federal Reserve Bank notes. The back design of the $100 note features five allegorical figures.

Back Designs of Series 1918 Blue Seals are as follows:
Series 1918, $500, De Soto discovering the Mississippi, as on the $10 First Charter, national bank note.
Series 1918, $1,000, American eagle with flag.
Series 1918, $5,000, Washington resigning his commission, as on the $1,000 First Charter note.
Series 1918, $10,000, Embarkation of the Pilgrims, as on the $50 First Charter note.

The lengthy inscription in the lower border of the back design differs from that on the Federal Reserve Bank notes. It stipulates that the note is payable in gold, and reads:

"This note is receivable by all national and member banks and the Federal Reserve Banks, and for all taxes, customs and other public dues. It is redeemable in gold on demand at the Treasury Department of the United States in the city of Washington, District of Columbia, or in gold or lawful money at any Federal Reserve Bank."

U.S. postage and fractional currency

In 1862 the need for small coins to make change became acute. Following the suspension of specie payments by the large Northeastern banks and the federal Treasury late the previous year, coinage became widely hoarded and commanded premium values as compared to the government greenbacks. The result of this hoarding was extreme difficulty in making change for ordinary business transactions.

Private attempts to remedy the small change shortage were ingenious but proved futile. Neither municipal, corporate nor private scrip could completely replace the withdrawn subsidiary silver coinage on a nationwide scale and local expedients such as John Gault's encased postage were little more than temporary measures.

To relieve the citizenry of the "worthless paper trash" which was circulating, F.E. Spinner, Treasurer of the United States, convinced Congress of the necessity for a federal, fractional paper currency. He proposed that the U.S. issue these small notes in values less than $1 and in sufficient quantities to meet the demand for small change. Congress responded with the Act of July 17, 1862, which monetized the postage and other stamps of the United States.

The immediate effect of the law was a run on the U.S. post offices to secure stamps for change. By Aug. 21, however, the first notes of the belated postage currency issue reached circulation. Privately printed, these notes bore the imprints of the contemporary 5- and 10-cent postage stamps. Jefferson appears on the 5- and 25-cent issues and Washington on the 10- and 50-cent notes. Both perforate and imperforate varieties exist.

The reverse obligation on these notes states, "Exchangeable for United States Notes by any Assistant Treasurer or designated U.S. Depositary in sums not less than five dollars. Receivable in payment of all dues to the U. [sic] States less than five Dollars."

Because of the prevalence of counterfeiting, the designs of the successive fractional note issues were changed frequently. The fractional currency, which succeeded the makeshift (and some students contend illegal) postage currency, was issued in four series under authorization of the Act of March 3, 1863, which also provided that the Treasury Department print its own notes.

The so-called "Second Issue" (first issue under the latter act) consists of four notes in the same denominations as the earlier issue, but all bearing a bust of Washington in a bronze oval frame on obverse.

The reverse obligation was altered to read, "Exchangeable for United States Notes by the Assistant Treasurers and designated depositaries of the U.S. in sums not less than three dollars. Receivable in payment of all dues to the United States less than five dollars except customs." As with the postage currency, these notes were also receivable for U.S. postage stamps.

The third general issue added a 3-cent denomination, and each denomination has a different design. Washington appears on the 3-cent note; Spencer M. Clark, on the 5-cent issue; Washington, on the 10-cent bill; William Pitt Fessenden, on the 25-cent note; and either a seated figure of Justice or F.E. Spinner on the 50-cent issue. The Spinner note also exists with two distinct reverse varieties. The proposed 15-cent Grant-Sherman essay also exists in the form of uniface specimens.

The fourth general issue includes only 10-, 15-, 25- and 50-cent denominations. The 10-cent note bears a bust of Liberty; Columbia appears on the 15-cent issue; Washington, on the 25-cent bill; and Lincoln, Edwin Stanton or Samuel Dexter appear on the 50-cent bill.

The short fifth issue is confined to three notes: William Meredith, on the 10-cent note; Robert Walker, on the 25-cent bill; and William Crawford, on the 50-cent issue.

The small notes continued to circulate until the Resumption Act of Jan. 14, 1875, provided for their retirement by subsidiary silver coinage. In all, nearly $370 million worth of these small bills were issued, but most have long since been redeemed or destroyed. It is estimated that less than $5,000 face value remains available to collectors.

The summary tabulation below shows the extent and value of the five fractional note issues:

FIRST ISSUE
Aug. 21, 1862 to May 27, 1863

	Number of notes	Value
5 cent.....	44,857,780	$ 2,242,889.00
10 cent.....	41,153,780	4,115,378.00
25 cent.....	20,902,784	5,225,696.00
50 cent.....	17,273,344	8,631,672.00
Totals....	124,187,688	$ 20,215,635.00

SECOND ISSUE
Oct. 10, 1863 to Feb. 23, 1867

5 cent.....	55,896,522	$ 2,794,826.10
10 cent.....	61,760,843	6,176,084.30
25 cent.....	30,593,365	7,648,341.25
50 cent.....	13,090,464	6,545,232.00
Totals....	161,341,194	$ 23,164,483.65

THIRD ISSUE
Dec. 5, 1864 to Aug. 16, 1869

3 Cent	20,064,130	$ 601,923.90
5 Cent	13,140,055	657,002.75
10 Cent	169,761,345	16,976,134.50
15 Cent (Specimen)	9,016	1,352.40
25 Cent	124,572,755	31,143,188.75
50 Cent	73,470,853	36,735,426.50
Totals....	401,018,154	$ 86,115,028.80

FOURTH ISSUE
July 14, 1869 to Feb. 16, 1875

10 Cent	349,409,600	$ 34,940,960.00
15 Cent	35,361,440	5,304,216.00
25 Cent	235,689,024	58,922,256.00
50 Cent	154,799,200	77,399,600.00
Totals....	154,799,200	$ 77,399,600.00

FIFTH ISSUE
Feb. 26, 1874 to Feb. 15, 1876

10 Cent	199,899,000	$ 19,989,900.00
25 Cent	144,368,000	36,092,000.00
50 Cent	13,160,000	6,580,000.00
Totals....	357,427,000	$ 62,661,990.00

SUMMARY OF ALL ISSUES

3 Cent	20,064,130	$ 601,923.90
5 Cent	113,894,357	5,694,717.85
10 Cent	821,984,568	82,198,456.80
15 Cent (Specimen)	9,016	1,352.40
15 Cent	35,361,440	5,304,216.00
25 Cent	556,125,928	139,031,482.00
50 Cent	271,783,861	135,891,930.50
Totals....		1,819,223,300
		$368,724,079.45

United States small-sized paper money

The current small-sized notes were first issued in mid-1929, though some carry the series year designation of 1928. Issues in the small-sized category comprise United States notes, silver certificates, national bank notes, Federal Reserve Bank notes, Federal Reserve notes, and gold certificates.

United States notes

The $1 United States note was issued only in Series 1928. It features a portrait of Washington on the front and is the only small-sized $1 note to feature a red seal. The inscription is printed over the seal and states: "This note is legal tender at its face value for all debts public and private except duties on imports and interest on the public debt." The note also advises that "The United States of America will pay to the bearer on demand One Dollar." On the back on the $1 note a large "ONE" appears with smaller letters stating "ONE DOLLAR" over the larger "ONE."

The $2 note, featuring a portrait of Jefferson on the front and his home, Monticello, on the back, was first printed in the Series 1928 and was discontinued in 1966. Final series year for the $2 United States note was 1963A. Jefferson and Monticello remained on the $2 issues from the beginning to the end, but there were some changes in the inscription and the Treasury seal was relocated starting with the 1953 series. On this and later issues the seal is on the right, while on earlier issues it was on the left.

The first inscription says, "This note is legal tender at its face value for all debts public and private except duties on imports and interest on the public debt." Beginning with the 1953 series the inscription reads, "This note is a legal tender at its face value for all debts public and private," and on the 1963 and 1963A series the inscription advises, "This note is legal tender for all debts public and private." The motto "In God We Trust" was added to the $2 note beginning with the 1963 series, and with this same series the wording "Will pay to the bearer on demand" was removed.

The $5 note went through the same inscription and seal changes as did the $2 note. It features Lincoln on the front and the Lincoln Memorial on the back. The motto was added with the 1963 (final) series. The last delivery of $5 United States notes was in late 1967.

Benjamin Franklin is featured on the front of the $100 United States note, and the back features Independence Hall. First issued in Series 1966 (the only note to have that series year) it is the first note to use the newly redesigned Treasury seal. All United States notes have red seals and serial numbers.

Silver certificates

The small-sized silver certificates were issued in denominations of $1, $5 and $10 and were discontinued in 1963. The early issues stated that the notes were redeemable in silver dollars on demand — a clause later changed to "In silver payable to the bearer on demand." After the change it was possible to exchange silver certificates for silver bullion.

However, on June 24, 1967, President Johnson signed into law a bill which spelled the end of silver certificate redemption. The Treasury Department announced it would redeem the certificates until June 24, 1968, and one of the wildest "silver rushes" in American history was under way. Collectors, dealers and speculators bought all the silver certificates they could get their hands on, paying premium prices, then exchanging them for silver bullion to be sold back on the silver market.

Redemptions were made at the U.S. Assay Offices in San Francisco, Calif., and in New York, N.Y. During the final days of redemption, long lines of certificate holders lined the sidewalks around the assay offices to trade notes for silver before the deadline.

For small transactions, the assay offices issued small envelopes each valued at $1, containing .77-plus ounces of fine silver in the form of crystals or pellets. For larger transactions plastic bags of silver granules or bars of silver were used. The standard bar varied in weight from 1,000 to 1,100 ounces at $1.292929292 per fine troy ounce, raised to the next highest dollar. The exchanges had to be made in person because the assay offices were instructed not to exchange silver by mail.

It was possible, however, for the individual having large holdings of silver certificates to arrange with certain banks to perform the redemption, as a goodwill gesture. Not all banks, though, were willing to perform this service. The banks that did cooperate would contact a bank in New York City or San Francisco and arrange for that bank to send an agent to purchase the silver. The purchas-

ing agent in either of the two cities would ship the silver direct to the home bank's customer.

Although this mad rush to redeem silver certificates did deplete the numismatic stock somewhat, it also served to introduce additional persons to the hobby of numismatics, due to the great amount of publicity that newspapers gave the modern-day silver rush. Silver certificates, like other issues that have been discontinued, remain legal tender.

The $1 silver certificate portrays Washington on the front side. On the 1928 to 1928E series the Treasury seal is on the left and a large "ONE" is on the right. The back side is similar to the 1928 $1 United States note.

On the 1934 series silver certificate the Treasury seal changes from the left to right side and a large number "1" appears where the seal was on the left. A third design, for Series 1935-1957, reduces the size of the number "1" and the Treasury seal. On the second two designs, the reverse side features the Great Seal of the United States and a large "ONE." The motto "In God We Trust" was added to the reverse of some 1935G notes, and all of 1935H, 1957, 1957A and 1957B notes.

The $5 silver certificate portrays Lincoln on the front and the Lincoln Memorial on the back. The figure "5" and the Treasury seal, left and right sides respectively, are larger on the 1934 through 1934D series than they are on following series, 1953 through 1953C.

Alexander Hamilton is featured on the front of the $10 silver certificate, with the U.S. Treasury building on the back. On the first series, 1933, to the left of Hamilton is the Treasury seal and to the right "TEN" appears. The seal was placed upon the "TEN" for series 1934 through 1934D, and was replaced on the left by "10." On later series $10 notes, the seal and "10" are reduced in size from the previous issues.

The first $10 silver certificates stated "Ten Dollars payable in silver coin to the bearer on demand." This was changed for the 1934 through 1953B series and these notes read "Ten Dollars in silver payable to the bearer on demand."

The inscription on 1933 series $10 silver certificates says: "This certificate issued pursuant to sections of the Act of May 12, 1933, and is legal tender at its face value for all debts public and private." Later issues simply said, "This certificate is legal tender for all debts public and private."

All silver certificates have blue seals and serial numbers, with certain exceptions. Special notes were printed for use during North African and European invasions of World War II and these notes have blue serial numbers and yellow seals. These latter notes were printed as follows: $1, 1935A; $5, 1934 and 1934A; and $10, 1934 and 1934A. Special $1 silver certificates were printed, and overprinted with "HAWAII," for use in Hawaii and other islands during World War II. The "HAWAII" notes have brown seals and serial numbers.

A special printing (experimental) of the $1 notes was included in the series year 1935A. The United States was testing the quality of currency paper and used two types of paper for the experimental issue. Some of the notes are marked with a large "R" in the lower right side, and others with a large "S" in the lower right. Like the regular certificates, these notes have blue seals and numbers.

Small-sized national bank notes

Small-sized national bank notes were all of Series 1929, but were issued through 1935. Issued by hundreds of banks throughout the nation, all carry the signatures of the issuing bank's president and cashier, along with the signatures of the Register of the Treasury and the United States Treasurer. Designs are similar to designs on other small-sized notes of the same denomination. They were issued in denominations of $5, $10, $20, $50 and $100. All state "National Currency" at the top center of each note, and all have brown seals and brown serial numbers.

There are two types of the 1929 series national bank notes. Type one features the issuing bank's charter number in black at each end of the face of the note. These notes were numbered in sheets of six notes with identical numbers on each but different prefix letters: A, B, C, D, E and F from top to bottom.

The serial numbers ended with a suffix letter: A for the first 999,999 sheets, B for the second 999,999 sheets, and so on.

In 1933, a new method of numbering national bank notes was approved, effective on July 1. The sheets still contained six notes each but the numbers ran consecutively from one to six on the first sheet, seven through 12 on the second sheet, and so on, with prefix letters A and without a suffix letter. The bank charter number preceded the serial number in the upper right corner and followed the serial number in the lower left corner of the notes.

After the numbering sequence reached 999,999 the prefix letter changed to B. This sequence continued with one exception — the letter O was never used.

The notes carried the issuing bank's name, the city and state as well as the bold, black, charter number on both types. Also featured on both types were words stating that the notes were secured by United States bonds deposited with the Treasurer of the United States of America.

Records do not reveal the number of national bank notes issued by type and denomination to the issuing banks, nor do the records of outstanding notes give reliable information about the number of unredeemed notes. National bank notes have one thing in common with all other discontinued notes — they remain legal tender of the United States.

Federal Reserve Bank notes

Only one series of small-sized Federal Reserve Bank notes was issued, Series 1929. They are often confused with Federal Reserve notes and are often mistaken for national bank notes.

The confusion arises in part from design similarities and in part from the fact that plates for national bank notes were used to print the Federal Reserve Bank notes. To further complicate matters, they are inscribed "National Currency" across the top.

They were authorized by Act of Congress March 9, 1933, to permit the Federal Reserve Banks to issue currency equal to 100 percent of the face value of U.S. bonds, or 90 percent of the value of commercial paper, used as collateral.

The obligation to pay the bearer is the same as it is on the national bank notes, but the words, "or by like deposit of other securities," have been added below the United States of America at the top of the notes.

Series 1929 FRBNs were printed in denominations of $5, $10, $20, $50 and $100. They have brown seals and brown serial numbers. Although they carry the series year of 1929, the first notes were not delivered until March 11, 1933, and the last of the notes was delivered on Dec. 21 of that same year.

Federal Reserve notes

Federal Reserve notes are authorized by the Act of Congress of Dec. 23, 1917. These notes are issued by the Federal Reserve Banks. They were authorized in denominations of $5, $10, $20, $50, $100, $500, $1,000, $5,000 and $10,000. However, the printing of Federal Reserve notes in denominations of $500 and higher was discontinued by action of the board of governors of the Federal Reserve System on June 26, 1946.

Federal Reserve notes are obligations of the United States and were secured by the deposit with Federal Reserve agents of an

equivalent amount of collateral, consisting of
gold certificates or gold certificate credits
with the Treasurer of the United States; such
discounted or purchased paper as is eligible
under the terms of the Federal Reserve Act as
amended; and direct obligations of the United States.

Until 1968, Federal Reserve Banks were required to maintain a reserve in gold certificates or gold certificate credits equal to at
least 25 percent of these notes in actual circulation, including in this reserve the redemption fund (equal to not less than 5 percent of
the notes outstanding less the amount of gold
certificates held by the Federal Reserve agent
as collateral) which was deposited with the
Treasurer of the United States and any gold
certificates or gold certificate credits held as
collateral for Federal Reserve notes. This requirement was abolished in 1968.

Federal Reserve notes have always been
printed at the Bureau of Engraving and Printing — although this is not required by law —
the Federal Reserve Act merely stating that
the Comptroller of the Currency, under the
direction of the Secretary of the Treasury,
shall have the plates engraved and the notes
printed. The entire expense of engraving and
printing the notes is paid by the Federal Reserve Banks, and is credited to the Bureau's
revolving fund.

The number to be ordered is determined
by the board of governors of the Federal Reserve System, but the printing order is issued
by the Comptroller of the Currency. As the
volume of Federal Reserve currency fluctu-
ates, it is necessary to keep a large stock on
hand before issue. This reserve stock is kept
in the vaults of the Bureau until it is shipped
to the several banks.

The storage of these notes is not, strictly
speaking, a Bureau activity. The law requires
that the stock be kept in the Treasury, subtreasury, or a Mint until delivered to the
banks.

The packages of completed notes are delivered by the Currency Processing Division of
the Bureau to the Federal Reserve vault in
the main Bureau building and remains under
the control of the Bureau until shipment is
made to Federal Reserve banks. See Chapter
6 (Bureau of Engraving and Printing) for how
paper money is printed.

Bicentennial $2 notes

Federal Reserve note denominations increased by one April 13, 1976, when the Series 1976 $2 note was issued in commemora-
tion of the American Independence Bicentennial. Treasury Secretary William Simon

announced Nov. 3, 1975, that the note would
be reissued bearing Thomas Jefferson's portrait as on the $2 United States note, but with
a reverse depicting a scene from John Trum-
bell's "Signing of the Declaration of Independence." The April 13 release date was Jefferson's birthday.

Treasury officials hoped public acceptance
of the $2 bill would alleviate demand for the
$1 bill, thus relieving pressure on the Bureau
of Engraving and Printing. The $1 bill repre-
sents the bulk of the work of the BEP. However, the $2 note never became popular in
most areas of the United States, and today
most of the $2 FRNs rest in bank vaults.

The release of the note did trigger a new
collector's item — the postally canceled note.
U.S. Postal Service officials agreed to permit
collectors to attach stamps to the bills which
were then postally canceled on April 13 as a
first day issue, and later on other commemorative dates. Collectors today continue to issue and collect postally canceled notes.

Small-sized currency series

Since July 10, 1929, the date the small-
sized currency was first put into circulation,
the Bureau of Engraving and Printing has
printed and delivered the following series of
notes:

$1 silver certificates: Series 1928, 1928A,
1928B, 1928C, 1928D, 1928E, 1934, 1935,
1935A, 1935B, 1935C, 1935D, 1935E, 1935F,
1935G, 1935H, 1957, 1957A and 1957B.

$5 silver certificates: Series 1934, 1934A,
1934B, 1934C, 1934D, 1953, 1953A, 1953B
and (printed but not released) 1953C.

$10 silver certificates: Series 1933, 1933A,
1934, 1934A, 1934B, 1934C, 1934D, 1953,
1953A and 1953B.

$1 United States notes: Series 1928.

$2 United States notes: Series 1928, 1928A,
1928B, 1928C, 1928D, 1928E, 1928F, 1928G,
1953, 1953A, 1953B, 1953C, 1963 and
1963A.

$5 United States notes: Series 1928, 1928A,
1928B, 1928C, 1928D, 1928E, 1928F, 1953,
1953A, 1953B, 1953C and 1963.

$10 and $20 United States notes: Series
1928 (reported but unverified).

$100 United States notes: Series 1966 and
1966A.

$1 Federal Reserve notes: Series 1963,
1963A, 1963B, 1969, 1969A, 1969B, 1969C,
1969D, 1974, 1977, 1977A, 1981, 1981A and
1985.

$2 Federal Reserve notes: 1976.

$5 Federal Reserve notes: Series 1928,
1928A, 1928B, 1928C, 1928D, 1934, 1934A,

1934B, 1934C, 1934D, 1950, 1950A, 1950B, 1950C, 1950D, 1950E, 1963, 1963A, 1969, 1969A, 1969B, 1969C, 1974, 1977, 1977A, 1981, 1981A and 1985.

$10 Federal Reserve notes: Series 1928, 1928A, 1928B, 1928C, 1934, 1934A, 1934B, 1934C, 1934D, 1950, 1950A, 1950B, 1950C, 1950D, 1950E, 1963, 1963A, 1969, 1969A, 1969B, 1969C, 1974, 1977, 1977A, 1981, 1981A and 1985.

$20 Federal Reserve notes: Series 1928, 1928A, 1928B, 1928C, 1934, 1934A, 1934B, 1934C, 1934D, 1950, 1950A, 1950B, 1950C, 1950D, 1950E, 1963, 1963A, 1969, 1969A, 1969B, 1969C, 1974, 1977, 1981, 1981A and 1985.

$50 and $100 Federal Reserve notes: Series 1928, 1928A, 1934, 1934A, 1934B, 1934C, 1934D, 1950, 1950A, 1950B, 1950C, 1950D, 1950E, 1963A, 1969, 1969A, 1969B, 1969C, 1974, 1977 and 1981, 1981A and 1985.

$500 Federal Reserve notes: Series 1928, 1934, 1934A, 1934B and 1934C.

$1,000 Federal Reserve notes: Series 1928, 1934, 1934A and 1934C.

$5,000 and $10,000 Federal Reserve notes: Series 1928, 1934, 1934A and 1934B.

$5, $10, $20, $50 and $100 Federal Reserve Bank notes: Series 1929.

$5, $10, $20, $50 and $100 national bank notes: Series 1929.

$10 and $20 gold certificates: Series 1928 and (printed but not released) 1928A.

$50, $500 and $5,000 gold certificates: Series 1928.

$100, $1,000 and $10,000 gold certificates: Series 1928 and (printed but not released) 1934.

$100,000 gold certificates: Series 1934.

Barr notes

Barr notes are those signed by Secretary of the Treasury Joseph W. Barr, who served from Dec. 21, 1968, to Jan. 20, 1969. Appointed to fill out the unexpired term of Henry H. Fowler, Barr was replaced by Nixon appointee David M. Kennedy.

Born in Vincennes, Ind., Barr had been Undersecretary of the Treasury since April 1965. A former U.S. representative from Indiana, he joined the Treasury Department in 1961 as an assistant to the Secretary.

Barr, while serving as Treasury Secretary, was also governor for the United States on the International Monetary Fund, the International Bank for Reconstruction and Development, the Inter-American Development Fund, and the Asian Development Bank.

Following his short term as Treasury Secretary, Barr was a director of the American Society Corporation. After resigning that post, he joined the Franklin National Bank of New York to serve as chairman and chief executive officer.

Because Barr served such a short term as Secretary of the Treasury, one month, some felt those notes signed by Barr were issued in limited numbers and would soon become rare.

However, production of Barr notes did not stop on Jan. 20, 1969, when he resigned. It wasn't until June 4, 1969, that notes bearing the signature of Barr's successor, David Kennedy, came off the presses.

Barr notes are not considered rare by informed paper money collectors. The following chart shows how many Barr notes were delivered to the Federal Reserve Banks.

Barr note statistics

Federal Reserve District	Regular Notes	Star Notes
New York	123,040,000	3,680,000
Richmond	93,600,000	3,200,000
Chicago	91,040,000	2,400,000
Kansas City	44,800,000	None Printed
San Francisco	106,400,000	3,040,000
Total notes printed	**458,880,000**	**12,320,000**
Less spoilage[1]	27,532,800	547,200
Estimated total notes released	**431,347,200**	**11,612,800**

[1] Based on past reports, spoilage is estimated at 6 percent for regular notes and 4.5 percent for star notes.

Official serial number range

	Regular notes		Star notes	
New York	.B57 600 001G	B80 640 000H	B48 800 001*	B52 480 000*
Richmond	.E32 000 001F	E25 600 000G	E41 600 001*	E44 800 000*
Chicago	.G84 480 001H	G75 520 000I	G52 640 001*	
				G55 040 000*
Kansas City	.J19 200 001C	J64 000 000C	None printed	
San Francisco	.L76 800 001F	L83 200 000G	L43 040 001*	L46 080 000*

The first delivery of notes bearing Joseph Barr's signature took place on Jan. 16, 1969 (Richmond District), and the last delivery was Nov. 12, 1969 (New York District).

Features of current United States paper money

Plate position numbers

The small capital letter and number which appear in the upper left-hand corner just below the denomination numeral on the face of a bill comprise what is referred to as the plate position number. This item designates the position of the note on the 32-subject face plate from which a particular bill was printed.

Each modern 32-note sheet is split into four quadrants, with two vertical rows of four notes each. The upper left quadrant is No. 1, the lower left, No. 2; the upper right is No. 3, and the lower right, No. 4. Within the quadrant, the left four notes, from top to bottom, are A, B, C, D; the right row is E, F, G, H. Thus, a note with position number B3 would be in the upper right quadrant, left row, second note from top. An H1 note would be from the upper left quadrant, right row, fourth note from top.

Plate serial numbers

The small number in the lower right-hand corner relates to the face plate from which a note was printed. This is referred to as the plate serial number. This number is assigned in sequential order at the time the plate is manufactured. It can be used to determine the number of the press plate from which a particular note was printed. The letter preceding the plate serial number is always the same as the letter in the upper left-hand corner.

Series date

The series date on the face of each bill signifies the year in which the design of the note was adopted. The series does not change each calendar year; usually only when the basic design has a major revision. The capital letter following the series year indicates that a minor change was authorized in a particular series. Minor revisions usually occur when a new Secretary of the Treasury or Treasurer of the United States is appointed, and a corresponding change is made in the signature of one or both of these officials.

Size of currency

Currency of the present size was first issued in July 1929, replacing the old, large (7.50 by 3.125 inches) notes. The present size of a U.S. bill is 6.14 inches by 2.61 inches, and the thickness is .0043 inch. New notes stack 233 to an inch, not compressed, and weigh 490 notes to a pound. A million notes will weigh approximately 2,000 pounds and occupy approximately 42 cubic feet of space, with moderate pressure.

Serial numbers on small-sized currency

The two numbers, with prefix and suffix letters or "stars," in the upper right-hand and lower left-hand corners of all small-sized currency are referred to as serial numbers. The letters in the Federal Reserve Bank seal and the prefix letter of the serial numbers are always identical on Federal Reserve notes.

Serial numbers are designed to foil counterfeiters and to accommodate the large volume of notes printed by the Bureau of Engraving and Printing. No two notes of a class, denomination and series have the same serial number, except for error notes. Each serial number has eight digits and an alphabetical prefix and suffix letter.

When a new series of Federal Reserve

notes is initiated, a new number sequence generally begins (although serial numbers continued from Series 1977 to 1977A). The first of the sequence is 00 000 001A, with a prefix letter indicating the Federal Reserve district issuing the note. The second is 00 000 002A, the hundredth is 00 000 100A, the thousandth 00 001 000A, until the number 99 920 000A is reached, at which point the suffix letter changes to B and the numbering system starts over. The letter O is never used as a suffix letter because it could be confused with the digit 0.

Serial numbers do not advance sequentially from note to note on an individual sheet, but from sheet to sheet. On a sheet, the numbers advance 100,000 digits from note to note, since sheets are overprinted in 100,000-sheet runs.

On United States notes and silver certificates, the first note is numbered A 00 000 001A, continuing in numerical sequence with the prefix and suffix letters remaining the same. When the number A 99 999 999A is reached, the suffix letter A is retained and the prefix letter changes alphabetically until 25 blocks of 99 999 999 are printed, each with a different prefix letter of the alphabet from A to Z, omitting O.

Federal Reserve symbols

On the face of every Federal Reserve note, the black seal to left of the portrait identifies the particular Federal Reserve Bank which issued the bill. There are 12 Federal Reserve Banks (see Chapter 7), each identifiable by a letter and a number, with the letter corresponding to the number, as follows:

1	A	Boston
2	B	New York
3	C	Philadelphia
4	D	Cleveland
5	E	Richmond
6	F	Atlanta
7	G	Chicago
8	H	St. Louis
9	I	Minneapolis
10	J	Kansas City
11	K	Dallas
12	L	San Francisco

The Federal Reserve Bank number, which appears four times, is repeated in the upper and lower and the left and right sections of the bill for identification purposes. These numbers are particularly helpful in cases involving claims made by the public for redemption of burned or mutilated notes, when only portions of the notes remain.

The Great Seal of the United States

Both the obverse and the reverse of the Great Seal of the United States are reproduced on the backs of $1 bills. The Great Seal was adopted in 1782. Its obverse depicts an American eagle breasted by a shield with the national colors. The eagle holds in his right talon an olive branch of 13 leaves and 13 berries, symbolic of peace.

In his left talon he holds 13 arrows signifying the original Colonies' fight for liberty. A ribbon flying from the beak of the eagle is inscribed with the Latin motto, "E Pluribus Unum," which is translated "One out of many," in reference to the unity of the 13 Colonies as one government.

Over the eagle's head is a constellation of 13 five-pointed stars surrounded by a wreath of clouds.

The reverse of the seal depicts a pyramid, with the Roman numerals "MDCCLXXVI" on its base — 1776, the year of the Declaration of Independence. The pyramid represents permanence and strength. Its unfinished condition symbolizes that there was still work to be done to form a more perfect government and signifies the expectation that new states would be admitted to the Union.

The eye in the triangular glory represents an all-seeing Deity. The words "Annuit coeptis," translated as "He (God) has favored our undertakings," refer to the many interpositions the founding fathers saw of divine providence in the forming of the government. "Novus Ordo Seclorum," translated as "A new order of the ages," signifies a new American era.

"In God We Trust"

In October 1957, $1 silver certificates bearing the motto, "In God We Trust," were first placed in circulation.

The suggestion to include the motto on U.S. paper currency was presented to the Secretary of the Treasury George W. Humphrey in November of 1953 by Matthew H. Rothert of Camden, Ark. Like the Baptist preacher who wrote to the Secretary of the Treasury in 1861 suggesting mention of the Deity on U.S. coins (see Chapter 9), Rothert also directed his inquiry to the Secretary of the Treasury. He followed through with letters to several senators and representatives and to his personal friend, Thomas Weeks, Secretary of Commerce.

Rothert's idea came to him while he was attending church on Sunday morning in Chicago. As the collection plate was passed, it occurred to him that only the coins in the plate had this motto. He then thought that since U.S. paper money has a much wider circulation abroad than U.S. coins, a message about the country's faith in God could be easily carried throughout the world if it were on United States paper currency.

The 84th Congress passed Public Law 140 and it was signed into law by President Dwight D. Eisenhower on July 11, 1955. The law provided, "At such times as new dies for the printing of currency are adopted in connection with the current program of the Treasury Department to increase the capacity of the presses utilized by the Bureau of Engraving and Printing, the dies shall bear, at such place or places as the Secretary of the Treasury may determine to be appropriate, the inscription 'In God We Trust,' and thereafter this inscription shall appear on all United States currency and coins."

The $ sign

The origin of the $ sign has been variously accounted for, with perhaps the most widely accepted explanation being that it is the result of evolution, independently, in different places, of the Mexican or Spanish "P's" for pesos, or piastres, or pieces of eight. The theory, derived from a study of old manuscripts, is that the "S" gradually came to be written over the "P," developing a close equivalent to the $ mark, which eventually evolved. It was widely used before the adoption of the United States dollar in 1785.

Portraits on United States paper money

Listed by denomination

Denom.	Type of Note	Series	Portrait
3¢	Fractional Currency	3rd issue	George Washington
5¢	Postage Currency	1st issue	Thomas Jefferson
	Fractional Currency	2nd issue	George Washington
	Fractional Currency	3rd issue	Spencer M. Clark
10¢	Postage Currency	1st issue	George Washington
	Fractional Currency	2nd issue	George Washington
	Fractional Currency	3rd issue	George Washington
	Fractional Currency	5th issue	William M. Meredith
25¢	Postage Currency	1st issue	Thomas Jefferson
	Fractional Currency	2nd issue	George Washington
	Fractional Currency	3rd issue	William P. Fessenden
	Fractional Currency	4th issue	George Washington
	Fractional Currency	5th issue	Robert J. Walker
50¢	Postage Currency	1st issue	George Washington
	Fractional Currency	2nd issue	George Washington
	Fractional Currency	3rd issue	Gen. F. E. Spinner
	Fractional Currency	4th issue	Abraham Lincoln;
		4th issue	E. M. Stanton; or
		4th issue	Samuel Dexter
	Fractional Currency	5th issue	William H. Crawford
$1	Federal Reserve Note	1963 to date	George Washington
	Federal Reserve Bank Note	1918	George Washington
	Legal Tender Note	1862	Salmon P. Chase
	Legal Tender Note	1869-1928	George Washington
	Silver Certificate	1886-1891	Martha Washington
	Silver Certificate	1899	Lincoln & Grant
	Silver Certificate	1923-1957B	George Washington
	Treasury or Coin Note	1890-1891	Edwin M. Stanton
$2	Federal Reserve Bank Note	1918	Thomas Jefferson
	Federal Reserve Note	1976	Thomas Jefferson
	Legal Tender Note	1862	Alexander Hamilton
	Legal Tender Note	1869-1963A	Thomas Jefferson
	Silver Certificate	1886	General Hancock
	Silver Certificate	1891	William Windom
	Silver Certificate	1899	George Washington
	Treasury or Coin Note	1890-1891	Gen. James McPherson

Denom.	Type of Note	Series	Portrait
$5	Demand Note	1861	Alexander Hamilton
	Federal Reserve Note	1914 to date	Abraham Lincoln
	Federal Reserve Bank Note	1915-1929	Abraham Lincoln
	Legal Tender Note	1869-1907	Andrew Jackson
	Legal Tender Note	1928-1963A	Abraham Lincoln
	National Bank Note	1882	James Garfield
	National Bank Note	1902	Benjamin Harrison
	National Bank Note	1929	Abraham Lincoln
	Silver Certificate	1886	Ulysses S. Grant
	Silver Certificate	1899	Running Antelope
	Silver Certificate	1923-1953C	Abraham Lincoln
	Treasury or Coin Note	1890-1891	Gen. George Thomas
Denom.	**Type of Note**	**Series**	**Portrait**
$10	Demand Note	1861	Abraham Lincoln
	Compound Interest Treasury Note	1863-1864	Salmon P. Chase
	Interest Bearing Note, 3 year	1863	Salmon P. Chase
	Federal Reserve Note	1914	Andrew Jackson
	Federal Reserve Note	1928 to date	Alexander Hamilton
	Federal Reserve Bank Note	1915-1918	Andrew Jackson
	Federal Reserve Bank Note	1929	Alexander Hamilton
	Gold Certificate	1907-1922	Michael Hillegas
	Gold Certificate	1928	Alexander Hamilton
	Legal Tender Note	1862-1863	Abraham Lincoln
	Legal Tender Note	1869-1880	Daniel Webster
	Legal Tender Note	1901	Lewis & Clark
	Legal Tender Note	1923	Andrew Jackson
	National Bank Note	1902	William McKinley
	National Bank Note	1929	Alexander Hamilton
	Refunding Certificate	1879	Benjamin Franklin
	Silver Certificate	1878-1880	Robert Morris
	Silver Certificate	1886-1908	Thomas A. Hendricks
	Silver Certificate	1933-1953B	Alexander Hamilton
	Treasury or Coin Note	1890-1891	General Sheridan
$20	Compound Interest Treasury Note	1863-1864	Abraham Lincoln
	Federal Reserve Note	1914	Grover Cleveland
	Federal Reserve Note	1928 to date	Andrew Jackson
	Federal Reserve Bank Note	1915-1918	Grover Cleveland
	Federal Reserve Bank Note	1929	Andrew Jackson
	Gold Certificate	1882	James Garfield
	Gold Certificate	1905-1922	George Washington
	Gold Certificate	1928	Andrew Jackson
	Interest Bearing Note, 1 year	1863	Abraham Lincoln
	Legal Tender Note	1869-1880	Alexander Hamilton
	National Bank Note	1902	Hugh McCulloch
	National Bank Note	1929	Andrew Jackson
	Silver Certificate	1878-1880	Stephen Decatur
	Silver Certificate	1886-1891	Daniel Manning
	Treasury or Coin Note	1890-1891	John Marshall
$50	Compound Interest Treasury Note	1863-1864	Alexander Hamilton
	Federal Reserve Note	1914 to date	Ulysses S. Grant
	Federal Reserve Bank Note	1918-1929	Ulysses S. Grant
	Gold Certificate	1882	Silas Wright
	Gold Certificate	1913-1928	Ulysses S. Grant
	Interest Bearing Note, 1 year	1863	Alexander Hamilton
	Legal Tender Note	1862-1863	Alexander Hamilton
	Legal Tender Note	1869	Henry Clay
	Legal Tender Note	1874-1880	Benjamin Franklin
	National Bank Note	1902	John Sherman

Denom.	Type of Note	Series	Portrait
	National Bank Note	1929	Ulysses S. Grant
	Silver Certificate	1878-1891	Edward Everett
	Treasury or Coin Note	1890-1891	William H. Seward
$100	Compound Interest Treasury Note	1863-1864	George Washington
	Federal Reserve Note	1914 to date	Benjamin Franklin
	Federal Reserve Bank Note	1929	Benjamin Franklin
	Gold Certificate	1875-1882	Thomas H. Benton
	Gold Certificate	1928-1934	Benjamin Franklin
	Interest Bearing Note, 1 year	1863	George Washington
	Interest Bearing Note, 3 year	1864	General Scott
	Legal Tender Note	1869-1880	Abraham Lincoln
	National Bank Note	1902	John J. Knox
	National Bank Note	1929	Benjamin Franklin
	Silver Certificate	1878-1891	James Monroe
	Treasury or Coin Note	1890-1891	Commodore Farragut
$500	Federal Reserve Note	1914	John Marshall
	Federal Reserve Note	1928-1934	William McKinley
	Gold Certificate	1875-1922	Abraham Lincoln
	Gold Certificate	1928	William McKinley
	Interest Bearing Note, 3 year	1864	Alexander Hamilton
	Legal Tender Note	1862-1863	Albert Gallatin
	Legal Tender Note	1869	John Quincy Adams
	Legal Tender Note	1874-1880	Maj. Gen. Mansfield
	Silver Certificate	1878-1880	Charles Sumner
$1,000	Federal Reserve Note	1918	Alexander Hamilton
	Federal Reserve Note	1928-1934A	Grover Cleveland
	Gold Certificate	1875-1922	Alexander Hamilton
	Gold Certificate	1928-1934	Grover Cleveland
	Interest Bearing Note, 3 year	1863	Salmon P. Chase
	Legal Tender Note	1862-1863	Robert Morris
	Legal Tender Note	1869-1880	DeWitt Clinton
	Silver Certificate	1878-1891	William L. Marcy
	Treasury or Coin Note	1890-1891	Gen. George Meade
$5,000	Federal Reserve Note	1918-1934	James Madison
	Gold Certificate	1882-1928	James Madison
	Legal Tender Note	1878	James Madison
$10,000	Federal Reserve Note	1918-1934	Salmon P. Chase
	Gold Certificate	1882-1902	Andrew Jackson
	Gold Certificate	1928-1934	Salmon P. Chase
	Legal Tender Note	1878	Andrew Jackson
$100,000	Gold Certificate	1934	Woodrow Wilson

Portraits on U.S. paper money

Listed by name

ADAMS, John Quincy (1767-1848), sixth president of the United States. Born in Quincy, Mass., he served as American minister in the Netherlands, Berlin, St. Petersburg and London, as senator from 1803 to 1808 and was appointed secretary of state in 1817. Elected president in 1824, served until 1829. Elected to the House in 1831 where he served until his death in 1848.

$500 1869 United States (legal tender) note
$2 Southern Bank of Indiana, Terre Haute

ADAMS, Samuel (1722-1803). Born in Boston, he served as tax collector there from 1756 to 1764. He was elected to the Massachusetts legislature in 1765, serving until 1774. He was a leader in the agitation that led to the Boston Tea Party. Delegate to

the first and second Continental Congress, he signed the Declaration of Independence. He was lieutenant governor and then governor (1794-1797) of Massachusetts.
$10 1862 Arkansas Treasury Warrant
ALCORN, J.L., governor of Mississippi.
$1 1870 State of Mississippi, Jackson, Miss.
$2 1870 State of Mississippi, Jackson, Miss.
$3 1870 State of Mississippi, Jackson, Miss.
BAKER, E.D. (1811-?). Born in London on Feb. 24, 1811, he came to the U.S. in 1816, studied and practiced law in Springfield, Ill., served as state senator in 1840 and was elected to Congress in 1844. Baker was killed in the early days of the Civil War while commanding a Union brigade.
$5,000 1872 Currency Certificate of Deposit
BEAUREGARD, Gen. P.G.T. (1818-1893). Pierre Gustave Toutant de Beauregard was born near New Orleans, La. Graduated from West Point in 1838, he served through the Mexican War. He was superintendent of West Point at the outbreak of the Civil War; he resigned to enter the Confederate Army. He was in command at the bombardment of Fort Sumter and served at Bull Run, Shiloh and Corinth. He was manager of the Louisiana Lottery and commissioner of public works in New Orleans (1888).
$20 1863 State of Louisiana, Shreveport
BENJAMIN, Judah Philip (1811-1884). Born in St. Croix, British West Indies (some sources say St. Thomas, Virgin Islands), he entered Yale in 1825. He entered the U.S. Senate in 1852 and withdrew in 1861 to join the Confederacy. He served as attorney general, secretary of war and secretary of state in the Confederacy.
$2 Sept. 2, 1861 Confederate note
$2 June 2, 1862 Confederate note
$2 Dec. 2, 1862 Confederate note
$2 Apr. 6, 1863 Confederate note
$2 Feb. 17, 1864 Confederate note
BENNETT, Jonathan M., governor of Virginia.
$5 1862 Virginia Treasury note
BENTON, Thomas Hart (1782-1858), served in U.S. Senate (1821-1851) and in the U.S. House of Representatives (1853-1855). He was in favor of Western development and spoke out against slavery.
$100 1863, 1882 gold certificate

BOONE, Daniel (1734-1820). Born near Reading, Pa., in 1734, he made trips to Kentucky in 1767, 1769-1770. He guided settlers into Kentucky (1775) and erected a fort on the site of what is now Boonesboro. Served in Virginia legislature. After some years in Virginia he moved into what is now Missouri and secured a land grant.
$3 Clark's Exchange Bank, Springfield, Ill.
$10 Bank of Kentucky, Louisville, Ky.
$10 Bank of Louisville, Kentucky
BOUDINOT, Elias (1740-1821) born in Philadelphia. Opened law practice in Elizabethtown, N.J. Member and president of the Continental Congress. Member of U.S. Congress (1789-1795). Appointed Director of the Mint in October 1795 by Washington and served until July 1, 1805. Trustee of Princeton (1772-1821). Helped found American Bible Society in 1816 and served as its first president.
$2 1858 Merchants Bank, New Bedford, Mass.
$2 1858 Delaware City Bank, Delaware City, Kan.
$2 1859 Safety Fund Bank, Boston, Mass.
$2 1861 Bank of Penn Township, Philadelphia, Pa.
$2 1861 What Cheer Bank, Providence, R.I.
$5 1863 Belvidere Bank, Belvidere, N.J.
$20 18-- Augusta, Ga., Insurance and Banking Co.
$20 1832 Bank of Darien, Ga.
$20 1857 Augusta, Ga., Insurance and Banking Co.

BROWN, Joseph E., governor of Georgia.
$50 1862 The State of Georgia, Milledgeville
$100 1863 The State of Georgia, Milledgeville
BUCHANAN, James (1791-1868), 15th president of the United States. Born near Mercersburg, Pa., he graduated from Dickinson College in 1809. A volunteer in the War of 1812, member of the House from 1821 to 1831, U.S. minister to Great Britain from 1853-1856, he was elected president in 1856 and served until 1861.
$10 North Western Bank, Ringgold, Ga.
$20 Bank of Pittsylvania, Chatham, Pa.
$3 1856 Fontenelle Bank, Bellevue, Neb.
$5 1852 Omaha, Neb., City Bank and Land Co.
$5 1857 Bank of Tekama, Neb.
$5 1858 Bank of the District of Columbia
$5 1859 Union Bank of Columbia, Washington, D.C.

$5 1861 Monongahela Valley Bank, McKee's Port, Pa.
$5 18-- Bank of Crawford County, Pa.
$10 1857 New England Bank, Fairmount, Maine
$10 1857 Manufacturers Bank, Macon, Ga.

CALHOUN, John Caldwell (1782-1850). Born near Calhoun Mills, S.C., he graduated from Yale in 1804. A member of the House from 1811-1817, secretary of war (1817-1825), vice president from 1825 to 1832, senator (1832-1843), secretary of state (1844-1845), he championed slavery and the southern cause in Senate debates.
$2 1860 Eastern Bank of Alabama, Eufala
$2 Bank of the State of S. Carolina, Charleston
$5 Northern Bank of Alabama, Huntsville
$5 Bank of South Carolina
$10 Bank of East Tennessee, Knoxville
$10 Northern Bank of Alabama, Huntsville
$10 1862 Manufacturers Bank, Macon, Ga.
$10 1860 Farmers and Mechanics Bank, Savannah, Ga.
$20 1860 Farmers and Mechanics Bank, Savannah, Ga.
$25 Planters Bank of Fairfield, Tenn.
$100 Confederate note, April 17, 1862
$1,000 Confederate note, Montgomery issue, 1861

CHASE, Salmon Portland (1808-1873). Governor of Ohio, Secretary of the Treasury under Lincoln (1861-1864), he originated national banking system. Chief Justice of the Supreme Court (1864-1873).
$1 1862 legal tender
$10 1863, 1864 6 percent compound interest Treasury note
$10 1863 5 percent compound interest Treasury note
$20 1861 6 percent 2-year, interest-bearing Treasury note
$1,000 1861, 1864, 1865 7.3 percent 3-year interest-bearing note
$10,000 1918, 1928, 1934 Federal Reserve note
$10,000 1928, 1934 gold certificate

CLARK, Spencer M. (1810-1890), first chief of the National Currency Bureau, predecessor of the Bureau of Engraving and Printing, from 1862 to 1868. This is one of the more curious U.S. paper notes. An order from the Treasury Department directed an issue to honor Lewis and Clark, the famed explorers of the Northwest Territory. Instead, Spencer Clark, a $1,200-a-year chief clerk, interpreted the order to mean his image was to be placed on the note. Congress wanted to fire him, but Salmon P. Chase, the Secretary of the Treasury, intervened and saved his job. As a direct result of this action, Congress enacted a law forbidding the likeness of any living person on any obligation of the U.S.
5¢ fractional currency, third issue

CLARK, William (1770-1838), American explorer. The Lewis and Clark Expedition, in 1804, opened up the Louisiana Purchase to settlers.
$10 1901 legal tender (nicknamed "Buffalo") note

CLAY, Clement C. (1819-1882). Born in Huntsville, Ala., he graduated from the University of Alabama in 1835, and was admitted to the bar in 1840. He was elected to the Senate in 1853 and reelected in 1861, when he was expelled for "treasonable utterances." He became a member of the Confederate Senate.
$1 1862, 1863, 1864 Confederate note

CLAY, Henry (1777-1852). Born in Hanover County, Va., he practiced law in Lexington, Ky., and was elected to the Kentucky legislature in 1803. He acted as counsel for Aaron Burr in 1806. He was elected to the Senate in 1809, and served in the Senate and House until 1821. Reelected to the House in 1823 and serving until 1825, was secretary of state (1825-1829), senator (1831-1842), Whig candidate for president in 1832 and 1844, again senator (1849-1852).
$50 1869 United States (legal tender) note
$1 Farmers and Millers Bank, Milwaukee, Wis.
$2 American Bank, Baltimore, Md.
$2 Stonington Bank, Stonington, Conn.
$2 Shawnee Bank, Attica, Ind.
$5 Bank of Kentucky, Louisville, Ky.
$5 Farmers and Mechanics Bank, Shippensburg, Pa.
$20 City Bank of New Haven, Conn.

CLEVELAND, Stephen Grover (1837-1908). Twenty-second (1885-1889) and 24th (1893-1897) president of the United States, the only president to serve two non-consecutive terms. Born in Caldwell, N.J., he was mayor of Buffalo, N.Y. (1881-1882), governor of New York (1883-1885). He was defeated by Benjamin Harrison in his bid for president in 1888.
$20 1915, 1918 Federal Reserve Bank note

$20 1914 Federal Reserve note
$1,000 1928, 1934 Federal Reserve note
$1,000 1928, 1934 gold certificate
CLINTON, DeWitt (1769-1828). Born in Little Britain, N.Y., he graduated from Columbia College in 1786. He was elected to the Senate in 1798 and served until 1802, and again from 1806 to 1811. Elected mayor of New York in 1802 and serving three terms as governor of New York, he was the chief sponsor of the Erie Canal.
$1,000 1869, 1878, 1880 United States (legal tender) note
$1 Franklin Bank, Jersey City, N.J.
CONANT, Charles A. A leading proponent of the Philippine National Bank, Conant is considered to be the "Father" of the United States-Philippine currency system.
1 peso 1918, 1921 & 1924 Philippine national bank circulating notes
COURTS, D.W.
$5 1863 State of North Carolina, Raleigh, N.C.
$10 1863 State of North Carolina, Raleigh, N.C.
CRAWFORD, William H. (1772-1834). A senator from Georgia (1807-1813), he also served as secretary of war under President Madison (1815-1816) and Secretary of the Treasury (1815-1825).
50¢ fractional currency, fifth issue
CRITTENDEN, John Jordan (1787-1863). Born near Versailles, Ky., he was a senator (1817-1819, 1835-1841, 1842-1848 and 1850-1853). He also served as attorney general (1841, 1850-1853) and as governor of Kentucky (1848-1850).
$50 Commercial Bank of Kentucky, Paducah, Ky.
DAVIS, Jefferson (1808-1889). Born in Fairfield, Ky., he was appointed to West Point in 1824 and served in the army until 1835. He was elected to the House in 1845, resigned in 1846 to serve in the Mexican War. He was a senator (1847-1851), secretary of war (1853-1857), and again senator (1857-1861). Chosen president of the Confederacy Feb. 18, 1861, he fled from Richmond in 1865 and was captured and indicted for treason, but the government entered a nolle prosequi in 1868. He retired to his estate near Biloxi, Miss.
50¢ Apr. 6, 1863 Confederate note
50¢ Feb. 17, 1864 Confederate note
$1 1862 State of Missouri, Jefferson City, Mo.
$1, $2, $3, 1862 Arkansas Treasury Warrant
$50 Sept. 2, 1861 Confederate note

$50 Dec. 2, 1862 Confederate note
$50 Apr. 6, 1863 Confederate note
$50 Feb. 17, 1864 Confederate note
$100 Missouri Defense Bond
DECATUR, Stephen (1779-1820), Naval officer, hero of the "war" with Tripoli and War of 1812, killed in a duel with James Brown on March 20, 1820.
$20 1878, 1880 silver certificate
DEXTER, Samuel (1761-1816), Member of House (1793-1795), Senate (1799-1800), secretary of war (1800), secretary of Treasury (1801).
50¢ fractional currency, fourth issue
DOUGLAS, Stephen A. (1813-1861). Born in Brandon, Vt., he was elected to the House in 1843 and served until 1847. He was a senator (1847-1861), and a nominee for president in 1856.
$10,000 1872, 1875 currency certificate of deposit
$2 Bank of Ottawa, Ill.
$5 State Bank of Illinois, Shawneetown, Ill.
EVERETT, Edward (1794-1865), Born in Dorchester, Mass., he was appointed professor of Greek at Harvard at age 21. Elected to the House in 1824, he assumed the governorship of Massachusetts in 1835. He was U.S. minister to Great Britain and president of Harvard, and was appointed secretary of state (1852-1853), serving only four months. He was elected to the Senate in 1853 and served until 1854.
$50 1878, 1880, 1891 silver certificate
FARRAGUT, David Glasgow (1801-1870). Born in Tennessee, he was adopted by Commodore Porter in 1808. He served on the Union side during the Civil War and captured New Orleans without bloodshed; his distinguished service during the war earned him the rank of vice-admiral (1864) and admiral (1866), two ranks created specially for him by Congress.
$100 1890, 1891 Treasury note
FESSENDEN, William Pitt (1806-1869), Born in Boscawen, N.H., he was elected to the House (1841-1843) and Senate (1854-1864), and served as Secretary of the Treasury (1864-1865). He was elected to the Senate again in 1865 and served until 1869.
25¢ fractional currency, third issue
$10 national bank note, Second Charter
FILLMORE, Millard (1800-1874), 13th president of the United States. Born at Locke, N.Y., he was a member of the House (1833-1835, 1837-1843), and vice presi-

dent (1849-1850). He became president upon the death of Zachary Taylor (July 9, 1850), and was a presidential candidate in 1852.
$2 American Bank, Trenton, N.J.
$50 Northern Bank of Alabama, Huntsville, Ala.

FLOYD, John B. (1806-1863). Born in Smithfield, Va., he was governor of Virginia (1849-1852), secretary of war (1857-1860). He resigned to enter Confederate services as brigadier of volunteers.
$10 1862 Virginia Treasury note
$1,000 Commonwealth of Virginia bond

FRANKLIN, Benjamin (1706-1790). Born in Boston in 1706, he left there in 1723 for Philadelphia, where he was proprietor of a printing business and publisher of "The Pennsylvania Gazette" (1730-1748) and "Poor Richard's Almanac" (1725-1757). He was the Pennsylvania delegate to the Albany Congress in 1754 and a member of the second Continental Congress in 1775. He was on the committee to draft the Declaration of Independence and one of its signers.
$10 1863, 1864, 1865, 1875 national bank note, all charter periods (vignette: "Franklin Drawing Electricity from the Sky")
$10 1870, 1872, 1873, 1874, 1875 national gold bank note (vignette as above)
$10 1879 refunding certificate
$50 1874, 1875, 1878, 1880 United States (legal tender) notes
$100 1966 and all later series United States (legal tender) notes
$100 1914 and all later series Federal Reserve notes
$100 1929 Federal Reserve Bank note
$100 1929 National Bank note
$100 1928, 1928A gold certificate
$1 Merchants and Planters Bank, Savannah, Ga.
$1 1854 Bank of Anacastia, Washington, D.C.
$3 Bank of Manchester, Mich.
$3 Bank of Augusta, Ga.
$3 1860 Eastern Bank of Alabama, Eufala, Ala.
$3 Columbia Bank, District of Columbia
$5 Mechanics Bank, Memphis
$5 Roxbury Bank, Mass.
$10 Bank of the Republic, District of Columbia
$10 Eagle Bank of New Haven, Conn.
$10 Bank of Augusta, Ga.
$20 South Carolina Bank
$20 Mechanics Bank, Augusta, Ga.

$20 Central Bank of Alabama, Montgomery, Ala.
$1,000 Bank of the U.S., Philadelphia, Pa.
FULTON, Robert (1765-1815). Beginning his career as a painter, he later devoted himself to mechanics and engineering study. He invented the first practical steamboat, the *Clermont* (1807).
$2 1896 silver certificate (reverse)
GALLATIN, Albert (1761-1849). Born in Geneva, Switzerland, he came to America in 1780. He was elected to the Senate in 1793 and served as secretary of the Treasury under Jefferson (1801-1814), and later as U.S. minister to France and Great Britain.
$500 1862, 1863 United States (legal tender) note
GARFIELD, James A. (1831-1881), 20th president of the United States. Born in Orange, Ohio, he served in the Ohio state senate and later as a Civil War general. He was elected to the House (1863-1880) and was elected president in 1880. He was shot by Charles J. Guiteau in a Washington railroad station July 22, 1881, and died Sept. 19, 1881.
$5 national bank note, Second Charter
$20 1882 gold certificate
GRANT, Ulysses S. (1822-1885), 18th president of the United States. Born in Point Pleasant, Ohio, he graduated from West Point in 1843. He served in the Mexican War and was appointed brigadier general in 1861. He was in command at the Battle of Shiloh in the Civil War and received Lee's surrender at Appomattox Court House (April 9, 1865), and was promoted to the rank of general in 1866. He was elected president in 1868 and reelected in 1872.
15¢ fractional currency, fourth issue
$1 1899 silver certificate
$5 1886, 1891 silver certificate
$5 1896 silver certificate (reverse)
$50 1914 and all later issues Federal Reserve notes
$50 1918 Federal Reserve Bank note
$50 1929 national bank note
$50 1928 gold certificate
HAMILTON, Alexander (1754-1804), first Secretary of the Treasury. Born on island of Nevis, Leeward Islands, he studied at King's College (now Columbia University). He served through the Revolution as secretary and aide-de-camp to Washington. A member of the Continental Congress, he was Secretary of the Treasury from 1789 to 1795. He was instrumental

in defeating Aaron Burr for the presidency in 1801. He planned and initiated policies establishing the national fiscal system.
$2 1862 legal tender
$5 1861 demand note
$5 1862, 1863 legal tender
$10 1933 and all later series silver certificates
$10 1929 Federal Reserve Bank notes
$10 1928 and all later series Federal Reserve notes
$10 1929 national bank notes
$10 1928, 1928A gold certificates
$20 1869, 1875, 1878, 1880 legal tender notes
$50 1862 legal tender notes
$50 1863 6 percent compound interest treasury note
$50 5 percent interest-bearing note
$500 1861 7.3 percent three-year interest-bearing note
$1,000 1863, 1870, 1871, 1875, 1882, 1907, 1922 gold certificates
$1,000 1918 Federal Reserve note

HANCOCK, Gen. Winfield Scott (1824-1886), American Civil War general. He fought in the battles of Chancellorsville, Fredericksburg and Gettysburg and held off Pickett's charge at Gettysburg. He was defeated in his 1880 bid for president by James Garfield.
$2 1886 silver certificate

HARRISON, Benjamin (1833-1901), 23rd president of the United States. He was a Civil War general, senator (1881-1887) and served one term as president (1889-1893).
$5 national bank note, Third Charter (all types)

HARRISON, William H. (1773-1841), ninth president of the United States. Born in Charles City County, Va., he was secretary of the Northwest Territory in 1798 and governor of the Territory of Indiana (1801-1813). Serving in the House (1816-1819) and Senate (1825-1828), he was elected president in 1840 but died of pneumonia a month after his inauguration.
$1 Southern Bank of Indiana, Terre Haute

HENDRICKS, Thomas Andrew (1819-1885), vice president of the United States in 1885 under Grover Cleveland, serving for nine months. A member of the House (1851-1855) and Senate (1863-1869), he was elected governor of Indiana in 1872.
$10 1886, 1891, 1908 silver certificates

HENRY, Patrick (1736-1799). Born in Hanover County, Va., he served in the Virginia legislature in 1765 and as a member of the Continental Congress. He was twice elected governor of Virginia, 1776-1779 and again 1784-1786.
$10 Bank of Augusta, Ga.

HILLEGAS, Michael (1729-1804). Born in Philadelphia, Pa., he was first Treasurer of the United States (1775-1789).
$10 1907, 1922 gold certificate

HUNTER, R.M.T. (1809-1887). Born in Essex County, Va., he was educated at the University of Virginia. He was elected to the House (1837-1843, 1845-1847), Senate (1847-1861), and was secretary of state of the Confederate States of America. He later served as treasurer of Virginia (1874-1880).
$10 Sept. 2, 1861 Confederate note
$10 Sept. 2, 1862 Confederate note
$10 Dec. 2, 1862 Confederate note
$10 Apr. 6, 1863 Confederate note
$10 Feb. 17, 1864 Confederate note
$20 Sept. 2, 1862 Confederate note

JACKSON, Andrew (1767-1845), seventh president of the United States. Born in Waxhaw, S.C., he was a member of the House (1796-1797) and Senate (1797-1798), (1823-1825). He was elected president in 1828 and again in 1832. He refused to renew the charter of the Bank of the United States and withdrew government funds on deposit, ensuring the demise of that institution and opening the way for "wildcat" banking.
$1 Bank of East Tennessee, Knoxville
$1 Mechanics Bank of Memphis, Tenn.
$2 Corn Exchange Bank, Wapun, Wisc.
$3 Mechanics Bank of Memphis, Tenn.
$5 Mechanics Bank of Memphis, Tenn.
$5 Farmers and Merchants Bank, Cecil Co., Md.
$5 Bank of America, Clarksville, Tenn.
$5 Southern Bank of Tennessee, Memphis
$5 1869, 1875, 1878, 1880, 1907 United States (legal tender) note
$10 State of Tennessee, 1875
$10 Bank of Tennessee, Nashville
$10 1923 United States (legal tender) note
$10 1914 Federal Reserve note
$10 1915, 1918 Federal Reserve Bank note
$20 1929 national bank note
$20 1928, 1928A gold certificate
$20 1928 and all later series Federal Reserve notes
$50 6 percent two-year interest-bearing Treasury note

$10,000 1878 United States (legal tender) note

$10,000 1863, 1870, 1871, 1875, 1882, 1888, 1902 gold certificate

$3 Central Bank of Alabama, Montgomery, Ala.

$3 American Bank, Baltimore, Md.

$5 1862 Manufacturers Bank, Macon, Ga.

$5 Mechanics Bank, Concord, N.H.

$10 Mechanics Bank, Concord, N.H.

$1,000 Confederate States of America Montgomery issue, 1861

JACKSON, C.F., governor of Missouri who advocated secession immediately prior to the Civil War.

$3 1862 State of Missouri, Jefferson City, Mo.

JACKSON, George James.

$20 1836 Bank of Augusta, Ga.

JACKSON, Gen. T.J. (1824-1863). Born in Clarksburg, Va., he was admitted to West Point in 1842 and graduated in 1846. He served in the Mexican War under Gen. Winfield Scott, and resigned from the Army in 1852. He entered Confederate service at the outbreak of the Civil War and gained his nickname "Stonewall" from his stand at Bull Run. He was accidentally killed by his own men at the Battle of Chancellorsville in 1863.

$500 Feb. 17, 1864 Confederate note

JEFFERSON, Thomas (1743-1826), third president of the United States. Born in Goochland, Va., he graduated from the College of William and Mary in 1762 and was admitted to the bar in 1767. A member of the Virginia House of Burgesses (1769-1774) and the Continental Congress (1775, 1776), he was chairman of the committee that prepared the Declaration of Independence. He wrote and presented the first draft of the Declaration to Congress on July 2, 1776. He was governor of Virginia (1779-1781), U.S. minister to France (1785-1789), secretary of state (1790-1793), vice president (1797-1801), and president (1801-1809).

5¢ postage currency, first issue

25¢ postage currency first issue

$2 1869, 1874, 1875, 1878, 1880, 1917 and all later issues of United States (legal tender) notes

$2 1918 Federal Reserve Bank note

$2 1976 Federal Reserve note

$3 Farmers and Mechanics Bank, Milford, Del.

$5 1863 Real Estate Bank, Newport, Del.

$5 Bank of Kentucky, Louisville, Ky.

$20 State of Louisiana, New Orleans, La.

$10 Mechanics Bank, Concord, N.H.

5¢ Jersey City, N.J.

$5 Bank of Charleston, W. Va.

$5 Bank of Chester, Tenn.

$5 Monticello Bank, Va.

$10 Monticello Bank, Va.

$20 Bank of the Commonwealth, Richmond, Va.

$20 Monticello Bank, Va.

$100 Monticello Bank, Va.

KNOX, John J. (1828-1892), comptroller of the currency from 1872 to 1884.

$100 national bank note, Third Charter

LAFAYETTE, Marie Joseph Paul Yves Roch Gilbert du Motier (1757-1834). Entering French military service in 1771, he left to enter American service in the Revolutionary War in 1777 and was made major general in the Continental army. He returned to France in 1781.

$5 Southern Bank of Indiana, Terre Haute, Ind.

$5 Lafayette Bank, Massachusetts

$10 1837 Mississippi and Alabama Railroad Company, Brandon, Miss.

LAMAR, Mary.

$2½ 1862 The Exchange Bank, Edwards County, Ill.

LETCHER, John, governor of Virginia.

$100 1862 Virginia Treasury note

$1 1862 Virginia Treasury note

LEWIS, Meriwether (1774-1809). Born in Albermarle County, Va., he was private secretary to President Jefferson (1801-1803) and was named by him to lead an expedition to explore the Louisiana Purchase lands and selected William Clark as his partner. The Lewis and Clark Expedition (1804-1806) went up the Missouri River to its source, crossed the Great Divide and descended the Columbia River to the Pacific Ocean. He was governor of Louisiana from 1807 to 1809.

$10 1901 United States (legal tender) "Buffalo" note

LINCOLN, Abraham (1809-1865), 16th president of the United States. Born in Hardin County, Ky., he moved to Indiana (1816) and to Macon County, Ill., in 1830. He studied law in his spare time from 1831 to 1837 and was elected to Illinois legislature (1834-1841). He was a member of the U.S. House of Representatives (1847-1849) and was nominated for vice president in 1856, nominated for Senate in 1858 but lost. Elected president in 1860 and again in 1864. He was shot at Ford's Theatre by John Wilkes Booth on

Good Friday, April 14, 1864, and died early the next morning.
50¢ fractional currency, fourth issue
$1 1899 silver certificate
$5 1923 "Porthole" silver certificate
$5 1915, 1918 Federal Reserve Bank note
$5 1914 and all later series Federal Reserve notes
$10 1861 demand note
$10 1862, 1863 legal tender note
$20 1863 6 percent compound interest Treasury note
$20 1863 5 percent interest-bearing note
$100 1869, 1875, 1878, 1880 United States (legal tender) note
$500 1863, 1870, 1871, 1882, 1922 gold certificates
$1 1861 Merchants Bank, Trenton, N.J.
$1 1862 Bank of Commerce, Georgetown, D.C.
$1 1862 Lincoln Bank, Clinton, N.Y.
$2 1862 Lincoln Bank, Clinton, N.Y.

LIND, Jenny, (1820-1887), the "Swedish Nightingale." Appearing first in theater in Die Freischutz (1838), she was a court singer (1840) and studied in Paris under Garcia (1841). She toured Germany and gained popularity in London (1847-1848). She retired from the operatic stage in 1849 and devoted herself to concert singing and oratorio. She was engaged to sing in America by P.T. Barnum (1850-1852) and toured Europe, spending her last years in England and becoming a British subject in 1859.
$1 (var. written dates) Hartford Bank, Conn.
$1 (var. written dates) Stock Security Bank, Danville, Ill.

LONGFELLOW, Alice, Allegra and Edith.
$2 1861 Mechanics Bank, St. Louis, Mo.

LYON, Pat, an early fire engine builder of considerable fame.
$1 Augusta Insurance and Banking Co., Augusta, Ga.
$3 Bank of Washtenaw, Mich.

MADISON, Dolly (1768-1849). Dorthea (nee Payne) Madison was born in Guilford County, N.C., and married James Madison in 1794. She was a famous Washington hostess while her husband was secretary of state (1801-1809) and president (1809-1817).
$10 Pawtucket Bank, Epping, N.H.

MADISON, James (1751-1836), fourth president of the United States. He was born in Port Conway, Va., and graduated from Princeton in 1771. A member of the Continental Congress and Constitutional

Convention in 1787 and the House (1789-1797), he was secretary of state under Jefferson (1801-1809) and president (1809-1817).
$5,000 1878 United States (legal tender) note
$5,000 1863, 1870, 1871, 1872, 1882, 1888, 1928 gold certificates
$5,000 1918, 1928, 1934 Federal Reserve note
$5 Bank of Kentucky, Louisville, Ky.

MANNING, Daniel (1831-1887), prominent New York banker. He was Secretary of the Treasury under Cleveland (1885-1887).
$20 1886, 1891 silver certificates

MANSFIELD, Joseph King. Born in New Haven, Conn., in 1803, he graduated from West Point. He was made brigadier general early in the Civil War and was killed at the Battle of Antietam.
$500 1873, 1875, 1878, 1880 United States (legal tender) notes

MARCY, William L. (1786-1857). Born in Southbridge, Mass., he graduated from Brown University. He was comptroller for the state of New York (1823-1829), associate justice of the New York Supreme Court (1829-1831), senator (1831, 1832), governor of New York (1833-1839), secretary of war (1845-1849) and secretary of state under Franklin Pierce (1853-1857).
$1,000 1878, 1880, 1891 silver certificates

MARION, Gen. Francis (1732-1795). Born in Winyah, near Georgetown, S.C., he fought in the Revolutionary War in guerrilla warfare, earning the nickname "the Swamp Fox." Under instructions to get Marion, British General Sir Banastre Tarleton failed to even locate him. Finally Marion invited Gen. Tarleton to dinner at Marion's camp after Tarleton asked for an interview under a truce flag.
$10 Sept. 2, 1861 Confederate note
$5 State of S. Carolina, 1866 and 1872
$10 Bank of Kentucky, Louisville
$20 Bank of Kentucky, Louisville, Ky.
$50 Bank of Kentucky, Louisville, Ky.

MARSHALL, John (1755-1835). Born in Virginia, he was Chief Justice of the Supreme Court (1801-1835) and established the strength and power of the court.
$20 1890, 1891 Treasury or coin notes
$500 1918 Federal Reserve note
$1 Southern Bank of Indiana, Terre Haute, Ind.
$10 Stafford Bank, Dover, N.H.
$50 Farmers Bank of Schuylkill County, Pa.

MASON, James M., governor of Virginia
$50 1862 Virginia Treasury note
$1,000 Commonwealth of Virginia Bond
McCLELLAN, George B. (1826-1885). Educated at the University of Pennsylvania (1842-1844). Transferred to West Point and graduated 1846, the youngest in his class. Author and railroad executive. Succeeded Winfield Scott as general of the Union Army. Unsuccessful Democratic presidential candidate 1864. Governor of New Jersey 1877-1881.
10¢ 1863 Searsport Bank, Frankfort, Maine
$1 1862 Chicopee Bank, Springfield, Mass.
$2 1861 Merchants Bank, Trenton, N.J.
$20 1862 Rutland County Bank, Vt.
McCULLOUGH, Hugh (1808-1895), Secretary of the Treasury under Lincoln (1865-1869) and Arthur (1884-1885).
$20 national bank note, Third Charter (all types)
McKINLEY, William (1843-1901), 25th president of the United States. Born in Niles, Ohio, he served in the Civil War. He was a member of the House (1877-1883, 1885, 1891), governor of Ohio (1892-1896) and president (1897-1901). He was shot by Leon Czolgosz, an anarchist, in Buffalo, N.Y. Sept. 6, 1901 and died Sept. 14.
$10 national bank note, Third Charter (all types)
$500 1928 and all later series Federal Reserve notes
MEADE, George Gordon. Born in 1815, he became a major general in 1864 after serving and being wounded in the Civil War.
$1,000 1890, 1891 Treasury notes
MEMMINGER, Christopher Gustavus (1803-1888). Born in Germany, he came to the U.S. as a child. He was Secretary of the Treasury of the Confederacy (1861-1864).
$5 and $10 Sept. 2, 1861 Confederate note
$5 Dec. 2, 1862 Confederate note
$5 Apr. 6, 1863 Confederate note
$5 Feb. 17, 1864 Confederate note
MEREDITH, William Morris (1799-1873). Born in Philadelphia, Pa., he was Secretary of the Treasury (1849-1850) and attorney general of Pennsylvania (1861-1867).
10¢ fractional currency, fifth issue

MONROE, James (1758-1831), fifth president of the United States. Born in Westmoreland County, Va., he served in the American Revolution, as a member of the Continental Congress and senator (1790-1794). He was minister to France (1794-1796), governor of Virginia (1799-1802), one of the negotiators of the Louisiana Purchase (1803), minister to England (1803-1807), secretary of state (1811-1817), and secretary of war (1814-1815). He served as president from 1817 to 1825.
$100 1878, 1880, 1881 silver certificate
$4 Bank of Monroe, Monroe, Mich.
MORRIS, Robert (1734-1806). Born in England, he came to America in 1747 and favored the Colonial cause in the Revolution. He was a member of the Continental Congress and a signer of the Declaration of Independence. He served as superintendent of finance (1781-1784), founded and organized the Bank of North America (1782) and was a delegate to the Constitutional convention in 1787. He served in the Senate from 1789 to 1795.
$10 1878, 1880 silver certificates
$1,000 1862, 1863 United States (legal tender) notes
$1,000 Bank of U.S. note (lower right corner)
$10 Northampton Bank, Pa.
MORSE, Samuel Finley Breese (1791-1872). Born in Charleston, Mass., he was a portrait painter in Boston, Charleston and New York. He was founder and first president of the National Academy of Design and was a professor at New York University. He invented Morse code and the magnetic telegraph, sending the first message, "What Hath God Wrought?" on May 24, 1844.
$2 1896 silver certificate (reverse)
MOULTRIE, Gen. William (1730-1805). Born in Charleston, S.C., he was an American Revolutionary War general. He repulsed the British attack on Sullivan's Island, now Fort Moultrie, in Charleston Harbor in 1776 and served as a brigadier general in the Continental Army in 1776 and defended Charleston in 1779. He was governor of South Carolina (1785-1787, 1794-1796).
$5 1866 and 1872 State of South Carolina
OGLETHORPE, James Edward (1696-1785). Born in London, he planned a project for colonizing unemployed men freed from debtors prison on lands in America. He received a charter in 1732 for Colony of Georgia and accompanied the first band of emigrants there in 1733.
$5 1862 The State of Georgia, Milledgeville, Ga.

$5 Bank of Augusta, Ga.
$10 1836 Bank of Augusta, Ga.
PENN, William (1644-1718). Named trustee to manage the West Jersey Colony in America, he had an important part in framing its charter in 1677. He received a grant of land from Charles II from which he founded Pennsylvania in 1681.
$1 1857 Penn Township Savings Inst., Philadelphia
$2 1856 Bank of Newark, Del.
$5 18-- Erie, Pa., Bank
$5 1820 Stephen Girard, Banker, Philadelphia
$5 1841 Towanda Bank, Pa.
$5 1859 Fort Stanwix Bank, Oneida, N.Y.
$10 1826 Bank of Pennsylvania, Philadelphia
$10 1833 Bank of Pennsylvania, Philadelphia
$20 Piscatqua Exchange Bank, Portsmouth, N.H.
$20 Farmers Bank of Schuylkill County, Pa.
PETTUS, J.J., governor of Mississippi.
$100 State of Mississippi
$50 State of Mississippi
$20 State of Mississippi
$10 State of Mississippi
PEWELLE, A., a Pennsylvania merchant.
2¢ 1862 note of A. Pewelle, Reading, Pa.
3¢ 1862 note of A. Pewelle, Reading, Pa.
PICKENS, Lucy Holcombe, wife of Francis W. Pickens (1805-1869), governor of South Carolina who ordered the bombardment of Fort Sumter, triggering the Civil War.
$1 June 2, 1862 Confederate note
$100 Dec. 2, 1862 Confederate note
$100 Apr. 6, 1863 Confederate note
$100 Feb. 17, 1863 Confederate note
PIERCE, Franklin (1804-1869), 14th president of the United States. Born in Hillsboro, N.H., his father, Benjamin Pierce, fought in the Revolution. He served in the New Hampshire House, the House (1833-1837), and the Senate (1837-1843). He served as president from 1853 to 1857.
$10 Amoskeag Bank, Manchester, N.H.
POLK, Gen. Leonidas
$50 1863 State of Louisiana, Shreveport, La.
RALEIGH, Sir Walter (1552?-1618). A favorite of Queen Elizabeth, he was granted a patent to send an expedition exploring the American coast from Florida to North Carolina in 1584 and named the coast north of Florida "Virginia." He sent settlers to occupy Roanoke Island, N.C., in

1585, but the colony failed. With the death of Queen Elizabeth in 1603, he fell out of favor with the English court and was eventually beheaded at Whitehall.
$2 original and 1875 "Lazy Deuce" First Charter national bank note (on the reverse, Sir Walter Raleigh in England, 1585, exhibiting corn and smoking tobacco from America)
RANDOLPH, George Wythe (1818-1867). Born March 10, 1818. His father was governor of Virginia (1819-1822). His mother was the daughter of Thomas Jefferson. George W. Randolph entered the U.S. Navy as a midshipman in 1831. Studied law at the University of Virginia. He served as the Confederate States secretary of war from March 1862 to September 1863 when he was appointed envoy to France. He died at Edge Hill, Va., on April 4, 1867.
$100 Dec. 2, 1862 Confederate note
$100 Apr. 6, 1863 Confederate note
$100 Feb. 17, 1864 Confederate note
RECTOR, H.M., governor of Arkansas.
$5 1862 Arkansas Treasury Warrant
SCOTT, Gen. Winfield (1786-1866). Born near Petersburg, Va., he was promoted to general-in-chief of the U.S. Army in 1841, and was defeated by Franklin Pierce in his bid for president in 1852.
$100 1865 interest-bearing note
$1 1861 Bank of Otego, Otego County, N.Y.
$1 Farmers and Mechanics Bank, Easton, Pa.
$2 Merchants Bank, Trenton, N.J.
$3 Beverly Bank, Beverly, N.J.
$20 Rutland County, Vt., Bank
SEWARD, William H. (1801-1872). Governor of New York (1839-1843) senator (1849-1861) and a prominent antislavery advocate, he served as secretary of state (1861-1869) and was responsible for the purchase of Alaska.
$50 1891 Treasury note
SHELBY, Isaac (1750-1826). Colonel of militia in Virginia in 1780, he organized a Colonial force after the fall of Charleston and defeated the British at Kings Mountain. He served in the North Carolina legislature in 1781 and 1782 and settled in Kentucky in 1783, where he served as the first governor (1792-1796, 1812-1816). He helped defeat the British at the battle of the Thames on Oct. 5, 1813.
$5 Bank of Kentucky, Louisville, Ky.

SHERIDAN, Gen. Philip Henry (1831-1888). Born in Albany, N.Y., he graduated from West Point in 1853 and succeeded Sherman as commander in chief of the U.S. Army in 1884. He was promoted to general in 1888.

$5 1896 silver certificate (reverse)
$10 1890, 1891 Treasury or coin notes

SHERMAN, John (1823-1900). Born in Lancaster, Ohio, he practiced law in Mansfield and Cleveland. He served in the House (1855-1861) and Senate (1861-1877, 1881-1897), as Secretary of the Treasury (1877-1881) and secretary of state (1897-1898).

$50 national bank note, Third Charter (all types)

SHERMAN, William Tecumseh (1820-1891). Born in Lancaster, Ohio, he was brother of John Sherman and graduated from West Point in 1840. He was made brigadier general of volunteers in the Civil War (1861), served at Bull Run, under Grant at Shiloh and Corinth, and was promoted to major general in 1862. He was promoted to lieutenant general in 1866 and succeeded Grant as general and commander of the Army in 1869.

15¢ fractional currency (proof notes), fourth issue, never circulated

SPINNER, Francis Elias (1802-1890). After serving as president of the Mohawk Valley Bank in Herkimer, N.Y., he was elected to the House (1855-1861) and then appointed Treasurer of the United States by Lincoln (1861-1875). Considered the father of fractional currency.

50¢ fractional currency, third issue

STANTON, Edwin McMasters (1814-1869). Born in Steubenville, Ohio, he was attorney general (1860-1861), secretary of war (1862-1868). He refused to support President Johnson's policies after Lincoln's death and was dismissed in 1868. Johnson's impeachment was partially a result of Stanton's dismissal. He was appointed to the Supreme Court in 1869 but died before he could take his seat.

$1 1890, 1891 Treasury or coin notes
50¢ fractional currency, fourth issue

STEPHENS, Alexander Hamilton (1812-1883). Born near Crawfordville, Ga., he was elected to the Georgia legislature in 1834, the Senate in 1842, and the House (1843-1859). He served as vice president of the Confederacy (1861-1865). After the war he was imprisoned briefly and later elected to the Senate in 1866 but refused to take a seat. He was elected to the House in 1873 and served until 1882, and was elected governor of Georgia in 1883.

$20 1861, 1862, 1863, 1864 Confederate note

STUYVESANT, Petrus (1592-1672). Born in the Netherlands, he served in the Dutch army and in the employ of the Dutch West India Company. He lost his right leg in a campaign against the island of St. Martin in 1644. He was appointed director-general of New Netherlands and adjacent regions in 1646 and arrived in New Amsterdam in 1647. He expelled the Swedes from Delaware in 1655 and surrendered New Netherlands to the English in 1664.

$3 St. Nicholas Bank, New York, N.Y.

SUMNER, Charles (1811-1874). Born in Boston and graduated from Harvard Law School, he was elected to the Senate in 1852 and was an opponent of slavery. Serving in the Senate until 1874, he took a prominent part in impeachment proceedings against President Johnson and opposed Grant's re-election in 1872.

$500 1878, 1880 silver certificate

SUMTER, Gen. Thomas (1734-1832). Born near Charlottesville, Va., he was a lieutenant-colonel of South Carolina troops during the Revolution. He was elected to the House (1789-1793, 1797-1801) and Senate (1801-1810).

$5 1866 and 1872 State of South Carolina

TAYLOR, Zachary (1784-1850), 12th president of the United States. Born in Orange County, Va., he entered the U.S. Army as a first lieutenant and spent most of his army life in the West. He defeated Santa Anna at Buena Vista in 1847, ending the war in northern Mexico. He served as president from 1849 to 1850, and died after only a year and four months in office.

$10 Southbridge Bank, Southbridge, Mass.
$20 City Bank of New Haven, Conn.
$20 Bank of Tennessee, Nashville, Tenn.

THOMAS, Gen. George Henry (1816-1870). Born in Southampton County, Va., he graduated from West Point in 1840 and remained loyal to the Union during the Civil War. He was made brigadier general in 1861 and major general in 1862. He commanded the Army of the Cumberland in the battle of Chattanooga and in Sherman's Atlanta campaign in 1864. He was promoted to major general in the regular army and commanded the military division of the Pacific in 1869 and 1870.

$5 1890, 1891 Treasury or coin notes

TUCKER, J.C.
3¢ July 4, 1864 Townsend Bank, Brookline, N.H.
24¢ July 16, 1862 Tucker and Stiles scrip, Brookline, N.H.

VAN BUREN, Martin (1782-1862), eighth president of the United States. Born in Kinderhook, N.Y., he was attorney general of New York (1816-1819) and senator from New York (1821-1828), governor of New York (1829), resigning to become secretary of state (1829-1831). He served as vice president (1833-1837) and as president from 1837 to 1841.
$5 Mechanics Bank, Concord, N.H.

VANCE, Zebulon, governor of North Carolina.
$20 1863 State of North Carolina, Raleigh, N.C.

WALKER, Robert J. (1801-1869). After practicing law in Pittsburgh, Pa., and Natchez, Miss., he served in the Senate (1836-1845) and as secretary of the Treasury (1845-1849). He was the financial agent of the U.S. in Europe (1863-1864) and sold $250 million worth of U.S. bonds and prevented the sale of $75 million worth of Confederate bonds.
25¢ fractional currency, fifth issue

WARD, John E. (1814-1871). Mayor of Savannah, Ga., he was violently opposed to secession and left the South with the outbreak of the Civil War.
$10 1861 Confederate States of America note

WASHINGTON, George (1732-1799), first president of the United States. Born in Westmoreland County, Va., he was privately educated and gained experience as a surveyor by assisting in the survey of some Fairfax holdings in Shenandoah Valley. He was county surveyor in Culpeper County, Va. (1749). He was commissioned as district adjutant by Gov. Dinwiddie in 1752, later commissioned lieutenant colonel and sent with 150 men in 1754 to establish an outpost on the site of the present city of Pittsburgh. He served on Gen. Braddock's staff in 1755 and in the British expedition against Fort Duquesne. He was commissioned colonel and commander-in-chief of Virginia troops in 1755. He married Martha Custis in 1759 and joined the Virginia House of Burgesses the same year (1759-1774). He was a member of the first and second Continental Congress and was elected to command all Continental armies in 1775. He resigned his commission in 1783, but was called from retirement to preside at the Federal Convention in Philadelphia in 1787, and was chosen president of the United States under the new Constitution. He took his oath of office in New York City on April 30, 1789, and was unanimously re-elected in 1792. He declined a third term and retired from political life in 1797. He came out of retirement again to accept a commission as lieutenant general and commander-in-chief of the Army in 1798 and retained the commission until his death on Dec. 14, 1799.
3¢ fractional currency, third issue
5¢ fractional currency, second issue
10¢ postage currency, first issue
10¢ fractional currency, second and third issues
25¢ fractional currency, second and fourth issues
50¢ postage currency, first issue
50¢ fractional currency, second issues
$1 1869, 1875, 1878, 1880, 1917 and all later series United States (legal tender) notes
$1 1896, 1923 and all later series silver certificates
$1 1918 Federal Reserve Bank notes
$1 1963 and all later series Federal Reserve notes
$2 1899 silver certificates
$5 national bank notes, Second Charter (dated back and denomination backs, small vignette on reverse)
$20 1901, 1906, 1922 gold certificates
$100 1863 6 percent compound interest Treasury note
$100 1863 5 percent one-year interest-bearing note
$500 1861 7.4 percent three-year interest-bearing note
10-peso 1913 Philippine silver certificates
10-peso 1918, 1924, 1929, 1936, 1941 & Victory Series 66 Philippine Treasury certificates
10 peso 1921 & 1937 Philippine national circulating notes
Many Confederate, obsolete and broken bank notes

WASHINGTON, Martha (1732-1802). Wife of George Washington, she was born Martha Dandridge and married Daniel Parke Custis who later died. She married George Washington Jan. 6, 1759.
$1 1886, 1896 silver certificate
$5 Belknap County Bank, N.H.

WATTS, Thomas N., governor of Alabama
$50 1864 Alabama State note
$10 1864 Alabama State note

WEAVER, John.
$50 Commercial Bank of Alabama, Selma, Ala.
WEBSTER, Daniel (1782-1852). Born in Salisbury, N.H., he graduated from Dartmouth in 1801 and was admitted to the bar in Boston in 1805. He was a member of the House (1813-1817, 1823-1827) and the Senate (1827-1841, 1845-1850). He served as secretary of state from 1841 to 1843 and again from 1850 to 1852. He was an unsuccessful candidate for Whig nomination for the presidency in 1852.
$10 1869, 1875, 1878, 1880 United States (legal tender) "Jackass" note
$10 Thames Bank, Norwich, Conn.
$1 State Bank of Wisconsin, Milwaukee
$2 Bank of Peru, Ill.
$3 DuPage Co. Bank, Naperville, Ill.
$5 Farmers and Traders Bank, Charlestown, Ill.
$5 Shawnee Bank, Attica, Ind.
$20 Bank of Kentucky, Louisville, Ky.
WILSON, Woodrow (1856-1924), 28th president of the United States. Born in Staunton, Va., he graduated from Princeton in 1879 and was admitted to the bar and practiced in Atlanta, Ga., in 1882. After receiving his Ph.D. from Johns Hopkins in 1886, he taught history at Bryn Mawr and Wesleyan and political science at Princeton. He was president of Princeton from 1902 to 1910, and governor of New Jersey (1911-1913). He was elected president in 1912 and served until 1921.
$100,000 1934 gold certificate
WINDOM, William (1827-1891). Born in Belmont, Ohio, he moved to Minnesota and became the first senator from Minnesota (1870-1881, 1881-1883) after serving in the House (1859-1869). He was Secretary of the Treasury in 1881 and again from 1889 to 1891.
$2 1891 silver certificate
WRIGHT, Silas (1795-1847). After practicing law in Canton, N.Y., he was elected to the House (1827-1829) and served as Comptroller of New York (1829-1833), as senator from New York (1833-1844), and governor of New York (1845-1847).
$50 1882 gold certificate

Military payment certificates

Military payment certificates (MPCs) were used from 1946 to 1973. Prior to that time U.S. military personnel stationed overseas were paid in Allied Military Currency, produced by the major Allied countries, or in the currency of the country in which they were stationed.

The need for this system arose because of the necessity to transact business with the locals without risking the loss of large amounts of U.S. currency, which could be used anywhere in the world.

Another reason for the creation of Allied Military Currency was the possibility that the enemy might flood an occupied territory's economy with currency to induce high inflation, or ordering local banks to burn their money when Allied attack was imminent.

Allied Military Currency was used in countries being liberated from the Axis powers and the notes were denominated in the liberated country's currency. The local government was required to redeem it at a later date.

Personnel were allowed to convert that foreign currency into U.S. currency as individual needs or wishes required. But it wasn't long before the services accumulated foreign currencies far in excess of pay requirements and the MPC system was developed to protect the services from those surpluses of foreign currencies.

After the MPC system was developed in 1946, all U.S. servicemen, U.S. government civilian employees and U.S. citizens employed by U.S. firms abroad doing business under government contracts were paid in MPCs and were prohibited from holding U.S. currency of any type.

U.S. citizens in the employ of a company of the host country were paid in the local currency. The local population was prohibited from holding any MPCs, which could be used only at U.S. facilities such as post exchanges or ship's stores. The local population was thus effectively restrained from purchasing items at the discounted PX prices, a form of black marketeering control.

If a U.S. serviceman or citizen wanted to buy something in the local civilian market, he was required to convert his MPCs into the local currency. Regulations restricted both the amount and frequency of MPC conversions.

Many of the servicemen supplemented their supply of convertible currency by doing a brisk business in cigarettes, silk or nylon stockings, and candy. It was inevitable that many of the MPCs would then be found in the local economy in spite of strict controls. The usual route was through the black market established both by servicemen and by the local population. Servicemen sold items they had purchased at government-operated stores while local businessmen sold watches and jewelry to servicemen who were returning stateside.

When it was determined that an excessive amount of MPCs were in the local economy via the black market, the old series would be withdrawn and a new series issued. The conversion days (popularly known as "C-days") were unannounced and strictly controlled. All personnel would be restricted to station and only designated persons were allowed to make the exchange of new for old notes.

After C-day the old series was invalid and worthless. The only supply of MPCs available to collectors today are those MPCs that were inadvertently unredeemed by authorized holders, or those illegally held by black marketeers who were unable to convert their holdings.

In the 28-year history of military payment certificates a total of 13 series were used in 21 foreign places in 17 countries. Denominations ranged from five cents to $20. The $20 MPC was issued only in series 661,681 and 692.

The first seven series were printed by private contractors in the United States and overprinted by the Bureau of Engraving and Printing. The overprint consisted of adding the series, serial and control numbers to the pre-printed notes. The last six series were completely printed and separated by the BEP.

The first issue, series 461, was released on Sept. 16, 1946. It was followed in order by series 471, 472, 481, 521, 541, 591, 611, 641, 651, 661, 681 and 692. The last issue to circulate, series 692, was released on Oct. 7, 1970, and was withdrawn from use in South Vietnam on March 15, 1973; and series 651 in South Korea on Nov. 19, 1973, ending a short but interesting and colorful era in another currency system. However, two series, 691 and 701, have been printed and are available should an emergency arise.

How to detect counterfeit bills

Know your money by examining and becoming familiar with the bills you receive. Compare a suspected bill with a genuine one of the same denomination. Look at these features:

Portrait
Genuine: Appears lifelike and stands out distinctly from the fine screen-like background. The hairlines are distinct.

Counterfeit: Appears lifeless and the background is usually too dark. Portrait merges into the background. The hairlines are not distinct.

Color seal
Genuine: Saw-toothed points are even, clear and sharp.

Counterfeit: Saw-toothed points on the circumference are usually uneven, blunt and broken off.

Border
Genuine: The fine lines are clear, distinct and unbroken.

Counterfeit: The fine lines that crisscross are not clear or distinct.

Paper
Genuine: Printed on distinctive paper with visible, interspersed red and blue fibers.

Counterfeit: Printed on paper with no colored fibers evident, or with red and blue lines to simulate fibers.

Signatures on U.S. paper money

Hand-written or facsimile signatures lend an aura of authority to paper money. Most U.S. currency bears two signatures and some bears four. Only the postage currency, second issue of fractional currency, and 3-cent third issue fractional currency bear no signatures at all. In the following list, the first name shown is that of the Register of the Treasury, the second is that of the Treasurer of the United States.

National bank notes, in addition to the signatures of the Register and the Treasurer, bear the signatures of the bank president and the bank cashier. Federal Reserve Bank notes also have two additional signatures: those of two Federal Reserve officers.

Realizing that the signing of paper money would be a burdensome task, President Lincoln signed legislation allowing the Secretary of the Treasury to delegate selected personnel to sign the first demand notes for the Treasury officials. Seventy employees were assigned to this task, signing their own names, with a handwritten "For The" before the appropriate title. Within a very short time the words "For The" were engraved into the printing plates.

Starting with the issues of 1863, the signatures of the Treasury officials were engraved directly into the plates and the words "for the" dropped into obscurity. From 1862 to 1925 the signature of the Register of the Treasury appeared on all notes, after 1925 the signature of the Secretary of the Treasury appears with that of the Treasurer of the United States.

The full names of the Treasury officials and their terms in office can be found in the appropriate tables in Chapter 4.

Signatures on large-sized paper money

ALLISON/GILFILLAN —
National Bank Notes
1875: $1, $2, $5, $10, $20, $50, $100.
Legal Tender Notes
1878: $1, $2, $5, $10, $20, $50, $100, $500, $1,000.
ALLISON/NEW —
Legal Tender Notes
1875: $1, $2, $5, $10, $20, $500.
1875-A: $1, $2, $5, $10, $100.
1875-B: $1, $2, $5.
1875-C: $1.
1875-D: $1.
1875-E: $1.
National Bank Notes
1875: $1, $2, $5, $10, $20, $50, $100.
ALLISON/SPINNER —
Legal Tender Notes
1869: $1, $2, $5, $10, $20, $50, $100, $500.
1874: $1, $2, $50, $100.
1880: $500.
National Bank Notes, Orig. Series
$1, $2, $5, $10, $20, $50, $100.
ALLISON/WYMAN —
Legal Tender Notes
1875: $1, $2, $5, $50, $100, $500.
National Bank Notes
1875: $1, $2, $5, $10, $20, $50, $100.

BRUCE/GILFILLAN —
Gold Certificates
1882: $20, $50, $100.
Legal Tender Notes
1880: $1, $2, $5, $10, $20, $50, $100.
National Bank Notes
1875: $5, $10, $20, $50, $100.
1882 Brown Backs: $5, $10, $20, $50, $100.
Silver Certificates
1880: $10, $20, $50, $100, $500, $1,000.

BRUCE/JORDAN —
National Bank Notes
1875: $5.
1882: Brown Backs: $5, $10, $20, $50, $100.

BRUCE/ROBERTS —
Legal Tender Notes
1880: $5, $10, $20, $50, $100.
National Bank Notes
1882 Brown Backs: $5, $10, $20, $50, $100.
1882 Date Backs: $5, $10, $20, $50, $100.
1882 Denom. Backs: $5, $10, $20.
Silver Certificates
1891: $10, $20, $50.
1896: $1, $2, $5
Treasury or Coin Notes
1891: $1, $2, $5, $10, $20

BRUCE/WYMAN —
Gold Certificates
1882: $20, $50, $100.
Legal Tender Notes
1880: $1, $5, $10, $20, $50, $100.
National Bank Notes
1875: $5, $10, $20, $50, $100.
1882 Brown Backs: $5, $10, $20, $50, $100.
Silver Certificates
1880: $10, $20, $50, $100, $1,000.
CHITTENDEN/SPINNER —
Compound Interest Treasury Notes
All types, all denominations issued.
Interest-Bearing Notes
All types, all denominations issued.
Legal Tender Notes
1862: $1, $2, $5, $10, $20, $50, $100, $500.
1863: $2, $5, $10, $20, $50, $100, $500.
National Bank Notes, Orig. Series
$5, $10, $20, $50, $100.
COLBY/SPINNER —
Compound Interest Treasury Notes
All types, all denominations issued.
Interest-Bearing Notes
All types, all denominations issued.

National Bank Notes, Orig. Series
$1, $2, $5, $10, $20, $50, $100.
ELLIOTT/BURKE —
Federal Reserve Bank Notes
1918: $1, $2, $5, $10, $20.
Legal Tender Notes
1917: $1, $2, $5.
National Bank Notes
1902 Blue Seal, No Date
Back: $5, $10, $20, $50, $100.
Silver Certificates
1899: $1, $2, $5.
ELLIOTT/WHITE —
Legal Tender Notes
1880: $20.
1907: $5
National Bank Notes
1902 Blue Seal, No Date
Back: $5, $10, $20, $50, $100.
Silver Certificates
1899: $1, $5.
JEFFRIES/SPINNER —
National Bank Notes, Orig. Series
$1, $2, $5, $10, $20.
JONES/WOOD —
National Bank Notes
1902 Blue Seal, No Date
Back: $5, $10, $20.
LYONS/ROBERTS —
Gold Certificates
1882: $20, $50, $100.
1905: $20.
Legal Tender Notes
1880: $5, $10, $20, $50, $100, $500.
1901: $10.
Silver Certificates
1891: $10, $20, $50.
1896: $5.
1899: $1, $2, $5.
National Bank Notes
1882 Brown Backs: $5, $10, $20, $50, $100.
1882 Date Backs: $5, $10, $20, $50, $100.
1882 Denomination Backs: $5, $10, $20, $50, $100.
1902 Red Seal: $5, $10, $20, $50, $100.
1902 Blue Seal Date

Back: $5, $10, $20, $50, $100.
1902 Blue Seal No Date
Back: $5, $10, $20, $50, $100.
Treasury or Coin Notes
1895: $5.
LYONS/TREAT —
Gold Certificates
1882: $50, $100.
1905: $20.
Legal Tender Notes
1901: $10.
National Bank Notes
1882 Brown Back: $5, $10, $20.
1882 Denomination Back: $10, $20.
1902 Red Seal: $5, $10, $20, $50, $100.
1902 Blue Seal Date
Back: $5, $10, $20, $50, $100.
1902 Blue Seal No Date
Back: $5, $10, $20, $50, $100.
Silver Certificates
1899: $1, $2, $5.
NAPIER/BURKE —
Gold Certificates
1882: $100.
National Bank Notes
1902 Blue Seal Date
Back: $5, $10, $20, $50, $100.
1902 Blue Seal No Date
Back: $5, $10, $20, $50.
NAPIER/McCLUNG —
Gold Certificates
1882: $5, $100.
1906: $20.
1907: $10.
Legal Tender Notes
1901: $10.
1907: $5.
National Bank Notes
1882 Date Back: $5, $10, $20, $50, $100.
1882 Denomination Back: $5, $10, $20.
1902 Blue Seal Date
Back: $5, $10, $20, $50, $100.
1902 Blue Seal No Date
Back: $5, $10, $20, $50, $100.
Silver Certificates
1899: $1, $2, $5.

NAPIER/THOMPSON —
Gold Certificates
1882: $100.
1906: $20.
1907: $10.
Legal Tender Notes
1907: $5.
National Bank Notes
1902 Blue Seal Date
Back: $5, $10, $20, $50, $100.
1902 Blue Seal No Date
Back: $5, $10, $20, $50, $100.
Silver Certificates
1899: $1, $2, $5.
PARKER/BURKE —
Gold Certificates
1882: $100
1906: $20.
1907: $10.
1913: $50.
Legal Tender Notes
1901: $10.
1907: $5.
National Bank Notes
1902 Blue Seal Date
Back: $5, $10, $20, $50, $100.
1902 Blue Seal No Date
Back: $5, $10, $20, $50, $100.
Silver Certificates
1891: $20, $50.
1899: $1, $2, $5.
1908: $10.
ROSECRANS/HUSTON —
Gold Certificates
1882: $20, $50, $100.
Legal Tender Notes
1880: $1, $2, $5, $10, $20, $50, $100.
National Bank Notes
1875: $5, $10, $20, $50, $100.
1882 Brown Back: $5, $10, $20, $50, $100.
1882 Date Back: $5, $10, $20, $50, $100.
Silver Certificates
1880: $50, $100.
1886: $1, $2, $5, $10, $20.
Treasury or Coin Notes
1890: $1, $2, $5, $10, $100, $1,000.
1891: $20.

ROSECRANS/HYATT —
Gold Certificates
1882: $50, $100.
Legal Tender Notes
1880: $5, $10, $20, $50,
$100.
National Bank Notes
1882 Brown Back: $5,
$10, $20, $50, $100.
Silver Certificates
1886: $1, $2, $5, $10,
$20.
ROSECRANS/JORDAN —
Legal Tender Notes
1880: $5, $10, $20, $50,
$100.
National Bank Notes
1875: $5.
1882 Brown Back: $5,
$10, $20, $50, $100.
Silver Certificates
1886: $1, $2, $5, $10.
ROSECRANS/MORGAN
—
National Bank Notes
1882 Brown Back: $5,
$10, $20, $50, $100.
1882 Date Back: $5, $10,
$20.

ROSECRANS/NEBEKER —
Legal Tender Notes
1880: $1, $2, $5, $10,
$20.
National Bank Notes
1875: $10, $20, $50,
$100.
1882 Brown Back: $5,
$10, $20, $50, $100.
1882 Date Back: $5, $10,
$20, $50, $100.
Silver Certificates
1886: $1, $5, $10, $20,
$50, $100.
1891: $1, $2, $5, $10,
$20, $50, $100.
Treasury or Coin Notes
1890: $1, $2, $5, $10,
$20, $1,000.
1891: $1, $2, $5, $10,
$50, $100, $1,000
SCOFIELD/GILFILLAN
—
Legal Tender Notes
1878: $2.
1880: $1, $2, $5, $10,
$20.
National Bank Notes
1875: $1, $2, $5, $10,
$20, $50, $100.

Refunding Certificate
Only denomination $10.
Silver Certificates
1878: $10, $20, $50,
$100, $500, $1,000.
1880: $10, $20, $50,
$100, $500, $1,000.
SPEELMAN/WHITE —
Gold Certificates
1922: $10, $20, $50,
$100.
Legal Tender Notes
1901: $10.
1907: $5.
1917: $1, $2.
1923: $10.
National Bank Notes
1902 Blue Seal No Date
Back: $5, $10, $20, $50,
$100.
Silver Certificates
1899: $1, $2, $5.
1923: $1, $5.

TEEHEE/BURKE —
**Federal Reserve Bank
Notes**
1918: $1, $2, $5, $10,
$20.
Gold Certificates
1882: $100.
1906: $20.
1907: $10.
1913: $50.
Legal Tender Notes
1880: $20.
1901: $10.
1907: $5.
1917: $1, $2.
National Bank Notes
1882 Denomination
Back: $5, $10, $20.
1902 Blue Seal Date
Back: $5, $10, $20, $50,
$100.
1902 Blue Seal No Date
Back: $5, $10, $20, $50,
$100.
Silver Certificates
1891: $20.
1899: $1, $2, $5.

TILLMAN/MORGAN —
Legal Tender Notes
1880: $1, $2, $5, $10,
$20, $50, $100.
National Bank Notes
1875: $10, $20, $50,
$100.
1882 Brown Back: $5,
$10, $20, $50, $100.

1882 Date Back: $5, $10,
$20, $50, $100.
1882 Denomination
Back: $5, $10, $20.
Silver Certificates
1891: $1, $2, $5, $10,
$20, $50, $100, $1,000.
1896: $1, $2, $5.
Treasury or Coin Notes
1891: $1, $2, $5, $10,
$20, $1,000.
TILLMAN/ROBERTS —
National Bank Notes
1882 Brown Back: $5,
$10, $20, $50, $100.
1882 Date Back: $5, $10,
$20, $50, $100.
1882 Denomination
Back: $5, $10, $20.
VERNON/McCLUNG —
Gold Certificates
1882: $50, $100.
1906: $20.
1907: $10.
Legal Tender Notes
1880: $20.
1901: $10.
1907: $20.
National Bank Notes
1882 Date Back: $5, $10,
$20.
1902 Blue Seal Date
Back: $5, $10, $20, $50,
$100.
1902 Blue Seal No Date
Back: $5, $10, $20, $50,
$100.
Silver Certificates
1899: $1, $2, $5.
1908: $10.
VERNON/TREAT —
Gold Certificates
1882: $50, $100.
1906: $20.
1907: $10.
Legal Tender Notes
1880: $20.
1901: $10.
1907: $5.
National Bank Notes
1882 Brown Back: $5,
$10, $20, $50, $100.
1882 Date Back: $5, $10,
$20, $50, $100.
1882 Denomination
Back: $5, $10, $20.
1902 Red Seal: $5, $10,
$20, $50, $100.
1902 Blue Seal Date

Back: $5, $10, $20, $50, $100.
1902 Blue Seal No Date
Back: $5, $10, $20, $50, $100.
Silver Certificates
1891: $50.
1899: $1, $2, $5.

1908: $10.

WOODS/TATE —

National Bank Notes
1902 Blue Seal No Date
Back: $5, $10, $20.
Silver Certificates
1923: $1.

WOODS/WHITE —
Legal Tender Notes
1907: $5.
National Bank Notes
1902 Blue Seal No Date
Back: $5, $10, $20, $50.
Silver Certificates
1923: $1.

Notes

1. Information on First Charter National Bank Notes of $500 and higher is incomplete or not available.
2. Signatures on early legal tender notes were often transposed.
3. Legal tender notes of $5,000 and $10,000 were issued but all have been redeemed.
4. No records available for $1,000 legal tender notes.
5. 1880 $500 legal tender notes were issued with 8 or 10 signature combinations but only Allison/ Spinner, Allison/ Gilfillan and Lyons/ Roberts are known.

Signatures on U.S. fractional currency

ALLISON/NEW —
Third Issue: 50¢ (Type II)*
Fifth Issue: 50¢
ALLISON/SPINNER —
Third Issue: 15¢, 50¢

(Type II)
Fourth Issue: 10¢, 15¢, 25¢, 50¢ (Types I, II, III)
Fifth Issue: 10¢, 25¢
COLBY/SPINNER —
Third Issue: 5¢, 10¢,

15¢, 25¢, 50¢ (Types I, II, III)

JEFFRIES/SPINNER —
Third Issue: 5¢, 10¢, 15¢, 50¢ (Types I, II)

* This extremely rare variety with autographed signatures was produced long after this type note had been replaced by a later issue.

Signatures on small-sized paper money

BANUELOS/CONNALLY —
Federal Reserve Notes
1969-B: $5, $10, $20, $50.
1969-C: $1.
BANUELOS/SHULTZ —
Federal Reserve Notes
1969-C: $5, $10, $20, $50, $100.
1969-D: $1.
BUCHANAN/REGAN —
Federal Reserve Notes
1981: $1, $5, $10, $20, $50, $100.
CLARK/SNYDER —
Federal Reserve Notes
1934-D: $5, $10, $20, $50, $100.
1950: $5, $10, $20, $50, $100.
Legal Tender Notes
1928-F: $5.
1928-G: $2.
Silver Certificates
1934-D: $5, $10.
1935-D: $1.

ELSTON/KENNEDY —
Federal Reserve Notes
1969: $1, $5, $10, $20, $50, $100.
Legal Tender Notes
1966-A: $100.
GRANAHAN/BARR —
Federal Reserve Notes
1963-B: $1.
GRANAHAN/DILLON —
Federal Reserve Notes
1950-D: $5, $10, $20, $50, $100.
1963: $1, $5, $10, $20.
Legal Tender Notes
1953-C: $2, $5.
1963: $2, $5.
Silver Certificates
1935-H: $1.
1953-C: $5.
1957-B: $1.
GRANAHAN/FOWLER —
Federal Reserve Notes
1950-E: $5, $10, $20, $50, $100.
1963-A: $1, $5, $10, $20, $50, $100.

Legal Tender Notes
1963-A: $2.
1966: $100.
JONES/WOODS —
Federal Reserve Bank Notes
1929: $5, $10, $20, $50, $100.
National Bank Notes
1929: $5, $10, $20, $50, $100.
JULIAN/MORGENTHAU
Federal Reserve Notes
1934: $5, $10, $20, $50, $100, $500, $1,000, $5,000, $10,000.
1934-A: $5, $10, $20, $50, $100, $500, $1,000.
Legal Tender Notes
1928-B: $5.
1928-C: $2, $5.
1928-D: $2.
Silver Certificates
1928-E: $1.
1934: $1, $5, $10.
1934-A: $5, $10.
1935: $1.
1935-A: $1.

Gold Certificates
1934: $100, $1,000,
$10,000, $100,000

JULIAN/SNYDER —
Federal Reserve Notes
1934-C: $5, $10, $20,
$50, $100.
Legal Tender Notes
1928-E: $5.
1928-F: $2.
Silver Certificates
1934-C: $5, $10.
1935-C: $1.

JULIAN/VINSON —
Federal Reserve Notes
1934-B: $5, $10, $20,
$50, $100.
Legal Tender Notes
1928-D: $5.
1928-E: $2.
Silver Certificates
1934-B: $5, $10.
1935-B: $1.

JULIAN/WOODIN —
Silver Certificates
1928-D: $1.
1933: $10.

KABIS/CONNALLY —
Federal Reserve Notes
1969-A: $5, $10, $20,
$50, $100.
1969-B: $1.

KABIS/KENNEDY —
Federal Reserve Notes
1969-A: $1.

MORTON/BLUMENTHAL —
Federal Reserve Notes
1977: $1, $5, $10, $20,
$50, $100.

MORTON/MILLER —
Federal Reserve Notes
1977-A: $1, $5, $10.

NEFF/SIMON —
Federal Reserve Notes
1974: $1, $5, $10, $20,
$50, $100.
1976: $2.

ORTEGA/BAKER —
Federal Reserve Notes
1985: $1, $5, $10, $20,
$50, $100.

ORTEGA/REGAN —
Federal Reserve Notes
1981-A: $1, $5, $10,
$20, $50, $100.

PRIEST/ANDERSON —
Federal Reserve Notes
1950-B: $5, $10, $20,
$50, $100.
Legal Tender Notes
1953-A: $2, $5.
Silver Certificates
1935-F: $1.
1953-A: $5, $10.
1957: $1.

PRIEST/HUMPHREY —
Federal Reserve Notes
1950-A: $5, $10, $20,
$50, $100.
Legal Tender Notes
1953: $2, $5.
Silver Certificates
1935-E: $1.
1953: $5, $10.

SMITH/DILLON —
Federal Reserve Notes
1950-C: $5, $10, $20,
$50, $100.
Legal Tender Notes
1953-B: $2, $5.

Silver Certificates
1935-G: $1.
1953-B: $5, $10.
1957-A: $1.

TATE/MELLON —
Federal Reserve Notes
1928: $5, $10, $20.
Legal Tender Notes
1928: $2.
Silver Certificates
1928: $1.

WOODS/MELLON —
Federal Reserve Notes
1928: $50, $100, $500,
$1,000, $5,000, $10,000.
1928-A: $5, $10, $20,
$50, $100.
1928-B: $5, $10, $20.
Legal Tender Notes
1928: $5.
1928-A: $2.
Silver Certificates
1928-A: $1.
Gold Certificates
1928: $10, $20, $50,
$100, $500, $1,000,
$5,000, $10,000

WOODS/MILLS —
Federal Reserve Notes
1928-C: $5, $10, $20.
Legal Tender Notes
1928-A: $5.
1928-B: $2.
Silver Certificates
1928-B: $1.
Gold Certificates
1928-A: $10, $20.

WOODS/WOODIN —
Federal Reserve Notes
1928-D: $5.
Legal Tender Notes
1928: $1.
Silver Certificates
1928-C: $1

Signatures on Series 1914 Federal Reserve notes

The Series 1914 Federal Reserve large-sized notes are listed separately from the other large-sized notes because they bear the signatures of the Secretary of the Treasury and the Treasurer of the United States instead of the signatures of the Register of the Treasury and the Treasurer of the United States as all other large-sized paper money does.

GLASS/BURKE —
Federal Reserve Notes
1914 Blue Seal: $5, $10, $20, $50, $100,
$500, $1,000, $5,000, $10,000.

HOUSTON/BURKE —
Federal Reserve Notes
1914 Blue Seal: $5, $10, $20, $50, $100,
$500, $1,000, $5,000, $10,000.

McADOO/BURKE —
Federal Reserve Notes
1914 Red Seal: $5, $10, $20, $50.
1914 Blue Seal: $5, $10, $20, $50, $100,
$500, $1,000, $5,000, $10,000.

MELLON/WHITE —
Federal Reserve Notes
1914 Blue Seal: $5, $10, $20, $50, $100,
$500, $1,000, $5,000, $10,000.

U.S. Coins   9

Coins in use in America before 1793

The first coins in circulation in non-Spanish North America were standard French and English issues used in a variety of unsuccessful colonies ranging from the St. Lawrence River to the Caribbean. The colonists were not likely to have too much specie left after they purchased their supplies for the voyage, but what was left most certainly did come along, as the travelers did not dare to leave anything of value in a land to which they were likely never to return.

With the establishment of successful colonies in the early 1600s, the colonists began to trade both with their parent companies and the Spanish colonies of the Caribbean. The trade with England was highly restricted, and most English gold and silver that reached these shores soon returned to Europe in the form of taxes, custom duties, and profit for the companies. The trade with Latin America was much less formal (thanks to smuggling), and provided much of the circulating coinage for the colonies.

Because the Colonies could never acquire enough coinage of the homeland to fulfill their needs, they were eventually forced to produce some themselves. In 1652 the Massachusetts Bay Colony produced silver shillings, sixpence, and threepence, but at a reduced weight so that the coins would not be exported. Various designs were used over a 30-year period, but the date on the coins remained at 1652 as a polite fiction to imply that the coins were made at a time when there was no king, thereby not usurping the king's right to coin money. One die, for an Oak Tree twopence, was inexplicably dated 1662, but it is not known if this was a slip which accidentally revealed the true date of manufacture or a deliberate attempt at testing

the British government's willingness to suppress the coinage.

Seeing that there was (supposedly) a market for underweight coins in the Colonies, several speculators began issuing private tokens for export to these markets. Most of these issues were officially sanctioned in some fashion. In effect the speculators were given a license to counterfeit, in exchange for a percentage of the profits. Some of these circulated and some did not, depending upon the greed of the manufacturer and how badly he debased the coins. One of the more candid manufacturers, an American, changed the inscription of his unpopular copper threepence pieces to read VALUE ME AS YOU PLEASE.

Throughout the period of the Revolution and afterward, a large part of the supply of small change was made up of privately issued store card tokens. Most of these were made in England and were of better quality than the majority of the various state issues. Those issued by American merchants were allegedly payable at these stores, but the others were payable only at London or Liverpool or other equally distant places. These tokens circulated for several years after the establishment of the Philadelphia Mint, despite an effort to recoin them into U.S. money.

The Articles of Confederation, adopted in 1778, permitted the states to issue their own coinages, with Congress fixing a uniform "standard of weights and measures." Only three of the 13 states struck coins for circulation under the Articles of Confederation: Connecticut, Massachusetts and New Jersey. Vermont, the 14th state, struck coinage before it entered the union. Most of the state coinages were produced by private manufacturers under contract to the states, although Massachusetts operated its own Mint in 1787 and 1788. Connecticut authorized a Mint, but most of its coinage was struck privately.

The U.S. Constitution, however, brought an end to the state coinage. Article 1, Section 10, Paragraph 1 of the Constitution reads, "No state shall . . . coin money, emit bills of credit, make anything but gold or silver coin a tender in payment of debts." The sole right to coin money was granted to the federal government (although a loophole permitted private coinage until 1864, when the constitutional loophole was closed) by the ratification of the Constitution in 1788.

Federal coinage studies

A federal coinage system had been under study since the early 1780s. Two plans merit attention here. The first was submitted to Congress Jan. 15, 1782, by Superintendent of Finance Robert Morris. The proposal was probably written by Assistant Financier of the Confederation Gouverneur Morris (no relation to Robert Morris). The Morris proposal was a complicated one, substituting the British system of pounds, shillings and pence for a decimal system based on the Spanish milled dollar. The basic unit would be worth 1/1,440 of the Spanish dollar, a sum arrived at by determing the largest common divisor by which state currencies could be divided without a fraction. The denominations would have been copper 5-unit and 8-unit pieces, plus a silver cent worth 100 units, a silver quint worth 500 units and a mark worth 1,000 units. The cumbersome nature of the Morris system, however, gained little support.

Meanwhile, as Congress debated various monetary plans, it took one concrete step and authorized a copper coin. At this time, 1787, the four states were still producing copper coinage when they were joined by the federal government, still organized under the Articles of Confederation. Members of Congress, meeting in Philadelphia, recognized the need for a standard coinage and on April 21, 1787, ordered that a copper coin be produced by private contract but under federal inspection.

The resulting coins were the Fugio cents,

generally acknowledged to be the first coins of the United States government. They are named for the Latin legend FUGIO ("I Fly") that appears on the the coin's obverse. A sundial appears on the obverse, along with the legend MIND YOUR BUSINESS, stressing the importance of time and the need for small business ventures; 13 linked rings on the reverse signify the 13 states, surrounding the legends UNITED STATES and WE ARE ONE. James Jarvis, a Connecticut business, received a contract to strike 300 tons of the copper coins, or about 26,666,666 pieces. Jarvis began coinage of the cents in New Haven, Conn., shortly after approval by Congress, but had struck fewer than 400,000 Fugio cents by June 1, 1787, by which time coinage had ceased. The federal government voided Jarvis' contract for missing the December 1787 delivery date (the coins were not delivered until beginning in May 1788). The Fugio cents proved underweight and were unpopular with the public.

The second plan warranting attention was submitted to Congress by Alexander Hamilton, Secretary of the Treasury, on Jan. 21, 1791. In his proposal, Hamilton recommended the basic unit be a dollar. The denominations would have been a gold $10 coin, a gold dollar, a silver dollar, a silver tenth-dollar, a copper coin valued at one hundred to the dollar, and a second copper coin, valued at 200 to the dollar.

The Hamilton proposal was very similar to what Congress would approve in April 1792. Following Hamilton's proposal, Congress passed a resolution March 3, 1791, that a federal Mint be built, and President Washington in his third State of the Union speech agreed. Then, on April 2, 1792, Congress passed a law authorizing both a federal Mint and coinage. Ten denominations of coins, more than recommended by Hamilton, were approved: in gold were a $10 eagle, a $5 half eagle and a $2.50 quarter eagle; in silver were a dollar, half dollar, quarter dollar, disme (the "s" was dropped by 1793, with the 10-cent piece called a dime) and half disme; and in copper, a cent and half cent, neither of which had legal tender status.

History of U.S. Coinage

Since coinage began at the Philadelphia Mint in 1793, 21 denominations have appeared on the circulating and commemorative coins of the United States. In gold, there have been the $50 (commemorative and bullion coins only), the $25 (on the American

Eagle bullion coins), $20, $10, $5, $3, $2.50 and $1. Among silver coins (many later changed to copper-nickel by the Mint Act of 1965), there have been the silver dollar, the Trade dollar, the 50-cent coin, the quarter dollar, 20-cent coin, dime, half dime and 3-

cent coin. There have also been copper-nickel 5-cent, 3-cent and 1-cent coins; a bronze 2-cent coin; cents in copper, bronze, brass, steel and zinc; and a copper half cent.

Production of U.S. coinage began in earnest in 1793 with the production of copper half cents and cents. The striking of silver coinage began one year after copper coinage production. The Mint began striking silver half dimes, half dollars and dollars in 1794; and silver dimes and quarter dollars in 1796. Gold coinage began in 1795 with the half eagle and the eagle, followed by the quarter eagle in 1796.

During the earlier years of the U.S. Mint, not all denominations were struck in all years. In 1804, coinage of the silver dollar ceased with the striking of 1803-dated coins; dollar coinage was not resumed until 1836. A few gold eagles were struck in 1804, but coinage then ceased until 1838. No quarter eagles were struck from 1809 through 1820. Production of the other denominations was sporadic except for the cent; a fire prevented any 1815-dated cents from being produced, but otherwise the chain has been unbroken since 1793.

Meanwhile, as the country's borders and population grew, the monetary system grew with them. The denominations authorized in 1792 were no longer sufficient to meet the country's monetary needs. New denominations were authorized at the century's midpoint. In 1849, Congress authorized a gold dollar and a gold $20 double eagle (both under the Act of March 3, 1849). In 1851, a silver 3-cent coin was authorized to facilitate the purchase of 3-cent postage stamps (Act of March 3, 1851). A gold $3 coin was introduced in 1854 (Act of Feb. 21, 1853), again to help in the purchase of 3-cent stamps (in sheets of 100). A smaller cent was approved in 1857, replacing the large cent. The half cent was eliminated, also in 1857.

The American Civil War opened in 1861, causing massive hoarding of coinage and the neccesity of coinage substitutes like encased postage stamps, privately produced copper-alloy cent-like tokens and finally, the first federal paper money. More changes to U.S. coins began in 1864, when the composition of the cent was changed to 95 percent copper and 5 percent tin and zinc, and when a bronze 2-cent coin was introduced (both under the Act of April 22, 1864). A copper-nickel 3-cent coin was issued beginning in 1865 (Act of March 3, 1865) to replace the silver 3-cent coins (which was struck in decreasing numbers until the last coins were produced in

1873). In 1866, a copper-nickel 5-cent piece was introduced (Act of May 16, 1866); the silver half dime was eliminated after 1873.

The year 1873 brought many changes to the U.S. coinage system, because of a law called by some the "Crime of '73." The Act of Feb. 12, 1873, is called by numismatic historian Don Taxay "the most exhaustive [coinage act] in our history. Four denominations were abolished by the act: the 2-cent coin, the silver 3-cent coin, the half dime and the silver dollar. A Trade silver dollar was authorized for use by merchants in the Orient; a year later, Congress revoked the coin's legal tender status in the United States. The weights of the silver half dime, dime, quarter dollar and half dollar were increased. In effect, the law demonetized silver and placed the United States on a gold standard, triggering a national debate that would last for the next quarter century.

Another new denomination was authorized under the Act of March 3, 1875 — the silver 20-cent piece. The coin was struck for circulation in 1875-76, setting the record for the shortest-lived silver denomination in U.S. coinage history. Coinage of Proof 20-cent pieces continued in 1877-78, but for collectors only.

Meanwhile, the powerful silver interests in the United States, faced with the demonetization of silver left by the Crime of '73, fought in Congress. The resulting Act of Feb, 28, 1878, reinstituted the standard silver dollar abolished by the Act of Feb. 12, 1873. The specifications were unchanged from the silver dollar of 1837-73: an alloy 90 percent silver and 10 percent copper, weighing 26.73 grams. Obverse and reverse designs created by Mint Engraver George T. Morgan were selected for the dollar, today generally called the Morgan dollar (it was also called the Bland-Allison dollar, after the names of the congressmen responsible for the bill). Coinage of the Morgan dollar continued through 1904.

Coinage denominations in use continued unchanged through 1889, when the gold dollar and gold $3 denominations were struck for the last time.

The silver dollar was resurrected twice for circulation: in 1921, to continue through 1935; and in 1964, although the 1964 Peace silver dollars were all destroyed before entering circulation, after government support for them was withdrawn. The copper-nickel dollar was introduced in 1971, and a smaller dollar was issued briefly from 1979-81.

Since the Mint Act of 1875, only two new denominations have been authorized, neither for circulation. In 1915, a gold $50 coin was approved to commemorate the Panama-Pacific Exposition being held in San Francisco that year. More than 70 years later, in 1986, the $50 denomination was revived for the American Eagle bullion program. That same legislation (Act of Dec. 17, 1986, Public Law 99-185) also approved the United States' first $25 coin, the American Eagle half-ounce coin.

Designs

The story behind the designs of U.S. coinage is one of artistic experimentation and drone-like uniformity; of political necessity and political favoritism; of beauty tempered by the realities of the coining process.

The senators and representatives who approved the U.S. monetary system created design parameters that affect new U.S. coin designs even today, nearly 200 years after that initial legislation. The Mint Act of April 2, 1792, specified that certain design features and legends appear on the coins which were authorized. On one side of all coins was to be an impression symbolic of Liberty, plus the word LIBERTY and the year of coinage. For the silver and gold coins, an eagle and UNITED STATES OF AMERICA were to appear on the reverse. The denomination was to appear on the reverses of the half cents and cents.

For more than 115 years in the history of U.S. coinage, Liberty was portrayed by allegorical female figures, either a bust or a full-length portrait. Liberty's changing face through the years says a lot about the artistic abilities of the craftsmen employed on the Mint staff and the artists hired from outside to design certain coins. Some of the most attractive U.S. coins were designed by non-Mint employees, often in opposition to a jealous Mint engraving staff who seemed more concerned about whether the coin would stack than its physical beauty. Beautiful designs created by Mint staff engravers never went beyond the pattern stage in favor of the period of drone-like uniformity that characterized U.S. designs from the mid-1830s into the early 20th century.

The changing portrait of Liberty also reveals the embodiment of the "ideal woman" by the physical standards set by the American men of the time, and men have always dominated U.S. coinage design. The first coinage portraits of Liberty are "Rubenesque" by modern standards. The most recent allegorical figure of Liberty to appear on U.S. coins is on American Eagle gold bullion coins. They depict a reproduction of an 80-year-old design, "slimmed down" to resemble the trimmer woman championed by American advertising and dietary standards in the 1980s.

The 1793 half cents and cents introduced the allegorical themes used on U.S. coins: The half cent depicts a bust of Liberty with her hair flowing free. A Liberty Cap on a pole, a familiar symbol of Liberty in the American and French revolutions of the latter 18th century, rests on her right shoulder, giving the design its name: the Liberty Cap. On the first cents of 1793, another Flowing Hair Liberty appears. Contemporary reports claim Liberty looks frightened on the cent. The designs are somewhat crude by modern standards. However, the Liberty busts were cut directly into steel by hand. Mint technicians had no access to the modern equipment and techniques available to their counterparts today.

Since the Mint Act of 1792 required only the denomination to appear on the reverses of the copper coins, the Mint engravers had a free rein. The first half cents have a wreath on the reverse, a device used as late as 1958 on the reverse of the Lincoln cent in the form of two ears of wheat. The reverse device on the first cents lasted only months. A 15-link chain meant to represent the unity of the 15 states appears on the first 1793 cents. The chain was believed by the public to be a symbol of enslavement perceived to represent "a bad omen for Liberty." Changes in the design of both sides of the cent came rapidly. The Chain reverse was replaced by a wreath, then the obverse design of the "frightened Liberty" was replaced with a Liberty Cap design similar to that on the half cent. Thus, three distinct cents were struck with the 1793 date: the Flowing Hair Liberty, Chain cent; the Flowing Hair, Wreath cent; and the Liberty Cap, Wreath cent.

Additional design changes were instituted for the cent in 1796, when a Draped Bust design was introduced and used through 1807. Liberty appears without a cap, her hair falling over bare shoulders. Loose drapery covers Liberty's bust. Another Liberty Head design called the Classic Head design was used on the cent from 1808-14. It differs considerably from the earlier allegorical motifs, with Liberty wearing a ribbon inscribed with LIBERTY around her hair.

The Coronet design was introduced in 1816 on the large cent. This design would prove one of the more versatile of the 19th century.

A variation of the Coronet design would appear on both copper coins until 1857, and on most of gold denominations from the 1830s to the first decade of the 20th century. The design is similar on all of the coins, depicting Liberty wearing a coronet inscribed with the word LIBERTY.

Designs for the half cent were generally similar to the cent's designs, although the timetable for introduction was often different. The half cent used a Liberty Cap design until 1797, and from 1800-08 a Draped Bust design was used. The Classic Head design was used on the half cent from 1809-36 and the Coronet design was introduced in 1840.

Silver coins

The silver coins of the 18th century feature designs similar to those on the copper coins. The silver coins used a Flowing Hair design in 1794-95, and in 1795-96 a Draped Bust design was introduced on all silver coins. The Capped Bust design was used first for the half dollar in 1807, with the dime following in 1809, the quarter dollar in 1815 and the half dime in 1829. The eagles appearing on the reverse of the silver coins appeared in several forms, first in a Small Eagle design that some critics likened to a pigeon, then a Heraldic Eagle which was used on the dollar beginning in 1798, the half dollar in 1801 and the quarter dollar in 1804.

Allegorical Liberty figures with similar themes but somewhat different details were used on the early gold coins. A Capped Bust, Heraldic Eagle design was used from 1796-1807 for the quarter eagle, then replaced in 1808 with the one-year-only Capped Bust type. The Capped Head quarter eagle was struck between 1821-34. On the half eagle, the Capped Bust design was used from 1796-1807; the Small Eagle reverse was used from 1796-98, and a Heraldic Eagle design was used from 1795-1807, concurrently with the Small Eagle at first. The Capped Draped Bust was used on the half eagle from 1807-12, and the Capped Head, from 1813-29. The Classic Head design was used briefly, from 1834-38. For the $10 eagle, the Capped Bust design was used from 1795 to 1804, when the denomination ceased coinage. On the reverse of the $10 coin, the Small Eagle was used from 1795-97, and the Heraldic Eagle design was used from 1797 to 1804.

Major events

Several things took place in the mid-1830s that were to affect coinage designs for decades. Among them was the Act of Jan. 18, 1837, which eliminated the need for an eagle on the reverses of the half dime and dime.

The other event was the resumption of coinage of the silver dollar in 1836, and the adoption of a new design that eventually would appear on six different denominations, on some of them for more than half a century.

Production of the silver dollar resumed in 1836 with the Gobrecht dollar. The obverse depicts a Seated Liberty figure sitting on a rock, her body wrapped in robes. The reverse depicts a Flying Eagle design, first of four coins which would use a similar theme.

With the creation of the Seated Liberty design, a new age of uniformity ensued on U.S. coins. The Seated Liberty obverse design was introduced on the half dime and dime in 1837, the quarter dollar in 1838 and the half dollar in 1839. Wreaths were placed on the half dime and dime in 1837; eagles appeared on the new quarter dollar and half dollar; and the dollar received a new eagle design in 1840, with the Flying Eagle replaced by an eagle similar to those on the quarter and half dollar.

Gold coins, too, entered the uniform age of coin designs when the Coronet (sometimes called Liberty Head on gold coins) design was introduced in 1838 for the eagle, 1839 for the half eagle and 1840 for the quarter eagle. When the gold dollar and double eagle were introduced in 1849, the Coronet design was used for both. Like the silver coins, the gold coins would not break out of uniformity until the early 20th century, except for the dollar.

New theme

A new theme was introduced in 1854 on the gold dollar, replacing the Coronet figure. An Indian Head portrait by James B. Longacre was introduced, the first in a series of medallic tributes to the first native Americans that would last until shortly before the beginning of World War II. Ironically, the Indian was being used as a symbol of Liberty even as the American movement to push the Indians into increasingly smaller portions of the West grew. However, the gold dollar portrait was not a true Indian; Longacre simply placed an Indian headdress on the same Liberty figure he would use in many different versions. A slightly larger Indian Head was used beginning in 1856 on the gold dollar. The gold $3 coin depicts an Indian Head portrait, and the reverse depicts not an eagle but a wreath.

When the large cent was abandoned in 1857 for a smaller cent (see section titled "specifications"), a Flying Eagle design was placed on the obverse (the 1856 Flying Eagle cents are patterns, struck before Congress authorized a change in composition). This was the first non-human portrayal of Liberty, and the only time an eagle would appear on the cent. The obverse design was changed to an Indian Head design in 1859. Wreaths of various types appear on the two smaller cents.

Several non-allegorical designs began to appear on U.S. coins in the 1850s. On the silver 3-cent piece, a six-point star appears as the central obverse design; the reverse depicts the Roman numeral III inside what resembles a large letter "C." Shields appear on the obverses of the 2-cent piece and the first copper-nickel 5-cent piece. A Liberty Head design replaced the Shield design on the 5-cent coin in 1883. The silver dollar, abandoned in 1873 and reinstated in 1878, depicts a Liberty Head and an eagle (called the Morgan dollar).

The Seated Liberty coinage design was dusted off and placed on the short-lived 20-cent coin of 1875-78. However, the Seated Liberty design, used on most of the silver coins since 1836, was finally abandoned at the end of 1891. By this time, it was in use only on the dime, quarter dollar and half dollar. It was replaced in 1892 with a Liberty Head design by Chief Mint Sculptor-Engraver Charles Barber, who also created a Heraldic Eagle for use on the reverse of the quarter dollar and half dollar; the reverse wreath appearing on the Seated Liberty dime was maintained on the reverse of the "Barber" dime. The Barber designs remained in use through mid-1916.

The first two decades of the 20th century resulted in two major design trends for U.S. coins. One, beginning in 1907, resulted in what can be called the "Golden Age of U.S. Coin Designs." The other, beginning in 1909, was the first step away from the allegorical depictions that had characterized U.S. coins since 1793 in favor of medallic tributes to prominent political figures from American history.

The "golden age" began with the election of Theodore Roosevelt as president of the United States. Roosevelt, best-known among non-numismatists as a vibrant president who built the Panama Canal and advocated the carrying of a "big stick," did more to improve the aesthetics of U.S. coins than any other politician since Washington. He invited Augustus Saint-Gaudens, the premier U.S. sculptor of the day, to create coin designs Roosevelt hoped would relive the beauty of ancient Greece. Saint-Gaudens submitted designs for the cent, $10 eagle and $20 double eagle. Roosevelt choose from the submissions the designs for the two gold coins: The $10 coin depicts an allegorical Liberty Head

wearing an Indian headdress on the obverse, and a standing eagle on the reverse; the double eagle depicts a Standing Liberty facing the viewer on the obverse, and a Flying Eagle design for the reverse.

The Mint engraving staff, led by Barber, was not happy with the hiring of outside talent, even though Saint-Gaudens' double eagle design is considered by many collectors to be the finest ever portrayed on a U.S. coin. The first $20 coins struck in 1907 feature high relief features, an artistic creation that created problems in production. The coins required too many strikings of the press for efficient production, so the relief was lowered later in 1907. Saint-Gaudens, who had been in ill-health, was dead by this time and unable to protest the changes in the design.

The "golden age" continued in 1908, with new designs for the $2.50 quarter eagle and $5 eagle: an American Indian on the obverse, and a Standing Eagle on the reverse. These were the first true Indians to appear on U.S. coins. What made the designs so unusual, however, was their placement on the coin. The designs were created in the oxymoronic "incused relief." Often incorrectly referred to as incused, the designs are raised, but sunken into the fields so the highest points are level with the flat fields. This design feature was criticized, with some suggesting that the "incused" portions would permit enough germs to accumulate to prove a health hazard. The experiment also did not please Barber.

In 1913, the designs for the 5-cent coin were changed. An American Indian was placed on the obverse, and an American bison was placed on the reverse. The coin, known variously as the Indian Head, Bison or Buffalo 5-cent coin, is considered the most American of U.S. coin designs because of the two themes portrayed on the coin. The Indian design appearing on the obverse is probably the finest to be placed on a U.S. coin. Three Indians, Iron Tail, Two Moons and Chief John Tree, posed for designer James Fraser, who created a composite portrait.

More design changes were made in 1916, when the Barber designs for the dime, quarter dollar and half dollar were replaced in midyear (although no 1916 Barber half dollars were struck). The dime features a Winged Liberty Head on the obverse; the design is often called the "Mercury" dime, but Mercury was a Roman male god with wings on his ankles, while the figure on the dime is female and wears a winged cap. The reverse depicts a fasces.

The quarter dollar design introduced in 1916 proved controversial. The Standing Liberty figure had an exposed right breast, an anatomical feature which had also appeared on the allegorical figure of Electricity on the Series 1896 $5 silver certificate until it was replaced in 1899 with a less prurient American Indian vignette. Some citizens of the period deemed the design too revealing on the quarter dollar as well, so in 1917 the offending breast was covered with a coat of mail (both varieties of 1917 design exist). The reverse depicts a Flying Eagle; its position was modified slightly in 1917 when Liberty was given additional clothing. Amusingly, correspondence between Mint officials and designer A.A. Weinman refer to changes in the placement of the eagle but apparently do not mention the unclad Liberty. The coat of mail was added very quietly.

The Walking Liberty half dollar was also introduced in 1916. The obverse depicts a Walking Liberty figure, while the reverse depicts one of the most attractive eagles placed on a regular issue of U.S. coins.

In 1921, the Peace dollar replaced the Morgan, which had been briefly resurrected in 1921 (coinage ceased in 1904). The Peace dollar commemorates the peace which followed the end of World War I. It ceased coinage at the end of 1935 when the dollar denomination was abandoned.

The second coinage trend to begin in the early 20th century occurred in 1909 when Abraham Lincoln replaced the Indian Head on the cent. For the first time, a historical, non-allegorical figure was used on a circulating coin of the United States. Lincoln's 100th birthday was celebrated in 1909. His 150th birthday in 1959 resulted in the Lincoln Memorial replacing the two ears of wheat found on the Lincoln cents of 1909-58.

The trend continued in 1932, when the Standing Liberty quarter dollar was replaced with the Washington design on the bicentennial of Washington's birth. Thomas Jefferson replaced the American Indian in 1938 (the Treasury Department held a design contest), and Franklin Roosevelt was placed on the dime in 1946, a year after his death. Benjamin Franklin was placed on the half dollar in 1948, replacing the Walking Liberty designs. He was replaced in turn in 1964 by John F. Kennedy in a numismatic tribute to the assassinated president.

In 1971, a copper-nickel dollar coin was introduced bearing President Dwight D. Eisenhower's portrait on the obverse and allegorical figure of an eagle landing on Earth's moon, commemorating the *Apollo* moon landings.

The Bicentennial of the Declaration of Independence in 1976 brought changes to the reverses of the quarter dollar, half dollar and dollar. The reverse of the 1976 quarter dollar depicts a Revolutionary War drummer; the half dollar depicts Independence Hall in Philadelphia; and the dollar depicts the Liberty Bell superimposed over the moon. The designs reverted to their original versions in 1977.

In 1979, a new copper-nickel dollar sized between the quarter dollar and half dollar was introduced, replacing the Eisenhower dollar. The new design depicts feminist Susan B. Anthony and a reduced version of the moon-landing design. Anthony was the first non-allegorical U.S. woman to appear on a circulating coin. The choice was not a popular one, since many collectors had hoped a reincarnation of the Flowing Hair Liberty, designed by Chief Sculptor-Engraver Frank Gasparro especially for the smaller dollar, would appear. Letters from collectors focused on the supposed unattractiveness of Anthony, although those same writers apparently had never criticized the physical attributes of Lincoln (who, after all, was referred to as an ape in the press of his time before his assassination) and Washington. Ironically, a descendant of Anthony was critical of an early version of Gasparro's Anthony portrait as too "pretty" and not at all indicative of the woman's strong character; Gasparro modified the design before it was placed on the coin. However, the coin did not circulate well, mainly because of its similarity in size to the quarter dollar (many found the two denominations too close to each other in diameter). Poor public usage of the smaller dollar resulted in none being struck after 1981 (the 1979-80 coins were struck for circulation, and the 1981 coins were struck for collectors only).

The reintroduction of commemorative coins and the American Eagle bullion coins have brought renewed interest in coinage designs, and renewed controversy. Collectors and others have been critical of some of the designs on the commemorative coins (the two torchbearers on an early version of the 1984 Olympic $10 eagle were lampooned as "Dick and Jane running" by congressional members). Others, most notably the obverse of the 1986-W Statue of Liberty half eagle, designed by Chief Sculptor-Engraver Elizabeth Jones, have been praised. Jones, incidentally, helped to end the male domination of U.S. coinage designs as the first woman to serve as Chief Sculptor-Engraver of the U.S. Mint.

The reintroduction of two older designs on the American Eagle coins has proven controversial. The obverse of the silver dollar depicts the Walking Liberty half dollar obverse, enlarged for placement on the larger coin. A new Heraldic Eagle appears on the reverse.

The designs chosen for the gold bullion coins were even more controversial. Saint-Gaudens' obverse Liberty for the double eagle was chosen, but not until Treasury Secretary James A. Baker III ordered Liberty on a diet. The Mint engraver assigned to the project was ordered to reduce Liberty's apparent weight, by giving her slimmer arms and legs. Members of the Commission of Fine Arts decried the changes to what is considered a classic design. Members were also critical of the reverse, a Family of Eagles design by Dallas sculptor Miley Busiek. The legislation authorizing the gold coins mandated the Busiek design. Busiek had been an untiring champion of her design, which shows two adult eagles and two younger birds. She lobbied in Congress and the Treasury Department for months in a politically successful attempt to have her design placed on the bullion coins. She says the design reflects the values of the American family.

Currently, hobbyists are calling for new designs on circulating coins, which the Treasury Secretary may change without congressional approval after they have been in use 25 years.

The 25-year limitation was placed on the coinage system in the Act of Sept. 26, 1890. Until then, there were no limitations concerning the life of a coin design. This act is now a part of Title 31 of the U.S. Code.

The Lincoln cent has been in use since 1909 (the reverse, since 1959). The Jefferson 5-cent coin has been around since 1938, and the Roosevelt dime, since 1946. The Kennedy half dollar is approaching its 25th birthday, having been introduced in 1964. Mint officials, however, have publicly stated that to change coinage designs would cause hoarding of the old designs, thus generating a coinage shortage.

Specifications

The physical specifications of U.S. coins — metallic content, weights, diameters — have been ever changing. Changes were in response to increases and decreases in the prices of the metals contained in them; public unpopularity of large-diameter coins; and other factors.

Even before the first copper coins were struck in 1793, their weights were reduced under the Act of May 8, 1792. The modified weights are 6.74 grams for the half cent, and 13.48 grams for the cent (weights are given in grams for modern convenience; the early coinage laws specified the weights in grains). Weights for both copper coins were reduced in 1795, to 5.44 grams for the half cent, and to 10.89 grams for the cent.

The 1794-95 silver coinage was struck in a composition of 90 percent silver and 10 percent copper. When additional silver denominations were added in 1796, the composition for all five coins was changed to 892.427 silver and 107.572 copper, until additional change came in 1836-37.

Composition of the first gold coins is 916.667 gold and 83.333 copper and silver.

The only changes made to U.S. coins between the first decade of the 19th century and 1834 were to the designs. Then, on June 28, 1834, the weight of gold coins was reduced and the alloy changed for two years to 899.225 percent gold and 100.775 copper and silver. In 1836, the gold alloy was changed again, to 90 percent gold and 10 percent copper and silver, an alloy unchanged until 1873. Changes were made to silver coins in 1836 as well, when the silver content was changed to 90 percent silver and 10 percent copper, an alloy not abandoned until the mid-1960s.

The rising price of silver resulted in a reduction in weights for the silver coins during 1853 (except for the silver dollar). Arrows were added to both sides of the dates on the reduced weight half dimes, dimes, quarter dollars and dollars, a design feature used for 1853-54. The arrows were removed in 1855 although the weights of the silver coins remained the same.

Major changes to the country's copper coinage were made in 1857. The half cent was eliminated and the large copper cent was replaced during the year with a smaller cent composed of 88 percent copper and 12 percent nickel (Act of Feb. 21, 1857). Diameter of the old cent is approximately 29 millimeters; the new cent has a diameter of 19mm.

The weights of the Seated Liberty silver coinage increased in 1873, and once again arrows were placed at either side of the date for two years to signify the increased weight. At the same time, silver was dropped from the gold-coin alloy; the coins were now composed of 90 percent gold and 10 percent copper.

The next major compositional changes in U.S. coins were made during World War II. At the beginning of the United States' entry into World War II, several metals used in coinage became in critical supply. The first to change was the 5-cent coin, which had nickel removed in mid-1942 after some copper-nickel specimens were struck. The new composition was 56 percent copper, 35 percent silver and 9 percent manganese. The old alloy was resumed in 1946.

Also during the war, the composition of the cent changed. First, tin was removed late in 1942. Then, in 1943, a zinc-plated steel cent was introduced to conserve copper. The brass alloy of 95 percent copper and 5 percent zinc was resumed in 1944 through 1946. The 95 percent copper, 5 percent tin and zinc composition resumed in 1947 and continued until late 1962. Once again, tin was removed from the bronze alloy, turning the alloy into the same brass composition used in 1944-46.

The 175-year-old history of United States coinage was changed with the stroke of a pen on July 23, 1965. On that day President Lyndon Johnson signed into law the Coinage Act of 1965, the most sweeping changes to the U.S. coinage system since the Mint Act of 1873. The 1965 act eliminated silver in dimes and quarter dollars and reduced the silver content of the half dollars to 40 percent.

Special congressional hearings relative to the nationwide coin shortage were first held in 1964. Coin shortages had continually worsened in the decade prior to 1965 as a result of the population growth, expanding vending machine businesses, popularity of Kennedy half dollars and the worldwide silver shortage.

In the face of the worldwide shortage of silver, it was essential that dependence on silver for the production of coins be reduced. Otherwise the country would be faced with a chronic coin shortage.

As a result of studies conducted by both the Treasury and the Battelle Memorial Institute, a clad metal composed of three layers of metal bonded together was selected for the new coinage.

The dimes and quarter dollars were to be composed of two layers of 75 percent copper and 25 percent nickel bonded to a core of pure copper. The half dollars were to be composed of two layers of 80 percent silver and 20 percent copper bonded to a core of approximately 20 percent silver and 80 percent copper, such that the entire coin is composed of 40 percent silver.

The combination of copper-nickel and copper gave the new coins the required electrical conductivity, a necessary property for vending machines. The copper-nickel surfaces also continued the traditional silvery color of the coins. In addition, a clad metal would be much harder to counterfeit.

The legal weights of the coins were affected by the change in alloy. The new clad dime weight is 2.27 grams, the quarter dollar weighs 5.67 grams and the half dollar weighs 11.5 grams. With the elimination of silver from half dollars in 1971 and the introduction of a copper-nickel clad version, the weight was changed to 11.34 grams. The cladding of all coins constitutes approximately 30 percent of the coin by weight.

At first all of the strip was produced at the Olin Brass Division of Olin Mathison Chemical Corp. in East Alton, Ill. From there it was shipped to the U.S. Mints at Philadelphia and Denver and to the San Francisco Assay Office. As time had passed and the Mints built new facilities, more and more of the cladding was produced at the Mints. However, the Mint now buys all strip from outside manufacturers. Mint officials claim it is more efficient and less expensive to do so. In addition, the Mint buys some of its planchets from private contractors, including all of the copper-plated zinc cent planchets and all of the precious metals planchets for special programs like commemorative coins and the American Eagle bullion coins.

In an effort to maximize production of coinage, 1964-dated silver coins were struck into 1965. The Coinage Act of 1965 also made it mandatory that clad coins be dated not earlier than 1965. Therefore, all clad coins actually made in 1965 bear that date. The first clad dimes were struck in late December 1965 and were released March 8, 1966. The first clad quarter dollars were struck Aug. 23, 1965, and released Nov. 1, 1965. The first clad half dollars were released March 8, 1966, but were struck starting Dec. 30, 1965.

The 1965 date was retained until July 31, 1966, when the date was changed to 1966. Normal dating was resumed on Jan. 1, 1967.

The last great compositional change to U.S. circulating coinage came in mid-1982, when the brass cent was replaced with a cent of nearly pure zinc, plated with a thin layer of pure copper to retain its copper appearance. Rising copper prices were the cause. The switchover to the copper-plated zinc cent was made with few non-numismatists noting the difference.

When the American Eagle bullion coins were introduced in 1986, some numismatists were critical of the .9167 gold content, a composition they deemed "non-traditional"; there was some preference for a .900 gold content. However, the chosen composition is virtually identical to the alloy first used for U.S. gold coins, from 1795 to 1834. A new silver composition was introduced with the production of the .999 fine silver American Eagle dollar.

Pioneer gold coins

The pioneer gold issues in the United States are an interesting series of private enterprise and pioneer necessity. Most were produced privately and legally, since the Constitution prohibited the states but not individuals from striking gold coins. However, "pioneer" is a better adjective to describe the gold coins than "private" and "territorial." Some of the coins in California were struck by the U.S. Assayer, and thus are of federal issue and are not true private issues; some of the gold coins were struck in states, not U.S. territories, thus "territorial" is incorrect for many of the issues. "Pioneer" describes the spirit in which the coins were struck: as necessity issues, brought about by the inability of the federal government to provide sufficient quantities of coinage in areas of the country newly opened to settlement.

The pioneer gold coins can best be classified by the region in which they were made, as the years in which they were struck often overlap. These regions are the southern Appalachians, the western Rockies (including Utah, which was much larger then) and Colorado. The scarcity of these coins is primarily due to their often having an intrinsic value less than the face value. The coins were often unaccepted and eventually melted.

The first significant gold mines in the United States were in the mountainous backwoods of North Carolina and Georgia. Transporting the gold overland to the Philadelphia Mint was slow and dangerous, whereas shipping it around Cape Hatteras was fast but expensive and not without risk. As the miners wished to have the convenience of coined gold without the expense of shipping the raw gold to the Philadelphia Mint, two private mints were established in 1830 and 1831.

The first mint was opened by Templeton Reid at Gainesville, Ga. Probably because he had no competition he charged a high fee for processing the bullion into coins. A large quantity of gold was handled during this first and only year, but most of it was eventually melted down as were regular U.S. gold coins, due to the prevailing price ratio of gold to silver. He was forced out of business amid charges that he had debased the coins.

The following year a second mint was opened by the Bechtler family, at Rutherfordton in southwestern North Carolina. For years the company produced coins equal in value to regular U.S. gold, although little of it circulated as the bullion value of the gold was greater than the face value of the coins.

This situation improved after 1834 (ultimately the coinage was accepted), and the new weight coins were temporarily marked with the date Aug. 1, 1834. The founder of the firm died in 1842, and his son and nephew carried on until 1852, but by then their standards of quality had declined and they could no longer compete with the two federal branch Mints in Georgia and North Carolina.

While it was difficult to go from northern Georgia to Philadelphia in 1849, it was virtually impossible to get there from California. The quickest route from San Francisco to Philadelphia or New Orleans was by ship to Mexico or Central America and then overland to a second ship for the voyage north. Although the situation clearly called for a branch Mint in California, one was not officially opened until 1854. In the meantime more than a dozen companies were engaged at various times in the production of gold coins.

The most popular issues were the $5 and $10 denominations, as these were needed for use in daily commerce. Later, $20 coins and $50 slugs were made for use in large business dealings, this being an era when the value of a check was dependent not only upon the solvency of the issuer but of the bank as well.

In addition to the questionable coins from the do-it-yourself mints, there were also in circulation legal tender coins struck by either the U.S. Assayer or the U.S. Assay Office. The first of these were octagonal $50 coins (officially called ingots) struck by the firm of Moffat & Co. but bearing both the legend UNITED STATES OF AMERICA and the name and title of AUGUSTUS HUMBERT, UNITED STATES ASSAYER OF GOLD, CALIFORNIA, 1851 or 1852. Eagles and double eagles were produced in 1852 before the Moffat & Co. firm dissolved.

The government contract was taken over by a new private firm which was called the United States Assay Office of Gold. This semi-official Mint produced eagles, double eagles and $50 "ingots" until December 1853, at which time its facilities were closed for reorganization as the official San Francisco Mint. Because the new official Mint could not at first produce coins as fast as the old semi-official one, several private companies opened to compete with the new federal Mint through 1854 and 1855.

In addition to the shortage of large denomination coins there was always a shortage of small change for use in retail stores. Several small, anonymous companies therefore produced gold dollars, half dollars, and even quarter dollars using a number of different designs. These fractional coins were struck from 1852 to 1882; federal law in 1864 finally forbid private coinage of any sort. It has been suggested that the later strikes were never intended for circulation but were merely souvenirs of California.

A number of eagles and half eagles were struck in Oregon in 1849, despite the objections of the new territorial governor. Presumably his orders eventually prevailed, as the issue was not repeated.

The Mormon government issued $2.50, $5, $10 and $20 pieces in 1849, as well as half eagles in 1850 and 1860. This last issue was made of Colorado gold from the Pikes Peak area. Most of the early issues of Mormon gold did not receive widespread acceptance, as they were underweight by as much as 15 percent.

The last period of "legal" pioneer gold coins (i.e., issued before 1864), was the Pikes Peak gold rush of 1860-61. Only three major firms produced coins in these two years, although several unverified patterns are known. It is interesting to note that in 1862 the largest of these companies, Clark, Gruber and Co., sold its equipment to the federal government, which intended to open a branch Mint in Denver at this time. The specie hoarding of the Civil War presumably doomed this project, and a Denver Mint did not open until 1906.

Other pioneer gold issues are known for Alaska and the northwestern states, but these were primarily made as souvenirs and did not circulate as coinage.

Just like regular coinage, pioneer gold coins are subject to Gresham's Law. Those which are of full weight and value or better will be hoarded and probably melted, while those that are undervalued are spent as soon as possible so as to avoid getting stuck with the coin.

Commemorative coins

Commemorative coins — the most colorful coinage issues struck in the United States — are pure Americana, history of a great nation frozen into metal. Commemorative coins in the United States are historically significant and relatively new. They had their start just before the turn of the 20th century.

The Coinage Act of Aug. 5, 1892, made the issuance of all commemorative coins possible. Since then, a total of one quarter dollar, 50 different types of half dollars, five silver dollars, six gold dollars, two gold quarter eagles, two gold half eagles, one gold eagle and two $50 gold coins have been struck on a commemorative basis. However, in different varieties, dates and Mints, including Proof versions of the four latest programs, a total of 182 different coins would make up a complete set of commemorative coins (and more if one adds the prohibitively rare pre-1982 Proof versions).

It may sound odd that the start of coinage for commemorative purposes in the United States, one of the richest in the world, should stem directly from dire financial straits of an exposition commission. The Columbian Exposition half dollar issued in 1892 and 1893, honoring Christopher Columbus and the 400th anniversary of his first voyage to America, was the first commemorative coin struck in the United States. It was produced to help defray the expenses of the 1892 and 1893 Chicago World's Columbian Exposition. The half dollars struck at the Philadelphia Mint were sold at a cost of $1. The Columbian Exposition was also commemorated with the 1893 Isabella quarter dollar, the United States' only fully commemorative 25-cent coin (however, the 1932 Washington quarter dollar was authorized as a commemorative issue, and some argue that the 1976 Bicentennial quarter dollar also is commemorative in nature).

Between 1899, when the Lafayette-Washington dollar was struck (the 1900 on the coin refers not to the date of issue, but to the year of the Paris Exposition), and 1954, when the first period of commemorative production ceased, more than 150 U.S. commemorative coins were struck. Some commemorative issues were not completely sold and the balance was returned to the Mint and melted down. In the case of the Columbian half, many were just put into circulation by banks, which accounts for the condition in which they are often found. For both reasons, the quantity minted for many commemoratives is larger than the quantity available.

Not all of the issues honor events or persons of national importance. At least one, the 1936 Cincinnati Musical Center half dollar, honors a non-existent event — 50 years of Cincinnati as a music center — and depicts an individual, Stephen Foster, who had little connection with the city except for a brief stay there.

Most of the commemorative coins struck by the U.S. Mint were turned over to various celebration committees for face value, with profits going not to the federal government, but to the cause being commemorated on the coin. Committee officials noted that with the production of additional date and Mint mark varieties of a single issue, more sales to collectors could be generated, with additional funds raised. This increasingly unseemly series of commemorative coins honoring less than noteworthy events was finally brought to a brief end to new issues at the end of 1938. However, three coins were issued after the end of World War II: the Iowa Centennial half dollar, and two half dollars commemorating the contributions of two great black Americans — Booker T. Washington and George Washington Carver. However, a multitude of date and Mint mark varieties of the last two coins spelled an end to commemorative coinage for more than a quarter century.

No commemorative coins were struck from 1954 to 1982. Hundreds of applications for such coins had been made through the years, but government officials were reluctant to issue new coins. Then, in 1981, Congress found a nationally acceptable event that Treasury officials did not object to: the 250th birthday of George Washington in 1982.

Legislation was introduced in the House of Representatives on May 7, 1981 (another bill had been introduced in March and a second in April), authorizing a commemorative half dollar for the Washington birthday celebration, with modifications recommended by Treasury officials (including a 10 million coin limit). A similar bill was introduced in the Senate May 18. Passage came in the House on May 19; in the Senate, the bill was approved Dec. 9. President Reagan signed the bill into law Dec. 13, 1981. The Mint offered the 1982 Washington half dollar in Proof and Uncirculated versions through Dec. 31, 1985.

Even as legislators were arguing the merits of the Washington commemorative coin legislation, others in both houses were preparing legislation for a commemorative coin series honoring the 1984 Summer Olympic Games in Los Angeles. The first legislation met with strong opposition from the collecting community, Treasury officials and Rep. Frank Annunzio, D-Ill., chairman of the House Banking Subcommittee on Consumer Affairs and Coinage. The original Senate proposal called for 29 different coins (more when counting Proof and Uncirculated versions); it passed the Senate Dec. 9, 1981. Much of the controversy arose from the number of coins and the method in which they would be distributed. The bill called for the coins to be turned over to a private cartel, which would donate some funds to the U.S. Olympic team but keep the profits for themselves. Opponents said this was a return to the system that killed commemorative coin issues in 1938 and 1954.

Compromise

A legislative compromise was sought. First, a 17-coin proposal was proposed in the House; again, the Senate approved this measure, but not the House. Annunzio introduced a one-coin bill, with the coins to be sold by the U.S. Mint. Annunzio agreed to a compromise, proposing a three-coin program. In a convoluted series of congressional maneuvering, Annunzio's subcommittee approved the three-coin proposal, but the House Banking Committee substituted the 17-coin proposal already approved by the Senate. But Annunzio called for a floor debate and the three-coin proposal was approved by the House May 20, 1982. The Senate agreed to the smaller program July 1, and President Reagan signed the bill into law July 22.

The Annunzio proposal authorized a 1984 gold $10 eagle (first commemorative of that denomination) and 1983 and 1984 silver dollars, each to be offered in Proof and Uncirculated versions. The coins were marketed by the Mint, with surcharges of $10 from the sale of each silver dollar and $50 from the sale of each gold eagle going to United States Olympic Committee, the Los Angeles Olympic Organizing Committee and other athletic organizations. However, the Mint ultimately and legally offered 13 varieties, using Mint marks and different finishes, instead of the six Annunzio wanted, angering the Illinois legislator. The program was deemed successful by most. It raised $73,389,300 for the Olympic teams.

No 1985-dated commemorative coins were authorized. However, the centennial of the dedication of the Statue of Liberty was to take place in 1986. The Statue of Liberty had never appeared on a U.S. coin, although several foreign coins had earlier depicted the symbol of freedom and opportunity in the United States.

Annunzio introduced a bill on Jan. 3, 1985, calling for a 1986 gold $5 half eagle, a 1986 silver dollar and a 1986 copper-nickel half dollar. The Annunzio proposal restricted production of each coin to one Mint. With counting Proof and Uncirculated versions, there was a maximum total of six coins. Surcharges of $35 per gold coin, $7 per silver dollar and $2 per half dollar were earmarked for the restoration of the Statue of Liberty and the immigration facilities on Ellis Island. House approval came quickly, on March 3, 1985, but discussion of a silver bullion coin delayed passage in the Senate. The Senate approved an amended version of Annunzio's bill June 21; it included a silver bullion dollar. The House approved the amended version June 24, and Reagan signed the bill into law July 9. Like the Olympic program, the Statue of Liberty program proved successful as a fund-raising event. U.S. Treasurer Katherine D. Ortega had set a goal of $40 million in surcharges, but the Statue of Liberty program surpassed the Olympic program (in less time, with lower surcharges and fewer varieties of coins available) and raised $82,859,101 in surcharges as of April 30, 1987. Total sales were about $300 million.

The Bicentennial of the drafting of the U.S. Constitution is being celebrated in 1987 as this edition is going to press, and a commemorative coin program has been approved for the event. Again, the proposal was introduced by Rep. Annunzio, on Sept. 23, 1985. House approval was delayed until Oct. 1, 1986. The Senate approved the measure Oct. 16, 1986, and President Reagan signed the legislation into law Oct. 29.

The bill calls for a 1987 gold half eagle and a 1987 silver dollar. Surcharges of $35 from sales of each gold coin and $7 from the sale of each silver dollar are earmarked for retirement of the national debt.

(For a closer look at the legislative history of recent commemorative coin programs, see Chapter 3.)

The future of the U.S. commemorative coin remains in doubt, despite the four recent programs. Annunzio, whose approval of coinage matters has proven essential in the last four programs, insists that any future programs be of truly national character.

Commemorative coins, 1892-1986

Date	Title	Net Mintage	Designers
1892	Columbian Exposition	950,000	Barber, Morgan
1893	Columbian Exposition	1,548,300	Barber, Morgan
1893	Isabella quarter	24,191	Barber
1900	Lafayette dollar	36,000	Barber
1915-S	Panama-Pacific Exposition	27,134	Barber
1918	Illinois Centennial	100,000	Morgan, Sinnock
1920	Maine Centennial	50,000	de Francisci
1920	Pilgrim Tercentenary	152,000	Dallin
1921	Pilgrim Tercentenary	20,000	Dallin
1921	Missouri Centennial 2★4	5,000	Aitken
1921	Missouri Centennial, no 2★4	15,400	Aitken
1921	Alabama Centennial, with 2 x 2	6,000	Fraser
1921	Alabama Centennial, no 2 x 2	59,000	Fraser
1922	Grant Memorial, Star	4,250	Fraser
1922	Grant Memorial, No Star	67,350	Fraser
1923-S	Monroe Doctrine Centennial	274,000	Beach
1924	Huguenot Walloon Tercentenary	142,000	Morgan
1925	Lexington Concord Sesquicentennial	161,914	Beach
1925	Stone Mountain Memorial	1,314,000	Borglum
1925-S	California Diamond Jubilee	86,394	Mora
1925	Fort Vancouver Centennial	14,966	Fraser
1926	Sesquicentennial of American Independence	140,592	Sinnock
1926	Oregon Trail Memorial	47,925	Fraser
1926-S	Oregon Trail Memorial	83,000	Fraser
1928	Oregon Trail Memorial	6,000	Fraser
1933-D	Oregon Trail Memorial	5,008	Fraser
1934-D	Oregon Trail Memorial	7,000	Fraser
1936	Oregon Trail Memorial	10,000	Fraser

Date	Title	Net Mintage	Designers
1936-S	Oregon Trail Memorial..................	5,000	Fraser
1937-D	Oregon Trail Memorial..................	12,000	Fraser
1938	Oregon Trail Memorial..................	6,000	Fraser
1938-D	Oregon Trail Memorial..................	6,000	Fraser
1938-S	Oregon Trail Memorial..................	6,000	Fraser
1939	Oregon Trail Memorial..................	3,000	Fraser
1939-D	Oregon Trail Memorial..................	3,000	Fraser
1939-S	Oregon Trail Memorial..................	3,000	Fraser
1927	Vermont Sesquicentennial (Bennington) ...	28,108	Keck
1928	Hawaiian Sesquicentennial	10,000	Fraser, Beach
1934	Maryland Tercentenary	25,000	Schuler
1934	Texas Centennial......................	61,350	Coppini
1935	Texas Centennial......................	9,988	Coppini
1935-D	Texas Centennial......................	10,000	Coppini
1935-S	Texas Centennial......................	10,000	Coppini
1936	Texas Centennial......................	8,903	Coppini
1936-D	Texas Centennial......................	9,032	Coppini
1936-S	Texas Centennial......................	9,057	Coppini
1937	Texas Centennial......................	6,566	Coppini
1937-D	Texas Centennial......................	6,599	Coppini
1937-S	Texas Centennial......................	6,630	Coppini
1938	Texas Centennial......................	3,775	Coppini
1938-D	Texas Centennial......................	3,770	Coppini
1938-S	Texas Centennial......................	3,808	Coppini
1934	Daniel Boone Bicentennial..............	10,000	Lukeman
1935	Daniel Boone Bicentennial..............	10,000	Lukeman
1935-D	Daniel Boone Bicentennial..............	5,000	Lukeman
1935-S	Daniel Boone Bicentennial..............	5,000	Lukeman
1935	Daniel Boone Bicentennial same as 1934 but small 1934 added on reverse	10,000	Lukeman
1935-D	Daniel Boone Bicentennial..............	2,000	Lukeman
1935-S	Daniel Boone Bicentennial..............	2,000	Lukeman
1936	Daniel Boone Bicentennial..............	12,000	Lukeman
1936-D	Daniel Boone Bicentennial..............	5,000	Lukeman
1936-S	Daniel Boone Bicentennial..............	5,000	Lukeman
1937	Daniel Boone Bicentennial..............	9,800	Lukeman
1937-D	Daniel Boone Bicentennial..............	2,500	Lukeman
1937-S	Daniel Boone Bicentennial..............	2,500	Lukeman
1938	Daniel Boone Bicentennial..............	2,095	Lukeman
1938-D	Daniel Boone Bicentennial..............	2,095	Lukeman
1938-S	Daniel Boone Bicentennial..............	2,095	Lukeman
1935	Connecticut Tercentenary	25,000	Kreiss
1935	Arkansas Centennial...................	13,000	Burr, Kreiss
1935-D	Arkansas Centennial...................	5,500	Burr, Kreiss
1935-S	Arkansas Centennial...................	5,500	Burr, Kreiss
1936	Arkansas Centennial...................	9,650	Burr, Kreiss
1936-D	Arkansas Centennial...................	9,650	Burr, Kreiss
1936-S	Arkansas Centennial...................	9,650	Burr, Kreiss
1937	Arkansas Centennial...................	5,500	Burr, Kreiss
1937-D	Arkansas Centennial...................	5,500	Burr, Kreiss
1937-S	Arkansas Centennial...................	5,500	Burr, Kreiss
1938	Arkansas Centennial...................	3,150	Burr, Kreiss
1938-D	Arkansas Centennial...................	3,150	Burr, Kreiss
1938-S	Arkansas Centennial...................	3,150	Burr, Kreiss
1939	Arkansas Centennial...................	2,100	Burr, Kreiss
1939-D	Arkansas Centennial...................	2,100	Burr, Kreiss
1939-S	Arkansas Centennial...................	2,100	Burr, Kreiss

Date	Title	Net Mintage	Designers
1936	Arkansas Centennial (Robinson)..........	25,000	Burr
1935	Hudson, N.Y., Sesquicentennial	10,000	Beach
1935-S	San Diego, California-Pacific Exp.	70,000	Aitken
1936-D	San Diego, California-Pacific Exp.	30,000	Aitken
1935	Old Spanish Trail 1535-1935	10,000	Hoffecker
1936	Rhode Island Tercentenary	20,000	Carey, Benson
1936-D	Rhode Island Tercentenary	15,000	Carey, Benson
1936-S	Rhode Island Tercentenary	15,000	Carey, Benson
1936	Cleveland, Great Lakes Exposition........	50,000	Putnam
1936	Wisconsin Centennial...................	25,000	Parsons, Hawkins
1936	Cincinnati Musical Center	5,000	Ortmayer
1936-D	Cincinnati Musical Center	5,000	Ortmayer
1936-S	Cincinnati Musical Center	5,000	Ortmayer
1936	Long Island Tercentenary...............	81,773	Weinman
1936	York County, Maine, Centennial.........	25,000	Rich
1936	Bridgeport, Conn., Centennial...........	25,000	Kreiss
1936	Lynchburg, Va., Sesquicentennial	20,000	Keck
1936	Elgin, Illinois, Centennial...............	20,000	Rovelstad
1936	Albany, New York......................	17,658	Lathrop
1936-S	San Francisco-Oakland Bay Bridge........	71,369	Schnier
1936	Columbia, S.C., Sesquicentennial	9,000	Davidson
1936-D	Columbia, S.C., Sesquicentennial	8,000	Davidson
1936-S	Columbia, S.C., Sesquicentennial	8,000	Davidson
1936	Delaware Tercentenary.................	20,978	Schmitz
1936	Battle of Gettysburg 1863-1938	26,900	Vittor
1936	Norfolk, Va. Bicentennial...............	16,923	Simpson
1937	Roanoke Island, N.C., 1587-1937	29,000	Simpson
1937	Battle of Antietam 1862-1937	18,000	Simpson
1938	New Rochelle, N.Y., 1688-1938	15,251	Lathrop
1946	Iowa Centennial......................	100,000	Pietz
1946	Booker T. Washington	1,000,546	Hathaway
1946-D	Booker T. Washington	200,113	Hathaway
1946-S	Booker T. Washington	500,279	Hathaway
1947	Booker T. Washington	100,017	Hathaway
1947-D	Booker T. Washington	100,017	Hathaway
1947-S	Booker T. Washington	100,017	Hathaway
1948	Booker T. Washington	8,000	Hathaway
1948-D	Booker T. Washington	8,000	Hathaway
1948-S	Booker T. Washington	8,000	Hathaway
1949	Booker T. Washington	6,000	Hathaway
1949-D	Booker T. Washington	6,000	Hathaway
1949-S	Booker T. Washington	6,000	Hathaway
1950	Booker T. Washington	6,000	Hathaway
1950-D	Booker T. Washington	6,000	Hathaway
1950-S	Booker T. Washington	512,091	Hathaway
1951	Booker T. Washington	510,082	Hathaway
1951-D	Booker T. Washington	7,000	Hathaway
1951-S	Booker T. Washington	7,000	Hathaway
1951	Washington-Carver....................	110,018	Hathaway
1951-D	Washington-Carver....................	10,004	Hathaway
1951-S	Washington-Carver....................	10,004	Hathaway
1952	Washington-Carver....................	2,006,292	Hathaway
1952-D	Washington-Carver....................	8,006	Hathaway
1952-S	Washington-Carver....................	8,006	Hathaway
1953	Washington-Carver....................	8,003	Hathaway
1953-D	Washington-Carver....................	8,003	Hathaway
1953-S	Washington-Carver....................	108,020	Hathaway

Date	Title	Net Mintage	Designers
1954	Washington-Carver.....................	12,006	Hathaway
1954-D	Washington-Carver.....................	12,006	Hathaway
1954-S	Washington-Carver.....................	122,024	Hathaway
1982-D	George Washington.....................	2,210,458	Jones
1982-S	George Washington.....................	4,894,044	Jones
1983-P	Olympic dollar, Unc...................	294,543	Jones
1983-D	Olympic dollar, Unc...................	174,014	Jones
1983-S	Olympic dollar, Unc...................	174,014	Jones
1983-S	Olympic dollar, Proof.................	1,577,025	Jones
1984-P	Olympic dollar, Unc...................	217,954	Graham
1984-D	Olympic dollar, Unc...................	116,675	Graham
1984-S	Olympic dollar, Unc...................	116,675	Graham
1984-S	Olympic dollar, Proof.................	1,801,210	Graham
1986-D	Immigrant, Unc.	pending	Steever-Winter
1986-S	Immigrant, Proof......................	pending	Steever-Winter
1986-P	Ellis Island dollar, Unc.	pending	Mercanti-Peloso
1986-S	Ellis Island dollar, Proof............	pending	Mercanti-Peloso
1987-	Constitution dollar, Proof............	pending	Verani
1987-	Constitution dollar, Unc.	pending	Jovine

All coins listed above are half dollars unless otherwise indicated. All are .900 fine silver except for the 1986 Immigrant half dollar, which is copper-nickel clad. Known meltings have been subtracted where available.

Gold commemoratives

1903	Louisiana Purchase Jefferson dollar	17,375	Barber
1903	Louisiana Purchase McKinley dollar	17,375	Barber
1904	Lewis and Clark Exposition dollar	9,997	Barber
1905	Lewis and Clark Exposition dollar	10,000	Barber
1915-S	Panama Pacific Exposition dollar	15,000	Keck
1915-S	Panama Pacific Exposition $2.50	6,749	Barber
1915-S	Panama Pacific $50 Round	483	Aitken
1915-S	Panama Pacific $50 Octagonal.	645	Aitken
1916	McKinley Memorial dollar...............	9,977	Barber, Morgan
1917	McKinley Memorial dollar...............	10,000	Barber, Morgan
1922	Grant Memorial dollar With Star	5,000	Fraser
1922	Grant Memorial dollar Without Star	5,000	Fraser
1926	U.S. Sesquicentennial $2.50..............	45,793	Sinnock
1984-P	Olympic eagle, Proof..................	33,309	Peed/Mercanti
1984-D	Olympic eagle, Proof..................	34,533	Peed/Mercanti
1984-S	Olympic eagle, Proof..................	48,551	Peed/Mercanti
1984-W	Olympic eagle, Proof..................	381,085	Peed/Mercanti
1984-W	Olympic eagle, Unc.	75,886	Peed/Mercanti
1986-W	Statue of Liberty half eagle, Unc..........	pending	Jones
1986-W	Statue of Liberty half eagle, Proof	pending	Jones
1987-	Constitution half eagle, Unc.	pending	Jovine
1987-	Constitution half eagle, Proof............	pending	Jovine

Current coins

Lincoln cent

When the Lincoln cent made its initial appearance in 1909, it marked a radical departure from accepted styling, introducing as it did for the first time a portrait coin in the regular series. A strong feeling had prevailed against the use of portraits on the coins of the country but public sentiment stemming from the 100th anniversary celebration of Abraham Lincoln's birthday proved stronger than the long-standing prejudice.

The only person invited to participate in the formulation of the new design was Victor David Brenner. President Theodore Roosevelt was so impressed with the talents of this outstanding sculptor that Brenner was singled out by the president for the commission.

The likeness of Lincoln on the obverse is an adaption of a plaque Brenner executed several years prior which had come to the attention of President Roosevelt. In addition to prescribed elements — LIBERTY and the date — the motto IN GOD WE TRUST appeared for the first time on a U.S. cent. Of interest is that the Congress passed the Act of March 3, 1865, authorizing the use of this expression on U.S. coins during Lincoln's tenure of office.

A study of three models for the reverse resulted in the approval of a very simple design bearing two ears of wheat in memorial style. Between these, in the center of the coin, are the denomination and UNITED STATES OF AMERICA, while curving around the upper border is the national motto, E PLURIBUS UNUM.

Even though no legislation was required for a new design, approval of the Treasury Secretary was necessary. Franklin MacVeagh gave his approval July 14, 1909, and not quite three weeks later, on Aug. 2, the new cent was released to the public.

The original model bore Brenner's name. Prior to issuance, however, the initials VDB were substituted on the lower reverse because Mint officials felt the name was too prominent. After the coin was released, many protested that even the initials were conspicuous and detracted from the design. Because the coin was in great demand, and because making a change in size would have required halting production, the decision was made to eliminate the initials entirely, a simple engraving process. They were restored in 1918, and are to be found in minute form on Lincoln's shoulder.

More cents are produced than any other denomination, which makes the Lincoln cent a familiar item. In its life span this little coin has weathered two world wars, one of which was to change it materially. Metals play a vital part in any war effort. At the time of World War II the cent was composed of 95 percent copper and 5 percent tin and zinc. These metals were denied the Mint for the duration of the emergency, making it necessary to seek a substitute. After much deliberation, even including consideration of plastics, zinc-plated steel was chosen as the best in a limited range of suitable materials.

Production of this wartime cent was provided for in the act approved Dec. 18, 1942, which also set as the expiration date of the authority Dec. 31, 1946. Low-grade carbon

steel formed the base, to which a zinc plating .005 inch thick was deposited on each side electrolytically as a rust preventative. The same size was maintained but the weight was reduced from the standard 48 grains to 42 grains, due to the use of a lighter alloy. Operations commenced Feb. 27, 1943, and by Dec. 31 of that year the three Mints then functioning had struck an almost record-breaking number of cents, with the total reaching 1,093,838,670 pieces. The copper released was enough to meet the combined needs of two cruisers, two destroyers, 1,243 B-17 Flying Fortresses, 120 field guns and 120 howitzers; or enough for 1.25 million shells for the U.S. big field guns.

On Jan. 1, 1944, the Mints were able to adopt a modified alloy, the supply being derived from expended shell casings which when melted furnished a composition similar to the original but with only a faint trace of tin; the 6 grains dropped from the total weight were restored. The original alloy was resumed in 1947.

On Feb. 12, 1959, a revised reverse was introduced as a part of the 150th anniversary celebration of the Great Emancipator's birth. No formal competition was held. Frank Gasparro, then Assistant Sculptor-Engraver at the Mint in Philadelphia, prepared the winning entry, selected from a group of 23 models the engraving staff at the Mint had been asked to present for consideration. Again, only the Treasury Secretary's approval was necessary to make the change because the design had been in force for more than the required 25 years.

The imposing marble Lincoln Memorial in Washington, D.C., provides the central motif; the legends E PLURIBUS UNUM and UNITED STATES OF AMERICA form the rest of the design, together with the denomination. Gasparro's initials, FG, appear on the right near the shrubbery.

The composition of the smallest U.S. denomination was changed once more in 1962. Mint officials felt that deletion of the tin content would have no adverse effect upon the wearing qualities of the coin, whereas the manufacturing advantages to be gained with the alloy stabilized at 95 percent copper and 5 percent zinc would be of much benefit. Congressional authority for this modification is contained in the Act of Sept. 5, 1962.

As the price of copper rose along with the demand for cents, a resolution was introduced Dec. 7, 1973, giving the Treasury Secretary power to change the 1-cent alloy. It appeared the new alloy would be aluminum.

The bill met opposition from the vending machine industry and the medical profession, and when the price of copper took a downhill turn, Mint Director Mary Brooks announced aluminum cents would not be necessary. There was no change in the 1-cent alloy. However, 1,579,324 1974-dated aluminum cents were struck in 1973 as experimental pieces. Most were melted, although a few specimens given to congressional members and staff disappeared. One coin is housed in the National Numismatic Collections of the Smithsonian Institution, where it was given by a congressional staff member.

In a report made public in September 1976, the Research Triangle Institute recommended that cent production be terminated by 1980, due to increasing costs of manufacturing the cent and the poor circulation of the coin. However, in making the study public the Mint said that it did not endorse the recommendations of the report, nor did it plan to adopt the recommendations at that time.

In 1982, feeling the pressure of rising copper prices again, Mint officials decided to switch to a new alloy composed of a core of 99.2 zinc and 0.8 percent copper plated by pure copper (total composition, 97.5 percent zinc, 2.5 percent copper). Both the old alloy and new alloy were produced during the year at all minting facilities striking cents. Copper and brass producers sued the federal government, claiming the Treasury Secretary did not have the authority to alter the composition despite the earlier legislation. A federal judge ruled against the producers, however, and the cent remains composed of copper-plated zinc.

Jefferson 5 cents

The Thomas Jefferson 5-cent coin was released to the public Nov. 15, 1938, after a national contest for the obverse and reverse designs.

The coin was designed by Felix Schlag of Chicago, Ill. Born in Frankfurt, Germany, in September 1891, Schlag had won numerous prizes in nationwide competitions. He began his art studies in the Munich Academy in Germany and became an American citizen in 1929.

The obverse of the coin carries a profile of Thomas Jefferson. The reverse bears a likeness of Monticello, the president's historic home near Charlottesville, Va.

President Franklin D. Roosevelt was personally interested in the design of the Jefferson 5-cent coin. It was a result of his suggestion that the sculptor altered his original design so as to emphasize certain architectural features, particularly the two wings of the building at Monticello.

Although the law did not then require that the phrase IN GOD WE TRUST appear on the coin, it was placed there at the request of the Director of the Mint. This was the first time this motto had reappeared on the United States 5-cent coin since 1883.

In the years following the release of the coin, there was considerable interest nationally, and particularly on the part of the Michigan congressional delegation, to place on the Jefferson coin the initials of the sculptor, Felix Schlag. (Schlag died in Owosso, Mich., March 9, 1974. He was 82.)

The failure of the sculptor to "sign" his work is said to have been due to the fact that he didn't know he could. All other current issues of United States coins bear the initials of their sculptors.

Placing of the initials on the coin was an administrative decision of the Secretary of the Treasury, at the request of Assistant Secretary Wallace and Mint Director Eva Adams. The initials appear on the 5-cent pieces dated 1966 and subsequent issues.

Roosevelt dime

Almost immediately after President Franklin D. Roosevelt's death in the spring of 1945, letters came to the Treasury Department from all over the country in advocacy of his portrait being placed on a coin of the United States. The dime was most frequently suggested by reason of his having been identified with that coin through the March of Dimes drives for the Infantile Paralysis Fund.

The coinage laws prohibit the changing of a coin design more often than once every 25 years. The same laws empower the Director of the Mint with the approval of the Secretary of the Treasury, to cause new designs to be prepared and adopted at any time after the expiration of said 25-year period. The Winged Liberty Head design having been in use for more than the required time, the Treasury officials acceded to public sentiment and placed the likeness of President Roosevelt on the 10-cent piece. The new Roosevelt dime was released Jan. 30, 1946, the late president's birthday.

The obverse bears a portrait of Roosevelt, facing left and LIBERTY to his left. In the left field is IN GOD WE TRUST and in the lower right field the date.

On the reverse, in the center, is a torch with an olive branch on the left and an oak branch on the right.

Around the border is UNITED STATES OF AMERICA with ONE DIME below and across the lower field is E PLURIBUS UNUM.

The designer was John R. Sinnock, at that time the Mint's Chief Engraver. Known as one of the country's great artists in this highly specialized field, Sinnock produced outstanding medals of the presidential series, various commemorative medals and coins, and designs used on several of the medals for the nation's war heroes, including the Purple Heart.

Washington quarter

The Washington quarter dollar replaced the Standing Liberty quarter dollar in 1932. The Standing Liberty had not been issued for the 25 years required by law, thereby making an act of Congress necessary to issue the Washington quarter. Congress passed the authorization act March 4, 1931, to commemorate the 200th birthday of the first president.

John Flanagan, a noted New York sculptor, designed the coin. His work was chosen from approximately 100 models that were submitted. The Treasury Department worked in close cooperation with the Commission of Fine Arts in selecting the design. However, the commission did not agree with the Treasury Department on the final selection but as law gives the Secretary of the Treasury the right to the final selection, the work of Flanagan was chosen over the commission's objections. The first coins were issued for general circulation Aug. 1, 1932. The designer's initials, J.F., appear on the obverse.

The obverse side shows the head of Washington with LIBERTY around the top of the coin. The date is directly under the head and the motto IN GOD WE TRUST is to the lower left of the head.

The reverse side shows an eagle with wings spread standing on a shaft of arrows. Beneath the eagle are two sprays of olive leaves. Over the top are the words UNITED STATES OF AMERICA and centered directly under these words and above the head of the eagle are the words E PLURIBUS UNUM. The inscription QUARTER DOLLAR is at the bottom under the olive spray.

New plaster models were made for both sides of the quarter in 1977, altering the relief slightly so as to increase die life.

Kennedy half dollar

John Fitzgerald Kennedy was inaugurated president of the United States Jan. 20, 1961, and served not quite three full years of his term of office. His assassination Nov. 22, 1963, resulted in such an outpouring of public sentiment that President Lyndon Johnson, on Dec. 10, 1963, sent to Congress a request for legislation to authorize the Treasury Department to mint new 50-cent pieces bearing the likeness of his predecessor.

Congress gave its overwhelming approval to the president's recommendation and on Dec. 30, 1963, Public Law No. 88-256 was enacted directing the Mint to proceed with the production of the new design. The first of the John F. Kennedy half dollars for general circulation purposes were struck at the Mints in Philadelphia and Denver on Feb. 11, 1964. The half dollar was selected because this would add another presidential portrait to a coin of regular issue.

In the center of the obverse, or face of the coin, is a strong but simple bust of the late president. Above, and around the border is LIBERTY. Just below the bust is IN GOD WE TRUST, which appears on all United States coins of current issue. The date is at the bottom around the border.

The presidential coat of arms forms the motif for the reverse. It is the central part of the presidential seal, the only difference being that the words SEAL OF THE PRESIDENT OF THE UNITED STATES have been removed and in their place are inscriptions required by law to appear on all coins: the words UNITED STATES OF AMERICA, above, around the border, and the denomination, HALF DOLLAR, around the bottom border. Other requirements already incorporated in the coat of arms are the eagle, and E PLURIBUS UNUM, which appears on the ribbon above the eagle's head.

The Kennedy coin had its beginnings when official sculptors were engaged in preparing a new medal for the historic series of presidential pieces manufactured in bronze for sale to the public. Gilroy Roberts, nationally known Chief Sculptor-Engraver of the Mint, and a member of the Philadelphia staff for many years, worked on the likeness of the president, studying first many photographs to capture the character and personality of his subject. He then selected a single portrait and commenced placing his concept in a preliminary model. During the final stages, Roberts called at the White House and studied the president at work, at which time he completed the model.

After the president's death, when the decision was reached to honor him on a United States coin, the Roberts' portrait was adapted from the medal, lowered in relief and simplified for use on a smaller scale necessary for a coin. His initials G.R. appear on the truncated bust.

Frank Gasparro, himself a veteran member of the Philadelphia staff, executed the reverse of the presidential medal. The coat of arms of the president of the United States, an integral part of this design, was chosen as the companion side for the half dollar. Gasparro's initials F.G. appear at the lower right edge of the shield.

The presidential seal originated during the administration of President Rutherford B. Hayes, apparently as a rendering of the Great Seal of the United States. There was no known basis in law for the coat of arms and the seal which had been used by presidents since 1880 and which was reproduced on the presidential flag. President Truman, when he signed the Executive Order of Oct. 25, 1945, containing the official description, established for the first time a legal definition of the president's coat of arms and his seal. According to heraldic custom, the eagle on a coat of arms, unless otherwise specified in the heraldic description, is always made to face to its own right. There is no explanation for the eagle facing to its own left in the case of the president's coat of arms. To conform to heraldic custom, and since there was no authority other than usage for the former coat of arms, President Franklin Roosevelt had asked that it be redesigned. The designs reached Washington after the president's death.

In the new coat of arms, seal and flag, the eagle not only faces to its right — the direction of honor — but also toward the olive branches for peace which it holds in its right talon. Formerly, the eagle faced toward the arrows in its left talon — symbolic of war.

Initial distribution of this newly designed coin took place on March 24, 1964, in the usual manner, when 26 million were released by the Mints directly to the Federal Reserve Banks and Branches for simultaneous distribution through the commercial banking system.

The Research Triangle Institute report of 1976 recommended the elimination of the half dollar from the U.S. coinage system.

Mint officials reported in 1986 that no half dollars would be struck for circulation in 1987; the coin was only to be struck for use in Proof, Uncirculated and Souvenir Mint sets.

Eisenhower dollar

On Dec. 31, 1970, President Nixon signed into law the Bank Holding Company Act. Appended to the legislation were important amendments relating to coinage. Pertinent to this narrative is one which concerns the reissuance of the dollar denomination. Section 203 of the Act reads:

"The dollars initially minted under authority of Section 101 of the Coinage Act of 1965 shall bear the likeness of the late President of the United States Dwight David Eisenhower, and on the other side thereof a design which is emblematic of the symbolic eagle of the Apollo 11 landing on the moon."

The act further provided for the removal of all silver from the dollar denomination and its coinage in the copper-nickel clad composition. The language was qualified, however, to permit the Secretary of the Treasury to mint and issue not more than 150 million dollar pieces composed of 40 percent silver. Of these, 130 million were to be manufactured and sold in Uncirculated condition, and 20 million processed as Proof coins, with the widest possible distribution among citizens interested in acquiring a few each. Production of this denomination for general circulation is in the copper-nickel clad metal.

The coin was designed by the Mint's Chief Sculptor-Engraver, Frank Gasparro, whose initials appear on both sides of the coin. Reverse of the coin shows the bald eagle, symbolic of the *Apollo 11* spacecraft christened *Eagle* landing on the cratered surface of the moon, clutching an olive branch in both claws. The receding Earth appears above the eagle's head. The 13 stars circling the eagle represent the first states of the Union.

Gasparro began working on the obverse drawing for the coin in spring 1969. He settled on using a profile of the former president and general of the army because of an image Gasparro saw of the supreme commander of the allied armies in Europe as Eisenhower rode through New York City June 20, 1945.

Gasparro made a profile drawing immediately suitable to cut directly in steel and capture the facial features that had impressed him. When he was asked to design the Eisenhower dollar coin, he studied his first drawing of Eisenhower and some 30 other pictures before sketching his design for the obverse of the coin.

He began working on the reverse of the coin in October 1969.

On Nov. 1, 1971, the first Eisenhower dollars were released for circulation.

The Research Triangle Institute report of 1976 recommended a reduction in the size of the dollar coin. Several designs for a smaller coin were tested in 1976, but none was accepted at that time.

Bicentennial dollar varieties

Almost as soon as the first 1776-1976 Bicentennial Eisenhower dollars were struck, Mint officials realized that the design did not lend itself well to high-speed mass production. Minor changes were made on the obverse and major changes on the reverse to facilitate that mode of production. The changes created two varieties of dollars.

Variety 1 dollars have thick, block-style lettering with nearly closed E's and straight tails on the R's. Variety 2 dollars have thinner, more contoured lettering with more open E's and curved tails on the R's.

Two of the reverse details which, if memorized, will enable anyone to tell the variety without having both varieties for comparison are the last S in STATES and the relationship of the first U in UNUM to the first U in PLURIBUS.

On Variety 1 the tail of the last S in STATES is level with the center bar of the E. On Variety 2 the tail of the S barely reaches the top of the bottom bar of the E. On Variety 1 the first U of UNUM is almost directly below the first U of PLURIBUS while on Variety 2 it is between the L and U.

The Denver Mint Variety 1 dollars outnumber the Philadelphia coins by a ratio of approximately six to one.

Anthony dollar

President Carter signed the Susan B. Anthony Dollar Act into law Oct. 10, 1978, but not until after a long fight over the design. A smaller dollar coin, sized between the quarter dollar and the half dollar, was recommended by the Research Triangle Institute report in 1976. The same report recommended that the introduction of a smaller dollar coin coincide with the elimination of the half dollar.

The first design submitted for the dollar was an adaption by Frank Gasparro of the Flowing Hair large cent design, with a Flying Eagle design of Gasparro's creation on the reverse. Collectors almost universally panned the design at first, although supporters welcomed a return to more traditional, non-partisan coinage designs. Meanwhile, in Congress in 1978, a movement toward placing feminist Susan B. Anthony's portrait on the coin was growing (see Chapter 3 for the legislative history of the Anthony dollar) as the legislation for a smaller dollar advanced through both houses.

Many hobbyists lobbied against the Anthony proposal in favor of a more traditional, allegorical portrait. Ironically, Gasparro's Flowing Hair Liberty design became the darling of the hobby as support for the Anthony design grew in Congress.

The Senate passed the Anthony dollar bill Aug. 22, 1978, without dissent; the House passed the bill Sept. 26 with a vote of 368 to 38. The first coins were struck at the Philadelphia Mint Dec. 13, 1978, with 1979 dates. The Mint mark "P" was used for the first time since the Wartime 5-cent coins of World War II. Denver strikes were produced Jan. 9, 1979, and the San Francisco Assay Office began producing business strikes Feb. 2, 1979.

Despite Treasury hopes to save $30 million a year by reducing demand for the $1 Federal Reserve note, the Anthony dollar never caught on with the public, which claimed the coin was too similar in size to the quarter dollar. The vending industry, which had supported the change in size but fought against a more distinctive multi-sided coin, never fully converted vending machines to accept the new, smaller dollar. The coins were produced for circulation and collectors' sets in 1979 and 1980, and only for collectors in 1981. None have been produced since 1981 although the law authorizing the Anthony dollar is still valid.

In the fall of 1985 the Mint began offering Anthony dollar sets through its catalog of products. The response surprised many, as the Anthony dollars were among the most popular items in the catalog.

History of Mint marks

A Mint mark on U.S. coins is a small letter added to the design of the coin to show which Mint manufactured it. Mint marks on United States coins began with the act of March 3, 1835, establishing the first branch Mints: in New Orleans, La., Charlotte, N.C., and Dahlonega, Ga. The first Mint marks appeared in 1838.

When other branch Mints were established, coins struck there bore an appropriate Mint mark. The letters used to signify the various Mints are as follows:

"C" for Charlotte, N.C., (gold coins only), 1838-1861
"CC" for Carson City, Nev., 1870-1893
"D" for Dahlonega, Ga. (gold coins only), 1838-1861
"D" for Denver, Colo., 1906-present

"O" for New Orleans, La., 1838-1861; 1879-1909

"P" for Philadelphia, Pa., 1793-present

"S" for San Francisco, Calif., 1854-1955; as an Assay Office, 1968-present

"W" for West Point Bullion Depository, 1984-present (gold coins only)

With one four-year exception, U.S. coins struck at the Philadelphia Mint bore no Mint marks until 1979. The initial use of the "P" appears on the Jefferson, Wartime 5-cent pieces, struck from 1942 to 1945 in a silver alloy. The "P" Mint mark on these issues was designed to distinguish the silver alloy issues from regular copper-nickel 5-cent pieces; during the war, silver was less important strategically than copper or nickel.

With the passage of the Coinage Act of 1965, which gave the United States copper-nickel clad coinage, Mint marks were removed from coins dated 1965 and from subsequent issues until 1968. The move was designed to help alleviate a coin shortage by removing the distinction between coins struck at branch Mints and those struck in Philadelphia so collectors could not determine which were the more limited strikes.

Since the San Francisco Assay Office opened in 1965 for coinage purposes, after 10 years of inactivity, no coins struck there after 1965 bear Mint marks until 1968, when they were returned to all coinage.

With the announcement Jan. 4, 1968, that Mint marks would return to coinage, Mint Director Eva Adams made several changes in Mint mark application. First, to achieve uniformity, she directed that all Mint marks be placed on the obverse of the coins. The Mint mark, she announced, on the cent, 5-cent piece, dime and quarter dollar would be to the right of the portraits, while on the half dollar it would appear in the center under the portrait of Kennedy.

Second, she announced Proof coin sets would be manufactured at the San Francisco Assay Office and would bear an "S" Mint mark. Previously, all Proof sets were produced at Philadelphia and so had no Mint mark, except for some 1942 5-cent pieces. Proof sets were discontinued altogether after 1964 because of the coin shortage and revived in 1968.

Mint marks were again omitted from certain U.S. coins when cents were struck at the West Point Bullion Depository in 1974 and later, and when dimes were struck in San Francisco in 1975.

Major changes were made in Mint mark policy beginning in 1978. Mint officials in 1978 announced that the 1979 Susan B. Anthony dollar would bear the "P" Mint mark for Philadelphia business strikes. The list of coins to bear the "P" Mint mark grew in 1980, when all other denominations but the 1-cent piece received the new Mint mark.

A new Mint mark, a "W," the eighth, was added to the U.S. inventory in September 1983, when the West Point Bullion Depository began striking 1984-dated $10 gold eagles commemorating the Los Angeles Olympic Games. Although other coins were being struck at West Point, the Mint mark was not added to those denominations.

Additional changes were announced in 1984 when it was reported that beginning in 1985, the Mint mark would be placed on the master die instead of the working dies for all Proof coinage. This was to forestall production of errors similar to the Proof 1983 Roosevelt, No S dime and the 1982 Roosevelt, No P dime. Mint officials denied that business strike master dies would be Mint marked as well.

In 1986, Mint officials decided to add the Mint marks on all commemorative and Proof coins at the plasticene model stage. Thus, on these special collectors' coins, the Mint mark appears on all stages of models, hubs and dies.

Also in 1986, the S Mint mark of the Proof American Eagle silver dollar was placed on the reverse, to the left of the eagle's tail. Mint officials cited tradition for doing so.

Location of Mint marks

Following is a list of all regular U.S. coin issues and where the Mint mark on these coins is located.

Half cents — All coined at Philadelphia, no Mint mark.

Large cents — All coined at Philadelphia, no Mint mark.

Flying Eagle cents — All coined at Philadelphia, no Mint mark.

Indian cents — 1908 and 1909, under the wreath on reverse side.

Lincoln cents — Under the date.

Two cents, Three cents (copper-nickel) — All coined at Philadelphia, no Mint mark.

Three cents (silver) — All coined at Philadelphia, except 1851 New Orleans Mint — reverse side, at right.

Shield 5-cent pieces — All coined at Philadelphia, no Mint mark.

Liberty 5-cent pieces — All coined at Philadelphia except 1912-S and -D — reverse side to left of word CENTS.

Indian 5-cent pieces — Reverse side under words FIVE CENTS.

Jefferson 5-cent pieces until 1964 — Reverse side at right of the building.

Jefferson 5-cent pieces (1942-1945, silver) — above dome on the reverse side.

Jefferson 5-cent pieces from 1968 to present — on obverse under Jefferson's queue.

Half dimes — Reverse side either within or below the wreath.

Dimes — Old types, on reverse side below or within wreath; Winged Liberty Head type (1916-1945) on the reverse to left of base of fasces; Roosevelt type to 1964, left of bottom of torch on reverse; Roosevelt type from 1968 to present, on obverse above date.

Twenty cents — Reverse side under the eagle.

Quarter dollars — Old types, on reverse side under eagle; Standing Liberty type, on obverse to left of date; Washington type to 1964, on reverse under eagle; Washington type from 1968 to present, on obverse to right of Washington's queue.

Half dollars — 1838 and 1839 "O" Mint mark above date; other dates to 1915 on reverse under eagle; 1916 on obverse below motto, 1917 on obverse below motto and on reverse. After 1917 on lower left reverse. Franklin type, above bell beam; Kennedy type in 1964, near claw and laurel at left on reverse; Kennedy type from 1968 to present, on obverse under Kennedy portrait.

Dollars — Old types, on reverse under eagle; Peace type, on reverse at lower tip of the eagle's wing; Eisenhower, on obverse above the date. Anthony, on obverse to left of bust. American Eagle, Proof version only, on reverse to left of eagle's tail.

Trade dollars — On reverse under eagle.

Gold dollars — On reverse under wreath.

Quarter eagles — 1838 and 1839, over the date; other dates prior to 1907, on reverse under the eagle; Indian type (1908-1929), on reverse lower left.

Three dollar pieces — Reverse under the wreath.

Half eagles — Same as quarter eagles.

Eagles — Reverse under eagle; after 1907 at left of value.

Double eagles — Old types on reverse under eagle; Saint-Gaudens (after 1907) above the date.

American Eagle $50 — gold bullion coin, Proof version only, on obverse between second and third rays at right, below date.

Dates, Edge Designs, Mottoes, Symbols

Dates

The insertion of a chronological mark or word on coins was a practice known to the ancients, but carried out by them on their money in a different method from that pursued by more modern sovereigns.

As for the United States, the original Mint Act of 1792 established the requirement that the date appear on U.S. coins, and this legislation has remained unchanged since that time.

Actually, the date on U.S. coins serves a very useful purpose, in that with it on a coin, counterfeiting is made more difficult and enforcement authorities can isolate specific issues which may have been produced illegally.

Traditionally, all United States coins have been dated the year of their coinage, although this didn't always happen the first few years the Mint was in operation and in recent years. One commemorative coin, the Lafayette-Washington dollar, is considered by Mint officials to be undated. The date 1900 appears on the coin, but that refers to the Paris Exposition; the coin was actually struck in December 1899.

The policy of placing the date in which a coin is struck was interrupted, because of the coin shortage and the speculation in rolls and bags of coins which took place in 1964. As a result, Congress passed legislation so that after the calendar year 1964 coinage was produced, the Mint could still use the 1964 date.

Starting in 1965, therefore, all denominations of United States coinage continued to be struck with the 1964 date.

When the Coinage Act of 1965 was passed, it became mandatory that the Mint continue to use the 1964 date on all 90 percent silver coins (halves, quarters, and dimes). Therefore, all the 90 percent silver coins which were manufactured in 1964, 1965 and 1966 bear the 1964 date.

The last of the 90 percent silver quarters were struck in January 1966, the last of the dimes in February 1966, and the last of the halves in April 1966.

The Coinage Act of 1965 also made it mandatory that the clad coins be dated not earlier than 1965. Therefore, all the clad coins actually made in 1965 bear the 1965 date. All the clad coins made through July 31, 1966, bear the 1965 date.

The first clad dime was struck in December

1965, the first clad quarter dollar in August 1965, and the first clad half dollar in December 1965.

In December 1965, the decision was made to change the 1964 date on the 5-cent pieces and the cents to 1965, as one step in catching up on normal coin dating. From December 1965 through July 31, 1966, all cents and 5-cent pieces struck bear the 1965 date.

Starting on Aug. 1, 1966, and through Dec. 31, 1966, all denominations of United States coins minted during that period carried the 1966 date. Commencing Jan. 1, 1967, the Mints resumed normal dating procedures.

The usual process of dating was interrupted again in December 1974, when Mint Director Mary Brooks announced the date 1974 would continue on dollars, half dollars and quarter dollars produced in the first half of 1975. The date of 1975 appeared, however, on cents, 5-cent and 10-cent coins.

All dollars, half dollars and quarters struck after July 4, 1975, bore the 1776-1976 Bicentennial dates. Normal dating was resumed in 1977.

The Mint Director attributed the date freeze decision to the necessity of building a sufficient coin inventory to conduct business affairs of the nation.

In 1973, the Mint struck 1974-dated aluminum cents in an experiment made necessary because of Mint worries over rising copper prices. When rising copper prices caused Mint officials to finally change the composition of the cent in 1982, the Mint began striking 1982 cents in late 1981 to build up inventories.

Recent special coinage programs have caused Mint officials to strike coins with dates of following or preceding years. Production of Olympic coinage of 1984 gold eagles and 1984 silver dollars began in 1983 to produce an inventory for collector sales in 1984. Striking of the 1986-dated Statue of Liberty commemorative coins began in late 1985, again to produce an inventory. The production of the Proof 1986-dated American Eagle gold and silver bullion coins, however, did not begin until early 1987 in order to permit the Mint to strike sufficient quantities of the business strike versions.

Edge designs

Edge designs on U.S. coins are one of the more neglected aspects of the field of numismatics. Occasionally differences will be noted in the books, such as the change from lettered edge to reeded edge on 1836 Capped Bust half dollars, some distinctions on early large cents and, most surprising, Dr. W.Q.

Wolfson's discovery of the 1921 Morgan, Infrequently Reeded Edge dollars.

We say "surprising" because collectors generally take reeding for granted. About the only people who examine reeded edges are those trying to compare fakes with genuine coins. Otherwise, almost the only time somebody mentions the edge is when he discovers, accidentally, the words misspelled on early halves.

Mention became even rarer when the lettered edges gave place to reeding. The only published mention of reeding counts we know of was in "Bristles and Barbs" in April 1965, and "Coinology" in June 1969, both in *Coin World*, the first being instigated by Wolfson's aforementioned discovery published in *Coin World*'s "Fair to Very Fine" column in December 1964.

"Coinology" for June 11, 1969, reports that the number of reeds on Winged Liberty Head and Roosevelt dimes varies from 104 to 118, an average of 111, so the statement is made that the number of reeds will probably vary also on all other denominations. It also states that "reeding counts are important in the study of any coinage and should be considered seriously." If the statement that the numbers of reed varies in a series is true, it would make reeding less useful in studying fakes.

Both ornamented and lettered edges on coins to 1836 were made on a Castaing machine, consisting of two edge strips, one moving, the other not. Planchets were rolled between the two strips before going to the coining press. Occasional errors were caused by either the planchets or the movable strip slipping. The strips are known as "edge dies."

The same machine was used to make reeded edges up to 1836, reeds or grooves being used instead of letters. From 1836, a grooved collar was used as it still is, with the edge receiving the reeding at the same instance as the coin is produced. If the grooves were not the same in all collars, then the reeding would vary with the collar used. No detailed study has been made of such variations except for the 1921 Morgan, Infrequently Reeded Edge dollar, and the mention of variations in reedings on dimes. Grooved collars are called "collar dies."

Different strips were used on Castaing machines, also, resulting in differences or varieties of ornamentation, lettering and more. Edge varieties and edge errors are two different things, and always have been true whether the edges contain letters, ornamental devices, reeding or a combination of any two or all of them. We discuss varieties here, caused by changes in Castaing strips or collars as the case may be.

Half cents: Two leaf ornamentation in 1793; one leaf 1794 with both large and small lettering known; 1795, large letters or no letters (plain edges); 1796, plain edges only; 1797, medium and small letters, no leaf, and plain edge varieties, also a "Gripped" variety (rare); 1798 and after, plain edge only.

Large cents: 1793 Vine and bars; two leaves; one leaf pointing down; one leaf pointing up (leaves accompany lettered edges); 1794, one leaf up, one leaf down; 1795, lettered edge, plain edge, reeded edge; 1796 and 1797, plain and partially gripped edges; 1798, plain and reeded edges; 1799 and thereafter, all plain edges.

Five-cent pieces: 1882, normal plain edges, a few patterns known with five raised bars.

Half dimes: reeded from 1794 thereafter.

Dimes: reeded from 1796, with some changes in number of reeds from 1837 and possibly still varying through Winged Liberty Head and Roosevelt.

Quarters: Reeded from 1796 to now with probable variations over the years in number of reeds or spacing; from 1838 normal count is 119, but Walter Breen noted some 1876-CC with 153 reeds.

Half dollars: 1794 to 1806, lettered edge with words separated by stars, squares and circles, occasional lettering errors from slipping edge dies; 1807 to 1813, no star after DOLLAR: 1814-1831, with star; 1830 and 1831, varieties with diagonal reeding between words; 1830 to 1836, star after DOLLAR, varieties with vertical reeding between words; vertical reeding with no letters; 1837 and after, vertical reeding, with four different reeded collars used in 1837, and probably unstudied variations thereafter.

Silver dollars: Lettered edge through 1803 with small designs separating words; 1840-1935, reeded edge with varieties possible. Normal is 188 reeds. Only positively known variety is 1921 Morgan, P-Mint, with 154 reeds, known as 1921 Morgan, Infrequently Reeded Edge, discovered by Wolfson.

Trade dollars: Reeded edges with possibility of variations.

Gold dollars: Reeded edges with apparent variations between Mints and types, but not yet permanently identified.

Quarter eagles: Reeded edges from 1796; 1840 and after differ at branch Mints from P-Mint coins, the former having fewer reeds.

Three dollars: Reeded edges, with possible variations at branch Mints.

Half eagles: Same comment.

Eagles: To 1907, same comment. 1907-1911, 46 stars on edge; 1912-1933, 48 stars on edge (1912 with 46 stars possible but unknown as yet).

Double eagles: To 1907, reeded edge without important variations; 1907 Roman Numerals, large letters on patterns, medium letters on regular issue; 1907 Arabic Numerals, small letters.

American Eagle gold bullion coins: Reeded edges, no studies done.

Mottoes

In the act establishing the Mint the devices and legends for the new coins were prescribed as follows: "Upon one side of each of the said coins there shall be an impression emblematic of liberty with an inscription of the word LIBERTY and the year of the coinage; and upon the reverse of each of the gold and silver coins there shall be the figure or representation of an eagle, with the inscription, 'United States of America,' and upon the reverse of the copper coins there shall be an inscription which shall express the denomination of the piece."

E PLURIBUS UNUM

Two legends have appeared on many of the coins of the United States, the one from almost the beginning of the national coinage, and the other since the Civil War. Neither, however, has had an uninterrupted history, nor has either been employed on all the denominations of the series.

The motto E PLURIBUS UNUM was first used on U.S. coinage in 1796, when the reverse of the quarter eagle ($2.50 gold piece) presented the main features of the Great Seal, on the scroll of which this inscription belongs. The same device was placed on certain of the silver coins in 1798, and so the motto was soon found on all the coins in the precious metals. In 1834, it was dropped from most of the gold coins to mark the change in the standard fineness of the coins. In 1837 it was dropped from the silver coins, marking the era of the Revised Mint Code.

The Act of Feb. 12, 1873, made this inscription a requirement of law upon the coins of the United States. A search will reveal, however, that it does not appear on all coins struck after 1873, and that not until much later were the provisions of this act followed in their entirety. From facts contained in Mint records it would appear that officials did not consider the provisions of the law mandatory, but rather, discretionary. The motto does appear on all coins currently being manufactured.

The motto as it appears on U.S. coins means "One Out of Many," and doubtless has reference to the unity of the early states. It is said that one Colonel Reed of Uxbridge, Mass., was instrumental in having it placed on the coins.

IN GOD WE TRUST

From the records of the Treasury Department it appears that the first suggestion of the recognition of the Deity on the coins of the United States was contained in a letter addressed to the Secretary of the Treasury, by the Rev. M.R. Watkinson, Minister of the Gospel, Ridleyville, Pa., dated Nov. 13, 1861.

This letter states:

"One fact touching our currency has hitherto been seriously overlooked. I mean the recognition of the Almighty God in some form in our coins.

"You are probably a Christian. What if our Republic were now shattered beyond reconstruction? Would not the antiquaries of succeeding centuries rightly reason from our past that we were a heathen nation? What I propose is that instead of the goddess of liberty we shall have next inside the 13 stars a ring inscribed with the words 'perpetual union'; within this ring the all-seeing eye, crowned with a halo; beneath this eye the American flag, bearing in its field stars equal to the number of the States united; in the folds of the bars the words 'God, liberty, law.'

"This would make a beautiful coin, to which no possible citizen could object. This would relieve us from the ignominy of heathenism. This would place us openly under the Divine protection we have personally claimed. From my heart I have felt our national shame in disowning God as not the least of our present national disasters.

"To you first I address a subject that must be agitated."

Under date of Nov. 20, 1861, the Secretary of the Treasury addressed the following letter to the Director of the Mint:

"Dear Sir: No nation can be strong except in the strength of God, or safe except in His defense. The trust of our people in God should be declared on our national coins.

"You will cause a device to be prepared without unnecessary delay with a motto expressing in the fewest and tersest words possible this national recognition."

It was found that the Act of Jan. 18, 1837, prescribed the mottoes and devices that should be placed upon the coins of the United States, so that nothing could be done without legislation.

In December 1863, the Director of the Mint submitted to the Secretary of the Treasury for approval designs for new 1-, 2-, and 3-cent pieces, on which it was proposed that one of the following mottoes should appear: "Our country; our God"; "God, our Trust."

The Secretary of the Treasury, in a letter to the Director of the Mint, dated Dec. 9, 1863, states:

"I approve your mottoes, only suggesting that on that with the Washington obverse the motto should begin with the word 'Our,' so as to read: 'Our God and our country.' And on that with the shield, it should be changed so as to read: 'In God We Trust.' "

An act passed April 22, 1864, changing the composition of the 1-cent piece and authorizing the coinage of the 2-cent piece, the devices of which were to be fixed by the Director of the Mint, with the approval of the Secretary of the Treasury, and it is upon the bronze 2-cent piece that the motto IN GOD WE TRUST first appears.

The Act of March 3, 1865, provided that in addition to the legend and devices on the gold and silver coins of the United States, it should be lawful for the Director of the Mint, with the approval of the Secretary of the Treasury to place the motto IN GOD WE TRUST on such coins as shall admit of the inscription thereon. Under this act, the motto was placed upon the double eagle, eagle and half eagle, and also upon the dollar, half dollar and quarter dollar in 1866.

The Coinage Act of Feb. 12, 1873, provided that the Secretary of the Treasury may cause the motto IN GOD WE TRUST to be inscribed on such coins as shall admit of such motto.

When the double eagle and eagle of new design appeared in 1907, it was soon discovered that the religious motto had been omitted. In response to a general demand, Congress ordered it restored, and the Act of May 18, 1908, made mandatory its appearance on all coins upon which it had heretofore appeared. The motto appears on all gold and silver coins struck since July 1, 1908, with the exception of Barber dimes. It was not mandatory upon the cent and 5-cent coins, but could be placed thereon by the Secretary of the Treasury, or the Director of the Mint with the Secretary's approval.

The issuance of the cent in 1909 honoring the centennial of the birth of Abraham Lincoln brought the motto IN GOD WE TRUST to the smallest denomination U.S. coin. This was an appropriate tribute to Lincoln, one of the most deeply spiritual presidents.

Almost another three decades were to go by before the motto was carried over to the one remaining coin in the U.S. series that did not carry it, the 5-cent piece. In 1938, a design for this coin was chosen as a result of a nationwide competition. The design selected, honoring Thomas Jefferson, was executed by Michigan sculptor Felix Schlag. A feature on the obverse is the motto, IN GOD WE TRUST.

The act approved July 11, 1955, makes appearance of the motto IN GOD WE TRUST mandatory upon all coins of the United States. (For a history of the mottoes on paper money, see Chapter 8.)

Symbols

Eagle

The eagle was a favorite device of the United States' founding fathers before it was placed on U.S. national coinage. It appears on the Great Seal of the United States which was adopted in 1782. At this time the states established their own Mints and Massachusetts saw fit to place on the reverse of its coins a spread eagle with arrows and an olive branch in the claws.

When the Mint was established the devices and legends for the new coins were prescribed. It was ordered that "upon the reverse of each of the gold and silver coins there shall be the figure or representation of an eagle." However, the act of Jan. 18, 1837, removed the legal requirement for the half dime and dime. Subsequent gold and silver coins — the silver 3-cent coin, the gold dollar and the gold $3 coin — were not required to have an eagle on the reverse.

The eagle was added almost as an afterthought on one recent U.S. coin. The eagle on the reverse of the Franklin half dollar, introduced in 1948, is very small. The story that Franklin preferred the wild turkey over the bald eagle as a symbol of American pride is well known among collectors. The Liberty Bell is the most prominent device on the reverse of the Franklin half, with a diminutive eagle to the right of the bell.

Portraits

With the exception of the great statesman, Benjamin Franklin, and the great feminist, Susan B. Anthony, the only individuals whose images appear on regular issue U.S. coins have been U.S. presidents. The Indian used on the 5-cent piece introduced in 1913 is not the image of any individual but is a composite of several Indians studied by the designer (identified as Iron Tail, Two Moons and Chief John Tree). One of the most popular designs has been the Goddess of Liberty who appears on many of U.S. coins.

Use of "V" in Trust

In medieval times the letters "u" and "v" were used interchangeably. These letters were not given separate alphabetical listings in English dictionaries until about 1800. In recent times many sculptors have used the "V" in place of "U" for artistic reasons, such as, to represent the permanence and long time significance of their work. Artists who design coins may choose to spell "Trust" with a "V." All of the dollars of the Peace dollar design have this characteristic. From 1921 through 1935 the United States Mints made more than 190 million dollars of this type.

It is interesting to note that sometimes the "V" is similarly used in wording on public buildings.

Initials

The custom of placing the signature of the engraver upon a coin die dates from remote antiquity. Many Greek coins, especially in the creations produced by the cities of Sicily and Magna Graecia, are signed with the initials of the artist, and in some cases his full name. The same practice prevailed generally in the European countries. There were no initials on United States coins until the gold dollar appeared in 1849 with the initial of Longacre, L, on the truncation of the bust.

Other symbols

Arrows were sometimes used on U.S. coins to symbolize preparedness. Olive branches or leaves are found often also. Symbolizing peace, the olive branch is the international emblem of friendship and accord. The fasces on the reverse of the Winged Liberty Head dime has a bundle of rods with protruding ax as the central device. It has been since ancient times a symbol of official authority. Also on this dime, the winged cap on the Roman style Liberty Head symbolizes freedom of thought.

The newer Roosevelt dime bears some representative symbols also. In the center of the reverse is a torch signifying liberty bounded by an olive branch on the left and an oak branch signifying strength and independence on the right.

The Kennedy half dollar contains much symbolism. The presidential coat of arms forms the motif for the reverse. The coat of arms depicts the American eagle holding the olive branch in his right claw and arrows in the left. Symbolism derived from the 13 original states governs the number of olive leaves, berries, arrows, stars and cloud puffs. The upper part of the flag or shield upon the breast of the eagle represents the Congress binding the Colonies into an entity. The vertical stripes complete the motif of the flag of the United States. Each state of the nation is represented in the 50-star amulet which rings the whole.

Issue dates, designers, original engravers, models

Regular issue United States coins

Coin	Issue Dates	Designers	Original Engraver	Model or Source
Half cent	1793-1857			
Liberty Cap Left	1793	Obv: Eckfeldt	Eckfeldt	Dupre's Libertas Americana medal
		Rev: Eckfeldt.	Eckfeldt	Original design
Liberty Cap Right . . . (Large Head)	1794	Obv: Scot.	Scot	Similar to previous issue, but reversed
		Rev: Scot	Scot	Similar to previous issue
Liberty Cap Right . . . (Small Head)	1795-1797	Obv: Scot-Gardner.	Scot	Similar to previous issue
		Rev: Scot-Gardner	Scot	Similar to previous issue
Draped Bust.	1800-1808	Obv: Stuart-Scot.	Scot	Ann Willing Bingham (?)
		Rev: Scot-Gardner	Scot	Similar to previous issue
Classic Head	1809-1836	Obv: Reich	Reich	Unknown model
		Rev: Reich.	Reich	Original design
Coronet Type.	1840-1857	Obv: Scot-Gobrecht.	Gobrecht	Coronet Type large cent
		Rev: Reich-Gobrecht.	Gobrecht	Similar to previous issue
Large cent	1793-1857			
Flowing Hair,. . . . . . . Chain Rev.	1793	Obv: Voigt.	Voigt	Unknown model
		Rev: Voigt	Voigt	Fugio cent (?)
Flowing Hair,. . . . . . . Wreath Rev.	1793	Obv: Voigt-Eckfeldt	Eckfeldt	Similar to previous issue
		Rev: Eckfeldt.	Eckfeldt	Original design
Liberty Cap	1793-1794	Obv: Wright	Wright	Dupre's Libertas Americana medal, reversed
		Rev: Wright.	Wright	Similar to previous issue
Liberty Cap . . . . (Modified)	1794-1796	Obv: Wright-Gardner.	Scot	Similar to previous issue
		Rev: Wright-Gardner.	Scot	Similar to previous issue
Draped Bust.	1796-1807	Obv: Stuart-Scot.	Scot	Ann Willing Bingham (?)
		Rev: Wright-Scot	Scot	Similar to previous issue
Classic Head	1808-1814	Obv: Reich	Reich	Unknown model
		Rev: Reich.	Reich	Original design
Coronet Type.	1816-1835	Obv: Scot.	Scot	Unknown model
		Rev: Reich.	Reich	Same as previous issue
	1835-1839	Obv: Scot-Gobrecht.	Gobrecht	Similar to previous issue
		Rev: Reich.	Reich	Same as previous issue
	1839-1857	Obv: Scot-Gobrecht.	Gobrecht	Similar to previous issue
		Rev: Reich-Gobrecht.	Gobrecht	Similar to previous issue
Small cent	1856-Present			
Flying Eagle	1856-1858	Obv: Gobrecht-Longacre. .	Longacre	Titian Peale's design for dollar reverse, c. 1836
		Rev: Longacre.	Longacre	Reverse of $1 & $3 gold.
Indian Head.	1859-1909	Obv: Longacre.	Longacre	Possibly Longacre's daughter Sarah
		Rev: (Both) Longacre	Longacre	Original designs
Lincoln Head. . . . . . . (Wheat Rev.)	1909-1958	Obv: Victor D. Brenner . . .	C. Barber	Brenner's plaque
		Rev: Victor D. Brenner . . .	C. Barber	Original design
Lincoln Head. . . . . . . (Memorial Rev.)	1959-	Obv: Brenner.	C. Barber	Same as previous issue
		Rev: Gasparro.	Roberts	Lincoln Memorial
Two cents	1864-1873	Obv: Longacre.	Longacre	Original design
		Rev: Longacre.	Longacre	Original design

Coin	Issue Dates	Designers	Original Engraver	Model or Source
Silver 3 cents	1851-1873	Obv: Longacre	Longacre	Original design (three varieties)
		Rev: Longacre	Longacre	Original design (two varieties)
Copper-nickel 3 cents	1865-1889	Obv: Longacre	Longacre	Possibly Sarah Longacre
		Rev: Longacre	Longacre	Original design
Half dime	1794-1873			
Flowing Hair	1794-1795	Obv: Scot	Scot	Unknown model
		Rev: Scot	Scot	Original design
Draped Bust (Small Eagle)	1796-1797	Obv: Stuart-Scot	Scot	Ann Willing Bingham (?)
		Rev: Scot-Eckstein(?)	Scot	Similar to previous issue
Draped Bust (Heraldic Eagle)	1800-1805	Obv: Stuart-Scot	Scot	Same as previous issue
		Rev: Scot	Scot	Great Seal of the United States
Capped Bust	1829-1837	Obv: Reich-Kneass	Kneass	Unknown model (similar to dime by Reich)
		Rev: Reich-Kneass	Kneass	Original design (similar to dime by Reich)
Seated Liberty[2] (No Drapery)	1837-1840	Obv: Gobrecht	Gobrecht	Drawing by Thomas Sully
		Rev: Gobrecht	Gobrecht	Original design
Seated Liberty (With Drapery)	1840-1859	Obv: Gobrecht-Hughes	Gobrecht	Similar to previous issue
		Rev: Gobrecht	Gobrecht	Same as previous issue
Seated Liberty (Legend Obv.)	1860-1873	Obv: Gobrecht-Hughes- Longacre	Longacre	Similar to previous issue
		Rev: Longacre	Longacre	Original design
Copper-nickel 5 cents	1866-Present			
Shield Type	1866-1883	Obv: Longacre	Longacre	Original design
		Rev: Longacre	Longacre	Original design (two varieties)
Liberty Head	1883-1912	Obv: C. Barber	C. Barber	Unknown model
		Rev: C. Barber	C. Barber	Original design (two varieties)
Indian Head	1913-1938	Obv: James E. Fraser	C. Barber	Composite of three Indians
		Rev: James E. Fraser	C. Barber	"Black Diamond," Central Park Zoo
Jefferson Head	1938-	Obv: Felix Schlag	Sinnock	Bust by Houdon, c. 1789
		Rev: Felix Schlag	Sinnock	Monticello
Dime	1796-Present			
Draped Bust (Small Eagle)	1796-1797	Obv: Stuart-Scot	Scot	Ann Willing Bingham (?)
		Rev: Scot-Eckstein (?)	Scot	Similar to Scot's 1794 silver reverse
Draped Bust (Heraldic Eagle)	1798-1807	Obv: Stuart-Scot	Scot	Same as previous issue
		Rev: Scot	Scot	Great Seal of the United States
Capped Bust[3]	1809-1837	Obv: Reich	Reich	Unknown model
		Rev: Reich	Reich	Original design
Seated Liberty[2] (No Drapery)	1837-1840	Obv: Gobrecht	Gobrecht	Drawing by Thomas Sully
		Rev: Gobrecht	Gobrecht	Original design
Seated Liberty (With Drapery)	1840-1860	Obv: Gobrecht-Hughes	Gobrecht	Similar to previous issue
		Rev: Gobrecht	Gobrecht	Same as previous issue
Seated Liberty (Legend Obv.)	1860-1891	Obv: Gobrecht-Hughes- Longacre	Longacre	Similar to previous issue
		Rev: Longacre	Longacre	Original design
"Barber" Head	1892-1916	Obv: C. Barber	C. Barber	French medal designs
		Rev: Longacre	Longacre	Same as previous issue
Winged Liberty Head	1916-1945	Obv: Adolph A. Weinman	C. Barber	Elsie Kachel Stevens
		Rev: Adolph A. Weinman	C. Barber	Original design
Roosevelt Head	1946-	Obv: Sinnock	Sinnock	Original design
		Rev: Sinnock	Sinnock	Original design
Twenty cents	1875-1878	Obv: Gobrecht-Hughes- W. Barber	W. Barber	Seated Liberty dollar
		Rev: W. Barber	W. Barber	Original design
Quarter dollar	1796-Present			
Draped Bust (Small Eagle)	1796	Obv: Stuart-Scot	Scot	Ann Willing Bingham (?)
		Rev: Scot-Eckstein (?)	Scot	Similar to Scot's 1794 silver reverse

Coin	Issue Dates	Designers	Original Engraver	Model or Source
Draped Bust (Heraldic Eagle)	1804-1807	Obv: Stuart-Scot Rev: Scot	Scot Scot	Same as previous issue Great Seal of the United States
Capped Bust[4]	1815-1838	Obv: Reich Rev: Reich	Reich Reich	Unknown model Original design (c. 1807)
Seated Liberty (No Drapery)	1838-1840	Obv: Gobrecht Rev: Reich-Kneass-Gobrecht	Gobrecht Gobrecht	Drawing by Thomas Sully Similar to previous issue
Seated Liberty (With Drapery)	1840-1891	Obv: Gobrecht-Hughes Rev: Reich-Kneass-Gobrecht	Gobrecht Gobrecht	Similar to previous issue Same as previous issue
"Barber" Head	1892-1916	Obv: C. Barber Rev: C. Barber	C. Barber C. Barber	French medal designs Great Seal of the United States
Standing Liberty	1916-1930	Obv: Herman A. MacNeil Rev: Herman A. MacNeil	C. Barber C. Barber	Dora Doscher (two varieties.) Original design (two var.)
Washington Head	1932-	Obv: John Flanagan Rev: John Flanagan	Sinnock Sinnock	Bust by Houdon (1785) Original design
Bicentennial	1976	Obv: Flanagan Rev: Jack L. Ahr	Sinnock Gasparro	Same as regular issue Original design
Half dollar 1794-Present				
Flowing Hair	1794-1795	Obv: Scot Rev: Scot	Scot Scot	Unknown model Original design
Draped Bust (Small Eagle)	1796-1797	Obv: Stuart-Scot Rev: Scot-Eckstein	Scot Scot	Ann Willing Bingham (?) Similar to previous issue
Draped Bust (Heraldic Eagle)	1801-1807	Obv: Stuart-Scot Rev: Scot	Scot Scot	Same as previous issue Great Seal of the United States
Capped Bust[5] (50 C. Rev.)	1807-1836	Obv: Reich Rev: Reich	Reich Reich	Unknown model Original design
Capped Bust (50 Cents Rev.)	1836-1837	Obv: Reich-Gobrecht Rev: Reich-Gobrecht	Gobrecht Gobrecht	Similar to previous issue Similar to previous issue
Capped Bust (Half Dol.)	1838-1839	Obv: Reich-Gobrecht Rev: Reich-Gobrecht	Gobrecht Gobrecht	Same as previous issue Similar to previous issue
Seated Liberty	1839-1891	Obv: Gobrecht Rev: Reich-Gobrecht	Gobrecht Gobrecht	Drawing by Thomas Sully Similar to previous issue
"Barber" Head	1892-1915	Obv: C. Barber Rev: C. Barber	C. Barber C. Barber	French medal designs Great Seal of the United States
Walking Liberty	1916-1947	Obv: Adolph A. Weinman Rev: Adolph A. Weinman	C. Barber C. Barber	Roty's Sower design on French silver Original design
Franklin Head	1948-1963	Obv: Sinnock Rev: Sinnock	Roberts Roberts	Bust by Houdon (1778) Sesquicentennial half
Kennedy Head	1964-	Obv.: Roberts Rev: Gasparro	Roberts Roberts	U.S. Mint medal Seal of the president of the U.S.
Bicentennial	1976	Obv: Roberts Rev: Seth G. Huntington	Roberts Gasparro	Same as regular issue Independence Hall
Dollar (silver, clad) 1794-Present				
Flowing Hair	1794-1795	Obv: Scot Rev: Scot	Scot Scot	Unknown model Original design
Draped Bust (Small Eagle)	1795-1798	Obv: Stuart-Scot Rev: Scot-Eckstein (?)	Scot Scot	Ann Willing Bingham(?) Similar to previous issue
Draped Bust (Heraldic Eagle)	1798-1804	Obv: Stuart-Scot Rev: Scot	Scot Scot	Same as previous issue Great Seal of the United States
"Gobrecht"[6]	1836-1839	Obv: Gobrecht Rev: Gobrecht	Gobrecht Gobrecht	Drawing by Thomas Sully Drawing by Titian Peale
Seated Liberty	1840-1873	Obv: Gobrecht-Hughes Rev: Reich-Gobrecht	Gobrecht Gobrecht	Similar to pattern issue Reich's 1807 reverse for silver
"Morgan" Head	1878-1921	Obv: Morgan Rev: Morgan	Morgan Morgan	Anna W. Williams Original design
Peace type	1921-1935	Obv: Anthony DeFrancisci Rev: Anthony DeFrancisci	Morgan Morgan	Teresa C. DeFrancisci Original design

Coin	Issue Dates	Designers	Original Engraver	Model or Source
Eisenhower Head ...	1971-1978	Obv: Gasparro	Gasparro	Sketch by Gasparro (1945)
		Rev: Gasparro.............	Gasparro	Apollo 11 emblem
Bicentennial........	1976	Obv: Gasparro	Gasparro	Same as regular issue
		Rev: Dennis R. Williams....	Gasparro	Original design
Anthony Head......	1979-1981	Obv: Gasparro	Gasparro	Original design
		Rev: Gasparro.............	Gasparro	Apollo 11 emblem
Trade dollar..........	1873-1883	Obv: W. Barber............	W. Barber	Unknown model
		Rev: W. Barber............	W. Barber	Original design
Dollar (gold)	1849-1889			
Liberty Head	1849-1854	Obv: Longacre.............	Longacre	Possibly Sarah Longacre
		Rev: Longacre.............	Longacre	Original design
Indian Head[7]	1854-1889	Obv: Longacre.............	Longacre	Possibly Sarah Longacre
		Rev: Longacre.............	Longacre	Original design
Quarter eagle........	1796-1929			
Capped Bust Right ..	1796-1807	Obv: Scot.................	Scot	Martha Washington(?)
		Rev. Scot.................	Scot	Great Seal of the United States
Capped Bust Left....	1808	Obv: Reich	Reich	Unknown model
		Rev: Reich................	Reich	1789 Mott token
Capped Head Left[8] ..	1821-1834	Obv: Reich-Scot	Scot	Similar to previous issue
		Rev: Reich................	Reich	Same as previous issue
Classic Head	1834-1839	Obv: Kneass	Kneass	Reich's Classic Head cent
		Rev: Reich-Kneass........	Kneass	Similar to previous issue
Coronet type	1840-1907	Obv: Gobrecht	Gobrecht	Coronet type large cent
		Rev: Reich-Kneass-Gobrecht	Gobrecht	Similar to previous issue
Indian Head........	1908-1929	Obv: Bela Lyon Pratt	C. Barber	Unknown model
		Rev: Bela Lyon Pratt	C. Barber	Original design
Three Dollars	1854-1889	Obv: Longacre.............	Longacre	Possibly Sarah Longacre
		Rev: Longacre.............	Longacre	Original design
Half Eagle	1795-1929			
Capped Bust Right .. (Small Eagle)	1795-1798	Obv: Scot.................	Scot	Martha Washington(?)
		Rev: Scot.................	Scot	Original design
Capped Bust Right .. (Heraldic Eagle)	1795-1807	Obv: Scot.................	Scot	Same as previous issue
		Rev: Scot.................	Scot	Great Seal of the United States
Capped Bust Left....	1807-1812	Obv: Reich	Reich	Unknown model
		Rev: Reich................	Reich	1789 Mott token
Capped Head Left[8] ..	1813-1834	Obv: Reich-Scot	Scot	Similar to previous issue
		Rev: Reich................	Reich	Same as previous issue
Classic Head	1834-1838	Obv: Kneass	Kneass	Reich's Classic Head cent
		Rev: Reich-Kneass........	Kneass	Similar to previous issue
Coronet Type.......	1839-1908	Obv: Gobrecht	Gobrecht	Coronet type large cent
		Rev: Reich-Kneass-Gobrecht	Gobrecht	Similar to previous issue
Indian Head........	1908-1929	Obv: Bela Lyon Pratt	C. Barber	Unknown model
		Rev. Bela Lyon Pratt	C. Barber	Original design
Eagle................	1795-1933			
Capped Bust Right .. (Small Eagle)	1795-1797	Obv: Scot.................	Scot	Possibly Martha Washington
		Rev: Scot.................	Scot	Original design
Capped Bust Right .. (Heraldic Eagle)	1797-1804	Obv: Scot.................	Scot	Same as previous issue
		Rev: Scot.................	Scot	Great Seal of the United States
Coronet Type.......	1838-1907	Obv: Gobrecht	Gobrecht	Coronet Type Large Cent
		Rev: Reich-Kneass-Gobrecht	Gobrecht	$2.50, $5 Rev.
Indian Head........	1907-1933	Obv: Saint-Gaudens........	C. Barber	Unknown model
		Rev: Saint-Gaudens	C. Barber	Original design
Double eagle	1849-1933			
Liberty Head	1849-1907	Obv: Longacre.............	Longacre	Possibly Sarah Longacre
		Rev: Longacre.............	Longacre	Original design
Saint-Gaudens Type .	1907-1933	Obv: Saint-Gaudens........	C. Barber	Unknown model
		Rev: Saint-Gaudens	C. Barber	Original design

Coin	Issue Dates	Designers	Original Engraver	Model or Source
American Eagle bullion	. 1986-date			
American Eagle	. . . . . 1986-date			
Silver bullion	1986-date	Obv: Adolph A. Weinman . . .	Steever	Walking Liberty half dollar
		Rev: John Mercanti	Mercanti	Great Seal of the United States
Gold bullion	1986-date			
		Saint-Gaudens	Peloso	Double eagle design of 1907-33[9]
		Rev: Miley Busiek	Winter	Original design

Notes

1. When two or more names appear hyphenated as the designers, the first person created the design and the others modified it for artistic and/or personal reasons. Modifications of design and/or relief solely for striking purposes are not included.
2. Stars are not on the obverse of 1837 and 1838-O coins.
3. Smaller size (1828-37) engraved by Kneass.
4. Smaller size without E PLURIBUS UNUM (1831-1838) engraved by Kneass.
5. Slight modifications made in 1809 by Reich and in 1834 by Kneass.
6. All coins are patterns but some did circulate.
7. Small Head 1854-56; Large Head 1856-89.
8. Smaller size (1829-34) engraved by Kneass.
9. Saint-Gaudens' Liberty was "slimmed down" to meet modern standards of physical beauty, under the orders of Treasury Secretary James A. Baker III.

Engravers of United States coins

The following is a brief biography of any engraver of a regular issue U.S. coin, plus any Chief Sculptor-Engraver. Most were official Chief Engravers; others were employed by the Mint in other capacities.

VOIGT, Henry. In reality the chief coiner of the Mint, he engraved the 1793 Chain cent as a matter of expediency.

ECKFELDT, Adam. Later the second chief coiner and eventually the superintendent of the Mint, he was not officially employed by the Mint until July 1795. He performed various jobs before that date and engraved dies for the 1793 Wreath cent and the 1793 half cent, again out of necessity. He was connected with the Mint in some manner, either officially or unofficially, from 1792 to his death in 1852.

WRIGHT, Joseph. Chief Engraver of the U.S. Mint. Appointed in August 1793, he designed and engraved only the 1793 Liberty Cap cent before he died the following month of yellow fever. Not every authority, including the U.S. Mint, considers Wright a Chief Engraver, since the sole documentary evidence for his appointment is found in letters between government officials.

SCOT, Robert. Chief Engraver of the U.S. Mint. Appointed Nov. 23, 1793, many of his designs were adaptations of others'. Possibly his best design was the Heraldic Eagle reverse, based on the Great Seal of the United States. For all practical design purposes, he was replaced by John Reich in 1807, although he retained his position and did design several coins later in his term until his death in November 1823.

GARDNER, John Smith. Assistant Engraver of the U.S. Mint. Serving from November 1794 to March 1796, he prepared the modified head and wreath punches for 1795 half cents and cents, as well as the small Flowing Hair head for some 1795 half dollars.

REICH, John. Assistant Engraver of the U.S. Mint. Although officially Robert Scot's assistant, appointed April 1, 1807, he redesigned and engraved every denomination then being struck. Dissatisfied with the assistant's pay for the master's work, he resigned on March 31, 1817, and was not replaced in Scot's term.

KNEASS, William. Chief Engraver of the U.S. Mint. Appointed Jan. 29, 1824, he was greatly praised for his proficiency. He did much to improve and standardize the quality of coins then being struck. He suffered a crippling stroke on Aug. 28, 1835, after which the physical work of engraving was done by Christian Gobrecht. He died in office Aug. 27, 1840.

GOBRECHT, Christian. Chief Engraver of the U.S. Mint. Appointed second, or co-engraver in September 1835, to assist the ailing Kneass, he was Chief Engraver in practice until Kneass' death, and in name therafter from Dec. 21, 1840, until his own death on July 23, 1844. A talented engraver, he was unfortunately not as talented an artist; his Seated Liberty design had to be modified by Robert Ball Hughes in 1840. His Seated Liberty obverse was used on most silver coins until 1891, and his Coronet type obverse was used on gold coins from 1838 to 1908. His most stunning work was the Flying Eagle reverse for dollars and half dollars, a design which was used only on the Gobrecht dollars.

LONGACRE, James Barton. Chief Engraver of the U.S. Mint. Although he was a well-known portrait engraver at the time of his appointment on Sept. 16, 1844, he had no experience in die-sinking and it was many years before he became competent at it. He was the first Chief Engraver in 50 years to have the opportunity to create new denominations for circulation. His works include the 2-cent piece, the silver 3-cent piece, the copper-nickel 3-cent and 5-cent pieces, the $1, $3 and $20 gold pieces, as well as the small cent. Three of his designs survived into this century: the Indian Head cent, the Coronet double eagle, and the reverse of the dime, which was used from 1860 to 1916. He died in office on Jan. 1, 1869.

PAQUET, Anthony. Assistant Engraver of the U.S. Mint. Appointed Oct. 20, 1857, to help Longacre with die-sinking, he was soon designing patterns of his own and produced a modified reverse die for the 1861 double eagle. However, the design proved unsatisfactory and the coins were recalled after a limited production run at both the Philadelphia and San Francisco Mints. Although he left the position for other Mint work in 1864, he continued to produce occasional pattern dies until 1877.

BARBER, William. Chief Engraver of the U.S. Mint. Appointed in January 1869, following Longacre's death, he served until his own death on Aug. 31, 1879. His term saw the issuance of hundreds of pattern coins, including those for the Trade dollar and the 20-cent piece which he designed.

BARBER, Charles. Chief Engraver of the U.S. Mint. Assistant Engraver to his father William, he was virtually replaced by George Morgan in 1876 but nevertheless was promoted to Chief Engraver in 1879. He proved to be an excellent engraver but an unimaginative designer. He was responsible for the design of the 1883 5-cent piece without the word CENTS. The formality of his 1892 designs led to Theodore Roosevelt's use of outside artists for the new gold designs of 1907-1908, as well as for the Lincoln cent. Later, designs for the Indian Head 5-cent and the 1916 silver issues also came from outside sources. After engraving the last of these he died soon after, on Feb. 18, 1917.

MORGAN, George T. Chief Engraver of the U.S. Mint. Brought over from the British Royal Mint in 1876 as special engraver to help redesign the silver dollar, his design was chosen over William Barber's for the 1878 Bland-Allison dollar. The logical successor to William Barber, he was instead passed over in favor of William's son, Charles. After that he was demoted to Assistant Engraver, a position he maintained until 1917 when he was finally promoted to Chief Engraver. His term saw the revival in 1921 of the Morgan silver dollar, only to have it replaced in that same year by the Peace dollar. Morgan had the same problem engraving both designs: he made the relief too high on the earliest issues. Morgan died on Jan. 4, 1925, and with him the era of engravers appointed according to their political affiliations.

SINNOCK, John R. Chief Engraver of the U.S. Mint. Appointed Aug. 1, 1925, he served until his death on May 14, 1947. Formerly an Assistant Engraver to Morgan, he engraved the Washington quarter from Flanagan's design, and designed both the Franklin Roosevelt dime and the Franklin half dollar. The latter was engraved after his death. Apparently he was not well known outside numismatic circles and the Treasury, since his initials JS on the dime were attributed by some to Roosevelt's wartime ally, Joseph Stalin. When the Franklin half dollar was issued in 1948, the bust was initialed JRS, another example of how public opinion can affect coinage design.

ROBERTS, Gilroy. Chief Engraver of the U.S. Mint. Assistant to Sinnock, he succeeded him on July 22, 1948. He resigned on Oct. 8, 1964, for reasons of health, although he has since pursued a successful private career. He engraved the Franklin half dollar from Sinnock's design, and in late 1963 he prepared the obverse for the Kennedy half dollar. Once again the public overreacted to the designer's initials, many people mistaking the stylized GR for a hammer and sickle.

GASPARRO, Frank. Chief Engraver of the U.S. Mint. Serving as Chief Engraver from Feb. 23, 1965, to Jan. 16, 1981, he was formerly Assistant Engraver and designed the Lincoln Memorial reverse for the cent and the reverse of the Kennedy half dollar and the obverse and reverse of the Eisenhower dollar and Anthony dollar. It was he who adapted the artists' designs for the Bicentennial coinage into the final designs suitable for coinage.

JONES, Elizabeth. Chief Sculptor-Engraver of the United States. Serving as Chief Engraver from July 13, 1981, to present. Designer of the obverse and reverse for the 1982 George Washington commemorative half dollar and the obverse and reverse of the 1983 Olympic silver dollar. Designer of the 1986-W Statue of Liberty $5 half eagle. First woman to serve in the position of Chief Sculptor-Engraver.

Chief Engravers

Engraver	Term
Joseph Wright	Aug.-Sept., 1793
Robert Scot	Nov. 23, 1793-Nov., 1823
William Kneass	Jan. 29, 1824-Aug. 27, 1840
Christian Gobrecht	Dec. 21, 1840-July 23, 1844
James B. Longacre	Sept. 16, 1844-Jan. 1, 1869
William Barber	Jan. 1869-Aug. 31, 1879
Charles Barber	Late 1879-Feb. 18, 1917
George T. Morgan	Early 1917-Jan. 4, 1925
John R. Sinnock	Aug. 1, 1925-May 14, 1947
Gilroy Roberts	July 22, 1948-Oct. 8, 1964
Frank Gasparro	Feb. 23, 1965-Jan. 16, 1981
Elizabeth Jones	July 13, 1981-

How coins are made

United States coins have their beginnings in the private sector, where a number of companies produce some coinage planchets and all coils of strip metal the Mint purchases. The Mint produced its own strip metal as late as fiscal year 1982 at the Philadelphia Mint, but the operations were closed officially in fiscal 1983.

Basically, the coinage metals are assayed, melted and formed into slabs which are then rolled to the proper thickness. For clad coinage, bonding operations are required to bond the two layers of copper-nickel to the core of pure copper. The strip is then coiled and shipped to the Mint for blanking.

Some of the purchased material arrives in planchet form, ready to be coined, including the copper-plated zinc cent planchets used since 1982.

The blanking presses are simply punch presses similar to those found in any machine shop. They have a bank of punches (or rams) which travel downward through the strip and into a steel bedplate which has holes corresponding to the punches. The presses punch out planchets each time the punches make their downward cycle. The planchets made at this stage are slightly larger than the finished coins. Because of the shearing action of the punches, the planchets have rough edges. Most of the rough edges (or burrs) are removed during succeeding operations.

The planchets (also called flans or blanks) are next passed over sorting screens which are supposed to eliminate all of the defective planchets. Thin and incomplete planchets will fall through the screens. These rejected planchets are remelted.

During the finish rolling and blanking press operations the planchets have again been hardened and must now be softened. The planchets are passed through a cylinder which has spiral grooves in its walls. As the cylinder turns, the planchets are forced from one end to the other by the spirals. As they move along the cylinder walls, the planchets are heated to controlled temperatures, approximately 1400 degrees, changing their crystal structure to a softer state. Planchets are "frozen" into that state by a water quench bath. This annealing process prolongs the life of the coining dies by ensuring well-struck coins with lower striking pressures.

Type I planchets

Despite a protective atmosphere, annealing causes some discoloration on the surfaces of the planchets which must be removed. The planchets are tumbled against each other and passed through a chemical bath. Then they are dried by forced hot air. The planchets are now completed Type I planchets and if they happen to bypass the coining presses you will see them as flat disks.

The upsetting mill consists of a rotating wheel with a groove on its edge. The grooved edge of the wheel fits into a curved section (or shoe) which has a corresponding groove. The distance between the wheel and the shoe gets progressively narrower so that, as the planchet is rolled along the groove, a raised rim is formed on both sides of the planchet. This raised rim serves several purposes. It sizes and shapes the planchet for better feed at the press and it work-hardens the edge to prevent escape of metal between the obverse die and the collar.

The planchets are now called Type II planchets and are ready to be struck into coins.

Die preparation

The dies used for striking coins start out as an approved sketch of the coin in the Engraving Department at the Philadelphia Mint. The sculptor-engraver makes a plasticene (modeling wax) model in bas-relief from the sketch. The model will be anywhere from three to 12 times as large as the finished coin. Next, a plaster-of-paris negative is cast from the model. The negative is touched up and details are added. Then a plaster-of-paris positive is made. The positive is used as the model to be approved by the Mint Director and the Secretary of the Treasury. If pictures are required for such approval, they are taken of this positive.

When final approval is received another negative is made and a hard epoxy positive model is prepared. The epoxy model replaces the copper galvano once used by the U.S. Mint.

Epoxy to hub

The completed epoxy is then mounted on a Janvier transfer engraving machine. This machine cuts the design in a soft tool steel blank to the exact size of the coin, following the exact details of the epoxy, producing a positive replica of the model. This positive is called a "hub." The hub is then heat treated to harden it and is used in a hydraulic press to prepare a master die. The original hub is carefully stored in a safe place to ensure against loss of the original reduction.

Working hubs are made from the master die in the hydraulic press, and similarly hardened in the same way.

Working dies are made from the working hub in the same way. Pressing an image into a piece of soft tool steel hardens the metal, so annealing is usually needed to fully form the image. Two to three cycles may be required to properly impress all details into the steel.

The working dies for non-Proofs and commemoratives are now complete in every detail except the addition of the Mint mark, although not all dies are Mint marked. Mint marks are added by using a handpunch, although some are Mint marked at the initial modeling stage.

Coinage operations are performed in the coin press room. It is here that the little disks take on their final identity. They go into the presses as blanks and come out bearing the devices and inscriptions which make them coins of the realm.

Coining presses

Coining presses are designed for a fixed class of work, not for a specific denomination of coin. Dies and collars are interchangeable and striking pressures are adjustable for the various denominations and metals. The collar forms the wall of the coining chamber and one die forms the bottom. The dies impress the various designs and devices on the obverse and reverse for the coin while the collar forms the edge of the coin, square and smooth on cents and 5-cent pieces and reeded on the larger denominations. The collar, which is five-thousandths of an inch larger in diameter than the dies, is mounted on springs which allows slight vertical movement.

It is generally assumed that the reverse die is the lower (or anvil) die while the obverse die is the upper (or hammer) die; however, there are exceptions to this general rule. Both dies can be adjusted both horizontally and vertically. Horizontal adjustments center the design of the coin on the planchet. Vertical adjustments determine how well the dies are impressed into the planchet.

Planchets are fed by gravity from a basin attached to the press through a cylindrical tube. This tube will stack 20 or so planchets and from this stack the bottom planchet is fed into the press by the feed fingers.

The feed fingers are two parallel pieces of metal joined in such a way that they can open and close. On one end of the two pieces is a covered recessed slot and in the center is a hole. The lower die at this point is stationary. As the upper die moves downward it impresses the designs of both sides into the planchet and then completes its cycle by moving upward to its original position. Now the lower die starts to move upward, actuated by an eccentric cam, raising the struck coin out of the coining chamber.

At about the same time the feeder fingers, in a closed position, start to move forward with a planchet lying in the center hole. At this time the lower die reaches the top of its cycle, the recessed slot (ejection slot) slides over the struck coin, and pushes the coin away from the coining chamber. The cam action now causes the lower die to move downward to its stationary position.

The feed fingers have completed their forward movement and now the center hole is moving towards the coining chamber. Having imparted movement to the struck coin, that coin continues onward until it hits a shield which deflects it into the struck coin hopper. The feed fingers open, allowing the planchet to fall into the coining chamber. Then the feed fingers reverse direction to return to their original position.

At frequent times, while a press is in operation, the press attendant will pick up a finished coin for inspection. He makes the inspection under a magnifier and it reveals any defects made in the die during operation.

After the coins have been struck they are ready for a final inspection. After passing the inspection, they are counted in automatic machines, weighed and bagged. The bags are sewn shut and are ready for shipment to the Federal Reserve Banks for distribution.

The first coining presses in the Mint were hand operated which severely limited their output. Later presses were powered by steam boilers and capable of 55 strokes per minute. Still later presses, speeded up to 140 strokes per minute, were converted to accept dual dies which doubled the output. And still later some were converted to quadro, four dies, increasing capacity up to 560 per minute.

Not all the old-style coining presses are out of commission, however. The coining press that had its first job striking Carson City silver dollars in 1870 had another assignment over a century later, striking the official Nevada Bicentennial medal.

The old press, rebuilt and moved to the Nevada State Museum, was built in 1869 by the firm of Morgan and Orr of Philadelphia. It struck its first coin, an 1870-CC silver dollar, in the Carson City Mint Feb. 11, 1870.

Another example of the Mint recycling coining presses is the use of 20 dual presses, some retired from the Philadelphia Mint, to strike cents at the West Point Bullion Depository. To help ease the burden of the Bicentennial coins, the Mint received permission to use the West Point facility to manufacture coins. The old presses were moved there in late 1974.

West Point also has struck the 1984-W Olmpic gold eagles and the American Arts Gold Medallions.

Source: United States Mint

U.S. Mint Coinage Manufacturing Processes for Dimes, Quarters, Halves and Dollars

U.S. Mint Coinage Manufacturing Processes for Cents and Nickels

Specifications of U.S. coins

COIN / DATES OF ISSUE	GRAMS WGT.	TOL.	GRAINS WGT.	TOL.	DIA. (mm)	COMPOSITION	SPEC. GRAV.
HALF CENT							
1793-1795	6.739		104.000		23.50*	Pure copper	8.92
1795-1837	5.443		84.000		23.50*	Pure copper	8.92
1837-1857	5.443	0.227	84.000	3.50	23.50*	Pure copper	8.92
LARGE CENT							
1793-1795	13.478		208.000		28.50*	Pure copper	8.92
1795-1837	10.886		168.000		28.50*	Pure copper	8.92
1837-1857	10.886	0.454	168.000	7.00	28.50*	Pure copper	8.92
SMALL CENT							
1856-1864	4.666	0.259	72.000	4.00	19.30*	88 Cu, 12 Ni	8.92
1864-1873	3.110	0.259	48.000	4.00	19.05	95 Cu, 5 Zn & Sn	8.84
1873-1942	3.110	0.130	48.000	2.00	19.05	95 Cu, 5 Zn & Sn	8.84
1943	2.689/2.754	0.130	41.500/42.500***	2.00	19.05	Zinc-plated steel	7.80
1944-1946	3.110	0.130	48.000	2.00	19.05	95 Cu, 5 Zn	8.83
1947-1962	3.110	0.130	48.000	2.00	19.05	95 Cu, 5 Zn & Sn	8.84
1962-1982	3.110	0.130	48.000	2.00	19.05	95 Cu, 5 Zn	8.83
1982-	2.500	0.100	38.581	1.54	19.05	97.5 Zn,2.5 Cu****	7.17
TWO CENTS							
1864-1873	6.221	0.259	96.000	4.00	23.00*	95 Cu, 5 Zn & Sn	8.84
THREE CENTS (Cu-Ni)							
1865-1873	1.944	0.259	30.000	4.00	17.90*	75 Cu, 25 Ni	8.92
1873-1889	1.944	0.130	30.000	2.00	17.90*	75 Cu, 25 Ni	8.92
FIVE CENTS							
1866-1873	5.000	0.130	77.162	2.00	20.50*	75 Cu, 25 Ni	8.92
1873-1883	5.000	0.194	77.162	3.00	20.50*	75 Cu, 25 Ni	8.92
1883-1942	5.000	0.194	77.162	3.00	21.21	75 Cu, 25 Ni	8.92
1942-1945	5.000	0.194	77.162	3.00	21.21	56 Cu, 35 Ag, 9 Mn	9.25*
1946-	5.000	0.194	77.162	3.00	21.21	75 Cu, 25 Ni	8.92
TRIME (Silver)							
1851-1853	0.802	0.032	12.375	0.50	14.00*	750 Ag, 250 Cu	10.11
1854-1873	0.746	0.032	11.520	0.50	14.00*	900 Ag, 100 Cu	10.34
HALF DIME							
1794-1795	1.348		20.800		16.50*	900 Ag, 100 Cu	10.34
1795-1805	1.348		20.800		16.50*	892.427 Ag, 107.572 Cu	10.32
1829-1837	1.348		20.800		15.50*	892.427 Ag, 107.572 Cu	10.32
1837-1853	1.336	0.032	20.625	0.50	15.50*	900 Ag, 100 Cu	10.34
1853-1873	1.244	0.032	19.200	0.50	15.50*	900 Ag, 100 Cu	10.34

COIN / DATES OF ISSUE	GRAMS WGT.	GRAMS TOL.	GRAINS WGT.	GRAINS TOL.	DIA. (mm)	COMPOSITION	SPEC. GRAV.
DIME							
1796-1828	2.696		41.600		18.80*	892.427 Ag, 107.572 Cu	10.32
1828-187	2.696		41.600		17.90*	892.427 Ag, 107.572 Cu	10.32
1837-1853	2.673	0.032	41.250	0.50	17.90*	900 Ag, 100 Cu	10.34
1853-1873	2.488	0.032	38.400	0.50	17.90*	900 Ag, 100 Cu	10.34
1873-1964	2.500	0.097	38.581	1.50	17.91	900 Ag, 100 Cu	10.34
1965-	2.268	0.091△	35.000	1.40△	17.91	75 Cu, 25 Ni on pure Cu	8.92
TWENTY CENTS							
1875-1878	5.000	0.097	77.162	1.50	22.50*	900 Ag, 100 Cu	10.34
QUARTER DOLLAR							
1796-1828	6.739		104.000		27.00*	892.427 Ag, 107.572 Cu	10.32
1831-1837	6.739		104.000		24.26*	892.427 Ag, 107.572 Cu	10.32
1837-1853	6.682	0.065	103.125	1.00	24.26*	900 Ag, 100 Cu	10.34
1853-1873	6.221	0.065	96.000	1.00	24.26*	900 Ag, 100 Cu	10.34
1873-1947	6.250	0.097	96.452	1.50	24.26	900 Ag, 100 Cu	10.34
1947-1964	6.250	0.194	96.452	3.00	24.26	900 Ag, 100 Cu	10.34
1965-	5.670	0.227△	87.500	3.50△	24.26	75 Cu, 25 Ni on pure Cu	8.92
1976	5.750△	0.200△	88.736△	3.09△	24.26	40% silver clad**	9.53
HALF DOLLAR							
1794-1795	13.478		208.000		32.50*	900 Ag, 100 Cu	10.34
1796-1836	13.478		208.000		32.50*	892.427 Ag, 107.572 Cu	10.32
1836-1853	13.365	0.097	206.250	1.50	30.61*	900 Ag, 100 Cu	10.34
1853-1873	12.441	0.097	192.000	1.50	30.61*	900 Ag, 100 Cu	10.34
1873-1947	12.500	0.097	192.904	1.50	30.61	900 Ag, 100 Cu	10.34
1947-1964	12.500	0.259	192.904	4.00	30.61	900 Ag, 100 Cu	10.34
1965-1970	11.500	0.400△	177.472	6.17△	30.61	40% silver clad**	9.53
1971-	11.340	0.454△	175.000	7.00△	30.61	75 Cu, 25 Ni on pure Cu	8.92
1976	11.500	0.400△	177.472	6.17△	30.61	40% silver clad**	9.53
DOLLAR							
1794-1795	26.956		416.000		39.50*	900 Ag, 100 Cu	10.34
1796-1803	26.956		416.000		39.50*	892.427 Ag, 107.572 Cu	10.32
1840-1935	26.730	0.097	412.500	1.50	38.10	900 Ag, 100 Cu	10.34
1971-1978	22.680	0.907△	350.000	14.00△	38.10	75 Cu, 25 Ni on pure Cu	8.92
1971-1976	24.592	0.984△	379.512	15.18△	38.10	40% silver clad**	9.53
1979-1981	8.100	0.300△	125.000	5.000△	26.5	75 Cu, 25 Ni on pure Cu	8.92
TRADE DOLLAR							
1873-1883	27.216	0.097	420.000	1.50	38.10	900 Ag, 100 Cu	10.34
GOLD DOLLAR							
1849-1854	1.672	0.016	25.800	0.25	13.00*	900 Au, 100 Cu & Ag	17.16
1854-1873	1.672	0.016	25.800	0.25	14.86*	900 Au, 100 Cu & Ag	17.16
1873-1889	1.672	0.016	25.800	0.25	14.86*	900 Au, 100 Cu	17.16
QUARTER EAGLE							
1796-1808	4.374		67.500		20.00*	916.667 Au, 83.333 Cu & Ag	17.45
1821-1827	4.374		67.500		18.50*	916.667 Au, 83.333 Cu & Ag	17.45
1829-1834	4.374		67.500		18.20*	916.667 Au, 83.333 Cu & Ag	17.45
1834-1836	4.180	0.008	64.500	0.13	18.20*	899.225 Au, 100.775 Cu & Ag	17.14
1837-1839	4.180	0.016	64.500	0.25	18.20*	900 Au, 100 Cu & Ag	17.16
1840-1873	4.180	0.016	64.500	0.25	17.78*	900 Au, 100 Cu & Ag	17.16
1873-1929	4.180	0.016	64.500	0.25	17.78*	900 Au, 100 Cu	17.16
THREE DOLLARS							
1854-1873	5.015		77.400		20.63*	900 Au, 100 Cu & Ag	17.16
1873-1889	5.015	0.016	77.400	0.25	20.63*	900 Au, 100 Cu	17.16
FOUR DOLLARS (Pattern issue)							
1879-1880	7.000*		108.026*		21.59*	857 Au, 43 Ag, 100 Cu*	16.67*
HALF EAGLE							
1795-1829	8.748		135.000		25.00*	916.667 Au, 83.333 Cu & Ag	17.45
1829-1834	8.748		135.000		22.50*	916.667 Au, 83.333 Cu & Ag	17.45
1834-1836	8.359	0.017	129.000	0.26	22.50*	899.225 Au, 100.775 Cu & Ag	17.14
1837-1840	8.359	0.016	129.000	0.25	22.50*	900 Au, 100 Cu & Ag	17.16
1840-1849	8.359	0.016	129.000	0.25	21.54*	900 Au, 100 Cu & Ag	17.16
1849-1873	8.359	0.032	129.000	0.50	21.54*	900 Au, 100 Cu & Ag	17.16
1873-1929	8.359	0.016	129.000	0.25	21.54*	900 Au, 100 Cu	17.16
EAGLE							
1795-1804	17.496		270.000		33.00*	916.667 Au, 83.333 Cu & Ag	17.45
1838-1849	16.718	0.016	258.000	0.25	27.00*	900 Au, 100 Cu & Ag	17.16
1849-1873	16.718	0.032	258.000	0.50	27.00*	900 Au, 100 Cu & Ag	17.16
1873-1933	16.718	0.032	258.000	0.50	27.00*	900 Au, 100 Cu	17.16
DOUBLE EAGLE							
1850-1873	33.436	0.032	516.000	0.50	34.29	900 Au, 100 Cu & Ag	17.16
1873-1933	33.436	0.032	516.000	0.50	34.29	900 Au, 100 Cu	17.16

AMERICAN EAGLE BULLION COINS

DENOM.	GRAMS WGT.	OUNCES WGT.	MM DIA.	COMPOSITION	OUNCE ALLOY WGTS.
$1	31.103	1.000	40.1	.999 Ag	
$5	3.393	0.1091	16.5	916.7 Au, 3.0 Ag, 5.33 Cu	1.000 Au 0.003 Ag 0.006 Cu
$10	8.483	0.2727	22	916.7 Au, 3.0 Ag, 5.33 Cu	0.250 Au 0.008 Ag 0.015 Cu
$25	16.966	0.5455	27	916.7 Au, 3.0 Ag, 5.33 Cu	0.500 Au 0.016 Ag 0.029 Cu
$50	33.931	1.091	32.7	916.7 Au, 3.0 Ag, 5.33 Cu	1.000 Au 0.033 Ag 0.058 Cu

*   — Unofficial data.
** — Consists of layers of 800 Ag, 200 Cu bonded to a core of 215 Ag, 785 Cu.
*** — Cents struck on steel planchets produced in 1942 weigh 41.5 grains, while those struck on planchets produced later in 1943 weigh 42.5 grains.
****— Consists of a planchet composed of 99.2 percent zinc and 0.8 copper, the whole plated with pure copper.
Δ   — Not specified by law, established instead by the Director of the Mint.
Au, Gold; Ag, Silver; Cu, Copper; Mn, Manganese; Ni, Nickel; Sn, Tin; Zn, Zinc.

Proof, Uncirculated production

The following information outlines the differences in production procedures for Proof and Uncirculated coins.

Blanking
Proof: Extra care used in blanking.
Uncirculated: High speed.

Annealing
Proof: Single layer of blanks moved through a special furnace on a slow-moving belt.
Uncirculated: Blanks processed in a high capacity rotary furnace capable of holding 4,000 pounds at a time.

Burnishing blanks
Proof: Burnished to a high luster with shot.
Uncirculated: Self-burnishing only.

Deoxidation treatment, drying
Proof: Use of freon and deoxidation.
Uncirculated: Not treated.

Inspection
Proof: Blanks inspected by hand by pressmen prior to stamping.
Uncirculated: Blanks not inspected by hand.

Coinage dies
Proof: Coinage dies polished to a high luster by hand prior to use and buffed during use to maintain luster.
Uncirculated: Dies not polished.

Press feed
Proof: Press hand-fed one at a time and blanks struck twice or more.
Uncirculated: High speed, automatic presses used; coins struck once.

Retrieval from press
Proof: Coins retrieved individually.
Uncirculated: Coins retrieved in bulk.

Handling of struck coin
Proof: Coins specially handled in small boxes.
Uncirculated: Coins handled in bulk.

Visual inspection
Proof: Visual inspection done individually.
Uncirculated: Visual inspection limited.

Precautions in packaging room
Proof: Special lighting, air conditioning, dust control in room; employees wear white gloves.
Uncirculated: Standard accommodations and atmosphere prevail.

Packaging
Proof: Coins packaged by hand in sonic sealed cases.
Uncirculated: Sealed in automatic heat sealer.

Annual proof coinage since 1817

The following series of charts is meant to show the quantities struck of U.S. Proof coins from 1817 to the present. In years prior to 1860, when Proof mintages were small and were not recorded, an asterisk marks those issues that are known or are thought to exist. In many instances from 1860 to 1922 the figures shown are approximate, the result of incomplete records, restrikes and the melting of unsold Proofs.

From 1817 to 1859, Proof coins were made in small batches whenever a number of orders had accumulated. An appropriate pair of dies, sometimes new but often used, was polished and used to strike the required number of coins. This is why many early Proof issues may show many varieties among only a dozen or so coins known. These Proof dies were usually returned to general use, where they would result in prooflike coins until the polished surfaces wore down. Occasionally the die chosen for use was overdated.

During these early years the most popular Proof coins were the half cent and later the silver dollar. It could be that these two coins represented, respectively, the cheapest and the most impressive (from the aspect of size) Proof coins. It could also be that the regular issues of these two coins were small, and collectors thought the Proofs would be good investments. Collecting complete Proof sets was popular from 1840 to 1848, although this fad was not revived until the late 1850s.

Beginning in 1860 the Mint produced Proof coins in quantity in anticipation of selling them, rather than producing them on demand. As a rule, a small but uniform number of gold Proofs and a much larger but also uniform number of silver Proofs were made. As no records were kept of the number of non-silver minor coin Proofs issued before 1878, they are commonly assumed to be equal to the silver Proofs of the same year.

This assumption may be drastically wrong, as it is apparent from the 1878 figures that the minor coins were much more popular. It has been suggested that these Proof minor coins were frequently given as Christmas presents to children. If so, we can probably assume that many of these were spent as soon as possible.

Exceptions to the uniform number plan are many, and can usually be logically explained. Coinage laws usually took effect during the middle of a year, and the new or discontinued issues would be produced for only a part of that year. Issues which were being phased

out, such as gold dollars in the 1880s, were popular as investments. Others, such as the Trade dollar, continued on in Proof form after regular coinage had been suspended. In 1883 a large number of each of the three varieties of 5-cent pieces was produced, unlike the 1864 cents where the number of Proof coins struck was proportionate to the varieties of regular coins issued.

Regular production of Proofs was suspended after 1915, with the exceptions of cents and 5-cent pieces in 1916 and a few Proofs of the half dollar and dime in 1916 and of the cent, 5-cent piece and quarter dollar in 1917. A few, perhaps as many as 25, Morgan dollars were struck in Brilliant Proof in 1921. Approximately three of each of the 1921 and 1922 Peace dollars were struck in Matte Proof. The Proof 1922 Peace dollars were of the same high relief as the 1921 Peace dollar and of a slightly different design from the 1922 business-strike Peace dollar. Any alleged 1922 Proof must match the design of a 1921 coin exactly.

The production of Proofs was resumed in 1936, with the total mintage of each coin dependent upon orders. It may be a comment upon the relative popularity of the designs that the Washington quarter dollar was the one usually ordered least. World War II brought about a second suspension of Proof coinage, but not before the wartime metal shortages created a new curiosity, the Proof 1942-P Jefferson 5-cent coin with a "P" Mint mark.

In 1950 the production of Proof coins was again resumed, but now the coins were available only in complete sets. From 1950 to mid-1955 the coins were packaged in individual cellophane envelopes, stapled together across the openings. This arrangement was meant to serve as a shipping device only, but many people left the coins in the package where rust from the staple could damage the coins. Beginning in mid-1955 the coins were sealed in a soft plastic "flat-pack," similar to the packaging currently being used for Uncirculated Mint sets. This series of Proofs continued through 1964.

In 1965, during a coin shortage when the Mint did not have the time to produce Proof sets, the Mint instead made available to collectors "Special Mint sets." These consisted of Uncirculated coins, packaged like the Proofs of previous years. In 1966-67 a long, hard plastic holder was used instead. These three Special Mint sets were sold at $4 per set, an increase over the $2.10 price of a 1950-64 Proof set.

In 1968, when the coin shortage was over and Mint marks were returned to coins, it was decided to strike Proof sets at the San Francisco Assay Office, formerly the San Francisco Mint. Various coins had been struck at this facility since 1964, but without Mint marks to prevent hoarding. These five-coin sets were packaged in a larger, hard plastic case and were issued at $5 per set.

When the Philadelphia and Denver Mints began producing copper-nickel clad Eisenhower dollars for circulation in 1971, the San Francisco Assay Office began striking silver-clad dollars for collectors in Proof and Uncirculated conditions. Beginning with 1973 a copper-nickel clad dollar became part of the regular Proof set. In 1979, the Anthony dollar replaced the Eisenhower dollar; it was removed from sets beginning in 1982. Special Prestige Proof sets containing an Olympic silver dollar were sold in 1983 and 1984 at $59 each. A 1986 Prestige Proof set contains the five regular coins, the Ellis Island dollar and Immigrant half dollar.

With the introduction of the Olympic gold eagle, Mint officials eventually decided to strike Proof eagles at each of the four minting facilities: Philadelphia, Denver, San Francisco and the initial Olympic gold plant, West Point.

Another change for Proofs took place in 1985. Since Mint marks were first used in 1838, the marks have been punched into the individual working dies. However, the inadvertent release of a 1983 Proof dime with no "S" Mint mark prompted Mint officials to place the Mint mark on the master die in an attempt to prevent this type of error from occuring again. In 1986, the Mint mark was included on the plasticene model stage for all Proof coins and commemoratives; thus, the Mint mark appears at every stage of the modeling and die-making process.

Miscellaneous notes

Proof $10 eagles dated 1804 are restrikes made in 1834-35, for inclusion in Proof sets meant to be given as diplomatic presents. The 1804 dollar was first struck at this time for this occasion, also in Proof. The 1804 dollar was restruck in Proof in the late 1850s. The Proof dollars of 1801-03 were first struck at this time.

Many different Proof issues before 1880 were restruck in Proof one or more times. In some instances, as with the 1873 $3 gold piece, there are more coins of this date known than were "officially" struck.

	1817	1818	1819	1820	1821	1822	1823	1824	1825	1826
Half Eagles	-0-	-0-	-0-	*	*	-0-	*	*	*3	*
Quarter Eagles	-0-	-0-	-0-	-0-	*	-0-	-0-	*	*	*
Half Dollars	*1	*	*	*	*	*	*	*	*	*
Quarter Dollars	-0-	*	-0-	*	*	*	*2	*	*	-0-
Dimes	-0-	-0-	-0-	*	*	*	*2	*	*	-0-
Cents	*	*	*	*	*	*	*2	-0-	*	*
Half Cents	-0-	-0-	-0-	-0-	-0-	-0-	-0-	-0-	*	*

	1827	1828	1829	1830	1831	1832	1833	1834	1835	1836
Half Eagles	*	*5	*	*	*	*	*	*6	*	*
Quarter Eagles	*	-0-	*	*	*	*	*	*7	*	*
Silver Dollars	-0-	-0-	-0-	-0-	-0-	-0-	-0-	-0-	-0-	*8
Half Dollars	*	a	*	*	*	*	*4	*4	*4	*9
Quarter Dollars	*4	*	-0-	-0-	*	*	*	*	*	*
Dimes	*	*	*	*	*	*	*	*	*	*
Half Dimes	-0-	-0-	*	*	*	*	*	*	*	*
Cents	*	*	*	*	*	*	*	*	*	*
Half Cents	-0-	*	*	-0-	*4	*	*	*	*	*4

	1837	1838	1839	1840	1841	1842	1843	1844	1845	1846
Eagles	-0-	*	*10	*	*	*	*	*	*	*
Half Eagles	*	*	*	*	*	*	*	*	*	*
Quarter Eagles	*	-0-	-0-	*	*12	*	*	*	*	*
Silver Dollars	-0-	*8	*8	*4	*4	*4	*4	*4	*4	*4
Half Dollars	*	*	*11	*	*	*	*	*	*	*
Quarter Dollars	*	*	*	*	*	*	*	*	*	*
Dimes	*	*	*	*	*	*	*	*	*	*
Half Dimes	*	*	*	*	*	*	*	*	*	*
Cents	*	*	*	*	*	*	*	*	*	*
Half Cents	-0-	-0-	-0-	*4	*4	*4	*4	*4	*4	*4

	1847	1848	1849	1850	1851	1852	1853	1854	1855	1856
Double Eagles	-0-	-0-	1[13]	*[14]	-0-	-0-	-0-	-0-	-0-	*
Eagles	*	*	-0-	-0-	-0-	-0-	-0-	-0-	*	*
Half Eagles	*	*	-0-	-0-	-0-	-0-	-0-	-0-	*	*
Three Dollars	-0-	-0-	-0-	-0-	-0-	-0-	-0-	*	*	*
Quarter Eagles	*	*	*	-0-	-0-	-0-	-0-	*	*	*
Gold Dollars	-0-	-0-	*	-0-	-0-	-0-	-0-	*[17]	*	*
Silver Dollars	*[4]	*[4]	*[4]	*[4]	*[4]	*[4]	*[15]	*	*	*
Half Dollars	*	*	*	*	-0-	*	*[16]	*	*	*
Quarter Dollars	*	*	*	*	*	*	*[16]	*	*	*
Dimes	*	*	*	*	*	*	*[16]	*	*	*
Half Dimes	*	*	*	*	*	*	*[16]	*	*	*
Three Cents (S)	-0-	-0-	-0-	-0-	*	*	-0-	*	*	*
Cents	*	*	*	*	-0-	*	-0-	*	*	*[18]
Half Cents	*[4]	*[4]	*[4]	*	*	*[4]	-0-	*	*	*[4]

	1857	1858	1859	1860	1861	1862	1863	1864	1865
Double Eagles	-0-**	59	66	35	30	50			25
Eagles	*	*	*	50	69	35	30	50	25
Half Eagles	*	*	*	62	66	35	30	50	25
Three Dollars	*	*	*	119	113	35	39	50	25
Quarter Eagles	*	*	*	112	90	35	30	50	25
Gold Dollars	*	*	*	154	349	35	50	50	25
Silver Dollars	*	*[20]	*	1,330	1,000	550	460	470	500
Half Dollars	*	*	*	1,000	1,000	550	460	470	500
Quarter Dollars	*	*	*	1,000	1,000	550	460	470	500
Dimes	*	*	*	1,000	1,000	550	460	470	500
Half Dimes	*	*	*	1,000	1,000	550	460	470	500
Three Cent (S)	*	*	*	1,000	1,000	550	460[21]	470	500
Three Cent (N)	-0-	-0-	-0-	-0-	-0-	-0-	-0-	-0-	400
Two Cents	-0-	-0-	-0-	-0-	-0-	-0-	-0-	100[22]	500
Cents	*[19]	*	*	1,000	1,000	550	460	470[23]	500
Half Cents	*[4]	-0-	-0-	-0-	-0-	-0-	-0-	-0-	-0-

	1866	1867	1868	1869	1870	1871	1872	1873	1874
Double Eagles	30	50	25	25	35	30	30	25[25]	20
Eagles	30	50	25	25	35	30	30	25[25]	20
Half Eagles	30	50	25	25	35	30	30	25[25]	20
Three Dollars	30	50	25	25	35	30	30	25[26]	20
Quarter Eagles	30	50	25	25	35	30	30	25[25]	20
Gold Dollars	30	50	25	25	35	30	30	25[25]	20
Trade Dollars	-0-	-0-	-0-	-0-	-0-	-0-	-0-	865[27]	700
Silver Dollars	725	625	600	600	1,000	960	950	600[25]	-0-
Half Dollars	725	625	600	600	1,000	960	950	1,150[28]	700
Quarter Dollars	725	625	600	600	1,000	960	950	1,140[29]	700
Dimes	725	625	600	600	1,000	960	950	1,400[30]	700
Half Dimes	725	625	600	600	1,000	960	950	600[25]	-0-
Five Cents	125	625[24]	600	600	1,000	960	950	1,100[25]	700
Three Cent (S)	725	625	600	600	1,000	960	950	600[25]	-0-
Three Cent (N)	725	625	600	600	1,000	960	950	1,100[25]	700
Two Cents	725	625	600	600	1,000	960	950	1,100[31]	-0-
Cents	725	625	600	600	1,000	960	950	1,100[25]	700

	1875	1876	1877	1878	1879	1880	1881	1882	1883
Double Eagles	20	45	20	20	30	36	61	59	92
Eagles	20	45	20	20	30	36	42	44	49
Half Eagles	20	45	20	20	30	36	42	48	61
Three Dollars	20[4]	45	20	20	30	36	54	76	89
Quarter Eagles	20	45	20	20	30	36	51	67	82
Gold Dollars	20	45	20	20	30	36	87	125	207
Trade Dollars	700	1,150	510	900	1,541	1,987	960	1,097	979
Silver Dollars	-0-	-0-	-0-	1,000[33]	1,100	1,355	975	1,100	1,039
Half Dollars	700	1,150	510	800	1,100	1,355	975	1,100	1,039
Quarter Dollars	700	1,150	510	800	250[34]	1,355	975	1,100	1,039
Twenty Cents	1,200	1,150	510	600	-0-	-0-	-0-	-0-	-0-
Dimes	700	1,150	510	800	1,100	1,355	975	1,100	1,039
Five Cents	700	1,150	510[32]	2,350	3,200	3,955	3,575	3,100	17,421[35]
Three Cent (N)	700	1,150	510[32]	2,350	3,200	3,955	3,575	3,100	6,609
Cents	700	1,150	510[32]	2,350	3,200	3,955	3,575	3,100	6,609

	1884	1885	1886	1887	1888	1889	1890	1891	1892
Double Eagles	71	77	106	121	102	41	55	52	93
Eagles	45	67	60	80	72	45	63	48	72
Half Eagles	48	66	72	87	94	45	88	53	92
Three Dollars	106	110	142	160	291	129	-0-	-0-	-0-
Quarter Eagles	73	87	88	122	92	48	93	80	105
Gold Dollars	1,006	1,105	1,016	1,043	1,079	1,779	-0-	-0-	-0-
Trade Dollars	(10)[36]	(5)[36]	-0-	-0-	-0-	-0-	-0-	-0-	-0-
Silver Dollars	875	930	886	710	832	811	590	650	1,245
Half Dollars	875	930	886	710	832	711	590	600	1,245
Quarter Dollars	875	930	886	710	832	711	590	600	1,245
Dimes	875	930	886	710	832	711	590	600	1,245
Five Cents	3,942	3,790	4,290	2,960	4,582	3,336	2,740	2,350	2,745
Three Cent (N)	3,942	3,790	4,290	2,960[37]	4,582	3,336	-0-	-0-	-0-
Cents	3,942	3,790	4,290	2,960	4,582	3,336	2,740	2,350	2,745

	1893	1894	1895	1896	1897	1898	1899	1900	1901
Double Eagles	59	50	51	128	86	75	84	124	96
Eagles	55	43	56	78	69	67	86	120	85
Half Eagles	77	75	81	103	83	75	99	230	140
Quarter Eagles	106	122	119	132	136	165	150	205	223
Silver Dollars	792	972	880	762	731	735	846	912	813
Half Dollars	792	972	880	762	731	735	846	912	813
Quarter Dollars	792	972	880	762	731	735	846	912	813
Dimes	792	972	880	762	731	735	846	912	813
Five Cents	2,195	2,632	2,062	1,862	1,938	1,795	2,031	2,262	1,985
Cents	2,195	2,632	2,062	1,862	1,938	1,795	2,031	2,262	1,985

	1902	1903	1904	1905	1906	1907	1908	1909	1910
Double Eagles	114	158	98	90	94	78[38]	101[40]	67	167
Eagles	113	96	108	86	77	74[39]	116[40]	74	204
Half Eagles	162	154	136	108	85	92	167[41]	78	250
Quarter Eagles	193	197	170	144	160	154	236	139	682
Silver Dollars	777	755	650	-0-	-0-	-0-	-0-	-0-	-0-
Half Dollars	777	755	670	727	675	575	545	650	551
Quarter Dollars	777	755	670	727	675	575	545	650	551
Dimes	777	755	670	727	675	575	545	650	551
Five Cents	2,018	1,790	1,817	2,152	1,725	1,475	1,620	4,763	2,405
Cents	2,018	1,790	1,817	2,152	1,725	1,475	1,620	4,793[42]	2,405

	1911	1912	1913	1914	1915	1916	1917	1921	1922
Double Eagles	100	74	58	70	50	-0-	-0-	-0-	-0-
Eagles	95	83	71	50	75	-0-	-0-	-0-	-0-
Half Eagles	139	144	99	125	75	-0-	-0-	-0-	-0-
Quarter Eagles	191	197	165	117	100	-0-	-0-	-0-	-0-
Silver Dollars	-0-	-0-	-0-	-0-	-0-	-0-	-0-	*	*
Half Dollars	543	700	627	380	450	*	-0-	-0-	-0-
Quarter Dollars	543	700	613	380	450	-0-	*	-0-	-0-
Dimes	543	700	622	425	450	*	-0-	-0-	-0-
Five Cents	1,733	2,145	3,034[43]	1,275	1,050	600	*	-0-	-0-
Cents	1,733	2,145	2,848	1,365	1,150	1,050	*	-0-	-0-

	1936	1937	1938	1939	1940	1941	1942
Half Dollars	3,901	5,728	8,152	8,808	11,279	15,412	21,120
Quarter Dollars	3,837	5,542	8,045	8,795	11,246	15,287	21,123
Dimes	4,130	5,756	8,728	9,321	11,827	16,557	22,329
Five Cents	4,420	5,769	19,365	12,535	14,158	18,720	57,200[44]
Cents	5,569	9,320	14,734	13,520	15,872	21,100	32,600

Sold in complete sets only, 1950-1986

Year Minted	Sets Sold	Selling Price	Face Value	Year Minted	Sets Sold	Selling Price	Face Value
1950	51,386	2.10	.91	1954	233,350	2.10	.91
1951	57,500	2.10	.91	1955	378,200	2.10	.91
1952	81,980	2.10	.91	1956	669,384	2.10	.91
1953	128,800	2.10	.91	1957	1,247,952	2.10	.91

Year Minted	Sets Sold	Selling Price	Face Value
1958	875,652	2.10	.91
1959	1,149,291	2.10	.91
1960	1,691,602	2.10	.91[45]
1961	3,028,244	2.10	.91
1962	3,218,019	2.10	.91
1963	3,075,645	2.10	.91
1964	3,950,762	2.10	.91

Production Suspended during 1965, 1966, 1967

Year Minted	Sets Sold	Selling Price	Face Value
1968	3,041,506	5.00	.91[46]
1969	2,934,631	5.00	.91
1970	2,632,810	5.00	.91[47]
1971	3,220,733	5.00	.91[48]
1972	3,260,996	5.00	.91
1973	2,760,339	7.00	1.91
1974	2,612,568	7.00	1.91
1975	2,845,450	7.00	1.91[49]
1976	4,123,056	7.00	1.91[49]
1977	3,236,798	9.00	1.91
1978	3,120,285	9.00	1.91
1979	3,677,175	9.00	1.91[51]
1980	3,554,806	10.00	1.91
1981	4,063,083	11.00	1.91

Year Minted	Sets Sold	Selling Price	Face Value
1982	3,857,479	11.00	.91[52]
1983	3,138,765	11.00	.91[53]
1984	2,746,321	11.00	.91
1985	3,362,662	11.00	.91
1986*	2,288,632	11.00	.91

* Sales through Feb. 25, 1987; still offered at press time.

Special Mint Sets

1965	2,360,000
1966	2,261,583[50]
1967	1,863,344

40% Silver Clad Dollars
Struck in San Francisco

	Uncirculated	Proof
1971	6,868,530	4,265,234
1972	2,193,056	1,811,631
1973	1,883,140	1,013,646
1974	1,900,156	1,306,579

Notes

1. 1817 50¢: Only one Proof known, with overdate 1817/3.
2. 1823 1¢, 10¢, 25¢: Exists with overdate, 1823/2.
3. 1825 $5: Struck from the regular overdated dies. 1825/4, (one known) and 1825/1, (two known).
4. (Various dates): Known to have been restruck at least once.
5. 1828 $5: Includes at least one overdate, 1828/7.
6. 1834 $5: Includes both old and new types (with and without motto).
7. 1834 $2.50: Includes both old and new types (see above).
8. 1836, 38, 39 $1S: All are Gobrecht dollars which were struck in Proof in several different varieties, many of which were restruck in later years. A good many of the originals were placed in circulation.
9. 1836 50¢: Includes both lettered edge coins and reeded edge patterns.
10. 1839 $10: Proofs are of the type of 1838, with large letters and different hair style.
11. 1839 50¢: Includes all three varieties, Capped Bust and Seated Liberty with or without drapery.
12. 1841 $2.50: Nine known, several of them circulated or otherwise impaired.
13. 1849 $20: The one known trial strike still surviving is a Proof.
14. 1850 $20: One Proof was once owned by the engraver, Longacre, but it cannot presently be found.
15. 1853 $1S: All Proofs are restrikes, made 1864-5.
16. 1853 50¢; 25¢; 10¢; 5¢S: All Proofs are of the new weight, with arrows (and rays on the 25¢ and 50¢).
17. 1854 $1G: Includes both Coronet and Indian Head.
18. 1856 1¢: Includes several large cents and many hundreds of Flying Eagle cents. The F.E. type was restruck in later years.
19. 1857 1¢: Includes both types.
20. 1858 $1S: Estimated that 80 pieces were struck, some of them possibly at a later date.
21. 1863 3¢S: Proofs struck from an overdated die, 1863/2, were struck in 1864.
22. 1864 2¢: Includes Small and Large Motto varieties. The Small Motto in Proof is rare.
23. 1864 1¢: Breakdown by varieties; thought to be about 300 to 350 copper-nickel and about 100 to 150 bronze coins without the designer's initial L. Bronze coins with the L are rare in Proof, possibly 20 or less struck.
24. 1867 5¢N: Approximately 25 Proofs struck with rays on reverse, (type of 1866), and 600 without rays, (type of 1868-83).
25. (Most 1873 Proofs): All Proofs are of the relatively Closed 3 variety.
26. 1873 $3: All original Proofs are of the more Open 3 variety. There were two restrikings with the Closed 3 and one with the Open 3.
27. 1873 $1T: All Proofs are of the Open 3 variety.
28. 1873 50¢: No Arrows, Closed 3: 600. With Arrows, Open 3: 550.
29. 1873 25¢: No Arrows, Closed 3: 600. With Arrows, Open 3: 540.
30. 1873 10¢: No Arrows, Closed 3: 600. With Arrows, Open 3: 800.
31. 1873 2¢: All originals have the Closed 3. It is estimated that 500 restrikes were made, all of them with an Open 3.
32. 1877 Minor coinages: Estimates for this year vary considerably, usually upwards. For lack of any records, the number shown is that of the silver Proofs of this year, conforming with the method used in the preceding years. These figures may be considerably low (see foreword).

33. 1878 $1S: Includes 700 of the 8 Tail Feathers variety and 300 of the 7 Tail Feathers, flat eagle breast variety. Beware of any early strike, prooflike surface Morgan dollar being sold as a Proof.
34. 1879 25¢: This figure is official, but may be wrong. The true number might be near or equal to 1,100.
35. 1883 5¢N: It has been estimated that 5,419 Shield type; 5,219 Liberty Head type without CENTS; and 6,783 Liberty Head type with CENTS were struck. Other estimates exist.
36. 1884-85 $1T: Struck in Proof in the Mint for private distribution by person or persons unknown. Not listed in the Mint Report.
37. 1887 3¢N: Many struck from an overdated die, 1887/6.
38. 1907 $20: Figure shown is for Coronet coins. An unknown number of Saint-Gaudens type coins of pattern or near-pattern status were also struck in Proof.
39 1907 $10: Figure shown is for Coronet coins. An unknown number of Indian Head patterns were also struck in Proof.
40. 1908 $20 and $10: All Proofs have the motto IN GOD WE TRUST on the reverse.
41. 1908 $5: All are Indian Head type.
42. 1909 1¢: Includes 2,175 Indian Head type; 420 Lincoln Head type with VDB; and 2,198 Lincoln Head without VDB on reverse.
43. 1913 5¢N: Does not include the five privately struck 1913 Liberty Head 5-cent coins. The Indian Head Proofs are thought to break down into 1,520 Bison on Mound and 1,514 Bison on Plain.
44. 1942 5¢N: Includes 29,600 pre-war alloy (no Mint mark), and 27,600 war-time alloy (with P Mint mark).
45. 1960 1¢: Includes Large and Small Date varieties. As in the regular issues, the Small Date is the scarcer.
46. 1968 10¢: Some Proof sets contain dimes which were struck from a Proof die without a Mint mark. This was an engraver's oversight and is not a filled die. It has been unofficially estimated that only 20 specimens from this die are known. Beware of sets opened and reclosed with "processed" P-Mint coins inserted. Check the edge of the case for signs of tampering.
47. 1970 10¢: Same engraver's oversight as above. Official estimate is that 2,200 sets were released with this error.
48. 1971 5¢N: Same type of error as above. Official estimate of 1,655 sets released.
49. Including Bicentennial quarters, halves and dollars.
50. 1966 5-cent piece: Two Proof Jefferson 5-cent pieces were struck to mark the addition of designer Felix Schlag's initials, F.S., to the obverse design. One coin was presented to Schlag; the other was retained by the Mint.
51. 1979 Proof set: The Anthony dollar replaced the Eisenhower dollar. During latter 1979, a new, clearer Mint mark punch was used on the dies. Sets with all six coins bearing the new Mint mark command a premium.
52. 1982 Proof set: A new Mint mark punch with serifs was introduced.
53. 1983 10-cent piece: Some 1983 sets were issued with dimes missing the S Mint mark, similar to errors in 1968, 1970, 1971 and 1975.

Branch Mint Proofs

Until 1968, branch Mint Proofs were rare. From 1968 to 1983, all Proofs were struck in San Francisco. Since 1984, Proofs have been produced in Philadelphia, Denver, San Francisco and West Point for commemorative and bullion coin programs.

1838-O half dollar: It is thought that 20 specimens were struck as souvenirs in honor of the opening of the New Orleans Mint. No regular issue coins of this date and Mint were struck, and it is possible that these were struck in 1839.

1839-O half dollar: Three or four known.

1844-O half eagle: One known, reason for issue unknown.

1844-O eagle: Same comments as for half eagle.

1852-O eagle: Three pieces known, reason for issue unknown.

1853-O eagle: Mintage unknown, reason for issue unknown.

1854-S double eagle: One known, in the Smithsonian Institution. Struck in honor of the opening of the San Francisco Mint.

1855-S quarter dollar: One known, presumably struck to celebrate the beginning of silver coinage at the San Francisco Mint.

1855-S half dollar: Three known, same occasion as for the quarter dollar.

1856-O half dime: One known, reason for issue unknown.

1860-O half dime: Three known, reason for issue unknown.

1861-O half dollar: Three to six known, probably struck under the authority of either the State of Louisiana or the Confederate States of America.

1870-CC silver dollar: Mintage unknown, possibly struck to mark first Carson City dollar coinage.

1875-S 20 cents: Six to seven known, probably struck to celebrate the first (or last) year of this denomination at this Mint.

1879-O silver dollar: Two now known of 12 struck to celebrate the re-opening of the New Orleans Mint.

1882-CC silver dollar: Mintage unknown, reason for issue unknown.

1883-CC silver dollar: Mintage unknown, reason for issue unknown.

1883-O silver dollar: One now known of 12 struck for presentation to various local dignitaries. Occasion uncertain.

1884-CC silver dollar: One reported, reason for issue unknown.

1891-O quarter dollar: Two known, probably struck to celebrate the resumption of fractional silver coinage at this Mint.

1893-CC silver dollar: 12 struck for presentation to Mint officials to mark the closing of the Carson City Mint.

1894-S dime: Twenty-four struck for private distribution by the superintendent of the San Francisco Mint. Ten are currently known, including two circulated pieces.

1895-O half dollar: Issued to mark reopening of New Orleans Mint.

1899-S half eagle: One or two known, reason for issue unknown.

1906-D dime: Struck in honor of the opening of the Denver Mint.

1906-D eagle: Struck in honor of the opening of the Denver Mint.

1906-D double eagle: Two now known of 12 struck in honor of the opening of the Denver Mint.

1907-D double eagle: One known, possibly struck as a specimen of the last year of this design.

Regular issue U.S. coins, 1793-1987

Foreword

The following mintage figures are a listing of the number of non-Proof coins struck in each year and each Mint, and which theoretically were released into circulation and thereby made available to collectors. In cases where a certain number of coins in a production run were melted at the Mint, the amount is subtracted from the total and/or footnoted.

In many instances the figures given are reconstructions and may be inaccurate. Prior to about 1950 the generally accepted source of mintage figures was the *U.S. Mint Report*. Since the *Mint Report* for many years was simply a bookkeeper's record of how many coins were issued in a particular year, the figures given often had no relation to the actual number of coins struck. In the last two decades much investigation has been done into the actual number of coins struck with each date. The following is a compilation from many sources.

Prior to 1860, production of Proof coins was small and no Proof mintage figures were kept. From 1860 on, Proof figures were kept for gold and silver coins only, as minor coins were considered unimportant. Beginning in 1878 records were kept for the minor coins as well.

Sources used in compiling these figures include: *The Annual Report of the Director of the Mint for 1973*; *A Guide Book of United States Coins*, by R.S. Yeoman; *Scott's Comprehensive Catalogue and Encyclopedia of U.S. Coins*, by Don Taxay; and the many works of Walter Breen.

(Note: Mint marks are listed in alphabetical order, not in order of the establishment of the respective Mints. Either system is logical, but the alphabetical is the one now in common use.)

	1793	1794	1795	1796	1797
Eagles	-0-	-0-	5,583	4,146	14,555[4]
Half Eagles	-0-	-0-	8,707	6,196	3,609
Quarter Eagles	-0-	-0-	-0-	1,395	427
Silver Dollars	-0-	1,758	203,033[2]	72,920	7,776
Half Dollars	-0-	23,464	299,680	934	2,984
Quarter Dollars	-0-	-0-	-0-	6,146	-0-
Dimes	-0-	-0-	-0-	22,135	25,261
Half Dimes	-0-	7,756	78,660	10,230	44,527
Cents	110,512[1]	918,521	538,500	473,200[3]	897,510
Half Cents	35,334	81,600	139,690	1,390	127,840

	1798	1799	1800	1801	1802
Eagles	1,742	37,449	5,999	44,344	-0-
Half Eagles	24,867[5]	7,451	37,628	-0-	53,176
Quarter Eagles	1,094	-0-	-0-	-0-	3,035
Silver Dollars	327,536[6]	423,515	220,920	54,454[7]	41,650[7]
Half Dollars	-0-	-0-	-0-	30,289	29,890
Quarter Dollars	-0-	-0-	-0-	-0-	-0-
Dimes	27,550	-0-	21,760	34,640	10,975
Half Dimes	-0-	-0-	24,000	33,910	13,010
Cents	1,841,745	42,540	2,822,175	1,362,837	3,435,100
Half Cents	-0-	-0-	202,908	-0-	20,266

	1803	1804	1805	1806	1807
Eagles	15,017	3,757	-0-	-0-	-0-
Half Eagles	33,506	30,475	33,183	64,093	84,093[1]
Quarter Eagles	-0-	3,327	1,781	1,616	6,812
Silver Dollars	85,634[7]	-0-[8]	-0-[10]	-0-	-0-
Half Dollars	188,234	-0-	211,722	839,576	1,051,576[12]
Quarter Dollars	-0-	6,738	121,394	286,424	140,343
Dimes	33,040	8,265	120,780	-0-	165,000
Half Dimes	37,850	-0-	15,600	-0-	-0-
Cents	3,131,691	96,500[9]	941,116	348,000	829,221
Half Cents	92,000	1,055,312	814,464	356,000	476,000

	1808	1809	1810	1811	1812
Eagles	-0-	-0-	-0-	-0-	-0-
Half Eagles	55,578	33,875	100,287	99,581	58,087
Quarter Eagles	2,710	-0-	-0-	-0-	-0-
Silver Dollars	-0-	-0-	-0-	-0-	-0-
Half Dollars	1,368,600	1,405,810	1,276,276	1,203,644	1,628,059
Quarter Dollars	-0-	-0-	-0-	-0-	-0-
Dimes	-0-	51,065	-0-	65,180	-0-
Half Dimes	-0-	-0-	-0-	-0-	-0-
Cents	1,007,000	222,867	1,458,500	218,025	1,075,500
Half Cents	400,000	1,154,572	215,000	63,140[9]	-0-

	1813	1814	1815	1816	1817
Eagles	-0-	-0-	-0-	-0-	-0-
Half Eagles	95,428	15,454	635	-0-	-0-
Quarter Eagles	-0-	-0-	-0-	-0-	-0-
Silver Dollars	-0-	-0-	-0-	-0-	-0-
Half Dollars	1,241,903	1,039,075	47,150	-0-	1,215,567
Quarter Dollars	-0-	-0-	89,235	-0-	-0-
Dimes	-0-	421,500	-0-	-0-	-0-
Half Dimes	-0-	-0-	-0-	-0-	-0-
Cents	418,000	357,830	-0-	2,820,982	3,948,400
Half Cents	-0-	-0-	-0-	-0-	-0-

	1818	1819	1820	1821	1822
Eagles	-0-	-0-	-0-	-0-	-0-
Half Eagles	48,588	51,723	263,806	34,641	17,796[13]
Quarter Eagles	-0-	-0-	-0-	6,448	-0-
Silver Dollars	-0-	-0-	-0-	-0-	-0-
Half Dollars	1,960,322	2,208,000	751,122	1,305,797	1,559,573
Quarter Dollars	361,174	144,000	127,444	216,851	64,080
Dime	-0-	-0-	942,587	1,186,512	100,000
Half Dimes	-0-	-0-	-0-	-0-	-0-
Cents	3,167,000	2,671,000	4,407,550	389,000	2,072,339
Half Cents	-0-	-0-	-0-	-0-	-0-

	1823	1824	1825	1826	1827
Eagles	-0-	-0-	-0-	-0-	-0-
Half Eagles	14,485	17,340	29,060	18,069	24,913
Quarter Eagles	-0-	2,600	4,434	760	2,800
Silver Dollars	-0-	-0-	-0-	-0-	-0-
Half Dollars	1,694,200	3,504,954	2,943,166	4,004,180	5,493,400
Quarter Dollars	17,800	24,000	148,000	-0-	-0-[14]
Dimes	440,000	100,000	410,000	-0-	1,215,000
Half Dimes	-0-	-0-	-0-	-0-	-0-
Cents	68,061[9]	1,193,939	1,461,100	1,517,425	2,357,732
Half Cents	-0-	-0-	63,000	234,000	-0-

	1828	1829	1830	1831	1832
Eagles	-0-	-0-	-0-	-0-	-0-
Half Eagles	28,029	57,442	126,351	140,594	157,487
Quarter Eagles	-0-	3,403	4,540	4,520	4,400
Silver Dollars	-0-	-0-	-0-	-0-	-0-
Half Dollars	3,075,200	3,712,156	4,764,800	5,873,660	4,797,000
Quarter Dollars	102,000	-0-	-0-	398,000	320,000
Dimes	125,000	770,000	510,000	771,350	522,500
Half Dimes	-0-	1,230,000	1,240,000	1,242,700	965,000
Cents	2,260,624	1,414,500	1,711,500	3,539,260	2,362,000
Half Cents	606,000	487,000	-0-	2,200[15]	154,000[16]

		1833	1834	1835	1836	1837
Eagles		-0-	-0-	-0-	-0-	-0-
Half Eagles		193,630	707,601[17]	371,534	553,147	207,121
Quarter Eagles		4,160	117,370[18]	131,402	547,986	45,080
Silver Dollars		-0-	-0-	-0-	-0-[19]	-0-
Half Dollars		5,206,000	6,412,004	5,352,006	6,546,200[20]	3,629,820
Quarter Dollars		156,000	286,000	1,952,000	472,000	252,400
Dimes		485,000	635,000	1,410,000	1,190,000	1,042,000[22]
Half Dimes		1,370,000	1,480,000	2,760,000	1,900,000	2,276,000[23]
Cents		2,739,000	1,855,100	3,878,400	2,111,000	5,558,300
Half Cents		120,000[16]	141,000[16]	398,000[16]	-0-[21]	-0-

		1838	1839	1840	1841	1842
Eagles	(P)	7,200	38,248[27]	47,338	63,131	81,507
	O	-0-	-0-	-0-	2,500	27,400
Half Eagles	(P)	286,588	118,143	137,382	15,833	27,578
	C	19,145	17,235	19,028	21,511	27,480
	D	20,583	18,939	22,896	30,495	59,608
	O	-0-	-0-	38,700	50	16,400
Quarter Eagles	(P)	47,030	27,021	18,859	-0-[31]	2,823
	C	7,908	18,173	12,838	10,297	6,737
	D	-0-	13,674	3,532	4,164	4,643
	O	-0-	17,781	33,580	-0-	19,800
Silver Dollars	(P)	-0-[19]	-0-[19]	61,005[29]	173,000[29]	184,618[29]
Half Dollars	(P)	3,546,000	3,334,560[28]	1,435,008	310,000	2,012,764
	O	-0-[24]	162,976	855,100	401,000	957,000
Quarter Dollars	(P)	832,000[25]	491,146	188,127	120,000	88,000
	O	-0-	-0-	-0-	452,000	769,000
Dimes	(P)	1,992,500	1,053,115	1,358,580	1,622,500	1,887,500
	O	406,034[26]	1,323,000	1,175,000	2,007,500	2,020,000
Half Dimes	(P)	2,255,000	1,069,150	1,344,085	1,150,000	815,000
	O	115,000[26]	981,550	935,000	815,000	350,000
Cents	(P)	6,370,200	3,128,661	2,462,700	1,597,367	2,383,390
Half Cents	(P)	-0-	-0-	-0-[30]	-0-[30]	-0-[30]

		1843	1844	1845	1846	1847
Eagles	(P)	75,462	6,361	26,153	20,095	762,258
	O	175,162	118,700	47,500	81,780	571,500
Half Eagles	(P)	611,205	340,330	417,099	395,942	915,981
	C	44,353	23,631	-0-	12,995	84,151
	D	98,452	88,982	90,629	80,294	64,405
	O	101,075	364,600	41,000	58,000	12,000
Quarter Eagles	(P)	100,546	6,784	91,051	21,598	29,814
	C	26,096	11,622	-0-	4,808	23,226
	D	36,209	17,332	19,460	19,303	15,784
	O	368,002	-0-	4,000	62,000	124,000
Silver Dollars	(P)	165,100[29]	20,000[29]	24,500[29]	110,600[29]	140,750[29]
	O	-0-	-0-	-0-	59,000	-0-
Half Dollars	(P)	3,844,000	1,766,000	589,000	2,210,000	1,156,000
	O	2,268,000	2,005,000	2,094,000	2,304,000	2,584,000
Quarter Dollars	(P)	645,600	421,200	922,000	510,000	734,000
	O	968,000	740,000	-0-	-0-	368,000
Dimes	(P)	1,370,000	72,500	1,755,000	31,300	245,000
	O	50,000	-0-	230,000	-0-	-0-
Half Dimes	(P)	1,165,000	430,000	1,564,000	27,000	1,274,000
	O	-0-	220,000	-0-	-0-	-0-
Cents	(P)	2,425,342	2,398,752	3,894,804	4,120,800	6,183,669
Half Cents	(P)	-0-[30]	-0-[30]	-0-[30]	-0-[30]	-0-[30]

		1848	1849	1850	1851	1852
Double Eagles	(P)	-0-	-0-[33]	1,170,261	2,087,155	2,053,026
	O	-0-	-0-	141,000	315,000	190,000
Eagles	(P)	145,484	653,618	291,451	176,328	263,106
	O	35,850	23,900	57,500	263,000	18,000
Half Eagles	(P)	260,775	133,070	64,491	377,505	573,901
	C	64,472	64,823	63,591	49,176	72,574
	D	47,465	39,036	43,984	62,710	91,584
	O	-0-	-0-	-0-	41,000	-0-

		1848	1849	1850	1851	1852
Quarter Eagles	(P)	8,886[32]	23,294	252,923	1,372,748	1,159,681
	C	16,788	10,220	9,148	14,923	9,772
	D	13,771	10,945	12,148	11,264	4,078
	O	-0-	-0-	84,000	148,000	140,000
Gold Dollars	(P)	-0-	688,567	481,953	3,317,671	2,045,351
	C	-0-	11,634	6,966	41,267	9,434
	D	-0-	21,588	8,382	9,882	6,360
	O	-0-	215,000	14,000	290,000	140,000
Silver Dollars	(P)	15,000[29]	62,600[29]	7,500[29]	1,300[29]	1,100[29]
	O	-0-	-0-	40,000	-0-	-0-
Half Dollars	(P)	580,000	1,252,000	227,000	200,750	77,130
	O	3,180,000	2,310,000	2,456,000	402,000	144,000
Quarter Dollars	(P)	146,000	340,000	190,800	160,000	177,060
	O	-0-	16,000	396,000	88,000	96,000
Dimes	(P)	451,500	839,000	1,931,500	1,026,500	1,535,500
	O	-0-	300,000	510,000	400,000	430,000
Half Dimes	(P)	668,000	1,309,000	955,000	781,000	1,000,500
	O	600,000	140,000	690,000	860,000	260,000
Three Cents (S)	(P)	-0-	-0-	-0-	5,447,400	18,663,500
	O	-0-	-0-	-0-	720,000	-0-
Cents	(P)	6,415,799	4,178,500	4,426,844	9,889,707	5,063,094
Half Cents	(P)	-0-[30]	43,364[15]	39,812	147,672	-0-[30]

		1853[34]	1854	1855	1856	1857
Double Eagles	(P)	1,261,326	757,899	364,666	29,878	439,375
	O	71,000	3,250	8,000	2,250	30,000
	S	-0-	141,468	879,675	1,189,780	970,500
Eagles	(P)	201,253	54,250	121,701	60,490	16,606
	O	51,000	52,500	18,000	14,500	5,500
	S	-0-	123,826	9,000	68,000	26,000
Half Eagles	(P)	305,770	160,675	117,098	197,990	98,188
	C	65,571	39,283	39,788	28,457	31,360
	D	89,678	56,413	22,432	19,786	17,046
	O	-0-	46,000	11,100	10,000	13,000
	S	-0-	268	61,000	105,100	87,000
Three Dollars	(P)	-0-	138,618	50,555	26,010	20,891
	D	-0-	1,120	-0-	-0-	-0-
	O	-0-	24,000	-0-	-0-	-0-
	S	-0-	-0-	6,600	34,500	14,000
Quarter Eagles	(P)	1,404,668	596,258	235,480	384,240	214,130
	C	-0-	7,295	3,677	7,913	-0-
	D	3,178	1,760	1,123	874	2,364
	O	-0-	153,000	-0-	21,100	34,000
	S	-0-	246	-0-	71,120	69,200
Gold Dollars	(P)	4,076,051	1,639,445[39]	758,269	1,762,936[40]	774,789
	C	11,515	-0-	9,803	-0-	13,280
	D	6,583	2,935[39]	1,811	1,460[40]	3,533
	O	290,000	-0-	55,000	-0-	-0-
	S	-0-	14,632[39]	-0-	24,600[40]	10,000
Silver Dollars	(P)	46,110[29]	33,140	26,000	63,500	94,000
	O	-0-	-0-	-0-	-0-	-0-
Half Dollars	(P)	3,532,708[35]	2,982,000	759,500	938,000	1,988,000
	O	1,328,000[35]	5,240,000	3,688,000	2,658,000	818,000
	S	-0-	-0-	129,950	211,000	158,000
Quarter Dollars	(P)	15,254,220[36]	12,380,000	2,857,000	7,264,000	9,644,000
	O	1,332,000[36]	1,484,000	176,000	968,000	1,180,000
	S	-0-	-0-	396,400	286,000	82,000
Dimes	(P)	12,173,010[37]	4,470,000	2,075,000	5,780,000	5,580,000
	O	1,100,000[37]	1,770,000	-0-	1,180,000	1,540,000
	S	-0-	-0-	-0-	70,000	-0-
Half Dimes	(P)	13,345,020[38]	5,740,000	1,750,000	4,880,000	7,280,000
	O	2,360,000[38]	1,560,000	600,000	1,100,000	1,380,000
Three Cents (S)	(P)	11,400,000	671,000	139,000	1,458,000	1,042,000
Cents	(P)	6,641,131	4,236,156	1,574,829	2,690,463[41]	17,783,456[42]
Half Cents	(P)	129,694	55,358	56,500	40,430[15]	35,180[15]

		1858	1859	1860	1861	1862
Double Eagles	(P)	211,714	43,597	577,611	2,976,387[47]	92,098
	O	35,250	9,100	6,600	17,741[48]	-0-
	S	846,710	636,445	544,950	768,000[49]	854,173
Eagles	(P)	2,521	16,093	15,055	113,164	10,960
	O	20,000	2,300	11,100	-0-	-0-
	S	11,800	7,000	5,000	15,500	12,500
Half Eagles	(P)	15,136	16,814	19,763	688,084	4,430
	C	38,856	31,847	14,813	6,879[50]	-0-
	D	15,362	10,366	14,635	1,597	-0-
	O	-0-	-0-	-0-	-0-	-0-
	S	18,600	13,220	21,200	18,000	9,500
Three Dollars	(P)	2,133	15,638	7,036	5,959	5,750
	S	-0-	-0-	4,408[45]	-0-	-0-
Quarter Eagles	(P)	47,377	39,444	22,563	1,272,428	98,508
	C	9,056	-0-	7,469	-0-	-0-
	D	-0-	2,244	-0-	-0-	-0-
	S	-0-	15,200	35,600	24,000	8,000
Gold Dollars	(P)	117,995	168,244	36,514	527,150	1,361,355
	C	-0-	5,235	-0-	-0-	-0-
	D	3,477	4,952	1,566	-0-[51]	-0-
	S	10,000	15,000	13,000	-0-	-0-
Silver Dollars	(P)	-0-[43]	256,500	217,600	77,500	11,540
	O	-0-	360,000	515,000	-0-	-0-
	S	-0-	20,000	-0-	-0-	-0-
Half Dollars	(P)	4,226,000	748,000	302,700	2,887,400	253,000
	O	7,294,000	2,834,000	1,290,000	2,532,633[52]	-0-
	S	476,000	566,000	472,000	939,500	1,352,000
Quarter Dollars	(P)	7,368,000	1,344,000	804,400	4,853,600	932,000
	O	520,000	260,000	388,000	-0-	-0-
	S	121,000	80,000	56,000	96,000	67,000
Dimes	(P)	1,540,000	430,000	606,000[46]	1,883,000	847,000
	O	290,000	480,000	40,000[46]	-0-	-0-
	S	60,000	60,000	140,000[46]	172,500	180,750
Half Dimes	(P)	3,500,000	340,000	798,000[46]	3,360,000	1,492,000
	O	1,660,000	560,000	1,060,000[46]	-0-	-0-
Three Cents (S)	(P)	1,604,000	365,000	286,000	497,000	343,000
Cents	(P)	24,600,000	36,400,000[44]	20,566,000	10,100,000	28,075,000

		1863	1864	1865	1866	1867
Double Eagle	(P)	42,760	204,235	351,175	698,745[59]	251,015
	O	-0-	-0-	-0-	-0-	-0-
	S	966,570	973,660	1,042,500	842,250[60]	920,750
Eagles	(P)	1,218	3,530	3,980	3,750	3,090
	O	-0-	-0-	-0-	-0-	-0-
	S	10,000	2,500	16,700	20,000[61]	9,000
Half Eagles	(P)	2,442	4,220	1,270	6,700	6,870
	O	-0-	-0-	-0-	-0-	-0-
	S	17,000	3,888	27,612	43,920[62]	29,000
Three Dollars	(P)	5,000	2,630	1,140	4,000	2,600
	S	-0-	-0-	-0-	-0-	-0-
Quarter Eagles	(P)	-0-[53]	2,824	1,520	3,080	3,200
	S	10,800	-0-	23,376	38,960	28,000
Gold Dollars	(P)	6,200	5,900	3,700	7,100	5,200
	S	-0-	-0-	-0-	-0-	-0-
Silver Dollars	(P)	27,200	30,700	46,500	48,900	47,900
	O	-0-	-0-	-0-	-0-	-0-
	S	-0-	-0-	-0-	-0-	-0-
Half Dollars	(P)	503,200	379,100	511,400	744,900	449,300
	O	-0-	-0-	-0-	-0-	-0-
	S	916,000	658,000	675,000	1,054,000	1,196,000
Quarter Dollars	(P)	191,600	93,600	58,800	16,800	20,000
	O	-0-	-0-	-0-	-0-	-0-
	S	-0-	20,000	41,000	28,000	48,000
Dimes	(P)	14,000	11,000[55]	10,000	8,000	6,000
	O	-0-	-0-	-0-	-0-	-0-
	S	157,500	230,000	175,000	135,000	140,000
Half Dimes	(P)	18,000	48,000[55]	13,000	10,000	8,000
	S	100,000	90,000	120,000	120,000	120,000

		1863	1864	1865	1866	1867
Five Cents	(P)	-0-	-0-	-0-	14,742,500	30,909,500[64]
Three Cents (S)	(P)	21,000[54]	12,000[55]	8,000	22,000	4,000
Three Cents (N)	(P)	-0-	-0-	11,382,000	4,801,000	3,915,000
Two Cents	(P)	-0-	19,847,500[56]	13,640,000	3,177,000	2,938,750
Cents	(P)	49,840,000	52,973,714[57]	35,429,286	9,826,000	9,821,000

		1868	1869	1870	1871	1872
Double Eagles	(P)	98,575	175,130	155,150	80,120	251,850
	CC	-0-	-0-	3,789	17,387	26,900
	O	-0-	-0-	-0-	-0-	-0-
	S	837,500	686,750	982,000	928,000	780,000
Eagles	(P)	10,630	1,830	3,990	1,790	1,620
	CC	-0-	-0-	5,908	8,085	4,600
	O	-0-	-0-	-0-	-0-	-0-
	S	13,500	6,430	8,000	16,500	17,300
Half Eagles	(P)	5,700	1,760	4,000	3,200	1,660
	CC	-0-	-0-	7,675	20,770	16,980
	O	-0-	-0-	-0-	-0-	-0-
	S	52,000	31,000	17,000	25,000	36,400
Three Dollars	(P)	4,850	2,500	3,500	1,300	2,000
	S	-0-	-0-	-0-[65]	-0-	-0-
Quarter Eagles	(P)	3,600	4,320	4,520	5,320	3,000
	S	34,000	29,500	16,000	22,000	18,000
Gold Dollars	(P)	10,500	5,900	6,300	3,900	3,500
	S	-0-	-0-	3,000[66]	-0-	-0-
Silver Dollars	(P)	162,100	423,700	415,000	1,073,800	1,105,500
	CC	-0-	-0-	12,462	1,376	3,150
	O	-0-	-0-	-0-	-0-	-0-
	S	-0-	-0-	-0-[67]	-0-	9,000
Half Dollars	(P)	417,600	795,300	633,900	1,203,600	880,600
	CC	-0-	-0-	54,617	153,950	257,000
	O	-0-	-0-	-0-	-0-	-0-
	S	1,160,000	656,000	1,004,000	2,178,000	580,000
Quarter Dollars	(P)	29,400	16,000	86,400	117,200	182,000
	CC	-0-	-0-	8,340	10,890	22,850
	O	-0-	-0-	-0-	-0-	-0-
	S	96,000	76,000	-0-	30,900	83,000
Dimes	(P)	464,000	256,000	470,500	906,750	2,395,500
	CC	-0-	-0-	-0-	20,100	35,480
	O	-0-	-0-	-0-	-0-	-0-
	S	260,000	450,000	50,000	320,000	190,000
Half Dimes	(P)	88,600	208,000	535,600	1,873,000	2,947,000
	S	280,000	230,000	-0-	161,000	837,000
Five Cents	(P)	28,817,000	16,395,000	4,806,000	561,000	6,036,000
Three Cents (S)	(P)	3,500	4,500	3,000	3,400	1,000
Three Cents (N)	(P)	3,252,000	1,604,000	1,335,000	604,000	862,000
Two Cents	(P)	2,803,750	1,546,500	861,250	721,250	65,000
Cents	(P)	10,266,500	6,420,000	5,275,000	3,929,500	4,042,000

		1873[68]	1874	1875	1876	1877
Double Eagles	(P)	1,709,800	366,780	295,720	583,860	397,650[77]
	CC	22,410	115,000	111,151	138,441	42,565[77]
	O	-0-	-0-	-0-	-0-	-0-
	S	1,040,600	1,214,000	1,230,000	1,597,000	1,735,000[77]
Eagles	(P)	800	53,140	100	687	797
	CC	4,543	16,767	7,715	4,696	3,332
	O	-0-	-0-	-0-	-0-	-0-
	S	12,000	10,000	-0-	5,000	17,000
Half Eagles	(P)	112,480	3,488	200	1,432	1,132
	CC	7,416	21,198	11,828	6,887	8,680
	O	-0-	-0-	-0-	-0-	-0-
	S	31,000	16,000	9,000	4,000	26,700
Three Dollars	(P)	-0-[69]	41,800	-0-[75]	-0-[53]	1,468
Quarter Eagles	(P)	178,000	3,920	400	4,176	1,632
	S	27,000	-0-	11,600	5,000	35,400
Gold Dollars	(P)	125,100	198,800	400	3,200	3,900
Trade Dollars	(P)	396,635	987,100	218,200	455,000	3,039,200
	CC	124,500	1,373,200	1,573,700	509,000	534,000
	S	703,000	2,549,000	4,487,000	5,227,000	9,519,000

		1873[68]	1874	1875	1876	1877
Silver Dollars........	(P)	293,000	-0-	-0-	-0-	-0-
	CC	2,300	-0-	-0-	-0-	-0-
	O	-0-	-0-	-0-	-0-	-0-
	S	700[70]	-0-	-0-	-0-	-0-
Half Dollars.........	(P)	2,616,350[71]	2,359,600	6,026,800	8,418,000	8,304,000
	CC	337,060[71]	59,000	1,008,000	1,956,000	1,420,000
	O	-0-	-0-	-0-	-0-	-0-
	S	233,000[71]	394,000	3,200,000	4,528,000	5,356,000
Quarter Dollars.......	(P)	1,483,160[72]	471,200	4,292,800	17,816,000	10,911,200
	CC	16,462[72]	-0-	140,000	4,944,000	4,192,000
	O	-0-	-0-	-0-	-0-	-0-
	S	156,000[72]	392,000	680,000	8,596,000	8,996,000
Twenty Cents........	(P)	-0-	-0-	38,500	14,750	-0-[53]
	CC	-0-	-0-	133,290	10,000[76]	-0-
	S	-0-	-0-	1,155,000	-0-	-0-
Dimes..............	(P)	3,945,700[73]	2,940,000	10,350,000	11,460,000	7,310,000
	CC	31,191[73]	10,817	4,645,000	8,270,000	7,700,000
	O	-0-	-0-	-0-	-0-	-0-
	S	455,000[73]	240,000	9,070,000	10,420,000	2,340,000
Half Dimes	(P)	712,000	-0-	-0-	-0-	-0-
	S	324,000	-0-	-0-	-0-	-0-
Five Cents	(P)	4,550,000	3,538,000	2,097,000	2,530,000	-0-[53]
Three Cent (S)	(P)	-0-[53]	-0-	-0-	-0-	-0-
Three Cent (N)	(P)	1,173,000	790,000	228,000	162,000	-0-[53]
Two Cent............	(P)	-0-[74]	-0-	-0-	-0-	-0-
Cents...............	(P)	11,676,500	14,187,500	13,528,000	7,944,000	852,000

		1878	1879	1880	1881	1882
Double Eagles	(P)	543,625	207,600	51,420	2,220	590
	CC	13,180	10,708	-0-	-0-	39,140
	O	-0-	2,325	-0-	-0-	-0-
	S	1,739,000	1,223,800	836,000	727,000	1,125,000
Eagles	(P)	73,780	384,740	1,644,840	3,877,220	2,324,440
	CC	3,244	1,762	11,190	24,015	6,764
	O	-0-	1,500	9,200	8,350	10,820
	S	26,100	224,000	506,250	970,000	132,000
Half Eagles..........	(P)	131,720	301,920	3,166,400	5,708,760	2,514,520
	CC	9,054	17,281	51,017	13,886	82,817
	O	-0-	-0-	-0-	-0-	-0-
	S	144,700	426,200	1,348,900	969,000	969,000
Three Dollars........	(P)	82,304	3,000	1,000	500	1,500
Quarter Eagles.......	(P)	286,240	88,960	2,960	640	4,000
	S	178,000	43,500	-0-	-0-	-0-
Gold Dollars	(P)	3,000	3,000	1,600	7,620	5,000
Trade Dollars........	(P)	-0-[78]	-0-[78]	-0-[78]	-0-[78]	-0-[78]
	CC	97,000	-0-	-0-	-0-	-0-
	S	4,162,000	-0-	-0-	-0-	-0-
Silver Dollars........	(P)	10,508,550[79]	14,806,000	12,600,000	9,163,000	11,100,000
	CC	2,212,000	756,000	591,000	296,000	1,133,000
	O	-0-	2,887,000	5,305,000	5,708,000	6,090,000
	S	9,774,000	9,110,000	8,900,000	12,760,000	9,250,000
Half Dollars..........	(P)	1,377,600	4,800	8,400	10,000	4,400
	CC	62,000	-0-	-0-	-0-	-0-
	O	-0-	-0-	-0-	-0-	-0-
	S	12,000	-0-	-0-	-0-	-0-
Quarter Dollars.......	(P)	2,260,000	14,450	13,600	12,000	15,200
	CC	996,000	-0-	-0-	-0-	-0-
	O	-0-	-0-	-0-	-0-	-0-
	S	140,000	-0-	-0-	-0-	-0-
Twenty Cents.........	(P)	-0-[53]	-0-	-0-	-0-	-0-
Dimes..............	(P)	1,678,000	14,000	36,000	24,000	3,910,000
	CC	200,000	-0-	-0-	-0-	-0-
	O	-0-	-0-	-0-	-0-	-0-
	S	-0-	-0-	-0-	-0-	-0-
Five Cents	(P)	-0-[53]	25,900	16,000	68,800	11,473,500
Three Cents (N).......	(P)	-0-[53]	38,000	21,000	1,077,000	22,200
Cents...............	(P)	5,797,500	16,228,000	38,961,000	39,208,000	38,578,000

		1883	1884	1885	1886	1887
Double Eagles	(P)	-0-[53]	-0-[53]	751	1,000	-0-[53]
	CC	59,962	81,139	9,450	-0-	-0-
	S	1,189,000	916,000	683,500	-0-	283,000
Eagles	(P)	208,700	76,890	253,462	236,100	53,600
	CC	12,000	9,925	-0-	-0-	-0-
	O	800	-0-	-0-	-0-	-0-
	S	38,000	124,250	228,000	826,000	817,000
Half Eagles	(P)	233,400	191,030	601,440	388,360	-0-[53]
	CC	12,958	16,402	-0-	-0-	-0-
	O	-0-	-0-	-0-	-0-	-0-
	S	83,200	177,000	1,211,500	3,268,000	1,912,000
Three Dollars	(P)	900	1,000	800	1,000	6,000
Quarter Eagles	(P)	1,920	1,950	800	4,000	6,160
Gold Dollars	(P)	10,800	5,230	11,156	5,000	7,500
Trade Dollars	(P)	-0-[78]	-0-[78]	-0-[78]	-0-	-0-
Silver Dollars	(P)	12,290,000	14,070,000	17,786,837	19,963,000	20,290,000
	CC	1,204,000	1,136,000	228,000	-0-	-0-
	O	8,725,000	9,730,000	9,185,000	10,710,000	11,550,000
	S	6,250,000	3,200,000	1,497,000	750,000	1,771,000
Half Dollars	(P)	8,000	4,400	5,200	5,000	5,000
	O	-0-	-0-	-0-	-0-	-0-
	S	-0-	-0-	-0-	-0-	-0-
Quarter Dollars	(P)	14,400	8,000	13,600	5,000	10,000
	O	-0-	-0-	-0-	-0-	-0-
	S	-0-	-0-	-0-	-0-	-0-
Dimes	(P)	7,674,673	3,365,505	2,532,497	6,376,684	11,283,229
	O	-0-	-0-	-0-	-0-	-0-
	S	-0-	564,969	43,690	206,524	4,454,450
Five Cents	(P)	22,952,000[80]	11,270,000	1,472,700	3,326,000	15,260,692
Three Cent (N)	(P)	4,000	1,700	1,000	-0-[53]	5,001
Cents	(P)	45,591,500	23,257,800	11,761,594	17,650,000	45,223,523

		1888	1889	1890	1891	1892
Double Eagles	(P)	226,164	44,070	75,940	1,390	4,430
	CC	-0-	30,945	91,209	5,000	27,265
	S	859,600	774,700	802,750	1,288,125	930,150
Eagles	(P)	132,924	4,440	57,980	91,820	797,480
	CC	-0-	-0-	17,500	103,732	40,000
	O	21,335	-0-	-0-	-0-	28,688
	S	648,700	425,400	-0-	-0-	115,500
Half Eagles	(P)	18,202	7,520	4,240	61,360	753,480
	CC	-0-	-0-	53,800	208,000	82,968
	O	-0-	-0-	-0-	-0-	10,000
	S	293,900	-0-	-0-	-0-	298,400
Three Dollars	(P)	5,000	2,300	-0-	-0-	-0-
Quarter Eagles	(P)	16,006	17,600	8,720	10,960	2,440
Gold Dollars	(P)	16,501	28,950	-0-	-0-	-0-
Silver Dollars	(P)	19,183,000	21,726,000	16,802,000	8,693,556	1,036,000
	CC	-0-	350,000	2,309,041	1,618,000	1,352,000
	O	12,150,000	11,875,000	10,701,000	7,954,529	2,744,000
	S	657,000	700,000	8,230,373	5,296,000	1,200,000
Half Dollars	(P)	12,001	12,000	12,000	200,000	934,245
	O	-0-	-0-	-0-	-0-	390,000
	S	-0-	-0-	-0-	-0-	1,029,028
Quarter Dollars	(P)	10,001	12,000	80,000	3,920,000	8,236,000
	O	-0-	-0-	-0-	68,000	2,640,000
	S	1,216,000	-0-	-0-	2,216,000	964,079
Dimes	(P)	5,495,655	7,380,000	9,910,951	15,310,000	12,120,000
	O	-0-	-0-	-0-	4,540,000	3,841,700
	S	1,720,000	972,678	1,423,076	3,196,116	990,710
Five Cents	(P)	10,715,901	15,878,025	16,256,532	16,832,000	11,696,897
Three Cent (N)	(P)	36,501	18,125	-0-	-0-	-0-
Cents	(P)	37,489,832	48,866,025	57,180,114	47,070,000	37,647,087

		1893	1894	1895	1896	1897
Double Eagles	(P)	344,280	1,368,940	1,114,605	792,535	1,383,175
	CC	18,402	-0-	-0-	-0-	-0-
	S	996,175	1,048,550	1,143,500	1,403,925	1,470,250
Eagles	(P)	1,840,840	2,470,735	567,770	76,270	1,000,090
	CC	14,000	-0-	-0-	-0-	-0-
	O	17,000	107,500	98,000	-0-	42,500
	S	141,350	25,000	49,000	123,750	234,750
Half Eagles	(P)	1,528,120	957,880	1,345,855	58,960	867,800
	CC	60,000	-0-	-0-	-0-	-0-
	O	110,000	16,600	-0-	-0-	-0-
	S	224,000	55,900	112,000	155,400	354,000
Quarter Eagles	(P)	30,000	4,000	6,000	19,070	29,768
Silver Dollars	(P)	378,000	110,000	12,000[82]	9,976,000	2,822,000
	CC	677,000	-0-	-0-	-0-	-0-
	O	300,000	1,723,000	450,000	4,900,000	4,004,000
	S	100,000	1,260,000	400,000	5,000,000	5,825,000
Half Dollars	(P)	1,826,000	1,148,000	1,834,338	950,000	2,480,000
	O	1,389,000	2,138,000	1,766,000	924,000	632,000
	S	740,000	4,048,690	1,108,086	1,140,948	933,900
Quarter Dollars	(P)	5,444,023	3,432,000	4,440,000	3,874,000	8,140,000
	O	3,396,000	2,852,000	2,816,000	1,484,000	1,414,800
	S	1,454,535	2,648,821	1,764,611	188,039	542,229
Dimes	(P)	3,340,000	1,330,000	690,000	2,000,000	10,868,533
	O	1,760,000	720,000	440,000	610,000	666,000
	S	2,491,401	-0-[81]	1,120,000	575,056	1,342,844
Five Cents	(P)	13,368,000	5,410,500	9,977,822	8,841,058	20,426,797
Cents	(P)	46,640,000	16,749,500	38,341,574	39,055,431	50,464,392

		1898	1899	1900	1901	1902
Double Eagles	(P)	170,395	1,669,300	1,874,460	111,430	31,140
	S	2,575,175	2,010,300	2,459,500	1,596,000	1,753,625
Eagles	(P)	812,130	1,262,219	293,840	1,718,740	82,400
	O	-0-	37,047	-0-	72,041	-0-
	S	473,600	841,000	81,000	2,812,750	469,500
Half Eagles	(P)	633,420	1,710,630	1,405,500	615,900	172,400
	O	-0-	-0-	-0-	-0-	-0-
	S	1,397,400	1,545,000	329,000	3,648,000	939,000
Quarter Eagles	(P)	24,000	27,200	67,000	91,100	133,540
Silver Dollars	(P)	5,884,000	330,000	8,830,000	6,962,000	7,994,000
	O	4,440,000	12,290,000	12,590,000	13,320,000	8,636,000
	S	4,102,000	2,562,000	3,540,000	2,284,000	1,530,000
Half Dollars	(P)	2,956,000	5,538,000	4,762,000	4,268,000	4,922,000
	O	874,000	1,724,000	2,744,000	1,124,000	2,526,000
	S	2,358,550	1,686,411	2,560,322	847,044	1,460,670
Quarter Dollars	(P)	11,100,000	12,624,000	10,016,000	8,892,000	12,196,967
	O	1,868,000	2,644,000	3,416,000	1,612,000	4,748,000
	S	1,020,592	708,000	1,858,585	72,664	1,524,612
Dimes	(P)	16,320,000	19,580,000	17,600,000	18,859,665	21,380,000
	O	2,130,000	2,650,000	2,010,000	5,620,000	4,500,000
	S	1,702,507	1,867,493	5,168,270	593,022	2,070,000
Five Cents	(P)	12,539,292	26,027,000	27,253,733	26,478,228	31,478,561
Cents	(P)	49,821,284	53,598,000	66,821,284	79,609,158	87,374,704

		1903	1904	1905	1906	1907
Double Eagles	(P)	287,270	6,256,699	58,919	69,596	1,824,703[84]
	D	-0-	-0-	-0-	620,250	842,250[84]
	S	954,000	5,134,175	1,813,000	2,065,750	2,165,800[84]
Eagles	(P)	125,830	161,930	200,992	165,420	1,443,305[85]
	D	-0-	-0-	-0-	981,000	1,030,000[85]
	O	112,771	108,950	-0-	86,895	-0-
	S	538,000	-0-	369,250	457,000	210,500[85]
Half Eagles	(P)	226,870	392,000	302,200	348,735	626,100
	D	-0-	-0-	-0-	320,000[83]	888,000[83]
	O	-0-	-0-	-0-	-0-	-0-
	S	1,855,000	97,000	880,700	598,000	-0-
Quarter Eagles	(P)	201,060	160,790	217,800	176,330	336,294
Silver Dollars	(P)	4,652,000	2,788,000	-0-	-0-	-0-
	O	4,450,000	3,720,000	-0-	-0-	-0-
	S	1,241,000	2,304,000	-0-	-0-	-0-

		1903	1904	1905	1906	1907
Half Dollars	(P)	2,278,000	2,992,000	662,000	2,638,000	2,598,000
	D	-0-	-0-	-0-	4,028,000	3,856,000
	O	2,100,000	1,117,600	505,000	2,446,000	3,946,600
	S	1,920,772	553,038	2,494,000	1,740,154	1,250,000
Quarter Dollars	(P)	9,669,309	9,588,143	4,967,523	3,655,760	7,192,000
	D	-0-	-0-	-0-	3,280,000	2,484,000
	O	3,500,000	2,456,000	1,230,000	2,056,000	4,560,000
	S	1,036,000	-0-	1,884,000	-0-	1,360,000
Dimes	(P)	19,500,000	14,600,357	14,551,623	19,957,731	22,220,000
	D	-0-	-0-	-0-	4,060,000	4,080,000
	O	8,180,000	-0-	3,400,000	2,610,000	5,058,000
	S	613,300	800,000	6,855,199	3,136,640	3,178,470
Five Cents	(P)	28,004,935	21,401,350	29,825,125	38,612,000	39,213,325
Cents	(P)	85,092,703	61,326,198	80,717,011	96,020,530	108,137,143

		1908	1909	1910	1911	1912
Double Eagles	(P)	4,427,809[86]	161,215	482,000	197,250	149,750
	D	1,013,250[86]	52,500	429,000	846,500	-0-
	S	22,000[86]	2,774,925	2,128,250	775,750	-0-
Eagles	(P)	374,870[87]	184,789	318,500	505,500	405,000
	D	1,046,500[87]	121,540	2,356,640	30,100	-0-
	S	59,850[87]	292,350	811,000	51,000	300,000
Half Eagles	(P)	999,719[88]	627,060	604,000	915,000	790,000
	D	148,000[88]	3,423,560	193,600	72,500	-0-
	O	-0-	34,200	-0-	-0-	-0-
	S	82,000[88]	297,200	770,200	1,416,000	392,000
Quarter Eagles	(P)	564,821	441,760	492,000	704,000	616,000
	D	-0-	-0-	-0-	55,680	-0-
Silver Dollars	(P)	-0-	-0-	-0-	-0-	-0-
	S	-0-	-0-	-0-	-0-	-0-
Half Dollars	(P)	1,354,000	2,368,000	418,000	1,406,000	1,550,000
	D	3,280,000	-0-	-0-	695,080	2,300,800
	O	5,360,000	925,400	-0-	-0-	-0-
	S	1,644,828	1,764,000	1,948,000	1,272,000	1,370,000
Quarter Dollars	(P)	4,232,000	9,268,000	2,244,000	3,720,000	4,400,000
	D	5,788,000	5,114,000	1,500,000	933,600	-0-
	O	6,244,000	712,000	-0-	-0-	-0-
	S	784,000	1,348,000	-0-	988,000	708,000
Dimes	(P)	10,600,000	10,240,000	11,520,000	18,870,000	19,350,000
	D	7,490,000	954,000	3,490,000	11,209,000	11,760,000
	O	1,789,000	2,287,000	-0-	-0-	-0-
	S	3,220,000	1,000,000	1,240,000	3,520,000	3,420,000
Five Cents	(P)	22,684,557	11,585,763	30,166,948	39,557,639	26,234,569
	D	-0-	-0-	-0-	-0-	8,474,000
	S	-0-	-0-	-0-	-0-	238,000
Cents	(P)	32,326,367	115,063,470[89]	146,798,813	101,176,054	68,150,915
	D	-0-	-0-	-0-	12,672,000	10,411,000
	S	1,115,000	2,618,000[89]	6,045,000	4,026,000	4,431,000

		1913	1914	1915	1916	1917
Double Eagles	(P)	168,780	95,250	152,000	-0-	-0-
	D	393,500	453,000	-0-	-0-	-0-
	S	34,000	1,498,000	567,500	796,000	-0-
Eagles	(P)	442,000	151,000	351,000	-0-	-0-
	D	-0-	343,500	-0-	-0-	-0-
	S	66,000	208,000	59,000	138,500	-0-
Half Eagles	(P)	916,000	247,000	588,000	-0-	-0-
	D	-0-	247,000	-0-	-0-	-0-
	S	408,000	263,000	164,000	240,000	-0-
Quarter Eagles	(P)	722,000	240,000	606,000	-0-	-0-
	D	-0-	448,000	-0-	-0-	-0-
Silver Dollars	(P)	-0-	-0-	-0-	-0-	-0-
	S	-0-	-0-	-0-	-0-	-0-
Half Dollars	(P)	188,000	124,230	138,000	608,000	12,292,000
	D	534,000	-0-	1,170,400	1,014,400	2,705,400[94]
	S	604,000	992,000	1,604,000	508,000	6,506,000[94]
Quarter Dollars	(P)	484,000	6,244,230	3,480,000	1,840,000[92]	22,620,000[95]
	D	1,450,800	3,046,000	3,694,000	6,540,800[92]	7,733,600[95]
	S	40,000	264,000	704,000	-0-	7,504,000[95]

		1913	1914	1915	1916	1917
Dimes.............	(P)	19,760,000	17,360,230	5,620,000	40,670,000[93]	55,230,000
	D	-0-	11,908,000	-0-	264,000[93]	9,402,000
	S	510,000	2,100,000	960,000	16,270,000[93]	27,330,000
Five Cents	(P)	60,849,186[90]	20,664,463	20,986,220	63,497,466	51,424,029
	D	9,493,000[91]	3,912,000	7,569,500	13,333,000	9,910,800
	S	3,314,000[91]	3,470,000	1,505,000	11,860,000	4,193,000
Cents..............	(P)	76,529,504	75,237,067	29,090,970	131,832,627	196,429,785
	D	15,804,000	1,193,000	22,050,000	35,956,000	55,120,000
	S	6,101,000	4,137,000	4,833,000	22,510,000	32,620,000

		1918	1919	1920	1921	1922
Double Eagles	(P)	-0-	-0-	228,250	528,500	1,375,500
	D	-0-	-0-	-0-	-0-	-0-
	S	-0-	-0-	558,000	-0-	2,658,000
Eagles	(P)	-0-	-0-	-0-	-0-	-0-
	S	-0-	-0-	126,500	-0-	-0-
Half Eagles..........	(P)	-0-	-0-	-0-	-0-	-0-
Quarter Eagles	(P)	-0-	-0-	-0-	-0-	-0-
	D	-0-	-0-	-0-	-0-	-0-
Silver Dollars........	(P)	-0-	-0-	-0-	45,696,473[96]	51,737,000
	D	-0-	-0-	-0-	20,345,000[96]	15,063,000
	S	-0-	-0-	-0-	21,695,000[96]	17,475,000
Half Dollars..........	(P)	6,734,058	962,000	6,372,000	246,000	-0-
	D	3,853,040	1,165,000	1,551,000	208,000	-0-
	S	10,282,000	1,552,000	4,624,000	548,000	-0-
Quarter Dollars	(P)	14,240,000	11,324,000	27,860,000	1,916,000	-0-
	D	7,380,000	1,944,000	3,586,400	-0-	-0-
	S	11,072,000	1,836,000	6,380,000	-0-	-0-
Dimes..............	(P)	26,680,000	35,740,000	59,030,000	1,230,000	-0-
	D	22,674,800	9,939,000	19,171,000	1,080,000	-0-
	S	19,300,000	8,850,000	13,820,000	-0-	-0-
Five Cents	(P)	32,086,314	60,868,000	63,093,000	10,633,000	-0-
	D	8,362,000	8,006,000	9,418,000	-0-	-0-
	S	4,882,000	7,521,000	9,689,000	1,557,000	-0-
Cents..............	(P)	288,104,634	392,021,000	310,165,000	39,157,000	-0-[97]
	D	47,830,000	57,154,000	49,280,000	-0-	7,160,000
	S	34,680,000	139,760,000	46,220,000	15,274,000	-0-

		1923	1924	1925	1926	1927
Double Eagles	(P)	566,000	4,323,500	2,831,750	816,750	2,946,750
	D	1,702,250	3,049,500	2,938,500	481,000	180,000
	S	-0-	2,927,500	3,776,500	2,041,500	3,107,000
Eagles	(P)	-0-	-0-	-0-	1,014,000	-0-
	S	-0-	-0-	-0-	-0-	-0-
Half Eagles..........	(P)	-0-	-0-	-0-	-0-	-0-
Quarter Eagles	(P)	-0-	-0-	-0-	446,000	388,000
	D	-0-	-0-	578,000	-0-	-0-
Silver Dollars........	(P)	30,800,000	11,811,000	10,198,000	1,939,000	848,000
	D	6,811,000	-0-	-0-	2,348,700	1,268,900
	S	19,020,000	1,728,000	1,610,000	6,980,000	866,000
Half Dollars..........	(P)	-0-	-0-	-0-	-0-	-0-
	D	-0-	-0-	-0-	-0-	-0-
	S	2,178,000	-0-	-0-	-0-	2,392,000
Quarter Dollars	(P)	9,716,000	10,920,000	12,280,000	11,316,000	11,912,000
	D	-0-	3,112,000	-0-	1,716,000	976,400
	S	1,360,000	2,860,000	-0-	2,700,000	396,000
Dimes..............	(P)	50,130,000	24,010,000	25,610,000	32,160,000	28,080,000
	D	-0-[103]	6,810,000	5,117,000	6,828,000	4,812,000
	S	6,440,000	7,120,000	5,850,000	1,520,000	4,770,000
Five Cents	(P)	35,715,000	21,620,000	35,565,100	44,693,000	37,981,000
	D	-0-	5,258,000	4,450,000	5,638,000	5,730,000
	S	6,142,000	1,437,000	6,286,000	970,000	3,430,000
Cents..............	(P)	74,723,000	75,178,000	139,949,000	157,088,000	144,440,000
	D	-0-	2,520,000	22,580,000	28,020,000	27,170,000
	S	8,700,000	11,696,000	26,380,000	4,550,000	14,276,000

		1928	1929	1930	1931	1932
Double Eagles	(P)	8,816,000	1,779,750	-0-	2,938,250	1,101,750
	D	-0-	-0-	-0-	106,500	-0-
	S	-0-	-0-	74,000	-0-	-0-
Eagles	(P)	-0-	-0-	-0-	-0-	4,463,000
	S	-0-	-0-	96,000	-0-	-0-
Half Eagles	(P)	-0-	662,000	-0-	-0-	-0-
Quarter Eagles	(P)	416,000	532,000	-0-	-0-	-0-
Silver Dollars	(P)	360,649	-0-	-0-	-0-	-0-
	D	-0-	-0-	-0-	-0-	-0-
	S	1,632,000	-0-	-0-	-0-	-0-
Half Dollars	(P)	-0-	-0-	-0-	-0-	-0-
	D	-0-	1,001,200	-0-	-0-	-0-
	S	1,940,000	1,902,000	-0-	-0-	-0-
Quarter Dollars	(P)	6,336,000	11,140,000	5,632,000	-0-	5,404,000
	D	1,627,600	1,358,000	-0-	-0-	436,800
	S	2,644,000	1,764,000	1,556,000	-0-	408,000
Dimes	(P)	19,480,000	25,970,000	6,770,000	3,150,000	-0-
	D	4,161,000	5,034,000	-0-[103]	1,260,000	-0-
	S	7,400,000	4,730,000	1,843,000	1,800,000	-0-
Five Cents	(P)	23,411,000	36,446,000	22,849,000	-0-	-0-
	D	6,436,000	8,370,000	-0-	-0-	-0-
	S	6,936,000	7,754,000	5,435,000	1,200,000	-0-
Cents	(P)	134,116,000	185,262,000	157,415,000	19,396,000	9,062,000
	D	31,170,000	41,730,000	40,100,000	4,480,000	10,500,000
	S	17,266,000	50,148,000	24,286,000	866,000	-0-

		1933	1934	1935	1936
Double Eagles	(P)	445,000[98]	-0-	-0-	-0-
Eagles	(P)	312,500[99]	-0-	-0-	-0-
Silver Dollars	(P)	-0-	954,057	1,576,000	-0-
	D	-0-	1,569,500	-0-	-0-
	S	-0-	1,011,000	1,964,000	-0-
Half Dollars	(P)	-0-	6,964,000	9,162,000	12,614,000
	D	-0-	2,361,400	3,003,800	4,252,400
	S	1,786,000	3,652,000	3,854,000	3,884,000
Quarter Dollars	(P)	-0-	31,912,052	32,484,000	41,300,000
	D	-0-	3,527,200	5,780,000	5,374,000
	S	-0-	-0-	5,660,000	3,828,000
Dimes	(P)	-0-	24,080,000	58,830,000	87,500,000
	D	-0-	6,772,000	10,477,000	16,132,000
	S	-0-	-0-	15,840,000	9,210,000
Five Cents	(P)	-0-	20,213,003	58,264,000	118,997,000
	D	-0-	7,480,000	12,092,000	24,814,000
	S	-0-	-0-	10,300,000	14,930,000
Cents	(P)	14,360,000	219,080,000	245,388,000	309,632,000
	D	6,200,000	28,446,000	47,000,000	40,620,000
	S	-0-	-0-	38,702,000	29,130,000

		1937	1938	1939	1940
Half Dollars	(P)	9,522,000	4,110,000	6,812,000	9,156,000
	D	1,676,000	491,600	4,267,800	-0-
	S	2,090,000	-0-	2,552,000	4,550,000
Quarter Dollars	(P)	19,696,000	9,472,000	33,540,000	35,704,000
	D	7,189,600	-0-	7,092,000	2,797,600
	S	1,652,000	2,832,000	2,628,000	8,244,000
Dimes	(P)	56,860,000	22,190,000	67,740,000	65,350,000
	D	14,146,000	5,537,000	24,394,000	21,198,000
	S	9,740,000	8,090,000	10,540,000	21,560,000
Five Cents	(P)	79,480,000	19,496,000	120,615,000	176,485,000
	D	17,826,000	12,396,000[100]	3,514,000	43,540,000
	S	5,635,000	4,105,000	6,630,000	39,690,000
Cents	(P)	309,170,000	156,682,000	316,466,000	586,810,000
	D	50,430,000	20,010,000	15,160,000	81,390,000
	S	34,500,000	15,180,000	52,070,000	112,940,000

		1941	1942	1943	1944
Half Dollars	(P)	24,192,000	47,818,000	53,190,000	28,206,000
	D	11,248,400	10,973,800	11,346,000	9,769,000
	S	8,098,000	12,708,000	13,450,000	8,904,000
Quarter Dollars	(P)	79,032,000	102,096,000	99,700,000	104,956,000
	D	16,714,800	17,487,200	16,095,600	14,600,800
	S	16,080,000	19,384,000	21,700,000	12,560,000
Dimes	(P)	175,090,000	205,410,000	191,710,000	231,410,000
	D	45,634,000	60,740,000	71,949,000	62,224,000
	S	43,090,000	49,300,000	60,400,000	49,490,000
Five Cents	(P)	203,265,000	107,662,000[101]	271,165,000	119,150,000[103]
	D	53,432,000	13,938,000	15,294,000	32,309,000
	S	43,445,000	32,900,000	104,060,000	21,640,000
Cents	(P)	887,018,000	657,796,000	684,628,670[102]	1,435,400,000
	D	128,700,000	206,698,000	217,660,000[102]	430,578,000
	S	92,460,000	85,590,000	191,550,000[102]	282,760,000

		1945	1946	1947	1948
Half Dollars	(P)	31,502,000	12,118,000	4,094,000	3,006,814
	D	9,996,800	2,151,000	3,900,600	4,028,600
	S	10,156,000	3,724,000	-0-	-0-
Quarter Dollars	(P)	74,372,000	53,436,000	22,556,000	35,196,000
	D	12,341,600	9,072,800	15,338,400	16,766,800
	S	17,004,001	4,204,000	5,532,000	15,960,000
Dimes	(P)	159,130,000	255,250,000	121,520,000	74,950,000
	D	40,245,000	61,043,500	46,835,000	52,841,000
	S	41,920,000	27,900,000	34,840,000	35,520,000
Five Cents	(P)	119,408,100	161,116,000	95,000,000	89,348,000
	D	37,158,000	45,292,200	37,822,000	44,734,000
	S	58,939,000	13,560,000	24,720,000	11,300,000
Cents	(P)	1,040,515,000	991,655,000	190,555,000	317,570,000
	D	226,268,000	315,690,000	194,750,000	172,630,500
	S	181,770,000	198,100,000	99,000,000	81,735,000

		1949	1950	1951	1952
Half Dollars	(P)	5,614,000	7,742,123	16,802,102	21,192,093
	D	4,120,600	8,031,600	9,475,200	25,395,600
	S	3,744,000	-0-	13,696,000	5,526,000
Quarter Dollars	(P)	9,312,000	24,920,126	43,448,102	38,780,093
	D	10,068,400	21,075,600	35,354,800	49,795,200
	S	-0-	10,284,004	9,048,000	13,707,800
Dimes	(P)	30,940,000	50,130,114	102,880,102	99,040,093
	D	26,034,000	46,803,000	56,529,000	122,100,000
	S	13,510,000	20,440,000	31,630,000	44,419,500
Five Cents	(P)	60,652,000	9,796,000	28,552,000	63,988,000
	D	36,498,000	2,630,030	20,460,000	30,638,000
	S	9,716,000	-0-	7,776,000	20,572,000
Cents	(P)	217,775,000	272,635,000	294,576,000	186,765,000
	D	153,132,500	334,950,000	625,355,000	746,130,000
	S	64,290,000	118,505,000	136,010,000	137,800,004

		1953	1954	1955	1956
Half Dollars	(P)	2,668,120	13,188,203	2,498,181	4,032,000
	D	20,900,400	25,445,580	-0-	-0-
	S	4,148,000	4,993,400	-0-	-0-
Quarter Dollars	(P)	18,536,120	54,412,203	18,180,181	44,144,000
	D	56,112,400	42,305,500	3,182,400	32,334,500
	S	14,016,000	11,834,722	-0-	-0-
Dimes	(P)	53,490,120	114,010,203	12,450,181	108,640,000
	D	136,433,000	106,397,000	13,959,000	108,015,100
	S	39,180,000	22,860,000	18,510,000	-0-
Five Cents	(P)	46,644,000	47,684,050	7,888,000	35,216,000
	D	59,878,600	117,136,560	74,464,100	67,222,640
	S	19,210,900	29,384,000	-0-	-0-
Cents	(P)	256,755,000	71,640,050	330,580,000	420,745,000
	D	700,515,000	251,552,500	563,257,500	1,098,210,100
	S	181,835,000	96,190,000	44,610,000	-0-

		1957	1958	1959	1960
Half Dollars	(P)	5,114,000	4,042,000	6,200,000	6,024,000
	D	19,966,850	23,962,412	13,053,750	18,215,812
	S	-0-	-0-	-0-	-0-
Quarter Dollars	(P)	46,532,000	6,360,000	24,384,000	29,164,000
	D	77,924,160	78,124,900	62,054,232	63,000,324
	S	-0-	-0-	-0-	-0-
Dimes	(P)	160,160,000	31,910,000	85,780,000	70,390,000
	D	113,354,330	136,564,600	164,919,790	200,160,400
	S	-0-	-0-	-0-	-0-
Five Cents	(P)	38,408,000	17,088,000	27,248,000	55,416,000
	D	136,828,900	168,249,120	160,738,240	192,582,180
	S	-0-	-0-	-0-	-0-
Cents	(P)	282,540,000	252,525,000	609,715,000	586,405,000
	D	1,051,342,000	800,953,300	1,279,760,000	1,580,884,000
	S	-0-	-0-	-0-	-0-

		1961	1962	1963	1964[1045]
Half Dollars	(P)	8,290,000	9,714,000	22,164,000	273,304,004
	D	20,276,442	35,473,281	67,069,292	156,205,446
	S	-0-	-0-	-0-	-0-
Quarter Dollars	(P)	37,036,000	36,156,000	74,316,000	560,390,585
	D	83,656,928	127,554,756	135,288,184	704,135,528
	S	-0-	-0-	-0-	-0-
Dimes	(P)	93,730,000	72,450,000	123,650,000	929,360,000
	D	209,146,550	334,948,380	421,476,530	1,357,517,180
	S	-0-	-0-	-0-	-0-
Five Cents	(P)	73,640,000	97,384,000	175,776,000	1,024,672,000
	D	229,342,760	280,195,720	276,829,460	1,787,297,160
	S	-0-	-0-	-0-	-0-
Cents	(P)	753,345,000	606,045,000	754,110,000	2,648,575,000
	D	1,753,266,700	1,793,148,400	1,774,020,400	3,799,071,500
	S	-0-	-0-	-0-	-0-

		1965[104]	1966[104]	1967[104]	1968
Half Dollars	(P)	65,879,366	108,984,932	295,046,978	-0-
	D	-0-	-0-	-0-	246,951,930
	S	-0-	-0-	-0-	-0-[53]
Quarter Dollars	(P)	1,819,717,540	821,101,500	1,524,031,848	220,731,500
	D	-0-	-0-	-0-	101,534,000
	S	-0-	-0-	-0-	-0-[53]
Dimes	(P)	1,652,140,470	1,382,734,540	2,224,007,320	424,470,000
	D	-0-	-0-	-0-	480,748,280
	S	-0-	-0-	-0-	-0-[53]
Five Cents	(P)	136,131,380	156,208,283	107,325,800	-0-
	D	-0-	-0-	-0-	91,227,880
	S	-0-	-0-	-0-	100,396,001
Cents	(P)	1,497,224,900	2,188,147,783	3,048,667,100	1,707,880,970
	D	-0-	-0-	-0-	2,886,269,600
	S	-0-	-0-	-0-	258,270,001

		1969	1970	1971	1972
Clad Dollars	(P)	-0-	-0-	47,799,000	75,890,000
	D	-0-	-0-	68,587,424	92,548,511
	S	-0-	-0-	-0-[106]	-0-[106]
Half Dollars	(P)	-0-	-0-	155,164,000	153,180,000
	D	129,881,800	2,150,000[105]	302,097,424	141,890,000
	S	-0-[53]	-0-[53]	-0-[53]	-0-[53]
Quarter Dollars	(P)	176,212,000	136,420,000	109,284,000	215,048,000
	D	114,372,000	417,341,364	258,634,428	311,067,732
	S	-0-[53]	-0-[53]	-0-[53]	-0-[53]
Dimes	(P)	145,790,000	345,570,000	162,690,000	431,540,000
	D	563,323,870	754,042,100	377,914,240	330,290,000
	S	-0-[53]	-0-[53]	-0-[53]	-0-[53]
Five Cents	(P)	-0-	-0-	106,884,000	202,036,000
	D	202,807,500	515,485,380	316,144,800	351,694,600
	S	120,165,000	238,832,004	-0-[53]	-0-[53]
Cents	(P)	1,136,910,000	1,898,315,000	1,919,490,000	2,933,255,000
	D	4,002,832,200	2,891,438,900	2,911,045,600	2,655,071,400
	S	544,375,000	690,560,004	525,130,054	376,932,437

		1973	1974	1975[109]	1976[110]
Clad Dollars	(P)	2,000,056[107]	27,366,000[108]	-0-	117,337,000
	D	2,000,000[107]	45,517,000[108]	-0-	103,228,274
	S	-0-[106]	-0-[106]	-0-	-0-[111]
Half Dollars	(P)	64,964,000	201,596,000[108]	-0-	234,308,000
	D	83,171,400	79,066,300[108]	-0-	287,565,248
	S	-0-[53]	-0-[53]	-0-	-0-[111]
Quarter Dollars	(P)	346,924,000	801,456,000[108]	-0-	809,784,016
	D	232,977,400	353,160,300[108]	-0-	860,118,839
	S	-0-[53]	-0-[53]	-0-	-0-[111]
Dimes	(P)	315,670,000	470,248,000	585,673,900	568,760,000
	D	455,032,426	571,083,000	313,705,300	695,222,774
	S	-0-[53]	-0-[53]	-0-	-0-[53]
Five Cents	(P)	384,396,000	601,752,000	181,772,000	367,124,000
	D	261,405,400	277,373,000	401,875,300	563,964,147
	S	-0-[53]	-0-[53]	-0-	-0-[53]
Cents	(P)	3,728,245,000	4,232,140,523	5,451,476,142	4,674,292,426
	D	3,549,576,588	4,235,098,000	4,505,275,300	4,221,592,455
	S	317,168,010	409,421,878	-0-	-0-[53]

		1977	1978	1979	1980
Clad Dollars	(P)	12,596,000	25,702,000	360,222,000[112]	27,610,000
	D	32,983,006	33,012,890	288,015,744	41,628,708
	S	-0-[53]	-0-[53]	109,576,000	20,422,000
Half Dollars	(P)	43,598,000	14,350,000	68,312,000	44,134,000[117]
	D	31,449,106	13,765,799	15,815,422	33,456,449
	S	-0-[53]	-0-[53]	-0-[53]	-0-[53]
Quarter Dollars	(P)	468,556,000	521,452,000	515,708,000	635,832,000[117]
	D	256,524,978	287,373,152	489,789,780	518,327,487
	S	-0-[53]	-0-[53]	-0-[53]	-0-[53]
Dimes	(P)	796,930,000	663,980,000	315,440,000	735,170,000[117]
	D	376,607,228	282,847,540	390,921,184	719,354,321
	S	-0-[53]	-0-[53]	-0-[53]	-0-[53]
Five Cents	(P)	585,376,000	391,308,000	463,188,000	593,004,000[117]
	D	297,313,422	313,092,780	325,867,672	502,323,448
	S	-0-[53]	-0-[53]	-0-[53]	-0-[53]
Cents	(P)	4,469,930,000	5,558,605,000	6,018,515,000	7,414,705,000
	D	4,194,062,300	4,280,233,400	4,139,357,254	5,140,098,660
	S	-0-[53]	-0-[53]	-0-[53]	-0-[53]

		1981	1982	1983	1984
Clad Dollars	P	3,000,000[118]	-0-	-0-	-0-
	D	3,250,000	-0-	-0-	-0-
	S	3,492,000	-0-	-0-	-0-
Half Dollars	P	29,544,000	10,819,000	34,139,000	26,029,000
	D	27,839,533	13,140,102	32,472,244	26,262,158
	S	-0-[53]	-0-[53]	-0-[53]	-0-[53]
Quarter Dollars	P	601,716,000	500,931,000	673,535,000	676,545,000
	D	575,722,833	480,042,788	617,806,446	546,483,064
	S	-0-[53]	-0-[53]	-0-[53]	-0-[53]
Dimes	P	676,650,000	519,475,000[114]	647,025,000	856,669,000
	D	712,284,143	542,713,584	730,129,224	704,803,976
	S	-0-[53]	-0-[53]	-0-[53]	-0-[53]
Five Cents	P	657,504,000	292,355,000	561,615,000	746,769,000
	D	364,801,843	373,726,544	536,726,276	517,675,146
	S	-0-[53]	-0-[53]	-0-[53]	-0-[53]
Cents	(P)	7,491,750,000	10,712,525,000[113]	7,571,590,000	8,151,079,000
	D	5,373,235,677	6,012,979,368[113]	6,467,199,428	5,569,238,906
	S	-0-[53]	-0-[53]	-0-[53]	-0-[53]

		1985	1986	1987	
Half Dollars	P	18,706,962	13,107,633	— —[119]	
	D	19,814,034	15,366,145	— —[119]	
	S	-0-[53]	-0-[53]	-0-[53]	
Quarter Dollars	P	775,818,962	551,199,333	— —	
	D	519,962,888	504,298,660	— —	
	S	-0-[53]	-0-[53]	-0-[53]	
Dimes	P	705,200,962	682,649,693	— —	
	D	587,979,970	473,326,974	— —	
	S	-0-[53]	-0-[53]	-0-[53]	

		1985	1986	1987
Five Cents	P	647,114,962	536,883,493	— —
	D	459,747,446	361,819,144	— —
		-0-[53]	-0-[53]	-0-[53]
Cents	(P)	4,951,904,887	4,491,395,493	— —
	D	5,287,399,926	4,442,866,698	— —
	S	-0-[53]	-0-[53]	-0-[53]

Notes

1. 1793 1¢: Flowing Hair Obverse, Chain Reverse: 36,103; Flowing Hair Obv., Wreath Rev.: 63,353; Liberty Cap Obv.; Wreath Rev.: 11,056.

2. 1795 $1S: Flowing Hair type: 160,295; Draped Bust type: 42,738.

3. 1796 1¢: Liberty Cap: 109,825; Draped Bust: 363,375.

4. 1797 $10: Mintage includes both reverse types.

5. 1798 $5: Mint Report of 24,867 coins includes Small Eagle reverse coins dated 1798, as well as Heraldic Eagle coins dated 1795, 1797, and 1798. This mixture of mulings is the result of an emergency coinage late in 1798 after the Mint had been closed for a while due to yellow fever. Quantities struck of each are unknown and can only be guessed at.

6. 1798 $1S: Mintage includes both reverse designs.

7. 1801, 1802, and 1803 $1S: All three dates were restruck in Proof in 1858 with a plain edge, using obverse dies made in 1834-5 and the reverse die from the Class I 1804 dollar, which was also made in 1834. Due to the scandal caused by the private issue of 1804 dollars in 1858, these coins were not offered for sale to collectors until 1875, by which time their edges had been lettered.

8. 1804 $1S: Although the Mint Report lists 19,570 dollars for this year it is assumed that they were all dated 1803. They were first struck in 1834-5 for inclusion in diplomatic presentation sets. A few pieces, possibly flawed Proofs or production overruns, reached collectors via trades with the Mint or in circulation and the coin was popularized as a rarity. In 1858 the son of a Mint employee used the obverse die prepared in 1834 and a newly prepared reverse die plus a plain collar to secretly strike 1804 dollars, a few of which were sold to collectors. While the Mint had intended to do exactly the same thing with dollars dated 1801-04, they were forced to cancel the project due to the public scandal over the privately-issued 1804s. The privately struck coins were recalled, and all but one (which went to the Mint Cabinet) were allegedly melted. Instead, they and the plain edged 1801-03s were put in storage and offered for sale in 1875, by which time their edges had been mechanically lettered.

9. 1804, 23 1¢, and 1811 ½¢: Counterfeits, called restrikes, exist which were made outside the Mint, using old, genuine but mismatched Mint dies.

10. 1805 $1S: The 321 dollars listed in the Mint Report for 1805 were older dollars which were found in deposits of Spanish-American silver and which were re-issued through the Treasury. On the basis of this misinformation a few coins have been altered to this date in the past.

11. 1807 $5: Old type: 32,488; new type: 51,605.

12. 1807 50¢: Old type: 301,076; new type: 750,500.

13. 1822 $5: Although the Mint Report says 17,796 coins were struck, only three pieces are known and it is likely that most of this mintage was from dies dated 1821.

14. 1827 25¢: Although the Mint Report lists a mintage of 4,000 pieces for this year, it is likely that all of these coins were dated 1825 except for a few Proofs. Later this date was unofficially (but intentionally) restruck at the Mint using an obverse die dated 1827 and a reverse die which had been used in 1819, and which had a Square Base 2 in 25¢, rather than the Curled Base 2 of the original 1827.

15. 1831, 49, 56, and 57 ½¢: Originally struck in Proof and Unc., the Proofs were restruck for collectors in later years.

16. 1832-35 ½¢: The figures shown are listed in the Mint Report for 1833-36 instead, but are assumed to be misplaced.

17. 1834 $5: Total of 732,169 coins struck. This includes 50,141, of the old head struck and released; 24,568 of the old head struck but melted; and 657,460 of the new head (and weight), all released.

18. 1834 $2½: Mintage includes 4,000 of the old head, of which most or all were melted. It may be that all survivors are Proofs and circulated Proofs.

19. 1836, 38, and 39 $1S: Gobrecht dollars, some patterns and some intended for circulation, were struck in these years, in quantities as high as 1,000 pieces. Also, some varieties were restruck in later years, making mintage figures questionable. Varieties exist with or without stars and/or the designer's name, some of them exceedingly scarce.

20. 1836 50¢: Mintage includes 6,545,000 Capped Bust, Lettered Edge coins and 1,200 pieces with a reeded edge and no motto E PLURIBUS UNUM. (The latter was actually a pattern of the design adopted the following year, but much of the mintage was placed into circulation.)

21. 1836 ½¢: Originally struck in Proof only, this date was restruck in Proof in later years to provide collectors with specimens of a coin that

was listed in the Mint Report but which couldn't be found in circulation. See #16.

22. 1837 10¢: Capped Bust type: 359,500; Seated Liberty without stars on obverse: 682,500.

23. 1837 5¢S: Capped Bust type: 871,000; Seated Liberty without stars on obverse: 1,405,000.

24. 1838-O 50¢: Twenty specimen pieces were struck to celebrate the opening of the New Orleans Mint.

25. 1838 25¢: Capped Bust type: 366,000; Seated Liberty type: 466,000.

26. 1838-O 10¢ & 5¢S: Both are of Seated Liberty design without stars (type of 1837). 1838 Philadelphia coins have stars, as do all others through 1859.

27. 1839 $10: Includes first design head (type of 1838) and modified head (type of 1840-1907).

28. 1839-P, O 50¢: Capped Bust type: (P): 1,362,160; O: 178,976. Seated Liberty type: (P): 1,972,400. (Note: Although Christian Gobrecht's half dollar design was slightly modified during 1839 by the addition of a small drapery fold beneath the elbow, the design was never as fully modified as the other Seated Liberty denominations were in 1840. In subsequent years individual dies would occasionally be overpolished, thus removing this small drapery fold. Coins struck from these inferior dies are sometimes referred to as having a "no-drapery design," when in fact no design change was intended or made.)

29. 1840-53 $1S: Proof restrikes exist for all dates.

30. 1840-48 and 1852 ½¢: Originally struck in Proof only, all dates were restruck in Proof for sale to collectors.

31. 1841-P $2.50: Struck in Proof only, possibly at a later date. Unlisted in Mint Report.

32. 1848-P $2.50: Approximately 1,389 coins were counter-stamped CAL. above the eagle to show that they were made from California gold. This was done while the coins were resting on an inverted obverse die on a worktable. This virtually eliminated distortion of the obverse, which will probably show on a genuine coin with a fake counter-stamp.

33. 1849 $20: One specimen in gold survives of a small number of trial strikes produced in December 1849. The dies were rejected, allegedly because of improper high relief, but in actuality to discredit Longacre in an attempt to force his removal. The attempt failed and Longacre eventually produced a second set of dies, but they were not completed until the following month and so they were dated 1850. The one known gold specimen is in the Smithsonian Institution and all others were melted.

34. 1853 Silver Coinage: In early 1853 the weight of all fractional silver coins was reduced by about 7 percent, to prevent hoarding and melting. To distinguish between the old and new weights, arrows were placed on either side of the date on the half dime through half dollar, and rays were put around the eagle on the quarter and half dollar. The rays were removed after 1853, and the arrows after 1855.

Much of the old silver was withdrawn from circulation and melted. The exception to all this was the silver 3-cent piece, which was decreased in weight but increased in fineness, making it intrinsically worth more than before and proportionate with the other fractional silver coins. No coins of the new weight were struck until 1854, at which time an olive branch and a cluster of arrows was added to the reverse.

35. 1853-P, O 50¢: All 1853-P and virtually all 1853-O 50¢ are of the new weight. Two or three 1853-O are known without the arrows and rays. Beware of alterations from 1858-O.

36. 1853-P, O 25¢: Without Arrows and Rays: (P): 44,200. With A&R: (P): 15,210,020; O: 1,332,000.

37. 1853-P, O 10¢: Without Arrows: (P): 95,000. With Arrows: (P): 12,078,010; O: 1,100,000.

38. 1853-P, O 5¢S: Without Arrows: (P): 135,000; O: 160,000. With Arrows: (P): 13,210,020; O: 2,200,000.

39. 1854-P, D, S $1G: (P): Coronet 736,709; Indian (small head) 902,736. All 1854-D&S are Coronet design.

40. 1856-P, D, S $1G: All P&D-Mint are Indian (large head); all S-Mint are Indian (small head).

41. 1856 1¢: More than 1,000 1856 Flying Eagle cents were struck in Proof and Unc., in this and later years. As they were patterns they are not included in the Mint Report or this figure.

42. 1857 1¢: Large cents: 333,456; small cents: 17,450,000.

43. 1858 $1S: It is estimated that 80 Proofs were struck, some of them possibly at a later date.

44. 1859 1¢: This year only comes with a reverse design without a shield. All other Indian cents (1860-1909) have a shield.

45. 1860-S $3: Out of 7,000 coins struck, 2,592 pieces were not released because of short weight. They were melted in 1869 for use in other denominations.

46. 1860-P, O, S 10¢ & 5¢S: Beginning in 1860 (with the exception of the 1860-S dime), the half dime and dime were redesigned by eliminating the stars, moving the legend UNITED STATES OF AMERICA to the obverse, and using a larger, more elaborate wreath on the reverse. A number of fabrications with the obverse of 1859 and the reverse of 1860 (thereby omitting the legend USA), were struck by order of the Director of the Mint. These consist of half dimes dated 1859 or 1860, and dimes dated 1859. Although they are considered by some to be patterns, that designation is doubtful as the intentions of the Director were highly questionable.

47. 1861-P $20: A few trial pieces are known with a reverse as engraved by Paquet, with taller, thinner letters and a narrow rim. The design was judged unacceptable because the narrow reverse rim would not stack easily. See #49.

48. 1861-O $20: Mintage includes 5,000 coins struck by the USA; 9,750 by the State of Louisiana; and 2,991 by the Confederate States of America. It is impossible to prove the issuer of any given coin.

49. 1861-S $20: Mintage includes 19,250 pieces struck with the Paquet reverse and released into circulation. See #47. Most of these were recalled and melted during the next few years, but specie hoarding during the Civil War probably preserved a number of them until later years when the problem was forgotten.

50. 1861-C $5: Mintage includes 5,992 pieces coined by USA and 887 by CSA. It is impossible to prove the issuer.

51. 1861-D $1G: A small number were struck by the CSA.

52. 1861-O 50¢: Mintage includes 330,000 struck by the USA; 1,240,000 by the State of Louisiana; and 962,633 by the CSA. It is impossible to tell them apart. One obverse die is identifiable as having been used with the CSA reverse to strike four pattern coins, but there is no way of telling when that die was used with a regular reverse die or who issued the coins struck from it.

53. Struck in Proof only.

54. 1863 3¢S: It is possible that all of these non-Proofs were dated 1862. Proof coins dated 1863/2 were struck in 1864. Obviously these were hard times at the Mint.

55. 1864-P 10¢, 5¢S & 3¢S: These figures, like many others in the years 1861-1871, are highly controversial due to extraordinary bookkeeping methods used in the Mint in this era.

56. 1864 2¢: Struck with Large and Small Motto IN GOD WE TRUST.

57. 1864 1¢: Mintage includes 13,740,000 copper-nickel and 39,233,714 bronze pieces. The bronze coins come without and with the designer's initial L, which appears on all subsequent issues. The 1864 variety with L is the scarcer.

58. 1866 Coinage: It was decided to add the motto In God We Trust to the reverse of all double eagles, eagles, half eagles, silver dollars, half dollars and quarter dollars beginning in 1866. Early in the year, before the new reverse dies had arrived, the San Francisco Mint produced $20, $10, $5, and 50¢ coins without the motto. These are regular issue coins and are not patterns or errors. They are not to be confused with a peculiar set of Philadelphia Mint silver coins without motto, consisting of two dollars, one half, and one quarter, which was clandestinely struck inside (but not by) the Mint for sale to a collector. A set of one of each of these was stolen in 1967 and never recovered. Beware of regular coins with motto and/or Mint mark removed.

59. 1866-P, S $20: When the reverse of the double eagle was altered to include the motto there were also a few minor changes made in the scrollwork, the most prominent being the change in the shield from flat-sided to curved.

Check any alleged 1866-S NM $20 for this feature.

60. 1866-S $20: Includes 120,000 coins Without Motto.

61. 1866-S $10: Includes 8,500 coins Without Motto.

62. 1866-S $5: Includes 9,000 coins Without Motto.

63. 1866-S 50¢: Includes 60,000 coins Without Motto.

64. 1867 5¢: Struck with rays on reverse (type of 1866) and without rays (type of 1868-83).

65. 1870-S $3: Not included in the Mint Report, supposedly one piece was struck for inclusion in the cornerstone of the new San Francisco Mint. One piece is known in a private collection, and the present whereabouts of the cornerstone piece is unknown. It is possible there is only one piece.

66. 1870-S $1G: 2,000 coins were struck without a Mint mark. It is unknown if they were melted and recoined or released as is and included in the Mint Report figure of 3,000 coins.

67. 1870-S $1S: Not listed in the Mint Report, a few pieces may have been struck as souvenirs of the opening of the new Mint.

68. 1873 Coinage: Early in the year a relatively closed style of 3 was used in the date on all denominations. In response to complaints that the 3 looked like an 8, a new, more open 3 was introduced. Most types were struck with both styles, except for those which were created or discontinued by the Coinage Act of February 12, 1873. This law created the Trade dollar and eliminated the standard silver dollar and the silver 5-cent and 3-cent pieces, as well as the 2-cent piece. The weight of the dime, quarter, and half dollar were slightly increased, and the heavier coins were marked by arrows for the remainder of 1873 and all of 1874.

69. 1873 $3: Struck in Proof only, later restruck in Proof more than once.

70. 1873-S $1S: Presumably all or most were melted at the Mint after production of standard silver dollars was suspended.

71. 1873-P, CC, S 50¢: Without Arrows: (P): 801,200; CC: 122,500; S: 5,000. With Arrows: (P) 1,815,150; CC: 214,560; S: 228,000. (Note: The 1873-S Without Arrows is unknown in any condition in any collection. Presumably they were all melted with the 1873-S silver dollars. Beware of any regular 1873-S with the arrows removed. The difference in weight between the two issues is insignificant, and useless in checking a suspected altered coin.)

72. 1873-P, CC, S 25¢: Without Arrows: (P): 212,000; CC: 4000. With Arrows: (P): 1,271,160; CC: 12,462; S: 156,000.

73. 1873-P, CC, S 10¢: Without Arrows: (P): 1,568,000; CC: 12,400. With Arrows: (P): 2,377,700; CC: 18,791; S: 455,000. (Note: Only one 1873-CC Without Arrows is known, all others presumably melted.)

74. 1873 2¢: Originally struck in Proof only early in 1873 with a Closed 3. Later restruck in Proof with an Open 3.

75. 1875 $3: Struck in Proof only, later restruck in Proof.

76. 1876-CC 20¢: Virtually all remelted at the Mint. A few escaped, possibly as souvenirs given to visitors.

77. 1877 $20: In this year the master hubs were redesigned slightly, raising the head and changing TWENTY D. to TWENTY DOLLARS.

78. 1878-P, 1879-85 $1T: The P-Mint Trade dollars from 1878 to 1883 were struck and sold in Proof only. Ten 1884 and five 1885 coins were struck in Proof in the Mint for private distribution, by person or persons unknown. They are not listed in the Mint Report.

79. 1878-P $1S: Three slightly different designs were used for both the obverse and reverse of this date, including some dies with the second designs impressed over the first. All 1878-CC&S are from the second designs. Most 1879-1904 dollars are of the third design, except for some second design reverses on 1879-S and 1880-CC coins. New, slightly different master hubs were prepared for 1921.

80. 1883 5¢N: Shield type: 1,451,500; Liberty Head type Without CENTS on reverse: 5,474,300; Liberty Head With CENTS on reverse: 16,026,200.

81. 1894-S 10¢: Twenty-four specimen strikings were made for private distribution by the Superintendent of the San Francisco Mint.

82. 1895 $1S: Apparently virtually all business strike coins were never issued and were probably melted in the great silver melt of 1918. One circulated business strike coin has been authenticated. Beware of altered dates and removed Mint marks.

83. 1906-D & 1907-D $5: These were, of course, struck at the Denver Mint. This is the only design which was struck at both Dahlonega and Denver.

84. 1907-P D, S $20: Coronet: 1,451,786 P-Mint and all D&S-Mint coins. Saint-Gaudens type: 11,250 medium-high relief, Roman Numeral date coins and 361,667 lower-relief, Arabic date coins. A few extremely-high relief patterns were also made.

85. 1907-P, D, S $10: Coronet: 1,203,899 P-Mint and all D&S-Mint coins. Indian Head type: 239,406.

86. 1908-P, D, S $20: Without motto In God We Trust: (type of 1907) (P): 4,271,551; D: 663,750. With motto: (type of 1909-33) (P): 156,258; D: 349,500; S: 22,000.

87. 1908-P, D, S $10: Without motto In God We Trust: (type of 1907) (P): 33,500; D: 210,000. With motto: (type of 1909-33) (P): 341,370; D: 836,500; S: 59,850.

88. 1908-P, D, S $5: Coronet: 421,874 P-Mint coins. Indian Head type: 577,845 P-Mint and all D&S-Mint coins.

89. 1909-P, S 1¢: Indian Head: (P): 14,368,470; S: 309,000. Lincoln Head with designer's initials V.D.B.: (P): 27,994,580; S: 484,000. Lincoln Head without V.D.B.: (P): 72,700,420; S: 1,825,000.

90. 1913 Liberty Head 5¢: Five unauthorized pieces were struck by person or persons unknown, using Mint machinery and dies. All five accounted for. Beware of forgeries. (See also #91)

91. 1913-P, D, S Indian Head 5¢: Variety 1, with the bison standing on a solid mound: (P): 30,992,000; D: 5,337,000; S: 2,105,000. Variety 2, the Bison on Plain variety, with the base of the mound recessed so as to protect the Mint mark and FIVE CENTS: (P): 29,857,186; D: 4,156,000; S: 1,209,000.

92. 1916-P, D 25¢: Barber Head type: 1,788,000 P-Mint and all D-Mint. Standing Liberty type: 52,000 P-Mint.

93. 1916-P, D, S 10¢: Barber Head type: (P): 18,490,000; S: 5,820,000. Winged Liberty Head type: (P): 22,180,080; D: 264,000; S: 10,450,000.

94. 1917-D, S 50¢: With Mint mark on obverse (type of 1916): D: 765,400; S: 952,000. On reverse (type of 1918-47): D: 1,940,000; S: 5,554,000.

95. 1917-P, D, S 25¢: Variety one (type of 1916, with partially nude figure): (P): 8,740,000; D: 1,509,200; S: 1,952,000. Variety two (type of 1918, with fully clothed figure and eagle higher on reverse): (P): 13,880,000; D: 6,224,400; S: 5,552,000.

96. 1921-P, D, S $1S: Morgan type: 44,690,000 P-Mint and all D&S Mint. Peace type: 1,006,473 P-Mint. The 1921 Peace dollars, (and a very few Proof 1922s), are of a higher relief than the 1922-35s.

97. 1922 "Plain" 1¢: No cents were struck in Philadelphia in 1922. Some 1922-Denver cents are found with the Mint mark missing due to obstructed dies. Beware of altered coins.

98. 1933 $20: This issue was officially never released, so the coins are considered illegal to own. A few are reported to exist, including one at the Smithsonian Institution. Most late date gold never filtered down through the banks and so it was returned to the Mint for melting.

99. 1933 $10: Very few of these were issued, perhaps several dozens known. Beware of counterfeits.

100. 1938-D 5¢: Indian Head: 7,020,000. Jefferson: 5,376,000.

101. 1942-1945-P, D, S 5¢: To conserve nickel during the war, the composition of the 5-cent piece was changed to a 56 percent copper, 35 percent silver, and 9 percent manganese alloy. Coins of this alloy were marked with a large Mint mark over the dome of Monticello, including those from Philadelphia. They consist of some 1942-P, all 1942-S, and all 1943-45 coins. The 1942 Philadelphia coins were made either way, as follows: C-N: 49,789,000; C-S-M: 57,873,000. Many war nickels have been melted for their silver content.

102. 1943-P, D, S 1¢: All 1943 cents were made of zinc-plated steel. A few 1943 bronze and 1944 steel cents were made by accident. Many fakes of these have been produced. Test any suspected off-metal 1943 or 1944 cent with a magnet to see if it has been plated, and check the date for alterations. Cents struck on steel planchets produced in 1942 weigh 41.5 grains, while those struck on planchets produced later in 1943 weigh 42.5 grains.

103. 1944 5¢: Copper-nickel 1944 5-cent coins without a Mint mark are counterfeits made for circulation, as are any 1923-D or 1930-D dimes. Not all counterfeits are of rare dates, meant to sell at high prices.

104. 1964-67 Coinage: All coins dated 1965-67 were made without Mint marks. Many coins dated 1964-66 were struck in later years.

105. 1970-D 50¢: Struck only for inclusion in Mint sets. Not a regular issue coin.

106. S-Mint clad dollars: Struck only for sale to collectors. In 1971-72 struck in 40 percent clad silver in Proof and Unc. for individual sale. Beginning in 1973 a copper-nickel clad dollar was added to the Proof sets.

107. 1973-P, D $1C: Struck only for inclusion in Mint sets. Not a regular issue coin. 1,769,258 Mint sets sold. 439,899 excess dollars melted, presumably of near-equal distribution. 21,641 coins were kept for possible replacement of defective sets and may be melted.

108. 1974-dated dollars, half dollars and quarters: Includes coins struck in calendar years 1974 and 1975.

109. 1975-dated dollars, half dollars and quarters: Absolutely none struck. 1975 Proof and Mint sets contain Bicentennial dollars, half dollars and quarters.

110. 1976-dated dollars, half dollars and quarters: Includes coins struck in calendar years 1975 and 1976.

111. 1976-S dollars, half dollars and quarters: Includes copper-nickel clad Proofs sold in 1975 and 1976 six-piece Proof sets, and 40 percent

silver clad Proofs
lion pieces of each
See section about 1
mintage figures.

112. Susan B. Anthony d
replacing larger Eisenh
delphia Mint dollars had

113. Composition of cent chan̠ ̠ ̠ ̠ ̠ ̠ent
copper, 5 percent zinc to 9 ̠ ̠ zinc, 2.5 percent copper (composed ̠ a planchet of 99.2 percent zinc, 0.8 percent copper, plated with pure copper). Some 1982 cents were struck in late 1981.

114. Some 1982 dimes were released without a Mint mark, although dimes have been Mint marked since 1980. Distribution of the coins, many found in the Sandusky, Ohio, area, indicates they were from the Philadelphia Mint.

115. 1964 Peace dollar: A total 316,076 silver dollars of the Peace design were struck at the Denver Mint, but were subsequently melted when it was decided not to issue the coins and when a silver shortage occurred. Rumors indicate a few coins may have survived, but the coins are illegal to own.

116. 1974 aluminum cent: During the 1973 copper shortage, 1,579,324 1974-dated aluminum Lincoln cents were struck experimentally. Most were subsequently melted, but a few given to congressional members and staff disappeared. One specimen is held in the National Numismatic Collections at the Smithsonian Institution. Many 1974 privately-plated cents resembling the aluminum cents are known.

117. The P Mint mark, placed on the 1979 Anthony dollar, was added to all 1980 denominations from the Philadelphia Mint except for the cent.

118. Susan B. Anthony dollars were sold in three-coin sets only in 1981. None were released into circulation.

119. 50¢ The Mint announced in 1986 that it would produce 1987 Kennedy half dollars for Uncirculated sets, Proof sets and Souvenir Mint sets only. Mint officials said there were no plans to strike 1987 Kennedy half dollars for circulation.

Varieties of Anthony dollars
Eisenhower dollars
and Kennedy half dollars

Coin World frequently receives letters from its readers asking for a complete listing of Anthony dollars, Eisenhower dollars or the Kennedy half dollars, or all three. These requests are quite understandable, as the three series have been issued in such variety that 62 different Kennedy halves were struck through 1987, 32 different Eisenhower dollars were struck by 1978, and 13 Anthony dollars were issued 1979-81.

The following lists include only those coins which are generally available to collectors.

The occasional errors such as the 90 percent silver 1965 halves and the 40 percent silver 1974-D dollars are not included, as these coins were never meant to be struck or released.

Kennedy half dollars
90 Percent Silver

1964	Unc.
1964	Proof
1964-D	Unc.

40 Percent Silver Clad

1965	Unc.
1966	Unc.
1967	Unc.
1968-D	Unc.
1968-S	Proof
1969-D	Unc.
1969-S	Proof
1970-D (Unc. sets only)	Unc.
1970-S	Proof

Copper-Nickel Clad

1971	Unc.
1971-D	Unc.
1971-S	Proof
1972	Unc.
1972-D	Unc.
1972-S	Proof
1973	Unc.
1973-D	Unc.
1973-S	Proof
1974	Unc.
1974-D	Unc.
1974-S	Proof
1977	Unc.
1977-D	Unc.
1977-S	Proof
1978	Unc.
1978-D	Unc.
1978-S	Proof
1979	Unc.
1979-D	Unc.
1979-S	Proof
1980-P	Unc.
1980-D	Unc.
1980-S	Proof
1981-P	Unc.
1981-D	Unc.
1981-S	Proof
1982-P	Unc.
1982-D	Unc.
1982-S	Proof
1983-P	Unc.
1983-D	Unc.
1983-S	Proof
1984-P	Unc.
1984-D	Unc.
1984-S	Proof
1985-P	Unc.
1985-D	Unc.
1985-S	Proof
1986-P	Unc.
1986-D	Unc.
1986-S	Proof
1987-P (Unc. sets only)	Unc.
1987-D (Unc. sets only)	Unc.
1987-S	Proof

Bicentennial Reverse
Copper-Nickel Clad

1776-1976	Unc.
1776-1976-D	Unc.
1776-1976-S	Proof

40 Percent Silver Clad

1776-1976-S	Unc.
1776-1976-S	Proof

Eisenhower dollars
Copper-Nickel Clad

1971	Unc.
1971-D	Unc.
1972	Unc.
1972-D	Unc.
1973 (Unc. sets only)	Unc.
1973-D (Unc. sets only)	Unc.
1973-S	Proof
1974	Unc.
1974-D	Unc.
1974-S	Proof
1977	Unc.
1977-D	Unc.
1977-S	Proof
1978	Unc.
1978-D	Unc.
1978-S	Proof

40 Percent Silver Clad

1971-S	Unc.
1971-S	Proof
1972-S	Unc.
1972-S	Proof
1973-S	Unc.
1973-S	Proof
1974-S	Unc.
1974-S	Proof

Bicentennial Reverse
Copper-Nickel Clad

1776-1976, Var. 1	Unc.
1776-1976, Var. 2	Unc.
1776-1976-D, Var. 1	Unc.
1776-1976-D, Var. 2	Unc.
1776-1976-S, Var. 1	Proof
1776-1976-S, Var. 2	Proof

40 Percent Silver Clad

1776-1976-S, Var. 1	Unc.
1776-1976-S, Var. 1	Proof

Anthony dollars
Copper-Nickel Clad

1979-P	Unc.
1979-D	Unc.
1979-S	Unc.
1979-S, Filled S	Proof
1979-S, Clear S	Proof
1980-P	Unc.
1980-D	Unc.
1980-S	Unc.

1980-S	Proof
1981-P	Unc.
1981-D..........................	Unc.
1981-S	Unc.
1981-S	Proof

Uncirculated sets

Uncirculated sets contain examples of each business-strike coin struck within a given year. Coins are struck no differently than the circulation strikes.

The United States Mint first offered Uncirculated Mint sets, dated 1947, in 1948. Later, after the 1947 sets sold out, 1948 coinage was offered. Before 1960, the sets were individually packaged in cardboard folders; each set contains two specimens of each coin struck that year.

Beginning in 1959, sets were packaged in polyethylene packets. During the coin shortage of the mid-1960s, Special Mint sets were struck in lieu of Proof sets and Uncirculated sets in 1965, 1966 and 1967. Uncirculated set production resumed in 1968. Philadelphia and Denver Eisenhower dollars were added to the set in 1973, which were replaced in 1979 by three Anthony dollars. No Uncirculated sets were issued in 1982 and 1983 for what Mint officials said were budget-reduction reasons. Congress passed a law in 1983, however, requiring annual sales of Uncirculated sets.

Uncirculated set statistics

Year Minted	Sets Sold	Selling Price	Face Value
1947	12,600	$ 4.87	$ 4.46
1948	17,000	4.92	4.46
1949	20,739	5.45	4.96
1950	None	—	—
1951	8,654	6.75	5.46
1952	11,499	6.14	5.46
1953	15,538	6.14	5.46
1954	25,599	6.19	5.46
1955	49,656	3.57	2.86
1956	45,475	3.34	2.64
1957	34,324	4.40	3.64
1958	50,314	4.43	3.64
1959	187,000	2.40	1.82
1960	260,485	2.40	1.82
1961	223,704	2.40	1.82
1962	385,285	2.40	1.82
1963	606,612	2.40	1.82
1964	1,008,108	2.40	1.82
1965	2,360,000	4.00	.91
1966	2,261,583	4.00	.91
1967	1,863,344	4.00	.91
1968	2,105,128	2.50	1.33
1969	1,817,392	2.50	1.33
1970	2,038,134	2.50	1.33
1971	2,193,396	3.50	1.83
1972	2,750,000	3.50	1.83
1973	1,767,691	6.00	3.83
1974	1,975,981	6.00	3.83
1975	1,921,488	6.00	3.82
1976	1,892,513	6.00	3.82
1977	2,006,869	7.00	3.82
1978	2,162,609	7.00	3.82
1979	2,526,000	8.00	4.82
1980	2,815,066	9.00	4.82
1981	2,908,145	11.00	4.82
1984	1,832,857	7.00	1.82
1985	1,710,571	7.00	1.82
1986	1,119,957	7.00	1.82

Source: United States Mint

Bicentennial sets

The 1976 Bicentennial of American Independence was numismatically celebrated with changes in the reverse designs of the Washington quarter dollar, Kennedy half dollar and Eisenhower dollar. Copper-nickel versions of all three were issued for circulation and for the regular Proof set.

Collectors were offered two three-coin sets of the same coins struck in a 40 percent silver composition, in Proof and Uncirculated versions. The silver collectors' coins were first offered Nov. 15, 1974, at prices of $15 for the Proof set and $9 for the Uncirculated set. In the 12 years of sales for the two three-coin sers, from November 1974 to Dec. 31, 1986, prices for the three-coin sets were changed no fewer than five times due to rising and falling silver prices. Mint officials reduced the prices for the Proof set Jan. 19, 1975, to $12. On Sept. 20, 1979, Mint officials suspended sales of the Bicentennial Uncirculated set because of the rising price of silver; the bullion value of the three coins in the set exceeded the Mint's price of $9. Sales of the Bicentennial Proof set were suspended in December 1979 as silver rose to even greater heights. When sales of the two Bicentennial sets were resumed in Aug. 4, 1980, the prices rose to $15 for the Uncirculated sets and $20 for the Proof sets. Falling silver prices permitted the introduction of lower prices Sept. 1, 1981: $15 for the Proof set, $12 for the Uncirculated set. In September 1982, prices for the coins dropped even lower — to $12 for the Proof set, and $9 for the Uncirculated set.

Prices maintained those levels until sales of the sets ceased: in 1985 for the Proof set, and on Dec. 31, 1986, for the Uncirculated set.

Final mintages are 3,998,621 for the Proof set, and 4,908,319 for the Uncirculated set.

Source: United States Mint

Errors

10

Error coins and paper money

Error coins and paper money are products of the United States Mint and the Bureau of Engraving and Printing that Treasury officials would rather did not exist. An error coin or note deviates from the norm as a result of a mishap in the minting or printing processes; in effect, an error represents a "substandard" product of the agency that produced it. Some collectors prefer these substandard items, however, over normal coins and notes.

Although it sometimes may seem that the Mint and the BEP produce inordinate amounts of error coins and notes, the numbers are generally relatively small when compared to the total numbers of pieces released. Those small numbers in part account for the values some collectors place on error numismatic material. Of course, values for error coins and paper money depend on the same factors affecting normal numismatic merchandise: supply, demand and condition. Obviously, errors are in very short supply when compared to total mintages. However, error collectors represent a fraction of the total number of collectors, so demand is less for most items. Some error coins, such as the 1955 Lincoln, Doubled Die cent, because of press publicity and dealer promotion, "cross over" and become popular with general collectors; thus, demand is higher for a fixed supply, and the values are correspondingly higher. Condition is important, although error collectors seem less concerned with "perfection" than other collectors.

Rare does not necessarily mean great value. Many error coins, struck in small quantities, are available for a few dollars. Even errors which are considered unique are often available for only several dollars. Unfortunately, many persons not familiar with errors, including some dealers, place unrealistically high values on error coins and notes.

Any discussion of error coins and notes must include a discussion of varieties. A numismatic variety is defined as the difference between individual dies or hubs of the same basic design or type, or between plates (in the case of paper money). The differences between two varieties of the same type are generally intentional; the 1917 Standing Liberty quarter dollar with Liberty baring her breast is a different variety than the 1917 Standing Liberty quarter with Liberty's breast covered by a coat of chain mail, for example, although both have the same basic design.

Can an error also be a variety? There are some who believe so, especially for certain die errors. Some die error coins have been accepted as varieties and are considered by many as part of the regular series; among these are the 1955 and 1972 Lincoln, Doubled Die cents, the 1937-D Indian Head, Three-Legged 5-cent piece, and others. Others believe that no distinction should be made between varieties or errors; they believe that *all* errors are varieties.

Error coins and notes can be found in circulation, unlike many other collectors' items. Some collectors go to banks and obtain large quantities of coins or notes to search through; coins and notes not bearing errors are returned to the bank. Many errors, particularly of the minor classification, can be discovered simply by going through pocket change and wallets. All it takes are sharp eyes and a knowledge of what to look for.

Error coins

The minting of a coin is a manufacturing process, and should be fully understood by anyone interested in collecting and studying error coins (see Chapter 9, "How coins are made"). Many forms of alteration and damage received outside the Mint resemble certain types of errors, but none precisely duplicate genuine Mint errors. Collectors who understand the minting process should be better able to distinguish between errors and damage and alteration than collectors who have never studied the manufacturing process.

The causes of error coins will be discussed in the section that follows. The section is split into three parts — die errors, planchet errors and striking errors — followed by definitions of common forms of alteration and damage.

Die errors are those produced due to a mishap involving the die or hub. Planchet errors are the result of defective or improper planchets, and striking errors are created during the actual coining.

Die errors

BIE: The term commonly used for minor errors affecting the letters of the word LIBERTY on Lincoln cents. A small break in the die between the letters, especially BE, often resembles the letter I, hence the BIE designation. Such errors are much more common on the coins of the 1950s and early 1960s than more recent issues. Collectors tend to be less interested in such errors in the 1980s than they were 20 years ago.

Clashed dies: When during the striking process two dies come together without a planchet between them, the dies clash (come into direct contact). Depending on the force with which the dies come together and the designs, a portion of the obverse design is transferred to the reverse, and a portion of the reverse is transferred to the obverse. Coins struck from the clashed dies will show signs of the transferred designs. Although the cause of this type of error occurs during the striking process, the die is affected; thus it is considered a die error.

Cuds: A "cud" is a type of major die break. It occurs when the die breaks at the rim and a piece of the die falls out of the press. The metal of coins struck from that die flows up into the missing area, resulting in a raised blob of metal bearing no image; these are called "cud" errors. The side of the coin opposite the cud is weak and indistinct; this is because metal flows along the path of least resistance, preferring to travel into the broken area and not the recesses of the other die. A retained cud occurs when the die breaks at the rim, but the piece does not fall out. Coins struck from these dies show the break, but also depict the image inside the break.

Die breaks, chips, cracks, gouges, scratches: Dies, like any other piece of steel, are subject to all sorts of damage that leave raised areas on coins. Breaks and cracks are similar, appearing on coins as raised lines. A die break affects a larger area than the die crack, and often breaks result in pieces of the die falling out (see "cud"). A die chip occurs when a small portion of the die breaks away, while gouges and scratches generally occur when a foreign object scores the surface of the die.

Doubled dies: If during the hubbing and die making process (see Chapter 9), a misalignment between hub and partially completed die occurs, overlapping, multiple images may appear on the die. Coins struck from that die will show overlapping images as well. Die doubling on coins with raised designs feature a rounded second image; on coins with incused designs, the second image is flat and shelf-like. At the corners of the overlapping images, there are distinct "notches" on coins with raised designs. A tripled die is caused by the same misalignment, but bears a tripled image.

Engraving errors: While more common on the dies of the 18th and 19th centuries, engraving errors have been made on modern dies. On the earlier dies, numerals and letters were often recut to strengthen the design, punched in upside down or otherwise out of alignment, and sometimes, wrong letters or numbers were punched into the die. On more modern dies, engraving errors include the use of the wrong size Mint mark by mistake and Mint marks placed too close to design elements or too far from their intended locations. Other engraving errors, discussed in separate sections, included doubled dies, overdates and multiple Mint marks.

Filled dies: The Mint is a factory, and like most metal-working factories, has more than its share of dirt, grease and other lubricants, and metal filings. The recessed areas of the dies sometimes fill up with a combination of this foreign material, preventing the metal of the coins from flowing into the incused areas. This results in weak designs or missing design details. Probably the most common type of error.

Multiple Mint marks: Mint marks are punched into each individual working die (beginning in 1986, all Proof and commemorative coins have the Mint mark placed on the plasticene model) by hand with mallet and punch. Several blows to the punch are needed to properly sink the Mint mark into the die. If the punch is not properly placed after the first blow, a multiple image may result. These are commonly known as doubled D and doubled S Mint marks, for the Denver and San Francisco Mints.

Overdates: When one or more numerals in the date are engraved, sunk or hubbed over a different numeral or numerals, both the orginial date and the second date can be seen. Examples include the 1943/2-P Jefferson 5-cent piece, the 1942/1 Winged Liberty Head dime and the 1958/7 Lincoln cent. Another overdate occurs when two dies with the same date, but of different varieties, are used. Prime examples of this are the 1960 Lincoln, Large Date Over Small Date cents.

Over Mint marks: A form of multiple Mint mark, but when punches of two different Mints are used. Examples include the 1944-D/S Lincoln cent and the 1938-D/S Jefferson 5-cent piece.

Polished dies: Mint employees polish dies to extend their working life and to remove such things as clash marks, die scratches, dirt and grease. If the die is polished too much, details may be erased, or small raised lines may appear on the coins. Most over-polished errors have little value, but there are exceptions, including the 1937-D Indian Head, Three-Legged 5-cent piece.

Rotated dies: Most U.S. coins have the obverse and reverse sides oriented so each side is upright when rotated vertically. The alignment between the two is 180 degrees. However, if the dies are aligned at anything other than 180 degrees, the dies are considered rotated. Coins rotated 5 degrees or less are considered within tolerance levels by Mint employees.

Worn dies: Dies have a set life, based on the hardness of the coinage metal being struck and the striking pressures involved. When a die wears beyond a certain point, details around the rim tend to flow into the rim, while other details weaken. The surface of the die becomes scarred, as though it was very heavily polished. Worn die errors rarely have collector value.

Planchet errors

Alloy errors: All U.S. coins are produced from alloyed metals, mixed when molten to strict specifications. If mixed incorrectly, the metals may cool in non-homogeneous form, with streaks of different metals appearing on the surface of the coin.

Damaged planchets: Planchets are subject to various sorts of damage, including cracks (not to be confused with die cracks), holes and major breaks.

Fragments, scrap struck: Small pieces of coinage metal — fragments and scrap left over from the blanking process — sometimes fall between the dies and are struck. Fragments must be struck on both sides and weigh less than 25 percent of a normal coin's weight to qualify as a struck fragment. Planchet scrap is generally larger than a fragment, and usually has straight or curved edges as a result of the blanking process.

Incomplete planchets: Often, though erroneously, called a "clip," an incomplete planchet results from a mishap in the blanking process. If the planchet strip does not advance far enough after a bank of punches rams through the metal, producing planchets, the punches come down and overlap the holes where the planchets were already punched out. Where the overlapping takes place, there is a curved area that appears to be "missing" from the planchet. The word "clip," commonly used, suggests a piece of the planchet was cut off, which is not the cause. "Clip," when properly used, refers to the ancient process of cutting small pieces of metal from the edges of precious metals coins for the bullion; that is why U.S. gold and silver coins have lettered or reeded edges, to make it more difficult to clip a coin.

An "incomplete clip" occurs when the punch does not completely punch a planchet out, but leaves a circular groove. If the strip advances improperly, planchets overlapping the incomplete punch will bear a curved groove; the groove remains visible after the coin is struck.

Most incomplete planchet errors have a "signature" known as the Blakesley effect. The area of the rim 180 degrees opposite the "clip" is weak or non-existent since the rim-making process in the upset mill is negated by the "clip." The lack of pressure in the upset mill at the clip results in improper formation of the rim on the opposite side (see Chapter 9, "How U.S. coins are made").

Laminations: During the preparation of the planchet strip, foreign materials — grease, dirt, oil, slag or gas — may become trapped just below the surface of the metal. Coins struck from this strip later may begin to flake and peel since adhesion is poor in the location of the trapped material. The Jefferson, Wartime 5-cent pieces are particularly susceptible to lamination, due to the metals used during war metal emergency.

Split planchets: Planchets can split due to deep internal laminations, or in the case of clad coinage, because of poor adhesion of the copper-nickel outer layers to the copper core. Planchets may split before or after striking. Those splitting before generally exhibit weak details due to lack of metal to fill the dies, while those split afterwards usually depict full detailing. On non-clad coins, the inner portion of the split shows parallel striations typical of the interior structure of coinage metal.

Thick and thin planchets: Planchets of the wrong thickness are produced from strip that was not rolled properly. Too little pressure can result in planchet stock that is too thick; too much can result in a thin planchet. If the rollers are out of alignment on one side, a tapered planchet — one that is thicker on one side than the other — is created.

Unplated planchets: New in U.S. coinage, unplated planchets became possible in 1982 with the introduction of the copper-plated zinc cent. The zinc-copper alloy planchets are plated after they are punched from the strip, but some planchets miss the plating process. Coins struck on the unplated planchets are grayish-white in color. Beware of cents which have had their plating removed after leaving the Mint.

Wrong metal, planchet, stock: There are several major types of errors in this series. A wrong metal error is a coin struck on a planchet intended for a different denomination of a different composition. This includes 5-cent pieces struck on cent planchets, cents struck on dime planchets, and higher denominations struck on cent and 5-cent planchets.

A second type is the wrong planchet error, defined as a coin struck on a planchet of the correct composition, but the wrong denomination. These include quarter dollars struck on dime planchets, half dollars struck on quarter and dime planchets, and dollars struck on other clad planchets.

A third type is the wrong planchet stock error. It occurs when clad coinage strip rolled to the thickness of one denomination is fed into the blanking press of another denomination; the diameter is correct, but the thickness is greater or less than normal. The most common appears to be quarter dollars struck on planchet stock intended for dimes.

A fourth, rarer form is the double denomination. It occurs when a coin is struck on a previously struck coin, such as a cent struck over a dime. Since the U.S. Mint strikes coins for foreign governments, it is possible to find in circulation U.S. coins struck on planchets intended for foreign coins, as well as coins struck on previously struck foreign coins.

Another rare type of wrong metal error is the transitional error. It occurs as the composition of a coin changes. Some 1965 coins are known struck on silver planchets of 1964 composition, while some 1964 coins were struck on clad planchets (1964 coins were struck through 1965, with planchets for both types of coins available side by side).

One fact true for all errors of this broad category is that the planchets must be of an equal size or smaller than the intended planchet. A 5-cent planchet, for example, would not fit between the dies of the smaller cent.

Striking errors

Broadstrikes: If the surrounding collar is pushed below the surface of the lower die during the moment of striking, the metal of the coin being struck is free to expand beyond the confines of the die. The design of the coin is normal at center, but as it nears the periphery, becomes distorted due to the uncontrolled spread of metal.

Brockage and capped die strikes: If a newly struck coin sticks to the surface of one of the dies, it acts as a die itself — called a die cap — and produces images on succeeding coins. The image produced by any die is the direct opposite on a coin, and brockages are no different. Since the image is raised on the coin adhering to the die, the image on the brockage is incused and reversed — a true mirror image. The first brockage strikes, perfect mirror images and undistorted, are most prized. As additional coins are struck from the capped die, the die cap begins to spread and thin under the pressures of striking, distorting its image. At some point, as the die cap becomes more distorted, the coins struck cease to be brockages and are known as capped die strikes. While a brockage image is undistorted or relatively so, images on capped die strikes are increasingly malformed. Although the image is still recognizable, the design expands, producing an image that can be several times the actual size of a normal image. Finally, the die cap breaks off or is pounded so thin it ceases to affect succeeding strikes. Sometimes, the die caps fall off early and in a relatively undistorted state. Die caps resemble bottle caps, with the metal wrapping around the surface of the die. Die caps are very rare and collectible, much more so than capped die strikes.

Double and multiple strikes: Double strikes are coins struck more than once. If the coin rotates slightly between strikes, but remains inside the collar, two images will appear on both sides of the coin. The first strike will be almost totally obliterated by the second strike, and the first strike will be flattened and have almost no relief. Sometimes, a struck coin will flip — somewhat like a pancake on a hot griddle — and fall upside down onto the surface of the die; thus, the second strike has an obverse image obliterating the original reverse, and a reverse image flattening the first obverse image. If the coin falls partially outside the dies after the first strike, the second image is only partial. The partial second strike obliterates the original image beneath it, but the rest of the first strike is undistorted, except in the immediate vicinity of the second strike. A saddle strike is generally not a true double strike, but usually the result of having a planchet fall partially between two pairs of dies on a multi-die press. Saddle strikes have two partial images, and an expanse of unstruck planchet between the struck areas.

What happens twice can happen three times or more, though rarely. However, examples of coins struck three or four times are known.

Indented errors: An indented error is a coin struck with another coin or planchet lying partially on its surface. The area covered by the planchet does not come into contact with the die, and thus is blank if indented by a planchet, or shows a partial brockage if indented by a struck coin. The most desirable of the indented errors are larger coins with the indentation of a smaller planchet centered on one side.

Machine, strike doubling: A form of doubling, this is probably the most common type of Mint error and is considered non-collectible by a majority of hobbyists. Some noted authorities do not consider it an error, but believe it to be a form of Mint-caused damage since it occurs immediately *after* the strike. The most common cause is a certain looseness of the die or other parts in the press which causes the die to bounce across the surface of the newly struck coin. In bouncing, the die shoves the metal of the raised designs to one side, creating the doubled image. On coins with raised designs, the doubling is flat, like a shelf.

Off-center coins: If a planchet lies partially outside of the dies during the striking, it re-ceives an off-center strike. Each coin struck off center is unique, but due to the large numbers available, are very inexpensive in the lower denominations. Off-center coins with dates are more valuable than coins without dates. Generally, on dated coins, the greater the off-center strike, the more it is worth. Some collectors collect off-center coins by their "clock" positions. Hold the coin with portrait upright and look for the direction the strike lies. If it is at 90 degrees, the strike is at 3 o'clock; if it lies at 270 degrees, the strike is at 9 o'clock.

Partial collar: Often known as "railroad rim" errors, the edge, not the rim, is the portion of the coin affected. It occurs when the collar is pushed somewhat below the surface of the lower die, so that the upper portion of the coin is free to expand beyond the confines of the collar, while the lower portion is restrained. On coins struck from a reeded collar, partial reeding exists on the area restrained by the collar. The error gets the nickname railroad rim from its appearance — the coin, viewed edge-on, resembles the wheel from a railroad car.

Struck-through errors: Filled-die errors and indented coins are related to struck-through errors, which occur when foreign objects fall between die and planchet during striking. In addition to the grease of a filled-die error and the planchet of an indented error, pieces of cloth, metal fragments, wire, slivers of reeding, wire bristles (from wire brushes used to clean dies, resembling staples), die covers and other objects. Sometimes, an incused letter or number of a die will fill up with grease, which solidifies under constant pressure. If the blob of grease — shaped like a letter or number — drops out of the die, it may be struck into the surface of the coin, leaving the impression of the affected letter or number. The most collectible struck-through errors are those with the foreign object still embedded into the surface of the coin.

Uniface errors: If two planchets fall between the same dies at the same time, one side of each will be prevented from coming into contact with the dies. One side of each will have a normal image, while the other side — facing the other planchet — will be blank. Uniface errors can also occur on indented coins.

Weak strikes: Weak strikes often resemble coins struck from grease-filled dies, but can be identified. They occur either when the press has been turned off — it tends to cycle through several strikings, each with less pressure than the previous — or when the press is being set up by the operators who test the placement of the dies at lower coining pressures. On reeded coins, weak strikes generally have poorly formed reeding (it is strong on filled dies). Depending on the pressure used, the image may be only slightly weak, or practically non-existent, or any stage in between.

Altered and damaged coins

A coin is subjected to a variety of abuses once it leaves the safety of the U.S. Mint. It can receive unintentional damage during normal use that alters the appearance of the coin. Intentional alteration can change the appearance even more drastically, whether the coin was altered by someone just experimenting or by someone who deliberately planned to change the appearance of a coin to deceive a collector or buyer.

To the informed, damaged and altered coins do not resemble Mint errors. The minting process leaves definite signatures on the surfaces of a coin that cannot be duplicated inadvertently in circulation or in the workshop of the coin alterer. The uninformed, however, often mistake damaged or altered coins for Mint errors. Those persons often have mistaken ideas about the values of error coins, believing all errors to worth a great deal. When told that the altered coins are worth face values only, many non-collectors may become discouraged and decide not to continue in the hobby.

Altered and damaged coins have no numismatic value.

A good place to begin to learn about the minting process is to read the section titled "How U.S. coins are made" in Chapter 9 of the *Coin World Almanac*. There are also several books about error coins available from coin dealers and book stores (see Chapter 21 about numismatic books). Most have sections about the production of U.S. coins, and how to distinguish between errors and altered or damaged coins. Joining an error coin club is a good idea as well (see Chapter 20).

Education is important. The following descriptions are of damaged and altered coins most likely to cause confusion for the non-specialist in error coins.

Acid-treated coins: Coins which have been soaked in an acid solution or have had acid poured over them are thinner than unaltered coins. The thinness of the acid-treated coin depends on the strength of the acid and the duration of the treatment. Some will be so thin the edge will be sharp and knife-like. The acid-treated coin will still have visible design elements, although the designs will be somewhat weakened (the longer the treatment, the weaker the design). Coins which have had acid poured over them may exhibit channels were the acid flowed. If more acid flows over one area, it may be thinner than another area which had less contact with the acid.

Added Mint mark: A coin with an added Mint mark is a form of alteration made deliberately to defraud a buyer. The most common form of added Mint mark is one that has been cut from a common coin and added to the Philadelphia version of a rarer coin. Close examination of this kind of added Mint mark will show a sharp line between the field and the Mint mark; metal flow lines found ascending from the field onto the Mint mark on an unaltered coin are not present on this form of alteration.

Another form of added Mint mark was discovered in recent years. The person altering the coin drills a small hole from the edge of a coin to the point where the Mint mark would be found if it had one. Then, a specially made tool with a small, Mint mark-shaped form, is inserted into the hole. Pressure is applied to the Mint mark form from the inside, forcing the surface of the metal to raise in the shape of the Mint mark. Flow lines may be found on this type of alteration. To detect, examine the edge below the Mint mark carefully for any signs of damage left by drilling the hole.

A crude form of added Mint mark is forming by cutting the shape of the Mint mark directly into the surface of the coin. The knife marks are generally clear. Few added Mint marks of this type can pass muster.

Glue: The application of a thin layer of transparent glue to the surface of a coin can cause a very deceptive appearance. The design is visible through the glue, and the hardened glue often resembles raised metal. Sometimes, the person altering the coin will press another coin into the wet glue, and let it dry. Once dry, the coins are pried apart and the glue remaining on one coin will have incused, mirror-image details from the other coin. One U.S. cent seen by *Coin World's* Collectors' Clearinghouse department personnel had dried glue with the incused image of a Canadian cent embedded on the coin. Most glues can be dissolved with clear acetone, an ingredient used in fingernail polish removers. The acetone can then be rinsed off of the coin.

Hammered edge: Often, coins will be found with a diameter slightly smaller than normal and a high, thick rim. This is done by placing the coin on its edge and hammering away at it. Sometimes, on larger coins, the edge can be hammered flat and the center of the coin cut away, providing the alterer with an inexpensive ring after all the rough edges are polished away. On coins with reeded edges, the reeding is often beaten smooth.

Lucky piece coin: Most persons have seen lucky piece coins, generally cents, which are embedded in a surrounding aluminum holder which has advertising or other writing on it. Force is required to squeeze the coin into the hole in the middle of the holder. Generally, the edge is distorted and made somewhat concave; if removed from the holder, the odd appearance of the edge can fool the untrained eye. The legends on the holder are generally stamped into the metal at the same time that the coin is forced into the hole. If the stamping dies overlap the coin, some of the legend can be stamped onto the coin. Again, if removed from the holder, the raised lettering can appear to be an original portion of the design.

1943 bronze cents: America's entry into World War II brought about sacrifice from every quarter, including the United States Mint. Copper became a critical war supply and little could be spared for cent coinage. Extensive testing in 1942 resulted in a zinc-plated steel cent that was used in 1943 only. About a dozen known bronze 1943 cents were struck in error, on planchets remaining from 1942 coinage. Thousands of collectors believe they own one of the dozen pieces, however. Many thousands of steel cents were plated with copper. They can easily be distinguished from genuine 1943 bronze cents by use of a magnet. A magnet will pick up a steel cent, but not a genuine bronze cent. Lack of magnetic properties does not mean the coin is genuine, however. Compare the 3 in the date of a genuine 1943 steel cent to the 3 on a suspected 1943 bronze cent. If the tail of the 3 does not extend the same distance, the coin is probably an altered 1948 cent (the alterer cuts away the left half of the 8). Struck-counterfeit 1943 bronze cents exist as well, so any coins passing all of the above tests should be sent to one of the several authentication services for professional evaluation.

Sandwich coin: Two or more coins are placed in a stack between the jaws of a bench vise. Pressure is applied, squeezing the coins together. Design elements will transfer from one coin to the other, creating a false double-struck coin. Unlike a genuine double strike, however, the additional image will be incused and reversed. Most sandwich coins will be distorted as a result of the pressure applied by the vise. Sandwich coins can also be produced by striking the stack of coins with a hammer. (The term sandwich coin was also used in the mid-1960s to describe the then new clad coinage.)

Slanted digits: Certain coins, in particular the Lincoln cent, can be damaged by parts in an automatic wrapping machine in such a way that the date resembles an overdate error. Feed fingers in the wrapping machine scrape across the surface of the cent, shoving the metal in the last digit to one side. A slight image of the last digit remains, with the displaced metal sitting above. On some specimens, the displaced metal may resemble the numeral 1 sitting over the ghost of another numeral.

Texas coins: Coins with diameters slightly greater than normal and with proportionally larger designs cannot be struck under the conditions in effect at the U.S. Mint. Nicknamed a Texas coin (for large), the altered pieces are produced by placing the coin between two pieces of leather and striking them with a hammer. The leather somehow causes the entire design to expand, not just the diameter. Some distortion is usually present, although it may be slight.

Wood-blocked cent: Coins which have strongly flattened features, plus peripheral lettering and numbers that extend into a flattened rim, have probably been placed between two blocks of wood and struck with a hammer.

Paper money errors

The production processes necessary to produce U.S. paper money, like the minting sequence, are subject to various forms of failure that can lead to error notes. The similarities do not end there. An understanding of the paper money production processes is essential for any serious collector of paper money errors (see Chapter 8). The ink on U.S. paper money can be altered after the notes enter circulation, both accidently and deliberately; some forms of alteration may resemble errors. Other forms of alteration are possible, too.

The causes of paper money errors will be discussed in the next section, to be followed by a discussion of the most commonly seen forms of altered and damaged notes. The error note section is presented in three sections: first and second printing errors, overprinting errors, and fold and cutting errors.

The basic production sequence is the first, or back printing, followed by the second, or face printing. Initial trimming and cutting comes next, followed by the application of the overprinting and additional trimming steps.

First and second printing errors

Blanket impression: Called "offset printing" by hobbyists, and blanket impression by BEP personnel, this is probably the most common type of printing error. A blanket impression is a mirror-image ink impression on the wrong side of the note; a reversed image of the face design will appear on the back, and a reversed image of the back design will appear on the face. Although it may appear that the wayward ink has "bled" through the paper, blanket impressions occur during one of the printing processes. Basically, sheets of currency paper pass between two huge rotating cylinders, one containing inked printing plates and the second a flexible surface that forces the paper into the ink-filled intaglio lines of the plates. If the paper is torn or folded, a portion of the inked printing plates may come into direct contact with the impression cylinder. The impression cylinder picks up ink from the plate cylinder and deposits it on next dozen or so sheets, on the side opposite the side being printed. The image is reversed because the ink lying on the surface of the impression cylinder is normally oriented (the printing plates have a mirror image). Blanket impressions may affect one entire side, or just a small portion of the design. Overprinting blanket impressions are known, but are much rarer than first and second printing blanket impressions. The cause is the same. The use of the term "blanket impression" is technically more accurate than "offset printing"; offset is a printing method, the kind used to produce this edition of the *Coin World Almanac*, and different from intaglio printing.

Board breaks: A board break occurs when a depression is created in the surface of the impression cylinder. The paper opposite the depression is not forced into the ink-filled intaglio lines of the printing plate, and therefore there is an unprinted area on an otherwise normal note. Board breaks generally affect small areas, although larger breaks are known.

Double denominations: Considered the ultimate in error notes, a double denomination note has face and back printings for two different denominations, like a $5 face and a $10 back. The back printing, since it is first, is the correct denomination. The error occurs when the uniface sheet is fed into the wrong press for the face printing, picking up a different denomination than from that of the back. All such notes are rare and are very collectible.

Double printings: Double printings can occur if a sheet of currency paper is inadvertently fed through through an intaglio printing press twice. The entire image may be doubled. If the press stops in the middle of a printing pass and the partially printed sheet is deliberately fed into the press again to restart it, a doubled image can also occur. In the case of the latter cause, the note may have one complete printing and a partial second printing. A rarer form is for the second image to be upside down relative to the first image. Both face and back can have a doubled printing. Plate check numbers are rarely the same.

Incomplete printing: Any portion or all of the back or face printings may be missing from a note. If two sheets ride through a press stuck together, one sheet does not come into contact with the printing plates. This can occur during the second printing step, which means the note will have a back printing (done first), but no face printing; or, can occur during the back printing, which means the note will have no back image, but will have a face printing. Those with no face printing are visually more spectacular, since the black and green overprinting is applied over a white, blank face. Improperly or incompletely inked plates can also cause an incomplete printing, with only a portion of the design usually missing. Folded or torn sheets, or scrap paper falling between a portion of the sheet and the printing plate can also cause partial or complete failure to print note surfaces. If an uninked plate comes in contact with the paper, an impression of the uninked design can be seen.

Ink smears: Called "sly wipes" by BEP personnel, ink smears occur when the surface of the inked printing plate is not properly wiped before printing to remove excess ink from the surface of the plate. Older presses were wiped by an automatically-fed roll of coarse paper, while the modern presses now in use at the Bureau use a "water-wipe" system which sprays a solution of water and caustic soda over the plate to wash away excess ink. On the note, an ink smear is just that — a smear of ink, black (on the face) or green (on the back), obscuring a portion of the design of the note. The smear occurs at the same instant the note is printed, and is not applied afterward. Beware of ink applied to the surface of a note after it reaches circulation.

Inverted printings: Occurs when a sheet with a back printing is rotated 180 degrees and fed into a press for the second printing. The face is upside down in relation to the back. Often incorrectly called an "inverted reverse," "inverted face" is the technically-correct term.

Off-register printing: Occurs when a currency sheet is fed into the press improperly aligned for one pass. The ink is deposited out of register in relation to the printing on the opposite side. Later, when cut into an individual note, the cuts may be made through the unaligned image so that one side of the note looks off center. Notes with the face off-registered generally have the overprinting in the correct location for the note, but not for the face image.

Printed through foreign matter: One of the causes of an incomplete printing, the foreign matter, generally a scrap of paper, sometimes sticks to the surface of the finished note. The note may appear normal to a casual viewer, but the shape of the scrap material should be visible. If the scrap is *gently* lifted, an unprinted area the same size and shape as the foreign matter will appear on the note. Notes with the foreign matter remaining attached are more collectible than notes on which the scrap is missing, leaving only the incomplete printing.

Overprinting errors

Double overprints: These occur much in the same way that a doubled first and second printing error occurs. The half sheet of currency paper is fed through the Currency Overprinting and Processing Equipment twice, picking up one complete overprint and a second partial or complete overprint.

Ink smears: The result of excess ink on the overprint wheels or the smudging of fresh overprint ink. Smears can be black or green, depending upon what stage of the overprinting is affected.

Inverted overprints: When a half sheet of currency paper is rotated 180 degrees before being fed into the COPE press, the overprint is applied upside down on the face. A major epidemic of inverted overprints occurred in 1976 and 1977, resulting in hundreds of such notes being released. So many were released that it was possible to collect a complete, 12-note Federal Reserve District set of $1 inverts of the same series date.

Misaligned overprint: Half sheets must be properly aligned for the overprinting to be perfectly located. If a half sheet is fed into the COPE press off center, the overprint will be misaligned in one or more directions. A small degree of latitude is permitted before a misaligned overprint error becomes collectible; generally, the overprint needs to be touching a portion of the second printing design to be collectible. Not to be confused with off-register notes, which appear similar but are the result of an error during the first or second printing steps.

Mismatched serial numbers, letters: Several mishaps can cause the prefix or suffix letters or numbers in the serial numbers on an individual note to be mismatched. The five digits on the far right of the serial number wheels decrease automatically (serial numbers are printed from the highest number to the lowest), but the three digits at the left and the prefix and suffix letters must be changed manually. A digit in the automatically turning wheels can stick in one position, or the person resetting the manual numbers or letters, or the automatic numerals at the beginning of a press run, can make a mistake and set the wrong digit. Any number or letter can be mismatched, and a simple comparison of the left serial number and right serial number will reveal the mismatched digit.

Missing and incomplete overprints: Missing and incomplete overprints may occur when scrap falls between the overprint wheels and the currency half sheet, or due to a fold or tear in the paper. Since the green overprint is applied before the black overprint (only seconds apart), one color can be normal and the other missing or incomplete. This can happen if the mishap occurs before the second overprinting step.

Overprint on back: If a currency half sheet is turned end over end, so the back faces the overprinting wheels, the overprint is applied on the back. Because the overprint is missing from the face, the blank areas of the face printing remain unprinted.

Partially turned digit: If one of the digits in the serial number wheel fails to decrease properly, a partial digit may appear on the overprint. Sometimes, the digit sticks in the partially-turned position and a series of notes are overprinted with the partial digit.

Same serial numbers: If all the digits in a serial number wheel fail to decrease, a series of notes bearing the same serial number may be printed. To be collectible, at least two notes with the identical serial numbers must be saved. The notes must be from the same series date, have indentical prefix and suffix letters, and must be the same denomination.

Scrap through overprint: Like the scrap paper or other foreign matter that remains attached to a note, affecting the first or second printings, notes with the overprint on a piece of scrap that remains attached are more collectible than those where the scrap has fallen off. A unique note of this type had the overprint printed through a Band-Aid brand bandage backing which remained attached to the note.

Wrong stock note: If a sheet of currency of one denomination with both first and second printings is mixed in with sheets of another denomination, the overprint for the wrong denomination is applied to the wayward sheet. Since the location of the overprint differs for each denomination, it may appear to be misaligned on the note. Collectible only if the immediately preceding and succeeding notes of the different denomination are saved. Otherwise, the note is visually indistinguishable from a misaligned overprint note in appearance.

Fold and cutting errors

Fold and cutting errors cannot be as neatly categorized as the two other major types of paper money errors, since each fold and cutting error is unique. The large sheets of paper used to print U.S. paper money notes are prone to folding at any time during the production process: first printing, second printing, trimming or overprinting.

Small folds extending vertically from note edge to edge are called gutter folds. They can affect the back, face, or both sides, depending on when the fold took place. Folds at the corners can obscure a portion of the design of either side, or the overprint; when unfolded, a portion of one side may appear on the other side. Major folds can drastically alter the appearance of the note, leaving huge unprinted areas and areas where a portion of one side is printed over the other side, or where a portion of the overprint is placed on the back.

If the fold remains closed during the several cutting and trimming stages, then extraneous paper may exist along one or several edges. Some fold and cutting errors are so large that when unfolded, a portion of another note above, below or beside the main note remains attached.

Values of fold and cutting errors depend on the size of the fold, the complexity of the fold, appearance, and general numismatic factors, including supply and demand, and condition.

Altered and damaged notes

Paper and ink are much more fragile media than brass, copper-nickel and zinc-copper, alloys found in pocket change today, and thus exhibit different types of damage. Notes are also subject to both accidental and deliberate alteration, the latter to either deceive a collector or cashier, or as a lark.

Education about the production processes necessary to make paper money is as important to the paper money collector as knowledge about minting techniques is to the coin collector. There are several general books available about paper money which cover the production of paper money, and the section in Chapter 8 of this edition of the *Coin World Almanac* briefly discusses the production process. Membership in syngraphic organizations is encouraged as well.

The following descriptions are of altered and damaged notes most likely to deceive the unknowing person.

Added ink smears: Smeared ink other than the black and two greens used on modern U.S. paper money was almost certainly added after the note left the BEP; some green and blacks could also have been added. There is no easy method to distinguish between an ink smear that was placed on the note at the BEP and ink added afterward if there is no obvious color difference. This is where experience and knowledge play a hand.

Altered denomination: Persons altering the denomination of a note prey on the public's ignorance about whose portrait appears on paper money, and the fact — shown by government studies — that a majority of persons never examine notes passing through their hands to determine whether they are authentic. The most common method of altering the denomination is to cut several corners bearing the denomination from several notes, and glue four corners to a note of a lower denomination. Some alterers cut the denominational legend from the bottom of a note and glue that in place over the lower denomination. This is not a numismatic type of alteration, but is used to deceive persons handling large quantities of money.

Bank teller stamps: Tellers in banks and other persons who handle large sums of money often stamp the band surrounding a stack with an inked seal of some sort. The stamp often has a date or other numbers on it. If the stamp is placed over the edge of the band onto the top note, untrained persons may believe the ink appearing on the note is a part of the original printing.

Erased ink: The ink used in printing U.S. paper money is erasable like any other ink on paper. Note alterers can use a soft eraser or an electric eraser to remove any portion of the face or back design, or the overprint. Erasers wielded skillfully can recreate missing overprints, board breaks, notes printed through scrap and related printing errors. However, use of an eraser generally damages the fibers of the paper beneath the erased ink. Close examination, particularly through a magnifying glass or microscope, may reveal the broken fibers.

Fake double denomination: The ability to recreate the ultimate in errors offers a note alterer potentially high profits. A *Coin World* staff member once saw a purported large-sized double denomination error that appeared to have been faked. Someone took two notes and "peeled" away one side of each. The two notes were then joined together to create the double denomination fake. The note was in Poor condition, and the joint between the halves was visible along the edges, which were in a flaked condition.

Political messages: Paper money is an excellent medium to spread political messages among the public. The most popular message seems to be a rubber stamp inked onto a note, reading "This note is not legal tender." This stamp is probably used by individuals who believe paper money unbacked by gold or silver is illegal, and who advocate a return to specie currency. Other political messages have been seen as well.

VIP photographs: Novelty notes with the photograph of a Hollywood celebrity, entertainer, politician or other "newsworthy" person pasted over the center vignette are sold by a number of firms. The BEP has never issued a note bearing a portrait of King Kong, or even Elvis Presley.

Water-wipe ink fading: The BEP began using water-wipe presses — using a caustic soda solution to clean excess ink from the plates instead of dry paper — in the early 1980s. To do so, the Bureau reformulated the ink to not break down under the solution. The formula was created, but BEP officials found that after the notes reached circulation, the ink on the back faded very quickly, particularly if the note became wet. It was necessary to again reformulate the ink, and the problem appears to have been corrected.

Wrong-color backs: The green ink on the back of U.S. paper money is made of blue and yellow pigments. When exposed to an acidic atmosphere the yellow pigment is sometimes destroyed, leaving only the blue. When exposed to an alkali, such as the bleach in detergent when a note is washed, the blue pigment may be destroyed, leaving the yellow pigment. Blue back and yellow back notes deceive many non-collectors who find it difficult to believe that one of the pigments can disappear and leave the design and paper unaffected. The back design remains the same, but is in either blue or yellow ink. The yellow back notes should not be confused with gold certificates, which normally have a yellow-gold back.

Collectors' Clearinghouse

One of the longest running regular features of *Coin World* is its weekly Collectors' Clearinghouse page, devoted mainly to reports of newly discovered error and variety coinage. The Collectors' Clearinghouse department was founded in 1960, shortly after publication of *Coin World* began. Its first editor, James G. Johnson, served in that capacity for nearly 15 years.

The Collectors' Clearinghouse staff through the years has answered tens of thousands of letters regarding error coins and paper money, varieties, normal coins and notes, and exonumia. Some of the more interesting finds are illustrated and discussed in the weekly full-page column, which, with the letters to the editor column and U.S. coin "Trends," represents one of the most popular features of the newspaper.

Readers may send coins and notes to the Collectors' Clearinghouse for examination and an explanation, whether errors or not. Collectors are asked not to send more than three or four items per letter unless given specific permission to send larger packages of material. If the reader wishes to have his material returned by insured or registered mail, he should send sufficient return postage. Readers not sending material and requesting information only are asked to include a large, self-addressed, stamped envelope. All inquiries should be addressed to Collectors' Clearinghouse, *Coin World*, P.O. Box 150, Sidney, Ohio 45365.

Counterfeit coins

Counterfeit coins exist. That simple truth may be as frightening to a professional numismatist as to a neophyte collector, for any counterfeit coin is potentially deceptive. A hobbyist's best defense against counterfeit coins is knowledge — about the coining process and about counterfeits. It helps also to have a dealer who is both trustworthy and knowledgeable about counterfeit coins.

There are two basic types of counterfeit coins. One was produced to deceive the public by passing in circulation as genuine. Counterfeits of this type have plagued coiners since the first coins were produced. The second category of counterfeit is the type meant as a fraudulent numismatic item, designed to deceive the unwary collector, dealer or numismatist for illicit monetary gain.

The best way to learn about counterfeit coins is to examine them and compare the frauds to genuine coins of the same type and date in order to learn about the characteristics of both. Since possession of counterfeit coins is illegal in the United States, few collectors have opportunities to examine the fakes. However, the American Numismatic Association sponsors an annual week-long course in counterfeit detection at its Summer Seminar, held in Colorado Springs, Colo. The ANA Certification Service maintains a counterfeit coin reference collection which federal officials have generally ignored, since the fakes are used as an educational tool. Students attending the course (which is taught in beginning and advance levels) have the opportunity to examine counterfeit coins (and their first cousins, altered coins) through microscopes. Genuine coins are used for comparison purposes. The cost of the course is cheap when compared to the cost of a counterfeit coin. Details about future Summer Seminars are available by writing to the ANA at 818 N. Cascade Ave., Colorado Springs, Colo. 80903. The ANA also sells several books about counterfeit coins, compiled from

illustrated articles written by the ANACS staff.

If you are uncertain about the authenticity of any numismatic item, do not buy it. If the dealer refuses to send the coin to an authentication service such as ANACS or the International Numismatic Society Authentication Bureau, be wary of buying the coin. Most reputable dealers will have no problems with sending a coin to ANACS for authentication. You may, however, have to pay the authentication fee; such an "insurance policy" is well worth the nominal cost, especially for a coin valued at hundreds or even thousands of dollars.

Some counterfeits are very deceptive. During the last 10 years, for example, a fairly rare coin was sold in several auctions by reputable companies and purchased by knowledgeable dealers and collectors. The coin turned out to be a counterfeit of such exceptional quality that many persons were fooled. As is standard in such practices, the money paid for the coin was refunded down the line, with each company and individual returning the money that had been paid for the coin.

The following information focuses on the numismatic counterfeit. No one article can teach everything there is to know about counterfeit coins, especially when unaccompanied by photographs. However, the information in this article provides the collector with some basic knowledge.

Replicas

The replica is a form of counterfeit generally not intentionally deceptive, but potentially so. Most replicas are not illegal, although the passage of the Hobby Protection Act of 1973 regulates modern replicas in the United States.

A replica is generally a cast duplicate of an obsolete coin, token or medal that originally had been produced by private individuals or companies. Replicas are intended as inexpensive souvenirs; rarely is the original intention deceptive in nature. Almost every Colonial and state coin or token illustrated in the front section of *A Guide Book of United States Coins* has been produced in replica form, legally. Some even have the word "copy" — which is now required by the Hobby Protection Act — "replica" or some abbreviation of either word stamped into or cast onto the coin, often on the edge. The problem arises when "copy" or "replica" is filed from the surface of a replica.

Some points to look for:

Most replicas are cast, so there is probably a thin line of metal along the center of the edge. The thin line is left by the joint between the two molds in which the molten metal is poured into during the casting process. The joint line, however, can be filed away.

The casting process usually leaves a rough, textured or porous surface.

Cast counterfeits are produced by the same methods and have the same characteristics as cast replicas. However, the cast counterfeits are produced to deceive a buyer into thinking he is purchasing a genuine numismatic item.

Electrotypes

An electrotype is a type of counterfeit so popular in the 19th century that even employees of the United States Mint produced them for sale to willing collectors who knew what they were buying. An electrotype is an inexpensive copy of what is generally a rare, expensive coin unavailable to most collectors.

Electrotypes are two thin shells of metal bearing the image of a particular coin, wrapped around a non-precious metal planchet for inner strength. The shells are made by an electroplating process, in which a wax or plaster cast of the original coin is suspended in a solution of acidic copper sulphate along with a copper anode. A weak electric current is passed through the solution, causing small copper particles from the anode to adhere to the graphite-coated cast until a thin copper shell bearing the cast's image is formed.

An electrotype can be identified fairly easily by examining the edge for signs of where the two shells were joined or by weighing the item.

Electrotypes are considered collectible by many, particularly those produced by the U.S. Mint employees in the mid-19th century. However, production of new electrotypes is frowned upon by modern collectors and dealers. *Coin World* will not accept advertising for electrotypes.

Die-struck counterfeits

There are a number of advantages to a counterfeiter in employing fake dies. The most obvious, of course, is that counterfeit dies allow an almost exact duplication of Mint production methods, making their detection more difficult.

Also the use of counterfeit dies allows the counterfeiter a much greater latitude in his efforts. Not only can he reproduce a greater number of identical coins, he can also duplicate the rarer coins without actually being in possession of one. He can create mules at will. And error coins such as off-center strikes, rotated reverses, multiple strikes, clipped planchets, thick and thin planchets, railroad rims or partial collars and many others can be created by duplicating the very Mint procedures, or Mint equipment malfunctions, that would cause those errors inside the Mint itself.

Though the physical characteristics, and even the edges, will often faithfully reproduce the characteristics of a genuine coin, the design details and field will often reveal the origin. Logically, then, in order to detect this type of counterfeit, you must know, at the very least, the rudiments of making the fake dies.

Machine-engraved dies are often made by use of machines similar, if not identical, to the Contamin portrait lathes and the Janvier reducing machines used in most Mints.

A tracing tool follows the contours of the coin as the coin rotates about its axis. The tracing tool, through linkages, duplicates the movements of the tracing point with a cutting tool on a soft steel blank. As long as the rotation of the coin and blank remain constant — this being a one-to-one transfer step — the design being reproduced will be identical to the original. However, should the relationship change, the design details will be different. They may be wider or narrower than the original.

After the reproduction is finished the field will consist of circular rings left by the cutting tool. The counterfeiter must polish out those rings, leading to the possibility of also removing parts of the design. On the other hand, if he doesn't do the job well enough, some of those marks may still remain on the die. So, if you spot a coin that has more or less concentric rings on its surface, you would be justified in thinking that it is a product of machine-engraved dies.

Dies can also be made by impacting the coin into a soft steel blank by use of an explosive charge, a heavy press, or any other means that will impart a sudden, tremendous pressure. Impact dies can have many obvious imperfections. Large coins do not impact evenly across their surface. The impact tends to spread the coin, especially silver and copper coins which are relatively soft. This spreading results in design details that are broader than normal and, quite often, slightly doubled near the edges. Attempts to touch up the dies can be made but careful inspection will usually reveal, not only the remaining defects, but the attempt to correct those defects. Quite often the first clue to an impact die is the fact that the design details are sharper near the center than at the edges.

Students of U.S. coinage have studied the rarer coins extensively. For example, specialists have identified the dies used to strike the 1909-S Lincoln, VDB cent, a classic scarce coin. By carefully examining thousands of coins, specialists know the proper shape of the "S" Mint mark and the letter "B" in the VDB intitials. Die gouges and scratches appearing on most examples of certain rare coins have been documented and cataloged. The ANA Summer Seminar courses in counterfeit detection include discussions of these die "signatures" for many rare and scarce numismatic items. One *Coin World* staff member who attended such a course finds his notes invaluable. The ANA, as noted, sells two books which include dozens of articles and hundreds of photographs of die characteristics of genuine and counterfeit coins.

Altered coins

An altered coin is a genuine coin which has had some element changed so that it resembles a rare and thus more expensive variety.

The methods of alteration are many. Thousands of 1943 Lincoln cents, produced on a steel planchet to conserve copper for the war effort, have been plated with copper to resemble the very rare 1943 bronze cent. The third digit on some 1903 Liberty Head 5-cent coins has been changed into a 1 to resemble the 1913 Liberty Head 5-cent coin, a classic rarity. Mint marks have been added to many 1909 Lincoln, VDB cents to resemble the coin's rarer San Francisco counterpart. Mint marks have been removed from many branch Mint 1895 Morgan silver dollars to "create" the scarce Philadelphia Mint version. The list is long.

Some forms of alteration are discussed elsewhere is this chapter.

Like with counterfeit coins, it helps to know about the coin-production process and the characteristics of genuine coins to fight the menace of altered coins. Know what you are buying, or else find a trustworthy and knowledgeable dealer. Otherwise, a "great buy" may turn out to be nothing of the sort.

A Numismatic Chronology

11

A numismatic chronology

The purpose of this chronology is to present in a simple and easy-to-scan form the bare outlines of world numismatics, with special emphasis on the period of history which has seen Christian-dated coins.

Every region of the globe is represented, with a view to presenting those facts that might have seemed noteworthy to the average coin user in a given time and country. The facts presented are of general interest and illustrative of each coin-issuing authority's history.

United States

1782 Resolution by Congress that favors establishment of a Mint. Feb. 21, 1782, Committee submits report, "Resolved, that Congress approve of the establishment of a Mint; and, that the superintendent of Finance, be, and hereby is directed to prepare and report to Congress a plan for establishing and conducting the same."

1785 July 6, "Resolved, that the money unit of the United States of America be one dollar. Resolved, that the smallest coin be a copper, of which 200 shall pass for one dollar."

1786 October, "It is hereby ordained by the United States in Congress assembled, that a Mint be established for the coinage of gold, silver and copper money."

1787 Fugio cents struck, first coins authorized by the United States.

1792 Act of Congress to establish Mint, April 2. Same act authorizes eagle, half eagle, quarter eagle, silver dollar, half dollar, quarter dollar, 10 cents, 5 cents, cent, half cent. David Rittenhouse appointed Director of the Mint. U.S. Mint building erected, first U.S. government structure. Half dimes are first coin struck under Constitution. First metal purchased by Mint for coinage purposes — six pounds of copper.

1793 Cents and half cents struck for first time for general circulation. Albion Cox appointed as first assayer. Joseph Wright named first Mint engraver, Henry Voigt first chief coiner.

1794 Silver dollars, half dollars and half dimes struck for circulation.

1795 Gold half eagles and eagles struck for first time. Mint comes under Department of Treasury instead of Department of State. E PLURIBUS UNUM used on U.S. coins.

1796 Quarter eagles, quarter dollars and dimes struck for first time for circulation.

1804 First U.S. virgin gold received at Mint, valued at $11,000, from Cabarrus County, N.C.

1816 Steam engine installed at Philadelphia Mint.

1817 Proof coins struck at U.S. Mint.

1829 July 4, cornerstone laid for Mint at corner of Chestnut and Juniper streets, Philadelphia.

1835 Act of March 3 establishes Mints in New Orleans, La.; Dahlonega, Ga.; and Charlotte, N.C.

1836 Steam coinage presses introduced in U.S. Mint.

1837 Charlotte, N.C., Mint opened, John H. Wheeler superintendent. Seated Liberty dimes and half dimes issued from Philadelphia.

1838 Branch Mints open in New Orleans and Dahlonega, Ga. U.S. Mint establishes "Cabinet of Coins."

1848 Gold discovered in California; California gold deposited at Mint.

1849 First gold dollars for circulation minted. Gold dollar and double eagle authorized by Act of Congress March 3.

1850 Gold double eagle of this year first to bear initials of designer. First double eagles released for circulation.

1851 Silver 3-cent piece released; first coin with limited legal tender value. Three-cent silver coin of this year lowest silver content of U.S. coin to date — .750 fine. Authorized March 3.

1852 Act of Congress, July 3, establishes San Francisco Mint.

1853 Reduced weight silver coins issued. $3 gold coin authorized Feb. 21. Act of Congress authorizes assay office in New York.

1854 First coins issued by San Francisco Mint. First $3 gold coins minted. Three-cent silver coins, .900 fine, issued. New York Assay Office established at 30-32 Wall St.

1857 Flying Eagle cents issued, first of small diameter cents. It was authorized Feb. 21; 12 percent nickel, issued 1857-1858. Foreign coins demonetized.

1858 American Numismatic Society formed. Numismatic and Antiquarian Society of Philadelphia organized. Proof sets offered.

1859 Longacre's Indian Head cent introduced.

1861 Demand notes, authorized July 17 and Aug. 5. Specie payments suspended Dec. 21.

1862 Government issues legal tender notes beginning March 10. Denver Mint established April 21; superintendent appointed; Mint serves as assay office until 1906, when coins first issued. Postage currency commences July 17.

1863 National bank notes authorized; gold certificates first authorized. First deposit of gold at Denver Mint Sept. 24; George W. Lane first assayer-in-charge until July 1, 1867. Fractional currency authorized March 3. Large private outpouring of tokens to relieve coin shortage.

1864 Motto IN GOD WE TRUST appears on coins for first time, on the 2-cent piece authorized April 22. Cent first of that denomination to bear initials of designer. Bronze cents authorized; private tokens banned.

1865 Copper-nickel 3-cent piece authorized April 3.

1866 Motto IN GOD WE TRUST appears on regular silver coin for first time. Abe Curry first superintendent of Carson City Mint. Shield 5-cent pieces first copper-nickel 5-cent coins, struck May 16.

1867 Carson City Mint erected. Sandstone used from Nevada State Prison quarry. Cost, $300,000.

1869 Carson City Mint opens July 1.

1870 Carson City Mint issues coins. Act of Congress establishes Boise City, Idaho, assay office.

1873 Mint made a bureau of Treasury Department. E PLURIBUS UNUM and IN GOD WE TRUST prescribed for coinage by statute. Director of the Mint located in Washington, D.C. James Pollock first Superintendent of the Mint. Trade dollars issued, authorized Feb. 12. Standard silver dollar discontinued, bimetallism effectively ended.

1874 Assay office in Helena, Mont., approved by Congress May 12. Cornerstone laid Oct. 1.

1875 20-cent coins issued. Authorized March 3. Resumption Act of Jan. 14 provides for immediate retirement of fractional currency with subsidiary silver and redemption of greenbacks on and after Jan. 1, 1879.

1878 Large-size silver certificates authorized Feb. 28.

1879 Specie payments resumed Jan. 1; greenbacks and gold at par.

1882 Assay office opens Jan. 3 at St. Louis.

1887 Trade dollar demonetized.

1888 *The Numismatist* first issued; Dr. George F. Heath editor.

1891 American Numismatic Association organized.

1892 First commemorative coin is Columbian half dollar.

1897 Feb. 19 act provides for assay office in Deadwood, S.D.

1898 April 20: Assay office opened, Deadwood, S.D. Assay Office opened in Seattle, Wash., on July 15; F.A. Wing assayer in charge.

1899 George Washington portrayed for first time on U.S. coin, on Lafayette dollar (with date of 1900).

1900 June 1, enactment of legislation for the mintage of commemorative coins. U.S. goes off bimetallism standard.

1903 Commemorative gold coins, Louisiana Purchase Exposition dollars, struck.

1906 First coins from Denver Mint.

1907 Saint-Gaudens eagles and double eagles first struck.

1908 First minor coinage at a branch Mint.

1909 Portrait of actual person, Lincoln, on first coin for general circulation. First cent to have mottoes IN GOD WE TRUST and E PLURIBUS UNUM.

1912 American Numismatic Association chartered by Congress.

1913 Federal Reserve Act becomes law, authorizes issuance of Federal Reserve notes. Indian Head 5-cent piece minted.

1915 Panama-Pacific coins first commemoratives to carry the mottoes IN GOD WE TRUST and E PLURIBUS UNUM.

1921 Coins and medals under jurisdiction of Commission of Fine Arts. Thomas E. Kilby portrayed on Alabama Centennial half dollar, first living person identified on a coin of the U.S. Peace silver dollar designed by Anthony De Francisci. Coins were first struck in December and released to circulation Jan. 3, 1922.

1924 Julius Guttag starts National Coin Week.

1929 First small-size paper money issued.

1932 George Washington portrayed on U.S. coins of regular issue for first time, quarters.

1933 Act issued prohibiting minting of gold coins; Treasury calls in all gold.

1938 First coin from large-scale design competition, Jefferson 5-cent piece.

1942 Mint mark P designated Philadelphia for first time, 5-cent pieces.

1943 Zinc-coated steel cents issued.

1946 Roosevelt dime issued.

1948 Franklin-Liberty Bell half dollar issued.

1955 IN GOD WE TRUST made mandatory on all U.S. coins and paper money.

1961 Office of Domestic Gold and Silver Operations created; Leland Howard first director.

1962 Tin removed from 1-cent piece.

1963 Kennedy half dollars authorized.

1964 Date 1964 frozen on coinage. Kennedy half dollars struck.

1965 Coinage Act of 1965: copper-nickel cladding on dimes and quarters replaces silver; half dollar clad in reduced silver content alloy. Joint Commission on Coinage established.

1966 Initials of Felix Schlag placed on Jefferson 5-cent piece.

1967 $2 note discontinued by Treasury.

1968 U.S. Proof coins resumed. Silver certificates cease to be redeemed for silver, General Services Administration begins selling silver on the market. Gold backing removed from paper money.

1969 New Philadelphia Mint dedicated. Mary T. Brooks becomes Director of the Mint.

1970 Federal appellate court rules United States is legally warranted to inscribe its coins and currency with IN GOD WE TRUST. GSA conducts silver sale. Eisenhower dollar legislation becomes law.

1971 Mint begins production of silverless Kennedy half dollars, in Denver. First Eisenhower dollar struck March 31. Technicians install new Currency Overprinting and Processing Equipment (COPE) at the Bureau of Engraving and Printing. First dollar devaluation.

1972 President approves transfer of old San Francisco Mint building to Treasury for restoration as Mint working facility and museum. ANA's Certification Service opens in Washington with Charles Hoskins as director.

1973 Second dollar devaluation. President Nixon signs bill providing for Bicentennial coinage, Oct. 31, with manufacture to begin in 1975. Hobby Protection Act becomes law Dec. 12.

1974 President Ford signs bill ending ban on U.S. citizens' ownership of gold, as of Dec. 31, 1974.

1975 First of the nation's Bicentennial coins roll off the presses in the Mints, both copper-nickel clad copper and 40 percent silver, Uncirculated and Proof.

1976 After extended hearings, reports and studies, the $2 bill returns, bearing Trumbull's "Signing of the Declaration of Independence" on the reverse.

1977 Pre-Bicentennial designs resumed. Citizen-members barred from U.S. Assay Commission. Stella Hackel named Director of the Mint.

1979 First Susan B. Anthony dollars issued for circulation.

1980 Mint accepts orders for American Arts Gold Medallions, first gold struck by the Mint in almost half a century.

1981 Section 314-b of the Economic Recovery Act restricts use of collectibles in IRA and Keogh retirement plans.

1982 Mint strikes silver commemorative half dollar marking the 250th anniversary of George Washington's birth, first commemorative coin struck since 1954. Copper-plated zinc cents introduced.

1983 U.S. Mint begins striking 1983 and 1984 Olympic commemorative coinage, and decides to use a W Mint mark on the 1984 gold eagle produced at West Point. Discovery of 1982 No P dime focuses public attention on hobby.

1984 Mint releases 1984 Olympic $10 eagle, first U.S. gold coin struck since 1933. Public attention focuses on hobby as media reports discovery of 1983 Doubled Die cent. U.S. Mint resumes sales of Uncirculated sets.

1985 President Reagan signs an executive order banning the importation of South African Krugerrands effective Oct. 11. A pre-issue discount offering by the U.S. Mint in December results in complete sell-out of the 1986-dated Statue of Liberty gold half eagle commemorative coins. U.S. Mint offers 1986 Ellis Island silver dollar and Immigrant copper-nickel half dollar at pre-issue discount prices.

1986 American Eagle gold bullion coins, the first non-commemorative gold coins struck for U.S. consumption since 1933, issued in October, followed by the release in November of the American Eagle silver bullion dollar. Sales of Statue of Liberty commemorative coins result in record surcharges being delivered to the Statue of Liberty restoration project. Treasury officials approve the first major changes to U.S. paper money in decades with the decision to incorporate anti-counterfeiting devices on all Federal Reserve notes in early 1987. Fort Worth, Texas, is selected as the site for the Bureau of Engraving and Printing's Western printing plant, which will give the federal government two currency producing plants for the first time in the BEP's 125-year history.

1987 U.S. Mint reports strong sales of Uncirculated souvenir sets in light of plans not to issue the Kennedy half dollar for circulation.

(Note: See Chapter 1 for a more detailed chronology of 1984-1987)

Canada
(Official types, major "national" tokens)

1670 First regal French silver, 5, 15 sols "Gloriam regni tui dicenti" coinage of Louis XIV, copper 2 deniers.

1717 Copper 6, 12 deniers, Louis XV.

1721-22 Copper 9 deniers colonial coinage.

1728 Billon marque, half marque enter circulation.

1813 "Holey dollar," cut and counterstamped Spanish dollars issued by the governor of Prince Edward Island.

1815 Magdalen Island token penny of Sir Isaac Coffin.

1823 Nova Scotia copper half-penny token introduces types issued through 1840.

1837-52 Bank and bouquet copper token coinages, Upper Canada, Quebec.

1843 New Brunswick tokens.

1856 Arbutus copper Nova Scotia tokens of Victoria.

1858 Silver 5, 10, 20 cents, bronze cent, Canada, young head of Victoria.

1861 Decimal bronze cent, half cent, New Brunswick.

1862 Silver 5, 10, 20 cents, New Brunswick; gold 10, 20 dollars, British Columbia.

1865 Bronze cent, silver 5, 10, 20 cents, gold 2 dollars, Newfoundland.

1870 New Confederation silver coinage of Canada.

1871 Prince Edward Island bronze cent, English inscription obverse.

1876 Large bronze cent introduced of Canadian Confederation type.

1911 Pattern dollar for Canada, George V, "Dei gratia" omitted on first coins of this reign.

1912 Normal inscriptions resumed, new gold 5 and 10 dollar Canadian coins join sovereigns of British type, minted 1908-1919-C.

1920 Small bronze cent replaces older large cent.

1922 Pure nickel round 5 cents replaces small silver 5 cents.

1935 Silver Jubilee of the reign of King George V sees silver dollar finally introduced, and begins ongoing series of commemorative coins for Canada.

1937 New coins of George VI, first wholly redesigned reverses.

1938 Small bronze cent introduced in Newfoundland.

1942 Tombac brass replaces nickel in Canadian 5 cents, coin struck on a 12-sided planchet.

1943 Canada first to issue coinage with international telegraphic code reverse dots and dashes, "We win when we work willingly" around edge of tombac "Victory" 5 cents.

1944 Chrome-plated steel 5 cents, victory reverse.

1946 Nickel 5 cents resumed, 12-sided.

1947 Last Newfoundland coins.

1951 First commemorative in 5-cent denomination marks anniversary of the isolation of nickel as a recognized element.

1967 Centenary of Confederation, completely redesigned coinage, bronze 1 cent through gold 20 dollars.

1968 Pure nickel replaces silver in Canadian coinage, 50 cents and the 1 dollar coins are reduced in size as well.

1971 British Columbia centenary sees re-introduction of large-size silver dollar, along with regular issue small pure nickel dollar.

1973 Montreal Mayor Drapeau and the Canadian government begin the issue of the first silver $5 and $10 Olympic coins, to be followed by six more four-coin sets for worldwide distribution, to aid in financing the XXI Olympiad held in 1976 in this city.

1976 Joining the 28 silver $5 and $10 Olympic coins are two new gold $100 pieces, struck in .5833 fine for sale as Unc.; .9166 fine in Proof. Measuring 27 and 25 millimeters respectively, the gold coins are offered at a premium over face.

1977 Silver Jubilee silver dollar, gold $100 of Elizabeth II. New, reduced diameter bronze 1-cent piece announced by Royal Canadian Mint. The 16.05mm new cent will be smaller than the existing 10-cent piece.

1979 Smaller bust of Queen Elizabeth II adopted on 1 cent. International trade coin, 31.1 gram, .999 fine gold, 1 ounce Maple Leaf coin issued for first time.

1980 1-cent coin reduced in weight.

1981 Mint begins manufacture of seven-piece Proof sets.

1982 Cent depicts smaller bust and becomes 12-sided coin. 5 cents changed to copper-nickel composition. Paper money adopts raised-print Braille for the blind.

1984 Canadian flax content in paper money replaced with U.S. cotton.

1985 Calgary Winter Olympic coin series unveiled.

1986 Royal Canadian Mint introduces half-ounce Maple Leaf. Maurice Lafontaine

succeeds James Corkery as Mint master.

1987 Smaller size dollar coin struck to replace dollar bill.

Mexico

1521 Following Cortez' capture of Tenochtitlan, now Mexico City, the territory was organized as a Spanish possession. The Aztec Indians were found using cacao bean and beaten copper "hoe money" in daily commerce.

1536 The Mexico City Mint, oldest in the New World, begins coinage of silver in quarter and half reales, 1-, 2-, 3- and 4-real denominations. An issue of copper 2 and 4 maravedis was an unsuccessful experiment, which saw hundreds of the coins thrown in Lake Texcoco.

1556 The reign of King Philip II saw the introduction of the 8-real crown, to be struck in various designs through 1897, becoming a world coin of international circulation and universally admired reliability. The silver coins became known as "cobs," from a Spanish expression "cabo de barra," cut from a bar; their weight was all-important, the actual shape of any one coin a matter of indifference.

1665 Gold coinage began in Mexico during Charles II's reign.

1732 Fully round coins struck within a collar. These are known to Spanish collectors as "dos mundos," or two worlds type from the crowned hemispheres on the reverse; English-speaking collectors know them as the "Pillar dollar," ancestor of the U.S. dollar.

1772 Portrait 8 reales struck for King Charles III.

1808 Following Ferdinand VII's ouster by Napoleon's brother Joseph, Mexican loyalists, as will be done throughout the Spanish empire, rally to Ferdinand and begin striking coins with his portrait at Mexico and a dozen new Mints.

1811 The revolt of Father Morelos sees a variety of cast and struck crude emergency coins, beginning a complex era of loyalist and revolutionary coinages.

1814 Copper coins in denominations of ⅛, ¼ and ½ real struck, to replace private tokens and provide small change.

1822 Following the independence of Mexico under liberator Augustin de Iturbide, imperial coinage began in Augustin's new Mexican empire, bearing the eagle of Aztec legend, seated on a nopal cactus.

1823 Following the overthrow of the empire, a republic was proclaimed, the beginning of a century of turbulence, misrule and civil struggle. A profile hook-necked eagle killing a serpent replaces Iturbide's crowned eagle on the 8-reales piece.

1824-97 Coinage of uniform "Liberty Cap" 8-reales pesos and minor silver.

1829 Copper national coinage in ⅛ and ¼ real denominations. Copper issues of individual states had begun in 1824.

1841 The first pattern decimal 1-centavo piece struck but not adopted.

1863 San Luis Potosi strikes silver decimal 5- and 10-centavo coins.

1864 The Congress of Notables invites Archduke Maximilian of Austria to ascend the throne of a second Mexican empire during the French intervention of Napoleon III. A decimal centavo in copper was issued by the imperial government.

1866-67 Imperial silver coinage of 5, 10 and 50 centavos struck in 1866, the handsome Maximilian peso in 1866 and 1867. The emperor was captured and ordered shot by President Benito Juarez.

1869 A republican copper centavo placed in circulation, although the silver coins were still being struck in real denominations.

1869-73 "Balance type" coin with value expressed as 1 peso; some decimal minor coins as well.

1870 Balance type gold coinage, 1 peso through 20 pesos.

1882 Copper-nickel briefly introduced in 1-, 2- and 5-centavos denominations.

1898 8 reales finally abandoned in favor of a new Liberty Cap peso.

1899 A new small size bronze centavo.

1905 A major monetary reform adopts the gold standad and introduces a new coinage in bronze, silver and gold, bearing a facing eagle and inscription ESTADOS UNIDOS MEXICANOS.

1910 Last of the large size pesos, called the "Caballito" from the equestrian liberty on the obverse introduced.

1918 Size of the peso, weight and fineness reduced. New issue is .800 fine, succeeded by a similar coin of .720 fineness in 1920. This was the start of a gradual disappearance of silver in the coinage in this and other denominations.

1936 Copper-nickel 5 and 10 centavos issued.

1942 Portrait and other scenic views placed on 5 and 20 centavos, beginning a trend toward greater variety of design for all coins.

1947 Morelos peso issued, .500 fine. The succeeding pesos drop to .100 fine by 1957.

1950 A commemorative 5 pesos marking the completion of the southeastern railway continues a modern commemorative series (that began in 1921) which still continues. The sizes of all coins are now reduced, .300 fine 25 and 50 centavos, 1 peso struck.

1954-55 Brass and bronze 5-, 10-, 20- and 50-centavo minor coins join the already brass 1 centavo in circulation; 5 pesos silver coin, .720, and 10 pesos, .900 fine, make their debut.

1964 Copper-nickel, smaller 25 centavos and 50 centavos replace bronze pieces.

1968 A silver 25-pesos introduced, .720 fine.

1970 Bronze coinage reduced further in size; copper-nickel adopted for the 1 peso, with a new copper-nickel 5 pesos planned for 1971. All reverses redesigned to bear an outline-form archaic Aztec treatment of the profile Mexican eagle.

1974 New small-size copper-nickel 20 centavos portrays revolutionary leader Madero, continuing trend toward smaller and smaller coins.

1976 Plans are announced for a .720 fine silver 100 pesos, designed to stimulate the silver mining industry.

1977 Numismatic excitement high as tiny copper-nickel 10 centavos dated 1974, 1975 and 1976 are released; seven-sided copper-nickel 10 pesos appear dated 1974, 1975 and 1976; 1977-dated silver 100 pesos are struck and released.

1980 Design of Aztec dragon adopted for 5-peso coin reverse. Copper-nickel composition commences for 20-peso production.

1981 Gold bullion coins of quarter, half, and 1 ounce pure gold, .900 fine, issued as international trade coins.

1982 Devaluation of peso to 50, then 100 to one U.S. dollar takes place due to high inflation. 50-peso coins issued in copper-nickel.

1983 Design of Almec culture adopted on new bronze 20-centavos coin. Design of Palenque adopted on reverse of new steel 50 centavos.

1984 Libertad of .999 fine silver dated 1982

released, replacing .925 fine silver Onza trade coin.

1985 Mexico Mint becomes an autonomous institution.

Central America
GUATEMALA

1824 Guatemala Mint strikes coinage of Central American Federation.

1829 Provisional coinage of 1 real, federation type with STATE OF GUATEMALA.

1859 Beginning of President Rafael Carrera's standardized real-peso coinage.

1869 Attempt at decimal peso of 100 centimos; 25 centimos struck, public reacts negatively.

1870 Decimal peso of 100 centavos decreed, abandoned the following year.

1881 Another decimalization attempt, four denominations struck, in copper and silver. Copper centavo overstruck on the 1871 issue.

1912 Last national coinage in real denominations, a copper-nickel coin first struck in 1900 as the economy began floundering.

1915 Copper provisional coinage.

1923 Amid a collapse of the currency, aluminum bronze 1 and 5 pesos issued.

1926 Thorough overhaul of the Guatemalan finances sees introduction of the gold and silver quetzal of 100 centavos.

1943 President Jorge Ubico causes an international incident by issuing a new 25-centavo piece to mark inauguration of the national palace, with a map reverse showing British Honduras as a part of Guatemala.

1965 Silver coinage replaced with copper-nickel-zinc.

BRITISH HONDURAS (Belize)

1864 Decimal system adopted.

1871 Private ¼-real tokens issued by importer John Jex.

1885 Copper cents introduce a new decimal colonial coinage, the first in this hemisphere south of Canada in the British colonial holdings.

1894 Silver coinage, 5 cents to 50 cents begun.

1914 Medium size bronze cent appears.

1946 Last silver coinage of British Honduras.

1954 Cent further reduced, scalloped edge after 1956.

1973 Premier George Price engineers sudden name change of the colony to Belize after the former capital, traditional coin designs modified to reflect the change.

1974 New coinage, first change in designs since 1894 announced, name of the colony, under internal self-government, changed to Belize. Franklin Mint strikes all-new series featuring birds of Belize, denominations expressed in words. Traditional designs with royal portrait continued after loyalist protest over new bird coin designs. One-, 5- and 10-dollar coins in bird series.

1975 Bird series continued with numerical values on reverse, royal types to continue as well.

1978 First 25 dollars of silver and of copper-nickel, and 250-dollar gold produced.

1981 World Food Day coins issued, part of international series.

NICARAGUA

1825 Provisional silver of Central American Federation type.

1878 First regular coinage, copper-nickel centavo.

1880 Silver decimal coins, 1 peso of 100 centavos.

1912 Overhaul of coinage introduces the silver cordoba of 100 centavos, copper-nickel coinage replaces silver in 1939.

1943 Brass shell case alloy replaces copper-nickel on three denominations.

1965 Central Bank becomes bank of issue.

1967 Famed Nicaragua-born Spanish language poet and writer Ruben Dario honored on gold 50-cordoba coin.

1974 Aluminum 5 and 10 centavos in Food and Agriculture Organization (FAO) series join the range of coins in circulation.

1980 One-year issue of copper-nickel 5 cordobas.

1981 Participates in FAO international issues with 1, 10 and 25 centavos in aluminum.

1982 Nickel-clad steel 50 centavos replaces former copper-nickel composition.

HONDURAS

1823 Coins of Spanish royalist and Mexican imperial type struck at Tegucigalpa Mint, presumably to suit all factions.

1832 Provisional Central American type coinage in base silver and copper.

1871 Republican silver decimal coinage.

1879-1920 Great coinage chaos, old dies of every type used to strike copper centavo coins.

1931 New coinage of the lempira, equal to 100 centavos.

1967 Copper-nickel coinage replaces silver.

EL SALVADOR

1828 Provisional coins and countermarked issues.

1889 Copper-nickel 1 centavo with Morazon portrait.
1892 Decimal peso-centavo silver coinage.
1909 Short-lived ¼ real copper struck and quickly recalled.
1925 Commemorative silver and gold coins for the fifth centenary of San Salvador in new unit, the colon.
1943 Large silver 25 centavos struck during World War II nickel shortage.
1953 Small size silver, 25 centavos equal a U.S. dime.
1970 Copper-nickel coins replace silver in circulation.
1974 Nickel-brass coinage includes 3-centavo coin last issued in 1915.
1975 Nickel-clad steel introduced for 5, 10, 25 centavos.
1976 Brass 1 centavo produced.
1977 Copper-nickel 5, 10 and 50 centavos increased to 2-millimeter coins from 1.65mm thickness.
1984 Copper-nickel 1 colon introduced as regular issue coin.

COSTA RICA
1831 Central American type coins struck, "CR" Mint mark.
1841 Star countermark applied to foreign coins in circulation.
1845 Woman's head and tree reverse countermarks on old Spanish 2 reales.
1846 One-real and 2-real dies used to validate colonial cob coins still in active circulation.
1850 Decimal silver, expressed in fractions to agree with old real coinage value.
1865 Decimal copper-nickel and silver coins.
1896 New currency unit, the colon of 100 centimos.
1935 Issues of the Banco Internacional in copper-nickel.
1937 Banco Nacional.
1954 Banco Central stainless steel coinage, first in the hemisphere.
1974 Gold, silver Conservation coinage released.
1975 Pure nickel 5, 10 and 20 colones, first circulating commemoratives.
1979 Five centimos changes to brass composition.
1982 Aluminum adopted as new composition for 10 and 25 centimos; stainless steel for the 50 centimos and 1 and 2 colon.

PANAMA
1904 First coinage, highlighted by tiny 2½ centesimos and huge half balboa.
1930 Silver coins in U.S. sizes and weights.

1931 First silver balboa issued.
1966 Copper-nickel-clad copper coinage of U.S. type replaces smaller silver coins in circulation.
1971 A new denomination, 20 balboas, issued in silver, first as a commemorative for the 150th anniversary of Central American independence, then as what the government of Panama has described as a regular issue.
1975 Franklin Mint strikes all-new portrait coinage including a 5-balboa piece, 2½ centesimos "pill" in new designs.
1975 First gold coinage, struck by Franklin Mint.
1976 Franklin Mint produces platinum 150 balboas with Bolivar head.
1979 Denomination of 200 balboas, 9.5 grams of .980 platinum, begins production.
1981 Denomination of 50 balboas of 5.37 grams of .500 gold begins production.

South America
(Countries listed alphabetically)

ARGENTINA
1813 United Provinces of Rio de la Plata coinage with radiant sun, reales or soles.
1822 Province of Buenos Aires and other chaotic provincial coinages.
1838 Confederated Argentine Republic coins.
1881 Modern unified bronze, silver and gold coinage of the republic decreed.
1896 Copper-nickel coinage becomes general coin in circulation until 1942.
1952 Copper-nickel-clad steel, first in hemisphere.
1970 New coinage, 100 old pesos equal one new.
1974 Inflation's advance leads to reappearance of small size aluminum-bronze 1 peso.
1983 Aluminum adopted for 10- and 50-centavos coins.
1985 Introduces austral currency in an effort to stop inflation.
1986 Notgeld-type paper "provincial bonds" appear as small change in circulation.

BOLIVIA
1573 Potosi Mint established on the fabulous "hill of silver."
1841 Republican silver and gold silver soles; gold scudos.
1864 Decimal boliviano of 100 centavos.
1883 First copper-nickel 5, 10 centavos.
1893 Copper-nickel "caduceus" coins, a type in use through the 1940s.

1951 Bronze bolivianos.
1965 Copper and nickel-clad coinage.
1977 A 200 pesos bolivianos of 23.3 grams of .925 silver issued as part of the international issue for the "International Year of the Child."
1984 Inflationary 100,000-peso notes issued.

BRAZIL

1822 Independent imperial coins of Dom Pedro I.
1831 Dom Pedro II, types of earlier reign.
1853 Modern imperial silver coinage.
1867-68 Portrait silver and copper introduced.
1871 Nickel minor coins introduced.
1889 Republic declared, monetary instability advances.
1900 400th anniversary commemoratives sets a trend. Huge 4,000 reis with the discoverer Pedro Alvares Cabral largest silver coin in hemisphere's history.
1922 First centenary of independence sees beginning of a distinguished series of national commemoratives, continuing through the next decade.
1942 President Getulio Vargas decrees new coinage, the cruzeiro of 100 centavos. Minor coins continue to bear his portrait; 1, 2 and 5 cruzeiros bear a remarkably detailed relief map of Brazil.
1956 Aluminum coins introduced as runaway inflation begins its inroads.
1967 After years of financial chaos, the military government decrees a coinage reform, introducing the heavy cruzeiro, equal to 1,000 old cruzeiros. New coinage of stainless steel and pure nickel.
1972 Re-introduction of commemoratives in nickel, silver and gold to mark the 150th anniversary of Brazilian independence.
1975 Silver 10 cruzeiros marks anniversary of Central Bank, leads to accusations of favoritism in distribution and Mint director's ouster.
1980 Manufacture begins of stainless steel 5- and 10-cruzeiros coins.
1981 Manufacture begins of stainless steel 20 cruzeiros.
1986 Cruzado currency introduced in an attempt to slow inflation.

CHILE

1749 Santiago Mint created.
1817 "Chile Independiente" coinage of republic.
1851 Decimal peso of 100 centavos introduced.
1895 Condor standing on mountain peak coinage, designed by French engraver O. Roty; standard design of fluctuating fineness, weight and size through 1941.
1920 Subsidiary coinage in copper-nickel, retaining Roty design.
1942 Bronze peso and minor coins, O'Higgins portrait type.
1954 Aluminum coinage; inflation advances.
1960 New escudo of 100 centesimos, valued at 1,000 old pesos.
1971 Rapid inflation of the escudo after election of Marxist president Allende.
1975 New peso introduced valued at 1,000 escudos.
1978 New 1 peso and 50 centavos issued composed of aluminum-bronze.

COLOMBIA

1627 Santa Fe de Bogota Mint authorized, operated sporadically.
1729 Popayan Mint established, few coins initially struck.
1758 Popayan in regular production.
1811 Cartagena royal coinage.
1815 Independent coinage of Nueva Granada.
1820 Name Colombia on coins, soon replaced by combinations and variations on the old name Nueva Granada.
1862 United States of Colombia decimal coinage, copper, copper-nickel, silver and gold.
1886 Republic of Colombia established as the official title of the country.
1892 Columbus portrait 50 centavos for anniversary of New World's discovery.
1907 Copper-nickel "paper money" 1, 2 and 5 pesos introduced to withdraw depreciated paper currency.
1917 Centavo denominations replace the above coinage.
1930 Last regular gold coinage.
1953 Last regular silver coin, 20 centavos.
1968 First 20th century commemorative marks Eucharistic Congress.
1969 Nickel-clad steel coins introduced.
1978 New denomination, 2 peso, appears. Design changes on 100 and 500 peso oro bank notes.
1979 20-centavo coin the size of 25 centavos of the 1920s is released.
1980 Newly designed 5-, 500- and 750- peso coins are released.
1981 A 30,000-peso coin is issued.

ECUADOR

1824 Royalist Cuzco Mint established.
1836 After emergence from union in Great Colombia, republic of Ecuador coins are issued.

1858 Brief experiment with Latin Monetary Union coins, 5 francos struck.
1872 Decimal sucre of 100 centavos adopted.
1927 Small size sucre introduced.
1937 Nickel sucre and minor coins.
1964 Nickel-clad steel coinage.
1980 New 5- and 20-sucre notes are produced.

BRITISH GUIANA (GUYANA)
1809 Coins of George III, Dutch guilder unit.
1816 More finely struck guilder coinage.
1891 Silver 4 pence struck for "British Guiana - British West Indies"; the English type 4 pence had been in circulation as the equivalent of the quarter guilder during the reign of William IV and Victoria.
1967 Decimal coinage of 1 dollar divided into 100 cents, issued by the new Bank of Guyana.
1970 Copper-nickel dollar portrays slave insurrection leader Cuffy as Guyana joins FAO coin program.
1976 All new coinage portrays historical figures, wildlife of Guyana.

DUTCH GUIANA-SURINAME
1762 Copper duit of the Society of Suriname.
1962 Autonomous coinage of Juliana; Suriname now self-governing as a part of the kingdom of the Netherlands.
1976 Gold, silver coins mark Independence anniversary.

FRENCH GUIANA
1780 Billon 2 sous of Louis XVI.
1718 Billon 10 centimes, Louis XVIII.
1846 Billon 10 centimes, Louis-Philippe.

PARAGUAY
1845 First coinage, a copper 1/12 real with lion seated before a pole crowned with a liberty cap.
1870 After devastating wars with her neighbors, Paraguay issued first decimal coins, in copper centesimo denominations of 1, 2 and 4 centesimos.
1889 Only crown-sized silver peso issued.
1925 Copper-nickel small pesos and multiples lead to gradual decay of the coinage.
1944 New aluminum-bronze coins in new currency based on 100 centimos to 1 guarani.
1953 Scalloped-edge aluminum bronze centimo issue.
1968 President Alfredo Stroessner issues commemorative coins for the centenary of the war of the triple alliance against Paraguay, waged by Brazil, Argentina and Uruguay in the 19th century.
1973 Veritable flood of German-struck commemorative "coins" begins in honor of Olympics, popes, world leaders, Indian cultures and other unrelated matters.
1974 Stainless steel regular coinage of 1 through 50 guaranies honors heroes of Paraguayan history.
1977 Bank notes are replaced with stainless steel 1-, 5-, 10- and 50-guarani coins.

PATAGONIA
1874 Fantasy 2-centavos copper coin struck by eccentric Frenchman "Orlie-Antoine I," self-proclaimed "king of Araucania and Patagonia." Silver pesos appear years later, products of a Berlin coin dealer.
1889 The adventurer Julius Popper strikes gold coin-weights in the name of the "Company of the gold-washers of the south."

PERU
1568 Lima Mint first established, coinage sporadic.
1684 More or less regular coinage at Lima Mint.
1822 Republican 8 reales struck at Lima Mint.
1824 The above coin systematically restruck with Spanish crown by Royalists.
1825 Regular republican coinage in real denominations.
1855 Decimal silver sol of 100 centavos introduced.
1880 Brief Latin Monetary Union style coinage of silver pesetas and 5 pesetas at Lima.
1898 The gold libra, or pound, first struck.
1918 A distinctive copper-nickel coinage of 5, 10 and 20 centavos introduced with the obverse date spelled out in words.
1935 Central Reserve Bank of Peru begins coinage emissions in bank note style, ". . . will pay to the bearer one half sol . . ."
1942 Brass replaces copper-nickel in minor coins.
1966 New, unified design brass coinage, reduced sizes. Silver commemorative 20 soles for the naval combat with Spain in 1866 begins a continuing commemorative series in various denominations of silver.
1971 Copper-nickel and silver coins for 150th anniversary of Peruvian independence recall earlier struggle of the would-be liberator, the Indian Tupac Amaru.

1975 New, tiny brass sol and half sol mark inflationary trend.

1986 Government purchases precious metals with hard assets to avoid creditor embargos.

URUGUAY

1840 Copper decimal coinage in centesimo denominations introduced.

1844 Silver peso fuerte struck during historic siege of Montevideo.

1877-95 Silver peso-centesimo coinage.

1901-51 Radiant sun centesimo coins in copper-nickel and copper.

1930 French-designed coins and notes for the centenary of independence.

1953 Artigas-portrait centesimo coinage begun at the outbreak of a steadily worsening inflationary spiral.

1969 Radiant sun of earliest coinage reappears on aluminum bronze 1-, 5- and 10-peso coins. Spectacularly modernistic 1,000-peso silver crown struck to mark the U.N. Food and Agricultural Organization's world-wide coin plan.

1975 Monetary reform attempts to halt inflation. New peso introduced, exchanged for 1,000 old pesos. 150th anniversary of the struggle for independence marked by new 5-peso coin.

1981 Coins of 2 new pesos in copper-nickel-zinc, 5 new pesos in copper-nickel-aluminum, and 10 new pesos of copper-nickel released. Largest coin denomination ever issued in the country, a 5,000 new pesos of silver issued as a commemorative.

VENEZUELA

1802 Royal coinage at Caracas.

1817 First coinage by independence forces at the start of a long struggle.

1843 After leaving the union of Great Colombia, the first distinctive Venezuela coinage of copper ¼, ½ and 1 centavos issued.

1858 Handsome French-designed real coinage struck.

1873 Brief centavo-venezolano coinage.

1879 Latin Monetary Union coinage, 100 centimos to one bolivar, equal to the French franc. Gold and silver coinage with bolivar head struck.

1965 Last silver bolivar issued, nickel 1 and 2 bolivares and minor pure nickel 25 and 50 centimos introduced.

1973 Large 10 bolivar commemorative issued for centenary of the national coinage with the head of the liberator, Simon Bolivar.

1977 Nickel composition coins depict denominations in larger numerals to stop confusion with silver issues of earlier years.

The Caribbean Islands
(Islands listed alphabetically)

BAHAMAS

1806 Half penny of George III struck for the Bahamas.

1966 New decimal coinage replaces British coins in use; Bahamas dollar of 100 cents, coins in nickel-brass, copper-nickel, pure nickel and silver, from 1 cent to 5 dollars.

1971 New name, Commonwealth of the Bahamas.

1973 Independence greeted by new coin types and a silver 10-dollar piece.

1978 Central bank discontinues acceptance of large quantities of gold coins for redemption.

BARBADOS

1788 Pineapple penny, copper, with Negro crowned with Prince of Wales's plume on obverse.

1792 Similar penny and additional half penny with colony's badge, the British king as Neptune in a marine car drawn by seahorses.

1973 New coinage and notes.

BERMUDA

1616 Sommer Islands "Hogge money" issued for the new colony on Bermuda.

1793 Half penny of George III issued for Bermuda.

1959 Silver 5-shilling crown struck, bearing a map of the island group.

1970 Decimal coinage in bronze and copper-nickel, 100 cents to one dollar.

1984 J. David Gibbons appointed chairman of the Bermuda Monetary Authority.

BRITISH CARIBBEAN TERRITORIES, EASTERN GROUP

1955 Decimal coins in bronze and copper-nickel released for Barbados, British Guiana, Windward, Leeward islands and Trinidad-Tobago.

BRITISH COLONIES

1820-22 Anchor money, silver fractions of a Spanish dollar in one-sixteenth, used in the West Indian colonies. Many cut and counterstamped coins in this same region.

CUBA

1870 Revolutionary provisional coinage, five centavos to one peso struck, probably at the Potosi, Bolivia, Mint.

1897 "Souvenir" silver peso struck in the U.S. to dramatize Cuban independence aspirations.

1898 Revolutionary committee issues similar coin with denomination ONE PESO.

1915 During the period of peak prosperity and booming economic speculation later recalled as the "dance of the millions" a full range of copper-nickel, silver and gold Cuban coinage is created. Silver 20 and 40 centavos struck to accommodate Spanish peseta denominations of this value still circulating.

1934 Following the overthrow of the first Cuban dictator, General Gerardo Machado, the new silver peso struck is dubbed the "A.B.C." type for the secret society which led in Machado's overthrow.

1951 Melting for the bullion value of millions of A.B.C. pesos held as reserve backing for silver certificates creates a modern rarity.

1952 Silver commemoratives struck for the 50th anniversary of the republic.

1953 Commemorative coinage for the centenary of Jose Marti, Cuba's national hero, includes 25-centavo and 50-centavo coins for the first time.

1962 The Kremnica Mint in Czechoslovakia strikes copper-nickel coins for the new Communist regime of Fidel Castro in 20- and 40-centavo denominations.

1975 Silver 5, 10 pesos announced marking 15th anniversary of the communization of the island's banking system.

CURACAO AND NETHERLANDS ANTILLES

1821 Silver real introduced.

1900 Dutch denominations begin to circulate with a silver ¼ guilder.

1944 U.S. Mints strike Dutch denominations with Curacao inscription during World War II for exiled Queen Wilhelmina.

1952 New coinage, still of older Dutch type for self governing Netherlands Antilles, including Curacao, Aruba, Bonaire, Saba and Sankt Maarten.

1970 Wholly redesigned Netherlands Antilles coinage, pure nickel replacing silver in higher denominations.

DANISH WEST INDIES

1708 Gold ducat of King Frederik IV struck for Danish West India Company.

1740 Copper and silver skilling coinage with royal monogram and ship reverse begin their long circulation.

1816 Small base silver 2-, 10- and 20-skilling coins with royal arms introduced.

1859 Base silver decimal coins of 100 cents to one daler introduced under King Frederik VII.

1904 Multiple good silver, nickel, bronze and gold coinage of Christian IX, based on a 20 cents equals one franc equals 100 bit standard.

1913 Last Danish coin, bronze 1 cent of Christian X. Islands sold to the U.S. in 1917.

DOMINICAN REPUBLIC

1844 Revolt against Haiti sees issue of a brass quarter real.

1877 Brass and small copper-nickel coinage during a period of great unrest.

1891 Latin Monetary Union coinage of the silver franco of 100 centesimos.

1897 Base silver peso of 100 centavos issued.

1937 Restoration of national financial independence after foreign tutelage and U.S. occupation as new bronze, coppernickel and silver coinage on American standard enters circulation.

1955 The 25th anniversary of the Trujillo dictatorship marked by the first gold coin struck in the hemisphere officially in accord with the U.S. official value of $35 per ounce; face value 30 pesos.

1967 Copper-nickel replaces silver in circulation.

1969 Copper-nickel peso marks 125th anniversary of 1844 revolt against Haitian occupiers.

1972 Silver crown-sized peso returns as commemorative issue, 25th anniversary of Central Bank.

1974 Gold 30 pesos returns for 12th Central American and Caribbean games in greatly reduced size, reflecting rise in gold prices.

1975 Historic 10-reales crown of 16th century recalled on silver 10 pesos marking the first coin struck in Hispaniola.

EAST CARIBBEAN

1970 Copper-nickel and Proof silver specimens of 4-dollar crown-sized coins released to commemorate the inauguration of the Caribbean Development Bank. Antigua, Barbados, St. Kitts, Dominica, Grenada, Montserrat, St. Lucia and St. Vincent, all represented with new coat-of-arms obverses.

1972 Cayman Islands coinage of decimal type.

FRENCH COLONIES
1717 Six- and 12-denier bronze coins of Louis XV designed for colonial commerce.
1721 Bronze 9-denier added.
1740 Billon 12 denier struck.
1767 Same denomination in bronze.
1758 Billon "sou marque" which is to see extended circulation all over the West Indies, where it becomes familiar as the "black dog."
1825 King Charles X strikes yellow bronze 5 and 10 centimes for the colonies.
1839-44 Louis-Philippe continues colonial bronze coinage.
1897 Martinique creates 50-centime and 1 franc copper-nickel coinage, a type secured by precious metal deposited in the colonial treasury. Issued also in 1922.
1903 Similar promissory coinage in copper-nickel for Guadeloupe.

HAITI
1802 Silver escalin denominations struck for the French Republic under the self-governing colony of Governor-General Toussaint l'Ouverture.
1807 President Henry Christophe creates a decimal currency, one gourde equals 100 centimes.
1814 Republic in southern Haiti issues base decimal coinage in denominations interchangeable with the Spanish American real.
1828 Copper coinage of fasces type begun by President J. P. Boyer, ruler of the whole island of Hispaniola.
1850 Imperial coinage of former president Faustin Soulouque, now emperor Faustin I.
1863 Reformed copper coinage of restored republic, President Fabre Geffrard.
1881 Silver gourde coinage of Latin Monetary Union fineness and weight, but not denomination, issued by President Salomon.
1904 President Nord Alexis begins copper-nickel coinage in sizes still current in the coinage of Jean-Claude Duvalier today.

JAMAICA
1869 Copper-nickel farthing, half penny and penny introduced.
1937 Alloy changed to nickel-brass.
1969 Decimal coinage after five years of independence within Commonwealth.
1972 Ten-dollar commemorative of 10 years independence issued in silver.

PUERTO RICO
1895 Silver peso worth five Spanish pesetas introduced by the colonial power.
1896 Silver minor coins introduced.

TRINIDAD AND TOBAGO
1966 New decimal coins, 100 cents equal one dollar.
1969 Copper-nickel dollar struck for FAO coin plan.

WINDWARD ISLES
1731 Six, 12 sols silver, Louis XV.

Europe
(Countries arranged by region)

ENGLAND
500-575 Beginning of Anglo-Saxon silver sceat coinage.
c. 765 Beginning of silver penny coinage, kingdoms of Kent, Mercia, etc.
c. 786 Pennies of kings of Wessex, later kings of all England.
885 Beginning of Viking coinages in England.
1257 Experimental gold penny of Henry III, worth 20 silver pennies.
1278 Introduction of silver groat, 4 pence; silver half penny and farthing.
1344 Introduction of gold florin, half and quarter florin; noble and parts.
1465 Rose noble introduced in gold, 120 grains valued at 10 shillings. Former gold noble replaced with angel of 80 grains.
1485 Reign of Henry VII, which saw a gold sovereign of 20 shillings and the silver testoon, or shilling.
1543 Start of the systematic debasement of the English coinage by Henry VIII.
1561 First attempt at milled, machine-struck coinage by French engraver Eloye Mestrelle, during reign of Elizabeth I; three-half pence and three-farthing coins introduced.
1601 Silver coinage restored to full fineness, pre-Henry VIII debasement.
1604 Gold unite introduced, lighter weight gold pound.
1613 Harrington farthings, licensed copper coinage, first such in England.
1631 Nicholas Briot actively seeks milled coinage.
1649 Commonwealth coinage, English inscriptions.
1648-72 Seventeenth century token issues, in absence of official copper coins.
1660 Restoration of Charles II, last hammered coinage.
1662 Milled coinage officially adopted.

1695 Great Silver Recoinage begins, removal of worn and clipped coinage from circulation.

1797 Steam machinery produced "cartwheel" twopence and penny.

1804 Bank of England dollar, overstruck on Spanish 8 reales.

1811 Bank of England token 3 shillings, 18 pence, 9 pence.

1816 Complete recoinage, token silver, new gold sovereign, half-sovereign.

1860 Copper penny, half penny and farthing replaced by bronze coinage.

1920 Silver coinage reduced to .500 fine, new quaternary alloy.

1925 End of regular gold coinage.

1937 New 12-sided threepence in nickel-bronze introduced.

1947 Silver replaced by copper-nickel, small threepence discontinued.

1956 Farthing discontinued.

1967 Half penny discontinued.

1968 First decimal denominations introduced alongside pre-decimal coins.

1971 Full decimalization, 100 new pence to one pound.

1972 Crown returns as 25 new pence for anniversary of royal wedding. New coin is twice the size of 50 new pence.

1977 British public, collectors greet Silver Jubilee crowns and medals with record enthusiasm.

1978 Liberalized policy on gold coin importation.

1979 Sir Christopher Wren is portrayed on new 50-pound note. Royal Mint weathers a strike by workers for one week in October.

1980 Sixpence ceases to be legal tender on June 30.

1981 Wedding of Prince Charles and Lady Diana Spencer is marked with commorative crowns.

1982 Value Added Tax (VAT) is added to all sales of coins more than 100 years old. A new 20-pence coin is introduced.

1984 Half penny production ceases. £1 bank note ceases production and is replaced by £1 coin already in circulation.

1986 £2 coin introduced as a commemorative issue.

1987 Britannia gold bullion coin program schedule to be introduced.

SCOTLAND

1124 Silver pennies of King David I.

1249 Silver half penny and farthing introduced by King Alexander III.

1329 David II introduces silver groat, half-groat.

1460 Billon plack, half-plack of James III, first copper, "black money."

1513 James V, billon bawbee (sixpence) and divisions.

1542 Reign of Mary sees many coinage innovations and types based on the royal marriages both in Scotland and abroad.

1553 Silver testoon and divisions.

1567 Silver ryal or dollar, and its two-third and one-third divisions, King James VI.

1555-56 Billon hardhead, 1½ pence, billon penny.

1572 Silver merk, half-merk.

1578 Silver 2 merks, merk.

1581 Silver 2, 4, 8, 16 shillings.

1603 James VI, as James I of Great Britain, France and Ireland, introduces 60-shilling crown of English design, first Scots-English interchangeable coin type.

1706 Ten-shillings and 5-shillings Scots, last of the distinctively Scottish coins under Queen Anne.

1937 Scottish crest reappears on British coinage as a tribute to the queen, the former Lady Elizabeth Bowes-Lyon.

1968 Scots thistle appears on new decimal 5 pence.

1984 Great Britain's 1-pound coin features Scotland.

ANGLO-AMERICAN COINAGE

1652 Nominal date on "NE," New England, Willow, Oak and Pine Tree coinage of Massachusetts.

1658 Proprietory coinage of Lord Baltimore in Maryland colony.

1688 Tin 1/24 part real, so-called "Florida token" in the southern colonies.

1722 Rosa Americana copper coinage under George I.

1774 Regal copper half pennies in Virginia, George III.

IRELAND

c. 995 Sihtric, Norse king of Dublin, issues first silver pennies, imitations of Aethelraed II types struck in England.

c. 1185 Anglo-Irish coinage begins in the name of John, Lord of Ireland, son of Henry II of England.

c. 1204 "Triangle coinage" of John as King of England, lord of Ireland.

1461 Silver groat introduced by Edward IV.

1536 The Irish harp first appears on coins of Henry VIII.

1553 Shilling appears under Mary I.

1646 The only two gold coins to be struck in Ireland, a pistole and double pistole, are issued as part of the "Inchiquin money" issue, which began in 1642.

c. 1670 "St. Patrick" copper farthings and half pennies in circulation. Many of these will appear with Mark Newby in Colonial New Jersey in 1681.

1689 Brass emergency "gun money," with some denominations dated by the month as well as the year, issued by exiled King James II, during an attempt to regain the British throne.

1728-36 Widespread issue of private copper tokens.

1760 "Voce populi" tokens appear, privately issued, later transported in some numbers to the American Colonies.

1804 Bank of Ireland tokens begin with 6-shilling crown.

1823 Last Anglo-Irish coinage, George IV penny and half penny.

1928 Percy Metcalfe designs new national coinage, eight new reverses with a uniform Irish Free State obverse featuring the harp. Metcalfe's work was the result of an international artistic competition in which seven artists participated.

1966 First commemorative, silver 10 shillings, marks 50th anniversary of Easter Rising.

1969 First two decimal coins enter circulation.

1970 New seven-sided 50 decimal pence struck with design of former farthing.

1971 Decimalization completed.

1977 First Irish Mint since 1691 opened by Central Bank at Sandyford, Co. Dublin.

1980 Twenty-pound notes are reduced in size by one-third.

FRANCE
(Since accession of Hugues Capet)

956 Hugues Capet, Duke of France, issues silver denier and billon obole, which were to become standard coins in succeeding reigns.

987 Hugues Capet becomes king, continues denier coinage.

1226 Louis IX (St. Louis) strikes gold coins: Ecu d'or (also called denier d'or a l'Ecu), l'agnel d'or and the royal d'or. Silver coinage reform sees introduction of gros tournois, valued at 12 denier old coinage. The once fine silver denier is lapsing into a billon coinage.

1285 Phillip the Fair creates petite royal d'or.

1303 Adds chaise d'or. The term "d'or" indicates gold; first word describes the coin's obverse design, in this case the king on the royal throne, "chaise."

1328 Phillip of Valois adds parisis d'or; pavillon d'or. All of these medieval gold issues are named for their designs.

1350 John the Good introduces the mouton d'or, with the lamb of God.

1360 Adds the franc a cheval, with figure of the king charging on horseback, in silver.

1396 After one of France's first excursions into adventure in Italy, French-style coins in Genoese denominations are struck in the Genoa Mint.

1413 Billon grossus added to French coinage by Charles VI.

1417 Heaume d'or shows king in armor and helmet.

1421 Salut d'or added to gold denominations.
(After 1415, English king Henry V struck French-style coinage during his war in France.)

1436 Charles VII introduces gold ecu de la couronne.

1461 Louis XI, the "Spider king," creates billon douzain and billon liard. The liard, originally valued at three denier, became a familiar copper coin in later years.

1483 Charles VIII introduces the billon hardi.

1494 Further military intervention in Italy sees coins struck in the name of King Charles VII struck in 10 Italian Mint cities, from Pisa to Naples.

1513 Louis XII introduces circulating portrait coins, the silver teston and half teston.

1515 The glittering reign of Francois I sees pattern portrait coin in many denominations, circulating silver testons of several designs, as well as billon hardi "black money" coinage. Much Italian coinage in this reign.

1550 Henri II introduces gold portrait Henri d'or.

1560 Franco-Scots coinage issued during brief reign of Francois II, husband of Mary, Queen of Scots; gros d'argent, silver coin with its half and its quarter.

1576 Reign of Henri III, cut short by assassination in France's troubled period, sees portrait silver piefort of the franc.

1594 Henri IV enters Paris after civil strife, sets path for stability and French unity. Earlier coin types become increasingly standardized.

1640 French gold becomes fixed as Louis d'or and multiples under Louis XIII.

1641 Louis d'Argent or Louis blanc, the silver crown of 60 sols known abroad as the ecu is introduced. French coinage is now essentially fixed in general pattern of issue until the great revolution.

1642 French invasion of Spanish Catalonia extends Louis XIII's coin types to the County of Barcelona.

1643 Louis XIV, whose long reign consolidated royal power and fixed the coinage in the general Louis d'or-silver ecu system. French culture, language and influence become all-pervading as a result of Louis' splendor, his military campaigns and the magnificence of his court at Versailles.

1685 The heavy ecu carambole is introduced for use in occupied Flanders; the coin is valued at 80 sols, rather than the 60 or the regular ecu.

1717 Louis XV's reign sees the first coinage for the French colonies in general, the 12 and 9 denier coppers of 1717 and 1721; as well as specialized coin for the Antilles and French India.

1774 Louis XVI, last of the pre-revolutionary rulers of France. First period coinage follows closely that of his predecessors.

1791 Following the revolution, a brief "constitutional period" precedes the reign of terror and the republic. The constitutional coinage began in 1791; the new title "king of the French" and value of six livres are distinguishing marks. Copper and brass coins are struck, partly from looted church bells.

1793 Following execution of Louis XVI, first republican coinage of France is released, followed by a rapid inflation of the increasingly useless assignat paper currency, ostensibly guaranteed by a blanket mortgage of the national domain.

1795 Franc adopted as the chief unit of a decimal coinage, made up of 100 centimes or 10 decimes.

1803 First portrait coins of Napoleon Bonaparte, first consul of the republic. Silver quarter and half franc, franc, 2 and 5 francs silver, 20 and 40 francs gold.

1804 Beginning of imperial coinage of Napoleon I, lasting until the "hundred days" coins of 1815.

1808 Bronze 5 centimes, billon 10 centimes introduced; Napoleon emperor.

1814-15 Restoration of the house of Bourbon, retention of the franc coinage.

1830 Louis Philippe, royal arms replaced by value in wreath. Propaganda coins of pretender Henri V appear, 1831, joined later by Napoleon II, bearing date "1816."

1848 Second republic sees massive issues of medals, jetons and a large pattern coinage before its replacement by the Prince President, Louis-Napoleon as authoritarian ruler in 1851.

1852-70 Second empire of Napoleon III. Copper 1, 2, 5 and 10 centimes join regular silver coinage, gold 50 and 100 francs replace the top value 40 francs of earlier issues.

1870-1940 Third republic maintained the Latin Monetary Union standards, established as an international standard by Napoleon III in 1867 until the general collapse of European currencies after World War I.

1903 Nickel 25-centime coinage introduced.

1904 Similar coin prepared with 22 sides in an attempt to reduce danger of confusion with 1-franc piece.

1914 Holed nickel Lindauer type coins begun, continued in various metal through 1946.

1933 Small Bazor type 5 franc in nickel, quickly withdrawn due to extensive counterfeiting.

1940 French defeat in World War II leads to Parliament calling aged Marshal Philippe Petain, hero of Verdun in the earlier war, to head the new French state.

1941 First coinage of "Vichy" France.

1945 Fourth French republic.

1950 Currency reform, new aluminum bronze and copper-nickel coinage.

1958 Fifth republic of Gen. Charles de Gaulle.

1960 New "heavy franc," equal to 100 old francs, introduced.

1965 Crown-sized coinage resumed with a revival of the Dupre design of Hercules, the republic and justice, first used in 1795.

1970 Silver abandoned in 5-franc coins.

1974 New 50-franc crown to supplant 10-franc silver; new abstract map 10 franc in base metal to be prepared for active circulation.

1979 The 2-franc coin is reinstated.

1982 First commemorative coin issued in nation's history.

1986 Commemoratives honor centennial of the Statue of Liberty in New York Harbor.

1987 Platinum, palladium, silver and silver piefort coins honor LaFayette.

SPAIN

711 Muslim invasion marked by a gold solidus dated 93 A.H. begins a long and complex Moorish coinage in Spain, which continues until the 15th century.

814 Carolingian coinage in Barcelona, silver dinero of Louis the Pious.

874 Independent coinage of the Counts of Barcelona begins with a silver dinero of Wilfredo.

991 Ampurias coinage of Count Hugo I, billon dinero. Billon becomes a major coinage metal of the Spanish principalities.

1018 Gold mancuso struck by Berenguer Ramon I, count of Barcelona.

1035 Kingdom of Leon coinage begins with silver dinero of Fernando I.

1054 Kingdom of Navarra, billon dineros of Sancho IV.

1063 Kingdom of Aragon's coinage initiated by Sancho I Ramirez.

1065 Kingdom of Castile coinage begun with dinero and obolo coins of Alfonso VI.

1157 Gold maravedi with Latin inscriptions of Fernando II of Leon.

1158 Castilian gold dobla, Moorish inscription and design with added cross.

1238 Kingdom of Valencia, liberated by El Cid Campeador, begins coinage of billon dineros under Jaime I.

1282 Sicilian gold and silver coinage under kings of Aragon, golden age of Catalan culture and influence.

1284 Sancho VI of Castile creates the billon cornado.

1297 Sardinia under Aragonese rule, silver real coinage.

1350 Silver real introduced in Castile by Pedro I, the Cruel.

1379 The billon "agnus dei" or blanca created by Juan I of Castile.

1406 Large gold coin of 20 doblas under Juan II of Castile.

1458 Gold escudo struck by Juan II of Aragon.

1469 Fernando V and Isabel, coinage gradually stabilizing around copper maravedi, silver real and gold excelente.

1492 Last Moorish stronghold, Granada, falls to Fernando and Isabel; gold 20 excelentes struck, probably to commemorate the final victory of the reconquest.

1580 Brief royal union with Portugal.

1636 Vast monetary confusion during the reign of Felipe IV, extensive and repeated revaluation of copper coinage by countermarking.

1643 During invasion of northern Spain, Louis XIV strikes coinage as Count of Barcelona.

1705 War of the Spanish Succession sees coins struck in Barcelona for claimant Carlos III of Hapsburg; coinage elsewhere for Felipe V of the new Bourbon dynasty.

1808 Jose Napoleon, brother of the French emperor, imposed as king of Spain. Coins struck for Jose Napoleon and Fernando VII, the legitimate king in guarded exile in France.

1809 French occupation coinage introduces "en Barcelona" peseta, struck in three silver and one gold denominations, which provided important future direction for Spain's monetary development.

1825 Emancipation of the Spanish colonies in South and Central America complete as Potosi Mint, in present day Bolivia, strikes the last Spanish style silver 8 reales.

1837 First Carlist war produces coins of Don Carlos V, pretender to the throne.

1864 Coinage reform under Isabel II introduces the decimal silver escudo, divided into 100 centimos. Distinctive Philippine peso-centimo gold and silver coinage created.

1869 The Provisional Government announces adoption of the peseta, on the standard of the Latin Monetary Union, divided into 100 centimos.

1873 Coinage of third Carlist pretender Don Carlos VII.

1895 Colonial coinage for Puerto Rico, 1 peso equals 5 pesetas.

1933 First coinage of the second Spanish Republic.

1937 Civil War causes a proliferation of local and regional emergency coinage and notes, Vienna Mint strikes first coins for Franco's Nationalist government.

1940 Aluminum minor coinage introduced.

1966 Continued growth and prosperity marked by issue of silver 100-peseta coin.

1975 Following the death of Generalissimo Francisco Franco, Council of the Realm drafts legislation for new portrait coinage of King Juan Carlos I.

1976 Royal portrait appears on Spanish coinage, new royal arms on 5, 50 pesetas. Copper-nickel 100 pesetas introduced, all coins with star date 1976, authorization date 1975.

1978 The country observes its first National Coin Week.

1982 A new, crowned M Mint mark is introduced.

PORTUGAL

1641 Coinage of Joao IV, the restorer of Portuguese independence, in silver and copper.

1642 Countermarking of earlier coinages begun.

1656 Gold coinage resumed under Afonso VI.

1683 Finely-styled coinage of Pedro II.

1686 Countermarking of earlier Portuguese coinages.

1722 Portrait coinage introduced by Joao V, gold only. These pieces were a favorite overseas, where they were dubbed "Joes."

1750 Similar portrait gold of Jose I, the real "Joe."

1777 Portrait gold coinage of Maria I and Pedro III.

1786 Widow's veil gold of Maria alone.

1811 Bronze portrait coinage of prince regent Joao.

1826 Brief coinage of Pedro IV, actually independent emperor Pedro I of Brazil.

1828 Usurpation of the throne by Dom Miguel, formerly the regent for his absent brother.

1833 Portrait coins of Miguel's niece, Maria da Gloria, as Maria II.

1837 Portrait silver coinage, beginning with the coroa of 1,000 reis.

1847 Countermarked bronze "G.C.P." coinage.

1882 Smaller sized portrait bronze coinage of Luis I, titles in Portuguese.

1898 Commemorative silver 200, 500 and 1,000 reis mark the fourth centenary of Vasco da Gama's discovery of the sea route to India.

1900 First copper-nickel coinage of 50 and 100 reis.

1908 Following the assassination of Carlos I and crown prince Luis Felipe, Manoel II becomes king; Latin titles resumed on the coinage.

1912 After the coup against king Manoel in 1910, the first republican coin is struck on a new standard of 100 centavos to one escudo.

1914 First crown-sized silver escudo commemorates the revolution of 1910.

1924 Small aluminum-bronze escudo struck.

1927 Nickel-bronze escudo coinage under Dr. Antonio da Oliveira Salazar's New State.

1928 First of many commemoratives of the New State, a silver 10 escudos recalling Portuguese victory over the Moors at Ourique in 1139.

1932 Silver 2½, 5 and 10 escudos introduced.

1942 Small bronze X, XX centavos revive old Roman numeral denominations.

1953 The 25th anniversary of Salazar's financial reforms is marked by a new 20 escudos silver coin.

1963 Copper-nickel replaces silver in 2½-, 5- and 10-escudo denominations.

1968 Fifty-escudo silver commemoratives begin.

1969 Bronze replaces nickel-bronze in 1½-escudo coins.

1971 Aluminum appears in the 10-centavo coinage.

1978 The first circulating coin since 1974 military coup, a new denomination 25 escudos, appears.

1981 The government releases 1977 dated copper-nickel coins.

ITALY

569 Anonymous gold solidi of the dukes of Beneventum.

650 Anonymous ⅓ solidus of Lucca.

772 Papal coinage begins under Adrian I.

934 Fatimid Arab gold coinage of Palermo, Sicily.

935 Gisnulf I issues Cufic type 1 tari at Salerno.

1042 Amalfi Cufic coinage.

1102 Norman gold tari struck at Messina.

1190 Gold grosso d'oro of emperor Frederick II, St. Vultus, Lucca Mint.

1197 Frederick II strikes gold 1½ augustales, in the style of the ancient Roman coinages.

1200 Anonymous cross and castle coinage of the doges of Genoa.

1252 Florence issues the famed florin, which soon becomes a widely imitated world gold trade coin, with its standing Christ and lily reverse.

1266 Coinage of the house of Anjou, Naples Mint.

1280 Doge Giovanni Dandolo issues the first of the famous Venetian gold ducat series, with the figure of the doge kneeling before Christ.

1340 Florins struck by the republic of Siena.

1431 Scudo d'oro struck for Sardinia by Louis I.

1441 Lionel d'Este issues gold ducat.

1445 Mantua coinage of Luigi II Gonzaga.

1495 French coinage in Naples; gold zecchino struck by the republic of Pisa.

1500 Silver testone of Francesco II Gonzaga, Mantua; French coinage in Milan.

1523 Coinage designs by Benevenuto Cellini for Pope Clement VII.

1534 Spanish King Charles V issues coins in Milan as this city continues to play its unhappy role as an international battleground.

1552 Coinage of the dukes of Modena.

1707 Milanese coinage of Austrian emperor Charles VI.

1726 With the death of Grand Duke Gian Gastone, the long association between the house of Medici and Florence comes to an end.

1749 Charles of Spain produces coinage as King of the Two Sicilies.

1759 Ferdinand IV of Bourbon begins his long years of coinage as King of the Two Sicilies.

1768 Venice strikes new bust type tallero in silver.

1797 Republic of Venice surrendered to Napoleon, soon after seized by Austria.

1798 Napoleon creates Ligurian Republic, coinage of Genoa Mint.

1799 Turin Mint strikes coins for Piedmont Republic after the house of Savoy retreats to Sardinia.

1800 Coinage of the Subalpine Republic, silver 5 francs.

1803 Napoleon's client Louis I of Bourbon begins coinage for the kingdom of Etruria after deposition of the grand duke of Tuscany.

1804 Coinage of the Italian republic, Bonaparte, president, Milan Mint.

1805 Beginning of the coins of principality of Lucca and Piombino under Napoleon's sister Elisa and her husband Felice.

1807 Napoleonic coinage for the new kingdom of Italy, 100 centesimi to the silver lira, forerunner of later united Italian coinage.

1809 Marshal Murat succeeds Joseph Bonaparte as king of the Two Sicilies; establishes decimal coinage.

1814 Siege silver coinage of Zara on the Adriatic coast.

1815 After Napoleon's overthrow, the duchy of Parma is given to his sometime empress Marie Louise, who issues centesimi-lira coinage.

1816 Papal coinage, interrupted by the Roman Republic of 1798 and by the captivity of the Pope in France, resumes under Pius VII. Victor Emanuel I, restored as king of Sardinia-Piedmont, strikes decimal centesimi-lira coinage.

1835 New decimal coinage of the 100 baioc-chi-one scudo type introduced by Pope Gregory XVI.

1848-49 This year of revolutionary upsurge sees new coinages in Venice, Rome and Lombardy, all striving toward a unified Italy.

1859 Italian unification advances as the last coins of Leopold II of Tuscany, Francesco II of the Two Sicilies and Robert of Parma are struck. Victor Emanuel II, "elected king" coinage of Tuscany; Bologna Mint strikes silver 5 lire with head of Victor Emanuel II, king of Italy.

1861 After the Florence Mint has struck a commemorative 5 lire on the occasion of his proclamation as king of Italy, Victor Emanuel II begins the definitive unified Italian coinage, struck at Turin, Naples, and later Milan and Rome.

1870 Last papal coinage at the Rome Mint until 1929; Italian coinage commences at this Mint.

1894 Copper-nickel 20 centesimi introduced as an unsuccessful experiment in small size, non-silver coinage.

1900 Outstanding numismatist Victor Emanuel III becomes king upon the murder of his father Umberto I. Victor Emanuel III is to spend a lifetime in the compilation of the "Corpus Nummorum Italicorum," the exhaustive catalog of all coins ever struck in Italy.

1911 The 50th anniversary of the kingdom of Italy is commemorated by a four-coin set in gold, silver and bronze.

1922 Pure nickel 1- and 2-lire "good for -" token coins issued, joining the 1918 20 centesimi and the 1919 50 centesimi in an increasingly non-precious metal post-war coinage.

1923 The first anniversary of the fascist march on Rome is marked by two gold commemoratives.

1929 Following the Treaty of the Lateran, papal coinage is resumed as the state of the Vatican City is created.

1931 Devaluation of the lire sees new, smaller format coins struck in gold, silver and bronze with the usual classical motifs.

1936 Following the annexation of Ethiopia and the proclamation of the empire, a redesigned imperial coinage in gold, silver, pure nickel and bronze is struck.

1939 Stainless steel, used in coinage for the first time as "acmonital," replaces nickel; aluminum-bronze replaces bronze in Italian coinage.

1943 After King Victor Emanuel III brings about the overthrow of Mussolini and fascism, the last regularly issued coins of the kingdom of Italy are issued.

1946 Following the artfully manipulated referendum of June, the new Italian republic issues a new aluminum coinage of 1, 2, 5 and 10 lire. Millions are struck; most disappear from circulation immediately, to reappear as the stuffing of Swiss-produced cloth covered buttons.

1951 New small-size aluminum coins are struck as the financial erosion of Italy under the republic continues.

1954 Stainless steel coins are minted again in 50 lire and next year 100-lire denominations.

1957 Aluminum-bronze 20 lire introduced.

1958 Silver returns in the 500-lire coin.

1961 Italian commemoratives begin again with a silver 500 lire for the first centenary of unification under Victor Emanuel II.

1970 A new 1,000-lire denomination celebrates the centenary of Rome as the capital of united Italy.

1972 The tiny republic of San Marino resumes Italian-style coinage in "annual series."

1974 A nationwide coin shortage, caused by unknown factors, sees Italians reduced to using candy, teabags, telephone tokens and even Kleenex as coin substitutes. Import-export limits are established on the lire due to inflation and loss of capital within the country. Stainless steel 100 lire honors radio inventor Marconi, replacing silver 500 lire originally proposed.

1975 Coinage shortages cause the acceptance of plastic tokens in commerce.

1976 Controversy swirls around announced plans to strike and sell at several times face value the 1974 silver Marconi 500 lire; San Marino 500 lire "outside annual series." Emergency 100- and 500-lire notes are declared illegal.

1977 Bronze 200-lire coin commences.

1982 A 500-lire coin is produced of bronze and acmonital composition.

1986 "New lira" denominations introduced, dropping the last three zeros as a reaction to inflation.

GERMANY

1554 Imperial decree established the fine Cologne mark as coinage measure, a weight of silver weighing 233.855 grams.

1618-23 "Kipper and wipper" period of debasement, inflation and the proliferation of Mints resulting in monetary chaos.

1690 Leipzig Convention established standard of 12 taler to the fine mark.

1747 Austria abandons 1690 standard, adopts a lesser standard of 13⅓ taler to the fine mark.

1750 Prussia adopts "Graumann standard," 14 taler to the fine mark.

1753 Austria and Bavaria announce "conventionstaler," 10 to the fine mark, a standard adopted by most German states, "ad normam conventionis."

1806 Abolition of Holy Roman Empire and resulting monetary disorganization.

1809 Kronentalers appear in Bavaria, similar to earlier issues in the former Austrian Netherlands, 9.08 to the fine mark.

1837 Bavaria leads south-central German states at the Munich Convention to adopt the gulden as the standard coinage unit, equal to 24½ gulden to the fine mark, or two gulden to one taler. Saxony leads Thuringian states into Dresden Convention, adopting the Graumann standard of 14 taler to the fine mark; the system already in use by Prussia and seven other states.

1838 Dresden and Munich groups agree on an integrated standard of 14 taler equaling one Cologne fine mark equaling 24½ gulden; two taler equaling 3½ gulden.

1857 Monetary union based on "zollfund," metric pound of 500 grams or half-kilogram, equal to 30 vereinstaler; gold coinage of one krone and half krone established at 50 kronen to the zollfund.

1873 Unification of coinage in the new German empire; silver and gold coinage, bronze subsidiary coins on a new one mark to 100 pfennig standard. Surviving vereinstaler to circulate as 3 marks.

1890 First colonial coins, for the German East Africa Company.

1894-95 Bird of Paradise coins of German New Guinea Company.

1904 New German East Africa coinage under Imperial administration.

1908 Beginning of 3-mark coinage, commemorative issues under same decree.

1909 Copper-nickel coins on Mexican peso standard for German treaty port of Kiautschou.

1915 World War I iron minor coinage begins.

1916 Coins struck for emergency use in German East Africa.

1918 State authorized notgeld in Braunschweig begins flood of such necessity coins and notes.

1923 Catastrophic inflation, ending in new rentenmark currency reform.

1924 Adoption of the reichsmark.

1925 Commemorative 3- and 5-mark series begins.

1945 "Denazified" zinc coins under Allied occupation.

1948 Monetary reform in western occupation zones; aluminum coins in east zone.

1949 Bank Deutscher Laender begins issuing coins in west.

1950 Bronze and brass-clad steel coinage of the German Federal Republic, coppernickel 50 pfennig.

1951 Silver 5 deutsche mark in circulation in Western zones. Copper-nickel 2 marks causes confusion among users, sees one year of striking.

1952 Silver 5 deutsche mark honoring Nuremberg's Germanisches Museum begins long, distinguished series of Federal Republic commemoratives.

1956 First coinage bearing the title of the German Democratic Republic, supplants earlier issues inscribed merely "Germany."

1966 First commemoratives of the German Democratic Republic, or East Germany.

1969 "Magnimat" copper-nickel clad nickel 2 deutsche mark with Adenauer portraits enters circulation in Federal Republic.

1972 Tons of recycled silver used in series of 10 deutsche mark coins honoring the XX Olympiad, first issue with improper legend "In Germany," rather than the Olympic non-national "In Muenchen."

1975 "Magnimat" material introduced for 5 deutsche mark. Only silver coins now are commemoratives in Federal Republic.

1986 Point-of-sale system cashless economy experimented with in Munich and in West Berlin.

THE NETHERLANDS

750 Gold triens of Duurstede, one of the earliest recognizable coinages in what was to become the Netherlands.

1200-1576 Separate provincial coinages of the several provinces which came together to produce the modern Dutch nation. The denominations were to include the gold mouton d'or and the gold florin.

1576 The United Provinces coinage begins, soon to be more or less standardized in the familiar gold ducats, silver ducatoons or rijders, and a number of smaller silver and copper coins, generally bearing a Mint mark or coat-of-arms identifying the provincial Mint at which the coins were struck.

1794 As the traditional world began to come apart under the revolutionary assault of the events in France after 1789, the Low Countries become a battlefield, reflected in such siege coinages as those struck in Maastricht in 1794 and in the city of Luxemburg in 1795.

1795 A triumphant Napoleon sees to the organization of the Batavian Republic, replacing the Stadholders of the house of Orange. Gold, silver and copper coinages continue along familiar lines; only the dates setting the coins of the Batavian Republic aside from those issued earlier.

1806 The emperor Napoleon places his younger brother Louis on the throne of a new kingdom of Holland as Lodewijk Napoleon I.

1808 A regular issue of portrait coins of the new kingdom is begun.

1818 Following the elevation of the last Stadholder as King Willem I of the new kingdom of the Netherlands, a decimal coinage of 100 cents to the gulden is begun; the largest silver piece is the 3 gulden.

1819 Regular gold coinage begins with the 10 gulden.

1840 The crown size 2½ gulden replaces the older 3 gulden as the largest silver coin in circulation.

1848 Gold "Negotiepenning" equal to 20, 10 and 5 gulden struck as trade coins.

1875 Regular gold coinage resumed under Willem III.

1907 Copper-nickel 5 cents introduced.

1933 Last portrait gold coinage.

1941 Zinc minor coins struck by German occupiers.

1948 All new bronze and pure nickel coinage after the liberation.

1954 The silver gulden reappears in smaller size than earlier issues.

1959 The silver "rijksdaalder" or 2½ gulden in silver is reintroduced.

1960 The gold ducat of the old United Provinces is again struck as a trade coin.

1967 Pure nickel 1 and 2½ gulden coins replace silver.

1970 The 25th anniversary of the liberation is marked by a silver 10-gulden commemorative coin, the beginning of a series in this denomination.

1980 First coinage produced for Beatrix as queen.

1982 One-cent coin abolished March 31.

BELGIUM

1790 The historic coinage of the then Austrian Netherlands is interrupted by the rebellion coinage in copper, silver and gold.

1815 Necessity copper coinage in the name of Napoleon, later Louis XVIII, in Anvers, Antwerp.

1831 After a period of unhappy union with the Netherlands, an independent kingdom of Belgium is proclaimed, Leopold of Saxe-Coburg-Gotha becomes "Leopold premier," a double-meaning title. He is both the first Leopold and the first king of the new kingdom.

1832 The first coins are issued, a copper 10 centimes and a silver 5 francs, the latter bearing Leopold's laureate head.

1834 Gold pattern 20 and 40 francs struck.

1848 Beginning of new, bare head coinage in silver, first gold coinage issued.

1860 Copper-nickel 20 centimes struck.

1901 Holed copper-nickel coinage under Leopold II, 5, 10 centimes; 25-centime piece added in 1908.

1915 Zinc coinage issued under the German occupation, 5, 10 and 25 centimes. Necessity coinage, Belgian notgeld of iron with unusual brass plated obverse, copper-plated reverse issued in occupied Ghent.

1918 Zinc 50 centimes struck with central hole.

1922 In the post-war period of financial uncertainty, pure nickel 50 centimes, 1 and 2 franc pieces are struck, still inscribed "good for -" to temporarily replace paper money, as in France, Italy, Luxembourg and Romania in this adjustment period.

1930 In an attempt to replace lower value paper money, a pure nickel coinage of 5, 10 and 20 francs is begun, with a new additional denomination of the belga, equal to 5 francs.

1935 A silver 50 francs is struck to mark the centenary of Belgian railroads, with a regular issue in this denomination appearing in 1939.

1941 Introduction of zinc minor coins under the German occupation, 5, 10, and 25 centimes, 1 and 5 francs eventually struck.

1944 Allied armies entering Belgium issue zinc plated steel 2 francs, the unused planchets of the U.S. zinc-steel Lincoln cent.

1948 Following liberation, a new coinage is begun, highlighted by a 100 francs with the busts of the nation's four kings.

1951 Baudouin I becomes king after a confused era of collaborationist charges against Leopold III. A new and innovative coinage is gradually created, including 50-franc silver commemoratives in 1958 and 1960; and a copper-nickel 10 francs in 1969, uniquely without obverse inscription around the king's head.

1976 Silver commemorative 250 francs in separate French and Flemish types honors 25th anniversary of King Baudouin I.

1979 New coins replace minor denomination circulating notes.

1980 The 25-franc 150th anniversary coin is struck, design determined by competition.

1981 The 25-centime denomination is abolished.

LUXEMBOURG

1795 Cast copper siege coins issued by the Austrian defenders against the French invaders.

1854 In personal union with the Netherlands' King Willem III, Grand Duke of Luxembourg, a copper coinage of 2½, 5 and 10 centimes is begun.

1890 Following the death of Willem III, his daughter is prevented from becoming Luxembourg's ruler by the Salic law; the succession goes to the elderly Adolphe of Orange-Nassau, ruling duke of Nassau, Germany, disposed in 1866.

1901 Portrait copper-nickel 5, 10 centimes of Adolphe.

1908 Issue of a slightly larger 5 centimes under William IV.

1915 Zinc coinage under the German occupation, holed types.

1918 Iron occupation coins enter circulation.

1924 Pure nickel "bon pour," good for- coinage of 1, 2 francs.

1939 Moselle-Frankisch name "Letzeburg" appears on the coinage.

1946 After liberation from a second German occupation, a commemorative set of 20, 50 and 100 francs in silver celebrates the 600th anniversary of the medieval warrior-king John the Blind.

1963 The millenary of Luxembourg sees the striking of a commemorative 250-franc coin in silver; only after striking is it discovered that the coinage laws do not provide for this denomination.

1964 New coinage under grand duke Jean.

1978 The country courts world gold trade by removing 100 percent added gold tax.

1986 Gold bullion Golden Lion 1-ounce legal tender trade coin issued.

CENTRAL EUROPE

1828 Coinage of independent Greece resumes, one phoenix equals 100 lepta; coins struck on the island of Aegina, where ancient Greek coinage began about 700 B.C.

1848 Kossuth rebellion sees coins with Hungarian inscriptions.

1857 Austrian empire adopts new florin silver coinage, one florin equals 100 kreuzer.

1867 First coinage of autonomous Romania, in copper.

1867 Prince Michael, Obrenovich III issues Serbian copper coins.

1868 Following the compromise with Austria, Hungary begins distinctive coinage, one forint equals 100 krajczar.

1881 Bulgarian coinage, one lev equals 100 stotinki under Prince Alexander I. Romania becomes a kingdom.

1882 Milan I, King of Serbia, issues first gold coins.

1892 New Austro-Hungarian standard of coinage; 100 heller (Hungarian 100 filler) to one silver corona, (German krone, Hungarian Korona).

1906 Montenegro begins coinage, 100 para to one perper.

1910 Montenegro declared a kingdom, commemorative gold issued.

1917 Iron fenigow coins from embryonic kingdom of Poland, first Polish coinage since the 1850s.

1920 Yugoslavia created, adopts Serbian standard, 100 para equals one dinara.

1921 Czecho-Slovakia begins coinage, 100 haleru equals one koruna.

1922 Estonian mark coins; Latvian coinage of 100 santimu equals one lats begun.

1923 Poland consolidates several monetary systems into 100 groszy equals one zloty system.

1924 After a disastrous inflation, new Austrian coinage of 100 groschen equals one schilling adopted.

1926 Hungary adopts new coinage, 100 filler equals one pengo, "pengo" an adaptation of the term "clinking." Albania commences coinage, 100 qindar ari equals one franka ari.

1939 Independent Slovakia begins coinage, 100 halierov equals one koruna, "Ks."

1941 Independent state of Croatia in former Yugoslavia issues a single zinc 2 kune on standard of 100 banica equals one kuna.

1945-46 Inflation and Communist takeovers in Romania and Hungary begin.

1946 New Hungarian forint currency replaces pengo, which had experienced the worst inflation in history.

1946 Austria resumes schilling coinage interrupted by the Nazi Anschluss.

1947 Zinc first coinage of communist Albania replaces Italian occupation coinage in aluminum-bronze, stainless steel, silver.

1947 Czechoslovakia introduces new reduced size coins of prewar design; royal reform coinage of Romania's Michael I enters circulation.

1948 First communist coins of the Romanian Peoples Republic.

1949 Polish coinage resumed, minus royal crown on the White Eagle, in the name of the Polish Republic; soviet-style emblem replaces Kossuth arms of Hungary on Peoples Republic issues.

1951 Communist Peoples Republic Bulgarian coinage begins.

1953 New aluminum coins for Peoples Federated Yugoslav Republic; Czechoslovak monetary reform brings new types and designs.

1954 First Greek postwar coinage in aluminum and copper-nickel bears King Paul's likeness.

1955 Start of the long run of Austrian modern commemoratives.

1958 Polish Peoples Republic title appears on coins.

1962 Bulgarian monetary reform.

1963 First new Bulgarian commemoratives, Socialist Federated Yugoslav coinage.

1964 Polish commemorative series begun; new communist Albanian coins in aluminum, a gift of Red China.

1966 Poland begins issue to collectors of limited runs of pattern "Proba" coins, rejected designs for commemoratives; Romania issues new coinage in the name of the Romania Socialist Republic.

1966   Royal Greek coins of Constantine II.
1967   Beginning of present-day system of Hungarian commemoratives.
1970   Czechoslovakia silver commemoratives launch new series.
1971   Greek royal arms of exiled King Constantine II replaced by symbol of ex-colonels' junta.
1973   New republican Greek coins of the junta.
1975   Redesigned Greek coins of post-junta era; Austria fixes upon 100-schilling denomination for silver commemoratives.
1976   Gold 1,000 schilling marks Austria's Millenary; first new gold type in country since 1938.
1979   Yugoslavia ceases legal tender status of 1965-dated 5-, 10- and 50-dinar notes.
1980   Poland begins a "Kings of Poland" coin series.
1981   Austria introduces a gold-colored 20 schilling coin.
1985   Austria bars South African Krugerrand importation.
1986   Bullion non-legal tender Helvetias minted in Switzerland.

DENMARK

1537   Crown-sized gulden in silver of King Christian III.
1541   Silver 1 mark.
1563   Klippe emergency coinage of the Seven Years War.
1564   Square gold gulden or krone minted.
1572   Silver speciedaler struck by Frederik II.
1591   Heavy gold Portugaloser struck by Christian IV.
1602   Copper coinage of 2 pennings, Christian IV.
1608   Silver double speciedaler, liondaler and gold sovereign minted.
1644   First coinage with Hebrew inscription and Latin combination, "Jehova the just judge."
1655   Goldkrone struck under Frederik III.
1659   Commemorative double krone issued with hand from clouds hacking a Swedish arm reaching for Denmark's crown.
1670   Silver speciedaler struck to mark the death of Frederik III and the accession of Christian V, beginning a long series of such coinages.
1688   Gold coinage with view of the fortress of Christiansborg in Guinea.
1708   Two ducats struck for the Danish West India Company.
1771   Trade piaster struck in imitation of the Spanish Pillar dollar, with circular

Danish and Norwegian arms replacing the two globes.
1808   Serious inflation leads to silver and copper, including the copper roof of the church of Our Lady in Copenhagen, used in dwindling-sized coins.
1813   National Bank tokens struck in copper.
1854   Last speciedaler of Frederik VII, silver rigsdalers form currency.
1873   New Scandinavia coinage of 100 ore to the silver krone, Christian IX.
1888   First commemorative under the new system, the 25th year of the reign.
1920   Copper-nickel 10- and 25-ore pieces replace silver, a consequence of the post-war economic crunch.
1941   Zinc minor coinage under the German occupation, 1, 10 and 25 ore; aluminum 2 and 5 ore.
1960   Copper-nickel replaces aluminum-bronze for the 1-krone piece; a new 5-kroner regular issue is begun in the same metal.
1960   A new bronze 5 ore replaces zinc; a silver 5 kroner marking the silver wedding anniversary of the royal couple begins another series.
1967   Silver 10-krøner commemoratives begin with wedding coins of princess Margrethe and princess Benedikte.
1973   New coinage of Queen Margrethe II includes copper-clad steel 5 ore.
1976   New Mint construction begins.
1980   10-kroner coin and 20-kroner bank note introduced.

NORWAY

1546   Silver crown-size gulden of Christian III.
1629   Thick double speciedaler struck by Christian IV.
1660   Gold ducat issued by Frederik III.
1704   First "reisedaler" or travel daler, specially struck to pay expenses of Danish king Frederik IV's trips to his Norwegian domain.
1819   Speciedaler of Carl XIV Johan, the former French Marshal Bernadotte, now king of Sweden and Norway.
1874   Transitional coinage struck for the change-over to the decimal 100 ore equals one krone currency.
1875   First regular issue krone coins struck.
1906   After achieving independence, Norway and her new King Haakon VII mark the occasion with a commemorative 2 kroner.
1910   Only issue of Norwegian gold, 20 and 10 kroner St. Olav coins.

1917 Iron replaces bronze in the 1, 2 and 5 ore coins during World War I.

1920 Copper-nickel minor coinage replaces silver; center holes make their appearance on coins not designed for them.

1925 Copper-nickel holed coins issued, designed around holes.

1941 Zinc and iron coinage of minister-president Vidkun Quisling's regime.

1942 London Mint strikes nickel-brass coinage for the use of the government in exile in the Faroe Islands.

1951 New post-war coins without center holes.

1958 Completely redesigned coinage with bird and animal reverses under new King Olav V.

1964 Silver 10 kroner commemorating the 150th anniversary of the Norwegian constitution.

1970 New 25 kroner marks the 25th anniversary of liberation from the German occupation.

1974 Redesigned coinage of King Olav V.

1981 Ole-Robert Kolberg becomes the new Director of the Mint.

1983 The 5 and 25 ore, and 10-kroner coins are withdrawn from circulation.

SWEDEN

995 Nordic coinage along English and Byzantine lines at Sweden's Hedeby Mint.

999 First Swedish coinage, King Olof Skotkonung.

c. 1150 "Penningar" bracteate coinage.

1478 First dated Swedish coins, ortug and half ortug.

1521 Reign of Gustaf Vasa, founder of a new dynasty for independent Sweden.

1534 Silver daler issued with standing figure of the king.

1556 Square klippe silver ore coinage.

1568 Gold gulden of Erik XIV, Hebrew name "Jehovah" out of clouds on reverse.

1598 Jehovah-name silver coinage, under regent Karl.

1606 Large silver 20 marks of Karl IX.

1611-32 Reign of Gustaf II Adolf sees Sweden caught up in the Thirty Years War on the continent.

1624 Square klippe emergency copper coinage.

1632 Queen Kristina issues silver riksdaler with standing figure of Christ.

1644 Massive copper "plate money" issues begin, valued in equivalence to the silver coins drained out of the kingdom to redeem fortresses held by the Danes.

1656 Gold ducat coinage under Karl X Gustaf; plate money continues.

1670 Portrait-type 8 marks in silver, similar to English coinage of Charles II, struck by Karl XI.

1661 Large copper circular ore coinage begins.

1697 Beginning of the reign of Karl XII, "Alexander of the North" and the exhausting wars of his reign.

1706 "Alchemy ducat" of gold allegedly produced by "the chemical art."

1715 Beginning of the emergency copper "Goertz dalers" named for the hated finance minister who was assassinated after a period of inflation.

1721 Commemorative riksdaler in silver issued by Fredrik I honoring the Protestant Reformation in Sweden.

1720 Coinage of 1, ½ ore coppers over old Goertz dalers.

1759 Last copper plate money issued under King Adolf Fredrik.

1810 Beginning of coinage under Karl XIII, Napoleon's candidate who deposed king Gustaf IV Adolf in 1809. Karl XIII adopts French Marshal Bernadotte as his heir, prince Karl Johan.

1818 Coinage of Bernadotte as Karl XIV Johan.

1821 Another Reformation commemorative riksdaler issued.

1835 Skilling banco token copper coinage.

1856 Decimal ½, 1, 2 and 5 ore copper coins of Oscar I.

1861 Decimal silver ore coins of Karl XV in style of Oscar's 1855 coinage, alongside the earlier issue of riksdalers riksmynt, struck until 1873.

1868 International currency gold coinage of Karl XV, one carolin equals 10 francs.

1873 Decimal system of the Scandinavian krona of 100 ore under Oscar II.

1897 Coronation commemorative 2 kronor begins a long series in this denomination.

1906 Following the independence of Norway, the royal motto on the coinage becomes "Sweden's Welfare," rather than "Welfare of the Brother Peoples."

1917 Iron is adopted for World War I 1, 2 and 5 ore.

1920 Copper-nickel replaces silver in 50, 25 and 10 ore.

1935 A commemorative 5 kronor marks the 500th anniversary of Sweden's Riksdag, or Parliament.

1942 New low-silver coinage, iron reappears in the lowest three values.

1952 New ultra-modern designs on the coinage of Gustaf VI Adolf, first modernistic royal portrait in the world.
1959 Smaller 5-kronor commemoratives begin with the 150th anniversary of the constitution.
1962 Copper-nickel replaces silver in the Swedish coinage.
1975 Constitution commemorative introduces silver 50 kroner.
1976 After many delays, new series of minor coins released for King Carl XVI Gustaf, 5 ore through 5 kronor.
1981 The 5 ore issued in brass.

FINLAND
1860 After groundwork by Minister of Finance J.V. Snellman, the grand duchy of Finland, under the rule of the Russian czar, adopts its own coinage of the Finnish markkaa of 100 pennia.
1917 Following the overthrow of the czar, uncrowned double eagles appear on the Finnish coinage.
1918 A single copper 5 pennia with Communist emblems is uttered by the Red forces during the Civil War. Normalized coinage of the new republic begins.
1926 Only gold coinage of modern Finland, 200, 100 markkaa.
1928 Aluminum-bronze 5, 10 markkaa.
1931 Aluminum-bronze 20 markkaa.
1941 Holed 5, 10 pennia, wartime issue.
1943 Iron war issues, 25, 50 pennia, 1 markkaa.
1951-52 The XV Olympic Games in Helsinki marked by a silver 500 markkaa.
1952 New aluminum-bronze, iron post war coinage.
1960 Silver 1,000 markkaa honors minister Snellman, founder of the coinage.
1963 Coinage reform, one new markkaa equals 100 old.
1967 First silver 10 markkaa honors 50th anniversary of independence. Currency devalued.
1969 Aluminum replaces the bronze 1 penni of the reform currency. Aluminum penni; copper-nickel 1 markkaa.
1972 Aluminum-bronze 5 markkaa.
1977 Aluminum 5 pennia.
1979 Production of penni ceases.
1983 Aluminum 10 pennia.
1984 Braille added to 10-markaa note to aid the blind.

GREENLAND
1922 Cryolite Mining and Trading Company copper-nickel tokens struck at the Copenhagen, Denmark, Mint.

1926 Royal coinage in copper-nickel and aluminum-bronze.
1944 Brass 5 kroner of 1926 design struck at Philadelphia Mint during the German occupation of Denmark.
1957 Aluminum-bronze 1 kroner struck with crowned polar bear coat-of-arms for the Royal Greenland Company.
1960 Same design struck in copper-nickel.

ICELAND
1926 Bronze, copper-nickel coinage under Iceland's King Christian X; 100 aurar to one krona.
1930 The millenary of Iceland's parliament, the Althing, is marked by commemorative coinage in silver and bronze.
1940 London Mint strikes bronze and copper-nickel of 1926 type without Mint mark during the German occupation of Denmark.
1942 Zinc wartime coinage struck.
1946 First bronze, aluminum-bronze coins of the republic.
1958 Nickel-brass replaces aluminum-bronze.
1961 A gold 500 kronur struck, commemorating Icelandic intellectual leader Jon Sigurdsson.
1967 Copper-nickel 10 kronur introduced.
1968 Copper-nickel 50 kronur marks 50th anniversary of sovereignty.
1969 Nickel-brass 50 aurar, 5 kronur in copper-nickel introduced.
1970 Aluminum 10 aurar, regular issue copper-nickel 50 kronur struck.
1974 Silver and gold coinage commemorates the 1100th anniversary of Iceland's settlement.
1976 The 1 krona is altered to aluminum from nickel-brass.
1981 Marine designs introduced on all circulating coinage.

RUSSIA (Soviet Union)
1704 First modern ruble of Peter the Great replaces archaic issues.
1764 Distinctive Siberian copper coinage, Catherine the Great.
1796 Paul I issues non-portrait coins with penitential inscription "Not unto us but unto thy Name, O Lord."
1834 First modern commemorative coin, ruble with Czar Alexander I memorial.
1828 Beginning of world's first regular platinum coinage, 3, 6 and 12 rubles, ending in 1845.
1902 Experimental international patterns of ruble-franc equivalency.
1917 Last Russian imperial coinage, fol-

lowed by vast flood of paper civil war necessity currency.

1921 New coinage of the Russian Soviet Federated Socialist Republic, R.S.F.S.R.

1923 Gold chervonetz, 10 rubles, first Soviet gold coin struck.

1924 Coinage begins in the name of the Union of Soviet Socialist Republics.

1961 "New ruble" coinage begun.

1965 First Soviet commemorative, victory in World War II anniversary.

1975 A 10-ruble chervonetz issued, first gold coin since 1923.

1977 An issue of 28 coins commemorating the Moscow Olympics commences in a four-year series.

1980 Last year of 10-ruble chervonetz production.

British Colonies
ISLE OF MAN

1709 Cast copper penny, half penny introduced by the Earl of Derby.

1721 Struck coppers of similar type.

1758 Copper penny, half penny of the duke of Atholl.

1786 Regal copper coinage of King George III.

1798 "Cartwheel" type regal coppers.

1811 Silver and copper private bank tokens issued during small change famine caused by the Napoleonic wars.

1839 Manx coinage on sterling system begins under Victoria.

1971 Complete U.K. type decimal coinage, half penny through 50 new pence with designs drawn from Manx history.

1973 Gold coinage, half pound through 5 pounds with Viking king reverse, Pobjoy Mint.

1974 Churchill commemorative crown begins prolific issues struck by Pobjoy Mint.

1976 Redesigned coinage eliminates "new" in new pence.

1983 Plastic notes introduced into circulation.

1984 Enters world bullion market with introduction of gold Angel coin.

LUNDY

1929 World-wide numismatic stir follows the actions of Martin Coles Harman, Lundy's owner, in issuing his own bronze coins, 1 and half puffin, named for the seabirds which breed on the island. Hauled into the Devonshire court, he was fined £5 for violating the Coinage Act of 1870.

CHANNEL ISLANDS, JERSEY

1834 French currency replaced with British in distinctively Jersey denomination series.

1841 First of the new coins issued, copper 1/13, 1/26, 1/52 shillings.

1866 Bronze coins, smaller sizes, in similar denominations.

1877 Conversion to standard United Kingdom denomin- ations, still uniquely stated as 1/12, 1/24, 1/48 shillings.

1949 The liberation from German occupation in 1945 is commemorated by a bronze 1/12 shilling piece.

1957 A new ¼ shilling nickel-brass coin introduced, 3 pence equivalent.

1966 The conquest of England by the duke of Normandy, of which Jersey was a part, is commemorated by three commemoratives, including the first regal 5-shilling copper-nickel crown.

1968 First decimal coins appear.

1971 Decimal range completed, ½ new penny to 50 new pence.

GUERNSEY

1830 Distinctive copper coinage of 1 and 4 doubles, relics of the medieval double tournois, still money of account until 1921.

1834 Eight doubles added to series.

1864 Bronze replaces copper.

1956 Redesigned bronze coins and new scalloped 3 pence.

1966 Round-cornered square copper-nickel 10-shilling Norman Conquest commemorative with portrait of William, Duke of Normandy.

1968 Decimal coinage begins, full range of bronze and copper-nickel complete by 1971.

1977 "New" dropped from pence denomination coins.

1985 First £2 commemorative coin introduced.

GIBRALTAR

1802-20 Private copper token coinage in circulation.

1841 Copper 1, 2 quart regal coins of Victoria.

1842 Half-quart completes roster of Gibraltar coinage, which ends in 1861.

1967 Copper-nickel crown issued.

1971 Famed Barbary ape appears on new crown of 25 new pence, start of ongoing crown series.

1975 Issues first gold coin.

MALTA
1521 Gold coinage of Philippe Villiers, grand master of the Order of St. John of Jerusalem, formerly based in the kingdom of Jerusalem and later on the island of Rhodes.

1553 Copper piccioli coinage under grand master Claude de la Sengle.

1566 The great Grand Master Jean de la Valette begins bronze grano coinage (followed by the tari types in 1567) with reverse inscription "not bronze but faith."

1723 First crown-sized silver coin, the 2 scudi of Antonio Manoel de Vilhena.

1798 Last coinage of the Order under Grand Master Ferdinand Hompesch; Malta conquered by Napoleon's forces, the Order withdraws, eventually relocates in Rome.

1798-1800 Siege of Malta, ingot necessity coinage under French general Vaubois.

1866 The British colonial government issues a distinctive third-farthing to approximate old grani coins, along with earlier British type third-farthings already in circulation.

1902 Edward VII third-farthing.

1913 Last Malta third-farthing under George V.

1961 The Sovereign Military Order of Malta, long domiciled in Rome, resumes a symbolic coinage struck by a small Mint set up in the palace in Rome.

1972 After the attaining of independence from Britain in 1964, a new decimal coinage of 1,000 mils or 100 cents to one Malta pound is begun.

IONIAN ISLANDS
1819 Copper obol coinage under British colonial rule.

1834 Silver 30-lepta coinage.

CYPRUS
1879 Copper piastre coinage of Victoria, first coins for the island since the medieval kingdom under the Lusignan rulers and the Venetians.

1901 Silver coinage begun, with a modified "Jubilee" head of Victoria used only on the Cyprus coinage.

1928 Crown sized 45-piastre coin commemorates 50 years of British rule.

1934 Copper-nickel scalloped 1, ½ piastre.

1947 Piastre denominations replaced by shilling types in copper-nickel.

1955 Decimalization, 1,000 mils to one Cyprus pound.

1963 Decimal issues by the new Republic of Cyprus.

1970 First crown issued after independence, 500 mils in copper-nickel for the FAO coin program.

1984 Mil coin denominations replaced by nickel-brass 1, 2, 5, 10 and 20 cents, and aluminum half cent.

ST. HELENA
1821 Copper half penny struck by the East India Company.

1974 Crown-sized copper-nickel 25 pence marks the anniversary of the E.I.C. royal charter.

1977 Silver Jubilee of Queen Elizabeth II sees crowns for St. Helena and dependency, Tristan da Cunha.

MAURITIUS AND REUNION
1779 Billon coinage of Louis XVI, Isles de France and Bourbon.

1810 Silver 10-livre crown for the Iles de France (Mauritius) and Bonaparte, (earlier Ile de Bourbon, still later the colony of Reunion).

1816 Ile de Bourbon billon 10 centimes of Louis XVIII.

1822 Base silver 50 and 25 sous issued by the Mauritius treasury.

1877 Decimal silver and bronze Victorian coinage, 100 cents to the Mauritius rupee.

1896 French Reunion nickel 1 franc, 50 centimes.

1934 First Mauritius 1 rupee in silver.

1939 Beginning of separate rupee-cent coinage for Seychelles.

1948 Aluminum colonial 1, 2 francs for French Reunion.

1955 Aluminum-bronze higher denominations in Reunion.

1971 Independence coinage of Mauritius, crown-sized 10 rupees bears the extinct dodo bird.

1972 Aluminum FAO minor coins, new copper-nickel seven-sided 5 rupee coins join Seychelles coinage.

1976 Independent coinage of Seychelles portrays President Mancham.

Near East, Africa
(Countries arranged by regions)
ISLAMIC COINAGES, NEAR EAST, NORTH AFRICA, RELATED AREAS
630-720 Anonymous ⅓ solidus coinages of the Caliphs.

660-750 Gold dinar coinage of the Umayyad caliphs of Damascus.

750-1517 Coinage of the Abbasid caliphs of Baghdad.

969-1173 Coinage of Egypt's Fatimid caliphs.

756-1024 Renewal of Umayyad coin types in Muslim Cordoba, Spain, by a refugee of the Umayyad house.

1040-1308 Seljuk Turkish empire coinage, Asia Minor and neighboring areas.

1056-1147 Coins of Spain's Almoravid Muslim rulers.

1130-1269 Almohad rulers, another splinter group of North African origin in Spain. Saracenic bezant gold coinage of the Crusaders' Latin Kingdom of Jerusalem, types of Muslim derivation.

1192-1300 Coinage of Shahs of Afghanistan.

1259 Last Jerusalem bezants of Latin Kingdom under Conrad and Conradin.

1451 Ottoman gold sequins of Muhammad II.

1502 Gold Ashrafis of Persian shah Ismail I.

1600 Gold of sultans of Morocco.

1773 Last coins of the khanate of Krim, Crimea, in South Russia.

1786 Modern round gold coin struck at Madrid, Spain, Mint for Morocco.

1789 Napoleon's invasion of Egypt sees 1, ½ and ¼ sequin coinage of Turkish type.

1823 Fath Ali Shah in Persia issues gold tomans with equestrian portrait.

1844 Abdul Mejid modernizes Turkish coinage, "Medjidieh dollar" struck.

1855 Distinctive coinage in Tunisia.

1876 Modernization of Persian coinage under Shah Nasr ud-Din.

1882 Round silver machine-struck coins of Morocco's Hasan I.

1885 Sudan coins of the Mahdi, Muhammad Ahmad.

1887 Coins of the khalifa Abdullahi, the mahdi's successor.

1891 Start of modern Afghan coinage under Amir Abd ur-Rahman.

1893 Modern copper coinage in Morocco.

1894 Coppers of Fessul bin Turkee, Imam of Muscat and Oman.

1904 Independent Yemen coinage of imam Yahya bin Muhammad Hamid ad-Din.

1916 First coins of Egypt of sultan Hussein Kamil.

1920 Last coins of Ottoman Turkey under Muhammad VI. Fuad, sultan of Egypt, issues his silver coins.

1921 French mandate issues Bank of Syria coin.

1922 First Turkish republic coinage. Fuad now king in Egypt.

1923 Hejaz coinage in bronze, silver and gold of Hussein ibn Ali.

1924 First coinage of the state of Great Lebanon, French mandate.

1925 Provisional coins of Abdul Aziz ibn as-Saud at occupied Mecca Mint. Reza Shah proclaimed ruler in Persia, solar year adopted.

1927 Distinctive Hebrew, English, Arabic coinage issued in Britain's Palestine Mandate, first coins to bear abbreviated name, "Land of Israel." Gold Pahlavi adopted by Reza Shah in Persia.

1931 First coinage in Iraq under King Faisal I

1934 Latin alphabet, western dates only on Turkish coinage.

1937 First coins of the "Kingdom of Saudi Arabia."

1940 Modern copper-nickel coinage in Muscat and Oman under Sultan Sa'id bin Taimur.

1947 Coinage of the independent Syrian republic.

1949 First coinage of the Hashemite kingdom of the Jordan, "of Jordan," 1955. French-type coinage in Algeria.

1952 Republic of Lebanon independent coinage; also kingdom of Libya.

1954 Egyptian republic coinage.

1956 King Muhammad V strikes Moroccan 500 francs after French protectorate is abolished. New coinage of Independent Sudan.

1958 United Arab Republic established, union of Egypt, (UAR coins 1958) and Syria (separate UAR coins, 1959).

1959 Following the murder of King Faisal II, Republic of Iraq coinage begins. Turkey introduces stainless steel coinage.

1960 Maldive Islands introduce new larin-rupee coinage. First distinctive republican Tunisia coinage in aluminum, aluminum-bronze.

1961 Kuwait strikes first independent coinage.

1962 Following breakup of UAR, Syrian Arab Republic strikes first coinage.

1963 Under Egyptian tutelage, Yemen Arab Republic begins coinage in the territory it is able to hold during continuing war with Imam's government.

1964 First independent coins of Algeria, federation of South Arabia.

1965 Coinage of oil-rich Bahrain, 1,000 fils to one dinar.

1966 Qatar and Dubai coinage issued, 100 dirham to one ryal.

1970 New Oman coinage based on Saidi ryal of 1,000 baizah.

1971 Following bloody revolution, "Democratic Yemen" coinage is struck for the former Federation of South Arabia. UAR (Egypt) adopts name, "Arab Republic of Egypt."

1973 Coinage of United Arab Emirates in Arabian gulf, former Trucial States, including Abu Dhabi, Dubai, Sharjah, Ajman, Umm al-Qaiwain, Fujairah and Ras al-Khaimah. One dirham equals 100 fils; 1,000 fils equals one dinar.

1972 Proclamation of loose union followed by identical eagle on coinage of Egypt, Libya and Syria.

1976 Iran adopts new Imperial calendar, year 2535 on new coins.

1979 Iranian currency no longer depicts monarch after overthrow of the Pahlavi dynasty.

ISRAEL

1948 Israel, only weeks old, strikes provisional aluminum 25 mils.

1949 Israel issues new 1,000 prutah to Israel pound coinage. Tenth anniversary of the independence of Israel sees beginning of commemorative coinage with copper-nickel 1 pound, silver 5 pounds.

1960 New Israeli coinage of 100 agora to one pound.

1985 Devalued Israeli sheqel coins issued in changeover to new sheqel monetary system.

SUB-SAHARAN AFRICA, ISLANDS

300-850 Coinage of the kingdom of Axum, ancestor of Ethiopia.

1755 Mozambique Portuguese gold coins.

1762 Angola Portuguese silver coins.

1791 Decimal coins for freed slave colony of Sierra Leone, "Lion on Rock" type.

1797 "Free trade to Africa by order of Parliament" coins of the Gold Coast, Ackey denominations.

1815 "Missionary coins" of Griqua Town, South Africa.

1833 American Colonization Society issues 1-cent copper coin for Liberia.

1842 Silver onca ingot-coinage for Maria II, Mozambique.

1847 Copper coins of republic of Liberia.

1874 Thomas Francois Burgers gold "staatspond," first official coin in South Africa, (old South African Republic, the Transvaal).

1881 Sultanate of Zanzibar issues gold, silver and copper riyal coins.

1883 French West African tokens, brass 10, 5, 1 centimes.

1887 Coinage of the Independent State of the Congo under personal rule of the king of the Belgians, Leopold II. Holed copper, unholed silver.

1888 Coins of the Imperial East Africa Company at Mombasa, rupee denominations.

1890 Comoro islands sultan's coinage, franc standard: first copper of the new German East Africa Company.

1891 First Italian tallero for Eritrea.

1892 Coins for President S.J.P. Kruger in the restored South African Republic, Mints in Berlin, Germany, Pretoria, South Africa.

1893 German East Africa silver coinage, company administration.

1894 Modern Ethiopian coinage in silver and copper under Menelik II.

1896 First regular issue silver coinage in Liberia.

1897 British East Africa pice-rupee standard.

1902 Last independent South African Republic coinage, the "Veld pond" at Pilgrim's Rest, Transvaal.

1904 New German East Africa coinage under the administration of the German Foreign Office.

1906 British East Africa aluminum 1 cent, silver 25, 50 cents. First regular issue aluminum coin in the world.

1907 Aluminum 1/10 penny, British West Africa-Nigeria.

1909 Belgian Congo's first coins under Belgian, rather than personal rule by Leopold II. Italian Somalia coinage begins on besa-rupia standard.

1913 Silver and copper-nickel coinage for British West Africa-Nigeria.

1916 Emergency coinage in the defense territory of German East Africa under General Paulus von Lettow-Vorbeck. The Tabora Railway shops produce both brass and copper 20- and 5-heller pieces as well as a 15 rupien gold coin.

1918 Italian Eritrea issues a "tallero veneto" in imitation of the standard Maria Theresia taler.

1920 Large franc denominations in copper-nickel in the Belgian Congo.

1921 Following hoarding of silver coins for jewelry purposes, brass coins replace silver in British West Africa.

1923 Pretoria Mint reopens to strike a full range of coins for the Union of South Africa (established 1910).

1924 First French coins for the former German colonies of Togo and Cameroon.

1929 Modern Portuguese coins for Sao Tome

e Principe, islands in the gulf of Guinea.

1930 New Portuguese coinage for Cape Verde Islands.

1931 New bronze, nickel coinage of Haile Selassie I of Ethiopia.

1932 New Southern Rhodesia coins.

1933 Modern coinage for Portuguese Guinea.

1935 Portuguese Mozambique introduces new silver standardized coins, adding copper-nickel and bronze in 1936, beginning a long colonial coin standard which was to permeate the rest of Portuguese colonial history.

1942-43 Coinage of the Free French in various African colonies, led by French Equatorial Africa under Governor General Felix Eboue.

1943 Pretoria, South Africa, Mint coinage for Belgian Congo for exile government.

1944 New Ethiopian coinage in bronze and silver under restored emperor.

1946 Portuguese Guinea marks fifth centenary of discovery with standard type commemorative coins.

1948 Standardized Angola Portuguese colonial coinage. French empire begins coinage explosion of standard-obverse Bazor type coins in many African, Indian and Pacific ocean colonies; initial types 1 and 2 francs in aluminum, aluminum-bronze and nickel added in 1960s in surviving colonies such as the Comoro islands.

1949 Cape Verde standardized Portuguese colonial coins.

1950 Italian trusteeship coinage for Somalia, 100 centesimi to one somalo.

1954 Last coins of Southern Rhodesia.

1955 Federation of Rhodesia and Nyasaland coins issued.

1958 Independent Ghana sets type for African coinages with new sterling-type coins portraying the "Osagyefo" Dr. Kwame Nkrumah.

1959 Coinage begins for former French Guinea, Federation of Nigeria. New unified coinage of the Equatorial African States begins.

1960 New coins for independent Cameroon, emission bank of Rwanda and Burundi; long-independent Liberia issues new bronze, copper-nickel and silver sets.

1961 South Africa decimal coins, 100 cents (Afrikaans, sent) to one rand; Katanga, Mali and the unified coinage of the West African States begins.

1964 French colonial coins of the Comoro become the first to bear a living fossil, the famed coelacanth fish; new independence coins in East Africa, Zambia, Rhodesia, Sierra Leone and Malawi.

1965 Malagasy republic coins in Madagascar introduces stainless steel to Africa; Ghana decimal coins; South Africa, new, smaller bronze, nickel and silver rand-cent/sent coins.

1966 Coins of Gambia, Kenya, Botswana, Tanzania and Uganda.

1967 Somali republic begins coinage; new 100 makuta to one zaire coinage, Congo. South Africa introduces gold Krugerrand coin and enters bullion market.

1968 Zambia, former Northern Rhodesia, begins decimal coinage.

1969 Ill-fated, short lived aluminum coins of republic of Biafra during the epic struggles of the Nigerian assault on the Ibos; new coins of the republic of Equatorial Guinea, formerly Spanish.

1970 Rhodesian decimalization.

1971 After break-up of the Equatorial African States unified currency, the new nickel 100 francs of Gabon, Central African Republic, Popular Republic of the Congo and Chad begins; decimal coins in Malawi, 100 tambala to one kwacha; decimalization in Gambia, 100 bututs to one dalasi; nickel coins introduced in place of silver in Portuguese colonies.

1973 Decimalization in Nigeria, 100 kobo to one naira; new Mauritania coinage of five khoum to one ouguiya.

1974 New decimal coins for Swaziland.

1975 Dissolution of the Portuguese empire leads to new currencies in Guinea-Bissau, Angola, Sao Tome and Mozambique.

1978 Madagascar Democratic Republic issues 10- and 20-ariary coins at five francs to the ariary. Uganda notes drop design depicting Idi Amin.

1979 South African circulating coinage design changes.

1980 Zimbabwe issues six denominations of coins, first issue for country. South Africa issues 1/10, 1/4 and 1/2 Krugerrands.

1981 South Africa introduces metal-plastic threads into paper money.

1985 Many countries ban importation of South African Krugerrand as a protest against racially-segregating apartheid policy.

India, Southeast Asia And Related Areas

(Countries arranged by region)

INDIA

1000-1300 Gold coinage of Chola.

1193 Coins of Sultan Muhammad, Delhi.

1302 Royal gold coinage of Bengal.

1495 First Portuguese colonial gold under Manoel I, Goa.

1540 Unusual but distinctive octagonal coinage in Assam.

1556 Innovative coinage of the great Mughal ruler Akbar.

1600 Portcullis silver coinage of Elizabeth I of England enters India to compete with Spanish silver reales.

1605 Portrait coinage of Sultan Jahangir, considered heretical by strict Muslims, who also emphatically disapproved of the appearance of the ruler's wine goblet on the coinage. Famed zodiac gold coinage issued.

1671 Silver 1, 2 speciedalers struck for the Danish East India Company.

1672 First British silver coined at Bombay, a city given by the King of Portugal as a wedding gift to King Charles II.

1677 "The rupee of Bombaim" struck under authority of Charles II.

1700 Beginning of the Muslim type coinage of the Nizams of Hyderabad.

1719 Gold coinage at Diu under Portugal's King Joao V.

1724 Dutch East India Company coinage in Cochin.

1730 Mughal type coinage under the French at Mahe in the name of Sultan Ahmad Shah Bahadur.

1735 British United East India Company, (E.I.C.) silver and lead coinage of Bombay.

1750 Gold mohar coinage in Nepal.

1751 French coinage of the Pondichery Mint in the name of Mughal Sultan Ahmad Shah Bahadur.

1760 Dutch East India Company gold coinage at Negapatam.

1765 E.I.C. coinage begins in Bengal, similarly in Bombay.

1768 Arcot-type French coinage at Mahe.

1791 Modern, machine-struck copper coinage produced by Matthew Boulton for E.I.C. in Bombay.

1794 Machine-struck copper for Calcutta.

1803 Madras struck E.I.C. modern copper.

1807 Silver pagoda coinage with figure of god Vishnu, Madras.

1811 Crown-sized double rupee struck over Spanish 8 reales at Arcot.

1824 Modern copper E.I.C. pice coinage for Bengal.

1833 First all-India coinage by E.I.C., 1/12 anna, ½ pice, ¼ anna, and half anna. These denominations become the standard through decimalization in 1957.

1835 All-India silver portrait coinage, gold mohur coins of "William IIII, king."

1839 Closing of French India Pondichery Mint.

1840 First portrait coinage of Victoria by E.I.C.

1841 State coinage of Kutch bears the name of Victoria.

1846 Last coinage of Danish India, Tranquebar.

1860 Following the great Indian mutiny and demise of the E.I.C., direct rule by Britain sees first all-India "Victoria Queen" silver, copper 1862.

1871 Modern machine-struck Portuguese colonial copper at Goa.

1877 Portrait coins of Victoria as empress of India.

1887 Standardized Victoria empress coins issued by Dewas and Dhar states.

1892 Bikanir state issues standardized portrait rupee; Hyderabad halli sicca coins struck.

1901 Gateway coinage introduced in Hyderabad.

1902 Modern gold in Gwalior, machine-struck silver in Indore.

1903 Bare-head all-India coinage of Edward VII.

1904 Modern copper coinage in Travancore.

1907 Edward VII copper-nickel 1 anna with scalloped edge struck.

1911 Modern silver coinage in Travancore; "pig" rupee of George V recalled.

1917 Modern sharply-struck coins in Kutch, in the name of George V.

1919 An attempt is made to replace smaller silver coinage with copper-nickel 8-, 4-, 2-anna pieces. The 8 anna, or half-rupee, is at once extensively counterfeited.

1942 Nickel-brass 2, 1 and ½ anna wartime coinage.

1943 Holed bronze 1 pice introduced.

1945 Rajkot state strikes last state gold coin, 1 mohur.

1947 Pure nickel rupee, half and quarter rupee, tiger reverse.

1950 First coinage of independent India.

1957 Decimalization introduces a rupee of 100 naya paisa.

1964 Subsidiary coinage now called simply paisa; first aluminum coin issued, and first commemorative rupee, half rupee honors Jawaharlal Nehru.

1969 Undated Gandhi commemoratives introduce new silver 10 rupees.

1974-75 Trend toward larger commemoratives, 20, 50 rupees; copper-nickel and aluminum small denominations begin to multiply.

1978 High-value notes of 1,000, 5,000 and 10,000 rupees demonetized to curb corruption.

PAKISTAN, BANGLADESH

1948 First coinage of the government of Pakistan.

1961 Beginning of decimalization, 100 pice, later paisa to one rupee.

1964 English legends omitted on Pakistani coinage.

1969 Copper-nickel replaces pure nickel in the higher denominations.

1973 Following bloody massacres and civil war, Bangladesh is born. A new coinage begins, based on the taka of 100 poisha.

CEYLON, SRI LANKA

1747-93 Silver, tin, lead and copper coinage of the Netherlands East India Company.

1801 First English coinage for Ceylon, crude dump types with Dutch denominations.

1802 Modern, machine-struck copper coinage.

1815 Copper stuiver-denominations and pattern silver rix dollar struck.

1823 Countermarked Arcot rupee and quarter rupee released to circulation.

1830 Reign of William IV sees circulation of British type half farthing and silver 1½ pence pieces in Ceylon.

1870 Decimal rupee adopted, 100 cents to one rupee; copper coinage struck.

1892 First silver decimal coinage, 50, 25 and 10 cents.

1909 Square copper-nickel 5-cent coin introduced.

1943 Wartime nickel-brass 50, 25 cents.

1957 First distinctive Ceylon independent coins, Buddhist commemorative issue.

1963 Full range of decimal coins, aluminum, nickel-brass and copper-nickel struck.

1972 First coinage with new national designation, Sri Lanka.

BURMA

1852 Silver peacock rupee coinage of King Mindon Min.

1865 Peacock copper quarter anna struck.

1866 Gold lion coinage.

1878 Copper quarter anna of the last king, Thibaw.

1949 Copper-nickel and pure nickel rupee standard coinage issued by newly independent Burma.

1952 Decimal rupee of 100 pyas adopted.

1966 Aluminum coinage with portrait of Gen. Aung San, founder of the republic.

1983 Issues 10 pyas bronze FAO coin for international series.

THAILAND

1767 Silver bullet money introduced by liberator-king Taksin.

1782 Bangkok dynasty introduces bullet coins struck with central ridge from two hammer blow striking.

1860 Modern silver tical coinage of King Phra Chom Klao, Mongkut.

1862 Tin minor coinage.

1865 Cast copper minor coinage.

1874 Royal monogram type struck copper.

1876 Portrait silver coins of King Phra Maha Chulalongkorn, undated.

1887 Portrait type copper struck.

1897 Copper-nickel decimal satang coins struck.

1902 Dates appear on the silver portrait coinage.

1908 Holed bronze 1 satang appears, 100 satangs to one baht.

1939 New national designation, "Muang Thai" or "land of the Thai" officially adopted in place of the former Siam.

1942 Tin replaces silver and bronze in the minor coinage.

1946 Royal portrait coinage resumed in tin.

1950 Aluminum-bronze minor coinage begins under King Pumiphol.

1961 The first Thai commemorative marks the world tour of the royal couple.

1963 The first recent crown-sized silver coin issued to mark the king's 36th birthday, 20 baht.

1970 Large silver 50 baht commemorates the 20th anniversary of the World Buddhist Fellowship.

1972 New polygonal 5-baht copper-nickel coin released.

1976 Silver 100-, 150-baht commemoratives joined by copper-nickel at 1 baht, beginning of a flood of modern commemoratives.

1978 Demonetization of 5-baht coin caused by counterfeiting.

CAMBODIA

1846 Gold rooster-obversed fuang struck by King Ong Harizak.

1847 Silver pagoda quarter and 1 tical.

1860 Franc standard coinage of King Norodom I, bronze 5 centimes through 4

francs silver, with a trade dollar or piastre equal to the Mexican peso.

1953 Aluminum three-coin set issued after
the restoration of independence, 10, 20
and 50 centimes.

1959 Similar coins issued in denominations
of 100 sen to 1 riel.

1975 Controversy is aroused by the release
through a numismatic distributor of
50,000-riel gold coins authorized by the
now-vanished Lon Nol regime; dispute
centered on the terms "legal tender"
and "face value," another argument
was raised over the "rate of exchange"
for the worthless currency of a vanished
government.

1981 Moneyless economy experimented with
by Kmer Rouge government.

LAOS

1952 Holed aluminum set of three coins, 10,
20 and 50 centimes.

1980 Exchange of 100 old kips for one new
kip.

VIETNAM

The early coins of Vietnam resemble
those of China, the square holed circular cash coins, which were cast under
the Le dynasty until 1789; by the Tay-
son rebels in southern Vietnam; and by
the Nguyen dynasty established by
Nguyen Anh in 1802. The ingots and
circular Vietnam issues are not considered true coins.

1802 Cast square-holed copper and zinc
dong coinage begins under Emperor
Gia-Long.

1883 Proclamation of a French protectorate
ends independence of Vietnam, which
already had lost Cochin-China in 1862-
67.

1884 Coinage of the heroic nationalist emperor Ham-Nghi.

1889-1926 Vietnam, its central region of Annam theoretically sovereign under
French protection, continues to issue
coins through the reign of emperor Bao
Dai, 1926-1945.

1945 Following the abdication of the emper-
or, the Communist-led Viet-Minh follow his earlier declaration of independence from France. The first aluminum
20 xu coin is released.

1946 Aluminum 5 hao and 1 dong, bronze 2-
dong coins struck, the latter two with
Ho Chi Minh's portrait.

1953 The state of Vietnam, with ex-emperor
Bao Dai at its head, issues three aluminum coins, 10, 20 and 50 xu.

1960 After the deposition of Bao Dai, the
new republic of Vietnam issues an aluminum 50 su and copper-nickel 1 dong
with the portrait of president Ngo
Dinh-diem.

1964 Following the murder of Ngo Dinh-
diem, republican coins with rice plant
obverse are issued in copper-nickel.

1968 Nickel-clad steel coinage released.

1971 An aluminum 1 dong issued in connection with the FAO coin program.

1975 Forcible unification of South and
North Vietnam as a newly united Communist state.

1979 North and South Vietnamese notes replaced with new dong notes.

COLONIAL INDOCHINA

1875 Old French 1-centime coins, holed, are
released to circulation, valued at 1
sapeque, for the new colony of Cochin
China.

1879 Square-holed 2-sapeque coinage in
bronze joins a large bronze centime and
silver 10, 20 and 50 centimes and a pattern trade dollar, the piastre with inscription "French Cochin China."

1885 Similar coinage is introduced for the
whole of French Indochina, which now
includes Cambodia, "Annam," Tonkin
and Laos.

1896 Smaller, holed 1 centime adopted.

1931 New Liberty Head piastre.

1935 Lindauer-designed bronze half centime
introduced.

1938 Holed nickel-bronze 5 centimes issued.

1939 Pure nickel and copper-nickel 10, 20
centimes struck.

1940 Following the collapse of France, locally produced zinc 1 centimes are issued,
followed by several aluminum denominations.

1945 Returning over Vietnamese protest, the
French issue aluminum and copper-
nickel coins of pre-war design.

1947 The last French issue is released, a copper-nickel 1 piastre struck in the name
of the still-born Indochinese Federation.

The Orient
(Countries arranged by region)

CHINA

B.C.

c. 1200 First spade coins, bronze "pu" types.

480 "Ming Tao" sword coinage, bronze.

c. 220 "Pan Liang" half-ounce coins, circular
with square hole, Ch'in Dynasty.

118 "Wu Ch'u" coinage of Han Dynasty.

A.D.

7 Usurper Wang Mang issues knife type coins, gold-inlaid inscriptions.

618 "Kai Yuan" circular coins with square holes; T'ang dynasty sets pattern for centuries of square-holed coinage which ends only after the new republic is in power, 1911. Similar coins will be in use in Japan, Korea and Vietnam centuries after.

c. 1264 "Wen Sheng," frugal currency bronze tablet coins of Southern Sung dynasty during Mongol invasions.

c. 1280 Paper money issued under Mongol Yuan dynasty, inflation and counterfeiting rampant.

1837 Manchu army issues circular "god of longevity" dollar for Taiwan.

1851 T'ai P'ing rebellion coins of the "Great kingdom of Heavenly Peace" and multiple-cash brass coins of Ch'ing (Manchu) Hsien Feng emperor.

1861 Round silver dollars of Fukien province.

1889 Modernization of Canton Mint. Kwangtung province sees famed "dragon dollars" and subsidiary coinage begin about 1890, soon copied in all China.

1912 First republican coinage, "memento" dollars.

1914 Yuan Shih-kai dollar becomes standard coin.

1915 Announcement of restoration of the empire with President Yuan as the Hung Hsien emperor, effective 1916, sees pattern and commemorative coinage issues.

1928 Kweichow province strikes first coin to show automobile in commemoration of the first motor road in the province.

1931-2 First Communist army coins for territories occupied during the Civil War.

1932 Standard national dollar in silver, famed "birds over junk - rising sun" type modified to show the sailing junk only in the next year.

1936 New, non-silver coinage in bronze and pure nickel.

1937 Japan begins full-scale invasion, Chiang Kai-Shek holds out amid civil war caused by Communists, continuing inflation.

1949 After defeat of Japan, Communist takeover proceeds amid bitter war. U.S. Mint at San Francisco restrikes millions of 1898-dated Mexican pesos for Chiang to pay his troops after inflationary collapse of the national currency.

1949 Nationalist government of Chiang Kai-Shek resumes coinage on Taiwan (Formosa).

1955 First aluminum coinage of the Communist People's Republic of China.

1965 Copper-nickel, silver and gold commemoratives mark centenary of Dr. Sun Yat-Sen's birth in Taiwan coinage, beginning of commemoratives for important anniversaries such as the birthdays of President Chiang Kai-Shek.

1979 Peoples Republic issues its first gold coin.

1980 Peoples Republic introduces copper-zinc coinage.

1982 China Mint issues gold bullion Panda coins.

1987 Bullion gold Panda coins carry Mint mark for first time.

JAPAN

708 First coins of native Japanese type cast, "Wado Kaichin" coinage made of copper mined in Musashi province under empress Genmyo. This is the first of 12 early coins called "dynastic sen."

765-950 Rest of dynastic coinage, from "Mannen Tsuho" through "Kengen Saiho" in 958.

1584 "Mumei Obankin" issued under warlord Toyotomi Hideyoshi.

1593 First "Eiraku sen," Japanese copies of China's Ming dynasty "Yung Le" cash coins cast, rapidly take over Japan's internal commerce.

1599 Tokugawa Ieyasu established "Kinza" Mint for gold coins, "Ginza" for silver.

1626-1862 Kanei Tsuho" cash type coinage.

1832 Debased gold and silver coins issued in inflationary period.

1835 Oval cast copper "Tempo Tsuho" coinage begun.

1853 Commodore Perry and his "black ships" begin opening Japan after 200 years of isolation. Japanese gold flows out of country.

1870 Osaka Mint comes into operation, striking modern gold, silver and copper circular coins. New monetary system, one yen equal to 100 sen along American lines.

1889 Copper-nickel introduced for 5-sen coins.

1938 Aluminum war time coinage.

1944 Coinage in tin and porcelain.

1945 Clay "toka" coinage planned, blocked by production bottlenecks, at war's ending.

1946 Coinage reform under Allied occupation, brass 50 sen.

1948 Coin inscriptions now read left to right.

1955 Pure nickel and silver coins introduced.

1964 Olympic Games commemoratives see return of silver crown, 1,000-yen piece; first use of Western dates since pattern yen of 1873.

1976 Copper-nickel 100 yen marks emperor's 50th year, fourth commemorative in this metal and denomination.

1982 500-yen notes replaced with copper-nickel coin.

1984 10,000-yen notes released due to inflation.

1986 Issues commemorative coins sold by lottery system marking 60th year of reign of Emperor Hirohito.

KOREA

996 "Kon Won" cast cash-type coinage of King Song Jong.

1100 Heavy cast cash coin production.

c. 1400 New coinage of Yi dynasty, "Sip Chon" issues begun.

1625 "Cho Son" cast coins.

1633 First stabilized currency "Sang Pyong" coins, often called "Yop Chon," issued well into the 19th century.

1885 Pattern for round, modern coinage of Korea introduced by Paul Georg von Mollendorf, Mint Director from Germany, on a yang-mun standard.

1886 Pattern warn-mun coins in copper, tin and gilt copper.

1892 Actual coinage of modern round pieces on 100 fun-one yang, soon overcome by a flood of officially-struck and counterfeit quarter-yang nickels.

1899 "Russian" 100 chon to one won coinage types prepared, some issued in 1901.

1905 Definitive Phoenix coinage on chon-won standard begun.

1910 Korean coinage ends with annexation to Japan.

1959 Following liberation, Communist invasion and war, coinage resumed on hwan standard.

1966 After overthrow of Syngman Rhee government, new won coinage begins.

1975 The 30th year of the restoration of Korea's sovereignty and independence is marked by a copper-nickel commemorative 100 won of South Korea.

Japanese states in occupied China.

1933 First coinage on 100 fen to one yuan coinage in new state of Manchukuo.

1934 Coinage in the name of the Kang Teh emperor, former Hsuan Tung ruler of China until 1911.

1937 Autonomous East Hopei government of Wen Ju-keng issues Chi-tung coins in five fen-yuan denominations.

1938 Autonomous federated government of Inner Mongolia issues coinage.

1941 Federal Reserve Bank of China issues three aluminum coins from Peking.

1945 Red fiber coinage, necessity issue of World War II.

Pacific Region
(Countries arranged by region)

AUSTRALIA

1813 "Holey dollar," pierced and counterstamped Spanish dollar issued in New South Wales.

1852 Adelaide Assay Office gold pounds, ingots struck.

1853 Fort Philip gold coinage.

1855 Sydney Mint gold coins Victoria 1-, ½-pound pieces.

1871 British style gold coins.

1872 Melbourne Mint gold coinage.

1900 Perth Mint regular gold coinage.

1910 First distinctive Australian silver coins of Edward VII.

1911 Bronze penny, half penny issued.

1927 First Australian commemorative coin, Canberra florin.

1937 Complete redesign of the coinage, first crown issued.

1942 Some World War II coins struck in U.S. Mints.

1966 Decimal coinage, 100 cents to the Australian dollar, silver 50 cents.

1969 Polygonal copper-nickel 50 cents joins minor copper-nickel and bronze coins.

1970 First decimal commemorative, Captain Cook's voyages.

1980 Currency futures market opens. Commences coining of $200 gold Koala coin.

1984 Dollar coin replaces dollar bill in circulation.

1986 Issues Proof 1987 Nugget gold bullion coins to preview gold bullion issue.

NEW ZEALAND

1933 First distinctive New Zealand coins, silver threepence to halfcrown.

1935 Waitangi commemorative crown struck.

1940 Bronze coinage of penny, half penny.

1947 Copper-nickel replaces silver in coinage.

1949 Crown commemorates aborted royal visit.

1967 Decimal coinage, 100 cents to one New

Zealand dollar, commemorative dollar series begun.

1982 A new portrait of Queen Elizabeth II is adopted on notes.

NEW GUINEA

1894-1895 Coinage of the German New Guinea Company, 100 pfennig to 1 Neu-Guinea Mark.

1929 Pattern coinage for the Territory of New Guinea.

1935 Regular coinage begins on sterling system.

1975 New decimal coinage, 100 toea to 1 kina.

COOK ISLANDS

1970 Commemorative 1 dollar begins decimal coinage.

HAWAII

1847 Copper 1 cent issued by King Kamehameha III.

1883 Silver dime through dollar coinage of King Kalakaua I.

FIJI

1934 Sterling-standard coinage of George V, half penny through florin.

1942 Some World War II coinage struck at U.S. Mints.

1969 Decimal coinage, 100 cents to $1.

TONGA

1967 Decimal coinage of 100 seniti to one pa'anga, portrait of late Queen Salote Tupou III.

1967 Coronation coinage of new King Taufa'ahau Tupou IV begins commemorative coin series.

1977 Ingot-shaped coin issued.

WESTERN SAMOA

1967 Decimal coins of 100 sene to one tala.

1969 Commemorative tala series begins with Robert Louis Stevenson coin.

TUVALU

1976 Formerly known as the Ellice Islands, Tuvalu opens its coinage history with a seven-coin set in bronze and copper-nickel, 1 cent through $1, featuring wildlife and sealife of this Pacific region.

MALAYA-EAST INDIES AREA

896 Hindu coinage in Java.

1297 Gold coins of the sultans of Acheh, Sumatra.

1601 Dordrecht, Netherlands, strikes first trade dollar of 8 reales for the United Amsterdam Company, forerunner of long "VOC" coins soon to follow.

1686 First Batavia gold ducats appear.

1728 Silver ducatoons of the United East India Company.

1786 Silver 3-gulden crowns.

1799 Batavian Republic coinage for the Indies.

1807 Indies coins of Louis Napoleon, King of Holland.

1814 First coins of kingdom of the Netherlands for the Indies.

1913 Copper-nickel 5 cents, first new type in decades.

1936 Holed type 1 cent, bronze.

1943 Aluminum and tin alloy Japanese occupation coinage.

1945 Last Dutch coinage for the Indies.

1949 Aluminum French colonial coinage for New Caledonia; French Oceania.

1951 First coins of independent Indonesia.

1962 Distinctive Indonesian coins for Riau islands and New Guinea, "West Irian."

1966 Silver 100-franc crown struck by the Paris Mint for New Hebrides, jointly administered with the British.

1967 New pure nickel coinage for New Caledonia, 10, 20, 50 francs; for New Hebrides, 10, 20 francs; 10, 20 and 50 francs for French Polynesia.

1970 Nickel-brass 1, 2 and 5 francs for New Hebrides.

1972 First of continuing coinage for French-administered islands by Overseas Emission Institute.

1975 Gold-on-silver coin of Solomon Islands repudiated by island government.

1977 Regular minor coinage for Solomons struck by Britain's Royal Mint.

1981 New Hebrides becomes Vanuata; issues new national currency — the vatu.

BRITISH MALAYA-EAST INDIES

1783 East India Company coins for Fort Marlbro, Sumatra, during Napoleonic wars.

1787 E.I.C. coins for Pulu Penang, cent-rupee standard.

1811-15 E.I.C. coins for occupied Java.

1841 Sir James Brooke's Sarawak copper kapang.

1845 First coins for the Straits Settlements under E.I.C.; 1862, "India-Straits."

1863 Copper coinage for Raj of Sarawak.

1863 Beginning of British Hong Kong coinage.

1866 Hong Kong Mint dollars.

1882 British North Borneo Company coinage begun.

1892 Sarawak issues world's only holed por-

trait coin, 1 cent with portrait of Sir Charles Brooke, rajah.
1903 Straits Settlements dollar struck.
1907 Straits dollar reduced size.
1935 Nickel alloys appear in Hong Kong coinage, replacing silver.
1939 New coinage under the Commissioners of Currency, Malaya.
1953 Coinage bears name Malaya and British Borneo.
1960 New copper-nickel Hong Kong dollar issued.
1967 New separate coinages for Malaysia, Brunei and Singapore.
1980 Singapore substitutes pure nickel for silver in $10 coins. Hong Kong Commodities Exchange begins gold futures trading.

PHILIPPINES
1803 Crude copper quarto coinage for Spanish King Charles IV.
1833 Counterstamped pesos of the New World in circulation.
1861 Distinctive centavo-peso coinage of gold, Isabel II.
1864 Silver denominations struck.
1897 Only peso struck for Philippines of Spanish type, Alfonso XIII.
1903 Centavo-peso coins under U.S. sovereignty.

1907 Reduced size silver coinage to halt export and melting of larger coins.
1936 Establishment of the Commonwealth of the Philippines, three commemoratives.
1937 Coinage of the Commonwealth of the Philippines.
1947 Restoration of the Republic commemorated by MacArthur peso, half peso.
1958 First minor coinage of the republic.
1961 Jose Rizal commemoratives begin an ongoing series.
1967 All new coinage with Tagalog or Filipino inscriptions, 100 sentimos to one piso.
1975 Redesign of coinage introduces square sentimo, scalloped 5 sentimos, 5 piso in pure nickel, and silver 25 and 50 piso, the latter in Proof sets. This set was partially struck for the Philippines by four different Mints in the U.S., Canada, Britain and West Germany.
1983 Piso devalued.
1984 1982-dated Reagan-Marcos commemorative appears in numismatic market, unannounced officially as released. Piso devalued by President Marcos due to flight of capital.
1986 Contracts future commemorative coin production with Pobjoy Mint rather than the Franklin Mint.

Dates on coins

There is an old vaudeville joke that goes, in one of its variations, something like this:
Stooge: "Look at this old coin."
Straight man: "How do you know it's old?"
Stooge: "Because of the date on it — 635 B.C."
The humor, of course, is that it would be impossible to date a coin with a B.C. date before Christ was actually born. But, for collectors of coins of the world, the possibility for date confusion is very real.
In the earliest days of coinage, dates, if used, generally refer to the regnal year or some other contemporary measure — for instance, the third year of reign of such-and-such emperor.

Dating coins by Anno Domini (A.D. — "year of our Lord") dates did not begin until the late 14th century. Coins dated in Christian era years from the 1300s are very rare, and the numbers appear as Roman numerals. Dates using Arabic numerals, those we are used to seeing today, did not appear until a century later. The use of Roman numerals for dating coins has risen and fallen in popularity. The latest manifestation is on the gold American Eagle bullion coins issued by the United States beginning in 1986.
Collectors of early modern world coins or

Islamic coins must be aware of a basic difference in calendars. In the West, we are currently in the 20th century of the Christian era, and dates are expressed as "1987" and so on.
However, coins dated using Arabic numerals but the Mohammedan calendar (A.H. or "Anno Hegira," the year of Mohammed's flight to Medina from Mecca) are currently in the 1400s.
Many novice collectors have been embarrassed to discover that their coin dated 1320 is actually from A.D. 1902.
To complicate matters, the Mohammedan

calendar is based on lunar years of 354 days, compared to the 365.25 days in the current Gregorian calendar, so it is not simply a matter of subtracting 622 from the A.D. date. To determine the Christian date from the Hegira date, multiply the Hegira date by 0.97, then add 622.

Year 1 A.H. began July 16, A.D. 622. The year 1000 A.H. corresponds to A.D. 1591; 1300 A.H. to A.D. 1882; 1400 A.H. to A.D. 1980.

However, a calendar based on a solar year was introduced into Iran and Afganistan about A.D. 1920. To convert dates from these countries, add 621.

Other major calendar systems, such as the Chinese lunar calendar, rarely use Arabic numerals to express the date, and the chance for confusion is less.

Collectors of modern Israeli coins may find dates in the 5700s, but these are not relics from the future; they are based on the Hebrew dating system.

Collectors of world coins can avoid confusion by becoming familiar with the various dating systems. However, a coin dated 635 B.C. is still a fake.

World Coins 12

World coin collecting

Many numismatists start their collections with coins, tokens, medals or paper money from their own country. Those items from other countries in the collection are the beginning of a "world collection."

The ancient Greeks collected their own coins, and the Romans collected those of the Greeks. As coin collecting emerged in Europe at the time of the Renaissance the attitude was that current coinage was too barbaric, and that collecting should be limited to that of the ancient world. In 18th and 19th century Europe, it was considered proper that a gentleman should have a cabinet of ancient Roman and Greek coins included somewhere in his study.

Due to lack of published knowledge, these collections tended to have many curious artifacts which were not numismatically related. The pattern for serious collecting, which is beneficial to the collector in any area of numismatics, did not become refined until the late 19th century.

Numismatics can be an adjunct to several disciplines. In many universities, particularly in Europe, courses in numismatics are required of archaeology and history majors. Others finding numismatics of interest are those studying art, economics, religion, languages or metallurgy.

We may want to establish the date the first coin was made. Like the game of chess, coins evolved, and we cannot say that in accordance with a specific edict of king so-and-so, on a certain date, were coins patented. Gold, silver and other metals represented value, and were bartered in the form of small bars or ingots, or round discs.

Later, someone stamped a weight on these pieces and they passed at fixed values. When the issuing place and king left their marks on these previously blank discs, coins can be considered in use. It is believed that the transition took place in about the seventh century B.C., probably independently in China and Lydia, Asia Minor.

Cultures generally issuing ancient coins which modern collectors study were the Greeks, Celts, Romans, Bactrians and occupants of India and China.

The medieval period begins about A.D. 476, with the fall of the Western Roman Empire. Modern coins generally date from 1500 onward.

Two distinct inventions divide modern coins, and many collectors limit their collections by these boundaries. Movement from hammered coinage to coins struck under pressure in a collar in England in 1662 marks one division, and was a definite step forward in the quality of coins produced.

At the end of the 18th century and the beginning of the 19th century the Industrial Revolution brought along with it steam pressure to operate minting machinery, allowing for more pressure for striking coins, and speedier production.

Famous men who interested themselves in coins, Mint machinery and production methods include Copernicus, Michelangelo and James Watt.

Until the 18th century, the hobby of coin collecting, again like chess, was considered reserved for nobility. Others who held coins were in circumstances where they usually had to spend them.

Hoards of coins which are found around the world today tell archaeologists the nature of the owner. If a hoard of 100 coins represents a time span of five years, with many duplicates, most all from one place and one ruler, it can be assumed the owner was a merchant or banker. On the other hand, if the 100 coins were without duplicates, spanning a couple hundred years, several rulers from many countries, we can speculate that the hoard was part of an early collection.

There have been many coins found in the western Soviet Union, between the Black Sea and the Baltic Sea. Some were Scandinavian coins, others from the Mediterranean area. What would these coins tell us? There was a trade route from the Black Sea, up the Dnieper River, overland about 70 miles to the Duna River and on to the Baltic at Riga. Merchants plying this route might lose or spend some coins, bury them in case of attack, or die with them in their possession — to be found a few centuries later and studied by modern numismatists.

Such hoards of coins would represent varied countries and rulers, spanning many years.

Until recent years, most Mints did not encourage sale of their coins outside of their country, directly from the Mint. Times have changed, and Mints, or central banks or trade agencies of governments, eagerly seek buyers for their coins in the world-wide coin collecting fraternity. Sale of paper money in this manner is just beginning to gain a degree of acceptance by central banks.

How to begin

How does one collect coins of the world?

One way is to acquire a representative coin for each country or place that struck coins; a more ambitious method would be to include a coin of each ruler in each country.

One can limit himself to coins of certain metal, or certain denominations, or size, or certain years. Hence, one collector seeks only coins struck in bronze; or only 20-cent pieces; or only 18 millimeters; or only his birth year.

Topical collecting can lead the numismatist into coin zoos (dogs, birds, fish, elephants) or trees, plants and flowers, bells, folklore, religion, medicine or music. Other subjects could be maps, chess, space (particularly popular on medals), sports, Christmas, ships, aviation, explorers or, in combination with the stamp hobby, seeking coins on stamps.

Doctors who collect coins have diagnosed ailments of rulers appearing on ancient coins.

Some collectors feel they must strive for completeness, and seek all denominations issued by certain countries, or each date and Mint mark of each type. The difficulty in this endeavor is that many scarce coins will be hard to locate, and expensive when found.

Some collectors concentrate only on coins of Proof quality — with polished, mirror-like surfaces. Others want coins that have been circulated.

Emergency coins, paper money and tokens issued by cities, nations or in prisoner of war camps are the goal of other collectors. This can become a highly specialized field, collecting to the exclusion of other numismatic items. History books and catalogs can weave a fascinating story of deprivation caused by war and economic disruption.

Non-circulating coins

Since 1950 the collector of world coins has become the target of opportunists who see the value of catering to collectors. The move started with Mints offering Proof sets at prices above face value plus costs, to add at the beginning what might be anticipated prices in a few years. When collectors began to complain that many coins offered in the early 1960s were not circulating as legal tender in the country whose name appeared on the coins, steps were taken by governments and private firms to see that a decree accompanied contracts for such coins which did not circulate.

Collectors were beset with legal tender coins which, in some instances, would have resulted in the death penalty for a citizen of the country named on the coin should he try to spend it in his local post office. Many of these coins appear separately in some modern catalogs under the heading of "noncirculating legal tender coins."

Today coins and paper money are offered by entities not recognized by the United Nations, often operating on the sovereign territory of another nation or visible as land only at low tide.

Starting in 1968, the Food and Agriculture Organization, a branch of the United Nations, extended a plan they had been fomenting with stamps. Various nations would place a food theme on stamps, coins and paper money and proceeds from the sale of those items would go to the FAO to help needy nations develop agriculture programs. The FAO plan was intended to last three years; in mid-1984 it numbered more than 1 billion coins, issued by more than 94 nations, with no indication of a cutoff date.

Introduced in the summer of 1974 was the Conservation Coinage Collection, intended to highlight endangered animals in numerous nations. Proceeds from sale of coins were to be allocated to those nations taking part in the program to further protection for the endangered animals.

Initially, the program was to include the following countries (followed in parentheses the name of the endangered animal they seek to protect): Mauritius (flycatcher, blue swallowtail butterfly, kestrel); Indonesia (Komodo dragon, Javan tiger, orangutan); Tanzania (cheetah, southern giraffe, black rhino); Costa Rica (great anteater, green turtle, manatee); Nepal (great Indian rhino, monal pheasant, red panda); and Thailand (white-eyed river martin, Sumatran rhino, brow-antlered deer). At least 24 nations participated in this program to issue uniform size gold and silver coins, three coins per country.

Where may collectors get coins of the world? While other portions of this almanac tell of coin prices as high as $725,000, a satisfying start on world coin collecting can come from coins which may cost less than 25 cents.

One can try writing Mints around the world. If you have the time and patience, the anticipation of waiting for coins in an envelope with colorful stamps from other continents can add to your collecting pleasure.

Do I have to collect coins to build a world numismatic collection? Not by any means, experienced numismatists will tell you. Sought by collectors are military and civilian decorations issued by royalty and military organizations; unit insignia of military and naval organizations; ration tokens and tickets; paper money from around the world, both emergency and regular issue; odd and primitive money; even gas and electric tokens and street car and bus tokens and tickets.

After you have embarked on your collecting plans, join a local club whose members share your interest; join a national organization, such as the American Numismatic Association and numerous specialty groups; display your collection and learn the background information on pieces in your collection. Before long, you will become an expert and others will seek you out for the advice you can offer them.

By all means, subscribe to *Coin World*. It has a special International section each week and a pull-out *World Coins* supplement with the last issue of each month.

Canadian numismatics

History of the Royal Canadian Mint

An expanding population, development of new areas and business growth were key factors in Canada's decision to issue its own money in 1858.

A popular early Canadian "money" was the beaver pelt. As the population grew, a mixture of coinage from America, England, France, Spain and other countries came into use. This ultimately proved unsatisfactory, bringing the decision to coin a national Canadian currency.

Canada adopted a decimal system similar to the American system. All Canadian coinage from 1858 to 1907 was struck at the Royal Mint, London, or, under its supervision, by a private concern in Birmingham, England.

In the closing years of the 19th century, the idea of establishing a Mint in Canada was formulated, one of the main reasons being that, at that time, gold production in British Columbia and the Yukon reached unprecedented levels and was being exported to the United States.

Promoters of the plan to establish a Mint believed that this would stabilize the price of gold. Also, government and banking reserves had always been held in gold coins of another country, or in bullion, and it was maintained that a policy of keeping reserves in domestic coinage should be inaugurated.

The subject of Canada having its own Mint was taken up with the British government by W.S. Fielding, then Minister of Finance for the dominion. Canada had never possessed its own gold currency and authorities felt that Canadian gold coins would not be circulated to any extent outside the dominion and that even locally the demand would be limited.

It would therefore be advantageous to the dominion to be able to strike a universally-accepted coin such as the sovereign. Since this could only be done by the Royal Mint or a branch of the Royal Mint, it was agreed that a branch would be established in Ottawa.

On May 2, 1901, Fielding gave notice to the House of Commons of a resolution for the provision of $75,000 as an annuity for the maintenance of a branch of the Royal Mint in Canada. Founded on this resolution, the Ottawa Mint Act was passed and received royal assent on May 23, 1901.

In negotiations with the British government, it was decided that provision be made for a coinage of 20 million pieces a year, and for the refining of gold on a small scale.

In 1905 construction began, and by 1907 the building was completed and machinery installed. The Ottawa Mint Proclamation in

1907, issued under the Imperial Coinage Act of 1870, fixed Jan. 1, 1908, as the formal date for the establishment of the Ottawa branch of the Royal Mint. On Jan. 2, 1908, Governor-General Earl Grey struck the first coin.

An Act of Parliament was passed in 1931 which established the Royal Canadian Mint as a branch of the Department of Finance on Dec. 1 of that year, and the staff of the Mint was transferred from the Imperial service to the Canadian civil service.

A committee was appointed in 1968 to draft the legislation to establish the Mint as a corporate body. Under Part X of the Government Organization Act, 1969, assented to on March 28, 1969, the Mint was established as a Crown corporation on April 1, 1969.

RCM today

The Royal Canadian Mint is recognized as one of the largest and most versatile Mints in the world. It is responsible for the production and supply of circulating Canadian coinage.

The Royal Canadian Mint's activities span many fields, including the design and production of coins, medals, tokens and die production. It has gained recognition throughout the industry for its advanced technology and its standards of quality.

Over the years, the corporation has been awarded significant international contracts and seeks increases in contract volume. In its continuing effort for innovative excellence, the Royal Canadian Mint is actively competing in the international coin market against other national and private mints.

Some recent export customers include the Bahamas, Bangladesh, Barbados, Cayman Islands, Costa Rica, El Salvador, Israel, Nepal, Nicaragua, Panama, Portugal, Trinidad and Tobago and Turks and Caicos Islands.

The Mint refinery's main function is to refine newly-mined gold bullion received from Canadian mines, much of which is made into .9999 fine Maple Leaf gold bullion coins. Subsidiary functions are to refine jewelry, scrap, placer deposits, fused metals and worn coin received from the Bank of Canada, and silver bearing materials received from other government departments and other divisions of the Mint.

Maurice LaFontaine is Master of the Royal Canadian Mint.

Facilities

The Royal Canadian Mint maintains its administrative offices at the Ottawa Mint in the capital city of Ottawa. The main production facilites include the Ottawa Mint, on Sussex Drive, which is equipped with furnaces and manufacturing equipment to handle most alloys. Production includes the supply of Canada's precious metal and commemorative coins, as well as medals and numismatic products for Canada and foreign countries. In addition, Ottawa Mint's activities include melting, rolling and refining gold, and the production of planchets and tokens. Its capacity is 300 million coins per year on a one-shift-per-day basis. The facility was shut down for a period to be modernized and was re-opened for production in 1986.

The Winnipeg Mint

The formal inauguration of Canada's new Winnipeg Mint in Manitoba ranked as one of the major numismatic happenings in North America in 1976.

Formally opened by Canada's Minister of Supply and Services, Jean-Pierre Goyer, on April 30, the $20 million facility is capable of producing 2.1 billion coins per year on a three-shift basis.

The Winnipeg Mint produces circulating coinage for Canada and contracted circulating coinage for foreign countries. Numismatic coins are produced at the Ottawa Mint.

Capable of meeting Canada's coinage need far into the future, the Winnipeg Mint's capacity is utilized in the production of foreign coins and blanks. Canadian officials made clear at the Mint opening that Canada, a substantial factor in the world coin market in the past, intends to expand that effort.

Orders for Canadian Uncirculated sets are acceptable each year commencing Jan. 1. Included in the set are the dollar, 50-, 25-, 10-, 5- and 1-cent pieces.

Correspondence should be directed to the Royal Canadian Mint, P.O. Box 470, Ottawa, Ontario K1N 8S5, Canada.

All orders must be accompanied by a certified check, post office money order or credit card in United States funds, payable to the Royal Canadian Mint.

The National Collection

The National Collection of coins and paper money is housed at the Bank of Canada, at 234 Wellington Street, Ottawa, Ontario. The emphasis is on Canadian material, but there is a selection of coins of other countries from all periods of numismatic history.

The National Collection of Medals is at the Public Archives of Canada in Ottawa. All types of medals, chiefly Canadian, are kept here, and ocassionally displays on a timely theme are exhibited. The National War Museum in Ottawa has an extensive collection of war medals and decorations.

The first steps toward establishing a national showplace took place in 1880 when the Dominion government purchased a Montreal numismatist's collection.

For many years the Parliamentary Library and the Public Archives of Canada were repositories for numismatic items accumulated from gifts to the Crown and other sources. A full-time curator was appointed in 1963.

Experts say the Bank of Canada now has the largest and most complete collection of Canadian coins, tokens and paper money in existence.

A sizeable addition was the acquisition of the bulk of the collection of Canadian coins, tokens and paper money formed by J. Douglas Ferguson of Rock Island, Quebec, considered the outstanding private collection of Canadian numismatic material in the world.

The Dominion's currency history spans approximately three centuries, broken down by authorities into the French Colonial, the English Colonial, and the post-Confederation periods. Coins and currency from each era are featured in the Bank of Canada's Numismatic Collection.

The first coins were struck for Canada in 1670 and the first paper money issued in 1675. A colorful paper money chapter was written in the late 1600s when playing cards became the first form of paper money in the Western Hemisphere. A shortage of metallic currency for French Canada forced its leaders to make money out of playing cards.

Mexico

Of all the countries in the Western Hemisphere, Mexico can safely boast one of the most colorful numismatic histories, traceable to the pre-coinage era of the Aztec and other native empires of the Americas.

Primitive money was used in exchange by local tribes and most notably by the Aztec Empire. Here copper miniature hoes and spades were used as exchange in much the same way as knife money was used in early China. Other primitive Aztec money included cocoa beans, colored beads, cowry shells, jade figures and quills filled with gold dust.

The Mixtecs used various shaped terracota beads, often engraved with images. Both the Mixtecs and the Aztecs used miniature bells of copper, both with and without clappers inside.

Organized as a Spanish possession after the successful conquest initiated by Hernan Cortez, Mexico became one of the richest gold, silver and copper mining areas in history, providing a worldwide trade coinage in both gold and silver through three centuries.

The historic Mexico City Mint began production in 1536 with silver quarter and half reales, 1, 2, 3 and 4 reales, issued in the name of Spain's rulers Carlos (later Holy Roman Emperor Charles V) and his mad aunt Juana.

An early copper coinage was unsuccessful, although research seems to indicate that the Indians were content to earn a few coins, drop tools until the coins were used up, stopping produce marketing until the coins were spent. This tendency, rather than any unpopularity of copper, may have led to suspension of the striking of these small denominations.

The silver coin of 8 reales, the famed "piece of eight," saw introduction in 1556 under King Philip II, one of the series of crude, irregularly shaped "cob" coins, struck more as true weights of silver than as fully round, modern coins. This "real de a ocho" became the lineal ancestor of the U.S. silver dollar, remaining legal tender in the U.S. until 1857 as the "Spanish Milled Dollar."

Gold coinage began in 1665 under the last of the Hapsburg kings, Charles II. The next major innovation was the perfecting of fully round "Columnario" or "Dos Mundos" coins, named for their design of two worlds symbolizing the Spanish empire, flanked by the Pillars of Hercules.

These new round coins, beginning with the 1732 date, have been faked extensively, particularly the early dates. This design was superseded by the royal bust type in 1772 under Bourbon King Charles III, which continued under Charles IV and Mexico's last Spanish ruler, Ferdinand VII.

Mexican independence was achieved in 1821. After the revolts of Fathers Hidalgo and Morelos, in this period of uncertainty, revolutionary emergency coinages in copper and silver first appeared.

The first definitive coins of the newly independent nation were the imperial issues of Emperor Augustin I Iturbide. Here appeared the Mexican eagle, crowned, seated upon a nopal cactus, similar to the bird in the Aztec legend of the founding of Mexico City, but without the snake of later designs.

Augustin's gold and silver coins were replaced in 1823 by the first republican coinage, the Hookneck or Profile eagle types which yielded in turn to the facing eagle, used until the 1940s. A number of Mints produced a uniform gold and silver coins, with small denomination copper coins issued by Mexico's states in a wide variety of designs.

The Second Empire of Emperor Maximilian saw new imperial decimal copper, silver and gold, again presenting a crowned eagle, supported by the Hapsburg griffins on the peso and gold 20 pesos. After the overthrow and death of Maximilian, the republic was restored. The decimal 1-peso coin was longed called the 8 reales as a trade coin.

The year 1905 saw the next major overhaul of the coinage, with new sizes and designs for the only remaining Mint, that of Mexico City. The silver types endured with minor changes through four decades. Gold coins first introduced in 1905 are still a regular offering on the bullion coin market, having been struck as late as 1948 for the tiny 2½ pesos; the 5 pesos was last dated 1955, the 10 and 20 pesos, 1959. Bullion quarter-, half- and 1-ounce coins called "onza oro puro" of .900 fine gold were issued in 1981.

Mexico's first commemoratives were struck in 1921 for the first centenary of independence, a silver crown-size 2 pesos with eagle in profile, and a large and heavy 50 pesos which was struck until recently and now is a prime gold bullion coin on world markets, known familiarly as the "Centenario."

Beginning in 1947, silver content in Mexico's coinage began a series of changes, which ended in the adoption of bronze for all minor coins in the mid-1950s, and copper-nickel after 1970. By 1977, copper-nickel 10, 20 and 50 centavos, 1, 5 and 10 pesos were in exclusive use.

Date and design varieties on the most recent Mexican coins provide considerable interest for collectors, as have delays in releasing some denominations, such as the tiny 10 centavos and seven-sided 10 pesos, known to have been struck since 1974 but only appearing years after.

Mexico's commemoratives blossomed in

the 1950s, with eight major silver types appearing to honor railway construction, independence struggle heroes, and 19th and 20th century patriots. Most were produced in goodly numbers and are available on the market at reasonable cost.

Mexico's last silver coins were the 1972 25-peso piece with facing bust of President Benito Juarez, the 100 pesos of 1977, struck to encourage the nation's silver mining industry, and the one troy ounce Libertad coins beginning in 1982.

A footnote to Mexican coinage is the 1913-1917 emergency money, struck in a wide range of metals during the revolution which followed the long dictatorship of President Porfirio Diaz.

These crude, locally struck or cast pieces are highlighted by famous coins like the Durango "Muera Huerta," or "Death to Huerta" peso and the massive gold 60 pesos of Oaxaca, today classic rarities of Mexican numismatics.

On Oct. 6, 1983, a new branch Mint was opened in the silver mining town of San Luis Potosi.

The Uncirculated Mint Set Program began in 1977. The address in Banco National de Mexico, S.A., Division Internacional, I. la Catoalica 44, Mexico 1, D.F.

The Mexico Mint was converted into an autonumus institution having independent status under the law, with its own assets, by a presidential decree dated Dec. 26, 1985.

Under the decree the Mint is still the minting center of coins ordered by the Mexican Congress and authorized by the Bank of Mexico. However, the Mint can now design and produce medals for the Mexican government, commemorative medals for official or private use, bars and plaques of precious metals as authorized by the Secretariat of Finance and the Bank of Mexico, and foreign coinage by order of the Mexican government or directly by the foreign government.

World Olympic coins

More than 1,000 years before Christ worshippers gathered in the sacred valley in Elis, on the western coast of Greece, to pay homage to their gods. Soon the festivals included game competitions, held at the tomb or before the funeral pyre of those being remembered. As the entire community joined in, and competition extended to neighboring towns, the Olympics evolved.

Coroebus of Elis was the first victor named in the oldest records available, 776 B.C. Sport

competition was added from time to time, with the first games recorded on a coin in 480 B.C., a silver tetradrachm struck at Messana, Sicily.

The piece weighs 17.5 grams, measures 25 millimeters in diameter, and depicts the race of a biga, a two-horse chariot, with Nike flying overhead, on the obverse. On the reverse is the inscription MEZZENION.

The games in 356 B.C. are recalled by a silver tetradrachm depicting a small rider astride a prancing horse. Zeus is shown on the reverse of the piece. The irregular coin measures 22 to 25mm, weighs 14.2 to 14.5 grams, struck in Macedonia.

Wrestlers grappling for the best hold appear on the obverse of a silver stater of Aspendus, Pamphylia, struck between 373 and 350 B.C. An athlete aiming a sling is shown on the reverse. The coin measures 22mm; averaging 10.7 to 11 grams in weight.

The earliest known dated Olympic medal is a gold medal award to a victor in the A.D. 242 games held in Rome. Gordian III, the Roman emperor, dedicated the games to the memory of Alexander the Great.

On June 23, 1894, it was agreed that the first modern games would be held in Athens in 1896.

First prize medals awarded Olympic competitors are 60mm in diameter, .925 fine silver, plated with at least six grams of fine gold; 3mm thick. Second place medals are .925 fine silver; bronze medals, also 60mm, go to the third place winners.

The Olympic Games have increased in participation since 1896, with 42 events joined by 13 nations and 285 athletes in 1896 to the Los Angeles Olympics of 1984, hosting 141 nations and more than 8,000 athletes.

An Olympiad is a four-year period beginning with the end of the games competition, such as the final day of the Montreal Games, 1976; at that time, the 22nd Olympiad, Moscow 1980, began.

Games are named for the city where performed, not the nation. Many collectors make a distinction between Olympic commemorative coins struck by the host nation and those struck by other nations. The XXIV Olympiad Summer Games will take place in Seoul, South Korea, in 1988. The XV Winter Games will take place in Calgary, Alberta, Canada, that year.

FAO Ceres medals

Beginning in 1971, the United Nations Food and Agriculture Organization started a program of Ceres medals, portrayed by women all over the world, to highlight the crucial role that women play in meeting world food needs.

In the order of release, the names of women portraying Ceres to date have included:

Indira Gandhi
Olave Baden-Powell
Angela Christian
Coretta Scott King
Germaine Tillion
Sonia Navas
Michele Morgan
Marie-Therese Basse
Mother Teresa
Iris Murdoch
Kathleen Kenyon
Matsuyo Yamamoto
Attiya Inayatullah

Margaret Mead
Jacqueline Auriol
Shirley Temple Black
Irene de Borbon de Parma
Dechhen Wangchuck
Aziza Hussein
Gloria Steinem
Thangam Philip
Julia Ojiambo
Alva Myrdal
Margot Fonteyn de Arias
Vittoria Nuti Ronchi
Barbara Ward

Dr. Fatima Abdel Mahmoud
Lillian Carter
Dorothy Nyembe
Grace of Monaco
Sirimavo Bandaranaike
Farah Pahlavi
Alpine shepherdess
Cicely Williams
Helen Newton Turner
Pauline Jewett
Queen Sirikit of Thailand
Portrait of Roma as
   Ceres on denarius

A Primer of ancient coins

Coinage in any land will tell an observer much about the people who issued and used it. A nation's religious beliefs, politics, artistic sense, sport, wars and above all its basic sense of priorities will emerge in the coinage.

The peoples of the ancient world, of Greek city-states and their colonies, of Rome with its long-enduring empire, the ancient Jews and the Byzantines, left a numismatic record of their hopes, fears and ambitions that has been unequaled in later ages. They were to create a wealth of design that to this day is considered a model of beauty and excellence.

Coinage had its roots in Asia Minor during the seventh century, in the bean-shaped blobs of electrum, a natural alloy of gold and silver, issued by Greek settlements along the Aegean coast. These earliest attempts at a metal medium of exchange were crude and simple, marked only by striations or punches.

It was left to the kings of Lydia in southern Asia Minor to refine these beginnings into recognizeable coins. Croesus, whose wealth assured him a permanent place in legend, launched a bimetallic coinage during his reign, 560-546 B.C., by stamping a lion facing a bull on the obverse of the gold staters.

The Mediterranean world, very much of a community in this era, was to accept these new coins, establishing the basic principle that a good coin, of reliable weight and fineness, of easily recognized type, was clearly superior to a commodity offered in barter.

By the early years of the seventh century, the idea of coinage had spread to the Greeks, whose city-states possessed a resilient, dynamic civilization of unequaled artistic consciousness, a consciousness which permeated every aspect of their citizens' daily lives.

Coinage in Europe is believed to have begun with the silver "turtle" staters of Aegina, a small island in the Saronic gulf south of Athens, about the beginning of the seventh century B.C. The Aegina coins set the basic form of ancient Greek coinage, and deserve some examination.

In a world in which many were illiterate, symbols rather than actual inscriptions were of the greatest importance. A simple, clearly recognizable emblem, a bird, animal, god, plant or figure from a shared mythology was of the utmost importance in making coins acceptable in such a world.

Thus, the Aegina turtle, Athenian owl, Corinthian winged horse, Theban shield and the Eretrian gorgon head became metallic purity "trademarks," guaranteeing the recognition and acceptance of the coins upon which they were featured.

Another advantage of such symbolic coinage was that merchants could demand payment in, let us say, Athenian "owls," thus assuring a return of such coins to their city of issue. More than 1,400 Mints were to see operation in ancient Greece, producing a coinage of silver staters, drachms and their many divisions and multiples.

Gold was seldom coined, except in sieges and emergencies. Bronze was not in general circulation, as many carried coins in their mouths, and the development of purses of various sorts was clearly required before copper alloy coinage could gain much popularity. Silver was the only acceptable metal in commerce and trade.

Greek coinage

Greek or Hellenistic coinage was to spread from the coast of Asia Minor to Greece itself, from there to lower Italy, Sicily, what is now the south of France, Spain and North Africa. After Alexander the Great's conquests, Greek-type coinage was to span the known world from what is now Morocco to Bactria in present-day Afghanistan.

Greek coins mirrored the strongly held esthetic ideals of the people they served. Their strong, detailed designs provided an example still pursued in the complex, mechanized world of today.

Numismatists agree that the most beautiful Greek coinages were those of "Magna Graecia," the colonies in southern Italy and Sicily. On the mainland of the "boot" were Mint cities such as Metapontum and Croton, which evolved a beautiful system which saw a simple figure such as the Apollo tripod and ear of barley in relief on one side of the broad, thin coins, with a reiteration of the feature in intaglio on the reverse.

Syracuse in Sicily produced large, heavy 10-drachm coins, decadrachms which set a standard of excellence in design seldom exceeded. Even under siege the designers produced coins of consummate beauty.

Designers such as Euainetos, Kimon, Eumenes and Eucleidas engraved and signed coins that made them immortal in the field of numismatic art. Kimon's commemorative decadrachm marking the naval victory over supposedly invincible Athens carried a head of Arethusa believed by many to be one of the ultimate designs of all time.

The Acragas decadrachm with its two eagles tearing a captured hare; the Mende tetradrachm with the god of wine Bacchus reclining on a donkey; the man-faced bull on the coins of Sicilian city-state of Gela; and the Hercules and lion coins of Tarentum could all be mentioned as outstanding examples of the magnificent numismatic art that attracts collectors to ancient Greek coins today as in centuries past.

Collectors entering the Greek field would do well to arm themselves with a selection of good reference books, a classical atlas and a willingness to study and to learn. It would also be highly advisable to find a knowledgeable and reliable dealer, who can distinguish genuine coins from counterfeits.

The item of expense should also be squarely faced. A Syracusan decadrachm set a record price of $273,000 in a coin auction in Europe during 1974. While most collectors will steer clear of this type of coin, many nice Greek coins in acceptable condition remain at reasonable prices.

Roman coinage

The long and diverse coinage of Rome developed rather late in the history of the Republic, with barter playing a key role until the expansion of the state brought Rome into contact with coin-producing Greek cities in Italy.

The development of Roman coinage mirrored the basic outlook of the Roman mind. While the Greeks sought beauty in all things, the Roman sought practicality, law and power. The first coins of Rome were the cast bronze "aes grave" bearing the image of the double-faced god Janus.

These early coins weighed a pound each and must have been cumbersome in daily use. As time went by, the bronze coinage was gradually reduced to smaller sizes. During the third century B.C., silver didrachms were being struck for Rome by Mint towns in the Campanian plain, and the long career of Roman coinage was under way.

Design features of Roman Republic silver included scenes from the mythical founding of the city, Romulus and Remus suckled by the she-wolf, the rape of the Sabine women, and events of the early wars.

The expanding Roman state was continually at war, making large coin issues a practical necessity to pay soldiers and purchase supplies. As a result Republican silver coins are relatively plentiful and inexpensive, ideal for a collector of moderate means.

Roman coins acted as propaganda for their day. Victories, sporting events, public buildings and political events were all commemorated in a seemingly endless procession of coin types.

The Roman Mint was under the patronage of the goddess Juno Moneta, the personification of money and financial probity. She was one of a number of personified virtues, including hope, security, joy, fertility and abundance, to name only a few of the many that were to adorn the reverses of hundreds of different coins.

Portraits of persons rather than gods were uncommon on Greek coinage until after the time of Alexander the Great; they were unknown on Roman coins until the latest era of the Republic, the Imperatorial period.

In the first century B.C., portraits of living men began to adorn coins, often as a form of personal propaganda for aspiring leaders such as Pompey the Great, Marc Antony and above all Caius Julius Caesar. These imperatorial coins foreshadowed the imperial portrait coins that began with Augustus in the beginning of the Christian era.

Collectors have eagerly sought the coins of this period, largely because of their historic importance. Especially sought have been Caesar's portrait coins and the now rare issues of the several conspirators who assassinated him. A popular piece is the denarius of Brutus, bearing the daggers of the killing and significant inscription, the "Ides of March."

The empire struck coins for four centuries in gold, silver, orichalcum, copper and bronze. Billon, a base silver alloy, was used in provincial Mints in the Near East. Generally, the gold coins, the aureus and solidus, are scarce and high priced. Silver coins are relatively inexpensive, and often are found like the gold in excellent condition.

This is because the precious metal coins tended to be hoarded, leaving the base metal coins, the sestertius, follis and their relations, to bear the brunt of most daily commerce. This has resulted in making bronze coins in the higher categories rather scarce, as they circulated until nearly smooth from handling. Few well-preserved specimens have survived.

The coins of the Roman emperors are masterpieces of portraiture, especially in the early reigns. The engravers plainly sought realistic and sometimes merciless likenesses. It is doubtful that any modern dictator would tolerate the pitiless realism with which Mint engravers highlighted the gross, perverted features of Nero or the vicious vacuousness of Caligula.

One attraction of Roman coins is the historical documentation they represent. The great names of Augustus, Trajan, Hadrian or Marcus Aurelius; the names of tyrants, such as Nero, Caracalla or Heliogabalus; the record of wars, conquests, triumphs and tragedies all are brought to life by these pieces of numismatic history.

As with the Greek series, a collector starting out in the field of Roman coins needs to prepare himself for some study. A knowledge of Latin helps but is really not an absolute necessity. The collector should acquire a small working library of popular-priced books and a historical reference, and go at it; the expense can be kept reasonable, and great satisfaction achieved.

It helps again, to patronize a professional numismatist of integrity and knowledge. In perhaps no other field is it truer that "if you don't know your coins, know your dealer."

There are various ways to go about assembling a representative Roman collection. One of the most logical and popular is to start by seeking one coin of each emperor. With a few exceptions, short-lived or would-be rulers, this goal can be reached at moderate expense.

Collectors can thank the efficiency of the ancient Mint masters for this. They worked fast to introduce new coins for a new ruler. Didius Julianus, for example, bought the throne in A.D. 193 and held it only a few months, but the Mints produced 19 portrait coin types of this emperor, as well as coins portraying his wife and daughter.

Judaic coinage

Another branch of ancient coin collecting which enjoys a great popularity is the historic Judaic coinage. Coinage of Judaea goes back to the fifth century B.C. when Greek type coinage began.

The rule of the Maccabees produced a more national coinage of simple but attractive style, succeeded by the Hellenistic-Roman types of the Herodian client kings.

Perhaps the most beautiful and significant coins before the rebirth of Israel in our time are the bronze and silver coins of the First Revolt, which ended with the Romans' destruction of the Temple in A.D. 70. Their simple and harmonious designs are in strange contrast to the violence and ultimate defeat of the Revolt.

Coins of the first century's Bar-Kochba War evoke a feeling of communion with this last outburst of the Jewish longing for independence and the restoration of Jerusalem and the Temple. The Temple's facade and sacred instruments adorn the coins, many overstruck on contemporary Roman issues.

Byzantine coinage

The basic unit of Byzantine coinage was the gold solidus, or nomisma, the latter often struck in a characteristic cupped shape. There was little silver in circulation; such denominations as the miliaresion and hexagram enjoyed, at best, a limited life.

The emperor Anastasius I decreed a unified bronze coinage in 498, with the actual denomination in multiple nummi expressed on each coin. Byzantine bronze was issued in considerable quantities, and is still available at quite reasonable prices.

Collectors of Byzantine coinage have a standard volume available to them, *Byzantine Coins and Their Values*, by David R. Sear. It was printed by B. A. Seaby Ltd., Audley House, 11 Margaret St., London W1N 8AT, Great Britain.

Collectors would be well advised to study all Byzantine gold coins with great attention, however, as counterfeits, even in museum collections, are plentiful, as one might expect from a coinage which spanned a large part of the world in its time.

With something to offer to every segment of collecting taste, ancient coins are undoubtedly on the rise. Interest in art, history and even profit spurs activity in the field; and it can safely be said that for expansion of an individual's knowledge, few areas of numismatics can offer as much as the systematic collecting of ancient coins of all types.

Foreign coin production in the U.S.

To facilitate collecting of foreign coins struck at the U.S. facilities, this format supplements the United States Mint charts.

Coins struck at United States Mint facilities 1977-87 are listed by country. United States Mint facilities did not strike any foreign coins in 1985, 1986 or through May 1987.

DOMINICAN REPUBLIC

1978	50 centavos...	Philadelphia	732,000
1979	50 centavos...	Philadelphia	300,000
1979	50 centavos...	San Francisco	5,015
1980	50 centavos...	Philadelphia	554,000
1981	50 centavos...	Philadelphia	1,000,000
1982	50 centavos...	Philadelphia	1,300,000
1978	25 centavos...	Philadelphia	995,000
1979	25 centavos...	Philadelphia	1,785,000*
1979	25 centavos...	San Francisco	5,015
1980	25 centavos...	Philadelphia	504,000
1981	25 centavos...	Philadelphia	2,600,000
1982	25 centavos...	Philadelphia	3,200,000
1978	10 centavos...	Philadelphia	6,490,000
1979	10 centavos...	San Francisco	5,015
1980	10 centavos...	Philadelphia	600,000
1981	10 centavos...	Philadelphia	4,400,000
1982	10 centavos...	Philadelphia	6,000,000
1978	5 centavos...	Philadelphia	4,984,000
1979	5 centavos...	San Francisco	5,015
1981	5 centavos...	Philadelphia	5,300,000
1982	5 centavos...	Philadelphia	4,500,000

1978	1 centavo....	Philadelphia	5,980,000
1979	1 centavo....	San Francisco	5,015
1981	1 centavo....	Philadelphia	200,000
1978	1 peso	Philadelphia	80,000
1979	1 peso	San Francisco	5,015
1981	1 peso	Philadelphia	20,000

HAITI

1979	50 centime ...	San Francisco	2,000,000

PANAMA

1980	10 balboa.....	Philadelphia	5,000,000
1979	½ balboa	Philadelphia	1,000,000
1980	½ balboa	Philadelphia	1,000,000
1982	½ balboa	Philadelphia	1,500,000
1984	½ balboa	Philadelphia	350,000
1979	¼ balboa	Philadelphia	2,000,000
1980	¼ balboa	Philadelphia	2,000,000
1982	¼ balboa	Philadelphia	3,148,000
1984	¼ balboa	Philadelphia	5,000,000
1982	1/10 balboa..	Philadelphia	7,740,000
1984	10 centesimo..	Philadelphia	7,750,000
1982	5 centesimo..	Philadelphia	8,400,000

1983	5 centesimo..	Philadelphia	5,500,000
1984	5 centesimo..	Philadelphia	2,000,000
1977	1 centesimo..	West Point	10,000,000
1978	1 centesimo..	West Point	10,000,000
1979	1 centesimo..	West Point	10,000,000
1980	1 centesimo..	West Point	10,000,000
1981	1 centesimo..	West Point	10,000,000
1982	1 centesimo..	West Point	2,000,000

1983	1 centesimo..	Philadelphia	20,000,000
1984	1 centesimo..	Philadelphia	25,000,000

PERU

1977	1 sol........	Philadelphia	2,100,000

PHILIPPINES

1977	5 sentimo ...	Philadelphia	1,088,000

*Struck in 1978, dated 1979.

Summary of foreign coinage by U.S. Mints, by country.

Country	Number of pieces produced	Country	Number of pieces produced
Argentina (blanks).............	64,058,334	Hawaii[1].......................	1,950,000
Australia.....................	168,000,000	Honduras....................	115,929,500
Belgian Congo	25,000,000	Indo-China...................	135,270,000
Belgium	25,000,000	Israel.......................	91,000
Bolivia	30,000,000	Korea	295,000,000
Brazil (blanks)	406,249,266	Liberia	56,744,679
Canada......................	85,170,000	Mexico	91,076,840
China	39,720,096	Mexico (blanks)..............	175,714,411
China, Republic of (Taiwan)	428,172,000	Nepal	195,608
Colombia....................	133,461,872	Netherlands..................	562,500,000
Costa Rica	131,798,820	Neth. E. Indies...............	1,716,368,000
Cuba.......................	496,559,888	Nicaragua...................	26,080,000
Curacao	12,000,000	Panama (Republic)	222,809,191
Dominican Republic...........	105,474,297	Peru........................	761,067,479
Ecuador	214,451,060	Philippines..................	3,483,718,169
El Salvador..................	226,695,351	Poland	6,000,000
Ethiopia	375,433,730	Saudi Arabia	124,712,574
Fiji	4,800,000	Siam (Thailand)..............	20,000,000
France......................	50,000,000	Surinam (Netherlands Guiana) ...	21,195,000
Greenland	100,000	Syria	7,350,000
Guatemala..................	7,835,000	Venezuela...................	306,762,944
Haiti	90,324,000	Totals (42 countries)	11,250,839,109

[1] Coined prior to Aug. 21, 1959, when Hawaii became the 50th State of the Union.

Foreign coins manufactured by U.S. Mints, through Dec. 31, 1983

Calendar year	Number of pieces produced	Calendar year	Number of pieces produced
July 1, 1875-Dec. 31, 1905	155,896,973	1927	3,650,000
1906	10,204,504	1928	16,701,000
1907	45,253,047	1929	34,980,000
1908	29,645,359	1930	3,300,120
1909	11,298,981	1931	4,498,020
1910	7,153,818	1932	9,756,096
1911	7,794,406	1933	15,240,000
1912	6,244,348	1934	24,280,000
1913	7,309,258	1935	109,600,850
1914	17,335,005	1936	32,350,000
1915	55,485,190	1937	26,800,000
1916	37,441,328	1938	48,579,644
1917	25,208,497	1939	15,725,000
1918	60,102,000	1940	33,170,000
1919	100,269,195	1941	208,603,500
1920	99,002,334	1942	307,737,000
1921	55,094,352	1943	186,682,008
1922	7,863,030	1944	788,498,000
1923	4,369,000	1945	1,802,376,004
1924	12,663,196	1946	504,528,000
1925	13,461,000	1947	277,376,094
1926	14,987,000	1948	21,950,000

Calendar year	Number of pieces produced	Calendar year	Number of pieces produced
1949	156,687,940	1967	176,196,206
1950	2,000,000	1968	416,088,658
1951	25,450,000	1969	348,653,046
1952	45,857,000	1970	483,988,392
1953	193,673,000	1971	207,959,692
1954	19,015,000	1972	392,723,895
1955	67,550,000	1973	295,408,674
1956	38,793,500	1974	373,293,733
1957	59,264,000	1975	762,126,363
1958	152,575,000	1976	562,372,000
1959	129,647,000	1977	13,188,000
1960	238,400,000	1978	30,846,000
1961	148,500,000	1979	15,530,090
1962	256,485,000	1980	19,658,000
1963	293,515,000	1981	23,520,000
1954	— —	1982	37,788,000
1965	— —	1983	25,500,000
1966	7,440,000	Total	11,280,156,346

Source: United States Mint

World monetary units

Country	Basic unit Name	Symbol or abbreviation	Divisional (fractional) unit Name	Symbol or abbreviation
United States of America	Dollar	$	Cent	¢
Afghanistan	Afghani	Af.	Pul	
Africa, Equatorial States: Cameroon, Central African Republic, Equatorial Guinea, Chad, Congo and Gabon	Communaute Africaine franc	CFA fr. Financiere	Centime	
Africa, West (Monetary Union): Benin, Ivory Coast, Mali, Niger, Senegal, Togo, and Burkina Faso	Communaute Financiere Africaine franc	CFA fr.	Centime	
Albania	Lek		Qindar	
Algeria	Dinar	DA	Centime	Cme
Andorra	Diner		Pesetas	
Angola, People's Republic of	Kwanza		Lwei	
Argentina	Austral	$	Centavo	ctv.
Australia	Dollar	$	Cent	c
Austria	Schilling	$	Groschen	g
Bahamas	Dollar	B$	Cent	B¢
Bahrain	Dinar	BD	Fils	
Bangladesh	Taka	Tk.	Poisha	
Barbados	Dollar	BDS$	Cent	¢
Belgium	Franc	F or BF	Centime	C
Belize	Dollar	$	Cent	
Bermuda	Dollar	BD$	Cent	¢
Bhutan	Ngultrum		Chetrum	
Bolivia	Peso Boliviano	$b	Centavos	
Botswana	Pula	P	Thebe	t
Brazil	New Cruzeiro	Cr.$	Centavo	
Brunei	Dollar		Sen	
Bulgaria	Leva		Stotinki	
Burma	Kyat	K	Pya	P
Burundi	Franc	F	Centimes	
Cambodia	Riel	£	Sen	
Canada	Dollar	$	Cent	¢
Cape Verde, Republic of	Escudo	Esc. or $	Centavo	
Caribbean Territories, Eastern Group: Grenada, Montserrat and Antigua, Dominica, Grenada, St. Kitts, St. Lucia, Monstserrat, St. Vincent	East Caribbean Dollar	E.C.$	Cent	¢

Country	Basic unit Name	Symbol or abbreviation	Divisional (fractional) unit Name	Symbol or abbreviation
Cayman Islands	Dollar	$	Cent	¢
Chile	New Peso	$	Centavo	¢
China, Mainland	Yuan	RMB Y	Jiao, Fen	
Taiwan	New Taiwan Dollar	NT $	Cent	¢
Colombia	Peso	$ or P	Centavo	c., ¢, or Ctv.
Comoros, Republic of	Franc	F	Centime	
Congo	Franc	F	Centine	
Cook Islands	Dollar	$	Cent	c
Costa Rica	Colon	C or ¢	Centimo	¢
Cuba	Peso		Centavos	
Cyprus	Pound	C£	Mil	m
Czechoslovakia	Koruna	Kcs	Haler	h
Denmark	Krone	Kr. of kr.	Ore (ore)	(O)
Djibouti, Republic of	Franc	F	Centime	
Dominica	Dollar	E.S.$	Cent	c
Dominican Republic	Peso	RD $	Centavo	ctv or ¢
Ecuador	Sucre	S/	Centavo	ctv.
Egypt, Arab Republic of	Pound	£.E.	Piastre, millime	P.T. & Mill.
El Salvador	Colon	C or ¢	Centavo	¢
Equatorial Guinea	Franc			
Ethiopia	Birr	Br. $	Cent	ct
Falkland Islands	Pound		Pence	
Fiji	Dollar	$	Cent	¢
Finland	Markka	mk	Penni	p.
France	Franc	F	Centime	C or Cme.
French Guadeloupe, Guiana, and Martinique	Franc	F	Centime	
French Polynesia: Austral, Leeward, Marquezas and Windward Islands; and Tuamotu group	Colonies Francaises du Pacifique franc	CFP fr.	Centime	
Gambia, The	Dalasi	D	Butut	b
Germany, Democratic Republic of	Mark		Pfennig	
Germany, Federal Republic of	Deutsche Mark	DM	Pfennig	Pf.
Ghana	Cedi	NC	Pesewa	P
Gibraltar	Pound		Pence	P
Greece	Drachma	Dr.	Lepton	l
Greenland	Krone		Ore	
Guatemala	Quetzal	Q	Centavo	¢
Guernsey	Pound		Pence	
Guinea-Bissau, Republic of	Peso		Centavo	
Guinea, Republic of	Franc			
Guyana	Dollar	G$	Cent	¢
Haiti	Gourde	G	Centime	¢
Honduras	Lempira	L.	Centavo	¢ or cto.
Hong Kong	Dollar	HK$	Cent	¢
Hungary	Forint	Ft.	Filler	Fill.
Iceland	Krona	kr. or Kr.	Aurar	aur. or au.
India	Rupee	Re. (Rs.)	Paisa	p.
Indonesia	Rupiah	Rp.	Sen	
Iran	Rial	Rl. (Rls.)	Dinar	
Iraq	Dinar	ID	Fils	
Ireland, Republic of	Pound	IR£	Penny	P.
Isle of Man	Pound		Pence	P.
Israel	Sheqel	I£	Agora	Ag.
Italy	Lira	L. or Lit.	Centesimo	
Jamaica	Dollar	$	Cent	c
Japan	Yen	Y	Sen	
Jersey	Pound		Pence	
Jordan	Dinar	J.D.	Fils	FLS.
Kenya	Shilling	Sh.	Cent	ct.
Kiribati	Dollar		Cent	
Korea, Republic of	Won	W	Chon	

Country	Basic unit		Divisional (fractional) unit	
	Name	Symbol or abbreviation	Name	Symbol or abbreviation
Kuwait	Dinar	KD	Fils	
Laos	Kip			
Lebanon	Livre	L£ or LL	Piastre	LP or PL
Lesotho	Maloti		Sente	
Liberia	Dollar	$	Cent	
Libya	Dinar	L.D.	Dirham	
Liechtenstein	Swiss Franc		Frank	
Luxembourg	Franc	fr. or F	Centime	Ct.
Macao	Pataca	$	Avos	
Madagascar, Democratic Republic of.	Ariary	FMG	Franc	Ct.
Malawi	Kwacha	K	Tambala	T
Malaysia	Ringgit	$	Sen.	¢
Maldive Republic	Rupee		Laari	l
Mali	Franc	MF		
Malta	Pound	£M	Cent, Mil.	
Mauritania, Islamic Republic of	Ouguiya		Khoum	
Mauritius	Rupee	Re	Cent	
Mexico	Peso	$	Centavo	¢
Monaco	Franc	NF	Centime	Cme
Mongolian People's Republic	Tukhrik		Mongo	
Morocco	Dirham	DH	Centime	C
Mozambique	Metica	Esc. or $	Centavo	
Nepal	Rupee	Re.	Paisa	P.
Netherlands	Guilder	f.	Cent	c
Netherlands Antilles (Curacao)	Guilder	NAF	Cent	ct.
New Caledonia	Colonies Francaises du Pacifique franc.	CFP fr.	Centime	
New Zealand	Dollar	$	Cent	c.
Nicaragua	Cordoba	C$	Centavo	¢
Nigeria	Naira	N	Kobo	K.
Norway	Krone	Kr.	Ore	
Oman	Rial	ORl	Baisa	
Pakistan	Rupee	Rs.	Paisa	Ps.
Panama, Republic of	Balboa	B/.	Centesimo	¢
Papua New Guinea	Kina		Toea	
Paraguay	Guarani	G	Centimo	ctmo.
Peru	Sol		Centavo	ct.
Philippines	Piso	P	Sentimo	s.
Poland	Zloty	Zl.	Grosz	Gr.
Portugal	Escudo	Esc. or $	Centavo	
Qatar	Riyal	QDR	Dirham	
Reunion	Franc	Fr.	Centime	
Romania, Socialist Republic of	Leu	n.a.	Bani	n.a.
Rwanda, Republic of	Franc	FRW.	Centime	
Saint-Pierre et Miquelon	Communaute Financiere Africaine franc	CFA fr.	Centime	
San Marino	Lira	£	Centesimi	
St. Thomas & Prince Islands	Dobra	Esc.	Centimo	
Saudi Arabia	Riyal	SR	Ghirsh, halalah	
Seychelles	Rupee	SR.	Cent	Cts
Sierra Leone	Leone	Le.	Cent	c
Singapore	Dollar	S$	Cent	¢
Solomon Islands	Dollar		Cent	
Somali Republic	Shilin	Sh. So.	Senti	
South Africa, Republic of	Rand	R	Cent	c
Spain	Peseta	Pta. (Pts.)	Centimo	ctmo.
Sri Lanka	Rupee	Rs.	cent	Cts.
Sudan, Republic of the	Pound	£S, LSd, or LS.	Piastre, millim	m/m
Suriname	Gulden	Sf	Cent	ct (cts)
Swaziland	Lilangeni		Cent	
Sweden	Krona	Kr. or kr.	Ore	

Country	Basic unit Name	Symbol or abbreviation	Divisional (fractional) unit Name	Symbol or abbreviation
Switzerland	Franc.	Fr.	Rappen	C.
Syrian Arab Republic	Pound	L.S.	Piastre	P.S.
Tanzania, United Republic of	Shilingi	sh., shs.	Senti	
Thailand	Baht	B, b	Satang	stg.
Timor	Escudo	Esc. or $	centavo	
Tokelau	Tala			
Tonga	Pa'anga	T$	Seniti	
Trinidad and Tobago	Dollar	T&T$	Cent	¢
Tunisia	Dinar	DT	Millim	M
Turkey	Lira	TL.	Kurus	Krs.
Turks and Caicos Islands	Crown			
Tuvalu	Dollar		Cent	
Uganda	Shilling	Sh.	Cent	ct.
Union of Soviet Socialist Republics	Ruble		Kopek	
United Arab Emirates	Dirham		Fil	
United Kingdom	Pound	£	Pence	p.
Uruguay	New Peso	N$	Centesimo	
Vanuatu	Franc.	F	Vatu	
Vatican City	Lira	L.	Centesimo	
Venezuela	Bolivar	B.	Centimo	c/or c
Vietnam	Dong		Hao, Xu	
Western Samoa	Tala	WS$	Sene	
Yemen, Arab Republic	Riyal		Fil	
Yemen, People's Democratic. Republic of	Dinar	S.Y.£	Fil	
Yugoslavia	New Dinar	Din.	Para	
Zaire	Zaire	Z	Makuta	k, s
Zambia	Kwacha	K	Ngwee	n
Zimbabwe (Rhodesia)	Dollar	Rh $	Cent	c

Values of foreign monetary units

During the period 1950-1971 the values of most of the "strong" foreign monetary units remained stable in relation to the U.S. dollar, and fluctuated only within 1 percent of the official value, which was defined through the International Monetary Fund. For example, the Belgian franc was set at 2 cents throughout this period. Devaluations and revaluations upwards of the foreign units were declared at infrequent intervals, and still the valuations fluctuated within 1 percent. For example, the British pound was fixed at $4.03 from 1940 to 1949 when it was devalued to $2.80, remaining stable at this rate until 1967 when it was again devalued to $2.40 (or one penny equalled 1 cent on the pre-decimal British system).

Between 1934 and 1971 the U.S. fixed the price of gold at $35 an ounce, and on this basis most countries fixed the value of their monetary units. This system began to disintegrate when the U.S. dollar was divorced from its gold backing, and a free market was established in gold bullion, after which the price of gold began to climb steeply. The start of the present chaos in foreign exchange began in August 1971 when the U.S. dollar began to decline in relation to the stronger foreign currencies, culminating in the first official devaluation of the U.S. dollar in December 1971. During this period, for example, the normally unstable British pound climbed from $2.40 to $2.60, but fell back to about $2.35 in the middle of the next year

when it was allowed to "float" in value on the international exchanges. Another devaluation of the dollar in February 1973 brought about the final collapse of the stable exchange rates experienced during the previous 15 years.

Before 1967, a large number of countries linked their monetary units to the British pound, but when the pound was devalued in 1967, many of them did not devalue, and thus started the disintegration of the former sterling area. Many of these countries did not devalue with the U.S. dollar in 1971 or 1973 either. For example, the Libyan dinar had the same value as the British pound from 1950 to 1967 — $2.80 — but was not devalued with the British pound in 1967, remaining at $2.80 and not devalued to $2.40. However, when the U.S. dollar was devalued in December 1971, the Libyan dinar was not devalued, so its value rose in proportion to the devalued U.S. dollar, to $3.04. In February 1973, the dollar was again devalued, but not the Libyan dinar, which rose from $3.04 to $3.38, and this has remained near this value to the present.

Thus, the Libyan dinar, a stable, oil-backed currency, rose from $2.80 to $3.38 due to the devaluations of the pound and the dollar. The British pound by 1976 only $1.29, or $2.09 less than the Libyan dinar. Before 1967, both had the same value of $2.80.

The devaluations of the dollar were expressed in terms of the official valuation of the troy ounce of pure gold, $35, from 1934 to 1971, $38 from 1971 to 1973, and $42.22 from 1973 to the present. The first devaluation was 7.89 percent and the second one was 10 percent.

The strongest monetary units did not devalue with the U.S. dollar, and additionally revalued their currency units upwards. For example, the West German Deutsch mark was fixed at DM4.20 to the dollar from 1948 to 1961. It was upvalued in 1961 to DM4 to the dollar, or from 23.8 cents to 25 cents. In the late 1960s it had risen to 27 cents. After the two devaluations of the U.S. dollar and further upvaluations of the Deutsch mark, it has risen to its 1987 value of 55 cents.

Four categories

The monetary units of the world can be divided into four categories: the "strong" units which have risen above their pre-1971 values in terms of the U.S. dollar; the units which were devalued with the U.S. dollar either both times or once only, whose units have the same, or nearly the same value in terms of the U.S. dollar of before 1971; the "weak" units which have been devalued further than the two devaluations of the dollar.

The fourth group of currencies are those of the Communist countries, which are not allowed to be exchanged on the international currency markets, and which have artificial values in terms of the U.S. dollar. Sometimes these countries have an official valuation together with a special, lower valuation for tourists exchanging strong units for the Communist ones.

Thus, the international monetary situation is, at present, an extremely complex problem compared with the pre-1971 period. Some countries have not only one but two or more different values for their monetary units. For example, in India, in December 1971, the rupee was officially valued at 13⅔ cents, but was exchanged against U.S. dollars locally at 12 cents. However, if one exchanged dollar notes on the streets unofficially, the rupee was worth only 10 cents, and if fairly large amounts were negotiated on the black market, it was worth only eight cents. This situation is common with most of the very weak currencies.

Before 1971, the monetary units had stable values, fluctuating daily by not more than 1 percent, and often the unit maintained the same value for as long as 20 years. All this is changed now, and values are subject to almost daily changes, some of them violent. The monetary units of different countries must be watched from day to day to verify their current values.

Quotations of currency values may be found in financial publication such as the *Wall Street Journal* or from foreign exchange specialists such as Manfra, Tordella & Brookes Inc., 30 Rockefeller Plaza, New York, N.Y. 10112. Some currencies are traded in the financial markets, and quotes may be gotten from a number of sources.

Modern world Mint marks

(Since 1500)

Listings of world Mint marks have appeared in *World Coins* and several editions of *How to Order Foreign Coins*. Suggestions for additions have been welcomed and several hundred included in later published formats. Readers wishing to have additional Mint marks and symbols of Mints included in later editions may write *Coin World* (Attention: World Mint marks), P.O. Box 150, Sidney, Ohio 45365.

Use of Mint marks

The use of Mint marks to indicate the place of origin of a coin is almost as old as coinage itself.

Ancient Greek city-states struck coins which bear the symbol of the city: the owl, turtle, bull, fish. In addition to identifying the city of origin, the mark on the coin also served as advertising, telling the world the main product of that city.

Mint marks have appeared on coins in the form of animals, flowers, letters, numbers, stars and rosettes. Instances are even recorded where a Mint counterstamp indicated a re-validation of a coin from another Mint site for local use.

The usefulness that a Mint mark serves perhaps must be interpreted by each Mint authority. To one it would be a means of tracing a coin that was below a standard fineness or weight; to another, a source of checking on coinage when Mints were leased to private enterprises. Placement of Mint marks have indicated a change of metal (1942-1945 U.S. 5-cent piece, for example).

Mint marks have sometimes denoted more than simply what Mint produced a coin. As an example, in ancient Roman times Mint marks often were composed of several letters, some of which identified the Mint and others that identified the specific shop within the Mint that struck the piece being examined.

In the modern world, coins may be issued by a Mint in one country for use in another. The Royal Canadian Mint and the British Royal Mint are two examples of Mints producing coins for many other nations, sometimes using a Mint mark if requested by the contracting government, and without a Mint mark in other cases.

Issues of the Philippines may display the Mint mark BSP for Bangko Sentral Pilipinas at some times, D for the Denver Mint in the United States for coins of 1944-45, S for the coins struck at the San Francisco Mint between 1903-1947, FM for the private Franklin Mint, and others, as many issues are contracted to foreign firms or government agencies.

Arrangement of the list

The arrangement is simplified to: Mint letter or symbol, the Mint, the nation it served, its approximate dates of operation with the Mint mark shown. A Mint need not be located in the nation for which it produces coins.

Some room for error is found in the dates of operation, which in some cases are only educated guesses. Dates of operation do give a range of dates where first and last dates have been seen or reliably reported.

If a Mint is still in operation and used the Mint letter given in recent years, an asterisk (*) appears after its name.

The Mint name given is normally that applied by the nation whose coins are being struck. For example Austrian coins struck at the "E" Mint are called Karlsburg strikings,

yet Hungarian coins from the same Mint are Gyulafehervar strikes; today the city is called Alba Julia by Romania, as it was by many Transylvanians for whom coins were once struck. In 1646 the same Mint used the A-I (Alba Iulia) Mint mark. Confusing? Yes, but our simplified list is designed to eradicate many such problems.

Many privy marks (Mint masters', engravers', etc., personal symbols) are not included in this compilation. Those included are mainly substitutes for a Mint letter or designator. Several Mint marks are the full name of the Mint as shown on coins. In other cases an impressed countermark is used as the "Mint mark" in this list.

Styles changed in Mint marks through the centuries. In 1539 France adopted a unified system of Mint marks throughout the kingdom. Austria abandoned its hodgepodge of privy marks and substituted uniform national marks in 1780. Letters of the alphabet are principally used as Mint marks in the Western world, but symbols from owl to lion are also used.

Wherever the inclusion of privy mark, countermark or signature was considered needful to identify a coin, the symbol was added to the list. Some deduction on the user's part is necessary. For full information, readers are urged to consult the references cited.

Mint mark placement

Often these are placed prominently on the obverse beneath a bust or other central device. They may appear on obverse or reverse divided by some device, e.g. AH (shield) GS. Often they are found in the coin's lower portion, a favorite spot being the dead-center-bottom point beneath the bow of a wreath. They may appear just within the lower extremity of a beaded circle or wreath.

Infrequently privy marks are on or below the truncation of a bust, but this place is usually reserved for "signatures" of engraver or designer, most of which are not included here.

Although small, Mint marks may be found after a few moments' careful study.

— A —

A Ackroyd & Best Ltd. private Mint in England (East Africa) 1920

A with horizontal bar at top Aix en Provence (France) 1481-1502, 1506-1515

A Alamos (Mexico) 1864-1895

A Amberg (Bavaria) 1763-1794

A Ancona (Papal States) 1740-1798

A Ancona (Roman Republic) 1798-1799, 1848-1849
A Angra (Azores)
A Appledore-Barnstable (England) 1645-1646
A Augsburg (City of Augsburg) 1763-1765
A Augsburg (Holy Roman Empire) 1713-1714
A Avila (Spain)
A Beaumont-le-Roger (France) 1942-1944
A Berlin * (Germany, Brandenburg, Prussia, Silesia) 1750-date
A Berlin (Brazil) 1913
A Clausthal (Hanover) 1832-1849
A Clausthal (Westphalia) 1833-1849
A Compiegne (France) 1572-1594
A Corbeil (France) 1655-1658
A Hall (Holy Roman Empire) 1765-1774
A Hirsch private Mint in Berlin (Uruguay) 1901. Full name was Hirsch Messing und Kupferwerke.
A London (England) 1582-1584
A Paris (France) 1539-1655, 1659-1897
A Paris * (many nations)
A Philadelphia (Dominican Republic) 1897. All minted in Philadelphia with dies furnished from Paris.
A San Francisco (Indo-China) 1934-1940. Minted in San Francisco with Paris markings.
A Schwabach (Brandenburg-Ansbach) 1755. Indicates coins struck for Sayn-Altenkirchen.
A Vienna (Austria) 1765-1872
A Vienna (Austrian Netherlands) 1788-1789
A inverted Vilnius, (Vilna, Wilno) (Lithuania) 1601
AA Marseilles (France) 1690-1715
AA Metz (France) 1662-1690, 1715-1794, 1796-1802
A-B Graubunden (Geneva) 1842
AB Strassburg (Switzerland) 1850, 5 rappen only.
A.B. Geneva (Geneva) 1847
A-C Arx Claudiopolis (Transylvania)
AC and rose Vienna (Austria) 1670-1676
A-D Diu (Portuguese India)
A and E ligate Aix and Marseilles (France)
A.E. Breslau (Silesia, Prussia) 1743-1751
A-F Fogaras (Transylvania) circa 1670
A.G.P. Cleve, Rhineland (Prussia) 1742-1743
AH-AG Karlsburg (Transylvania) 1765-1776
A.H.E. Breslau (Silesia, Prussia) 1743-1751
AH-GS Karlsburg (Austria) 1777-1780
A-I Karlsburg (Transylvania) circa 1646
A.K. Dusseldorf (Julich-Berg) 1749-1766
A-K Graz (Holy Roman Empire) 1767-1770
A.L. Turin (Subalpine Republic) 1800-1801

ALOST Alost (Alost, Belgium, "Monnaie Fictive") 1821, 1833
A.L.S. Berlin (Prussia) 1749
AM Annensk (Russia)
A-M Malaca (Portugal)
ANCO Ancona (Papal States) 1513-?
ANCONA Ancona (Papal States) 1796-1797
A.P. Fermo (Roman Republic)
AP Glatz (Holy Roman Empire) 1627-1628
AP Goa (Portuguese India) 1831
A-P Vienna (Holy Roman Empire) 1630
A.P. Warsaw (Poland) 1772
AR Arras (France) 1640-1658
AR and rat Arras (France) 1640-1658
ARBOGA Arboga (Sweden) 1626-1627
ARBOGENSIS Arboga (Sweden) 1627-1628
Areq Arequipa (Peru) 1836-1839
ARGOR Argor private Mint in Chiasso * (Rwanda, Burundi, Congo) 1961-present. Full name Argor S.A. Lavorazione, Chiasso, Switzerland.
As Alamos (Mexico) 1864-1895
a-S Hall (Austria) 1765-1767
A-S Hall (Austria) 1765-1774
A.S. Mannheim (Bavaria) 1778-1793
ASCOLI Ascoli (Papal States) 1797-1798
ASCOLI Ascoli (Roman Republic) 1798-1799
AS-IE Vienna (Austria) 1745
A-T Posen (Poland) 1651-1667
A.T. Tiflis (Georgia) 1812-1832
A-T Wschowa (Poland) 1646-1650
AW Compiegne (France) 1572-1594
AW Vienna (Austria) 1762-1779
AYACUCHO Ayacucho (Peru) 1881-1882
A-Z Zalanta (Transylvania)

— B —

B Appledore-Barnstable (England) 1645-1646
B crowned Avesta (Sweden) 1711-1713
B Bacaim (India)
B Bahia (Brazil) 1695-1831
B Bahia (Portugal) 1714-1805. Gold only.
.B. Barcelona (Barcelona) 1709-1711
B Barcelona (Spain) 1700-1746, 1814-1851
B Bayreuth (Brandenburg-Bayreuth) 1766-1768
B Bayreuth, Franconia (Prussia) 1796-1804
b Beaucaire (France) 1418-1423
B Beaumont-le-Roger (France) 1943-1958
B Beauvais (France) 1433-1435
B Bern * (Switzerland) 1853-date
B Bogota * (Colombia) 1652-date
B Bologna (Italy) 1860-1861
B Bologna (Papal States) 1826-1859
B Bombay (India)
B or b Bourges (France) 1419-1540
B Breslau (Prussia, Silesia) 1750-1826
B Briot's coinage (England, Scotland) 1631-1639

B and crescent Bordeaux (France) 1494
B Bristol (England) 1696-1697
B Bromberg (Poland) 1598-1606. Known as Bydgoszcz today.
B Brunswick (Brunswick) 1850-1860
B Brunswick (Westphalia) 1809-1813
B Brussels (France, Netherlands) 1593, 1821-1830
B Brussels (Spanish Netherlands) 1874
B Brussels (Switzerland) 1874
B Bucharest (Romania) 1879-1885
B Budapest (Hungary)
B Buenos Aires (Argentina) 1880's
B Burgos (Spain) 1580?-1680
B Dieppe (France) 1592-1594
B Dresden (Prussian occupation of Saxony) 1756-1759
B Dresden (Saxony) 1861-1872
B Ensisheim (Holy Roman Empire) 1601-1629
B Hannover (Brunswick) 1860-1871
B Hannover (East Friesland) 1823-1825
B Hannover (Germany) 1866-1878
B Hannover (Hanover) 1821-1866
B Kormoczbanya (Hungary) 1777-1780
B Kremnitz (Austria) 1766-1867
B Kremnitz (Austrian Netherlands) 1788-1798
B Mannheim (Bavarian Palatinate, or Pfalz) 1802
B Pointe-de-l'Arche (France) 1655-1658
B Regensburg (Regensburg) 1809
B Rouen (France) 1593-1655, 1659-1858
B Vienna (Holy Roman Empire) 1707-1743
B Vienna (Germany) 1938-1944
B Unknown (Brandenburg-Ansbach) 1786
B and acorn Bologna (France) 1806-1813
B and acorn Bologna (Italy) 1806-1813
BA Bahia (Brazil)
BA Barcelona (Spain) 1958
BA ligate Basel (Switzerland)
B-A Bayonne (France) 1494
Ba Bogota * (Colombia) 1652-present
BAMBERG Bamberg (Bishopric of Bamberg) 1795-1800
BARCELONA Barcelona (Spain) 1808-1814
BARCINO Barcelona (Barcelona) 1613-1651, 1708-1710, 1789
BAYREUTH Bayreuth (Brandenburg-Ansbach) 1779-1783
BAYREUTH Bayreuth (Brandenburg-Bayreuth) 1754-1766
BB Bydgoszcz (Poland) 1600
BB Strasbourg (France) 1696-1870
B-C Chaul (Portuguese India)
B.C.C.R. San Jose (Costa Rica) 1951-1963 Mark of Banco Central de Costa Rica.
BD monogram Bearn (France) circa 1675-1704

BEL Basel, Fribourg, Vaud (Swiss cantons) 1826-1846
B.H. Frankfurt (Free City of Frankfurt) 1808
BH Liegnitz Ohlau (Holy Roman Empire) circa 1621
B (rosette) H Regensburg (Prince Primate of Germany) 1802-1812
BH Unknown (Schleswig-Holstein) 1706
BI ligate Birmingham (Italy) 1893-1894
B.I.C.R. Philadelphia (Costa Rica) 1935
B.I.D. Aurich (Prussia) 1747-1748. For Dedekind, Mint master.
BK Moscow (Russia)
B-L Nagybanya (Austria) 1765-1771
BM Bankovaya Moneta Mint in St. Petersburg (Russia) 1796-1801
B.N.C.R. London (Costa Rica) 1942-1948 (except on the 1944-1946 brass and bronze 25 centimos)
B.N.C.R. San Jose (Costa Rica) 1944-1946 (on brass and bronze 25 centimos. For Banco Nacional de Costa Rica)
BN and T Turin (Italy) 1864
Bo Bilbao (Spain) 1821
BO Brandenburg-Onolzbach (Brandenburg-Ansbach) 1752-1753
BOGOTA Bogota * (Colombia) 1824-present
BOLOGNA Bologna (Italy) 1859-1860
BON Bologna (Bologna Republic) 1796-1798. Usually occurs in exergue as BON DOCET.
BON DOCET Bologna (Papal States) 1781-1784
BONON DOCET Bologna (Papal States) 1780-1781, 1795-1796
BONONIA Bologna (Cispadane Republic) 1797
BONONIA Bologna (Papal States) 1503-?, 1730-1756
BONONIA DOCET Bologna (Papal States) 1513-?, 1778-1779, 1784, 1795-1796
BONONIA MATER Bologna (Papal States) 1796
BP Budapest (Egypt) 1929
BP Budapest * (Hungary) 1919-date
BPS-IK Prague (Bohemia) 1780
BR monogram Bristol (England) 1643-1645
BRAB. Z Antwerp (Austrian Netherlands) 1692-1700
BRAB.Zc Antwerp (Austrian Netherlands) 1643-1656, 1685
B-S Bromberg (Poland) 1646
BS Burgos (Spain)
BSP Bangko Sentral ng Pilipinas * (Philippines)
B.S. Rostock (Rostock) 1842-1862
B-T Bistritz (Transylvania)
B-V Nagybanya (Austria) 1772-1780
B-W Kuttenberg (Austria) 1711-1712
BW and crossed swords Kuttenberg (Bohemia) 1702-1716

BW and star Wurzburg (Austria) 1680-1694

BZ Brunn (Holy Roman Empire) 1624

BZ Glogau (Holy Roman Empire) 1623-1624

BZ Neisse (Silesia) 1624

BZ Olmutz (Holy Roman Empire) 1620-1622 (BZ was Balthasar Zwirner, who moved frequently)

— C —

C Bucharest (Romania) 1870

C Cadiz (Spain) 1808-1815

C Caen (France) 1655-1658, 1693-1772

C Calcutta (India)

C Camora (Portugal)

C Cassel (Westphalia) 1810-1813

C Castelsarrasin (France) 1914, 1943-1946

C Cataluna (Spain). Was a portable Mint which operated in Reus, Tarragona, and Palma de Mallorca during the Napoleonic wars (1808-1815).

C Cayenne (French Guiana)

C Ceuta (Morocco)

C Charlotte, N.C. (USA) 1838-1861

C Chester (England) 1696-1697

C Chihuahua (Mexico) 1821

Gothic C Chinon or Cremieu (France). Chinon 1418-1422, Cremieu 1419-1423.

C Cibinium (Transylvania)

C Civita Vecchia (Roman Republic) 1798-1799

C Clausthal (Brunswick) 1814-1831

C Clausthal (Hanover) 1813-1834

C Clausthal (Westphalia) 1810-1811

C Cleves (Prussia) 1751-1806

C Cochim (Portuguese India)

C Coruna (Portugal)

C Cuenca (Spain)

C Cuiaba (Brazil) 1823-1833

C Culiacan (Mexico) 1846-1905

C Cuzco (Spanish America) 1798

C Dresden (Saxony) 1779-1804

C Frankfurt-Main (Germany) 1866-1879

C Guenzburg (Holy Roman Empire) 1765-1774

C Karlsburg (Austria) 1762-1764

C Krakow (Poland) 1681

C Ober-Hessen (Ober-Hessen) 1807, 1814-1821

C Ottawa (Canada, Jamaica, Newfoundland, Dominican Rep., England) 1908-1947

C Prague (Austrian Netherlands) 1792-1798

C Prague (Holy Roman Empire) 1765-1856

C Reus in Catalonia (Spain) 1809-1814. Used with assayer initials MP or SF.

C Spoleto (Roman Republic)

C St. Lo (France) 1539-1653, 1659-1693

C Surabaya (Dutch East Indies) 1837

C Vienna (Holy Roman Empire) 1766-1780

C and lion Geneva (France)

CA and pennant Brandenburg (Prussia) 1594

CA Camora (Portugal)

CA Chihuahua (Mexico) 1811-1816

Ca Chihuahua (Mexico) 1814-1822, 1831-1895

CA (A inside C) Cuenca (Spain) 1627-1634

C-A Karlsburg (Austria) 1746-1766

C-A Vienna (Holy Roman Empire) 1774-1780

CA Zaragoza (Spain) 1556-1707

C-AE (AE ligate) Frankfurt am Main (Free City of Frankfurt) 1618-1636

C.A.M. Central American Mint Ltd., private Mint, San Salvador (El Salvador) 1892-1894

CAMPEN Campen in Overyssel (Campen) 1639-1672

CAMPENSIS Campen in Overyssel (Campen) 1578-1597

CARACAS Caracas (Venezuela) 1817-1821

CARL Carlisle (England, obsidional) 1645

CB Brieg (Silesia) 1669-1713

C-B Chaul (Portuguese India)

CB Churfurstenthum Bayern (Bavaria) 1765-1767

C-B Clausenburg (Transylvania)

CB Kormoczbanya (Hungary) 1705-1711

CB Kronstadt (Hungary) 1660

CB Regensburg (Regensburg) 1809

CC (first C is backward) Besancon (France) 1693-1772

C-C Kaschau (Transylvania)

CC Carson City (USA) 1870-1893

CC Genoa (France) 1803

C-C Olmutz (Holy Roman Empire) 1619-1620

CC linked uncertain (England) circa 1645

CCS St. Viet (Holy Roman Empire) 1689-1699

C.D. Munich (Bavaria) 1790. For Cajetan Destouches, die cutter at Munich 1784-1807

CE Ceuta (Morocco)

Ce Real del Catorce (Mexico) 1863-1869

C-E-A-R-A on star Ceara (Brazil) 1834

C-F Fogaras (Transylvania)

CG-AK Graz (Holy Roman Empire) 1767-1772

CG-AR Graz (Austria) 1767

C.G.-L. Nuremberg (Bishopric of Bamberg) 1750

CH monogram Chalons (France) 1591-1595

CH Chihuahua (Mexico) 1831-1895

CH Pressburg (Austria) 1697-1718

CH Vienna (Holy Roman Empire) 1610-1616

CHI in circle Valcambi Mint - Switzerland (Panama)

C.H.H. Hanover (Hanover) 1813-1818

C.H.I. Berlin (Prussia) 1749-1763
chi-loe Chiloe Islands (Chiloe Islands under Spanish occupation of Antonio Quintan-illa) 1818-1822
CHST Chester (England) 1644-1645
C-I Cibinium (Transylvania)
C.I. Olkusz (Poland) 1767
Ci-Bi Hermannstadt (Hungary) circa 1613
C II M St. Petersburg (Russia)
CIVITA VECCH Civita Vecchia (Papal States) 1797
CIVITA VECCHI Civita Vecchia (Papal States) 1797
CIVITA VECCHIA Civita Vecchia (Papal States) 1797
C-K Vienna (Holy Roman Empire) 1765-1774
CL Genoa (France) 1806-1814
CL and prow Genoa (France) 1811-1814
CL script Lucca (Duchy of Lucca) 1835
CLITUNNO Spoleto (Roman Republic) 1798-1799
C-Lo Colombo (Dutch Ceylon)
C-Lo Colombo (Portuguese Ceylon)
C.L.-R Bayreuth (Brandenburg-Bayreuth) 1742-1765
C.L.S. Dusseldorf (Julich-Berg) 1767-1770
CM monogram Calcutta (Mombasa) 1888
C/M Calcutta (Mombasa)
C-M Cibinium (Transylvania)
C-M Kaschau (Transylvania)
CM Kaschau (Hungary) 1704-1707
CM Kremnitz (Austria) 1779
C-M Sestroretsk (Russia)
C.M. Suzun (Russia)
CM Vienna (Holy Roman Empire) 1609-1612
Cn Culiacan (Mexico) 1846-1905
C.N. Krakow (Poland) 1528-1534
Co Coimbra (Portugal)
Co Cuzco (Peru) 1826-1840
CO Hall in Tyrol (Teutonic Order) circa 1613-1618
COPIAPO Copiapo (Copiapo) 1865
CORDOBA Cordoba (Argentina) 1844-1854
CR Coruna (Portugal)
C (shield) R Olkusz (Poland) 1593-1595
CR San Jose (Central American Rep., Costa Rica) 1828-1850
C-S Konigsberg (East Prussia) 1718-1743
CS St. Viet (Holy Roman Empire) 1689-1699
C.S.H. Pressburg (Austria) 1705-1711
CUNDINAMARCA I.F. Bogota (New Granada, Colombia) 1813-1821
CUZ or CUZO plain Cuzco (Peru) 1824-1840
CUZCO Cuzco (South Peru)
Cuzco Cuzco (Spanish America)
CUZO monogram Cuzco (Peru)

CV Clausenburg (Hungary) 1659
C.v.C Brunswick (Brunswick) 1821-1850
CVG-AK Graz (Holy Roman Empire) 1767-1772
CVG-AR Graz (Austria) 1767
CW monogram Brunn (Holy Roman Empire) 1623-1627
CW and heart Copenhagen (Denmark) 1700-1747
CWF Wschowa (Poland) 1551-1603. Initials mean: Civitas Wschoviensis Fecit.
CWF Wurschbauer's coinage (Transylvania)

— D —

D Aurich (East-Friesland under Prussia) 1750-1806
D Aurich (Prussia) 1744
D Dahlonega (USA) 1838-1861
D Damao (Portuguese India)
D Danzig (Danzig) 1535
D Denver * (USA) 1906-1964, 1968-present
D Dresden (East Friesland during Prussian occupation) 1758
D Durango (Mexico) 1811-1822, 1824-1895
D Dusseldorf, Rhineland (Prussia) 1816-1848
D Edinburg (Scotland) 1351-1358
D Graz (Holy Roman Empire) 1765-1772
D Lyons (France) 1539-1655; 1659-1858
D Munich * (Germany) 1872-date
D Salzburg (Austria) 1800-1809
D Surabaya (Dutch East Indies) 1832
D Stuttgart (Zurich) 1842-1848
D Vienna (Bishopric of Breslau) 1753-1773
D Vienne in Dauphiny (France) 1655-1658
D-B Damao (Portuguese India)
DB Schwyz (Schwyz) 1843-1846
D-D Diu (Portuguese India) 1765-1828
DI Diu (Portuguese India) 1851
DIO Diu (Portuguese India) 1841
D-O Diu (Portuguese India)
Do Durango (Mexico) 1824-1895
D.P.Z. Lubeck (Lubeck) 1758-1769
DROZ.F Boulton private Mint, Birmingham (Bermuda) 1793. Name is for Jean Pierre Droz, engraver.
D-S St. Viet (Holy Roman Empire) 1622
D-S Vienna (Holy Roman Empire) 1624-1637
Dt Dordrecht (Dutch Indies)
D:S Vilna (Lithuania) 1582
DVB Neisse (Holy Roman Empire) 1624-1625

— E —

E Dresden (Germany) 1872-1887
E Edinburgh (England) 1707-1709
E Enkhuizen (Dutch Indies)
E Ekaterinburg (Russia)
E Eskilstuna * (Sweden)
E Evora (Portugal) 1642-1688

E Exeter (England) 1696-1697
E Gyula Fehervar (Hungary)
E Karlsburg (Austria) 1765-1867
E Karlsburg (Austrian Netherlands) 1791-1798
E Konigsberg (Prussia) 1750-1798
E London (England) 1544-1547
E Mehen-sur-Loire (France) 1655-1658
E Muldenhutte (Germany) 1877-1953
Roman E Southwark (England) 1547-1549
E Tours (France) 1539-1655, 1659-1772
E-B unknown Privy mark (Brandenburg-Ansbach) 1786
EBOR York (England) 1644-1645
E.C. Dresden (Saxony) 1764-1778
E.C. Leipzig (Saxony) 1753-1763
EC-SK Vienna (Austria) 1766
E.D.C. Dresden (Saxony) 1764-1778
E.D.C. Leipzig (Saxony) 1753-1763
E.G.N. Berlin (Prussia) 1725-1749
EL York (England) 1531-1545
El R.D. CATORCE in box Real del Catorce (Mexican Revolutionary) 1811
EM Ekaterinburg (Russia)
Eo Mo Tlalpan in Estado de Mexico (Mexico) 1828-1830
ETR Florence (Etruria) 1803-1859
ETRUR Florence (Etruria) 1801-1803
EV Evora (Portugal)
EVGVBII unknown (Papal States) 1730-1769
Evm-D Kremnitz (Austria) 1741-1765, 1767-1780
EVOR Evora (Portugal)
EvS-AS Prague (Bohemia, H.R.E.) 1765-1773
EvS-IK Prague (Holy Roman Empire) 1774-1780
EX Exeter (England) 1644-1645

— F —

F Angers (France) 1539-1738
F Dresden (Saxony) 1845-1858
F Falconer's coinage (Scotland) circa 1630-1640
F or f Figeac (France) 1420-1442
F Florence (Italy) circa 1861
F and mountain Florence (Italy) 1861
F Fontenay-le-Comte (France) 1420-1431
F Fraustadt (Poland) 1598-1606. Known as Wschowa today.
F Glarus 1806-7
F Guenzburg (Holy Roman Empire) 1744-1805
F Hall (Austrian Netherlands) 1786-1798
F Hall (Austrian Venetia) 1802
F Hall (Holy Roman Empire, Tyrol) 1765-1807
F Magdeburg (Prussia) 1750-1806
F Ober-Hessen (Ober-Hessen) 1803-1807
F Stuttgart * (Germany and West Germany) 1872-present

F-A Vienna (Holy Roman Empire) 1774-1780
FABRIAN Fabriano (Papal States) 1513-?
FANI Fano (Papal States) circa 1492
FANO Fano (Papal States) circa 1492, 1797
F.E. Mannheim (Bavarian Palatinate) 1802
FERA Ferrara (Papal States) 1753
FERMANO Fermo (Papal States) 1798
FERMO Fermo (Papal States) 1796-1797
FERMO Fermo (Roman Republic) 1798
FERRA Ferrara (Papal States) 1750
FERRAR Ferrara (Papal States) 1750
FERRARA Ferrara (Papal States) 1744-1753
FERRARIA Ferrara (Papal States) 1492-?
FERRARIAE Ferrara (Papal States) 1744
FF Altona (Denmark) 1842
FF and orb Altona (Denmark) circa 1839-1848
FIRENZE Florence (Sardinia, Italy) 1859-1861
FK and heart Copenhagen (Denmark) 1835-1848
FLOR Florence (Etruria) 1807
FLORENTIAE Florence (Etruria) 1803-1806
FM monogram Franklin private Mint, Yeadon, Pa. (Tunisia, Panama) 1965-1969
FM monogram Franklin private Mint * Franklin Center, Pa. (Bahamas, Jamaica, Trinidad & Tobago, Cayman Islands, many others)
F.N or FN Breslau (Austria, Silesia) 1703-1723
F.N. or FN Oppeln (Austria, Silesia) 1600-1703
FOG Fogaras (Transylvania)
FOLIGNO Foligno (Papal States) 1793-1795
F.P. Cattaro (Ragusa) 1548-1549, 1562-1563
F.Q. Scutari (Venetian Republic) 1442
F.R. Brunswick (Brunswick) 1814-1820
FS monogram Prague (Bohemia) 1721-1727
F.S. Santa Fe de Bogota (Spanish America)
FVLG Foligno (Papal States) 1513-?
FVLGINIA Foligno (Papal States) 1523
FVLGW Foligno (Papal States) 1523
FVLI Foligno (Papal States) 1513
FVLIGNIO Foligno (Papal States) 1796
FVLIGNO Foligno (Papal States) 1793-1797
FVLIGNO Foligno (Roman Republic) 1798
F.W.oF. Dresden (Saxony, Poland) 1734-1763

— G —

G Dresden (Saxony) 1833-1844, 1850-1854
G Fort Gelria in Pulicat (Dutch India)
G Galle (Dutch Ceylon) 1783-1793
G J. R. Gaunt private Mint, Birmingham (Br. West Africa) 1920
G Geneva (France) 1799-1805
G and lion Geneva (France) 1799-1805

Gothic G   Genoa (France) 1526-1527
G   Glatz (Holy Roman Empire) 1637-1640
G   Glatz (Prussian Silesia) 1807-1809
g G   Glatz (Holy Roman Empire) circa 1628
G   Goa (Portuguese India) 1762-1774
G   Goerz, or Gorizia (Gorizia) 1733-1802
G   Goias (Brazil) 1823-1833
G   Granada (Spain) 1588-1679
G   Graz (Holy Roman Empire, Austria) 1655-1766
G   Grenoble (France) 1489-1503
G   Guadalajara (Mexico)
G   Guatemala (Guatemala) 1733-1776
G   Guenzburg (Austria) 1764-1765, 1771-1780
G   Guenzburg (Burgau) 1764-1779
G   Guenzburg (Constance) 1772
G   Karlsruhe * (Germany) 1872-present
G   Krakow (Poland) 1766-1767
G   Nagybanya (Austria, Hungary) 1766-1851
G   Nagybanya (Austrian Netherlands) 1792-1797
G   Poitiers (France) 1539-1789
G   Schwabach (Brandenburg-Ansbach) 1752-1785
G   St. Veit (Holy Roman Empire) 1675-1688
G   Stettin in Pomerania (Prussia) 1750-1806
G-A   Goa (Portuguese India) 1750-1769
Ga   Guadalajara (Mexico) 1812-1895
GC   Guadalupe y Calvo (Mexico) 1843-1851
GCP countermark   Porto (Portugal) 1847
GCS   St. Veit (Holy Roman Empire) 1668-1675, 1689-1699
GCVS   St. Veit (Holy Roman Empire) 1689-1699
G.E or GE   Prague (Austria, Bohemia) 1694-1711
GEL   Harderwijk in Gelderland (Batavian Republic) 1799-1806
GEND   unknown (Ghent, Belgium "Monnaie Fictive") 1821, 1833
GERONA   Gerona (Gerona obsidional issues) 1809
GFN   Nuremberg (Brandenburg-Bayreuth) 1704
G-G   Bydgoszcz (Poland) 1642-1651
G-G   Guatemala (Guatemala) 1733-1776
G.H.   Breslau (Austria) 1706-1711
GH   Breslau (Silesia) 1659-1662
GH and double lily   Breslau (Silesia) circa 1637-1657
G.H.L.M.   unknown (Hesse-Darmstadt) 1819
G.H.S.M.   unknown (Hesse-Darmstadt) 1819
G-J.R.   Gaunt & Son, England (British West Africa)
G.K.   Cleve (Prussia) 1740-1755
G-K   Graz (Austria) 1767-1772
G.M   Mantua (Mantua in Italy obsidional issues) 1848

GM   Sesterbek in Finland (Russia)
Gn   Culiacan (Mexico) 1884-1885. Die error for Cn.
C.N. (Mint official)   Frankfurt (Frankfurt) 1765
GN   Krain-Carniola (Holy Roman Empire) 1623-1624
GNA   Gerona (Gerona in Spain obsidional issues) 1808
GN-BW   Bamberg (Bamberg)
G.N.(W.)P.B.   Wurzburg (Wurzburg)
GO (O inside G)   Guanajuato (Mexico) 1812-1822
Go   Guanajuato (Mexico) 1824-1900
GOA   Goa (Portuguese India) 1787-1880
G.P.   Krakow (Poland) 1646-1650
G-R   Graz (Holy Roman Empire) 1665-1672, 1746-1767
GR   Olmutz (Holy Roman Empire) 1621-1623
GS   St. Veit (Holy Roman Empire) 1675-1688
GSVS   St. Veit (Holy Roman Empire) 1689-1699
GTK   Vienna (Austria) 1761
GUB   Gubbio (Papal States) 1732
GUBBIO   Gubbio (Roman Republic)
GVAIANA   Angostura provisional Mint (Guiana Province, Venezuela) 1811-1817. Mark appears as part of legend: PROVINCIA DE GVAIANA.
GVB   Gubbio (Papal States) 1738-1756
GVBBIO   Gubbio (Papal States) 1730-1760, 1788-1797
GVBBIO   Gubbio (Roman Republic)
GW   Glatz (Holy Roman Empire) 1640-1660
GYF   Gyulafehervar (Hungary) 1868-1871
GYF or GY.F.   Karlsburg (Austria) 1868-1871

— H —

H   Amsterdam (Dutch Indies)
H   Birmingham * (England, Canada, Austria, Egypt and other nations) 1860-present
H   Birmingham (Belize)*
H   Birmingham (Italy) 1866-1867
H   Darmstadt (Germany) 1872-1882
H   Dresden (Saxony) 1804-1812
H   Guenzburg (Austria, Holy Roman Empire) 1765-1805
H   Guenzburg (Austrian Netherlands, Luxemburg) 1788-1797
H   Guenzburg (Burgau) circa 1781-1805
H   Hall (Holy Roman Empire, Tyrol) 1746-1805, 1975, 1977
H   Heaton private Mint, Birmingham (Ecuador) 1890
H   Heaton private Mint, Birmingham (Nicaragua) 1880-1915
H   Hermannstadt (Transylvania) 1551-1552
H script   H. le Heus Mint in Amsterdam (Netherlands) 1814-1816

H La Rochelle (France) 1539-1837
H and castle London (England) 1509-1526
H-A Hall (Holy Roman Empire) 1746-1805
H-A Hall (Austria) 1746-1765
HA Moscow (Russia)
HB monogram Brunswick (Hesse-Cassel, Hesse-Darmstadt, Marburg) 1572-1610. Appears with and without trefoil.
HB monogram Dresden (Saxony) 1553-1591
HCK Graz (Holy Roman Empire) 1655-1660
HEATON Heaton private Mint in Birmingham (Bulgaria) 1881
HEATON Heaton private Mint in Birmingham (Ecuador) 1872, 1884-1886.
HEATON Heaton private Mint, Birmingham (Romania)
HEATON Heaton private Mint, Birmingham (Venezuela) 1852, 1858
HF ligate Huguenin Freres, Le Locle * (Switzerland) present
HG Glatz (Holy Roman Empire) 1629
H-G Karlsburg (Austria) 1765-1777
H G St. Veit (Holy Roman Empire) 1627-1632
HG ligate St. Veit (Holy Roman Empire) 1627-1632
HGP St. Veit (Holy Roman Empire) circa 1635
HH Hildburg Hausen (Saxe-Hildburghausen) 1772, 1778, 1781
H.K. Rostock (Rostock) 1862-1864
Hk Harderwijk (Dutch Indies)
H L St. Veit (Holy Roman Empire) 1693
HL Teschen (Silesia) 1620-1649
HL and TA Altona Mint (Schleswig-Holstein) 1850-1851
Hn Hoorn (Dutch Indies)
Ho Hermosillo (Mexico) 1861-1895
HOL and rosette Dordrecht in Holland (Batavian Republic) 1799-1806
HOL and star Enkhuizen in Holland (Netherlands) 1796-1803
HOL and star Hoorn in Holland (Netherlands) 1803-1809
HP monogram Glatz (Holy Roman Empire) 1628-1631
HR Breslau (Silesia) 1619-1631
HR Glatz (Holy Roman Empire) 1631-1636
H-R Glogau (Holy Roman Empire) 1621
HR Glogau (Holy Roman Empire) 1621
H (shield) R Krakow (Poland) 1595-1598
HR unknown (Egypt) 1917
H - S Hermannstadt (Transylvania)
H-S Karlsburg (Austria) 1777-1780
HS St. Veit (Holy Roman Empire) 1631-circa 1670
H S Vienna (Holy Roman Empire) 1657-1658 (talers only)
HS and triangle Vienna (Austria) circa 1657

HT Breslau (Holy Roman Empire) 1623-1624
HT Vienna (Austria) 1651
HT-BZ Neisse (Silesia) 1624
HUGUENIN Huguenin Freres, Switzerland private Mint (Latvian coins, etc.)
H-W Riga (Riga) 1625-1650
HZ and hooked bar Breslau (Silesia) 1635

— I —

I Bombay (India, Australia, England) 1918-1943
I Calcutta (Australia) 1916-1918
I Graz (Holy Roman Empire) 1765-1770
Is Hamburg (Germany)
I. Ilcussia (Poland) 1600. Now called Olkusz.
I Jaffna (Dutch Ceylon) 1783-1793
I Limoges (France) 1539-1837
(I) Prague (Holy Roman Empire) 1668-1688
IA Graz (Holy Roman Empire) 1694-1711
IAEN Jaen (Spain) 1454-1474
IAK Hall (Austria) 1684-1746
IAN Graz (Holy Roman Empire) 1670-1692
I.A.P. Prague (Austria) 1711-1732, 1735-1740
IAP Prague (Holy Roman Empire) 1711-1713
IB Danzig (Danzig) 1650-1670
I.B. Warsaw (Poland) 1811-1830
IB-FL Nagybanya (Austria) 1765-1771
IB-IV Nagybanya (Austria) 1772-1780
I.C. Dresden (Saxony) 1779-1804
I-C Glogau (Holy Roman Empire) circa 1621
I-C and arms Plan (county of Schlick) 1627-1640
IC Vienna (Holy Roman Empire) 1766-1780
IC-FA or I.C.-F.A. Vienna (Holy Roman Empire) 1774-1780
I.C.G. Esens in Ostfriesland (Prussia) 1746, for Gitterman, Mint master.
IC-IA Vienna (Holy Roman Empire) 1780
I.C.M. Cleve (Royal Prussian Asiatic Society) 1751
ICO counterstamp Ico in Ceara (Brazil) 1829-1832
IC-SK or I.C.-S.K. Vienna (Holy Roman Empire) 1765-1773
I.D.B. Dresden (Prussian occupation of Saxony) 1756-1759
I.E.C. Dresden (Saxony) 1779-1804
I.F. Bogota (New Granada, Colombia) 1819-1820
IF Gunzburg (Holy Roman Empire) 1744-1805
I.F.oF Leipzig (Saxony) 1763-1765
I.G. Earl of Arran private Mint (Scotland) 1517-1519, 1553-1554
I.G.G. Leipzig (Saxony) 1752

IGR Prague (Holy Roman Empire) 1713-1714

IGR St. Veit (Holy Roman Empire) 1679-1689

I.G.S. Dresden (Saxony) 1716-1734, 1813-1832

IGW Graz (Holy Roman Empire) 1669-1671

IH Danzig (Danzig) 1658-1687

IH Glogau (Holy Roman Empire) 1623

IH Neisse (Holy Roman Empire) 1624

I-I Elbing (Thorn) 1630-1639

II Glogau (Holy Roman Empire) 1625

II Niort (France) 1420-1427

I-I Thorn (Thorn) 1630-1639

IIE and rose St. Polten (Austria) circa 1590-1637

IIE St. Polten (Holy Roman Empire) 1624-1625

IIH Glogau (Holy Roman Empire) 1623

IIH Neisse (Holy Roman Empire) 1624

IIL Prague (Holy Roman Empire) 1717

IIM Izhorsk (Russia) 1811-1821

IIP St. Veit (Holy Roman Empire) 1699-1717

I-K Graz (Holy Roman Empire) 1765-1767

I-K Vienna, (Austria) 1767

IK-SC Vienna (Austria) 1767 only (error for IC-SK)

ILD Lerida (Spain) 1809

IMH Vienna (Holy Roman Empire) 1680-1736

I.Milton. F. John Milton private Mint, London (Barbados) 1788

IP St. Veit (Holy Roman Empire) 1699-1717

IR St. Veit (Holy Roman Empire) 1679-1689

IS St. Veit (Holy Roman Empire) 1631-1657

I.-S. Warsaw (Poland) 1811

IsM Ihora (Russia)

I.T. Augsburg (City of Augsburg) 1740-1745

ITOR Tortosa (Spain) 1808-1811

IW Graz (Holy Roman Empire) 1669-1671

IZV Vienna (Austria) 1761-1765

— J —

J Hamburg * (Germany) 1873-present

J Jubia (Spain) about 1816

J Paris (Westphalia) 1808-1809

J Surabaya (Dutch East Indies) 1837-1839

J.A. Augsburg (City of Augsburg) 1708-1725

JA Jubia (Spain) about 1816

JAEN Jaen (Spain) about 1454-1474

JAPP Jose Policarpo Patino private Mint in Cordoba (Cordoba province, Argentina) 1843

JP John Pinches, London (Bahamas)

— K —

K and orb Altona (Danish West Indies) 1859. K is initial of Krohn, engraver.

K Bordeaux (France) 1539-1878

K Boulton private Mint, Birmingham (Bahamas) 1806. Initial is for Conrad Kuchler, engraver.

K Goerz (Gorizia) 1733-1802

K Kampen (Dutch Indies)

K King's Norton (East Africa) 1914

K Kormoczbanya (Hungary, Transylvania) 1767-1776

K Krain-Carniola (Holy Roman Empire) 1623-1624

K Krakow (Poland) 1600-1606

K Kremnitz (Austria) 1760-1763

K London (England) 1547-1549

K St. Gallen (St. Gallen) 1810-1817. Privy mark of Erasmus Kunkler, Mint master.

K Vienna (Holy Roman Empire) 1774-1780

K.A Moscow (Russia)

KB Kormoczbanya (Hungary, Transylvania) 1632-1765, 1848, 1868-1918

K-B or K.B. Kremnitz (Austria, Holy Roman Empire) 1703-1715, 1718-1780, 1848 (Kremnitz is the German name for the Hungarian Kormoczbanya; now known as Kremnica, Czechoslovakia)

KB Krupp private Mint, Berlin (Italy) 1894

KB Kormoczbonya (Bulgaria)

K-D Kremnitz (Austria) 1765

KM Copenhagen (Denmark)

KM Kaschau (Hungary, Transylvania) 1763-1765

KM Kolyvan (Siberia) 1764-1781

K-M Kremnitz (Austria) 1763-1765

(KM) Kuttenberg (Holy Roman Empire) 1702

KN King's Norton * (England, many other nations) 1910-present

KN Krain-Carniola (Holy Roman Empire) 1623-1624

K-O Koloszvar (Transylvania)

Kr Kremnica Mint (Slovak Republic) 1940-1945.

K-S Kis-Selyk (Transylvania)

KV Klausenburg (Hungary, Transylvania) 1705

— L —

L Bayonne (France) 1539-1837

L Lahore (India) circa 1943-1945

L Leipzig (Saxony) 1761-1762

L crowned Lille (France) 1686-1693

L Lima (Peru, Spanish America) 1722

L Limoges (France) 1423-1429, 1485-1498

L Lisbon (Portugal)

L Lobzenica (Poland) 1626

L Loches (France) 1419- circa 1442

L London (Albania)

L London (England)

.L. Lublin (Poland) 1598-1606

L unknown (Persia) 1931. L on upper bow of reverse wreath on 5-krans piece from Persia dated AH 1309.

LA Laon (France) during the League

L.A.B. Hanover (Hanover) 1819

LANDI Lucca (Duchy of Lucca) 1833-1838

LA PAZ La Paz (Bolivia) 1853-1858

LASS WASK Sahla (Sweden) 1682

LAVY Vittorio Paroletti private Mint at Turin (Subalpine Republic) 1800-1801

L.B. Hannover (Hanover) 1819-1824

LB Lisbon (Portugal)

LE York (England) 1531-1545

LERIDA Lerida (Lerida obsidional issues) 1809

LIMA Lima * (Spanish America, Peru) 1659-present (sporadic appearances)

LIMA London (Great Britain) 1743-1758

LIMAE monogram Lima (Peru, Spanish America)

LM monogram Lima (Peru)

L*M or L-M Lima (Spanish America) 1659-1749

LMA monogram Lima (Spanish America) 1751-1772

LME monogram Lima (Spanish America)

LOBZ Lobzenica (Poland) 1627

LR Lima (Peru)

LS monogram and hammer Florence (Etruria) 1803-1807

LT Tarascon (France) 1483-1508

— M —

M Aargau (Aargau) 1807-1808

M Danzig (Danzig) 1808-1812

M Glogau (Holy Roman Empire) 1621

M on a bar Graz (Holy Roman Empire, Styria)

M crowned Madrid (Spain) 1728-1850

M Madrid (Spain) 1597-1663, 1704-1726

M Manila (Philippines) 1920-1942

M Maranhao (Brazil) 1834-1835

M Malbork (Poland) 1600-1602.

Gothic M Mazeres (France) 1419

M Medellin (Colombia)

M Mediasch (Transylvania)

M Melbourne (Austria, England) 1872-1931

M Mendoza (Argentina) 1823-1824

M Mexico (Mexico) 1535-1542

M Milan (Austria, Austrian Italy) 1780-1859

M Milan (Eritrea) 1890

M and inverted cup Milan (France) 1804-1814

M Milan (Italy) 1807-1814, 1861-1875, 1887

M Milan (Lombardy) 1848

M. Milan (Sardinia) 1859-1860

M Milmanda (Portugal)

M John Milton private Mint, London (Barbados) 1788, 1792

M Minas Gerais (Portugal) 1724-1738

M Minas Gerais (Brazil) 1810-1828

Gothic M Mirabel (France) 1418-1422

Gothic M Mouzon (France) 1419-1429

M Monaco (Monaco) 1837-1838

M Moscow (Russia) 1701-1775

M Salzburg (Holy Roman Empire) 1803-1806

M Toulouse (France) 1539-1837

M Unknown privy mark (Bishopric of Augsburg) 1744

M-A Malaca (Portugal)

Ma Manila (Philippines under Spain)

MA ligate Marseilles (France) 1786-1858

M-A Moscow (Russia)

MACER Macerata (Roman Republic) 1798-1799

MACERATA Macerata (Papal States) 1797

MACERATA Macerata (Roman Republic)

MACHIA Marches (Papal States) 1513-?

MAE monogram Lima (Spanish America, Peru) 1772-1824, 1828-1855

MAIORICA Palma on Majorca (Spain) circa 1580-1723

MARC Marches (Papal States) 1492-?

MARCHIA Marches (Papal States) 1513-?

MATELICA Matelica (Papal States) 1797-1798

MB ligate Birmingham (Mombasa)

MB Brieg (Silesia, Holy Roman Empire) 1693-1697

M - BN Milan (Italy) 1861-1875

M.C. Brunswick (Brunswick) 1813-1814, 1820. Means Munz Commission and was used in periods of absence of a Mint master.

M-C Cibinium, or Hermannstadt (Transylvania)

M-C Kaschau (Transylvania)

MC Monaco (Monaco) 1837-1838

MD ligate Madrid (Spain) 1616-1628

M-E Mozambique (Mozambique)

ME. Tlalpan (Mexico)

MEDELLIN Medellin (Colombia) 1862-1888

MF Unknown (Schleswig-Holstein) 1787

MFDFLLIN Medellin (Colombia) 1929

MF-MF Olmutz (Holy Roman Empire) 1626-1633

.MH. or M-H Bromberg (Poland) 1670-1673

MH St. Veit (Holy Roman Empire) 1624-1625

MH Vienna (Holy Roman Empire) 1680-1736

MI and duck Unknown (Silesia) circa 1637-1657

MI Milmanda (Portugal)

MK (Gothic M) Krakow (Poland) 1444-1492. Initials are for Latin name: Moneta Krakoviensis.

MM monogram Mantua (Austria) 1796

MM Moscow (Russia)

MM Munkacs (Hungary, Transylvania) 1705-1706
MM Vienna (Austria) 1680-1694
M. M-A Moscow (Russia)
MMW Breslau (Silesia) 1694
Mo Mexico * (Mexico) 1542-present
Mo Six coins struck for Mexico in New Orleans, Denver, San Francisco and Philadelphia, all carrying Mexico City Mint marks. 1949
MONT'ALTO Montalto (Papal States) 1797
MONTALTO Montalto (Papal States) 1707, 9177 (error date)
M-P (Gothic M) Poznan (Poland) 1386-1444. Initials are for Latin name: Moneta Posnaniensis.
M-P Wurzburg (Wurzburg) 1764
M-S Danzig (Danzig) 1539. Initials are for Moneta Sigismundi.
MS Mediasch (Hungary, Transylvania) 1627
(MV) Prague (Holy Roman Empire) 1688-1694
M.V. Warsaw (Poland) 1792
MW or M.W. Warsaw (Poland) 1651, 1792. Initials mean Mennica Warszawska (Warsaw Mint).
MW or MWB Warsaw (Russia) 1834-1857
M:X Mexico (Mexico) 1733
Mxo Mexico (Mexico) 1679-1712

— N —

N Montpellier (France) 1539-1794
N Nagybanya (Holy Roman Empire) 1780
N Nantes (France) 1491-1540
N Naples (Italy) 1861-1867
N in circle Nikolsburg (Holy Roman Empire) 1627-1628
N Norwich (England) 1696-1697
N Nuremberg (City of Nuremberg) 1760-1773
N above VOC Negapatnam (Dutch India)
N backward above VOC Negapatnam (Dutch India)
N and IV Negapatnam (Dutch India)
N-B or N.B. Nagybanya (Austria, Hungary, Transylvania) 1630-1851
N - BN Naples (Italy) 1863-1867
N-E Nagy-Enyed (Transylvania)
NG Guatemala (Guatemala) 1776-1822, 1825-1862
NICOPENS Nykoping (Sweden) 1629
NICOPENSIS Nykoping (Sweden) 1707-1709
No-Ro, NoR, RoN.R., or N-R Bogota (Colombia) circa 1621-1820
NR Bogota (Colombia) 1656-1722, 1772-1811
NR Leon (Nicaragua)
N-S.R. Nurnberg Mint (Eichstadt) 1764

— O —

O Clermont (France) 1572, 1591-1594, 1610-1772
O Moulins (France) 1549-1555
O New Orleans (USA) 1838-1861, 1879-1909
O Oaxaca (Mexico) 1858-1893
O crowned between pillars Oaxaca (Oaxaca Revolutionary) 1812 (With various letters: A, O, R, BL or V)
O Oravicza (Austria, Holy Roman Empire) 1812-1816 (located in Sziklova)
O Orleans (France) 1420-1442
O Oswiecim (Poland) 1563
O Riom (France) 1555-1591, 1594-1772
O St. Pourzain (France) 1539-1549
Oa Oaxaca (Mexico) 1858-1893
OERTEL Oertel private Mint in Berlin (Germany, Prussia, China) 1892-1906. Fantasy coins, etc., only made, possibly also after 1906. Full name was Berliner Medaillen-Munze Otto Oertel.
oF Dresden (Saxony, Poland) 1734-1764
oFERRAL Dresden (Saxony, Poland) 1734-1764
O.H.K. Hamburg (Free City of Hamburg) 1761-1805
O-M Rotterdam (Rotterdam) 1694
OM ligate Strasbourg (Italy, Spain) OM Strasbourg (Italy) 1866-1867
OM Strasbourg (Italy) 1867
OM and 8-point star Oeschger-Merdoch private Mint in Barcelona (Spain) 1865-1890
ONATE Onate (Spain) 1875. A Carlista Mint.
O-O Diu (Portuguese India)
O.S.R.N. Zacatlan (Mexico) 1812-1813
OX Oxford (England) 1642-1646
OXA Oaxaca (Mexico) 1813-1814
oXM Mexico (Spanish America) 1536-1821
OXON Oxford (England) 1644

— P —

P Aix en Provence (France) 1503-1506, 1517-1538
P in circle Ancona (Papal States) 1512
P Dijon (France) 1539-1772
P Lima (Spanish America) 1568-1571, 1575-1588
(P) London (England) 1643-1644
P Oporto (Portugal) 1642-1663, 1688-1714
P Palma (Majorca)
P Pamplona (Spain) 1651-1658, 1788-1855 (latter period with Navarre arms)
P Parma (Parma) 1858
P Pernambuco (Brazil)
P at center of cross Perpignan (France) 1463-1494

P Perth (Australia, Great Britain) 1899-1931, 1986
P. Perugia (Papal States) 1795, 1798
P Perugia (Roman Republic) 1799
P Philadelphia (USA) 1942-1945, 1979-present
P Philadelphia (Netherlands, Curacao, other nations) 1940-1945
P Pont St. Espirt (France) 1419-1442
P Popayan (Colombia) 1772-1820
P Port-au-Prince (Haiti)
P Poznan (Poland) 1598-1609, 1616.
P Potosi (Spanish America) circa 1555-1773
P Prague (Austria, Bohemia) circa 1761
P over VOC Pulicat (Dutch India)
PAL over VOC Pulicat (Dutch India)
PARMA Parma (Papal States) 1503-?
PASCO Pasco (Peru) 1844, 1855-1857
PB Ensisheim (Holy Roman Empire) 1601-1629
PC Aix en Provence (France) 1503-1506, 1517-1538
PC Pontefract (Pontefract, England, obsidional issues) 1648
P.C.B. Frankfurt (Frankfurt) 1765
PERGOLA Pergola (Papal States) 1796-1797
PERGOLA Pergola (Roman Republic)
PERVGIA Perugia (Papal States) 1796-1798
PERVGIA Perugia (Roman Republic)
PERVSIA Perugia (Papal States) 1517
PERVSIA AVGVSTA Perugia (Papal States) 1795
P.F.C. Perugia (Roman Republic)
PHILA Philadelphia (Ecuador)
PHILADELPHIA Philadelphia (Ecuador) 1895
PHILA USA Philadelphia (Ecuador)
PI Graz (Holy Roman Empire) 1712-1756
Pi San Luis Potosi (Mexico) 1829
PI/SAV/R Pisa (Papal States) 1520
PISIS Florence (Etruria) 1803-1806
P*L Lima (Spanish America) 1565-
PL London (Australia) 1951
PLAC. Piacenza (Papal States) 1522
PLACENTIA Piacenza (Papal States) 1513-
P.M. Dusseldorf (Julich-Berg) 1771-1783
PM Manila (Culion Leper Colony) 1920-1930
(PM) Prague (Holy Roman Empire) 1694, 1710-1711
PM Pobjoy * (Isle of Man)
PN or Pn Popayan (Colombia) 1758-1822
PO Oporto (Portugal)
PORT Oporto (Portugal)
POTOSI Potosi (Bolivia) 1852-1853
P.P. Pampeluna (Spain) 1837
P four times in angles of cross Oporto (Brazil) 1693-1699
P.R. Dusseldorf (Julich-Berg) 1783-1804

PR 809 counterstamp Goa (Portuguese India) circa 1831
P-R Prague (Austria, Bohemia) 1746-1767
PROVINCIA DE GVAIANA Ciudad Bolivar (Spanish America) 1813-1815
PS St. Veit (Holy Roman Empire) 1625-1628
PS-IK Prague (Holy Roman Empire) 1774-1780
P-T Poitiers (France) 1494
PTS monogram Potosi (Argentina) 1813-1815
PTS monogram Potosi (Bolivia) 1767-1825, 1834-1841, 1872-?
PW Pressburg (Austria) 1710-1718

— Q —

Q Chalons-sur-Saone (France) 1539-1700
Q Narbonne (France) 1700-1710
Q Perpignan (France) 1710-1837
Q Weissenfels (German States) 1686
QUITO Quito (Ecuador) 1833-1862

— R —

R Avignon (France)
R Beaucaire (France)
(R) London (England) 1644-1645
R London (France) 1815. On 20 francs gold only.
R Nisme (France) 1655-1658
R Orleans (France) 1700-1794
R Rennes (France) 1491-1540
R Rio de Janeiro (Brazil, St. Thomas and Prince Is., Angola) 1765-1777, 1811-1834
R Rio de Janeiro (Portugal) 1703-1822. Gold only.
R Rioja (Argentina) 1842-1843
R Riom (France) 1422-1431
R Romans (France) 1419-1441
R crowned Romans (France) 1523-1539
R Rome (Eritrea) 1890-1896, 1918
R crowned Rome (France) 1812-1814
R crowned and wolf Rome (France) 1811-1814
R Rome (Italian Somaliland) 1909-1925
R Rome * (Italy) 1870-present
R. Rome (Italy) 1911
R and anchor Rome (Italy) 1902. Gold 20 lire only. Anchor indicates Eritrean gold.
R Rome (Papal States until 1870, Vatican City, San Marino, Albania)
R Rome (Albania)
R. Rome (Roman Republic)
.R. Rome (Roman Republic)
R St. Andre de Villeneuve (France) 1539-1654, 1659-1699
R Wolschot private Mint in Antwerp (Antwerp) 1814
R and lis Ghent (France) 1815
RA Rioja (Argentina) 1824-1826
RAV Ravenna (Papal States) 1745-1753
RAVEN Ravenna (Papal States) 1745

RAVENE Ravenna (Papal States) 1513-?
RAVENN Ravenna (Papal States) 1745
RAVENNA Ravenna (Papal States) 1745
RAVENNAE ANTIQUAE Ravenna (Papal States) 1744
REGIUM AEMILIA Reggio Emilia (Papal States) 1513-?
REGIUM LEPIDI Reggio Lepidi (Papal States) 1513-?
RIOXA Rioja (Argentina) 1821-1823
ROM Rome (Papal States) 1738-1760
ROMA Rome (Papal States) 1503-1738
ROMA Rome (Roman Republic) 1800
ROMA Rome (Somalia) 1950
ROMANI Rome (Papal States) 1785-1796
ROMANO Rome (Papal States) 1750-1758, 1781-1797
RONCIGLIOE Ronciglione (Papal States) 1799
RONCIGLION Ronciglione (Papal States, Roman Republic) 1799
RONCIGLIONE Ronciglione (Papal States) 1799
RONNC Ronciglione (Papal States, Roman Republic) 1799

— S —

S. Danzig (Danzig) 1733
S Dresden (Saxony) 1813-1832
S Durlach (Baden) 1763-1779
S Gunzburg (Holy Roman Empire) 1762-1780
S Hall in Tyrol (Holy Roman Empire) 1765-1780
S Hanover (Hanover) 1839-1844
S Helsinki * (Finland) 1917-present
S Reims (France) 1690-1772
S and Holy cloth Reims (France) 1679-1690
S and Phial Reims (France) 1679-1690
S San Francisco * (USA) 1856-1955, 1968-present
S San Francisco (Australia, Fiji, Netherlands East Indies, many other nations)
S Santiago (Chile) 1744-1818
S Saumur (France) 1420-1431
S Schmollnitz in Slovakia (Austria) 1763-1816
S Schmollnitz in Slovakia (Galicia-Lodomeria) 1774
S Schwabach (Brandenburg-Ansbach) 1764-1785
S Schwabach (Brandenburg-Bayreuth) 1769
S Schwabach (Prussia) 1792-1794
S Solothurn (Helvetian Republic) 1798-1801
S Utrecht (Dutch Indies)
S crowned between pillars Sombrerete de Vargas (Mexico Revolutionary) 1810-1812
S Stockholm (Sweden) 1593
S Suermond (Netherlands) 1820-1822
S Sydney (Australia) 1871-1926
S Troyes (France) 1539-1679

S crowned Troyes (France) 1679-1690
S-A Danzig (Danzig) 1614-1621
SA Pretoria (South Africa) 1923-1932
"SA" Sandsfoot Castle Mint (England) 1644 (sometimes called Salisbury Mint)
SAGUR Sagur (Circars) 1825-1835
SAHLABERG Sahla (Sweden) 1688-1740. Variations of the name.
Sa Surabaya (Dutch Indies)
SB Sahla (Sweden) 1688
S-B Schassburg (Transylvania)
S.B. Thorn (Thorn in Poland) 1764-1768
S-C Gunzburg (Holy Roman Empire) 1765-1774
SC-G Gunzburg (Austria) 1765
SCHWABACH Schwabach (Brandenburg-Ansbach) 1754-1765, 1773-1774, 1779
SD Santo Domingo (Spanish America)
SE Santiago del Estero (Argentina)
SE Seville (Spain)
SER. under 3 mountains counter-mark Serena (Chile) circa 1817-1823
SEVERINO San Severino (Papal States) 1796
S-F Guenzburg (Austria) 1789-1797?
SF Guenzburg (Holy Roman Empire, Further Austria) 1775-1780. The most famous appearance of this privy mark is under the bust of the Maria Theresa taler, still being struck today. In this sense, SF also stands for all Mints which have struck the "Maria." These include Brussels 1937-1957; London 1936-1961; Birmingham 1949-1955; Paris 1935-1957; Bombay 1940-1941; Florence 1814-1828; Vienna 1827-present; Venice 1836-1866; Prague 1836-1842; Milan 1820-1859; Rome 1936-1940 and Leningrad.
S.F. Santa Fe de Bogota (Spanish America)
S.F. Frankfurt (Frankfurt) 1765
S. FELICIANO Foligno (Papal States) 1793
S-G Guenzburg (Austria) 1764-1765
S.G.H. Dresden (Saxony) 1804-1812
SGV Madrid (Philippines)
SH Graz (Holy Roman Empire) 1664-1666
SHS Breslau (Silesia) 1667-1683
S-IE Vienna (Austria) 1745
SIBER Lausanne (Vaud) 1845
SK Vienna (Holy Roman Empire) 1774-1780
SK-PD Kremnitz (Austria) 1774-1780
SLP San Luis Potosi (Mexico) 1863
SM St. Petersburg (Russia) 1796-1801
SM Santa Marta (Colombia)
S.M. in beaded oval Santa Marta (Venezuela Revolutionary) 1810, 1813, 1820-1821
S-M-O-M in angles of Maltese Cross Order of Malta Mint in Rome * (Sovereign Military Order of Malta) 1965-present

So (o above S) Santiago * (Chile) 1751-present
So Do Santo Domingo (Spanish America)
SOHO Mathew Boulton private Mint in Birmingham (England, Bahamas, Monneron tokens, East India Company, etc.) 1788-1806
SP St. Petersburg (Russia) 1798-1800
S-P Santo Domingo (Spanish America)
SP Sao Paulo (Brazil) 1825-1832
SPB St. Petersburg (Livonia-Estonia) 1757
SPB St. Petersburg (Russia) 1736-1917
SPOLETVM VMB CAP Spoleto (Papal States) 1797
S.P.Q.N. Nurnberg (Nurnberg) 1745.
S.P.Q.W. Wurzburg (Bavaria) 1815-1864.
S.P.Q.W. Wurzburg (Wurzburg) 1749, 1755, 1773-1778
SR (R above S) Santander (Spain) 1821
S-S Prague (Holy Roman Empire) 1765-1773
S. SEVERI San Severino (Papal States) 1797
S. SEVERINO San Severino (Papal States) 1796-1798
ST monogram Stockholm (Sweden) 1945-1959
ST Strickling (Blomberg) 1820-1840
ST. BERNARD unknown (St. Bernard "Monnaie Fictive") 1821, 1833
STIGH KOHL Sahla (Sweden) early 18th century
STOCKHOLM Stockholm (Sweden) 1566-1575
STORA KOPPARBERGSLAGH Stora Kopparbergs-Bergslag, private Mint in Fahlun (Sweden) 1719-1791. Name appears in many variations, as STORE KOPPARBERGSL, STORY KOPPARBERGZLAGENS, etc.
S-V Szeben-Varos (Transylvania)

— T —

T Canterbury (England) 1526-1532, 1549
t Canterbury (England) 1549-1550
Gothic T Chalons-sur-Marne (France) 1412-1440
T Nantes (France) 1551-1837
Gothic T Ste. Menehould (France) 1392-1412
T Ste. Menehould (France) 1539-1551
T Tabora (German East Africa) 1916. Recent evidence proves this T mark also stood for the Lulanguru Mint on part of the German East Africa gold 15 rupie coins only.
T Tarascon (France) 1483-1508
T Tegucigalpa (Hondura, Central American Republic)
T Tlalpujahua (Mexico) 1811-1813
T Toledo (Spain)
T Toro (Portugal)
T Trincomalee (Dutch Ceylon) 1789-1793
T Tui (Portugal)

T Turin (Italy) 1861-1870
T Turin (France) 1540-1549
TARAPACA Tarapaca (Chile) 1891
T.B. Turin (Savoy) 1519-1535
TB ligate Turin (Italy) 1861
T and BN Turin (Italy) 1861-1870
TC monogram Bristol (England) 1549
TERNI Terni (Papal States) 1797
TIVOLI Tivoli (Papal States) 1797
TL Tarascon (France) 1483-1508
T.L. Tegucigalpa (Honduras) 1823
T.L.B. Krakow (Poland) 1658-1685
T.L.B. Ujazdow or Warsaw (Poland-Lithuania) 1656-1683 (T.L.B. was Titus Livius Boratyni, Concessionaire of the Krakow and Ujazdow Mints.)
T.M. Bologna (Papal States) 1816-1818
TM Feodosia (Taurida, or Crimea) 1787-1788
TM monogram Rome (Papal States, Roman Republic) 1796-1799, 1807
T.M. Rome (Papal States, Roman Republic) 1796-1799
T and NB Turin (Italy) 1863
T and NB (B inverted) Turin (Italy) 1863
TOR-SA counterstamp Tortosa (Tortosa in Spain obsidional issues) circa 1809
TRA Utrecht (Batavian Republic)
TRAI Utrecht (Netherlands, etc.) 1738-1797
TRANSI Kampen in Overyssel (Batavian Republic) 1799-1806
TS Guenzburg (Holy Roman Empire) 1762-1788
TS-IF Guenzburg (Holy Roman Empire) 1797
TW Wyon private Mint, London (British Guiana) 1813. Initials for Thomas Wyon, engraver.

— U —

U Amiens (France) 1571-1578
U and St. Erik Stockholm * (Sweden) 1959-present
U Troyes (France) 1690-1772
U Turin (France, French Italy) 1538-1544, 1802-1814
U and heart Turin (France) 1803-1814
U and heart Turin (Republic of Italy) 1802-1804

— V —

V Lauer private Mint in Nuremburg, Germany (Orange Free State, Transvaal patterns) 1888-1890
V Nuremberg (Brandenburg-Ansbach) 1727-1732
V Surabaya (Dutch East Indies) 1833-1837
V Troyes (France) 1690-1772
V Turin (France) 1539-1540
V Valencia (Portugal)

v Valencia (Spain) 1707, 1811
v Valona (Albania)
v Venice (Austria) 1797-1866
v Venice (Italy, Napoleonic Kingdom) 1807-1813
v Venice (Venetia prov. government) 1848
v Vienna (Albania and others) 1926-1928
v Vilalon (Spain) 1454-1474
v Villefranche-de-Rouergue (France) 1422-1540
v Vilnius (Lithuania) 1528, 1601-1602
Va Valdivia (Chile)
V.A. Valdivia (Chile) 1822
VA Valencia (Portugal)
VA monogram Vilnius (Lithuania) 1616
VALD. under 3 mountains counter-mark Valdivia (Chile) circa 1817-1823
VALLADOLID Valladolid (Mexico) 1813
VALP. under 3 mountains counter-mark Valparaiso (Chile) circa 1817-1823
VC Hall in Tyrol (Holy Roman Empire) 1775-1780
VC Vienna (Austria and others) circa 1590-1637
V between c - o Negapatnam (Dutch India)
VC-S Hall in Tyrol (Austria) 1774-1780
VET.M. Venice (Venice) 1762
V-I flanking crossed pennants Poznan (Poland) 1594-1595
VITERBO Viterbo (Papal States) 1796-1798
VM Sagan (Holy Roman Empire) 1625
VMB CAP Spoleto (Papal States) 1797
V between o - o Pulicat (Dutch India)
VS-K Prague (Austria) 1774-1780
VS-S Prague (Austria) 1765-1773
V over VOC monogram Pulicat (Dutch India)

— W —

w Arras (France) 1792-1793
w Breslau (Holy Roman Empire, Breslau City) 1624-1635
w Breslau (Prussia) 1743
w Breslau (Silesia) until 1750
w Goerz (Gorizia) 1747
w Lille (France) 1685-1858
w Milan (Italy) 1861. On copper centesimo actually an inverted M.
w Surabaya (Dutch East Indies) 1839-1843
w Vienna (Austria and others) 1650-1658, 1781
w Vienna (Austrian Netherlands)
w Vilnius, Wilno (Lithuania) 1601
WA Archbishop Wareham (England) 1504-1533
w James Watt and Co. private Mint in Birmingham (Egypt) 1886-1887, 1891, 1896-1898, 1900, 1905
w James Watt and Co. in Birmingham (several nations)
w Soho (Malaysia)

w West Point, N.Y. (collector coins 1984-present)
w Weymouth (England) 1644
w Wschowa (city of Wschowa) 1526-1608
w Wyon private Mint, London (British Guiana) 1813
WATT James Watt and Co. private Mint in Birmingham (several nations)
WESTF Enkhuizen in West Friesland (Netherlands and others) 1731-1741, 1761-1771, 1791-1796
WESTF Hoorn in West Friesland (Netherlands and others) 1720-1731, 1751-1761, 1781-1791
WESTF Medemblijk in West Friesland (Netherlands and others) 1741-1751, 1771-1781
WESTFRI Enkhuizen in West Friesland (Batavian Republic) 1799-1806
W/HR Breslau (Silesia) 1626-1627
WI Vienna (Austria and others) 1746-1771
W.M. Warsaw (Poland) 1792. Warszawska Mennica.
WS monogram Bristol (England) 1546-1549
WW Wyon private Mint, London (Venezuela) 1843. William Wyon, engraver.
W. WYON Wyon private Mint, London (Venezuela) 1843. Name is for William Wyon, engraver; Mint was owned by Peter Wyon.

— X —

x Aix-en-Provence (France) 1548-1578
x Amiens (France) 1578-1772
x Besancon (France) 1739. This is actually two "C's" back to back. See entry under C.
x Villefranche (France) 1539-1548
XB Archbishop Rotherham (England) 1480-1500
XX Vilna (Lithuania) 1616. This is actually inverted V superimposed over normal V.

— Y —

Y Bourges (France) 1539-1772
y London (England) 1552
Roman Y London (England) 1549-1550
Y York (England) 1696-1697

— Z —

z Batavia (Dutch East Indies) 1800-1808
z Grenoble (France) 1539-1772
z Saint Pourcain (France) 1529-1531. This privy mark of Mint master Pierre Monachy was used at the end of legends until the Mint was transferred to Montferrand in January 1531.
z Surabaya (Dutch East Indies) 1809-1819
z Zacatecas (Mexico)
z Zagreb (Croatia) 1849. Count Jelacich Mint.

Z Zaragoza (Spain) 1700-1746
Z Zator (Poland) 1563
Z Zongolica (Mexico Revolutionary) 1812 Coins are inscribed SONGOLICA.
ZACATECAS Zacatecas (Spanish America)
Z.B. Cattaro (Ragusa) 1427-1429, 1453-1456
Z.B. Venice (Venice) circa 1751
Z-B Zalathna Banya (Transylvania)
ZECCA.V Venice (Venetian Republic) 1797
ZEL Middelburg in Zeeland (Batavian Republic) 1799-1806
ZEL Middleburg in Zeeland (Netherlands, etc.) 1725-1799
Zs Zacatecas (Mexico) 1810-1822, 1824-1905
Z*V Venice (Venetian Republic) 1797
Z.V. Venice (Venetia Prov. government) 1848-1849

— No Mark —
(Reported where this is significant to the understanding of a series only)
Auschwitz (Galicia-Pomerania) 1794
Bombay * (India)
Brussels (Italy) 1866
Cagliari (Island of Sardinia) 1812
Ceylon government Mint (Ceylon) 1811-1816. Mint master was A. Bertolacci.
Local private Mints in Ceylon (Ceylon) 1801-1809. Mints operated by Adriaan Pieter Blume, Jurgen Arnoldus Hikken and Chinna T. C. S. Chitty, respectively. All crude work.
Cordoba (Cordoba province of Argentina) 1845-1854
Denver (USA) 1965-1967
Dresden under Prussian occupation (Prussia)
Genoa (Genoa Republic) 1814
Genoa (Ligurian Republic) 1798-1805
Gibbs private Mint in Belleville, N.J. (Liberia) 1833. One cent token.
Goerz (Gorizia) 1733-1736
Hall (Tyrol) 1739, 1809
Heaton private Mint in Birmingham (Tuscany) 1859
Kou-Pei Mint in Kalgan (Inner Mongolia) 1938
Kremnitz (Hungary malcontents) 1704-1707
Lisbon (Brazil) 1715-1746, 1752-1760, 1768-1805
Lisbon (Maranhao province) 1749
Lisbon * (Portugal) 1640-present
London (Canada) 1858-1907
London (Portugal) 1830. Copper 5 and 10 reis. These were circulated on Terceira Island in 1831.
Mantua (Mantua in Italy obsidional issues) 1796, 1799 (French siege June-July, 1796; Austro-Russian siege 1799-1801)

Milan (Cisalpine Republic) 1800-1801
Milan (Duchy of Parma) 1830
Milan (San Marino) 1864-1875
Osaka (Russia) 1916. Absence of moneyer letters distinguishes Osaka on 10 and 15 kopecks of 1916 only.
Ottawa * (Canada) 1908-present
Palma Nova (Palma Nova in Italy obsidional issues) 1814
Paris (Italy) 1862-1866
Parma (Duchy of Parma) 1854-1858
Philadelphia (France) 1944. Brass occupation 2 francs only.
Philadelphia * (USA) 1793-present
Porto (Portugal) 1833-1834
Rio de Janeiro * (Brazil) 1751-1752, 1868-present
Rome (Eritrea) 1891-1896
Rome (Papal States) 1784
Sandyford (Ireland)
San Francisco (USA) 1965-1967
Soho Mint in Birmingham (Ceylon) 1802
Surabaya (Netherlands) 1816, 1818, 1821
Tarragona (Spain). During Napoleonic wars.
Tehran * (Iran) 1876-present
Turin (Piedmont Republic) 1799
Turin (Sardinia) 1814-1815
Turin (Savoy) 1799-1800
Venice (Austrian Venetia) 1798-1802
Venice (Venetia Prov. government) 1848
West Point, N.Y. (U.S.; Centavo, Panama, 1974)
Wyon private Mint, London (Venezuela) 1852

— Special Symbols —
& Aix-en-Provence (France) 1578-1786
+ Nuremberg (Nuremberg) 1655-1716
0 (numeral) London (England) 1600
1 (numeral) London (England) 1601
2 (numeral) London (England) 1602
9 Rennes (France) 1539-1772
9 lying on its back to left of regnal year Surat (Surat) 1748
45 Farrukhabad (Circas) 1802-1845
99 Dinan (France)
99 Nantes (France) 1539-1956
    Krakow (Poland) 1588-1595
    Lublin (Poland) 1597

— Symbols —
Acorn York (England) 1526-1530
Three acorns Vilnius (Lithuania) 1580
Anchor Nicholas Briot coinage (England) 1638-1639
Anchor Genoa (Sardinia) 1824-1860
Anchor London (England) 1597-1600, 1628-1629, 1638-1639, 1658-1660
Anchor Paris Commune Mint (France) 1871. Used March 18 to May 29, 1871 only.

Anchor is privy mark of Zephyrin Camelinat, Mint master; he fled to England 1871, returning to France 1885.

Angel's head Brussels (Austrian Netherlands) 1607-1693, 1711-1716, 1744-1745, 1758-1794. This mark is referred to as a human head in several publications.

Aquaduct Segovia (Spain) circa 1550-1868

Arrow Mitau (Courland) 1599-1607

Arrow shaped mark Warsaw (Poland between the world wars)

Axe, Battle Amsterdam (Netherlands) 1875-1887

Ball and 4 lis Sandsfoot Castle (England) 1644. Sometimes called Salisbury Mint. This mark has also been attributed to Weymouth Mint.

3 wavy bars Valladolid (Spain) ?-1588

4 wavy bars Valladolid (Spain) 1588?-1651

Bell London (England) 1643-1645

Bird Sandsfoot Castle (England) 1643-1644. Same remarks as ball and 4 lis Mint mark.

Bird, supposed to be a bat Valencia (Spain) 1700-1746

Bird and St. Michel head Brussels * (Belgium, Congo, Rwanda, others) 1963-present

Boar's head Sandsfoot Castle (England) 1643-1644

Open book Aberystwyth (England) 1638-1642

Bow Durham House Mint (England) 1548-1549

Shallow bowl or cup Cuenca (Spain) Ferdinand III (1230-1252) until Charles and Johanna (1516-1555)

Bugle Truro (England)

Bull's head Toro (Portugal)

Caduceus Utrecht * (Netherlands) 1815-present

Calvary cross London (England) 1625-1626

Cardinal's hat and keys York (England) 1531-1545

Cask (or tun) London (England) 1592-1595, 1615-1616, 1636-1638

Castle Exeter (England) 1645

Castle London (England) 1569-1571, 1627-1628

Castle Sandsfoot Castle (England) 1643-1644

Castle Tournai (Spanish Netherlands) 1576-1616

Castle Weymouth (England) 1643-1644

Chalice La Coruna (Spain)

Child or star Utrecht (Netherlands East Indies) 1827-1843

Club Annaberg (Saxony) 1533-1539

Cock Batavia (Dutch East Indies) 1745-1807. Originally (1745-1751) this was privy mark of Mint master Paulus Dorsman,

but continued in use until 1807. Appears on gold coins only.

Cock Hoorn in Westfrisia (Netherlands) 1751-1761

Cock Medemblik in Westfrisia (Netherlands) 1741-1751

Conch shell Travancore, India Mint.

Cornucopia Paris * (France, etc.) 1898-present. Used in conjunction with other symbols, as torch, wing or owl.

Cornucopia Vincennes (France)

Cow Pau (France) 1539-1794

Crane Kampen in Overyssel (Netherlands) 1752-1754

Crane Harderwijk in Gelderland (Netherlands) 1752-1757

Crane Vienna (Austria) circa 1637-1657

Crescent Mysore (Mysore) 1806-1812

Crescent Pondichery (Pondichery) 1817-1839?

Cross Namur (Spanish Netherlands) 1579

Cross above crossed keys Riga (Poland) 1588-1591

Cross patee Bristol (England) 1643

Cross patee Oxford (England) 1644

Cross and 4 annulets Sandsfoot Castle (England) 1643-1644

Crown Bombay (Surat) 1825

Crown Combe Martin (England) 1647-1648

Crown Copenhagen (Denmark)1842-1855?

Crown London (England) 1635-1636, 1660-1662

Crown Paris (France) 1422-1436

Crowned M Madrid * (Spain)

Diamond shape Bombay * (India)

Diamond shape with small incuse dot in center Hyderabad * (India)

Dog running Riga (Riga) 1609-1620

Dot Bombay (India)

Dot London (Poland) 1925. Silver 2 zloty only.

Dot Perth * (Australia) 1941-present

Three dots Valladolid (Spain)

Eagle's head Turin (Sardinia) 1816-1861

Eagle Hall * (Austria)

Heraldic eagle Kampen in Overyssel (Netherlands) 1763-1807

Ear of corn Harderwijk in Gelderland (Netherlands) 1782-1806

Eye London (England) 1645

Feline head Weymouth (England) 1643-1644

Fish Banaras (India) 1775-1819

Fish and caduceus Utrecht (Netherlands) 1974

Two fishes and mast Utrecht (France) 1811-1814

Fish Utrecht (France) 1811-1814. See above.

Floriate cross Oxford (England) 1643-1644

Flower Nicholas Briot private Mint (England) 1631-1632

5-petal flower Chester (England) 1644-1646
Flower Mitau (Courland) 1596-1600
Jasmin flower to right of regnal year Murshidabad (India) 1769-1785
Fleur de lis Utrecht (Holland-Belgium) 1838-1845
Foot Marseilles (France) 1539-1542
Fox Harderwijk in Gelderland (Netherlands) 1731-1732
Grapes in bunch Weymouth or Sandsfoot Castle (England) 1643-1644
Halberd Amsterdam (Netherlands) 1888
Hammer Florence (Etruria) 1803-1807. Alone on gold coins only; also occurs with other symbols.
Hammer Eskilstuna * (Sweden)
Crossed hammers Kongsberg * (Norway, Denmark)
Crossed hammers Kuttenberg (Holy Roman Empire) 1633-1635
Hand Antwerp (Austrian Netherlands) 1608-1620, 1679-1683, 1707-1729, 1744-1758
Hand Antwerp (Spanish Netherlands) 1543-1598
Hand with tiny cross Brussels (Austrian Netherlands) 1712-1715
Hand London (England) 1590-1592
Hand and Tower Tournai (Austrian Netherlands) 1645-1665
Harp London (England) 1632-1633 and 1525-1549
Heart Copenhagen * (Denmark, Iceland, Greenland)
Heart flying a pennant Elbing (Elbing) 1628
Heart pierced by arrow Elbing (Elbing) 1628
Heart London (England) 1629-1630
Helmet Sandsfoot Castle (England) 1643-1644
Helmet Weymouth (England) 1643-1644
Herring-buss Enkhuizen in Westfrisia (Netherlands) 1761-1771
Herring-buss Medemblik in Westfrisia (Netherlands) 1771-1781
Hill Harderwijk in Gelderland (Netherlands) 1732-1748. On copper doits.
Horse with feet on hill Harderwijk in Gelderland (Netherlands) 1732-1748. On silver ducatoons.
Knot ecclesiastic (England) Archbishop Bourdier 1454-1486
Paschal lamb Amiens (France) 1423-1455
Lamb's head with St. Michel head Brussels (Belgium) 1960-1963
Lamp and apple Milan (Duchy of Parma) 1815-1832
Leaf on stem Vilna (Poland) 1584-1589
Leopard Rouen (France) 1420-1449
Three leaves on stems Vilna (Poland) 1580-1595

Lily Bruges (Austrian Netherlands) 1643-1700, 1707-1709
Lily Bruges (Spanish Netherlands) 1545-1593
Lily Joachimsthal (county of Schlick) 1526. This symbol was the privy mark of Caspar von Mergenthal, the Mint master.
Double lily St. Polten (Austria, etc.) 1625
Line-across-hexagon Sherritt private Mint, Fort Saskatchewan, Canada * (Syria) 1968-present

Lion rampant Bruges (Austrian Netherlands) 1744-1754
Lion London (England) 1566-1567
Lion right Namur (Austrian Netherlands) 1707-1715
Lion rampant Sandsfoot (England) 1643-1644
Lion rampant Weymouth (England) 1643-1644
Two lions Weymouth (England) 1643-1644
Lion York (England) 1642-1644
Lis Canterbury and Durham (England) 1509-1526
Lis London (England) 1526-1551, 1558-1560, 1567-1570, 1604-1605, 1623-1624
Lis Oxford (England) 1642-1646
Lis Sandsfoot Castle (England) 1643-1644
Lis Weymouth (England) 1643-1644
Lotus Madras (Arcot) 1759-1835
Lozenge Oxford (England) 1644
Mercury staff Utrecht (Netherlands)
Negroid head London (England) 1626-1627

Newborn infant Utrecht (Holland-Belgium) 1815-1818
Orb Altona (Danish West Indies) 1859
Orb and star Altona (Danish West Indies) 1860
Orb Altona (Denmark)
Orb Nuremberg private counter Mints (jetons of 16th-18th century)
Owl Athens (Greece) 1833, 1842-1844
Pear-like object Sandsfoot Castle (England) circa 1643. Also attributed to Salisbury and Weymouth.
Pear Worcester (England) 1644-1646
Three pears Worcester (England) 1644-1646
Pearl (or dot) King's Norton (Israel)
Pellets Bristol (England) 1643-1645
Pellets Oxford (England) 1642-1646
Pellets Shrewsbury (England) 1642
Crossed pennants over orb Brandenburg (Prussia) 1586
Crossed pennants Danzig (Danzig) 1538
Crossed pennants Krakow (Poland) 1585-1595
Piratini arms in oval Piratini Republic Mint in Rio Grande do Sul (Brazil) 1833-1845

Plume (small, broad) Bristol (England) 1643-1645

Plume Chester (England) circa 1645?

Plume London (England) 1630-1631

Plume Lundy (England) 1645-1646

Plume, bands at bottom Oxford (England) 1642-1646

Plume Shrewsbury (England) 1642

Pomegranate Granada (Spain)

Portcullis London (England) 1566, 1633-1634

Rat Arras (Spanish Netherlands) 1582-1591

Ring (or beaded circle) Marienburg (Poland) 1592-1601. Shown with triangle 1592-1593.

Rooster Utrecht (Netherlands) 1975

Rooster Vienna (Austria) circa 1608-1619

Rose Calcutta (Arcot) 1759-1835

Rose Canterbury (England) 1509-1526, 1549

Rose Exeter (England) 1643-1645

Rose London (England) 1526-1544, 1549-1551, 1565, 1604-1605, 1620-1621, 1631-1632

Rose Truro (England) 1642-1643

Rosette Batavia (Dutch East Indies) 1745-1751. Silver only.

Rosette Dordrecht in Holland (Netherlands) 1607-1806

Rosette Enkuizen in Westfrisia (Netherlands) 1791-1796

Rosette Hoorn in Westfrisia (Netherlands) 1781-1791

Rosette Oxford (England) 1643-1645

Rosette Sandsfoot Castle (England) 1643-1644

Rosette Weymouth (England) 1643-1644

St. Erik head Stockholm, Sweden Mint.

St. Michel head Brussels * (Belgium) 1960-present

St. Michel head Brussels * (Congo, Rwanda, others) 1964-present

Scallop shell Corunna (Spain)

Scepter London (England) 1646-1648

Scimitar Baroda, India Mint.

Scissors, points down Poona (Poona, Peshwa coinage)

Scroll Sandsfoot Castle (England)

Sheaf Chester (England) 1644-1646

Three sheaves Chester (England)

Shell Chambery (Savoy) 1423-1434

Shield of Majorca Palma (Majorca, Balearic Islands) 1678-1707, 1808, 1821, 1823

Shield of Navarre Pamplona (Spain) 1788-1855 (occasionally with letter P)

Shield of Tarragona Tarragona (Tarragona obsidional issues) 1809

Shield of Utrecht Utrecht in Utrecht (Netherlands) 1738-1797

Split diamond Hyderabad (India)

Two stars (on coin edge) Brussels (Russia) 1897-1899

Star Enkuizen in Holland (Netherlands) 1796-1803

Star Hoorn in Holland (Netherlands) 1803-1809

Star London (England) 1611-1612, 1640-1641

Star Maastricht (Austrian Netherlands) 1794

Star Madrid (France) 1916. On bronze 10 centimes only: indicates planchets made at Madrid, with striking at Paris.

Star Munich (Austria) 1705-1714

Star (on coin edge) Paris (Russia) 1896-1899

Star Weymouth (England)

3-pointed star Jubia (Spain) 1866-1868

4-pointed star Segovia (Spain)

5-pointed star Hyderabad * (India) 1963-present

5-pointed star Lucca (Duchy of Lucca) 1826-1841

5-pointed star Maastricht (Austrian Netherlands) 1604-1619

5-pointed star Maastricht (Spanish Netherlands) 1549-1597

5-pointed star Manila (Spanish Philippines) 1881-1897

5-pointed star Nevers (France) 1422-1435

5-pointed star Oxford (England) 1644

6-pointed star Batavia (Dutch East Indies) 1744-1745

6-pointed star Le Puy (France) 1420-1423, 1429

6-pointed star Madrid * (Spain) 1850-present

6-pointed star Jerusalem, Israel Mint.

7-pointed star Seville (Spain) 1850-1863

8-pointed star Barcelona (Spain) 1850-1868

5-rayed star Batavia (Dutch East Indies) 1840-1843

5-rayed star Surabaya (Dutch East Indies) 1840-1843

Sun London (England) 1645-1646, 1649-1657

Sunface Indore (Indore) 1773-1902

Sword Amsterdam (Netherlands) 1846-1874

Thunderbolt Poissy (Bulgaria)

Thistles and lion Scottish Mint (England) 1637-1642

Torch Utrecht (Holland-Belgium) 1818-1838

Tower London (England) 1612-1613

Tower Middelburg in Zeeland (Netherlands) 1601-1799

Tower Mons (Austrian Netherlands)

Tower Mons (Spanish Netherlands) 1581-1587

Tower Tours (France) 1422-1540

Tree Herzogenbusch (Austrian Netherlands) 1602-1616

Tree Herzogenbusch (Spanish Netherlands) 1581-1597

Tree Vienna (Austria) circa 1608-1619
Tree trunk Harderwijk in Gelderland (Netherlands) 1758-1776
Trefoil London (England) 1613, 1624
Triangle London (England) 1639-1640
Triangle in circle London (England) 1641-1643
Triangle Moscow (Russia)
Triangle Neuburg am Inn (Austria) ?-1705
Triangle within Triangle Thorn (Thorn) 1659
Trident Kutch, India Mint

Trident to left of regnal year Masulipa-tam (Masulipatam) 1751-1754
Trident Paris Commune Mint (France) 1871. On silver five francs only.
Trisul Shahpur (Shahpur)
Turnip Enkhuizen in Westfrisia (Netherlands) 1731-1741
Turnip Hoorn in Westfrisia (Netherlands) 1720-1731
Wings Danzig (Danzig) 1612-1613
Zigzag line Poissy (France, other nations) 1922-1926

Indian State Mint Marks

Bhopal	Bundi, Kotah	Jaipur	Dewas
Bhopal	Jhalawar	Jodhpur	Indore
Bikanir	Bhartpur, Narwar	Jodhpur	Indore
Chhatarpur Orissa	Bikanir	Jodhpur	Mewar
Gwalior	Jaipur	Jodhpur	Narwar
Srinagar, Jalaun	Jodhpur	Karauli	Tonk
Alwar	Alwar	Karauli	Datia
Dholpur	Bhopal	Karauli	Dholpur
Gwalior	Bhartpur	Kishangarh	Jalaun, Kuchawan
Saugor	Dholpur, Tonk	Jhalawar	Jodhpur
Datia	Gwalior	Tonk	Seondha
Datia	Jaipur	Bikanir	Srinagar, Kunch
Datia	Srinagar, Jalaun, Kunch, Mandla	Bikanir	Bikanir
Dewas	Tonk	Bikanir	Jhansi
Gwalior	British East India Co.	Dewas	Karauli
Jalaun, Mandla	Bhartpur	Rewah	Mewar
Jhansi	Mewar	Saugor	Mewar
Bijawar, Chhatarpur	Mewar	Bikanir	Poona
Bikanir	Tonk	British East India Co.	Seondha
Jalaun	Datia	Dewas, Indore	Indore
Datia, Orchha	Kunch, Mandla, Saugor	French East India Co.	Jaipur
Gwalior	Ajmir	Bundi, Kotah	Tonk
Gwalior	Alwar		Awadh, British East India Co.
	Dewas		

Plate courtesy *Catalogue of the Coins in the Indian Museum Calcutta*, volume IV, published for the trustees of the Indian Museum in Oxford at the Clarendon Press, 1928, and *Coins of the World 1750-1850* by William D. Craig, Western Publishing Co.

English hallmarks

Laws and regulations affecting English hallmarks

A comprehensive study of the complete legislation with regard to the ancient art of goldsmithing and silversmithing might well fill several volumes. The laws passed are many, and invariably written in great detail. Here we will attempt merely to give in a very concise form the highlights or most important acts and laws that influenced the production of old silver.

The year 1180 commemorates the earliest mention of a guild or fraternity with regard to silversmithing. However, little importance is attached to it as the association was purely a voluntary one and had but few laws to govern it. After its inauguration, the founders were fined for being irregularly established without a proper license from the king.

As early as the year 1238, many inferior goldsmiths took advantage of their trade and produced silver of a very much lower standard than was used for government coins. These pieces were marketed for the same price as those of the correct alloy. Because of these numerous frauds, Henry III ordered the mayor and aldermen of the city of London to choose six of the most discreet goldsmiths to superintend the craft. This order was duly obeyed and in the succeeding years these men were in turn followed by others in the so-called offices of superintendents or wardens.

The wardens were given more and more power as time went on and in 1300 were authorized to assay every silver vessel produced, to ascertain whether or not it contained the correct proportion of silver and alloy. They became known as "gardiens."

In the year 1327 the Guild of London Goldsmiths became regularly incorporated by royal charter, under the title of "The Wardens and Commonalty of the Mystery of Goldsmiths of the City of London." The most important legislation enacted by this congress was that requiring every silversmith to use a particular hallmark of his own.

The second "Statutum de Moneta" in 1335 declared that inasmuch as counterfeit money had been imported by foreigners, plate was not to be exported without official license in order to protect the coin within the realm of the people. It is interesting to note here that the only means of exit from England officially allowed was from Dover, at which place foreigners were searched and then permitted to depart from England.

A statute passed in 1363 commanded that no goldsmith should work gold or silver into a wrought article unless it was of the alloy of good sterling. In the succeeding years, numerous by-laws were enacted in regard to the trade, all of varying importance.

The guild was reincorporated by charter in 1392 with vastly extended powers. In the provinces there is also evidence of the existence of similar guilds. These, however, will be discussed in detail in their proper place.

During the reigns of Henry VIII and Edward VI the silver coinage in England had been scandalously debased to the extent that in 1551, the coin minted consisted of only three ounces of silver to every pound weight of coins. But in 1560, an act of Elizabeth definitely established the Sterling Standard of 11 ounces 2 dwt. This is the equivalent of 92.5 percent pure silver. In order to correct the existing evil state of the coinage at this time, all existing base money was recalled by royal proclamation on February 19, 1560.

In order to stop the melting of coins for use in silverware, a law was passed in 1696 raising the silverware standard above the coin standard to 11 ounces 10 dwt. (95.8 percent). Pieces made of this standard were to be stamped with a new mark and known as Britannia silver.

But in 1719 the old standard of 11 ounces 2 dwt. was revived since wares of this content were proven to be more durable than the softer Britannia ware and the higher standard did not accomplish its purpose. Silversmiths merely added pure silver to coin silver to increase the standard. The higher or Britannia standard was not abolished but left to the discretion of individual silversmiths. It is interesting to note that the silver standard of 1719 has never changed since. This same act, which was one of the most important recorded in the annals of the guild, also imposed a tax of sixpence per ounce on all silver made in Great Britain. This is the first known mention of any duty on plate, but because of the ineffectuality of collecting the duty, this act was repealed in 1757. In its place a law was passed which required a license to be purchased by every goldsmith and silversmith, for which a nominal fee was charged.

The duty on plate was reimposed in 1784

and continued until 1890. The head of the reigning sovereign was punched on the piece in order to denote that the full duty had been paid.

In 1890 the duty on silver was repealed, and the use of the sovereign's head was discontinued.

Hallmarks

Because of the correct and continued use of hallmarks on English silver, the collector and research student of today is able to trace the complete ancestry of nearly any piece made subsequent to 1300. However, let it not be thought that hallmarks were ever originally used for any other purpose than to prevent fraud. On all pieces made from the beginning of the 14th century, a series of hallmarks was to be impressed denoting the quality of the piece made, and indicative of the individual maker.

The leopard's head mark was first established in 1300 and may be said to be the earliest known hallmark on English silver. In 1363 the name was changed and this particular mark was called a king's mark. Through an error in translation from the French, the name leopard was applied to the head as depicted in the hallmark, but actually the figure used was that of the head of a lion. From 1478 to the George II era there was a crown on the leopard's head. After this time, however, the size of the head was diminished and again through an error in reading the original laws of the guild, the crown was omitted.

Maker's mark

This mark is next in chronological order to the leopard's head. The act of 1363 ordained that every master goldsmith should have a mark of his own which was to be impressed on each piece after it had been assayed. The first maker's marks were generally flowers, animals, hearts, crosses, or other symbols generally selected in allusion to the maker's name. It is probably because most of the population at this time was illiterate that this form of mark was used. Shops in London of this period were rarely advertised by name since so few people were able to read. Therefore, we may assume that the earliest silversmiths imitated the styles of shopkeepers in advertising or hallmarking their own products. This system fell into disuse in the 17th century and by the time of Charles II, initials and letters were used. During the years of the Britannia standard many makers used two individual marks, in order to distinguish silver

made of one standard from the other. This caused so much confusion that in 1739 a statute decreed that all silversmiths should use the first initials of their Christian name and surname. At this time all previous marks were discontinued.

Date letters

Although there has been definite proof of the use of the date letter on silver as early as 1500, the first actual mention is in 1629. From this time on, date letters were used with sufficient frequency to enable one to fill in the missing years, and so be able to determine the exact year in which a piece was made. The use of the date letter was arranged in cycles of 20 years using the letters A to U or V, but excluding J. At the end of each 20 years, a different type of letter was used and the cartouche was changed. It must be mentioned here that dates that one often finds engraved on a piece of silver are of but little help in determining the actual year in which a piece was created, as many pieces were given or bequeathed and the date inscribed signified the time of the presentation, not the time of making.

Lion passant

This mark was adopted as the official stamp at the Goldsmiths Hall in London in 1544. All London silver made since then must have this mark.

Lion's head erased and "Britannia"

The only importance to be attached to these two marks is that they denoted pieces made of the higher standard and were used for only 23 years, from 1697 to 1720. It is because of the short term of use of these marks that pieces bearing the Britannia are rare and always sought after by collectors.

Sovereign's head

This mark should be found on all plate assayed in England from 1784 to 1890 as it was required to be used to denote the payment of duty by the silversmith to the crown. This mark is actually the head in profile of the reigning king or queen.

Thus the use of these marks enables us to identify the place, year, and maker of old silverware. Wyler, Seymour B., *The Book of Old Silver - English, American, Foreign*, Crown Publishers, New York, pp. 6-10.

Bank notes and other paper money

Not as old as coins but equally fascinating to many are bank notes and other forms of paper money. Checks, stock and bond certificates and even deposit slips and check writing machines are also collected with paper money.

Our purpose here will be to introduce the subject matter on a general basis.

Early notes

Marco Polo brought back to Italy tales of paper money in circulation in China. In 806, 400 years before Marco Polo, Emperor Hien Tsung issued certificates of deposit to merchants, who then had to carry only the paper and not the heavy metal it represented. The earliest notes known to us date from the Ming Dynasty, 1368, when notes made of mulberry bark were issued.

Emergency notes are known to have been issued during the siege of the Alhama in Spain in 1483 and in Granada, Spain, in 1490.

Bank of Stockholm notes in Sweden date from 1661, considered the earliest circulating bank notes in Europe.

Topics

Choices offered in topic collecting are almost as wide in paper money as in coins. There are few genuine, intentional commemorative notes, but they can be found. Some collectors seek bank buildings on notes; others could parallel the coin themes of ships, animals, fruit, trees, women, portraits and even coins and Mints on notes.

Advanced collectors might seek variety of note manufacture methods, including offset, intaglio or engraved notes or lithographic.

The paper money collector has two sources of delight not shared with most coin collectors: serial numbers and signatures. One to four signatures are often found on notes, and as one of the these signatures may change, endless combinations become available to the specialist.

Numbers and letters found on notes can include engraving plate numbers, serial letter combinations, issue-date changes and easiest of all, a serial number. Collectors observe the color of the number; height of the figures; and then may check for palindromes, numbers reading the same both ways, popularly called "radar notes." The more digits in a number, the more difficult this becomes. A number 1441 may be easy to find; more difficult would be 123454321.

Housing

The collector of paper money of the world experiences the same problems of the collector of notes of the United States when he must decide how to store and arrange his collection.

Since notes are not as durable as coins and folding and handling can reduce their desirability, it is important to keep the notes flat and yet in view.

Plastic sheets are made in several sizes, including 8½-by-11-inches, with two, three or four pockets, to hold notes of varying sizes. Also smaller wallet-size holders are made, as well as single plastic pockets slightly larger than the notes to be handled.

Other useful tools for studying your notes are a magnifying glass, a ruler with millimeter readings and a good eye for color shades.

Grading

The grade indicated by many sellers and catalogers of notes is a tool for determining how worn a note is, or how far from being Uncirculated it may be. A crisp note may be worth twice as much as one with a single fold. Once a note has several folds, is dirty, has torn corners and ragged edges, it is probably worth face value only if still circulating, and very little more if obsolete, unless it is extremely rare.

These remarks on condition are not intended to lead the paper money collector to believe that only Uncirculated notes are collectible. Many collectors want a note that has genuinely seen circulation; others will take a worn note, with the expectation of replacing it when a note in better condition becomes available. The collector who turns down notes for the Uncirculated issues may wait a long time; meanwhile, prices may increase for even the worn notes.

Some grade paper money in the same terms by which coins are graded. Others have devised a percentage scale, with a 100 percent note Uncirculated, and the amount of wear indicated by lesser figures; a 90 percent note would be better than a 70 percent note.

Emergency money

Siege notes, issued in times of emergency, have been mentioned already. Collectors of world notes often encounter other emergency notes which should be reviewed.

At least a dozen countries of Europe issued emergency money in the 1914-1923 period of World War I and the aftermath. In France they are called monnaies de necessite and in Germany and Austria, notgeld, emergency money. Many cities issued these; others were issued by the army, the railways or the post offices.

Collectors often separate the emergency issues from inflation issues. The latter appeared first in late 1922, and by 1923 in Germany the issues reached such enormous sums that a single note might represent more than the entire indebtedness of the German people in August 1914. Even more rampant inflation was known in Hungary in 1946.

In some cases, governments have been known to bring out of storage notes not issued for many years and overprint them with new dates and values.

Other specialized forms of emergency money are cited as postage stamp money, encased and unencased; military payment certificates; invasion money; guerrilla issues; prisoner of war camp money; and issues from concentration and displaced persons camps.

Other uses of paper money

Economists can point to the printing press and its unlimited yield of paper money as a major cause of inflation and monetary woes of many a nation. Paper money does not have to reach the point of spiraling inflation.

Paper money can represent 100 percent hard money; that is, $100 worth of gold is on deposit in a bank, with a $100 note issued and the statement that the note is redeemable for $100 in gold.

In practice, the tendency of governments has been that with a gold reserve of $100, notes might be issued in sums of $200 or $500 or $1,000 or more, backed by the same $100 in gold; or eventually, no gold at all.

A study of paper money issues will reveal various names for notes, many based on the type of backing; gold note, silver note, even copper coins depicted on a note, to denote copper coin backing. Other notes found will be treasury note; certificate of deposit; Federal Reserve note; in France, "billets de confiance," (notes of confidence); gold or silver certificates.

During the French Revolution, and in 1923 in Germany, land was the backing of assignates and rentenmark notes, respectively. Also in 1923 in Germany, there were notes backed by wood, rye, gas, electricity and other tangible commodities.

To readily identify paper money of the United States in circulation in war zones during World War II, United States silver certificates were used to pay troops in the Pacific and North African theaters of operation with distinctive markings.

Had there been a takeover by the enemy, the money could have been immediately disclaimed and redemption refused, if it was believed the enemy would benefit.

Printers

Some government printing facilities might print bank notes for other governments. Often the name of the printer, government or private, appears on the one side or the other of the note in very small letters.

Private firms which have printed notes around the world include:

American Bank Note Co., New York
British American Bank Note Co, Ottawa, Canada
Barclay and Fry Ltd., England
Blades, East & Blades Bank Note Engravers
Bouligay & Schmidt, Mexico
Bradbury Wilkinson & Co., New Malden, Surrey, England
Calicografia e Cartevalori, Milano, Italy
Canadian Bank Note Co., Ltd., Ottawa, Canada
Charles Skipper & East, England
Chosun Textbook Printing, Co. Ltd., South Korea
Chung Hwa Book Co., China
Commonwealth Banknote Co., Melbourne, Australia
Continental Banknote Co., New York
E.A. Wright, Philadelphia, Pa.
J. Enschede & Son, Haarlem, the Netherlands
Franklin-Lee Bank Note Co.
Forbes Lithograph Manufacturing Co., Boston, Mass.
Homer Lee Bank Note Co., New York
Hong Kong Banknote Co., Hong Kong
Hong Kong Printing Press, Hong Kong
Giesecke & Devrient, Berlin, Leipzig & Munich, Germany
International Bank Note Co., London
Jefferies Bank Note Co., Los Angeles
Nisson & Arnold, London
Orell Fuessli, Zurich
Beijing Bureau of Engraving and Printing, Beijing (Peking), China
Perkins, Bacon & Co. Ltd., London
St. Luke's Printing Works, London
Saul Soloman & Co., Cape Town, South Africa
Security Banknote Co., New York
Shanghai Printing Co., Shanghai, China
State of California Bureau of Printing, Sacramento, Calif.
Stecher-Traung Lithograph Corp., San Francisco, Calif.

Thomas de la Rue Ltd., Basingstoke, England
Tokyo Printing Co., Tokyo
Union Printing Co., Shanghai
Union Publishers and Printers Fed. Inc.,
  Shanghai
Waterlow & Sons Ltd., London

Waterlow Bros. & Layton Ltd., London
Watson Printing Co.
Western District Banknote Fed. Inc., Shang-
  hai
William Brown & Co., London
W.W. Sprague & Co., Ltd., England

World coinage report, 1984

Total coinages by nation for calendar year 1984. Source is "World Coinage Report 1980-
1984" issued by the United States Mint. Countries not listed either did not strike coins in 1984
or did not make information available.

Country	Rank	Coinage
United States	1	17,845,500,340
China, People's Republic	2	5,859,600,000
Japan	3	2,788,850,000
Germany, Federal Republic	4	1,494,160,000
Mexico	5	1,450,694,000
Brazil	6	1,213,518,000
Canada	7	1,180,732,241
Spain	8	872,500,000
Netherlands	9	776,000,000
France	10	689,200,000
China, Taiwan	11	610,000,000
India	12	560,077,700
United Kingdom	13	494,210,699
Australia	14	468,596,225
Bangladesh	15	429,632,000
South Africa	16	362,265,836
Argentina	17	334,918,560
Sri Lanka	18	305,000,000
Indonesia	19	230,205,000
Sweden	20	219,314,549
Italy	21	201,232,121
Austria	22	177,554,000
Korea	23	170,724,400
Portugal	24	166,107,281
Pakistan	25	163,430,000
Thailand	26	155,124,770
Switzerland	27	148,263,000
Greece	28	145,137,000
Ghana	29	139,041,425
Norway	30	128,499,500
Israel	31	114,031,270
Chile	32	110,000,000
Finland	33	98,098,200
Singapore	34	84,071,000
Peru	35	78,437,000
Hong Kong	36	76,548,000
Colombia	37	75,670,478
Turkey	38	58,318,291

Country	Rank	Coinage
Ireland	39	51,878,000
Paraguay	40	50,000,000
New Zealand	41	48,835,000
Dominican Republic	42	44,720,000
Nepal	43	39,405,062
Panama	44	37,850,000
Malaysia	45	36,756,000
Jordan	46	29,100,000
El Salvador	47	25,000,000
Jamaica	48	23,213,600
Guatemala	49	22,000,000
Tanzania	50	20,000,000
Botswana	51	15,000,000
Iceland	52	13,000,000
Netherlands Antilles	53	8,795,000
Madagascar	54	8,700,000
Barbados	55	8,414,457
Sudan, Rep. of	56	6,612,000
Oman	57	6,000,000
Mozambique	58	5,670,000
Swaziland	59	4,280,000
Seychelles	60	4,200,000
Fiji	61	4,160,000
Liberia	62	4,000,000
San Marino	63	3,516,920
Belgium	64	3,200,000
Luxembourg	65	3,000,000
Vatican City	66	1,710,000
Guyana	67	1,000,000
Malta	68	412,250
Malawi	69	351,325
Gambia	70	240,000
Uruguay	71	153,800
Bahamas	72	14,491
Trinidad & Tobago	73	4,927
Morocco	74	200
Total		**41,006,455,918**

Government Coinage Mints of the World

Country	Name of mint	Address
United States	Office of Director of the Mint	633 Third St. NW, Washington, D.C. 20220
Do	Philadelphia Mint	Independence Mall, Philadelphia, Pa. 19106
Do	Denver Mint	320 W. Colfax St., Denver, Colo. 80204
Do	San Francisco Assay Office (production)	155 Hermann St., San Francisco, Calif. 94102
Do	West Point Bullion Depository	West Point, N.Y. 10996
Afghanistan	Afghan National Mint	Baricote, Kabul
Argentina	Sociedad del Estado Casa de Moneda	Avenida Antardida Argentina s/n; Buenos Aires
Australia	Royal Australian Mint	Deakin, A.C.T. 2600
Austria	Osterreichisches Hauptmunzamt	Am. Heumarkt I Postfach 225, A-1031 Vienna
Belgium	Monnaie Royale de Belgique	Boulveard Pacheco 32, B-1000 Bruxelles
Bolivia	Casa de la Moneda de Potosi	Potosi
Brazil	Casa da Moeda	Praca da Republica, 173, Rio de Janeiro

Country	Name of mint	Address
Canada...............	Royal Canadian Mint.....................	Ottawa, Ontario, K1N 8V5
Do.................	do......................................	Winnipeg, Manitoba
Chile...............	Casa de Moneda de Chile................	Avada. Portales s/n. Int. Quinta Normal, Santiago
China...............	China Mint Company	Yau An Men Xin An Nan, Jia-1 Beijing, China
Taiwan..............	Central Mint...........................	Taoyuan 333, Taiwan
Colombia...........	Casa de Moneda	Apartado Aereo 16814 Bogota
Czechoslovakia........	Czechoslovak State Mint..................	Mennicy, Kremnica, CSSR
Denmark.............	Den Kongelige Mont	Solmarksvej 5, 2600 Glostrup
Egypt	Mint House.............................	Cairo
Finland..............	Suomen Rahapaja	Box 114, SF-00161 Helsinki 16
France	Administration des Monnaies et Medailles...	11, Quai de Conti 75270, Paris 6E
Do.................	Monnaie de Paris Etablissement de Pessac....	Pessac
Germany, East.........	Staatsmunzamt DDR.....................	Berlin, DDR
Germany, West........	Bundesschuldenverwaltung................	D-6380 Bad Homburg v.d. Hohe 1, Germany
Greece	Bank of Greece, Banknote Printing Works	Odos El Venizelou 21, P.O. Box 105, 133 Athens.
Guatemala............	Casa de Moneda	Avenida de Petapa No. 43-81, Zona 12, Guatemala City
Hungary.............	Allami Penzverdo.......................	1450 Budapest, Ulloi Ut 102 Pf. 6
India................	India Government Mint	Shahid Bhagatsing Road, Fort Bombay 400023
Do.................	do......................................	Alipore, Calcutta
Do.................	do......................................	Hyderbad, Andhra Pradesh
Indonesia............	Perum Peruri..........................	Jalan Palatehan No. 4, Blok K-V, Kebayoran Baru, Jakarta
Iran.................	Mint of Central Bank of Iran..............	Avenue Saltanatabad, Tehran
Ireland	Currency Centre	P.O. Box 61, Sandyford, Dublin 14
Israel...............	Israel Mint (new mint)..................	Myriam Habashmonait St., Jerusalem
Italy	La Zecca..............................	Via Principe Umberto, 4, Rome
Japan	Mint Bureau	1-79, Tenma 1-chome, Kita-ku, Osaka, 530
Do.................	Tokyo Branch	3277, 1 chome, Nishiugamo, Toshima-ku, Tokyo-to, Tokyo
Do.................	Hiroshima Branch	Itsukamachi, Saheki-gun, Hiroshima Prefecture
Do.................	Kumamoto Sub-branch (refining, etc.)	Shinminami, Sendanbata-cho Kumamoto City, Jumamoto Prefecture
Korea, Republic of	Kyeongsan Mint, Government.............. Printing & Mint Agency..................	Aplyang-Meyeon, Kyeongsan, Kyeongsangbukdo
Malaysia..............	Kilang Wang	Bank Negara, Shah Alam, Selangor
Malta	Order of Malta Mint.....................	Via Condotti, Rome, Italy
Mexico..............	Casa de Moneda (old mint)...............	Calle de Apartado No. 13, Mexico 1, D.F.
Do.................	Casa de Moneda (new).................	Calu. Legaria No. 631, Mexico 10, D.F.
Nepal	His Majesty's Mint, Dharahara	Bhimsenstambha, Kathmandu
Netherlands...........	's Rijks Munt..........................	P.O. Box 2407, 3500 GK, Utrecht
Nigeria	Nigerian Security Printing and Minting....... Co., Ltd..........................	P.O. Box 3053, Victoria Island, Lagos
Norway	Den Kongelige Mynt	Postboks 53, N-3601, Kongsberg
Pakistan.............	Pakistan Mint..........................	Baghban Pura, Lahore (Punjab)
Peru	Casa Nacional de Moneda................	Jiron Junin 791, Lima 1
Philipines............	Mint and Gold Refinery	Security Plant Complex, Central Bank of the Phillipines, East Ave., Quezon City
Poland	Mennica Panstwowa	ul. Pereca 21, 00-958 Warsaw
Portugal	Casa de Moeda	Avenida Dr. Antonio Jose de Almeida, 1000 Lisbon
Romania	State Mint, Socialist Republic of Romania	Treasury Dept., Bucarest
Singapore	Singapore Mint	249 Jalan Boon Lay, Jurong, Singapore, 22
South Africa, Republic of	South African Mint	P.O. Box 464, Pretoria, 0001
Spain	Fabrica Nacional de Moneda y Timbre.......	Jorge Juan 106, Madrid 9
Sudan	Sudan Mint...........................	P.O. Box 5043, Khartoum South
Sweden	Myntverket	Box 401, S631 06 Eskilstuna 1
Switzerland	Swiss Federal Mint.....................	28, Bernastrasse, Bern 3003
Thailand.............	Royal Mint	110/7 Praidiphat Road, Bangkok
Turkey	Darphane ve Damga Matbaasi	Yildiz Besiktas, Istanbul
United Kingdom........	Royal Mint	Tower Hill, London, E.C. 3
Do.................	Royal Mint	Llantrisant, Pontyclun, Mid Glamorgan, Wales
U.S.S.R.............	Leningrad Mint........................	Leningrad, Russia
Yugoslavia............	National Bank of Yugoslavia	Bulevar, Revolucije 15, P.O. Box 1010, 11001 Belgrade

Precious Metals

13

Gold

Chemical symbol: Au
Atomic number: 79
Atomic weight: 196.967
Density: 18.88 times the weight of
an equal volume of water

Gold, the precious and magical yellow metal, has been known and valued by men and women since the dawn of civilization. Egyptian, Etruscan, Assyrian and Minoan cultures all valued gold. Gold coinage began in Lydia (modern-day Turkey) in 700 B.C.

Early gold coinage

The first gold coins were not struck from pure gold, but from a gold and silver alloy called electrum, found in Lydia. In addition to hosting the earliest gold coins made from electrum in 700 B.C., Lydia was also the site of the first pure gold coinage, during the sixth century B.C. Lydia was followed in the same century by gold pieces created by Persian rulers. These were called darics, after King Darius I.

Other rulers of the ancient world, such as Philip and Alexander the Great of Macedon, as well as Lysimachus of Thrace, issued widely circulating gold coins. The Romans issued gold coinage, the so-called aurei, beginning in Caesar's time.

After the fall of Rome, the Byzantine Empire became the important outlet for gold coins. The Byzantines struck their coins in more than 10 Mints throughout the empire.

The early Middle Ages saw the decline of gold coinage in the West. Monetary gold came back into use with the Crusades; the most notable example of the revival is the augustalis, issued during the 13th century by Frederick II of Hohenstaufen. In 1252, Florence issued the gold florin, followed by gold coinage issued in France, Bohemia, Hungary, the Low Countries and Spain. In 1284 Venice issued what became the most popular coin for more than 500 years, the ducat, or zecchino.

In 1343, England issued its first major gold coin, the florin, followed in 1344 by the noble. The English later struck the angel and the crown, in 1663 the guinea, and in 1816 the sovereign. Germany struck the gulden, Spain the excellente and France a variety of gold coins, following England's lead.

The first gold coins in the United States were authorized in 1792 after the Republic was formed.

Sources of gold

The Egyptians obtained gold from the earliest times in Nubia, a region in northeastern Africa, modern-day Sudan and Egypt. The Greeks went as far away as India, the Urals, and the mountains and rivers of Asia Minor to obtain gold. Most of the gold used in the Roman Empire came from Spain, then Hungary and Transylvania, and finally Dalmatia (now Yugoslavia, on the Adriatic coast) and the eastern Alps.

After the fall of the Roman Empire, gold circulation was greatly diminished in the West. From the 10th to the 15th centuries, the gold that was used came from Bohemia (part of modern-day Czechoslovakia), Silesia (part of modern Poland), Transylvania and Hungary. In the 18th century Siberia and the Urals became important gold-producing regions.

The first half of the 19th century was marked by a large production of gold in Russia and by gold discoveries in Georgia, North Carolina, and finally, in 1848, the extensive finds in California. Gold production in Australia began around this time as well, followed in 1885 by finds in South Africa, and in 1897 by production in the Klondike, a gold-rich region in northwestern Canada.

Gold mining and refining

Two techniques are usually used to recover gold from its place in nature — placer mining, used to extract gold from rivers and streams; and lode mining, used to take gold out of hard rock.

Placer mining, named after the alluvial deposits, or "placers" of gold found in the beds of streams, was the most common and productive method of gold mining until the 1920s. The principle is to separate gold from river gravel by washing it with water. The gold, mixed with the river gravel, is washed through a series of sluice boxes, each containing crossbars at the bottom. As the water and gravel pass through the boxes, which are slanted downward to employ the force of gravity, the gold sinks to the bottom and lodges behind the crossbars.

An important derivative of this basic placer mining is dredging. A continuously working chain of buckets brings gravel up from the riverbed onto a ship, where it is broken, screened, and washed through sluices.

Extracting gold from solid rock, or lode mining, uses the same processes common to all underground mining. Entry into the ground is gained by breaking the rock by drilling and blasting; the gold ore is broken away from the surrounding rock in a transportable size, and hauled out of the mine.

These processes of mining yield an impure gold, containing amounts of silver, copper and other metals. Two methods are most commonly used to extract gold from its metal relatives — a chemical process using chlorine, and the electrolytic process, first used in United States Mints.

In the chlorine process, the impure gold is heated until it becomes molten. Chlorine is bubbled through the molten gold, converting the silver to silver chloride, which can be skimmed off the top of the liquid solution. Unlike the electrolytic process, this chlorine method does not extract platinum from the impure gold.

The electrolytic process involves suspending plates of pure gold alternately with plates of impure gold in a cell containing a solution of gold chloride and hydrochloric acid. The impure gold plates are made the anode, the pure gold plates are the cathode. Through the liquid, a current of electricity is passed from the anode plates to the cathode plates. The gold dissolves from the anodes and is precipitated on the cathodes. The other metals that were combined with the impure gold dissolve in the liquid, except the silver, which is converted into insoluble chloride and falls to the bottom of the cell. The gold which precipitates on the cathode plates is washed and melted into bars. This process yields gold that is more than .999 fine, or 99.9 percent pure.

Measure of worth

Gold is valued not only for its beauty, but for its high resistance to corrosion, malleability and longevity. Gold will not readily combine with other metals. It is one of the greatest conductors of electricity.

A cubic foot of solid gold weighs about 1,200 pounds. The standard gold brick, or bullion bar, contains 1,000 troy ounces, or nearly 68.5 pounds avoirdupois.

The purity of gold is measured in fineness, parts of gold per 1,000. Pure gold is called 24 karat. A small quantity of silver will reduce the yellowish color of gold, and with added quantities it will develop a greenish color. Copper added will deepen the gold color. A pure white alloy is obtained by adding platinum, nickel or zinc; this is called white gold or jeweler's gold, and can also be produced by alloying yellow gold with palladium.

The rise and fall of the gold standard

Because gold is durable and highly malleable, it can be hammered into almost any shape and precisely divided into any size or unit of weight. Since it can be stamped into coins of a precise weight, the values of all other goods could, in the early days of gold coinage, be measured in terms of units of gold. Eventually gold became the absolute standard of value.

Although gold is very dense, its high value compared with its weight and bulk increased the risk of its being stolen. Nevertheless, by the 16th century and even much later, some gold-holding citizens kept their fortunes of gold in their own houses. But most people eventually became accustomed to leaving their gold for safekeeping in the goldsmiths' vaults, where it was well-protected. The goldsmiths would issue a receipt for the gold received.

Before long, gold-holding citizens realized it was much easier, when it came time to make a purchase or pay a debt, to simply issue an order to the goldsmith to pay over the gold to whomever they owed, rather than to transfer the gold itself. The recipient of the order, again, might find it easier to leave the gold he was to receive at the goldsmith's and in turn issue orders to the goldsmith to pay specific amounts of gold to still a third person. Thus, all these monetary transactions took place without the actual gold leaving the goldsmith's vault. This was the origin of bank notes and checks.

As this new paper money began to circulate on its own, goldsmiths discovered they could issue paper promises that exceeded the value of the gold in their vaults. Since this made the medium of exchange more abundant, trade flourished as the amount of money increased to meet its needs. When paper money became too abundant and exceeded the goods available in the market, it was withdrawn from circulation and exchanged for gold; when paper money became too scarce, gold was returned to the banks and exchanged for its paper representative.

The goldsmiths were gambling that everyone wouldn't demand his gold at once. Since this was a good risk, in nearly every country these new banks went on expanding their credit until the amount of bank note and demand deposit liabilities, that is, the amount of money, was several times the amount of gold held in the banks' vaults.

For centuries this alternating appearance (when paper money was cashed in) and disappearance (when gold was exchanged for paper money) of gold was the only stabilizing factor in a radically fluctuating market. Paper notes were issued freely by goldsmiths, money changers, merchants and bankers. No government could control the system; gold was the only stabilizing influence on the market. As the international monetary system became more complex, more and more governments used this traditional method of balancing and stabilizing international trade and backing up domestic currency with gold.

Gold stands firm

From these origins came the gold standard. First adopted by Great Britain in 1821, it was the system under which governments issued paper money which was backed by, and exchangeable for, gold. The amount of money circulating in a country depended upon the amount of gold it had.

The gold standard had several advantages. Since governments couldn't legally increase the money supply without obtaining more gold, citizens were thought to be protected from politically attractive, printing-press inflation. The threat that people would demand gold for their paper tended to act as a damper on politicians.

The gold standard was also supposed to keep a nation's payments to, and receipts from, foreigners automatically in rough balance. Suppose a country bought from foreigners, or imported, more than it exported over a long period. The country would pay out much more gold than it received, which would reduce the amount of money circulating at home. A smaller money supply would, in turn, tend to reduce the prices of things the country produced. Lower prices would make the country's goods and services more attractive to both foreign and domestic buyers. This would encourage purchases by foreigners, or exports, and discourage purchase from them.

Since everyone accepted gold as a medium of exchange, the gold standard also tended to create certainty in international trade by providing a fixed pattern of exchange rates, that is, the rate or price at which the currency of one country is exchanged for currency of another country.

But since the money supply depended on the amount of gold a country had, less money in circulation could mean less domestic business and more unemployment. In other words, the gold standard may not allow enough flexibility in the supply of money. And, since it provided a fixed pattern of exchange rates, the gold standard made it difficult for any nation to isolate its economy from depression or inflation in the rest of the world.

Most major nations of the world had adopted the gold standard by the 1870s. The United States was one of the last, officially adopting it in 1900.

Some countries at this time were using a close relative of the gold standard, the gold exchange standard. In this system, gold was not exported or imported at all. One country would offer to buy and sell the currency of another gold-standard country at a fixed price in the paper currency of the country making the offer. This was much cheaper than the full gold standard since the expense of transporting the gold was eliminated.

1919 and after

World War I spelled an effective end to the gold standard. War-induced inflation caused most nations to change to inconvertible currency or to restrict gold export.

At any other time the gold standard might have supplied its own automatic corrective: inflation at home would have meant that gold, in itself, was a more profitable export than goods, and a partial drain of gold abroad would thus normally have resulted in a contracted volume of money at home, making it necessary to reduce imports until a balance of trade had again been reached by an intensification of cheaper exports.

But the expense of war caused Great Britain and other countries to spend gold profusely to buy arms from the United States.

At the end of World War I, all currencies were inflated, and there was a severe shortage of gold. Most of the world's stock had gone into hiding; half of it was in the United States reserve and the rest was in private hands. Inflation had driven the cost of gold mining up until it approached and sometimes exceeded the official price of gold. Convinced a return to the gold standard would solve the world's monetary ills, the nations of the Atlantic trading community agreed to return to the gold standard in the 1920s.

The stock market crash in 1929 killed this last valiant effort to remain on the gold standard. In 1931, Britain went off the gold standard after using up her gold reserve in an attempt to defend her overvalued pound.

When President Roosevelt signed the Gold Reserve Act of 1934, the United States officially abandoned the gold standard. The dollar was no longer convertible to gold and gold could not be exported. The government prohibited the manufacture of gold coins, the private hoarding of gold and the use of gold as money or in lieu of money.

Gold having a recognized special value to collectors of rare and unusual coins, including gold coins made prior to April 4, 1933, were exempted from delivery to the U.S. Treasury, including U.S. and foreign coins. All other gold coins, gold certificates, and gold bullion were required to be turned in to the Treasury.

At the same time the Secretary of the Treasury issued a public announcement that, beginning February 1, 1934, the Treasury would buy any and all gold delivered to any U.S. Mint, or any Assay office in New York or Seattle, at the rate of $35 per fine troy ounce. An exhausted nation in the depths of a depression jumped at the offer; wedding rings, gold plates and jewelry poured into the Treasury. By the end of 1934 gold was coming into the Philadelphia Mint at the rate of $1.5 million worth a month.

In October 1933 President Roosevelt announced he would establish a government market for gold, and on January 31, 1934, he froze the price at $35 an ounce, thereby devaluing the dollar 40.94 percent. The result was a literal flood of gold pouring into the United States from foreign countries. The onslaught of gold made the government real-ize it had nowhere to put it, so the gold vaults of Fort Knox, Ky., were built in 1935.

By October 1939, the United States had well over half the world's stock of gold.

Dethroning the king

With the founding of the United Nations after World War II, representatives of 44 nations met in conference at Bretton Woods, N.H., in July 1944, to form the International Monetary Fund. The IMF is a specialized agency affiliated with the UN, designed to stabilize international monetary exchange rates in lieu of the gold standard. It has no power to dictate national monetary policies.

The members of the IMF, it was decided, would all deposit quotas in the fund, only one-quarter of which had to be in gold, and the rest in their own currencies. From this fund members could purchase with their own national currencies the gold or foreign exchange they needed.

The IMF, then, became the world's largest source of quickly available international credit. By June 1972, the 124-nation fund had provided $24.6 billion in short-term financial assistance.

Only the United States decided to keep its currency convertible at all times into gold. The U.S. pledged at Bretton Woods to convert foreign holdings of dollars into gold on demand at the fixed rate of $35 an ounce. The other countries could hold and count dollars as part of their reserves as if dollars were gold. Thus the dollar became the center of the world's monetary system.

Each member of the IMF was required to maintain the dollar or gold parity ($35 an ounce) of its currency by buying its currency when the price fell to 1 percent below parity or selling if the price rose 1 percent above parity.

The London gold market reopened in 1954 after World War II had forced its close in 1939. From 1954 to 1957, the price of gold on the London market fell consistently below $35 an ounce. Private demand for gold was composed almost entirely of industrial-artistic use and hoarding in countries where savings are traditionally held in gold.

Despite the growth in industrial use of gold and that gold, at a fixed price, was cheap in comparison to other commodities, private demand generally did not absorb all newly mined gold and the gold purchased from Communist stocks during this time. Except when the monetary authorities purchased gold to maintain its price at $35 an ounce, most countries bought relatively little gold, and instead built up their dollar holdings.

The gold drain

The system ran into difficulty in 1958 when the United States saw its first significantly large balance of payments deficit. This is a name given to the excess in the amount of dollars going abroad for foreign aid, for investments, for tourist expenditures, for imports, and for other payments, in comparison to the amount of dollars coming in for payments of U.S. exports to foreign countries. This meant a heavy drain on U.S. gold supply.

The balance of payments deficit persisted into 1960. Rumors began to spread in October that the United States might devalue the dollar (by raising the price of gold) to slow the gold drain. The first sharp gold panic swept the world's monetary trading centers. Under pressure from a sudden and widespread demand for gold, the market price jumped in London from $35 to $42 an ounce.

The crisis was eased temporarily as the U.S. Treasury transferred $135 million in gold to the London market, and as the Bank of England intervened as a substantial seller. This flood of gold forced the price back down to $35 by the spring of 1961.

Relief was short-lived. The supply of new gold coming into the London market began to fall in midsummer of 1961 as the two largest producers of gold, Canada and South Africa, began to add their newly mined gold to their monetary reserves. Demand for gold continued to rise, though, as the U.S. balance of payments deficit continued. The price of gold began to creep upward again.

In the autumn of 1961, the United States proposed that other nations join it to maintain the price of gold at a reasonable level. This was the birth of the London gold pool, a group formed to try to stabilize the gold market and avoid excessive swings in the price of gold that would lead to a loss of confidence in many foreign currencies.

The central banks of eight nations joined the gold pool — Belgium, France, Italy, Switzerland, the Netherlands, West Germany, the United Kingdom and the United States. Each contributed a quota to the pool, with the United States matching their combined payment. The Bank of England acted as agent for the group, given the right to draw on the pool and to sell gold if the price rose too high.

In November 1961, the first sales were made. The price of gold fell and the sales by the pool were recovered in later purchases. By February 1962, all the members of the gold pool had been repaid.

The price was temporarily under control, but the U.S. gold drain continued. To defend the dollar on foreign markets, President Johnson signed legislation in early 1965 to drop the 25 percent requirement for gold backing of commercial banks' deposits at Federal Reserve banks. This bill freed about $5 billion of the country's remaining $15 billion gold stock for additional sale to dollar-holding foreign governments. The requirement that paper currency in circulation be backed 25 percent by gold remained.

Despite United States efforts, in 1966 and 1967 private demand began to exceed the supply of gold available at $35 an ounce. During this time massive losses from official stocks occurred. The rate of expansion of gold production in South Africa, which had been increasing for 15 years, came to a halt in 1966. With rising production costs the outlook for a greatly increased supply of gold didn't look favorable, especially at a fixed price of $35 an ounce. Greatly aggravating this drop in free world gold production in 1966 was the Soviet Union's decision to discontinue its by-then-customary gold sales.

As production of gold decreased, demand climbed, particularly from gold speculators who had entered the market in significant numbers with the gold crisis of 1960. These speculators tried to take advantage of the worsening U.S. balance of payments deficit by purchasing large amounts of gold, which they expected to increase in price.

The two-tier system

In the five months preceeding March 1968, speculation absorbed nearly $3 billion in gold, almost all of which was lost by the gold pool countries, primarily the U.S. Unwilling to suffer such losses in the future, the gold pool members instituted the two-tier system.

The system, outlined in a Washington meeting of the gold pool nations on March 16-17, 1968, set up new guidelines governing the future of gold. On one level, the $35 an ounce price of gold was maintained. At this price, transnational governmental authorities agreed to the unlimited exchange of gold among themselves. On the second level, a free market in gold was established which could fluctuate to reflect whatever the value of gold really was. Three conditions effectively achieved this segregation:

1. An agreement among monetary authorities to trade gold among themselves at an official price of $35 an ounce.
2. Agreement to supply no more gold to private markets from official stocks.
3. Agreement to buy little or no gold from private sellers.

The concept of Special Drawing Rights (SDRs) was introduced at the March meeting and adopted later in 1969 and 1970. SDRs are a form of "paper gold" to be used in the same manner as gold, dollars or other currencies to settle debts between nations. The SDRs were distributed to members of the International Monetary Fund in proportion to their economic importance in the world economy. Designed to protect gold reserves, SDRs could be used to settle international payment deficits that would have otherwise drawn on these reserves. SDRs were given the value in gold of one U.S. dollar, which, at the official price of $35 an ounce, would buy 0.888671 gram of fine gold.

U.S. domestic policy changed to conform to the new system. The Treasury announced it would no longer purchase gold in the private market, nor would it sell gold for industrial, professional or artistic uses. Domestic producers were permitted to sell and export freely to foreign buyers as well as to authorized domestic users. Domestic consumers regularly engaged in an industry, profession or art in which gold is required were permitted to continue to import gold or to purchase gold from domestic producers.

The U.S. government also removed the remaining 25 percent gold backing from paper money in circulation, freeing another $750 million to stabilize the gold market.

The price of gold on the free-market tier began to rise. On May 17, 1968, it touched $40 an ounce on the London market. In July, however, the price fell again when the French government tried to bolster the franc and rumors spread that South Africa would be selling some of its newly mined gold on the free market. In October, the U.S. and other major nations in the IMF agreed to provide a mechanism for sales of newly mined gold to monetary authorities, but only when the free market price reached or fell below the official price of $35 an ounce.

Dollar devaluation

The economic crisis of the United States worsened as the balance of payments deficit persisted. As a result, on Aug. 16, 1971, President Nixon announced the United States was freeing the dollar for devaluation against other currencies by suspending the full convertibility of foreign-held dollars into gold. This inconvertibility meant no foreign government could convert dollars into Treasury-held gold; thus, the tie between the dollar and gold was severed.

The devaluation of the dollar occurred Dec. 18, 1971, and was accomplished by raising the official price of gold from $35 to $38 an ounce. Other currencies were juggled up or down into a new pattern of exchange rates. Throughout 1972 the price of gold on the free market climbed until it leveled off in December at $61 an ounce.

Economists and monetary authorities almost unanimously regarded the 8.57 percent devaluation of the dollar as inadequate. And since the dollar was no longer exchangeable for gold, it made little difference that the price at which the Treasury did not sell gold was raised from $35 to $38 an ounce.

Another devaluation was forced, then, in February 1973. Treasury Secretary George Shultz announced that the dollar would be devalued 10 percent against Special Drawing Rights (and so against gold) with the official monetary price of gold raised from $38 to $42.22 an ounce.

The price of gold on the London market took a sharp leap upward, breaking through the $100 an ounce barrier on May 14, 1973. Official stocks of gold were virtually frozen because no central bank would give up gold at the official price of $42.22 an ounce when the free market price had climbed so far above it.

The king is dead

Five and a half years after its birth, the two-tier gold system was abandoned by central bank officials Nov. 10, 1973. The system had out-lived its usefulness since it was made when the dollar was still convertible into gold; there was no point in continuing it when the central banks of other nations could not buy gold from the U.S. Treasury with dollars, as the original agreement had allowed for.

By abandoning the system the central bank officials, from Belgium, West Germany, Italy, the Netherlands, Switzerland, Britain and the U.S. relegated gold to the status of commodity, with no special monetary status, opening the way for increased international dependence on Special Drawing Rights.

Two months later the International Monetary Fund met in Rome to finalize the demotion of gold. The IMF's Committee of Twenty decided to adopt a new world currency plan that would end all relationship between Special Drawing Rights and gold. It would be replaced by a "basket" of 14 of the world's strongest paper currencies. The value of SDRs would be based on an average value of a portfolio of these currencies, including the dollar, the British pound, French franc, West German mark, Japanese yen, and a sampling of other currencies. The scheme was approved in June 1974.

The IMF Group of Ten (the U.S., Britain, France, West Germany, Italy, Belgium, the Netherlands, Sweden, Canada and Japan) met in June 1974, and gave gold a new function in the monetary world. Gold stocks stored in the vaults of central banks, it was decided, could be used by economically distressed countries as security for international loans, expanding their borrowing power.

Though this was perfectly legal before, it was economically unfeasible under the two-tier system since no nation was ready to risk its gold as loan collateral at the official price of $42.22 when the market price was four times that. It was agreed the pledged gold could be valued at a price much closer to the free-market quote than to the official level.

President Ford signed a bill Aug. 20, 1974, lifting the 40-year-old restrictions on U.S. citizens' holding of gold. Americans, as of Dec. 31, 1974, would be permitted to buy, hold and sell gold without restriction, as they would deal in any other commodity.

After Ford signed the bill, Treasury Under Secretary Jack F. Bennett commented that the U.S. "might feel free to sell gold from official stocks" directly to domestic buyers. Bennett noted that unless there was such a source of gold inside the country, most of the gold purchased would have to be imported, thus further distorting the U.S. balance of payments deficit.

Gold, once the undisputed king of the international monetary system, was now reduced to the status of another commodity. Still as durable, malleable, and beautiful as it always was, gold's value now rests in the hands of the gold dealers of London, Paris, Zurich and the United States.

In the hobby . . .

Gold coinage, authorized soon after the Republic was formed, had been gradually phased out until the end was spelled out in 1933 when it became illegal to manufacture gold coins or to use gold as money or in lieu of money (See GOLD CHRONOLOGY).

With the gold acts and orders of 1933 and 1934, designed to centralize the gold reserves of the country into the hands of the government, restrictions on collecting gold coins were very stringent. The government wanted to make sure no one was "collecting" gold coins for their gold content rather than for their numismatic value; hence, all gold coins were called in except for those "having a recognized special value to collectors of rare and unusual coin," according to the Treasury.

A determination was made on each individual gold coin presented to the Treasury for a ruling, including gold coins made before and after 1933. The criterion for a pre-1933 coin was whether or not it had "recognized" special collector value on April 4, 1933. That for coins struck after 1933 was whether they had "true numismatic value," based on the number issued, the purpose for which they were issued, the condition of the coin, the Mint mark if any, and all other factors concerning the issue.

Foreign coins struck after 1933 and issued in large quantities or for the purpose of providing a market for gold, or simply as a money-making device, were denied entry.

These strict regulations were relaxed somewhat in 1954 when the Treasury amended the gold regulations. The amendment provided that any gold coin made prior to 1933 would be considered a rare gold coin. Any struck after 1933 would not be considered rare unless a specific determination to the contrary was made by the Treasury Department.

As a numismatic authority, the Treasury called on the Curator of Numismatics of the United States National Museum.

These regulations and the stricter ones made in 1933 still gave the Treasury no control over gold held by U.S. citizens outside the United States. The coin market abroad was flooded with counterfeits and restrikes of coins made before 1933, making it difficult for the Treasury to determine whether the coins held abroad were actually those ruled exempt under Treasury Department rulings.

Restrictions on U.S. citizens holding gold abroad began Jan. 14, 1961, when President Eisenhower issued an executive order prohibiting the holding of gold abroad by any persons subject to the jurisdiction of the United States. An exception was made for gold coins, again, "of recognized value to collectors of rare and unusual coin."

ODGSO is born

Before October 9, 1961, the function of administering the gold and silver regulations was assigned to the Bureau of the Mint. On that date, a Treasury Department order created the Office of Domestic Gold and Silver Operations (ODGSO) and placed it in the Office of the Undersecretary for Monetary Affairs.

The ODGSO reported directly to the Deputy Undersecretary for Monetary Affairs until April 1, 1969, when it was placed under the new position of Assistant Secretary (Economic Policy).

The primary functions of ODGSO were to:

1. Assist in the formulation of policies regarding the control of gold.
2. Administer the Treasury gold regulations to include the issuance of licenses or other authorizations for the acquisition, possession, ownership, importation, exportation, and uses of gold for industrial, professional and artistic purposes. The office also issued licenses or other authorizations for the importation of gold coins, medals and bars of exceptional numismatic value.
3. Maintain statistical data on the production and uses of gold.

The first director of ODGSO was Leland Howard. He retired Dec. 30, 1966, but remained as an adviser until Thomas Wolfe was named the new director in June 1967.

The new office went to work soon after its creation when President Kennedy, on July 20, 1962, proclaimed that acquiring gold coins abroad was illegal for subjects of the United States. Citizens were ordered to bring home or to dispose of any rare gold coins they held abroad by Jan. 1, 1963.

The proclamation also prohibited the importation of any rare gold coins except under licenses issued by the ODGSO.

Not all pre-1933 gold coins, then, were admissible for import any longer, a partial reinstitution of the 1933 regulations, reflecting the United States gold drain.

The ODGSO also ruled illegal the holding of mutilated gold coins, with any solder on the coin or the drilling of a hole constituting mutilation; and restrikes, which were "subject to forfeiture in the hands of purchasers, no matter how innocent."

The White House commented the action had been taken to prevent large-scale counterfeiting and restriking of rare gold coins in Europe, Argentina and India. Coin dealers reacted with a mixture of suspicion and hostility at the new ruling.

Paper money collectors received a break soon after, however. Another amendment to the gold regulations was issued allowing the holding and importation without license of U.S. gold certificates issued before Jan. 30, 1934. These certificates were issued by the government as a form of paper currency beginning in 1865 and were redeemable on demand in gold. Since it became a crime to hold gold after 1934, the certificates could no longer be cashed in after that date; the certificates themselves, indeed, were supposed to be turned in to the Treasury in 1934.

The government realized that many certificates were still out, in the hands of collectors, since they were no good as currency. The 1964 ruling made their possession legal since they posed no threat to the U.S. gold reserves.

Collectors of gold medals were informed of regulations governing their aspect of numismatics on June 26, 1964. The Treasury issued a release clarifying the acquisition of "fabricated gold":

" 'Fabricated gold,' " the Treasury stated, "is gold processed or manufactured gold in any form which: a) has a gold content the value of which does not exceed 90 percent of the total domestic value of such processed or manufactured gold; and b) has in good faith, and not for the purpose of evading or enabling others to evade the provisions of the Acts, the Orders, or the Regulations in this part, been processed or manufactured for some one or more specific and customary industrial, professional or artistic uses. Hence, to qualify as a fabricated gold object an article must pass all three of the following tests:

"1. The value of the gold content may not exceed 90 percent of the total value.
"2. The article must be manufactured in good faith.
"3. The article must be for specific and customary industrial, professional or artistic uses.

"Award medals which are specially manufactured medals, presented to an individual in recognition of a worthy achievement, may be imported into the United States by the individual receiving the award, that is, the original recipient of the medal."

More regulations governing gold medals were spelled out in an Aug. 21, 1965, Treasury Department order legalizing the possession of rare gold bars:

"The Director, Office of Domestic Gold and Silver Operations, may issue or cause to be issued licenses or other authorizations, permitting the acquisition, holding, transportation and importation of gold bars which the Director is satisfied have been of recognized special value to collectors of numismatic items in all times since prior to April 5, 1933. Gold bars manufactured after Dec. 31, 1900, shall be presumed to not be of such recognized special value to collectors."

The directive continued: "The manufacture of gold medals (other than special award medals) and the plating of coins are not customary industrial, professional or artistic uses of gold within the meaning of the regulations and, accordingly, such uses of gold and the acquisition or possession of any gold medals (other than special award medals) and gold-plated coins are not authorized by the regulations or any licenses issued pursuant thereto. Without limitation the following are not deemed to be of customary industrial, professional or artistic uses of gold:

"1. The plating of any coins.

"2. The manufacture of any gold medals other than special award medals, or,

"3. The acquisition, holding, transportation, importation or exportation of any gold-plated coins or gold medals other than special award medals."

The ODGSO was called into court early in 1966 to defend its determination of "rare and unusual coin" by Stack's, one of the largest coin dealers in the U.S. The dispute arose when Stack's was denied a license to import a gold coin collection from Amsterdam.

In the extensive and secret hearings, ODGSO disclosed its criterion to determine whether a coin has "exceptional numismatic value" was the ratio between the market value of the coin and its gold bullion content. This was the first public admission by ODGSO of how import licenses were awarded.

Stack's lost the fight Oct. 31, 1966, when the Treasury Deputy Undersecretary for Monetary Affairs upheld the ODGSO position and Stack's was not allowed to import the collection.

The ODGSO did rule, however, on March 21, 1966, that a set of Proof 1965-dated South African gold coins were of exceptional numismatic value and could be licensed for import. In 1968, though, ODGSO ruled against a request for an import license for a set of 1968-dated South African gold coins, taking a turnabout from its former ruling.

Regulations ease

A gradual easing of gold regulations began in 1969, after the U.S. and other International Monetary Fund nations set up the two-tier system for the gold market. On April 26, the Treasury announced that no more licensing would be required for pre-1934 gold coins "of legitimate issue from any nation." The change was made to remove what the Treasury called an "inconsistency" in regulations on imported pre-1934 gold coins, which generally had to have licenses, and those regularly traded within the U.S.

The new ruling freed over 250 additional gold coin issues to come into the U.S. ODGSO Director Thomas Wolfe said the pre-1934 coins constituted 95 percent of all licenses.

The ban continued on importation of all gold coins struck after 1960 except for those

already licensed, including: 1961, 500 kronur, Iceland; 1960, 20 pounds, Israel; 1961, 10 scudi, 5 scudi, Malta; 1960, pound and half pound, South Africa; 1961, 1962, 1963, 1964, 1965, rand and two rand, South Africa, all Proof; 1961, 500 piastres, 1962, 250 piastres, Turkey.

The regulations governing coins minted after 1934 remained the same.

Early in 1970 ODGSO granted permission for the importation of one complete six-coin set of Yemen 1969 gold coins and allowed two Israel 1969 gold 100-pound "Shalom" coins to come into the country.

Regulations on gold medals were eased in April 1971. Licenses would be issued for the acquisition, holding, transportation and exportation of gold-plated coins or gold medals which were either antique or for public display by an institution serving the public.

The amendment also authorized the ODGSO to license foreign subsidiaries of U.S. corporations to manufacture gold medals for sale to persons not subject to the jurisdiction of the United States.

Mexican gold coins caused difficulty for the ODGSO after the office allowed importation of coins struck between 1934 and 1959. The flood of restrikes coming from Mexico caused the office to reverse its ruling three months after it was made, and place a ban on importation of all gold coins of Mexico dated since 1933.

The ruling did not stand for long. On Dec. 17, 1973, ODGSO ruled "any gold coin legally issued, dated between 1934 and 1959, may now enter the United States without the formality of applying for a license." The ruling liberated many gold coins of Mexico, Iran, 100 franc pieces of Switzerland dated 1934 and 1939, a four-coin Coronation set of the United Kingdom dated 1937 and gold sovereigns of earlier years restruck in this period, as long as they were dated 1959 or earlier.

But at the same time all coins struck since 1960 were barred, including some for which licenses previously had been granted. So some gold coins that had been legal were now illegal for import. Counterfeit coins and gold bullion or bars continued to be denied passage into the United States.

With President Ford's signature on the bill allowing U.S. citizens to buy, hold and sell gold without restriction ended the back and forth battle between the ODGSO and coin collectors and dealers. All gold coins, as of Dec. 31, 1974, are legal for American citizens to hold. The confusion of regulations raging since 1934 has been cleared and closed. Treasury Secretary William E. Simon announced the abolition of the ODGSO in August 1975. The remaining gold responsibilities of the agency were transferred to the Treasury's Assistant Secretary for International Affairs.

'Gold rush'
European gold dealers, anticipating a "gold rush" by Americans after it became legal once again for them to own gold, were dismayed when this failed to come about. Indeed, the price of gold, which reached $195.25 on Dec. 27, 1974, actually slipped to 186.75 on Dec. 31, and continued to tumble to $175.25 on Jan. 2, 1975.

Free to buy and own gold after a hiatus of more than 40 years, Americans found themselves unfamiliar with the precious metal as an investment medium. They were further aswailed with the prevailing official concept that gold was a "barbarous" medium, reflecting the Keynsian philosophy that remained heavily entrenched in government circles.

The government's role in thwarting citizens' speculating in gold became apparent when Sen. William Proxmire, D-Wis., chairman of the powerful Senate Banking Committee, announced that he would introduce legislation for the sale of 25 million ounces of gold from the government stockpile in 1975.

When a previously authorized 2 million ounces of 400-ounce gold bars were offered at auction on Jan. 6, however, the market showed little interest. Only one-third of the gold offered was taken. The sale had the effect of depressing the London price of gold from $173.50 to $169.50; however, two days later in jumped back to $180.25, registering the sharpest one-day price rise on record.

General Services Administration and International Monetary Fund auctions, together with the importation of tons of gold by refugees following the fall of South Vietnam and Cambodia had a bearish effect on the market throughout 1975 and most of 1976. On July 20, the price plunged to a 31-month low of $107.75, following a second IMF auction.

Inflation heats up
The Carter election victory and the OPEC energy crunch resulted in a turn-around in the gold price and the gold market, so that by Jan. 4, 1978, the gold price registered a 2½-year high of $172.50 at the morning fix in London.

In April Sens. Jesse Helms, R-N.C., and Barry Goldwater, R-Ariz., introduced the American Arts Gold Medallion Act of 1978 as an alternative to the mostly unsuccessful GSA auctions. Meantime, the International-Gold Corp. (Intergold), the marketing arm of the South African gold mining industry, was aggressively marketing the Krugerrand 1-ounce bullion coin throughout the world.

Higher inflation, increasing U.S. trade deficits and a weakening dollar drove the London morning fix for gold to $223.50 by Oct. 3, 1978. Nine months later, on July 18, 1979, it was fixed at $303.85. The gold price continued to escalate through the year, reaching the all-time record high of $850 on Jan. 21, 1980.

(For a discussion of the Americans Art Gold Medallions and the American Eagle gold and silver bullion coins, see Chapter 14, "Bullion Coins.")

Gold chronology

1782
Thomas Jefferson reports finding a lump of gold ore on the north side of the Rappahannock River in Virginia.

1792
April 2 — Authorizing act issued to strike U.S. gold eagle ($10, standard weight 270 grains, .91666 fineness), half eagle ($5, standard weight 135 grains, .91666 fineness), and quarter eagle ($2.50, standard weight 67.5 grains, .91666 fineness). Dollar defined as a unit containing 24.75 grains of fine gold or 371.25 grains of fine silver (exchange rate between the two metals set at 15 to one.)

1799
Gold discovered in Cabarrus County, North Carolina.

1802
Gold discovered in South Carolina.

1821
Britain adopts the gold standard.

1827
Indians recovering gold near Coker Creek, Tennessee.

1833
Samples of gold found near Georgetown, Texas.

1834

June 28 — Authorizing act issued to change the standard weight of the eagle to 258 grains, .899225 fineness; the half eagle to 129 grains, .899225 fineness; and the Quarter Eagle to 64.5 grains, .899225 fineness.

Standard definition of dollar changed; redefined as unit containing 23.2 grains of fine gold (changed from 24.75 grains). Silver definition unchanged, remains at 371.25 grains of fine silver in one dollar. Exchange rate becomes 16 to one.

Gold mining town of Dahlonega, Ga., built.

1837

Jan. 18 — Authorizing act issued to change fineness of eagle, half eagle, and quarter eagle to .900. Exchange rate becomes 15.988 to one.

1848

Jan. 24 — Gold discovered by James W. Marshall, who was erecting a sawmill in partnership with Captain John A. Sutter on American River, a branch of the Sacramento, near Coloma, Calif.

1849

March 3 — Authorizing act issued to strike U.S. gold double eagle ($20, standard weight 516 grains, .900 fineness), and $1 gold coin (25.8 grains, .900 fineness).

1853

Feb. 21 — Authorizing act issued to strike $3 gold coin (77.4 grains, .900 fineness).

1863

March 3 — Authorizing act issued to produce gold certificates.

1865

November 13 — First U.S. gold certificates issued.

1867

International monetary conference in Paris. Delegates vote to adopt the gold standard.

1869

Sept. 24 — Financial "Black Friday" in New York, caused by an attempt by Jay Gould, financier and speculator, and James Fisk, Erie railroad magnate, to corner the gold market. Gold touched $163.50 per ounce. To bring the price down and foil the financiers' scheme, the Secretary of the Treasury ordered the sale of $4 million in government gold, forcing the price down to $133 and causing a panic in the securities market.

1873

U.S. drops silver dollar from the list of coins to be struck at the Mint; effectively ends bimetallism.

1890

Sept. 26 — $1, $3 gold coins ordered discontinued.

1896

July 8 — William Jennings Bryan, Democratic candidate for president, delivers his impassioned "Cross of Gold" speech at the Democratic National Convention in Chicago, calling for restoration of the bimetallic (silver and gold) standard.

1900

Bimetallism legislation repealed; Gold Standard act passed, officially placing the United States on the gold standard. Gold dollar of 25.8 grains, .900 fine becomes the unit of value; all other forms of currency maintained at parity with the gold dollar.

1902

June 28 — Authorizing act issued to strike $1 gold commemorative coins (25.8 grains, .900 fineness) for the Louisiana Purchase Exposition.

1904

April 13 — Authorizing act issued to strike $1 gold commemorative coins (25.8 grains, .900 fineness) for the Lewis and Clark Exposition.

1915

Jan. 16 — Authorizing act issued to strike $50 (1,290 grains, .900 fineness), $1 (25.8 grains, .900 fineness) and quarter eagle (64.5 grains, .900 fineness) commemorative gold coins for the Panama-Pacific International Exposition.

1916

Feb. 23 — Authorizing act issued to strike $1 gold commemorative coins (25.8 grains, .900 fineness) in honor of President William McKinley.

1925

March 3 — Authorizing act issued to strike quarter eagle gold commemorative coins (64.5 grains, .900 fineness) for the Sesquicentennial Exhibition.

Nations of the Atlantic trading community agree to return to the gold standard after inflated post-World War I currency had caused its demise; Britain returns to the gold standard.

1929

Oct. 29 — Stock market crash marks the end of post-World War I prosperity. Depression begins.

1931

Britain goes off the gold standard.

1933

June 5 — The United States goes off the gold standard.

April 5 — (Executive Order 6102), August 28 (Executive Order 6260), December 28 (Order of the Secretary of the Treasury) — Government prohibits the manufacture of gold coins, private hoarding of gold and the use of gold as money or in lieu of money. Gold coins having a recognized special value to collectors of rare and unusual coin, including gold coins made prior to April 5, 1933, are exempted from delivery to the U.S. Treasury, including U.S. and foreign coins. All other gold coins, gold certificates and gold bullion are required to be turned in to the Treasury.

1934

Jan. 31 — Executive Order freezes the price of gold at $35 an ounce, up from its former $20.67 an ounce, thereby devaluing the dollar 40.94 percent.

1942

President Roosevelt issues an Executive Order closing all gold mines in the United States.

1944

July — Articles and agreements of the International Monetary Fund, a specialized agency affiliated with the United Nations, signed at Bretton Woods, New Hampshire.

1945

Federal Reserve requirement to hold title to gold in an amount greater than or equal to 40 percent of outstanding Federal Reserve notes plus 35 percent of commercial bank deposits with Federal Reserve banks revised; requirement lowered to 25 percent of the total combined sum of Federal Reserve liabilities.

1946

Ban against gold mining lifted.

1954

London gold market reopens after 15 years of inactivity.

Amendment to gold regulations issued; gold coins made prior to April 5, 1933, both foreign and domestic, declared to be of special value to collectors of rare and unusual coins. Gold coins made after 1933 are presumed not to be rare unless determined otherwise by the Treasury Department.

1958

United States runs a significantly large bal-

ance of payments deficit; currency of 14 nations becomes convertible for non-residents.

1960

October — Gold panic sweeps world's monetary trading centers. Free market price of gold jumps from $29.67 to $35 an ounce in London. As a result, eight-nation Gold Pool formed.

1961

Jan. 14 — President Eisenhower issues an Executive Order prohibiting U.S. citizens from purchasing or holding gold abroad in any form except numismatic gold coins. Gold owned by U.S. citizens, residents and corporations abroad must be sold before June 1, 1961.

1962

July 20 — President Kennedy proclaims no person subject to the jurisdiction of the U.S. can acquire gold coins abroad except under Treasury Department license, and no gold coins can be imported without a license. Prohibits ownership abroad of any kind of gold coins. Citizens ordered to bring back to the U.S. or to dispose of any rare gold coins held abroad by Jan. 1, 1963.

September — Treasury Department, for the first time in 17 years, moves a large amount of gold from Fort Knox to the Treasury's Assay Office in New York City to meet foreign demand for U.S. gold bullion.

1963

Jan. 3 — Treasury Secretary Dillon clarifies phrase "customary industrial, professional or artistic use" in Part 54, Title 31; adds definition reading: "Customary industrial professional or artistic use means the use of gold in industry, profession or art, in a manner, for a purpose, in a form, and in quantities in which gold is customarily used in industry, profession or art."

June 26 — Treasury Department clarifies rules on fabricated gold.

Aug. 13 — Customs agents confiscate 21 gold coins from the Witte Museum's $50,000 Albert Hirschfeld collection in San Antonio, Texas, saying the coins were illegally imported.

1964

April 24 — Treasury Department removes all restrictions on the acquisition or holding of gold certificates issued by the U.S. prior to Jan. 30, 1934.

Nov. 30 — Monetary gold reserves drop $75 million for the week ended Nov. 25.

1965

Jan. 7 — France announces its government will convert $150 million of its currency reserves into gold by buying the gold in the United States.

Jan. 13 — U.S. monetary gold reserves drop $200 million in the week ended Jan. 13.

February 19 — Senate passes legislation to repeal requirement for 25 percent gold backing of commerical banks' deposits at Federal Reserve banks. Bill would free about $5 billion of the country's $15 billion gold stock for additional sale to dollar-holding foreign governments and for future growth of the domestic money supply.

March 4 — President Johnson approves and signs legislation freeing $5 billion in U.S. gold in an effort to maintain the stability of the dollar in the world market. Leaves in effect the required 25 percent gold backing of the paper currency in circulation.

Aug. 21 — Treasury Department order issued, allowing the importation, transporting, holding and exportation of numismatically valued gold bars, with license. Also clarifies rules regarding gold medals and gold-plated coins.

1966

April 27 — Chancellor of the Exchequer announces in Parliament that Great Britain will forbid the use of gold in the making of medallions, plaques, medals and other articles. The new order also bars United Kingdom residents from holding more than four gold coins minted after 1837, except with official permission.

1967

March — Treasury reports gold stock at lowest level since 1938.

March — French government lifts restrictions on the import and export of gold, ending restrictions in effect since September 1939.

March 23 — South African 1966 Proof gold coins are not admissible into the U.S. as collectors' items, the ODGSO rules.

June — Thomas W. Wolfe appointed acting director of ODGSO.

Aug. 2 — Gold reserves reach 29-year low as gold goes into the Treasury's stabilization fund, which handles sales of U.S. gold to foreign nations.

Nov. 18 — Britian devalues the pound, from $2.80 to $2.40

Nov. 27 — Dollar remains strong; Gold Pool members pledge support of the $35 an ounce gold price.

December — U.S. moves almost $1 billion in gold bullion, half going to London to prevent price rise on gold.

1968

Feb. 7 — Treasury reports reserves of gold have dropped to the lowest level since 1937.

Feb. 9 — House Banking and Currency Committee recommends passage of administration bill to remove the 25 percent gold cover from U.S. paper money.

March 17 — Treasury amends gold regulations; Treasury will no longer purchase gold in the private market, nor will it sell gold for industrial, professional or artistic uses. Domestic producers are permitted to sell and export freely to foreign buyers as well as to authorized domestic users. The amendment authorizes domestic users regularly engaged in an industry, profession or art in which gold is required may continue to import gold or to purchase gold from domestic producers within the limits of their licenses or authorization in the gold regulations.

March 17 — Central Banks announce the formation of a two-tier price system for gold. Under the new plan, the price of gold would remain at $35 an ounce in transactions between cooperating governments, while it will be permitted to seek its own price in the private market.

March 20 — With President Johnson's signature on the bill removing gold backing from U.S. paper money, the Treasury transfers $750 million to the Exchange Stabilization Fund. Gold prices fall on European markets.

April 7 — Gold remains stable at about $37-$38 an ounce in London.

April 16 — Treasury issues new gold regulations, noting the ODGSO will accept applications for licenses submitted by persons wishing to buy and sell gold for authorized industrial, professional and artistic uses; that persons, including banks, may, without a license, buy gold for the account of persons licensed and offer storage and safekeeping services for licensed persons; and that persons holding licenses may continue to acquire newly mined gold or to import gold for authorized uses. All transactions in gold with foreign monetary authorities are prohibited.

April 19 — ODGSO grants temporary permission to import a 1967 Canadian $20 gold coin so it can be displayed at the Northwest Central States Numismatic Association show.

May 2 — Gold reaches a record high of $39.35 an ounce in London.

May 17 — Gold tops $40 an ounce in London; pound falls to its lowest point since 1967, $2.3853.

May 30 — Treasury reports gold stockpile lowest since 1936, at $10.547 billion.

July 9 — Attempts by the French government to bolster the franc and rumors that South Africa would be selling some of its newly mined gold on the free market brings gold prices below $40 in London.

July — ODGSO denies a license for the importation of gold coins of South Africa dated 1968.

October — U.S. and other leading industrial nations in the International Monetary Fund reach an accord providing a mechanism for limited sales of newly minted gold to monetary authorities, but only when the free market price is at or below the official price of $35 an ounce.

1969

Feb. 24 — Sensitive world gold market reacts to President Nixon's visit to Europe and drives the price of gold up to $46.33 in Paris.

March 5 — Devaluation-jittery Frenchmen drive gold up to $47 an ounce in Paris.

April 25 — ODGSO allows import of gold coins made before 1934 without a license.

June 5 — ODGSO revises medal regulations; permits licenses to be issued for the acquisition, holding, transportation and exportation of gold-plated coins or gold medals which are either antique or are for public display by an institution serving the public.

July 30 — Swiss bankers confirm that South Africa is unloading sizable quantities of gold on the bullion market in Zurich.

Nov. 6 — Free market gold drops to $39 an ounce in London.

Nov. 24 — Gold drops to $37.90; attributed to general world monetary stability partly caused by the revaluation of the German mark.

Nov. 28 — Treasury rules after December 31 it will no longer be possible to deposit gold for exchange into gold bars at U.S. Mints and Assay Offices.

Dec. 2 — Gold drops five cents below the International Monetary Fund ceiling of $35.35.

1970

January 8 — Gold reaches a 12-year low of $34.95 in London.

April 8 — ODGSO grants permission for the import of one complete six-coin set of Yemen 1969 gold coins, to be donated to and become part of the permanent collection of the Smithsonian Institution.

December — Gold price up to $41.90 in New York.

1971

April 1 — United Kingdom lifts all gold coin and medal restrictions; gold coin can again be freely bought, sold and held.

April 19 — Treasury amends gold regulations, authorizing the Director of ODGSO to license foreign subsidiaries of U.S. corporations to manufacture gold medals for sale to persons not subject to the jurisdiction of the U.S. Also removes restrictions on the gold plating of any coins and the acquisition, holding, transportation, importation, or exportation of any gold-plated coins.

July 12 — Thomas Wolfe, director of the ODGSO, determines Mexican gold coins struck between 1934 and 1959 are eligible for import into the U.S., with license.

July 22 — Gold regulations amended, prohibiting the trading of gold in any form on commodity exchanges, and the acquisition of American or foreign gold coins of any description for speculative purposes. Reaffirms existing regulations.

Aug. 15 — President Nixon frees the dollar for devaluation against other currencies by cutting its tie with gold and halts the conversion of foreign-held dollars into gold.

Oct. 21 — Treasury Department places a ban on importation of all gold coins of Mexico dated since 1933. Designed to prevent the importation of restrikes.

Dec. 18 — President Nixon announces an 8.57 percent devaluation of the U.S. dollar. The devaluation would be accomplished by a $3 increase in the price of gold, from $35 to $38 an ounce.

1972

March 13 — House postpones for a week the bill to devalue the dollar.

March 21 — Dollar devaluation bill passes the House without proposed amendment to permit U.S. citizens to own gold.

March 22 — Sen. Peter Dominick (R-Colo.) introduces a Senate bill to allow private ownership of gold.

April 3 — President Nixon signs bill to devalue the dollar.

May 8 — Treasury Department formally adopts the $3 increase in the price of monetary gold to $38 an ounce.

May 17 — Gold climbs to $57.75 on the London exchange.

May 29 — Gold closes at $58.55 in London. Common date gold coins advancing on the average of $5 in value in two weeks.

June 6 — Gold goes through $60 mark.

July — Dealer reports common date Double Eagles up from $80 to $95 over a five week period.

Aug. 2 — Gold at $70 an ounce in London.

Aug. 22 — Private ownership of gold endorsed by the Republican National Convention meeting in Miami, Fla.

Oct. 12 — Industrial demand for gold softens, speculative pressure subsides, South Africa announces increased gold reserves; price of gold in London falls.

November — Treasury announces U.S. firms will be permitted to trade in gold futures on the new Winnipeg Commodity Exchange when it opens in mid-November, but "only to an extent consistent with their licenses."

Nov. 15 — Winnipeg Commodity Exchange opens, world's first commodities market in gold futures.

Nov. 20 — Gold levels off at $61 in London.

1973

January — ODGSO clarifies regulations on gold coin jewelry.

Feb. 12 — Treasury Secretary George Shultz announces the dollar is devalued 10 percent; official price of gold raised to $42.22 an ounce.

Feb. 23 — Gold at $95 an ounce in London, up $10 overnight.

April 1 — Japanese government allows its citizens to buy, sell, hoard and own gold.

April 4 — Senate OKs legislation ending ban on private ownership of gold, an amendment to President Nixon's 10 percent devaluation of the dollar (Par Value Modification Act).

May 14 — Gold breaks through $100 barrier, closing at $102.50 an ounce in London.

May 29 — Gold-holding amendment to Par Value Modification Act fails in the House.

June 1 — Gold at $119 an ounce in London.

July 12 — Senate approves free ownership of gold, an amendment to the Bicentennial coinage bill.

Aug. 14 — Gold drops to $95.50 in London.

Nov. 10 — Central Banks end two-tier gold system following a Berne, Switzerland, meeting. Price of gold drops to $90.

Nov. 28 — Gold rallies, up to $97.25 in London.

Dec. 17 — ODGSO rules any gold coin legally issued, dated between 1934 and 1959, may now enter the United States without the formality of applying for a license. Gold coins issued after 1959 assumed not to be rare.

1974

January 3 — Gold jumps, at $121.25 an ounce in London.

January 8 — Continues rise, at $126.50.

January 18 — More than 750 attend a two-day symposium in New Orleans sponsored by the National Committee to Legalize Gold.

January 21 — Gold reaches $161.31 in the Paris Bourse. Double eagles priced at $238.

January 30 — Gold drops to $135 in London.

Feb. 5 — G. Drake Jacobs of Aspen, Colo., files suit challenging the constitutionality of the U.S. Gold Regulations and the Trading with the Enemy Act under which the regulations were promulgated.

Feb. 10 — Gold closes at $146 an ounce in London.

Feb. 21 — Gold, silver, platinum and copper break all world records. Gold at $160 in London, a new world record fixing for that market.

Feb. 26 — Gold crests at $188 in Paris.

March 27 — Gold searches for a new floor price, settles at $174.

April 3 — Gold leaps to $197 in Paris, fixed at London at a record $179.50.

May 3 — Gold steady at $169 in London.

May 29 — Senate approves an amendment allowing citizen ownership of gold as of Sept. 1, 1974. Tacked on to a bill authorizing $1.5 billion in funds to the International Development Association.

May 30 — Gold jumps to $161 in London.

June 11 — Treasury Secretary William E. Simon says he believes President Nixon will probably end restrictions on U.S. gold ownership by the end of the year.

June 11 — Finance leaders in the Group of Ten industrial nations meet; decide to use gold stocks as security for international loans by economically distressed countries; agree that the pledge metal could be valued at a price much closer to the free-market quote than to the official level, the price determined as a result of agreement between the borrower and the lender.

June 11 — Committee of Twenty of the International Monetary Fund meets, approves new scheme for valuing the Standard Drawing Rights in terms of a "basket" of currencies, including the U.S. dollar, British pound, French franc, West German mark, Japanese yen and a sampling of other currencies on international monetary markets.

June 18 — House Banking and Currency Committee votes to amend the International Development Association bill with a measure to permit U.S. citizens to own gold after Dec. 31, 1974.

July 2 — House passes International Development Association bill, with gold ownership amendment.

July 4 — Gold prices slump to $129 an ounce in London.

July 31 — House passes IDA bill with gold ownership amendment; goes to President Nixon for his signature.

Aug. 1 — Gold price at $159.40 in London.

Aug. 14 — President Ford signs legislation lifting 40-year ban on U.S. citizens' holding of gold. The law will take effect at the end of December, unless the President decides to speed up the process by declaring an earlier date.

Aug. 20 — ODGSO director Thomas Wolfe says gold coins may be ordered by American citizens if coin firms are willing to place names on mailing lists in anticipation of coming legalization of holding gold by U.S. citizens.

Aug. 27 — Treasury Department invites congressmen to Fort Knox Sept. 23.

Sept. 11 — Rep. Philip M. Crane (R-Ill.) introduces a bill prohibiting authorization by the Secretary of the Treasury or the president to sell gold from the American stockpile.

Sept. 23 — A seven-man congressional inspection team and nearly 100 reporters inspect the Fort Knox Bullion Depository.

October 10 — Several major U.S. brokerage houses announce plans to enter gold trading market at the end of 1974.

October 17 — ODGSO denies rumor that the Treasury is considering a Bicentennial gold coin, claiming such a coin would be illegal under current laws.

October 24 — Gold prices rise past $160 per ounce level, amid rumors of Middle Eastern dollar manipulations.

October 24 — California legislature prepares bill regulating gold dealings in post-ban days. Several coin dealers object to restrictions.

November 8 — Gold price hits $183 per ounce in London, leading to speculation of $200 gold by the end of the year.

November 8 — Federal Trade Commission orders jewelry replicas of pioneer gold coins marked with COPY in incuse lettering.

November 8 — New York Stock Exchange contemplates establishment of a gold trading center after the end of the gold ban.

November 11 — Gold climbs to $188.25 per ounce. Treasury Secretary denies there will be a delay in the legalization of gold.

November 20 — Last minute opposition to

the freeing of gold sees the introduction into Congress of bills delaying gold ban lifting.

November 20 — Great Britain resumes striking of sovereigns for release through Bank of England.

Dec. 3 — U.S. Treasury announces plans for sale of 2 million ounces of gold bullion on Jan. 6, 1975. Sale intended to ease the balance of payments deficit which would result from U.S. citizens buying gold from overseas.

Dec. 5 — Federal Reserve Board Chairman Arthur Burns urges delay in lifting of gold ban, fearing that Americans will withdraw savings to buy gold.

Dec. 19 — Proposal for Canadian gold Olympic coin receives unexpected endorsement from postmaster-general, minister responsible for Olympic coin program.

Dec. 27 — Gold reaches $195.25 per ounce in London, expected to reach $200 by the end of the year.

Dec. 27 — France to revalue its gold reserves to near-market level shortly after the first of the year.

Dec. 27 — Philippines reported to be considering a legal tender gold coin for 1975.

Dec. 31 — Striking of Panamanian 100-balboa gold coin at Franklin Mint marks end of U.S. gold ban.

Dec. 31 — President Ford inaugural medal struck in gold for public sale, first such medal since 1933.

Dec. 31 — Gold prices drop sharply in first day of legalized gold in America.

1975

Jan. 2 — Gold drops to $175.25 per ounce from Dec. 31 close of $186.75, confusing metal market experts. Profit-taking blamed.

Jan. 6 — U.S. Treasury opens bids on 2 million ounces of gold in 400-ounce bars. Demand so small that only 753,600 ounces sold, at an average price of $165.67 per ounce. Lowest bid accepted is $153 per ounce. Treasury Secretary delighted at the "failure" of the sale.

Jan. 8 — London gold market jumps from $169.50 to $180 per ounce, despite the lack of interest shown in the U.S. Treasury gold sale. Gold experts unable to explain trend.

Jan. 15 — Gold prices settle down near $175 per ounce level, stay there for several weeks.

Jan. 19 — U.S. hobby leaders meet at American Numismatic Association round table; Mint Director says that the rumors of the death of the Bicentennial gold coin are greatly exaggerated.

January — Gold imports for the month of January more than double those for December. Most of increase thought to be for industrial purposes, rather than speculative.

Jan. 31 — Gold closes at $176.05 per ounce.

Feb. 10 — GAO audit verifies U.S. gold supplies. U.S. Mint controls called "adequate."

Feb. 19 — Gold prices spurt upwards to $184.50 per ounce, highest price since Jan. 2. Rumors of changes in European central bank operations blamed.

Feb. 28 — Gold closes at $182 per ounce.

March — Twelve rare Adelaide Assay Office gold pounds found to be missing from the Library of New South Wales, Sydney, Australia. The genuine coins had been replaced by worthless modern replicas.

March 31 — Gold closes at $176 per ounce.

April 15 — United Kingdom bans sale of newly minted sovereigns to U.K. residents, making them available only to overseas buyers.

April 15 — U.S. Treasury announces updated gold regulations in wake of legalization.

April 15 — Gold drops to $164 per ounce, several dollars below the official figure used to value French gold reserves. Speculators disappointed when France does not step in to buy gold at the unofficial "floor" price.

April 30 — Gold closes at $167 per ounce.

May — Several bills introduced into U.S. House and Senate calling for a Bicentennial gold coin. Legislation receives ANA support.

May 30 — U.S. Treasury announces upcoming sale of an additional half million ounces of gold on June 30.

May 30 — Gold closes at $167.20 per ounce.

May — Following the fall of South Vietnam and Cambodia, tons of gold come to light as refugees leave Southeast Asia.

June 2 — The Treasury Department announces it will sell about a half million of its 276 million ounces of gold on hand, in bars of 250 ounces each. Gold prices on world markets fall.

June 30 — The General Services Administration opens bids for the Treasury gold auction; in contrast with the Jan. 6 sale, Treasury calls interest in the June sale "substantial," with 41 sucessful bidders for 499,500 ounces of gold at $165.05 per ounce. Largest successful bidder is Swiss Bank Corporation of Zurich (140,000 ounces).

Aug. 11 — Gold lists two-month low in London, $161.90 per ounce.

Aug. 27 — Office of Domestic Gold and Silver Operations abolished; functions remaining after the lift of the gold ban are transferred to the Treasury's Assistant Secretary for International Affairs. J. H. Nisenson named Deputy Director of Gold Market Activities.

Aug. 29 — The International Monetary Fund announces it will sell about $1.1 billion of its gold for the benefit of poor nations, permitting central banks to buy 25 million ounces at market-related prices. Markets begin decline.

Sept. 19 — Gold plunges to year's low of $135.00.

Nov. 28 — Charles Heim, publisher of *Heim's Investment Letter*, says outlook for gold is "negative." Price stands at $138.15 in London.

Dec. 19 — The IMF Group of Ten meets in Paris, discusses possibility of reducing amount of gold to be auctioned from 25 million ounces to 17.5 million.

Dec. 31 — Thomas Wolfe, former Director of the Office of Domestic Gold and Silver Operations, begins a government-sponsored study of world gold and silver markets.

1976

Jan. 8 — Franklin Mint strikes first gold coin of the Netherlands Antilles.

Jan. 30 — Gold continues to slide, closing month of January at $128.40 per ounce in New York.

Feb. 27 — Gold steady for February, closing at monthly average of $130.81 per ounce in New York.

March 31 — Stack's sells five gold coins from the Garrett collection for $408,000; total sale brings more than $2.3 million.

April 21 — Jesse Owens receives first $100 gold Canadian Olympic gold coin presented to an American.

April 28 — International Monetary Fund anticipates beginning its gold sales in May, planning to auction off 25 million ounces over the next four years.

May 19 — Australians gain the right to own, buy and sell gold.

June 2 — IMF auctions 780,000 ounces of gold at a common price of $126 per ounce. The "Dutch auction" system adopted, permitting all successful bidders to receive gold at the same price. Next auction set for July 14.

July 7 — Internal Revenue Service rules that trades of investment coins qualify as "like kind" exchanges and thus are not taxable transactions. The ruling involved a trade of five lots of Mexican 50-peso gold coins for six and a half lots of Austrian 100-corona coins. Since both lots were restrikes, their value depended on their gold content; thus, though the pieces differed in size and gold content, their nature was the same.

July 20 — Gold plunges to 31-month low on London gold exchange, with a closing fix of $107.75, following second IMF auction.

Sept. 15 — IMF sells 780,000 ounces of gold at $109.40 per ounce; market responds by moving up $2.75 to $114 per ounce.

Sept. 29 — American Stock Exchange proposes to set up affiliate to trade in gold bullion options.

Oct. 27 — Thomas Wolfe, former ODGSO chief, believes gold price has bottomed out and should move up in years ahead, based on increased industrial demand and other factors.

Nov. 15 — Gold climbs to $139.20 on London exchange, in wake of Carter election victory; boom replaces gloom among speculators.

Oct. 1 — President Ford signs Gold Labeling Act into law. The bill reduces tolerances permitted in gold products.

1977

Feb. 9 — American Stock Exchange continues to promote its gold and silver commodity options program while awaiting Commodity Futures Trading Commission approval. Also plans a spot market in gold and silver.

March 15 — London gold market appears to level at $140 to $150 per ounce during first weeks of March.

March 30 — Gold reaches high of $153.55 per troy ounce; slips to $149.95 five days later.

April 6 — Bidders pay an average of $149.18 per troy ounce in IMF gold sale. Rep. Henry S. Reuss, D-Wis., urges Treasury to release U.S. gold for auction to "cool" price.

April 13 — South Africa revalues gold from "official" $42.40-per-ounce price to market-related price. The move benefits the nation's gold mines by eliminating the time they must wait between receiving the "official" price and getting the difference between it and the actual selling price from the government.

April 23 — Historic Reed Mine in Cabarrus County, N.C., the first gold mine in the U.S., is opened to the public. Restoration includes 300 feet of original shafts.

May 11 — Gold futures trading on New York's COMEX and Chicago's IMM triple in volume from the previous year, with 171,849 contracts traded in March.

June 1 — Canada announces plans to strike 300,000 $100 22-karat gold coins for the Silver Jubilee of Queen Elizabeth II. IMF sells 525,000 ounces of gold at $143.32.

June 15 — International Precious Metals Institute holds its first international conference at New York's World Trade Center.

June 29 — North Carolina's gold rush days are recalled in three dioramas depicting the minting cf gold coins at the Charlotte Mint Museum.

Oct. 10 — London price of gold reaches two-year high of $157.15 per troy ounce.

Oct. 30 — President Carter signs "gold clause" bill, permitting U.S. citizens to enter into contracts specifying payment in gold, or in dollars based on the value of gold.

1978

Jan. 4 — Gold opens at 2½-year high of $172.50 at the morning fix in the London gold market.

March 28 — Weak dollar combined with energy crunch drive London gold price upward to $183.20 per troy ounce.

April 20 — Treasury announces plans to sell 1.8 million troy ounces of stockpiled gold to prop up the U.S. dollar; gold responds with a price drop of more than $10.

April 20 — Sen. Jesse Helms, R-N.C., and Barry Goldwater, R-Ariz., co-sponsor Gold Medallion Act of 1978 as an alternative to stockpile auctions.

Aug. 1 — London's major gold merchants set the morning fix at $207.50 per troy ounce.

Oct. 4 — U.S. gold coin imports averaged 236,000 ounces during the first seven months of 1978, 76 percent ahead of the previous year's imports of these items.

Oct. 3 — Gold breaks upward to $223.50 in London, as U.S. trade deficits continue to take their toll on the dollar.

1979

July 18 — London gold prices shatter $300 barrier as price is fixed at $303.85.

Sept. 29 — Gold sells for $400.20 in Hong Kong as world paper currencies register distress.

Sept. 29 — Appropriations legislation for funding American Arts Gold Medallion program is signed by President Carter.

Dec. 12 — Price of gold continues climb to $462.50 per troy ounce.

1980

Jan. 3 — Gold price continues upward to $634 per troy ounce.

Jan. 21 — All-time record price of $850 reached in gold trading; Comex silver trades for $50.35 per troy ounce.

April 15 — Gold price slips below $500, to $495.50 per ounce.

June 16 and July 1 are the opening dates for ordering half-ounce American Arts Gold Medallions honoring Marian Anderson and the 1-ounce pieces commemorating artist Grant Wood.

1981

Feb. 11 — Gold price continues slippage to $490 per troy ounce.

June 24 — London price of gold drops off plateau, to $460 level.

July 8 — Gold price falls through $400 as it is fixed in London at $397.75, the lowest price since Nov. 27, 1979; prime interest rate climbs to 20.5 percent.

Sept. 16 — The U.S. Gold Commission meets to consider returning to the gold standard, and other questions relating to the yellow metal. Rep. Ron Paul, R-Texas, and Lewis Lehrman of New York are the only members of the 16-person commission known to favor this move.

1982

Feb. 17 — Study by the Aden sisters predicts return to $850 gold by 1984; $3,600-to-$4,500 gold by 1986.

March 12 — Gold price falls to $322 under pressure of high interest rates.

March 24 — Reduction in prime rate bounces the gold price upward to $411.50 for the first time since Jan. 8.

1983

Jan. 18 — Gold tops $500 for the first time in 22 months, as it trades at $502.50 on the New York Commodity Exchange.

Feb. 22 — Gold price tumbles from $503.50 to $485.50 in a single day's trading on the Comex.

Feb. 29 — J. Aron & Co. wins marketing contract for American Arts Gold Medallions; accents bullion nature of pieces by renaming them "U.S. Gold."

April 2 — Designs approved for 1983 U.S. Gold, commemorating poet Robert Frost and artist Alexander Calder.

May 25 — Rep. Ron Paul introduces legislation which proposes that the International Monetary Fund sell gold at the spot price to the United States, rather than increasing the U.S. contribution to the fund.

May 31 — The price of gold drops $23.90, to $412 per troy ounce on the Comex; price future is "confused" as a bill to ban Krugerrand sales is introduced in Congress.

Aug. 17 - J. Aron & Co. vice president Arnold Reishman reports satisfaction with share U.S. Gold has carved in slow gold bullion market.

Sept. 13 — The United States Mint strikes the first Olympic gold eagle at West Point, N.Y. This is the first gold coin struck by the U.S. Mint in 50 years, and is the first to bear the "W" Mint mark.

1984

Jan. 9 — Price of gold drops to $365.90 on the Comex in New York as the U.S. dollar gains strength against world currencies.

June 20 — The U.S. Treasury terminates its U.S. Gold distribution contract with J. Aron & Co. The Treasury absorbs $2 million advertising costs, while J. Aron will reimburse $1.3 million for material on hand.

July 25 — Gold plunges to an almost-two-year low of $333.50 on the Comex; experts anticipate lower price levels.

Oct. 17 — A U.S. Senate and House committee drops a bill which would prohibit the importation of Krugerrands and Soviet Union gold coins.

Oct. 17 — A bill introduced in the final days of the 98th Congress to continue the American Arts Gold Medallion program is modified to make the issue legal tender $20 one-ounce gold coins showing the Statue of Liberty on one side and a family of eagles on the other.

Dec. 12 — U.S. Mint officials, after five weeks of telemarketing, report a "planned, smooth rise in sales of American Arts gold medallions.

1985

Jan. 16 — Chairman Frank Annunzio of the House Consumer Affairs and Coinage subcommittee introduces legislation authorizing the sale of gold and silver coins to commemorate the Centennial of the Statue of Liberty.

Feb. 27 — Jammed telephone lines for ordering American Arts Gold Medallions (U.S. Gold) result in an extension of the ordering date beyond Jan. 31.

June 19 — House passes legislation that would impose immediate sanctions against South Africa, including the importation of Krugerrands.

July 3 — Senate passes Statue of Liberty commemorative coin bill with an amendment calling for a 1-ounce silver bullion coin to follow the Statue program.

July 17 — Bullion dealers report the Canadian Maple Leaf is overtaking the Krugerrand in the bullion market.

July 24 — The Senate passes its version of the anti-apartheid act containing a U.S. bullion coin amendment.

Aug. 14 — South Africa halts release of its worldwide sales figures for Krugerrands.

Sept. 25 — President Reagan issues executive order for economic sanctions against the government of South Africa and requests the Treasury Department to report on the feasibility of minting U.S. gold bullion coins.

Oct. 11 — President Reagan signs executive order banning importation of the Krugerrand.

Dec. 4 — Passage by the House of gold bullion coinage legislation is blocked at the Treasury Department's request, to provide an opportunity to amend the bill to conform with Treasury recommendations

Dec. 18 — House passes gold bullion coin legislation already approved by the Senate on Dec. 2.

Dec. 17 — President Reagan signs legislation authorizing the minting of four gold bullion coins — one-ounce $50, half-ounce $25, quarter-ounce $10 and tenth-ounce $5 face values — to be struck from newly mined domestic gold.

1986

March 12 — Mint Director Donna Pope predicts sales of 2.2 million ounces of gold bullion coins and 4 million ounces of silver bullion coins in first year at House Appropriations subcommittee hearing.

June 11 — U.S. Mint Director Donna Pope reveals all four gold bullion coins will carry a revised Augustus Saint-Gaudens double eagle design, with Texas sculptor Miley Biesek's "Family of Eagles" design for the reverse.

July 23 — The Royal Canadian Mint reports 8 million ounces of Maple Leaf gold bullion coins have been sold since their introduction in 1979, through the end of 1985 — 1985 sales increased 87.4 percent over 1984.

Aug. 13 — U.S. Mint defines criteria for gold bullion coin wholesalers, who must have a net worth in excess of $50 million and liquid assets of $10 million. Minimum purchases of 5,000 ounces of gold, 50 million ounces of silver will be required.

Sept. 8 — Though the Mint schedules its ceremonial striking of the new bullion coins for Sept. 8, sales are being delayed until Oct. 20 to permit an inventory buildup.

Sept. 9 — The ban against importation of the South African Krugerrand, due to expire, is extended by President Reagan.

October — Twenty-five U.S. and foreign firms are selected by the Treasury Department to make the market for the American Eagle gold bullion coins.

Nov. 5 — American Eagle gold bullion coin orders empty Mint valults, with 558,000 ounces moving out in two days.

November — Three-week sales total for American Eagle gold coins climbs to 820,500 ounces, or 1,253,000 coins.

Nov. 26 — "Eaglemania" continues: Retail premiums range from 6.7 to 16.9 percent for one-ounce coins; 49.2 to 81.8 percent for half-ounce coins; 57.6 to 82.5 percent for the quarter ounce; and 69.9 to 84.7 percent for the tenth-ounce.

November — U.S. Mint reports that for the first time in seven weeks, demand for 1-ounce gold bullion coins fell below supply on Dec. 1. Total sales of all four coins climbs to 1,278,750 ounces or 1,932,000 coins.

Dec. 3 — Sales of American Eagle gold coin year-end production goals set at 1.4 million 1-ounce, 50,000 half-ounce, 600,000 quarter-ounce and 650,000 tenth-ounce pieces.

Dec. 24 — 1986 Proof American Eagle gold coin sales exceed $187 million; Proofs to be offered in some denominations in 1987.

1987

Jan. 7 — Supply of all four denominations of American Eagle gold coins exceeded demand on Dec. 23 for the second week in a row. Total produced amounts to 1,607,250 ounces, or 2,675,000 coins.

Jan. 14 — Mint reaches gold bullion production goals; sells 1,312,500 1-ounce coins, 486,500 half-ounce coins, 587,000 quarter-ounce coins and 825,000 tenth-ounce coins, for a total of 1,787,750 ounces.

Jan. 21 — Coinage subcommittee hears Jan.5 that eight U.S. distributors bought 34 percent of gold bullion coins; the balance were sold to 17 foreign dealers.

March 25 — Great Britain announces it will enter the gold bullion coin market in 1987, with a gold "Britannia" to be issued in 1-ounce and three fractional-ounce sizes, joining similar programs operated by South Africa, Canada, the United States, Australia, the Isle of Man and China.

Monthly gold prices

(Dollars per troy ounce)

	Engelhard Industries			Handy and Harman	London final
	Low/date	High/date	Average	Average	Average
1984					
January......	365.10/24	383.00/3	371.29	370.89	370.89
February.....	376.00/14	399.25/28	386.36	385.96	385.92
March.......	385.75/28	405.85/5	394.66	394.26	394.26
April........	376.20/30	387.20/1	381.98	381.66	381.36
May.........	371.90/8	386.80/30	377.68	377.26	377.40
June	368.30/18	394.15/1&5	378.06	377.66	377.66
July.........	335.40/23	370.40/2	346.84	346.44	347.47
August	339.40/1	354.40/14	348.09	347.69	347.68
September ...	335.65/17	348.15/24	341.31	341.09	341.09
October......	333.90/31	348.90/3	340.57	340.10	340.17
November ...	329.40/28&30	350.85/13	341.54	340.86	341.18
December....	307.90/20	332.40/4	319.50	319.74	320.16
1985					
January......	298.15/28	308.40/18	303.19	302.79	302.79
February.....	284.65/25	304.55/14	299.22	298.82	299.10
March.......	287.65/1	330.80/1	304.34	303.94	303.94
April........	317.15/4	334.65/15	325.31	324.90	325.27
May.........	310.00/6	326.90/14	316.46	316.07	316.37
June	312.40/10	325.80/19	316.89	316.49	316.49
July.........	308.65/2	327.90/31	318.20	317.80	317.22
August	320.20/6	341.30/19&28	330.46	330.23	329.79
September ...	316.65/18	329.65/26	323.18	322.62	323.35
October......	322.65/1	328.15/22	326.24	326.02	325.84
November ...	322.35/8	331.50/26	325.64	325.47	325.30
December....	315.90/11	330.00/31	322.76	322.42	321.72
1986					
January......	326.70/2	363.40/16	345.78	345.49	345.38
February.....	331.75/14	352.80/25	339.60	339.33	338.89
March.......	336.00/3	353.30/21	345.74	345.42	345.70
April........	333.50/1	346.60/23	340.84	340.55	340.44
May.........	339.10/20	345.75/9	342.80	342.46	342.38
June	337.15/17	348.75/12	343.12	342.79	342.72
July.........	342.70/2	357.90/31	349.17	348.85	348.34
August	358.90/5	388.40/11,13	377.24	376.85	376.60
September ...	393.65/2	435.90/22	419.37	419.01	417.73
October......	401.40/31	438.50/8	423.91	423.62	423.51
November ...	381.15/24	411.15/10	398.74	398.81	397.55
December....	388.30/9	397.07/1	392.58	391.22	390.92
1987					
January......	400.48/5	423.83/19	409.81	408.26	408.26
February.....	391.51/18	408.29/2	402.85	401.32	401.12
March.......	405.34/3	425.58/30	410.46	408.91	408.91

Source: Bureau of Mines

Silver

Chemical symbol: Ag
Atomic number: 47
Atomic weight: 107.88
Density: 10.49 times the weight of
an equal volume of water

Silver, the brilliant white metal, is second only to its sister gold in malleability. It is harder than gold, has a high resistance to corrosion, and is an excellent conductor of heat and electricity.

Silver was used for decorative purposes as far back as 4000 B.C., as a standard of value by 3500 B.C., and was widely used in coinage by 450 B.C.

The leading world producer of silver has been Mexico since 1900. Mexico, the United States, Canada and Peru produce more than two-thirds of the world's total of silver. The world's largest silver mine is the Real de Monte y Pachuca, in Hidalgo, Mexico.

In the United States, Idaho is the leading producer of silver; in Canada the topmost producers are Ontario, British Columbia and the Yukon territory.

Silver mining and refining

Most of the silver presently mined occurs in the native condition, that is, as an alloy of silver and some other metals. Most of this native silver is finely dispersed throughout other metals. Traditional mining techniques, then, are used to bring silver out of the ground.

Silver can be extracted from its ores using a variety of methods. The amalgamation process involves treating ores with water and mercury; the cyanidation process uses pulverized ore that is treated with sodium cyanide. Crude silver can be smelted, yielding a gold-silver alloy called dore.

Since gold and silver often occur together, as in forming dore, several methods are employed to separate and purify them. Electrolysis is one (see GOLD), the parting method is another. In the latter, the dore or very high-purity gold and silver bullion is bathed with hot concentrated sulfuric or strong nitric acid and the silver dissolves. Once the gold is removed, the silver is precipitated using ferrous sulfate, copper or iron.

The crime of silver

The following appeared in large part in a Federal Reserve Bank of San Francisco Monthly Review supplement, reprinted in *Coin World*, in 1969. It has been updated to include significant events of the 1970s and '80s.

By William Burke and Yvonne Levy

Populist orators, finding no rational explanation for the grinding deflation that racked the nation's economy before the turn of the century, argued that hard times were the result of a monstrous conspiracy organized by London bankers and their Wall Street minions. When asked for evidence, these orators automatically cited the "Crime of 1873" — the (temporary) demonetization of silver.

"A crime, because it has brought tears to strong men's eyes and hunger and pinching want to widows and orphans. A crime because it is destroying the honest yeomanry of the land, the bulwark of the nation. A crime because it has brought this once great republic to the verge of ruin, where it is now in imminent danger of tottering to its fall." (*Coin's Financial School*)

The Populists denounced this "crime" so fervently because they equated the dethronement of silver with a deliberate policy of deflation. In their eyes, the "crime" was compounded in 1900 with the formal adoption of the gold standard, and it was only partly assuaged in the 1930s with the discarding of gold as a domestic means of payment and the adoption of a silver-purchase program.

Yet in the late 1960s when the Treasury ceased redeeming silver certificates in silver and began to mint quarters and dimes out of baser metals, few observers if any suggested that the republic was on the verge of ruin. Aside from a few nostalgic editorials, the news of this final dethronement of monetary silver was confined to the financial pages.

The nation easily survived this latest episode in silver's checkered career, in large part because the turn-of-the-century monetary battles had eventually led to the enactment of the Federal Reserve Act, and thus to the institution of flexible methods of monetary control. But more to the point, this time it was silver's rebirth as an industrial and artistic material that contributed to its problems as a monetary metal.

Silver today

Speculative excesses undoubtedly have helped drive silver prices upward in the last few decades but a more basic reason for this upsurge is the deficit in the major sources of supply — Western mines and Treasury stockpiles — in relation to the significant increase in the worldwide demand for silver. Because of its varied characteristics — silver is foremost in electrical and thermal conductivity, highest in optical reflectivity, and second only to gold in ductility — the white metal has gained new luster among dentists as well as debutantes, and among spacemen as well as shutterbugs.

This latest episode has been closely involved with the metal's dazzling price performance during the decade of the 1960s. The major episodes in silver's earlier monetary history, by way of contrast, were products of prolonged price declines for silver, and for everything else, in the Great Depression of the 1890s and the even greater catastrophe of the 1930s. So, just as the "Crime of '73" epitomized the earlier time of monetary troubles, the virtual repetition of that act may well typify silver's new-found period of prosperity.

Yesterday's silver

Since a major chapter in silver's long emotion-drenched monetary history came to a close in the 1960s, some perspective may be gained from a review of the legislative highlights. The record dates back to 1792 when the new nation set up two units of value: a gold dollar containing 24.75 grains of pure gold and a silver dollar containing 371.25 grains of pure silver.

Silver's monetary value of $1.2929 per ounce, although not defined in such terms in the law, could be derived by dividing the number of grains in an ounce (480) by the number of grains of pure silver in the silver dollar (371.25). Silver's monetary value was still measured in the same way in the 1960s but that apparently was the only sign of stability that could be found in the metal's volatile behavior.

The Founding Fathers — specifically Alexander Hamilton — had opted for a bimetallic standard, with the unit of account and all types of money kept at a constant value in terms of gold and also in terms of silver. Practically, however, an alternating standard developed because of the implacable workings of Gresham's Law, the principle that bad money drives good money out of circulation. Although the relative values of the two metals *at the Mint* were constant by legal definition, the relative values in commodity markets fluctuated continuously, producing "bargain" prices at the Mint now for one metal and again for the other; the metal that was overvalued at the Mint consistently drove out of monetary use the metal that was undervalued for such purposes.

The original 15-1 Mint ratio of silver to gold (by weight of equivalent value) was below the market ratio existing at that time and the consequent gold outflow tended to make silver the nation's standard money until the 1830s. Gold was then revalued, however, and the resultant 16-1 Mint ratio caused a reversal of the situation and led to a disappearance of silver.

Debts and debtors

Then came the Civil War — and then came the losing 30-year battle on the part of debtor groups to maintain prices at the high wartime levels at which they had contracted their debts. The postwar price decline had developed partly because of the cessation of the war-induced demand for commodities and partly because of the sudden build-up in farm surpluses resulting from the rapid expansion of the trans-Mississippi West — but also because of a shift in monetary policy toward contraction of the paper currency and resumption of specie payment.

The struggle of Populist farmers and other debtors to restore wartime price levels through currency inflation was led initially by the Greenbackers. That doughty group, which demanded the redemption of war bonds in paper and not in gold, suffered a crucial defeat when the administration resumed specie payments in 1879. But even before that event the inflationists had arrived at the view that they could attain their ends by injecting silver into the monetary system at an inflated ratio.

In accordance with Gresham's Law, silver at the 16-1 Mint ratio had been undervalued and had long since disappeared from circulation. In fact, such a long time had elapsed since any silver had been presented to the Mints for coinage that Congress in 1873 stopped the further minting of the standard silver dollar and thereby effectively demonetized silver. Whether deliberately or through oversight, Congress simply failed to include in a long, very detailed and technical revision of the coinage laws any provision for the continuing coinage of the standard (371.25-grain) silver dollar. Thus was the "Crime of '73" perpetrated.

No cries of outrage greeted the event at the time it occurred, since every ounce of silver was then worth $1.30. But within three years the situation altered drastically. The price of silver dropped to $1.16 and below, on the heels of a glut occasioned by the opening of new mines in Nevada and the closing of silver markets in the new gold-standard countries of western and southern Europe.

The Populists cried conspiracy, for if silver could have been coined freely at the old 16-1 ratio the debtors could have paid their debts with the easier-to-earn white metal. In order to repair the ravages of the crime, therefore, these inflationists demanded that Congress restore the free and unlimited coinage of silver at the old 16-1 ratio.

The best they could obtain, however, was the passage of the Bland-Allison Act of 1878, which required the Treasury to buy not less than $2 million of silver every month for coinage or for backing of silver certificates. But the net increase in currency, which amounted to $253 million in the 1879-90 period, failed to match the hopes of the backers of this legislation; the new silver certificates simply took the place of national bank notes which were being retired in connection with the reduction of the national debt.

The price of silver dropped to $0.94 within the following decade, so the inflationists demanded that more be done. This time the best they could accomplish was the passage of the Sherman Silver Purchase Act of 1890, in a trade whereby Westerners voted for a tariff bill which they disliked while Easterners voted for a silver bill which they feared.

The Sherman Act directed the Secretary of the Treasury to buy 4.5 million ounces of silver bullion — almost the entire domestic production — every month. The bullion was to be paid for through the issue of new legal-tender Treasury notes, which were to be redeemable in either gold or silver — a provision which permitted an "endless chain" of gold withdrawals in the panic of 1893.

Despite these efforts, the Sherman Act did not succeed in its purpose. It failed to raise the price of silver, and moreover it failed to increase the amount of money in circulation and to reverse the steady decline in farm prices. (Sen. Sherman's influence was far more lasting in the antitrust field.)

President Cleveland and other gold supporters wanted to abandon silver to its fate and to adhere formally to the gold standard. The silverites, on the other hand, continued to favor the unlimited coinage of silver and the pegging of the silver price at the traditional 16-1 ratio. For a while, Cleveland had his way; faced with the panic of 1893 and with a substantial gold outflow which reduced the gold reserve below the tacitly recognized floor of $100 million, he forced through Congress the repeal of the Silver Purchase Act. Yet this led to his repudiation by his own party and to the mighty Populist upsurge

which in 1896 brought William Jennings Bryan to the verge of the presidency.

Gold on the throne

Nonetheless, within four years the money question was no longer at the center of public controversy — in fact, was hardly in the public eye at all. Early in 1900 the victorious "goldbugs" secured the passage of an act providing that the gold dollar of 25.8 grains nine-tenths fine should be the unit of value and that all other forms of currency should be maintained at parity with this dollar. (Parity was to be maintained through a $150-million gold reserve which the Treasury would hold available for the redemption of paper money.) Then, later in 1900, Bryan's second defeat sealed the doom of silver as a dominant political issue.

The issue died out simply because of the long-awaited reversal of the downward trend in prices. Between 1896 (the low point) and 1914, the general price level increased 40 percent. But inflation and farm prosperity were achieved not through the Populists' chosen instrument, silver, but rather through several unexpected developments — developments related to the metal which they detested (gold) and to the center of the gold "conspiracy" which they despised (the city).

New gold discoveries in South Africa and North America, along with the development of new processes for extracting the precious metal from the ore, flooded the world with gold during these critical years. Over two decades, the amount of gold coinage increased by half, and thereby permitted a corresponding expansion of the currency supply. After 1896, therefore, the gold inflation helped bring about the happy situation which the farmers for so long had tried to win with silver. The evidence was apparent on every hand — wheat rising from 72 cents a bushel in 1896 to 98 cents a bushel in 1909, corn rising from 21 cents to 57 cents, and so on throughout list.

But the American city itself, and not simply the gold inflation, saved the American farmer. Throughout that golden age, the foreign market for many of his products sharply declined. Yet his income situation sharply improved, because of the very thing that was cited as evidence of his political submergence — the great increase of the urban population. In 1890, 4.6 million American farms supplied a domestic urban population of 22 million; in 1910, 6.4 million farms supplied 42 million city-dwellers. The larger, more efficient, and more mechanized farms which developed over those two decades produced an increasing part of their total produce for the home market (and less for the foreign market), under far stabler and more advantageous conditions of transportation and finance than had prevailed in the past. And yet this favorable trend — labeled "From Pathos to Parity" by one historian — was achieved without any aid from the Populists' favorite weapon, silver inflation.

Silver in the '30s

The second major development in silver's dramatic history occurred in another major period of deflation — the 1930s. Once again a movement arose to halt a prolonged deflationary spiral by restoring currency values to the level at which wartime and postwar debts had been contracted. And once again a remedy was proposed, in the Thomas Amendment to the Agricultural Adjustment Act of 1933, that envisioned both the printing of more paper money and unlimited coinage of silver. The Amendment, in addition, authorized increased open-market purchases of government securities and a reduction in the gold content of the dollar.

The last-named of these alternatives received the most emphasis in the early New Deal days. Under the authority of the Gold Reserve Act of 1934, the value of the dollar was fixed at 59.08 percent of its formerly established (1900) value in terms of gold.

But much to the surprise of the theorists who influenced the administration's decision — theorists who posited a close relationship between the price level of commodities and the gold content of the monetary medium — the price level did not automatically respond. True enough, the wholesale price index increased somewhat in line with the general expansion of demand following the Depression low, but the increase was only about half of what the inflationists expected in view of the 41 percent reduction in the gold content of the dollar. Silver inflation, therefore, was brought forward as a supplement to the incomplete gold inflation — and as an answer to the perennial legislative demand to "do something for silver."

Since 1873, the downward trend in the price of silver had been interrupted only twice, during the silver-purchase period around 1890 and again during World War I. After the turn of the century, in fact, the market price rarely exceeded one-half the nominal Mint value.

Silver had remained in a monetary limbo with respect to new acquisitions; some was used for subsidiary coins, some circulated in the West in the form of standard silver dollars, and a roughly fixed stock of silver certificates remained as a relic of the 1890s. Thus, by the 1930s, only about 650 million ounces were in use as coin or as currency backing at the Treasury.

Government purchase

At the end of 1933, with the market price of silver standing at about 44 cents an ounce — 75 percent above the Depression low — unlimited purchase of newly minted silver was initiated at $0.6464 an ounce under the authority granted by the Thomas Amendment. But inflationist pressure then brought about even further action, in the form of the Silver Purchase Act of 1934. Under its terms, the Secretary of the Treasury was directed to purchase silver at home and abroad until the market price reached the traditional Mint price of $1.2929 an ounce, or until the monetary value of the Treasury's silver stock reached one-third of the monetary value of its gold stock. The support price at which purchases were made was changed on several different occasions during the ensuing dozen years; originally $0.6464, it was eventually set at $0.9050 in 1946.

Under the authority of the silver-purchase legislation of the 1930s and subsequent Presidential proclamations the Treasury acquired some 3,200 million ounces of silver — about half of it in the four-year period 1934-37, and the remaining half of it in the subsequent quarter-century. A minor part (about 110 million ounces) consisted of silver that was "nationalized" in mid-1934, when the administration required nonmonetary silver to be turned in at $0.5001 per fine ounce, so as to capture the profits expected to be realized from the increased government purchase price. About 2,210 million ounces consisted of metal purchased abroad at prevailing market prices, and the remaining 830 million ounces consisted of newly minted domestic silver.

Until 1955, the Treasury support price for newly mined domestic silver was higher than the market price, so the U.S. government purchased domestic metal at the higher price while U.S. silver-using industries purchased low-priced foreign metal. But from 1955 to late 1961, the market price approximated the support price, and silver users then began to purchase some supplies from the Treasury as well as from foreign and domestic mines.

In little more than a quarter-century, the Treasury purchased $2 billion in silver and sextupled the physical quantity used as currency or held in stockpiles. Nevertheless, the silver program during that period failed to achieve either of the objectives specified in the 1934 Silver Purchase Act: a market price equal to the monetary value of $1.2929, or a one-to-three ratio of the monetary stocks of silver and gold.

Prior to the 1960s and to the upsurge of world demand, market pressures failed to push prices above the $0.5001 floor. Meanwhile, the ratio of monetary silver to monetary gold stocks — both at their nominal monetary values — failed to reach the one-to-three target figure. (The ratio ranged around one-to-five in the pre-war period, then rose to one-to-seven as a consequence of the early postwar gold inflow, and finally dropped to one-to-four during the following decade as gold began to flow out instead of in.) Then, when silver's supporters achieved the price upsurge they wanted, it turned out to be a mixed blessing indeed.

On its way up

Eventually, the market accomplished what a century's legislation could not do for the cause of silver price support. In the late 1950s, world consumption of silver increased about 4 percent annually, while world production rose only about 1.5 percent annually. Sales from Treasury stockpiles filled the gap — and held the price line — for almost a decade, but the depletion of stocks finally brought the process to a halt.

The first scene in a long drawn-out final act occurred in late 1961. By that time, the worldwide industrial and coinage demand for silver approximated 300 million ounces annually, about half of which was American demand, whereas worldwide production approximated 235 million ounces annually, about one-sixth of which was from American mines. The gap had to be filled by sales from the Treasury's "free silver" stocks — that is, stocks that were not earmarked for currency backing or coinage.

The Treasury's supply of free silver had reached its peak in early 1959 at 222 million ounces. But by the end of 1960, half that supply was gone and by late 1961, only 22 million ounces were left. There remained, however, nearly 1,700 million ounces in a bullion reserve held against the issuance of part of the nation's paper currency. About one-fourth was held against $5 and $10 silver certificates, and the remainder was used to support $1 and $2 silver certificates. The larger denominations could have been issued in the form of Federal Reserve notes, but then-existing legislation authorized only silver certificates for the smaller denominations.

The legislative stage was thus set for the beginning of the final act. In November 1961,

President Kennedy wrote Treasury Secretary Dillon, "I have reached the decision that silver metal should gradually be withdrawn from our monetary reserves" — and with that, he instructed the Secretary to suspend further sales of the Treasury's free silver, to suspend the use of free silver for coinage, and to obtain the silver required for coinage needs through the retirement from circulation of $5 and $10 silver certificates. By this measure, some 400 million ounces of the total reserve of 1,700 million ounces were released for coinage purposes. (Interpreting the President's statement as a Treasury withdrawal from the supply side of the market, the market responded with a 10 percent jump in price the very next day, and with a further 30 percent rise the following year.)

The next scene occurred with the passage of Public Law 88-36 (June 1963). The Act repealed the Silver Purchase Act of 1934 and subsequent silver legislation, repealed the tax on transfers of interest in silver bullion, and confirmed the redeemability of silver certificates for silver dollars or bullion at the monetary value of $1.2929 an ounce. But in particular, it authorized the issuance of Federal Reserve notes in the smaller denominations, thereby providing for the eventual elimination of silver as backing for $1 and $2 bills. The new policy, in effect, "provided for the eventual demonetization of silver except for its use in subsidiary coinage."

In congressional hearings which preceded the passage of this new law, Secretary Dillon argued that the new legislation would not mean the disappearance of the silver dollar, since the Treasury had ample supplies of "cartwheels" and other traditional coins. But the market felt otherwise, and soon thereafter staged the dramatic epilogue to the Act of 1963 — the great silver rush of '64.

Part of the explanation was the inability of the Philadelphia and Denver Mints to keep up with the public's burgeoning demand for coin. The amount of circulating coin, which had increased roughly 50 percent in the first postwar decade, more than doubled in the following decade because of the heavy toll levied by vending machines, sales taxes, school lunches, parking meters and coin telephones — and because of the insatiable demands of the growing band of coin collectors and speculators.

The Mints, intent on supplying the public demand for minor coin, had not minted standard silver dollars during the entire post-war periods; in fact, the last of these "cartwheels" came out in 1935. Yet, for some time, there appeared to be no problem. Out of a total supply of 485 million silver dollars, about one-third were circulating in 1950, and about two-thirds in 1960. But then the outflow increased sharply, and accelerated even more in the months following the enactment of the new silver legislation.

Only 28 million "cartwheels" were left in Treasury hands at the beginning of 1964. Many of them went into circulation by early March, and then, when the House Appropriations Committee rejected a Treasury request for authorization to begin minting these pieces again, the rush was on. In two weeks' time the Treasury shipped out more than 11 million pieces to the tradition-loving Western states — and meanwhile distributed more than three million pieces to a jostling, haggling crowd which besieged the Treasury building in search of choice "Morgan" dollars of turn-of-the century vintage.

Out of the temple

Only 2.9 million "cartwheels" were left when, in the *Wall Street Journal's* description, "Secretary Dillon drove the money changers out of his temple." Exercising the option open to him under the terms of the 1963 legislation, the Secretary decreed that silver certificates thenceforth would be redeemable only in silver bullion at the monetary value of $1.2929 per ounce. Holders of silver certificates could continue to exercise their legal right to demand an amount of silver precisely equal to the silver content of a standard silver dollar, but they would be assured of getting only several slivers of metal in an envelope instead of a coin of considerable numismatic value.

Still, most observers continued to feel that silver dollars represented only a special case, and that a silver shortage was practically out of the question in the foreseeable future. In his 1963 congressional testimony, Secretary Dillon argued that, with the passage of the proposed legislation, the government's silver reserves would "assure an adequate supply of silver to meet our coinage requirements for the next 10 to 20 years." But over the next two years alone, consumption of silver came to exceed all earlier expectations, and it became readily apparent that even the Act of 1963 had failed to provide a lasting solution to the Treasury's problems.

Production of silver in this country had fallen short of U.S. consumption consistently throughout the postwar period, but the gap began to widen appreciably after 1958. In fact, domestic production actually declined slightly from 1958 to 1963, while domestic consumption for coinage and industrial use rose sharply, from 124 to 222 million ounces. As a result, the annual deficits increased from a sizeable 100 million ounces or so in the 1950-58 period to an even more substantial 187 million ounces in 1963. But then, in 1964 the deficit jumped to 289 million ounces, as production remained level in the face of a soaring demand of 326 million ounces.

Moreover, the same type of situation existed elsewhere, as total world consumption (outside the Soviet Bloc) grew to more than two and one-half times total new production. With total metal usage at 556 million ounces, the world supply deficit in 1964 amounted to 338 million ounces.

Foreign sources came to fill less and less of the U.S. deficit over the 1958-63 period, because of the expanding needs for the metal abroad. At the same time, returns of lend-lease silver which had been shipped out during World War II dropped steadily, from a peak of 103 million ounces in 1958 to zero in 1963. In making up the growing deficiency, Treasury stocks receded by 523 million ounces in the five-year period, to 1,583 million ounces in 1963.

In 1964, moreover, foreign demand actually comprised a drain on Treasury stocks, and this country became a net exporter of silver for the first time since the lend-lease shipments of World War II. Total exports during the year amounted to 110 million ounces, more than triple the 1963 figure, while imports declined from 64 to 55 million ounces. In meeting both this new export demand and the soaring domestic demand, Treasury stocks of the metal dropped 23 percent in 1964 alone, to 1,214 million ounces.

Hungry industries

An increase in industrial consumption of silver — mainly for use in photographic film, electronic components, and storage batteries — helped to intensify the growing shortage. Industrial consumption in this country, which had dropped from an annual average of 100 million ounces in the early 1950s to 86 million ounces in 1958, rose by more than 5 percent annually over the next five years, and then jumped 11 percent more in 1964, to 123 million ounces.

Overseas, the expansion in industrial consumption had been even more impressive, particularly in West Germany and Japan. Between 1950 and 1958, foreign industrial consumption doubled and by 1964 it increased again by half to 163 million ounces. Thus a shortage existed from industrial demands alone, since world industrial consumption exceeded total mine production by 71 million ounces in 1964.

The sharp upsurge in silver usage took place even in the face of a 40 percent increase in silver prices between November 1961 and June 1963. The demand for silver evidently was quite inelastic — unresponsive to an increase in price — because no known alternative equaled its high electrical and heat conductivity, resistance to corrosion and sensitivity to light.

Consumption of silver for photographic film, plates and sensitized paper — the largest single market in this country for the metal — increased at an annual rate of about 2 percent between 1959 and 1963, and then jumped 20 percent, to 40.3 million ounces, in 1964 alone. The photographic industry's consumption would have increased even more rapidly had it not learned to economize on its supplies. By extracting silver from photographic solutions used in developing film, for example, it was able to reclaim as much as 10 million ounces in 1964.

Under the stimulus of the sharp run-up in silver prices, the photographic industry also accelerated its research aimed at the development of substitutes. In many of silver's most important applications, however, no other material could be found with silver's unique ability to record an image when exposed to light. (The only major alternative was the use of electrostatic copying methods in office equipment.) Because silver was all but indispensable to the photographic process, its use in this field tended to increase with the continued growth of the industry.

The electrical-equipment and electronics industry represented another rapidly growing outlet. Consumption of silver in these fields rose almost 50 percent between 1959 and 1964, from 20.5 to 30.3 million ounces, and, as a result, the electrical industry surpassed silverware and jewelry to become silver's second market.

Unequalled as an electrical conductor, silver's use as an electrical contact had expanded until it could be found in practically every on-off switch and electrical appliance. Silver-wire contact relays also were at the heart of most computers and almost every piece of telephone and aviation equipment. Besides, suitable substitutes were not available for applications accounting for perhaps three-fourths of the entire market — primarily voltage connections for space vehicle guidance systems, military electronic systems and the like.

Consumption in brazing alloys and solders,

another rapidly growing field, expanded from 10.5 million ounces in 1959 to 15.8 ounces in 1964. During World War II the use of silver alloys as industrial joining metal gained impetus in the manufacture of shells, gun parts and ordnance. After the war, silver brazing alloys became important in air-conditioning and refrigeration equipment, electrical appliances, and automobile parts — in fact, in virtually every end-product where joining or bonding was involved. An entirely new application also arose: silver-infiltrated tungsten for rocket fuels, as well as silver brazing alloys capable of withstanding heat and pressures generated at supersonic speeds. For these applications, which require high temperature soldering, substitution of other materials was completely impractical.

Consumption of silver in storage batteries, a relatively new use, almost tripled between 1959 and 1964, reaching nine million ounces. Batteries utilizing silver (in association with zinc or cadmium) can be recharged, and they are very useful for applications requiring high output in relation to weight, for example in spacecraft and portable tools and appliances. Because these batteries rely on the chemical reactivity of silver, the substitution of other materials again was impractical.

For all these reasons, the industrial demand for silver expanded inexorably in the early '60s, even in the face of stable or declining demand for the metal in its more traditional uses. (Silver consumption for silverware and jewelry had actually declined, as a result of the rising price of sterling silver and the increasing acceptance of modern design.) But industry had to meet much of its rapidly increasing needs through the redemption of silver certificates. With each dollar exchangeable for .7734 ounces of silver, the availability of Treasury supplies held the market price at $1.2929, the level first reached in September 1963. But because of this drain and additional withdrawals for speculative holdings and inventories, redemptions totaled 141 million ounces in 1964.

Coinage pull

Nevertheless, by far the largest drain on Treasury stocks resulted from the tremendous expansion in silver usage for coinage. The actual silver crisis might have been delayed for years had not a terrific coin shortage developed. Consumption of silver for U.S. coinage began to rise sharply in 1961, and doubled over the next two years, reaching 112 million ounces in 1963. Even with this, the demand could not be met, and the coin shortage turned critical around mid-1964.

At one time limited to relatively few geographical areas to particular coins, and to particular seasons of the year, the shortage eventually became a general problem affecting the entire economy. Merchants found it difficult, and in some instances impossible, to make change. Banks, unable to satisfy their customers' requests for coin, found it necessary to ration their supplies. In fact, coin rationing was instituted down the line — from the Mints, to the Federal Reserve, to the commercial banks, to the public.

A new type of entrepreneur, "the money merchant," appeared on the scene, acquiring coins by the bagful and selling them to the highest bidder. The American Bankers Association staged a "Calling All Coins" campaign, in an attempt to bring to market the large supply of coins stored in the nation's piggy banks. And one chain of food stores conceived of the idea of issuing scrip, in denominations of 1, 5, and 10 cents, redeemable at the company's stores. (The chain dropped the plan when it found that it might be violating federal law.)

Some observers blamed the shortage on the growing use of some 12 million automatic coin-operated vending and service machines — ranging from parking meters and telephone pay stations to machines that dispense hot and cold drinks, sandwiches, candy, cigarettes, music and laundry and drycleaning services — and upon the growing coin requirements of toll roads, sales taxes and school lunches. Other observers simply traced the shortage to the burgeoning demands of a rapidly growing population and a rapidly expanding economy.

According to Treasury officials, the expansion in coin production should have been more than adequate to compensate for all these developments. From fiscal 1959 through fiscal 1964, the Mint had nearly tripled the production of coins, from 1.6 to 4.3 billion pieces — yet during that same period, population had increased only 8 percent, gross national product 28 percent and vending machine sales by 47 percent. Furthermore, the 48 billion coins available for circulation provided an average of 240 coins for every man, woman and child in the entire country.

The Committee on Government Operations, investigating the coin shortage, drew attention to the problem of availability as opposed to the actual supply of coins. Large amounts had been placed in circulation, but large amounts had been withdrawn, by businessmen anxious to assure themselves of an adequate supply for the needs of trade, by the nation's 8-to-10 million coin collectors — and by speculators, who bought up new coin by the roll, by the bag and even by the ton in the hope of profiting from a possible increase in the price of silver or coin. Incidentally, vending industry spokesmen argued in their own defense that only about $22 million remained in their machines at any one time, even though the machines swallowed some $3,500 million in coins every year.

As commercial banks found themselves with less and less coin, the "flowback" of coin returned to the Federal Reserve Banks had dropped sharply, from 11.4 billion coins in fiscal 1962 to only 6.7 million pieces in fiscal 1964. Deliveries of new coin from the Mint had risen, but the added supply had been more than offset by the drying up of return flows from circulation.

Coin shortage

By mid-1964, the return flow had shrunk to the point where it was less than the amount of new coin received from the Mint, whereas in more normal times the return flow was nine times as great as Mint deliveries. Consequently, the Reserve Banks were unable to deliver coin on request and had to ration the limited supply.

The rise in the price of silver to $1.2929 an ounce — that is, the development of a situation where the silver dollar was worth a dollar of silver — had encouraged the run on the Treasury's depleted stock of silver dollars, as described above. Thus, broad new public interest in coins was stimulated when the Treasury found itself with less than 3 million "cartwheels" and, amidst great publicity, was forced to restrict redemption of silver certificates to bullion.

Whatever the reasons for the coin shortage, Treasury officials decided that it could be overcome only by a rapid and substantial increase in production. By flooding the economy with coins, they hoped to convince those who held them for speculative reasons that the market would soon be saturated.

The Treasury previously had planned to boost production at the existing Mint facilities gradually over time, while waiting for the completion of the new Philadelphia Mint authorized by Congress in 1963. This new Mint was designed to have as much production capacity as the Denver and old Philadelphia Mints combined.

Events, however, forced the adoption of another approach. In mid-1964, the Treasury placed its two operating Mints on a round-the-clock seven-day-a-week intensified "crash program" in an attempt to double the annual production of coins from 4 to 8 billion in a year's time. It pushed into production all possible equipment and facilities — including the San Francisco Assay Office, which was assigned to produce annealed planchets for 5-cent coins and cents — and also purchased metal strip for coinage from private industry. Moreover, it obtained congressional authorization to continue the 1964 date on new coins indefinitely, so that it could flood the market with 1964 coins and thus destroy the incentive for dealers and hoarders to divert such coins from normal commercial uses.

As 1964 drew to a close, the Treasury was well along in its crash program. During that calendar year the Mint produced 5.5 billion coins, compared with 3.4 billion the year before — and in the second half of the year, it produced as many coins as in all of 1962. But about 203 million ounces of silver were consumed during 1964's rapid upsurge of Mint production. In fact, about 73 million ounces alone went into the production of some 200 million Kennedy half dollars, which collectors, hoarders and souvenir hunters snapped up as soon as they went into circulation.

By early 1965, the Director of the Mint was able to report a definite improvement in the coin situation. Businessmen were able to get through 1964, including a busy Christmas, without an actual crisis, even though consumer spending was up $26 billion (7 percent) for the year. The shortage of cents, which at one point had been critical, was completely relieved, while the shortage of nickels was almost over. Nonetheless, shortages continued in the minor silver coins, and the half dollar was not circulating at all.

At the same time, the problem of silver supplies had grown more acute. By June 1965, consumption for coinage purposes was running at a 300-million-ounce annual rate, and the Treasury's supply was down to 1,000 million ounces.

The Treasury thus faced the prospect of total depletion of its stocks within a relatively short period of time. In that event, the Mints would have had to stop coining dimes, quarters and halves of the kind then in use. The Treasury would no longer be able to offer silver to all comers at $1.2929 an ounce. The price of the metal could rise beyond $1.3824 — the point at which the silver content of these minor coins would be equal to their face value — and coins would begin to disappear from circulation. Obviously, drastic new action was required.

Demonetization of silver

The soaring industrial and coinage demand for silver and the rapid depletion of the government's silver stock forced the Treasury in May 1965, to make a momentous decision: "The world and the U.S. silver supply and production situation and outlook do not warrant continuation of the large-scale use of silver in the U.S. coinage," (*Staff Study of Silver and Coinage*).

Moreover, the Treasury argued for a once-and-for-all change; otherwise, subsidiary silver coinage undoubtedly could suffer from difficult transitional problems and from the fear in future changes in silver content.

On the basis of technical studies, the Treasury recommended copper-nickel clad on a copper core as the best metal for a new and permanent subsidiary coinage. This material had several desirable characteristics — ability to provide uninterrupted service as a medium of exchange; acceptability to the public in terms of weight, color, wearing qualities and operation in vending machines; ease and certainty of production; cost and availability; and compatibility with present coinage.

Copper-nickel was already the most widely used coinage material in the world. It was familiar as the basis for the American 5-cent piece, and it had circulated side by side with silver coinage in high-denomination coins in the United Kingdom. Coins of copper-nickel clad on a copper core could operate readily in vending machines without the difficulty, expense and inconvenience of modifying existing rejectors. Furthermore, the Mint had made sizeable production runs using the copper-nickel material and had not encountered any serious difficulties.

According to the Treasury, the cost of the alloy — 45 cents a pound, based on 33-cent copper and 79-cent nickel — would be much less than silver at $18.81 a pound. Coinage at the projected fiscal 1965 rate would require approximately 5,355 short tons of copper and 1,785 short tons of nickel annually. In both cases, the tonnages would represent a small fractional part of total domestic consumption and could be drawn from surpluses in the strategic stockpile.

Many of these Treasury recommendations were contained in the legislation which President Johnson submitted to Congress in June 1965, and which was passed soon thereafter as Public Law 89-91, the Coinage Act of 1965. In the president's words, the legislation was designed to "insure a stable and dignified coinage, fully adequate in quantity and in its specially designed technical characteristics to the needs of our 20th century life."

The need for this legislation was evident: "There is no dependable or likely prospect that new, economically workable sources of silver may be found that could appreciably narrow the gap between silver supply and demand. ... The one part of the demand for silver that can be reduced is governmental demand for use in coinage."

Under the Coinage Act, some 90 percent of the silver formerly used for coinage would be made available for other purposes. The new half dollar was a composite — an outside layer (80 percent silver, 20 percent copper) clad on an alloy core (21 percent silver, 79 percent copper). To the naked eye the coin would be almost indistinguishable from the old half dollar, but it would be 40 percent instead of 90 percent silver.

The new dimes and quarter dollars, although identical in size and design to the former 90 percent silver coins, were made silverless. Each of these also was a composite — an outer layer (75 percent copper, 25 percent nickel) clad on a core of pure copper. The legislation did not call for any change in the silver dollar, but it specified that none be minted for five years.

The government's readiness to sell silver bullion from its stocks at $1.2929 an ounce had previously provided protection against the melting of silver coins, since it effectively prevented the price of silver from rising above the face value of the coins. Now, since the Treasury intended the silver coins to circulate alongside the new coins, the Act provided further protection for the silver coinage by authorizing the Secretary of the Treasury to prohibit the melting, treating or export of any U.S. coin. Again, to discourage hoarding it stipulated that any .900-fine coins minted after the law's enactment would be inscribed with the date 1964.

Finally, the legislation authorized the President to establish a Joint Commission on the Coinage, a 24-man body representing the legislative and executive branches as well as the general public. The commission, when convened, would be expected to make recommendations on such matters as the economy's need for coins, technological developments in metallurgy and coin-selector devices, the supply of the various metals, the future of the silver dollar, and the government's future role in maintaining the price of silver.

Public opinion — as expressed in the congressional hearings which preceded the passage of the Coinage Act — was virtually unanimous in regard to the need for reducing the silver content of the nation's subsidiary coinage. Emotions ran high, however, on the question of "how much," as would be expected from the diversity of interests with a stake in silver's future.

Users and producers

Silver users, anxious to have ample supplies of the metal available at stable or declining prices, wanted silver to be completely eliminated from the coinage. They pointed out that total world production could fall 100 million ounces below annual industrial demand alone, so that even under the most favorable circumstances, Treasury stocks could disappear within a half-decade.

In their analysis, silver-consuming industries projected a sharp reduction world-wide in silver usage for coinage. In this country, Mint requirements could drop perhaps 90 percent from the 1965 peak to about 30 million ounces; in other countries coinage requirements could drop 50 percent, also to about 30 million ounces. (Most countries throughout the world had already eliminated or drastically reduced the use of silver for coinage.) However, consumers projected an increase in world-wide industrial consumption to 360 million ounces by 1970, even assuming a reduced growth rate in that segment of the market. The resultant world-wide demand, 420 million ounces annually, would substantially exceed the projected supply, which (optimistically) could be estimated at about 340 million ounces from mine production and secondary sources.

Silver producers took a somewhat different view of the future. Fearing that a sharp swing away from silver might trigger a price break, they argued for the retention of silver in the coinage to the maximum extent feasible. They claimed that the supply deficit had been abnormally inflated in 1964 by the hoarding of well more than 100 million ounces in the form of Kennedy halves and speculative stocks; furthermore, they claimed on the basis of current exploration that world mine production could increase by one-fourth or more within several years' time. (They were right on the first count, but wrong on the second.) Thus, they argued that increased mine production along with the gradual recovery of the 1,800 million ounces of silver outstanding in coins would permit the retention of some silver in both the half dollar and the smaller denominations.

Western legislators argued that Treasury stocks would soon be depleted unless the government permitted the price of silver to rise in a free market. Moreover, they felt that the Treasury approach failed to attract increased production and thereby in effect aggravated the coin shortage. Thus, the Western governors conference in 1965 resolved "that Congress provide for retention of silver in reduced amounts in all coins now silver, that an affirmative program be adopted to increase exploration for and development of domestic silver supplies, and that silver be permitted to seek its own price in the market place."

The vending industry, with its $3.5-billion annual take in coins, wanted coins that would be "compatible" with the nation's 12 million coin-operated merchandising devices. About half of these machines tended to reject coins that lacked the correct electrical properties, and major changes in them could require several years' time and could cost perhaps $100 million. Furthermore, the industry wanted coins that would pose no inconvenience to the consuming public, which plunked 30 billion pieces into these machines annually for more than 12 billion cups of coffee, milk and soft drinks, about 4.5 billion candy bars, and numerous other goods and services.

Finally, almost every company with a material in any way suitable for coinage — from aluminum to zirconium — pressed its claim for inclusion in the new coinage.

Actually, the Coinage Act, like the new coinage, was a composite containing something for nearly everyone. For Western silver producers, silver kept at least a stake in the coinage, with the new half dollars requiring at least 15 million ounces per year. Producers were also assured a minimum of $1.25 per ounce for their silver supplies.

Silver users did not get an entirely silverless coinage, but they did get silverless dimes and quarters. In addition, the continued redemption of silver certificates by the Treasury provided an effective ceiling on the price — at least for awhile. The vending industry also was well enough satisfied, because the copper-nickel and copper coins had the same electrical properties as the silver coins and worked in existing machines.

To the marketplace

Considering the persistence of the coin shortage, the release of the new coins apparently did not come a moment too soon. Despite the continued expansion in production of silver coins under the "crash program," Federal Reserve inventories of quarters had shrunk to only 15 million pieces for the entire nation prior to the 1965 Christmas season.

But with the help of the new Coinage Act — which authorized the reactivation of coin production at the San Francisco Assay office, the construction of new facilities, and the acquisition of necessary metallic strip, equipment and supplies — the Mint was able to achieve an unprecedented production rate. In November 1965, the Mint released more than 230 million new clad quarters, and scheduled the release of that many more pieces every single month — four times the highest production rate ever previously attained. These new coins carried the economy safely through the Christmas season without a crisis.

In early 1966, when almost 700 million new quarters already were in circulation and the first new dimes and half dollars were about to be released, Assistant Treasury Secretary Wallace told a Senate subcommittee that "the supply of our most vital coins is in better shape now than in any comparable period during the last 10 years. . . . There is no shortage of those coins most vital to the transaction of business." Flow-back and inventories at the Federal Reserve banks had increased in all denominations except the half dollar. But relatively few of the latter were in circulation, despite the production of 480 million Franklin halves in the 1948-63 period and of almost that many Kennedy halves in the following several years.

The Treasury scheduled total production for the fiscal 1965-67 period at 34 billion coins — enough to provide every person in the country with 180 additional pieces. Its objective was to manufacture enough of the new clad coins to replace over a relatively brief period all of the 13 billion old dimes and quarters then in circulation.

The steps taken under the new Coinage Act were successful in overcoming the nationwide coin shortage, but failed to halt the drain on the Treasury's silver supplies.

As 1966 advanced, in fact, the feeling grew that the Treasury might not be able to hold the line until the completion of the transition to the new coinage. The Treasury used only 54 million ounces for coinage in 1966, as against the 1965 peak of 320 million ounces, but its stocks continued to decline as both domestic and foreign industrial users increased their demands. So Treasury stocks dropped, and then dropped some more — from 1,218 million ounces in December 1964 to 804 million ounces in December 1965, and then to 594 million ounces in December 1966.

Moreover, an ominous threat existed in the form of the silver certificates that had not yet been turned in for redemption. At the end of 1966, all but 154 million of the 594 million ounces in the Treasury's holdings were earmarked for redemption of certificates.

The Administration acted to meet this situation by introducing a new piece of silver legislation in March 1967. (As P.L. 90-29, it became law on June 24.) The law authorized the Treasury to write off $200 million in certificates — on the assumption that at least that amount had been lost, destroyed or held in collections, and thus would not be turned in for redemption. In addition, it limited the time for the redemption of certificates to one year after the passage of the legislation. Any stocks then remaining, aside from 165 million ounces earmarked for the strategic stockpile, could be sold at not less than $1.2929.

The crisis would not wait, however, as the Treasury was hit by an unprecedented flood of orders for silver bullion during the spring. (During the first half of May alone, 33 million ounces flowed out — much of it out of the country.) Thereupon, the Treasury turned for advice to the Joint Commission on the Coinage. That 24-man commission — composed of 12 members of Congress concerned with silver policies, along with four members from the executive branch and eight public members appointed by the president — had been organized under the terms of the 1965 legislation to formulate long-range coinage plans for the post-silver era. Its first meeting was held in May 1967 when it was hastily convened to make recommendations dealing with the Treasury's current dilemma.

Immediately following the commission's May 18 meeting, the Treasury moved to assure the continued availability of silver to the U.S. market by discontinuing silver sales to other than "legitimate domestic concerns" and by invoking its statutory authority to prohibit the melting or export of coins. The result was the creation of a dual market. While the dealer price in New York remained at $1.30 an ounce, silver prices on the dealer and exchange markets abroad rose sharply.

Then, as soon as the President signed the new law on June 24, the Treasury wrote off $150 million of certificates, thereby freeing 116 million ounces of previously earmarked silver stocks and raising its free stocks to 135 million ounces. But the spread between the unrestricted price on world markets and the Treasury price proved to be too wide to be long maintained. With the London price fluctuating around the $1.70-level in early July producers quite naturally sold their supplies in the premium markets while industrial

users turned increasingly to the Treasury for their purchases.

By mid-July, the Mint had produced 8¼ billion new dimes and quarters — virtually duplicating the entire old stock of circulating silver dimes and quarters — and it was minting more of these clad coins at a 3.1-billion annual rate. Thus the problem of transition appeared solved: even if all other silver coins followed the silver dollars out of circulation, enough clad coins would be available in circulation and in inventory to meet the foreseeable needs of a growing economy.

At that point, following the Commission's second meeting on July 14, the Treasury halted all sales of silver at the old monetary value of $1.2929, and announced that it would sell thereafter only two million ounces a week, with the General Services Administration handling the sales at the metal's going market price. This reduction in Treasury offerings by itself would have pushed prices upward. But by an unfortunate coincidence, the very next day the copper strike shut down nearly all nonferrous-metals refineries, and thereby pulled off the market, for almost nine months' time, a large part of the normal refinery supply of silver.

Prices surge

These two developments in combination created an explosive price situation. The New York price immediately jumped from the old $1.29 ceiling to $1.87 an ounce, and after a brief period of stability, it surged upward again during the international financial crises of late 1967 and 1968. In June 1968, the New York price reached a whopping $2.56½ an ounce.

These rousing price developments, along with the Treasury's June 24 deadline for redemption of silver certificates, set the stage for one final silver rush. In the *Wall Street Journal's* description, "Newcomers needn't pack picks, shovels, and Klondike maps, but just have wads of paper money (silver certificates, to be specific), a future contract, and taxi fare to the nearest Federal Reserve bank." In May and June especially, when half of the final year's redemptions occurred, long lines of people formed early each morning at the New York and San Francisco Assay Offices to make the guaranteed .77-ounce-per-dollar exchange. (Those with $1,300 or more first had to exchange their certificates for a receipt at the Federal Reserve Bank.)

Altogether, 77 million ounces left the Treasury's coffers during this final silver rush — roughly three times more than had been expected on the basis of the earlier pace of redemptions. But with that transfer out of the way — and with allowances made for certain supplies earmarked either for the strategic stockpile or for the last small remnant of the silver-coinage system, part-silver Kennedy halves — the Treasury by late 1968 had about 250 million ounces left in bullion and coins.

The Treasury's one remaining commitment, then, was to help make up the deficiency in the nation's industrial consumption of silver — the difference between total annual consumption of roughly 50 million ounces. The deficiency was covered by the continuation of weekly GSA sales in the amount of two million ounces, the purpose being to maintain sales at a level that will have a neutral effect on prices.

In March 1970, the GSA reduced the number of ounces of silver at its sales to 1.5 million ounces a week. The sales were halted November 10, 1970.

In any event, demonetization was in effect completed on June 24, 1968, when the right to redeem silver certificates for silver was finally terminated. The transition of the last several years has brought about a slight change in the composition and appearance of the nation's coins and currency, but it in no way affects their value as a means of payment. Silver meanwhile remains a commodity, but it is no longer money.

Silver in the West

As a major mining center, the West has always had a vital interest in the fortunes of silver. And on frequent occasions since the opening of the Comstock Lode, the white metal has dominated the regional as well as the national stage. The voice of silver has been heard in the halls of Congress; and the economy, the society and the politics of the West have harkened to its voice.

Prosperity has been only a fitful visitor to silver mining camps, however. Prices have fluctuated violently over the years, while the long-term trend of output and employment has been downward. But, as of today, the versatile metal can bask in the upsurge of industrial demand which — along with the speculation which accompanied depletion of Treasury stocks — has caused prices to triple within the past several decades. In the context of this new situation, the silver camps of the West are bustling with new life.

The birth of the nation's silver industry occurred in the Washoe Hills of Nevada in 1858, as thousands of miners rushed across the Sierra from the already failing placers of California's Mother Lode to stake a claim in the fabulously rich Comstock Lode. Over the next twenty years, the Comstock bonanza helped finance the Civil War, provided the foundation for a transcontinental railroad, and established San Francisco as a glittering and opulent metropolis. By the time the lode played out at the end of the century, the bonanza had yielded over $200 million worth of silver and almost as much in gold.

But Comstock was only one of a series of rich silver finds. In the late 1860s, there was Black Hawk Canyon (Colorado), Cottonwood Canyon (Utah), Butte (Montana), and Owyhee County (Idaho). The 1870s and 1880s saw the development of the great silver deposits at Leadville, Colo., as well as the mines in the Calico District of California.

From this series of beginnings, the Western states, as the center of U.S. mining activity, soon made this country the world's leading silver producer. (After 1900, however, Mexico took first place.) Colorado and Montana, topping the roster of producing states in 1900, accounted at that time for 60 percent of the domestic total of about 58 million fine ounces. Utah, Idaho, and Arizona were next — and then came Nevada, despite the virtual exhaustion of the Comstock.

Western states have dominated the industry during this century; in 1966 they supplied almost 80 percent of the 44 million ounces produced domestically. Idaho's share began to rise dramatically in the late 1930s, and in recent years has produced almost half of the United States' silver; in 1986, it produced about 47.8 percent of the new silver mined in the United States. Most of it emanates from the rich silver-base deposits of the Coeur d'Alene District in northern Idaho, the home of the nation's three largest silver mines.

In 1986, the second largest producer of U.S.-mined silver was Nevada, with about 12.5 percent of the total. Arizona was a close third, about 12.4 percent. Montana produced about 10 percent of the total ounces of new silver mined in the United States in 1986.

Silver since 1970

Silver market manipulations in the 1970s by the heirs of oil magnate H. Lamarr Hunt once again spotlighted the white metal and resulted in a financial crisis in January 1980.

Traders on the Commodity Exchange in New York became aware in late 1973 of an anonymous source that had been taking delivery on silver contracts bought on the Comex.

An estimated 30 million ounces had been taken out of the market by mid-February of the following year, when the source of this activity was identified as Texas millionaire Nelson Bunker Hunt.

The 20 million ounces he accepted in December 1973 was the equivalent of about one year's production at Idaho's Coeur d'Alene mining district, and one source estimated the paper profits from his "squeeze" operation at $200 million in the U.S. market and $78 million in London.

Commodity brokers already expressed concern over Hunt's activities. Trusting that delivery will be taken on a relatively small number of contracts at any given time, they normally maintain only a small percentage of bullion to cover these contracts.

Faced with a large demand for delivery of contracts, they were forced to go into the market and buy silver at the rapidly escalating market price, which had moved from $2.80 an ounce in October 1973 to $5.70 early in the second week of February 1974.

Silver traders sought congressional aid to stabilize the market, without avail, estimating that the silver holdings accumulated by Hunt and his brother, Herbert, amounted to 50 million ounces, close to half the 117 million ounces held by the U.S. Treasury at the time.

The Hunt brothers' efforts to corner the silver market continued until January 1980, when the price on the Comex in New York closed at just under $50. The price of silver nosedived to $10.80 on March 27, 1980, and Hunt's broker, the New York based Bache Group, issued a call to the brothers for $100 million margin, which they failed to meet.

Bache Vice President Elliot J. Smith revealed that the firm met the margin call by selling the silver, and that the Hunt family still owed an unspecified amount of money to the brokerage firm.

At the order of the Securities and Exchange Commission, however, trading in Bache stock was suspended in the midafternoon of Thursday, March 27.

The Commodities Futures Trading Commission rejected a request by Bache that silver trading be closed and an administrative price be arranged for settling contracts.

CFTC Chairman James M. Stone commented that the commission's primary job is "to protect small customers and commercial users. We are not here to protect large speculators," he said.

The only grounds for suspending silver trading, according to Stone, would be if it appeared supply and demand were not the chief regulators of the marketplace. "And that has not happened," he said. He also

noted that permanent position limits, which would curb the speculation in which the Hunts participated, were being investigated.

Stone said CFTC investigators currently were looking into several troubled brokerages — including Bache — to be sure they don't dip into other investors' funds to cover their possible losses.

A later recapitulation indicated that Hunt lost an estimated $1 billion in paper profits after the price of silver plummeted to $10.30 in four days. The squeeze left him $33 million in debt to the Bache Group; $10 million to Paine Webber, another brokerage firm; and $4 million to St. Louis broker A.G. Edwards.

His biggest debt, however, was to Engelhard Mineral & Chemical Co., with whom he had a contract to buy 19 million ounces of silver at $35 an ounce, paying $665 million for metal which was worth only $270 million following the price drop.

Hunt escaped from this commitment by giving Engelhard 8.5 million ounces of silver worth $121 million, together with oil and drilling rights in Canada's Beauford Sea, which had a value of $350 to $700 million.

It was also learned as a result of the debacle, that Hunt was a 6.5 percent owner of the Bache Group, which sustained losses of $50 million, and faced an SEC investigation to determine whether the firm acted in the interest of all of its stockholders when it became involved in Hunt's silver deals.

Silver Thursday

As the full skein of financial embarrassments resulting from "Silver Thursday" was unravelled, it became apparent that ACLI Commodity Services and ContiCommodites Corp. were among those also affected by the credit they had given to the Hunts, as well as 10 banks and many other firms.

In an unprecedented move for a commodity exchange, Comex put together a revealing "Chronology of Activities of the Silver Market from September 1979 to March 1980," which detailed the extent of both individual and brokerage firm holdings in silver during this period, as well as the action taken by the exchange to increase minimum margins and limit the number of positions held by individuals, in an attempt to avoid a "squeeze" on the market.

Federal Reserve Board Chairman Paul A. Volcker subsequently encountered strong hostility when he appeared before a House committee to justify the authorization by the Fed of $1 billion in Fed loans to cover their losses from the collapse of the silver market.

At one time, Volcker revealed, the Texas brothers controlled two-thirds of the 170 million ounces of silver in circulation throughout the world.

A forced sale of these holdings, he argued, would not be in the interest of the brothers' creditors, and would shake the entire U.S. economy.

A wide-ranging two-year investigation of the Hunt brothers by the SEC concluded in July 1982 with a citation for a minor disclosure violation.

The SEC accused Nelson Bunker and Herbert L. Hunt of failing to file reports disclosing that they had acquired more than 5 percent of the stock of Bache Group Inc.

The Hunts agreed to a consent judgment in which they promised not to violate SEC regulations in the future, but neither admitted nor denied that they had done so in the past.

The Hunts dropped a multimillion-dollar lawsuit they had filed against the SEC, which accused government investigators of violating federal privacy laws during their probe.

The chief victim of the silver market "squeeze" was, of course, the white metal itself, which never has experienced substantial price recovery, and still lies like an albatross in the Hunts' portfolio.

Silver chronology

1792
April 2 — Authorizing act issued to strike U.S. silver dollar (standard weight 416 grains, .89224 fine), half dollar (standard weight 208 grains, .89244 fine), quarter dollar (standard weight 104 grains, .89244 fine), dime (standard weight 41.6 grains, .89244 fine) and half dime (standard weight 20.8 grains, .89244 fine). Dollar defined as a unit containing 24.75 grains of fine gold or 371.25 grains of fine silver (exchange rate between the two metals set at 15 to 1).

1834
Standard definition of gold dollar changed to unit containing 23.2 grains of fine gold; silver unchanged at 371.25 grains. Silver-gold ratio becomes 16 to 1.

1837
Jan. 18 — Authorizing act issued to change silver dollar standard weight to 412.50 grains, .900 fine; half dollar standard weight changed to 206.25 grains, .900 fine; quarter dollar changed to 103.125 grains, .900 fine; dime changed to 41.25 grains, .900 fine; half dime to 20.625 grains, .900 fine. Exchange rate becomes 15.988 to one.

1851
March 3 — Authorizing act issued to strike silver 3-cent piece, standard weight 12.375 grains, .750 fine.

1853
Feb. 21 — Half dollar standard weight changed to 192 grains, quarter dollar to 96 grains, dime to 38.4 grains, half dime to 19.2 grains. All remain .900 fine.

1854
Three-cent piece changed to 11.52 grains, .900 fine.

1859
Silver discovered in Comstock Lode in Nevada.

1860
Decade sees silver finds in Black Hawk Canyon, Colo.; Cottonwood Canyon, Utah; Butte, Mont.; and Owyhee County, Idaho.

1873
Feb. 12 — Authorizing act issued to strike silver Trade dollar, 420 grains, .900 fine. Half dollar changed to 192.9 grains, .900 fine; quarter dollar changed to 96.45 grains, .900 fine; dime changed to 38.58 grains, .900 fine. Half dime and 3-cent piece discontinued.

Standard silver dollar discontinued; bi-metallism effectively ended.

1875
March 3 — Authorizing act issued to strike 20-cent piece, 77.16 grains, .900 fine.

1878
May 2 — Twenty-cent piece discontinued.

Bland-Allison Act passed, requiring Treasury to buy not less than $2 million in silver every month for coinage or for backing silver certificates.

1887
March 3 — Trade dollar officially discontinued.

1890
Sherman Silver Purchase Act passed, directing the Secretary of the Treasury to buy 4.5 million ounces of silver bullion every month.

1896
July 8 — William Jennings Bryan delivers "Cross of Gold" speech calling for a restora-

tion of the bimetallic (silver and gold) standard.

1900
Bimetallism legislation repealed, Gold Standard Act passed, officially placing the U.S. on the gold standard. Gold dollar of 25.8 grains, .900 fine becomes the unit of value; all other forms of currency maintained at parity with the gold dollar.

1920
Jan. 10 — Silver reaches an all-time high of $1.37 an ounce, caused by speculation and world-wide monetary devaluation.

1923
Silver reaches an all-time low of 24 cents an ounce.

1933
June 5 — U.S. goes off the gold standard.
Thomas Amendment to Agricultural Adjustment Act passed, authorizing unlimited coinage of silver.

1934
Silver Purchase Act passed, directing the Secretary of the Treasury to purchase silver at home and abroad until the market price reaches the Mint price of $1.2929 an ounce, or until the monetary value of Treasury silver stock reaches one-third of the monetary value of its gold stock.

1935
Minting of silver dollars halted.

1961
November — President Kennedy orders Secretary of the Treasury to suspend further sales of Treasury's free silver, to suspend the use of free silver for coinage, and to obtain coinage silver through the retirement from circulation of $5 and $10 silver certificates. Silver begins upward price climb.

1962
Oct. 20 — Silver hits 42-year high in New York, $1.22 per ounce.

1963
March 13 — Silver stands at $1.28; when it reaches $1.2929 it becomes profitable to turn in silver certificates in exchange for silver bullion.
June 4 — Silver Purchase Act repealed; tax on transfers of interest in silver bullion repealed, $1 and $2 silver certificates to be gradually retired. Treasury is authorized to issue Federal Reserve notes in smaller denominations and is required to hold an amount of silver equal in monetary value (at $1.2929 an ounce) to the face value of all silver certificates outstanding.

July 8 — Silver reaches $1.29 in New York, the "numismatic melting point" at which speculators could profit by converting silver certificates to silver and then selling the silver.

Dec. 30 — Authorizing act issued to strike Kennedy half dollars, 90 percent silver, 10 percent copper.

1964
Jan. 29 — Treasury announces silver dollars depleted from the Treasury at the rate of 700,000 per week as citizens cash in silver certificates in exchange for silver dollars.

Feb. 11 — First Kennedy half dollars struck.

March 20 — House Appropriations Committee refuses to give Treasury funds to strike more silver dollars.

March 23 — Less than three million silver dollars left in the Treasury; long lines form outside the Treasury building as people wait to buy silver dollars.

March 24 — First Kennedy half dollars issued.

March 26 — Treasury Secretary Douglas Dillon issues an order saying citizens who want to exchange $1 silver certificates for a dollar's worth of silver will have to go to New York or San Francisco, and that the Treasury will redeem the certificates in silver bullion rather than in silver dollars.

April — Mints go on stepped-up schedule in an attempt to double the annual production of coins to ease the coin shortage. Treasury obtains permission to continue the 1964 dates on new coins indefinitely to stop hoarding.

June 17 — Senate Appropriations Committee approves striking of 45 million silver dollars.

Aug. 3 — President Johnson signs legislation to provide for the striking of the first silver dollars since 1935. Peace dollar design to be used.

Sept. 3 — President Johnson signs a bill authorizing the Secretary of the Treasury to continue using the date 1964 on all coins minted from this time on until he decides the coin shortage is over.

November — Government announces no more Proof or Mint sets will be made after 1964 until the coin shortage is over.

Dec. 28 — Mint Director Eva Adams says silver dollars will not be considered for striking until after the coin shortage is over.

484 Precious Metals — Silver Chronology

1965

May 15 — President Johnson directs the Bureau of the Mint to strike 45 million silver dollars before June 30.

May 25 — Treasury announces it has decided against minting any new silver dollars at this time, after a conference with the White House.

June 3 — President Johnson sends proposal to Congress calling for the elimination of silver from dimes and quarters and a reduction of silver in the Kennedy half dollars; asks Congress to reopen the San Francisco Mint for all coin processes; and for authorization to prohibit exportation, melting or treating U.S. coins.

June 24 — New coinage bill passes the Senate without change.

July 14 — House passes coinage bill with amendments: no Mint marks to be used on the new coins, and no Mint marks for five years; there will be no silver dollars for five years; the coins are to be dated with the year of issuance or coinage unless the Treasury Secretary decides this will contribute to a coin shortage; the President may enlarge the membership of the proposed Joint Commission on the Coinage to 24; and the Secretary of the Treasury has standby authority to prohibit the use of coins as security on loans.

July 23 — President Johnson signs the Coinage Act of 1965, providing for new dimes and quarters to be three-layered "sandwich" coins with faces of the same copper-nickel alloy now used in 5-cent coins, 75 percent copper, 25 percent nickel, and bonded to a core of pure copper; and for the silver content of the Kennedy half to be reduced from 90 to 40 percent. Bill includes House amendments as well as Senate provisions.

Aug. 23 — First clad coins, 25-cent pieces, struck at the Philadelphia Mint; these are also the first coins to bear the 1965 date.

Nov. 1 — Treasury releases first clad quarters to Federal Reserve banks for circulation.

1966

March 8 — Bureau of the Mint releases clad dimes and 40 percent silver half dollars for circulation.

June — Treasury Secretary Henry Fowler announces "the coin shortage is over."

July 7 — Treasury Department says all U.S. coins manufactured after Aug. 1, 1966, will be dated 1966, and on Jan. 1, 1967, current annual dating of coins will be resumed.

July 12 — Treasury Department announces new regulations: mutilated silver coins will be purchased at the Philadelphia and Denver

Mints at approximately the going price of silver bullion.

July 26 — Hearings begin on a proposal to sell the three million silver dollars in the Treasury Department's vaults at face value to the American Cancer Society and the American Heart Fund for resale to coin collectors at a profit. The Treasury Department voices its opposition to the bill.

Aug. 27 — Royal Canadian Mintmaster predicts silver will disappear from Canadian coins within two years.

November — *American Metal Market* newspaper predicts silver prices will rise to between $1.50 and $1.80 an ounce in 1967.

Nov. 2 — Treasury reports the silver stockpile continues to diminish, dropping by almost three million ounces during the five-day period from Oct. 28 to Nov. 2.

Nov. 17 — Treasury reports silver stockpile down to 608.5 million ounces.

Dec. 1 — Stockpile down to 601.3 million ounces.

Dec. 24 — Canadian Finance Minister announces Canada will drop silver from most of its coinage, changing to nickel, in 1968. Silver is to be retained in the dollar.

1967

Jan. 3 — Treasury announces its stockpile is at 591.9 million ounces.

March 1 — Treasury reports its stockpile dropped 45 million ounces in the first two months of 1967.

March 17 — Treasury Secretary Fowler asks Congress for the power to free the remaining silver held by the Treasury as backing for silver certificates.

April 10 — Treasury stock of silver down to 524.9 million ounces.

May 18 — Treasury Department discontinues immediately sales of silver to any buyers other than legitimate domestic concerns which use silver in their businesses. The Treasury also invokes its power to prohibit the melting, treatment and export of silver coins. The announcement creates a two-price system for silver; silver jumps to $1.60 an ounce in London markets.

June 2 — Canada announces it is changing to the manufacture of nickel 10- and 25-cent pieces.

June 5 — Senate passes a measure allowing the Treasury to write off lost or destroyed silver certificates and to free for other use the silver now held against the certificates, and to allow the Bureau of the Mint to return Mint marks to U.S. coins.

June 24 — President Johnson signs bill authorizing the eventual end of the redemption of silver certificates with silver bullion, and authorizing the Mint to restore Mint marks to U.S. coinage. The Treasury Department will stop redeeming silver certificates with bullion in a year. The Treasury also now has permission to begin the write-off of an obligation to hold 116 million ounces of silver against $200 million worth of silver certificates believed lost, destroyed or held by collectors.

July 14 — Treasury announces it will no longer keep the price of silver at $1.2929, saying it believes there are enough new clad coins in circulation to serve the nation's commerce even if all of the silver coins drop out of circulation. Silver sales from the Treasury stockpiles will now be handled by the General Services Administration (GSA) and will be limited to two million ounces a week at the going market prices (over $1.71 an ounce in London).

July 18 — New York silver quotations reach $1.87 an ounce. Coin dealers who are buying silver certificates for redemption in silver report a booming business.

Aug. 4 — GSA begins selling silver on a competitive bid basis.

Aug. 21 — Silver dollars in Uncirculated and circulated bags of $1,000 offered on the New York Mercantile Exchange.

Aug. 30 — New York Mercantile Exchange reports silver dollar market is brisk, with Uncirculated bags opening at $2,160 and circulated at $1,895 for $1,000 face. GSA reports about 10 million ounces of silver have been sold at its weekly sales since they began.

Oct. 12 — Treasury Department announces beginning Nov. 1 silver bars issued in exchange for silver certificates will be of fineness of .996 and .998 rather than the .999 fine bars presently issued.

Oct. 13 — GSA reports a sharp rise in silver prices, at $1.7715 an ounce for silver stores at West Point Bullion Depository.

Oct. 24 — New record set for silver price in New York markets as a dealer pays $20,000 for a contract of 10,000 ounces on the Commodity Exchange.

Nov. 8 — London reports an all-time high for silver, $1.951 per ounce.

Nov. 18 — Britain devalues the pound, from $2.80 to $2.40, causing increased silver speculation and a rise in early December prices to $2.17 an ounce in New York.

Nov. 22 — Treasury says it has enough silver to redeem all the silver certificates presented to them before the June 24, 1968, cutoff date for redemption.

Dec. 11 — U.S. to resume selling .999 fine silver to industrial consumers.

1968

Jan. 4 — First coins struck with Mint marks since those dated 1964.

Jan. 19 — Silver steady in New York at $2.07 an ounce.

Handy & Harman Review of the Silver Market terms 1967 market "confused, unpredictable."

Feb. 2 — Treasury reports it redeemed only $8 million worth of silver certificates during the first seven weeks of 1968.

March 1 — Joint Commission on the Coinage recommends governmental melting of silver dimes and quarters. Process in full swing soon after in the Philadelphia and Denver Mints and the San Francisco Assay Office.

March 25 — GSA announces prices ranging from $2.03 to $2.13 an ounce in its sales.

April 3 — Treasury reports the government has melted enough silver coins to produce 403,726.2 ounces of silver.

April 29 — Coin silver derived from melted coins will be sold to industrial users, the Treasury says. Sale of .999 fine silver is suspended; the GSA will sell a million ounces of .996 fine silver to .998 fine silver each week, beginning May 3, in addition to a million ounces of .897 to .900 fine coinage silver.

June 24 — Deadline for redeeming silver certificates for silver bullion. Silver certificates remain legal tender.

June 25 — Total Treasury silver estimated at 482 million ounces.

July 15 — Joint Commission on the Coinage meets to work out a plan for the disposition of the 2.9 million rare silver dollars still held in the Treasury vaults.

Sept. 10 — GSA announces the sale of 452,000 ounces of silver to 12 firms in category B, the portion set aside for small business concerns. Handy & Harman price per ounce stands at $2.220.

Oct. 16 — Silver continues month-long retreat; stands at $1.92 per ounce in London.

Oct. 31 — Silver prices show inclination to firm up; New York spot price at $1.933.

Dec. 5 — Joint Commission on the Coinage meets to consider a new non-silver dollar; recommends the 2.9 million silver dollars now held by the Treasury be sold on a bid sale basis at minimum fixed prices.

Dec. 20 — Treasury Secretary Fowler says the Joint Commission on Coinage has recommended minting non-silver clad half dollars to replace the existing 40 percent silver half dollar, and to make the current ban on melting silver coins permanent.

1969

Feb. 13 — Silver hits a 15-month low of $1.76 per ounce on the New York and Chicago exchanges.

March 14 — Spot silver at $1.79 in Chicago.

May 12 — Treasury Department lifts ban on melting and exporting silver coins following a meeting of the Joint Commission on the Coinage. The Commission also recommended minting a non-silver half dollar and a non-silver dollar, as well as selling the 2.9 million silver dollars remaining in the Treasury. Treasury also to reduce the amount of silver offered at its weekly auction from two million ounces to 1½ million.

June 17 — Silver slides to $1.59 an ounce in London, the lowest price since the British devalued the pound in 1967.

July 10 — Rep. James A. McClure and 146 other representatives propose the Treasury resume minting a 40 percent silver dollar with the likeness of Dwight D. Eisenhower on it. Sen. Peter Dominick introduces a similar measure in the Senate, joined by 20 other senators.

August — Members of the Chicago Board of Trade approve the establishment of a futures market in silver, calling for trading in units of 5,000 troy ounces at not less than .999 fineness.

Sept. 9 — GSA auction sets a new sales record, selling more than 14 million ounces of silver.

Sept. 22 — Silver advances, spot price in New York at $1.82 an ounce, with the one-year future price moving to $2.038.

Oct. 6 — Bill calling for a silverless Eisenhower dollar, a silverless half dollar and machinery for the sale of the 2.9 million silver dollars held in the Treasury fails to pass the House.

Oct. 7 — Senate joint resolution introduced to mint copper-nickel dollar Eisenhower coins.

Oct. 15 — Treasury reports its stock of coinage silver dropped by almost four million ounces during the week of Oct. 8 to 15.

Nov. 10 — Wright Patman, chairman of the House Banking and Currency Committee, confirms he opposes any silver in the Eisenhower dollars.

Nov. 17 — Office of Domestic Gold and Silver Operations chief Thomas Wolfe indicates GSA silver sales will probably be halted in a year.

Dec. 2 — Silver prices rise in GSA sale; prices at $1.9121.

1970

March 4 — Senate and House leaders reach a compromise agreement on a plan to mint 150 million 40 percent silver dollars and an undetermined number of copper-nickel dollar coins, all with the likeness of President Dwight D. Eisenhower. The conferees also agree that the Treasury will continue through Nov. 10 sales of silver at the rate of 1½ million ounces a week, and that the Office of Emergency Planning will transfer to the Mint 25.5 million ounces of surplus silver no longer needed in the nation's stockpile to be used for coinage.

March 19 — Senate passes Eisenhower dollar bill; House Banking and Currency Committee chairman Wright Patman maintains his opposition to striking silver dollar coins.

April 9 — Silver prices continue to falter, closing at season's low of $1.85 an ounce.

April 29 — Silver continues to slide, closing at $1.663 an ounce in New York.

May 13 — Joint Commission on the Coinage votes in favor of a silver Eisenhower dollar. Patman says he will use his influence to block House passage of the legislation for the remainder of the year.

June 4 — Federal Reserve Board proposes that banks stop counting silver coins they hold in their vaults as part of their reserve requirements.

June 17 — Senate approves a bill to authorize further adjustments in the amount of silver certificates outstanding, and to include Federal Reserve Bank notes and national bank notes in the estimates of notes that are irretrievable as a result of being lost or in collections.

September — Senate approves the Bank Holding bill, onto which is tacked authorization to strike 150 million Eisenhower 40 percent silver dollars.

Oct. 9 — *Federal Register* notes that effective Nov. 10 the U.S. Mints and Assay Offices will no longer accept deposits of silver for exchange into bars.

Nov. 10 — GSA silver auctions end with the Franklin Mint buying the last silver sold by the Treasury, marking the end of the government's 194-year role in the silver market.

Nov. 24 — Both the Senate and the House make concessions; passage of the Eisenhower dollar bill, tied onto revisions in the Banking Holding Company bill, draws nearer.

Dec. 8 — Senate-House conferees reach agreement on the Eisenhower dollar bill; approve coinage amendments authorizing the Mint to produce Eisenhower dollar coins in silver and copper-nickel, and half dollars in copper-nickel. Bill now goes before the Senate and House.

Dec. 18 — Senate unanimously passes Eisenhower dollar bill, following House passage the previous day.

Dec. 31 — President Nixon signs Eisenhower dollar bill, marking the first dollar coin issued since 1935. The Mint is to produce over a four or five year period 150 million 40 percent silver coins for sale at premium prices and an undetermined number of copper-nickel clad dollars for general circulation. The bill also eliminates the 40 percent silver content from the half dollar and authorizes minting copper-nickel clad coins in an effort to achieve general circulation of the half dollar; and authorizes the GSA to sell the 2.9 million silver dollars now in the vaults of the Treasury, on a bid basis. Most of the dollars to be offered for sale are Carson City specimens, 90 percent silver, minted between 1878 and 1891.

1971

Jan. 25 — First trial strikes for new Eisenhower dollar performed at the Philadelphia Mint.

Jan. 29 — Treasury announces Eisenhower dollars of 40 percent silver will sell for $10 per coin in Proof and $3 per coin in Uncirculated. Orders will be accepted beginning July 1.

Feb. 1 — Handy & Harman releases annual Review of the Silver Market, noting that the world silver markets were still dominated by speculators in 1970 for the fourth year in a row. The report also comments that with the end of GSA silver sales the price of silver dropped rather than climbed, contrary to expectations.

Feb. 3 — Denver Mint begins producing copper-nickel half dollars.

March 31 — First silver Eisenhower dollars struck at the San Francisco Assay Office.

April 1 — The Royal Canadian Mint begins accepting orders for its British Columbia Commemorative silver dollar.

April 1 — Trading in silver coin futures begins on the New York Mercantile Exchange, with the contract covering U.S. dimes, quarters and half dollars minted in 1964 or before.

May 17 — West Coast Commodity Exchange begins listing U.S. silver coins as a new commodity futures contract.

May 28 — New York Mercantile Exchange reflects softening silver prices; closing price slips to $1,205 for July delivery of a $1,000 face silver coin contract.

June 6 — A GSA spokesman says he expects as many as 15 million bids on the silver dollars being held in the Treasury.

June 29 — Prices drop on the New York Mercantile Exchange; $1,155 per bag of $1,000 face U.S. silver coins on July contracts.

July 2 — Prices bounce back; $1,175 per bag of $1,000 face U.S. silver coins on July contracts.

Oct. 5 — Silver slips to a four and a half year low, closing at $1.331 an ounce in New York.

Oct. 27 — Silver closes at below $1.30 an ounce in New York.

Nov. 1 — First Eisenhower dollars released for circulation.

Nov. 3 — Downward trend continues; silver at $1.27 an ounce for November futures.

Dec. 6 — The Treasury's 2.9 million Carson City silver dollars are transferred to the U.S. bullion depository in West Point, N.Y., as a major step toward public sale of the coins in about a year.

1972

Feb. 16 — San Francisco Federal Reserve bank official William Burke notes in a *Coin World* article that many traders are now referring to silver ironically as a "semi-precious metal." He notes that from a quotation of $1.80 an ounce at the time of the last Treasury sale in November 1970, the price went down instead of up, as many had expected, reaching $1.31 an ounce in October 1971.

March 27 — Trade begins on silver coin contracts in the Chicago Open Board of Trade.

April 12 — Sustained price advance peaks; reaches $1.65 an ounce in New York.

May 19 — Senator Jacob K. Javits presents testimony on a bill he sponsored to authorize the Secretary of the Treasury to make grants to Eisenhower College, Seneca Falls, N.Y., out of proceeds from the sale of Proof Eisenhower dollars sold by the Mint.

June 8 — Senate passes bill to supply 10 percent of the proceeds from the sale of Proof Eisenhower dollars to the Eisenhower College.

July 17 — Silver reaches a two-year high of $1.80 in New York.

Sept. 5 — Silver prices slide to $1.772 in New York.

Sept. 25 — The Silver Institute, Inc., sponsors an exhibition of the silver coins issued by over 30 nations in the past 10 years for those attending the International Monetary Fund meeting in Washington, D.C.

Oct. 31 — Bids open for Carson City silver dollar sale; public may submit bids for the

1882, 1883, and 1884 coins produced at the now obsolete Carson City Mint. Minimum acceptable bid placed at $30 for each coin, with bids limited to one coin of each year.

Nov. 3 — Coin firm Stack's of New York calls for a Securities and Exchange Commission investigation of the GSA and its use of the terms investment and investments in its Carson City silver dollar sale brochure. SEC later declares the GSA claims are beyond the jurisdiction of the SEC.

1973

Jan. 3 — GSA announces inspection of Carson City dollars complete, meeting standards set for Uncirculated coins.

Jan. 17 — Federal Trade Commission refuses to intervene at the request of Professional Numismatists Guild in the fight against advertising use of the term "silver dollar" for silverless coins.

Feb. 2 — A total of 700,000 Carson City dollars sold for $30 each.

Feb. 27 — Silver continues to rise; at $2.381 in London.

March 15 — Senator Jacob Javits introduces another bill to provide money from the sale of Eisenhower Proof dollars for the Eisenhower College, Seneca Falls, N.Y. Similar legislation introduced in 1972 died in the 92nd Congress.

April 17 — Senate Banking, Housing and Urban Affairs committee approves bill providing $1 from the sale of each Proof Eisenhower dollar to the Eisenhower College.

April 19 — Wright Patman introduces Eisenhower College bill in the House.

April 30 — GSA sells 70,000 more Carson City dollars, at $30 each.

May 2 — Senate approves bill allocating $1 from the sale of each Eisenhower Proof silver dollar to Eisenhower College.

June 8 — GSA announces it will auction off 2 million ounces of reclaimed silver obtained from Defense Department projects, not part of the national stockpile. Silver coin futures drop by as much as $50 a bag.

June 20 — GSA sells first of 2 million ounces of silver on a competitive bid basis, selling a total of 1,240,000 ounces.

Aug. 1 — Mint Director Mary Brooks announces there will be no 1973-dated copper-nickel Eisenhower dollars for general circulation.

Aug. 3 — Rep. Chalmer P. Wylie introduces bill to make an outright grant of $6 million to both the Eisenhower College and the Rayburn Library.

Oct. 31 — GSA closes bids on sales of Car-

son City dollars dated 1880, 1881, and 1885; bids total $14,071,958.

Dec. 10 — Royal Canadian Mint unveils first four silver coins in the Montreal Olympic commemorative series.

1974

Jan. 8 — Spot silver prices reach $3.40 in New York.

Jan. 21 — Silver soars to $3.97 in London.

Feb. 10 — Silver futures stand at $4.815 in London.

Feb. 14 — Silver at $4.427 an ounce in London.

Feb. 21 — Silver breaks world price record at $5.965 in London.

April 1 — GSA opens bidding for what is expected to be its last Carson City dollar sale.

April 11 — Silver drops; closes at $4.27 in New York.

April 17 — Silver bounces back, at $4.828 in New York for May futures.

May 3 — Silver shows new strength; at $5.501 an ounce in London.

June 5 — Silver Institute releases figures showing the rising price of silver in April drove 1,480,053 ounces of pre-1965 U.S. silver coins into the melting pot.

July 16 — Mint Director Mary Brooks announces the Park Hill section of Denver will be the site of the new Denver Mint.

July 22 — Rep. Wright Patman again introduces a bill authorizing grants from the sale of Eisenhower Proof dollars to the Eisenhower College in Seneca Falls, N.Y. The bill also gives power to the Bureau of the Mint to change the alloy and weight of the 1-cent piece. Patman's last Eisenhower College bill met defeat under a House rule technicality Aug. 3, 1973.

Aug. 3 — Eisenhower College bill wins House Banking and Currency committee OK.

Aug. 21 — The Pacific Commodities Exchange in San Francisco launches trading in silver futures with a new "mini-contract" for delivery of 1,000 troy ounces of silver.

Aug. 21 — The GSA says there are no plans for the present about disposing of the remaining one million Carson City silver dollars held by the Treasury.

Sept. 11 — Silver slips to $3.89 an ounce in New York. Mining stocks in both gold and silver drop.

Sept. 18 — Silver falls back to $3.87 an ounce. The Silver Institute reports substantial melting of silver coins by U.S. refiners during August.

Sept. 25 — House passes bill including a provision for $9 million grant to the Eisenhower College at Seneca Falls, N.Y., tapped from the proceeds of the sale of 40 percent silver Proof Eisenhower dollars.

Sept. 26 — Eisenhower College bill passes Senate, goes to president for signature.

Oct. 10 — Las Vegas blackjack dealer brings 1974-D Eisenhower dollar struck on 40 percent silver planchet to *Coin World* offices. U.S. Mint confirms that a quantity of copper-nickel clad dollar planchets unfit for striking into Proofs had been shipped from San Francisco to Denver, accidentally including an unknown number of 40 percent silver planchets intended for Proof or Uncirculated collector coins.

Oct. 10 — U.S. Bicentennial 40 percent silver coins to go on sale Nov. 15 through Jan. 31, 1975. Price of three-piece Proof sets $15, Uncirculated set $9, limit of five sets of each per customer.

Nov. 13 — Presentation set of 40 percent silver Bicentennial coins presented to President Ford at White House ceremonies.

Nov. 20 — Senate passes appropriations bill releasing Eisenhower dollar funds for Eisenhower College and Sam Rayburn Library.

1975

Jan. 10 — Royal Canadian Mint employees strike for higher wages, delaying production of third series of silver Olympic coins.

Jan. 19 — U.S. Mint reduces price of three-piece, 40 percent silver Bicentennial Proof set from $15 to $12 per set. Quantity limit removed and ordering deadline extended to July 4, 1976, for Proof and Uncirculated Bicentennial sets.

Feb. 19 — GSA considering new plans for the disposal of approximately one million Carson City silver dollars left unsold in earlier sales. Coins may be put in storage for future sale.

February — Handy & Harman, precious metal dealer, releases annual review of the previous year's metal markets. Refers to 1974 as "the most chaotic period in the history of the world's silver markets."

March 2 — Royal Canadian Mint strike ends. Production of silver Olympic coins to resume.

April 23 — U.S. Mint begins striking 40 percent silver Bicentennial coins for release on July 4, 1975.

June 24 — The newly organized Commodity Futures Trading Commission imposes new stringent regulations to protect public against fraud in transactions involving gold and silver bullion and bulk silver and gold coins. Exchange members must now file reports on silver market activities.

July 16 — Silver Institute credits the 1974 increase in use of silver for coinage to the Olympic Coin Program, which put Canada in first place as a user of silver for coins.

Oct. 1 — Bureau of Mines reports domestic industrial silver consumption increased seven million ounces above the first quarter of 1975; new mine production remains unchanged.

Oct. 31 — Bureau of the Mint taps over one million ounces of its silver stocks between Aug. 1 and Oct. 31 to produce 40 percent silver Bicentennial coins, Bureau of Mines reports.

Dec. 17 — Japanese exports of silver bullion at 219.7 metric tons during the first nine months of 1975.

1976

Feb. 11 — A-Mark Coin Co., Beverly Hills, Calif., spends $7.3 million to acquire the dollar hoard of LaVere Redfield.

April 1 — Indian government announces exporters of silver will be required to have a license, to be granted on a quota system. Before, India had permitted unlicensed export of silver. Prices rise in New York in response to the news.

April 12 — *Wall Street Journal* reports silver experts show optimism about an increase in use of silver as the economy improves.

Aug. 26 — Indian government decrees that all exports of silver be channeled through the State Trading Corporation.

Sept. 8 — The House Armed Services Committee votes to reinstate the bill permitting the sale of 118 million ounces of silver from the national stockpile after silver has been eliminated from an earlier stockpile sale bill.

Oct. 2 — The 94th Congress adjourns without having taken action on pending legislation authorizing disposal of silver deemed in excess of stockpile objectives.

Dec. 31 — Handy & Harman estimates industrial consumption of silver increased about 6 percent during 1976 to an estimated 167.5 million ounces compared to a revised figure of 157.7 million ounces in 1975.

World consumption for industrial and coinage uses combined, excluding Communist-dominated areas, amounted to about 442 million ounces about 7 percent ahead of Handy & Harman's revised 1975 figure.

Industrial consumption rose about 8 percent over the previous year, to some 395 million ounces; consumption for coinage decreased by the same percentage to 27 million ounces, from 29.2 million ounces in 1975.

An unexpected boost was given to silver supplies in 1976 as a result of the demonetizing and melting of 28,000,000 ounces of German coins.

1977

Jan. 12 — The Silver Institute reports coins supplied the ingredients for 4,579,119 ounces of silver refined in the U.S. during November 1976, the second month in a row that substantial quantities of coins were supplied to refiners of .999 fine silver.

Feb. 23 — Handy & Harman's 61st annual report on the silver market anticipates little change in conditions in 1977, with a somewhat higher price for the year.

March 9 — Rep. Silvio Conte, R-Mass., introduces a bill to release 118 million troy ounces of silver from the national stockpile. Experts have little expectation the bill will pass in 1977.

March 28 — Silver price marches to $4.983 per troy ounce in a bid to break the $5 barrier; yields to profit-taking in the next few days.

April 27 — Hecla Mines' Philip Lindstrom sees silver demand growing in 1977, and higher prices in the long term.

May 1 — J. Aron Commodities Corp. researchers believe inflation could carry silver to as high as $5.50 per ounce during 1977; they believe a price well above $5 will be required to free a substantial amount of silver coins for the refiners.

July 20 — Coinage consumed 10 percent of the silver mined in 1976, with 180 types issued by 72 countries, according to the Silver Institute. Canada, France, Austria, the German Federal Republic and Belgium were the major producers, with the United States sixth.

July 20 — Sen. James McClure, R-Idaho, introduces a bill which would set strategic stockpile objectives based on average annual import deficits. This would require a one- or two-year supply of silver for emergencies.

1978

March 8 — The price of silver on the Commodity Exchange in New York gains 35 cents since March 6, to clear the $5 price barrier.

June 7 — Sen. Gary Hart, D-Colo., proposes a silver stockpile sales target of 15 million ounces as a compromise between the Carter administration's request to sell 62.5 million ounces and other Western senators' opposition to any sale.

Oct. 17 — Silver price climbs to $5.945 on the Comex; warehouse stocks are down by nearly 10 million ounces.

1979

Jan. 3 — Silver consumption for the third quarter of 1978 (37.3 million ounces) was 5.9 million ounces, or 13.6 percent, lower than the second quarter.

Feb. 20 — The price of silver climbs to a record $7.94 on the Comex, in response to political and military tensions.

May 2 - Mint Director Stella Hackel says she would consider striking a silver commemorative coin for the Olympics in 1984.

July 25 — Rep. Larry McDonald, D-Ga., introduces bill that would authorize the purchase of 140 million ounces of silver over the next six years, calling silver "the first of the strategic metals the world will run out of."

Aug. 8 — The House is considering three silver bills: An administration request for the sale of 15 million ounces; a bill introduced by Rep. Silvio Conte, R-Mass., to sell all 139.5 million ounces in the stockpile; and the bill by Larry McDonald, to increase the stockpile by 240 million ounces.

Sept. 4 — Silver climbs to a record $11.02 on the Comex in New York.

Dec. 12 — Silver price on the Comex crosses $20, as it is traded for $20.08.

1980

Jan. 2 — House votes to keep silver stockpile intact.

Jan. 18 — Silver price soars to an all-time record of $50.35 in trading on Comex.

Jan. 28 — The Chicago Board of Trade joins Comex in halting silver trading for a three-month period to stabilize prices at $33-$36.50 level.

April 9 — Silver prices tumble below $20; Hunts fail to meet $100 million margin call.

May 7 — Commodity Futures Trading Commission probes the Hunt family's role in the "Great Silver Runup."

May 21 — The Federal Reserve approves more than $800 million in bailout loans to the Hunt family.

July 9 — The Silver Institute reports the Soviet Union was the world's major silver producer in 1979, mining 49.8 million tons, 400,000 tons more than Mexico produced.

Nov. 26 — The General Services Administration is accepting bids for 140,173.29 ounces of silver reclaimed by the Veterans Administration and refined by the New York Assay Office.

1981

April 1 — The Reagan administration announces plans to sell 139.5 million ounces of stockpiled silver.

May 27 — The Commodity Futures Trading Commission fails to pin a market manipulation "rap" on the Hunt brothers.

June 24 — House subcommittee on Seapower and Strategic and Critical Materials seeks to block Reagan administration's proposal to sell stockpiled silver.

July 8 — Sen. James McClure, R-Idaho, voices opposition to the sale of silver in the strategic stockpile.

Oct. 14 — First General Serices Administration sale of stockpiled silver draws few successful bidders.

Nov. 11 — Interior Secretary James Watt joins Republican Senators McClure and Symms and Reps. Craig and Hansen of Idaho in opposition to the silver stockpile sell-off.

Nov. 25 — Idaho Senators James McClure and Steven Symms introduce legislation to halt weekly silver stockpile sales and turn any excess silver into commemorative coins.

Dec. 9 — GSA suspends Nov. 25 auction after not accepting any bids at the two previous weekly auctions.

Dec. 30 — President signs Defense Appropriations Act with amendment that halts the sale of strategic silver for six months to permit a study of GSA sales and alternate disposal methods.

1982

Feb. 10 — General Accounting Office calls silver bullion coin sales a viable alternative to stockpile auctions.

March 8 — Spot price of silver drops to $6.85 on the Comex in New York.

May 19 — Seventy-seven nations issued 180 different silver coin types during 1981, including 14 that did not issue any the previous year.

July 7 — The U.S. Mint begins accepting orders for Washington commemorative silver half dollars.

July 7 — The use of silver for coins and medals in the first quarter of 1982 was down 100,000 ounces from the same quarter in 1981; but the 900,000 ounces consumed was 50 percent greater than that used in the fourth quarter of the previous year.

Sept. 15 — The price of silver reaches $8.465 per ounce, high for the year on the Comex on Aug. 26.

Oct. 14 — The Treasury Department announces plans to strike 1983 and 1984 .900 fine silver dollar Proof coins together with a 1984 Proof gold coin, to commemorate the 1984 Summer Olympic Games in Los Angeles. The silver coins will be struck at the San Francisco Assay Office and will bear an "S" Mint mark.

1983

Jan. 19 — Washington commemorative half dollar sales exceed 5 million.

Feb. 16 — Bureau of the Mint announces availability for future purchase of P, D and S Uncirculated 1983 and 1984 silver Olympic commemorative dollars.

Feb. 23 — Secretary Watt tells silver miners that the silver stockpile disposal is still "under review" by the Interior Department.

May 18 — Mint officials announce the availability of Prestige Proof sets in 1983 and 1984, each of which will contain specimens of the 1983-S and 1984-S Proof Olympic commemorative dollars.

June 29 — The Ad Hoc Committee for American Silver recommends that the 137.5 million ounces of silver in the stockpile be reduced to zero through the sale of silver bullion coins.

Oct. 5 — A joint survey by the Ad Hoc Committee for American Silver and the Silver Institute shows strong public interest in silver bullion coins struck from stockpiled silver.

Nov. 2 — Domestic silver usage during the first half of 1983, at 59 million ounces, was down 8 percent from the same period in 1982.

Dec. 14 — The Treasury launches a feasibility study for marketing bullion coins struck from stockpiled silver; no action is likely before 1985.

1984

Jan. 9 — Silver plummets to $7.79 as the U.S. dollar overwhelms foreign currencies.

May 23 — The House Armed Services Committee recommends the sale of 10 million ounces of stockpiled silver, leaving open the possibility of minting coins from the silver.

June 13 — Two separate measures introduced in Congress could pave the way for Americans to buy newly-minted Morgan dollars this year.

July 18 — Industrial consumption of silver for the first quarter of 1984 was 30.7 million ounces, up 5 percent from a year ago, according to the Bureau of Mines.

July 25 — World Mints in 1983 used nearly 500,000 more ounces of silver for coinage than in 1982, with 77 countries issuing 264 coin types, according to the Silver Institute.

Dec. 5 — Mexico's new silver bullion coin, the Libertad, is selling beyond expectations, with the 1983 version released Nov. 1 and a new method of pricing due to be introduced with the release of the 1985 coin.

1985

June 21 — The Senate passes the Statue of Liberty coin program with an amendment calling for a 1-ounce silver bullion coin to follow the Statue program.

July 9 — President Reagan signs bill authorizing the striking of a 1-ounce silver bullion coin and four gold bullion coins.

1986

Jan. 29 — Silver Users Association executive calls the failure of silver prices to move up as interest rates and the dollar weakened the "biggest surprise" of 1985.

March 12 — Mint Director Donna Pope predicts 4 million ounces of silver bullion coins will be sold during their first year of production to a House Appropriations subcommittee.

May 23 — Clayton silver mine in Idaho's Coeur d'Alene district joins Hecla's Lucky Friday and Sunshine mines in closing down because of unprofitable silver prices.

June 18 — Mexico releases 1986 Libertad silver coin; mintage of the 1985 date was 2,015,000 pieces. Mintages were limited to 1 million for 1982, 1983 and 1984.

June 25 — Silver bullion coin features A.A. Weinman's Walking Liberty design on the obverse; a new Heraldic Eagle design by John Mercanti on the reverse.

Aug. 20 — Mint announces plans to strike Proof specimens of its 1986 silver bullion coins, with Mint marks. Uncirculated strikes will carry no Mint mark.

Sept. 3 — Ceremonial striking of the first silver bullion coin is tentatively set for Oct. 29 at the San Francisco Assay Office.

Nov. 24 — The Mint releases American Eagle silver bullion coins to 27 authorized bulk dealers and marketmakers.

Dec. 3 — Mint expands production of silver bullion coins from the San Francisco Assay Office to the Denver Mint, with an end-of-the-year goal of 5 million pieces.

Dec. 3 — Preliminary orders for Proof 1986 silver bullion coins climb to 624,743.

Dec. 10 — Sales of Proof gold bullion coins amount to $168,117,400; Proof silver, $18,962,055, for a total of $187,079,055.

Dec. 14 — Gold and silver Proof coin sales pass $200 million mark.

1987

Jan. 14 — 1986 silver bullion coin production exceeds 5 million-coin goal by 96,000 pieces.

March 11 — The Mint reports the sale of 7,286,000 silver bullion coins since the program began Oct. 29; projects a need for 18-24 million ounces of silver in 1987.

Monthly silver prices

(Dollars per troy ounce)

	Handy and Harman, New York			London spot		
	Low/date	High/date	Average	Low/date	High/date	Average
1984						
January......	7.90/11	8.58/3	8.18	7.90/9	8.96/3	8.20
February.....	8.70/13	9.81/28	9.13	8.64/7, 14	9.86/28	9.11
March.......	9.34/23	10.04/5	9.65	9.39/23	10.11/5	9.65
April........	8.90/30	9.62/2	9.22	8.96/30	9.74/2	9.25
May.........	8.63/8	9.26/29	8.97	8.58/8	9.20/29	8.95
June	8.33/27	9.44/1	8.74	8.36/26-28	9.38/4	8.77
July.........	6.90/27	8.30/2	7.42	6.92/30	8.30/2	7.45
August	7.09/1	7.92/15	7.61	7.02/1	7.92/15	7.60
September ...	7.02/17	7.64/26	7.26	6.98/18	7.65/24	7.24
October......	7.14/9	7.66/3	7.32	7.10/10	7.61/3	7.29
November ...	7.02/30	7.80/13	7.49	7.05/30	7.85/7	7.50
December....	6.26/20	7.14/4	6.69	6.22/20	7.10/5	6.67
1985						
January........	5.80/7	6.37/31	6.10	5.83/7	6.33/31	6.09
February.....	5.60/25	6.32/14	6.07	5.45/25	6.32/15	6.08
March.......	5.57/12	6.74/27	6.01	5.52/12	6.66/29	5.95
April........	6.16/24	6.72/11	6.46	6.12/24	6.75/15	6.45
May.........	6.02/28	6.65/14	6.28	6.00/29	6.56/20	6.26
June	6.07/3	6.39/18	6.17	6.06/5	6.42/19	6.17

	Handy and Harman, New York			London spot		
	Low/date	High/date	Average	Low/date	High/date	Average
July	5.90/3	6.36/29	6.10	5.89/3	6.34/31	6.08
August	6.11/6	6.38/16	6.25	6.11/7	6.40/28	6.25
September	5.88/18	6.16/24,25	6.05	5.89/18	6.22/2	6.06
October	6.03/1	6.33/3	6.19	6.00/1	6.36/4	6.18
November	6.00/8	6.28/25	6.13	6.04/8	6.25/25,26	6.12
December	5.71/11	6.08/3	5.89	5.76/18	6.10/2	5.89
1986						
January	5.73/2	6.20/27	6.05	5.75/3	6.31/16	6.06
February	5.61/28	6.03/3	5.87	5.67/28	6.04/3	5.88
March	5.33/31	5.77/17,18	5.64	5.55/10	5.79/13	5.66
April	5.05/28	5.47/11	5.23	5.03/29	5.48/14	5.22
May	4.87/20	5.25/30	5.11	4.85/20	5.23/8	5.09
June	5.01/27	5.38/10	5.15	5.04/27	5.43/12	5.15
July	4.99/21	5.11/8	5.05	4.97/23	5.11/2,9	5.04
August	5.11/27	5.51/11	5.22	5.05/1	5.49/11	5.21
September	5.19/2	6.00/22	5.68	5.21/1,2	6.03/22	5.67
October	5.55/15,17	5.81/22	5.67	5.51/17	5.82/22	5.65
November	5.24/26	5.81/10	5.60	5.25/25	5.84/14	5.57
December	5.27/30	5.47/15	5.36	5.28/30,31	5.50/1	5.37
1987						
January	5.36/7	5.68/27	5.53	5.36/7	5.73/28	5.52
February	5.39/18	5.57/2,9	5.49	5.39/18	5.56/6	5.48
March	5.45/2,3	6.31/31	5.68	5.43/2	6.31/31	5.56

Source: Bureau of Mines; Handy and Harman

Platinum

Platinum is one of the rarest and most precious of metals. Each year, from 70 to 80 tons of platinum reach the free world market, compared to 10,000 tons of silver and 1,000 tons of gold. Ninety-five percent of the world's supply of platinum is mined in only two countries — South Africa and the Soviet Union — and it requires eight tons of ore to yield a single ounce of platinum.

Platinum's great strength, high melting point and unique catalytic properties have made it vital to industry, and its rarity and purity have created a demand for it in the jewelry industry as well.

Much stronger than gold, 1 troy ounce of platinum can be spun into a wire two miles long. It is all but impervious to acids; it does not tarnish; and will not melt, except at extraordinary temperatures. Moreover, as a catalyst, platinum is one of those rare elements capable of triggering a chemical reaction in another substance, while remaining unchanged in the process. And, since it doesn't oxidize, platinum has been used by the National Bureau of Standards to make weights that will remain accurate forever.

Until the late 18th century, platinum was considered a nuisance. Though traces of it have been found in ancient Egyptian inlays, artisans of the time probably believed it was some form of silver. Pre-Columbian Indians forged jewelry from copper alloys, but it was the Spanish who officially reported its "discovery" in the 16th century. They found it mixed with gold and called it "platina" — little silver. Most of the time, they threw the heavy metal back into the river, to permit it to "ripen" into gold.

The only "commercial" use made of platinum at this time was in the creation of counterfeit gold pieces, which were actually platinum coated with gold. When discovered by authorities, these imitation coins were thrown into the sea.

In the early 1700s, European metallurgists began to experiment with platinum for use in industry, but the metal's high melting point — 3,216 degrees Fahrenheit — proved frustrating to them. It wasn't until 1782, when scientists developed new techniques for melting platinum, that the metal became a useful material for artisans. People became interested in platinum because it has the sheen of silver, does not tarnish, and its metallic bonding makes it stronger than gold. Scientists continued to experiment with the metal, and in the early 1800s they discovered that platinum had five related metals in its group — palladium, rhodium, iridium, osmium and ruthenium. These were sometimes known as the "exotic" metals, because of their super-rarity. Today, many of these related metals are mixed with platinum to create special alloys that resist melting in the 3,000-4,000 degree Fahrenheit temperature range.

As a jewelry metal, the platinum vogue rached its peak in the United States in the jazz age of the 1920s, the era of Jean Harlow and platinum blondes. The icy-white metal was favored for its durability and nobility. Far harder than gold, it resists the nicks and scratches of daily wear; and, unlike silver, it never has to be polished to retain its lustrous sheen.

Platinum is much stronger than gold or silver, and so it is the preferred metal for holding fine stones and weaving delicate designs. It is also heavier, and is the purest of the precious jewelry metals. Most platinum is 95 percent pure, while sterling silver is 92.5 percent, and 18-karat gold is only 75 percent.

Ironically, it was platinum's very unique physical and chemical properties that brought about its eclipse as the country's premier jewelry metal in the 1940s. When World War II began, platinum was declared a strategic metal of critical importance to the national defense, and its sale as a jewelry metal was critically limited. Because the sources of platinum are limited to only a few countries, and it would be difficult to obtain in the event of a protracted war or other national emergency, the United States maintains 453,000 ounces of it in the National Defense Stockpile, and has a current goal of increasing this amount to 1,310,000 ounces.

While the vogue for platinum jewelry in America disappeared almost half a century ago, its popularity in Japan continues to rival or exceed that of gold to this day.

Ninety percent of platinum's use is as an industrial and decorative metal. Experts say that today platinum is used in one out of five products. In catalytic converters, the platinum catalyst changes noxious auto fumes into carbon dioxide amd water vapor. In 1983, platinum use in this area in the United States alone accounted for 32 percent of total worldwide fabrication demand.

Outside the United States, the British are moving toward banning leaded gasoline, and Germany and other countries are setting new air quality standard laws. In both cases, their next step is the installation of catalytic converters in automobiles, thereby opening a large market for platinum abroad.

Platinum also is essential in the manufacture of fertilizer, pacemakers, cancer-combating drugs, industrial rubies (used in lasers), high-grade optical glass, fiberglass and razorblades.

One of the most promising new areas for platinum is its use as a catalytic electrode coating in fuel cells, which are electrochemical devices that generate electricity. Fuel cells today are used in space shuttles and some military applications. Experiments with these cells are now being conducted by public utilities in New York City and Tokyo, to supply electricity to their city power grids.

Ninety-five percent of today's platinum is mined in South Africa and the Soviet Arctic, with Canada and Colombia producing most of the balance. Another potential source of the metal will be "recycled" platinum taken from catalytic converters in junked cars. The converters are removed by the wrecker and sent to a plant where the platinum is stripped off chemically. This process, which yields only a small amount of platinum per converter, promises to be an important resource for the future, because of the sheer volume of converters available for recycling.

Platinum has become a relatively recent investment medium, and its future looks bright. Institutional investors, banks and investment managers are showing an interest in platinum because of its bullish long-term fundamentals, and platinum bullion coins and investment ingots are appearing in banks and brokerage houses, as well as at coin dealers. Importantly also, a futures market is being established in Japan that will deal only in platinum.

Bullion Coins 14

Bullion coins

Bullion coins are a popular investment — and to a lesser extent, collectible — medium. But just what is a bullion coin? How is it different from any other precious metal coin?

The dictionary definition of "bullion" is "uncoined precious metal of precious metal fineness," so at first glance, the term "bullion coin" seems to be self-contradictory. For our purposes, bullion coin can be defined as a non-circulating legal tender coin intended for sale for its precious metal content rather than for face value or at a collector's premium.

However, this brings us to the even murkier world of the "Proof bullion coin," which is a collectible version of the "Uncirculated" bullion coin. Proof bullion coins are generally issued in limited mintages and at significant premiums above the precious metal value.

From the earliest days of coinage to well into the 20th century, coinage was tied to the value of the metal in which it was struck. In theory, a silver or gold coin's face value (denomination) was representative of its weight.

Since the time of the death of the Austrian empress Maria Theresia in 1780, restrikes of a 42.5 millimeter, .8333 fine silver taler dated 1780 depicting her portrait have been minted by at least 15 Mints, most of them outside Austria.

Prior to the mid 1970s legalization of gold ownership by U.S. citizens, this coin was accepted internationally, not only in Europe, but in areas of the world where a firm local coinage did not or does not now exist. In particular, these included southeastern Africa and the countries around and including Saudi Arabia.

The Maria Theresia taler, as it is called, can be found with many types of chop marks and other banker test marks, indicative of a coin which was being accepted in international trade. It was not the only coin which enjoyed this wide acceptance. However, it is by far the best known. An estimated 800 million of the coins have been struck to date.

The U.S. silver Trade dollar struck from 1873 to 1885, widely considered a bullion coin, was another example of a silver bullion coin used throughout the world for trade. The coin was intended for use in the Orient.

As recently as the mid-1960s in the United States, 90 percent silver coinage was issued for circulation; gold coinage stopped in 1933. Today, no nation on Earth issues a circulating silver or gold coin.

With a worldwide market in silver and gold where prices change daily, money can be made (and lost) in speculation. The stage was now set for government-issued bullion coins.

The Republic of South Africa in 1967 struck 50,065 pieces of a coin called the "Krugerrand." Like the 1-rand and 2-rand pieces still being struck by South Africa, the Krugerrand is composed of .917 fine gold. The gold rand had a gross weight of 3.99 grams; the Krugerrand 33.9 grams. The Krugerrand contains a full ounce of gold where the rand contained about an eighth ounce and the 2-rand about a quarter ounce.

(As a footnote, South Africa was at the time withdrawing from circulation silver coins minted from 1923-1964 and replacing them with pure nickel coinage. An .800 fine silver 1-rand coin was being struck concurrently with the gold rand.)

Through 1969, Krugerrand annual mintages held below 50,000 pieces. In 1970, the mintage jumped to 242,000, including for the first time 10,000 Proof versions. From 1971-73, Krugerrand mintages hovered around half a million pieces, with fewer than 10,000 Proofs.

In 1974, the mintage jumped to 3,180,075 pieces. This jump, which was to be sustained for the next decade, is attributable in large part to a single act — the Aug. 14, 1974, signing by President Gerald Ford of legislation lifting a 40-year ban on the ownership of gold by United States citizens.

Intergold

Today, the gold bullion coin industry is a multi-billion-dollar-a-year business. Credit can largely be given to one organization — the International Gold Corp.

Intergold, as the International Gold Corp. was known in the marketplace until its reorganization in 1986 into the Gold Information Center, was the marketing arm of the South African Chamber of Mines, the semi-official consortium responsible for distribution of the Krugerrand.

Intergold established offices worldwide with the goal of educating the investing public about gold in general, bullion coins especially and Krugerrands specifically. The measure of Intergold's success can be seen in that during the early 1980s, the Krugerrand commanded as much as 80 percent of the world's gold bullion coin market.

But two factors in 1984-85 beyond Intergold's influence combined to bring down the Krugerrand as the undisputed king of bullion coins. First, the price of gold stayed relatively flat and many investors shied away from tangibles. Second, and perhaps most devastatingly, the Krugerrand became identified as a symbol of South Africa's apartheid policy of racial discrimination.

Paul Kruger, for whom the Krugerrand is named and whose effigy appears on the coins' obverse, laid the foundation of apartheid government. South Africa was much in the news and the idea of political and economic sanctions to persuade South Africa to change its policy took hold popularly and in Congress.

It was perhaps inevitable that, when no fewer than 10 pieces of legislation introduced in Congress in 1985 called for some restriction on the importation of Krugerrands into the United States, the Reagan administration which had staunchly defended against sanctions finally acceded. Reagan on Oct. 1, 1985, signed an executive order banning the importation of the Krugerrand effective Oct. 11. No restrictions were placed on Krugerrands already trading within the United States.

However, the death knell had sounded. By late 1985 and early 1986, nearly every major market for the Krugerrand had been affected by government bans or banking agreements. Krugerrands are still traded by bullion coin investors, but the net effect of the prolonged debate about the morality of South Africa's policies and the destabilizing effect of months of doubt severely dulled the coin's sheen. The Royal Canadian Mint, which had introduced its .9999 fine Maple Leaf in 1979, was ready to grab the throne.

In 1984, despite growing pressures against South Africa, the Krugerrand still held about two thirds of the gold bullion coin market worldwide. By early 1986, that distinction belonged to the Maple Leaf.

The market

The bullion coin market is different from the numismatic market to which many collectors are accustomed. The bullion coin market operates in a tier system structured something like a ziggurat, with the issuing authority at the top. The issuing government produces and then distributes the coins in large quantity through a narrow system of large distributors. Distributors in turn sell to wholesalers, who sell to a network of retailers, who then sell to the public. There is, of course, nothing to prevent a distributor or wholesaler from also being a retailer.

At each step down on the ziggurat, the field widens. Let's say a government sells to 10 distributors (these numbers are simply to show how the marketing system works). Each distributor sells to 10 wholesalers, for a total of 100 wholesalers. Each wholesaler then sells to 10 retailers, for a total of 1,000 retailers.

The tiered distribution system (ziggurat) is often referred to as the "pipeline." It is the supply system to the consumer — the bullion coin investor. During a program start-up, such as with the Maple Leaf in 1979 and to a more dramatic extent the American Eagle in 1986, the period spanning the first release of the coins to the time when the pipeline is filled can often be rather turbulent.

Supply limitations can cause high premiums for a short time, but barring any sustained artificial restrictions on supply, the "open valve" effect subsides in a matter of a few months.

The ziggurat's most important function is in providing a buy-back market. Bullion coins are investments; investments must have a degree of liquidity. Governments will sell coins into the pipeline but will not buy them back.

It is the ziggurat structure which enables a ready two-way market in bullion coins. Large distributors absorb buy-backs while at the same time hedging their positions in the marketplace and hold the coins until the market turns favorable. A small dealer, such as a coin shop or local bank, would place a serious strain on its liquidity if it were compelled to buy and hold coins from an investor taking a profit. And investors would not likely purchase coins for investment that could not be resold for profit.

Legal tender

No aspect of bullion coins is quite so important nor quite so difficult to explain as legal tender status. Just what, in fact, constitutes a legal tender bullion coin is the matter of no little debate, and seems to change from nation to nation.

Legal tender status for a bullion coin distinguishes it, at least in the mind of the collector or investor, from the many privately-issued bullion pieces on the market. It is a badge of honor and legitimacy.

As an example, the American Arts Gold Medallion series of 1980-84, although issued by the United States Mint under congressional mandate, was not afforded legal tender status. The distinction between "official," which they are, and "legal tender," which they are not, may seem trivial to the point of an argument of semantics. However, the investors who were expected to purchase a minimum of a million ounces of the medallions every year stayed away in droves. The program is today largely seen as a failure.

The American Arts Gold Medallions were designed with the investor in mind, the larger piece containing 1.00 ounce of fine gold and the smaller 0.50 ounce. However, the pieces of 1980-81 have a "medal-like" appearance. Obverses are portraits of the artist with the name above the bust. Reverses show a scene reminiscent of the artist with the legend AMERICAN ARTS COMMEMORATIVE SERIES and the date of issue around. The edges are plain.

In 1982 the pieces were altered to give them a more "coin-like" appearance. Reeded edges and rim beading were added. Dates were moved into the field. The legend UNITED STATES OF AMERICA was added to the obverse and ONE OUNCE GOLD or ONE HALF OUNCE GOLD was added to the reverse.

In comparison to the Krugerrand, the later American Arts Gold Medallions certainly looked like bullion coins. The Krugerrand has a reeded edge and beading. The obverse has a portrait of Paul Kruger and SUID-AFRIKA • SOUTH AFRICA; the reverse the date, and the legends KRUGERRAND

and FYN GOUD 1 OUNCE FINE GOLD around a springbok design.

Marketing attempts for the sale of the American Arts Gold Medallions included the name U.S. Gold, which was given the program by J. Aron & Co., the firm that contracted in 1983 to be the prime distributor of the U.S. Mint-produced gold medallions. The public did not respond to this marketing attempt. The Mint set up a telephone ordering system which was also unsuccessful.

Maple Leaf

The Canadians did not overlook the success of the South African Krugerrand or the failure of the American Arts Gold Medallions program. The Canadians studied the U.S. experiment and did extensive market research in the U.S. — their largest single market potential at start-up. The study showed that a legal tender status coin with reeded edges was what the public wanted.

The Royal Canadian Mint introduced its .9999 fine gold Maple Leaf in 1979 in 1-ounce, quarter-ounce and tenth-ounce sizes. The Maple Leaf is the purest gold bullion coin in the world with a fineness of .9999 gold.

Production of the Maple Leaf gold bullion coins has at times consumed over half of all the gold produced by Canadian gold mines.

In 1985 sales of the Maple Leaf reached 1.878 million ounces, an 87.4 percent increase over 1984. This amounted to a 65 percent share of the worldwide market for gold bullion investment coins in 1985. Bans on importation of the Krugerrand and other government and private sector sanctions against South Africa played a major role in driving the gold-buying public to the Maple Leaf.

In June 1986 the half-ounce Maple Leaf gold bullion coin was introduced. Denominations assigned to the coins are $50 for the 1-ounce piece, $20 for the half-ounce piece, $10 for the quarter-ounce piece and $5 for the tenth-ounce piece.

The distribution system used for the sale of the Canadian Maple Leaf gold bullion coins involves approximately 25 primary distributors selected and recognized as being actual coin marketers, those who could make a two-way market and give the coin liquidity.

According to the 1986 Royal Canadian Mint Report, since the introduction of the bullion coins in 1979, 12.7 million coins have been produced using 9.5 million ounces of gold.

American Eagle

The United States gold and silver bullion coin program began with the release of the American Eagle gold bullion coins on Oct. 20, 1986.

The gold coins are being produced in sizes and denominations of 1-ounce $50, half-ounce $25, quarter-ounce $10 and tenth-ounce $5.

The gold bullion coins consist of .917 fine gold. The 1-ounce pieces are produced with guaranteed weight planchets, each containing a full ounce of .999 fine gold. The fractional pieces are produced with average weight planchets.

Designs on the gold bullion coins include a modified Saint-Gaudens Liberty design on the obverse and the "Family of Eagles" design by Dallas sculptor Miley Busiek on the reverse.

In addition to the Uncirculated gold bullion coins, a Proof 1-ounce version was issued during a one-month sales period ending Dec. 1, 1986. The Proof coin was priced at $550.

The 1-ounce, $1 silver American Eagle bullion coin was issued with first-strike ceremonies Oct. 29, 1986. The silver coins contain 1 troy ounce of .999 fine silver. The design includes A.A. Weinman's Walking Liberty design on the obverse and the Heraldic Eagle design of John Mercanti on the reverse.

A Proof version of the silver bullion coin was offered along with the offer for the gold bullion coin at $21 each. The "S" Mint mark appears on the reverse of the Proof silver bullion coin.

In the six months after the issue of the gold bullion coins, more than 2.3 million ounces had been sold. Silver bullion coin sales topped 9 million in just six months after issue.

Bulk distributors of the gold bullion coins include 26 distributors who purchase the bullion coins from the United States Mint at a percentage over the spot price of gold. Silver bullion coin distributors number approximately 30.

The American Eagle silver bullion coins are made from silver in the National Strategic Stockpile. Authorizing legislation specified that gold for the bullion coins must come from newly mined U.S. gold, unless it is not available. The Treasury Department used gold reserves for the program start-up and purchased on the open market when available in the U.S. and from countries which are signatories to the General Agreement on Tariffs and Trade (GATT).

Bullion coin programs exist in a number of other countries. China's gold Panda bullion coins are issued in sizes of 1-ounce, half-ounce, quarter-ounce, tenth-ounce and twentieth-ounce. The coins were first issued in 1982 with panda designs that change with each new issue. The China Pandas consist of .999 fine gold and are produced at the Shanghai and Shengyang Mints by the China Mint Company. While ostensibly bullion issues, the China Panda gold coins carry a numismatic premium due to low mintages. The coins are legal tender and carry nominal face values.

Mexican bullion coins include the .999 silver 1-ounce Libertads issued each year since 1982 (the first, dated and struck in 1982, were not released until 1984). The coins are legal tender.

The Australian gold bullion program began in 1986 with the issue of Proof Australian Nugget .9999 fine gold bullion coins in 1-ounce, half-ounce, quarter-ounce and tenth-ounce sizes. Each coin carries a depiction of a different Australian gold nugget. The 1986 coins were the first in the world to be produced in Proof .9999 fine gold. The regular issue gold bullion coins were issued in 1987.

Britain's gold bullion program was scheduled to be initiated in 1987 with the issue of the 1-ounce legal tender Britannia .9166 fine gold coin. Fractional issues in sizes half-ounce, quarter-ounce and tenth-ounce were scheduled to be issued later in 1987.

The Isle of Man bullion program was launched in 1983 with the issue of the 1-ounce platinum Noble. A tenth-ounce piece was issued in 1984.

Private bullion pieces

A variety of gold and silver bullion pieces are produced by private firms. The majority of these pieces are 1-ounce .999 fine silver round or rectangular bars, often called "art bars." Some private mints produce rounds with reeded edges which have the appearance of bullion coins issued by governments. Pieces in different sizes and shapes exist, as well as similar products produced in gold. Many of these products depict artistic renderings of past coinage designs, and should not be confused with actual coinage. These pieces are neither official government bullion issues nor legal tender, and should not be confused with government bullion coin programs.

Official state bullion issues exist. California, South Dakota and Texas have issued a variety of silver and gold bullion pieces. Many of these bullion pieces are exempt from state sales taxes.

Name/country of issue Denomination	Fineness	Gold weight[1]	Total weight[1]	Diameter	Edge
American Eagle[2]/United States					
$50	.9167[3]	1.00	1.091	32.7mm	Reeded
$25	.9167[3]	0.50	0.545	27.0mm	Reeded
$10	.9167[3]	0.25	0.273	22.0mm	Reeded
$5	.9167[3]	0.10	0.109	16.5mm	Reeded
Britannia[2]/Great Britain[4]					
£100	.9167	1.00	NA	NA	NA
£50	.9167	0.50	NA	NA	NA
£25	.9167	0.25	NA	NA	NA
£10	.9167	0.10	NA	NA	NA
China Panda[2]/China					
100 yuan	.9999	1.00	1.00	32.05mm	Reeded
50 yuan	.9999	0.50	0.50	27.00mm	Reeded
25 yuan	.9999	0.25	0.25	21.95mm	Reeded
10 yuan	.9999	0.10	0.10	17.95mm	Reeded
5 yuan	.9999	0.05	0.05	13.92mm	Reeded
Angel[2]/Isle of Man					
£50	.9167	10.00	10.90	63.00mm	Reeded
£25	.9167	5.00	5.45	50.00mm	Reeded
£5	.9167	1.00	1.09	32.76mm	Reeded
£2.50	.9167	0.50	0.54	27.0mm	Reeded
£1.25	.9167	0.25	0.27	22.0mm	Reeded
£50 pence	.9167	0.10	0.109	16.5mm	Reeded
£25 pence	.9167	0.05	0.054	15.0mm	Reeded
Krugerrand[2]/South Africa					
Krugerrand	.9167[5]	1.00	1.091	32.7mm	Reeded
Half Krugerrand	.9167[5]	0.50	0.545	27.0mm	Reeded
Quarter Krugerrand	.9167[5]	0.25	0.273	22.0mm	Reeded
Tenth Krugerrand	.9167[5]	0.10	0.109	16.5mm	Reeded
Maple Leaf[2]/Canada					
$50	.9999	1.00	1.00	30.0mm	Reeded
$20	.9999	0.50	0.50	25.0mm	Reeded
$10	.9999	0.25	0.25	20.0mm	Reeded
$5	.9999	0.10	0.10	16.0mm	Reeded
Nugget[2]/Australia					
$100	.9999	1.00	1.00	32.08mm	Reeded
$50	.9999	0.50	0.50	25.08mm	Reeded
$25	.9999	0.25	0.25	20.08mm	Reeded
$15	.9999	0.10	0.10	16.08mm	Reeded
Noble[2]/Isle of Man					
£100	.9995	10.00	10.00	63.00mm	Reeded
£50	.9995	5.00	5.00	50.00mm	Reeded
£10	.9995	1.00	1.00	32.76mm	Reeded
£5	.9995	0.50	0.50	27.00mm	Reeded
£2.50	.9995	0.25	0.25	22.00mm	Reeded
£1	.9995	0.10	0.10	16.50mm	Reeded
American Eagle silver dollar[2]/United States					
$1	.9999	1.00	1.00	40.6mm	Reeded

[1] Troy ounces
[2] Legal tender
[3] Composition is 91.67 percent gold, 3.0 percent silver and 5.33 percent copper.
[4] To begin in mid-1987.
[5] Composition is 91.67 percent gold, 8.33 percent copper.

Large silver bullion pieces

By Ronald J. Gillio

Throughout history, large silver commemoratives have been avidly sought by collectors, from ancient Greek decadrachms to Germanic multiple talers. This tradition was revived in modern times by Panama, which issued 20-balboa coins, minted from 4.16 troy ounces of .925 fine silver, from 1971 through 1979. The next step was taken by the Falkland Islands with the issuance of £25 coins in 1985 commemorating "100 Years of Self Sufficiency"; these contain 4.82 troy ounces of .925 fine silver.

The first breakthrough of the 5-ounce barrier was produced by the China Mint Company in 1985 for the Hong Kong International Coin Show, featuring a panda design, minted from .999 fine silver, measuring 65 millimeters (2.5 inches) in diameter. This was evidently the magic combination — 5 troy ounces, .999 fine silver, 2.5 inches diameter — which captured the public's interest and inspired dozens of new issues. Most pieces are made by official government Mints, though some are minted privately for governments. The majority have no legal tender status as coins, but are considered silver bullion medals. There are also a few "colossal" silver bullion pieces authorized by individual states, such as Texas and South Dakota. And even larger pieces are appearing weighing in at 6, 10, 12 and even 16 troy ounces! Virtually all are Proofs.

We have tabulated almost 60 pieces, and would like to invite readers to advise us of any issues we missed or new issues so that updated listings can be published from time to time, perhaps including price trends. Your comments and information will be greatly appreciated. Send comments to Ronald J. Gillio Inc., 1013 State St., Santa Barbara, Calif. 93101.

Country	Mint	Date	Denom.	Oz.	Fine.	Dia.	Mintage	Status*	Description
Albania	Budapest	1987	50 leke	5.34	.925	65	15,000	LT	2,600th anniversary of Durres Harbor
Austria	Vienna	1986	5 unzen	5.00	.999	— —	1,050	NLT	500th anniversary of world's first dollar
Austria	Vienna	1986	5 unzen	5.00	.999	65	2,500	NLT	Maria Theresia "Grand" taler
Austria	Vienna	1987	5 unzen	5.00	.999	65	1,000	NLT	Maria Theresia "Grand" taler
China	Shanghai	1985	— —	5.00	.999	— —	1,400	NLT	Sinkiang Province (Chinese Turkestan)
China	Shanghai	1985	— —	5.00	.999	— —	1,000	NLT	Hong Kong International Coin Show
China	Shanghai	1986	— —	12.00	.999	80	1,000	NLT	Panda — Hong Kong Coin Expo
China	Shanghai	1986	— —	5.00	.999	— —	2,000	NLT	Panda — ANA Convention
China	Shanghai	1986	50 yuan	5.00	.999	— —	3,000	LT	120th birthday of Dr. Sun Yat-Sen
China	Shanghai	1987	100 yuan	12.00	.999	80	3,000	LT	"Celestial Express" railroad
China	Shanghai	1987	— —	5.00	.999	— —	2,000	NLT	Cash vault protector
China	Shanghai	1987	— —	5.00	.999	— —	1,500	NLT	"Longevity"
Egypt	Cairo	1987	— —	5.00	.999	65	500	NLT	Queen Nefertiti
Egypt	Cairo	1987	— —	5.00	.999	65	500	NLT	King Tutankhamen
Egypt	Cairo	1987	— —	5.00	.999	65	500	NLT	Queen Cleopatra VII
Equador	Budapest	1987	50 reales	5.00	.999	65	1,000	NLT	Galapagos Island turtle
Falkland Islands	BRM	1985	25 pounds	4.82	.925	— —	20,000	LT	100 years of self-sufficiency
Greenland	Budapest	1987	5 piasters	5.00	.999	65	800	NLT	Polar Bear
Hungary	Budapest	1986	5 uncia	5.00	.999	65	2,550	NLT	Madonna and Child
Hungary	Budapest	1986	— —	5.00	.999	65	1,000	NLT	Treasures of Hungary U.S. exhibit
Hutt River	Johnson-Matthey	1986	100 dollars	6.00	.999	— —	2,000	LT	Statue of Liberty centennial

Country	Mint	Date	Denom.	Oz.	Fine.	Dia.	Mintage	Status*	Description
Hutt River	Johnson-Matthey	1987	100 dollars	6.00	.999	— —	1,000	LT	America's Cup
Isle of Man	Pobjoy	1987	5 crowns	5.00	.999	65	7,500	LT	America's Cup
Isle of Man	Pobjoy	1987	10 crowns	10.00	.999	75	5,000	LT	America's Cup
Japan	Osaka	1987	— —	6.00	.999	68	1,000	NLT	13th International Coin Festival Tokyo
Liechtenstein	Vienna	1986	10 taler	5.00	.999	65	2,500	NLT	Vaduz Castle
Mexico	Mexico City	1985	— —	10.00	.999	— —	unknown	NLT	Statue of Liberty
— —	Johnson-Matthey	1985	— —	10.00	.999	— —	unknown	NLT	Statue of Liberty
Mexico	Mexico City	1986	— —	10.00	.999	— —	unknown	NLT	Statue of Liberty
Mexico	Mexico City	1986	5 onzas	5.00	.999	— —	10,000	NLT	450th anniversary of Mexico City Mint
Mexico	Mexico City	1986	5 onzas	5.00	.999	— —	100	NLT	Catholic Cathedral
Mexico	Mexico City	1987	5 onza	5.00	.999	— —	unknown	NLT	Statue of Liberty
Mexico	Mexico City	1987	5 onzas	5.00	.999	— —	500	NLT	Legends — Volcanos (plain edge)
Mexico	Mexico City	1987	5 onzas	5.00	.999	— —	500	NLT	Legends — Volcanos (milled edge)
Mexico	Mexico City	(1987)	40 reales	5.00	.999	— —	4,800	NLT	"Piece of Eight"
Mexico	Mexico City	1987	— —	16.00	.999	— —	500	NLT	U.S. Constitution
Mexico	Mexico City	1987	— —	12.00	.999	— —	5,000	NLT	Panda's fifth birthday
Namibia	Budapest	1987	5 unzen	5.00	.999	65	2,500	NLT	Elephants — Equestrian Statue
Netherlands	Utrecht	1986	5 daalder	5.00	.999	— —	2,500	NLT	400th Anniversary of Trade Ducat
Panama	Franklin	1971-79	20 balboas	4.16	.925	— —	various	LT	Simon Bolivar
Singapore	Singapore	1985	— —	5.00	.999	65	500	NLT	Chinese junk "Keying"
Singapore	Singapore	1986	— —	5.00	.999	— —	1,000	NLT	Halley's comet
Singapore	Singapore	1986	— —	5.00	.999	65	850	NLT	100th anniversary of train service
Singapore	Singapore	1986	— —	5.00	.999	— —	5,500	NLT	Year of the tiger
Singapore	Singapore	1987	— —	5.00	.999	— —	4,000	NLT	Year of the rabbit
Singapore	Singapore	1987	— —	12.00	.999	— —	1,500	NLT	Singapore International Coin Convention
S. Dakota	Tri-State	1987	— —	5.00	.999	— —	unknown	NLT	Bison
S. Dakota	Tri-State	1987	— —	10.00	.999	— —	unknown	NLT	Bison
Switzerland	Bern	1986	5 unzen	5.00	.999	65	1,000	NLT	Helvetia — Eternal Pact
Switzerland	Huguenin	1986	5 unzen	5.00	.999	65	1,500	NLT	Helvetia — Eternal Pact
Switzerland	Huguenin	1987	5 unzen	5.00	.999	65	2,500	NLT	Helvetia — Matterhorn
Texas	North America	1986	— —	5.00	.999	— —	2,000	NLT	Texas Sesquicentennial
Texas	North America	1986	— —	12.00	.999	— —	2,500	NLT	Texas Sesquicentennial
Tonga	Pobjoy	1987	2 pa'anga	5.00	.999	65	7,500	LT	America's Cup
Tonga	Pobjoy	1987	10 pa'anga	10.00	.999	75	5,000	LT	America's Cup
Turks & Caicos	Valcambi	1986	50 crowns	4.37	.925	63	20,000	LT	Columbus
W. Germany	Hamburg	(1986)	5 reichsmark	5.00	.999	— —	2,500	NLT	60th anniversary of Graf Zeppelin
W. Germany	Hamburg	1987	— —	5.00	.999	70	1,000	NLT	750th anniversary of Berlin
W. Samoa	Singapore	1986	25 dollars	5.00	.999	— —	25,000	LT	Kon-Tiki
W. Samoa	Singapore	1987	25 dollars	5.00	.999	— —	50,000	LT	America's Cup

* Some pieces are given legal tender status by the government of the nation in which they were struck. LT = legal tender, NLT = not legal tender.

Bullion value of gold coins

Price of Gold Per Troy Ounce

Gross Weight (grams)	Fineness	Pure Gold Weight (Troy Ounces)	Country	Date	Denomination	$300	$325	$350	$375	$400	$425	$450	$475	$500	$525
33.875	.900	.980	Austria	1915	100 corona	294.00	318.50	343.00	367.50	392.00	416.50	441.00	465.50	490.00	514.50
18.273	.900	.5288	Canada	1967	$20	158.64	171.86	185.08	198.30	211.52	224.74	237.96	251.18	264.40	277.62
32.166	.999	1.00	Canada	1979	$50	300.00	325.00	350.00	375.00	400.00	425.00	450.00	475.00	500.00	525.00
13.34	.5833	.2493	Canada	1976	$100	74.79	81.03	87.26	93.49	99.72	105.95	112.19	118.42	124.65	130.88
16.9665	.9166	.50	Canada	1976	$100	150.00	162.50	175.00	187.50	200.00	212.50	225.00	237.50	250.00	262.50
16.965	.9166	.50	Canada	1977-1979	$100	150.00	162.50	175.00	187.50	200.00	212.50	225.00	237.50	250.00	262.50
41.66	.900	1.205	Mexico	1921-1947	50 pesos	361.50	391.63	421.75	451.88	482.00	512.13	542.25	572.38	602.50	632.63
33.93	.9166	1.00	South Africa	1967-1979	Krugerrand	300.00	325.00	350.00	375.00	400.00	425.00	450.00	475.00	500.00	525.00
7.99	.9166	.2354	Great Britain	1902-1931	sovereign	70.62	76.51	82.39	88.28	94.16	100.05	105.93	111.82	117.70	123.59
4.18	.900	.1209	USA	1908-1929	$2.50	36.27	39.29	42.32	45.34	48.36	51.38	54.41	57.43	60.45	63.47
8.359	.900	.2418	USA	1908-1929	$5	72.54	78.59	84.63	90.68	96.72	102.77	108.81	114.85	120.90	126.95
16.718	.900	.4837	USA	1908-1933	$10	145.11	157.20	169.30	181.39	193.48	205.57	217.67	229.76	241.85	253.94
33.436	.900	.9675	USA	1908-1932	$20	290.25	314.44	338.26	362.81	387.00	411.19	435.38	459.56	483.75	507.94

Bullion value of silver coins

Price of Silver per Troy Ounce

Gross Weight (Grams)	Fineness	Pure Silver Weight (Troy Ounces)	Denomination	Date	7.00	7.50	8.00	8.50	9.00	10.00	11.00	12.00	12.50	13.00	13.50
United States															
26.73	.900	.77344	$1	1840-1935	5.41	5.80	6.19	6.57	6.96	7.73	8.51	9.28	9.67	10.05	10.44
12.50	.900	.36169	.50	1873-1964	2.53	2.71	2.89	3.07	3.26	3.62	3.98	4.34	4.52	4.70	4.88
6.25	.900	.18084	.25	1873-1964	1.27	1.36	1.45	1.54	1.63	1.81	1.99	2.17	2.26	2.35	2.44
2.50	.900	.07234	.10	1873-1964	.51	.54	.58	.61	.65	.72	.80	.87	.90	.94	.98
5.00	.350	.05626	.05	1942-1945	.39	.42	.45	.48	.51	.56	.62	.68	.70	.73	.76
11.50	.400	.14792	.50	1965-1970	1.04	1.11	1.18	1.26	1.33	1.48	1.63	1.78	1.85	1.92	2.00
Canada															
23.328	.800	.600	$1	1935-1967	4.20	4.50	4.80	5.10	5.40	6.00	6.60	7.20	7.50	7.80	8.10
23.328	.500	.375	$1	1971-Date	2.63	2.81	3.00	3.19	3.38	3.75	4.13	4.50	4.69	4.88	5.06
(Non-Circulating)															
11.664	.800	.300	.50	1920-1967	2.10	2.25	2.40	2.55	2.70	3.00	3.30	3.60	3.75	3.90	4.05
5.832	.800	.150	.25	1920-1967	1.05	1.13	1.20	1.28	1.35	1.50	1.65	1.80	1.88	1.95	2.03
5.832	.500	.0937	.25	1967-1968	.66	.70	.75	.80	.84	.94	1.03	1.12	1.17	1.22	1.26
2.333	.800	.060	.10	1920-1967	.42	.45	.48	.51	.54	.60	.66	.72	.75	.78	.81
2.333	.500	.037	.10	1967-1968	.26	.28	.30	.31	.33	.37	.41	.44	.46	.48	.50

Gold, Platinum, Silver Prices

	Troy ounce	Fineness	6/4	6/5	6/8	6/9	6/10
GOLD+ (Spot)	1.0000	.999	$452.75	$453.50	$456.55	$452.65	$455.65
*American Eagle $50 (asked)++	1.0000	.917	—	$478.50	$474.00	—	$477.00
Austrian 100-corona (asked)++	0.9803	.900	—	$449.00	$444.00	—	$450.00
British sovereign (Elizabeth, new)++	0.2354	.917	—	$111.00	$110.00	—	$111.00
*Canadian Maple Leaf (asked)++	1.0000	.999	—	$472.00	$468.00	—	$475.00
*Isle of Man Angel+++	1.0000	.917	—	$472.00	$468.00	—	$475.00
*People's Republic of China Panda (asked)++	1.0000	.999	—	$545.00	$543.00	—	$549.00
Mexican 50 Peso (asked)++	1.2057	.999	—	$554.00	$547.00	—	—
*South African Krugerrand (asked)	1.0000	.917	$453.75	$465.75	$452.00	$460.00	$459.00
PLATINUM+++ (Spot)	1.0000	.999	$571.10	$571.10	$571.10	$582.40	$583.70
*Isle of Man Noble+++	1.0000	.999	$596.00	$596.00	$610.45	$616.77	$615.00
SILVER+ (Spot)	1.0000	.999	$7.680	$7.840	$7.670	$7.800	$7.770
American Eagle Dollar++	1.0000	.999	—	$9.90	$9.70	—	$9.84
*Mexican Libertad++	1.0000	.999	—	$9.90	$9.70	—	$9.84
United States silver coins $1,000 bag (asked)		.900	$5780.00	$5770.00	$5625.00	$5785.00	$5765.00
United States silver half dollars $1,000 bag (asked)++		.400	—	$2300.00	$2225.00	—	$2300.00

+++ Source: N.Y Mercantile Exchange
* Fractional bullion coins exist
C Markets closed

+ Source: Handy & Harman
++ Source: Manfra, Tordella and Brookes
+++ Source: Pobjoy Mint

Example of listing that appears weekly in COIN WORLD comparing actual published prices of gold, silver and platinum bullion with popularly traded bullion coins.

American Arts Gold Medallions
Striking, sales and melting figures*

Year	Size	Portrait	Number struck	Number sold	Number melted
1980	1-ounce	Grant Wood	500,000	312,709	187,291
	½-ounce	Marian Anderson	1,000,000	281,624	718,376
1981	1-ounce	Mark Twain	141,000	116,371	24,629
	½-ounce	Willa Cather	200,000	97,331	102,669
1982	1-ounce	Louis Armstrong	420,000	409,098	10,902
	½-ounce	Frank Lloyd Wright	360,000	348,305	11,695
1983	1-ounce	Robert Frost	500,000	390,669	109,331
	½-ounce	Alexander Calder	410,000	74,571	335,429
1984	1-ounce	Helen Hayes	**35,000	33,546	**1,454
	½-ounce	John Steinbeck	**35,000	32,572	**2,428

* The number melted is the number sold subtracted from the number struck. Number sold is in effect the final net mintage. Audited figures supplied by the United States Mint.

** The 1984 issues began with a striking of 20,000 pieces in each weight and to demand from then on, accounting for the relatively low melt figures.

Grading

15

Grading of coins and paper money

Grading.

Probably no other subject has been more hotly debated in American numismatists by collectors, and investors. Since the dealer first charged more for one specimen of a coin than for another of the same type, date and Mint mark simply because the second had less wear than the other, there has been controversy.

What is grading and why the controversy?

The grade of a coin (note, medal or token) represents what professional numismatist and researcher Dr. Richard Bagg aptly called its "level of preservation" in a 1977 collection of readings about grading that he co-edited. The grading controversy arises both from disagreements over the grade of a coin and the often enormous differences in price between two specimens of the same type and date of a U.S. coin, even when the only difference lies in the placement of one or two marks or surface abrasions from contact with other coins, commonly referred to as "bag marks."

The grade measures the amount of wear, natural mishaps and other surface degradation a coin has received after leaving the coining press. The more wear and surface marks a coin has received, the less it is worth compared to other specimens of the same coin with less surface degradation.

However, not all coins have received circulation wear since they were struck. These coins are called Uncirculated or Mint State, and rather than being easier to grade because there are no points of wear to determine, the coin becomes much harder to grade if it has received no wear.

A non-collector unexposed to the intricacies of grading might be expected to show surprise at this last statement. After all, he might think, it seems logicial that a coin which has received less wear is worth more than one which has received more wear. But if a coin hasn't received any wear, how can it be different from other unworn specimens of the same coin? Suffice to say, there are graduated levels of Mint State, as many as 11 (from Mint State 60 to Mint State 70), determined by such factors as contact marks, luster and depending on the grading standard being used, the strength of the strike and toning. Therein lies the heart of the controversy.

This chapter discusses the grading of U.S. coins in three parts: a background section about grading, a history of grading and written descriptions of grading levels. The chapter also discusses the grading of paper money and foreign coins, in lesser detail since there is less controversy in those areas.

Grading: What's involved?

Richard Bagg, in *Grading Coins: A Collection of Readings* which he co-edited in 1977 with James J. Jelinski, described the grade of a coin as its "level of preservation." It is not entirely accurate to call grading the charting of wear on a coin, since the very definition of an Uncirculated coin (also called Mint State) is "a coin which has seen no circulation" (in *Official American Numismatic Association Grading Standards for United States Coins*) and a coin with "no wear" (in *New Photograde: A Photographic Grading Guide for United States Coins*). However, Uncirculated coins are subject to other forms of surface degradation other than circulation wear.

A coin becomes subject to external factors

affecting its surface from the moment it leaves the press. The moment a coin is struck, it is pushed from the surface of the lower die. (Prior to 1836, the coin was removed manually by a nimble-fingered press operator; after the widescale mechanization of the Mint, mechanical fingers have shoved the newly struck coin from the die.) The coin then falls into a bin of other coins. When the coin hits the previously struck coins lying in the bin, the portion of its surface coming into contact with the other coins will probably be marred. Then, as the coins are bundled into bags for shipment to banks, the coins will scrape, scratch and bump each other.

Contact marks

The collisions between coins create a variety of surface marks called "contact marks" or "bag marks," the first factor concerning grading to be discussed. A contact mark may range in severity from a light, minor disruption of the coin's surface, to a large, heavy scrape. Generally, the bigger and heavier the coin, the larger and more unsightly the contact marks, due to the heavier weight of the coins.

The placement of contact marks plays a major role in determining at what level of Mint State a coin may be categorized. For example, marks that are clearly visible in the field of a coin, or on the cheeks, chin or forehead of a Liberty Head device, are more distracting than marks of equal severity hidden in curls of Liberty's hair or the wing feathers of the eagle found on the reverse of many U.S. coins.

The size of contact marks also plays a role in determining the proper Mint State level. Larger marks, of course, are more distracting than smaller marks. Remember, however, that a contact mark 1 millimeter long is less distracting on a large coin such as a silver dollar (diameter of 38.1mm) than it is on a smaller coin such as a silver half dime (diameter of 15.5mm).

The number of contact marks also play a significant role in determining the proper level of a Mint State coin. A coin with numerous contact marks is less appealing to the eye than a coin with one or two distracting marks. The diameter of the coin plays a role here too. A silver dollar with five contact marks scattered across its surfaces may be judged appealing; a much smaller half dime with five contact marks may be judged less appealing, since the half dime has a smaller surface area in which the marks may lay.

Luster

Another factor involved in determining the level of Mint State and high-level circulated grades is luster. "Luster is simply the way light reflects from the microscopic flow lines of a coin," according to ANA grader/authenticator Michael Fahey in "Basic Grading," a reprint from his series of articles in the American Numismatic Association's *The Numismatist*. James L. Halperin, in his *NCI Grading Guide*, defines luster as, "The brightness of a coin which results from the way in which it reflects light."

Luster is imparted to the surfaces of a coin at the moment of striking. The immense pressures used in the coining process create flow lines, the microscopic lines that trace the paths the metal took while filling the crevices of the die that compose the designs.

A coin with full luster is generally one which has a bright, shiny surface (although toning, to be discussed later, may obscure full luster), caused by the light reflecting off the surface of the coin. If the luster has been disturbed, the light reflects from the surface of the coin differently; the coin may appear dull.

Circulation wear erases the microscopic flow lines which cause the luster. Heavy cleaning, or cleaning with a substance that removes a microscopic layer of the surface metal, will also damage the flow lines and disrupt or eliminate the luster of a coin.

A Mint State coin cannot be lackluster. At best, an Uncirculated coin without full luster can be no higher than Mint State 63 under the American Numismatic Association grading standards. However, high-level circulated coins may show small patches of luster in protected areas.

Wear vs. friction

Once a coin enters the channels of commerce, it begins to receive wear. A man reaches into his pocket to pull out some change and his fingers rub across the surfaces of the coin, creating wear. A coin is thrown into a cash register drawer where it bumps against other coins, creating more wear. A dime is used as an inpromptu screwdriver, damaging the edge and creating more wear.

The amount of wear a coin receives determines its grade among the circulated grade levels. The high points of a design are usually the first to depict wear, since they are the most exposed. Then the raised inscriptions and date depict wear, and finally, the flat fields.

Circulation wear erases design details, ultimately to the point where only the slightest design features are visible to the naked eye.

The separate curls of hair tend to merge, the eagle's feathers are rubbed out and the inscriptions begin to disappear into the fields.

Coins with only the slightest hint of wear are called About Uncirculated, a term which, if studied closely, defies logic (a coin is either Uncirculated or it is not). Then, in descending order, are Extremely Fine, Very Fine, Fine, Very Good, Good, About Good, Fair (and many years ago, Poor). Some of the higher circulated grades are broken into several levels to denote, for example, an Extremely Fine coin of higher quality than another legitimate Extremely Fine coin.

Many hobbyists differentiate between circulation wear and another form of wear labeled "friction." According to Halperin in *NCI Grading Guide,* friction is "A disturbance which appears either on the high points of a coin or in the fields, as a result of that coin rubbing against other projections." It is often referred to as cabinet friction, a term applied to the minute wear a coin received when sliding back and forth in the drawer of a cabinet used for storage by earlier numismatists.

Friction does disturb the luster of the coin, but it should not disturb the metal underneath. If it does, the disturbance falls into the category of wear. It may be difficult for a novice to distinguish between the two. However, a close examination of the suspected friction should reveal whether the metal itself has been disturbed, and not just the surface luster.

Some grading standards permit coins with friction to be Mint State. For example, the ANA distinguishes between a coin with circulation wear and one with friction wear, permitting Mint State coins to possess small amounts of friction.

Strike

Strike is "The sharpness of detail which the coin had when it was Mint State," according to Halperin; Fahey defines it as "the evenness and fullness of metal-flow into all the crevices of a die."

The amount of pressure used to strike a coin controls the sharpness of a strike. Design elements may also affect the strike; if two large design features are centered on both sides of the same coin, there may not be enough metal to flow into every little crevice of the design, thus leaving some details weak and ill-defined

A coin with a sharp strike has sharp design details. For example, the curls of hair on Liberty's head are strong and distinct. The feathers on the eagle's wings and breast are clearly

visible. All of the other design details, legends and other elements are sharp and well-defined.

A coin with a weak strike has weak and ill-defined design details. It may look worn, since design details are missing from the high points of a coin. However, luster is unimpaired. Lower striking pressures may not force the metal into the deepest crevices of the die (the highest point on the coin), thus the weaker design details.

The American Numismatic Association does not take strike into consideration when determining the grade of a coin. The ANA uses a technical grading system, which considers only those factors taking place after the strike.

However, most dealers consider strike an important part of a coin's grade. An Uncirculated coin relatively free of marks and with full luster may still be placed at the lower end of the Mint State scale if it has a weak strike.

Strike does affect the value of a coin. A coin with a sharp strike will generally have a higher value than a coin with a weak strike, all other factors being equal. ANA graders acknowledge that while strike does not affect the grade under the ANA standards, it does affect the value.

Toning and color

As coins age, the original color changes in reaction to the environment. The original red of copper coins becomes brown (or green; witness the copper of the Statue of Liberty, which once had a deep copper color). Silver coins may tone into any color of the rainbow, depending on enviromental factors. Gold is a more stable metal and even when immersed in seawater for centuries, generally shows little change in tone and color.

Many years ago, toned coins, particularly silver coins, were judged unattractive. Silver coins were "dipped," placed into a chemical solution that removed the toning and restored the shiny surface by stripping away the outer surface of the silver or the dirt.

However, in the last decade in the United States, attractively toned coins are more appreciated from an aesthetic viewpoint. A silver dollar with rainbow toning may bring a considerable premium because of the its coloration. Still, coins which exhibit unattractive tarnish (a form of toning) are still considered to be lesser specimens.

Because attractively toned coins bring higher prices, some unscrupulous individuals have devised ways of artificially toning coins. Some use the bluing materials used by gunsmiths. Others bake their coins in ovens using various substances to impart different colors.

Novices will find it difficult to judge between natural toning and artificial toning. Experience is important here. An individual who has looked at a large number of coins will find that he can determine at a glance whether the toning is natural or whether it looks "odd."

Other factors

There are other factors involved in grading that under some grading standards, do not affect the grade but may affect the value. Under such standards, those same factors affect both the grade and the value of the coin.

Among these factors are die scratches, not to be confused with "hairline" scratches. Die scratches are thin raised lines on a coin, resulting from minute scratches in the surface of the die. A hairline is a thin scratch into the surface of a coin.

A close examination of a coin's surface through a magnifying glass should indicate whether a line on a coin is raised, and thus a die scratch, or incused, making it a hairline scratch.

Hairlines tend to affect the value more than die scratches. The ANA will not lower the grade of a coin for die scratches, since the scratches took place before the striking. Other grading standards, however, will lower the grade of a coin for more extensive, distracting die scratches.

Adjustment marks are often found on older U.S. silver and gold coins. Planchets (unstruck coins) were individually weighed before striking. If found to be a little overweight, the excess gold or silver was filed away.

The striking pressures often did not obliterate the adjustment marks, which may resemble a series of parallel grooves. Under ANA standards, adjustment marks do not affect the grade, although they may affect value. Under other standards, adjustment marks may affect both the grade and the value.

Grading history

As any regular reader of letters to the editor of any numismatic publication can tell you, grading is one of the most frequent and most hotly debated issues of all. One series of letters appearing in a monthly magazine, the *American Journal of Numismatics,* concerning a major auction, pits the dealer, the consignor of the coins and a bidder against each other in a grading dispute. However, the series of letters did not run in a recent issue of *Coin World,* but in two issues of the magazine dated November and December 1868. Nothing is new under the sun.

The grading of Edward Cogan, the first full-time coin dealer in the United States, has been described by modern numismatist John W. Adams as on the "conservative end of the spectrum." Therefore, his letter to the editor of the *American Journal of Numismatics* published in the November 1868 issue is enlightening. Cogan had attended the Oct. 28-29, 1868, auction of the collection of J. Colvin Randall, conducted in Philadelphia by Mason & Co. It was, incidentally, Ebenezer Locke Mason's first public auction.

Cogan's first letter was critical of the grading in the auction. Among the quarter dollars, he noted that "five or six of them [were] described as Proofs, without stating that they were considerably injured by circulation." Three dimes, dated 1796, 1798 and 1800, "were much over-described," Cogan said. "In regard to the Cents, I regret to say that many of them were ridiculously over-described — in the earlier dates especially," he added.

Mason was angered by Cogan's comments, and penned a letter in response that appeared in the December *AJN.* He wrote that Cogan's comments were "very vague and indefinite," basically complaining that Cogan had failed to note that some coins were described accurately. Mason notes that in regards to one 1793 Flowing Hair, Chain, AMERI. cent mentioned by Cogan as bringing the low price of $1.25, the coin was cataloged as "Poor." Mason asks, "Is that coin over-described?"

Cogan, responding in a second letter, also appearing in the December issue, records a conversation he had with the consignor, J. Colvin Randall, whom he told that a 1793 cent described as Uncirculated was a "long way" from being Uncirculated. Randall replied, according to Cogan, "Why, it is Uncirculated for a 1793 cent."

Rarity and wear

What this dispute shows is that even 119 years ago, grading was a subject taken very seriously by collectors and dealers. The letters indicate that there was even less standardization concerning grading terms than there is today. There were, however, fewer grades.

A perusal of several issues of the *American Journal of Numismatics* in 1866-67 reveals about a half dozen grading terms in use: Good, Very Good, Fine, Very Fine, Uncirculated; in addition, Proof and nearly Proof appear.

As Cogan noted in his two letters, some catalogers in the 1860s graded not only by the amount of wear on a coin, but by its rarity. Mason even admitted that "a spot so indistinct that a microscope would scarcely make the defect observable, [on] such excessively rare coins, in this condition, were usually described as uncirculated." Mason noted that the practice of omitting mention of such wear "had been customary with all persons cataloguing collections . . . on coins very nearly unique."

The practice of grading by a combination of wear and rarity was still in force at the end of the 1870s, some 11 years after the Cogan-Mason letters. In W. Elliot Woodward's Oct. 15-16, 1879, auction, for example, a 1796 Draped Bust quarter dollar is described as "Fair for this date." In the same auction, the cataloger says a 1799 Draped Bust cent "may be fairly called very fine for date; extremely rare."

Woodward was also using a greater number of grading terms in his auction catalogs of 1879-82: Good, Very Good, Fine, Very Fine, Nearly Uncirculated, Almost Uncirculated, Uncirculated and Brilliant Uncirculated, among others.

Beginnings of codification

It wasn't until a decade later, in the 1890s, that U.S. numismatists began to seriously consider codification of standard grading terms. Richard Bagg and James J. Jelinski cover this issue in quite some detail in their *Grading Coins: A Collection of Readings.* The 1977 book compiles articles from various numismatic publications, beginning with *The Numismatist* in February 1892.

A February 1892 article by J. Hopper is perhaps one of the earliest in a national publication concerning grading. In it, Hopper lists 12 grade levels, describing three of them: Mint Brilliant Proof, Mint Proof, Uncirculated, Extremely Fine, Very Fine, Fine, Very Good, Good, Very Fair, Fair, Poor and Very Poor.

He defines both levels of Proof as conditions; today, most numismatists consider Proof to represent a method of manufacture and not a grade, although most will recognize that not all Proofs are equal in quality. The other level he identifies are Uncirculated ("showing no abrasion or wearing . . . yet not [necessarily having] the sharp impression of the first strikes as the dies tire").

Of the lower grades, he notes that from Good and lower "are often disappointing, the terms applied misleading, until being understood, being used by dealers to describe a certain state of preservation."

In February 1913, some members of the American Numismatic Association began pressing for the ANA "to take some stand with reference to issuing some kind of statement classifying coins so that all dealers that catalogue and sell coins at auction must use the same classification."

The editor of *The Numismatist,* in the February 1913 issue, reprints a 1910 statement by ANA Secretary H.O. Granberg. The statement might have been written today except for the lack of any grades between Very Fine and Uncirculated. It is a concise and serious attempt to persuade dealers to ethically describe coins they are selling so that the buyer knows about any problems the coins may have. Granberg describes in detail eight levels of preservation: Proof, Uncirculated, Very Fine, Fine, Very Good, Good, Fair and Poor. Granberg recommends coins that have been cleaned should be noted as such, and suggests split grading for obverse and reverse where necessary.

In a departure from the catalogs of the latter half of the 19th century, Granberg recommends against grading a piece by its rarity. "Terms, such as 'good for piece' should never be used unless the reason why is stated as well," he writes.

A decade and a half later, ANA members were still calling for standardized grades. One writer in November 1927 calls for standard classifications and notes that when he was younger, he had been cheated by a dealer who sent him an 1866 Shield 5-cent coin graded Fine but advertised as Uncirculated. ". . . I concluded this sort of establishment was too big for my schoolboy orders of three or four dollars." This statement might have been written today by a young collector.

Adding more grades

During this period, a new-old grade between Very Fine and Uncirculated was being used more often — Extremely Fine. The grade had been used before, but apparently not by everyone. The lists of grades published in the ANA's journal in the first two decades of the 20th century left a huge gap between Very Fine and Uncirculated. In 1928, a writer in *The Numismatist* defined Extremely Fine: "A coin which is perfect in all details of design, except that its luster is gone or else the signs of wear show on the more exposed parts. Otherwise, the coin must show details as strong as when first struck."

However, Extremely Fine did not catch on quickly. In late 1930s the first edition of Wayte Raymond's *The Standard Catalogue of United States Coins and Tokens* was published. The hard-cover book was the "Red

Book" of its day. A writer in the November 1939 issue of *The Numismatist* recommends that the *Standard Catalogue* "be the accepted authority on the classification of coins as to their condition." The *Standard Catalogue* recognized seven conditions: Proof, Uncirculated, Very Fine, Fine, Very Good, Good and Fair. Very Fine is described as "From circulation, but no signs of wear," and Fine is described as "Slightest sign of wear, but still an attractive piece."

It was not until the 17th edition, published in 1954 and dated 1954-55, that the Raymond book listed Extremely Fine as a grade. It is described as "A new coin displaying only the lightest rubbing or friction on the highest parts." Very Fine is now described as "Showing only slight evidence of circulation," and the definition for Fine is basically unchanged in meaning.

By now Raymond's book had some serious competition, R.S. Yeoman's "Red Book," formally called *A Guide Book of United States Coins.* The 1954-55 *Guide Book* lists six levels of condition: Proof, Uncirculated, Very Fine, Fine, Very Good and Good. The text notes, however, that grades such as Extremely Fine and About Uncirculated "are terms frequently used to describe the degree of wear between Very Fine and Uncirculated."

Sheldon system

The greatest innovation in the grading of U.S. coins in the post-war period came, however, not in the *Standard Catalogue* or *Guide Book,* but in a book about the large cents of 1793-1814 first published in 1949. The title of that first edition is *Early American Cents* and its author was Dr. William H. Sheldon. Dr. Sheldon was already nationally famous, though not for his numismatic contributions. He devised a method of physically classifying three main types of human physiology: ectomorph, endomorph and mesomorph.

He is best known to numismatists, however, as the creator of the numerical system of grading, what some now call the Mint State system. In his 1949 *Early American Cents* (called *Penny Whimsy* in subsequent editions), Sheldon devised a numerical grading scale of 1-70, with 70 representing the perfect coin and 1 representing a coin in the poorest possible condition. Sheldon devised 10 basic levels of condition, several of which were broken into various sublevels; from poorest to best, Sheldon's grades were: Basal State, Fair, Very Fair, Good, Very Good, Fine, Very Fine, Extremely Fine, About Uncirculated and Mint State.

The system was designed specifically for large cents. When Sheldon first devised the system, which he called "quantitative grading of condition," an MS-70 cent was worth 70 times the value of the same variety in Basal State 1 condition. Sheldon wrote that "For at least three grades of condition, ... there appears to be some relationship between value and conventional descriptions of condition." These levels were Fair, Good and Fine. According to Sheldon, a coin in Fair 2 condition was worth about twice a coin in Basal State 1 condition. A Good 4 coin was worth twice a Fair 2 coin. A Fine 12 coin was worth about three times a Good 4 coin.

Sheldon listed three levels of Mint State or Uncirculated: MS-60, MS-65 and MS-70.

Sheldon's system was innovative at the time, but intended strictly for the early large cents. Not long after the book was first published, changing prices made his theory of the relationship between numerical grade and value obsolete.

During the late 1950s the grade About Uncirculated began to receive greater recognition and use. However, *The Standard Catalogue,* which ceased publication in the 1950s, never used the AU grade. Yeoman's *Guide Book* did not recognize About Uncirculated until the 1978 edition, published in 1977.

In an article appearing in the May 1956 issue of *The Numismatist,* Loyd B. Gettys and Edward M. Catich attempted to define the line drawn between Uncirculated coins and those those which are not. In "'AU' or 'BU'" the two illustrate with photographs the high points of wear for each U.S. coin type. In a later article, the same is done for commemorative coins.

Brown and Dunn

Another major event took place in 1958 — the publishing of the first grading guide in book form. Martin R. Brown and John W. Dunn published *A Guide to the Grading of United States Coins,* a book known today as "Brown and Dunn." The first edition had no illustrations; in 1961, a revised edition was published containing a single photograph for each major coin type.

Brown and Dunn recognized seven grades of U.S. coins in their early editions: Good, Very Good, Fine, Very Fine, Extremely Fine, About Uncirculated and Uncirculated. The authors note that for Uncirculated coins, "there are grades." Like Sheldon who recognized three levels of Mint State, the authors recognize that not all Uncirculated coins are equal in condition. Coins which are free of marks and defects, they say, "are more desirable." The Brown and Dunn book was eventually recognized as the official grading guide of the ANA.

In the fourth edition, published in 1964, Brown and Dunn included line illustrations for each grade in each major coin type, a feature all subsequent editions have maintained.

Meanwhile, dealers began to use Sheldon's numerical system of 1-70 for other series of coins other than early large cents. Paramount International Coin Co., then with its headquarters in Ohio, is generally credited with introducing the Mint State system to Morgan silver dollars, in the late 1960s and early 1970s. Later, Paramount began "using the quantitative grading method of describing most of the lots in this sale" (May 10, 1971, mail-bid sale).

Another major movement in U.S. coin grading came in 1970 with the publication of James F. Ruddy's *Photograde.* Unlike the Brown and Dunn book, Ruddy used photographs instead of line illustrations. The book contains black-and-white photographs of every major coin type in each of seven circulated grade levels: About Good, Good, Very Good, Fine, Very Fine, Extremely Fine and About Uncirculated. No photographs were used for Uncirculated coins.

Ruddy's *Photograde* was designated in 1972 as the official grading guide of the American Numismatic Association. It would be designated as such until 1977, when the ANA took a giant step forward and published its own grading guide.

ANA grading guide

As noted, members of the ANA had been calling for an official ANA grading standards almost since it was founded in 1892. The adoption of the Brown and Dunn and *Photograde* volumes as official ANA grading guides proved to be temporary measures. In 1973, ANA President Virginia Culver asked dealer Abe Kosoff to attempt to standardize grading. "Our goal was to standardize grading by defining significant degrees of wear and establishing guide lines so that the various grades may be easily identified," Kosoff wrote in the introduction. "Now, after four years of effort on the part of many, there is an easy-to-use and officially approved set of standards which everyone can apply to the grading of United States coins. Now the confusion in grading caused by multiple systems and biased private opinions should be eliminated."

The 1977 edition of *The Official American Numismatic Association Grading Standards for United States Coins,* visually, appears to be a combination of Brown and Dunn, using

line illustrations, and the Sheldon system, using a 1-70 numerical system. The first edition recognized three levels of Mint State (MS-60, MS-65 and MS-70). The circulated levels recognized were Choice About Uncirculated 55, AU-50, Choice Extremely Fine 45, EF-40, Choice Very Fine 30, VF-20, Fine 12, Very Good 8, Good 4 and About Good 3.

Two second editions were published, both with line illustrations. The first, published in hard-cover in 1981, recognized two additional levels of Mint State: MS-67 and MS-63. A revised second edition, was published in soft-cover in 1984.

A new, third edition of the ANA grading guide was published in April 1987, shortly before this edition went to press. The new ANA guide eliminates the line illustrations and substitutes black-and-white photographs. It also recognizes changes made by the ANA Board of Governors in June 1986.

During the mid- to late-1970s, numismatic organizations began grading coins for a fee, providing a certificate. The International Numismatic Society Authentication Bureau began grading coins in December 1976, several months after it began authenticating coins. The INS is based in Washington, D.C., and unlike ANACS, will examine foreign coins in addition to U.S. coins.

Probably what is the major step taken by the ANA concerning grading began March 1, 1979, when the ANA Certification Service began grading coins for a fee and providing third-party certificates noting a grading opinion. ANACS was founded June 22, 1972, to provide third-party opinions concerning the authenticity of a coin. Staff members would examine coins to determine whether they were genuine, counterfeit or altered.

The decision to begin grading coins for a fee was a revolution for ANA, and a controversial revolution at that. Many collectors welcomed what they called independent, non-biased grading opinions. Others, including dealers, questioned the grading ability and experience of the ANACS personnel doing the grading.

As ANACS began grading more and more coins, it soon became a profit center for the association. Some dealers began trading exclusively in ANACS-graded materials. The ANA Board of Governors expanded the number of Uncirculated grades from the three found in the first edition of the ANA grading guide to five, recognizing the intermediate grades of MS-67 and MS-63.

ANACS began receiving competition from other third-party graders. Private grading companies were formed, although ANACS continued to lead the pack of third-party grading services. Until early 1986, that is.

In February 1986, a group of dealers formed the Professional Coin Grading Service. Like ANACS, the PCGS used a modified version of William Sheldon's 1-70 scale, with a major change. Now, instead of three or five levels of Mint State, PCGS used 11 levels: MS-60, -61, -62, -63, -64, -65, -66, -67, -68, -69 and -70. Many collectors, and some dealers, were outraged. No one, they claimed, could consistently and accurately distinguish between single levels of Mint State. No matter. PCGS rapidly overtook ANACS to become the largest (by volume) third-party grading service.

In June 1986, the ANA Board of Governors, faced with a loss of revenue by the channeling of coins to PCGS that once would have been sent to ANACS, recognized all 11 levels of Mint State, plus About Uncirculated

58, and authorized their use by ANACS. The ANA Board of Governors stipulated, however, that ANA authenticator-graders, could not use the intermediate levels of MS-61, -62, -64, -66, -68 and -69 until a specimen of a specific coin in that grade was purchased and placed into the ANACS reference grading set. That decision was modified in February 1987 when the ANA Board voted to permit the use of representative grading sets based on general design types, not specific design types. A portrait coin in a specific grade, for example, may now be used to grade various portrait coins. For example, a Seated Liberty half dollar might be used to grade all denominations of Seated Liberty coinage once a specimen is located.

The latest change in ANACS operations came as this book was going to press. The ANA Board approved a proposal to permit ANACS to begin grading ancient and world coins effective July 1, 1987.

Grading of coins and paper money

The following guides are not presented as grading systems, but as introductions to the terminology of grading and its usage.

U.S. coins

A few words regarding grading usage. When two grades are linked together by a virgule — as in Mint State 65/63 — it means that the coin has two grades; the first grade represents the obverse and the second, the reverse. When two grades are linked by a hyphen — as in Mint State 65-63 — it means that the grade for both sides is indeterminate and lies somewhere between the two grades given. Sometimes, a combination of both usages will appear, as in MS-60/60-63, meaning the obverse grades MS-60 and the reverse somewhere between MS-60 and -63.

Plus signs are used by many to indicate a coin slightly better than the numerical graded indicated, but not as good as the next numerical grade. A coin graded MS-60+ is better than an MS-60 coin, but not as good as an MS-63 coin.

Many dealers and collectors use adjectives instead of numerals, or combine adjectives and numerals when speaking about Mint State coins. A superb or superb gem coin is generally MS-67, and a gem coin is usually MS-65. Some dealers use choice to describe an MS-63 coin, and others use choice for an MS-65 coin. Mint State 60 coins are generally refered to as Uncirculated or Brilliant Uncirculated; sometimes an MS-60 coin is called typical Uncirculated. Collectors should deter-

mine what adjectival "system" the dealer uses when no numerals are present because of the disagreement over what the adjectives represent numerically.

Buyers should remember that different dealers use different systems.

Grading guide

Proof: Many persons in the hobby maintain that Proof represents a method of manufacture only, and not a grade; this is the traditional belief, held by most. However, others believe that since numerals are often assigned to Proof coins, there are different qualities of Proof coins; in effect, different grades. A circulated Proof is often called an "impaired Proof." Proof is rarely abbreviated, and never in *Coin World* articles.

Brilliant Proof coins are struck on highly-polished planchets, using slower, high-pressure presses; coins are struck two or more times to bring up greater detail in the design. (See Pages 321-323 for additional information about the manufacture of Proof coins.)

Mint State and **Uncirculated:** The two terms are used interchangably to describe a coin which has no wear. Mint State is most often used with numerals.

The numerical Mint State system so widely used in the current rare coin market is based on a system created by Dr. William H. Sheldon for the U.S. large cents of 1793-1814. When the numerical system began to spread to other series, three levels of Mint State were used: Mint State 60, for an Uncirculated coin of average luster, strike and marks; MS-65, an Uncirculated coin of above average quality; and MS-70, a perfect coin as regards luster, strike and marks.

As prices of rare coins began to rise in the later years of the 1970s, dealers began paying more for certain Mint State coins than for others; the price range between an MS-60 coin and an MS-65 coin grew. To account for the rising prices, two additional levels of Mint State were created: MS-63, for a coin located between MS-60 and MS-65; and MS-67, for a coin better than MS-65, but not perfect.

In the mid-1980s, the price gap between MS-63 and MS-65 grew. Coins that were superior MS-63 specimens were bringing better prices than an "average" MS-63 coin, but still less than an MS-65 coin. Thus was born the MS-64 grade, first used for Morgan and Peace silver dollars. An earlier supporter of MS-64 was the National Silver Dollar Roundtable, an organization of dealers specializing in silver dollars.

In February 1986, the Professional Coin Grading Service, a private grading service comprising rare coin dealers, began operations. The company adopted an 11-point Mint State grading system for all series of U.S. coins: MS-60, -61, -62, -63, -64, -65, -66, -67, -68, -69 and -70. Within a few months, the private firm became the largest coin grading service in the United States. The American Numismatic Association, which had previously been the largest grading service, became second by volume of coins submitted for grading.

The ANA Board of Governors recognized all 11 levels of Mint State in June 1986, but stipulated that ANACS could not use the new intermediate grade levels until reference grading sets containing the coins were built. The ANA did not codify the 11 levels until the April 1987 publication of the third edition of its *Official ANA Grading Standards for United States Coins.*

The descriptions were written by Kenneth E. Bressett, director of education for the ANA. The following descriptions reprinted here are published with the permission of the ANA:

MS-70: The perfect coin. Has very attractive full original luster of the highest quality for the date and Mint. No contact marks are visible under magnification. There are absolutely no hairlines or scuff marks. Attractive and outstanding eye appeal. Copper coins must be bright with full original color and blazing luster.

MS-69: Must have very attractive full original luster for the date and Mint, with no more than two small non-detracting contact marks. Absolutely no hairlines or scuff marks can be seen. Attractive with exceptional eye appeal. Copper coins must be bright with full original color and blazing luster.

MS-68: Attractive full original luster for date and Mint, with no more than four light scattered contact marks. No hairlines or scuff marks show. Exceptional eye appeal. Copper coins must have lusterous original color.

MS-67: Has full original luster for date and Mint. May have three or four very small contact marks and one more noticeable but not detracting mark. On comparable coins, one or two small single hairlines may show under magnification or one or two partially hidden scuff marks may be present. Eye appeal is exceptional. Copper coins have lusterous original color.

MS-66: Must have above average quality full original Mint luster, with no more than two or three noticeable contact marks. A few very light scuffmarks showing on frosted surfaces or in the field. The eye appeal must be above average for the date and Mint. Copper coins display full original color and tone.

MS-65: Shows attractive average quality of luster for the type. A few small scattered contact marks or two larger marks may be present, and one or two small patches of hairlines may show under magnification. Noticeable scuff marks may show on the high points of the design. Overall quality is above average and overall eye appeal is very pleasing. Copper coins must have full original color and tone.

MS-64: Full average luster for the type is necessary. Several small contact marks in groups, as well as one or two heavy marks may be present. One or two small patches of hairlines may show under low magnification. Noticeable scuff marks might be seen throughout the design or in the field. Average overall quality with a pleasing eye appeal. Copper coins may be slightly dull but show original color.

MS-63: Mint luster may be slighly impaired. Numerous small contact marks, and a few scattered heavy marks may be seen. Small hairlines are visible without magnification. Several detracting scuff marks may be present throughout the design or in the fields. The general quality is slightly below average, but overall the coin is rather attractive. Copper pieces will retain parts of the original color.

MS-62: An impaired or dull luster may be

evident. Clusters of small marks are seen throughout with a few large marks or nicks in the prime focal areas. Hairlines may be very noticeable. Large unattractive scuff marks might be seen on major features, and the quality may be noticeably below average. Overall eye appeal is generally acceptable. Copper coins will show a diminished color and tone.

MS-61: Mint luster may be diminished or noticeably impaired, and the surface has clusters of large and small contact marks throughout. Hairlines could be very noticeable. Scuff marks may show as unattractive patches on large areas or major features. Small rim nicks may show, and the quality may be noticeably poor. Eye appeal is quite unattractive. Copper pieces will be generally dark and possibly spotted.

MS-60: Unattractive, dull or washed-out Mint luster may mark this coin. There may be many ugly or large contact marks, or damage spots, but absolutely no trace of wear. There could be heavy concentrations of hairlines, or unattractive large areas of scuff marks. Rim nicks may be present, and eye appeal is very poor. Copper coins may be dark, dull and spotted.

Uncirculated is usually abbreviated as Unc.; it often appears as Brilliant Uncirculated, abbreviated as BU. Sometimes used with numerals, generally as Unc. 60, and so on. Some dealers use a plus sign to indicate a coin better than one level of Mint State, but not as good as the next level.

About Uncirculated: This is a coin with only the barest traces of wear on the high points of the design. It is abbreviated AU and often appears with numerals as AU-50, AU-55 and AU-58. The term has gained acceptance despite seeming inconsistency. Some people in the hobby still say that no coin can be About Uncirculated — it is either Uncirculated or it's not. Some use Almost Uncirculated, although all three U.S. grading guides use About.

The AU-58 grade has been described as an MS-63 coin with just the slightest hint of wear. It should have fewer contact marks than lower level Mint State coins: MS-60, MS-61 and MS-62.

Extremely Fine: Light overall wear on highest points, but with all design elements sharp and clear distinguishes this grade. It is abbreviated by most hobbyists as EF, although a few use XF. It appears with numerals as EF-40 and EF-45.

Very Fine: The coin has light to moderate even wear on surface and high points of de-

sign. Abbreviated VF, it appears with numerals as VF-20 and VF-30. Infrequently used are VF-25 and VF-35.

Fine: The wear is considerable although the entire design is still strong and visible. It is not abbreviated unless with numeral as in F-12.

Very Good: The design and surface are well worn, main features are clear but flat. Abbreviated as VG, it is used with numeral as VG-8. Infrequently used is VG-10.

Good: Design and surface are heavily worn, with some details weak and many details flat. It is abbreviated only when used with numeral, G-4; infrequently used is G-6. Ironically, a coin in Good condition is not a "good" coin to collect; a Good coin is generally the lowest collectible grade.

About Good: The design is heavily worn with surface fading into rim, many details weak or missing. Abbreviated as AG, it is used with a numeral as AG-3. Few coins are collectible in About Good condition. Dealers also use the terms Fair and Fair 3 to describe a coin in this state of preservation.

Ancient and foreign coins

The grading of foreign and ancient coins is described differently from those of the United States, as is paper money. The terms are similar to those used with coins of the United States; however, the Sheldon system is not to be considered as a single standard for universal numismatic usage. It does find wide use with Canadian coins, however.

Ancient coins

Ancient coins are graded in a different set of terminology from modern foreign coins. The grading which is outlined in David Sear's books *Greek Coins and Their Values, Roman Coins and Their Values* and *Byzantine Coins and their Values* is generally accepted as the guideline for this field by collectors, dealers and numismatists in countries all over the world.

It should be kept in mind by readers that the opinion and interpretation of these grades may vary from dealer to dealer.

Fleur-de-Coin: It is considered to be synonymous with the U.S. coin term "Mint State." The coin is as it was struck, without wear. This does not mean that a weakly struck coin does not fall into this catagory. Such a piece is still "as struck." A coin is not considered to be FDC if it has surface problems such as corrosion, pitting or scratches. Patina is not considered a reason to treat an ancient coin as less than FDC. Original Mint luster on ancient coins is quite rare and not necessarily expected on coins in this grade.

Superb: This grade has caused much confusion in recent years due to its use by various auction houses to mean either of two things. Sear originally identified it as the French word which translated to mean Extremely Fine. Many of the most important auction houses in both the United States and abroad have been utilizing it separately from EF within their catalogs, as a grade where a coin does not exhibit wear, but is less than perfect "as struck." When used separately from EF, Superb is better than EF, but less than a perfect FDC.

Extremely Fine: In ancient coins, the EF designation is given to coins which have only very minor wear, and only on the high points of detail. All original detail is still sharp and clear beyond these high points. If these were modern U.S. coins, they would grade About Uncirculated.

Very Fine: This designates a coin where design is still in sharp relief; however, more progressive wear has begun. If a portrait is depicted, fillets between individual hairs begin to disappear. This is still a coin with great detail, which a collector would be proud to possess.

Fine: Advancing wear, particularly in the raised areas of design and loss of much detail, are present in the Fine grade. The coin must still have significant detail on surfaces, and not be worn smooth, leaving, as an example, only the profile of a personification's bust. Edges of designs are still sharp and all coin inscriptions are completely legible to the degree which they existed when struck.

Fair: Heavy wear may now leave only the outline of former designs. All details have been worn to blend into the remaining design. Flattening along the edges has taken portions of border lettering. Other surface problems may exist.

Mediocre: The coin is able to be identified, with some of the design still recognizable. Inscriptions may no longer be readable in their entirety.

Poor: The coin may appear to be as if dredged from a river bed, or have heavy corrosion from perhaps burial. It may or may not have enough detail to be identified.

World coins

Grading standards for modern world coins lack any definitive studies which are accepted to be the guide to the terms to be used. This dilemma surfaces especially within auctions and fixed-price sales of foreign coins within the United States, where dealers who attempt to adopt standards used on U.S. coins find themselves grading drastically more liberally than for the same coins when offered by their foreign counterparts.

Some have attempted to define grading terms for foreign coins in such texts as *World Coin Catalogue* by Simon and Schuster and *Standard Catalog of World Coins* by Krause Publications. On the other hand such popular books as *Fell's International Coin Book* and *Current Coins of the World* by Richard Yeoman avoid the subject entirely.

The most satisfactory way to approach the terminology is to examine how coins are described when sold by coin dealers in the countries from which they originate.

The following list of terms was compiled based on terms accepted by the well-known firms of: B.A. Seaby Ltd., London; Spink & Son Ltd., London; Schweizerischer Bankverein, Basel, Switzerland; Bank Leu, Zurich, Switzerland; Munzen und Medaillen A.G., Basel, Switzerland; Dr. Busso Peus Nachf. Munzhandlung, Frankfurt-am-Main, West Germany; Emporium Hamburg, Hamburg, West Germany; and Jacques Schulman B.V., Amsterdam, the Netherlands.

Proof: Proof coins are struck on highly-polished planchets, using slower, high-pressure presses. The coins are struck more than once to bring up greater detail on the coin.

Proof-like: Not to be confused with the U.S. term prooflike, this is a quality of choice Uncirculated coins, not business strikes, whose surfaces are not as bright as those of Proofs. These are struck using selected dies and planchets and on slower moving presses than for circulation strikes. These are not highly polished.

Fleur-de-Coin and **Uncirculated:** Two terms used interchangably to describe a coin which is "as struck" — without wear. Further adjectives may be used to note contact marks and other problems.

Extremely Fine: Commonly misunderstood by U.S. coin dealers, this grade describes a coin with only the highest points showing wear. The grade About Uncirculated is only used on U.S. and on Canadian coins. A foreign EF coin equates to an AU coin, as described generally for U.S. coins.

Very Fine: Light to moderate wear appears on the surfaces of the coin. All design elements are still visible, yet beyond the point of EF wear.

Fine: The wear becomes more considerable, with high points of the coin possibly gone. Still quite attractive, with the entire design strong and visible.

Very Good: Design and surface show much wear; however, the coin is quite identifiable and all legends are readable. Denticles, if present, and the rim are becoming flat.

Good: Heavy wear may leave just the outline of the designs. Legends must still be readable; however, denticles will be flat.

U.S. paper money

A formal, hobby-wide grading system for U.S. paper money is non-existent. Two individuals attempted to establish a set of "guidelines" for the grading of U.S. paper money during the 1960s, and Guy A. Cruse created a system in 1970. Herbert J. Kwart published a 44-page pamphlet, *United States Paper Money Grading Standard,* in June 1984, using a numerical system. The earlier systems apparently never achieved widespread acceptance, and Kwart's system has not caught on.

Paper money grading standards in print before Kwart's had basically consisted of those used in three catalogs. Gene Hessler's *The Comprehensive Catalog of U.S. Paper Money* lists notes in three conditions — New, Extra Fine and Fine — and describes six, including Very Fine, Very Good and Good in addition. *Paper Money of the United States,* by Robert Friedberg, lists three grades — New or Uncirculated, Very Fine and Very Good — plus describes Fine. Krause Publications' *Standard Catalog of United States Paper Money* lists three grades — Crisp Uncirculated, Extremely Fine and Fine — but does not define them.

Minor differences in opinion among the authors of the books are apparent. Hessler writes that notes in Very Good condition "are usually not desirable unless the notes are very rare or extremely scarce," but Friedberg prices most large-sized notes in Very Good. The Krause catalog assumes that readers know what the three grades it uses represent, for it does not describe them.

The following guide is an introduction to the grading of paper money, but is not meant to serve as a grading system.

New and **Uncirculated:** Both terms are interchangable, and often preceded by Crisp. A New note cannot show any folds, creases or tears, but may show bank teller handling, including pinholes. Notes that have the image well-centered on each side and even margins bring a premium over more typical notes. A Crisp Uncirculated note is abbreviated CU.

Extremely Fine: A note in this condition must retain crispness, but may have a light center fold or light corner fold. Tears and major stains are not permitted. Abbreviated as EF, or sometimes as XF.

Very Fine: Some crispness must remain, but a note in Very Fine condition is permitted two to four folds and corner creases. A Very Fine note has seen moderate circulation, but is still attractive to the eye and touch. Several small stains or one larger stain are permitted, but should not detract from the general appearance of the note. No tears are permitted.

Fine: Horizontal and vertical folds and creases are well defined. Most of the crispness is gone from a Fine note, and some limpness may be noticeable. A Fine note has seen considerable circulation and may have a minor tear or two. It may have some larger, more noticeable stains detracting from the note's general appearance.

Very Good: Well worn, with considerable folding and limpness. Note may be dirty, but not filthy. The print may have worn away along the heavy creases.

Good: Note is ragged and dirty, and may have holes, large tears, missing corners and considerable wear and damage.

Coins as Investments 16

Coins as investments

By Q. David Bowers

Q. David Bowers, a regular columnist for COIN WORLD, is an owner of Bowers and Merena Galleries, Wolfeboro, N.H. He has written extensively about the subject of coin investment, with his book "High Profits From Rare Coin Investment" now in its 11th edition. A numismatist since 1953, the author served as president of the Professional Numismatists Guild from 1977-79 and of the American Numismatic Association from 1983-85.

"The more things change, the more they are the same" — an old saying. And, perhaps this is nowhere truer than with the subject of rare coin investment. It was my privilege to write about coin investment for previous editions of the *Coin World Almanac*. Re-reading these recently, I could not help but note a comment made nine years ago:

"At any given time — including right now — it is difficult to survey the current coin market and have confidence that there are indeed many excellent values remaining — purchases with ample room for future price appreciation from an investment viewpoint."

History shows that a given $1,000 invested in choice Uncirculated United States coins in 1978 would have doubled or tripled by 1980, two years later! However, in subsequent years the prices rolled back, and today there are certain pieces which cost little more than they did back in 1978.

The coin hobby, of which investment plays an important part — has been likened by some to an industry. Like a chameleon, the field of coins and coin investment is always changing. Collecting rare coins is different now from what it was 10 years ago, much different from what it was 20 years earlier, and bears only a slight resemblance to the field a decade more distant. Undoubtedly, 10 years from now we'll see changes which would amaze us if we could only know of them in advance!

Having been involved in numismatics for more than three decades (my gosh, doesn't that sound impressive!) — actually since 1953 — I have had a front-row seat during the changing panorama of persons, places, things and events. And, I must say, it has been a lot of fun!

I was one of the first to emphasize the investment aspect of rare coins. Indeed, a monthly investment program instituted by my firm in 1958 was the first in the coin field.

Back in 1953, or in 1963, or in any other point in time I can remember, the future was not certain. This situation is not unique to the coin market. Look at today's newspaper and survey the stock prices. Are there any good buys? On one hand you can reason that all the good buys have already been bought by people who know more than you do — and that everything is priced "just right." The more you study the situation, the more apt you are to become confused! And yet, you know that three years from now if you could look at today's paper you would find items which did very, very well in the stock market and, of course, items which did poorly.

In the meantime, millions of dollars are spent annually by people seeking advice in the stock market. This is the stuff that keeps investment newsletters in business. So it is with coins. It seems people are always willing to pay for predictions of the future. Never mind that the predictions may not turn out as hoped. Undoubtedly there was "an unforeseen reason" that a prediction did not materialize, but, of course, the person doing the predicting is not responsible.

Are there any bargains left in the coin market? After all, coin prices have risen quite sharply in recent decades. What $2,000 buys in coins this year might have cost only $500 10 years ago. So, 10 years ago there were many investment opportunities, and those fortunate enough to buy coins back then did well. But what about right now?

At any given time we have to deal with today — not yesterday. While "the good old days" are fun to think about, and while it certainly is nostalgic to look through old issues of *Coin World* to see all of the "bargains," the fact is that we now have to deal with the present — right now. I personally believe that the present offers the investor many opportunities. Indeed, the opportunities today are in my mind much better than they were in 1979-1980, a peak in the market cycle for many popular coins. This peak will be discussed later.

In my book *High Profits From Rare Coin Investment* (available from your local coin dealer or from the ANA library) I raised the question: "How high is high? How far can coin prices go?"

Future unknown

My answer is that the future is unknown and that no one can predict it with accuracy. As stated, millions of dollars are spent in the quest for future knowledge, but even the United States government, with enormous resources at its disposal, cannot figure out what the interest rate, employment rate or inflation rate will be even six months from now, let alone five or 10 years from now! Similarly, one cannot predict coin prices with accuracy. However, on a comparative basis it can be said with certainty that coin prices have a long, long way to go in relation to prices of rarities in other fields.

Right now many classic American rarities can be purchased for $50,000 to $100,000. During the 1983-87 years such pieces as examples of the 1894-S dime, 1876-CC 20-cent piece, 1838-O half dollar, $4 Stellas of 1880, original 1915-S Panama-Pacific sets and other legendary properties have sold for less than $100,000. It may be significant to note that "Juliet's Nurse," a painting by Turner, sold at auction for close to the figure realized for the entire Eliasberg Collection of United States gold coins ($12.4 million was realized for this collection when it was auctioned in 1982), a collection which contained one of

every date and Mint mark of United States gold issue from the dollar through the double eagle!

Examples of the 1918 24-cent airmail stamp with inverted plane have sold as high as $200,000, and yet 100 examples of this stamp were distributed to collectors. By contrast, there are many famous coins of which approximately 100 are in collector's hands which sell for $1,000 to $10,000 each! This is not to say that the aforementioned painting or the famous stamp are overpriced. Rather, it merely reflects that classic numismatic items may have quite a way to go.

For the price of $5,544,000 paid for a rather obscure painting, "Portrait of Juan de Pareja," by artist Velasquez a few years ago, one could spend a lifetime collecting United States Colonial and early American coins, half cents, large cents, small cents and all issues from 2-cent pieces through silver dollars, acquire a complete or nearly complete collection, and have lots of money left over! Such an exhibition would fill a large volume of description. Are coins overpriced? You can judge for yourself.

Actually, the answer is not as simple as that. Within any given market, there are some pieces which are probably overpriced and others which are probably bargains. The object of the present article is to make you aware of how such can be identified — not to identify them specifically, but to point out such elements as coin cycles, market changes, popularity and the like. Then you can think for yourself. In any investment market — coins included — the buyer who is knowledgeable makes the greatest profits. My aim is to set you on the road to knowledge.

Days gone by

It always takes a measure of courage to buy at the current market price. It is easy to look back at catalogs published in 1953, 1958, 1962, 1974 or some other early year and determine by hindsight that the right thing to have done would have been to mortgage your house, borrow on your life insurance, and do everything else you could to put every last penny into the rare coin market. And, if you did, your stake would have multiplied many times in the years since.

Looking over a catalog I issued in 1956, I see many bargains which seem to be unbelievable: Uncirculated Indian cents of the early 1900s priced at $1.25 each (about 1/100 of today's price!), a 1931-S Uncirculated cent at $2 (described as a "fast climbing item" — climb fast it did, and now it is worth approximately 100 times that price!), Proof copper-nickel 3-cent pieces in the 1880s at $5.50 to $6.50 each (less than 1/100 of today's price!), and so on. If you had invested, say, $1,000 in such items back in 1956, today you would have approximately $100,000 in replacement value.

(Note: In this edition of the *Coin World Almanac* I use numerical grading, the ANA official grading standards scale. For now, in 1987, its use is widespread. In earlier editions of this work, and also earlier editions of published reference works such as *A Guide Book of United States Coins,* grading was adjectival. Because of this change, certain price comparisons may be approximate rather than precise. Further, today, in 1987, the Uncirculated and Proof grade categories are split into various numerical subdivisions, whereas years ago the catalogs simply listed coins as "Uncirculated" or "Proof" without any distinction being made for exceptional or inferior coins with those categories.)

Uncirculated Liberty Head 5-cent pieces at $5 were plentiful in my 1956 catalog. In 1978, when I wrote my article for an earlier edition of the *Coin World Almanac,* I noted that "the same coins are worth in the $100 range." Now that same Liberty Head 5-cent piece, if choice Uncirculated, would cost you in the $1,000 range!

A Proof 1880 Trade dollar at $34 was available from me in 1956. By 1978 the price had climbed to $1,500, leading me to state that "whoever purchased it in 1956 can be happy now!" Today he or she can be even happier, for the same choice Proof 65 1880 Trade dollar sells in the $8,000 to $10,000 range! Indeed, certain of the 1978 prices are now appearing to be great bargains, but in 1978 all these were "fully priced." Similarly, in the previous edition of this almanac, prepared in 1984, I noted that a Proof 1880 Trade dollar was then selling in the $4,000 range — but now, in 1987, the price has more than doubled.

Back in 1956 when I issued my "bargain" catalog, the coins were not bargains then. The telephone did not ring off the hook, and the mailman did not have to make five trips to my door each day. Rather, sales came in at a normal rate. No one said, "Send me 10 1880 Trade dollars at $34 each." Indeed, it was hard enough to sell even one piece to a customer! From the viewpoint of a dealer, these coins required the same effort to sell then that they do now. Each piece had to be graded, properly described and priced to be competitive.

The reason I mention this is that I do not want to imply that the days of 1956 (or any other earlier year) were times in which coins were parceled out to just a favored few, and that such "bargains" were not really available. They were available, and if you had the inclination you could have bought virtually all the coins you wanted. We are dealing with reality, not theory. Back in 1956 it would have been appropriate for me to have written an article asking, "Are prices too high?" After all, $34 was a lot of money for a Proof 1880 Trade dollar at the time, and there were probably individuals among my clients who remembered when they were available for just $5 each! I did not have the faintest dream, not the foggiest notion, that such a piece would ever sell for more than $8,000! Nor did I know that the price I was charging for an 1879 gold $4 Stella, $995, would be just 1/40 of the price it would sell for nearly 30 years later.

All of this emphasizes the fact that we must now think of the present and what opportunities it offers. The past is interesting to contemplate, but it is gone. I posit that the present offers many opportunities. While I do not expect that a Proof 1880 Trade dollar purchased at, say, $9,000 will be worth 100 times more 30 years from now — this would price the piece at close to $1 million — I do feel that there is ample room left for price movements among certain issues.

Price cycles

When analyzing coin investment it is important to realize that all series run in cycles. In the 1976 issue of the *Coin World Almanac* I said: "Right now gold coins are 'hot' and sell very well. At the same time, Indian cents are 'quiet' and there is no rush to buy them."

In the 1977 issue, I reported that: "Gold coins are now 'quiet' and Indian cents are more active! Perhaps in 1980 the situation will reverse itself again."

In the 1978 edition, I wrote: "Gold coins have indeed picked up in activity, particularly scarcer issues. Indian cents remain active as well. Perhaps a few years from now gold coins will become intensely active and Indian cents will become quiet once more."

In mid-1984, when I wrote my comments for the 25th anniversary edition of the *Coin World Almanac,* I noted that "gold coins are 'quiet,' with very little activity among common or bullion-type issues, especially in comparison with the activity of the recent past. Indian cents are neither active nor dormant but, rather, are somewhere in between. Moving to other series, I note that Colonial coins are very quiet. Large cents and half cents, never the scene of frenzied activity, are moderately active in keeping with interest by collectors. The same goes for Indian and Lincoln cents. United States 'type' coins are fairly quiet but seem to be stirring. These were the heroes of the 1979-1980 boom market. Commemoratives are fairly active at levels less than they were several years ago. Silver dollars are very active, 'down' from 'extremely active' a few years ago, but still a lot of buying and selling is going on. Silver dollars form a special category, for they, more than any other series, are an investment medium."

Now, in 1987, gold coins are very active, with great interest for common and rare coins alike. Bullion-type issues are especially popular, with interest focused on the gold American Eagles issued by the United States Mint for the first time in the autumn of 1986. Half cents and large cents are extremely active, and my own recent auctions, together with the Robinson S. Brown Jr. collection sold by Superior Galleries in 1986, have seen numerous price estimates shattered. Indian cents and Lincoln cents remain quiescent as do Colonial coins, although I notice some interesting stirrings in the latter series. United States "type" coins are very active and are a centerpiece in the market. Likewise, commemoratives are among the hottest series, in sharp contrast with the situation three years ago. Silver dollars remain active, but the market is more selective. Highly publicized issues such as an 1881-S Morgan dollar in Mint State 65 grade are down sharply from what they were as recently as a year ago, but truly scarce issues — 1879-CC, 1893-CC, 1895 Proof, 1895-S, 1896-S, being examples — are in extremely strong demand.

Over the years coin cycles have occurred in every series. I have seen them again and again and again — and I'll see them more in the future.

While the long-term trend of rare numismatic coins has been upward, on a short-term basis (less than five to 10 years) market activities are often subject to cycles. Prior to a study I published in February 1964, to my knowledge no one had ever written about the subject of coin cycles before. Since then numerous references have appeared in the numismatic press.

While cycles need not be of primary concern to the long-term investor who diversifies his holdings across many areas, they are nevertheless worthy of study and give the explanation of why a coin can sometimes be worth less this year than it was last year. This can be a sharp advantage so far as buying is concerned. Unquestionably, it is more advisable to buy at a low or valley in the cycle than it is at the top of a peak.

In the field of coin collecting and investing nearly every series has had its turn in the limelight. Commemorative half dollars have gone through a number of well-marked cycles over the years. United States gold coins have waxed and waned in popularity — with a huge increase in interest in value taking place during the years 1973-74, followed by a slump in 1975-76, a gathering of interest in 1977 and 1978, and new high prices in 1979-1980. I noted in 1984 that commemoratives were "fairly active at levels less than they were several years ago," but now, in 1987, the levels of years earlier have been surpassed, and commemoratives once again are breaking into new pricing ground.

During the 1940s, 1950s, 1960s rolls and Proof sets underwent many cycles. Certain type coins (different major designs of United States coinage) have faded and sharpened in interest from time to time. Early Proof sets from 1858 through 1916 have been immensely popular in one market and then have had few buyers in another. Each in its day has been the "hottest" series.

Each has had short-term cyclical characteristics in addition to long-term price growth. A typical short-term cycle in coin investment has a number of characteristics. If you check through old coin magazines and fixed-price lists you will see that certain things repeat themselves. Most coin prices can be plotted easily using standard methods of business statistics and economics.

The anatomy of a coin cycle

The performance of coin "X" is typical. It may be a roll, it may be a commemorative, it may be a type coin, it may be a foreign Proof set, it may be one of many different coins or sets which have commanded the attention of investors during the past few decades. The time span of each "stage" varies. Due to the availability of monthly publications, cycles prior to 1960 used to take longer than they do now. Beginning in 1960 *Coin World* was published on a weekly basis, a few years later *Numismatic News* and the *Coin Dealer Newsletter* joined the same publishing frequency. During the 1960s teletypewriter services, something formerly reserved for newspaper offices and stock brokers, became a familiar sight in many coin dealerships. The long distance telephone has also contributed to the speed at which a cycle takes place. In today's market a cycle may occur in a matter of months or even weeks.

Stage I. The market for coin X is not particularly active. Some dealers price X for $12 each; some for $11. One dealer offers a group of 10 X for $99.50. At a convention, a sharp buyer who knows that a dealer has had trouble selling his large holding of X succeeds in buying 375 pieces of X for only $8.50 each. In various numismatic publications there are few, if any, dealers stating realistic buying prices for X. In other words, there just isn't much life to X at all.

Popular psychology being what it is, there isn't much support for X on the behalf of anyone. A dealer is apt to say "X is dead, so I am not even interested in discussing buying any for stock." A collector might say: "Why should I bother collecting items like X, there doesn't seem to be much interest in them and apparently they would be a poor investment — I don't see any buy ads and the last dealer I talked to said he couldn't care less about X."

Stage II. Some alert persons note that X is selling for $10 and $12 and has been selling at that price for quite some time, without any extensive market activity and without any increase in price. In fact, as time wears on the price weakens as dealers give discounts and special deals to move unwanted X items out of stock.

In the meantime item "Y," which is not as scarce as X but which is in a currently popular field, sells for $25. Dealers are publishing many ads offering to buy Y, and many are offering close to the $25 retail price. Item Y is hard to buy in quantities as most people owning Y are busy watching the price go up! Other investors have been watching X stagnate price-wise, decide that X is underpriced and start buying. Dealers are contacted by telephone, by letter, by personal contact in shops and at conventions, and by any other feasible means. The formerly unwanted large supply of X is now dried up!

Stage III. Having bought all of the X available at $10 and $12, collectors and investors are now willing to pay $14 or $15 and say so in print and in voice. Dealers run "wanted to buy" ads for X offering $13.50 for all specimens submitted, knowing that a dollar or two profit awaits them for each X acquired. These "buy" advertisements prompt thousands of collectors and dealers and other investors to start thinking about X. After all, why is X selling for a super-bargain $15 when Y, which is not as scarce, finds a ready market at a new high price of $30?

Stage IV. X becomes a hot item! Everyone is talking about X. Everyone wants to buy X. There are not enough X to go around. The price of X rises to $20, and then to $25, and then to $30. Meanwhile, many sell their supply of Y to raise money to buy X. Y drops in value to $18.

Stage V. Those who bought X at prices from $8.50 to $12 each find the $30 price very attractive. Some sell. Others hold out for a higher price. The great activity in X has lessened somewhat as investors turn to other things. X advances to $30.50 and then to $31. Noting that the market is not rising as sharply as before, thousands of X are now sold by many different investors and speculators. The first ones to sell realize $30 to $31 each. Some of the later ones have to be satisfied with $27, and a few are only able to get $25. At this $25 point, the supply curve intersects with the demand curve and the price stabilizes — for a while.

Stage VI. At the new $25 price very few people want to invest in X. It takes fortitude to buy on a falling market, and they have just seen the price fall from $31 down to $25. Other investors, who missed the higher profit, now sell additional X for less than $25. The market is sluggish. X is now available in quantity for $22 each. If you are in the market for a large quantity, you may be able to drive a hard bargain and buy some X for $19.50. A story is told of a large metropolitan convention in which the investor helped a dealer unload 243 pieces of X by offering him $18.50 each — an unheard of low price in the recent market. In other words, stage VI brings us back to stage I. The cycle is complete!

The preceding illustration is remarkably typical of many, many past coin price movements, particularly those of the past two or three decades. Each cycle seems to take place at a succeedingly higher plateau. In the next cycle, X will start out at $19.50 and may rise to a new high of $50 before settling back at, say $35.

While knowledge of earlier cycles is not particularly critical to the long-term investor (except that a knowledge of cycles will permit buying "dead" series at favorable prices and perhaps passing by "hot" coins until they settle in price somewhat), it is of vital importance to the short-term buyer. Any purchaser who keeps in mind the fact that coins are subject to cyclical variations will have little cause to worry. Anyone who takes the time to research the investment market of recent years will notice various definite cycles and will gain a valuable insight into coin price behavior. This work will pay off in being able to recognize cycles that are yet to come. There is no short-cut to this research. You will not be able to calculate cycles by reading today's advertisements, as very few advertisements mention price drops.

The cycle theory fits neatly many price movements over the years — but not all. Do you know, for example, that there was a series that was extremely "hot" over 110 years ago in the 1860s and which hasn't been on the "most active" list since then? Skeptical? Don't be. I'm speaking of medals honoring George Washington — the hottest item in the numismatic market of the 1860s.

Today in the 1980s Washington medals are the domain of the specialized collector of Colonial and early American coins and are hardly in the mainstream of numismatics. Anyone buying certain expensive Washington medals in the 19th century to hold them for price increases in certain instances might still be waiting!

In 1978 in the *Coin World Almanac* I noted: "It would be difficult to foresee a boom in common day gold coins which would equal the 1973-1974 activity. The explanation for that activity was a special circumstance — tremendous interest on behalf of the public, fueled by heavy advertising from bullion firms and others not previously in professional numismatics. It is doubtful if a situation like this will recur."

Little did I know back in 1978 that a situation like that indeed would recur, except that the names of the players would be different and the circumstances contributing to the situation would involve other factors. But, the net result was that prices of gold coins far outstripped the almost unbelievable 1973-74 activity of just a few years earlier.

In 1975 and 1976 there was a general market slump. In 1977 interest gathered momentum, in 1978 it increased further, and by 1979 there was a full-scale rush toward rare coins, a frenetic activity which culminated in 1980 when coin prices reached a peak.

Coming together all at once in 1979-1980 were many factors. The price of gold bullion rose to brush the $900 per ounce mark, a historic high, providing much glittering excitement. Silver touched $50 at one point, creating so much interest that many dealers were faced with long lines of people selling the precious metal. In the process, numerous dealers made hundreds of thousands or millions of dollars' worth of profits. The logical place to spend these profits was to make a "splash" in the rare coin market — by buying scarce and rare pieces, thus driving the prices upward.

Dollar questioned

Back in 1979-1980 the American dollar was called into question, especially when Arab oil interests demanded payment in gold. During the administration of President Jimmy Carter we had the reality of double-digit inflation. The oil crisis and the Organization of Petroleum Exporting Countries caused additional concern. "Tangible assets" became a new and popular investment medium, and many banks, pension funds, financial advisers and others in the world of finance became attracted to the field.

The success of coin investment became publicized. Previously, coin investment was primarily the domain of numismatists — knowledgeable collectors. During the 1979-80 period we had a great outreach to the public though advertisements in popular magazines, television programs, seminars and other ways — which brought many new investors into the fold. As the supply of scarce coins remained the same, there was no alternative but a rise in price as more and more people scrambled to spend money.

In 1984 I wrote that coin prices had drifted lower, and many issues were selling half or a third of what they brought in the top of the market. Now, in 1987, the market has strengthened considerably, and while certain high-priced rarities are still not bringing 1980 values, by and large scarce "type" coins, rare dates and Mint marks, and most other things in higher condition levels, particularly MS-65 and Proof 65, are selling for as much or more as they did back then. I sense a resurgence of interest by the collector. Driven to the sidelines by the dominance of the investor in 1980, and by controversies concerning grading interpretations and market prices during the 1980s, the typical collector almost faded from the scene. Now, the collector, representing the true ultimate "consumer" of a coin, is coming back — and I as well as numerous other professionals look for a healthy market, collector-oriented, in the years to come.

Market cycles are not unique to the coin market. Earlier I observed that uncertainty is part of the game of stock investment. The stock market runs in cycles, and an entire library could be filled with studies in the subject, none of which particularly points the way clearly as to what one should do next month! The field of rare books, rare prints, art, commemorative plates and other fields of collectibles likewise show cyclical tendencies. In general, the more investors there are in a field, the sharper the cycles tend to be. When a field is composed of pure collectors, with investment considerations nowhere to be seen, then cyclical considerations are either absent or consist only of changes, usually slight within a given short-term period, in the numbers of collectors attracted to the area.

The knowledge of coin cycles is valuable in that it helps explain certain price movements. However, cycles don't tell everything. As noted, anyone buying certain expensive Washington medals in the 19th century would have long since died of old age waiting for the next cycle peak! And, sometimes cyclical effects can be observed but not acted on. Take my example of the 1973-74 market which I viewed as a temporary phenomenon — never dreaming that the prices of a later era, 1979-80, would make certain earlier prices appear to be bargains!

Cycles can be an aid to buying and selling. If an area seems to be more popular than it should be and if prices have risen at an unnatural rate, then stop to think about it. Was the run-up in price caused by an increased number of collectors (for the collector is the ultimate "consumer" of a coin), or was it caused by investors selling to other investors, accompanied by lots of advertising promotion? If the answer is that there are more collectors, then "not to worry," as they say. However, if the price increase was fueled by promotional considerations with very little in the way of numismatic or collector activity, then watch out! It might indeed be the time to sell.

Conversely, a person seeking to buy will do best when the market is quiet. This was noted in my earlier illustration of a coin cycle. Now, in 1987, it is a truly wonderful time to buy Colonial and early American coins. Lincoln cents and Indian cents are likewise inexpensive. Scarce dates and Mint mark varieties of Seated Liberty silver coins, while not inexpensive and while subject to a fair amount of interest, still are far from being "hot." It is a low or nearly low point in the cycle for such pieces, and activity seems to be at a small percentage of its potential. And yet, the rarity, numismatic considerations, romance and appeal of the coins remain. Sooner or later the activity will again build, prices will rise and anyone buying now will be in the driver's seat. In the field of paper money, the market is likewise quiet today, as it is in California fractional gold pieces and a number of other disciplines. It takes a strong-willed individual to buy against the tide, to make an investment in a market when a given series is quiet, but the historical record vividly demonstrates that such times are far and away the most profitable acquisition opportunities.

Similarly, the prices of numerous rarities, "type" coins, patterns, large-size United States paper money, and certain other series are at a low point, probably temporary.

With whom you do business

Most of the problems I have observed in the coin investment field today have had to do with buyers who invested only for the sake of investment and who completely ignored the collecting aspect. In 1984, news accounts told of certain rare Canadian coins advertised for close to $100 each in daily newspapers, while at the same time such pieces were commonly available for about $15 in coin shops. When I was president of the American Numismatic Association (1983-85), I saw many letters from coin buyers who bought, for example, "rare" Morgan silver dollars from promotional outfits at prices many multiples of what they would have paid had they purchased from an established professional numismatist. Often such promotional offerings are overpriced or sharply overgraded, or worse, even counterfeit.

In recent times there have been many abuses in the field of financial planning. An investigation conducted by the Federal Trade Commission in 1986 revealed, for example, that naive investors were being sold Walking Liberty half dollars billed as "MS-65" for hundreds of dollars each, whereas in reality the coins were not even Mint State (Uncirculated) and were worth $10 to $15 each.

The same investigation showed, as one of many examples, a group of coins sold for $10,000 which had a true numismatic retail value of perhaps $2,000. The coins were overpriced and overgraded. In other instances, coins are properly graded and are given good numismatic descriptions, but the prices charged are significantly more than what the buyer would have paid had the sale been arranged through an established professional numismatic firm.

I recall one instance in which an investor paid $15,000 for a scarce Trade dollar, a coin that an investment adviser had purchased a few weeks earlier for $4,000. In another instance, a 1652 Massachusetts Oak Tree shilling was called "Uncirculated" and bought by an investor for $8,000. When the investor tried to sell it shortly thereafter, it realized just $2,000.

To avoid this and other abuses it is always advisable in my opinion to buy from a dealer with established numismatic credentials. The fact that you are reading the *Coin World Al-*

manac probably means that you are somewhat familiar with coins, or have an interest in becoming so. As a start, when you pick one or more dealers be sure they are in good standing with the American Numismatic Association. If a firm is a very large one, then membership in the Professional Numismatists Guild indicates that the dealer has pledged not to sell counterfeit coins, has pledged to grade properly, and has subscribed to a rigid code of ethics. Also there is the protection that in the event of a dispute the organization will take fast and effective action on your behalf.

Of course, there are thousands of smaller dealers who, because of capital requirements or length of time they may have been in business, have not been able to meet the membership requirements of the Professional Numismatists Guild but who may be equally fine to deal with. Perhaps the best way to learn about which dealers are good and which ones are not is to join a local coin club and ask others in the hobby, particularly the old-timers. There is usually a feeling of sentiment one way or the other toward professionals in the business — and a little conversation on this point may pay you great rewards.

Quality, not quantity

For investment purposes, in my opinion, quality is preferable to quantity. I consider it better, for example, to have 10 $50 coins (representing a total investment of $500) than 500 $1 coins or 50 $10 coins. One reason for this is that the dealer's margin of profit is usually less on a more expensive coin for there is less handling. For a $50 coin a dealer will often pay $35 to $40 or so — say 70 to 80 percent of the purchase price. However, for a $1 coin the dealer might want to pay just 30 cents to 50 cents, because there is so much handling involved. Obviously, when time comes for you to sell your investment it is better to own a piece in which the dealer's margin of profit is less.

Another precept is to invest with the long term in view. If you buy coins today and sell them just three months from now or a year from now you are making money just for the dealer — which is fine for the dealer, but which isn't fine for you! Considering that most dealers and major auction houses operate on a margin of 20 to 25 percent, it is only rarely that you can buy and resell at a profit within a space of a year or so. However, if you hold coins for five to 10 years, then the dealer's margin of profit becomes less significant, and most of the profit goes into your own pocket.

Grading is another important — actually vital — consideration. When you purchase coins for investment you are faced with the uncertainty of what they will do in the future. Will they go up in value or won't they? Of course, we both hope that they will. Why add to this the uncertainty of whether or not your coins are in the correct condition? Instead, be very sure you are buying the grade value you expect, the grade you are paying for.

In recent years many coins have been "treated" and "processed." Lower grade coins have been given the false appearance of "Uncirculated" or "Proof." There is a lot of money to be made by selling processed, treated and over-graded coins. Such operations prey on the bargain seeker.

An Extremely Fine 1853 Coronet cent, a coin worth, say, in the $40-50 range, if "processed" and wrongly sold as "Uncirculated" for $100 (just a fraction of the going price for true Uncirculated), is no bargain at $100. In fact, you would be overpaying by a factor of two or three! And yet it is continually amazing to see how many collectors, particularly new ones, fall into such a trap. While dealers are sometimes reluctant to discuss "processed" coins, if you want a discussion concerning this subject you can talk with the representatives of numismatic publications. Grading is a big problem. I might mention that ethical dealers do not "process" coins. Your best protection is to buy from an ethical dealer.

In summary, it costs no more, in fact it is infinitely cheaper in the long run (when the time comes to sell your coins) to buy properly graded coins. Otherwise you are just kidding yourself and are impairing the chances for the success of your investment. I don't mean to be negative in a discussion which perhaps should be 100 percent positive, but I do want to clarify this situation and make you aware of it. In many years of buying millions of dollars worth of collections I have seen large sums of money lost by collectors who are hoodwinked in this regard. "There is no Santa Claus in numismatics," Lee Hewitt (founder of the *Numismatic Scrapbook Magazine*) once wrote. This is one of my favorite quotations.

If you are uncertain about coin grading, do some "comparison shopping." The same coin advertised as "Uncirculated" at $10 and $15 can be a better buy at $15 than $10 if, for instance, the $15 is really Uncirculated and the $10 is really Extremely Fine.

In the mid-1980s, a market developed for so-called "certified" coins. Some of these pieces were accompanied by fancy certificates issued by the American Numismatic Association Certification Service or by more than a dozen individual private grading services. Some were given "guaranteed grades" and were firmly sealed in plastic capsules or "slabs." While the intention of the coin graders was good, the prospective buyer must remember that grading is only part of a coin's value.

Indeed, in an informational pamphlet the ANA itself noted, for example, that certain coins graded as MS-63 might have a market value of About Uncirculated 55 or less, while others graded MS-63 might be worth as much as MS-65 coins. This is because other factors intervene, such as the quality of striking, presence or absence of toning, quality of the planchet, centering and overall aesthetic appeal. Time and time again I have seen two coins, each "certified" as MS-65, bring vastly different values. In a letter to *Coin World,* one West Coast appraiser told of evaluating a group of MS-65 Morgan silver dollars, all of which had the correct MS-65 "technical" grade, but yet the market values ranged from $400 all the way up to $1,200.

Further, grading interpretations have changed over a period of years. In February 1986, the board of governors of the ANA issued an official announcement stating that numerous coins certified as MS-65 by the ANA Grading Service several years earlier were, upon recertification at the changed grading interpretations of 1986, only MS-60 to MS-63. Thus, depending on the date of an ANA certificate, one certificate may be more "valuable" or accurate than another.

Similarly, there have been problems with encapsulated coins. At a convention in 1987, I saw a 1910-D Indian Head gold $10 eagle which had a "guaranteed grade" of MS-63 on it. Once the coin was on the market, a "recall notice" was issued, stating that it was a typographical error, and that the coin was just barely MS-60. Similarly, around the same time it was announced that tens of thousands of dollars' worth of coins had been given erroneous grades, and that when the attention of a particular service was called to these, it was generously buying them back. The only fly in the ointment — and this situation was pointed out by Martin Paul in an advertisement in *Coin World* — is that those people buying certified coins might not know whether they have one of the "mistakes" or whether they have a properly graded one.

The bottom line of all of this is that while certified and encapsulated coins may be fine

and dandy, grading is still a matter of opinion, experts can and do differ, and even when experts agree on the grade of a coin, the market value may vary because of such other aspects as toning, striking, aesthetic appeal and so on. So, don't be a slave to someone else's formulas or guarantees. As noted, think for yourself, do some comparison shopping, and be sure that what you want is in the grade you want and is priced as you want it to be.

A guide to the "Guide Book"

In past editions of the *Coin World Almanac* I have given commentaries about *A Guide Book of United States Coins,* issued by the Western Publishing Co. This has been a popular feature, and I continue it in the present article. I have at my fingertips the 1987 edition. It is important to remember that this edition, while dated 1987, was actually released in July 1986 and contains prices compiled in some instances in 1985. So, certain prices may be two years behind the cover date.

The following are some of my own personal feelings concerning United States coins, their availability, some interesting situations, and their price structure in comparison to *Guide Book* value.

Colonial coins

The term "Colonial" coins refers to issues of the Colonies, various copper coins of the states, pieces pertaining to President George Washington, and other issues, mostly of the 1790s and earlier, commonly grouped under the "Colonial" heading.

Colonial coins have never been in the limelight for investors. Even the most common of Colonial coins are apt to be rare in comparison to later United States issues. Thus, few if any dealers have ever had quantities available for promotion or speculation. Very little advertising has been devoted to them. The result is a field which offers pure numismatic enjoyment at prices which are very reasonable in comparison to the rarity of the pieces. Even great rarities are apt to be inexpensive in relation to later series. Take for example the 1774 Virginia "shilling" piece in silver. It is believed that just six pieces are known, and yet a Proof lists in the *Guide Book* for $16,500, less than one-tenth of an 1804 silver dollar (of which 15 pieces are known). 1737 and 1739 Higley copper threepence pieces are listed in the $5,000 range, and yet no more than a couple dozen exist of each variety. Uncirculated 1776 Continental dollars in pewter catalog $9,000 to $12,000 each, and yet often the span of a year or more will elapse between offerings. An entire wonderland of numismatic fascination is in store for the numismatist desiring to collect copper coins of Massachusetts, Connecticut, New Jersey or Vermont of the 1785-1788 years. Often great rarities can be purchased for just a few hundred dollars each. These coins, made from hand-cut dies and struck under primitive circumstances, have lots of "character," as a perusal of the *Guide Book* will quickly point out. I have studied the Vermont copper series for a number of years and am still fascinated when I see a well-worn piece even of a common variety. No two pieces are ever alike.

From an investment perspective, my recommendation for Colonial coins is to build a collection. Do not buy duplicates; rather, acquire one each of as many different as you can find. If you are collecting state copper coins, then the grade of Fine to Very Fine would be a good condition objective unless examples of certain rare varieties are obtainable only in lower grades (as is sometimes the case). If you are of an intellectual turn of mind, enjoy numismatics and want a generous helping of history with what you collect, Colonial coins can indeed be a nice collection and investment combined, an ideal situation.

U. S. copper coins

In my opinion, United States half cents and large cents are very reasonably priced, even low priced in nearly all instances. As a challenge I suggest putting together a set of large cents of the later era, 1816-1857. If you can buy such pieces in MS-60 condition and pay no more than the *Guide Book* values, your complete or nearly complete set should be worth a substantial premium over what you paid — even if you paid "full retail." With a few exceptions, such pieces are seldom seen. The investor market has largely overlooked such pieces, resulting in bargains for the astute buyer.

The same situation is observable for Flying Eagle, Indian, and early Lincoln cents. Certain of these issues are cheaper now than they were 20 years ago — a remarkable situation! The investment market has leaned toward silver and gold issues, leaving many bargains among copper and bronze coins. When buying Indian and Lincoln cents in higher grades, be picky about condition. There are many cleaned and "processed" pieces which are apt to trap the unwary purchaser.

The formation of a set of early Lincoln cents in Uncirculated grade with full Mint color would be quite a challenge. When completed, it should be an excellent investment if

held for a few years. The Matte Proof issues are not as good for investment, in my opinion, for these have received much investment emphasis in the past and have risen sharply in price. However, certain of the branch Mint issues of the 1909-1929 era in particular have been nearly completely overlooked by investors and yield some superb possibilities. The 1915-D Lincoln cent, priced $110 in MS-63 grade, is sufficiently scarce that if you advertised to pay $500 each, I doubt if you could buy more than two or three dozen within a given year's time! I am not recommending that you do this, for if you are seeking these they will probably cost you little more than the catalog valuation. However, it does illustrate their true rarity.

The great investment opportunity in copper coins lies in grades from Extremely Fine 40 to MS-60. Such pieces have been overlooked by investors and offer many bargains to prospective purchasers. The same is true of many issues among silver coins.

U.S. silver coins

The field of United States silver coins comprises many different issues. Silver 3-cent pieces (1851-1873) are mainly collected by design type rather than by dates. As a result, certain scarce dates can be obtained for reasonable prices in comparision to common issues. In a recent study for a book, I noted that the 1856 silver 3-cent piece in choice Uncirculated grade is several times rarer than than the 1855 of the same denomination, although the mintage of the 1856 is 10 times greater! Here is a "sleeper." Bargains can be obtained in coins graded from EF-40 through MS-60. Often an MS-60 coin will be available for a tiny fraction of the MS-65 price. Many early issues are not priced in MS-65 preservation in *A Guide Book of United States Coins*. To obtain prices, auction records must be consulted.

Copper-nickel 3-cent pieces from 1865-1889 appeal mainly to the type collector. Not many people saved them by date sequence. While prices of copper-nickel 3-cent pieces and higher grades are lower than they were a few years ago, right now I feel that they are "fully priced" for the most part. This is not one of my recommended areas.

Copper-nickel 5-cent pieces include Shield, Liberty, Indian and Jefferson types. Among the issues I like are Liberty Head 5-cent pieces in the grades of Extremely Fine, MS-60 and MS-65. In the latter grade, be sure that there is no rubbing, friction or other impairments, for many pieces sold as "MS-65" — equal to choice Uncirculated — are not quite what is hoped once they are examined in person. True MS-65 5-cent pieces are sharply undervalued. Among Indian (also called Buffalo or Bison) 5-cent pieces, most issues in higher grades are difficult to evaluate, for grading criteria are not well-defined, and striking plays a part. If you are an advanced numismatist, then forming an MS-65 set can be a great challenge. However, if you are a beginner I suggest you leave this alone.

Jefferson 5 cents from 1938 onward cost in many instances no more than they did 20 years ago, a bargain situation comparable to Indian cents. I view as a good investment a set of dates and Mint marks from 1938 through the 1960s. Such a set will cost you in the range of $200 and is easily obtained. Be sure, however, that such key issues as the 1939-D, 1942-D and others are really MS-65.

Half dimes of the 1795-1873 era are quite attractively priced in comparison to values of just a few years ago. I particularly like MS-60 issues in the 1840s and 1850s, especially if a given piece has a low mintage or some other unusual characteristic.

In general, the field of MS-65 and Proof 65 coins of the 19th century is still the domain of the investor. Well-heeled collectors can participate, but the cost of entry is high, and it is often the situation that several MS-60 specimens of a given issue can be purchased for the price of a single MS-65. There are some advantages that rare dates can often be purchased for just slightly more than "type" issues.

Among dimes, I like Seated Liberty issues of scarcer dates in EF grade. I like Barber dimes in grades of Fine through MS-60, with Extremely Fine being a great bargain, in my opinion. Among Winged Liberty Head dimes, there will probably be no better time than the present to pick up Uncirculated specimens of such key issues as 1916-D, 1921, 1921-D and the overdates. I like MS-60 and, in some instances, also MS-65 for these. If you can find a 1942/1 Overdate in MS-65 at the $2,500 *Guide Book* price, you have purchased a major rarity. Here is a coin which should be worth closer to $10,000!

Twenty-cent pieces are mainly collected by design types. Most seem to be fully priced at the moment from an investment viewpoint.

Among quarter dollars I like Extremely Fine Seated Liberty issues of common dates. These are quite rare — probably at least 10 times rarer than comparable issues in the dime series. I also like Barber quarter dollars in grades from Fine through About Uncirculated. I like Washington quarter dollars of the

1932-50 era in MS-65 grade. Some of the earlier Mint mark issues in particular will probably be much higher in price a few years from now.

Among half dollars, I feel that there are good values in VF, EF and AU Seated Liberty coins with common dates and especially in Barber half dollars from Fine through AU, the latter being some of the greatest sleepers in the American series. Walking Liberty half dollars of later dates in MS-65 condition will probably continue their strength, simply because these pieces are of a beautiful design and have a broad base of popularity.

The silver dollar market always has its ups and downs. I am presently engaged in a detailed study of Morgan and Peace dollars and hope to have a book about the subject on the market within the next year. In general, certain common Morgan silver dollars, issues such as 1881-S, seem to be higher priced than the *collector* market would warrant; this is particularly true of coins in MS-65 grade. On the other hand, scarce Carson City Mint issues, Proofs and other coins which are legitimately scarce or rare sell for much lower values in proportion. I feel that the grade MS-63 yields a better value at today's prices than MS-65, simply because MS-65 coins are largely priced that way in response to the investor segment of the market. Peace silver dollars of the 1925-35 era have been neglected for many years, and in MS-65 grade there are many rarities and many sleepers, so for this series, a close study of the MS-65 category is recommended.

Trade dollars are mostly collected by type. Choice Proof-65 specimens of the 1873-77 years are rarer than catalog values indicate, much rarer than those of the 1878-83 years. However, the later issues have the appeal of being Proof-only pieces, which strengthens their market. In general I like all Proof 65 Trade dollars.

Gold coins

Now seems to be a good time to buy gold coins. The market is more active than it was a few years ago, but there are still many bargains to be had. I recommend forming a gold type set. Rather than picking the most common of each issue, pay a little more and get a scarce date or variety. As an example, the *Guide Book* notes that an MS-60 specimen of an 1853 Coronet gold dollar is worth $1,200, whereas an 1876 Indian Head gold dollar in the same preservation is listed at $1,700, and yet the 1876 is at least 50 to 100 times rarer! Curiously, in 1984, an MS-60 example of the 1853 gold dollar was listed at $750, and the

1876 was listed at $1,800. In the intervening years, the catalog value of the common issue has risen sharply, while the rarer issue has declined. Thus, the bargain aspect of the 1876 is greater than ever! Just by reading these words you have a great advantage over most investors, for most investors will not take the time to do any research. If they did, then an MS-60 example of the 1876 gold dollar would list for $10,000.

Among $2.50 quarter eagles, $5 half eagles and $20 double eagles, it is not hard to find a scarce New Orleans, Carson City of San Francisco Mint issue for little more than a common piece. Go for them!

The field of gold coins in general offers many opportunities for the collector and investor. For those who can afford it, probably today offers some of the most wonderful opportunities imaginable for building sets of gold dollars, quarter eagles and other specialties. The number of museum and other collections coming on the market have made the available supply of rarities greater than it was 10 or 20 years ago, and yet the prices are not much higher in certain instances. These opportunities will not last long, in my opinion.

Commemoratives

Commemorative issues have always been popular, although the prices have fluctuated over a period of time. My recommendation is to go for a set of commemorative half dollars by design types. I recommend MS-63 condition, simply because such pieces are not a great deal more expensive than MS-60 coins but, in many instances, are much, much less expensive than MS-65 pieces. Again, as in silver dollars, the price for MS-65 coins has been artificially inflated by investor demand, making MS-63 coins seem to be bargains by comparisons.

Other numismatic areas

For the investor with a roving eye, there are many diverse series worthy of consideration. The field of tokens and medals offers many possibilities, although you must be prepared to buy many reference books and to become involved in deep study, actually a very pleasant experience. Civil War tokens, Hard Times tokens and other specialties have rewarded many investors in the past. And because such pieces are not recognized by the "average" dealer, there is always the possibility of buying a truly rare die variety for little more than you would have to pay for a common issue.

United States paper money is another field. Six or seven years ago it became a popular investment medium, with the result that many collectors were frightened away. After investors left the market, prices fell. Today there are many issues that can be obtained for a fraction of what they sold for in 1979-80. Included are numerous scarcities and rarities, classic issues and the like. Here is a very fertile field for the inquiring investor. Coins of Hawaii, patterns and other pieces associated with the American series are likewise worthy of investigation.

Holistic relationship

I encourage you to have a holistic relationship with numismatics. By this I mean that the whole is worth more than the sum of the parts. A modest amount of time spent by you reading and studying coins, plus some intelligent buying, will not only reward you with a nice coin collection but should over a period of time give you much collecting enjoyment and the possibility for really super investment. Along the way, build a numismatic library. In fact, don't wait until you have bought a lot of coins. Start on your library first! If you contemplate spending $5,000 for coins, then spend at least $500 for a basic library. There is no substitute for knowledge, and a library can literally be worth its weight in gold. There are more excellent numismatic references available now than at any other time in the history of our hobby.

When contemplating an investment, consider its past price movement. This can be done by referring to old issues of *A Guide Book of United States Coins* and other data. If the prices seem to be unnaturally high, then beware. On the other hand, if prices are attractively low in comparison to other years, now may be a good time to buy.

Learn about grading. *Photograde* and the *Official ANA Grading Standards for United States Coins* are essential in this regard. There are probably more abuses and complaints in the field of grading than in any other in the numismatic hobby. Grading is not only important, it is absolutely essential. Don't rely upon others to do grading for you. Learn about it yourself!

Learn about different dealers, their techniques and how they compare with each other. Consult with other numismatists. When buying, do comparison shopping. If you consider coins to be strictly an investment you probably will do well providing you buy the coins from an established numismatic source and differentiate between speculative coins and numismatic coins. If you consider coins to be an investment and collection combined you will do even better!

Your knowledge gained in being a collector will enable you to be more careful and more intelligent with your coin purchases. This will result in a better performance of what you buy. It might seem strange for you to read this, but the best investment performances I've ever seen in the field of numismatics have been turned in by collectors, not by investors! There may be a few exceptions, but such exceptions are occasional.

Further, the coins themselves will provide countless hours of enjoyment. Actually, with coin collecting and investment combined you can literally have your cake and eat it too.

Your favorite hobby can also be your best investment!

Ten years from now, toward the end of 1997, hopefully I will be writing about coin investment and will be discussing a future market. At that time we can look back on 1987 and see what happened. Between now and then there will be fortunes made in coin collecting, and there will be money lost as well. Just as in any field, some will prosper and some will not. The difference between the haves and the have-nots is summarized by one word: knowledge. In addition, right now you have the advantage of a low point in the market cycle for many series. Investigate it!

Coin World Trends

Trends, a regular feature of *Coin World*, is a market trend compiled from many different sources of pricing information, keeping demand and rarity in mind. Some examples include dealer price lists, both buy and sell, the American Teleprocessing Corp. teletypewriter service, Information Networks Inc. teletypewriter service, advertisements, auction prices realized, realistic private transactions and any additional information personally acquired. Variances in grading coins between dealers and also collectors or investors is an important consideration in determining values. *Coin World* neither buys nor sells coins, but does report a specific composite or trend of coin values, which may or may not represent individuals or dealers buy and sell prices.

The U.S. Trends to follow were published in *Coin World* in June 1987; the Canadian Trends in May 1987. U.S. Trends are updated on a biweekly rotation by Trends Editor Keith M. Zaner. Canadian Trends are compiled for *Coin World* by James Charlton.

Coins are listed by denomination from smallest to largest, and within each denomination by date. Values are listed by condition (About Good — AG-3; Good — G-4; Very Good — VG-8; Fine — F-12; Very Fine — VF-20; Extremely Fine — EF-40; About Uncirculated — AU-50; Mint State — MS-60, MS-63, MS-65; and Proof strikes — Prf-65). Proof coins, Proof sets, Mint sets, Year sets, Brilliant Uncirculated rolls and commemoratives have separate listings where applicable.

Trends is aware of the 11 Mint State and Proof grades used today numerically from 60 to 70 of the Sheldon scale. Trends will continue to monitor the activity level as well as the hobby demand for these grades. At such time when these grades are fully acclimated and accepted by hobbyists and investors alike, Trends will add the necessary grading categories to the present Trends list of MS-60, MS-63, MS-65, Proof 60, Proof 63 and Proof 65. Further information concerning the 11 grades from 60 through 70 can be found in Chapter 15.

U.S. Trends

Half Cents

Large Cents

	AG-3	G-4	VG-8	F-12	VF-20	EF-40
1793 Chain....	900.	1700.	2450.	3800.	6500.	11750.
1793 Wreath..	425.	800.	1075.	1650.	2750.	6250.
1793 Lib. Cap.	775.	1600.	2500.	3400.	5800.	---
1794 All Vars.	75.00	145.	240.	365.	750.	1800.
1795 Pl. Edge.	67.50	125.	225.	350.	600.	1650.
1795 Let. Ed...	100.	180.	300.	550.	1300.	2550.
1796 Lib. Cap.	87.50	160.	275.	500.	875.	2400.
1796 Dr. Bust.	50.00	95.00	190.	350.	650.	1700.
1797.........	32.50	47.50	100.	145.	330.	950.
1797 Stemless.	50.00	87.50	175.	320.	585.	2300.
1798 1st Hair Style.......	23.50	42.50	92.50	150.	380.	1000.
1798 98/97....	65.00	130.	260.	325.	850.	2900.
1799.........	465.	925.	1750.	3650.	5750.	---
1799/8.......	500.	1075.	1900.	4000.	6000.	---

	G-4	VG-8	F-12	VF-20	EF-40
1800.........	35.50	46.00	100.	290.	615.
1800/1798 1st....	44.50	65.00	200.	545.	1400.
1801.......	27.75	35.00	100.	290.	595.
1801 3 Err....	82.50	185.	335.	1050.	2450.
1801 1/000 ...	43.50	80.00	165.	400.	835.
1801 1/100 over 1/000 ...	55.00	125.	210.	435.	935.
1802.........	26.75	34.50	85.00	285.	565.
1802 stemless .	29.50	46.00	100.	290.	605.
1802 1/000 ...	36.00	58.50	125.	360.	725.
1803.........	23.00	32.50	82.50	270.	580.
1803 stemless .	30.75	49.50	105.	310.	760.
1803 1/100 over 1/000 ...	38.50	60.00	135.	360.	825.
1804.........	500.	800.	1550.	2850.	6250.
1805.........	27.75	49.50	92.50	300.	605.
1806.........	49.50	87.50	245.	520.	925.
1807 Lg Fract..	25.75	42.50	87.50	285.	585.
1807/6 Lg 7 ...	26.00	43.00	97.50	320.	640.
1808 Classic ..	34.00	46.50	100.	310.	730.
1809.........	67.50	140.	345.	775.	1625.
1810.........	28.50	45.00	100.	300.	640.
1810 10/09	28.50	45.00	90.00	300.	640.
1811.........	69.00	105.	225.	535.	1100.
1811/0........	77.50	130.	260.	610.	1400.
1812 All Vars..	28.50	45.00	87.50	300.	645.
1813.........	39.50	75.00	145.	385.	825.
1814 All Vars..	29.00	45.00	92.50	320.	665.

	G-4	VG-8	F-12	VF-20	EF-40	MS-60
1816 Coronet..	8.00	14.25	21.50	40.00	95.00	370.
1817 13 Stars..	6.50	10.75	16.00	33.50	82.50	295.
1817 15 Stars.	11.25	20.00	29.50	70.00	285.	1100.
1818.........	6.50	10.75	15.50	33.50	82.50	275.
1819 All Vars..	7.00	11.00	15.75	33.50	82.50	285.
1819/8........	10.65	17.50	25.00	55.00	215.	475.
1820 All Vars..	6.50	10.75	16.00	33.50	87.50	285.
1820/19....	10.75	14.25	18.00	45.00	195.	435.
1821.........	13.50	27.00	60.00	165.	575.	---
1822.........	6.00	11.25	23.75	52.50	150.	485.
1823.........	45.00	90.00	200.	425.	1250.	---
1823/2........	40.00	80.00	175.	365.	1200.	4250.
1824.........	7.00	13.00	32.50	67.50	325.	2250.
1824/2........	15.00	30.00	52.50	165.	450.	---
1825.........	6.00	11.25	19.50	47.50	210.	1100.
1826.........	6.00	11.25	19.50	40.00	95.00	280.
1826/5........	28.00	45.00	90.00	200.	525.	1400.
1827.........	6.00	10.25	14.00	39.00	87.50	290.
1828 Lg. Date.	6.00	9.00	13.50	37.50	87.50	255.
1828 S. Date..	7.90	13.50	22.50	47.50	210.	560.
1829 Lg. Lts...	6.00	10.75	16.00	38.50	90.00	300.
1830 Lg. Lts...	5.75	9.50	13.50	33.50	82.50	295.

Half Cents

	AG-3	G-4	VG-8	F-12	VF-20	EF-40
1793 Flwg Hr..	625.	1250.	1650.	2700.	3650.	7250.
1794 Lib Cap..	82.50	245.	370.	550.	1125.	2250.
1795 All Vars..	77.50	210.	270.	450.	850.	2050.
1796 w/pole..	2200.	3600.	5500.	8000.	14500.	---
1797 Pl. Ed....	100.	285.	325.	565.	1025.	2150.
1797 Let. Ed..	310.	485.	750.	1500.	3600.	---

	G-4	VG-8	F-12	VF-20	EF-40	AU-50
1800 Dr. Bust.	24.25	35.50	50.00	110.	260.	500.
1802/0	290.	410.	785.	2900.	---	---
1803.........	25.25	36.00	55.00	115.	360.	900.
1804 All Vars.	23.25	30.50	42.50	85.00	275.	450.
1805 All Vars..	23.25	31.50	43.50	87.50	295.	460.
1806 All Vars..	23.25	30.50	42.50	85.00	275.	450.
1807.........	23.25	32.50	47.50	100.	320.	550.
1808.........	23.25	32.50	47.50	115.	410.	---
1808/7	70.00	115.	300.	650.	900.	---
1809 Classic ..	21.00	26.50	30.50	38.50	80.00	155.
1809/6	21.00	26.50	30.50	38.50	145.	305.
1810.........	23.00	36.50	54.00	160.	380.	560.
1811.........	115.	200.	345.	850.	1750.	---
1825.........	22.00	27.50	31.50	50.00	145.	285.
1826.........	20.50	26.50	30.00	38.50	80.00	235.
1828 13 Stars.	20.00	23.00	29.00	34.00	55.00	140.
1828 12 Stars..	24.25	37.00	47.50	80.00	260.	435.
1829.........	20.00	23.00	29.00	34.50	50.00	130.
1831 Original and Restrikes						
1832.........	20.00	23.00	29.00	34.00	50.00	130.
1833.........	20.00	23.00	29.00	34.00	50.00	110.
1834.........	20.00	23.00	29.00	34.00	50.00	110.
1835.........	20.00	23.00	29.00	34.00	50.00	105.
1836 Orig and Restrikes Proof - Proof 63 $4400.						

	G-4	VG-8	F-12	VF-20	EF-40	MS-60
1840-49 Originals and Restrikes Proofs Only Br Hair						
1849 Lg. Date.	29.00	32.00	42.50	55.00	70.00	355.
1850.........	29.00	32.00	40.50	50.00	65.00	260.
1851.........	25.50	30.00	38.50	45.00	60.00	205.
1853.........	25.50	30.00	38.50	45.00	60.00	205.
1854.........	26.00	30.50	39.00	49.50	62.50	200.
1855.........	26.00	30.50	39.00	47.50	60.00	195.
1856.........	29.00	32.00	40.50	50.00	65.50	215.
1857.........	33.50	40.00	52.50	61.50	67.50	250.

LARGE CENTS

	G-4	VG-8	F-12	VF-20	EF-40	MS-60
1831 All Vars..	5.50	8.25	11.75	27.50	55.00	290.
1832 All Vars..	5.75	8.50	12.50	33.50	75.00	290.
1833	5.25	8.00	11.75	27.50	82.50	250.
1834 All Vars..	6.00	9.00	13.50	32.00	65.00	250.
1835 All Vars..	6.25	9.50	14.00	33.50	67.50	260.
1835 Type 36..	5.40	7.25	11.25	32.00	55.00	245.
1836	5.25	8.50	15.00	32.00	80.00	255.
1837 All Vars..	5.25	7.00	9.25	24.50	52.50	250.
1838	5.25	6.75	11.00	18.75	50.00	240.
1839 Type 38..	6.00	9.00	13.50	32.00	70.00	280.
1839/6	155.	225.	435.	875.	2350.	— —
1839 Silly Hd..	8.60	12.75	18.50	38.50	90.00	615.
1839 Booby Hd	6.00	10.25	16.75	36.00	87.50	435.
1839 All Vars..	5.85	10.25	15.00	28.50	67.50	240.
1840 All Vars..	5.15	7.25	9.00	18.50	42.50	230.
1841 Sm Date .	5.20	7.25	11.50	21.50	67.50	235.
1842 All Vars..	5.15	7.25	8.50	15.15	42.50	230.
1843 Petite Sm Let	5.15	5.75	7.50	15.15	41.00	230.
1843 Mature Lg Let......	5.15	9.00	13.50	22.25	50.00	230.
1843 Petite Lg Let......	13.50	20.50	46.50	77.50	195.	690.
1844	5.00	6.25	8.00	14.15	40.00	220.
1844/81	14.50	20.00	26.00	70.00	190.	— —
1845	5.00	6.25	8.00	14.15	40.00	205.
1846 All Vars..	5.00	6.25	7.75	13.65	37.50	205.
1847 All Vars..	5.00	5.50	8.00	14.65	41.00	220.
1848	5.00	5.50	7.25	13.40	37.50	205.
1849	5.00	5.50	7.25	13.40	40.00	205.
1850	5.00	5.50	7.25	13.00	37.50	205.
1851	5.00	5.50	7.25	13.00	37.50	205.
1851/81	12.75	15.50	17.25	38.50	90.00	385.
1852	5.00	5.50	7.25	13.00	37.50	205.
1853	5.00	5.50	7.25	13.00	37.50	205.
1854	5.15	5.75	7.50	13.00	37.50	205.
1855 All Vars..	5.25	6.75	9.25	13.15	37.50	220.
1856 All Vars..	5.20	6.00	7.60	13.65	37.50	205.
1857 Sm. Date.	32.00	41.00	51.00	66.50	97.50	285.
1857 Lg. Date .	27.50	33.00	46.00	54.00	92.50	385.

Flying Eagle Cents

	G-4	F-12	VF-20	EF-40	AU-50	MS-60	MS-65
1856	1400.	1875.	2250.	2575.	2900.	3250.	6150.
1857	8.50	12.00	25.00	52.50	125.	180.	2050.
1858 Lg Lt....	8.55	13.40	25.75	70.00	145.	210.	2100.
1858 Sm Lt ...	8.55	13.00	25.50	66.50	135.	195.	2100.

Indian Head Cents

	G-4	F-12	VF-20	EF-40	AU-50	MS-60	MS-65
1859 Var. 1 ...	3.50	7.10	19.25	54.50	130.	180.	1250.
1860 Var. 2 ...	3.50	5.00	10.00	21.00	46.50	90.00	775.
1861	8.50	13.00	23.00	45.00	79.00	145.	1050.
1862	2.75	4.00	8.25	17.00	39.50	82.50	575.
1863	2.25	3.50	7.50	16.75	37.00	77.50	575.
1864	8.00	11.75	16.50	25.00	47.50	100.	800.
1864-L Var. 3..	25.00	40.00	80.00	115.	185.	300.	1050.
1864	3.25	6.40	14.00	22.00	31.50	52.50	485.
1865	3.00	6.10	13.25	19.50	27.75	48.00	510.
1866	18.00	30.00	45.00	72.50	110.	160.	575.

Indian Head Cents

	G-4	F-12	VF-20	EF-40	AU-50	MS-60	MS-65
1867	18.00	30.00	45.00	72.50	110.	160.	575.
1868	18.00	30.00	45.00	72.50	110.	160.	575.
1869	23.00	62.50	92.50	150.	195.	275.	850.
1869/8	87.50	190.	320.	425.	625.	815.	2350.
1870	18.00	55.00	85.00	110.	155.	245.	725.
1871	24.00	65.00	90.00	130.	160.	260.	775.
1872	33.50	70.00	115.	155.	230.	385.	925.
1873	8.00	13.50	25.25	43.50	58.50	87.50	590.
1874	8.00	13.25	24.50	42.50	55.00	82.50	525.
1875	8.00	13.25	25.00	42.75	56.00	85.00	550.
1876	14.00	24.00	42.50	60.00	75.00	140.	615.
1877	145.	275.	450.	690.	900.	1300.	4900.
1878	14.00	22.50	45.00	61.50	77.00	160.	615.
1879	2.50	4.50	9.00	18.00	28.00	42.00	480.
1880	1.65	2.50	4.00	11.25	17.00	33.00	385.
1881	1.60	2.50	4.00	10.50	18.00	33.00	385.
1882	1.60	2.50	4.00	10.50	16.00	33.00	385.
1883	1.60	2.60	4.00	10.50	19.00	34.00	390.
1884	1.40	3.50	6.50	13.00	21.00	39.50	440.
1885	2.35	6.25	11.00	20.00	28.50	55.00	460.
1886	2.00	4.50	7.00	14.50	24.00	47.50	440.
1887	.85	1.45	2.50	8.00	15.25	28.50	385.
1888	.85	1.45	2.50	8.00	14.75	28.50	385.
1889	.85	1.45	2.50	8.00	14.50	28.50	385.
1890	.85	1.45	2.50	8.00	14.00	26.00	385.
1891	.85	1.45	2.50	8.00	13.90	26.00	385.
1892	.85	1.45	2.50	8.00	14.00	26.00	385.
1893	.85	1.45	2.50	8.00	13.90	26.00	410.
1894	1.15	3.75	6.25	11.75	19.00	32.00	440.
1895	.75	1.20	2.50	6.75	13.50	26.00	380.
1896	.75	1.20	2.50	6.75	13.00	26.00	380.
1897	.75	1.20	2.50	6.75	13.00	26.00	380.
1898	.75	1.20	2.50	6.75	13.00	25.50	380.
1899	.75	1.20	2.50	6.75	13.00	25.50	380.
1900	.70	.95	1.40	5.50	11.00	25.00	365.
1901	.70	.95	1.40	5.50	11.00	25.00	365.
1902	.70	.95	1.40	5.50	11.00	25.00	365.
1903	.70	.95	1.40	5.50	11.00	25.00	365.
1904	.70	.95	1.40	5.50	11.00	25.00	365.
1905	.70	.95	1.40	5.50	11.00	25.00	365.
1906	.70	.95	1.40	5.50	11.00	25.00	365.
1907	.70	.95	1.40	5.50	11.00	25.00	365.
1908	.70	.95	1.40	5.50	11.00	25.00	365.
1908-S	16.50	23.00	30.00	45.00	80.00	140.	700.
1909	1.00	1.75	2.75	7.00	13.75	26.50	425.
1909-S	89.00	115.	135.	170.	240.	330.	900.

Lincoln Cents

	G-4	VG-8	F-12	VF-20	EF-40	MS-60	MS-65
1909 VDB	1.50	1.75	2.10	2.35	3.00	10.00	45.00
1909-SVDB* ..	200.	220.	245.	265.	300.	415.	1000.
1909	.50	.60	.80	1.20	2.00	11.25	52.50
1909-S	32.50	35.00	40.00	52.50	82.50	130.	275.
1910	.16	.21	.35	.75	1.50	12.75	60.00
1910-S	5.00	5.50	7.50	9.00	17.50	70.00	315.
1911	.20	.25	.50	1.10	2.50	14.75	72.50
1911-D	2.95	3.25	4.75	9.50	25.00	87.50	345.
1911-S	8.25	9.25	11.75	15.75	29.00	110.	525.
1912	.40	.50	1.45	2.90	5.75	19.00	77.50
1912-D	3.25	4.00	5.50	10.00	30.00	105.	390.
1912-S	8.00	8.75	11.00	14.50	27.50	100.	525.
1913	.30	.40	1.00	2.50	6.00	18.75	77.50
1913-D	1.40	1.75	2.50	6.00	18.00	70.00	365.
1913-S	5.00	5.75	7.00	10.50	22.00	87.50	675.
1914	.30	.40	1.25	2.60	6.50	45.00	165.
1914-D*	46.50	60.00	85.00	150.	365.	725.	1850.
1914-S	7.50	9.00	10.50	15.00	29.50	140.	1100.
1915	.85	1.00	2.65	6.00	25.00	77.50	225.

532   **Coins as Investments — U.S. Trends**

LINCOLN CENTS

	G-4	VG-8	F-12	VF-20	EF-40	MS-60	MS-65
1915-D	.55	.70	1.50	2.65	7.75	35.00	365.
1915-S	5.50	6.50	7.75	10.00	23.50	85.00	675.
1916	.15	.20	.30	.75	1.70	9.50	62.50
1916-D	.25	.35	.60	1.25	5.50	42.50	265.
1916-S	.65	.80	1.10	2.00	6.35	49.00	380.
1917	.15	.20	.30	.70	1.55	11.00	67.50
1917-D	.20	.30	.60	1.70	4.75	42.50	250.
1917-S	.21	.32	.62	1.55	4.60	49.00	360.
1918	.15	.20	.30	.70	1.55	11.00	65.00
1918-D	.21	.32	.62	1.70	4.75	42.50	245.
1918-S	.25	.35	.55	1.55	4.55	49.00	350.
1919	.15	.20	.30	.75	1.40	8.00	62.50
1919-D	.20	.33	.55	1.30	3.15	37.50	150.
1919-S	.19	.25	.40	1.00	2.35	29.50	210.
1920	.15	.20	.30	.75	1.50	8.50	62.50
1920-D	.20	.27	.50	1.25	3.50	43.50	185.
1920-S	.20	.25	.50	1.15	2.90	47.50	360.
1921	.17	.21	.40	1.05	3.00	34.50	135.
1921-S	.60	.80	1.10	2.50	9.50	105.	925.
1922 Pl.*	125.	165.	210.	350.	675.	2650.	8250.
1922-D	3.00	3.75	5.75	9.00	17.50	67.50	335.
1923	.12	.16	.25	.70	2.00	8.00	60.00
1923-S	1.15	1.40	2.25	3.75	14.00	170.	925.
1924	.12	.16	.25	.75	2.40	19.00	87.50
1924-D	8.00	8.75	10.00	17.50	38.00	210.	800.
1924-S	.60	.75	1.15	1.90	6.50	92.50	700.
1925	.12	.16	.20	.60	1.25	7.50	52.50
1925-D	.20	.35	.65	1.05	3.75	42.00	365.
1925-S	.16	.25	.45	.80	3.50	52.50	535.
1926	.12	.17	.21	.60	1.25	7.00	48.50
1926-D	.20	.30	.60	1.05	3.50	40.00	350.
1926-S	1.40	1.75	2.75	3.75	9.50	82.50	575.
1927	.12	.17	.23	.60	1.20	7.15	47.50
1927-D	.20	.30	.50	.75	2.35	24.00	310.
1927-S	.40	.60	.90	1.80	5.00	50.00	525.
1928	.11	.16	.22	.55	1.15	6.00	47.50
1928-D	.20	.30	.50	.75	2.25	19.50	235.
1928-S	.25	.35	.60	1.25	2.75	40.00	385.
1929	.11	.16	.25	.40	.75	5.00	32.50
1929-D	.20	.30	.40	.70	1.25	13.25	135.
1929-S	.15	.20	.30	.55	1.00	7.25	73.00
1930	.10	.15	.20	.55	.80	4.00	27.00
1930-D	.13	.20	.40	.75	1.40	9.25	77.50
1930-S	.17	.25	.35	.65	.95	5.75	55.00
1931	.45	.60	.75	.95	1.45	14.00	75.00
1931-D	1.75	2.00	2.50	3.25	7.00	39.00	220.
1931-S	27.50	29.50	30.50	32.50	36.00	56.50	140.
1932	1.10	1.25	1.50	1.95	2.50	14.75	54.00
1932-D	.70	.80	.90	1.25	1.50	12.25	60.00
1933	.75	.90	1.10	1.40	2.00	13.50	70.00
1933-D	1.50	1.75	2.00	2.75	3.15	19.50	67.50

	F-12	VF-20	EF-40	MS-60	MS-65
1934	.18	.25	.55	2.00	12.25
1934-D	.30	.65	1.50	16.00	57.50
1935	.12	.18	.45	1.25	6.00
1935-D	.18	.30	.60	2.50	12.50
1935-S	.18	.30	.70	6.50	55.00
1936	.12	.18	.35	.80	4.75
1936-D	.18	.25	.40	1.30	7.25
1936-S	.18	.30	.55	1.35	7.65
1937	.12	.18	.35	.75	4.75
1937-D	.18	.30	.40	1.25	5.90
1937-S	.18	.30	.40	1.00	8.50
1938	.12	.18	.35	.85	5.50
1938-D	.25	.30	.50	1.25	6.90
1938-S	.40	.45	.70	1.35	10.00
1939	.12	.18	.35	.50	3.40
1939-D	.40	.45	.70	1.65	10.25
1939-S	.20	.30	.45	.90	7.45
1940	.07	.12	.19	.40	3.20
1940-D	.12	.18	.25	.60	3.90
1940-S	.12	.18	.25	.85	5.10
1941	.07	.12	.19	.45	3.50

LINCOLN CENTS

	F-12	VF-20	EF-40	MS-60	MS-65
1941-D	.07	.12	.30	1.35	7.25
1941-S	.12	.18	.30	1.80	8.50
1942	.07	.12	.19	.35	2.65
1942-D	.07	.12	.19	.40	3.00
1942-S	.12	.18	.45	3.00	16.00
1943	.18	.20	.32	.42	2.50
1943-D	.20	.25	.38	.85	4.35
1943-S	.20	.25	.38	1.30	6.50
1944	.07	.12	.19	.27	1.30
1944-D	.07	.12	.19	.30	1.40
1944-S	.07	.12	.19	.30	1.65
1945	.07	.12	.19	.30	1.20
1945-D	.07	.12	.19	.30	1.75
1945-S	.07	.12	.19	.33	1.45
1946	.07	.12	.19	.24	1.20
1946-D	.07	.12	.19	.26	1.25
1946-S	.07	.12	.19	.30	1.35
1947	.07	.12	.19	.32	1.45
1947-D	.07	.12	.19	.30	1.30
1947-S	.12	.18	.22	.31	1.65
1948	.07	.12	.19	.30	1.35
1948-D	.07	.12	.19	.35	1.55
1948-S	.12	.18	.23	.50	1.80
1949	.07	.12	.19	.55	2.05
1949-D	.07	.12	.19	.50	2.00
1949-S	.12	.18	.24	.85	3.75

	VF-20	EF-40	MS-60	MS-65	Proof-65
1950	.12	.19	.35	1.30	39.00
1950-D	.07	.13	.24	1.15	— —
1950-S	.12	.25	.40	1.30	— —
1951	.12	.28	.40	1.35	24.50
1951-D	.07	.13	.24	1.10	— —
1951-S	.18	.25	.55	2.30	— —
1952	.12	.19	.35	1.20	18.75
1952-D	.06	.13	.29	1.15	— —
1952-S	.12	.19	.40	1.65	— —
1953	.07	.13	.19	1.05	10.75
1953-D	.06	.13	.28	1.15	— —
1953-S	.12	.19	.29	1.20	— —
1954	.16	.26	.32	1.40	7.00
1954-D	.06	.13	.19	1.00	— —
1954-S	.07	.13	.22	1.10	— —
1955	.06	.13	.19	.95	5.00
1955 Dbl. Die	300.	350.	665.	3100.	— —
1955-D	.06	.13	.19	.90	— —
1955-S	.15	.19	.30	1.20	— —
1960 SD	.60	.85	1.50	4.25	12.00
1960-D SD	.04	.06	.15	.85	— —
1972 Dbl. Die	97.50	105.	190.	265.	— —

	Proof-65		Proof-65
1975-S	4.25	1980-S	1.50
1976-S	2.50	1981-S Var. I	1.50
		1982-S	2.50
1977-S	2.50	1983-S	8.50
1978-S	2.55	1984-S	9.00
1979-S Var. I	1.95	1985-S	7.00

MS-65 Lincolns, 1956 to 1982, are valued at 10¢ to 40¢; Proofs, 1956 to 1960 at $1.50 to $3; Proofs 1961 to 1974-S at $1.25.
* Beware of Struck Counterfeits.

Two Cent Pieces

	F-12	VF-20	EF-40	AU-50	MS-60	MS-65	Prf-65
1864 Sm Motto	78.00	120.	200.	315.	525.	2750.	
1864 Lg Motto	5.90	12.00	27.50	54.50	125.	800.	1750.
1865 All Vars.	5.50	12.00	27.50	55.00	130.	785.	1325.
1866	5.60	14.00	30.50	56.00	140.	800.	1325.

2-cent pieces

	F-12	VF-20	EF-40	AU-50	MS-60	MS-65	Prf-65
1867 All Vars..	5.60	14.00	32.00	58.50	150.	850.	1325.
1868	7.60	14.50	34.50	61.50	165.	875.	1325.
1869 All Vars..	8.60	15.50	39.00	65.00	235.	950.	1325.
1870	16.00	32.50	62.50	87.50	260.	1050.	1335.
1871	18.75	38.00	75.00	125.	280.	1150.	1350.
1872	130.	215.	315.	435.	700.	2600.	1400.
1873 Closed 3 Proofs Only							3000.
1873 Open 3 Restrike Proofs Only							3250.

Three Cent Nickel Pieces

	F-12	VF-20	EF-40	AU-50	MS-60	MS-65	Prf-65
1865	4.50	6.50	13.50	34.00	85.00	1100.	3100.
1866	4.50	6.50	13.50	34.00	80.00	1100.	1200.
1867	4.50	6.50	13.50	34.00	80.00	1100.	1175.
1868	4.55	6.50	13.75	34.50	80.00	1100.	1175.
1869	4.75	6.75	14.75	35.00	85.00	1100.	1200.
1870	5.50	7.00	15.00	37.00	95.00	1125.	1200.
1871	7.25	8.50	18.00	39.00	105.	1150.	1240.
1872	7.00	7.75	17.00	38.00	100.	1175.	1240.
1873 All Vars.	6.75	7.50	16.00	37.00	95.00	1175.	1225.
1874	6.75	7.50	17.00	40.00	100.	1175.	1225.
1875	10.25	13.25	25.00	65.00	140.	1225.	1250.
1876	13.50	18.25	31.00	75.00	150.	1275.	1275.
1877 Proofs Only	—	—	—	—	—	—	3400.
1878 Proofs Only	—	—	—	—	—	—	2200.
1879	52.50	62.00	77.50	130.	220.	1325.	1275.
1880	77.50	90.00	105.	165.	265.	1350.	1325.
1881	5.85	6.85	16.50	36.00	80.00	1100.	1225.
1882	67.00	83.00	97.50	145.	230.	1375.	1300.
1883	185.	225.	250.	285.	380.	1575.	1325.
1884	325.	350.	400.	465.	575.	1650.	1350.
1885	440.	490.	525.	600.	725.	1800.	1375.
1886 Proofs Only	—	—	—	—	—	—	1650.
1887/6 Proofs Only	...	—	—	—	—	—	1700.
1887	250.	270.	315.	375.	500.	1600.	1375.
1888	45.00	54.50	62.50	105.	255.	1325.	1350.
1889	65.00	80.00	95.00	140.	245.	1400.	1375.

Shield Nickels

	VG-8	F-12	VF-20	EF-40	AU-50	MS-60	MS-65
1866 Rays	13.00	18.00	29.00	68.00	155.	290.	3150.
1867 Rays	14.25	20.00	35.00	77.50	165.	310.	3300.
1867 No Rays .	7.00	8.75	12.00	25.00	43.50	115.	2300.
1868	7.00	8.75	12.00	25.00	43.50	115.	2200.
1869	7.00	9.00	12.25	26.00	46.50	120.	2225.
1870	7.75	10.00	15.00	33.00	49.00	125.	2250.
1871	29.00	37.50	60.00	90.00	160.	275.	2500.
1872	7.75	10.25	15.00	33.00	60.00	140.	2250.
1873 All Vars.	7.75	10.75	15.50	34.00	62.50	145.	2300.
1874	7.75	11.00	16.50	39.00	67.50	145.	2300.
1875	11.00	15.25	25.00	49.00	80.00	160.	2350.
1876	11.00	14.75	22.50	40.00	70.00	145.	2325.
1877	785.	885.	975.	1075.	1175.	1550.	4000.
1878	550.	600.	675.	750.	800.	950.	3150.
1879 All Vars.	270.	315.	340.	450.	490.	580.	2450.
1880	315.	335.	375.	475.	515.	615.	2500.
1881	190.	225.	265.	350.	410.	490.	2400.
1882	6.75	8.75	11.25	25.00	43.50	115.	2250.
1883 All Vars.	6.85	9.00	12.25	26.00	45.00	120.	2275.
1883/2	50.00	75.00	110.	175.	245.	400.	2400.

Liberty Head Nickels

	VG-8	F-12	VF-20	EF-40	AU-50	MS-60	MS-65
1883 No Cents..	2.60	3.15	4.50	6.00	10.50	40.00	650.
1883 Cents....	6.50	8.75	15.00	33.50	62.00	110.	1225.
1884	7.25	10.85	18.75	35.00	72.50	135.	1300.
1885	200.	300.	425.	625.	775.	1000.	2250.
1886	55.00	115.	170.	220.	290.	425.	1800.
1887	6.50	10.00	15.00	32.00	61.50	115.	1200.
1888	8.50	12.50	20.50	41.50	80.00	130.	1300.
1889	5.00	8.50	14.50	30.00	62.50	115.	1200.
1890	6.00	9.00	17.00	32.50	64.00	125.	1275.
1891	4.55	8.50	13.50	33.50	62.50	115.	1200.
1892	5.00	8.75	15.50	33.00	64.00	125.	1250.
1893	4.25	8.00	14.75	31.00	62.50	125.	1275.
1894	7.00	13.00	22.00	57.50	92.50	145.	1400.
1895	3.25	7.00	14.00	29.00	63.50	110.	1175.
1896	3.75	8.50	16.00	33.50	67.50	115.	1250.
1897	1.25	3.90	7.75	21.00	59.00	100.	1175.
1898	1.40	4.60	8.25	22.00	60.00	100.	1135.
1899	.70	3.10	6.25	19.00	49.00	95.00	1150.
1900	.65	3.00	5.00	15.50	40.00	90.00	1100.
1901	.65	3.00	5.00	15.50	40.00	90.00	1100.
1902	.65	3.00	5.00	15.50	40.00	90.00	1100.
1903	.65	3.00	5.00	15.50	40.00	100.	1100.
1904	.65	3.00	5.00	15.50	40.00	90.00	1100.
1905	.65	3.00	5.00	15.50	40.00	90.00	1100.
1906	.65	3.00	5.00	15.50	40.00	90.00	1100.
1907	.65	3.00	5.00	15.50	40.00	90.00	1100.
1908	.65	3.00	5.00	15.50	40.00	90.00	1100.
1909	.70	3.25	6.00	18.25	46.50	95.00	1125.
1910	.65	3.00	5.00	15.50	40.00	90.00	1100.
1911	.65	3.00	5.00	15.50	40.00	90.00	1100.
1912	.65	3.00	5.00	15.50	40.00	95.00	1100.
1912-D	1.25	4.25	8.50	40.00	87.50	225.	2000.
1912-S	40.00	52.50	150.	340.	430.	575.	2250.
1913 Extremely Rare - 5 known Proof 63 $350,000.							

Buffalo Nickels

	VG-8	F-12	VF-20	EF-40	AU-50	MS-60	MS-65
VARIETY 1							
1913 Var. 1 ..	3.15	3.50	6.00	9.85	17.00	30.00	425.
1913-D Var. 1 .	6.50	8.00	10.75	17.50	30.00	60.00	650.
1913-S Var. 1..	10.50	14.25	21.50	32.00	45.00	82.50	850.
VARIETY 2							
1913 Var. 2 ..	3.25	4.00	6.00	10.25	19.50	32.00	615.
1913-D Var. 2 .	35.00	39.00	48.00	57.50	90.00	175.	1750.
1913-S Var. 2..	65.00	90.00	100.	140.	210.	300.	2450.
1914	4.25	5.50	7.25	12.00	25.50	48.00	615.
1914-D	27.50	36.50	50.00	81.00	105.	220.	1500.
1914-S	5.40	8.50	15.00	26.50	39.00	87.50	1550.
1915	3.25	3.75	5.25	10.00	21.00	42.50	675.
1915-D	7.00	15.75	29.00	41.00	57.50	115.	1550.
1915-S	12.00	17.50	50.00	90.00	130.	225.	1900.
1916 All Vars.	.95	1.50	2.50	4.25	12.50	32.50	635.
1916-D	5.25	8.00	18.75	38.50	60.00	125.	1250.
1916-S	3.50	6.00	16.25	34.00	58.00	115.	1325.
1917	1.00	1.55	3.00	7.50	19.00	39.50	665.
1917-D	5.25	10.50	35.50	70.00	105.	200.	2050.
1917-S	5.00	10.75	33.00	57.50	95.00	210.	2300.
1918	1.10	2.00	5.00	14.50	29.50	62.50	880.
1918/17-D	410.	600.	1050.	2600.	4800.	7500.	26000.
1918-D	6.00	11.75	50.00	76.50	140.	265.	2550.
1918-S	4.50	10.50	33.00	67.00	115.	210.	2450.

BUFFALO NICKELS

	VG-8	F-12	VF-20	EF-40	AU-50	MS-60	MS-65
1919	.75	1.25	2.50	6.00	18.00	35.00	730.
1919-D	6.00	13.75	57.50	85.00	145.	315.	2300.
1919-S	3.50	7.75	38.50	66.00	110.	275.	3400.
1920	.70	1.20	2.25	6.25	18.75	36.00	725.
1920-D	4.00	9.25	46.50	76.00	140.	285.	3350.
1920-S	2.60	5.00	25.50	67.50	105.	175.	4000.
1921	1.00	1.80	5.25	16.50	31.50	69.00	810.
1921-S	17.00	39.00	130.	340.	460.	725.	3175.
1923	.60	1.00	1.90	5.75	14.00	33.00	730.
1923-S	2.00	4.35	22.50	41.00	68.00	135.	3900.
1924	.65	1.05	2.50	7.75	23.00	47.00	760.
1924-D	3.00	6.00	37.50	61.00	130.	190.	1900.
1924-S	6.25	13.50	185.	365.	500.	780.	2750.
1925	.65	1.05	2.35	5.75	16.50	32.00	680.
1925-D	5.25	10.50	41.50	64.00	135.	260.	2000.
1925-S	2.75	5.50	20.00	40.00	72.50	190.	3100.
1926	.45	.80	1.60	4.00	13.00	28.50	665.
1926-D	3.35	8.00	45.00	77.50	97.50	145.	2350.
1926-S	6.00	10.50	60.00	265.	450.	675.	3900.
1927	.45	.80	1.40	3.90	13.25	29.50	675.
1927-D	1.50	2.25	10.00	31.00	50.00	86.00	1300.
1927-S	1.00	1.75	12.00	38.00	58.00	150.	1550.
1928	.45	.80	1.50	4.00	13.75	29.50	650.
1928-D	1.05	1.75	5.85	11.75	23.50	40.00	875.
1928-S	.65	1.25	2.75	9.75	24.50	57.50	1050.
1929	.45	.80	1.25	2.85	11.00	27.50	535.
1929-D	1.05	1.50	3.25	10.00	23.00	44.50	1050.
1929-S	.45	.85	1.40	7.00	16.50	32.50	925.
1930	.45	.80	1.10	3.25	12.00	27.50	350.
1930-S	.60	1.05	1.50	6.00	22.00	42.50	635.
1931-S	3.50	3.85	4.50	8.50	23.00	47.50	525.
1934	.40	.50	1.00	2.65	10.00	22.50	330.
1934-D	.45	.85	2.50	7.50	18.00	45.00	445.
1935	.35	.50	.80	1.50	7.00	17.00	210.
1935-D	.60	1.00	1.65	3.75	11.00	41.50	575.
1935-S	.40	.65	1.20	2.75	10.50	22.50	280.
1936	.35	.50	.90	1.50	6.00	14.00	140.
1936-D	.45	.60	1.00	2.25	8.00	16.50	175.
1936-S	.40	.55	1.00	2.00	9.50	17.50	215.
1937	.35	.50	.90	1.50	5.50	11.50	94.50
1937-D	.45	.60	1.15	2.10	7.50	14.50	125.
1937-D 3 Legs	85.00	95.00	130.	170.	285.	475.	5100.
1937-S	.55	.65	1.20	2.20	7.65	15.00	130.
1938-D	.50	.60	1.00	2.00	6.50	12.00	70.00
1938-D/S	4.25	5.25	6.75	9.00	14.75	23.50	130.

Jefferson Nickels

	F-12	VF-20	EF-40	AU-50	MS-60	MS-65	Prf-65
1938	.25	.35	.60	.80	1.10	4.00	165.
1938-D	.95	1.10	1.50	2.50	3.25	7.00	—
1938-S	1.50	2.10	2.50	2.90	3.85	8.25	—
1939	.15	.25	.40	.80	1.00	3.25	145.
1939-D	2.75	4.50	6.75	17.00	25.00	47.50	—
1939-S	.75	1.00	3.45	7.00	15.85	30.00	—
1940	.07	.15	.25	.55	.90	2.55	130.
1940-D	.10	.20	.40	1.25	1.80	4.25	—
1940-S	.10	.25	.55	1.00	1.75	3.95	—
1941	.07	.15	.25	.40	.75	2.10	95.00
1941-D	.10	.20	.40	1.30	2.25	4.85	—
1941-S	.10	.25	.50	1.65	2.50	6.00	—
1942	.10	.15	.20	.60	1.00	3.00	95.00
1942-P	.60	1.10	2.50	3.50	9.50	17.50	475.
1942-S	.38	.55	1.85	8.00	13.75	35.00	—
1943-P	.60	.80	1.60	3.00	9.00	16.50	—
1943-D	.60	.80	1.05	1.85	3.15	8.15	—
1943-S	.75	1.00	1.85	2.35	3.40	9.00	—
1944-P	.60	.80	1.10	2.10	3.65	10.00	—
1944-P	.60	.80	1.35	2.10	4.15	10.00	—

JEFFERSON NICKELS

	F-12	VF-20	EF-40	AU-50	MS-60	MS-65	Prf-65
1944-D	.60	.80	1.60	2.30	6.10	16.00	—
1944-S	.60	.80	1.60	2.20	6.00	15.00	—
1945-P	.60	.80	1.35	2.10	3.60	13.75	—
1945-D	.60	.80	1.75	2.15	4.65	11.75	—
1945-S	.60	.80	1.20	1.85	3.65	9.50	—
1946	.07	.15	.20	.30	.45	1.85	—
1946-D	.10	.15	.20	.35	.60	3.25	—
1946-S	.20	.25	.40	.50	.55	3.50	—
1947	.07	.15	.20	.30	.40	1.70	—
1947-D	.08	.15	.25	.50	.65	2.05	—
1947-S	.08	.15	.20	.30	.60	2.00	—
1948	.07	.10	.20	.28	.45	1.80	—
1948-D	.10	.25	.45	.60	.80	2.65	—
1948-S	.10	.25	.45	.55	.70	2.10	—
1949	.15	.20	.25	.45	.75	2.95	—
1949-D	.10	.15	.25	.50	.80	2.65	—
1949-S	.30	.35	.50	.90	1.25	3.20	—
1950	.35	.40	.55	.85	1.30	3.05	72.50
1950-D*	4.75	4.85	5.00	5.30	5.75	8.25	—
1951	.07	.15	.25	.45	.70	2.65	56.50
1951-D	.07	.15	.25	.65	.85	2.50	—
1951-S	.25	.40	.60	1.25	1.90	4.25	—
1952	.07	.08	.10	.20	.45	2.10	34.50
1952-D	.07	.15	.25	.75	1.15	3.35	—
1952-S	.10	.15	.25	.35	.80	2.30	—
1953	.07	.08	.10	.20	.26	1.10	24.50
1953-D	.07	.10	.15	.21	.24	1.25	—
1953-S	.15	.20	.25	.28	.40	1.45	—
1954	.07	.08	.10	.15	.19	1.25	11.00
1954-D	.07	.08	.10	.15	.19	1.35	—
1954-S	.07	.08	.10	.19	.24	1.35	—
1955	.24	.30	.35	.50	.60	2.00	8.15
1955-D	.07	.08	.10	.15	.19	1.25	—

	MS-60	MS-65	Prf-65		MS-60	MS-65	Prf-65
1956	.19	.75	2.50	1957	.19	.75	1.25
1956-D	.19	.75	—	1957-D	.19	.75	—

	VG-8	F-12	EF-40	AU-50	MS-60	MS-65	Prf-65
1958	.06	.08	.17	.19	.24	1.45	2.25

	MS-60	MS-65	Prf-65		MS-60	MS-65	Prf-65
1958-D	.19	.75	—				
1959	.19	.75	1.00	1971	.13	.35	—
1959-D	.19	.75	—	1971-D	.13	.35	—
1960	.19	.75	.75	1971-S	—	—	.80
1960-D	.19	.75	—	1972	.13	.35	—
1961	.19	.75	—	1972-D	.13	.35	—
1961-D	.19	.75	—	1972-S	—	—	.95
1962	.19	.75	.60	1973	.13	.35	—
1962-D	.19	.75	—	1973-D	.13	.35	—
1963	.19	.75	.60	1973-S	—	—	.95
1963-D	.19	.75	—	1974	.13	.35	—
1964	.19	.75	.60	1974-D	.13	.35	—
1964-D	.19	.75	—	1974-S	—	—	.95
1965	.13	.35	—	1975	.13	.35	—
1966	.13	.35	—	1975-D	.13	.35	—
1967	.13	.35	—	1975-S	—	—	.95
1968-D	.13	.35	—				
1968-S	.13	.35	.40	1976	.13	.35	—
1969-D	.13	.35	—	1976-D	.13	.35	—
1969-S	.13	.35	.40	1976-S	—	—	.50
1970-D	.13	.35	—	1977	.13	.35	—
1970-S	.13	.35	.45	1977-D	.13	.35	—
				1977-S	—	—	.55

* Beware of Struck Counterfeits

Three Cent Silver

	VG-8	F-12	VF-20	EF-40	AU-50	MS-60	MS-65
1851 Var. 1	9.30	13.00	21.00	45.00	95.00	185.	2400.
1851-O	16.75	25.00	49.00	88.00	220.	445.	3350.
1852	9.30	13.00	21.00	45.00	95.00	195.	2400.

3-cent pieces

	VG-8	F-12	VF-20	EF-40	AU-50	MS-60	MS-65
1853........	9.30	13.00	21.00	45.00	95.00	195.	2400.
1854 Var. 2 ...	12.50	17.00	35.00	85.00	215.	365.	3300.
1855........	19.00	32.50	57.50	105.	235.	420.	3550.
1856........	10.85	15.75	31.50	82.50	190.	355.	3350.
1857........	11.00	16.00	32.50	85.00	180.	345.	3300.
1858........	11.00	15.75	31.50	82.50	175.	340.	3250.
1859 Var. 3 ...	11.50	15.85	27.00	50.00	115.	195.	2000.
1860........	11.50	15.50	26.50	50.00	115.	195.	2000.
1861........	11.50	15.85	27.00	50.00	115.	195.	2000.
1862 All Vars..	11.50	15.85	27.00	50.00	115.	195.	2000.

	AU-50	MS-60	MS-63	MS-65	Prf-60	Prf-63	Prf-65
1863 All Vars..	375.	495.	1000.	2500.	510.	1025.	2650.
1864........	375.	495.	1000.	2550.	510.	1025.	2700.
1865........	415.	515.	1025.	2700.	540.	1100.	2725.
1866........	385.	495.	1000.	2500.	510.	1025.	2650.
1867........	440.	555.	1050.	2650.	580.	1125.	2725.
1868........	415.	505.	1050.	2650.	525.	1125.	2725.
1869 All Vars..	480.	530.	1100.	2725.	540.	1225.	2750.
1870........	375.	480.	1100.	2725.	485.	1225.	2750.
1871........	375.	480.	1100.	2725.	485.	1225.	2800.
1872........	515.	580.	1175.	2800.	590.	1325.	2850.
1873 Proof Only Closed 3.........................							3750.

Half Dimes

	AG-3	G-4	VG-8	F-12	VF-20
1794 Flwg Hr..	320.	640.	920.	1175.	2050.
1795........	295.	540.	700.	900.	1525.
1796/5 Dr Bst..	415.	730.	875.	1150.	2400.
1796 All Vars..	375.	690.	810.	1000.	1800.
1796 Likerty ..	375.	690.	810.	1050.	1950.
1797 15 Sts. ...	350.	640.	790.	1000.	1700.
1797 16 Sts. ...	365.	665.	810.	1050.	1725.
1797 13 Sts. ...	400.	705.	850.	1150.	1900.
1800 Herd Eag	190.	490.	610.	750.	1025.
1800 Libekty ..	195.	500.	625.	760.	1050.
1801........	245.	540.	710.	900.	1375.
1802........	—	—	—	—	—
1803 All Vars..	230.	515.	660.	825.	1100.
1805........	330.	630.	800.	875.	1775.

	G-4	F-12	VF-20	EF-40	MS-60
1829 Cap Bust.	11.75	21.50	44.00	92.50	395.
1830........	11.75	21.50	44.00	87.50	380.
1831........	11.75	21.50	44.00	92.50	360.
1832........	11.75	21.50	44.00	92.50	380.
1833........	11.75	21.50	44.00	87.50	360.
1834........	11.75	21.50	44.00	97.50	360.
1835 All Vars..	11.75	21.50	44.00	92.50	380.
1836 All Vars..	11.75	21.50	44.00	92.50	360.
1837 sm 5c....	18.50	40.00	90.00	245.	1300.
1837 lg 5c.....	11.75	21.50	44.00	92.50	360.

Liberty Seated Type

	G-4	F-12	VF-20	EF-40	MS-60
1837 All Vars..	23.00	52.50	75.00	215.	635.
1838-O N Star .	67.50	145.	325.	600.	—

SEATED HALF DIMES

	G-4	F-12	VF-20	EF-40	MS-60
1838 Stars No Dr. All Vars .	4.60	8.00	26.00	52.50	390.
1839 No Dr....	4.60	8.00	23.00	49.00	330.
1839-O No Dr..	9.00	18.00	31.00	62.50	460.
1840 No. Dr...	4.60	8.00	23.00	49.00	400.
1840-O No Dr..	9.00	21.00	37.50	67.50	600.
1840 Dr......	19.50	50.00	90.00	175.	750.
1840-O Dr.....	25.00	77.50	115.	375.	—
1841........	4.60	8.00	23.00	45.50	240.
1841-O	10.00	22.50	40.00	80.00	590.
1842........	4.60	8.00	23.00	45.50	250.
1842-O	21.50	47.50	150.	350.	—
1843........	4.60	8.00	23.00	44.00	235.
1844........	4.60	8.00	23.00	45.50	335.
1844-O	77.50	165.	350.	675.	—
1845........	4.60	8.00	23.00	44.00	235.
1846........	115.	235.	450.	1000.	—
1847........	4.60	8.00	23.00	44.00	235.
1848 All Vars..	4.60	8.00	23.00	44.00	235.
1848-O	12.00	27.50	47.50	90.00	470.
1849/8	13.00	27.50	55.00	95.00	385.
1849 All Vars..	4.60	8.00	21.00	44.00	240.
1849-O	20.00	47.50	175.	335.	—
1850........	4.60	8.00	19.50	44.00	280.
1850-O	11.00	24.00	67.50	115.	675.
1851........	4.90	8.00	19.50	42.50	270.
1851-O	7.00	19.00	45.00	95.00	635.
1852........	4.60	8.00	19.50	42.50	270.
1852-O	21.00	55.00	115.	260.	—
1853 No Arr...	25.00	50.00	75.00	150.	470.
1853-O No Arr.	140.	250.	415.	750.	—
1853 Arr.....	4.15	7.00	15.50	40.50	265.
1853-O Arr....	6.00	10.75	28.50	60.00	385.
1854 Arr......	4.15	7.00	15.50	40.50	265.
1854-O Arr....	5.85	9.50	27.50	65.00	475.
1855 Arr......	4.15	7.00	20.00	40.50	265.
1855-O Arr....	15.00	25.00	50.00	125.	500.
1856 No Arr...	4.25	7.25	15.25	28.00	240.
1856-O No Arr.	9.00	20.00	37.50	87.50	790.
1857........	4.25	7.25	15.25	31.50	240.
1857-O	9.00	13.75	30.00	72.50	535.
1858........	4.25	7.15	15.25	32.50	240.
1858-O	8.50	13.25	32.00	75.00	460.
1859........	9.00	22.00	29.00	50.00	250.
1859-O	14.75	21.50	34.00	82.50	460.
1860 Leg	4.00	8.00	15.50	28.00	240.
1860-O	4.00	16.00	20.00	45.50	320.
1861........	4.00	8.00	15.50	28.00	190.
1862........	4.00	8.00	15.50	28.00	190.
1863........	115.	160.	240.	360.	520.
1863-S	15.00	33.00	49.00	135.	600.
1864........	260.	315.	400.	600.	1600.
1864-S	29.00	60.00	85.00	260.	650.
1865........	180.	290.	365.	585.	1100.
1865-S	12.00	28.00	49.00	130.	700.
1866........	175.	275.	300.	475.	590.
1866-S	12.00	28.00	49.00	130.	610.
1867........	325.	435.	515.	635.	950.
1867-S	14.50	32.50	72.50	150.	480.
1868........	25.00	75.00	135.	245.	520.
1868-S	5.35	7.85	24.00	50.00	530.
1869........	5.85	17.50	24.50	45.00	340.
1869-S	4.85	7.85	17.50	47.50	385.
1870........	5.85	8.60	17.50	32.00	205.
1870-S (unique) MS-60 $253000.					
1871........	4.35	7.85	17.50	30.00	200.
1871-S	9.50	32.00	42.50	75.00	320.
1872........	4.35	6.50	17.50	30.00	190.
1872-S in wr...	5.60	8.60	17.50	30.00	190.
1872-S Below..	5.60	8.60	17.50	30.00	190.
1873........	4.35	6.50	17.50	30.00	190.
1873-S	8.50	15.00	27.50	45.00	295.

Early Dimes

	G-4	VG-8	F-12	VF-20	EF-40
1796 Dr Bust..	1000.	1225.	1700.	2250.	3450.
1797 16 sts. ...	790.	950.	1275.	1775.	2650.
1797 13 sts. ...	790.	950.	1275.	1775.	2650.
1798/97 All Vars	475.	575.	975.	1750.	2400.
1798 All Vars..	425.	525.	710.	925.	1525.
1800	425.	525.	710.	925.	1525.
1801	425.	525.	710.	950.	1600.
1802	600.	785.	1250.	2300.	4750.
1803	455.	525.	685.	925.	1525.
1804 All Vars..	850.	1200.	2000.	3300.	4500.
1805 All Vars..	425.	500.	675.	850.	1475.
1807	425.	500.	675.	915.	1625.

	G-4	VG-8	F-12	VF-20	EF-40
1809 Cap Bust.	82.50	145.	275.	415.	700.
1811/9	42.50	70.00	100.	210.	425.
1814 S.D......	30.00	60.00	97.50	185.	440.
1814 L.D......	15.00	21.50	45.00	85.00	355.
1820 Lg. O	12.25	15.25	28.50	85.00	300.
1820 Sm. O	12.25	15.25	28.50	85.00	300.
1821 S.D......	16.50	22.50	45.00	90.00	325.
1821 L.D......	12.25	15.25	28.50	85.00	300.
1822	250.	415.	600.	870.	1400.
1823/2 All Vars	11.50	15.25	22.50	85.00	275.
1824/2	17.50	25.00	40.00	115.	350.
1825	11.50	15.25	22.50	85.00	275.
1827 All Vars..	11.75	15.25	22.50	85.00	275.
1828 L.D......	23.50	32.50	52.50	150.	365.

	G-4	VG-8	F-12	VF-20	EF-40	MS-60
1828 S.D......	24.50	39.00	75.00	110.	265.	1600.
1829 Sm. 10c ..	16.50	24.00	35.00	95.00	200.	985.
1829 Lg. 10c..	32.50	55.00	87.50	145.	400.	1175.
1830 All Vars..	9.00	11.00	17.50	48.00	150.	700.
1831	9.00	11.00	17.50	48.00	150.	700.
1832	9.00	11.00	17.50	48.00	150.	900.
1833 All Vars..	9.00	11.00	17.50	48.00	150.	700.
1834 All Vars..	9.00	11.00	17.50	48.00	150.	700.
1835	9.00	11.00	17.50	48.00	150.	700.
1836	9.00	11.00	17.50	48.00	150.	700.
1837	9.00	11.00	17.50	48.00	150.	700.

Liberty Seated Type

	G-4	VG-8	F-12	VF-20	EF-40	MS-60
1837 No Stars All Vars.....	20.00	38.00	52.50	100.	230.	875.
1838-O	26.50	52.50	77.50	195.	375.	1900.
1838 Sm Stars.	19.00	29.00	45.00	75.00	180.	1000.
1838 Lg Stars .	6.75	10.00	15.50	19.50	57.50	425.
1839	6.75	10.00	15.50	25.00	47.50	345.
1839-O	8.00	16.50	21.00	37.50	77.50	440.
1840 No Dr....	5.25	6.25	11.25	17.25	45.00	345.
1840-O No Dr..	7.75	16.00	19.00	37.50	90.00	850.
1840 Dr.......	32.50	53.50	78.50	150.	235.	—
1841	5.00	6.00	11.25	17.25	33.50	280.
1841-O	8.25	17.00	21.50	40.00	90.00	900.
1842	5.00	6.50	11.25	16.25	35.00	280.
1842-O	8.50	13.50	19.00	29.00	100.	—
1843	5.00	6.00	9.50	25.00	35.00	280.
1843-O	30.00	45.00	70.00	175.	435.	—

SEATED DIMES

	G-4	VG-8	F-12	VF-20	EF-40	MS-60
1844	25.00	40.00	60.00	105.	275.	—
1845	5.00	6.00	9.00	26.50	37.50	280.
1845-O	15.00	25.00	47.50	135.	325.	—
1846	50.00	77.50	120.	225.	400.	—
1847	12.00	20.00	31.50	55.00	115.	900.
1848	9.00	13.50	18.50	42.50	72.50	750.
1849	5.75	8.75	16.00	30.00	45.00	430.
1849-O	7.60	11.00	47.50	95.00	175.	5000.
1850	6.00	8.00	13.00	27.00	50.00	295.
1850-O	8.25	10.50	26.50	60.00	100.	925.
1851	5.00	6.00	12.25	23.50	40.00	280.
1851-O	8.50	13.00	26.50	75.00	155.	1550.
1852	5.00	6.00	12.25	25.00	40.00	280.
1852-O	11.00	17.50	32.50	82.50	175.	1650.
1853 No Arr..	28.00	45.00	77.50	155.	250.	425.
1853 Arr.....	3.00	3.50	6.00	13.75	37.50	325.
1853-O Arr...	6.25	12.00	23.50	38.00	95.00	825.
1854 Arr.....	3.00	6.25	9.00	13.75	37.50	450.
1854-O Arr...	3.00	3.50	6.00	13.75	40.00	370.
1855 Arr.....	3.50	6.25	9.00	13.75	40.00	365.
1856 S.D. No Arr......	3.50	7.25	14.00	20.00	37.50	340.
1856 L.D.....	7.60	12.00	17.00	22.50	50.00	350.
1856-O	7.00	11.00	17.50	28.00	77.50	625.
1856-S	62.50	97.50	125.	215.	265.	—
1857	3.40	5.25	6.50	12.75	37.50	280.
1857-O	5.00	8.00	9.50	20.00	55.00	440.
1858	3.40	5.00	6.50	12.75	37.50	280.
1858-O	12.75	21.00	57.50	97.50	115.	625.
1858-S	60.00	90.00	105.	185.	360.	—
1859	3.50	5.25	7.50	25.00	55.00	400.
1859-O	7.00	13.00	20.00	29.50	60.00	430.
1859-S	57.50	75.00	135.	225.	350.	—
1860-S	20.00	30.00	50.00	100.	190.	—
1860 Legend ..	4.90	8.00	9.50	22.50	35.00	235.
1860-O	235.	365.	475.	835.	1525.	4700.
1861 All Vars..	4.75	7.75	8.75	13.75	34.00	230.
1861-S	27.50	43.00	75.00	145.	190.	1350.
1862	4.75	7.75	8.75	13.75	34.00	230.
1862-S	24.50	39.00	60.00	120.	150.	1100.
1863	190.	290.	450.	520.	615.	825.
1863-S	19.00	30.00	45.00	70.00	115.	1050.
1864	175.	280.	465.	560.	690.	1000.
1864-S	16.50	25.00	38.50	62.50	100.	1050.
1865	220.	350.	550.	620.	790.	1150.
1865-S	16.50	22.00	42.50	80.00	165.	—
1866	255.	375.	625.	690.	890.	1200.
1866-S	17.00	23.00	38.00	60.00	110.	1025.
1867	330.	475.	740.	880.	1050.	1700.
1867-S	19.00	24.00	41.00	70.00	125.	1050.
1868	8.75	12.50	22.50	35.00	67.50	365.
1868-S	11.00	16.00	23.00	50.00	87.50	390.
1869	13.00	17.50	28.00	60.00	92.50	370.
1869-S	7.00	10.50	16.00	28.00	77.50	415.
1870	5.00	6.00	9.00	20.00	47.50	290.
1870-S	90.00	135.	165.	210.	350.	925.
1871	4.75	5.50	7.75	13.25	37.50	355.
1871-CC	490.	625.	925.	1350.	2450.	—
1871-S	6.50	10.50	23.00	45.00	75.00	545.
1872	4.50	5.25	7.50	10.75	35.00	290.
1872-CC	275.	485.	625.	750.	1400.	—
1872-S	14.50	19.00	50.00	95.00	180.	715.
1873 Cl 3	9.00	14.00	18.50	22.50	38.00	225.
1873 Op. 3 ...	14.50	21.50	38.00	67.50	97.50	625.
1873-CC (Unique)						
1873 Arr.....	8.50	13.00	22.00	50.00	90.00	555.
1873-CC Arr...	525.	685.	1150.	1850.	3000.	—
1873-S	14.00	15.50	25.50	52.00	97.50	875.
1874	9.00	14.50	25.50	52.00	97.50	585.
1874-CC	875.	1050.	1850.	2350.	3850.	—
1874-S	16.50	27.00	48.50	72.50	145.	710.
1875 No. Arr. .	3.10	3.75	5.25	9.00	18.75	215.

Seated dimes

	G-4	VG-8	F-12	VF-20	EF-40	MS-60
1875-CC Under Wr.	5.25	8.50	18.50	28.00	55.00	220.
1875-CC in Wr.	5.00	7.75	16.00	25.00	45.00	215.
1875-S Below Wr.	3.00	3.50	5.25	8.55	19.50	210.
1876	3.00	3.50	5.25	8.55	18.50	205.
1876-CC	3.00	3.50	5.25	8.55	22.50	205.
1876-S	4.75	5.25	9.25	13.75	24.50	235.
1877	3.00	3.50	5.25	8.55	18.50	205.
1877-CC	3.00	3.50	5.25	8.55	23.00	205.
1877-S	5.00	5.50	9.50	14.00	26.00	240.
1878	3.00	3.50	5.25	8.55	18.50	205.
1878-CC	32.50	55.00	75.00	125.	175.	475.
1879	140.	190.	250.	300.	340.	525.
1880	95.00	145.	175.	215.	265.	450.
1881	95.00	145.	175.	240.	295.	500.
1882	3.00	3.50	5.25	8.55	18.50	220.
1883	3.00	3.50	5.25	8.55	18.50	205.
1884	3.00	3.50	5.25	8.55	18.50	205.
1884-S	7.60	13.50	20.00	28.00	47.50	365.
1885	3.00	3.50	5.25	8.55	18.50	205.
1885-S	135.	180.	245.	330.	450.	1000.
1886	3.00	3.50	5.25	8.55	18.50	195.
1886-S	28.50	39.00	50.00	72.50	105.	465.
1887	3.00	3.50	5.25	9.00	18.50	195.
1887-S	3.00	3.50	5.25	9.00	18.50	195.
1888	3.00	3.50	5.25	9.00	18.50	195.
1888-S	3.00	3.50	5.25	9.00	18.50	195.
1889	3.00	3.50	5.25	9.00	18.50	195.
1889-S	10.50	14.00	21.50	30.00	57.50	265.
1890	3.00	3.50	5.25	9.00	18.50	195.
1890-S	8.75	15.50	24.50	40.00	65.00	255.
1891	3.00	3.50	5.25	9.00	18.50	205.
1891-O	3.25	3.75	5.50	9.15	19.50	245.
1891-S	3.50	4.00	5.65	10.15	19.50	265.

Barber Dimes

	G-4	VG-8	F-12	VF-20	EF-40	AU-50	MS-60
1892	2.25	3.40	6.00	8.65	19.00	43.00	130.
1892-O	4.65	5.90	8.15	13.50	25.50	54.50	145.
1892-S	22.00	29.00	40.00	55.00	77.50	125.	205.
1893	4.30	5.40	8.15	11.50	22.50	45.50	135.
1893-O	12.00	16.00	45.00	65.00	70.00	80.00	195.
1893-S	5.40	6.50	12.25	21.00	27.50	55.00	170.
1894	6.15	9.00	40.00	47.50	62.50	77.50	185.
1894-O	28.00	35.00	67.50	110.	215.	465.	790.
1894-S Extremely Rare - 24 Struck Proof 60 $50,000.							
1895	49.00	56.50	110.	135.	185.	265.	470.
1895-O	135.	170.	220.	265.	365.	500.	775.
1895-S	13.50	16.50	26.50	36.50	42.50	70.00	190.
1896	4.90	6.00	13.00	18.75	32.50	55.00	140.
1896-O	36.00	47.50	85.00	100.	170.	300.	500.
1896-S	30.50	37.50	62.50	80.00	125.	225.	365.
1897	1.95	2.90	4.00	6.00	18.00	43.00	135.
1897-O	31.00	40.00	70.00	92.50	180.	290.	525.
1897-S	7.15	9.25	16.50	28.50	46.00	75.00	190.
1898	1.20	1.45	3.15	5.50	16.50	40.50	135.
1898-O	3.40	4.75	10.75	22.00	37.00	67.50	240.
1898-S	3.15	4.00	8.90	16.50	33.50	55.00	165.
1899	1.20	1.45	3.15	5.50	16.50	40.50	130.
1899-O	2.90	3.90	9.50	21.00	39.00	67.00	240.
1899-S	3.15	3.90	9.00	19.00	27.50	52.50	155.
1900	1.20	1.45	3.15	5.50	16.50	40.50	130.
1900-O	4.50	6.50	16.50	25.00	45.00	100.	255.
1900-S	2.00	2.50	5.10	8.00	22.00	50.00	165.
1901	1.20	1.45	3.15	5.50	16.50	40.50	130.
1901-O	2.00	2.60	5.25	16.00	38.50	100.	255.
1901-S	29.00	37.50	70.00	125.	200.	350.	625.

Barber dimes

	G-4	VG-8	F-12	VF-20	EF-40	AU-50	MS-60
1902	1.20	1.45	3.15	5.50	16.50	40.50	130.
1902-O	2.05	2.50	5.10	12.50	26.50	62.50	205.
1902-S	3.25	5.15	11.50	23.75	48.50	90.00	205.
1903	1.20	1.45	3.15	5.50	16.50	40.50	130.
1903-O	2.00	2.35	4.50	8.00	24.00	61.50	200.
1903-S	25.50	31.00	48.50	70.00	130.	250.	485.
1904	1.20	1.45	3.15	5.50	16.50	40.50	130.
1904-S	18.50	23.50	41.00	65.00	120.	235.	445.
1905	1.20	1.45	3.15	5.50	16.50	40.50	130.
1905-O	2.00	2.85	6.15	13.50	25.50	52.50	155.
1905-S	1.85	2.65	4.50	9.00	24.00	57.50	190.
1906	1.20	1.45	3.15	5.50	16.50	40.50	130.
1906-D	2.00	2.85	4.85	8.50	21.50	50.00	155.
1906-O	1.90	3.75	9.25	18.00	27.50	52.50	160.
1906-S	1.80	2.80	5.75	11.50	26.00	52.50	165.
1907	1.20	1.45	3.15	5.50	16.50	46.50	130.
1907-D	1.50	2.15	5.15	9.50	24.00	52.50	160.
1907-O	1.50	2.15	5.15	8.50	20.50	46.50	130.
1907-S	1.90	2.40	5.50	12.00	27.00	60.00	190.
1908	1.20	1.45	3.15	5.50	16.50	40.50	130.
1908-O	1.35	1.65	4.65	6.25	19.50	46.50	130.
1908-O	1.90	2.90	10.00	19.75	32.50	65.00	185.
1908-S	1.45	2.05	4.75	9.25	23.50	52.50	165.
1909	1.25	1.45	3.15	5.50	16.50	40.50	130.
1909-D	2.50	4.65	11.25	20.50	34.00	67.50	180.
1909-O	1.85	2.45	5.25	15.00	25.50	52.50	155.
1909-S	2.50	4.75	12.50	21.00	36.00	70.00	195.
1910	1.20	1.45	3.15	5.60	16.50	40.50	145.
1910-D	1.50	2.30	4.75	12.75	27.00	62.50	180.
1910-S	1.75	2.40	7.75	15.50	26.50	60.00	160.
1911	1.20	1.60	3.15	5.50	16.35	40.00	130.
1911-D	1.20	1.60	3.35	5.75	16.50	40.50	130.
1911-S	1.30	1.85	4.50	7.15	18.75	52.50	145.
1912	1.20	1.60	3.15	5.50	16.35	40.00	130.
1912-D	1.20	1.40	3.50	5.65	16.50	40.50	155.
1912-S	1.30	1.65	4.50	7.75	19.00	52.50	165.
1913	1.20	1.60	3.15	5.50	16.35	40.00	130.
1913-S	6.50	9.75	25.00	45.00	87.50	150.	285.
1914	1.20	1.60	3.15	5.50	16.35	40.00	130.
1914-D	1.20	1.60	3.50	5.65	16.50	40.50	135.
1914-S	1.30	1.65	4.50	8.25	23.50	52.50	155.
1915	1.20	1.60	3.15	5.50	16.35	40.00	140.
1915-S	1.30	1.70	5.50	10.50	27.00	60.00	170.
1916	1.20	1.60	3.15	5.50	16.35	40.00	140.
1916-S	1.20	1.45	3.05	7.50	16.50	40.50	155.

Mercury Dimes

	VG-8	F-12	VF-20	EF-40	AU-50	MS-60	MS-65
1916	2.45	3.75	5.75	8.50	14.25	21.00	265.
1916-D	385.	725.	1000.	1250.	1800.	2350.	3900.
1916-S	3.00	4.75	8.00	13.50	19.50	32.50	270.
1917	1.55	2.05	4.50	5.75	11.25	17.50	225.
1917-D	2.75	6.00	12.50	29.00	55.00	85.00	725.
1917-S	1.85	2.85	5.00	7.50	17.50	32.50	275.
1918	1.55	3.40	8.00	19.00	32.50	50.00	265.
1918-D	2.00	3.15	7.50	17.50	33.50	58.00	730.
1918-S	1.55	3.00	5.50	10.25	21.50	37.00	550.
1919	1.50	2.50	4.50	5.85	12.75	23.00	335.
1919-D	2.40	4.85	12.00	26.00	58.00	110.	900.
1919-S	2.25	3.70	10.15	22.50	58.00	125.	790.
1920	1.30	2.00	4.00	5.50	11.25	17.00	265.
1920-D	1.75	3.25	6.00	11.25	25.50	57.50	780.
1920-S	1.75	3.00	5.85	10.25	21.50	55.00	635.
1921	25.00	55.00	115.	320.	565.	710.	1700.
1921-D	36.00	80.00	170.	350.	580.	700.	1750.
1923	1.35	2.00	5.00	9.00	17.00	265.	
1923-S	1.85	3.15	6.25	16.50	36.50	67.50	690.

MERCURY DIMES

	VG-8	F-12	VF-20	EF-40	AU-50	MS-60	MS-65
1924	1.40	2.00	4.00	6.75	16.75	37.50	350.
1924-D	1.60	3.25	7.25	15.00	36.00	80.00	475.
1924-S	1.60	2.95	6.00	13.00	33.50	77.50	750.
1925	1.30	1.90	3.50	5.90	14.25	32.50	325.
1925-D	3.50	7.00	19.00	55.00	120.	215.	740.
1925-S	1.80	2.95	6.00	14.75	42.00	96.50	675.
1926	1.30	1.70	3.50	4.65	8.00	15.75	250.
1926-D	1.65	3.25	5.25	11.00	25.50	57.50	550.
1926-S	6.50	12.50	25.00	66.00	180.	435.	1650.
1927	1.30	1.70	3.50	4.50	8.00	15.75	245.
1927-D	2.15	4.00	10.00	28.00	68.50	150.	650.
1927-S	1.60	2.50	4.50	10.00	28.50	67.50	800.
1928	1.30	1.70	3.25	4.50	8.00	16.25	250.
1928-D	2.50	5.00	11.75	27.50	57.50	115.	450.
1928-S	1.55	2.35	4.00	8.50	22.50	45.00	440.
1929	1.25	1.70	3.00	4.00	7.00	12.00	100.
1929-D	2.25	3.50	5.50	7.85	16.75	35.00	175.
1929-S	1.35	2.50	3.50	4.60	11.00	36.50	210.
1930	1.40	1.75	3.25	4.50	10.00	18.00	140.
1930-S	2.50	3.75	5.00	9.50	33.50	60.00	315.
1931	1.55	2.50	4.00	7.50	16.00	29.50	160.
1931-D	7.00	8.50	14.00	25.50	48.50	80.00	285.
1931-S	3.00	3.75	5.00	10.00	29.00	57.50	290.
1934	.85	1.00	1.25	2.10	5.00	14.50	58.50
1934-D	1.55	1.75	3.00	5.00	15.50	27.00	110.
1935	.85	1.00	1.25	2.00	4.00	12.00	57.50
1935-D	1.30	1.65	3.00	6.00	17.00	32.50	155.
1935-S	1.10	1.30	1.75	3.00	5.50	20.00	90.00
1936	.85	1.00	1.25	2.00	2.75	10.00	50.00
1936-D	1.10	1.30	1.75	4.00	10.00	25.00	105.
1936-S	1.10	1.30	1.50	2.75	6.25	16.00	58.50
1937	.85	1.00	1.25	2.00	2.75	10.00	45.00
1937-D	1.10	1.30	1.75	2.75	5.75	21.00	115.
1937-S	1.10	1.30	1.50	2.50	5.50	15.00	62.50
1938	.85	1.00	1.25	2.00	3.50	12.00	50.00
1938-D	1.35	1.50	2.00	3.00	8.50	17.50	93.00
1938-S	1.30	1.50	1.85	3.00	6.00	12.00	57.00
1939	.85	1.00	1.25	2.15	3.25	11.00	44.50
1939-D	1.00	1.25	1.50	2.05	4.00	12.00	50.00
1939-S	1.50	1.75	2.00	2.50	6.00	15.50	66.50
1940	.85	1.00	1.25	1.50	2.25	9.50	38.00
1940-D	.85	1.00	1.25	1.65	4.25	11.00	44.00
1940-S	.85	1.00	1.25	1.50	2.75	10.75	42.50
1941	.85	1.00	1.25	1.50	2.30	9.50	34.50
1941-D	.85	1.00	1.25	1.65	3.25	11.25	44.50
1941-S	.85	1.00	1.25	1.65	3.50	11.00	45.00
1942/1	160.	180.	205.	235.	350.	850.	2075.
1942/1-D	180.	205.	225.	275.	390.	950.	2300.
1942	.85	1.00	1.25	1.40	2.25	9.50	34.50
1942-D	.85	1.00	1.25	1.50	2.80	11.00	42.50
1942-S	.85	1.00	1.25	1.50	3.55	14.25	55.00
1943	.85	1.00	1.25	1.40	2.25	9.50	34.50
1943-D	.85	1.00	1.25	1.50	2.75	10.50	38.50
1943-S	.85	1.00	1.25	1.50	3.00	11.50	40.00
1944	.85	1.00	1.25	1.40	2.25	9.50	34.50
1944-D	.85	1.00	1.25	1.50	2.75	10.50	37.00
1944-S	.85	1.00	1.25	1.50	2.75	11.00	37.50
1945	.85	1.00	1.25	1.40	2.25	9.50	45.00
1945-D	.85	1.00	1.25	1.50	2.75	11.00	37.50
1945-S	.85	1.00	1.25	1.50	2.75	11.50	38.00
1945 Micro S	1.35	1.50	2.50	3.65	6.75	15.00	60.00

Roosevelt Dimes

	VG-8	VF-20	EF-40	AU-50	MS-60	MS-65
1946	.70	.80	.90	1.10	1.55	3.00
1946-D	.70	.80	1.10	1.30	2.25	4.50
1946-S	.70	.80	1.30	1.50	2.50	6.15
1947	.70	.80	1.00	1.35	2.10	4.00

ROOSEVELT DIMES

	VG-8	VF-20	EF-40	AU-50	MS-60	MS-65
1947-D	.80	.95	1.45	1.90	2.85	6.40
1947-S	.70	.80	1.10	1.35	2.85	6.15
1948	.70	.80	1.00	1.50	4.00	10.25
1948-D	.80	.95	1.45	2.75	4.75	10.00
1948-S	.70	.80	1.15	1.45	4.60	9.85
1949	.90	1.10	1.85	4.00	10.50	27.00
1949-D	.75	1.05	1.45	3.75	6.50	12.75
1949-S	1.05	1.75	2.50	8.00	18.50	60.00

	VG-8	VF-20	EF-40	AU-50	MS-60	MS-65	Prf-65
1950	.70	.80	.90	1.50	2.75	5.85	75.00
1950-D	.70	.80	.90	1.45	2.70	5.75	—
1950-S	.95	1.15	1.50	4.50	14.00	22.00	—
1951	.70	.80	.90	1.25	1.95	3.40	62.50
1951-D	.70	.80	.90	1.20	2.00	3.70	—
1951-S	.95	1.15	1.65	3.00	9.00	19.00	—
1952	.70	.80	.90	1.15	2.00	3.40	40.00
1952-D	.70	.80	.90	1.25	2.10	3.80	—
1952-S	.85	1.00	1.15	1.45	3.50	8.30	—
1953	.70	.80	.90	1.35	1.75	4.00	22.00
1953-D	.70	.80	.90	1.10	1.35	3.25	—
1953-S	.70	.80	.90	1.10	1.45	2.80	—
1954	.70	.80	.90	1.05	1.45	2.85	8.75
1954-D	.70	.80	.90	1.05	1.25	2.70	—
1954-S	.75	.85	.95	1.15	1.40	2.70	—
1955	.90	1.10	1.20	1.40	2.05	4.10	7.50
1955-D	.80	.90	.95	1.15	1.60	2.85	—
1955-S	.80	.90	.95	1.10	1.45	2.95	—
1956	.70	.80	.90	1.05	1.25	2.40	2.50
1956-D	.70	.80	.85	1.00	1.20	2.30	—
1957	.70	.80	.95	1.05	1.35	2.40	2.25
1957-D	.70	.80	.95	1.10	1.60	2.90	—
1958	.75	.85	1.05	1.20	1.55	2.80	2.50

	MS-60	MS-65	Prf-65			MS-60	MS-65	Prf-65
1958-D	1.25	2.40	—		1972-D	.25	.65	—
1959	1.20	2.10	1.75		1972-S	—	—	.95
1959-D	1.40	2.50	—		1973	.25	.65	—
1960	1.00	2.05	1.70		1973-D	.25	.65	—
1960-D	.95	2.05	—		1973-S	—	—	.75
1961	.90	1.80	1.60		1974	.25	.65	—
1961-D	.90	1.80	—		1974-D	.25	.65	—
1962	.90	1.80	1.50		1974-S	—	—	.75
1962-D	1.15	2.25	—		1975	.25	.65	—
1963	.90	1.75	1.50		1975-D	.25	.65	—
1963-D	.90	1.75	—		1975-S	—	—	.75
1964	.90	1.75	1.50		1976	.25	.65	—
1964-D	.90	1.75	—		1976-D	.25	.65	—
1965	.30	.70	—		1976-S	—	—	.75
1966	.30	.70	—		1977	.20	.65	—
1967	.30	.70	—		1977-D	.20	.65	—
1968	.30	.70	—		1977-S	—	—	.60
1968-D	.30	.70	—		1978	.20	.65	—
1968-S	—	—	.75		1978-D	.20	.70	—
1969	.35	1.00	—		1978-S	—	—	.60
1969-D	.25	.65	—		1979	.20	.65	—
1969-S	—	—	.75		1979-D	.20	.65	—
1970	.25	.65	—		1979-S	—	—	.60
1970-D	.25	.65	—		1980	.20	.50	—
1970-S	—	—	.95		1980-D	.20	.50	—
1971	.25	.65	—		1980-S	—	—	.60
1971-D	.25	.65	—		1981	.20	.50	—
1971-S	—	—	.95		1981-D	.20	.50	—
1972	.25	.65	—		1981-S	—	—	.60

Twenty Cent Pieces

	F-12	VF-20	EF-40	AU-50	MS-60	MS-65	Prf-65
1875	77.50	130.	215.	340.	675.	5400.	8300.
1875-CC	75.00	150.	235.	385.	825.	5500.	—

20-cent pieces

	F-12	VF-20	EF-40	AU-50	MS-60	MS-65	Prf-65
1875-S 8-10							
Proofs known	61.00	92.50	140.	315.	650.	5350.	21500.
1876	125.	200.	290.	485.	875.	5650.	8500.
1876-CC 12-15 known			27500.	35000.	68500.	—	—
1877 Proofs only (350)							10500.
1878 Proofs only (600)							9500.

Early Quarters

	G-4	VG-8	F-12	VF-20	EF-40	MS-60
1796 Dr Bust						
Sm Eag.....	2900.	3350.	4850.	8250.	12000.	22000.
1804 Herd Eag	655.	800.	2000.	3850.	—	—
1805	180.	215.	385.	860.	1550.	5750.
1806/5	175.	200.	350.	830.	1475.	9600.
1806	175.	200.	365.	825.	1400.	5600.
1807	175.	200.	340.	820.	1375.	5550.
1815 Cap Bust.	36.00	45.00	75.00	260.	525.	1950.
1818/5	39.50	50.00	95.00	285.	550.	2150.
1818	36.00	45.00	75.00	260.	525.	1900.
1819 All Vars..	36.00	45.00	70.00	215.	500.	1900.
1820 Sm. O	36.00	45.00	70.00	215.	500.	2000.
1820 Lg. O....	36.00	47.50	72.50	215.	500.	1900.
1821	36.00	45.00	70.00	215.	500.	1900.
1822 All Vars..	51.00	68.50	140.	325.	600.	2050.
1822 25/50c...	375.	535.	690.	1300.	2250.	3850.
1823/2 Extremely Rare - Proof $46200.						
1824/2	57.50	77.50	115.	285.	525.	—
1825 All Vars..	36.00	45.00	70.00	225.	480.	1950.
1827 Both Types - Extremely Rare						
1828 All Vars..	36.00	45.00	70.00	230.	480.	1950.
1828 25/50c...	62.50	97.50	175.	270.	675.	3000.
1831 No Motto						
All Vars.....	23.75	29.00	42.50	87.50	180.	900.
1832	23.75	29.00	42.50	87.50	180.	900.
1833	25.25	31.00	51.50	115.	435.	1750.
1834	23.75	29.00	42.50	87.50	200.	1000.
1835	23.75	29.00	42.50	87.50	180.	900.
1836	23.75	29.00	42.50	87.50	180.	900.
1837	23.75	29.00	42.50	87.50	180.	900.
1838	23.75	29.00	42.50	87.50	190.	950.

Liberty Seated Quarters

	G-4	VG-8	F-12	VF-20	EF-40	MS-60
1838 No Dr....	7.50	13.00	21.50	48.50	135.	1500.
1839 No Dr....	7.50	13.25	21.50	48.50	135.	1300.
1840-O No Dr..	7.50	13.25	21.50	48.50	130.	1300.
1840 Dr	18.75	32.50	50.00	87.00	180.	—
1840-O Dr.....	20.00	40.00	65.00	90.00	190.	1250.
1841	37.00	67.50	87.50	130.	215.	1000.
1841-O	15.50	27.50	40.00	67.50	160.	1250.
1842 S.D. Proofs only Proof 63 $23100.						
1842 L.D.....	70.00	87.50	115.	170.	285.	—
1842-O S.D....	250.	405.	655.	1200.	2400.	—
1842-O L.D....	12.50	18.25	28.00	45.00	70.00	1125.
1843	8.50	14.00	19.75	32.50	60.00	605.
1843-O	15.50	28.00	42.50	75.00	160.	—
1844	7.00	13.00	18.75	37.50	70.00	655.
1844-O	7.50	14.00	20.50	45.00	87.50	1050.
1845	7.00	13.00	18.75	35.00	70.00	665.
1846	8.50	13.50	19.50	35.00	70.00	640.
1847	7.00	13.00	18.75	35.00	70.00	630.

SEATED QUARTERS

	G-4	VG-8	F-12	VF-20	EF-40	MS-60
1847-O	20.00	37.50	68.50	105.	190.	—
1848	22.50	36.50	70.00	95.00	175.	—
1849	14.00	19.75	42.50	67.50	85.00	1050.
1849-O	350.	495.	720.	1475.	2600.	—
1850	23.75	37.00	55.00	75.00	115.	975.
1850-O	15.50	27.50	50.00	80.00	100.	950.
1851	26.25	39.00	60.00	87.50	125.	665.
1851-O	135.	175.	325.	575.	1100.	—
1852	35.00	47.50	75.00	95.00	145.	640.
1852-O	150.	180.	335.	525.	1025.	—
1853/52	165.	210.	285.	375.	525.	2350.
1853 A&R	6.85	13.00	19.00	36.00	110.	740.
1853/4 A&R..	45.00	77.50	115.	210.	425.	2300.
1853-O A&R..	14.25	20.00	34.00	60.00	145.	1350.
1854 Arr.	6.10	12.75	17.25	24.00	65.00	575.
1854-O Arr.						
All Vars.....	7.85	14.25	24.00	39.00	75.00	1150.
1855 Arr.....	6.10	12.75	17.25	24.00	65.00	575.
1855-O Arr....	35.00	49.00	75.00	130.	285.	—
1855-S Arr...	32.50	44.00	65.00	115.	265.	—
1856 No Arr..	6.00	11.75	17.50	23.00	45.00	405.
1856-O	9.00	15.00	22.75	45.00	80.00	1050.
1856-S All						
Vars	28.00	42.50	75.00	115.	235.	515.
1857	6.15	11.75	17.50	23.00	42.50	405.
1857-O	7.25	12.25	19.00	25.00	52.50	975.
1857-S	40.00	67.50	115.	200.	410.	—
1858	6.15	11.75	17.50	23.00	42.50	405.
1858-O	9.75	15.50	25.25	50.00	85.00	1075.
1858-S	35.00	42.50	115.	150.	400.	—
1859	7.50	12.50	18.50	27.50	53.00	680.
1859-O	17.00	27.00	42.50	65.00	92.50	1100.
1859-S	80.00	105.	140.	275.	425.	—
1860	6.15	11.75	17.50	23.00	42.50	465.
1860-O	14.00	20.00	35.00	55.00	85.00	950.
1860-S	92.50	145.	250.	415.	750.	—
1861	6.15	11.75	17.50	23.00	42.50	405.
1861-S	55.00	75.00	120.	195.	350.	—
1862	6.40	12.00	18.00	24.00	45.00	475.
1862-S	47.50	65.00	105.	175.	315.	—
1863	23.75	33.50	50.00	77.50	135.	540.
1864	55.00	70.00	105.	155.	210.	605.
1864-S	135.	175.	310.	425.	775.	—
1865	50.00	65.00	93.50	125.	195.	780.
1865-S	70.00	90.00	135.	245.	350.	1475.
1866 Only One Known (PROOF)						
1866 Motto	175.	225.	345.	475.	625.	925.
1866-S	145.	190.	285.	405.	650.	1800.
1867	110.	145.	200.	265.	375.	730.
1867-S	95.00	145.	195.	275.	400.	—
1868	96.00	105.	140.	225.	325.	755.
1868-S	50.00	72.50	95.00	145.	200.	1550.
1869	175.	215.	335.	400.	550.	1025.
1869-S	65.00	92.50	130.	215.	320.	925.
1870	45.00	60.00	90.00	155.	225.	865.
1870-CC	1200.	1700.	2100.	3000.	4200.	—
1871	31.00	42.50	57.50	100.	160.	645.
1871-CC	750.	875.	1300.	2150.	3500.	—
1871-S	220.	260.	360.	495.	710.	1750.
1872	23.50	32.50	55.00	77.50	135.	595.
1872-CC	280.	385.	525.	880.	—	—
1872-S	215.	350.	405.	615.*	835.	3750.
1873 Cl 3	80.00	105.	165.	240.	355.	—
1873 Op 3	27.50	35.00	60.00	90.00	160.	480.
1873-CC NO ARR. 2 known MS-60 $205000.						
1873 Arr.	10.25	16.00	24.50	57.50	125.	765.
1873-CC Arr...	700.	875.	1350.	2650.	4250.	—
1873-S Arr.	17.50	26.50	40.00	68.00	170.	1100.
1874 Arr.	10.25	16.00	24.50	62.50	125.	815.
1874-S Arr.	14.50	20.00	35.00	68.00	150.	925.
1875	6.35	11.25	16.25	22.50	55.00	315.
1875-CC	55.00	65.00	120.	225.	420.	1350.
1875-S	22.50	39.00	55.00	95.00	185.	490.

SEATED QUARTERS

	G-4	VG-8	F-12	VF-20	EF-40	MS-60
1876	6.25	11.00	16.00	21.50	52.50	310.
1876-CC	6.90	15.00	28.50	37.50	70.00	465.
1876-S	6.35	11.25	16.25	22.50	55.00	335.
1877	6.25	11.00	16.00	21.50	52.50	310.
1877-CC	6.80	14.25	26.00	37.50	80.00	525.
1877-S All Vars	6.50	12.00	22.50	31.50	52.50	350.
1878	6.35	11.25	16.25	22.50	52.50	320.
1878-CC	19.00	28.50	50.00	85.00	120.	505.
1878-S	45.00	67.50	110.	165.	295.	1200.
1879	115.	135.	150.	175.	310.	530.
1880	115.	140.	155.	180.	315.	545.
1881	125.	145.	160.	205.	310.	565.
1882	130.	150.	160.	205.	315.	635.
1883	125.	145.	160.	205.	310.	565.
1884	140.	160.	185.	250.	370.	655.
1885	125.	145.	160.	205.	315.	565.
1886	215.	245.	260.	295.	395.	700.
1887	145.	155.	170.	220.	330.	590.
1888	145.	155.	170.	220.	330.	590.
1888-S	7.25	12.25	18.00	24.00	41.50	430.
1889	125.	145.	160.	205.	325.	590.
1890	57.50	65.00	76.50	92.50	205.	605.
1891	6.50	11.25	17.00	26.50	42.50	310.
1891-O	115.	135.	170.	275.	470.	—
1891-S	8.00	13.25	21.00	38.00	50.00	325.

Barber Quarters

	G-4	VG-8	F-12	VF-20	EF-40	AU-50	MS-60
1892	2.70	3.60	9.00	16.00	44.00	90.00	250.
1892-O	4.00	6.25	10.50	20.50	57.50	135.	260.
1892-S	13.00	16.00	24.00	42.50	75.00	170.	325.
1893	2.70	3.85	9.00	16.00	44.00	90.00	230.
1893-O	3.30	5.50	11.25	20.50	55.00	145.	255.
1893-S	3.40	5.75	12.50	23.00	57.50	145.	265.
1894	2.70	3.85	9.00	16.00	44.00	90.00	230.
1894-O	3.30	5.50	11.25	20.50	52.50	145.	255.
1894-S	3.30	5.50	11.25	20.50	57.50	145.	265.
1895	3.00	3.85	9.00	16.00	44.00	90.00	230.
1895-O	3.60	5.60	12.50	20.50	52.50	150.	325.
1895-S	3.85	5.85	13.50	27.50	65.00	145.	265.
1896	3.00	3.85	8.75	20.50	46.50	110.	230.
1896-O	3.85	6.25	14.00	35.00	95.00	340.	650.
1896-S	190.	240.	475.	725.	1150.	2150.	2900.
1897	2.45	3.20	8.00	15.25	40.00	85.00	225.
1897-O	6.10	9.75	15.00	40.00	105.	375.	675.
1897-S	9.00	12.25	18.00	42.50	90.00	220.	290.
1898	2.45	3.20	8.00	15.25	40.00	85.00	225.
1898-O	3.35	6.00	11.75	27.50	67.50	200.	400.
1898-S	3.35	5.65	10.50	21.50	50.00	160.	290.
1899	2.45	3.20	8.00	15.25	40.00	85.00	225.
1899-O	4.00	6.25	11.75	24.00	57.50	195.	320.
1899-S	7.15	9.25	14.50	29.50	60.00	175.	290.
1900	2.30	2.95	7.50	15.00	40.00	85.00	225.
1900-O	4.40	6.90	12.75	28.00	67.50	205.	330.
1900-S	4.25	6.50	10.50	19.50	47.50	145.	255.
1901	2.30	2.95	7.50	15.00	40.00	85.00	225.
1901-O	9.50	12.50	27.50	55.00	120.	360.	665.
1901-S	900.	1150.	1675.	2350.	3450.	5500.	7750.
1902	2.30	2.95	7.50	15.00	40.00	85.00	220.
1902-O	3.35	5.45	10.50	25.50	52.50	155.	310.
1902-S	7.40	9.50	13.75	29.00	70.00	175.	295.
1903	2.30	2.95	7.50	15.00	40.00	85.00	220.
1903-O	3.35	5.25	10.50	25.50	57.50	185.	255.
1903-S	7.25	9.25	13.25	29.50	75.00	190.	310.
1904	2.30	2.95	7.50	15.00	40.00	85.00	220.
1904-O	4.15	6.75	13.75	31.00	90.00	365.	600.

BARBER QUARTERS

	G-4	VG-8	F-12	VF-20	EF-40	AU-50	MS-60
1905	2.30	2.95	7.50	15.00	40.00	85.00	220.
1905-O	4.15	6.75	13.50	28.00	55.00	145.	275.
1905-S	5.50	7.50	12.75	24.00	47.50	140.	260.
1906	2.30	2.95	7.50	15.00	40.00	85.00	220.
1906-D	2.70	3.45	9.00	17.50	44.00	120.	245.
1906-O	2.55	3.70	11.25	20.50	47.50	120.	240.
1907	2.30	2.95	7.50	15.00	40.00	85.00	220.
1907-D	2.55	3.45	9.00	16.50	46.50	120.	250.
1907-O	2.55	3.45	8.50	16.00	44.00	115.	235.
1907-S	3.35	4.55	10.00	17.50	50.00	130.	285.
1908	2.30	2.95	7.50	15.00	40.00	85.00	220.
1908-D	2.55	3.55	8.00	16.00	44.00	115.	235.
1908-O	2.55	3.55	8.00	15.00	44.00	115.	235.
1908-S	7.00	8.25	15.00	29.50	70.00	185.	310.
1909	2.30	2.95	7.50	15.00	40.00	85.00	220.
1909-D	2.55	3.55	8.00	15.50	44.00	115.	235.
1909-O	8.50	12.25	27.00	60.00	140.	285.	460.
1909-S	3.05	3.70	8.00	16.00	47.50	130.	290.
1910	2.30	2.95	7.50	15.00	40.00	85.00	220.
1910-D	2.70	3.70	8.50	18.50	47.50	125.	255.
1911	2.30	2.95	7.50	15.00	40.00	85.00	220.
1911-D	2.70	3.70	10.00	17.50	47.50	110.	235.
1911-S	2.70	3.70	9.25	16.50	46.50	125.	270.
1912	2.30	2.95	7.50	15.00	40.00	85.00	225.
1912-S	2.45	3.70	8.50	18.50	50.00	130.	290.
1913	10.60	14.25	42.00	105.	335.	525.	1200.
1913-D	2.45	3.70	8.25	18.50	47.50	120.	245.
1913-S	280.	340.	550.	850.	1450.	2050.	2850.
1914	2.30	2.95	7.50	15.00	40.00	85.00	225.
1914-D	2.30	3.70	8.00	16.00	40.00	85.00	230.
1914-S	13.00	16.50	32.50	88.00	205.	350.	600.
1915	2.30	2.95	7.50	15.00	40.00	85.00	245.
1915-D	2.30	3.20	8.00	16.00	40.00	85.00	230.
1915-S	3.00	3.85	11.25	20.50	47.50	115.	245.
1916	2.30	3.20	7.50	15.00	40.00	85.00	235.
1916-D	2.30	3.20	8.00	15.25	46.50	90.00	240.

Standing Liberty Quarters

	G-4	F-12	VF-20	EF-40	AU-50	MS-60	MS-65
1916 Var. 1	1025.	1275.	1400.	1800.	2200.	2950.	4750.
1917 Var. 1	9.50	11.75	26.50	52.50	92.50	150.	1175.
1917-D Var. 1	14.75	22.50	48.50	85.00	110.	165.	1215.
1917-S Var. 1	13.75	20.00	45.00	75.00	115.	175.	1250.
1917 Var. 2	12.50	18.25	21.50	35.00	60.00	110.	1000.
1917-D Var. 2	17.75	42.50	55.00	85.00	110.	155.	1125.
1917-S Var. 2	17.65	28.00	48.00	68.50	94.00	140.	1135.
1918	14.25	20.50	29.50	44.00	75.00	140.	1110.
1918-D	20.50	35.50	49.00	75.00	120.	190.	1150.
1918-S	13.00	21.00	25.00	42.00	75.00	140.	1075.
1918/7-S	965.	1550.	2050.	2800.	4850.	7250.	22500.
1919	23.00	39.50	45.00	60.00	85.00	145.	1000.
1919-D	42.00	96.00	125.	205.	280.	475.	1900.
1919-S	41.00	79.50	105.	180.	250.	400.	1750.
1920	13.00	17.00	20.00	33.00	56.00	125.	975.
1920-D	21.50	48.00	69.00	95.00	145.	200.	1150.
1920-S	15.00	22.50	26.50	44.00	72.50	140.	1000.
1921	50.00	115.	145.	205.	290.	380.	1200.
1923	13.00	18.75	21.50	36.00	60.00	130.	1000.
1923-S	85.00	160.	220.	335.	425.	500.	1200.
1924	13.00	17.50	21.75	36.00	60.00	130.	1000.
1924-D	22.00	40.00	57.50	82.50	100.	140.	1015.
1924-S	14.00	22.50	24.50	39.00	69.00	145.	1075.
1925	2.60	5.25	13.65	24.00	55.00	115.	965.
1926	2.60	5.25	13.50	24.00	55.00	115.	980.
1926-D	5.00	12.00	20.00	42.50	72.50	120.	990.
1926-S	4.00	11.85	19.50	49.50	85.00	175.	1150.

STANDING QUARTERS

	G-4	F-12	VF-20	EF-40	AU-50	MS-60	MS-65
1927	2.60	5.25	13.50	23.85	55.00	120.	965.
1927-D	6.75	11.50	25.00	52.50	80.00	145.	1015.
1927-S	6.75	44.00	120.	440.	725.	1275.	5250.
1928	2.85	5.25	13.50	23.85	55.00	115.	990.
1928-D	3.50	7.75	16.25	33.00	65.00	135.	1025.
1928-S	2.70	5.75	13.75	26.50	60.00	125.	985.
1929	2.60	5.25	13.50	23.85	55.00	110.	950.
1929-D	4.25	11.00	16.00	30.00	60.00	125.	980.
1929-S	2.60	5.25	13.50	24.50	55.00	110.	965.
1930	2.60	5.25	13.50	23.00	55.00	110.	950.
1930-S	2.60	5.25	13.50	24.25	55.00	105.	960.

Washington Quarters

	G-4	F-12	EF-40	AU-50	MS-60	MS-65
1932	2.75	4.00	7.00	12.25	27.00	425.
1932-D	31.50	42.50	160.	265.	425.	3500.
1932-S	27.50	32.50	50.00	97.50	235.	1850.
1934	2.80	3.50	5.00	7.85	30.00	150.
1934-D	3.00	5.50	11.75	23.00	82.50	800.
1935	1.75	2.50	4.00	6.85	19.50	140.
1935-D	2.00	3.50	11.50	22.50	75.00	750.
1935-S	2.00	3.75	7.00	16.00	60.00	500.
1936	1.75	2.50	4.00	6.85	18.50	145.
1936-D	2.25	3.25	27.50	77.50	225.	1400.
1936-S	2.00	4.00	8.75	19.00	60.00	375.
1937	1.75	2.90	4.50	8.50	21.00	150.
1937-D	2.00	2.75	8.00	14.00	37.00	340.
1937-S	4.00	5.35	16.00	42.50	82.50	720.
1938	2.85	3.85	10.75	23.00	50.00	430.
1938-S	3.15	7.00	9.75	19.00	45.00	400.
1939	1.75	2.65	4.25	6.00	12.00	75.00
1939-D	2.00	3.50	7.50	11.75	24.50	210.
1939-S	3.50	4.00	9.50	23.00	52.50	350.
1940	1.75	2.40	3.85	6.00	11.50	46.50
1940-D	2.95	5.25	11.00	24.00	62.00	400.
1940-S	2.00	2.80	4.25	7.00	16.00	52.50
1941	1.60	2.00	3.50	4.00	7.75	27.00
1941-D	1.60	2.00	3.75	6.75	16.50	49.00
1941-S	1.60	2.00	3.50	6.50	14.75	50.00
1942	1.60	2.00	3.10	4.00	6.00	18.75
1942-D	1.60	2.00	3.20	5.50	10.25	27.50
1942-S	1.60	2.00	4.00	16.00	47.50	165.
1943	1.60	2.00	3.40	3.75	6.00	18.50
1943-D	1.60	2.00	3.10	6.00	13.25	30.00
1943-S	1.60	2.00	3.50	12.75	28.00	105.
1944	1.60	2.00	2.85	3.75	5.00	15.75
1944-D	1.60	2.00	2.60	5.75	10.00	24.75
1944-S	1.60	2.00	2.60	5.85	10.25	27.25
1945	1.60	2.00	2.35	3.75	5.05	17.50
1945-D	1.60	2.00	2.60	4.50	6.50	18.25
1945-S	1.60	2.00	2.60	4.35	6.90	17.75
1946	1.60	2.00	2.35	2.70	4.10	7.75
1946-D	1.60	2.00	2.60	3.35	4.95	9.75
1946-S	1.60	2.00	2.60	4.25	6.75	12.75
1947	1.60	2.00	2.35	3.50	6.00	11.00
1947-D	1.60	2.00	2.60	4.25	6.50	12.00
1947-S	1.60	2.00	2.60	4.50	6.75	13.75
1948	1.60	2.00	2.35	2.65	4.00	7.25
1948-D	1.60	2.00	2.60	3.35	5.75	11.00
1948-S	1.60	2.00	2.60	3.65	7.25	12.75
1949	1.60	2.00	3.50	7.00	16.50	32.50
1949-D	1.60	2.00	2.60	5.00	7.50	14.50

	F-12	EF-40	AU-50	MS-60	MS-65	Prf-65
1950	2.00	2.35	2.85	3.85	8.00	130.
1950-D	2.00	2.35	2.50	3.80	9.75	——
1950-S	2.00	2.35	4.50	7.85	15.75	——

WASHINGTON QUARTERS

	F-12	EF-40	AU-50	MS-60	MS-65	Prf-65
1951	2.00	2.35	2.55	3.75	7.25	82.50
1951-D	2.00	2.35	2.55	3.70	6.25	——
1951-S	2.00	2.35	5.75	10.50	17.25	——
1952	2.00	2.35	2.50	3.55	6.25	65.00
1952-D	2.00	2.35	2.50	3.65	7.00	——
1952-S	2.00	2.35	4.50	8.15	13.50	——
1953	2.00	2.35	2.80	4.00	7.50	33.00
1953-D	2.00	2.35	2.50	3.45	6.00	——
1953-S	2.10	2.85	3.50	3.90	7.50	——
1954	2.00	2.35	2.50	3.35	5.35	16.00
1954-D	2.00	2.35	2.50	3.35	5.25	——
1954-S	2.00	2.35	2.65	3.50	5.75	——
1955	2.00	2.35	2.45	3.35	4.90	11.50
1955-D	2.35	2.75	3.00	4.10	6.50	——

	MS-60	MS-65	Prf-65		MS-60	MS-65	Prf-65
1956	2.35	4.00	5.75	1957	2.35	3.75	4.50
1956-D	2.35	3.75	——	1957-D	2.35	3.75	——

	F-12	EF-40	AU-50	MS-60	MS-65	Prf-65
1958	1.70	1.95	2.35	3.15	4.00	5.50

	MS-60	MS-65	Prf-65		MS-60	MS-65	Prf-65
1958-D	2.25	3.40	——	1970-D	.35	.95	——
1959	2.25	3.40	4.00	1970-S	——	——	.75
1959-D	2.25	3.40	——	1971	.35	.95	——
1960	2.20	2.90	3.75	1971-D	.35	.95	——
1960-D	2.20	2.90	——	1971-S	——	——	.75
1961	2.50	4.25	3.55	1972	.35	.95	——
1961-D	2.20	2.90	——	1972-D	.35	.95	——
1962	2.20	2.90	3.55	1972-S	——	——	.75
1962-D	2.20	2.90	——	1973	.30	.90	——
1963	1.90	2.75	3.55	1973-D	.30	.90	——
1963-D	1.90	2.75	——	1973-S	——	——	.75
1964	1.90	2.75	3.50				
1964-D	1.90	2.75	——	1974	.30	.90	——
1965	.40	1.00	——	1974-D	.30	.90	——
1966	.40	1.00	——	1974-S	——	——	1.00
1967	.40	1.00	——	1976	.30	.90	——
1968	.40	1.00	——				
1968-D	.45	1.05	——	1976-D	.30	.90	——
1968-S	——	——	.75	1976-S	——	——	.75
1969	.40	1.00	——	1976-S Silver	.90	1.90	2.50
1969-D	.50	1.10	——	1977	.30	.90	——
1969-S	——	——	.75	1977-D	.30	.90	——
1970	.35	.95	——	1977-S Pf.	——	——	.75

Early Half Dollars

	AG-3	G-4	VG-8	F-12	VF-20	EF-40
1794 Flwg Hr..	550.	1250.	1700.	2350.	4150.	6600.
1795 All Vars..	195.	350.	450.	650.	1250.	2150.
1795 3 Lvs....	400.	725.	1050.	1800.	3350.	7850.
1796 15 Stars Drp Bust....	7000.	9750.	12500.	16250.	22000.	32500.
1796 16 Stars..	7000.	9750.	12500.	16250.	22000.	——
1797 15 Stars..	7000.	9750.	12500.	16250.	22000.	——

	G-4	VG-8	F-12	VF-20	EF-40	MS-60
1801 Herd Eag	160.	245.	425.	725.	1600.	——
1802	145.	225.	390.	675.	1475.	7500.
1803 Sm. 3....	105.	165.	220.	490.	740.	4500.
1803 Lg. 3....	77.50	120.	185.	365.	725.	6250.
1805/4	175.	250.	400.	700.	1575.	6500.
1805 All Vars..	75.00	95.00	150.	310.	585.	4500.
1806/5	87.50	130.	205.	440.	685.	4500.
1806 Inv..	145.	215.	315.	490.	875.	6200.
1806 All Vars..	75.00	95.00	150.	310.	585.	4500.
1807	75.00	95.00	150.	310.	575.	4500.

Half Dollars
Turban Head

	G-4	VG-8	F-12	VF-20	EF-40	MS-60
1807 Sm Stars.	60.00	85.00	165.	300.	525.	1800.
1807 Lg Stars.	43.00	52.50	110.	200.	425.	1750.
1807 50/20	38.50	50.00	72.50	180.	400.	1700.
1808/7	38.50	42.50	51.50	120.	285.	1200.
1808 All Vars.	32.50	37.00	42.50	75.00	240.	950.
1809 All Vars.	31.50	37.00	47.00	75.00	240.	950.
1810	28.00	35.00	41.50	67.50	230.	950.
1811 Sm 8	28.00	35.00	41.50	57.50	190.	850.
1811 Lg 8	28.00	35.00	41.50	67.50	195.	850.
1812/1	30.00	50.00	65.00	115.	250.	1025.
1812 All Vars.	27.50	34.50	41.50	67.50	175.	850.
1813 All Vars.	27.50	34.50	41.50	70.00	180.	930.
1814 All Vars.	27.50	35.00	43.50	72.50	265.	1150.
1814/3	45.00	52.50	70.00	100.	300.	1250.
1815/2	675.	800.	1150.	1650.	2400.	6750.
1817/3	80.00	125.	220.	340.	675.	2300.
1817 All Vars.	24.00	30.50	46.50	65.00	175.	835.
1818/7	24.00	30.50	39.50	52.50	180.	960.
1818 All Vars.	24.00	30.50	39.50	50.00	160.	805.
1819/8	24.00	30.50	39.50	57.50	175.	840.
1819 All Vars.	24.00	30.50	33.50	50.00	160.	860.
1820/19	31.50	40.00	50.00	140.	250.	1000.
1820 All Vars.	31.00	39.00	46.00	72.50	225.	860.
1821	31.00	36.50	42.50	60.00	130.	835.
1822 All Vars.	24.00	36.50	39.50	60.00	130.	835.
1822/1	45.00	57.50	105.	175.	300.	1350.
1823 All Vars.	24.00	30.50	33.50	46.50	125.	820.
1824/1	24.00	30.50	39.50	64.00	185.	830.
1824/4	26.50	33.00	41.00	77.00	195.	860.
1824 All Vars.	22.50	26.50	30.50	36.50	130.	830.
1825	22.50	26.50	30.50	36.50	79.00	785.
1826	22.50	26.50	30.50	46.50	82.50	790.
1827/6	22.50	26.50	33.50	62.50	165.	975.
1827 Sq. 2.	22.50	26.50	30.50	36.50	79.00	785.
1827 Crl. 2.	26.00	32.50	39.50	60.00	80.00	790.
1828 All Vars.	22.50	26.50	30.50	36.50	79.00	775.
1828 Lg. 8s.	24.00	30.50	33.50	46.50	80.00	855.
1828 Sm. 8s	22.50	26.50	30.50	36.50	79.00	855.
1829/7	22.50	26.50	30.50	42.50	85.00	985.
1829 All Vars.	22.50	26.50	30.50	36.50	79.00	760.
1830 Lg O	22.50	26.50	30.50	36.50	79.00	750.
1830 Sm O	22.50	26.50	30.50	36.50	79.00	750.
1831	22.50	26.50	30.50	36.50	79.00	750.
1832 Normal	22.50	26.50	30.50	36.50	79.00	750.
1832 Lg Lets	24.50	30.50	39.50	62.50	160.	875.
1833	22.50	26.50	30.50	36.50	79.00	750.
1834 All Vars.	22.50	26.50	30.50	36.50	79.00	750.
1835	22.50	26.50	30.50	36.50	79.00	750.
1836 All Vars.	22.50	26.50	30.50	36.50	79.00	750.

Half Dollars
Reeded Edge

	G-4	VG-8	F-12	VF-20	EF-40	MS-60
1836 50 CENTS	465.	550.	750.	1000.	1650.	5000.
1837 50 CENTS	25.50	32.50	39.00	59.00	140.	825.
1838 Half Dol.	25.50	32.50	39.00	59.00	140.	825.
1838-O Only 20 Struck Extremely Fine $40700.						
1839 All Vars.	25.50	32.50	39.00	59.00	140.	825.
1839-O	140.	190.	250.	400.	650.	2850.

Liberty Seated
Halves

	G-4	VG-8	F-12	VF-20	EF-40	MS-60
1839 No Dr	40.00	55.00	88.00	180.	525.	5850.
1839 Dr	21.00	37.50	53.00	100.	165.	430.
1840 Sm Let	25.00	40.00	58.00	95.00	160.	510.
1840-O	20.50	32.00	50.50	77.50	110.	560.
1841	30.00	45.00	83.00	145.	285.	1250.
1841-O	14.50	26.25	35.00	63.00	110.	775.
1842-O SD	575.	825.	1250.	2250.	4000.	——
1842 SD	30.00	47.50	73.00	92.50	130.	825.
1842-O LD	14.50	26.25	35.00	62.50	135.	535.
1843	14.50	24.25	37.50	58.50	95.00	435.
1843-O	14.50	26.25	40.50	62.50	130.	545.
1844	14.50	24.25	34.00	44.50	85.00	435.
1844-O	14.50	24.25	32.00	40.50	72.50	510.
1844-O Dbl Dt.	50.00	65.00	86.00	150.	350.	1300.
1845	28.00	40.00	63.00	110.	185.	850.
1845-O	14.50	24.25	34.00	50.00	125.	550.
1846 SD	15.50	26.25	35.00	52.50	77.50	535.
1846 TD	18.50	28.50	38.00	57.50	98.00	695.
1846/Hor. 6	125.	165.	235.	365.	550.	1900.
1846-O MD	16.75	26.25	34.00	42.00	130.	595.
1847	14.50	24.25	32.00	38.00	67.50	495.
1847-O	14.50	25.25	34.50	40.50	87.50	675.
1847/6	——	2350.	3250.	4050.	5300.	——
1848	32.50	48.50	69.00	120.	240.	1125.
1848-O	17.00	29.00	37.50	44.50	90.00	725.
1849	20.00	25.50	36.50	55.00	135.	1000.
1849-O	18.00	27.00	37.75	62.50	145.	675.
1850	87.50	115.	155.	265.	400.	1275.
1850-O	17.00	26.25	37.00	50.00	135.	695.
1851	100.	145.	225.	360.	560.	1375.
1851-O	16.50	30.50	51.50	75.00	170.	675.
1852	120.	185.	275.	415.	575.	1475.
1852-O	42.50	65.00	115.	185.	315.	1400.
1853-O No Arrows (Only 3 known - Beware Alterations)						
1853 A&R	14.00	23.50	40.50	82.50	200.	1750.
1853-O A&R	18.00	30.50	60.50	135.	355.	2250.
1854 Arr.	12.50	23.00	31.50	40.00	97.50	740.
1854-O Arr.	11.50	22.00	30.50	39.50	90.00	650.
1855 Arr.	17.50	29.00	38.00	58.00	155.	1100.
1855-O Arr.	11.50	25.00	31.50	42.00	90.00	740.
1855-S Arr.	310.	485.	685.	1375.	2800.	——
1856 No Arr.	11.00	21.75	28.50	45.00	57.50	420.
1856-O	11.00	21.75	29.00	45.00	57.50	495.
1856-S	30.00	47.50	65.50	165.	290.	1300.
1857	11.00	21.75	28.50	38.00	57.50	420.
1857-O	16.50	25.00	38.00	62.50	135.	825.
1857-S	40.00	60.00	83.00	185.	365.	1400.
1858	11.00	21.75	28.50	38.00	57.50	420.
1858-O	11.00	19.00	26.00	34.00	60.00	525.
1858-S	17.00	30.00	45.50	130.	265.	825.
1859	16.00	25.00	36.00	47.50	75.00	485.
1859-O	11.00	21.75	29.00	39.00	58.00	495.
1859-S	17.00	30.00	47.00	100.	225.	750.
1860	18.50	29.00	43.00	62.50	97.50	775.
1860-O	15.00	22.00	34.00	46.50	72.50	510.
1860-S	25.00	36.00	47.00	61.50	120.	535.
1861	11.00	21.75	28.50	38.00	67.50	435.
1861-O	16.00	25.00	37.75	52.50	80.00	460.
1861-S	13.50	25.75	32.00	41.50	71.00	600.
1862	25.00	37.00	53.00	110.	200.	700.
1862-S	11.50	22.25	30.50	39.00	70.00	525.
1863	17.50	26.00	35.00	60.00	125.	600.
1863-S	11.50	22.25	30.50	39.00	70.00	525.
1864	20.00	27.00	43.00	72.50	165.	625.
1864-S	14.50	22.25	35.00	50.00	80.00	525.
1865	21.00	28.00	43.00	67.50	145.	725.
1865-S	11.50	22.25	30.50	50.00	75.00	525.
1866-S	65.00	85.00	135.	275.	450.	4100.

SEATED HALVES
MOTTO ABOVE EAGLE

	G-4	VG-8	F-12	VF-20	EF-40	MS-60
1866 Motto ...	15.00	25.00	38.00	65.00	145.	440.
1866-S Motto..	12.00	22.00	31.50	45.00	82.50	475.
1867	23.00	38.00	53.00	125.	200.	440.
1867-S	12.00	22.00	31.50	37.00	80.00	475.
1868	30.00	45.00	63.00	140.	250.	600.
1868-S	14.50	27.50	36.50	43.50	145.	480.
1869	15.00	24.00	32.50	48.00	85.00	435.
1869-S	14.25	25.75	34.00	45.00	175.	500.
1870	21.00	32.50	48.00	77.50	165.	410.
1870-CC	550.	750.	1200.	2400.	4000.	--
1870-S	15.00	27.00	38.00	60.00	150.	525.
1871	17.50	25.00	37.50	62.50	120.	385.
1871-CC	85.00	135.	205.	390.	600.	--
1871-S	12.00	21.60	27.50	36.50	72.50	635.
1872	16.00	24.00	36.50	52.50	80.00	345.
1872-CC	40.00	65.00	135.	250.	400.	1500.
1872-S	24.50	39.00	60.50	110.	255.	1050.
1873 Closed 3..	23.00	43.00	63.00	97.50	180.	535.
1873 Open 3 N.A. MS-63 $11000.						
1873-CC	82.50	145.	240.	385.	615.	2550.
1873 Arr.....	16.50	22.00	33.50	70.00	205.	750.
1873-CC Arr...	70.00	95.00	190.	285.	485.	1650.
1873-S Arr...	42.50	67.50	110.	195.	375.	1300.
1874 Arr.....	16.50	22.00	33.50	66.00	160.	775.
1874-CC Arr..	150.	285.	435.	675.	1075.	--
1874-S Arr...	32.00	45.00	72.50	160.	330.	1550.
1875	11.00	21.25	27.50	39.00	62.50	345.
1875-CC	18.50	30.00	50.50	80.00	175.	480.
1875-S	15.00	27.00	45.50	65.00	130.	360.
1876	11.00	21.25	27.50	34.50	60.00	345.
1876-CC	14.00	26.00	38.00	62.50	100.	560.
1876-S	11.00	21.25	27.50	34.50	60.00	360.
1877	11.00	21.25	27.50	34.50	60.00	345.
1877-CC	15.00	27.00	38.00	59.00	97.50	500.
1877-S	11.25	21.50	28.50	35.50	59.00	410.
1878	16.50	36.00	50.50	77.50	135.	425.
1878-CC	200.	250.	450.	765.	1350.	2600.
1878-S	3750.	4750.	5750.	7000.	8750.	21000.
1879	170.	205.	250.	285.	350.	750.
1880	155.	180.	215.	270.	300.	675.
1881	155.	180.	210.	240.	280.	675.
1882	185.	210.	270.	310.	390.	750.
1883	165.	190.	225.	270.	330.	725.
1884	200.	235.	285.	330.	410.	825.
1885	190.	225.	275.	320.	400.	800.
1886	225.	265.	325.	375.	435.	825.
1887	250.	290.	350.	410.	515.	900.
1888	160.	185.	220.	260.	330.	685.
1889	160.	185.	220.	270.	335.	695.
1890	165.	190.	230.	285.	350.	700.
1891	45.00	62.50	92.50	130.	210.	475.

Barber Halves

	G-4	VG-8	F-12	VF-20	EF-40	AU-50	MS-60
1892........	13.00	16.75	28.00	54.00	135.	280.	495.
1892-O	72.50	95.00	150.	225.	340.	500.	840.
1892-S	85.00	115.	155.	225.	335.	490.	875.
1893........	9.00	11.50	26.50	52.50	125.	280.	500.
1893-O	14.00	17.75	39.50	85.00	225.	355.	660.
1893-S	40.00	50.00	78.00	190.	285.	430.	810.
1894	6.50	8.75	24.75	54.00	125.	280.	485.
1894-O	6.50	9.75	26.50	62.00	195.	315.	560.
1894-S	6.50	9.25	25.00	59.50	190.	300.	550.
1895........	6.50	8.75	24.25	45.00	120.	275.	480.

BARBER HALVES

	G-4	VG-8	F-12	VF-20	EF-40	AU-50	MS-60
1895-O	6.50	9.50	25.00	56.00	160.	330.	585.
1895-S	13.10	16.85	32.50	80.00	200.	340.	600.
1896	7.25	10.25	28.00	55.50	125.	285.	500.
1896-O	13.15	18.50	42.00	90.00	260.	480.	1000.
1896-S	40.00	47.50	78.00	170.	310.	495.	1150.
1897	4.50	7.00	21.50	37.50	110.	235.	470.
1897-O	35.00	46.00	74.00	205.	355.	650.	1375.
1897-S	62.50	87.50	135.	180.	330.	510.	1200.
1898	4.50	7.00	21.50	37.50	110.	235.	470.
1898-O	12.00	15.25	30.00	70.00	200.	365.	580.
1898-S	6.75	9.50	24.00	52.50	160.	320.	555.
1899	4.50	7.00	21.50	37.50	110.	230.	455.
1899-O	6.85	10.00	25.00	62.00	200.	320.	575.
1899-S	6.75	9.50	24.00	52.50	160.	300.	550.
1900	4.50	7.00	20.50	37.50	110.	230.	455.
1900-O	6.75	9.50	24.00	65.00	215.	350.	640.
1900-S	6.75	9.25	23.50	52.50	160.	300.	550.
1901	4.50	7.00	20.50	37.50	110.	230.	470.
1901-O	7.25	10.25	27.50	62.00	240.	445.	1025.
1901-S	10.50	14.75	39.50	110.	340.	650.	1350.
1902	4.50	7.00	20.50	37.50	110.	230.	470.
1902-O	5.65	8.00	23.50	45.00	155.	340.	675.
1902-S	5.65	8.00	23.50	52.50	165.	345.	600.
1903	4.50	7.00	20.50	37.50	110.	230.	470.
1903-O	5.40	8.00	23.50	45.00	145.	315.	570.
1903-S	5.40	8.00	23.50	52.50	180.	410.	825.
1904	4.50	7.00	20.50	37.50	110.	230.	470.
1904-O	7.75	10.75	28.00	70.00	240.	440.	1050.
1904-S	9.50	12.50	40.00	105.	300.	550.	1015.
1905	8.00	10.00	29.00	67.50	170.	300.	600.
1905-O	8.75	10.75	31.50	77.50	220.	400.	800.
1905-S	4.65	7.50	23.50	52.50	160.	315.	570.
1906	4.50	7.00	20.50	37.50	110.	230.	470.
1906-D	4.65	7.50	23.50	42.50	125.	260.	480.
1906-O	4.65	7.50	23.50	45.00	135.	275.	530.
1906-S	4.65	7.50	23.50	52.50	145.	295.	550.
1907	4.50	7.00	20.50	37.50	110.	230.	470.
1907-D	4.65	7.50	23.50	42.50	125.	260.	480.
1907-O	4.65	7.50	23.50	42.50	125.	270.	530.
1907-S	4.65	8.75	24.25	57.00	200.	300.	560.
1908	4.50	7.00	20.50	44.00	140.	300.	545.
1908-D	4.65	7.50	22.50	42.50	115.	235.	480.
1908-O	4.65	7.50	22.50	42.50	125.	250.	480.
1908-S	4.65	8.50	23.50	54.00	160.	300.	560.
1909	4.50	7.10	21.50	37.50	110.	230.	470.
1909-O	7.25	9.00	26.50	62.50	210.	420.	690.
1909-S	4.65	7.75	23.00	45.00	155.	340.	745.
1910	7.25	9.75	27.00	62.00	200.	380.	610.
1910-S	4.65	7.75	22.50	45.00	150.	295.	550.
1911	4.50	7.00	20.50	37.50	110.	230.	470.
1911-D	4.65	7.50	22.50	45.00	145.	280.	530.
1911-S	4.65	7.50	22.50	45.00	145.	300.	550.
1912	4.50	7.00	20.50	37.50	110.	230.	470.
1912-D	4.65	7.50	22.00	42.50	115.	235.	470.
1912-S	4.65	7.50	22.50	45.00	145.	300.	550.
1913	14.75	16.85	35.00	77.50	190.	395.	785.
1913-D	4.55	7.50	22.50	54.00	145.	255.	470.
1913-S	4.55	7.75	25.00	65.00	155.	340.	700.
1914	16.75	23.50	54.00	115.	270.	500.	825.
1914-S	4.55	7.35	23.00	54.50	145.	310.	550.
1915	16.25	18.75	37.50	80.00	205.	415.	790.
1915-D	4.50	7.00	20.50	37.50	110.	245.	455.
1915-S	4.55	7.15	21.50	45.00	115.	260.	505.

Liberty Walking Half Dollars

	VG-8	F-12	VF-20	EF-40	MS-60	MS-63	MS-65
1916........	18.75	44.50	95.00	160.	380.	685.	2500.
1916-D	16.50	25.00	58.50	125.	350.	670.	2300.

WALKING HALVES

	VG-8	F-12	VF-20	EF-40	MS-60	MS-63	MS-65
1916-S	35.00	100.	205.	325.	700.	1300.	4700.
1917	6.50	8.50	17.00	27.50	145.	425.	1450.
1917-D Obv.	13.00	25.00	65.00	145.	440.	850.	3850.
1917-D Rev.	9.75	16.50	38.50	110.	475.	950.	4200.
1917-S Obv.	17.00	33.00	140.	320.	800.	1450.	5850.
1917-S Rev.	6.75	12.75	19.50	37.50	250.	525.	4850.
1918	7.50	14.00	36.50	100.	350.	575.	3200.
1918-D	8.00	15.00	40.00	120.	590.	1150.	5400.
1918-S	6.60	10.75	21.50	42.00	285.	725.	4050.
1919	12.50	24.50	94.50	340.	975.	1900.	5100.
1919-D	9.50	25.50	105.	400.	1700.	3250.	12500.
1919-S	9.00	18.00	80.00	355.	1500.	3150.	10500.
1920	6.50	8.50	18.50	40.00	235.	485.	3050.
1920-D	7.75	17.00	83.00	300.	875.	1550.	5800.
1920-S	7.00	12.00	34.00	120.	700.	1400.	4250.
1921	58.50	160.	410.	890.	1600.	2200.	4500.
1921-D	76.50	200.	465.	950.	1950.	2750.	6250.
1921-S	15.75	38.00	225.	1050.	5500.	8250.	27500.
1923-S	8.35	14.00	32.00	140.	745.	1400.	5300.
1927-S	6.50	9.00	22.00	75.00	600.	1250.	5000.
1928-S	6.75	9.50	23.00	87.50	650.	1300.	5500.
1929-D	6.65	8.75	16.00	65.00	365.	680.	2400.
1929-S	5.90	8.00	12.00	57.50	350.	700.	2650.
1933-S	6.60	9.25	11.50	47.50	335.	715.	2900.
1934	4.75	5.00	6.00	9.50	77.50	185.	775.
1934-D	4.85	5.50	9.50	27.00	165.	340.	1350.
1934-S	5.00	5.75	8.75	18.00	310.	625.	1950.
1935	4.50	4.75	6.00	9.00	60.00	130.	490.
1935-D	4.75	5.50	9.50	23.00	180.	325.	1900.
1935-S	4.75	5.50	8.25	20.00	230.	400.	1600.
1936	4.50	4.75	6.00	7.75	54.00	125.	425.
1936-D	4.75	5.50	8.65	15.75	120.	225.	790.
1936-S	4.75	5.50	8.65	15.75	145.	250.	1250.
1937	4.50	4.75	6.00	8.25	57.00	140.	475.
1937-D	5.75	6.00	12.50	32.50	235.	300.	1100.
1937-S	5.00	5.50	8.65	18.75	170.	260.	1050.
1938	5.00	5.50	7.00	12.50	87.50	185.	900.
1938-D	19.00	24.50	36.00	92.50	360.	675.	1700.
1939	4.00	4.60	6.10	19.50	80.00	170.	500.
1939-D	4.75	5.60	7.25	12.50	77.50	145.	550.
1939-S	5.75	6.00	8.00	14.50	120.	205.	650.
1940	4.00	4.60	5.00	7.00	49.00	125.	440.
1940-S	4.00	4.60	7.00	12.00	67.50	175.	875.
1941	4.00	4.60	5.00	6.00	46.50	115.	360.
1941-D	4.00	4.60	6.00	6.50	62.50	155.	450.
1941-S	4.00	4.60	6.25	8.00	210.	480.	1400.
1942	4.00	4.60	5.00	6.00	46.50	115.	350.
1942-D	4.00	4.60	6.00	7.00	65.00	220.	475.
1942-S	4.00	4.60	6.00	7.75	110.	290.	600.
1943	4.00	4.60	5.00	6.00	46.50	110.	350.
1943-D	4.00	4.60	6.00	6.50	67.50	225.	525.
1943-S	4.00	4.60	6.00	7.00	105.	305.	675.
1944	4.00	4.60	5.00	6.00	46.50	110.	360.
1944-D	4.00	4.60	6.00	6.90	60.00	190.	420.
1944-S	4.00	4.60	6.00	7.25	68.50	210.	1100.
1945	4.00	4.60	5.00	6.00	47.50	110.	355.
1945-D	4.00	4.60	6.00	6.90	56.50	150.	400.
1945-S	4.00	4.60	6.00	7.25	67.50	155.	480.
1946	4.00	5.25	6.25	6.75	48.00	120.	400.
1946-D	5.75	7.00	8.00	12.00	57.50	120.	375.
1946-S	5.25	5.50	6.00	7.50	66.50	140.	450.
1947	5.25	5.50	6.00	8.00	72.50	145.	425.
1947-D	5.25	5.50	6.00	7.75	67.50	120.	440.

Franklin half dollars

	F-12	VF-20	EF-40	AU-50	MS-60	MS-65	Prf-65
1949	4.50	6.00	7.00	11.00	34.50	120.	——
1949-D	4.50	6.10	7.25	11.50	35.00	125.	——
1949-S	6.00	8.00	16.50	29.75	87.50	290.	——
1950	4.25	5.10	6.00	9.00	31.50	69.00	675.
1950-D	4.00	5.00	5.85	8.75	22.50	72.50	——
1951	3.00	3.50	4.25	6.50	14.00	38.00	400.
1951-D	3.00	5.85	6.85	10.00	31.00	120.	——
1951-S	3.00	4.65	5.00	9.75	29.00	87.50	——
1952	3.00	3.50	4.25	5.00	13.00	27.00	265.
1952-D	3.00	3.50	4.25	5.50	10.50	31.00	——
1952-S	3.00	4.75	6.00	14.75	31.00	82.50	——
1953	4.50	5.50	7.00	12.25	23.00	66.00	200.
1953-D	3.00	3.50	4.25	5.00	10.75	34.00	——
1953-S	3.00	4.00	5.75	7.50	19.50	67.50	——
1954	3.00	3.50	4.10	4.35	9.75	22.50	120.
1954-D	3.00	3.50	4.25	4.75	8.75	22.25	——
1954-S	3.00	4.00	5.75	7.50	14.25	47.50	——
1955	6.50	7.00	9.00	10.75	14.00	25.50	97.50
1956	4.25	4.50	5.00	6.75	10.50	22.50	62.50
1957	3.25	4.25	4.75	5.00	8.25	18.50	47.50
1957-D	3.25	4.00	4.50	4.75	7.25	16.75	——
1958	3.50	4.25	5.00	6.75	8.25	18.00	67.50
1958-D	3.00	3.50	4.10	4.75	7.50	17.00	——
1959	3.00	3.50	4.10	4.85	7.50	16.90	42.50
1959-D	3.00	3.50	4.10	5.00	8.00	17.00	——
1960	3.00	3.50	4.10	4.65	7.00	16.75	35.00
1960-D	3.00	3.50	4.10	4.65	6.50	16.75	——
1961	3.00	3.50	4.10	4.50	7.00	16.75	27.50
1961-D	3.00	3.50	4.10	4.50	6.50	16.75	——
1962	3.00	3.50	4.10	4.50	6.25	14.25	26.00
1962-D	3.00	3.50	4.10	4.40	6.25	14.00	——
1963	3.00	3.50	4.00	4.15	6.00	14.00	26.00
1963-D	3.00	3.50	4.00	4.15	5.75	14.00	——

Mint State 65 Franklin Half Dollars with "Fully Struck Bell Lines" on the reverse are worth considerably more than the MS-65 prices listed.

Kennedy Half Dollars

	MS-60	MS-65	Prf-65		MS-60	MS-65	Prf-65
1964	3.50	6.25	14.50	1976	.85	1.95	——
1964-D	3.75	6.50	——	1976-D	.85	1.95	——
1965	2.25	4.50	——	1976-S	——	——	2.00
1966	1.95	4.20	——	1976-S Silver	2.25	4.00	4.50
1967	2.00	4.25	——	1977	.95	2.10	——
1968-D	1.90	4.00	——	1977-D	.95	2.10	——
1968-S	——	——	4.50	1977-S	——	——	2.00
1969-D	1.90	4.00	——	1978	1.00	2.35	——
1969-S	——	——	4.50	1978-D	1.00	2.30	——
1970-D	14.75	25.50	——	1978-S	——	——	2.50
1970-S	——	——	12.00	1979	.85	1.90	——
1971	.95	2.25	——	1979-D	.85	1.90	——
1971-D	.95	2.25	——	1979-S Var. 1.	——	——	2.00
1971-S	——	——	2.90	1980	.85	1.90	——
1972	.95	2.25	——	1980-D	.85	1.90	——
1972-D	.95	2.25	——	1980-S	——	——	1.50
1972-S	——	——	2.90	1981	1.00	2.10	——
1973	.95	2.00	——	1981-D	.85	1.85	——
1973-D	.95	2.00	——	1981-S Var. 1.	——	——	1.75
1973-S	——	——	3.00	1982-S	——	——	4.00
1974	.85	1.95	——	1983-S	——	——	6.50
1974-D	.85	1.95	——	1984-S	——	——	11.00
1974-S	——	——	3.00	1985-S	——	——	11.00

Franklin Half Dollars

	F-12	VF-20	EF-40	AU-50	MS-60	MS-65	Prf-65
1948	5.50	7.00	8.50	10.00	18.00	39.00	——
1948-D	4.50	5.25	6.50	9.50	13.50	42.50	——

Silver Dollars

	AG-3	G-4	VG-8	F-12	VF-20	EF-40
1794	3300.	6350.	8750.	14500.	23000.	45000.
1795 94 Ty.	375.	725.	800.	1250.	2150.	3700.
1795 Bust	300.	690.	775.	1100.	1600.	3200.
1796	300.	660.	750.	1100.	1550.	2800.
1797 9x7 S.L.	650.	975.	1350.	1850.	3450.	7500.
1797 9x7 L.L.	250.	640.	740.	1000.	1550.	2850.
1797 10x6	250.	640.	740.	1000.	1550.	2800.
1798 13 St. Sm. Eag.	275.	785.	975.	1500.	2000.	3450.
1798 15 St. Sm. Eag.	500.	950.	1450.	1900.	2500.	5750.
1798 Heraldic .	125.	290.	425.	540.	700.	1375.
1799	125.	290.	425.	540.	700.	1375.
1799/98	125.	290.	425.	540.	700.	1375.
1799 8x5 Stars	180.	380.	550.	810.	1075.	1675.
1800	140.	300.	435.	550.	740.	1400.
1801	200.	350.	450.	625.	925.	1700.
1802/1	140.	300.	435.	575.	790.	1475.
1802	170.	345.	440.	585.	875.	1625.
1803 Lg. 3	140.	300.	435.	560.	745.	1425.
1803 Sm. 3	140.	300.	435.	560.	745.	1425.

1804 Three Varieties-MS-60 $308000.

Liberty Seated Dollars

	G-4	VG-8	F-12	VF-20	EF-40	MS-60
1840 No Motto	95.00	145.	165.	205.	390.	1000.
1841	67.50	87.50	140.	155.	370.	925.
1842	65.00	85.00	135.	150.	335.	900.
1843	65.00	85.00	135.	150.	305.	900.
1844	130.	155.	205.	325.	535.	1250.
1845	160.	200.	255.	350.	490.	1600.
1846	67.50	87.50	140.	160.	325.	925.
1846-O	105.	145.	190.	270.	475.	2050.
1847	65.00	82.50	135.	150.	300.	900.
1848	170.	240.	285.	390.	530.	1750.
1849	95.00	145.	185.	260.	390.	1125.
1850	235.	305.	410.	525.	1025.	3800.
1850-O	185.	260.	350.	475.	890.	4000.

1851 Rare Only 1300 Struck Original MS-63 $11000.
1852 Rare Only 1100 Struck MS-60 $7500.

1853	90.00	125.	170.	205.	400.	1150.
1854	365.	475.	625.	1000.	1600.	3450.
1855	345.	450.	600.	900.	1400.	3300.
1856	125.	165.	195.	235.	625.	1650.
1857	120.	155.	185.	220.	605.	1550.

1858 Rare Only 80 Proofs Struck Proof 63 $7750.

1859	135.	195.	245.	365.	520.	1650.
1859-O	65.00	90.00	135.	150.	340.	790.
1859-S	170.	245.	275.	390.	615.	3550.
1860	150.	190.	280.	340.	525.	1700.
1860-O	65.00	90.00	135.	150.	315.	725.
1861	200.	300.	390.	435.	825.	2150.
1862	185.	275.	365.	410.	615.	2050.
1863	130.	185.	245.	330.	505.	1800.
1864	115.	170.	240.	325.	490.	1750.
1865	92.50	165.	215.	265.	415.	1750.
1866 Motto	95.00	160.	215.	275.	430.	1600.
1867	92.50	160.	220.	270.	425.	1600.

Seated $1

	G-4	VG-8	F-12	VF-20	EF-40	MS-60
1868	90.00	155.	220.	265.	435.	1500.
1869	70.00	115.	165.	220.	355.	1000.
1870	70.00	115.	165.	210.	345.	1000.
1870-CC	235.	285.	440.	525.	775.	3350.
1870-S 7-12 known	——	——	40500.	55000.	——	
1871	70.00	115.	165.	215.	365.	900.
1871-CC	1000.	1200.	2400.	3050.	4750.	——
1872	75.00	100.	145.	165.	290.	900.
1872-CC	725.	965.	1200.	1450.	2550.	6500.
1872-S	125.	200.	290.	500.	735.	3500.
1873	87.50	115.	185.	265.	425.	1200.
1873-CC	1400.	1650.	2350.	3500.	5500.	——

1873-S Unknown in any collection

Morgan Dollars

	F-12	VF-20	EF-40	AU-50	MS-60	MS-63	MS-65
1878 8TF	16.00	18.00	21.00	32.50	60.50	130.	1700.
1878 7TF	13.00	15.75	17.00	22.50	57.50	81.50	1250.
1878 7/8F	17.50	19.50	24.00	38.25	67.50	150.	1950.
1878-CC	25.00	30.00	36.50	47.50	130.	220.	1200.
1878-S	14.00	16.00	18.00	23.00	55.00	105.	700.
1879	10.75	12.25	15.00	19.50	42.00	77.50	1300.
1879-CC	39.00	75.00	185.	475.	1300.	2250.	9200.
1879-O	10.75	12.25	17.75	21.50	54.00	165.	2150.
1879-S	12.75	15.75	17.50	23.00	53.00	79.00	425.
1880	10.75	12.25	14.75	18.50	38.00	72.50	915.
1880-CC	36.50	52.50	82.50	115.	180.	320.	1275.
1880-O	10.75	12.25	17.85	23.00	56.50	195.	2550.
1880-S	12.75	15.75	17.75	22.75	47.00	79.00	420.
1881	10.75	12.50	14.75	19.25	35.00	73.50	915.
1881-CC	70.00	80.00	90.00	140.	245.	390.	1350.
1881-O	10.65	12.25	15.75	17.00	28.00	80.00	1225.
1881-S	12.50	15.50	18.00	23.50	40.00	81.00	405.
1882	10.65	12.25	16.00	19.25	35.00	73.50	800.
1882-CC	29.00	35.00	50.00	70.00	110.	235.	850.
1882-O	10.65	12.25	15.10	17.50	28.50	73.50	975.
1882-S	14.25	16.50	20.00	25.75	49.00	81.00	430.
1883	10.75	12.50	15.25	18.75	34.50	72.00	655.
1883-CC	24.75	35.00	50.00	67.50	105.	220.	835.
1883-S	10.75	12.50	15.15	17.00	24.50	62.50	425.
1884	10.75	13.50	15.25	20.00	34.50	100.	890.
1884-CC	34.00	47.50	62.50	77.50	105.	230.	835.
1884-O	10.75	12.50	15.35	17.50	24.50	62.50	420.
1884-S	15.00	18.00	34.00	210.	1550.	3500.	34500.
1885	10.75	12.50	15.25	17.75	24.50	62.50	425.
1885-CC	170.	180.	190.	220.	275.	425.	1300.
1885-O	10.75	12.50	15.25	17.25	24.50	62.50	425.
1885-S	14.75	17.50	21.50	46.50	145.	265.	1600.
1886	10.75	12.50	15.25	17.75	24.50	63.50	425.
1886-O	11.75	14.75	19.50	47.50	330.	735.	4750.
1886-S	16.50	20.00	25.75	37.50	185.	325.	1950.
1887	10.75	12.50	15.00	17.00	26.00	65.50	415.
1887-O	11.50	12.50	17.50	23.75	51.00	92.50	1500.
1887-S	13.75	15.50	19.50	26.00	87.50	245.	1750.
1888	10.75	12.50	15.10	17.00	24.50	69.00	550.
1888-O	10.75	14.00	15.00	18.50	24.00	90.00	685.
1888-S	17.25	20.75	26.50	40.00	195.	340.	2000.
1889	10.75	12.40	14.75	16.50	27.50	70.50	800.
1889-CC	155.	275.	515.	2100.	5400.	8600.	26500.
1889-O	12.00	14.50	17.50	23.50	87.50	255.	3350.

MORGAN DOLLARS

	F-12	VF-20	EF-40	AU-50	MS-60	MS-63	MS-65
1889-S	18.00	22.50	25.50	42.50	165.	315.	1500.
1890	10.75	13.00	15.50	18.25	28.00	92.50	1250.
1890-CC	24.00	31.50	41.00	75.00	245.	440.	1750.
1890-O	12.25	15.50	17.00	23.00	50.00	110.	1650.
1890-S	14.00	15.50	17.25	26.50	76.50	150.	965.
1891	12.00	15.00	16.50	33.50	73.50	160.	1750.
1891-CC	24.50	33.50	45.00	76.50	240.	425.	1700.
1891-O	12.50	15.00	17.50	28.00	77.50	215.	4350.
1891-S	14.75	16.00	18.50	25.50	79.00	155.	960.
1892	14.50	17.00	20.00	37.50	160.	365.	2550.
1892-CC	31.00	50.00	76.00	180.	400.	615.	2200.
1892-O	13.25	15.50	17.75	38.50	135.	400.	3900.
1892-S	15.50	40.00	140.	650.	4150.	7600.	34000.
1893	37.50	45.00	71.50	135.	325.	625.	3000.
1893-CC	55.00	130.	270.	440.	835.	1750.	9250.
1893-O	38.50	77.50	185.	335.	1000.	2150.	24000.
1893-S	750.	1200.	2750.	7500.	16000.	28000.	65000.
1894	175.	215.	280.	525.	850.	1375.	10750.
1894-O	15.00	17.50	26.00	67.50	450.	1050.	15750.
1894-S	18.00	36.50	67.50	155.	385.	685.	2950.
1895 Very Rare-Proof 67 $40000.							
1895-O	38.50	72.50	180.	425.	1950.	5100.	41000.
1895-S	67.50	135.	320.	500.	975.	1550.	10000.
1896	10.75	13.50	15.00	17.00	26.50	73.50	450.
1896-O	12.50	14.50	19.50	77.50	690.	1400.	35000.
1896-S	14.00	35.00	100.	225.	550.	865.	6150.
1897	10.75	13.50	15.50	17.50	26.50	78.00	590.
1897-O	13.25	15.00	19.00	42.50	360.	950.	9000.
1897-S	14.00	15.50	17.00	22.50	74.00	190.	900.
1898	10.75	13.50	15.50	17.25	26.50	72.50	535.
1898-O	13.50	16.00	17.50	22.50	28.00	73.50	485.
1898-S	14.25	17.50	22.50	41.00	190.	375.	1800.
1899	23.75	30.00	43.00	62.50	87.50	210.	1300.
1899-O	13.00	14.00	15.00	22.00	26.50	75.00	490.
1899-S	15.25	18.00	22.25	52.50	150.	375.	1800.
1900	11.75	13.00	15.00	17.25	25.50	68.00	565.
1900-O	13.50	14.25	15.75	21.50	27.50	74.00	480.
1900-S	14.00	16.75	19.50	41.00	130.	335.	1400.
1901	21.50	27.00	38.00	185.	850.	2300.	41000.
1901-O	14.50	17.00	19.00	22.50	27.00	75.00	950.
1901-S	15.50	19.00	27.00	60.00	285.	650.	3450.
1902	10.75	13.50	15.25	25.00	55.00	120.	1500.
1902-O	13.50	14.25	16.00	21.50	26.50	74.00	520.
1902-S	23.50	35.00	65.00	95.00	240.	435.	1900.
1903	10.75	12.75	15.25	23.25	52.00	100.	850.
1903-O	140.	170.	180.	210.	265.	400.	1000.
1903-S	15.50	42.50	165.	585.	1700.	3100.	8000.
1904	10.75	16.00	17.50	30.25	87.50	275.	1775.
1904-O	14.00	16.50	17.50	21.00	25.50	65.00	430.
1904-S	21.25	40.00	115.	385.	860.	1850.	5150.
1921	9.85	10.00	10.50	12.00	24.50	56.50	425.
1921-D	10.00	10.25	11.00	13.50	37.50	81.50	1150.
1921-S	10.00	10.25	10.75	13.00	31.50	91.50	1400.

Peace $1

	F-12	VF-20	EF-40	AU-50	MS-60	MS-63	MS-65
1924-S	12.75	14.50	17.75	39.50	170.	450.	3350.
1925	11.25	13.50	14.25	15.50	34.50	67.50	725.
1925-S	11.50	13.65	15.45	30.00	135.	335.	2450.
1926	10.00	13.75	15.50	19.00	49.00	115.	1000.
1926-D	10.00	14.00	16.50	26.50	67.50	165.	1500.
1926-S	9.85	12.50	14.75	19.00	49.00	120.	1125.
1927	14.50	16.25	18.00	28.50	100.	250.	2150.
1927-D	14.50	15.85	25.00	60.00	235.	585.	3800.
1927-S	14.65	16.00	21.75	49.00	150.	335.	2350.
1928	92.50	100.	115.	155.	245.	410.	2650.
1928-S	14.45	16.45	21.50	40.00	145.	365.	2700.
1934	14.50	16.50	20.00	28.00	90.00	235.	1850.
1934-D	14.75	16.25	20.25	30.00	105.	345.	2600.
1934-S	16.25	35.00	140.	400.	1300.	2150.	8000.
1935	11.75	14.30	16.75	21.00	61.50	160.	1175.
1935-S	11.65	14.00	17.25	45.00	175.	410.	2150.

Eisenhower Dollars

	MS-60	Prf-65
1971	1.90	—
1971-D	1.90	—
1971-S 40% Silver	5.00	7.50
1972	2.00	—
1972-D	1.85	—
1972-S 40% Silver	7.75	9.00
1973	4.00	—
1973-D	4.10	—
1973-S Clad Proof	—	4.25
1973-S 40% Silver	10.00	55.00
1974	1.65	—
1974-D	1.65	—
1974-S Clad Proof	—	3.75
1974-S 40% Silver	7.65	15.00
1976 Var. I	2.15	—
1976 Var. II	1.65	—
1976-D Var. I	1.85	—
1976-D Var. II	1.65	—
1976-S Var. I Clad Proof	—	3.25
1976-S Var. II Clad Proof	—	4.75
1976-S 40% Silver	6.75	10.00
1977	1.85	—
1977-D	1.80	—
1977-S Clad Proof	—	4.00
1978	1.60	—
1978-D	1.60	—
1978-S Clad Proof	—	4.00

Peace Type Dollars

	F-12	VF-20	EF-40	AU-50	MS-60	MS-63	MS-65
1921	24.50	29.00	36.50	55.00	250.	420.	4500.
1922	9.65	10.50	11.50	12.50	25.00	57.50	650.
1922-D	9.85	11.25	12.50	14.50	43.50	95.00	1100.
1922-S	9.75	11.10	12.35	14.75	45.00	110.	1500.
1923	9.65	10.50	11.50	12.50	25.00	57.50	625.
1923-D	9.85	11.50	12.65	15.75	41.50	120.	2100.
1923-S	9.75	11.10	12.35	15.65	43.50	135.	2500.
1924	10.75	13.50	14.50	15.50	34.50	67.50	725.

Anthony Dollars

	MS-60	Prf-65
1979-P	1.60	—
1979-D	1.60	—
1979-S	1.70	7.00
1979-S Var 2 Clear S	—	75.00
1980-P	1.60	—
1980-D	1.60	—
1980-S	1.85	6.90
1981	2.50	—
1981-D	2.50	—
1981-S	2.50	7.00

Trade Dollars

	F-12	VF-20	EF-40	MS-60	MS-65	Prf-65
1873	70.00	95.00	180.	585.	7300.	8850.
1873-CC	135.	200.	425.	1250.	7450.	—
1873-S	75.00	120.	210.	900.	7400.	—
1874	80.00	130.	190.	615.	7100.	8800.
1874-CC	67.50	92.50	175.	690.	7100.	—
1874-S	63.50	80.00	160.	585.	7150.	—
1875	200.	310.	525.	1350.	8050.	8900.
1875-CC	65.00	80.00	185.	620.	7100.	—
1875-S	63.50	78.00	150.	585.	7100.	—
1876	65.00	80.00	160.	615.	7150.	8800.
1876-CC	72.50	145.	340.	1100.	7100.	—
1876-S	63.50	80.00	170.	585.	7100.	—
1877	65.00	80.00	155.	765.	7550.	8900.
1877-S	63.50	80.00	160.	585.	7100.	—
1877-CC	85.00	175.	330.	825.	7300.	—
1878 Proof - Only 900 Struck						9100.
1878-CC	345.	585.	975.	7750.	47500.	—
1878-S	63.50	80.00	160.	625.	7100.	—
1879 Proof - Only 1541 Struck						9100.
1880 Proof - Only 1987 Struck						9100.
1881 Proof - Only 960 Struck						9250.
1882 Proof - Only 1097 Struck						9100.
1883 Proof - Only 979 Struck						9250.
1884 Proof Only - 10 Known						52500.
1885 Proof Only - 5 Known						105000.

U.S. Gold Dollars

	F-12	VF-20	EF-40	MS-60	MS-65
1849 Op. WR L Type I	140.	150.	180.	720.	7600.
1849 Cl. WR.	140.	150.	180.	700.	7450.
1849-C Cl. WR.	290.	400.	815.	3600.	—
1849-D	265.	400.	780.	2600.	10000.
1849-O	155.	170.	315.	1750.	7300.
1850	145.	155.	180.	690.	7150.
1850-C	375.	600.	1125.	4300.	—
1850-D	345.	555.	1000.	4100.	—
1850-O	255.	340.	500.	1800.	10250.
1851	140.	145.	175.	680.	7050.
1851-C	275.	340.	490.	1600.	10500.
1851-D	280.	375.	815.	2550.	11000.
1851-O	185.	195.	220.	730.	7250.
1852	140.	145.	175.	680.	7050.
1852-C	270.	365.	725.	1700.	11500.
1852-D	340.	625.	1025.	4000.	—
1852-O	155.	190.	225.	800.	10000.
1853	140.	155.	180.	680.	7050.
1853-C	255.	365.	825.	4250.	—
1853-D	340.	700.	1500.	4500.	17500.
1853-O	155.	185.	240.	690.	7200.
1854	140.	145.	175.	680.	7100.
1854-D	550.	860.	2000.	7750.	—
1854-S	295.	365.	605.	1850.	7600.
1854 Type II	175.	295.	500.	5000.	26500.
1855	175.	295.	500.	5000.	26500.
1855-C	800.	1300.	2200.	7250.	—
1855-D	1700.	2450.	6250.	—	—
1855-O	475.	660.	800.	6350.	—

GOLD $1.00

	F-12	VF-20	EF-40	MS-60	MS-65
1856-S	500.	685.	875.	6000.	—
1856 Up 5 Type III	155.	175.	250.	750.	6350.
1856 Sl. 5	135.	145.	180.	625.	5700.
1856-D	2800.	4600.	7650.	—	—
1857	135.	145.	175.	620.	5950.
1857-C	300.	575.	975.	4100.	—
1857-D	325.	650.	1175.	5650.	—
1857-S	330.	475.	700.	—	—
1858	135.	145.	185.	620.	5800.
1858-D	375.	625.	1325.	5900.	—
1858-S	340.	400.	600.	—	—
1859	145.	160.	220.	700.	5750.
1859-C	305.	390.	875.	3200.	9000.
1859-D	450.	750.	1475.	4450.	—
1859-S	355.	385.	490.	—	—
1860	160.	175.	195.	630.	5850.
1860-D	2250.	3600.	5250.	17500.	—
1860-S	295.	320.	490.	1150.	6350.
1861	135.	145.	175.	635.	5750.
1861-D	4650.	7000.	9500.	26000.	67500.
1862	135.	145.	175.	635.	5750.
1863	310.	390.	585.	1900.	6700.
1864	290.	365.	480.	755.	5900.
1865	290.	365.	500.	985.	6250.
1866	290.	365.	500.	900.	5900.
1867	300.	415.	525.	985.	6150.
1868	260.	280.	390.	725.	5850.
1869	305.	325.	525.	975.	5900.
1870	260.	270.	360.	850.	5950.
1870-S	290.	465.	600.	1850.	6300.
1871	260.	270.	360.	735.	6000.
1872	270.	285.	385.	755.	6550.
1873 Cl. 3	300.	350.	775.	2100.	—
1873 Op. 3	135.	145.	175.	600.	5650.
1874	135.	145.	175.	600.	5650.
1875	1975.	2250.	3150.	7650.	20500.
1876	215.	250.	270.	935.	6400.
1877	170.	200.	220.	755.	6300.
1878	205.	220.	230.	805.	6350.
1879	170.	200.	220.	650.	5750.
1880	150.	170.	195.	640.	5650.
1881	150.	170.	195.	640.	5650.
1882	160.	175.	195.	645.	5700.
1883	150.	170.	195.	640.	5650.
1884	150.	170.	195.	640.	5650.
1885	150.	170.	195.	640.	5650.
1886	150.	170.	195.	640.	5650.
1887	150.	170.	195.	640.	5650.
1888	150.	170.	195.	640.	5650.
1889	150.	170.	195.	640.	5650.

Quarter Eagle $2.50 Gold

	F-12	VF-20	EF-40	AU-50	MS-60
1834 Classic Hd. N.M.	225.	265.	380.	835.	2000.
1835	225.	265.	380.	835.	2150.
1836	225.	265.	380.	835.	2000.
1837	225.	265.	380.	835.	2100.
1838	225.	265.	380.	835.	2100.
1838-C	475.	785.	1600.	2600.	5900.
1839/8	225.	265.	380.	835.	2300.
1839-C 9 Over 8	385.	525.	1000.	1800.	4850.

GOLD $2.50

	F-12	VF-20	EF-40	AU-50	MS-60
1839-D 9 Over 8.........	385.	615.	1175.	2550.	4950.
1839-O......	380.	415.	690.	1450.	3400.
1840 Coronet..	195.	220.	375.	615.	1250.
1840-C......	320.	460.	860.	1850.	— —
1840-D......	435.	1250.	3100.	5950.	— —
1840-O......	205.	235.	355.	575.	1400.
1841 Ext. Rare..	— —	— —	28500.	— —	— —
1841-C......	260.	375.	760.	1300.	2750.
1841-D......	460.	975.	2800.	4850.	6750.
1842........	340.	510.	1075.	— —	— —
1842-C......	400.	675.	1300.	2550.	— —
1842-D......	410.	875.	2175.	4700.	— —
1842-O......	265.	280.	750.	1450.	2550.
1843........	200.	220.	285.	355.	825.
1843-C Large Date.......	315.	430.	775.	1400.	2850.
1843-D......	315.	515.	860.	1525.	3050.
1843-O Small Date.......	200.	220.	270.	470.	910.
1844........	215.	335.	610.	1350.	1600.
1844-C......	295.	410.	700.	1925.	3500.
1844-D......	295.	550.	850.	1575.	2950.
1845........	200.	210.	240.	280.	840.
1845-D......	295.	560.	850.	1750.	3250.
1845-O......	500.	1000.	1700.	3650.	— —
1846........	220.	275.	505.	755.	1375.
1846-C......	420.	735.	1250.	1750.	4750.
1846-D......	405.	675.	975.	1600.	4550.
1846-O......	200.	230.	355.	630.	1400.
1847........	200.	230.	285.	600.	1050.
1847-C......	330.	365.	680.	1075.	3650.
1847-D......	355.	540.	825.	2000.	3950.
1847-O......	200.	230.	395.	775.	1550.
1848........	265.	485.	790.	950.	2400.
1848 CAL. Rare - Only 1389 Struck MS-65 $46500.					
1848-C......	330.	410.	775.	1525.	— —
1848-D......	355.	505.	850.	1500.	3100.
1849........	200.	255.	360.	610.	1000.
1849-C......	340.	410.	845.	1850.	3350.
1849-D......	380.	640.	1225.	1950.	4600.
1850........	180.	195.	270.	490.	860.
1850-C......	255.	410.	860.	1550.	3100.
1850-D......	295.	510.	950.	1600.	3850.
1850-O......	180.	245.	405.	655.	1100.
1851........	180.	195.	240.	305.	805.
1851-C......	295.	410.	860.	1675.	3600.
1851-D......	330.	535.	1000.	1875.	4800.
1851-O......	195.	215.	250.	345.	875.
1852........	200.	220.	270.	315.	815.
1852-C......	330.	360.	810.	1350.	2700.
1852-D......	370.	630.	1350.	2700.	4750.
1852-O......	185.	210.	270.	520.	1100.
1853........	180.	195.	220.	280.	790.
1853-D......	370.	580.	1350.	2350.	4600.
1854........	180.	195.	220.	280.	790.
1854-C......	295.	410.	775.	1350.	2700.
1854-D......	1250.	2500.	4600.	7750.	— —
1854-O......	180.	195.	220.	320.	850.
1854-S Ext. Rare - 246 Struck F-12 $15000.					
1855........	190.	205.	230.	300.	815.
1855-C......	580.	1075.	2000.	3000.	5000.
1855-D......	1850.	2900.	4700.	8900.	— —
1856........	190.	205.	240.	300.	815.
1856-C......	410.	575.	1050.	2500.	— —
1856-D......	3450.	5750.	10000.	19500.	39500.
1856-O......	195.	220.	400.	610.	1300.
1856-S......	195.	220.	330.	580.	1000.
1857........	185.	195.	260.	300.	815.

GOLD $2.50

	F-12	VF-20	EF-40	AU-50	MS-60
1857-D......	395.	890.	1425.	2050.	5100.
1857-O......	190.	205.	285.	480.	1050.
1857-S......	190.	205.	285.	505.	1400.
1858........	190.	205.	260.	345.	890.
1858-C......	295.	410.	760.	1650.	3350.
1859........	190.	205.	230.	305.	825.
1859-D......	465.	1050.	2150.	4250.	7000.
1859-S......	200.	265.	400.	740.	1300.
1860 Small Lets. & Arrhds.		185.	205.	260.	465.
1860-C......	295.	455.	890.	1550.	3300.
1860-S......	185.	205.	285.	545.	1050.
1861........	180.	195.	225.	325.	800.
1861-S......	230.	340.	600.	1200.	— —
1862........	185.	205.	230.	345.	1015.
1862-S......	425.	635.	950.	1600.	3050.
1863 Proofs Only - 30 Pcs. Struck Proof 65 $50000.					
1863-S........	190.	265.	685.	1350.	2550.
1864........	700.	1350.	4250.	6500.	— —
1865........	625.	1100.	1850.	3250.	— —
1865-S........	185.	205.	345.	700.	1200.
1866........	230.	450.	850.	1150.	— —
1866-S........	185.	205.	450.	1350.	1825.
1867........	185.	260.	485.	785.	1250.
1867-S........	185.	205.	445.	1075.	— —
1868........	185.	250.	355.	630.	975.
1868-S........	185.	205.	390.	785.	1300.
1869........	200.	250.	360.	545.	1000.
1869-S........	185.	205.	280.	565.	1100.
1870........	200.	275.	380.	565.	1000.
1870-S........	185.	205.	230.	550.	1450.
1871........	200.	250.	365.	500.	1000.
1871-S........	185.	210.	275.	480.	950.
1872........	205.	265.	485.	850.	1275.
1872-S........	195.	205.	280.	560.	900.
1873 Open 3...	180.	195.	230.	295.	820.
1873-S........	185.	220.	360.	700.	1300.
1874........	200.	245.	385.	550.	975.
1875 Very Rare - Only 420 Struck AU-50 $4850.					
1875-S........	185.	205.	365.	730.	1100.
1876........	200.	230.	330.	775.	1600
1876-S........	185.	205.	270.	650.	1375
1877........	315.	415.	625.	800.	147?
1877-S........	185.	205.	230.	285.	81?.
1878........	180.	195.	215.	270.	810.
1878-S........	180.	195.	215.	270.	810.
1879........	180.	195.	215.	270.	810.
1879-S........	185.	205.	270.	320.	840.
1880........	210.	230.	410.	550.	950.
1881........	650.	1300.	2250.	3650.	— —
1882........	240.	260.	405.	525.	915.
1883........	240.	260.	420.	555.	950.
1884........	240.	260.	420.	555.	950.
1885........	455.	700.	1300.	1800.	3350.
1886........	240.	250.	405.	525.	915.
1887........	240.	260.	405.	525.	915.
1888........	240.	260.	385.	425.	825.
1889........	240.	260.	385.	425.	825.
1890........	240.	260.	385.	425.	825.
1891........	240.	260.	385.	450.	835.
1892........	220.	255.	440.	565.	950.
1893........	235.	245.	260.	385.	805.
1894........	215.	250.	405.	525.	905.
1895........	180.	190.	240.	300.	805.
1896........	180.	190.	210.	255.	770.
1897........	180.	195.	235.	280.	780.
1898........	180.	190.	210.	255.	770.
1899........	180.	190.	215.	270.	800.
1900........	180.	190.	210.	255.	770.
1901........	180.	190.	210.	255.	770.

Gold $2.50

	F-15	VF-20	EF-40	AU-50	MS-60
1902	180.	190.	210.	255.	770.
1903	180.	190.	210.	255.	770.
1904	180.	190.	210.	255.	770.
1905	180.	190.	210.	255.	770.
1906	180.	190.	210.	255.	770.
1907	180.	190.	210.	255.	770.

Indian Head Type

	F-12	VF-20	EF-40	AU-50	MS-60	MS-65
1908	180.	195.	205.	225.	370.	4450.
1909	180.	195.	205.	225.	370.	4550.
1910	180.	195.	205.	225.	385.	4800.
1911	180.	195.	205.	225.	370.	4650.
1911-D	525.	650.	900.	1400.	2850.	8300.
1912	180.	195.	205.	225.	370.	4900.
1913	180.	195.	205.	225.	360.	4650.
1914	185.	200.	225.	255.	420.	5000.
1914-D	180.	195.	225.	275.	400.	4500.
1915	180.	195.	205.	225.	340.	4700.
1925-D	180.	195.	205.	225.	340.	4450.
1926	180.	195.	205.	225.	340.	4450.
1927	180.	195.	205.	225.	340.	4450.
1928	180.	195.	205.	225.	340.	4450.
1929	180.	195.	205.	225.	340.	4600.

Three Dollars Gold

	F-12	VF-20	EF-40	MS-60	MS-65
1854	440.	520.	665.	2900.	13850.
1854-D	5300.	7500.	15000.	42500.	—
1854-O	475.	560.	735.	3400.	14950.
1855	440.	505.	655.	3100.	13950.
1855-S	560.	725.	1025.	4500.	—
1856	440.	505.	700.	3250.	13650.
1856-S	465.	655.	800.	3400.	—
1857	440.	510.	700.	3200.	13900.
1857-S	635.	800.	1250.	4600.	—
1858	775.	950.	1400.	4200.	—
1859	440.	510.	675.	3050.	14500.
1860	440.	525.	725.	3100.	14850.
1860-S	635.	680.	975.	—	—
1861	535.	640.	750.	3950.	13850.
1862	535.	640.	850.	4050.	14300.
1863	550.	655.	750.	4050.	13850.
1864	560.	665.	800.	4150.	14700.
1865	740.	910.	1200.	5750.	23000.
1866	685.	690.	850.	4100.	15250.
1867	660.	665.	775.	4250.	15000.
1868	610.	660.	740.	4000.	15500.
1869	635.	700.	775.	4250.	15500.
1870	635.	690.	775.	4100.	15500.

1870-S Only One Known EF-40 $687500.

	F-12	VF-20	EF-40	MS-60	MS-65
1871	675.	690.	850.	4000.	15500.
1872	665.	665.	750.	3950.	15000.

1873 Open 3 Proofs Only 25 Struck
1873 Closed 3

	F-12	VF-20	EF-40	MS-60	MS-65
(All Restrikes).	2450.	3000.	4000.	9250.	—
1874	430.	505.	640.	2750.	13200.

1875 Proofs Only 20 Pieces Struck Proof 65 $125000.
1876 Proofs Only 45 Pieces Struck Proof 65 $32500.

GOLD $3.00

	F-12	VF-20	EF-40	MS-60	MS-65
1877	740.	810.	1850.	4400.	—
1878	430.	505.	635.	2700.	13150.
1879	515.	610.	675.	3000.	13350.
1880	540.	650.	800.	3150.	13350.
1881	610.	725.	1350.	3300.	14500.
1882	610.	635.	775.	3150.	13400.
1883	620.	635.	775.	3200.	14600.
1884	700.	775.	925.	3150.	13600.
1885	635.	700.	975.	4100.	14000.
1886	645.	675.	950.	3150.	13750.
1887	540.	550.	750.	3100.	13400.
1888	540.	550.	750.	3100.	13500.
1889	540.	550.	750.	3100.	13500.

Half Eagles $5.00 Gold

	F-12	VF-20	EF-40	AU-50	MS-60
1834 Classic Hd. Pl. 4	235.	285.	415.	975.	2650.
1834 Cr. 4	425.	650.	900.	—	—
1835	235.	285.	415.	960.	2400.
1836	235.	285.	415.	960.	2300.
1837	255.	300.	550.	1450.	2750.
1838	240.	290.	415.	1000.	2450.
1838-C	840.	1600.	2700.	4100.	—
1838-D	785.	1500.	2050.	3800.	—
1839 Coronet N.M.	235.	290.	390.	800.	2150.
1839-C	455.	750.	1375.	3500.	—
1839-D	415.	645.	1225.	2750.	5500.
1840	210.	295.	380.	700.	2150.
1840-C	420.	650.	1050.	3500.	—
1840-D	415.	645.	1000.	2850.	5750.
1840-O	295.	415.	600.	1750.	3900.
1841	195.	325.	450.	725.	2100.
1841-C	365.	490.	925.	2800.	5850.
1841-D	370.	490.	950.	2700.	5750.
1842 Small Letters	190.	280.	515.	2150.	—
1842-C Large Date	405.	500.	820.	2800.	—
1842-D S.D. S.L.	410.	500.	855.	3500.	—
1842-O	260.	330.	740.	2600.	—
1843	170.	200.	235.	385.	1550.
1843-C	410.	490.	925.	2900.	—
1843-D	395.	465.	900.	2500.	4900.
1843-O	225.	275.	525.	1425.	2950.
1844	180.	210.	320.	485.	1600.
1844-C	450.	675.	1050.	—	—
1844-D	415.	515.	725.	2950.	5100.
1844-O	260.	345.	420.	850.	2100.
1845	180.	210.	275.	425.	1550.
1845-D	415.	465.	750.	1800.	5000.
1845-O	290.	375.	535.	2625.	—
1846	170.	210.	255.	440.	1550.
1846-C	440.	725.	1525.	3550.	—
1846-D	425.	465.	725.	1750.	2900.
1846-O	305.	375.	500.	1700.	—
1847	170.	200.	235.	385.	1525.
1847-C	430.	620.	1100.	—	—
1847-D	460.	515.	960.	2950.	5150.
1847-O	425.	550.	1050.	2800.	—
1848	180.	250.	320.	765.	2000.
1848-C	440.	515.	1100.	3900.	—

GOLD $5.00

	F-12	VF-20	EF-40	AU-50	MS-60
1848-D	425.	465.	975.	3100.	5250.
1849	170.	210.	255.	735.	1775.
1849-C	390.	465.	735.	2000.	3950.
1849-D	400.	515.	1250.	3050.	––
1850	225.	310.	400.	925.	1900.
1850-C	390.	475.	800.	2200.	4050.
1850-D	400.	475.	1225.	3450.	––
1851	180.	250.	320.	500.	1850.
1851-C	370.	490.	825.	2150.	––
1851-D	375.	465.	760.	2000.	––
1851-O	315.	400.	510.	1650.	––
1852	170.	200.	235.	385.	1500.
1852-C	370.	490.	750.	1700.	3950.
1852-D	375.	490.	760.	1600.	3800.
1853	180.	250.	320.	500.	1700.
1853-C	370.	475.	750.	1600.	4650.
1853-D	375.	465.	725.	1300.	4400.
1854	190.	280.	360.	500.	1750.
1854-C	400.	495.	850.	1975.	3400.
1854-D	365.	460.	765.	1650.	3750.
1854-O	305.	365.	550.	1150.	2700.
1854-S EXTREMELY RARE - 268 Struck AU-55 $210000.					
1855	180.	250.	320.	500.	1650.
1855-C	400.	500.	775.	1525.	––
1855-D	410.	500.	825.	1950.	––
1855-O	370.	465.	790.	2050.	––
1855-S	190.	230.	500.	1275.	––
1856	175.	205.	250.	440.	1550.
1856-C	400.	490.	765.	1925.	5050.
1856-D	390.	485.	770.	2125.	4350.
1856-O	410.	525.	935.	––	––
1856-S	210.	290.	440.	2175.	––
1857	180.	210.	235.	385.	1550.
1857-C	345.	485.	765.	1850.	––
1857-D	400.	515.	785.	2100.	4950.
1857-O	355.	415.	600.	1625.	––
1857-S	210.	290.	425.	1150.	2650.
1858	225.	295.	370.	650.	1700.
1858-C	370.	465.	735.	1750.	––
1858-D	400.	515.	1000.	2350.	––
1858-S	335.	425.	725.	1725.	––
1859	230.	380.	525.	1400.	2100.
1859-C	365.	475.	765.	1975.	––
1859-D	415.	500.	755.	1950.	4850.
1859-S	450.	635.	1450.	2700.	––
1860	215.	330.	455.	1150.	2000.
1860-C	390.	620.	1400.	3600.	––
1860-D	400.	620.	1375.	3050.	5250.
1860-S	290.	460.	1225.	––	––
1861	170.	200.	215.	400.	1475.
1861-C	800.	1375.	2150.	4000.	––
1861-D	2850.	4500.	7000.	––	––
1861-S	435.	750.	1500.	––	––
1862	445.	675.	950.	2750.	––
1862-S	700.	1200.	2050.	––	––
1863	415.	675.	1125.	2600.	––
1863-S	355.	635.	1400.	––	––
1864	320.	400.	750.	1450.	2200.
1864-S	1150.	1750.	2800.	––	––
1865	415.	685.	1350.	2850.	––
1865-S	330.	625.	1325.	––	––
1866 Motto	340.	425.	775.	1100.	––
1866-S N.M.	360.	775.	1400.	––	––
1866-S Motto	290.	550.	950.	––	––
1867	285.	425.	750.	1675.	––
1867-S	370.	725.	1325.	––	––
1868	260.	440.	875.	1775.	––
1868-S	255.	400.	1050.	––	––

GOLD $5.00

	F-12	VF-20	EF-40	AU-50	MS-60
1869	340.	620.	925.	1575.	––
1869-S	300.	520.	1050.	––	––
1870	340.	545.	875.	1775.	––
1870-CC	1175.	2000.	4000.	––	––
1870-S	410.	875.	1575.	––	––
1871	355.	620.	960.	––	––
1871-CC	500.	815.	1175.	2550.	––
1871-S	255.	375.	825.	2125.	––
1872	330.	505.	775.	1250.	2250.
1872-CC	475.	750.	1350.	––	––
1872-S	255.	390.	975.	3100.	––
1873 Closed 3.	200.	235.	395.	700.	2050.
1873-CC	550.	825.	1450.	––	––
1873-S	365.	560.	975.	––	––
1874	355.	500.	825.	1450.	––
1874-CC	385.	575.	900.	1550.	––
1874-S	370.	665.	1225.	––	––
1875 Very Rare - 220 Pcs. Struck Proof 65 $72500.					
1875-CC	550.	840.	1250.	––	––
1875-S	225.	545.	1275.	––	––
1876	435.	875.	1125.	1600.	2150.
1876-CC	430.	700.	1075.	3050.	––
1876-S	465.	1000.	1850.	––	––
1877	420.	755.	975.	1400.	2750.
1877-CC	460.	750.	1175.	––	––
1877-S	200.	385.	625.	––	––
1878	155.	165.	250.	325.	450.
1878-CC	775.	1300.	2650.	––	––
1878-S	155.	165.	250.	350.	660.
1879	155.	165.	205.	275.	400.
1879-CC	275.	375.	785.	1075.	––
1879-S	185.	215.	260.	290.	400.
1880	155.	165.	180.	195.	325.
1880-CC	265.	365.	675.	800.	1500.
1880-S	155.	165.	180.	195.	325.
1881	155.	165.	180.	195.	325.
1881-CC	275.	410.	700.	1475.	2900.
1881-S	155.	165.	180.	195.	325.
1882	155.	165.	180.	195.	325.
1882-CC	240.	290.	350.	510.	1700.
1882-S	155.	165.	180.	195.	325.
1883	155.	165.	180.	240.	450.
1883-CC	270.	410.	715.	1500.	––
1883-S	200.	235.	285.	400.	650.
1884	155.	180.	205.	340.	715.
1884-CC	280.	450.	800.	1650.	––
1884-S	195.	275.	310.	480.	625.
1885	155.	165.	180.	195.	325.
1885-S	155.	165.	180.	195.	325.
1886	155.	180.	215.	250.	355.
1886-S	155.	165.	195.	210.	325.
1887 Proofs Only - 87 Pcs. Struck Proof 65 $28500.					
1887-S	155.	165.	180.	195.	325.
1888	175.	215.	260.	315.	880.
1888-S	185.	275.	325.	625.	––
1889	175.	300.	575.	785.	975.
1890	225.	400.	615.	1250.	––
1890-CC	185.	265.	300.	485.	790.
1891	155.	180.	205.	265.	750.
1891-CC	180.	235.	285.	430.	690.
1892	155.	165.	180.	195.	315.
1892-CC	180.	255.	300.	500.	870.
1892-O	350.	450.	625.	1250.	2650.
1892-S	155.	200.	260.	485.	940.
1893	155.	165.	180.	195.	315.
1893-CC	185.	230.	295.	560.	1350.
1893-O	180.	235.	310.	440.	890.
1893-S	155.	200.	220.	370.	425.
1894	155.	165.	180.	195.	315.

GOLD $5.00

	F-12	VF-20	EF-40	AU-50	MS-60
1894-O	155.	190.	355.	485.	720.
1894-S	255.	325.	475.	850.	——
1895	155.	165.	180.	195.	315.
1895-S	180.	265.	350.	950.	——
1896	155.	200.	230.	250.	385.
1896-S	180.	265.	325.	550.	1300.
1897	155.	165.	180.	195.	315.
1897-S	165.	190.	280.	485.	865.
1898	155.	165.	180.	195.	315.
1898-S	165.	180.	205.	225.	350.
1899	155.	165.	180.	195.	315.
1899-S	155.	175.	195.	215.	340.
1900	155.	165.	180.	195.	315.
1900-S	165.	190.	250.	350.	735.
1901	155.	165.	180.	195.	315.
1901-S	155.	165.	180.	195.	315.
1902	155.	165.	190.	205.	330.
1902-S	155.	165.	180.	195.	315.
1903	155.	165.	190.	205.	330.
1903-S	155.	165.	180.	195.	315.
1904	155.	165.	180.	195.	315.
1904-S	170.	205.	230.	265.	410.
1905	155.	165.	190.	205.	330.
1905-S	170.	205.	230.	265.	635.
1906	155.	165.	180.	195.	315.
1906-D	155.	165.	180.	195.	340.
1906-S	155.	175.	195.	215.	370.
1907	155.	165.	180.	195.	315.
1907-D	155.	165.	180.	195.	315.
1908	155.	165.	180.	195.	325.

Indian Head Type

	F-12	VF-20	EF-40	AU-50	MS-60	MS-65
1908	225.	235.	250.	275.	840.	7550.
1908-D	225.	235.	250.	285.	845.	7900.
1908-S	280.	305.	425.	590.	2450.	8750.
1909	225.	235.	250.	275.	815.	7800.
1909-D	225.	235.	250.	275.	800.	7650.
1909-O	315.	385.	875.	1450.	6350.	50000.
1909-S	275.	300.	375.	625.	1400.	13000.
1910	225.	235.	250.	275.	815.	7900.
1910-D	240.	250.	265.	380.	855.	8100.
1910-S	255.	285.	325.	600.	1900.	14000.
1911	225.	235.	250.	275.	800.	7700.
1911-D	295.	370.	485.	825.	4000.	——
1911-S	235.	260.	280.	340.	900.	8600.
1912	225.	235.	250.	275.	800.	7700.
1912-S	260.	290.	335.	675.	1750.	13000.
1913	225.	235.	250.	275.	800.	7700.
1913-S	290.	305.	395.	750.	2700.	——
1914	230.	240.	255.	305.	830.	7700.
1914-D	230.	240.	260.	315.	810.	7800.
1914-S	240.	245.	280.	420.	950.	——
1915	230.	240.	255.	295.	800.	7700.
1915-S	255.	280.	325.	700.	2500.	——
1916-S	235.	240.	270.	435.	900.	8650.
1929	——	——	3450.	4200.	6600.	16000.

Eagles - $10 Gold

	F-12	VF-20	EF-40	AU-50	MS-60
1838 Coronet N.M.	545.	775.	1750.	5850.	——

GOLD $10.00

	F-12	VF-20	EF-40	AU-50	MS-60
1839 Type of '38	420.	680.	1050.	2400.	6450.
1840	355.	415.	560.	1675.	——
1841	355.	415.	560.	1300.	——
1841-O	675.	1075.	2000.	——	——
1842	300.	390.	460.	1250.	——
1842-O	300.	390.	460.	1025.	3150.
1843	340.	415.	510.	1250.	——
1843-O	300.	390.	450.	785.	2250.
1844	465.	735.	1375.	2500.	——
1844-O	315.	415.	450.	1000.	2950.
1845	415.	545.	750.	1850.	——
1845-O	355.	480.	575.	1300.	——
1846	505.	610.	1450.	——	——
1846-O	355.	480.	535.	1275.	——
1847	300.	345.	430.	560.	2150.
1847-O	300.	345.	430.	605.	2200.
1848	315.	415.	535.	885.	3200.
1848-O	440.	600.	1175.	2050.	——
1849	300.	345.	430.	560.	2250.
1849-O	440.	675.	1125.	1525.	——
1850	300.	345.	430.	685.	2150.
1850-O	340.	455.	560.	900.	——
1851	340.	390.	535.	975.	2450.
1851-O	300.	345.	445.	850.	——
1852	315.	405.	560.	1400.	——
1852-O	400.	535.	850.	2350.	——
1853	300.	355.	425.	635.	2300.
1853-O	315.	390.	535.	1125.	——
1854	340.	405.	560.	1225.	——
1854-O	300.	345.	500.	1300.	——
1854-S	300.	345.	440.	850.	2550.
1855	300.	345.	440.	770.	2300.
1855-O	375.	475.	785.	2200.	——
1855-S	485.	700.	1375.	——	——
1856	315.	395.	485.	795.	2500.
1856-O	405.	520.	950.	1425.	——
1856-S	315.	340.	540.	825.	3300.
1857	340.	410.	625.	975.	——
1857-O	485.	585.	1125.	1950.	——
1857-S	385.	515.	660.	1075.	——
1858	——	2950.	5500.	——	——
1858-O	315.	385.	525.	875.	3450.
1858-S	485.	660.	1150.	——	——
1859	340.	405.	575.	1025.	——
1859-O	875.	1900.	3200.	——	——
1859-S	850.	1025.	1750.	——	——
1860	——	385.	560.	975.	2450.
1860-O	400.	505.	650.	1250.	3550.
1860-S	——	1325.	2250.	——	——
1861	305.	340.	395.	520.	2250.
1861-S	425.	560.	1000.	1325.	——
1862	315.	385.	525.	975.	——
1862-S	575.	725.	1400.	——	——
1863	——	1800.	3500.	——	——
1863-S	650.	825.	1450.	——	——
1864	675.	925.	1550.	——	——
1864-S	1225.	2800.	4050.	——	——
1865	675.	950.	1450.	——	——
1865-S	650.	875.	1500.	——	——
1866-S N.M.	835.	1600.	2400.	——	——
1866 Motto	550.	700.	850.	1800.	——
1866-S Motto	450.	635.	1125.	——	——
1867	675.	850.	1400.	——	——
1867-S	750.	1375.	2750.	——	——
1868	460.	625.	785.	2950.	——
1868-S	470.	670.	1325.	——	——
1869	675.	825.	1500.	——	——
1869-S	700.	875.	1450.	——	——
1870	575.	700.	1125.	——	——

GOLD $10.00

	F-12	VF-20	EF-40	AU-50	MS-60
1870-CC	1175.	2200.	4400.	—	—
1870-S	470.	585.	1550.	—	—
1871	—	1175.	1650.	—	—
1871-CC	650.	1000.	2000.	—	—
1871-S	—	685.	1350.	—	—
1872	—	1750.	3450.	—	—
1872-CC	650.	1050.	2200.	—	—
1872-S	425.	635.	1275.	—	—
1873	—	2700.	4500.	—	—
1873-CC	665.	1075.	1950.	—	—
1873-S	460.	660.	1175.	—	—
1874	320.	340.	415.	535.	955.
1874-CC	450.	660.	1600.	—	—
1874-S	450.	585.	1275.	—	—
1875 Ext. Rare - Only 120 Struck Proof 65 $120000.					
1875-CC	615.	825.	1500.	—	—
1876	—	1325.	2900.	—	—
1876-CC	675.	1125.	2800.	—	—
1876-S	450.	650.	1375.	—	—
1877	—	1375.	2550.	—	—
1877-CC	625.	925.	1500.	3100.	
1877-S	485.	690.	1400.	—	—
1878	270.	330.	395.	535.	800.
1878-CC	900.	1375.	1950.	—	—
1878-S	415.	575.	950.	—	—
1879	240.	280.	320.	370.	545.
1879-CC	2100.	2650.	4500.	—	—
1879-O	—	1550.	3000.	—	—
1879-S	240.	280.	300.	430.	530.
1880	235.	265.	275.	310.	410.
1880-CC	340.	435.	600.	850.	—
1880-O	—	350.	510.	950.	—
1880-S	240.	280.	295.	325.	470.
1881	230.	255.	260.	310.	410.
1881-CC	290.	405.	485.	700.	1650.
1881-O	290.	410.	500.	975.	—
1881-S	230.	255.	260.	320.	425.
1882	230.	255.	260.	305.	410.
1882-CC	—	495.	665.	1000.	2600.
1882-O	—	435.	560.	970.	—
1882-S	270.	330.	395.	535.	905.
1883	240.	280.	300.	335.	425.
1883-CC	310.	435.	565.	845.	2750.
1883-O	900.	1900.	2850.	4700.	—
1883-S	270.	330.	375.	535.	905.
1884	270.	340.	375.	485.	905.
1884-CC	345.	480.	565.	850.	—
1884-S	240.	325.	355.	485.	905.
1885	235.	280.	310.	345.	785.
1885-S	235.	280.	285.	390.	555.
1886	255.	330.	375.	480.	955.
1886-S	230.	260.	275.	310.	410.
1887	235.	280.	310.	345.	835.
1887-S	240.	280.	285.	335.	535.
1888	270.	320.	370.	470.	1100.
1888-O	230.	260.	275.	310.	495.
1888-S	230.	260.	275.	310.	425.
1889	305.	410.	450.	625.	955.
1889-S	230.	260.	275.	310.	410.
1890	270.	330.	375.	430.	630.
1890-CC	310.	345.	380.	450.	1025.
1891	235.	280.	310.	335.	520.
1891-CC	245.	275.	295.	355.	550.
1892	240.	265.	280.	310.	410.
1892-CC	305.	340.	395.	460.	1100.
1892-O	245.	300.	325.	335.	495.
1892-S	260.	305.	345.	370.	520.
1893	230.	260.	275.	320.	405.
1893-CC	305.	395.	420.	710.	1550.
1893-O	240.	280.	310.	355.	500.

Gold $10.00

	F-12	VF-20	EF-40	AU-50	MS-60
1893-S	260.	305.	345.	355.	520.
1894	230.	260.	275.	295.	390.
1894-O	230.	260.	275.	305.	450.
1894-S	240.	280.	365.	660.	1500.
1895	230.	260.	275.	295.	375.
1895-O	230.	260.	275.	295.	390.
1895-S	320.	380.	650.	900.	2250.
1896	235.	280.	295.	330.	435.
1896-S	320.	370.	435.	700.	2300.
1897	230.	260.	275.	295.	375.
1897-O	235.	280.	300.	355.	450.
1897-S	240.	280.	345.	450.	810.
1898	230.	260.	275.	295.	375.
1898-S	240.	280.	300.	415.	525.
1899	230.	260.	275.	295.	375.
1899-O	260.	305.	330.	380.	525.
1899-S	260.	305.	345.	355.	520.
1900	235.	270.	285.	310.	410.
1900-S	245.	305.	345.	450.	810.
1901	230.	260.	275.	295.	375.
1901-O	235.	280.	320.	345.	525.
1901-S	230.	260.	275.	295.	375.
1902	235.	280.	295.	320.	410.
1902-S	230.	260.	280.	300.	385.
1903	235.	280.	295.	320.	410.
1903-O	230.	260.	275.	295.	375.
1903-S	260.	320.	345.	350.	485.
1904	235.	265.	280.	300.	410.
1904-O	265.	330.	360.	370.	485.
1905	235.	275.	290.	310.	400.
1905-S	270.	305.	320.	420.	630.
1906	235.	275.	290.	310.	400.
1906-D	230.	260.	275.	295.	375.
1906-O	260.	320.	345.	405.	555.
1906-S	260.	305.	335.	350.	520.
1907	230.	260.	275.	295.	375.
1907-D	245.	280.	300.	335.	465.
1907-S	295.	335.	365.	420.	735.

Indian Head Type

	F-12	VF-20	EF-40	AU-50	MS-60	MS-65
1907 Wire Rim, Periods	—	—	—	5600.	10500.	24500.
1907 Rolled Rim, Periods MS-65 $35200.						
1907 No Prds.	485.	525.	540.	580.	780.	7200.
1908 N.M.	495.	550.	615.	735.	1075.	8100.
1908-D N.M.	495.	550.	595.	685.	1000.	7800.
1908 Motto	495.	510.	520.	545.	740.	7050.
1908-D	520.	560.	615.	690.	810.	8400.
1908-S	500.	580.	675.	790.	3150.	10750.
1909	485.	525.	540.	595.	780.	7150.
1909-D	495.	550.	590.	635.	915.	7500.
1909-S	495.	545.	570.	645.	1200.	7600.
1910	495.	510.	520.	535.	730.	7000.
1910-D	495.	510.	520.	535.	730.	7000.
1910-S	495.	515.	525.	570.	1050.	7500.
1911	470.	480.	490.	530.	730.	6950.
1911-D	570.	690.	900.	1200.	5000.	25000.
1911-S	485.	520.	545.	650.	2100.	8500.
1912	485.	505.	515.	535.	730.	7000.
1912-S	500.	535.	555.	620.	1600.	8150.
1913	470.	480.	490.	530.	730.	6975.
1913-S	515.	570.	630.	1050.	7000.	42500.
1914	480.	500.	510.	530.	740.	7050.

GOLD $10

	F-12	VF-20	EF-40	AU-50	MS-60	MS-65
1914-D	470.	480.	490.	530.	765.	7250.
1914-S	495.	510.	520.	600.	1150.	7600.
1915	485.	500.	510.	530.	750.	6850.
1915-S	500.	530.	555.	675.	2250.	19500.
1916-S	470.	480.	490.	590.	1075.	8200.
1920-S	——	——	7750.	9750.	14500.	55000.
1926	460.	475.	490.	520.	715.	6800.
1930-S	——	——	——	5500.	11500.	25500.
1932	460.	475.	490.	520.	715.	6750.
1933	——	——	——	——	50000.	140000.

Double Eagles $20 Gold

	VF-20	EF-40	AU-50	MS-60
1849 One Specimen U.S. Mint collection				
1850 N.M.	565.	655.	850.	1525.
1850-O	630.	720.	1300.	——
1851	570.	635.	775.	1350.
1851-O	620.	775.	1000.	2800.
1852	605.	660.	735.	1275.
1852-O	620.	740.	1000.	2400.
1853	565.	635.	735.	1375.
1853-O	630.	850.	1950.	——
1854	580.	655.	835.	2000.
1854-O V. Rare	19500.	32000.	50000.	——
1854-S	605.	670.	860.	2000.
1855	580.	655.	860.	1850.
1855-O	3300.	7500.	——	——
1855-S	565.	640.	860.	2200.
1856	565.	620.	830.	1850.
1856-O V. Rare	20500.	34000.	50000.	——
1856-S	565.	595.	735.	1575.
1857	605.	670.	975.	1900.
1857-O	875.	1900.	3200.	——
1857-S	565.	620.	860.	2350.
1858	605.	655.	950.	2400.
1858-O	900.	1450.	2750.	——
1858-S	565.	620.	860.	2400.
1859	775.	1250.	——	——
1859-O	2000.	4050.	6500.	——
1859-S	560.	645.	935.	3050.
1860	590.	655.	845.	1400.
1860-O	3200.	6750.	——	——
1860-S	605.	670.	960.	3150.
1861	565.	590.	735.	1325.
1861-O	950.	2650.	4800.	——
1861-S	605.	670.	985.	3100.
1862	705.	950.	1250.	3550.
1862-S	615.	715.	1150.	3300.
1863	590.	670.	1500.	——
1863-S	565.	635.	935.	2450.
1864	565.	670.	1350.	——
1864-S	605.	670.	1450.	——
1865	600.	650.	960.	2500.
1865-S	565.	620.	1350.	4000.
1866-S	690.	1000.	2650.	——
1866 Motto	560.	655.	960.	2450.
1866-S Motto	575.	685.	1000.	——
1867	515.	555.	690.	805.
1867-S	575.	670.	1150.	——
1868	630.	775.	1000.	2700.
1868-S	560.	655.	1100.	2500.
1869	560.	670.	935.	2450.
1869-S	545.	625.	860.	1675.

GOLD $20.00

	VF-20	EF-40	AU-50	MS-60
1870	575.	715.	1250.	——
1870-CC V. Rare	17500.	25000.	——	——
1870-S	540.	625.	935.	1675.
1871	600.	705.	1250.	2850.
1871-CC	1500.	3250.	4700.	——
1871-S	540.	625.	835.	1525.
1872	525.	585.	675.	820.
1872-CC	900.	1150.	2000.	3850.
1872-S	560.	630.	910.	1525.
1873 Closed 3.	725.	895.	1200.	2750.
1873 Open 3.	515.	555.	595.	755.
1873-CC	925.	1100.	2200.	——
1873-S	560.	630.	935.	1250.
1874	575.	660.	775.	1275.
1874-CC	620.	850.	1475.	3650.
1874-S	535.	585.	685.	800.
1875	575.	660.	805.	1050.
1875-CC	590.	710.	845.	1250.
1875-S	535.	585.	630.	765.
1876	525.	585.	630.	755.
1876-CC	595.	745.	895.	2050.
1876-S	525.	585.	630.	760.
1877 TWENTY DOLLARS	545.	625.	720.	780.
1877-CC	605.	755.	935.	2200.
1877-S	515.	545.	620.	820.
1878	530.	625.	720.	815.
1878-CC	785.	950.	1950.	——
1878-S	525.	600.	685.	805.
1879	545.	655.	815.	845.
1879-CC	850.	1050.	2300.	——
1879-O	2550.	3800.	4900.	12000.
1879-S	530.	605.	720.	805.
1880	545.	655.	860.	2300.
1880-S	545.	655.	885.	1475.
1881	2000.	5800.	7700.	——
1881-S	545.	655.	885.	1100.
1882	——	12000.	——	——
1882-CC	655.	720.	830.	1800.
1882-S	530.	605.	720.	1000.
*1883 Proofs Only 40 Struck - Proof 65 $68500.				
1883-CC	670.	745.	835.	1375.
1883-S	520.	550.	585.	740.
*1884 Proofs Only 71 Struck - Proof 65 $55000.				
1884-CC	670.	710.	835.	1575.
1884-S	520.	560.	680.	740.
1885	——	8250.	9750.	22000.
1885-CC	1000.	1575.	3450.	5550.
1885-S	525.	600.	640.	740.
1886	——	9250.	16000.	——
*1887 Proofs Only 121 Struck - Proof $35000.				
1887-S	545.	600.	670.	775.
1888	530.	605.	720.	780.
1888-S	530.	600.	640.	745.
1889	530.	600.	695.	775.
1889-CC	685.	875.	970.	1675.
1889-S	515.	540.	575.	725.
1890	545.	625.	670.	745.
1890-CC	670.	700.	790.	1525.
1890-S	545.	625.	820.	830.
1891	——	3200.	5250.	——
1891-CC	1400.	2050.	3750.	7150.
1891-S	505.	530.	565.	650.
1892	——	1200.	2350.	3300.
1892-CC	670.	735.	895.	1425.
1892-S	525.	540.	570.	655.
1893	515.	530.	565.	710.
1893-CC	675.	745.	935.	1900.
1893-S	525.	540.	570.	705.
1894	505.	530.	560.	640.

GOLD $20.00

	VF-20	EF-40	AU-50	MS-60
1894-S	515.	540.	570.	660.
1895	495.	530.	545.	625.
1895-S	505.	540.	570.	660.
1896	505.	530.	560.	640.
1896-S	515.	540.	570.	660.
1897	505.	530.	560.	640.
1897-S	505.	530.	555.	650.
1898	535.	550.	610.	740.
1898-S	495.	515.	540.	615.
1899	495.	515.	540.	615.
1899-S	505.	520.	555.	630.
1900	495.	515.	540.	615.
1900-S	495.	515.	540.	615.
1901	495.	515.	540.	660.
1901-S	525.	540.	570.	725.
1902	525.	540.	570.	750.
1902-S	520.	560.	585.	750.
1903	495.	515.	540.	615.
1903-S	515.	540.	570.	660.
1904	495.	515.	540.	615.
1904-S	495.	515.	540.	615.
1905	530.	600.	680.	805.
1905-S	525.	540.	570.	720.
1906	525.	540.	570.	725.
1906-D	515.	530.	560.	655.
1906-S	505.	520.	550.	625.
1907	495.	515.	540.	615.
1907-D	505.	520.	550.	625.
1907-S	500.	515.	545.	620.

	VF-20	EF-40	AU-50	MS-60	MS-63	MS-65
1921	——	8750.	11000.	19250.	29500.	
1922	550.	575.	605.	655.	1075.	3500.
1922-S	590.	655.	740.	1175.	2500.	4150.
1923	550.	575.	590.	640.	1090.	3600.
1923-D	550.	575.	590.	665.	1450.	3350.
1924	550.	575.	590.	640.	1050.	3075.
1924-D	——	950.	1250.	1950.	3000.	7750.
1924-S	——	——	1150.	1900.	3050.	8800.
1925	550.	575.	590.	640.	1075.	3100.
1925-D	——	——	1300.	2100.	3250.	8250.
1925-S	——	850.	1200.	2200.	3150.	——
1926	550.	575.	590.	660.	1090.	3250.
1926-D	——	——	1250.	2200.	3400.	——
1926-S	——	——	1050.	1750.	2300.	5900.
1927	550.	575.	590.	640.	1050.	3050.
1927-D - Extremely Rare MS-65 $290000.						
1927-S	——	——	3350.	7750.	14500.	24500.
1928	550.	575.	590.	640.	1050.	3050.
1929	——	——	——	7400.	11000.	——
1930-S	——	——	——	17750.	——	——
1931	——	——	——	14750.	23500.	——
1931-D	——	——	——	16750.	24500.	——
1932	——	——	——	17250.	26000.	38500.
1933 NOT LEGAL TO OWN.						

St. Gaudens Type

	VF-20	EF-40	AU-50	MS-60	MS-63	MS-65
1907 Ex. High Relief Proofs Only Proof 65 $265000.						
1907 H.R.- R.N. Wire Ed.	3000.	4250.	5700.	9000.	13000.	26500.
1907 H.R.- R.N. Flat Ed.	3050.	4400.	5800.	9100.	13250.	27000.
1907	550.	575.	590.	650.	1075.	3150.
1908	550.	575.	590.	650.	1025.	3025.
1908-D	575.	600.	625.	700.	1150.	3550.
1908 Motto	560.	590.	615.	725.	1100.	4300.
1908-D Motto	575.	605.	620.	725.	1200.	3800.
1908-S Motto	715.	925.	1200.	3300.	5250.	15250.
1909/8	550.	575.	685.	925.	2200.	4750.
1909	575.	610.	700.	775.	1325.	4100.
1909-D	655.	740.	1050.	2750.	5250.	27000.
1909-S	550.	575.	605.	675.	1125.	3550.
1910	550.	575.	605.	675.	1150.	3525.
1910-D	550.	575.	605.	675.	1125.	3550.
1910-S	550.	575.	605.	675.	1175.	3600.
1911	550.	580.	620.	710.	1225.	3750.
1911-D	550.	575.	605.	675.	1050.	3300.
1911-S	550.	580.	620.	700.	1185.	3650.
1912	550.	580.	620.	725.	1300.	3850.
1913	550.	580.	620.	720.	1325.	3850.
1913-D	550.	575.	595.	705.	1150.	3650.
1913-S	570.	605.	725.	1175.	2250.	4250.
1914	560.	590.	620.	725.	1225.	3850.
1914-D	550.	580.	620.	700.	1150.	3450.
1914-S	550.	575.	605.	665.	1100.	3350.
1915	560.	590.	605.	700.	1325.	3800.
1915-S	550.	580.	620.	685.	1100.	3300.
1916-S	550.	575.	605.	675.	1175.	3450.
1920	550.	580.	620.	665.	1150.	3700.
1920-S	——	7000.	8750.	13750.	21500.	——

Commemorative Half Dollars

	AU-50	MS-60	MS-63	MS-65
1892 Columbian	22.50	75.00	150.	1225.
1893 Columbian	20.00	74.00	145.	1200.
1893 Isabella 25¢	260.	560.	1100.	4500.
1900 Lafayette $1	375.	950.	2150.	13000.
1915 Pan-Pacific	260.	575.	1100.	4150.
1918 Illinois	65.00	135.	400.	1150.
1920 Maine	73.50	145.	410.	1450.
1920 Pilgrim	36.50	58.50	140.	850.
1921 Pilgrim	92.50	150.	260.	1600.
1921 Alabama 2x2	160.	375.	650.	3400.
1921 Alabama Plain	87.50	250.	525.	3200.
1921 Missouri Plain	240.	475.	950.	3850.
1921 Missouri 2x4	315.	515.	1025.	3900.
1922 Grant	52.50	135.	385.	1450.
1922 Grant Star	390.	775.	1700.	6900.
1923 Monroe	28.50	65.00	150.	2400.
1924 Huguenot	65.00	120.	385.	1150.
1925 Lexington	37.00	49.00	230.	1200.
1925 Stone Mtn.	28.00	44.50	115.	525.
1925 California	85.00	145.	420.	1250.
1925 Vancouver	300.	400.	575.	1850.
1926 Sesqui	29.00	45.00	135.	2150.
1926 Oregon	90.00	110.	300.	825.
1926-S Oregon	92.50	115.	285.	875.
1928 Oregon	155.	260.	360.	1300.
1933-D Oregon	190.	290.	390.	1550.
1934-D Oregon	105.	220.	310.	1775.
1936 Oregon	92.50	155.	290.	850.
1936-S Oregon	155.	240.	380.	1450.
1937-D Oregon	90.00	135.	330.	675.
1938 Oregon PDS	——	600.	850.	2550.
1939 Oregon PDS	——	1200.	1550.	4400.
1927 Vermont	175.	230.	330.	1800.
1928 Hawaiian	725.	1075.	1800.	5500.
1934 Boone	100.	120.	230.	650.
1934 Boone Set Sm. 4	——	925.	1375.	4000.
1935 Boone Set PDS	——	350.	680.	1500.

COMMEMORATIVE HALF DOLLARS

	AU-50	MS-60	MS-63	MS-65
1936 Boone Set PDS	——	350.	675.	1500.
1937 Boone Set PDS	——	675.	1000.	2500.
1938 Boone Set PDS	——	1200.	1350.	3200.
1934 Maryland	125.	165.	300.	1350.
1934 Texas	110.	140.	225.	525.
1935 Texas Set PDS	——	400.	670.	1550.
1936 Texas Set PDS	——	415.	695.	1575.
1937 Texas Set PDS	——	425.	735.	1700.
1938 Texas Set PDS	——	835.	1050.	2100.
1935 Ark. Set PDS .	——	275.	385.	3100.
1936 Ark. Set PDS .	——	275.	385.	3100.
1936 Ark. Single ...	79.00	89.50	145.	1050.
1937 Ark. Set PDS .	——	290.	400.	3150.
1938 Ark. Set PDS .	——	475.	710.	4100.
1939 Ark. Set PDS .	——	875.	1200.	6750.
1935 Conn........	190.	245.	500.	1300.
1935 Hudson	450.	575.	850.	2900.
1935-S San Diego ..	77.50	115.	195.	550.
1936-D San Diego ..	80.00	135.	210.	650.
1935 Spanish Trail .	600.	750.	950.	1850.
1936 Albany	235.	260.	365.	825.
1936 Bridgeport ...	135.	165.	225.	1000.
1936 Cincinnati Set.	——	815.	1200.	6650.
1936 Cincinnati (1) .	260.	280.	400.	2200.
1936 Cleveland	75.00	105.	200.	790.
1936 Columbia PDS	——	840.	1075.	2150.
1936 Columbia Sing.	225.	290.	330.	725.
1936 Delaware	210.	240.	465.	1400.
1936 Elgin, Ill.	195.	225.	330.	1050.
1936 Gettysburg ...	210.	235.	350.	1025.
1936 Long Island ..	67.50	90.00	155.	925.
1936 Lynchburg ...	185.	230.	290.	975.
1936 Norfolk	480.	535.	615.	850.
1936 Rhode Is. Sing.	95.00	120.	185.	900.
1936 Rhode Is. Set .	——	350.	535.	2750.
1936 Robinson	92.50	115.	275.	925.
1936 San Francisco	82.50	170.	205.	775.
1936 Wisconsin....	210.	245.	350.	785.
1936 York County..	200.	235.	330.	700.
1937 Antietam.....	335.	380.	550.	1100.
1937 Roanoke	165.	215.	315.	875.
1938 New Rochelle.	380.	425.	490.	1250.
1946 Iowa	82.50	97.50	155.	485.
1946 B.T. Wash. (3)	——	34.00	45.00	330.
1946 B.T. Wash. (1)	11.00	12.00	16.00	115.
1947 B.T. Wash. (3)	——	55.00	72.50	455.
1948 B.T. Wash. (3)	——	130.	160.	740.
1949 B.T. Wash. (3)	——	175.	235.	1200.
1950 B.T. Wash. (3)	——	155.	190.	950.
1951 B.T. Wash. (3)	——	85.00	130.	690.
1951 Wash.-Car. (3)	——	85.00	120.	670.
1951 Wash.-Car. (1)	11.00	13.00	15.00	115.
1952 Wash.-Car. (3)	——	115.	170.	790.
1953 Wash.-Car. (3)	——	135.	205.	840.
1954 Wash.-Car. (3)	——	95.00	115.	630.

1982 George Washington MS-65 $15.00 Proof-65 $15.00
1983 and 1984 Olympic silver dollar Proof 65 $25.00

Commemorative Gold Coins

	AU-50	MS-60	MS-63	MS-65
1903 La.Pur Jeff.$1	370.	635.	1350.	3600.

Commemorative Gold

	AU-50	MS-60	MS-63	MS-65
1903 La. Purchase McKinley $1	360.	630.	1400.	3650.
1904 Lew.&Clark $1	490.	1125.	2250.	6350.
1905 Lew.&Clark $1	515.	1150.	2300.	6450.
1915-S Pan-Pac $1 .	350.	675.	1450.	3900.
1915-S Pan-Pac $2.50............	850.	1700.	2950.	6500.
1915-S Pan-Pac $50 Rnd	20500.	29500.	37000.	47500.
1915-S Pan-Pac $50 Oct.........	16500.	23500.	28500.	39500.
1916 McKinley $1 ..	335.	740.	1400.	4750.
1917 McKinley $1 ..	350.	750.	1500.	4900.
1922 Grant Star $1 .	675.	1150.	2100.	4900.
1922 Grant Plain $1	625.	1125.	2075.	4800.
1926 Sesqui $2.50...	290.	565.	1050.	4150.

PROOF COINS
Proof-65

	1¢	5¢	10¢	25¢	50¢	$1.00
1859 CN	4700.	——	4350.	5400.	6450.	10750.
1860	2450.	——	3250.	5100.	6100.	10350.
1861	2550.	——	3250.	5050.	6050.	10450.
1862	2450.	——	3250.	5100.	6175.	10500.
1863	2450.	——	3350.	5150.	6150.	10400.
1864 CN	2400.	——	——	——	——	——
1864 BR	800.	——	3350.	5200.	6150.	10400.
1865	875.	——	3350.	5175.	6150.	10350.
1866	825.	6500.	3400.	4650.	5250.	10000.
1867 NR	800.	1900.	3400.	4500.	5250.	10000.
1868	800.	1800.	3300.	4500.	5250.	9950.
1869	975.	1800.	3300.	4550.	5350.	9900.
1870	825.	1800.	3200.	4450.	5300.	9850.
1871	825.	1950.	3200.	4450.	5275.	9750.
1872	825.	1800.	3200.	4450.	5275.	9750.
1873	750.	1800.	——	——	——	9800.
1873 NAR	——	——	3200.	4500.	5300.	——
1873 WAR ...	——	——	4300.	5600.	5800.	——
1874	750.	1800.	4300.	5600.	5800.	——
1875	775.	1800.	3150.	4450.	5250.	——
1876	775.	1800.	3150.	4400.	5200.	——
1877	5100.	3750.	3250.	4450.	5250.	——
1878	725.	2700.	3150.	4450.	5275.	——
1878 8TF	——	——	——	——	——	8250.
1878 7TF 2nd Rev.........	——	——	——	——	——	12750.
1879	725.	1825.	3400.	4650.	5350.	7550.
1880	625.	1700.	3400.	4650.	5325.	7300.
1881	660.	1700.	3450.	4650.	5350.	7300.
1882	660.	1700.	3250.	4650.	5375.	7300.
1883 Sh. 5c....	660.	1800.	3150.	4650.	5350.	7300.
1883 W.C.....	——	1650.	——	——	——	——
1883 N.C.....	——	2000.	——	——	——	——
1884	660.	1500.	3150.	4750.	5400.	7300.
1885	725.	1850.	3150.	4650.	5375.	7300.
1886	650.	1550.	3150.	4750.	5400.	7300.
1887	650.	1400.	3150.	4700.	5400.	7350.
1888	625.	1400.	3150.	4700.	5350.	7350.
1889	625.	1400.	3150.	4700.	5350.	7300.
1890	600.	1400.	3150.	4650.	5375.	7500.
1891	600.	1400.	3150.	4600.	5300.	7350.
1892	600.	1450.	2900.	3950.	5050.	7300.
1893	600.	1450.	2900.	4100.	5050.	7850.
1894	600.	1450.	2900.	4200.	5050.	7800.
1895	600.	1450.	2900.	4100.	5050.	32500.
1896	600.	1450.	2900.	4250.	5100.	7350.
1897	600.	1450.	2900.	4050.	5050.	7350.
1898	600.	1450.	2900.	3900.	5050.	7400.
1899	600.	1450.	2900.	3900.	5000.	7450.

Proof-65

	1¢	5¢	10¢	25¢	50¢	$1.00
1900	600.	1300.	2900.	3900.	5000.	7350.
1901	600.	1300.	2900.	3900.	5000.	8500.
1902	600.	1300.	2900.	3900.	5000.	7400.
1903	600.	1300.	2900.	3900.	5050.	7400.
1904	600.	1300.	2900.	3925.	5050.	7500.
1905	600.	1300.	2900.	3925.	5250.	— —
1906	600.	1300.	2900.	3950.	5050.	— —
1907	600.	1300.	2900.	3950.	5050.	— —
1908	600.	1300.	2900.	4100.	5100.	— —
1909 Ind.	600.	1325.	2900.	3925.	5050.	— —
1909 VDB	3500.	— —	— —	— —	— —	— —
1909 Pl.	1175.	— —	— —	— —	— —	— —
1910	1100.	1325.	2900.	4250.	5150.	— —
1911	1000.	1325.	2900.	4250.	5100.	— —
1912	925.	1325.	2900.	4150.	5075.	— —
1913 Var. 1	950.	3400.	2900.	4450.	5175.	— —
1914	1200.	2900.	3000.	4350.	5200.	— —
1915	1300.	3050.	3100.	4400.	5175.	— —
1916	1350.	3250.	— —	— —	— —	— —
1936	340.	2000.	1150.	1550.	3000.	— —
1937	140.	1900.	925.	440.	1650.	— —
1938	70.00	165.	850.	415.	1500.	— —
1939	56.00	145.	775.	290.	1275.	— —
1940	48.50	130.	600.	210.	1200.	— —
1941	41.50	95.00	590.	185.	1100.	— —
1942	41.50	95.00	590.	175.	1100.	— —
1942 T II	— —	475.	— —	— —	— —	— —

YEAR SETS

	Phila.	Denver	San Fr.	Price	Range
1940	335.	92.50	285.	640.	760.
1941	140.	240.	410.	645.	805.
1942	135.	295.	365.	640.	790.
1943	145.	285.	335.	610.	755.
1944	130.	230.	220.	495.	575.
1945	140.	210.	205.	430.	550.
1946	130.	125.	190.	370.	450.

MINT SETS

	Phila.	Denver	San Fr.	Price	Range
1947	365.	325.	50.00	685.	740.
1948	92.50	92.50	42.50	200.	225.
1949	135.	155.	360.	600.	650.
1950 No Sets Issued					
1951	52.50	180.	115.	315.	345.
1952	27.50	55.00	180.	235.	260.
1953	105.	35.00	75.00	180.	210.
1954	32.50	28.50	56.00	105.	120.
1955	50.00	13.50	5.35	62.50	68.50
1956	37.00	19.50	— —	51.50	56.50
1957	39.50	38.00	— —	70.00	77.50
1958	38.00	32.00	— —	65.00	70.00
1959	10.00	10.50	— —	18.00	20.50
1960	8.50	8.60	— —	15.50	17.10
1961	8.25	8.50	— —	15.00	16.75
1962	8.00	8.25	— —	14.00	16.25
1963	6.75	7.75	— —	14.00	15.75
1964	4.85	5.00	— —	9.15	9.75

	Price	Range		Price	Range
1965 SMS	3.85	4.25	1976-S 3 Pcs.		
1966 SMS	3.90	4.50	40%	10.00	11.00
1967 SMS	5.00	5.50	1976	4.65	5.65
1968 (PD&S)	2.60	3.05	1977	4.50	5.50
1969 (PD&S)	2.70	3.10	1978	4.50	5.40
1970 (PD&S)	17.00	18.75	1979	4.15	5.10
1971 (PD&S)	2.25	2.90	1980	5.30	6.00
1972 (PD&S)	2.20	2.90	1981	9.25	10.75
1973 (PD&S)	9.50	10.75	1984	3.50	4.50
1974 (PD&S)	4.60	5.50	1985	4.85	6.50
1975 (PD&S)	4.70	5.55	1986	6.75	8.00

BU ROLLS

	1¢	5¢	10¢	25¢	50¢
1934	155.	2800.	1900.	1850.	3900.
1934-D	1250.	4600.	2400.	— —	— —
1935	80.00	1500.	1250.	1175.	2900.
1935-D	200.	— —	3600.	— —	— —
1935-S	425.	2300.	1800.	— —	— —
1936	55.00	1000.	1200.	1150.	2800.
1936-D	85.00	1350.	2300.	— —	— —
1936-S	87.50	1400.	1700.	— —	— —
1937	34.00	915.	1150.	1250.	2900.
1937-D	67.50	925.	1800.	— —	— —
1937-S	45.00	1025.	1450.	— —	— —
1938	60.00	41.50	1275.	— —	— —
1938-D	65.00	140.	2450.	— —	— —
1938-D Buff	— —	950.	— —	— —	— —
1938-S	85.00	145.	2450.	— —	— —
1939	25.00	52.50	905.	690.	3800.
1939-D	77.50	1350.	915.	— —	3300.
1939-S	50.00	600.	1750.	— —	4350.
1940	23.50	21.25	790.	635.	3800.
1940-D	25.50	72.50	1150.	— —	— —
1940-S	39.00	74.00	940.	900.	2000.
1941	32.50	23.00	865.	265.	2300.
1941-D	105.	72.50	1400.	900.	4200.
1941-S	90.00	77.50	900.	675.	8400.
1942	17.50	22.75	890.	300.	2400.
1942-P Nickels	— —	430.	— —	— —	— —
1942-D	18.00	650.	1250.	475.	4750.
1942-S	200.	450.	1375.	2600.	5250.
1943	18.50	160.	855.	275.	2350.
1943-D	42.50	140.	1150.	625.	4750.
1943-S	65.00	170.	950.	1225.	5000.
1944	16.75	190.	825.	245.	2375.
1944-D	11.00	330.	1025.	440.	4200.
1944-S	8.75	290.	915.	490.	3950.
1945	16.50	195.	740.	240.	2375.
1945-D	12.25	185.	890.	350.	4000.
1945-S	12.75	140.	880.	310.	2950.
1946	7.75	12.00	67.50	225.	3250.
1946-D	8.50	16.50	140.	230.	2200.
1946-S	12.00	17.50	170.	250.	3600.
1947	10.50	10.50	130.	305.	3800.
1947-D	7.35	17.25	205.	300.	2800.
1947-S	8.75	15.00	210.	280.	— —
1948	10.50	11.25	325.	190.	425.
1948-D	11.25	19.00	245.	280.	290.
1948-S	18.00	15.00	320.	345.	— —
1949	19.50	14.00	710.	760.	1050.
1949-D	19.00	16.00	345.	325.	1025.
1949-S	47.50	46.00	1450.	— —	2350.
1950	13.75	35.00	170.	215.	800.
1950-D	8.50	230.	170.	220.	525.
1950-S	18.25	— —	780.	325.	— —
1951	16.50	13.75	110.	185.	325.
1951-D	9.85	23.00	100.	180.	700.
1951-S	23.25	40.00	450.	475.	665.
1952	18.50	20.00	92.50	160.	280.
1952-D	6.60	31.00	85.00	170.	265.
1952-S	20.50	17.75	225.	340.	685.
1953	5.75	5.50	72.50	160.	490.
1953-D	5.05	4.75	60.50	140.	235.
1953-S	11.25	11.00	65.00	190.	425.
1954	14.25	5.75	66.00	100.	195.
1954-D	3.85	7.00	54.00	80.00	170.
1954-S	3.90	9.00	59.50	140.	315.
1955	3.65	12.50	90.00	85.00	305.
1955-D	2.75	4.05	61.50	160.	— —
1955-S	12.50	— —	59.00	— —	— —
1956	3.00	3.00	49.50	72.50	230.
1956-D	2.30	3.15	48.50	72.50	— —

BU ROLLS

	1¢	5¢	10¢	25¢	50¢
1957	2.45	3.65	46.50	72.50	200.
1957-D	2.00	3.55	92.50	70.00	140.
1958	1.75	3.90	59.50	100.	200.
1958-D	1.70	2.95	48.50	80.00	165.
1959	1.00	3.05	40.50	72.50	160.
1959-D	1.00	2.60	50.50	72.50	175.
1960	.95	3.05	34.00	67.50	145.
1960-D	1.05	3.20	34.00	67.50	135.
1960 SD	81.50	—	—	—	—
1960-D SD	1.70	—	—	—	—
1961	1.05	3.25	33.00	72.50	140.
1961-D	.90	3.45	33.00	65.00	135.
1962	1.15	3.30	29.50	59.50	135.
1962-D	1.10	3.40	29.50	59.50	130.
1963	.90	2.70	28.50	58.50	120.
1963-D	.95	2.65	28.50	58.50	120.
1964	.80	3.45	28.00	58.50	65.00
1964-D	1.00	3.60	28.00	58.50	65.00

PROOF SETS

	Price	Range
1936 (3,837)	4850.	5400.
1937 (5,542)	3200.	3650.
1938 (8,045)	1600.	1850.
1939 (8,795)	1350.	1600.
1940 (11,246)	1100.	1400.
1941 (15,287)	935.	1175.
1942 ( ) (5 Pcs.)	925.	1100.
1942 (21,120) (6 Pcs.)	1300.	1575.
1950 (51,386)	510.	590.
1951 (57,500)	330.	425.
1952 (81,980)	205.	240.
1953 (128,800)	125.	155.
1954 (233,300)	70.00	78.00

PROOF SETS

	Price	Range
1955 (378,200) Flat	63.00	67.00
1956 (669,384)	32.00	38.00
1957 (1,247,952)	19.75	23.00
1958 (875,652)	25.00	28.50
1959 (1,149,291)	18.50	19.50
1960 (1,691,602)	18.25	19.25
1960 (Small Date Cent)	22.50	24.00
1961 (3,028,244)	17.00	18.25
1962 (3,218,019)	17.25	18.25
1963 (3,075,645)	17.50	18.50
1964 (3,950,762)	15.50	17.00
1968-S (3,041,509)	4.30	5.00
1969-S (2,934,631)	4.40	5.10
1970-S (2,632,810)	11.75	12.75
1971-S (3,220,733)	3.40	4.00
1972-S (3,260,996)	3.40	4.00
1973-S (2,760,339)	5.75	6.35
1974-S (2,612,568)	5.80	6.40
1975-S (2,845,450)	10.50	11.50
1976-S (4,123,056)	5.90	6.85
1976-S 3 piece (3,295,666)	15.50	16.50
1977-S (3,236,798)	4.75	5.50
1978-S (3,120,285)	6.00	6.75
1979-S (3,677,175) Var. I	8.00	8.75
1979-S Var. II	75.00	82.50
1980-S (3,547,030)	7.50	8.00
1981-S Var. I	7.25	8.40
1981-S Var. II	210.	240.
1982-S	4.75	5.40
1983-S	11.50	12.75
1984-S	16.50	18.00
1985-S	15.50	17.50
1986-S	11.45	12.75

Major U.S. Gold Type Coin Trend Values

GOLD DOLLARS

	F-12	VF-20	EF-40	AU-50	MS-60	MS-63	MS-65	PF-60	PF-65
Liberty Head Type 1 1849-1854	140.	145.	175.	185.	680.	1700.	3150.	—	—
Indian Head Type 2 1854-1856	175.	295.	500.	1600.	5000.	8500.	16500.	—	—
Indian Head Type 3 1856-1889	135.	145.	175.	185.	600.	1600.	2700.	1450.	9500.

QUARTER EAGLES

	F-12	VF-20	EF-40	AU-50	MS-60	MS-63	MS-65	PF-60	PF-65
Capped Bust Right - NS 1796	9100.	14500.	22000.	30000.	40000.	58500.	—	—	—
Capped Bust Right - 1796-1807	2750.	4000.	5150.	8750.	15750.	22500.	30000.	—	—
Capped Bust Left - Lg. 1808	8400.	13500.	20000.	28750.	44000.	60000.	135000.	—	—
Capped Bust Left - Sm. 1821-1834	2950.	3900.	5250.	7500.	13250.	17500.	24500.	—	—
Classic Head 1834-1839	225.	265.	380.	835.	2000.	4100.	11000.	—	—
Liberty Coronet 1840-1907	180.	190.	210.	255.	770.	1550.	4350.	1800.	16000.
Indian Head 1908-1929	180.	195.	205.	225.	340.	1100.	2600.	3000.	16250.

THREE DOLLARS

	F-12	VF-20	EF-40	AU-50	MS-60	MS-63	MS-65	PF-60	PF-65
Indian Head 1854-1889	430.	505.	635.	1050.	2700.	4600.	7750.	3500.	26500.

FOUR DOLLAR (Stella)

	F-12	VF-20	EF-40	AU-50	MS-60	MS-63	MS-65	PF-60	PF-65
Flowing Hair - 1879-1880	—	—	—	—	—	—	—	27500.	60000.

HALF EAGLES

	F-12	VF-20	EF-40	AU-50	MS-60	MS-63	MS-65	PF-60	PF-65
Capped Bust - Sm. Eag. 1795-1798	5150.	6900.	10250.	13500.	22500.	28500.	45000.	—	—
Capped Bust Right - HE 1795-1807	1125.	1650.	2750.	4300.	8400.	16750.	26500.	—	—
Capped Draped Bust 1807-1812	1100.	1600.	2350.	3950.	9000.	15250.	24000.	—	—
Capped Head 1813-1834	1400.	1950.	2900.	5100.	8900.	17500.	32500.	—	—
Classic Head 1834-1838	235.	285.	415.	960.	2300.	4750.	14000.	—	—
Liberty Coronet - NM 1839-1866	170.	200.	215.	385.	1475.	4000.	11750.	4900.	26000.
Liberty Coronet 1866-1908	155.	165.	180.	195.	315.	1200.	6000.	2500.	21000.
Indian Head 1908-1929	225.	235.	250.	275.	800.	2500.	4350.	3500.	20000.

EAGLES

	F-12	VF-20	EF-40	AU-50	MS-60	MS-63	MS-65	PF-60	PF-65
Capped Bust - Sm. Eag. 1795-1797	5750.	8200.	9850.	17000.	24000.	35000.	55000.	—	—
Capped Bust Right - HE 1797-1804	2100.	3000.	4500.	6800.	11750.	19500.	34500.	—	—
Liberty Coronet - NM 1838-1866	300.	340.	395.	520.	2150.	5750.	19500.	6650.	40500.
Liberty Coronet - 1866-1907	230.	255.	260.	295.	375.	1950.	7000.	3000.	29500.
Indian Head - NM 1907-1908	485.	525.	540.	580.	780.	2400.	4000.	—	—
Indian Head - 1908-1933	460.	475.	490.	520.	715.	2025.	3750.	5250.	31000.

DOUBLE EAGLES

	F-12	VF-20	EF-40	AU-50	MS-60	MS-63	MS-65	PF-60	PF-65
Liberty Coronet - NM 1849-1866	535.	560.	590.	735.	1275.	3050.	15500.	9500.	57500.
Liberty - (Twenty D.) 1866-1876	490.	515.	555.	595.	755.	2100.	9150.	7750.	51000.
Liberty - (Twenty Dollars) 1877-1907	470.	495.	515.	540.	615.	1250.	6550.	4750.	47500.
Saint-Gaudens - RN HR 1907	2750.	3000.	4250.	5700.	9000.	13000.	17500.	—	—
Saint-Gaudens - AN NM 1907-1908	525.	550.	575.	590.	650.	1025.	1750.	—	—
Saint-Gaudens - 1908-1933	525.	550.	575.	590.	640.	1050.	1775.	9000.	39000.

Major U.S. Type Coin (Copper and Silver) Trend Values

	G-4	VG-8	F-12	VF-20	EF-40	AU-50	MS-60	MS-63	MS-65	PF-60	PF-65
HALF CENTS											
Flowing Hair 1793	1250.	1650.	2700.	3650.	7250.	11500.	19000.	—	—	—	—
Liberty Cap 1794-1797	210.	270.	450.	850.	2050.	3000.	—	—	—	—	—
Draped Bust 1800-1808	23.25	30.50	42.50	85.00	260.	450.	700.	1200.	3850.	—	—
Classic Head 1809-1836	20.00	23.00	29.00	34.00	50.00	105.	215.	500.	2100.	—	—
Braided Hair 1840-1857	25.50	30.00	38.50	45.00	60.00	115.	195.	420.	1775.	—	4000.
CENTS - (Large)											
Chain 1793	1700.	2450.	3800.	6500.	11750.	25000.	—	—	—	—	—
Wreath 1793	800.	1075.	1650.	2750.	6250.	11000.	22000.	32000.	70000.	—	—
Liberty Cap 1793-1796	125.	225.	350.	600.	1650.	2650.	—	—	—	—	—
Draped Bust 1796-1807	23.00	32.50	82.50	270.	565.	900.	2000.	4300.	13500.	—	—
Classic Head 1808-1814	28.50	45.00	87.50	300.	640.	950.	2300.	5400.	14250.	—	—
Coronet Head 1816-1839	5.25	6.75	9.25	18.75	50.00	130.	240.	395.	2100.	—	—
Braided Hair 1840-1857	5.00	5.50	7.25	13.00	37.50	105.	205.	375.	1450.	2000.	6000.
CENTS - (Small)											
Flying Eagle 1857-1858	8.50	9.25	12.00	25.00	52.50	125.	180.	465.	2050.	1300.	4750.
Indian CN 1859	3.50	4.00	7.10	19.25	54.50	130.	180.	375.	1250.	625.	4700.
Indian CN 1860-1864	2.25	2.75	3.50	7.50	16.75	37.00	77.50	190.	575.	800.	800.
Indian AE 1864-1909	.70	.85	.95	1.40	5.50	11.00	25.00	60.00	365.	100.	600.
TWO CENTS											
1864-1873	3.50	4.00	5.50	12.00	27.50	54.50	125.	225.	785.	290.	1325.
THREE CENT NICKEL											
1865-1889	3.15	3.50	4.50	6.50	13.50	34.00	80.00	200.	1100.	205.	1175.
THREE CENT SILVER											
Var. I 1851-1853	8.00	9.30	13.00	21.00	45.00	95.00	185.	450.	2400.	—	—
Var. II 1854-1858	8.75	10.85	15.75	31.50	82.50	175.	340.	750.	3250.	800.	8000.
Var. III 1859-1873	9.25	11.50	15.50	26.50	50.00	115.	195.	400.	2000.	485.	2650.
NICKEL FIVE CENT											
Shield - Rays 1866-1867	10.50	13.00	18.00	29.00	68.00	155.	290.	485.	3150.	975.	6500.
Shield - No Rays 1867-1883	6.25	6.75	8.75	11.25	25.00	43.50	115.	275.	2200.	250.	1700.
Liberty Head - NC 1883	2.15	2.60	3.15	4.50	6.00	10.50	40.00	75.00	650.	245.	2000.
Liberty Head - WC 1883-1912	.40	.65	3.00	5.00	15.50	40.00	90.00	180.	1100.	205.	1300.
Buffalo Var. I 1913	2.95	3.15	3.50	6.00	9.85	17.00	30.00	66.50	425.	950.	3400.
Buffalo Var. II 1913-1938	.23	.35	.50	.80	1.50	5.50	11.50	21.00	70.00	525.	1900.
HALF DIMES											
Flowing Hair 1794-1795	540.	700.	900.	1525.	2250.	3300.	5900.	12500.	30000.	—	—
Draped Bust SE 1796-1797	640.	790.	1000.	1700.	2650.	4050.	6400.	14000.	36000.	—	—
Draped Bust HE 1800-1805	490.	610.	750.	1025.	2000.	2800.	5750.	13000.	30500.	—	—
Capped Bust 1829-1837	11.75	15.00	21.50	44.00	87.50	225.	360.	950.	4500.	—	—
Seated Liberty - NS 1837-1838	23.00	32.00	52.50	75.00	215.	330.	635.	900.	5750.	—	—
Std. Lib. - Stars 1838-1859.	4.25	5.10	7.15	15.25	28.00	80.00	235.	465.	3100.	700.	7300.
Seated Lib. - Arr. 1853-1855	4.15	5.00	7.00	15.50	40.50	82.00	265.	590.	3500.	—	—
Seated Lib. - Leg. 1860-1873	4.00	4.75	6.50	15.50	28.00	58.00	190.	415.	2250.	300.	3000.
DIMES											
Draped Bust SE 1796-1797	790.	950.	1275.	1775.	2650.	4000.	8400.	14500.	37000.	—	—
Draped Bust HE 1798-1807	425.	500.	675.	850.	1475.	2150.	4250.	8500.	23500.	—	—
Capped Bust lg. 1809-1828	11.50	15.25	22.50	85.00	275.	700.	1100.	2850.	8400.	—	—
Capped Bust sm. 1828-1837	9.00	11.00	17.50	48.00	150.	350.	700.	1500.	6200.	—	—
Liberty Std. - NS 1837-1838.	20.00	38.00	52.50	100.	230.	565.	875.	1450.	6500.	—	—
Lib. Seated - Stars 1838-1860	3.40	5.00	6.50	12.75	33.50	82.50	280.	650.	3300.	800.	4350.
Lib. Seated - Arr. 1853-1855	3.00	3.50	6.00	13.75	37.50	110.	325.	675.	4250.	—	—
Lib. Seated - Leg. 1860-1891.	3.00	3.50	5.25	8.55	18.50	46.50	195.	390.	2200.	325.	3150.
Lib. Seated - Arr. 1873-1874.	8.50	13.00	22.00	50.00	90.00	265.	555.	1100.	3900.	585.	4300.
Barber Type 1892-1916	1.20	1.40	3.05	5.50	16.35	40.00	130.	325.	2150.	325.	2900.
Mercury Type 1916-1945.	.65	.85	1.00	1.25	1.40	2.25	9.50	12.50	34.50	170.	590.
TWENTY CENT PIECE											
1875-1878	30.00	35.00	61.00	92.50	140.	315.	650.	1650.	5350.	950.	8300.
QUARTERS											
Draped Bust - SE 1796	2900.	3350.	4850.	8250.	12000.	15000.	22000.	24500.	50000.	—	—
Draped Bust - HE 1804-1807.	175.	200.	340.	820.	1375.	2500.	5550.	11500.	35000.	15500.	—
Lg. Bust Type 1815-28	36.00	45.00	70.00	215.	480.	1100.	1900.	4300.	13500.	—	—
Sm. Bust Type 1831-1838	23.75	29.00	42.50	87.50	180.	600.	900.	1900.	8500.	—	—
Liberty Seated - NM 1838-1865...	6.00	11.75	17.50	23.00	42.50	105.	405.	800.	5000.	425.	5050.
Liberty Seated - A&R 1853	6.85	13.00	19.00	36.00	110.	275.	740.	2350.	9500.	—	—
Liberty Seated - Arr. 1854-55	6.10	12.75	17.25	24.00	65.00	185.	575.	1250.	4850.	—	—
Liberty Seated - WM 1866-91	6.25	11.00	16.00	21.50	41.50	95.00	310.	725.	3900.	390.	4400.
Liberty Seated - Arr. 1873-74.	10.25	16.00	24.50	57.50	125.	320.	765.	1200.	4700.	700.	5600.
Barber Type 1892-1916	2.30	2.95	7.50	15.00	40.00	85.00	220.	600.	2950.	380.	3900.
Standing Liberty I 1916-1917	9.50	10.00	11.75	26.50	52.50	92.50	150.	440.	1175.	—	—
Stdg. Liberty II 1917-1930.	2.60	3.60	5.25	13.50	23.00	55.00	105.	300.	950.	—	—
HALF DOLLARS											
Flowing Hair 1794-1795	350.	450.	650.	1250.	2150.	3400.	10000.	20000.	57500.	—	—
Draped Bust SE 1796-1797	9750.	12500.	16250.	22000.	32500.	42500.	50000.	—	—	—	—
Draped Bust HE 1801-1807.	75.00	95.00	150.	310.	575.	1150.	4500.	9000.	27500.	—	—
Capped Bust Type 1807-1836	22.50	26.50	30.50	36.50	79.00	210.	750.	1450.	6500.	—	—
Capped Bust RE 1836-1839.	25.50	32.50	39.00	59.00	140.	330.	825.	1800.	8800.	—	—
Liberty Seated - NM 1839-66	11.00	19.00	26.00	34.00	57.50	115.	420.	1050.	5200.	500.	6050.
Liberty Seated - A&R 1853	14.00	23.50	40.50	82.50	200.	415.	1750.	4650.	15500.	—	—
Liberty Seated - Arr. 1854-55	11.50	22.00	30.50	39.50	90.00	235.	650.	1500.	6650.	—	—
Liberty Seated - WM 1866-91	11.00	21.25	27.50	34.50	59.00	120.	345.	1075.	5100.	450.	5200.
Liberty Seated - Arr. 1873-74	16.50	24.00	33.50	66.00	160.	375.	750.	1600.	6750.	850.	5800.
Barber Type 1892-1915	4.50	7.00	20.50	37.50	110.	230.	455.	1100.	4750.	490.	5000.
Walking Liberty 1916-1947	3.25	4.00	4.60	5.00	6.00	10.00	46.50	110.	190.	350.	1100.

DOLLARS

Flowing Hair 1794-1795	725.	800.	1250.	2150.	3700.	6500.	16500.	——	——	——
Draped Bust SE 1795-1798	640.	740.	1000.	1550.	2800.	5600.	12250.	22500.	56500.	——
Draped Bust HE 1798-1804.......	290.	425.	540.	700.	1375.	2950.	6800.	14500.	38500.	80000.
Seated Liberty - NM 1840-1866....	65.00	82.50	135.	150.	300.	390.	725.	1950.	9000.	1050. 10350.
Seated Liberty - WM 1866-1873 ...	70.00	100.	145.	165.	290.	400.	900.	2050.	9250.	1050. 9750.
Morgan Dollar 1878-1921........	9.70	9.80	9.85	10.00	10.50	12.00	24.00	56.50	185.	800. 7300.
Peace Dollar 1921-1935..........	9.55	9.60	9.65	10.50	11.50	12.50	25.00	57.50	315.	—— ——
U.S. Trade Dollar 1873-1885	41.50	55.00	63.50	78.00	150.	275.	585.	1500.	7100.	1000. 8800.

Canadian Trends

CANADA LARGE CENTS

VICTORIA

	VG-8	F-12	VF-20	EF-40	MS-60	BU MS-60
1858	25.00	30.00	40.00	50.00	150.	350.
1859	1.50	2.00	2.75	4.00	25.00	125.
1859 Re. N9...	25.00	32.00	42.00	60.00	125.	250.
1859/58 N9....	100.	150.	225.	325.	650.	1100.
1859/8 W9 ...	22.00	32.00	40.00	50.00	125.	275.
1876-H	1.50	2.50	3.50	6.00	30.00	125.
1881-H	2.50	3.50	5.50	9.00	45.00	150.
1882-H	1.35	2.25	3.00	5.00	25.00	90.00
1884	2.00	3.00	4.50	7.50	40.00	135.
1886	3.25	4.25	6.50	11.00	50.00	175.
1887	2.50	3.50	5.00	7.50	40.00	135.
1888	1.25	2.00	2.75	4.50	25.00	90.00
1890-H	4.50	8.00	11.00	18.00	90.00	250.
1891 LD	3.50	5.50	9.00	15.00	60.00	225.
1891 SD LL ...	35.00	50.00	65.00	90.00	325.	750.
1891 SD SL ...	30.00	40.00	50.00	70.00	200.	500.
1892	3.00	5.00	7.00	10.00	35.00	110.
1893	1.75	2.50	4.00	7.00	25.00	90.00
1894	4.50	7.50	10.00	16.00	90.00	200.
1895	3.00	5.00	7.00	8.00	60.00	160.
1896	1.40	2.00	3.00	4.50	25.00	90.00
1897	1.50	2.25	3.00	4.50	25.00	90.00
1898-H	3.50	5.00	7.00	9.00	65.00	175.
1899	1.50	2.25	3.00	5.00	25.00	90.00
1900	5.00	7.50	10.00	16.00	60.00	165.
1900-H	1.50	2.00	3.00	4.50	25.00	75.00
1901	1.25	1.75	2.25	4.00	20.00	65.00

EDWARD VII

	VG-8	F-12	VF-20	EF-40	MS-60	BU MS-60
1902	1.00	1.50	2.00	3.00	13.00	40.00
1903	1.25	1.75	2.50	4.00	18.00	50.00
1904	1.75	2.25	3.00	4.25	20.00	70.00

EDWARD VII

	VG-8	F-12	VF-20	EF-40	MS-60	BU MS-60
1905	3.00	4.50	6.00	8.00	30.00	115.
1906	1.25	1.50	2.50	4.25	18.00	50.00
1907	2.15	3.25	4.00	6.00	25.00	85.00
1907-H	7.50	10.00	15.00	25.00	75.00	200.
1908	2.50	3.50	4.50	6.50	22.00	60.00
1909	1.25	1.75	2.50	3.50	18.00	55.00
1910	1.10	1.50	2.25	3.25	16.00	50.00

GEORGE V

	VG-8	F-12	VF-20	EF-40	MS-60	BU MS-60
1911	1.25	1.60	2.25	4.25	18.00	55.00
1912	.90	1.25	1.75	3.25	15.00	50.00
1913	.90	1.25	1.75	3.25	14.00	40.00
1914	1.25	1.50	2.50	4.50	25.00	75.00
1915	.75	1.25	2.00	3.50	18.00	55.00
1916	.60	.90	1.25	2.50	13.00	40.00
1917	.50	.70	1.10	1.75	9.00	30.00
1918	.50	.70	1.10	1.75	9.00	30.00
1919	.50	.70	1.10	1.75	9.00	30.00
1920	.55	.75	1.15	1.85	11.00	35.00

SMALL CENTS

GEORGE V

	VG-8	F-12	VF-20	EF-40	MS-60	BU MS-60
1920	.20	.50	1.50	3.00	9.00	25.00
1921	.60	1.25	2.50	5.50	12.00	50.00
1922	8.00	10.00	15.00	20.00	100.	275.
1923	13.00	18.00	23.00	30.00	175.	500.
1924	4.00	5.00	7.00	10.00	80.00	225.
1925	12.00	15.00	20.00	30.00	135.	400.
1926	2.00	3.00	4.50	9.00	65.00	175.
1927	.70	1.10	2.25	4.50	25.00	100.
1928	.25	.35	1.25	2.25	10.00	35.00
1929	.25	.35	1.25	2.25	10.00	35.00
1930	1.75	2.25	3.25	6.50	30.00	100.
1931	1.00	1.25	2.25	3.50	23.00	75.00
1932	.20	.25	.60	2.25	10.00	35.00
1933	.20	.30	.60	2.25	10.00	35.00
1934	.25	.40	1.25	2.50	10.00	35.00
1935	.25	.40	1.25	2.50	10.00	35.00
1936	.25	.40	1.25	2.25	7.50	30.00

1936Dot (4 specimens known)
(Proof)................................ No Recent Sale

GEORGE VI

	VG-8	F-12	VF-20	EF-40	MS-60	BU MS-60
1937	.25	.40	.80	2.00	2.25	4.00
1938	.20	.25	.50	.80	3.00	7.00
1939	.20	.25	.50	.80	2.50	5.50
1940	.15	.20	.30	.60	1.50	3.50
1941	.15	.20	.35	.70	10.00	35.00
1942	.15	.20	.35	.70	8.50	30.00
1943	.15	.20	.35	.70	4.50	10.00
1944	.25	.35	.60	.70	10.00	30.00
1945	.15	.20	.30	.60	1.50	4.00

SMALL CENTS
GEORGE VI

	VG-8	F-12	VF-20	EF-40	MS-60	BU MS-60
1946.........	.15	.20	.30	.60	1.50	4.00
1947.........	.15	.20	.25	.60	2.25	5.00
1947 ML	.15	.20	.30	.60	1.50	3.50
1948.........	.15	.30	.55	.80	2.25	7.00
1949.........	.15	.20	.25	.40	1.50	2.75
1950.........	.15	.20	.25	.40	1.50	2.75
1951.........	.15	.20	.25	.40	.75	2.25
1952.........	.15	.20	.25	.40	.75	2.25

ELIZABETH II

	Mint.	VG-8	F-12	VF-20	EF-40	MS-60	BU MS-60
1953 no strap .	67.8	.15	.20	.30	.45	.75	2.00
1953 strap....	Incl.	1.00	1.50	2.00	3.50	15.00	30.00
1954 SS	22.1	.15	.20	.40	.75	2.00	5.00
1954 No SS ...	Incl.	Proof-Like Only			——	150.	225.
1955.........	56.4	——	.15	.20	.25	.60	1.50
1955 No SS ...	Incl.	35.00	50.00	85.00	150.	400.	750.

	Mint.	VF-20	EF-40	MS-60	BU MS-60
1956..........	78.6	.20	.30	.50	.90
1957..........	100.6	.20	.30	.50	.80
1958..........	59.3	.20	.30	.50	.80
1959..........	83.6	.15	.20	.25	.70
1960..........	75.7	.15	.20	.25	.70
1961..........	47.8	.15	.20	.25	.50
1962..........	227.2	.15	.20	.25	.35
1963..........	279.0	.15	.20	.25	.35
1964..........	484.6	.15	.20	.25	.35
1965 Sm Bds Type 1........	P 5	——	——	.75	1.50
1965 Sm Bds Type 2........	BI 5	——	——	.15	.30
1965 Lg Bds Type 3........	BI 5	——	——	.25	.50
1965 Lg Bds Type 4........	P 5	——	——	12.00	25.00
1966..........	183.6	——	——	.15	.20
1967..........	345.1	——	——	.15	.20
1968..........	344.7	——	——	.15	.20
1969..........	335.2	——	——	.15	.20
1970..........	311.1	——	——	.15	.20
1971..........	298.2	——	——	.10	.20
1972..........	451.3	——	——	.10	.20
1973..........	457.0	—·—	——	.10	.20
1974..........	692.0	——	——	.10	.20
1975..........	642.3	——	——	.10	.20
1976..........	701.1	——	——	.10	.20
1977..........	453.0	——	——	.10	.20
1978..........	911.1	——	——	.10	.20
1979..........	753.9	——	——	.10	.20
1980..........	911.8	——	——	.10	.15
1981..........	1,219.0	——	——	.10	.15
1982..........	911.0	——	——	.10	.15
1983..........	975.5	——	——	.10	.15
1984..........	838.2	——	——	.10	.15
1985..........	——	——	——	.10	.15
1986..........	——	——	——	.10	.15
1987..........	——	——	——	.40	.15

FIVE CENT SILVER
VICTORIA

	VG-8	F-12	VF-20	EF-40	MS-60	MS-63
1858 S.D......	8.00	13.00	18.00	30.00	225.	475.
1858 LD/SD ..	100.	135.	225.	300.	800.	1600.
1870 Flat Border	7.00	10.00	18.00	30.00	200.	400.

FIVE CENT SILVER
VICTORIA

	VG-8	F-12	VF-20	EF-40	MS-60	MS-63
1870 Raised Border	8.00	12.00	20.00	30.00	225.	425.
1871.........	7.00	10.00	18.00	30.00	175.	400.
1872-H.......	6.00	9.00	15.00	25.00	175.	425.
1874-H Plain 4	15.00	22.00	35.00	75.00	450.	1000.
1874-H Cross 4	9.00	13.00	18.00	30.00	375.	800.
1875-H SD	75.00	110.	160.	325.	1250.	2500.
1875-H LD....	100.	125.	200.	400.	1500.	3000.
1880-H	3.50	6.00	9.00	20.00	150.	375.
1881-H	4.50	7.00	12.00	22.00	175.	425.
1882-H	5.00	8.00	13.00	25.00	200.	450.
1883-H	10.00	18.00	25.00	45.00	400.	900.
1884-H	75.00	110.	160.	300.	1700.	3000.
1885.........	5.50	9.00	14.00	30.00	375.	900.
1886 L.D......	4.50	7.50	12.00	22.00	225.	500.
1886 S.D......	4.50	7.50	12.00	22.00	225.	500.
1887.........	12.00	18.00	27.00	50.00	350.	700.
1888.........	3.50	6.00	10.00	15.00	175.	300.
1889.........	15.00	25.00	35.00	75.	500.	800.
1890-H	4.50	7.00	12.00	20.00	200.	350.
1891.........	3.00	5.50	8.00	14.00	150.	300.
1892.........	4.00	7.00	13.00	20.00	225.	400.
1893.........	3.00	5.50	8.00	15.00	175.	325.
1894.........	10.00	17.00	25.00	50.00	325.	750.
1896.........	3.50	6.00	9.00	15.00	150.	300.
1897.........	3.50	5.25	9.00	15.00	150.	300.
1898.........	7.00	12.00	18.00	28.00	200.	500.
1899.........	2.25	4.00	5.50	11.00	125.	225.
1900 Oval O ..	2.25	4.00	5.50	11.00	150.	325.
1900 Round O.	15.00	25.00	35.00	60.00	425.	800.
1901.........	2.25	3.50	5.00	10.00	125.	225.

EDWARD VII

	VG-8	F-12	VF-20	EF-40	MS-60	MS-63
1902.........	2.00	3.00	4.00	7.50	45.00	80.00
1902 Lg. H....	2.50	3.50	5.50	10.00	50.00	90.00
1902 Sm. H ...	8.00	13.00	20.00	40.00	150.	300.
1903.........	4.50	6.50	12.00	20.00	275.	500.
1903-H	2.25	4.00	6.00	12.00	125.	225.
1904.........	2.25	4.00	6.00	11.00	125.	300.
1905.........	2.25	4.00	6.00	10.00	100.	250.
1906.........	2.00	2.75	4.00	7.00	100.	175.
1907.........	2.00	2.75	4.00	7.00	100.	175.
1908.........	4.50	7.50	14.00	24.00	125.	275.
1909.........	2.25	3.00	6.00	10.00	200.	375.
1910.........	1.50	2.00	3.50	7.00	75.00	135.

GEORGE V

	VG-8	F-12	VF-20	EF-40	MS-60	MS-63
1911.........	2.00	3.50	5.50	10.00	125.	250.
1912.........	1.35	2.25	4.00	6.00	75.00	125.
1913.........	1.35	2.25	4.00	6.00	45.00	75.00
1914.........	1.35	2.25	4.50	6.50	75.00	125.
1915.........	7.00	12.00	18.00	40.00	300.	550.
1916.........	3.75	5.50	8.00	15.00	125.	250.
1917.........	1.25	2.00	3.00	4.50	50.00	100.
1918.........	1.25	2.00	3.00	4.50	50.00	90.00
1919.........	1.25	2.00	3.00	4.50	50.00	90.00
1920.........	1.25	2.00	3.00	4.50	50.00	90.00
1921.........	1300.	2000.	3000.	4000.	14,000.	23,000.

FIVE CENT NICKELS
GEORGE V

	VG-8	F-12	VF-20	EF-40	MS-60	MS-63
1922.........	.35	.75	2.25	5.50	50.00	90.00
1923.........	.50	1.35	3.00	9.00	100.	225.
1924.........	.45	.75	3.00	7.00	75.00	150.
1925.........	25.00	35.00	55.00	150.	850.	1400.

FIVE CENT
GEORGE V

	VG-8	F-12	VF-20	EF-40	MS-60	MS-63
1926 N.6......	3.00	5.00	15.00	45.00	300.	550.
1926 Far 6....	75.00	110.	150.	325.	1500.	2500.
1927.........	.35	.75	3.00	6.00	60.00	125.
1928.........	.35	.75	3.00	5.50	50.00	90.00
1929.........	.35	.75	3.00	6.00	55.00	115.
1930.........	.35	.75	3.00	6.00	70.00	125.
1931.........	.35	.75	3.00	6.00	75.00	200.
1932.........	.35	.75	3.00	6.00	75.00	200.
1933.........	.50	1.25	3.50	9.00	100.	300.
1934.........	.35	.75	3.00	6.00	90.00	200.
1935.........	.35	.75	3.00	6.00	90.00	175.
1936.........	.35	.75	3.00	6.00	50.00	100.

GEORGE VI

	VG-8	F-12	VF-20	EF-40	MS-60	MS-63
1937 Dot	.35	.50	2.00	3.50	15.00	25.00
1938.........	.45	1.25	3.00	9.00	90.00	140.
1939.........	.30	.75	2.00	6.00	50.00	90.00
1940.........	.30	.50	1.35	3.50	22.00	45.00
1941.........	.30	.50	1.35	3.50	25.00	50.00
1942.........	.30	.50	1.35	3.50	20.00	40.00
1942 Tombac Beaver	.50	.75	1.25	2.00	3.00	7.00
1943 Tombac V	.25	.35	.50	.65	2.50	5.50
1944.........	.20	.35	.65	1.00	2.75	4.50
1945.........	.20	.35	.65	1.00	2.75	4.50
1946.........	.30	.40	.75	3.00	13.00	25.00
1947.........	.20	.30	.60	2.00	9.00	13.00
1947 M.L.	.20	.30	.60	2.00	8.00	13.00
1947 Dot.....	13.00	17.00	25.00	45.00	400.	700.
1948.........	.50	.75	1.25	3.50	21.00	35.00
1949.........	——	.20	.40	.75	4.50	9.00
1950.........	——	.20	.40	.75	4.50	9.00
1951 Com.....	——	.20	.40	.65	2.00	4.00
1951 Beaver	.20	.40	.75	1.25	3.25	7.00
1952.........	.20	.40	.60	1.25	3.25	5.00

ELIZABETH II

	Mint.	VF-20	EF-40	MS-60	MS-63
1953 No strap ...	16.6	.50	.90	3.50	5.50
1953 Strap.....	——	.65	1.25	4.50	8.00
1954 Steel	6.99	.75	1.50	5.50	10.00
1955 Nickel.....	5.35	.50	1.25	3.50	5.50
1956..........	9.39	.35	.60	2.00	3.50
1957..........	7.38	.35	.50	2.00	3.50
1958..........	7.60	.35	.50	2.00	3.50
1959..........	11.5	.30	.40	.80	1.50
1960..........	37.1	——	——	.50	.75
1961..........	47.8	——	——	.35	.45
1962..........	46.3	——	——	.35	.45
1962 Dbl. Dt.....	——	2.00	2.50	4.50	7.50
1962 Re-engr. Dt..........	——	——	——	——	4.00
1963 Round.....	43.9	——	——	.25	.35
1964..........	78.0	——	——	.25	.35
1964 Extra W.L.........	——	13.00	18.00	25.00	35.00
1965..........	84.8	——	——	.25	.35
1966..........	27.6	——	——	.25	.35
1967..........	36.8	——	——	.25	.35
1968..........	101.9	——	——	.25	.35
1969..........	27.0	——	——	.25	.35
1970..........	5.7	——	.30	.60	.75
1971..........	27.3	——	——	.20	.30
1972..........	62.4	——	——	.20	.30
1973..........	53.5	——	——	.20	.30
1974..........	94.7	——	——	.20	.30

FIVE CENT
ELIZABETH II

	Mint.	VF-20	EF-40	MS-60	MS-63
1975.........	138.8	——	——	.20	.30
1976.........	55.1	——	——	.20	.25
1977.........	89.1	——	——	.20	.25
1978.........	137.	——	——	.20	.25
1979.........	186.3	——	——	.20	.25
1980.........	134.9	——	——	.20	.25
1981.........	98.7	——	——	.20	.25
1982.........	64.9	——	——	.20	.25
1983.........	72.5	——	——	.20	.25
1984.........	84.0	——	——	.20	.25
1985.........	——	——	——	.20	.25
1986.........	——	——	——	.20	.25
1987.........	——	——	——	.20	.25

TEN CENTS
VICTORIA

	VG-8	F-12	VF-20	EF-40	MS-60	MS-63
1858.........	10.00	18.00	35.00	70.00	300.	550.
1870 Narrow "O".......	9.00	15.00	35.00	70.00	325.	550.
1870 Wide "O".......	10.00	20.00	40.00	80.00	350.	600.
1871.........	11.00	20.00	45.00	90.00	400.	700.
1871-H......	15.00	30.00	55.00	115.	550.	900.
1872-H......	55.00	100.	175.	300.	1100.	2000.
1874-H......	5.50	10.00	20.00	50.00	325.	500.
1875-H......	150.	250.	400.	800.	2500.	4500.
1880-H......	5.50	10.00	20.00	50.00	275.	500.
1881-H......	7.50	15.00	30.00	60.00	375.	600.
1882-H......	6.00	12.00	25.00	60.00	350.	600.
1883-H......	15.00	25.00	60.00	125.	900.	1500.
1884.........	115.	200.	400.	800.	3000.	5500.
1885.........	10.00	20.00	50.00	125.	900.	2000.
1886 Sm. 6....	9.00	16.00	35.00	70.00	450.	800.
1886 Lg. 6	10.00	20.00	45.00	125.	600.	900.
1887.........	15.00	30.00	75.00	175.	1250.	2500.
1888.........	4.50	8.00	20.00	45.00	300.	500.
1889.........	350.	600.	1200.	2000.	6000.	10,000.
1890-H......	10.00	18.00	35.00	80.00	425.	725.
1891 21 Leaves	10.00	18.00	40.00	90.00	500.	800.
1891 22 Leaves	9.00	18.00	35.00	80.00	450.	800.
1892.........	8.00	15.00	30.00	80.00	450.	750.
1893 Flat Top 3.....	12.00	22.00	50.00	100.	600.	1000.
1893 Round Top 3	350.	700.	1200.	2600.	6,500.	10,000.
1894.........	7.50	15.00	30.00	60.00	450.	850.
1896.........	4.50	9.00	18.00	45.00	325.	525.
1898.........	4.50	9.00	18.00	45.00	300.	600.
1899 Sm. D ...	4.00	7.50	15.00	40.00	250.	500.
1899 Lg. D....	7.50	15.00	30.00	70.00	400.	800.
1900.........	3.00	6.00	14.00	35.00	200.	400.
1901.........	3.00	6.00	14.00	35.00	200.	400.

EDWARD VII

	VG-8	F-12	VF-20	EF-40	MS-60	MS-63
1902.........	3.00	6.00	12.00	35.00	225.	500.
1902-H......	2.50	4.50	10.00	22.00	150.	250.
1903.........	6.00	12.00	30.00	85.00	650.	1500.
1903-H......	3.00	6.00	14.00	35.00	275.	500.
1904.........	4.50	9.00	22.00	60.00	350.	650.
1905.........	3.75	7.50	20.00	50.00	350.	700.
1906.........	2.25	4.50	11.00	30.00	250.	450.
1907.........	2.25	4.00	9.00	25.00	185.	400.
1908.........	4.50	9.00	23.00	55.00	325.	750.
1909 Large Leaves	3.00	7.50	15.00	40.00	350.	650.

TEN CENTS
EDWARD VII

	VG-8	F-12	VF-20	EF-40	MS-60	MS-63
1909 Broad Leaves	5.50	10.00	25.00	60.00	400.	700.
1910........	2.25	4.00	8.00	22.00	200.	350.

GEORGE V

	VG-8	F-12	VF-20	EF-40	MS-60	MS-63
1911........	7.00	14.00	22.00	65.00	225.	400.
1912........	2.25	3.25	8.00	18.00	200.	450.
1913 Small Leaves	1.50	3.00	7.00	15.00	200.	400.
1913 Broad Leaves	90.00	125.	275.	625.	3000.	4500.
1914........	1.50	3.00	6.00	13.00	200.	400.
1915........	5.00	10.00	30.00	110.	800.	1200.
1916........	1.50	2.25	4.00	10.00	150.	300.
1917........	1.50	2.25	4.00	7.50	100.	160.
1918........	1.50	2.25	4.00	7.50	100.	160.
1919........	1.50	2.25	4.00	7.50	100.	160.
1920........	1.50	2.25	4.00	7.50	100.	160.
1921........	2.15	3.00	5.50	12.50	110.	250.
1928........	1.50	2.50	5.50	10.00	90.00	200.
1929........	1.50	3.00	5.50	10.00	90.00	200.
1930........	2.25	3.00	5.75	12.00	110.	250.
1931........	1.50	3.25	5.50	10.00	100.	200.
1932........	2.25	4.00	7.50	15.00	150.	250.
1933........	3.00	5.00	10.00	25.00	200.	400.
1934........	4.50	7.00	13.00	50.00	525.	1200.
1935........	5.50	7.50	18.00	55.00	550.	1000.
1936........	1.50	2.25	4.00	8.00	65.00	110.
1936 with raised Dot (4 known) .... No Recent Sale						

GEORGE VI

	VG-8	F-12	VF-20	EF-40	MS-60	MS-63
1937........	2.25	3.00	4.00	8.00	20.00	30.00
1938........	1.50	3.00	4.00	10.00	80.00	150.
1939........	1.50	3.00	4.00	10.00	80.00	150.
1940........	.90	1.25	2.00	4.00	25.00	38.00
1941........	.90	1.50	4.00	8.00	60.00	125.
1942........	.90	1.50	2.50	6.00	45.00	70.00
1943........	.90	1.50	2.25	4.50	20.00	35.00
1944........	.90	1.50	2.50	5.00	40.00	70.00
1945........	.90	1.50	2.50	5.00	18.00	30.00
1946........	1.35	2.25	3.00	6.00	35.00	55.00
1947........	1.50	2.50	4.00	8.00	50.00	80.00
1947 Maple Leaf......	.80	1.50	2.25	3.75	18.00	30.00
1948........	3.75	5.00	10.00	20.00	110.	175.
1949........	.80	1.50	1.75	2.00	9.00	15.00
1950........	.80	1.50	1.75	2.00	8.00	11.00
1951........	.80	1.50	1.75	2.00	8.00	11.00
1952........	.80	1.50	1.75	2.00	8.00	11.00

ELIZABETH II

	Mint.	VF-20	EF-40	MS-60	MS-63
1953 No strap...	17.7	1.50	1.75	6.00	8.00
1953 Strap......	--	1.65	2.25	8.00	10.00
1954..........	4.49	1.65	3.00	10.00	15.00
1955..........	12.2	1.00	1.50	6.00	7.50
1956..........	16.7	1.00	1.50	5.00	6.00
1956 Dot	--	3.00	4.50	12.00	20.00
1957..........	16.1	.75	.85	2.25	3.00
1958..........	10.6	.75	.85	2.25	3.00
1959..........	19.6	--	.85	2.00	3.00
1960..........	45.4	--	--	1.50	2.00
1961..........	26.8	--	--	1.50	1.75
1962..........	41.8	--	--	1.50	1.75
1963..........	41.9	--	--	1.50	1.75
1964..........	49.5	--	--	1.50	1.75
1965..........	56.9	--	--	1.25	1.75
1966..........	34.3	--	--	1.25	1.75

TEN CENTS
ELIZABETH II

	Mint.	VF-20	EF-40	MS-60	MS-63
1967..........	68.7	--	--	1.25	1.50
1968 50% Silver .	55.8	--	--	.80	1.35
1968 Nickel.....	107.0	--	--	.35	.50
1969..........	7.04	--	--	.35	.50
1970 Nickel.....	5.2	--	--	.75	1.00
1971 Nickel.....	41.0	--	--	.25	.35
1972 Nickel.....	60.1	--	--	.25	.35
1973 Nickel.....	167.	--	--	.25	.35
1974..........	201.	--	--	.25	.35
1975..........	207.6	--	--	.25	.35
1976..........	95.0	--	--	.25	.35
1977..........	128.0	--	--	.25	.35
1978..........	170.3	--	--	--	.30
1979..........	236.9	--	--	--	.30
1980..........	169.7	--	--	--	.30
1981..........	123.4	--	--	--	.30
1982..........	93.4	--	--	--	.30
1983..........	111.0	--	--	--	.30
1984..........	119.0	--	--	--	.30
1985..........	--	--	--	--	.30
1986..........	--	--	--	--	.30
1987..........	--	--	--	--	.30

CANADA 20 CENTS
VICTORIA

	VG-8	F-12	VF-20	EF-40	MS-60	MS-63
1858.........	50.00	65.00	100.	175.	1000.	1800.

CANADA 25 CENTS
VICTORIA

	VG-8	F-12	VF-20	EF-40	MS-60	MS-63
1870.........	10.00	18.00	40.00	80.00	750.	1200.
1871.........	12.00	21.00	50.00	130.	900.	1800.
1871-H......	14.00	23.00	60.00	160.	900.	1400.
1872-H......	6.00	10.00	21.00	60.00	500.	900.
1874-H......	6.00	11.00	22.00	60.00	500.	1000.
1875-H......	175.	375.	850.00	1700.	5000.	10,000.
1880-H Narrow "O"....	30.00	60.00	140.	300.	1100.	2200.
1880-H Wide "O"....	85.00	150.	350.	650.	2700.	4000.
1881-H......	9.00	17.00	40.00	130.	750.	1300.
1882-H......	12.00	21.00	50.00	160.	900.	1500.
1883-H......	8.00	15.00	35.00	140.	900.	1500.
1885........	75.00	150.	275.	550.	3500.	5000.
1886........	10.00	20.00	50.00	175.	1000.	2000.
1887........	75.00	125.	275.	600.	3000.	5000.
1888........	10.00	18.00	45.00	125.	750.	1200.
1889........	80.00	160.	275.	750.	3000.	5500.
1890-H......	15.00	25.00	60.00	175.	1200.	2000.
1891........	45.00	75.00	175.	350.	1700.	2500.
1892........	9.00	15.00	35.00	125.	750.	1200.
1893........	65.00	125.	250.	500.	2000.	3000.
1894........	13.00	25.00	50.00	175.	1000.	1600.
1899........	5.00	9.00	22.00	65.00	550.	990.
1900........	4.00	8.00	20.00	60.00	500.	800.
1901........	4.00	8.00	21.00	60.00	550.	850.

EDWARD VII

	VG-8	F-12	VF-20	EF-40	MS-60	MS-63
1902........	4.50	9.00	25.00	75.00	600.	1000.
1902-H......	4.00	7.00	18.00	50.00	300.	500.
1903........	4.50	9.00	26.00	80.00	650.	1000.
1904........	10.00	23.00	75.00	200.	1100.	2000.
1905........	6.00	11.00	30.00	115.	900.	1700.
1906........	4.50	7.50	20.00	55.00	500.	800.
1907........	4.50	7.50	20.00	55.00	450.	750.
1908........	6.50	16.00	35.00	120.	700.	1000.
1909........	5.00	10.00	25.00	90.	700.	1100.
1910........	3.50	7.00	18.00	45.00	325.	550.

25 CENTS
GEORGE V

	VG-8	F-12	VF-20	EF-40	MS-60	MS-63
1911	10.00	22.00	45.00	110.	600.	1000.
1912	3.50	5.50	11.00	35.00	450.	800.
1913	3.50	5.50	11.00	35.00	400.	750.
1914	4.00	6.00	14.00	50.00	600.	1000.
1915	13.00	25.00	110.	300.	2500.	4000.
1916	3.50	6.00	12.00	30.00	300.	500.
1917	3.00	4.50	10.00	25.00	175.	350.
1918	3.00	4.50	10.00	25.00	175.	350.
1919	3.25	4.50	11.00	28.00	225.	400.
1920	3.25	4.50	10.00	25.00	225.	450.
1921	9.00	20.00	75.00	175.	1700.	2400.
1927	25.00	40.00	100.	250.	1500.	2300.
1928	3.25	4.50	10.00	30.00	225.	450.
1929	3.00	4.25	10.00	30.00	225.	450.
1930	4.00	6.00	12.00	30.00	325.	600.
1931	4.00	6.00	13.00	35.00	400.	700.
1932	4.50	7.00	15.00	40.00	350.	600.
1933	5.50	8.00	16.00	50.00	375.	650.
1934	6.00	9.00	23.00	65.00	550.	800.
1935	6.00	8.00	20.00	50.00	450.	700.
1936	3.25	4.50	10.00	25.00	200.	325.
1936 Dot	30.00	70.00	175.	400.	1500.	2500.

GEORGE VI

	VG-8	F-12	VF-20	EF-40	MS-60	MS-63
1937	3.50	4.00	5.00	8.00	25.00	37.50
1938	3.50	4.00	5.50	12.00	115.	175.
1939	3.50	3.50	5.00	11.00	115.	165.
1940	--	3.00	4.00	7.00	25.00	35.00
1941	--	3.00	4.00	7.00	30.00	45.00
1942	--	3.00	4.00	7.00	30.00	45.00
1943	--	3.00	4.00	7.00	30.00	45.00
1944	--	3.00	4.00	7.50	50.00	75.00
1945	--	3.00	4.00	6.00	23.00	35.00
1946	--	3.50	4.50	10.00	75.00	125.
1947	--	3.50	4.50	12.00	90.00	140.
1947 Dot	25.00	50.00	90.00	150.	500.	900.
1947 ML	--	3.00	4.00	5.00	23.00	35.00
1948	3.00	3.50	5.00	10.00	75.00	125.
1949	--	--	3.25	4.00	15.00	20.00
1950	--	--	3.25	4.00	12.00	20.00
1951	--	--	3.25	4.00	10.00	15.00
1952	--	--	3.25	4.00	10.00	15.00

ELIZABETH II

	Mint.	F-12	VF-20	EF-40	MS-60	MS-63
1953 Lg. Dt. no SS	10.4	3.00	3.50	4.50	7.00	10.00
1953 Sm. Dt. SS	--	3.00	3.50	5.00	10.00	12.00
1954	2.31	3.50	5.00	9.00	30.00	45.00
1955	9.5	--	3.00	3.50	6.00	8.00
1956	11.2	--	3.00	3.50	4.50	6.00
1957	12.7	--	--	3.00	4.00	5.50
1958	9.3	--	--	3.00	4.00	5.00
1959	13.5	--	--	--	4.00	5.00
1960	22.8	--	--	--	4.00	5.00
1961	18.1	--	--	--	4.00	5.00
1962	20.5	--	--	--	3.00	4.00
1963	21.1	--	--	--	3.00	4.00
1964	36.4	--	--	--	3.00	4.00
1965	44.7	--	--	--	3.00	4.00
1966	25.3	--	--	--	3.00	4.00
1967	48.8	--	--	--	3.00	3.50
1968 50% sil.	71.5	--	--	--	2.25	2.75
1968 Nickel	88.9	--	--	--	--	.80
1969 Nickel	133.0	--	--	--	--	.80
1970 Nickel	10.3	--	--	--	3.00	3.50
1971 Nickel	48.1	--	--	--	--	1.00
1972 Nickel	43.7	--	--	--	--	1.00

25 CENTS
ELIZABETH II

	Mint.	F-12	VF-20	EF-40	MS-60	MS-63
1973 RCMP Var. I Lg. Bust	--	--	60.00	75.00	100.	150.
1973 RCMP Var. II Sm. Bust	135.	--	--	--	--	.80
1974	192.	--	--	--	--	.80
1975	141.00	--	--	--	--	.80
1976	86.00	--	--	--	--	.80
1977	99.	--	--	--	--	.80
1978	176.	--	--	--	--	.75
1979	131.0	--	--	--	--	.70
1980	76.1	--	--	--	--	.70
1981	131.1	--	--	--	--	.70
1982	171.9	--	--	--	--	.70
1983	13.1	--	--	--	--	1.25
1984	119.2	--	--	--	--	.70
1985	154.4	--	--	--	--	.70
1986	--	--	--	--	--	.70
1987	--	--	--	--	--	.70

CANADA 50 CENTS
VICTORIA

	VG-8	F-12	VF-20	EF-40	MS-60	MS-63
1870 Without LCW under bust	500.	800.	1500.	2500.	12,000.	16,000.
1870 LCW	35.00	70.00	150.	275.	3500.	5500.
1871	45.00	110.	225.	450.	4000.	6500.
1871-H	70.00	140.	325.	700.	4500.	7500.
1872-H	35.00	70.00	135.	300.	4000.	6500.
1872-H Inverted A over V incl. above	80.00	150.	350.	700.	4500.	8000.
1881-H	35.00	75.00	150.	300.	3500.	6000.
1888	90.00	200.	400.	800.	4000.	7500.
1890-H	600.	1200.	2000.	4000.	18,000.	25,000.
1892	45.00	90.00	180.	400.	4000.	7000.
1894	200.	350.	800.	1600.	9000.	13,000.
1898	35.00	80.00	175.	350.	3500.	6000.
1899	75.00	150.	350.	900.	5500.	10,000.
1900	25.00	50.00	125.	275.	2500.	5000.
1901	30.00	55.00	140.	300.	3500.	6000.

EDWARD VII

	VG-8	F-12	VF-20	EF-40	MS-60	MS-63
1902	15.00	30.00	80.00	175.	1500.	2500.
1903-H	23.00	45.00	140.	250.	2300.	4000.
1904	90.00	175.	375.	750.	5500.	8000.
1905	100.	200.	450.	1000.	6500.	10,000.
1906	15.00	30.00	75.00	175.	1800.	2500.
1907	11.00	22.00	65.00	150.	1800.	2500.
1908	25.00	50.00	135.	300.	2100.	3300.
1909	15.00	35.00	80.00	250.	2000.	3500.
1910	11.00	22.00	65.00	200.	1500.	2500.

GEORGE V

	VG-8	F-12	VF-20	EF-40	MS-60	MS-63
1911	13.00	80.00	325.	750.	2000.	3200.
1912	7.00	20.00	75.00	200.	2000.	3000.
1913	7.00	20.00	70.00	200.	2000.	3000.
1914	25.00	75.00	225.	550.	3500.	6000.
1916	5.50	15.00	55.00	140.	1100.	1900.
1917	5.50	11.00	33.00	115.	750.	1400.
1918	5.00	11.00	28.00	100.	700.	1300.
1919	5.00	11.00	28.00	100.	700.	1300.
1920	5.00	11.00	30.00	135.	1000.	1700.
1921	8,000.	10,000.	12,000.	20,000.	35,000.	45,000.
1929	5.00	13.00	35.00	125.	900.	1700.
1931	9.00	23.00	70.00	200.	1700.	3000.
1932	40.00	100.	240.	500.	2300.	3800.
1934	15.00	35.00	100.	250.	1700.	3000.
1936	13.00	25.00	80.	225.	1300.	2000.

50 CENTS
GEORGE VI

	VG-8	F-12	VF-20	EF-40	MS-60	MS-63
1937	4.50	7.00	9.00	13.00	45.00	70.00
1938	5.00	10.00	25.00	35.00	250.	500.
1939	4.50	7.00	15.00	25.00	175.	350.
1940	3.50	4.50	5.50	7.00	35.00	55.00
1941	3.50	4.50	5.50	7.00	35.00	55.00
1942	3.50	4.50	5.50	7.00	35.00	55.00
1943	3.50	4.50	5.50	7.00	30.00	50.00
1944	3.50	4.50	6.00	8.00	35.00	55.00
1945	3.50	4.50	5.50	7.00	30.00	50.00
1946	4.00	5.50	7.50	12.00	80.00	135.
1946 Design in 6	20.00	25.00	45.00	110.	1200.	1800.
1947 St. 7	4.50	6.00	8.00	15.00	150.	250.
1947 Curved 7	4.50	6.00	8.00	15.00	150.	250.
1947 M.L. Str. 7	20.00	25.00	45.00	70.00	300.	450.
1947 M.L. Curved 7	1100.	1400.	1700.	2000.	3500.	5000.
1948	40.00	55.00	75.00	125.	250.	400.
1949	4.50	6.00	7.50	10.00	60.00	100.
1949 Hoof over 9	10.00	15.00	25.00	75.00	600.	800.
1950 No Design in 0	6.00	9.00	12.00	23.00	250.	450.
1950 Design in 0	3.00	3.50	4.00	4.50	13.00	23.00
1951	3.00	3.50	4.00	4.50	12.00	20.00
1952	3.00	3.50	4.00	4.50	12.00	20.00

ELIZABETH II

	Mint.	F-12	VF-20	EF-40	MS-60	MS-63
1953 Sm. Dt. No SS	1.63	3.00	4.00	4.50	9.00	15.00
1953 Lg. Dt. SS	——	4.00	5.00	6.50	30.00	45.00
1953 Lg. Dt. No S.S. (Mule)	——	8.00	15.00	23.00	135.	200.
1954	.506	5.00	6.00	10.00	30.00	40.00
1955	.753	4.50	6.00	8.00	23.00	35.00
1956	1.37	——	3.50	5.00	8.00	12.00
1957	2.17	——	3.00	3.50	5.50	8.00
1958	2.95	——	3.00	3.50	5.00	7.00
1959	3.09	——	3.00	3.50	4.50	6.50
1960	3.48	——	——	3.50	4.00	5.00
1961	3.58	——	——	3.50	4.00	5.00
1962	5.20	——	——	——	4.00	5.00
1963	8.34	——	——	——	4.00	5.00
1964	9.37	——	——	——	4.00	5.00
1965	12.6	——	——	——	4.00	5.00
1966	7.6	——	——	——	4.00	5.00
1967	4.2	——	——	3.50	4.00	5.00
1968 Nickel	3.4	——	——	——	.85	1.00
1969 Nickel	7.1	——	——	——	.85	1.00
1970 Nickel	2.4	——	——	——	.80	.90
1971 Nickel	2.16	——	——	——	.75	.85
1972	2.51	——	——	——	.75	.85
1973	2.54	——	——	——	.75	.85
1974	3.43	——	——	——	.75	.85
1975	3.4	——	——	——	.75	.85
1976	3.7	——	——	——	.75	.85
1977	.996	——	——	1.50	2.25	3.00
1978	3.3	——	——	——	——	1.00
1978 Rnd. Bds.	——	——	——	——	3.00	4.00
1979	3.4	——	——	——	——	.85
1980	1.5	——	——	——	——	.75
1981	2.1	——	——	——	——	.75
1982	2.23	——	——	——	——	.75
1983	1.17	——	——	——	——	.75
1984	1.50	——	——	——	——	.75

CANADA 50 CENTS
ELIZABETH II

	Mint.	F-12	VF-20	EF-40	MS-60	MS-63
1985	2.18	——	——	——	——	.75
1986	——	——	——	——	——	.75
1987	——	——	——	——	——	.75

SILVER DOLLARS
GEORGE V

	VF-20	EF-40	AU-50	MS-60	MS-63
1935 Jubilee	12.00	15.00	25.00	55.00	100.
1936	12.00	15.00	25.00	65.00	120.

GEORGE VI

	VF-20	EF-40	AU-50	MS-60	MS-63
1937	14.00	18.00	25.00	55.00.	110.
1938	30.00	40.00	65.00	160.	250.
1939 Royal Visit	8.00	10.00	12.00	20.00	35.00
1945	100.	125.	175.	350.	500.
1946	28.00	40.00	60.00	140.	225.
1947 Blunt 7	60.00	75.00	100.	175.	325.
1947 Ptd 7	125.	160.	250.	550.	800.
1947 Maple Leaf	175.	200.	300.	450.	700.
1948	550.	650.	800.	1100.	1400.
1949 Ship	13.00	15.00	20.00	35.00	50.00
1950	11.00	14.00	17.50	25.00	38.00
1950 Arnprior	20.00	25.00	40.00	75.00	100.
1951	10.00	12.00	14.00	20.00	30.00
1951 Arnprior	30.00	45.00	70.00	135.	200.
1952 Water Lines	10.00	12.00	15.00	20.00	30.00
1952 No Water Lines	11.00	14.00	18.00	25.00	45.00

ELIZABETH II

	VF-20	EF-40	AU-50	MS-60	MS-63
1953 Wire Edge No SS	8.00	9.00	11.00	16.00	25.00
1953 Flat Border SS	8.00	9.00	11.00	16.00	25.00
1954	11.00	13.00	16.00	22.00	35.00
1955	11.00	13.00	16.00	22.00	30.00
1955 Arnprior	100.	125.	150.	185.	225.
1956	13.00	15.00	20.00	35.00	45.00
1957	8.00	9.00	10.00	15.00	23.00
1957-1 Water Line	12.00	15.00	20.00	25.00	33.00
1958 Totem Pole	8.00	9.00	10.00	12.00	15.00
1959	7.00	8.00	9.00	10.00	12.00
1960	7.50	8.00	9.00	10.00	11.00
1961	7.50	8.00	9.00	10.00	11.00
1962	7.50	8.00	9.00	10.00	11.00
1963	7.50	8.00	9.00	10.00	11.00
1964 Confed. Mtgs.	——	——	8.00	9.00	11.00
1965 Sm. Bds. P. 5 Var. 1	——	——	8.00	9.00	11.00
1965 Sm. Bds. Bl. 5 Var. 2	——	——	8.00	9.00	11.00
1965 Lg. Bds. Bl. 5 Var. 3	——	——	9.00	10.00	11.00
1965 Lg. Bds. P. 5 Var. 4	8.00	9.00	10.00	14.00	16.00
1965 Med. Bds. P. 5 Var. 5	10.00	12.00	15.00	20.00	35.00

SILVER DOLLARS
ELIZABETH II

	VF-20	EF-40	AU-50	MS-60	MS-63
1966 Lg. Bds..........	——	8.00	9.00	10.00	11.00
1966 Sm. Bd...........	——	——	——	1200.	1400.
1967 Cent.......	8.00	9.00	10.00	11.00	12.00

NICKEL DOLLARS

	VF-20	EF-40	AU-50	MS-60	MS-63
1968........	5.5	——	——	——	1.25	1.50
1969........	4.8	——	——	——	1.25	1.50
1970 Man. ...	4.1	——	——	——	1.60	1.75
1971 B.C.	4.2	——	——	——	1.60	1.75
1972........	2.6	——	——	——	1.75	2.00
1973 P.E.I.	3.1	——	——	——	1.60	1.75
1974 Winn. ...	2.7	——	——	——	2.50	3.00
1975........	3.2	——	——	——	1.75	2.00
1976........	2.4	——	——	——	2.25	3.00
1977 Type I (Attd. Jewel - short lines)				5.00	7.00
1977 Type II (Det. Jewel - long lines)........				1.75	2.25
1977 Type III (Det. Jewel - short lines)				3.00	4.00
1978........	2.9	——	——	——	1.60	1.75
1979........	2.5	——	——	——	1.60	1.75
1980........	2.9	——	——	——	1.60	1.75
1981........	2.3	——	——	——	1.60	1.75
1982........	——	——	——	——	1.60	1.75
1982 Const....	13.3	——	——	——	1.60	1.75
1983........	2.26	——	——	——	1.45	1.70
1984........	——	——	——	——	1.40	1.60
1984 Cartier ..	——	——	——	——	1.40	1.60
1985........	——	——	——	——	1.40	1.60
1986........	——	——	——	——	1.40	1.60

OLYMPIC COINS - 1976

$5 1 .925 (.723 Troy ounces - Fine Silver) - 38mm
$10 1 .925 (1.44 Troy ounces - Fine Silver) - 45mm
Series I (Geographic Themes) issued 1973
$5 - Map of Canada or Kingston
$10 - Map of the World or Montreal
Series II (Olympic Motifs) issued 1974
$5 - Athlete or Wreath
$10 - Zeus or Temple
Series III (Early Cdn. Sports) issued 1974
$5 - Rowing or Canoeing
$10 - Bicycling or Lacrosse
Series IV (Track and Field Sports) issued 1975
$5 - Ladies Javelin or Marathon
$10 - Men's Hurdles or Ladies Shot Put
Series V (Water Sports) issued 1975
$5 - Diver or Swimmer
$10 - Sailing or Paddling
Series VI (Team and Contact Sports) issued 1976
$5 - Boxing or Fencing
$10 - Soccer or Hockey
Series VII (Souvenir Issues) issued 1976
$5 - Olympic Flame or Village
$10 - Olympic Stadium or Veledrome

	Price
$5 Loose (Series I only) BU........................	7.00
$10 Loose (Series I only) BU......................	14.00
$10 Map (Mule) 1974 instead of 1973 Encapsulated.................................	375.
$5 Encapsulated, series one to five, each	7.50
Encapsulated series six or seven, each...........	8.00
$10 Encapsulated, series one to five, each..........	15.00
$10 Encapsulated series six or seven, each..........	17.00
Custom or prestige set of four coins, series one to five ..	35.00
Custom or prestige set of four coins, series six or seven.	40.00
Proof set of four coins, series one to five...........	45.00
Proof set of four coins, series six or seven	50.00
Complete set series I to VII BU 300.; Proof...........	350.

FIVE DOLLARS GOLD
GEORGE V

	VF-20	EF-40	MS-60	MS-63
1912..........	175.	225.	375.	700.
1913..........	175.	225.	400.	750.
1914..........	500.	600.	875.	1600.

TEN DOLLARS GOLD
GEORGE V

	VF-20	EF-40	MS-60	MS-63
1912..........	450.	525.	800.	1600.
1913..........	475.	550.	850.	1700.
1914..........	550.	650.	1100.	2000.

CANADIAN SOVEREIGNS

Similar to Great Britain Sovereigns except for the "C" mint mark on the mound under the horse's hoof.

EDWARD VII

	F-12	VF-20	EF-40	MS-60	MS-63
1908-C	1300.	1700.	2500.	3000.	3500.
1909-C	250.	300.	400.	700.	1300.
1910-C	200.	225.	300.	700.	1200.

GEORGE V

	F-12	VF-20	EF-40	MS-60	MS-63
1911-C	110.	125.	135.	150.	250.
1913-C	500.	600.	750.	1200.	1800.
1914-C	250.	300.	400.	750.	1200.
1916-C	13,000.	16,000.	22,000.	25,000.	30,000.
1917-C	110.	125.	135.	200.	275.
1918-C	110.	125.	135.	200.	275.
1919-C	110.	125.	135.	200.	275.

COMMEMORATIVE GOLD COINS (PROOF)

	Mintage	Price Range
1967 Centennial $20 Proof (.900)	.280	260-270.
1976 Olympic $100 Unc. (.583)........	.572	125-135.
1976 Olympic $100 Proof (.917).......	.336	250-260.
1977 Jubilee $100 Proof (.917)	.181	270-280.
1978 Unity $100 Proof (.917)	.200	250-260.
1979 I.Y.C. $100 Proof (.917)	.250	250-260.
1980 Arctic $100 Proof (.917)	.132	260-275.
1981 "O Canada" $100 Proof (.917)	.250	260-275.
1979-86 Maple Leaf $50 (1 oz. 24K) at $460 U.S. Bullion		485-495.
1982 Canadian Constitution $100 Proof (.917)............................		250-260.
1983 Newfoundland $100 Proof (.917) ..		260-275.
1984 Cartier $100 Proof (.917)		280-290.
1985 National Parks Cent to $100 Proof (.917)............................		340-350
1986 Maple Leaf (½ oz. 24K)		250-260
1986 Peace $100 Proof...............	.917	250-260

PROOF-LIKE MINT SETS
CARD (1954-1960)
OR PLIOFILM HOLDER (1961-1968)

NOTE: First full year of issue 1954. Small quantity issued in card holder in 1953 and in cello envelopes in 1951 & 1952. Proof-Like silver dollars issued in individual cellophane envelopes from 1954 to 1961 and part of 1962 and then until 1964 in Pliofilm holders. Majority of sets received from the Mint in 1953 and earlier years are not Proof-like.

ELIZABETH II

		SETS		DOLLARS	
	Mint.	Pr.	Range	Pr.	Range
1954 with SS Cent......	.007	275.	300.	160.	180.
1954 with Strapless Cent........	——	450.	475.	——	——

SILVER DOLLARS

ELIZABETH II

	VF-20	EF-40	AU-50	MS-60	MS-63
1955.........	.006	200.	225.	140.	150.
Arnprior.....	——	325.	350.	280.	300.
1956.........	.009	110.	125.	85.00	95.00
1957.........	.018	50.00	60.00	30.00	35.00
1958.........	.018	50.00	55.00	30.00	35.00
1959.........	.031	25.00	30.00	15.00	18.00
1960.........	.064	19.00	21.00	13.00	15.00
1961.........	.098	17.00	19.00	11.00	12.00
1962.........	.200	15.00	16.00	10.00	11.00
1963.........	.675	13.00	14.00	9.00	10.00
1964.........	1.65	13.00	14.00	9.00	10.00
1965 (Pointed 5 Dollar)......	2.90	13.00	14.00	9.00	10.00
1965 (Blunt 5 Dollars).....	——	13.00	14.00	9.00	10.00
1966.........	.672	14.00	15.00	10.00	11.00
1967.........	.963	17.00	18.00	13.00	15.00
1968.........	.521-Sp.	2.25	2.35	1.75	2.00
1968 (no island).	——	8.00	9.00	4.50	5.50
1969.........	.326-Sp.	2.75	3.00	1.50	1.75
1970.........	.349	5.25	5.75	——	——
1971.........	.253	3.50	4.00	——	——
1972.........	.224	3.25	3.50	——	——
1973.........	.243	3.50	3.75	——	——
1973 with muled 25¢ (est. 400 sets)........	——	150.	175.	——	——
1974.........	——	3.50	4.00	——	——
1975.........	——	3.50	4.00	——	——
1976.........	——	5.25	5.75	——	——
1977.........	——	5.00	5.50	——	——
1977 S.W.L.....	——	8.00	10.00	——	——
1978.........	——	3.25	3.50	——	——
1978 Rd. beads..	——	8.00	10.00	——	——
1979.........	——	6.50	7.00	——	——
1980.........	——	11.00	12.00	——	——
1981.........	——	7.50	8.00	——	——
1982.........	——	6.50	7.00	——	——
1983.........	——	10.00	11.00	——	——
1984.........	——	6.50	7.50	——	——
1985.........	——	6.50	7.50	——	——
1986.........	——	6.00	7.00	——	——
1987.........	——	6.00	6.50	——	——

CASED PROOF-LIKE NICKEL DOLLARS

	Mint.	Pr.	Range
1970 Manitoba.................	.297	2.25	2.50
1971 B.C.....................	.182	2.25	2.50
1972........................	.143	2.25	2.50
1973 P.E.I...................	.175	2.25	2.50
1974 Winnipeg...............	.106	2.75	3.00
1975........................	.88	2.25	2.75
1976........................	.74	2.75	3.00

CASED PROOF (.500) SILVER DOLLARS

	Mint.	Pr.	Range
1971 B.C. Cent..............	.556	11.00	12.00
1972 Voyageur..............	.350	15.00	16.00
1973 R.C.M.P. Cent.........	.905	8.00	9.00
1974 Winnipeg Cent.........	.628	8.00	9.00
1975 Calgary Cent..........	.833	8.00	9.00
1976 Library...............	.484	12.00	14.00
1977 Jubilee...............	.745	9.00	10.00
1978 Comm. Games..........	.709	9.00	10.00
1979 Griffon...............	.826	14.00	15.00
1980 Polar Bear............	.539	23.00	25.00
1981 Trans-Canada R.R.......	——	47.00	50.00

CASED (.500) SILVER DOLLARS

		Pr.	Range
1982 Regina, Sask., Cent.............	——	20.00	21.00
1983 University Games..............	——	21.00	24.00
1984 Toronto 150th. Anniv...........	——	19.00	20.00
1985 Moose......................	——	18.00	20.00
1986 Vancouver Cent................	——	15.00	16.00
1987 16th Century Ship..............	——	15.00	16.00

SPECIMEN AND PROOF SETS

	Pr.	Range
1858 Victoria 1¢ to 20¢ (Sm. Date 5¢) (no case)..............	7000.	10,000.
1858 Victoria 1¢ to 20¢ (Lg. Date 5¢) (no case)................	8000.	11,000.
1858 Double set 1¢ to 20¢ in case.........	15,000.	20,000.
1870 Victoria 1¢ to 50¢ (no case).........	15,000.	20,000.
*1870 Victoria 1¢ to 50¢ in case double set ..	30,000	40,000
*1902H 5¢, 10¢, 25¢ in case................	8000.	10,000.
*1908 Edw. VII 1¢ to 50¢ in case.........	1500.	2000.
*1911 Geo. V 1¢ to 50¢ in case..........	7000.	8000.
*1911 - 1¢ to 50¢ Plus 1911C Sovereign and 1912 $5 & $10 (5-10 sets known) in case..........	25,000.	35,000.
1912 $5 and $10 gold pieces no case	12,500.	15,000.
1921 Geo. V 1¢ to 50¢ (no case)..........	90,000.	100,000.
1929 Geo. V 1¢ to 50¢ (no case)...........	10,000.	15,000.
1930 Geo. V 1¢ to 5-¢ (no case)..........	5000.	5500.
1934 Geo. V 1¢ to 50¢ (no case).........	8000.	10,000.
1936 Geo. V 1¢ to 50¢ (no case).........	7000.	9000.
*1937 Geo. VI 1¢ to $1 Brilliant in leather case	1200.	1500.
* 1937 sim. but in card case..............	1000.	1300.
1937 Semi-Matte, Card Case...........	700.	800.
*1937 1¢-25¢ mirror fields in leather case ...	700.	800.
*1938 in case.....................	9000.	12,000.
*1944 Geo VI 1¢ to 50¢ (no case)	9000.	12,000.
*1945 in leather case	4000.	5000.
*1946 in leather case	4000.	5000.
*1947 in leather case	7,000.	10,000.
*1947 ML (7 curved right 50¢) in leather case	7000.	8000.
*1948 in leather case	6000.	8000.
*1949 in leather case	2500.	3500.
*1950 in leather case	2500.	3500.
*1951 1¢ to $1 both 5¢ pieces no case	2500.	3500.
*1952 NWL in leather case	2500.	3500.
*1952 WL in leather case..............	2500.	3500.
*1953 No SS in leather case	1250.	1500.
*1953 SS in leather case	1250.	1500.
1964 in leather case	400.	550.
*1965 in leather case	400.	550.
*1967 Red case 1¢ to $1 & medal..........	20.00	30.00
*1967 1¢ to $1 black case gold coin removed....................	20.00	25.00
*1967 1¢ to $1 black case with $20 gold Proof	280.	290.

V.I.P. PRESENTATION SETS

Specially struck proof sets (1¢ to $1) for presentation to visiting dignitaries (very important people) to the Royal Canadian Mint, Ottawa and Canada. Black and other color leather cases used.

	Pr.	Range
1969 (2 known)......................	1700.	2000.
1970 (100 issued)	500.	600.
1971 (69 issued)	400.	500.
1972 (25 issued)	475.	500.
1973 (26 issued)	475.	500.
1974 (72 issued)	400.	500.
1975 (94 issued)	400.	500.
1976..............................	400.	500.
1977, 78, 79, 80 (no information - possibly issued)		

DOUBLE DOLLAR SPECIMEN SETS

Deluxe presentation sets (two $1 coins plus 50¢ to 1¢) in leather cases.

	Mint.	Pr.	Range
1971	.067	13.00	14.00
1972	.036	55.00	60.00
1973	.119	14.00	15.00
1974	.085	14.00	15.00
1975	.097	14.00	15.00
1976	.008	17.00	19.00
1977	.143	15.00	16.00
1978	——	15.00	16.00
1979	——	19.00	21.00
1980	——	30.00	32.00
1981	——	50.00	55.00
1982	——	25.00	28.00
1983	——	28.00	30.00
1984	——	35.00	40.00
1985	——	35.00	40.00
1986	——	34.00	38.00
1987	——	34.00	36.00

DOUBLE CENT 'PROOF-LIKE" SETS

Cased sets of 7 coins ($1 to 1¢ plus extra 1¢) 1971-1976
Specimen Condition 1977-1984

	Mint.	Pr.	Range
1971	.033	5.50	6.00
1972	.038	5.50	6.00
1973	.049	5.50	6.00
1974	.044	5.50	6.00
1975	.037	5.50	6.00
1976	.028	7.50	8.00
1977	.044	10.00	10.50
1978	——	5.50	6.00
1979	——	8.00	9.00
1980	——	11.00	12.00
1981	——	11.00	12.00
1982	——	11.00	12.00
1983	——	11.00	12.00
1984	——	11.00	12.00
1985	——	10.00	11.00

SPECIMEN COINS

Double struck coins, issued with unusually sharp detail, and either a Matte or a Brilliant, Mirror-Like surface. To distinguish specimen from Proof-Like coins, look for extreme sharpness of detail and smooth surface, particularly at the Queen's shoulder on recent issues, also square edge and rim and full reeding on issues dated 1858 to 1952.

LARGE CENTS

1858	850.
1859 (Narrow 9)	800.
1876H	750.
1882H	750.
1908	200.
1911	500.

SMALL CENTS

1921 or 1922, each.	500.
1923	900.
1924	300.
1925	850.
1926	450.
1927, 30, 31, 34 or 36, each	300.
1928, 29, 32, 33 or 38, each	250.
1937 Matte	75.
1937 Brilliant	125.
1944, 45, 46, 47 or 47ML, 48	100.
1949, 50, 51, 52 or 53 NSS each.	100.
1953 SS	175.
1964, 65, 70, 71, 72, 73, 74, 75, 76, 77, 78, 79 each	10.00

5 CENT SILVER

1858 Sm. Date	1100.
1858 Lg. Date	2500.
1870 Raised Border	1600.
1872H	3500.
1875H Lg. Date.	7500.
1880H	2500.
1881H	3000.
1890H	900.
1908	250.
1911	800.
1921	25,000.

5 CENTS NICKEL

1922, 34 or 38, 42 Tom., 43 Tom., each	300
1923	1000
1924	1400.
1927, 28, 29, 30 each	400.
1925	4000.
1926 Near 6	1500.
1931	2500.
1932, 1933, 1935	1000.
1936	500.
1937 Matte	90.
1937 Brilliant	125.
1944, 45, 47, 47ML, 49, each	150.
1946, 50 each	235.
1948	550.
1951 Commem., 51, 52, 53 NSS ea.	150.
1951 High relief	1500.
1953 SS	225.
1963, 64, 65, 70, 71, 72, 73, 74, 75, 76, 77, 78, 79 each	40.00

10 CENTS

1858	1000.
1858 Plain edge	1500.
1870 Narrow 'O'.	2500.
1871, 1872H, each	3000.
1880H, 82H, each	2000.
1908	550.
1911, 38, 46, each	1000.
1921	5000.
1928	1500.
1931	1600.
1934, 39, 44, 45, each	800.
1936, 47, 47ML, each	400.
1937 Matte	175.
1937 Brilliant	250.
1949, 53 SS, each.	225.
1941, 48, each	1200.
1950, 51, 52, 53 NSS, each.	150.
1964, 65, 70, 71, 72, 73, 74, 75, 76, 77, 78, 79 each	60.00

20 CENTS

1858	2300.

25 CENTS

1870	4000.
1871	3500.
1872H	3500.
1880H Wide 'O', 1902H, each.	6000.
1881H, 82H, each	3500.
1883H	4000.
1888	3700.
1900	2800.
1908	800.
1911, 41, 44, 45, 48, each.	1400.
1919	1200.
1921	9000.
1929	1500.
1934, 36, each	2400.
1937 Matte	225.

25 CENTS

1937 Brilliant	300.
1938, 47, each	1000.
1939, 47ML	550.
1946, 1948	600.
1949, 1973 Lg. Bust, each	225.
1950, 51, 52, 53LD, 53SD, each	225.
1962, 63, 64, 65, 70, 71, 72, 73, 74, 75, 76, 77, 78, 79 each	60.

50 CENTS

1870 LCW	6000.
1871H	16,000.
1872H	10,000.
1881H	5500.
1890	40,000.
1908	1000.
1911	4000.
1921	75,000.
1931	5000.
1932	9000.
1934	4000.
1936, 38, each	4000.
1937 Matte	225.
1937 Brilliant	400.
1944, 45, 46, 47 St.7, 47 Curved 7, 47 St.7 ML, each	1000.
1947 Curved 7 ML	6000.
1948	1500.
1949	250.
1950 Des. in 'O', 51, 52	400.
1953 SS, 53 NSS, each	250.
1963, 64, 65, 70, 71, 72, 73, 74, 75, 76, 77, 78 each	100.

SILVER DOLLARS

1911 (2 known)	—
1935, 36, each	4000.
1937 Matte	400.
1937 Brilliant	900.
1938	6000.
1939	1500.
1945, 46, 47 Bl.7, each	1800.
1947 Ptd. 7 or 1947 ML, each	3000.
1948	3500.
1949, 50, 51, 52, 53, each	900.
1952 NWL	1400.
1952 Arnprior	2500.
1964, 65, (var I, II, III, & IV) 67 each	275.
1966 Large beads	150.

GOLD COINS

$5 - 1912	5000.
$10 - 1912	10,000.

SOVEREIGNS ('C' MINT MARK)

1908C	4000.
1911C	2500.

NEWFOUNDLAND LARGE CENTS
VICTORIA

	VG-8	F-12	VF-20	EF-40	MS-60	BU MS-60
1865	2.00	3.00	5.50	11.50	135.	400.
1872-H	2.00	3.00	5.50	11.50	100.	250.
1873	2.00	3.00	5.50	11.50	150.	400.
1876-H	2.00	3.00	5.50	11.50	175.	450.
1880 Round 0 even dt.	1.50	3.00	5.50	11.00	125.	375.
1880 Round 0 low 0	2.00	4.00	7.00	12.00	135.	375.
1880 Oval 0	60.00	90.00	100.	200.	750.	1600.
1885	15.00	20.00	30.00	50.00	300.	600.

NEWFOUNDLAND LARGE CENTS
VICTORIA

	VG-8	F-12	VF-20	EF-40	MS-60	BU MS-60
1888	12.50	16.00	25.00	45.00	225.	500.
1890	1.60	2.75	4.50	8.00	125.	350.
1894	1.60	2.75	4.50	8.00	125.	350.
1896	1.60	2.75	4.50	8.00	125.	350.

EDWARD VII

	VG-8	F-12	VF-20	EF-40	MS-60	BU MS-60
1904-H	5.00	7.50	15.00	25.00	225.	600.
1907	1.50	2.50	4.75	10.00	150.	375.
1909	1.50	2.50	4.75	10.00	150.	375.

GEORGE V

	VG-8	F-12	VF-20	EF-40	MS-60	BU MS-60
1913	1.00	1.50	3.00	5.00	45.00	140.
1917-C	1.00	1.50	3.00	5.00	50.00	150.
1919-C	1.00	1.50	3.00	5.00	60.00	190.
1920-C	1.00	1.50	3.00	5.00	60.00	190.
1929	1.00	1.50	3.00	5.00	55.00	180.
1936	.75	1.25	2.50	4.00	30.00	125.

NEW FOUNDLAND SMALL CENTS
GEORGE VI

	VG-8	F-12	VF-20	EF-40	MS-60	BU MS-60
1938	.50	.75	1.50	3.00	20.00	45.00
1940	2.00	3.00	4.00	8.50	45.00	150.
1940 Re-engr. date	12.50	20.00	30.00	40.00	200.	475.
1941-C	.30	.50	.75	1.50	15.00	35.00
1942	.30	.50	.75	1.50	15.00	35.00
1943-C	.30	.50	.75	1.50	15.00	35.00
1944-C	1.40	2.00	3.00	4.00	35.00	100.
1947-C	.70	1.00	1.50	3.00	30.00	85.00

NEWFOUNDLAND FIVE CENTS SILVER
VICTORIA

	VG-8	F-12	VF-20	EF-40	MS-60	MS-63
1865	25.00	35.00	70.00	150.	1200.	2200.
1870	35.00	55.00	100.	200.	1500.	2500.
1872-H	26.00	40.00	75.00	175.	1000.	1300.
1873	35.00	50.00	115.	225.	1500.	2500.
1873-H	800.	1300.	2000.	3000.	7500.	10,000.
1876-H	70.00	115.	175.	350.	2500.	4500.
1880	30.00	45.00	90.00	175.	1200.	2300.
1881	20.00	30.00	50.00	150.	1000.	2000.
1882-H	15.00	25.00	45.00	115.	900.	1800.
1885	100.	150.	250.	500.	3000.	5000.
1888	23.00	35.00	60.00	150.	900.	1400.
1890	8.00	18.00	35.00	100.	800.	1400.
1894	8.00	18.00	35.00	100.	800.	1400.
1896	5.00	10.00	25.00	50.00	600.	1300.

EDWARD VII

	VG-8	F-12	VF-20	EF-40	MS-60	MS-63
1903	4.00	8.00	22.00	50.00	650.	1200.
1904-H	3.50	6.50	18.00	40.00	400.	800.
1908	2.75	5.50	14.00	35.00	350.	650.

GEORGE V

	VG-8	F-12	VF-20	EF-40	MS-60	MS-63
1912	1.75	3.25	8.50	25.00	350.	600.
1917-C	1.75	3.25	8.50	25.00	350.	600.
1919-C	2.50	5.50	14.00	35.00	500.	900.
1929	1.35	3.00	7.50	22.00	250.	450.

Newfoundland five cents silver
GEORGE VI

	VG-8	F-12	VF-20	EF-40	MS-60	MS-63
1938	1.00	1.25	2.75	6.00	115.	250.
1940-C	1.00	1.25	2.25	4.50	60.00	135.
1941-C	.65	1.00	1.35	2.75	25.00	50.00
1942-C	1.15	1.25	3.00	6.00	50.00	90.00
1943-C	.75	1.00	1.50	3.25	25.00	50.00
1944-C	1.00	1.50	2.50	4.50	50.00	150.
1945-C	.75	1.00	1.35	3.50	25.00	50.00
1946-C	250.	300.	400.	550.	2300.	3500.
1947-C	5.00	7.00	10.00	15.00	150.	250.

NEWFOUNDLAND 10 CENTS
VICTORIA

	VG-8	F-12	VF-20	EF-40	MS-60	MS-63
1865	15.00	30.00	75.00	150.	1800.	2500.
1870	150.	225.	400.	800.	5000.	7000.
1872-H	17.00	28.00	75.00	175.	1400.	2500.
1873	18.00	32.00	90.00	250.	2100.	4000.
1876-H	30.00	50.00	125.	350.	2500.	4000.
1880	28.00	50.00	125.	350.	3000.	4500.
1882-H	17.00	28.00	70.00	150.	1400.	2500.
1885	75.00	135.	325.	650.	3000.	5000.
1888	15.00	30.00	70.00	200.	1800.	3000.
1890	7.50	15.00	35.00	110.	1200.	2300.
1894	7.50	15.00	35.00	110.	1000.	2200.
1896	5.50	10.00	30.00	100.	1000.	1700.

EDWARD VII

	VG-8	F-12	VF-20	EF-40	MS-60	MS-63
1903	5.00	12.00	35.00	100.	1100.	2000.
1904-H	4.50	10.00	25.00	80.00	600.	1100.

GEORGE V

	VG-8	F-12	VF-20	EF-40	MS-60	MS-63
1912	2.50	6.00	15.00	50.00	600.	1000.
1917-C	2.00	4.00	10.00	30.00	500.	1100.
1919-C	3.25	6.50	15.00	50.00	600.	900.

GEORGE VI

	VG-8	F-12	VF-20	EF-40	MS-60	MS-63
1938	1.25	2.50	5.00	12.00	150.	300.
1940	1.15	2.35	4.50	10.00	125.	250.
1941-C	1.25	2.00	3.50	7.00	50.00	100.
1942-C	1.25	2.00	3.50	7.00	60.00	120.
1943-C	1.35	2.10	3.75	8.00	60.00	125.
1944-C	1.25	2.00	4.00	8.00	75.00	150.
1945-C	1.25	2.00	3.50	7.00	50.00	100.
1946-C	4.50	7.50	15.00	30.00	200.	300.
1947-C	2.25	4.00	8.00	18.00	110.	225.

NEWFOUNDLAND 20 CENTS
VICTORIA

	VG-8	F-12	VF-20	EF-40	MS-60	MS-63
1865	10.00	18.00	45.00	185.	1500.	2500.
1870	17.00	30.00	90.00	200.	2000.	3500.
1872-H	10.00	18.00	45.00	150.	1500.	2500.
1873	13.00	20.00	60.00	175.	1800.	3000.
1876-H	15.00	25.00	75.00	200.	2000.	4000.
1880	20.00	35.00	90.00	250.	2000.	4500.
1881	6.00	13.00	35.00	125.	1200.	2200.
1882-H	6.00	13.00	30.00	135.	1100.	2100.
1885	10.00	16.00	40.00	150.	1800.	2750.
1888	6.00	14.00	40.00	125.	1200.	2500.
1890	4.50	9.00	25.00	80.00	1000.	1800.
1894	4.50	10.00	25.00	80.00	1000.	1800.
1896 Sm.						
96	4.50	9.00	28.00	75.00	1000.	2000.
1896 Lg.						
96	6.00	15.00	35.00	110.	1100.	2200.

NEWFOUNDLAND 20 CENTS
VICTORIA

	VG-8	F-12	VF-20	EF-40	MS-60	MS-63
1899 Lg.						
99	5.00	10.00	28.00	80.00	1000.	2000.
1899 Sm.						
99	6.00	14.00	33.00	110.	1100.	2200.
1900	4.50	7.50	18.00	70.00	1000.	2000.

EDWARD VII

	VG-8	F-12	VF-20	EF-40	MS-60	MS-63
1904-H	9.00	20.00	65.00	175.	1200.	2300.

GEORGE V

	VG-8	F-12	VF-20	EF-40	MS-60	MS-63
1912	2.50	4.00	15.00	45.00	600.	1100.

NEWFOUNDLAND 25 CENTS

	VG-8	F-12	VF-20	EF-40	MS-60	MS-63
1917-C	2.25	3.50	8.00	15.00	150.	300.
1919-C	2.25	3.75	9.00	20.00	225.	450.

NEWFOUNDLAND 50 CENTS
VICTORIA

	VG-8	F-12	VF-20	EF-40	MS-60	MS-63
1870	12.50	20.00	50.00	200.	2000.	4200.
1872-H	12.00	20.00	50.00	200.	1800.	4000.
1873	16.00	25.00	60.00	250.	2500.	4500.
1874	12.00	20.00	55.00	225.	2500.	4500.
1876-H	20.00	35.00	100.	400.	3500.	6500.
1880	23.00	40.00	120.	450.	3000.	6500.
1881	12.00	25.00	75.00	300.	2500.	4500.
1882-H	10.00	18.00	45.00	225.	1800.	4000.
1885	12.00	20.00	65.00	250.	2500.	6000.
1888	15.00	30.00	90.00	400.	2500.	5500.
1894	9.00	15.00	50.00	225.	1800.	3500.
1896	8.00	13.00	35.00	175.	1800.	3000.
1898	7.50	12.00	40.00	175.	1800.	3000.
1899 Sm.						
Dt.	7.00	12.00	35.00	160.	1800.	3500.
1899 Lg.						
Dt.	7.50	12.00	35.00	160.	1800.	3500.
1900	6.00	12.00	35.00	135.	1300.	2800.

EDWARD VII

	VG-8	F-12	VF-20	EF-40	MS-60	MS-63
1904-H	5.50	7.50	23.00	75.00	500.	800.
1907	6.00	10.00	25.00	75.00	550.	800.
1908	5.50	8.00	20.00	50.00	500.	700.
1909	5.50	8.00	20.00	50.00	500.	700.

GEORGE V

	VG-8	F-12	VF-20	EF-40	MS-60	MS-63
1911	4.50	7.50	15.00	60.00	500.	700.
1917-C	4.50	6.50	13.00	35.00	300.	550.
1918-C	4.50	6.50	14.00	35.00	300.	550.
1919-C	4.50	6.50	14.00	35.00	300.	550.

NEWFOUNDLAND $2 GOLD
VICTORIA

	F-12	VF-20	EF-40	AU-50	MS-60	MS-63
1865	200.	250.	350.	500.	1200.	2400.
1870	200.	250.	350.	500.	1200.	2400.
1872	250.	375.	500.	900.	2400.	3500.
1880	1000.	1600.	2200.	3000.	4500.	7000.
1881	150.	200.	250.	350.	700.	1200.
1882-H	125.	175.	225.	300.	600.	1000.
1885	150.	200.	250.	350.	700.	1200.
1888	125.	175.	225.	300.	600.	1000.

NOVA SCOTIA
HALF CENTS

	VG-8	F-12	VF-20	EF-40	MS-60	BU MS-60
1861.........	5.00	8.00	11.00	15.00	60.00	125.
1864.........	5.00	8.00	11.00	15.00	60.00	125.

LARGE CENTS

	VG-8	F-12	VF-20	EF-40	MS-60	BU MS-60
1861.........	2.00	3.00	6.00	11.00	75.00	175.
1862.........	20.00	30.00	50.00	100.	300.	700.
1964.........	2.00	3.50	7.00	12.00	75.00	175.

NEW BRUNSWICK
HALF CENT

	VG-8	F-12	VF-20	EF-40	MS-60	BU MS-60
1861.........	45.00	60.00	90.00	125.	400.	850.

LARGE CENTS

	VG-8	F-12	VF-20	EF-40	MS-60	BU MS-60
1861.........	2.00	3.00	6.00	10.00	70.00	175.
1864.........	2.00	3.00	6.00	10.00	70.00	175.

FIVE CENTS

	VG-8	F-12	VF-20	EF-40	MS-60	MS-63
1862.........	28.00	50.00	125.	200.	1200.	2500.
1864.........	28.00	50.00	100.	200.	1200.	2500.

TEN CENTS

	VG-8	F-12	VF-20	EF-40	MS-60	MS-63
1862 recut "2"	25.00	40.00	100.	200.	1200.	2200.
1862.........	25.00	40.00	125.	200.	1200.	2200.
1864.........	25.00	40.00	100.	200.	1200.	2200.

TWENTY CENTS

	VG-8	F-12	VF-20	EF-40	MS-60	MS-63
1862.........	15.00	20.00	40.00	110.	1000.	1800.
1864.........	16.00	22.00	42.00	125.	1100.	2000.

PRINCE EDWARD ISLAND
LARGE CENTS

	VG-8	F-12	VF-20	EF-40	MS-60	BU MS-60
1871.........	1.25	2.00	5.00	12.00	120.	250.

Rarities 17

How a coin becomes rare

There are many factors which can make a particular issue coin rare. These include total mintage, the normal attrition of circulation, official and private meltings, and the level of collector interest at the time of issue.

The most important factor is total mintage. This figure sets the upper limit of potential collectible specimens. The actual number of specimens extant might sink to zero, but it will never rise above the total mintage figure (except for counterfeits and several issues of the 19th century which were restruck so flagrantly that even today more specimens are known than were "officially" minted).

In many instances the actual total mintage of an issue will never be definitely known, and not because of any illicit practices. For many years the United States Mint's bookkeeping consisted solely of recording the number of coins turned over to the Treasury during a calendar year, regardless of the actual year in which the coins were struck or of the date on the dies used to strike them.

Once the coins of a particular issue are released they begin to disappear. Coins are engraved, burnt, swallowed, buried by misers, placed in cornerstones and under masts, nailed to the aforesaid masts (a la *Moby Dick*), drilled for use as washers, made into rings and bracelets, and thrown into wishing wells. Although these deletions should normally occur in equal proportion to the number of coins in circulation, this is not always the case.

Many relatively common coins, such as 1889 dollars and 1916 dimes, have been altered in an attempt to disguise them as their more valuable counterparts that came from the branch Mints. Manufacturers of coin jewelry often prefer 1964 Kennedy halves over the later years because of the higher silver content.

Even pattern coins were subject to this selective destruction, as a large number of $4 gold Stellas were holed and made into earrings for presentation to the wives of congressmen, in an attempt to influence the husbands into approving the design.

Melting

In addition to the occasional random destruction of coins by accident or carelessness, coins have often been intentionally melted in wholesale lots for their bullion. The most zealous smelter of U.S. coins has always been the U.S. government, although private enterprise has contributed greatly to the death and dearth of coinage. During the great increases in bullion values during 1979-1980, millions of coins were melted privately as their intrinsic value increased dramatically in the space of several months. Occasionally the government's reasons have been aesthetic rather than intrinsic, as in the practice of recoining worn or mutilated coins.

Early U.S. silver coins, especially dollars, were often exchanged for worn Spanish colonial coins and the heavier dollars were then exported and melted. In 1834 the standard weight of each U.S. gold denomination was reduced, which resulted in most of the older coins being melted.

By 1853 the price of silver had risen to the point that all silver coins (except for the 3-cent piece) were worth more than their face value and were being privately melted. To combat this problem the government reduced the weight of the half dime through the half dollar by about 7 percent, except the dollar, which represented a hypothetical standard and was minted in only token quantities during this era. The new weight coins were marked with arrows at the date through 1855, not to inform the public of the change in weight, but to assist the Treasury in withdrawing the heavier coins for melting at a profit to the government.

In 1873, an otherwise insignificant increase was made in the weight of the dime, quarter dollar and half dollar. Once again arrows were placed at the date of the new weight coins, even though no withdrawal of the old coins was necessary. Nevertheless, many coins already struck at the branch Mints in the old weights were melted, resulting in several unknown or unique issues. Other denominations were discontinued after only six weeks production; in some cases only Proofs had yet been struck.

The Morgan silver dollar was never a necessary or popular coin, and much of the mintage was shipped directly into storage in the original Mint-sewn bags. More than 270 million of these surplus coins were melted after World War I, at which time presumably all 1895 non-Proof dollars were melted. One circulated non-Proof has been reported, possibly a souvenir presented to a visitor at the Mint.

Although large quantities of unwanted and unnecessary silver dollars had been melted in 1918, the silver interests in the United States were powerful enough to see to it that all of these coins were replaced through the striking of new coins. The result was the production of tens of millions of equally unwanted and unnecessary Morgan and Peace dollars in 1921 and subsequent years. Virtually all of these coins ended up in the Treasury's vaults, and for years these "common date" coins filled the limited demand for gifts and for circulation in the Western states.

This supply of coins might have lasted forever, at least until the price of silver rose above $1.29 per ounce, had it not been noticed that the Treasury was occasionally giving out older coins as well as the common dates of the 1920s. When it was discovered that a few bags of Seated Liberty dollars had been released at face value, thousands of collectors and speculators rushed to the Treasury to see what they might find. Within months the stock of silver dollars fell from hundreds of millions to less than 3 million, and several formerly scarce coins suddenly became common.

Virtually all of the nearly 3 million dollars retained by the Treasury were Uncirculated coins struck at the Carson City Mint. Most of these pieces were struck in the years 1882-1884, making these three dates uncommon, when compared to certain other Morgan dollars. After seven successive sales by the General Services Administration begining in October 1972, all of the coins were sold.

In many instances the heavy production of one denomination, such as silver dollars, was made at the expense of other denominations. See the mintage figures for dimes through halves of 1878-90 and for cents through halves of 1921-28 in the chapter about U.S. coins. The production of fractional silver increased after 1890 because of the Sherman Silver Purchase Act, not because of a decrease in the production of dollars. The production of dollars declined from 1893 to 1895 because of opposition to them from President Cleveland, who blamed them for the business panic of 1893.

Collector conservation

Once a coin has been struck, its best chance for survival is to be acquired by a collector who knows how to care for it. Prior to the 1820s there were very few collectors in the United States. Most of the Uncirculated coins from before this decade have come from the collections of Europeans who visited the United States Mint.

Once collecting became popular the collectors became aware of condition and wanted the best coins available. If the number of Proof coins of an earlier year was insufficient to meet the current demand, the Mint could often be induced to create a few more. In a few instances these semi-official restrikes were augmented with counterfeits produced outside the Mint from old dies, such as the 1804 "restrike" cent.

Throughout the remainder of the 19th century the several hundred collectors in the United States mainly concentrated on obtaining one specimen of each date for whatever denominations in which they were interested. Since this was often taken care of with a Proof, the Uncirculated coins were usually ignored. This was especially so for the branch Mints, as many dates from San Francisco and Carson City are unknown in Uncirculated condition. Non-silver minor coins are the easiest to collect, because they were all made in Philadelphia at a time when most collectors lived between Boston and Washington, D.C.

The national economy also has a great deal to do with the number of coins preserved from a particular era. During times of recession or depression, few coins are produced and few people have surplus cash to invest in BU rolls. Examples are the Great Depression of 1929-39 and the recessions of 1949 and 1958.

There are always exceptions to this rule, such as the 1931-S cents and 5-cent pieces which are more common in BU than one would expect, considering their low mintages. Either business was so bad that the coin never filtered down through the banks into circulation, or else some individual hoarded a great many of them. Other seemingly scarce issues, such as the 1950-D 5-cent piece and the 1955 half dollar, are common in BU because of speculators who were able to obtain the coins in bag quantities.

The number of collectors is never static, and an increased collector base places greater demand on supply. Generally, prices increase as the number of collectors grows, and drop if fewer persons are searching for the same coins.

Rarities can be caused by a whim of nature, an act of God, or the greed of man. Mintages have risen and fallen with the price of gold and the price of wheat. The lowly mosquito and the mighty politician have each been able to restrict production, in direct proportion to the venom of their sting. As long as coins are being struck there will always be an occasional rarity. They are, like gold, where you find them.

Famous collections

Matthew Adams Stickney

Matthew Adams Stickney was born Sept. 23, 1805, at Rowley, Mass., and died Aug. 11, 1894, in Salem, Mass.

He began collecting coins in 1823 and was probably the first person in America to form a systematic collection of the various dates in several series.

He assisted Sylvester S. Crosby in preparing his monumental work on U.S. Colonial, state and Washington coins in 1873-1875. Many of the Stickney coins were used to illustrate the Crosby book.

Some of the more famous coins in his collection included:

1787 New York Brasher doubloon, 1815 half eagle, 1804 silver dollar, 1776 cent of New Hampshire, the unique 1776 "Janus head" halfpenny, cent series of Massachusetts, Vermont, Connecticut, New York, New Jersey, many pattern pieces, world coins, Canada coins and medals, private and pioneer gold coins, plus numerous others.

The entire Stickney collection was sold by Henry Chapman June 25-29, 1907, with a total of 3,026 lots bringing $37,859.21.

William Forrester Dunham

William Forrester Dunham was born Oct. 3, 1857, at Barnard, Vt., and died Oct. 12, 1936, at the age of 79.

In early life Dunham was a school teacher, and later a wholesale and retail grocer. He studied pharmacy and became one of the leading druggists in Chicago. He retired from active business in 1916. He was a graduate of Tabor College, Iowa, and the University of Illinois.

Dunham was an ardent numismatist, beginning his collection early in life. He took an active interest in the affairs of the ANA and attended its conventions regularly. He served as a member of the ANA board of governors as well as chairman of the board. He was a charter member of the Chicago Coin Club.

Some of the items in his collection included:

1804 silver dollar, 1822 half eagle, 1852 half cent, 1802 half dime, Proof set of the gold coins of 1875, complete set of quarter eagles, complete set of $3 gold, largest collection of encased postage stamps ever formed, extensive collection of Hard Times tokens, Canada coins and medals, 2,500 varieties of Confederate paper currency, world gold, silver and platinum coins.

The collection was sold by B. Max Mehl June 3, 1941, with a total of 4,169 lots bringing $83,364.08.

Louis Eliasberg

On April 21, 1976, the Louis Eliasberg memorial exhibition, a complete date and Mint collection of United States coins, plus pattern coins, paper money, world coins and primitive means of exchange, opened as a Bicentennial feature at the Philadelphia Mint.

It was designated as a memorial exhibit in honor of its late owner who died Feb. 20, 1976. His sons, Louis Eliasberg Jr. and Richard Eliasberg, and his widow, Mrs. Lucille Eliasberg, officiated at the opening of the exhibit with Acting Mint Director Frank H. MacDonald.

The collection remained on display throughout the entire Bicentennial year and into America's third century.

Louis Eliasberg was life member 169 of the American Numismatic Association and a member of the Baltimore Coin Club.

In 1942 he startled the numismatic world by acquiring the famous collection formed by John H. Clapp. It cost more than $100,000 and at that time was the all-time high single cash transaction in the history of numismatics.

Eliasberg had a very nearly complete collection of regular-issue United States coins including a 1913 Liberty Head 5-cent piece and an 1804 silver dollar. The only pieces he was known to be missing were the 1841-O and 1797 16 Star obverse, Large Eagle reverse half eagles.

The Eliasberg gold coin collection was sold Oct. 27-29, 1982, by Bowers and Ruddy Galleries Inc., under the sobriquet "The United States Gold Collection" at the request of the family. However, it was widely known throughout the hobby that the coins being sold were from the Eliasberg collection and the news was eventually published in the numismatic press. The 1,074 lots brought more than $11.4 million, including two coins which each brought record prices of $652,000 — the unique 1870-S $3 gold piece and the 1822 half eagle.

"Colonel" E.H.R. Green

"Texas Colonel" Green was born Aug. 22, 1868, and died June 8, 1936. Before he reached the age of 20, his right leg was amputated 7 inches above the knee. Even so, he stood 6 feet, 4 inches, and weighed 300 pounds.

Green was the eccentric playboy son of the equally eccentric, but miserly, Hetty Green, the famous Wall Street financier and manipulator, known as the "Witch of Wall Street." She died July 3, 1916, and left her entire estate to her son and to a frightened, eremitic daughter, Sylvia Wilks.

Green reputedly spent $3 million a year on yachts, coins, stamps, pornography, orchid culture and Texas politics.

At the time of his death, Green's collection contained some of the finest and rarest numismatic pieces ever assembled by one person, including all five known 1913 Liberty Head 5-cent pieces plus a specimen of the 1913 Buffalo 5-cent piece in copper.

Josiah Kirby Lilly

The Josiah K. Lilly Collection specializing in United States and foreign gold coins was passed to the Smithsonian Institution after an act of Congress in 1968 gave the Lilly estate a tax credit of $5.5 million.

Included in the collection of 6,125 gold coins are 1,227 United States gold coins, among them an 1822 half eagle (three known)

and a 1797 half eagle with 16 star obverse; 1,236 Latin American coins; 3,227 European coins; and 243 Africa, Asia and Far East coins, all of which are in gold.

The only United States gold coin Lilly did not possess was the 1870-S $3 piece, which was owned by Louis Eliasberg.

Lilly also possessed an extensive collection of stamps which was sold for a total value of $3,123,127.

King Farouk

King Farouk was born in 1919. At the age of 17 he succeeded his father, King Fuad, as king of Egypt. He ruled Egypt from 1936 to 1952 when he was deposed and forced into exile.

King Farouk assembled one of the largest coin collections in the world. After he was deposed in 1952, his collection was seized by the Egyptian government and sold at public auction by Sotheby's of London, England.

An accumulator rather than a student of numismatics, Farouk's collection represented one of the finest ever assembled. There were about 8,500 coins and medals in gold and 164 in platinum. In addition, of course, were many copper and silver coins.

Among the pre-19th century items was a group of 19 Brazilian gold bars dating back to 1767. Also included were a few ancients of the Ptolemys of Egypt, some Roman aureii and some Roman gold bars of the fourth century A.D. Also represented were extensive selections from Europe, the Far East and an important selection of U.S. gold and patterns. The collection included a 1933 Saint-Gaudens double eagle, never officially released and considered illegal to own. U.S. authorities requested the coin be removed from the London auction, which it was, but it was not turned over and its location is unknown.

Many of the most famous U.S. and foreign rarities are still referred to as "ex Farouk" — from the Farouk collection.

John Andrew Beck

John A. Beck was born in Chestnut Ridge, Pa., Jan. 5, 1859. After attending St. Vincent's College, he and his brothers went into their father's salt-producing business, drilling for salt on the Ohio River.

When salt was more profitably produced by mining in the West, he sold out his salt and chemical interests and prospected for oil. He continued in this business until his death Jan. 27, 1924.

Beck began collecting coins when he was 10 years old. Major coins in his collection were acquired with the help of a prominent Philadelphia coin dealer, Henry Chapman.

The Beck collection contains an outstanding array of United States gold coins and other U.S. rarities. He considered his pioneer gold coins his most highly prized acquisitions.

Pioneer gold, a complete set of eagles, 1795-1804, commemorative gold, the 1861-D gold dollar, $4 Stellas and the rare 1900 Indian Head cent struck in gold comprise only part of this all-encompassing collection. He also possessed 531 1856 Flying Eagle cents.

Beck's collection remained intact until January 27, 1975, when the first portion of it was offered at public auction by the Trust Division, Pittsburgh National Bank, Pittsburgh, executors of the Beck estate. Three such sales were conducted by Abner Kreisberg Corp., in Beverly Hills, Calif., realizing $3,232,169. These sales were held Jan. 27-29, 1975 ($1,837,021); Feb. 12-13, 1976 ($741,816); and Feb. 14, 1977 ($653,332).

Arnold H. Kagan

Known both in Israel and the United States as builder, publisher, collector and numismatist, A.H. Kagan has many outstanding accomplishments to his credit. Where Rome's legions failed to ascend, Kagan built the cable railway linking historic Masada to the Judaean desert.

In less than 10 years, Kagan assembled the most complete collection of Israel's coins, medals and paper money in history, arranging them in 86 plastic panels which duplicate with actual coins and medals the pages of his standard reference, *Israel's Money and Medals*.

The 160-foot long exhibit, known as the Kagan-Maremba Collection, has been placed at the disposal of the Israel Government Coins and Medals Corp., and the American Israel Numismatic Association by Kagan, a long-time member of the American Numismatic Association.

Included are such rarities as the Utrecht die 100 prutot of 1954; various SPECIMEN pieces of the prutot series; three types of the 1960 eight grains one agora; commemorative rarities in all metals; and the rarest state, commissioned and presentation medals of the State of Israel. Since 1984, five rare medals have been added to the collection along with some Palestine Mandate pieces. The total value of the collection as of June 1987 exceeds $1.3 million.

For the past two years, the collection has been in the process of being refurbished. Plastic panels are being prepared to house the collection for display. Future plans include exhibit at various museums. When the refurbishing is completed, the weight of the collection is expected to approach 2,000 pounds.

Both in assembling the Kagan-Maremba Collection and in generously making it available to the world, Arnold H. Kagan has assured a prominent place for himself and his family in the numismatic history of the 20th century.

Garrett family collection

T. Harrison Garrett was a student at Princeton in the mid-1860s when he began collecting coins, beginning what was to become one of the major collections of U.S. coins and exonumia. Upon his death in 1888, he left the collection to his son Robert, who loaned it to Princeton University where it was on display for nearly 20 years.

Robert Garrett added to the collection until 1919 when he traded it to a brother, John Work Garrett, for art objects. J.W. Garrett was able to buy the pick of the Col. James W. Ellsworth Collection when it was sold in March 1923, including many 1792 patterns. Garrett died in 1942, and he continued his numismatic activity until shortly before then.

The Garrett collection was given to Johns Hopkins University in Baltimore, which sold duplicates in March 1976 in a Stack's auction, and consigned the bulk to Bowers and Ruddy Galleries which held a series of four auctions from 1979 to 1981. The coins sold by Bowers and Ruddy included *two* Brasher doubloons, many rare Colonial pieces, Washington medals, one of the greatest collections of 1792 pattern coinage assembled, a Proof 1795 silver dollar, an 1804 silver dollar and rare gold coins.

The four sales were held Nov. 28-29, 1979; March 26-27, 1980; Oct. 1-2, 1980; and March 25-26, 1981. Total prices realized was $25,235,360.

Virgil M. Brand

Virgil Michael Brand, born in Blue Island, Ill., in 1862, heir to one of the largest brewing businesses in Chicago, began collecting coins in 1889 when about 23 years old. His initial recorded purchases were of California gold issues, and by the time of his death in 1926, Brand had purchased more than 350,000 pieces. Some consider his collection to be among the greatest ever formed.

Brand purchased everything, refusing to specialize. He bought coins in all areas, from nearly every major dealer in the late 19th and early 20th centuries. He did so quietly, preferring to remain an unknown, unlike many prominent collectors of his era.

Following his death, Brand's two brothers, Horace and Armin, fought over the collection after failing to sell it intact. Dealers Henry Chapman and Burdette G. Johnson were hired in 1932 and 1933 to appraise the collection, and parts were sold through consignments and direct sales.

Many coins were given to Armin Brand's daughter, Jane, who kept them in her estate until her death. Bowers and Merena Galleries was selected to sell the Jane Brand Allen estate collection, doing so in two sales. The first, of American gold and copper coins, plus several foreign pieces, was held Nov. 7-8, 1983, realizing $1.9 million; the second, offering American coins and exonumia, sold June 18-19, 1984, for $1,417,977.

Sotheby Parke Bernet & Co. auctioned the bulk of Brand's estate of ancient and foreign coinage. Coins from the Soviet Union, Poland, Germany, Switzerland, France, Austria, Italy, England, Sweden, Finland and Portugal are just some of the countries represented taking place from July 1982 through October 1985 in 10 European sales totaling £4,514,334. The Brand auctions took place in New York, London, Amsterdam and Zurich. Also of note, Brand's numismatic book and literature auction realized $20,500 when it was auctioned by George Frederick Kolbe Aug. 13, 1983, in Los Angeles.

John L. Roper 2nd

Born Sept. 18, 1902, John L. Roper 2nd was an heir to a shipbuilding firm in Norfolk, Va., that gave him the money to build one of the major collections of Colonial and early American coinage of the 20th century. Roper died in April 1983.

The Dec. 8-9, 1983, auction of Roper's collection by Stack's included a half dozen Sommer Islands pieces, two New England silver pieces, 34 Massachusetts silver tree coins, plus copper and silver coins of most American Colonies and the early Confederation and federal issues. Fifteen Fugio coppers, five 1792 patterns and three Chain cents were also in the collection.

A second Roper sale, held March 20, 1984, offered paper money, Hard Times tokens and other items of numismatic Americana.

Emery May and R. Henry Norweb

Emery May Holden became interested in coins when she was about 9 years old in 1905 when she was given a half cent piece. R. Henry Norweb began collecting during his long diplomatic career in U.S. diplomatic service. Norweb died Oct. 1, 1983, and Mrs. Norweb died March 27, 1984.

Mrs. Norweb's collection of English gold coins is believed to be the greatest in the United States, and her collections of American Colonial, United States and Latin American coins were extensive as well.

The Norwebs were philanthropic in nature, and donated many rarities to museums. Among them were a 1913 Liberty 5-cent piece, given to the Smithsonian Institution in 1978, and a Brasher doubloon, given to the American Numismatic Society in 1969. A 52-piece collection of Colonial rarities was donated to the Smithsonian in 1982.

The legendary American portion of the Norweb collection will be sold at public auction in New York City by Auctions by Bowers and Merena Inc. The sale is scheduled to take place beginning in October 1987 with two additional sessions in 1988.

Amon G. Carter Jr.

Paper money collectors invariably think of Amon G. Carter Jr. when they think of great collections. His collection of Texas notes, including national bank notes, was undoubtedly the greatest in the world. Major U.S. rarities owned by Carter included a Series 1863 $1,000 legal tender note, an 1863 $100 legal tender note, an 1891 $100 "Open Back" Treasury note, and an 1874 $500 legal tender. Among the rarer nationals in the collection was an 1875 $100 note from the Deseret National Bank of Salt Lake City, Utah Territory, possibly the only First Charter $100 territorial national in existence.

Carter's coin collection contained such rarities as the Adams specimen 1804 silver dollar, a Very Fine 1870-S Seated Liberty silver dollar, the 1801, 1802, 1803 dollar restrikes and 1884 and 1885 Trade dollars, and many other rare pieces.

The coins were sold Jan. 18-21, 1984, by Stack's of New York, where the 1,798 lots brought more than $8 million including a 10 percent buyer's fee. His paper money collection is being sold at fixed prices by various dealers.

Carter, publisher of the *Fort Worth Star-Telegram,* which his father founded, died July 24, 1982, at the age of 62.

Robinson S. Brown Jr.

Robinson S. Brown Jr. from Louisville, Ky., began his hobby interests with stamps before moving on to coins.

He was fascinated with completing a set of

U.S. large cents by die varieties.

Determination played an important role in the success of his nearly-complete collection which is the second finest and most complete collection in the world, according to Brown. The collection assembled by Brown consisted of 1457 lots by Sheldon and Newcomb varieties of cents from 1793 through 1857. The collection of cents from 1816-1839 was complete while the collection by Newcomb variety from 1840-1857 is nearly complete.

The collection was sold at auction Sept.30-Oct.1, 1986, in West Hollywood, Calif., by Superior Galleries and realized a hammer price of $1,273,215. The catalog for the auction is destined to become the standard catalog of large cents.

Since the auction, Brown has begun to put together another large cent collection along with collecting other numismatic coins and tokens.

Wayne Miller

Wayne Miller, a Helena, Mont., coin dealer and collector, during a span of 16 years starting in the late 1960s acquired a complete set of Morgan and Peace silver dollars.

The characteristic that set his complete collection aside from others who have complete sets was the quality. The set included many of the finest known specimens, Proof Morgan dollars and several branch Mint Proof coins rarely seen were among the 160 pieces which made up the collection.

Miller had sold the collection in April 1984 to dealer David Hall, who was serving as a broker for an unnamed collector on the West Coast for a price believed to be in excess of $1 million.

The coin collection was subsequently sold at public auction by Superior Galleries, Jan.27-28, 1986 in Beverly Hills, Calif. and realized a hammer price of $1,109,375.

World's smallest, largest, oldest, and most beautiful coins

The smallest coins in the world were the gold "pinhead" coins used in Colpata, southern India, in 1800, which weighed as little as one grain, or 1/480 of a troy ounce.

Among the world's smallest coins are the following: Gold 1/32 dukat of Regensburg, about 1700, which bears no date; Nepal 1/100 gold mohar; and Nurnberg gold 1/32 dukat, about 1700, which bears no date.

Another contender for the world's smallest coin title is the silver Travancore chuckram, minted in 1860-1880. This tiny coin measures approximately 5.5 millimeters in diameter.

The Panama 2.5 centesimo of 1904, often called the "Panama pill," is perhaps the coin most often thought of as the world's smallest coin. The silver "pill" measures 10 millimeters in diameter and is less than 2 millimeters thick.

Also to be mentioned with the world's smallest coins is the bronze cash minted by the Indian state of Travancore until the mid-1940s. Obverse bears the Travancore arms (a conch shell) within an eight-pointed star, and on the reverse is the value. The coin measures 11 millimeters in diameter.

The bronze Amman cash of the Indian state Padukotah, depicting a Hindu god, measures 12 millimeters.

By comparison, the smallest U.S. coins are the Coronet gold dollar, minted from 1849-1854, with a diameter of 13 millimeters, and the silver 3-cent piece, minted 1851-1873, with a diameter of 14 millimeters.

The world's largest money, or primitive exchange tokens, is the stone money or fei (native name for stone money), from Yap Island. Yap is the name of an island in the Caroline Islands group in the South Pacific.

Yap stone money is made of limestone or calcite with diameters from 6 to 12 feet, sometimes weighing as much as 5 tons.

A hole about a sixth of the stone's diameter is made in the center of the circular-shaped fei. Through this hole a pole is inserted to make it easier for transportation. The value of the fei is determined by the fineness of the stone's grain and the size.

Yap stone money was owned by individual families and because of its bulk, when it was brought to the island it was plopped down in one spot and there it tended to remain.

When the stones were used to buy things, ownership changed but the position of the stone didn't. Everybody on the island always knew to whom the stones belonged.

With the beginning of the 1800s a series of conquerors occupied the island at various times and with them came new types of currency so stone money began losing its importance as a means of exchange. The stones became useful only in ceremonies.

Also to be reckoned with in considering the world's largest money is the Swedish plate money. In 1644 the Swedish copper 10-daler plate money was minted and attained a weight of up to 38.5 pounds.

The silver multiple talers (up to 12-taler pieces) of the Brunswick duchies and Saxe-Lauenburg rank with the world's largest silver coins. A single taler weighs about 29 grams, so a double would weigh approximately 58, a triple 87, 5 talers 145, 10 talers 290, and so on. A 1679 6-taler of Luneburg measures 97 millimeters.

Measuring 133 millimeters was the gold 200 mohurs of India. Pieces were issued under the rule of Shah Jahan, 1628-1658. Estimated at 70 ounces, no specimen is known to have survived.

Oldest coins are usually attributed to the electrum (alloy of gold and silver) staters of Lydia, in Asia Minor (now Turkey). Pieces were coined in about 700 B.C., probably in the reign of Candaules.

Chinese primitive money is now believed to be earlier but this date remains uncertain. A date of 1000 B.C. has been attributed to earlier Chinese spade money, or pu.

Results of a survey to determine "the world's prettiest crown" issued since 1900 were announced by Julius Weiss, *Cleveland Press* stamp and coin columnist, in 1967.

Promoted in *Coin World* and other numismatic publications, announcement of the survey also was carried by coin magazines in Sydney, Australia, as well as in U.S. newspapers from coast to coast, and was even carried over a European news wire service.

Collectors from more than 40 states, Canada, Germany and Mexico participated in the poll, and named the three numismatic "Beauty contest" winners as follows:

First place was won by a silver coin of Hungary, the 5-pengo crown, issued in 1938 in commemoration of the 900th anniversary of the death of St. Stephen.

The popular Mexican "Ferrocarril" 5-peso silver alloy coin, marking the opening of Mexico's Southeast Railway in 1950, was judged winner of second place.

The third choice of collectors who responded to the poll was the "Five Kings" 30-drachma piece of Greece, a 1963 issue which commemorated the 100th anniversary of the then-current Greek royal dynasty.

Also cited often by American collectors are the Saint-Gaudens U.S. $20 gold piece, the Walking Liberty half dollar and the Standing Liberty quarter dollar.

Rare coins achieve high prices

The numismatic market underwent a major transformation in the mid-1970s — the five-figure bid at auction became commonplace, and several times a year exceptional coins traded at $100,000 or more. A sellers' market was born in 1978, when in August two major collections were placed on the auction block, the N.M. Kaufman Collection, sold by the Rare Coin Company of America, and the Richard Branigan sale, auctioned by Bowers and Ruddy Galleries during the American Numismatic Association convention.

High prices were not unknown before 1978; there are nearly 225 prices $21,000 or higher listed in the 1978 edition of the *Coin World Almanac,* including 16 reaching $100,000 or more. The record-holder at that time was a 2,300-year-old coin, a silver decadrachm of Athens, Greece, which sold in 1974 for approximately $272,240 (U.S. figure computed from foreign funds). However, five-figure prices were still relatively uncommon; no Brasher doubloon had been sold at auction since 1907, when it brought $6,200; and the top price for a U.S. coin was the $225,000 paid in 1974 for the Idler specimen of the 1804 dollar restrike.

Look at how things have changed!

Historically, 112 coins have posted hammer prices of $100,000 or more at public auction. The top recorded auction price is $725,000, paid for one of the finest specimens of the Brasher doubloon.

The following listing is not strictly a chart of record auction prices, but a listing of every U.S. piece recorded by the *Coin World* staff as having brought very high prices at public auction, both in the United States and abroad. Foreign prices are calculated using a published exchange rate near the time of sale. Some exonumic items appear on the list, including several medals, but no high-priced paper money appears, although many specimens exist. Some specimens may appear more than once, reflecting the rapid turnover some top-level coins bring. In many cases, later sales of the same specimen are for lower prices than earlier sales, indicating the market has lower expectations currently than in 1978-1980. Researchers must be forewarned that different grades may be assigned the same specimen, particularly when it was sold at different times by different dealers.

A consistent style in descriptions has been adopted for U.S. coins appearing in the following chart. The date is followed by denomination, design or type, variety, if any, and condition, which appears in parentheses; pricing information and auction data follow. The dollar coin denomination is preceded by metallic content for clarity. If a date appears within parentheses, it means the date does not appear on the specimen itself, but is generally accepted as the year of issue or production. Coins listed like 1798/7 are overdates, while 5D/50 C. and similar listings represent a punching error in the denomination.

Coins "selling" at auction are not listed if it is known that they went back to the owner or were retained by the auction firm, even if a "selling" price was publicly announced. However, there may be coins listed that did not actually sell to a third party.

The listing is as complete as possible, but the sheer volume of coin sales ensures that some sales may be missing.

The price recorded is the hammer price, and does not include the buyer's fee charged by many firms, taxes or other charges added to hammer prices.

Description	Price	Auction
U.S. 1787 Brasher gold doubloon, Eagle's Wing (punch) (MS-63)	$725,000	Bowers & Ruddy-Garrett Nov. 28-29, 1979
U.S. 1787 Brasher gold doubloon, Eagle's Breast (punch) Very Fine	$625,000	Bowers & Ruddy-Garrett Mar. 25-26, 1981
U.S. 1822 $5 Capped Head gold (VF-30)	$625,000	Bowers & Ruddy-Oct. 27-29, 1982
U.S. 1870-S $3 Indian gold (EF-40)	$625,000	Bowers & Ruddy-Oct. 27-29, 1982
U.S. 1851 $50 Augustus Humbert, pioneer gold (Proof)	$500,000	Bowers & Ruddy-Garrett Mar. 26-27, 1980
U.S. 1907 $20 Indian, Roman Numerals, pattern, J-1776 unique (Proof 65)	$475,000	ANA-Bowers & Ruddy, Aug. 1, 1981
U.S. 1787 Brasher gold doubloon (AU-55)	$430,000	Auction '79-Rarcoa July 26-27, 1979
U.S. 1804 silver $1, Class III, Berg specimen (EF-40)	$400,000	Bowers & Ruddy-Garrett Mar. 26-27, 1980
U.S. 1913 Liberty 5-cent (Proof 63)	$350,000	Superior Galleries, Jan. 28-30, 1985
U.S. 1852/1 $20 Augustus Humbert, pioneer gold (Proof)	$325,000	Bowers & Ruddy-Garrett Mar. 26-27, 1980
U.S. 1855 $50 Kellogg & Co., pioneer gold (Proof)	$300,000	Bowers & Ruddy-Garrett Mar. 26-27, 1980
U.S. 1804 silver $1, Class I, Dexter-Bareford (Proof)	$280,000	Stack's-Bedford coll. Oct. 22-23, 1981
U.S. 1804 Bust silver $1 (MS-60+)	$280,000	Superior Galleries, Jan. 28-30, 1985
U.S. 1855 $50 Wass, Molitor & Co., pioneer gold (MS-65)	$275,000	Bowers & Ruddy-Garrett Mar. 26-27, 1980
U.S. 1849 $10 Cincinnati Mining & Trading Co., pioneer gold (EF-40)	$270,000	Bowers & Ruddy-Garrett Mar. 26-27, 1980
U.S. MCMVII (1907) Saint-Gaudens $20 gold Roman Numerals (Proof 65+)	$260,000	Auction '85-Superior, July 26-27
U.S. 1794 silver $1, Flowing Hair (MS-65)	$240,000	Stack's Jan. 18-21, 1984
U.S. 1854 $50 Kellogg & Co., pioneer gold (Proof)	$230,000	Bowers & Ruddy-Garrett Mar. 26-27, 1980
U.S. 1870-S Seated Liberty half dime, BU	$230,000	Auction '86-Superior, July 26, 1986
U.S. 1907 $20 Saint-Gaudens, Roman Numerals, Extremely High Relief (Proof 69)	$230,000	Auction '80-Paramount Aug. 14-15, 1980
U.S. 1907 $20 Saint-Gaudens, Roman Numerals (Proof 67)	$220,000	Bowers & Ruddy, Oct. 27-29, 1982
U.S. 1873-CC quarter dollar, Seated Liberty, No Arrows (MS-65)	$205,000	NERCA Sale - Apr. 10-12, 1980
U.S. 1830 $5 Templeton Reid, pioneer gold (EF-40)	$200,000	Bowers & Ruddy-Garrett Nov. 28-29, 1979
U.S. 1850 $50 F.D. Kohler, pioneer gold ingot (1,348.9 grains) (EF-40)	$200,000	Bowers & Ruddy-Garrett Mar. 26-27, 1980
U.S. 1792 Birch cent, pattern, J-4 (MS-63)	$200,000	Bowers & Ruddy-Garrett Mar. 25-26, 1981
U.S. 1825/4 $5 Capped Head gold (Proof 60)	$200,000	Bowers & Ruddy Galleries Oct. 27-29, 1982
U.S. 1907 $20 gold, Saint-Gaudens Ultra High Relief, Roman Finish (Proof)	$200,000	Stacks, Oct. 22-23, 1985
U.S. 1783 Nova Constellatio Mark, silver (MS-63, prooflike)	$190,000	Bowers & Ruddy-Garrett Nov. 28-29, 1979
U.S. 1804 silver $1, Class III, Berg-Garrett specimen (EF-40)	$190,000	Pullen & Hanks, Inc. Feb. 5-6, 1982
U.S. 1827/3 quarter dollar, Capped Bust, Large Size B-1, original (Proof)	$190,000	Bowers & Ruddy-Garrett, Mar. 26-27, 1980
U.S. 1804 silver $1, Class III, Adams-Carter (EF-40)	$180,000	Stack's Jan. 18-21, 1984
U.S. 1849 $5 Pacific & Co., pioneer gold (VF-30)	$180,000	Bowers & Ruddy-Garrett, Mar. 26-27, 1980
U.S. 1927-D $20 Saint-Gaudens (MS-65)	$180,000	Auction '84-Paramount July 25-26, 1984
U.S. 1879 $4 Coiled Hair Stella, pattern, J-1638 (Proof 65)	$175,000	Auction '80-Superior Aug. 14-15, 1980
U.S. 1907 $20 Saint-Gaudens, Roman Numerals (Proof 65)	$175,000	NERCA-Boston Jubilee July 24-265, 1980
U.S. 1795 Draped Bust $1 (Proof 63)	$170,000	Bowers & Ruddy-Garrett Mar. 26-27, 1980
U.S. 1804 Bust dollar, The Garrett specimen Class III (EF-40)	$170,000	Bowers & Merena, June 23-25, 1986
U.S. 1783 Nova Constellatio Quint, silver (MS-65, prooflike)	$165,000	Bowers & Ruddy-Garrett Nov. 28-29, 1979
U.S. 1829 $5 Capped Head, Large Date, Large Planchet (MS-65, prooflike)	$165,000	Bowers & Ruddy-Garrett Nov. 28-29, 1979
U.S. 1927-D $20 Saint-Gaudens (MS-65)	$160,000	Bowers & Ruddy-Oct. 27-29, 1982

U.S. 1815 $5 Capped Head gold (AU-55)	$150,000	Bowers & Ruddy-Garrett Nov. 28-29, 1979
U.S. 1875 $3 Indian gold (Proof)	$150,000	Stack's-Ullmer sale Dec. 1974
U.S. 1879 $4 Coiled Hair Stella, (Proof 65)	$150,000	Superior May 31-June 2, 1987
U.S. 1894-S dime, Barber (choice Proof)	$145,000	Auction '80-Rarcoa Aug. 14-15, 1980
U.S. 1855 $50 Kellogg & Co., Round, Reeded Edge, pioneer gold (Proof)	$140,000	Auction '79-Stack's July 26-27, 1979
U.S. 1855 $5 Kellogg & Co., Round, pioneer gold (Proof)	$140,000	Stack's Jan. 18-21, 1984
U.S. 1834 $2.50 Classic Head, No Motto (Proof)	$135,000	Bowers & Ruddy-Garrett Mar. 26-27, 1980
U.S. $10 (1849) undated Miners' Bank, pioneer gold (MS-65)	$135,000	Bowers & Ruddy-Garrett Mar. 26-27, 1980
U.S. 1879 $20 Quintuple Stella, pattern gold, J-1643 (Proof 65)	$135,000	NERCA sale Apr. 10-12, 1980
U.S. 1795 $10 Small Eagle, 12 Leaves (BU)	$130,000	Bowers & Ruddy-Garrett Oct. 1-2, 1980
U.S. 1830 $5 Templeton Reid, Reeded Edge, pioneer gold (EF-40)	$130,000	ANA '83-Kagin's Aug. 16-20, 1983
U.S. 1850 $50 Kellogg & Co., Round, pioneer gold (Proof 63)	$130,000	Auction '80-Paramount Aug. 14-15, 1980
U.S. 1910 $20 Saint-Gaudens, Roman Finish (Proof 69)	$125,000	NERCA sale - Apr. 10-12, 1980
U.S. 1796 $2.50 Without Stars gold (AU-55)	$125,000	Bowers & Ruddy-Garrett Mar. 26-27, 1980
U.S. 1855 $50 Kellogg & Co., pioneer gold (Proof 63)	$125,000	ANA '83-Kagin's Aug. 16-20, 1983
U.S. 1875 $3 Indian gold (Proof 63)	$125,000	Auction '81-Rarcoa July 23-24, 1981
U.S. 1793 cent, Chain AMERICA, S-3 (MS-65)	$120,000	Auction '80-Paramount Aug. 14-15, 1980
U.S. 1798/7 $10 Heraldic Eagle gold, 7X6 Stars (AU-55)	$120,000	Bowers & Ruddy-Garrett Oct. 1-2, 1980
U.S. 1821 $2.50 Capped Head gold (Proof)	$120,000	Bowers & Ruddy-Garrett Mar. 26-27, 1980
U.S. 1849 $10 Mormon, pioneer gold (AU-55)	$120,000	Stack's Jan. 18-21, 1984
U.S. 1849 $10 Pacific Company, pioneer gold (AU-50)	$120,000	Bowers & Merena, Inc. June 18-19, 1984
U.S. 1793 cent, Chain AMERICA, S-3 (MS-63)	$115,000	Bowers & Ruddy, Garrett I, Nov. 28-29, 1979
U.S. 1858 $10 Coronet gold (MS-67)	$115,000	Auction '80-Paramount Aug. 14-15, 1980
U.S. 1879 $4 Coiled Hair Stella, pattern, J-1638 (Proof 63)	$115,000	Bowers & Ruddy Garrett I Nov. 28-29, 1979
U.S. 1794 silver $1, Flowing Hair (MS-63)	$110,000	Steve Ivy-Charmont sale Aug. 11-14, 1983
U.S. 1828 $5 Capped Head, Perfect Date (MS-65)	$110,000	Auction '79-Stack's July 27, 1979
U.S. 1839 $10 Coronet gold (Proof 65)	$110,000	Bowers & Ruddy-Oct. 27-29, 1982
U.S. 1794 silver $1 (Uncirculated)	$110,000	Superior-1973
U.S. 1798 $5 Small Eagle gold (EF-40)	$110,000	Bowers & Ruddy-Garrett Nov. 28-29, 1979
U.S. 1884 $20 Liberty gold (Proof)	$110,000	Stack's Ullmer sale Dec. 1974
U.S. 1851 $20 Baldwin & Co., pioneer gold (VF-30)	$110,000	Bowers & Ruddy-Garrett Mar. 26-27, 1980
U.S. 1855 $50 Kellogg & Co., Round, Reeded Edge pioneer gold (Proof)	$110,000	Auction '84-Rarcoa July 25-26, 1984
U.S. 1858 $10 Coronet gold (Proof)	$110,000	Stack's Jan. 18-21, 1984
U.S. 1875 $3 Indian gold (Proof 63)	$110,000	Stack's Jan. 18-21, 1984
U.S. 1885 silver $1, Trade (Proof)	$110,000	Auction '80-Rarcoa Aug. 14-15, 1980
U.S. 1792 cent, Silver Center, pattern, J-1 (EF-45)	$105,000	Pine Tree Rare Coin Auction-GENA sale Sept. 18-21, 1974
U.S. 1831 $2.50 Capped Head gold (MS-65)	$105,000	Bowers & Ruddy-Garrett Mar. 26-27, 1980
U.S. 1838 $10 Coronet gold, No Motto (Proof)	$105,000	Paramount NASC sale, Feb. 14-15, 1975
U.S. 1855 $50 Kellogg & Co., Round, pioneer gold (Proof)	$105,000	Stack's Oct. 27, 1983
U.S. 1879 silver $1 "Schoolgirl," pattern, J-1608 (choice Proof)	$105,000	Bowers & Ruddy-Garrett Mar. 26-27, 1980
U.S. 1879 $4 Coiled Hair Stella, pattern, J-1638 (Proof 65)	$105,000	Superior Oct. 15, 1974
U.S. 1880 $4 Flowing Hair Stella, pattern, J-1657 (Proof 65)	$105,000	Auction '80-Superior, Aug. 14-15 1980
U.S. 1880-CC $20 Liberty gold, EF	$102,500	Auction '79-Superior July 26-27, 1979
U.S. 1829 $5 Capped Head, Small Date, Large Planchet	$100,000	Kagin's-MANA sale Nov. 1-2, 1974
U.S. $10 (1849) undated J.S. Ormsby, pioneer gold (F-12)	$100,000	Bowers & Ruddy-Garrett Mar. 26-27, 1980
U.S. $5 (1861) undated John Parsons & Co., pioneer gold (VF-20)	$100,000	Bowers & Ruddy-Garrett Nov. 28-29, 1979
U.S. $5 (1861) undated J.J. Conway & Co., pioneer gold (EF-45)	$100,000	Bowers & Ruddy-Garrett Nov. 28-29, 1979
U.S. 1875 $3 Indian gold (Proof 65)	$100,000	Bowers & Ruddy Galleries Oct. 27-29, 1982
U.S. 1879 $20 Quintuple Stella, Reeded Edge, pattern gold, J-1643 (Proof)	$100,000	Auction '79-Stack's July 27, 1979
U.S. 1885 silver $1, Trade (Proof 63)	$100,000	Stack's Jan. 18-21, 1984
U.S. 1915-S $50 Panama-Pacific, Octagonal (MS-65)	$100,000	Bowers & Ruddy-Garrett Mar. 26-27, 1980
U.S. 1855 $50 Kellogg & Co., FIFTY DOLLS, Reeded edge (Proof)	$98,500	Superior May 31-June 2, 1987.
U.S. 1783 bit, Nova Constellatio, silver (MS-65, prooflike)	$97,500	Bowers & Ruddy-Garrett Nov. 28-29, 1979
U.S. 1933 $10 Indian gold (MS-60)	$97,500	Stack's-Kahn sale Oct. 23-24, 1980
U.S. 1829 $5 gold, Large date (MS-65)	$95,000	Auction '85-Superior, July 26-27, 1985
U.S. 1849 $10 Cincinnati Mining & Trading Co., overstruck on J.S. Ormsby & Co. $10 (EF-40)	$95,000	Bowers & Merena, Inc. June 18-19, 1984
U.S. 1879 Coiled Hair Stella $4 gold (Proof 65)	$95,000	Superior Galleries, Jan. 28-30, 1985
U.S. 1915-S $50 Panama-Pacific, Round (MS-65)	$95,000	Bowers & Ruddy-Garrett Mar. 26-27, 1980
U.S. 1875 $10 Coronet gold (Proof 65)	$95,000	Bowers & Ruddy, Oct. 27-29, 1982
U.S. 1792 cent, Silver Center, pattern, J-1 (MS-63)	$95,000	Bowers & Ruddy-Garrett Mar. 25-26, 1981
U.S. 1776 dollar, Continental, silver, N-1-C (unique) (VG-8)	$95,000	Bowers & Ruddy-Garrett Oct. 1-2, 1980

U.S. 1924/1 $2.50 gold, Capped Bust, Left (gem BU)	$95,000	Auction '85-Rarcoa, July 26-27, 1985
U.S. 1880 $4 Coiled Hair Stella, pattern, J-1660 (Proof 65)	$93,000	Sotheby's-S. Hallock du Pont coll. Sept. 21, 1982
U.S. 1879 $4 Coiled Hair Stella, pattern, J-1638 (Proof 67)	$92,500	Bowers & Ruddy Galleries Oct. 27-29, 1982
U.S. 1883 $20 Liberty gold (Proof)	$92,500	Stack's-June 22, 1979
U.S. 1875 $3 Indian gold (Proof 65)	$91,000	Stack's-Garrett sale, Mar. 12-13, 1976
U.S. 1875 $10 Coronet gold (Proof)	$91,000	Stack's-Garrett sale Mar. 12-13, 1976
U.S. 1792 half disme, pattern, J-7 (MS-67)	$90,000	Auction '80-Paramount Aug. 14-15, 1980
U.S. 1792 cent, Birch, G.W. PT. (George Washington president), pattern, J-6 (choice Uncirculated)	$90,000	Bowers & Ruddy-Garrett Mar. 25-26, 1981
U.S. 1795 silver $1, Flowing Hair, B-7 (MS-65, prooflike)	$90,000	Stack's GNYNC Apr. 27-29, 1983
U.S. 1808 $2.50 Indian (gem Brilliant Uncirculated)	$90,000	Auction '84-Stack's July 25-26, 1984
U.S. 1849-C gold $1, Type I, Open Wreath (EF-40)	$90,000	Auction '79-Stack's July 27, 1979
U.S. 1849 $2.50 Mormon, pioneer gold (VF-20)	$90,000	Bowers & Ruddy-Garrett Mar. 26-27, 1980
U.S. 1854 gold $1, Type II (Proof)	$90,000	Bowers & Ruddy-Garrett Nov. 28-29, 1979
U.S. 1874 $10 Bickford gold, pattern, J-1373	$90,000	ANA-Bowers & Ruddy July 28-Aug. 1, 1981
U.S. 1875 $3 gold (Proof 65)	$90,000	Auction '85-Superior, July 26-27, 1985
U.S. 1876 Coronet Double Eagle Pattern, J-1490 (Proof 65)	$90,000	Auction 86-Superior, July 26, 1986
U.S. 1880 $4 Coiled Hair Stella, pattern, J-1660 (Proof 65)	$90,000	Bowers & Ruddy Galleries Oct. 27-29, 1982
U.S. 1891 $20 Liberty gold (Proof 63)	$90,000	Bowers & Ruddy-Garrett Mar. 26-27, 1980
U.S. 1910 $20 Saint-Gaudens gold (Roman Finish, choice Matte Proof)	$90,000	Bowers & Ruddy-Garrett Mar. 26-27, 1980
U.S. 1875 $3 gold (Proof 65)	$90,000	Superior May 31-June 2, 1987
U.S. 1823/22 quarter dollar, Wire Rim (Proof)	$87,500	Auction '80-Stack's Aug. 14-15, 1980
U.S. 1875 $3 gold (gem Proof)	$87,500	Stack's, Jan. 15, 1986
U.S. 1885 Trade $1 (Proof)	$87,500	Auction '84-Rarcoa July 25-26, 1984
U.S. 1885 Trade $1 (Proof)	$87,500	Superior, Hoffecker coll., Feb. 8-11, 1987
U.S. 1794 silver $1 (MS-60+)	$85,000	Auction '84-Paramount July 25-26, 1984
U.S. 1814 half dollar, Capped Bust, Lettered Edge struck in platinum, 50 C., O-107, J-44 (EF-40)	$85,000	Pine Tree Rare Coin Auction-GENA sale Sept. 18-21, 1974
U.S. 1819 $5 Capped Head, 5D/50 (MS-65)	$85,000	Bowers & Ruddy-Garrett Nov. 28-29, 1979
U.S. (1861) undated $2.50 John Parsons & Co., pioneer gold (VF-20) . .	$85,000	Bowers & Ruddy-Garrett Nov. 28-29, 1979
U.S. 1876-CC 20-cent, Seated Liberty (AU-55)	$85,000	Auction '80-Superior, Aug. 14-15, 1980
U.S. 1879 $20 Quintuple Stella, Reeded Edge, pattern gold, J-1643 (Proof)	$85,000	Stack's Jan. 18-21, 1984
U.S. 1901-S quarter dollar, Barber (MS-65)	$85,000	Auction '80-Stack's, Aug. 14-15, 1980
U.S. 1907 $20 Saint-Gaudens, Roman Numerals, High Relief (MS-69).	$85,000	Bowers & Ruddy Garrett II Mar. 26-27, 1980
U.S. 1909 $20 Saint-Gaudens (Matte Proof)	$85,000	Bowers & Ruddy-Garrett Mar. 26-27, 1980
U.S. 1909 $20 Saint-Gaudens (Roman Finish, choice Matte Proof). . . .	$85,000	Bowers & Ruddy Garrett II Mar. 26-29, 1981
U.S. 1914 $20 Saint-Gaudens (choice Matte Proof).	$85,000	Bowers & Ruddy-Garrett Mar. 26-27, 1980
U.S. 1920-S $10 Indian gold (MS-65).	$85,000	Stack's June 22, 1979
U.S. 1932 $20 Saint-Gaudens gold (MS-63).	$85,000	NERCA Apr. 10-12, 1980
U.S. 1933 $10 Indian gold (MS-65)	$85,000	Bowers & Ruddy Galleries Oct. 27-29, 1982
U.S. 1830 $10 Templeton Reid, pioneer gold (EF-40).	$82,500	Bowers & Merena June 18-19, 1984
U.S. 1885 Trade $1 (Proof 63).	$82,500	Auction '84-Superior July 25-26, 1984
U.S. 1875 $5 Coronet gold (Proof)	$81,000	Stack's-Garrett sale Mar. 12-13, 1976
U.S. 1804 quarter dollar, Draped Bust, B-1 (AU-55).	$80,000	Bowers & Ruddy-Garrett Mar. 26-27, 1980
U.S. 1829 $5 Capped Head, Large Planchet, B-1-A (Proof 67).	$80,000	Bowers & Merena Galleries Nov. 7-8, 1983
U.S. 1849 $10 Mormon, pioneer gold (VF-30).	$80,000	ANA '83-Kagin's Aug. 16-20, 1983
U.S. 1860 $20 Liberty gold (Proof 63)	$80,000	Bowers & Ruddy-Garrett Mar. 26-27, 1980
U.S. 1865 $20 Liberty gold (Proof 63)	$80,000	Bowers & Ruddy-Garrett Mar. 26-27, 1980
U.S. 1866 $20 Liberty gold (Proof 63)	$80,000	Bowers & Ruddy-Garrett Mar. 26-27, 1980
U.S. 1879 $4 Coiled Hair Stella, pattern, J-1638 (Proof 65)	$80,000	Stack's Jan. 18-21, 1984
U.S. 1883 $20 Liberty gold (Proof 67)	$80,000	Bowers & Ruddy Galleries Oct. 27-29, 1982
U.S. 1933 $10 Indian Head gold (MS-65)	$79,000	Paramount Sept. 14, 1981
U.S. 1850 $10 Baldwin & Co., "Horseman," pioneer gold (AU-50). . . .	$77,500	Bowers & Ruddy-Garrett Mar. 26-27, 1980
U.S. 1913 $20 Saint-Gaudens (choice Matte Proof).	$77,500	Bowers & Ruddy-Garrett Mar. 26-27, 1980
U.S. (1652) undated sixpence, New England (VF-30)	$75,000	Bowers & Ruddy-Garrett Oct. 1-2, 1980
U.S. 1737 Higley copper, WHEELE GOES ROUND (VF-30)	$75,000	Bowers & Ruddy-Garrett Oct. 1-2, 1980
U.S. 1783 shilling, Chalmers, With Rings (EF-40).	$75,000	Bowers & Ruddy-Garrett Oct. 1-2, 1980
U.S. 1796 half dollar, Draped Bust, 15 Stars (MS-60)	$75,000	Auction '80-Rarcoa Aug. 14-15, 1980
U.S. 1815 $5 Capped Head gold (MS-60).	$75,000	ANA '76-Stack's Aug. 24-28, 1976
U.S. 1826 $2.50 Capped Head gold (MS-60)	$75,000	Bowers & Ruddy-Garrett Mar. 26-27, 1980
U.S. 1829 $5 Capped Head, Large Planchet, B-1-A, C-1 (MS-65/67). . .	$75,000	Bowers & Ruddy Galleries Oct. 27-29, 1982
U.S. 1835 quarter dollar, Capped Bust, Reduced Size (Proof 63)	$75,000	Bowers & Ruddy-Garrett Mar. 26-27, 1980
U.S. 1841 $2.50 Coronet gold (Proof 63)	$75,000	Bowers & Ruddy Oct. 27-29, 1982

U.S. 1874 $10 gold, Judd 1373 (Proof 65/67).	$75,000	Auction '85-Paramount, July 26-27, 1985
U.S. 1884 $20 Liberty gold (Proof 65)	$75,000	Bowers & Ruddy Galleries Oct. 27-29, 1982
U.S. 1907 $20 Saint-Gaudens, Arabic Numerals (Matte Proof)	$75,000	Stack's Sale Dec. 7-8, 1979
U.S. 1912 $20 Saint-Gaudens (choice Matte Proof).	$75,000	Bowers & Ruddy-Garrett Mar. 26-27, 1980
U.S. 1815 $5 Capped Head gold (AU-58/MS-60)	$72,500	Auction '84-Paramount July 25-26, 1984
U.S. 1845 $5 Coronet gold (Proof 65).	$72,500	NERCA - Apr. 10-12, 1980
U.S. 1851 $5 Dunbar & Co., pioneer gold (EF-40)	$72,500	Auction '79-Rarcoa July 27, 1979
U.S. 1854 Kellogg & Co. $20 gold (Proof 63)	$72,500	Auction '85-Superior, July 26-27, 1985
U.S. 1854-D $3 Indian gold (MS-60)	$72,500	Auction '81-Rarcoa July 23-24, 1981
U.S. 1883 $20 Liberty gold (Proof).	$72,500	Stack's Garrett sale Mar. 12-13, 1976
U.S. 1884 $20 Liberty gold (Proof).	$72,500	Stack's Garrett sale Mar. 12-13, 1976
U.S. 1911 $20 Saint-Gaudens (choice Matte Proof).	$72,500	Bowers & Ruddy-Garrett Mar. 26-27, 1980
U.S. 1933 $10 gold, Indian Head (MS-63)	$72,000	Bowers & Merena Inc., June 23-25, 1986
U.S. 1889 $20 gold, Coronet (Proof 65)	$72,500	Superior May 31-June2, 1987.
U.S. 1933 $10 Indian gold (MS-60)	$71,000	Sotheby's Mar. 4, 1983
U.S. 1798 $5 Small Eagle gold (VF-30).	$70,000	Bowers & Ruddy Galleries Oct. 27-29, 1982
U.S. 1804 quarter dollar, Heraldic Eagle (MS-65, prooflike)	$70,000	Auction '80-Stack's Aug. 14-15, 1980
U.S. 1824 $5 Capped Head gold (MS-65).	$70,000	NERCA Apr. 10-12, 1980
U.S. 1827 quarter dollar, Capped Bust, original, Curled Base 2 (Proof)	$70,000	Auction '80-Stack's Aug. 14-15, 1980
U.S. 1828 $5 Capped Head gold (AU-50)	$70,000	Bowers & Ruddy, Garrett Nov. 28-29, 1979
U.S. 1838-O half dollar, Capped Bust, Reeded Edge (Proof).	$70,000	Stack's Feb. 10-13, 1982
U.S. 1933 $10 Indian Head gold (MS-63)	$70,000	Stack's Feb. 2-4, 1983
U.S. 1848 $2.50 Coronet gold, CAL. (MS-65)	$70,000	Bowers & Ruddy-Garrett Mar. 26-27, 1980
U.S. 1856-O $20 Liberty gold, (EF-40)	$70,000	Stack's Sale June 22, 1979
U.S. 1857 $10 Coronet gold (Proof)	$70,000	Bowers & Ruddy Oct. 27-29, 1982
U.S. 1874 $20 Liberty gold (Proof).	$70,000	Bowers & Ruddy-Garrett Mar. 26-27, 1980
U.S. 1875 $3 gold, choice Proof	$70,000	Stack's, Oct. 22-23, 1986
U.S. 1933 $10 gold, Indian Head, BU	$70,000	Stack's, May 2, 1986
U.S. 1933 $10 gold Indian Head, BU	$69,000	Stack's, Jan. 15, 1986
U.S. 1803 silver $1, restrike (Proof 63)	$68,000	Auction '84-Superior July 25-26, 1984
U.S. 1879 $4 Coiled Hair Stella, pattern, J-1638 (Proof 63)	$68,000	Stack's Oct. 27, 1983
U.S. 1796 $2.50 Capped Bust, With Stars (MS-65, prooflike)	$67,500	Auction '84-Stack's July 25-26, 1984
U.S. 1880 $4 Coiled Hair Stella, pattern J-1660, (Proof).	$67,500	Paramount 1975
U.S. 1880 $4 Coiled Hair Stella, pattern, J-1660 (Proof 65)	$67,500	Stack's Jan. 18-21, 1984
U.S. 1908 $20 Saint-Gaudens, With Motto (Proof 65)	$67,500	NERCA-Apr. 10-12, 1980
U.S. 1933 $10 gold Indian Head, choice BU	$66,000	Stack's, Oct. 22-23, 1986
U.S. 1795 Washington Peace medal	$65,000	Bowers & Ruddy-Garrett Mar. 25-26, 1981
U.S. 1798 silver $1, Draped Bust, Heraldic Eagle, Closed Date (MS-65)	$65,000	Bowers & Ruddy Garrett Mar. 26-27, 1981
U.S. 1798 $5 Capped Bust, Small Eagle (EF-40)	$65,000	Auction '83-Paramount July 29-30, 1983
U.S. 1815 $5 Capped Bust (AU-50)	$65,000	Bowers & Ruddy Galleries Oct. 27-29, 1982
U.S. 1821 $2.50 Capped Head (Proof 67).	$65,000	Auction '84-Stack's July 25-26, 1984
U.S. 1829 $5 Capped Head, Large Date (MS-65).	$65,000	ANA '76-Stack's Aug. 24-28, 1976
U.S. 1829 $5 Capped Head, Small Date, Small Planchet (AU-55)	$65,000	Bowers & Ruddy Garrett Nov. 28-29, 1979
U.S. 1850 $10 Baldwin & Co., "Horseman," pioneer gold, (superb gem Uncirculated)	$65,000	Auction '84-Rarcoa July 25-26, 1984
U.S. 1854 gold $1, Type II (Proof 63).	$65,000	Auction '83-Stack's July 29-30, 1983
U.S. 1859 $20 Liberty gold (Proof 65)	$65,000	Bowers & Ruddy Oct. 27-29, 1982
U.S. 1873 $20 Liberty gold (Proof 63)	$65,000	Bowers & Ruddy-Garrett Mar. 26-27, 1980
U.S. 1879 $20 Liberty gold (Proof 63)	$65,000	Bowers & Ruddy-Garrett Mar. 26-27, 1980
U.S. 1880 $4 Flowing Hair Stella, pattern, J-1657 (Proof 63)	$65,000	Bowers & Ruddy-Garrett Nov. 28-29, 1979
U.S. 1880 $4 Flowing Hair Stella, pattern, J-1657 (Proof 63)	$65,000	Auction '80-Stack's Aug. 14-15, 1980
U.S. 1880 $20 Liberty gold (Proof 63)	$65,000	Bowers & Ruddy Garrett II Mar. 26-27, 1980
U.S. 1886-O Morgan $1 (MS-69, prooflike).	$65,000	Superior Galleries, Jan. 27-28, 1986
U.S. 1892 $20 Liberty gold (Proof 63)	$65,000	Bowers & Ruddy-Garrett Mar. 26-27, 1980
U.S. 1895-O Morgan $1 (MS-67)	$65,000	Superior Galleries, Jan. 27-28, 1986
U.S. 1907 $10 Indian, Rolled Rim, With Periods, (MS-60)	$65,000	Kreisberg Gainsborough Sept. 24-26, 1980
U.S. 1907 $20 Liberty gold (Proof 63)	$65,000	Bowers & Ruddy-Garrett Mar. 26-27, 1980
U.S. 1907 $20 Saint-Gaudens, Arabic Numerals (Matte Proof 63).	$65,000	Bowers & Merena Galleries Aug. 3-5, 1983
U.S. 1933 $10 Eagle, choice BU	$65,000	Stack's, Oct. 22-23, 1985
U.S. 1802 silver $1, Draped Bust, restrike (Proof 63)	$64,000	Auction '84-Superior July 25-26, 1984
U.S. 1827 quarter dollar, Capped Bust, original (Proof 63)	$64,000	Stack's Nov. 9-10, 1983
U.S. 1876-CC 20 cents, Seated Liberty (MS-60)	$63,500	ANA 1975
U.S. 1870-S silver $1, Seated Liberty (VF-30)	$63,000	ANA '83-Kagin's Aug. 16-20, 1983
U.S. 1798/7 Capped Head $10 gold, Heraldic Eagle (Unc.).	$62,500	Stack's, Jan. 15, 1986

U.S. 1803 silver $1, Draped Bust, restrike (Proof)	$62,500	Stack's Jan. 18-21, 1984
U.S. 1880 $4 Flowing Hair Stella, pattern, J-1657 (Proof 65)	$62,500	Stack's Jan. 18-21, 1984
U.S. 1914 $5 Indian gold (Matte Proof 65)	$62,500	NERCA Apr. 10-12, 1980
U.S. 1914 $10 Indian gold (Proof 65)	$62,500	NERCA-Apr. 10-12, 1980
U.S. 1838-O half dollar, Capped Bust, Reeded Edge (Proof 60)	$62,000	Auction '79-Superior July 27, 1979
U.S. 1875 $10 Coronet gold (EF-45)	$62,000	ANA-NERCA July 29-Aug. 1, 1979
U.S. 1883 $20 gold (Proof 65+)	$62,000	Auction '85-Superior, July 26-27, 1985
U.S. 1795 $5 Capped Bust, Small Eagle (AU-55)	$60,000	Bowers & Ruddy-Garrett Nov. 28-29, 1979
U.S. 1796/5 half dime, Draped Bust, V-1 (MS-65)	$60,000	Bowers & Ruddy-Garrett Nov. 28-29, 1979
U.S. 1798/7 $10 Capped Bust, 7X6 Stars (AU-50)	$60,000	Auction '79-Rarcoa July 26-27, 1979
U.S. 1803 silver $1, Draped Bust, restrike (Proof 60)	$60,000	NERCA Apr. 10-12, 1980
U.S. 1819 $5 gold, 5D over 50, choice BU	$60,000	Auction '85-Stack's, July 26-27, 1985
U.S. 1822 quarter dollar, Capped Bust, 25/50 C. (Proof)	$60,000	Bowers & Ruddy-Garrett Mar. 26-27, 1980
U.S. 1827 $5 Capped Head (MS-65)	$60,000	Bowers & Ruddy-Garrett Nov. 28-29, 1979
U.S. 1828 quarter dollar, Capped Bust (MS-65)	$60,000	Bowers & Ruddy-Garrett Mar. 26-27, 1980
U.S. 1831 half cent, Classic Head, first restrike (Proof 65)	$60,000	Auction '80-Stack's Aug. 14-15, 1980
U.S. 1834 $2.50 Capped Head, Motto (AU-53)	$60,000	Bowers & Ruddy, Garrett Mar. 26-27, 1980
U.S. 1858 $5 Coronet gold (Proof 65)	$60,000	Stack's Dec. 1974
U.S. 1861-D Coronet half Eagle (MS-63)	$60,000	Mid-America — FUN, Jan. 8-9, 1987
U.S. 1876-CC 20 cents, Seated Liberty (MS-60)	$60,000	Auction '83-Stack's July 29-30, 1983
U.S. 1876-CC 20 cents (MS-65)	$60,000	Bowers & Merena Inc., Nov. 12-13, 1984
U.S. 1879 $4 Flowing Hair Stella, pattern, J-1635 (Proof)	$60,000	Kreisberg Gainsborough Sept. 24-26, 1980
U.S. 1901 $20 Liberty gold (Proof 63)	$60,000	Bowers & Ruddy-Garrett Mar. 26-27, 1980
U.S. 1908 $20 Saint-Gaudens, With Motto (choice Matte Proof)	$60,000	Bowers & Ruddy, Garrett II Mar. 26-27, 1980
U.S. 1909 $5 Indian gold, (Roman Finish Proof 69)	$60,000	NERCA Apr. 10-12, 1980
U.S. 1915 $20 Saint-Gaudens, (choice Matte Proof)	$60,000	Bowers & Ruddy-Garrett Mar. 26-27, 1980
U.S. 1927-D $20 Saint-Gaudens (MS-60)	$60,000	Superior Feb. 19-21, 1973
U.S. 1827/3 quarter dollar, Capped Bust, original (Proof 65)	$59,000	Bowers & Merena Galleries Nov. 9-10, 1983
U.S. 1796 $10 Capped Bust, Small Eagle (MS-63)	$58,000	Auction '80-Paramount Aug. 14-15, 1980
U.S. 1854 $20 Kellogg & Co., pioneer gold (Proof 65)	$58,000	ANA '82-Steve Ivy Aug. 17-21, 1982
U.S. 1830 $5 Templeton Reid, pioneer gold (VF-30)	$57,500	Bowers & Merena June 18-19, 1984
U.S. 1849 $10 Oregon Exchange Co., pioneer gold (AU-50)	$57,500	Auction '79-Rarcoa July 26-27, 1979
U.S. 1851 $20 U.S. Assay Office, K-5, pioneer gold (VF-30)	$57,500	Sotheby's Oct. 14, 1982
U.S. 1879 $4 Flowing Hair Stella, pattern, J-1635 (Proof 60+)	$57,500	Auction '80-Superior Aug. 14-15, 1980
U.S. 1920-S $20 Saint-Gaudens gold (MS-64)	$57,500	NERCA Apr. 10-12, 1980
U.S. 1921 $20 Saint-Gaudens gold (MS-65)	$57,500	Premier Sale, Jan. 30-31, Feb. 1-2, 1984
U.S. 1931 $20 Saint-Gaudens gold (MS-65)	$57,500	Auction '80-Rarcoa Aug. 14-15, 1980
U.S. 1849 $10 Oregon Exchange Co., pioneer gold (AU-50)	$57,500	Auction '79-Rarcoa July 26-27, 1979
U.S. 1863 $10, GOD OUR TRUST motto, pattern, J-349 (Proof)	$57,500	Bowers & Ruddy-Garrett Mar. 26-27, 1980
U.S. 1880 $4 gold, Flowing Hair Stella, gem BU	$57,500	Stack's, May 2-4, 1985
U.S. 1893-O silver $1, Morgan (MS-65, prooflike)	$57,500	Auction '80-Rarcoa Aug. 14-15, 1980
U.S. 1893-S Morgan $1 (MS-65)	$57,500	Superior Galleries, Jan. 27-28, 1986
U.S. 1902 $20 Liberty gold (Proof 63)	$57,500	Bowers & Ruddy-Garrett Mar. 26-27, 1980
U.S. 1920-S $20 Saint-Gaudens gold (MS-65)	$57,500	Auction '80-Rarcoa Aug. 14-15, 1980
U.S. 1931 $20 Saint-Gaudens gold (MS-60)	$57,500	Auction '80-Rarcoa Aug. 14-15, 1980
U.S. 1855 gold $1, Type II (Proof 67)	$57,000	Bowers & Ruddy Galleries Oct. 27-29, 1982
U.S. 1884 $20 Liberty gold (Proof)	$57,000	Stack's Feb. 2-4, 1983
U.S. 1885 gold $1, Type III (Proof 67)	$57,000	Bowers & Ruddy Galleries Oct. 27-29, 1982
U.S. 1879 $4 Coiled Hair Stella, pattern, J-1638 (Proof)	$56,000	Sotheby's Sept. 21, 1982
U.S. 1880 $4 Flowing Hair Stella, pattern, J-1657 (gem Proof)	$56,000	Auction '84-Rarcoa July 25-26, 1984
U.S. (1737) undated Higley copper, THE WHEELE GOES ROUND (Fine)	$55,000	Stack's Dec. 8-9, 1983
U.S. 1783 quint, Nova Constellatio, silver, Type II (AU-55, prooflike)	$55,000	Bowers & Ruddy-Garrett Nov. 28-29, 1979
U.S. 1793 cent, Wreath, S-9, C-9h (MS-65)	$55,000	Auction '83-Superior July 29-30, 1983
U.S. 1795 $5 Capped Bust, Small Eagle (MS-60)	$55,000	Auction '83-Stack's July 29-30
U.S. 1802 silver $l, Draped Bust, restrike, B-8 (Proof)	$55,000	Stack's Jan. 18-21, 1984
U.S. 1804 $2.50 Draped Bust, Heraldic Eagle (MS-65)	$55,000	Auction '81-Rarcoa July 23-24, 1981
U.S. 1819 $5 Capped Head gold, 5D/50 (MS-60)	$55,000	Auction '84-Stack's July 25-26, 1984
U.S. 1827 Capped Head half eagle (MS-65)	$55,000	Superior-Robert Lawson sale, June 3-6, 1985
U.S. 1828/7 $5 Capped Head (AU-55)	$55,000	Auction '80-Paramount Aug. 14-15, 1980
U.S. 1834 $2.50 Classic Head, No Motto (Proof)	$55,000	Auction '84-Rarcoa July 25-26, 1984
U.S. 1851 $5 Dunbar & Co., pioneer gold (EF-40)	$55,000	Stack's Jan. 18-21, 1984
U.S. 1854-D $3 gold (Unc. 60)	$55,000	Mid-America — FUN, Jan. 8-9, 1987
U.S. 1875 $5 Coronet gold (Proof 65)	$55,000	Bowers & Ruddy Galleries Oct. 27-29, 1982

U.S. 1877 $50, William Barber design, copper, pattern, J-1547 (choice Proof)	$55,000	Bowers & Ruddy-Garrett Mar. 26-27, 1980
U.S. 1875 $20 Liberty gold (Proof 63)	$55,000	Bowers & Ruddy Galleries Oct. 27-29, 1982
U.S. 1879 $4 Flowing Hair Stella, pattern, J-1635 (Proof 65)	$55,000	Auction '80-Rarcoa Aug. 14-15, 1980
U.S. 1907 $10 Indian, Rolled Rim, Periods (MS-65+)	$55,000	Auction '79-Paramount July 26-27, 1979
U.S. 1792 disme, Reeded Edge, copper, pattern, J-10 (AU-55).	$54,000	Bowers & Ruddy-Garrett Mar. 25-26, 1981
U.S. 1797 half dollar, Draped Bust, Small Eagle, 15 Stars (MS-60).	$54,000	Auction '81-Rarcoa July 23-24, 1981
U.S. 1879 $4 Flowing Hair Stella, pattern, J-1635 (Proof 65)	$54,000	Superior Galleries Feb. 2-3, 1981
U.S. 1897 $4 gold, Flowing Hair Stella (Proof 67)	$54,000	Bowers & Merena Inc., June 23-25, 1986
U.S. 1796 half cent, Liberty Cap (MS-65, prooflike)	$52,500	Auction '80-Stack's Aug. 14-15, 1980
U.S. 1798/7 $10 Capped Bust, Heraldic Eagle, 9x4 Stars (MS-65)	$52,500	Bowers & Ruddy-Garrett Oct. 1-2, 1980
U.S. 1815 $5 Capped Head gold (AU-50)	$52,500	Stack's Jan. 18-21, 1984
U.S. 1830 $2.50 gold, Capped Head (MS-65).	$52,500	Bowers & Ruddy-Garrett Mar. 26-27, 1980
U.S. 1849 $5 Pacific Co., pioneer gold (AU-55).	$52,500	Stack's Oct. 27, 1983
U.S. 1863 $2.50 Coronet gold (Proof).	$52,500	Garrett sale 1976
U.S. 1876-CC 20 cents, Seated Liberty (Proof)	$52,500	ANA '83-Kagin's Aug. 16-20, 1983
U.S. 1876-CC 20 cents, choice BU	$52,500	Auction '85-Stack's, July 26-27, 1985
U.S. 1879 $4 Coiled Hair Stella, pattern, J-1638 (Proof 65)	$52,500	Stack's Jan. 18-21, 1984
U.S. 1876 $20 Liberty gold (Proof)	$52,500	Bowers & Ruddy, Garrett Mar. 26-27, 1980
U.S. 1884 silver $1, Trade (Proof).	$52,500	Kreisberg sale 1976
U.S. 1893-S silver $1, Morgan (MS-65)	$52,500	Stack's Jan. 18-21, 1984
U.S. 1915-S $50 Panama-Pacific, Round, Octagonal (MS-60)	$52,500	Stack's Feb. 2-4, 1983
U.S. 1920 'S' Pristine Eagle, gem BU	$52,500	Stack's, Oct. 24-26, 1984
U.S. 1933 Indian Head Eagle, choice BU	$52,500	Stack's, Dec. 8-9, 1986
U.S. 1786 New Jersey, Date Under Plow Beam, copper M-8F (EF-40)	$52,000	Bowers & Ruddy-Garrett Oct. 1-2, 1980
U.S. 1795 $10 Capped Bust, Small Eagle (MS-63/MS-65+)	$52,000	Bowers & Ruddy Galleries Oct. 27-29, 1982
U.S. 1893-S silver $1, Morgan (MS-65)	$52,000	Kagin's-GENA Sept. 29-20, 1978
U.S. 1895 Morgan $1 (Proof 67)	$52,000	McIntire, Nov. 14-16, 1985
U.S. 1841 dime, Seated Liberty, No Drapery (EF).	$52,000	Kagin sale 1973
U.S. (1652) undated sixpence, New England (EF-40).	$51,000	Stack's Dec. 8-9, 1983
U.S. gold medal, Gen. Anthony Wayne, Battle of Stony Point, July 15, 1779	$51,000	Sotheby, Parke Bernet June 15, 1978
U.S. 1851 $50 U.S. Assay Office, Without 50, pioneer gold (MS-60).	$51,000	Auction '79-Stack's July 27, 1979
U.S. 1891-O quarter dollar, Barber (Proof)	$51,000	ANA-Steve Ivy Aug. 18-20, 1980
U.S. (1786) undated New Jersey copper, Geo. Washington motif (EF-40)	$50,000	Bowers & Ruddy-Garrett Oct. 1-2, 1980
U.S. 1795 $10 Capped Bust, Small Eagle (MS-60).	$50,000	Auction '83-Stack's July 29-30, 1983
U.S. 1795 $10 Capped Bust, Small Eagle (superb Uncirculated).	$50,000	Auction '84-Stack's July 25-26, 1984
U.S. 1801 silver $1, Draped Bust, restrike, B-5 (Proof)	$50,000	Stack's Jan. 18-21, 1984
U.S. 1803 Draped Bust $1, gem Proof	$50,000	Auction '86-Rarcoa, July 25, 1986
U.S. 1819 $5 Capped Head, 5D over 50, B-1-A (MS-63)	$50,000	Bowers & Merena Galleries Nov. 7-8, 1983
U.S. 1825 $2.50 gold, gem BU	$50,000	Stack's, March 20-22, 1985
U.S. 1827/3 quarter dollar, Capped Bust, original (Proof 65)	$50,000	Bowers & Merena June 19-21, 1984
U.S. 1829 $2.50 Capped Head	$50,000	Greater N.Y. Convention 1976
U.S. 1838-O half dollar, Capped Bust, Reeded Edge (Proof).	$50,000	Auction '84-Rarcoa July 25-26, 1984
U.S. 1842 quarter dollar, Seated Liberty (Proof)	$50,000	Stack's 1975
U.S. 1849-C gold $1, Type I, Open Wreath (AU-53).	$50,000	NERCA Jan. 7-9, 1982
U.S. 1849 $20 Mormon, pioneer gold (EF-40)	$50,000	Bowers & Ruddy-Garrett Mar. 26-27, 1980
U.S. 1851 $20 Baldwin & Co., pioneer gold (EF-40)	$50,000	Stack's Oct. 27, 1983
U.S. 1851 $50 Augustus Humbert, pioneer gold (AU-50)	$50,000	Bowers & Ruddy-Garrett Mar. 26-27, 1980
U.S. 1855 $3 Indian gold (Proof 67)	$50,000	NERCA Apr. 10-12, 1980
U.S. 1863 $2.50 Coronet gold (Proof 63)	$50,000	ANA '79-NERCA July 29-Aug. 1, 1979
U.S. 1863 $10 Coronet gold (Proof)	$50,000	Bowers & Ruddy-Garrett Mar. 26-27, 1980
U.S. 1877 $50, William Barber design, gold, pattern, J-1548	$50,000	The Austin Collection, May 31-June 1, 1974
U.S. 1880 $4 Flowing Hair Stella, pattern, J-1657 (Proof 65)	$50,000	Auction '79-Stack's July 26-27, 1979
U.S. 1880 $4 Flowing Hair Stella, pattern, J-1657 (Proof 67)	$50,000	Bowers & Ruddy Galleries Oct. 27-29, 1982
U.S. 1884 $20 gold (Proof 65).	$50,000	Auction '85-Superior, July 26-27, 1985
U.S. 1920-S $10 Indian gold (MS-65).	$50,000	Auction '80-Superior Aug. 14-15, 1980

World high prices

Athens, Attica, decadrachm, 470 B.C., EF, finest style.	$272,240	Bank Leu-Munzen & Medaillen May 28, 1974
Spain 1870, 100 pesetas, Proof	$190,000	Stack's Sept. 15-16, 1982
Islamic, Post Reform Umayyad gold dinar AH. 77, 697 A.D.	$184,000	Munzen & Medaillen Oct. 9, 1982

Roman aureus of Maxentius, 310-311 A.D.		
Rev: winged Victory offers orb to emperor, FDC.	$171,100	Bank Leu May 8-9, 1979
Roman aureus of Quintillus, 269-270 A.D.		
Rev: Concordia standing left, holds cornucopia		
and standards, EF.	$168,200	Schweizerischer Bankverein Apr. 19, 1980
Canada 1911 silver dollar pattern, 3 known MS65+.	$160,000	Auction '79-Paramount July 26-27, 1979
Naxos, Sicily, tetradrachm, 460 B.C.		
Obv: Bearded Head of Dionysus.		
Rev: Seated Silenus with shallow bowl. Superb	$155,000	Numismatic Fine Arts Sept. 17-18, 1981
Roman aureus of Allectus, London Mint, 286-293 A.D.		
Rev: Pax standing left, EF	$147,500	Bank Leu May 8-9, 1979
Austria seven-ducat, 1486, Archduke Sigismund, FDC.	$145,000	Swiss Bank Corp. Jan. 26-27, 1983
Seleucid, Syria, Antiochus III, gold octadrachm, circa 208-200 B.C.,		
Antioch Mint. Superb.	$140,000	Numismatic Fine Arts March 31, 1987
Syracuse, Sicily, decadrachm, signed by Kimon,		
Superb	$137,500	Schweiz. Bankverein Apr. 19, 1980.
Roman 5 aureii of Galerius Maximian.		
Rev: Mars advancing right.		
Arras hoard, EF.	$132,000	Sotheby's July 1, 1982
Seleucid, Syria, silver tetradrachm, 281-280 B.C. Pergamum Mint. EF		
Obv: Horned horse head right.		
Rev: Elephant right.	$130,000	Numismatic Fine Arts March 31, 1987
Syracuse, Sicily, decadrachm, 405-400 B.C.,		
signed by Kimon, Superb.	$126,506	Bank Leu-Munzen & Medaillen May 28, 1974
Austria double ducat of Maximilian I, 1513-1514, struck		
at Modena. EF.	$125,000	Swiss Bank Corp. Jan. 26-27, 1983
Russian 1825 Constantine I pattern ruble, smooth edge	$122,500	ANA-NERCA July 29-Aug. 1, 1979
Poland King Sigismund III, 1621, 100 gold ducats, EF	$120,000	Stack's Sept. 18, 1980
Syracuse, Sicily, tetradrachm, 410 B.C., signed by Eucleidis.		
Obv: Fast quadriga gallops left, crowned by winged Nike.		
Rev: Head of Athena, plumed helmet.	$110,140	Bank Leu May 13-14, 1986
Amphipoli, Macedon, tetradrachm, 420 B.C.		
Obv: Facing Apollo, curly locks.		
Rev: Hand held candle within square, Superb.	$104,633	Bank Leu May 13-14 , 1986
Rome aureus of Vespasian and Domitilla, A.D. 81-84.		
Rev: Bust of empress, EF.	$100,300	Bank Leu May 8-9, 1979
Roman aureus, Julia Titi, Rome Mint, 90 A.D.		
Rev: peacock, EF	$100,300	Bank Leu May 8-9, 1979
Australia 1855 half sovereign pattern of Queen Victoria, FDC.	$96,050	Spink Nov. 19-20, 1981
Seleucid, Syria, Antiochus III, circa 210 B.C., gold octadrachm.		
Seleucia on the Tigris Mint. Mint State	$95,000	Numismatic Fine Arts March 31, 1987
Seleucid, Syria silver tetradrachm 220-213 B.C. Sardes Mint. EF. . . .	$95,000	Numismatic Fine Arts March 31, 1987
Roman gold medal of Probus, 277 A.D., unique.		
Rev: Three standing figures, EF	$94,400	Bank Leu May 8-9, 1979
Roman eight aureii, Claudius Gothicus, 268-270 A.D.	$92,800	Schweizerischer Bankverein Apr. 19, 1980
Roman aureus of Didia Clara.		
Rev: Hilaritas standing left, EF.	$88,500	Bank Leu May 8-9, 1979
Salzburg, Austria, 25 ducaton 1594 in gold, EF.	$87,500	Spink's-Zurich 1981
Naxos, Sicily, silver tetradrachm 460 B.C. EF		
Obv: Head of Dionysus right		
Rev: Nude Ithyphallic Silenus squatting	$85,000	Numismatic Fine Arts March 31, 1987
Syracuse, Sicily, decadrachm, 400 B.C., signed by Kimon, EF	$82,831	Bank Leu-Munzen & Medaillen May 28, 1974
Spain, Philip III, 1613 50 reales, Segouia Mint	$82,280	Glendining's, May 27, 1987
England, Henry III, 1216-1272, gold penny of 20 pence.		
Obv: Bearded figure of king holding orb and sceptre	$83,233	Spink June 13, 1985
Pontus gold stater of King Pharnaces I, 185-160 B.C., FDC.	$82,000	Numismatic Fine Arts Mar. 25-26, 1976
Australia 1852 £1 Adelaide Govt. Assay Office, Superb	$81,900	Spink's Australia Nov. 19, 1980
Pontus gold stater of King Pharnakes I,		
185-170 B.C., Superb	$79,650	Bank Leu May 8-9, 1979
Scotland 1575 gold £20 of James VI, VF.	$79,200	Paramount July 29-30, 1983
Seleucid, Syria, Seleucus I, tetradrachm,		
Pergamon Mint, about 280 B.C., EF.	$78,313	Bank Leu May 28, 1974
Syracuse, Sicily, tetradrachm 410 B.C., EF		
Obv: Facing helmeted Athena.	$78,313	Bank Leu May 28, 1974

Roman aureus of Brutus, 43-42 B.C., an Asia Minor Mint EF	$76,700	Bank Leu May 8-9, 1979
Syracuse, Sicily, decadrachm, 480-479 B.C., quadriga and olive-crowned female, Demareteion, signed by Evrakoeio, VF	$76,250	Schweizerischer Bank Oct. 16, 1979
Naxos, Sicily, silver tetradrachm 460-B.C. Obv: Head of Bacchus right. Rev: Seated Silenus with shallow bowl, EF	$75,301	Bank Leu May 28, 1974
Roman gold medallion of 5 aureii of Constantius I, Chlorus, A.D. 293-305, Trier Mint. Rev: Mars advancing right. About EF	$75,000	NFA-Bank Leu May 16-18, 1984.
Roman gold medallion of 12 aureii, Gallienus. Obv: Half-length bust of Gallienus.	$75,000	Sfpink-London Oct. 9, 1984
Roman aureus, Carus and Carinus, A.D. 282-284. Rev: Concordia standing, FDC.	$73,750	Bank Leu May 8-9, 1979
Salzburg, Austria, 1504 Rubentaler, EF.	$72,500	Spink-Zurich, 1981
Hungary 50 ducats, 1677, 78 mm, unique	$71,000	Spink & Son.-Galerie de Monnaies 1973
Amphipolis, Macedon, tetradrachm, about 375 B.C., with facing Apollo, Superb.	$70,800	Bank Leu May 8-9, 1979
Seleucid, Syria, Timarchus 161 B.C., tetradrachm, Seleucia on the Tigres Mint. EF	$70,000	Numismatic Fine Arts March 31, 1987
Seleucid, Syria, Seleucis III, circa 226 B.C., gold octadrachm EF. Antioch Mint	$70,000	Numismatic Fine Arts March 31, 1987
Kamarina, Sicily, didrachm of 410 B.C., silver 8.32 grams	$68,000	1975
Roman aureus of Severina 270-275 A.D., Sisca Mint. Rev: Concordia standing, EF.	$67,850	Bank Leu May 8-9, 1979
Roman solidus of Fausta, 324-325 A.D. Rev: Salus standing facing, EF	$67,850	Bank Leu May 8-9, 1979
Scotland 1576 £20 of boy King James VI, VF.	$67,500	NASCA 1976
Australia 1887 £1 gold, Sydney Mint, FDC.	$67,100	Spink's Australia, Nov. 22, 1979
Roman aureus of Diadumenian, 217-218 A.D. Rev: Salus standing facing.	$65,825	1973
Athens, Attica, decadrachm 490-407 B.C., Fine/VF	$65,000	Vinchon Apr. 14, 1984
Catana, Sicily, silver tetradrachm 460-450 B.C., EF-VF	$65,000	Numismatic Fine Arts Sept. 17-18, 1982
Spain 100 pesetas, 1871, Amadeo I, Proof.	$65,000	Stack's Sept. 15-16, 1982
Thraco-Macedonian region, Acanthus? circa 525-510 B.C., electrum stater, nearly Superb. Obv: Lactating lioness kneeling left. Rev: Two incuses.	$65,000	Numismatic Fine Arts March 31, 1987
Modena, Italy, Francesco I d'este 1633 gold 12 scudi d'oro EF.	$63,250	Swiss Bank Jan. 27-29, 1981
Australia 1859 half sovereign, Sydney Mint EF	$63,180	Spink Australia Nov. 19, 1980
England 1703 gold five guineas, First Bust type	$63,180	1975
Roman aureus of Didius Julianus 193 A.D. Rev: Rector, holding globe, EF	$61,950	Bank Leu May 8-9, 1979
Roman solidus of Licinia Eudoxia Rev: Empress enthroned, Superb	$61,950,	Bank Leu, May 8-9, 1979
Roman aureus of Sextus Julius Saturnius about 280 A.D., struck in Alexandria	$61,500	1972
Roman medallion of 4 aurei, Maximian Hercules, Trier Mint	$61,083	Spink, London
Arcadia or Pheneos, Peloponnes, silver stater, about 350 B.C., EF. Obv: Bust of Demeter facing right. Rev: Hermes wakening	$60,577	Bank Leu May 13-14, 1986
First Jewish Revolt, shekel of Year 5 (A.D.70)	$60,000	Superior 1974
Roman aureus of Marius, 268 A.D., Cologne Mint. Rev: Empress enthroned, EF.	$59,305	1972
Roman half solidi of Crispus 319-320, Trier Mint. Rev: Captive and armament, EF.	$59,000	Bank Leu May 8-9, 1979
Archduke Ferdinand III, 100 ducats, 1629 Glatz Mint, King of Bohemia and Hungary, VF	$57,494	Sotheby's March 4, 1983
Roman aureus of Victorinus, 268-270 A.D., Cologne Mint. Rev: Bust of helmeted Roma facing right, EF.	$57,230	Bank Leu May 8-9, 1979
Naxos, Sicily, silver drachm, 540 B.C.,EF Obv: Bearded head of Bacchus left. Rev: Bunch of grapes. EF.	$57,228	Bank Leu May 28, 1974
England, Henry VII sovereign 1485-1509, Class B. Mint mark cross and fitchee. VF.	$56,880	Spink June 2, 1983
Australia, New South Wales 1813 Holey dollar, EF.	$56,500	Spink-Aust. Nov. 19-20,1981

Pantikapaion, Crimea, gold stater, 350 B.C.
Obv: Head of Pan facing left
Rev: Griffin with spear in teeth............................ $56,171 Bank Leu May 13-14, 1986
Italy, Victor Emanuel II, 1864-T 50 lire, EF .... $56,100 Swiss Bank Jan. 27-29, 1981
Roman aureus of Domitian and Domitia, 81-84 EF .... $56,050 Bank Leu May 8-9, 1979
Roman 2 solidii of Constantine the Great, 309-310 A.D.
Rev: Emperor standing right holds spear and orb, FDC......... $56,050 Bank Leu May 8-9, 1979
Zeugatania, Siculo-Punic tetradrachm, 360 B.C., EF
Obv: Head of Dido left.
Rev: Lion left, palm tree behind. EF .... $56,000 Num. Fine Arts Mar. 25-26, 1976
Naxos, Sicily, tetradrachm 430 B.C., EF $56,000 1975
Pantikapaion, Crimea, gold stater, 340 B.C., Superb .... $55,722 Bank Leu May 28, 1974
Roman aureus of Florianus, 275-276 A.D.
Rev: Sol drives fast quadriga right, EF...................... $55,460 Bank Leu May 8-9, 1979
Roman aureus of emperor Postumus, 259-268 A.D., Cologne Mint.
Rev: Hercules wrestles Nemian lion, EF .... $54,280 Bank Leu May 8-9, 1979
Akragas, Sicily, tetradrachm 415 B.C.
Obv: Crab and scylla.
Rev: Two eagles on hare, EF., test cut obverse .... $54,216 Bank Leu Apr. 25-26, 1978
Ionia electrum stater 500 B.C................................ $54,000 1975
Holy Roman Empire, Maximilian I half schauguldiner
1511, gold.. $53,300 Spink & Son and Galerie de Monnaies-1974
Roman aureus of Diadumenian.
Rev: Ruler standing with three legionary standards, Superb...... $52,867 Bank Leu May 13-14, 1986
Bologna, Italy, Gregory XIII (1572-1585) ducatone
da Un'ocia, year VIII, VF .... $52,800 Sotheby & Co.-June 12, 1974
Great Britain 1839 £5 gold pattern Una and the Lion .... $52,500 RARCOA Mar. 13-15, 1981
Phocis, Delphoi stater, 350-338 B.C.
Obv: Head of Demeter. Rev: Apollo Pythios seated. Superb ..... $52,500 Vinchon Apr. 14, 1984
England, Elizabeth I, royal, Fifth issue, Lombardic A
reverse. EF... $52,360 Spink Coin Auction June 4, 1980
Barca, Cyrenaica, tetradrachm, 360-B.C.,VF-EF .... $51,920 Bank Leu May 8-9, 1979
Roman aureus of Matidia 119 A.D.
Rev: Pietas with 2 small children, EF........................ $51,920 Bank Leu May 8-9, 1979
Roman aureus of Maximinus, 236 A.D.
Rev: Providentia with horn of plenty, EF .... $51,920 Bank Leu May 8-9, 1979
Selinus, Sicily, tetradrachm 409 B.C., Apollo and Artemus
in quadriga, river God Selinos, FDC .... $51,850 Swiss Bank Oct, 16, 1979
First Jewish Revolt, half shekel of Year 4 (A.D.69)
edge reveals traces of claw mount VF........................ $51,603 Bank Leu
Aenos, tetradrachm 394-392 B.C............................. $51,204 Bank Leu May 28, 1974
England 1820 pattern £5 by B. Pistrucci, Large Bust $51,030 1975
Thailand 1918 50-ticals bank note,.......................... $51,000 Spink & Son, Singapore Feb. 20-22, 1987
Roman aureus of Magnia Urbica, 282-284 A.D.
Rev: Concordia seated left, FDC........................... $50,740 Bank Leu May 8-9, 1979
England, Chas. I, Oxford triple unite 1643. Mint mark
small lis. Unc... $50,560 Spink's, London June 2, 1983
Bavaria 1869 one krone, Ludwig II, FDC .... $50,470 Spink & Son, Zurich June 18-19, 1980
Greece electrum stater of an unidentified barbarian tribe
with kneeling steer, 500 B.C. EF........................... $50,150 Bank Leu May 8-9, 1979
Syracuse, Sicily, decadrachm of the Euainetus type
385-380 B.C., EF....................................... $50,000 Numismatic Fine Arts-June 6, 1980
Ionia double siglos of Samos 394 B.C......................... $50,000 1975
Seleucid Empire tetradrachm of Alexander I Bala
154-144 B.C... $50,000 1975
Germany 20-ducat 1646 of Archduke Ferdinand Charles,
Hall Mint, EF .... $50,000 Swiss Bank Corp. Jan. 26-27, 1983
Seleucid, Syria, tetradrachm of Cleopatra-Thea, 126-125 B.C.
Ake-Ptolemais Mint. EF.................................. $50,000 Numismatic Fine Arts March 31, 1987
Seleucid, Syria, two and one-half stater of Demetrus I, 151-150 B.C.
Fleur-de-coin.. $50,000 Numismatic Fine Arts March 31, 1987

Potpourri 18

Ordering coins

Ordering coins from dealers is a simple matter. We assume the dealer has advertised or issued a price list. The buyer picks out the coin or coins he wants, and then reads the instructions at the beginning of the price list or the end of the advertisement.

If there is a minimum order the dealer will accept, the buyer must reach it or not buy from that dealer. If the dealer requires an added amount for postage, insurance and handling, the order must include it.

The instructions may say that a postal money order is required, or a bank certified check, or that a delay will be made to allow a personal check to clear the banks. The buyer will take note of all this, and do as instructed and be prepared to wait for his order, from two to four weeks, depending on distance from the dealer and how payment is made.

Half that time will be credited to the check clearing, and the other half to the time it takes for the mail to get the shipment through. This can be up to three weeks or so from coast to coast, after the check clears if that is the method of payment.

Wait at least three weeks before sending a query to the dealer, but it is justified after that time. However, it should be a tactful one and include a return envelope or government postcard for reply. There is no reason why a buyer can't write and ask for the date of mailing, so he can check with his local post office. No dealer would get mad at that.

Buying by mail is a two-way proposition, of course. The dealer should hold up his end. One of the biggest "blow-ups" on record was caused when a dealer didn't.

A California collector ordered a good-sized package of rolls from an Eastern dealer. The latter duly sent them by express, but didn't notify the buyer. The buyer didn't receive the coins, and wrote the dealer. The latter assumed the shipment would have arrived by that time, and did not answer the letter. The buyer got madder and madder, and complained to *Coin World*.

Final investigation disclosed that the shipment arrived at the nearest express office the day the agent went on vacation. He didn't notify the addressee, and his substitute thought he had. The vacation lasted a month, and there sat the coins, with nobody aware of it, and the buyer ready to sue everybody he could think of.

One little postcard from the dealer at shipment, or one polite query from the buyer asking when the coins were shipped and how, with a postcard for reply, would have avoided the whole mess.

Finally, to the buyer, do not forget to include your name and full address including zip code when sending the order, both inside and outside the envelope, preferably printed or typed. More disputes have been caused by the buyer's failure to include a legible or any return address than all other causes put together. And, strange as it may seem, some buyers have been known to forget to sign their check.

Just a few more tips to ensure that transactions go smoothly. If the seller says returns will be allowed for three, five or seven days or any other period, for unsatisfactory merchandise, he means it. If the buyer needs more time to get a coin authenticated or graded elsewhere, he should ask for it. He would also be wise to ask for a written guarantee of authenticity with the coin, if it's worth more than a few dollars.

Incidentally, the *Coin World* advertising

department has a policy that time limits are invalid if a coin should turn out to be counterfeit. But the buyer has to prove he didn't switch, if there is any question.

If an advertisement contains the phrase "prices subject to change without notice," in a period of fast-rising markets, the buyer should be prepared to get his check returned. If the coin is one-of-a-kind, he should also be prepared for a "sold-out" answer to his order.

Finally, in some cases it is wise for the buyer to phone the dealer for a confirmation of an order at a given price. The buyer should get the name of the person confirming the order at that price, and how many days he will be allowed to get the payment in.

Most transactions are simple, and most dealers and buyers are well-meaning and honest. There are a few exceptions on both sides. If either buyer or dealer should get "taken" once, they will be suspicious from then on, and that will make things harder for everybody thereafter. If both dealer and buyer stick to the "Golden Rule" the hobby and business of numismatics would be much more pleasant for everyone.

Whether buying or selling coins should be any different from buying and selling neckties or shoes is an interesting question. However, that there is a difference is one of the facts of life, and collectors would be advised to keep that in mind. It is true for all hobbies, and dealers who cater to hobbyists are likely to be different from those who sell the necessities of life.

Mailing coins

The Postal Service is usually blamed for lost coins. Most of the time the blame should be placed on the sender.

Mail, on its long and often arduous journey from sender to addressee, is subjected to much handling, by many people.

In most cases, it is recommended you write or call the person you are sending coins before doing so. Postal law permits individuals to keep unsolicited material, including coins, although that has never been a major problem in the hobby. Dealers, authenticators and other professional hobbyists expect to receive coins, but a letter asking permission to send coins is a courtesy and a form of protection. *Coin World* advertisers are required to accept mailings and to return them if not purchased.

The sender should provide as much protection as possible for his letters and packages. Enclose the coin in the readily available 2X2 coin envelopes or holders. Tape or staple the holders between cardboard. "Jiffy" bags are no longer acceptable by the post office for registered mail.

Include a letter identifying the coin(s) and stating the reason they are being sent. The person who is to examine the coins should not have to waste time trying to figure out why the coins were sent.

Your letter of transmittal should also include instructions for the return of the coins and sufficient return postage to provide whatever level of protection you wish.

Registered mail provides signature protection for the contents. That means that anyone handling the package en route must sign for it. Registered mail also provides for a de-

clared value up to the amount specified by the sender upon payment of the proper fee.

Insured mail can go via first class, third class or fourth class mail, although the sender must request first class mail if he prefers faster service. It provides indemnity for declared value but only up to $200. Contrary to popular belief, insuring a package does not guarantee delivery. It guarantees only that the sender will be reimbursed for loss in transit. Further, the sender is not guaranteed to recover the amount declared.

The Postal Service will often attempt to establish a value for the lost coins based on findings of a disinterested authority. This is one of the ways by which the Postal Service attempts to protect itself against fraud.

If the coin has no intrinsic value, it can be sent via certified mail. A receipt is issued to the sender and, for an additional fee, a return receipt can be obtained showing when, where and to whom the mail was delivered.

Both registered and certified mail are traceable from initial mailing to ultimate delivery.

Express mail ensures the fastest possible delivery, often overnight between larger communities. The initial cost is $10.75 for up to two pounds; rates increase with greater weight. Express mail is insured up to $50,000.

Whatever means of mailing is selected, be certain that the package is securely sealed. An authenticator's nightmare begins with the receipt of a package that is empty because the sender neglected to seal it properly.

Unless special arrangements have been made, limit the number of coins sent at any one time to three or four. The person to whom you are sending them will also be receiving coins from many others. He would be forced to ignore your large number of coins in order to satisfy a greater number of people who have complied with this basic tenet of courtesy. His only alternative to ignoring your coins would be to ignore all his other correspondents. So, no matter which avenue he chooses, he is automatically guilty of slighting someone.

Auctions — how to participate

The following section was prepared by Raymond N. Merena, with his associate, Q. David Bowers. Merena is president of Auctions by Bowers and Merena Inc., which with its predecessor firm, Bowers and Ruddy Galleries, is the holder of eight of the top 10 world's numismatic auction records, including that for the most valuable coin ever to cross the auction block, the 1787 Brasher doubloon at $725,000.

By Raymond N. Merena

Auctions may well be the truest test of coin values. A rare coin auction, nationally advertised and presented in an authoritative catalog, sets the stage for bidding competition. Ultimately, a coin (or any other object) is worth what someone will pay for it. An auction separates "the men from the boys," as they say, and results in a piece bringing its true value. Asking price, as reflected in dealers' price lists, may represent wishful thinking, where an actual auction transaction generally represents true value.

As such, the reader seeking what a coin is worth would do well to study auction prices realized. While one can point to all sorts of price lists, guides, market indexes, and the like, a list of auction prices realized is usually much more realistic. The situation, however, is not as simple as it sounds. When analyzing an auction list of prices it is important to know how the dealer graded his coins. And, as noted, it is important that the sale be widely advertised and made known to specialists in a given area. It is important to know whether or not reserves are disclosed. If a piece sold for, say, $10,000, but went back to the original owner, this is not as meaningful as knowing that it sold for $10,000 to an outside collector or dealer.

The usefulness of auction records is echoed by Walter Breen, who in his *Encyclopedia of United States Half Cents,* notes: "What of prices? I have no better answer at the moment than to list the top coins of each variety known to me, together with their auction records. In a market that is far more unstable than it was in previous decades, this seems to be the only sensible procedure. ... Values will be established by subsequent auction results. Fixed-price lists too often represent dealers' dreams; they may or may not change hands at the stated values, or in trade, or in negotiated agreement at lower (or sometimes higher!) figures. ..."

If you are a coin buyer you may wish to consider the advantages of auction. If you are a coin seller, some of what I have to say may be valuable to you. In the following paragraphs are some of my personal observations based upon cataloging and selling some of the most important collections ever to cross the auction block. First, let me discuss different types of "auctions," some of which are not auctions in true sense.

Mail-bid sales

Mail-bid sales have a rich numismatic tradition. B. Max Mehl, the famous Fort Worth, Texas, dealer, conducted many auctions during his long career, but as no participation by floor bidders was involved, and as all participation was by mail, the term "mail-bid sale" would be more appropriate today — even for such landmark events as his Dunham Collection which in 1941 stood as one the greatest cabinets of American coins ever dispersed. Although it was not announced at the time and, in fact, was kept a secret until Q. David Bowers unearthed information concerning it in the files of John Work Garrett (presently in Johns Hopkins University), Mehl bought the collection outright, so when it was "auctioned" he was simply soliciting bids on his own material, which points out another feature of certain auctions that will be discussed later.

The typical mail-bid sale, many of which appear in the pages of *Coin World* and other numismatic periodicals, consists of a listing of coins or other numismatic items for sale. Usually such descriptions are brief and consist of little more than the date, Mint mark (if any), and grade. Prospective buyers are invited to submit bids. Sometimes estimates are provided.

As is true of any auction sale, it is important to read the terms of sale stated by the seller. There are no standard rules in this regard, although some (*Coin World* for one) have suggested guidelines. Determine the following things:

What is my return privilege? If I disagree with the grade of a coin can I return it? If so, what is the time period involved? Do I have to pay for the lots immediately, or are credit terms given? Can I bid on several lots but limit my total purchases to a stated amount? What is the reputation of the auctioneer or seller? Are there any extra charges such as postage, handling, or a buyer's fee? If my bid is far higher than other bids received, will a reduction be made? What are the other policies of the seller?

Before submitting offers in a mail-bid sale, you must determine the total cost to you. If there is a buyer's fee of 10 percent added, and if you bid $100 on a coin, then your bill, before sales taxes and postage, will be $110. If you have in mind bidding a total of $100 (excluding taxes and handling), you would be better bidding somewhere around $90, for this will be closer to $100 when the 10 percent is added.

The terms for a mail-bid sale may include payment of state or local sales tax, postage and handling charges, some or all of these. These costs, too, must be factored into the total amount you wish to pay for a given item. In particular, sales taxes can be costly.

The bidding procedure is often outlined in the terms of sale. In some auctions the highest bid received takes the lot for the total amount of the bid, without regard to what the underbid might be. For example, if you bid $100 on a lot and the next highest bid is $50, you are charged the full $100 price. Other sellers may adopt some percentage increment over the next highest bid, whereby you pay an advance of 5 to 10 percent over the lower figure. In this example, you would pay, say, 10 percent over the next highest $50 bid, or a total of $55. This gives you the advantage of buying the piece at the lowest possible prices, almost as if it were a public sale and you were bidding in person.

Return privileges are an important consideration. While most auctions with floor bidding permit no returns by floor bidders, mail bids are often different. Read carefully to determine exactly what your rights and privileges are. For example, if you do not agree with the grade of a coin, can you return it within a certain period?

Some people conducting mail-bid sales permit telephone bids. In this way you can call the seller and determine what the bid level is at a given time and then submit your offers accordingly. Other mail-bid sales are strictly that, sales by mail with no telephone calls allowed.

Assuming that the pieces are properly graded — and proper grading must always be an important factor — bidding in a mail-bid sale can be a very enjoyable and profitable way to add to your collections. You are buying the coins you want at the prices you want to pay, an ideal situation.

Public auctions

Most larger auctions are of the public variety with in-person attendance by bidders in addition to bids by mail. An important difference between public auctions and mail-bid sales is that, with few exceptions, public coin sale auctioneers do not permit items to be returned. An exception might be in the case of authenticity, but not grading. Other auctioneers may have slightly more lenient rules for mail bidders but with the proviso that all sales to floor bidders are final without any possibility of return (except for reasons of authenticity). So, before bidding in a public auction, check the terms of sale carefully. If you are not familiar with the auctioneer or his grading standards, it may pay you to examine the coins in advance or give your bids to a dealer or fellow collector who will be attending the sale in person and who can view the lots beforehand.

Beginning shortly after 1980 it became the custom of American auction houses to charge a buyer's fee, often 10 percent, in addition to the "hammer price." This procedure had been in effect among art and antique auction houses for many years earlier. Soon, nearly all coin firms adopted this procedure. By this method, a coin which has a hammer price of $1,000 and which is sold for $1,000 at the sale has 10 percent added so that the invoice totals $1,100. This arrangement took root when the auction houses decided to split the commission between seller and buyer. Under such an arrangement, usually a smaller charge is levied to the seller.

Under the old system, if a coin brought $1,100, an auction house might charge the seller 20 percent, thus deducting $220 from the proceeds and giving the seller a check for $880. Under the system with a buyer's fee of 10 percent, if the hammer price is $1,000, the buyer still pays $1,100 ($1,000 plus 10 percent), while the seller gets $1,000 less 10 percent, or $900. Mathematically the auction house is at a very slight disadvantage (paying the consignor $20 more under this method than under the old method), but the idea of spreading the fee between buyer and seller is sufficiently popular that most sellers have adopted it. As the auctioneer will announce only the hammer price at the sale, be sure to do your calculations in advance so that you do not pay more than you want to once the buyer's fee is added.

Indeed, advance preparation on all fronts is suggested for participation in a public auction if you plan to attend in person. All auctions have a lot viewing period in which time the individual coins, paper money, and the like can be examined in detail. Take your auction catalog with you and make appropriate notes. If you agree with the grading and description, then a simple check mark can indicate this. On the other hand, if you feel that the coin is under-graded or over-graded, this can be noted as well. Sometimes two coins can be in an identical grade, but one will be more appealing due to the presence of attractive toning, the sharpness of strike, or some other consideration. Any extra factors that influence positively or negatively the value of a coin should be likewise noted.

Once you have completed lot viewing, then determine the price you want to bid on each lot. "Auction fever" is well known, and many are the bidders who later say they were carried away during the heat of a sale. While saving your bidding calculations until the sale takes place may have the advantage that you can gauge the market at the sale itself, a more leisurely view can be obtained if you do your calculations prior to the auction.

A simple way is to enter the maximum hammer price you want to pay into your catalog. As other people may see your catalog during the sale, you may wish to do this in code. There are several ways of doing this. One way is to put an irrelevant figure before and after the price you want to pay. In such an example, the number 75003 would indicate that you want to bid $500 once the first and last numbers were ignored. Or, you can use a letter substitution code whereby a word with 10 non-repetitive letters is used. As an example, the term HARDMONEYS would be used whereby H=1, A=2, R=3, and so on. The notation "MSS" in your auction catalog would indicate that you want to pay a maximum of $500 for the lot. Other 10 letter words I have seen used include CHARLESTON, TRADE QUICK, and BRICKMASON. In going over the ledgers of old-time collector S. Benton Emery recently, I found that around the turn of the present century he used the code INDUSTRYCO when making annotations.

When the sale time arrives, be there early. By this time you will have viewed the lots, done your homework so far as prices are concerned, and will have established credit with the auctioneer. Arrive early at the sale, sign a registration card, and determine where you want to sit in the audience.

Over the years, I have heard many ideas concerning the best place to be when a sale takes place. Ask a dozen veteran sale-attenders and you are apt to get a dozen different answers! One leading Maryland dealer invariably sits in the front row near the aisle. He figures that the auctioneer will see him first, will recognize his signals without mistake, and may give him precedence in case of a tie bid. Further, by sitting in the front row his hand movements, if done in front of his chest, cannot be observed by anyone in the rows behind, thus his bids are more confidential than would otherwise be the case.

A New York City dealer I know always sits in the front row, but slightly to the side so that he can watch other people in the front row. Still another dealer, this one from New Jersey, likes nothing better than to sit even with the first row but far off to the right, so he can watch the front row, watch the audience, but not have his own actions easily observed.

A leading California bidder, a gentleman who has attended many of our sales over the years, usually sits three or four rows back from the front. In this way, he can see the bidding action in the front rows and get a general idea of what's going on, but still his movements cannot be seen by many in the audience. Several other acquaintances like nothing better than to sit against the back wall so that they have a view of the audience in front of them. Who is bidding seems to be more important than the price paid, it would seem!

So, study the possibilities and the room layout, pick a place where the auctioneer can see you and where you will not be distracted by nearby doors or openings, and settle down for some serious bidding.

How to bid once you have found your seat is another area that is far from standard. Chances are that you will be provided with a card or a paddle with a number on it, such number representing that given to you when you registered at the door. The typical bidder will hold his paddle in the air until his maximum bid has been reached, at which time he will take it down, either owning the coin or not owning it as competition dictates. However, I have seen people stand up straight as an arrow, bidder paddle aloft toward the ceiling, looking like the Statue of Liberty. Other bidders will wildly wave the paddle high in the air to the left and to the right as if they were flagging down a runaway express train! Still others may keep the paddle in front of them for identification but indicate bids by a nod of the head, the lifting of a pencil, or a slight hand movement.

Don't get too complicated. There is nothing at all wrong with being discreet. If you want to create the least amount of attention, sit near the front where the auctioneer can see you and make slight movements while bidding. If the auctioneer fails to notice your bid, you can always call out, but if the auctioneer knows your specialty is in a particular area, chances are he will look directly at you when coins of your specialty come up. One of the functions of a commercial auctioneer is to know the audience.

Still other bidders will call out a price in an effort to frighten off competition. Time and time again in our sales, I have seen a coin open at, say, $2,000, go to $2,200, $2,400, $2,600, then to be interrupted by a shout, "four thousand dollars!" Of course, the person bidding $4,000 hopes that he will have frightened away all competition, which indeed may be the case. On the other hand, perhaps if he had bid in a more leisurely manner he would have obtained the coin for less. The theory is that another bidder, hearing the shout, would think that the bidder was prepared to go much higher, even if he might not be. It's like a game of poker!

In a large auction there may be many dozens of bidders in attendance. The auctioneer only has one pair of eyes, and with talking among the audience, sharp eyes and careful ears might not be able to detect all bids. So, if your bid is missed, be sure to call out at the time of sale. The auctioneer will usually reopen the lot and recognize your bid. If you wait until several lots have passed, however, the auctioneer may not do this. Or, if the auctioneer simply thinks you are daydreaming and should have been paying attention, he may elect not to reopen the lot. So, when bidding, be alert!

Mail bidding in public sales

Public auctions usually encourage participation by mail as well. My own firm, for one, encourages bidding by mail and devotes a special section of each catalog to instructions in this regard. If you bid by mail, be sure to read the terms of sale carefully, for mail bidding in an auction is different from ordering coins on approval or even from a fixed price list. In general, coins are to be paid for as soon as your invoice is received. One of the terms of sale in my own catalog is especially important — and this particular sale point is found in one form of wording or another in most other sale catalogs as well:

Any claims involving errors in the catalog must be made within three days of receipt of the coins. Grading is a subjective description that represents the opinion of the cataloger as to the state of preservation of a particular coin or lot. "Proof" is used to describe a method of manufacturing and it not a grade or condition. All such terms, including adjectival and numerical descriptions of coins and other numismatic items, are the opinion of the cataloger and are not an attribution. No warranty, whether expressed or implied, is made with repect to such adjectival or numerical descriptions, which can and do vary among experts.

In other words, if you are not certain about grading, then do not bid until you determine that the grade is what you want. The reason for this is that the sale will have floor competition as well, and the floor bidders will have examined the coins in person and will be bidding without a return privilege. If an auctioneer were to accept a mail bid of, say, $2,000 for a coin which is graded Mint State 65, but then after the sale took place the buyer wanted to return it, the auctioneer would not have any possibility to sell it elsewhere, for all the floor bidders would have long since gone home. There would be no alternative except to return the coin to the consignor as an unsold item. It would be far better to have not entered the mail bid at all, but, rather, let the coin sell in a floor competition where chances are good that it would have brought the same price or more.

Some auction houses offer special services for mail bidders. One of these is a "maximum expenditure" service. Under this procedure you can mark at the top of your bid sheet the total amount you wish to spend. You can then submit bids for amounts up to several times that of the maximum expenditure. A customer representative will personally attend to your bid sheet by bidding from the auction floor, or this may be handled by a computer (which keeps a running track of the sale as it progresses). In this way, you can bid on, say, $5,000 worth of coins and be assured of winning no more than $1,000 worth. This sharply increases your chances for success.

Another service is that called "one lot only" whereby if you wish to purchase only one example of a coin of which several examples appear in a sale, you can mark these on a list, and your bid will be entered progressively as the different lots appear in the catalog. Then when (and if) one lot is bought, your bidding will stop there. I remember one sale in which we had several dozen beautiful Uncirculated examples of the 1925 Vancouver commemorative half dollar. By bids such as this, clients could buy just one coin but could spread their chances of success by competing on many different lots until one was finally obtained.

When you bid by mail, be sure to do some homework before sending your bid sheet. Just as the floor bidder has to do, carefully calculate the most you want to pay. Remember that the buyer's fee, if there is one, applies to mail bidders as well as floor bidders, so govern your top bids accordingly. If the sale has many different items offered, you may wish to make up a "work sheet." In this way you can adjust and readjust your prices and the coins you bid on until you have it in final form. Then enter your bids on the bid sheet provided with the catalog.

I have found that it is best to write your bids in ink (not pencil, for pencil tends to blur), or type them, being sure there is no confusion among similar numbers such as 9 and 4 or 1 and 7. After you have filled out your bid sheet, then carefully recheck each and every bid. Remember, if you bid $500 on a lot by mistake, you may wind up owning it! The bid sheet is a legal contract, and when you sign your bid and send it in, you are bound to abide by the terms.

If you are new to an auction firm, a deposit and reference may be required. These deposits are refundable if your bids are not successful.

Be sure to send in your bid sheet as early as possible, this is for two reasons: First, this will help avoid any delays in the mail. Second, in the event of a tie bid, your bid will win if received first. As a further consideration, if the auctioneer has any questions when your bid sheet is received, he has time to contact you. It is always a good idea to put your telephone number on the bid sheet to aid in the event of such a possibility.

Floor-bid only auctions

Another type of auction, and one not frequently encountered, is that in which floor bids are accepted but for which no catalog is issued and there are no mail bids. Auctions conducted by the United States Custom Service, unclaimed packages at the post office, sheriffs' sales, and the like are examples. Sometimes some valuable coins can be acquired in this way. In such auctions, everything is usually sold "as is" without any re-

course at all, even if a coin proves to be counterfeit. So, before bidding, be sure you know what you are doing when it comes to the matter of authenticity, for if there is a problem later you will be out of luck. Still, this should not deter you from bidding, and if you do not know about authenticity yourself, then it may pay to enlist the aid of an expert.

Such sales are usually not advertised in coin periodicals, so the best way to find out about them is in local newspapers or in government publications. Your bank or attorney may be able to tell you of such events. They are few and far between, but occasionally nice pieces can be found.

Another type of floor-bid only sale is the country auction. Often an estate, a group of antiques, or the like will include some old coins, again usually offered on an "as is" basis. Such sales may be fun to attend, and you may walk away with some nice furniture or paintings, but probably the chance of finding a true bargain among coins is relatively slight, especially if you consider the time and expense involved in attending the sale.

Somewhat related are coin sales held by art auction houses. In this instance, read the terms of sale very carefully, for I have seen art auction house sale catalogs which give the bidder no recourse in the event a coin proves counterfeit, unless the bidder is alert enough to detect the counterfeit coin relatively quickly. Many such sales are sold "as is." As a result, most serious coin collectors do not consign coins to other than numismatic auction specialists, but occasionally art auction houses or antique auction houses will acquire coins as part of an estate or as a result of their reputation in the art or antique field. Such sales can offer excellent values, for often the catalogs are poorly distributed and are not widely advertised. However, grading is apt to be very erratic and, as noted, coins may be sold "as is."

Summary

Over the years, most large collections of United States coins, world coins, and paper money have been formed, at least in part, by bidding at auction. As noted earlier in the present text, auctions give you the ideal possibility of buying the pieces you want at the price you want to pay — not at the price someone else says you should pay. And, auctions represent the true value of a coin. While there may be occasional instances of unknowledgeable bidders bidding against other unknowledgeable bidders, by and large those attending numismatic auctions know what they are doing, and if you pay $2,000 for a coin, you have a reasonable assurance that the price represents the current market value at the time and place of sale.

Bidding in auctions requires some homework, and to be successful, you should be familiar with grading procedures and the grading practices of the dealer conducting the sale. You should read the terms of sale carefully and be prepared to abide by them, and you should spend time studying the pieces you want and formulating in advance the price you wish to pay.

B. Max Mehl, the famous Texas dealer, used to stress the OPPORTUNITIES that his sales presented. It is indeed the case that many extremely rare and one-of-a-kind pieces are available only at auction, and if you do not participate in the sale in which they are offered, you may do without them for a long time, if not forever. My recommendation is to become acquainted with different auction houses. Most offer their catalogs on a subscription basis. The price paid for the catalog includes a key to the prices realized which will be sent to you after the sale. Thus, not only do you have the chance to bid in an auction, but the prices realized list will give you a good view of market values (providing there are not undisclosed reserves or other situations not readily apparent).

For the collector interested in research, I highly recommend seeking out back issues of auction catalogs. How many times has an Uncirculated 1921-S half dollar appeared at auction? From the standpoint of auction appearances, what are the scarcest Seated Liberty silver dollars of the 1840s? According to auction prices, what is the current value of an Uncirculated 1915-S Panama-Pacific commemorative half dollar? A perusal of auction catalogs and prices-realized lists will provide such information and much other data as well. Dealers, who make their living by buying and selling coins, consider auction catalogs to be among their most valuable sources of information. You should do likewise.

Selling at auction

Sooner or later the time will come to sell your coins. There are several ways to sell them, and it would be to your advantage to check out the features of each. However, the frequency with which large collections cross the auction block indicates that those who have some of the most valuable numismatic property consider the auction route the best way to go. There must be reason for this, and some of the reasons are given herewith.

By offering your coins at auction, you expose your coins to tens of thousands of potential bidders. The firm conducting the sale typically will send out news releases and place advertisements, with the result that if you have a rare 1876-CC 20-cent piece, some German multiple talers, a pattern 1831 crown of King William IV, a Proof 1877 Indian cent, or a set of $1, $2, $5 "Educational" notes of 1896, readers of numismatic and other periodicals will be aware that they will be crossing the auction block. They are invited to send for a catalog at which time they will read the descriptions of these and other pieces. In addition to prospective bidders attracted by advertisements and publicity, a typical auction house has its own mailing list of thousands of proven buyers.

With such an array of potential buyers to choose from, chances are excellent that your coins will bring current market value. On the other hand, if you were to sell by fixed price, you probably could not expose your coins to more than a few dozen bidders if you spent all year doing so, and these bidders, if they are dealers, would want to buy the coins wholesale anyway. Then there are such considerations as security and safety involved in showing coins personally to many different buyers, not to overlook the value of your time. The auction route is simplicity itself. You ship the coins to the auctioneer, or if the coins are very valuable, the auctioneer may send a representative to call for them. Receipts are exchanged, then the next thing you do is to wait for your check to arrive in the mail.

Not all auction houses are the same. Before selecting a firm to sell your coins, do some investigating. If I were selling coins, here are some of the questions I might ask:

What is the commission rate? The typical commission rate charged by a large auction house may be 10 percent to the seller (plus a fee of 10 percent to the buyer). Other firms will advertise a lower commission. For items which are bulky or which involve fairly low value in relation to the catalog space occupied — numismatic books, certain tokens and medals and the like being examples — a higher fee may be charged.

The commission rate should be studied, but more important is the question: What do I get for the commission paid? It may be false economy to pick a lower commission rate if the firm does not do a good job for you. For example, if firm "A" sells a coin for $10,000 and charges you a 10 percent fee, this might be a better deal than firm "B" who charges you a 5 percent fee but the coin realizes just $7,000. It is the bottom line, the net results, that should interest you most. So, once you have established the fee, there are more questions to ask:

What type of advertising does the firm do? Does the firm acquire consignments and then forget about them, or does the firm pursue with great energy an advertising campaign offering your pieces? In my opinion, it is important that a sale be advertised so that prospective bidders have a chance to know about this. Such advertising is quite expensive, and not all firms do it.

Can I be sure my coins are being kept properly? Insist upon insurance coverage for your coins from the moment the auction firm takes possession of them. If your consignment is particularly large, you may wish to request an insurance certificate outlining the coverage. What type of security precautions will be taken? Will the firm be casual with your coins or careful with them?

What is the financial reputation of the firm? Is the company known for its financial strength? When settlement time comes (usually 45 days after the sale) will I be assured of receiving my check promptly? Does the firm have good financial and numismatic references?

What is the quantity and quality of the mailing list? How many catalogs will be distributed? And will they go to knowledgeable buyers? For example, 4,000 catalogs distributed to proven auction buyers will probably be more effective than 20,000 catalogs distributed to casual collectors, most of whom have never bid in an auction. Carefully ask about the quality and quantity of the mailing list.

When and where will the auction be held? Will it be held in a major metropolitan center or will it be held in a smaller community? Experience shows that a large city will usually yield better results than a smaller town, unless a major convention is being held in an out-of-the-way location. My own preference is to conduct auctions in New York or Los Angeles, for these seem to attract the most buyers, although sales in such places as Houston, Dearborn, Mich., and New Orleans have also done quite well, especially in conjunction with leading conventions.

Who will be cataloging the coins? Does the auction firm have leading numismatists who are prepared to attribute the coins, grade them properly, and write interesting and appealing descriptions concerning them? How have the past catalogs been received by the collecting fraternity? Ask to see some issues of older catalogs and carefully study them for style and content. Review the prices realized of former sales. "Nothing succeeds like success," it has been said, and chances are that the firm with the most successful track record in the past will be the most successful for you.

What outstanding coins and collections has the firm handled, and what prices have they brought? Again, check into the past and determine the track record of the firm in years gone by. If your collection will fit in nicely with those offered in the past, you know that the firm has bidders on its mailing list who want your type of material and who are prepared to pay good prices for it. You do not want to have an auction firm experiment or gain knowledge at your expense!

In any field, it pays to see a specialist, and when time comes to sell your coins, I personally recommend that you have an auction specialist handle them.

As is true of any method of selling, there are advantages and disadvantages to selling by auction. The disadvantage is that you do not know precisely what your coins will bring until they sell. Further, it is usually several months or so until you receive your funds (although cash advances are often available).

Some prospective consignors have hesitated to auction their coins, fearing tax consequences. In my opinion, the present tax rates in the United States on capital gains are sufficiently low that this should not be a factor in anyone's mind. It would be far better, in my opinion, to sell your coins and receive money that you can put into interest-bearing financial assets, if you choose.

There are many positive aspects of selling by auction. If you pay a 10 percent commission to the seller, and if the buyer pays a 10 percent fee, then if a coin brings $1,100 you net $900, or approximately 80 percent of the price. Dealers buying directly usually cannot operate on such a small margin of profit except, perhaps, for bullion-type coins and certain closely-traded items. If you have particularly scarce or rare pieces, it is often the situation that there will be a "fight" on the auction floor and new records will be set. Time and time again, I have seen pieces expected to bring $1,000 soar to $1,500, $2,000 or even more! As noted, when you sell your coins at auction, thousands of potential bidders have a chance to review your coins and consider bidding on them.

Auction! An effective way to sell them. Get involved in auctions. If you are a coin buyer, get on the mailing list of several coin auction firms. If you are thinking of selling, carefully consider the auction route.

Basic advertising policy

Coin World, Amos Press Inc.

P.O. Box 150, Sidney, Ohio 45365

The publisher offers advertising space for the purpose of bringing buyer and seller together for their mutual benefit. Years of publishing experience indicate the reader must be able to expect satisfactory service from the advertiser in order to respond to future advertisements. It is by giving such satisfactory service that advertisers can expect to continue productive advertising. Readers are reminded that all transactions are "two-way streets," and equity must exist for both parties for a satisfactory transaction.

Advertisements submitted which are not in the best interest of the advertiser specifically and of the trade generally, in the opinion of the publisher, or which may mislead readers, will be rejected. Customer checks of advertisers are periodically made by the publisher in a practical effort to assure accuracy and reliability of all advertisements. However, it is impossible to guarantee the reader's satisfaction with the advertiser's manner of doing business, and the reader is therefore reminded to exercise common sense in responding to any advertisement. The reader is also urged to exercise patience in awaiting response from an advertiser making allowances for mail transit time.

Coin World assumes no responsibility for representations made in advertisements.

Advance orders or futures

Advertisements offering coins or paper money which are not physically delivered into the hands of dealers at time of placing the advertisement will not be accepted. EXCEPTION: Advertisements will be accepted from governments or their officially appointed agents or distributors when such is the only source from which anyone may order the items. Dealers serving as official agents or distributors in the advance sale of such items are required to supply documentation of such appointment.

Fake, counterfeit or altered coins

Only genuine numismatic items may be offered for sale. The submission of an advertisement for publication is considered a warranty by the seller that all items offered are genuine. Any buyer of a fake or spurious item shall be entitled to full refund, and the normal return period shall be nullified.

Coin restrikes

Restrikes are numismatic items reproduced from the original dies or plates, but at a later date than appears on the item; the item must be restruck or reissued by the original issuing government authority, or authorized by decree or proclamation of the issuing government authority.

1. STRUCK FROM U.S. MINT DIES, whether inside or outside the Mint. Strictly speaking, these seem to be illegal, but they have a long history of collectibility, and many are listed in standard catalogs. They may be advertised in *Coin World,* always at the dealer's risk of the illegality.

2. COINS STRUCK FROM ORIGINAL DIES other than U.S. Mint dies, but for items which either circulated or were intended to circulate generally as money, making them coins rather than tokens, and with denominations usually on them; these include pioneer issues, the Confederate half dollar and cent, etc. These are acceptable for advertising, provided they are accurately described and identified as restrikes. Second or later restrikes must be distinguished from earlier restrikes in a permanent manner, such as metal used or appreciable difference in thickness, to be acceptable.

Any numismatic item created, designed or originally manufactured on or after March 1, 1963, which the owner wishes to advertise in *Coin World* as a restrike, must use the original dies on both obverse and reverse and make the impression transferral directly from die to planchet without otherwise making transferrals to any intermediate materials, dies, hubs, etc. Each piece must be indelibly labeled as a restrike.

It will be incumbent upon the advertiser to verify all facts concerning method and date of production.

Copies

Ads offering reproductions, imitations, replicas or copies of coins or other numismatic items are acceptable for advertising under the following conditions:

1. That such items are in compliance with the Hobby Protection Act and the U.S. Treasury's policy regarding coin replicas.

2. That the advertising copy or offer NOT contain false or misleading statements of the legal tender status of such items.

3. That the items be fully described in ads and samples of such items be submitted to *Coin World* with the initial ad.

4. That all items falling into this category must be clearly marked "COPY."

Cleaned coins

Cleaned coins are those from which something has been removed, such as tarnish, dirt, grit, carbon, and so on, but not including any of the metal which would fall into the whizzed category. Cleaned coins can be advertised but it must be clearly stated that the coin is cleaned.

Applying a new surface to a coin to change its appearance is the same as replating and not acceptable for advertising in *Coin World*. Applying lacquer or similar protective coating to prevent tarnish is traditionally permissible, if neither the appearance nor the grade of the coin is changed.

Coin grading and descriptions

Coins and numismatic material offered for sale shall be accurately described. *Coin World* recognizes *The American Numismatic Association Grading Standards for United States Coins, Photograde, The Numismatic Certification Institute Grading Guide* and *A Guide to the Grading of United States Coins* by Brown and Dunn as the accepted standard methods of grading U.S. coins. Advertisers who do not use any of these standard grading methods must describe, in each ad, accurately and in detail the method of grading used. Advertisers using any one of the standard methods need to make reference to the grading method(s) used in the ads. *Coin World* reserves the right to reject any ad using methods other than the four standard methods listed.

Coin World has adopted the following minimum standards for grading terms used in *Coin World* advertisements in order that buyer and seller can better communicate. Borderline Uncirculated must be minimum of About Uncirculated 55. Uncirculated, Brilliant Uncirculated and Select Uncirculated must be minimum of Mint State 60. Choice Uncirculated or Choice Brilliant Uncirculated must be a minimum of Mint State 63. Gem Uncirculated or Gem Brilliant Uncirculated must be a minimum of Mint State 65. Superb Brilliant Uncirculated must be a minimum of Mint State 67. Split grades such as MS-63/65 must fall back into the lowest adjective level. MS-63/65 may be described as Choice Brilliant Uncirculated or Choice Uncirculated.

Any advertiser placing an advertisement in *Coin World* agrees to adhere to these minimum standards. Advertisers found in violation may have their advertising privileges suspended or revoked at the discretion of *Coin World*.

Inspection and return period

All individual coins are to be shipped in holders which permit thorough inspection of coins. Any coin removed from holder is not returnable. Coins or numismatic material which the buyer finds to be unsatisfactory may be returned to the seller for full refund or replacement. Returns must be made within five days of receipt by the buyers, unless other return periods are specified in the advertisement. Refund or replacement will be made by the seller within seven days upon receipt of the returned item. Maximum return period allowed by advertisers is 30 days. The buyer MUST verify any extension of return period if coins are to be shipped to a grading service for verification.

Return postage on buy and trade ads

All advertisers who do not state "Write First" in their ads are expected to return merchandise postpaid. Refusal of packages at the post office may be grounds for suspension unless the ad indicates that confirmation is needed before shipping. If overgraded coins are to be returned at seller's or trader's expense, advertisement must so state.

Complaints

All advertisers will be notified of complaints received in writing from the readers and prompt adjustment by the advertiser, if warranted, and notification to the publisher will be expected as a condition of continued acceptance of advertising. Failure of any advertiser to correct the cause of a complaint, or satisfactorily explain the same, may result in suspension of advertising privileges at the discretion of *Coin World*.

Verification, inspection, financial statement

Acceptance of advertising for any item or service is subject to investigation and verification of the product or service, and of the claims made for it, in the advertisement submitted for publication.

Coin World will utilize its Customer Checking Service to verify the accuracy of the specified grade of advertised numismatic items. Collectors living throughout the United States, upon instruction from the publishers, place orders for merchandise advertsied.

The parcels are forwarded unopened to the publisher for examination of the contents.

Verification by the Customer Checking Service of an advertiser shipping overgraded coin(s) may result in suspension of advertising privileges at the discretion of *Coin World*.

The publisher reserves the right to require a current financial statement from any advertiser at any time.

Copy regulations

All advertisements submitted are subject to copy regulations contained in the rate card. By submitting advertising, the advertiser acknowledges that he is familiar with the advertising contract and copy regulations then in effect. Additional copies will be furnished upon request.

Layaway sales

Advertisers must write for complete policy requirements prior to offering layaways in ads.

Sold out

In the event an item is sold out, remittance will be returned within 48 hours. The advertiser will not hold the remittance pending

arrival of a new supply without obtaining permission of the buyer.

Reserve right to reject advertising

All advertising submitted is subject to publisher's approval. The publisher reserves the right to reject advertising, or suspend advertising privileges at the publisher's discretion.

Liability for contents of ads

Advertisers assume liability for all contents (including text representation and illustrations) of advertisement printed, and also assume responsibility for any claims arising therefrom.

Use of post office box

California law requires complete legal company name and full street address from which the business is actually being conducted. A post office box or phone number is not considered sufficient.

Coin World urges that complete information be included in all ads to promote uniformity and fairness between advertiser and reader.

Commercial numismatic publications

Following is a list of United States commercial numismatic publications and their addresses.

Bank Note Reporter
Krause Publications Inc.
Iola, Wis. 54945

Coin Prices
Krause Publications Inc.
Iola, Wis. 54945

Coin World
Box 150
Sidney, Ohio 45365

COINage
Miller Magazines Inc.
2660 E. Main St.
Ventura, Calif. 93003

Coins Magazine
Krause Publications Inc.
Iola, Wis. 54945

Error Trends Coin Magazine
P.O. Box 158
Oceanside, N.Y. 11572

Error-Variety News/ The Numismistake
3475 Old Conejo Road, C6
Newbury Park, Calif. 91320

Numismatic News
Krause Publications Inc.
Iola, Wis. 54945

World Coin News
Krause Publications Inc.
Iola, Wis. 54945

Exonumia

Col. Bill Murray is a COIN WORLD columnist whose column, the "New-mismatist," covers a wide variety of subjects of interest to the beginning collector. He is a member of the Numismatic Literary Guild and numerous other numismatic organizations. Murray has a special interest in exonumia.

By Col. Bill Murray, NLG
San Antonio, Texas

Among the first usages of the word exonumia was in correspondence between Russell Rulau and James Curto in the 1960s, but the subject matter included in the topic, according to some scholars, harks back to Roman

medallions of the second century. Today's definition of exonumia is "numismatic items (as tokens, medals or scrip) other than coins or paper money."

Tokens, medals and scrip are given as examples of items as exonumist might study or collect, but the field of exonumia includes a myriad of subjects. Some are inclusive within the three subjects enumerated, but additional areas of interest do exist. The collection of exonumia lends itself to topical collecting, and it is doubtful if any area of human endeavor is not represented by examples of exonumia. Such diverse fields as photography, politics and popes; lunches, lumber and liquor; sex, slavery and science; buses, bakers and boats; and coal, circuses and calendars have intrigued collectors over the years.

In this brief review of exonumia tokens, medals and scrip will be examined, but no attempt at an exhaustive dissertation is intended. Also, only exonumic items of the United States will be included.

Tokens

A token is usually a piece of durable material appropriately marked and unofficially issued for monetary, advertising, services or other purposes.

Early tokens in the United States emanated from England as a principal source but also were occasionally made locally or in other countries. Almost from the outset of colonization they were to be found in America. Sylvester S. Crosby in his book, *The Early Coins of America,* says, ". . . my intention has been to give . . . [information about] . . . those coins or tokens which were intended to serve as coins . . . in those parts of America which now constitute the United States."

These early tokens were needed because of a shortage of coinage. The tokens looked like and passed for money.

R.S. Yeoman's *A Guide Book of United States Coins* is another useful reference for Colonial tokens.

Store cards

One favorite type of token with collectors, the store card, is a token bearing a business name or address, and often intended as a local or ad-hoc medium of exchange as well as an advertisement for the issuer.

Generally accepted as the first store card in the United States is the Mott token, according to Rulau in his book, *Early American Tokens.* The token was issued by William and John Mott, who ". . . were importers, dealers and manufacturers of gold and silver wares, jewelry, watches and clocks. . . ."

Store cards have been popular with U.S. merchants ever since. Current store cards are being issued today. Rarely have they passed as money in recent years. However, both in the past and presently, they may be pure ad-

vertising pieces, or sometimes, called "good fors." They are redeemable and may be exchanged by the issuer for merchandise or a service. "Good fors" bear messages such as "Good for 5 cents in trade," "Good for one drink," "Good for a cup of coffee" or "Good for $10 on purchase of a piano."

Tokens *designed* to pass locally as currency, as previously indicated, have a tendency to appear during times when money is hard to come by. It is no surprise that such tokens were found in the Colonies, because of the economic policies of the mother country. Money was short.

Hard Times tokens came a bit later, during the period 1832-1844. They are normally of copper and about the size of the United States large cent. Rulau, in his definitive reference about the subject, *Hard Times Tokens,* says tokens were issued ". . . in a time when, to use of the phrases of the day, 'money was a cash article,' hard to get for daily needs."

He identifies five categories of Hard Times tokens. His categories are: 1. pieces referring to the Bank of the United States and the controversy surrounding it; 2. those with inscriptions relating to political and satirical situations of the era; 3. tokens with inscriptions and designs closely resembling the regular cent coinage, but with some differences in order to evade the counterfeiting laws; 4. store cards; and 5. die mulings — combinations with obverses and reverses of any of the preceding.

No organization dedicated to collectors of these early tokens exists, but an organization devoted primarily to the United States large cents and half cents, the Early American Coppers club, caters to collectors of early American tokens.

Civil War tokens issued during the Civil War when small change became scarce also was money of necessity. Civil War tokens, though often referred to as copperheads, were struck not only in copper but in brass and other alloys as well. Many of the off-metal varities were struck specifically for collectors and in small numbers.

The production and use of Civil War tokens was limited primarily to the Eastern and Midwestern states, but they were produced in prodigious numbers and are readily available to collectors today. Rare pieces, of course, demand premium prices.

Two general categories of Civil War tokens are identified — patriotics and store cards. Though thousands of varities exist, they are well cataloged and recent, updated catalogs have been published by the Civil War Token Society. The books are *U.S. Civil War Store Cards* and *Patriotic Civil War Tokens,* by George and Melvin Fuld.

A popular and generally more modern token is the transportation token. Transportation tokens — or vectures, as they are sometimes called — include items such as bus and street car tokens and tokens for toll roads and bridges and ferries. Tokens for a ride in a carriage, on a carousel, other amusement rides and in horsecars and taxis also exist.

The American Vecturist Association is an active organization. The monthly periodical, "The Fare Box," regularly updates listings for *The Atwood-Coffee Catalogue of United States and Canadian Transportation Tokens,* an important reference for transportation collectors. In addition to transportation tokens, the AVA monitors activities for collectors of parking tokens and car wash tokens.

Wooden money

Many collectors who specialize in wooden money can also be added to the list of exonumists. The science of wooden money collecting is called lignadenarics. Most people, however, still use the phrase "wooden money." While most of the pieces found in such a person's collection are round, and many are labeled "nickel," many more are rectangular. Any may be identified with different monetary denominations, such as 50 cents, $1, $10 and even more.

The first known use of wooden tokens in the United States was in Tenino, Wash., in 1931. The Tenino bank had failed, and Don Major, a local publisher, suggested the idea of issuing the wooden money for local use as an emergency measure.

Wooden pieces may be used for any of the purposes of other, non-wooden, tokens already discussed. Also we find some which are commemorative in nature, and frequently they are used in promotion of an event or person. Politicians often distribute them to promote their cause. For collectors they are inexpensive and are popular with many who have tight budgets. Two national wooden money organizations offer services to the collector: Dedicated Wooden Money Collectors and International Order of Wooden Money Collectors.

During World War II, rationing was a way of life. Practically all commodities were rationed. The Office of Price Administration was responsible for the program and issued ration stamps and coupons, usually in booklet form. The coupons for meat and processed food were issued in denominations of five points, 10 points and 20 points.

In 1944 tokens good for one point were issued to be used in making change for the meat and processed food coupons. These tokens were red or blue and were made of a tough fibrous material. They are 16 millimeters in diameter. Each has an outlined number 1 stamped in the center with two small letters on either side of the 1. The letters are found in various unexplained combinations such as MV, HH, UX, CH and HH. Perhaps this was an attempt to foil counterfeiters. A complete set requires 30 red tokens and 24 blue tokens. Only the red MV token can be considered scarce or costly. Most OPA token collectors also collect other ration material, but ration token collectors, per se, have their own national organization, the Society of Ration Token Collectors.

Medals

Medals as collector's items frequently seem to be the province of experienced collectors with a long background in coin collecting. The term medal is defined as "usually a piece of metal marked with a design or inscription made to honor a person, place or event, and is not intended to pass as money."

A medal may be a piece of metal hanging at the end of a ribbon, as commonly thought and given as a prize or award for some personal action such as winning a contest or for acts of heroism. The term medal encompasses much more than this type of award. Collectors of medals often collect them as art objects, and the art medal, so called, undoubtedly represents the zenith of numismatic art. Well-known American sculptors such as Augustus Saint-Gaudens, James Earle Fraser, Victor D. Brenner and Karen Worth are recognized for their work as medallic artists.

Probably the earliest definitive work concerning medals in the United States is C. Wyllys Betts' *American Colonial History Illustrated by Contemporary Medals.* His volume covers the period 1556-1786 and still is the basic reference for the era.

When discussing medals, one must reflect on the generalization of the definition and realize that not all medals will be paragons of the medalist's art. Many "lesser" medals exist which, because of their contribution to the recording of historial, parochial or topical subjects, are desired by collectors.

In his prize-winning book, *Medals of the United States Mint, The First Century, 1792-1892,* R.W. Julian lists, describes, discusses and illustrates United States medals under the following categories: Assay Commission,

Indian peace, presidential, military, naval, Mint and Treasury, personal, commemorative, school, agricultural, mechanical, scientific and professional, life saving, marksmanship, religious and fraternal and unclassified. The U.S. Mint is still producing medals today and will send a list of available medals for sale on request.

Not included in Julian's catalog, it may come as a surprise, are medals issued by the various military departments. Though authorized by the federal government or one of its executive branches, they were not designed nor struck at the Mint.

These last mentioned items are properly categorized under the general heading of medals but usually are listed in the sub-categories of decorations or awards. The study of medals includes consideration of at least the following: medalets, medallions, plaques, plaquettes, badges, decorations, awards and orders.

Scrip

Scrip is the last example included in the definition of exonumia. A good definition for scrip is: "tokens and paper currency, often in denominations of less than $1, issued as substitutes for currency to private persons or organizations."

Someone has devised the mnemonic "Substitute Currency Received in Payment" — SCRIP, probably because one often encounters the incorrect spelling as "script." There is no terminal "T" on the word scrip.

Coal companies, sutlers, lumber companies, prisons and an agency of the United States government (the Alaskan Rural Rehabilitation Corp.) are examples of issuing agencies. Paper scrip was used but often was replaced by metallic scrip which better withstood the damaging effects of hard, daily usage. Denominations issued may usually have less than $1, but $5 and $10 pieces are not uncommon. The U.S. government, or its agencies, have issued scrip. Most notable are military payment certificates provided for the armed forces in certain overseas locations.

One organization (National Scrip Collectors Association) is dedicated to scrip collecting with emphasis primarily on metallic coal and lumber scrip.

Three exonomic categories, properly included in a complete discussion of exonumia, depend on alteration of coins after they have left the Mint — love tokens, elongated coins and counterstamped coins. Two of these have sufficient following to have their own national organizations. The Love Token Society and The Elongated Collectors are the organizations involved.

Counterstamped coins are the simplest alteration, and the title clearly indicates what you might expect — the use of punches to make marks on the coins. United States collectors of counterstamps often direct their efforts towards coins where the counterstamp alters the coin into a presentation piece, a store card or some other use of the piece as a token. Large cents were often used in this fashion.

Love tokens

Love tokens may "mutilate" the coin as a piece of money, but most collectors collect love tokens because of their intrinsic beauty. A love token is a coin which has been altered by smoothing one or both surfaces and engraving initials, scenes, messages and so on thereon. The engraved coins were often given to an individual's loved one, hence the name given them.

Love tokens were especially popular in the 19th century, a time when the engraver's art was pervasive in the United States. Many of the names, monograms or scenes depicted are beautifully done. Often the engraving appears on the side opposite from the date because the date may have had significance to the originator.

An elongated coin is an oval medalet produced by a roller die using a coin, token or medal as a planchet — usually a cent.

Les Martin and Dottie Dow in their book, *Yesterday's Elongateds,* discuss the techniques of elongated "rolling." Elongated coins are dated from the World's Columbian Expositon in Chaicago during 1892-93. However, many people think the technique may have been developed before then, but to date, elongates from that exposition are the earliest that have been identified.

The typical elongated coin has been rolled with a die which impresses one side of the coin. The die has been engraved with a design, often commemorative, or a message. Subject matter, as Martin and Dow aver, "It's as wide-ranging as the imagination."

As can be inferred from previous discussion, exonumia lends itself to topical collecting. Geography frequently dictates the direction of a collection — a certain state, county or town of interest to the collector. Many individuals relate their collections to personal interests: business, hobby, a sport or other. Just a few examples will suffice: photography, good-luck pieces, insurance, boats, animals, religion, automobiles, flowers, dairies, banks and the United States Bicentennial.

Two organizations devoted to exonumia not specifically aligned with any of the special areas of exonumia previously discussed are the Token and Medal Society and the Active Token Collectors Organization. Both are important organizations serving the exonumist.

TAMS is the one organization catering to all aspects of exonumia. The *TAMS Journal* is professional in aspect and content. In addition to the regular issues of the journal, TAMS publishes supplementary issues which are catalogs of special topics of exonumia and most useful to the collector. Also, TAMS has published several quality books about various facets of the subject. R.W. Julian's book about the U.S. Mint medals is just one example.

ATCO is composed of several hundred members who are collectors of many types of tokens. Its publication affords a primary outlet for collectors to buy, sell or trade.

Among serious token collectors, trading is a way of life.

The magnitude and complexity of the study of exonumia eliminates the possibility of a single book covering the subject adequately. As a consequence, many books of specialized interest exist. The selected bibliography included in Chapter 21, "First the Book," was chosen to support this introduction to exonumia, but books and catalogs in profusion, devoted to special, individual aspects of exonumia are available.

Several of the organizations dedicated to exonumia maintain libraries related to the subject. In addition, the American Numismatic Association has many volumes about exonumia. Books can be borrowed by collector members of these organizations usually at the cost of postage and insurance. Addresses for these organizations can be found in Chapter 20, Organizations.

Hard Times tokens

The period between the end of the Revolutionary War and the beginning of the Civil War was marked by times of economic upheavals which were separated by periods of monetary stability. The infant government was attempting to cope with the westward expansion of the country, with animosity directed toward the United States by foreign powers, and the slow process of learning self-government.

The first United States Mint had been established in Philadelphia in 1792 but crude equipment and limited experience curtailed production. At the same time an ever-increasing population required more and more coins. During periods of economic stability coin production was able to keep up with use, but during periods of economic upheaval, hard money was taken out of circulation and hoarded.

By the early 1830s the lack of available coinage had almost reached the critical stage. Though tokens had been issued even before the Revolutionary War, mainly of an advertising nature, they had never been used in commerce to any great degree.

The extreme shortage of small change caused more and more merchants to use tokens in lieu of cents in ever greater numbers in their day-to-day business transactions. Privately issued token coinage was a preferable alternative to the barter system.

The Hard Times tokens consist of two main types: merchant's advertising tokens and political tokens.

The advertising tokens carry information about the location and type of business the merchant was engaged in. Most of them are of copper, bronze or brass but some were issued in other metals, such as Feuchtwanger's "American Silver" composition.

An interesting view of the practice of issuing token coinage is given in a paper read by Thomas Elder to the New York Numismatic Club on Jan. 8, 1915: "It is of interest to read that H.M. & E.I. Richards, of Attleboro, Mass., sold their tokens by the keg-full to their customers for from 60 to 75 cents per hundred."

Elder's statement helps make the practice understandable. Not only was the merchant able to make change for his customers, he bought the tokens at less than 1 cent each and knew that many would be lost or otherwise unredeemed, reducing his cost per token even more.

The tokens are generally about the size of the large cents of that period in which they were issued. For that reason they were accepted in commerce.

As the economy demanded small change which couldn't be provided in quantity by the Mints and was thus provided by merchants, so too did political actions result in another type of token coinage.

Champions of political causes and detractors of those same causes often issued tokens hoping thereby to advance their particular aims. Many of the political tokens centered around the refusal of President Jackson to renew the charter of the Bank of the United States.

Whatever the reason for issuing Hard Times tokens may have been, they do form an interesting and historical segment of numismatics.

Civil War tokens

The Civil War gave rise to numerous forms of emergency money, the variety and ingenuity of which have never been equaled. Early in 1862 all metallic currency was gradually withdrawn from circulation. During the war people feared the total devaluation of currency and started to hoard gold and silver. Finally even copper currency disappeared from circulation. The result was chaos for those conducting day-to-day business — there was simply no way to make change.

The first attempt was the use of ordinary U.S. postage stamps. But, because of their flimsy nature, stamps had a very short circulating lifespan. Next, the merchants issued small envelopes, generally with some advertising on the back, so the postage stamps would be afforded some degree of protection.

In 1862, John Gault patented a novel brass encasement for the stamps, with a mica cover, so the stamps were easily visible. These encased stamps, made by the Scoville Manufacturing Co. in Waterbury, Conn., with the merchant's advertising on one side, circulated widely. Their one disadvantage was that they cost more than face value to issue because the cost of manufacture of the case had to be added to the face value of the stamp.

Various forms of fractional, privately issued, paper money then appeared but, because it had no intrinsic value (and doubtful backing in many cases) it did not meet with wide acceptance. Cardboard scrip met with the same fate.

Finally the most popular and realistic form of emergency money, in the form of small copper tokens, began circulating extensively throughout the Northeast and Midwest in late 1862. These small coins, generally the size and weight of small bronze cents, met with immediate acceptance. The use soon spread to other states and cities.

Two general types of tokens were issued — the so-called "patriotic" tokens and the "tradesmen's" tokens. The patriotic series, mainly issued in and around New York, have patriotic slogans on the tokens but bear no merchant's advertising. Many of the pieces are in general imitation of the Indian cent. The tradesmen's (or merchant's) store cards were widely issued and usually bear the merchant's advertisement on one side and some patriotic symbol on the other.

The issue of Civil War tokens exceeded 25 million pieces, which amply filled the needs of the merchants. And the merchants were happy with the arrangement since the tokens not only advertised their business but also cost only 23/100ths of a cent to produce.

The tokens were undoubtedly a source of great relief and convenience, but their irresponsible character soon attracted the attentions of the federal government, because some of the merchants refused to redeem the tokens they had issued. Government attempts at issuing bronze coins and fractional currency were not sufficient to suppress the Civil War tokens then current. Finally, in 1864, an act of Congress forbid the practice of issuing money in any form. Thus ended another era.

The authoritative book about the subject of Civil War Tokens had long been Hetrich and Guttag's epic work *Civil War Tokens and Tradesmen's Cards,* published in 1924. They listed some 7,000 varieties but, at the present time, more than 11,000 different specimens (different die-metal varieties) are known to exist.

At present the most comprehensive works on the subject are the two books, *Patriotic Civil War Tokens* and *U.S. Civil War Store Card Tokens* by George and Melvin Fuld.

Storage and preservation

Coins and paper money change over time, and not for the better.

This simple maxim is too often neglected by collectors, dealers and investors, and received little coverage in the numismatic press until the late 1970s, when it was learned that most of the coin storage methods then in use tended to cause coins and notes to deteriorate instead of protecting the materials being stored. Deterioration is at odds with the long-accepted belief that the better the condition of a numismatic collectible, the more it is worth.

The greater awareness of coin storage and preservation has resulted in safer storage materials being offered. However, most coins sold, bought and stored are probably being held in a holder that does not offer much protection, or may even harm the coin.

In general, storage materials that are safe for coins are also safe for paper money, but common sense must be applied.

The following observations are based on a series of Collectors' Clearinghouse articles by Bernard Nagengast, a Sidney, Ohio, specialist in coin storage and preservation and a dealer in materials he says are safe for storage and handling.

Metal

Metals vary in their resistance to corrosion; however, all coinage metals can be affected. Gold is probably the most resistant coinage metal, being unaffected by most corrosive agents. A problem arises with some gold coins because they usually contain copper, and a poor mix can result in areas of high concentration of copper which can corrode, causing streaks, spotting and other surface blemishes.

Fortunately, this does not often occur. Gold coins are remarkably resistant to storage in dangerous coin holders, polluted atmospheres, and under other adverse conditions. Be careful with gold coins if you smoke, however. Tobacco will stain gold. Avoid handling gold coins with tobacco contaminated fingers, or blowing smoke on the coins, which can condense on the surface.

Silver is also quite resistant, but subject to tarnish, especially in the presence of sulfur compounds and nitrates. Since sulfur and nitrate compounds are frequent components of air pollution, modern times are especially hard on silver coins.

As with gold, silver U.S. coins contain copper. Since the percentage is about 10 percent, it is possible to oxidize copper at the coin's surface, resulting in green to blue corrosion. Attractive, irridescent patina is considered desirable on silver coins by some collectors. This patina results from complex chemical processes over a long period of time, thus the rainbow hues seen on some 19th century silver coins.

There have been modern day attempts to duplicate natural toning when it was discovered that such coins sometimes bring premium prices. By experimenting with various chemicals, some found that they could produce instant toning, and there are "midnight labs" in various parts of the country turning out these coins. Beware when toning is used to cover up rubbing on an Uncirculated coin or hairlines on a Proof coin.

Copper-nickel alloy is even more susceptible to chemical attack because of the 75 percent copper present. Not only is it affected by atmospheric contaminants, but it is also more subject to electrochemical action (battery action) than silver and gold. Small black spots, called "carbon spots," are sometimes seen. These are the result of oxygen cells, discussed later, or the result of a contaminant imbedded in the coin's surface, which later corrodes or oxidizes, or causes the surrounding metal to corrode or oxidize.

Copper is possibly the most fragile commonly used U.S. coinage material. Upon oxidation, it forms green to blue copper oxide. Copper alloy coins are very susceptible to carbon spots.

The atmosphere

This was touched on in the topic above, and it should be obvious by now that airborne gases can adversely affect a coin. Normal pollutants found in the air can cause long-term problems. They can combine with oxygen at the coin's surface. Artificial gases produced while a coin is in a plastic holder, coming from the plastic itself, can also have an adverse effect.

The atmosphere also contains moisture and dust, both dangerous to a coin's surface. Both are carriers of oxygen and other compounds, bringing them into intimate contact with the coin's surface. Since we don't have much direct control over the air around us, the only way to protect a coin from the atmospheric pollutants is to isolate it in a container that is airtight and inert, so the container itself won't contaminate the coin.

Contaminants

Coins are dirty, even when coming off the coinage press! Since the metal is rolled, punched, annealed, struck by dies and handled by various mechanical devices, even a Mint State or Proof coin will be contaminated with metallic particles, oil and grease, rag dust, bag dust, and other foreign material. Contaminants may even be imbedded in the surface from the rollers, dies and other mechanical devices.

Once the coins leave the Mint, they are further contaminated by counting machines, rolling machine, and handling by the collector himself. Collectors can contaminate a coin when they handle it — grease on fingers, dust particles in the air, dandruff or the surface the coin is laid on.

Coin holders themselves can contaminate the coin. They may contain dust particles picked up by static electricity from the air on surfaces. Many also contain paper or cardboard dust, highly dangerous to pristine coins. As discussed above, some plastic holders give off dangerous gases due to their volatility. Some release acetic, hydrochloric and other acids. Some "sweat" and the liquid coming out of the plastic is deposited on the coin.

Dust particles on the coins are dangerous not only because they themselves may be corrosive, but also because they can form oxygen cells. When a particle rests on a coin, it causes an oxygen deficiency at that point and this sets up an electrochemical reaction resulting in precipitation of corrosive compounds around the particle. A spot forms as a result, and the surface of the coin pits directly under the dust particle. Experience indicates that paper and cardboard dust particles are especially prone to forming oxygen cells.

Handling

Improper handling causes abrasion, decreasing the value of the coin itself and also exposes fresh metal which can oxidize and corrode. Although every collector should be aware of these facts, some can be seen carelessly handling coins. Don't allow coins to come in contact with each other if you value their long-term life.

Vibration from street traffic, footsteps and other sources can cause them to rub imperceptibly, and over a long period of time, rub marks may develop on the high spots. When you lay a coin down, be aware of the surface. Is it clean? If not, the coin may pick up contaminants. Coins stored in slide-type albums may develop "slide mark" abrasion on the high points from sliding the windows past the coins.

Storage materials

The factors described above will have an adverse effect on coins over time, but can be reduced and perhaps eliminated by careful selection of materials for storage or display. Length of time for storage needs consideration. A certain material may not harm the coin on a short-term level, but could be highly dangerous in the long term.

Common sense would dictate that it is unnecessary to spend a lot of time and money on a container if the coin is only being temporarily stored. Once the coin is in the hands of the collector who plans on keeping it for a

long time, it is foolish not to take the steps necessary to protect the coin.

One interesting fact about collecting is that people will often spend a fortune on a coin without a second thought about properly preserving it, risking the possibility of large financial losses if the coin deteriorates while they own it. Consider then that selection of a good holder is the coin owner's responsibility, simply because the previous owner or dealer probably didn't give it a thought.

The following statement may shock you, but it is a fact: many of the coin holders on the market are not suitable for long-term storage. The following discusses the most common coin holders and their suitability.

Coin albums: One expert on coin storage has said he has yet to see an album he would call satisfactory. The cardboard ones with plastic slides are bad because of the cardboard and paper, the abrasion possible with the plastic slides, and the fact that a large number of coins are exposed at the same time when the slides are pulled.

These albums also don't protect against the atmosphere or moisture since the cardboard is porous. Some newer albums are made of plastic, and although they eliminate the slides, they are also not suitable because the plastic itself is not inert. Some of them "sweat" over a period of time, causing tarnished or green corrosion. Coin boards without any covering should obviously never be used for high-grade coins.

Two-by-twos: Probably the most common coin holder is the cardboard 2-by-2-inch or 1.5-by-1.5-inch square container. They come as one piece usually, with a plastic window and are stapled or glued together with the coin in between. This holder is one of the most dangerous holders around. Many of the plastics used are dangerous, the holder is not airtight, and worst of all, many are badly contaminated with paper and cardboard dust on the surface of the plastic.

Even when wiped off, the holder still has microscopic dust particles which fly to the coin's surface when it is inserted. You would be amazed how big a spot a dust particle invisible to the naked eye can cause. Certainly these holders can be used for short-term transactions, but should never be used to store a collection for an extended period of time.

Flips: This is the name given to the 2-by-2-inch solid plastic holder. There are usually two sections hinged at the top, and one section contains a paper insert for labeling. Most are made of vinyl, a dangerous plastic because it can combine with oxygen to form compounds which will attack the coin.

Some are Mylar, a polyethylene derivative, and these are basically inert, but are moisture permeable. The mylars are reasonably safe for short-term storage though. There is a possibility of contaminating the interiors of the flips with paper dust from the inserts. Also, the flips do not seal at the top, thus the coins are exposed to the atmosphere.

Plexiglass: Three-layer plexiglass holders are available for single coins or sets. They are much better than most holders, but have the disadvantage of high cost. Plexiglass contains polymethacrylic acid, which can attack the coin's surface. The coins usually are loose in the holes and can rattle around, abrading the plastic and picking up dust from the plastic, thus the acid can come in contact with the coin. Plexiglass can also absorb moisture.

Polystyrene holders: Single coin or Proof and Mint holders, as well as roll tubes, are available. Made of clear brittle plastic, the holders usually snap together. Polystyrene is one of the few inert plastics and therefore can be considered safe. The edges of these holders, however, frequently do not seal airtight.

Preparation for storage

There is no point in storing a coin in a safe holder if the coin itself is contaminated with materials which can cause corrosion. All coins contain varying amounts of Mint oil and grease, counting machine grease, bag dust, and the dust particles from the air and from previous storage methods. This contamination should be removed before the coin is put into its final storage holder.

The coin should be dipped into a good solvent which will dissolve grease and oil and carry away dust. It is advisable to swish the coin in the solvent, and may be necessary to take a cotton swab to remove heavy accumulations of grease. Two dips should be used, an initial one of any good solvent (alcohol, trichloroethane) to remove most of the contamination, and a final rinse to neutralize the solvent and carry away final traces of contamination.

There are only two safe solvents which can be used for neutralizing. Both will evaporate readily and leave no residue on the coin. One is pure medical Benzene, available at a drug store. The other is Trichlorotrifluoroethane, which is not easily available, but has the advantage of being non-toxic, and completely non-flammable.

Benzene should be used with adequate ventilation since it is considered toxic and cancer-causing as well as being highly flammable. The solvents should be free of any water or contaminants.

After dipping the coin, let the solvent evaporate in the air and immediately insert it into the holder. It is best not to allow the coin to come in contact with anything other than the inside of the holder to prevent re-contamination with dust.

Once the coin is placed in an airtight, safe holder, it is irrelevant where the coin is stored, since atmosphere won't affect the coin itself. However, heat should be avoided, as well as sunlight.

Following these suggestions will not guarantee that a coin will not deteriorate, but they do suggest the best methods known to ensure that coins which are the pride and joy of a collector will survive for the lifetime of this and future generations of collectors.

Coin weights and measures

Weights and measures pertaining to coins are almost as numerous as coin types issued over the centuries. It is only natural that a nation would issue coins based on the weight system recognized by that government.

Ancient weights in many cases have been adapted to coin denominations. The shekel, a weight mentioned in the Old Testament, became a coin of the ancient Jews.

The British pound and Mexican peso are other examples of denominations named for weights.

The grains-ounces-pounds system of Great Britain was adapted for use by the American Colonies and the United States. The metric system was adopted later by the French and then almost all other countries of the world.

In Europe in the 16th, 17th and 18th centuries, as trade between nations brought coins of many denominations and metals from other countries into a merchant's counting room, special scales were developed to weigh each coin. Instead of a weight representing so many drachma, pennyweights or grams, the weight represented a gold French louis d'or, Spanish pistole or British sovereign. The boxes holding the scales and weights were often inlaid, quite ornate, and are collector's items today.

In Great Britain, three 1-penny coins equaled 1 ounce. Struck to such a fine tolerance were British halfpenny and penny coins that bank clerks counted coins by weighing them. Two hundred and forty 1-penny coins (£1) weighed 80 ounces, and triangular-shaped packages were prepared for sale to the public on the basis of weight, not counting machines.

An early system used to measure coins in England was to assign a number for each 16th of an inch of a coin; a coin measuring 1 inch in diameter was considered size 16; 1½-inches, size 24; 2 inches, size 32; and so on. U.S. numismatists adopted this system too, although it is no longer used.

Before the metric system, a Frenchman named Mionnet devised a series of concentric lines emanating from a common plane; whichever number line the coin met, when placed on the plane, such was the size of the coin.

The U.S. Mint Reports list coin diameters in both inches and millimeters, and coin weights in grains and grams.

Weights and measures

Following is a chart of coin weight and measure conversions. Included are conversion values for grams, grains, millimeters, centimeters and inches.

Gold, silver and platinum coins are usually weighed in grams or grains.

One gram equals:
.001 kilogram
15.43235639 grains
.002204622 pound, avoirdupois
.03527396 ounce, avoirdupois
.002679229 pound, troy
.03215075 ounce, troy

One grain equals:
.00006479 kilogram
.0647989 gram
.000142857 pound, avoirdupois
.002285 ounce, avoirdupois
.000173611 pound, troy
.002083 ounce, troy

One millimeter equals:
.03937 inch

One centimeter equals:
.3937 inch

One inch equals:
25.4 millimeters
2.54 centimeters
.0254 meter

Metric conversion

mm	inches	mm	inches	mm	inches
10	.39	27	1.06	44	1.73
11	.43	28	1.10	45	1.77
12	.47	29	1.14	46	1.81
13	.51	30	1.18	47	1.85
14	.55	31	1.22	48	1.89
15	.59	32	1.26	49	1.93
16	.63	33	1.30	50	1.97
17	.67	34	1.34	51	2.01
18	.71	35	1.38	52	2.05
19	.75	36	1.42	53	2.09
20	.79	37	1.46	54	2.13
21	.83	38	1.50	55	2.17
22	.87	39	1.54	56	2.21
23	.91	40	1.58	57	2.24
24	.95	41	1.61	58	2.28
25	.98	42	1.65	59	2.32
26	1.02	43	1.69	60	2.36

Specific gravity

A value of specific gravity is a basis for comparison of the density of differing masses; in numismatics, these are generally metals and their alloys. As in measuring temperature, various scales have been developed to measure density, but the most common and one of the easiest to determine is a specific gravity (sp. gr.) scale which, for solids and liquids, is expressed as a ratio of the mass of a body to the mass of an equal volume of water at 4° Celsius.

In the table of elements common to numismatics below, specific gravity values expressed are those given in the *CRC Handbook of Chemistry and Physics* and other basic scientific references. Values may differ slightly in some references (as from the Third Edition of *Coin World Almanac*) because of improved measuring methods and purification of test samples.

When specific gravities and proportions of given elements or alloys are known, it is a relatively simple matter to determine approximate correct weight of the given item (coin). In this manner, testing for genuineness can be done.

Dating from the ancient Greeks (Archimedes is given credit for discovering the principle in a bathtub); it is the oldest, and is still perhaps the best, method of quickly and accurately determining the probable composition of precious metal alloys. Unfortunately, those who could use it to best advantage are often deterred from using it because they mistakenly assume that it requires complicated laboratory techniques using sophisticated and expensive equipment, combined with the mathematical skills of an Einstein.

Not so! Even when done under "field" conditions, the basic equipment and mathematics are within the reach and comprehension of anyone who has completed elementary school.

The accuracy and the repeatability of test results is dependent more upon the care exercised by the person doing the testing than upon any other single factor. The test results will naturally be more accurate, and more consistently repeatable, if the equipment used is extremely sensitive and housed in a draft-free, temperature controlled environment, but such laboratory conditions are not absolutely essential — as long as you understand the limitations.

We will assume that most users of this equipment do not have those ideal laboratory conditions under which specific gravity testing can be done most accurately. The procedures outlined in these pages will be predicated on field conditions and must be recognized as having those limitations. The results probably would not survive a court challenge, but they will be accurate enough to give us an indication of whether or not a particular coin could possibly be composed of the proper alloy, or if it is more likely to be something entirely different than it should be.

We will be using an Ohaus "Cent-O-Gram" Balance, Model 311. This particular scale allows us to do both the old longhand method of specific gravity testing and the new method developed by Ohaus. The new method is a simple "GO-NO-GO" method which uses added buoyancy factor weights to eliminate all of the mathematics to arrive at the test result.

Size, weight and composition of most United States and foreign coins can be found in any number of books and periodicals, though it often takes considerable effort to locate the data. Comparison of that data and your test results will give you an idea of the probability of genuineness of the subject coin.

After a few pointers that will enable the average person to make the test results as accurate as humanly possible under less than ideal conditions, we will go into the methods of performing specific gravity tests on coins.

1. Observe good laboratory techniques as much as possible under existing conditions.
2. Locate the scale on the most stable surface available. A desk is less susceptible to vibrations than a folding table would be.
3. Eliminate stray air currents as much as possible. The balance can be housed in a cardboard box or other suitable container. If at all possible, put a plastic curtain over the opening of the box. Be careful not to breathe directly at the scale.
4. Use pure water whenever possible. The best water is steam distilled deionized water. Add a drop or two of Photo-Flo 200, household detergent, or any other good wetting agent. This helps to eliminate the air bubbles which normally cling to the coin and the suspension device.
5. Always be certain that the scale has been zeroed both before and after any weighing operation, or any time the scale is moved.
6. Always depress the right end of the beam after making adjustments for either zero balance or movement of the poises.
7. Above all, remember that specific gravity is not the final word in determining authenticity of a coin. It is just one more tool to be used.

Work slowly and carefully. Do not allow yourself to jump to any conclusion that could cloud your judgment. Remember, if there is any doubt about the genuineness of a coin after its specific gravity is determined, there are higher authorities to which you can send the coin.

In conjunction with specific gravity tests, one of the most useful tools any collector can acquire is an accurate vernier calipers. Accurate measurement of diameters and edge thicknesses of the subject coins can be valuable verification of the visual examination and the specific gravity testing.

Determining specific gravity

1. Zero the scale exactly and carefully.
2. Place the coin to be checked on the lower pan. Stop the swaying of the pan, but it is not essential that the pan be absolutely still.
3. Move the balance poises to the right until the beam returns to exact zero. Start with the heaviest poise and work downward (or forward), on the beam until you reach zero using the smallest of the four poises on the beam.
4. Read the combined total of the poises to arrive at the total weight of the coin in air.

5. Write that weight on a piece of paper.
6. Place the coin on the suspension device and immerse it in the water. Do not return the poises to zero, move them back only far enough to return the beam to the zero balance.
7. Read the new combined total of the poises. This is the weight of the coin in water. Mark this total on the sheet, immediately below the total marked down in step 4.
8. Subtract the weight of the coin in water (step 7) from the weight of the coin in air (step 4).
9. Divide the result of step 8 into the weight of the coin in air (step 4 divided by step 8).
10. The answer will be the specific gravity of the coin being checked.

When the weight and specific gravity of the subject coin is given, you need only compare those nominal figures with your test results. Bear in mind that specific gravity, like weight, is subject to tolerance limits. Also, your test results are subject to variances because of the conditions under which the testing was done, as well as an error factor for the balance itself.

If your test results are less than 0.5 above or below the nominal figure for a given alloy, consider that the test result is normal for that particular alloy. If your test result is more than 0.5 above or below the nominal figure, first be suspicious of your test result rather than being suspicious of the coin. Do the testing over one or more times to see if you arrive at the same result each time. If so, your test results are probably accurate and the coin is suspicious.

Now, suppose that you know what the alloy of the genuine coin is supposed to be but do not know the specific gravity figure for that alloy. Consult the table of elements which gives the specific gravity of the various metals in their pure forms. Multiply the specific gravity of each metal by the percentage of that metal in the alloy and add the results to get the specific gravity of the alloy.

For example: you know that the alloy normally contained 75 percent silver, 20 percent copper and 5 percent zinc.

(silver)	10.50 x .75 =	7.875
(copper)	8.96 x .20 =	1.792
(zinc)	7.133 x .05 =	0.357
		———
		10.024

is the specific gravity of the alloy.

Common elements

Element	Sym.	Sp. Grav.
Aluminum	Al	2.6989
Antimony	Sb	6.691
Beryllium	Be	1.848
Bismuth	Bi	9.747
Cadmium	Cd	8.650
Carbon	C	2.250[1]
Chromium	Cr	7.19[2]
Copper	Cu	8.96
Gold	Au	18.88[3]
Iron	Fe	7.874
Lead	Pb	11.35
Magnesium	Mg	1.738
Manganese	Mn	7.3[4]
Molybdenum	Mo	10.22
Nickel	Ni	8.902
Palladium	Pd	12.02
Platinum	Pt	21.45
Ruthenium	Ru	12.41
Silicon	Si	2.33
Silver	Ag	10.50
Tantalum	Ta	16.654
Tin	Sn	7.298[5]
Titanium	Ti	4.54
Tungsten	W	19.3
Vanadium	V	6.11
Zinc	Zn	7.133

[1] Carbon has three distinct ranges of specific gravity, depending upon its form. Amorphous carbon ranges from 1.8 to 2.1; diamonds have the highest, at 3.15 to 3.53.
[2] Average in the range of 7.18 to 7.20.
[3] Value for elemental gold. See "Specific gravity of gold and copper" below.
[4] Average in the range of 7.21 to 7.44.
[5] Gray tin has a specific gravity of 5.75; white tin has a specific gravity of 7.31. Value given is approximate value of combined white and gray in normally occuring proportions.

Specific gravity of gold and copper

Gold is the one metal which does not lend itself to this method of specific gravity determination. When gold is alloyed with copper there is an molecular interaction with the result that the specific gravity of the two metals in alloy is smaller than the specific gravity of the individual parts that were used to make up the alloy. The following is a table of the specific gravity figures of the most common gold-copper alloys.

Au %	Cu %	Sp. Gr.
99	01	19.099
98	02	18.883
97	03	18.672
96	04	18.465
95	05	18.264
94	06	18.066
93	07	17.873
92	08	17.684
91	09	17.499
90	10	17.317

Photographing coins

Home photography of coins is not only a very enjoyable contribution to your hobby, but it can also be much cheaper than commercially-produced prints. An added benefit is the knowledge that the photo is something you accomplished yourself. You didn't purchase the result; you created it.

The first consideration is the ultimate use of the photographs. If they are for your own enjoyment, eye-appeal is of primary importance. If the pictures are to be used for publication, contrast must be considered because some of the finer details will be lost in the creation of the dot pattern essential for printed material.

Once you have determined the use of your pictures, you are ready to consider your equipment. Photographs can be taken with any camera. The simplest box camera can do a respectable job, but is limited in application. The pictures will be the size, or smaller, than the coin. After the picture is taken you will have to rely on the person doing the processing for further enlargements.

Most modern pocket cameras or equivalent snapshot cameras will not focus closer than 3 or 4 feet. In order to shoot coins you must buy auxiliary close-up attachments, if available, for your particular camera.

The simple, fixed-focus cameras can be modified to increase their capability. Addition of a close-up lens has the same effect as bringing the coin closer to the lens while keeping it in focus, thus slightly enlarging the coin image.

By now you can appreciate some of the problems professional photographers run into. You've tried the available simple cameras and found them wanting. You are ready to consider better equipment.

One of the simplest camera set-ups consists of a good 35 millimeter single lens reflex camera with an automatic shutter. The camera is mounted by means of a support which contains a tripod screw on a pipe which is mounted on a rigid board base. Use of three or four spotlights in clamp-type holders provides a variable light source, although two lights are usually sufficient. The automatic lens system corrects exposures as the lights are moved to highlight the coin being photographed. The resulting photograph should show exactly what you saw through the lens. Ideally, though, you should shoot at least one test roll of film to establish the average exposure required for the lights and the film you have chosen.

The moveable lights allow you to bring out the needed contrasts to show the desired details of the coin. Contrast is the difference in density between the highlights of the subject, through the varying shades of gray, to the almost total black of the shadows. It lends a three-dimensional aura to what would otherwise be a flat appearing object.

If your tastes run along more expensive lines, or if you progress to the point where you want more detailed photographs of small areas of a coin, consider macrophotography.

Simply stated, macrophotography means that you get the greatly enlarged detail of the coin onto the negative without the intermediate step of the enlarger. You use the camera itself as an enlarger through the use of auxiliary lenses. One of the benefits of macrophotography can also be one of its drawbacks. The elimination of the enlarger means limitation of the size of the picture. Of course, you can still use an enlarger if you wish.

Photomicrography, which permits the enlargement of a very small area of the coin, involves coupling your camera to a microscope. Trial and error will permit you to accomplish this with any camera. Any camera with a removable lens can do the job, but a single lens reflex is still the best.

The limitations of both photomicrography and macrophotography lie only in the equipment used. The better the equipment, the better the results will be.

Those who make coin photography their profession use radically different equipment than those who do it as a hobby.

The *Coin World* photographer uses a Polaroid MP-3 Multipurpose Industrial View Camera with a 4X5 negative material. Auxiliary lenses and equipment include a Prontor 5-inch lens, a Prontor 3-inch lens and a Micro 35mm lens plus various extension tubes and barrels for microscope adaptation. The enlarger is an Omega Pro Lab 4X5 (condenser type) with a 135mm lens which is used in conjunction with 4X5 negatives and 80mm and 50mm lenses, used primarily with 35mm and 120 film sizes. The 50mm lens provides the greatest degree of enlargement.

Photographers are urged to use a fine grain film with fine grain developers for best results. Among these are Kodak Panatomic-X with an ISO of 32, or Kodak Plus-X with an ISO of 125. However, satisfactory results may be obtained with Kodak Tri-X with an ISO of 400.

Once you decide on a film, stay with it. If

you keep switching films, it only complicates your efforts to obtain consistent and acceptable results.

The fine grain film is an absolute must when making extreme enlargements. Generally, fine grain film is slower, meaning that longer exposures are required to gather the proper amount of light. In part, this can be overcome by use of better lights. But the longer exposures also mean that the camera must be absolutely steady when making those exposures. That, in turn, usually rules out hand-held cameras, or cameras mounted on home-made tripods.

Your best source of information is still your local camera store.

A record finder for your heirs

Soon after your death, documents and information bearing on your personal affairs may be urgently needed. You can make things easier for your heirs during that painful period by leaving them a guide to your files and records. Information that should be included follows:

Bank accounts — location of checkbook, records and bankbooks; bank officer's name and address.

Cemetery — location of deed to burial plot, if you have reserved one.

Current income and expenses — location of ledgers and records; name and address of your accountant.

Insurance — location of policies, names and addresses of agents.

Military service records — location of discharge certification and VA benefit information; regional office address of the Veteran's Administration.

Real estate — location of deeds and records on your house. When assets are jointly owned, any records bearing on the contributions of the survivor to the purchase price will help cut down the tax bill on your estate. Canceled checks and income tax returns are among the papers that may be helpful. Be sure to list the real estate management agent's name and address.

Safe-deposit box — number of box, location of keys and list of contents; bank's name and address.

Securities — who holds them, location of records, name and address of broker.

Social Security — your number, location of record of credits earned, regional address and phone number of Social Security office.

Will — location of duplicate copy, attorney's name and address.

Getting a copyright

Now that those coin stories you've worked so hard on have finally been published, you'll want to know about the Copyright Law, effective Jan. 1, 1978.

The Library of Congress has a publication that explains what the Copyright Law does for authors of literary, dramatic, musical and artistic works. For single free copies of Circular R99, which briefly describes the law, and Circular R1, *Copyright Basics,* write to the Copyright Office, Library of Congress, Washington, D.C. 20559.

Books, individual articles and short works of fiction, photographs and other illustrative works, music and dramatic works can all be copyrighted. Numismatic publications hold the copyrights to all materials produced by staff members and to all works from the outside commissioned "for hire." However, the publications hold only limited rights to materials from outside contributors if there was no agreement to produce "for hire" and if no explicit transfer of copyright was made.

Copyrighting a published work gives the holder certain legal rights to the work. No one may publish the work without the copyright holder's permission, although the fair use portion of the law permits sensible publication of small portions of a copyrighted work. The copyright is good for the author's life, plus 50 years. After then, the material becomes a part of the public domain and may be printed by anyone.

Among the exclusive rights the Copyright Law gives the owner of a copyright are:
• To sell or distribute the work.
• To transform or revise the work by dramatization, translation, or musical arrangement.
• To record the work.
• To perform the work publicly.
• Print, reprint, and copy the work.

Only the author or someone designated by the author can claim a copyright.

To obtain a copyright, you need to register a claim in the Copyright Office, Library of

Congress. The holder must fill out an application form, and send it along with a registration fee and one or more copies of the work to be copyrighted. The law protects uncopyrighted material from the moment it is produced, although when it is published, full protection can be obtained by placing a prominent notice of copyright (©, "Copyright," or "Copr."), plus name of the copyright holder and the year of publication.

How to prevent robberies

Coin collectors, because of the nature of their hobby, are often marks for burglars. The frequency of robberies for numismatists, as for other collectors of valuable objects, is an unhappy fact of life. Are you protecting your investment the best you can?

DO YOU:

Keep your coins in old cigar boxes?

Under your bed?

In the bottom drawer?

Pushed way back on the clothes closet shelf?

In suitcases?

Under the davenport or chairs?

In a piggy bank?

In your tool chest in the basement?

In a garbage can?

In the trunk in the attic?

In surplus shell cases?

In your jewelry box?

ARE YOUR:

Doors left unlocked or open?

Doors capable of being opened with a skeleton key, a pen knife, or a crowbar?

Windows open or unlocked?

Coins and other numismatic items insured for their full value?

Outside lights on when you answer the door at night?

Valuables locked in a safe which two people could carry?

DO YOU:

Permit strangers to enter your home to use your phone and copy your phone number?

Attend coin meetings, shows, conventions, or auctions without necessary security?

Carry with you high priced items and show them around?

Always buy high priced items and let everyone know?

Have a method of operation, a regular schedule of coming and going from your house?

DOES YOUR FAMILY:

Do your shopping on the same day every week, with the same stops, returning home at the same time?

Have the same schedule week in and week out? Could a stranger park his car in your neighborhood and watch your house without you noticing it?

Receive many phone calls where the caller asks for someone who doesn't live at your house?

Have your name on many lists of known coin collectors?

Go out after coin meetings, shows, or conventions, to have a drink or a hamburger, always at the same place with the same people?

Pass coins around among this group and talk about your collection or someone else's collection so everyone can hear about it?

IF YOU'RE A COIN DEALER, DO YOU:

Travel alone, leave your car while you stop and eat, leave your car unlocked?

Leave all your coins in your car while you check into a motel?

Leave your coins in your room while you eat or see the town?

Not bother to check into a security room before you check into your hotel room?

Know most hotels have safety deposit boxes for their guests' valuables, some of which will hold two large suitcases? Do you use them?

Have safety deposit boxes, one that you can get into on Saturday and another on Monday?

Have a burglar alarm on your house or store? Have its installers been checked out by the police? Does it have a direct line to the police?

Have a neighbor or relative keep an eye on your house or store while you are on vacation or at a coin show?

Leave your bourse table unlocked and unattended at a show while you visit other dealers?

Travel with a luggage carrier on top of your car so you can be easily tailed?

Have a bank offering a room or office where you might safely work on your coins without being disturbed or seen?

Have a bank with arrangements to make night deposits?

Park your car in the driveway after returning home from a show and carry your suitcases in, leaving your coins in the car?

Travel with other dealers?

Always leave a show during the break time when there's confusion and a shortage of trucks? Who watches your valuables while you hunt a truck?

Have panic buttons at strategic locations in your store?

Have a large enough safe, preferably a walk-in with the walls, ceiling and floor also part of the safe?

Become so preoccupied with the ticker tape you wouldn't notice customers, or notice being robbed?

Know someone could attach a homing device to your car and follow you for thousands of miles?

Know several cars could be following you, connected by walkie-talkies, interchanging positions so you don't become suspicious?

Think a burglar wouldn't know which coins to steal? Many are experts in their fields and know which coins command the highest prices on the market.

Know how long you could remain in business if your stock is stolen while you wait for the insurance company to settle up?

Museums 19

History of the national collection

The national numismatic collection, now housed in the Smithsonian Institution, had its beginnings soon after the United States was formed.

The history begins around 1818, when the Columbian Institute for the Promotion of Arts and Sciences was granted a charter from Congress. Located in Washington, D.C., the Institute had a small numismatic collection kept in the Institute's cabinets, not available to the public.

When the charter for the Columbian Institute expired in 1838, associates became members of the National Institution, and deposited their effects, books and papers in its cabinet.

The National Institution for the Promotion of Science, or the National Institute as it was later called, was organized on May 15, 1840, under the leadership of Joel Roberts Poinsett. Its purpose was to establish a national museum.

John Varden, however, must be given credit as the first to offer public exhibits featuring numismatic objects. He was an enterprising private citizen of Washington, D.C., who opened a small museum adjoining his home in 1836, with displays consisting of some 500 curiosities.

In 1840 Varden sold his collection to the National Institute for $1,500. The curator of the National Institute, Dr. Henry King, had the entire inventory of Varden's museum installed in the National Gallery Hall at the United States Patent Office. Varden accompanied the collection as an assistant.

For four years following its organization in 1840, the National Institute was exceedingly active and prosperous. In rooms made available at the Patent Office Building it gathered, under the name of the "National Cabinet of Curiosities."

Smithson fortune

In 1846 James Smithson, an English scientist, bequeathed his fortune, including many numismatic items, to the United States for the "increase and diffusion of knowledge." On Aug. 10, 1846, an act of Congress was signed by President Polk establishing the Smithsonian Institution and on May 1, 1847, the cornerstone of its first building was laid on the Mall.

During this time the National Institute failed to secure public recognition and in 1858 the transfer of its collection to the Smithsonian began, but was not completed until 1883.

When the centennial exposition of 1876 was held in Philadelphia, the Institution found that it had such an enormous quantity of material in its custody that it became necessary to move to a new building, the United States National Museum, now the Arts and Industries Building. George Brown Goode was appointed assistant secretary in charge of the museum.

In 1893 the entire numismatic collection was withdrawn from display and stored, after being crowded out by expanding natural history collections. During this time an attempt was made to assemble a general collection of currencies of the world and numismatic acquisitions were both numerous and varied.

One of the most outstanding groups of coins received was a collection of 28 Japanese gold and silver pieces, which came to the Museum in 1886 together with other relics once owned by Ulysses S. Grant.

Another major accession was a collection

of 2,025 Far Eastern coins bequeathed to the Smithsonian by George Bunker Glover in 1897.

Theodore Belote was appointed assistant curator in 1909. This provided a fresh opportunity for the development of numismatic collections in the Smithsonian, for Belote had a particular interest in this subject. Also, in the years from 1910 to 1914, with the addition of a new museum building for natural history, space was gradually relinquished for the numismatic exhibits. By 1914 Belote had finished selecting, classifying, cleaning and labeling coins and medals for the display.

During World War I and the early postwar years, the numismatic acquisitions were heavily weighted toward medals and decorations, including 1,200 Lincoln items covering nearly every phase of his life, assembled by Robert Hewitt.

Mint collection

The most important event of this period was the transfer of the Mint collection in Philadelphia to the Smithsonian. When Dr. T. Louis Comparette, curator, died suddenly in 1922 the Mint collection was closed to the public. At that time it was suggested that it be moved to Washington.

Formal acceptance by the Secretary of the Smithsonian Institution followed on Feb. 19, 1923. A total of 18,291 specimens was included in the transfer, increasing the holdings of the national numismatic collection from 21,523 to 39,814 items. In addition to the numismatic items, the Mint transferred 814 books selected by Belote from the specialized library at the Philadelphia Mint in 1924.

The history of the Mint collection officially started in June 1838, but its actual history goes back to the beginning of the Mint in 1792-1793. The Chief Coiner, Adam Eckfeldt, connected with the Mint since its inception, "led as well by his own taste as by the expectation that a conservatory would some day be established, took pains to preserve master-coins of the different annual issues of the Mint, and to retain some of the finest foreign specimens, as they appeared in deposit for recoinage."

Among the coins deposited by Adam Eckfeldt was, for instance, the Brasher doubloon. When a special annual appropriation was instituted for this purpose by Congress in 1838, the collection took permanent form and grew continuously.

The eagerness of the Mint assayers William E. Du Bois and Jacob R. Eckfeldt to complete the Mint collection contributed to its continued growth. Du Bois in his *Pledges of History*

(1846) mentions that after the collection was officially established in June 1838, it "has gone on in a continual augmentation ... specimens of new coinage, domestic or foreign, must be added as they appear."

In the same volume Du Bois also describes the early Mint exhibit, located at that time at 17th and Spring Garden streets in Philadelphia.

Data about the growth of the Philadelphia Mint collection may be gleaned from Mint records preserved in the National Archives as well as from occasional published notes and reports. Some early illustrations of coins from the cabinet are contained in Jacob R. Eckfeldt and William E. Du Bois' *A Manual of Gold and Silver Coins of All Nations, Struck Within the Past Century* (1842).

The first full catalog of the collection appeared in 1860 under the direction of James Ross Snowden. Titled *A Description of Ancient and Modern-Coins, in the Cabinet Collection at the Mint of the United States* (1860), it was prepared by George Bull, in charge of the cabinet, with the advice and assistance of Du Bois, at that time assistant assayer and curator of the cabinet.

In 1861 Snowden published *The Medallic Memorials of Washington in the Mint of the United States.* He was very much interested in this particular section of the cabinet and made every effort to enlarge it.

Notes about additions to the collections were published by W.E. Du Bois in *The United States Mint Cabinet,* where he mentions that "the whole number of coins and medals at this time [1874] is 6,484," and in *Recent Additions to the Mint Cabinet.*

In 1891, R.A. McClure, curator of the Mint collection, prepared *An Index to the Coins and Medals of the Cabinet of the Mint of the United States at Philadelphia,* published by the Superintendent of the Mint, O.C. Bobyshell; and in 1894 the *Philadelphia Telegraph* reported on "Late Additions" to the Mint cabinet: "8,000 coins were on display, the case of current coins stands to the left of the museum door, opposite the curator's desk."

With the completion of a new Mint in Philadelphia in 1902, described as "the finest building ever constructed for coinage purposes in the world," the cabinet was moved to the new location. It was reinstalled there in sumptuous surroundings and in new, rather ponderous exhibit cases.

The first and only formally recognized curator of the Mint collection was Dr. Thomas Louis Comparette, appointed to the post in 1905. (Various other people had been delegated to take care of the cabinet but without the curator title.) Comparette immediately made plans for expansion and improvement of the Mint collection.

"The most pressing needs appear to be a new catalog and a rearrangement of the coins in the cases," according to his comprehensive report about the numismatic collection.

In the same report he mentions, referring to the past, "An apparent tendency to give undue preference to rather expensive rarities for exhibitions as 'show pieces' has resulted in restricting the numerical development of the collection, in the increase of certain series at the expense of others, and especially in the neglect of the coins of lower denomination, which are much less attractive to the average visitor but necessary in order to gain a proper idea of the complete coinage of a given country or period and highly valued by the better informed.

"The more serious purpose better harmonizes with what is felt to be the worthier function of the collection, for the attitude of the cabinet has been from the first that of an educational institution," he recorded.

The preparation of the catalog took Comparette about seven years; it appeared in 1912 comprising 634 pages and 15 plates. In 1914 a so-called "third edition" followed with the same number of plates but expanded through additions to 694 pages. A most useful 106-page *Guide to the Numismatic Collection of the Mint of The United States at Philadelphia, Pa.* was published in 1913. In addition to the catalog Dr. Comparette published various papers, particularly in the field of ancient numismatics.

While in charge of the Mint cabinet Comparette expended considerable time and effort to mobilize support for the improvement of the collection. He attempted to obtain the support of President Theodore Roosevelt to secure for the cabinet the H.C. Hoskier collection of Greek and Roman coins when the owners who lived in South Orange, N.J., offered it for sale.

Comparette succeeded in obtaining the support of the Assay Commission of 1909; its committee on resolutions passed a motion recommending that the coin collection be improved and suggested the striking of artistic medals with the understanding that the profits from their sale should benefit the Mint collection. Similar resolutions were passed by the annual Assay Commissions meeting in subsequent years.

Reports about the growth of the collection were incorporated in the Director's *Annual Report* from 1910 through 1921 under the title "The State of the Numismatic Collection" (after 1917, "The Progress of the Numismatic Collection"). All these activities ended with Dr. Comparette's sudden death on July 3, 1922.

Transferring the collection

The idea of the transfer of the collection to Washington had been proposed as early as 1916 by Dr. George F. Kunz of New York, president of the American Scenic and Historic Preservation Society and one of the most active members of the American Numismatic Society. He discussed the idea with Dr. Charles D. Walcott, secretary of the Smithsonian, and with Director of the Mint Robert W. Wooley on April 4, 1916.

The lack of a curator after the death of Dr. Comparette and the closing of the Mint to the public because of a robbery at the Denver Mint (committed after thieves obtained information through a previous visit) were among the factors that persuaded Secretary of the Treasury Andrew W. Mellon to decide to transfer the collection to the National Museum in Washington, and he so notified Secretary Walcott in February 1923.

The secretary of the Smithsonian acknowledged Andrew Mellon's letter on Feb. 12 and delegated W. de C. Ravenel, director of the museum, and T. T. Belote, curator of history, to discuss the necessary arrangements for the transfer.

Formal acceptance of the collection by the secretary of the Smithsonian Institution followed on Feb. 19.

On Feb. 28, Theodore T. Belote was authorized to inspect the numismatic collection at the Mint in order to plan for its packing and transportation to the National Museum. He spent March 6 and 7 there and reported on March 8 to Miss M.M. O'Reilly, Acting Director of the Mint, his findings and recommendations.

Pressure, however, built up in Philadelphia against the proposed transfer. The *Philadelphia Ledger* of March 31 expressed great concern "that the Philadelphia Mint's invaluable collections of coins, medals and tokens is being boxed, ready for shipment to the National Museum in Washington. The collection which was begun with the inception of the Philadelphia Mint in 1792, is believed to be one of the finest in the world." Another editorial on the same subject appeared in the *Ledger* on April 1.

Various local organizations, and through them congressmen from the area, were mobilized in an intensive but futile action to reverse the Treasury Department's decision.

On a national level, however, the American Numismatic Association immediately supported the transfer. In an editorial comment which appeared in the May 1923 issue of *The Numismatist,* this position was made very clear:

"Taking a broad view of the matter, the National Museum in Washington is the logical place for the coin collection. It has been termed the Mint collection, though, strictly speaking, it is the national collection. The National Museum already has a collection of medals, and the merging of the two collections will be advantageous.

"The construction of the Mint Cabinet is such that it would be impossible to enlarge the space for the collection without remodeling the entire rotunda. This fact would prevent the material growth of the collection.... In the national Museum more space will probably be available, and perhaps more money for the purchase of additional specimens can be obtained.

"Washington is the home of our other national collections. ... The Capital City is a Mecca for sightseers and visitors, and the other collections will help to attract a larger number of visitors than a collection of coins alone could command.

"There is one phase of the matter that is worthy of reflection, but which may not have received consideration by the Treasury officials in reaching their decision. The late Dr. Comparette ... is said to have been greatly concerned ... about the apparent deterioration of the condition of the coins in the collection. The cause of this ... was believed to be due to an atmospheric condition ... on The Mall in Washington, all such conditions will be removed."

The editorial concludes that the closing of the Mints to visitors "is to be regretted more than the transfer of the collection from one city to another."

Concerned about the protests from Philadelphia, which multiplied during the month of April, Belote tried to obtain the active support of the national numismatic organizations.

He visited New York where he had a series of meetings on May 7 and 8 with Edward T. Newell, president of the American Numismatic Society, Moritz Wormser, president of the American Numismatic Association, and Howland Wood, curator of the American Numismatic Society's collections.

He obtained assurances that efforts would be made to have resolutions passed by the executive bodies of the two societies for presentation to the Secretary of the Treasury recommending the proposed transfer without delay.

As a result of these conferences, the Council of the American Numismatic Society passed a resolution favoring the transfer of the Mint collection to the Smithsonian, and on May 15 a letter to that effect was sent to the Secretary of the Treasury.

Howland Wood reported to Belote that: "Our Council passed a Resolution to write to Secretary Mellon favoring the transfer of the Mint collection to Washington, and a letter was sent to that effect on Saturday last. Also, the N.Y. Numismatic Club on Friday evening passed a similar Resolution. It looks now fairly favorable for the National Museum's getting it."

Similar action was taken by the New York Numismatic Club upon motion brought by Moritz Wormser at its May meeting. After obtaining the unanimous support of the board of governors of the American Numismatic Association as well, Wormser notified Andrew Mellon of this support.

In short sequence, Secretary Walcott informed Mellon on May 16 that "the National Museum has entirely perfected its plans for the acceptance and appropriate installation of the numismatic collection from the United States Mint" and asked whether the Secretary of the Treasury could advise him "of the exact time when transfer ... will be completed."

Actually, all arrangements for the transportation of the collection were completed without further delay. The shipment went forward by registered mail, insured and accompanied by Secret Service men. It arrived at the Smithsonian the next morning. It was formally "accessioned" as a transfer on June 13, 1923.

In 1931, the Smithsonian Institution numismatic collection was moved from poorly lighted quarters to a smaller, but much brighter area of the Arts and Industries building where it remained until its transfer to the Museum of History and Technology.

Theodore Belote, curator of the Division of History, remained in charge of the collections until 1948, and by this time the collection had increased to 54,175 pieces.

In 1948, Stuart Mosher was appointed acting curator of the division. He held this position until his death in February 1956. At the time of his death, the collection had a total of 64,522 pieces. This growth included the contribution of Paul Straub consisting of 1,860 gold and 3,886 silver coins.

From February through September 1956, Mendel Peterson served as acting curator of the division until Dr. Vladimir Clain-Stefanelli was appointed curator in October 1956, and Elvira Clain-Stefanelli was appointed as assistant curator in 1957 and associate curator in 1959. She now serves as executive director, a position to which she was named after the death of her husband in 1982.

In October 1964, the Hall of Monetary History and Medallic Art, in the newly built Museum of American History, became the home of the Smithsonian Institution collection.

In 1966, the Smithsonian started acquiring from the Bureau of Engraving and Printing, 306,275 "certified proofs" of just about everything the BEP has printed. The certified proofs of paper money, government documents and other inked impressions from new printing plates submitted to BEP officials for approval before the plates went into regular use were transferred to the Smithsonian when the BEP ran out of room to store a century's worth of printing treasures. This acquisition was completed in July 1984.

In 1968, after governmental maneuvering and eventual sanction, the Smithsonian acquired the Josiah K. Lilly collection of gold coins in exchange for a $5.5 million tax write-off for the Lilly estate. The collection contains 6,125 gold coins and is considered one of the finest gold coin collections in the world. The collection arrived at the Smithsonian June 13, 1968.

New exhibit

The Smithsonian opened a new exhibit, "The History of Money and Medals," July 12, 1972, showing the history of mankind as it is mirrored in coinage.

The exhibit was compiled in slightly more than six months. Containing more than 10,000 numismatic specimens arranged in 130 units, the display has something for everyone from the most knowledgeable scholars to children (coins for touching have been provided for the latter).

Vladimir and Elvira Clain-Stefanelli, co-curators of the Division of Numismatics for more than two decades, used for the central theme of the main display the evolution of the money economy as an integral aspect of the cultural, economic and social development of human society.

Significant contributions to the exhibit were made by private collectors and corpora-tions as well as by government agencies such as the Library of Congress, the Secret Service and the Mints of the United States, Britain and France.

Early in 1974 the Smithsonian and the American Bankers Association announced plans to mount a major Bicentennial exhibit concerning commercial banking in the Smithsonian's National Museum of History and Technology.

The exhibit opened to the public Sept. 18, 1975. It told the story of America's involvement in banking, from Colonial barter systems, when prices were expressed in beaver skins, to the sophisticated electronic techniques of today.

The exhibit was supplemented by an illustrated essay, "Two Centuries of American Banking," written by Mrs. Clain-Stefanelli and her husband.

The exhibit remained in place through the American Bicentennial celebration of 1976.

Important acquisitions

The year 1978 proved one of important acquisitions for the Smithsonian. Formal papers for the transfer of the Chase Manhattan Bank money collection, one of the most famous in the history of the United States, were signed on Jan. 16 by S. Dillon Ripley, secretary of the Smithsonian Institution, and David Rockefeller, chairman of the Chase Manhattan Bank.

The massive collection of coins, tokens, medals and paper money was formed by the American numismatic immortal, Farran Zerbe, who became the Chase Manhattan Museum's first curator.

On May 17, 1978, in a historic ceremony, the Treasury Department turned over to the Smithsonian a collection of 800 pieces of U.S. paper money with a numismatic value of more than $1 million. The collection, with a face value of $578,365.79, includes nearly one note for every issue of U.S. currency between the Civil War period and the early 1960s.

Three months later, in August, Mr. and Mrs. R. Henry Norweb donated a Proof specimen of the 1913 Liberty Head 5-cent piece — one of only five such pieces known — to the Smithsonian.

Death ends tenure

On Oct. 19, 1982, Dr. Vladimir Clain-Stefanelli, chairman of the Department of Applied Arts of the Smithsonian Institution and senior historian and curator of the National Numismatic Collection, died at

Georgetown University Hospital in Washington, D.C.

During the quarter of a century he was associated with the Smithsonian, Dr. Clain-Stefanelli's acumen and diplomacy were successful in increasing the size of the National Numismatic Collection more than tenfold, building it from a relatively insignificant collection of about 64,000 to one of the most outstanding in the world numbering close to 900,000 pieces.

On Dec. 28, 1982, Emery May Norweb donated a 52-piece collection of U.S. Colonial coins in memory of Dr. Vladimir Clain-Stefanelli.

In September 1983, Mrs. Elvira Clain-Stefanelli, who had served with her husband as co-curator and carried on the curatorial work they had shared prior to his death, was named to the new title of executive director of the National Numismatic Collection.

At the same time, Cory Gillilland was named curator for the Division of Numismatics, leaving her position as chief of the Bureau of the Mint's consumer affairs staff to assume her new post. She was associated with the Smithsonian's Division of Numismatics earlier, from 1965 to 1975. Her areas of responsibility include American and foreign medals.

In July 1984, the United States Mint transferred 114 Olympic coins, American Arts Gold Medallions, bronze and pewter national medals to the national collection. This was the largest transaction of its kind since 1923. Participating were Mint Director Donna Pope, Mrs. Clain-Stefanelli and Smithsonian officials Roger G. Kennedy and John Jameson.

On April 21, 1986, Dr. Richard G. Doty became the curator of Western Hemisphere Numismatics for the National Numismatic Collection. His responsibilities at the Smithsonian include the vast collections of U.S. paper money, foreign currency and financial documents. He also oversees the world token collection and the collections of medieval and Roman coinages. Prior to this position, Doty was curator of modern coins and paper money at the American Numismatic Society in New York.

The Smithsonian Institution's National Numismatic Collection is displayed in segments, often with themes or focusing upon current events or persons. The Museum of History and Technology, which houses the collection, is located on Constitution Avenue at 14th Street Northwest on the Mall. It is open to the public from 10 a.m. to 5:30 p.m. every day and is closed Christmas Day. There is no admission charge.

Other government displays

Numismatic displays contained in the various current U.S. Mints and restored facilities are discussed with the respective facility in Chapter 5.

American Numismatic Society

The American Numismatic Society Museum, Broadway between 155th and 156th streets in New York, is unique in being the first museum in the world devoted entirely to numismatics.

In honor of the society's 125th anniversary celebration in 1983, a new exhibition, "The World of Coins," was mounted with a wholly new approach to the story of money. It shows the use, value and design of money in a cross-cultural story, shedding light on such humanistic issues as economic development, trade patterns, social and political symbolism and the relationship of religion and public life.

The first annual exhibition of medallic and bas-relief works sponsored by the American Medallic Sculpture Association was held in the east hall in 1983, co-sponsored by the AMSA and the society. The east hall was restructured in 1984 and re-carpeted to provide for temporary displays, including those placed each fall since December 1984, in conjunction with the annual "Coinage of Americas" conference.

The society has pioneered in the use of the computer, integrating the computer facility into the exhibition experience in the refurbished west hall. The society's extensive holdings are in the process of being computerized with all of the relevant information available being included for the benefit of the researcher.

The ANS collection is large and representative. All fields are covered, but particularly important are the coins of ancient Greece and Rome, the Far Eastern series, and the Islamic issues. The medieval, modern and American groups are also distinguished.

By far the greater portion of the collection has been received through bequests and gifts both of collections and of single specimens. A relatively small proportion has been acquired by purchase.

The collection's great strength in the ancient Greek, Roman and Byzantine periods lies in the great collection bequeathed by Edward T. Newell, the society's president from 1916 until his death in 1941. Newell's collection, long known throughout the numismatic world for its quality, is especially rich in those series to which his scholarly publications were devoted — the coinages of Alexander the Great and his successors. Altogether his collection numbers more than 87,000 pieces.

The collection of ancient coins has been enriched also by the F. Munroe Endicott collection of Greek and Roman coins, the Richard Hoe Lawrence collection of Roman coins, the W. Gedney Beatty collection of Greek coins, the Harold W. Bell collection of Byzantine coins, the Gautier collection of Greek coins presented by an anonymous donor, the Abraham A. Rosen gift of Greek fractional silver and bronze coins and by many other gifts of whole groups or single coins.

A monumental bequest, with an estimated value of $500,000, was received from the estate of the late Robert F. Kelley, a former head of the U.S. State Department's East European Division. Amassed largely through $8 to $10 purchases from Turkish bazaars, Kelley's collection included 1,155 ancient Greek and Byzantine coins. Among the 855 Greek pieces were coins minted from the seventh to the first centuries B.C. The 300 Byzantine coins span the fourth century B.C. through the late 12th century A.D. All coins are of gold, silver or electrum.

In 1980 the society received the Arthur J. Fecht collection, 3,310 pieces of world gold coins, United States and modern foreign.

Coinage of the Far East is likewise well represented in the society's cabinets. The Chinese coins alone number more than 18,000 and constitute one of the largest collections of its kind in the world. The Far Eastern section derives its great strength from a large private collection, that of John Reilly Jr., one-time treasurer of ANS, which was presented to the society by his daughter. The collections of two famous numismatists, Henry A. Ramsden and Neil Gordon Munro, form important sections of the Reilly collection.

In the field of Islamic numismatics, the collection ranks among the leading in the world. Its growth from small beginnings began in 1917 with the gift by Edward T. Newell of both his own collection of more than 5,000 Islamic coins and that of Howland Wood of 6,000 odd specimens. The Durkee, A.F.R. Hoernle, W.H. Valentine, Longworth Dames, among other collections, have provided additions especially in the series for India.

An important adjunct to this section is a remarkable collection of Arabic glass weights built on a nucleus bequeathed the society by James B. Nies and expanded by gifts from Edward T. Newell and Louis H. Schroeder. With its extensive coverage of the entire Near and Middle Eastern world, this section of the society's cabinet contains much material for study and publication. Among the coins of the many dynasties in its trays there are some whose inscriptions add to historical record the name of a Mint or ruler otherwise unknown.

Coinages of the lands of America's forefathers have representative selections, strong in some sections, weaker in others. Thanks to gifts from J. Sanford Saltus and the bequest of Herbert E. Ives, there are important pieces in the English series. The medieval and later periods of Italy are well represented through the Herbert Scoville collection of more than 3,600 coins and collection of Florentine florins and Venetian ducats bequeathed by Herbert E. Ives. Poland and its history are well illustrated by the Alexandre Orlowski collection of more than 2,000 specimens.

Early Latin American coinages from Mexico and Peru are strong through gifts from Wayte Raymond, as are the cut and counterstamped pieces of the West Indies from the Julius Guttag collection.

Coinage struck in the 19th and 20th centuries is well represented through the gift of Wayte Raymond of the specimens gathered in preparation of his *Standard Catalogues* of contemporary coins.

The coinage of the United States naturally forms an important section of the society's cabinet. Notable sections have come from the J. Pierpont Morgan, William B. Osgood Field, and Elliott Smith collections. The society possesses such treasures as one of the four known specimens of the original Confederate half dollar, a gift of J. Sanford Saltus, and the press used by Augustus Bechtler in striking private gold coins in North Carolina, given by Julius Guttag.

One of the richest series is that of the United States copper cents struck between 1793 and 1857, the collection gathered by George H. Clapp and given by him to the society. The Colonial issues of Massachusetts are present with specimens from the Field collection, and the state coinages before the adoption of the Constitution are well represented.

Tokens, helpmates to coinages in times of stress, offer interesting sidelights to the history of periods of monetary crisis. The richest series of tokens in the collection are those of the "Hard Times" period in the United States, 1837-41, and the merchants' tokens of the Civil War period of the 1860s, including the Edward Groh collection of 5,286 specimens donated in 1900.

Although weak in medals of the Renaissance, the age in which medallic art was born, the collection has strength in later periods of its development. English medals from the period of Elizabeth from the Daniel Parish Jr. collection, Indian Peace medals from the Stephen H.P. Pell collection, Adm. Vernon medals from the L. McCormick-Goodhart collection, along with a good selection of medals designed by contemporary American and European sculptors, provide a record of the progress of medallic art. Of special interest as a development in modern medallic art is the complete series of porcelain medals made at the Meissen Porcelain Works since World War I, a gift from Louis H. Schroeder.

In 1978, Ira, Mark and Lawrence Goldberg gave 1,000 medals, trial strikes, models and dies of Karl Goetz.

Decorations of orders of knighthood and of governments for military or civil merit form a special section of the collection. It is one of the most comprehensive of such collections in the world. It was built on a nucleus given by J. Sanford Saltus and expanded by gifts from Harold E. Gillingham and others.

Paper money, which in the present century is more and more encroaching on coins as a medium of currency, is also present in the collection. The obsolete bank notes of the "wildcat" bank era of the United States, Continential notes of Revolutionary times, are supplemented with selections of foreign paper currencies and special series as prisoner of war money, occupational currency, and more. As have other fields, this section has benefited from donations, such as the 4,431 specimens of paper currency donated by Archer M. Huntington in 1914.

American Numismatic Association

The American Numismatic Association continually expands its collection of all numismatic items in the museum located at its Colorado Springs, Colo., headquarters. Presently, it holds an estimated 250,000 specimens.

Displays are mounted in the museum's entrance rotunda and eight galleries, all of which are open to the public free of charge. The entrance rotunda features the "Hall of Nations," a touching gallery for the visually-impaired. Here, coin models contributed by Mints throughout the world are mounted.

A separate gallery houses the ANA Numismatic Hall of Fame, while other permanent exhibits are mounted in the Americana I and Americana II galleries. Americana I houses displays of tokens, paper money and coins used by the Colonies and United States prior to the establishment of the U.S. Mint.

Coinage and paper money of the United States, including regular issue and commemorative coins and medals, are on permanent display in the Americana II gallery, where visitors also will find displays of Hard Times tokens, Civil War tokens and private issue gold coins.

Dedication of the Arthur Braddan Coole Oriental library in July 1983, prompted an exhibit of Far Eastern Numismatic material in the upper level of the west gallery of the ANA museum. Later in the year the American Medallic Sculpture Association's exhibition traveled from New York to ANA through a grant from the Lewis M. Reagan Memorial Foundation Inc. The exhibit was installed in the museum's hall of modern medallic art.

These were part of the program of temporary exhibitions which the ANA continues to install in its galleries. It has an ongoing program of improving collection storage facilities, expanding service through lectures and tours, and publicizing its collections.

Highlighting the Los Angeles Olympic Games was an exhibit in the ANA museum galleries, "The Olympic Games: A Numismatic Celebration." This was co-sponsored by the United States Olympic Committee and utilized the Stack's galleries, the museum's primary changing exhibits area. It opened in connection with the USOC's National Sports festival in Colorado Springs in June 1983.

Three special exhibits mounted include the Hall of Presidents, in which the famed Elliott Markoff collection of coins and presidential memorabilia can be found; the Colorado gallery, with displays that relate to the state's role in numismatics; and the Hall of Modern Medallic Art, a gift of the Franklin Mint.

Also integral to the ANA Museum is the Amos Memorial Theater, donated by the publishers of *Coin World*, in which educational talks, slide programs and films are presented, as well as other educational programs.

The ANA plans a large-scale reorganization of its permanent galleries following its hosting of the 50th anniversary congress of the Federation Internationale de la Medaille in 1987 in Colorado Springs.

Museums
UNITED STATES

California
BERKELEY. Judah L. Magnes Museum, 2911 Russell St., 94705. Jewish American Hall of Fame medal series, modern foreign coins and ancients. Open 10 a.m. to 4 p.m. Sunday through Thursday.

LOS ANGELES. Hebrew Union College Skirball Museum, 3077 University Mall, 90007. Ancient Jewish coins, medals, tokens and numismatic literature. Open only to scholars by appointment.

SAN FRANCISCO. Bank of California Money Museum, 400 California St., 94104. Gold rush period coins and ingots. Open 10 a.m. to 3:30 p.m. Monday through Thursday, 10 a.m. to 5 p.m. Friday, closed weekends and national holidays.

SAN FRANCISCO. Old Mint Museum, 5th and Mission Sts., 94103. Million dollars in gold bullion, United States coins, medals and paper money. Open 10 a.m. to 4 p.m. Monday through Friday; closed legal holidays. Free

SAN FRANCISCO. Wells Fargo Bank History Museum, 420 Montgomery St., 94104. Wells Fargo and Company history from 1852 to present. U.S. coins, paper money and modern foreign coins. Open 9 a.m. to 5 p.m. Monday through Friday, closed weekends and national holidays.

Colorado
COLORADO SPRINGS. American Numismatic Association, 818 N. Cascade Ave., 80903. U.S. and foreign coins, medals, tokens, paper money, medieval, ancients and a numismatic library. Open 8:30 a.m. to 4 p.m. Tuesday through Saturday, closed some national holidays. Tours by arrangement (303) 632-2646. Free.

COLORADO SPRINGS. Pioneers' Museum, 215 S. Tejon St., 80903. U.S. paper money and medals. Open 10 a.m. to 5 p.m. Monday through Saturday and 1 p.m. to 5 p.m. Sunday, closed national holidays. Free.

DENVER. Denver Museum of Natural History, City Park, 80205. Houses the gold boulder of Summitville. Open 9 a.m. to 5 p.m. daily. Closed Christmas.

DENVER. United States Mint, 320 West Colfax Ave., 80204. Million dollar gold display, coin production history, U.S. coins and paper money. Open 8 a.m. to 3:30 p.m. daily except Wednesday 9 a.m. to 3:30 p.m. Closed holidays. Free.

FORT COLLINS. Fort Collins Museum, 200 Mathews St., 80524. Coins, medals, tokens and paper money. Open 10 a.m. to 5 p.m. Tuesday through Saturday and noon to 5 p.m. on Sunday. Free.

Connecticut
HARTFORD. Raymond E. Baldwin Museum of Connecticut History, Connecticut State Library, 231 Capitol Ave., 06106. Joseph C. Mitchelson collection, U.S. coins and medals. Open 9 a.m. to 4:45 p.m. Monday through Friday, 9 a.m. to 1 p.m. Saturday. Closed state holidays. Free.

MYSTIC. Mystic Seaport, Inc., P.O. Box 6000, 06355. U.S. and foreign coins, medals and paper money. Available to scholars upon written request. Open 9 a.m. to 5 p.m. Monday through Friday. Closed holidays.

Delaware
DOVER. Delaware State Museum, 316 S. Governors Ave., 19901. U.S. coins, medals, tokens and paper money. Open 10 a.m. to 4:30 p.m. Tuesday through Saturday and 1 p.m. to 4:30 p.m. Sunday, closed national holidays. Free.

District of Columbia
WASHINGTON. B'nai B'rith Museum, 1640 Rhode Island St. N.W., 20036. Ancients. Open 10 a.m. to 5 p.m. Sunday through Friday, closed national and Jewish holidays. Free.

WASHINGTON. National Archives and Records Administration Exhibition Hall, 8th St. and Constitution Ave. N.W., 20408, where the Declaration of Independence, Constitution and Bill of Rights are permanently displayed. U.S. presidents and constitution medals. Exhibition Hall open daily 10 a.m. to 9 p.m. April 1 through Labor Day and 10 a.m. to 5:30 p.m. Labor Day through March 31, except Christmas.

WASHINGTON. Smithsonian Institution, National Museum of American History, Constitution Ave. between 12th and 14th Sts., N.W., 20560. Oriental, Islamic, U.S. and foreign tokens, orders and decorations, U.S. and foreign coins, paper money, medals, medieval and ancients, on display in the Hall of Monetary History and Medallic Art, third floor. Open 10 a.m. to 5:30 p.m. daily during the winter and 10 a.m. to 7:30 p.m. daily from April to first week of September. Closed Christmas Day. (202) 357-1798. Free.

Florida

KEY WEST. Mel Fisher Maritime Heritage Society Museum, 200 Greene St. Contains the treasures removed from the sunken Spanish treasure ship *Nuestra Senora de Atocha,* including gold and silver bars, ship's artifacts, jewels, etc. Open 10 a.m. to 5:30 p.m., seven days a week. Admission $5 for adults, $1 for children. Senior Citizens' discounts available.

PENSACOLA. T. T. Wentworth Jr. Museum, 8382 Palafax, 32594. U.S. coins, medals, paper money, foreign coins, paper money, medieval and ancients. Open 2 p.m. to 6 p.m. Saturday and Sunday. Free.

TALLAHASSEE. Museum of Florida History, R.A. Gray Bldg., 32399. 18th century Spanish coins from new world Mints, U.S. and foreign coins and paper money. Open 9 a.m. to 4:30 p.m. Monday through Friday, 10 a.m. to 4:30 p.m. Saturday and 1 p.m. to 4:30 p.m. Sunday. Closed Christmas. Free.

Georgia

DAHLONEGA. Dahlonega Courthouse Gold Museum, 1-A Public Square, 30533. Georgia's gold mining history, U.S. coins. Open 9 a.m. to 5 p.m. Tuesday through Saturday, 2 p.m. to 5:30 p.m. Sunday. Closed Mondays, Christmas and Thanksgiving. $1 adults, 50¢ for children under 12. Groups rates available.

DAHLONEGA. North Georgia College, 30597. A complete set of gold coins minted at the Dahlonega branch Mint. Open 8 a.m. to 5 p.m. Monday through Friday, closed Thanksgiving, July 4 and Christmas. Free.

FORT BENNING. National Infantry Museum, U.S. Army Infantry Center, 31905. U.S. and world service medals. Open Tuesday through Friday 10 a.m. to 4:30 p.m. and Saturday-Sunday 12:30 p.m. to 4:30 p.m.. Closed New Year's Day, Thanksgiving and Christmas. Free.

ROYSTON. Northeast Georgia Bank, 30662. J.H. Beasley collection of gold and silver coins from 1799 and paper money from 1861 to present. Open 9 a.m. to 1 p.m. and 3

p.m. to 5 p.m. Monday, Tuesday, Thursday and Friday; 9 a.m. to noon Saturday. Closed Wednesday, Sunday and holidays. Free.

Idaho

COEUR D'ALENE. Museum of North Idaho, P.O. Box 812, 83814. Idaho medals and tokens. Open 11 a.m. to 5 p.m. Tuesday through Saturday from April 1 to Oct. 31 and by appointment only during the winter. Closed on holidays. Donation admission.

Illinois

CHICAGO. Balzekas Museum of Lithuanian Culture, 6500 S. Pulaski Road, 60629. Lithuanian medals, medieval, ancients and numismatic literature. Closed Christmas and New Year's Day. Adults $2, children and senior citizens $1.

CHICAGO. Field Museum of Natural History, Roosevelt Road at Lake Shore Drive, 60605. 80 different varieties of money displayed. Open 9 a.m. to 5 p.m. daily. Closed Thanksgiving, Christmas and New Year's Day.

WATSEKA. Iroquois County Historical Society, Old Court House, 103 W. Cherry, 60970. Coins, medals, tokens and paper money. Open 10:30 a.m. to 4:30 p.m. Monday through Friday; 1 p.m. to 4:30 p.m. Saturday and Sunday April-Dec. Closed Christmas and weekends Jan.-March. Donation admission.

Indiana

BLOOMINGTON. Indiana University Art Museum, 47405. Ancient and Byzantine coins. Open Wednesday, Friday and Saturday 9 a.m. to 5 p.m.; Thursday 10 a.m. to 8 p.m. and Sunday 1 p.m. to 5 p.m. Closed major holidays. Free.

INDIANAPOLIS. U.S. Army Finance Corps Museum, Building 1, Fort Harrison, 46249. Military currency, U.S. and foreign paper money. Open 8 a.m. to 4:30 p.m. Monday through Friday; closed national holidays. Free.

Iowa

LAKE OKOBOJI. Higgins Paper Money Museum, Airport Rd., 51355. Iowa National Bank notes and U.S. paper money. Open Memorial Day through Labor Day, Tuesday through Sunday 11 a.m. to 5:30 p.m. Closed Monday.

MAXWELL. Community Historical Museum, 50161. U.S. and foreign coins and paper money. Open 2 p.m. to 5 p.m. Sundays only from May 30 to October. Closed during the winter. Free

Kansas

BALDWIN. Old Castle Museum, Baker University, 515 Fifth St., 66006. U.S. and foreign coins and U.S. paper money including Confederate notes and notes of Louisiana banks. Open 2 p.m. to 5 p.m. daily except Monday, closed Christmas and New Year's Day. Free.

LOGAN. Dane G. Hansen Memorial Museum, 67646. Medals, tokens, paper money and other related items. Open 9 a.m. to noon and 1 p.m. to 4 p.m. Monday through Friday, 9 a.m. to noon and 1 p.m. to 5 p.m. Saturday and 1 p.m. to 5 p.m. Sunday and holidays. Closed Christmas. Free.

LYONS. Coronado Quivira Museum, 105 W. Lyon, 67554. First medal of the Catholic missionary. Open Tuesday through Saturday 10 a.m. to noon and 1 p.m. to 5 p.m. and Sunday 2 p.m. to 5 p.m. Closed Monday, Thanksgiving, Christmas and New Year's Day. Free.

Kentucky

OWENSBORO. Owensboro Area Museum, 2829 S. Griffith Ave., 42301. Coins, tokens, paper money, Colonial currency, Confederate and obsolete bank notes. Open 8 a.m. to 4 p.m. weekdays, 1 p.m. to 4 p.m. Saturday and Sunday. Closed national holidays. Free.

Louisiana

SHREVEPORT. The R.W. Norton Art Gallery, 4700 block of Creswell Ave., 71106. U.S. coins, medals, paper money and foreign coins. Open 1 p.m. to 5 p.m. daily except Mondays, closed national holidays. Free.

Maine

BRUNSWICK. Bowdoin College Museum of Art, Walker Art Museum, 04011. World medals and ancients. Open July-Labor Day Tuesday through Saturday 10 a.m. to 8 p.m. Sunday 2 p.m. to 5 p.m. September-June Tuesday through Friday 10 a.m. to 4 p.m.; Saturday 10 a.m. to 5 p.m.; Sunday 2 p.m. to 5 p.m. Closed national holidays. Free.

Maryland

ANNAPOLIS. U.S. Naval Academy Museum, 21402. U.S. and world naval medals. Open 9 a.m. to 4:50 p.m. Monday through Saturday; 11 a.m. to 4:50 p.m. Sunday. Closed New Year's Day, Thanksgiving and Christmas. Free.

BALTIMORE. Baltimore Museum of Art, Art Museum Drive, 21218. U.S. medals.

Massachusetts

BOSTON. Museum of Fine Arts, Huntington Ave., 02115. Ancients and medals. Open Tuesday 10 a.m. to 5 p.m., Wednesday 10 a.m. to 10 p.m., Thursday through Sunday 10 a.m. to 5 p.m. Closed Mondays and holidays. Adults $5, senior citizens $4 and free to all on Saturdays from 10 a.m. to noon, children 16 and under free.

LYNN. Lynn Historical Society, 125 Green St., 01902. U.S. coins, medals, tokens and paper money shown by appointment. Open to scholars only 9 a.m. to 4 p.m. Monday through Friday and 1 p.m. to 4 p.m. Saturday. Closed national holidays.

SALEM. Peabody Museum of Salem, East India Square, 01970. Coins, medals, tokens and paper money. Stored items open to scholars only. Open to public 10 a.m. to 5 p.m. Monday through Friday, 1 p.m. to 5 p.m. Sunday. Closed Thanksgiving, Christmas and New Year's Day. $3 for adults, $1.50 children.

WORCESTER. American Antiquarian Society, Salisbury St. and Park Ave., 01609. U.S. paper money, medals and numismatic literature. Open to scholars only. Library open 9 a.m. to 5 p.m. Monday through Friday, closed legal holidays. Free.

Michigan

DETROIT. Detroit Historical Museum, 5401 Woodward Ave., 48202. Detroit and Michigan scrip and coins, U.S. coins, medals and paper money. Available to scholars only. Open 9:30 a.m. to 5:30 p.m. Wednesday through Sunday, closed Monday and Tuesday. Free.

Mississippi

STATE COLLEGE. Cobb Institute of Archeology, Mississippi State University, 39762. Ancient Greek, Roman and Jewish coins, especially those relating to the Bible, medals and numismatic literature. Open Monday through Friday with certain restrictions. Closed regular holidays. Free.

Missouri

COLUMBIA. Museum of Art and Archeology, University of Missouri-Columbia, 1 Pickard Hall, 65211. Permanent exhibit of Ancient coins. Extensive collection of numismatic literature. Open 8 a.m. to 5 p.m. Tuesday through Friday, noon to 5 p.m. Saturday and Sunday. Closed some holidays. Free.

INDEPENDENCE. Truman Library, 64050. U.S. coins and medals on display; U.S. and foreign paper money in study collections only. Open to public 9 a.m. to 5 p.m. daily, closed Christmas, Thanksgiving and New Year's Day. $1.50 admission.

ST. LOUIS. Concordia Historical Institute, 801 De Mun Ave., 63105. Lutheran anniversary medals, foreign coins, medals, paper money and medieval. Shown by appointment. Open 8:30 a.m. to 4:30 p.m. Monday through Friday. Free.

ST. LOUIS. Mercantile-Newman Money Museum, Mercantile Tower, 7th and Washington Streets, 63101. Eric Newman collection of coins and currency, numismatic literature, U.S. coins, U.S. and foreign paper money and money changers. Open 9 a.m. to 4 p.m. Monday through Friday except holidays. Free.

ST. LOUIS. Washington University Gallery of Art, Forsyth and Skinker Campus, 63130. More than 1,000 Greek and Roman coins shown by appointment to scholars.

Nebraska

BOYS TOWN. Philamatic Center, P.O. Box 1, 68010. U.S. and foreign coins, paper money, medals and ancients. Open 8 a.m. to 4:30 p.m. Monday through Saturday, 9 a.m. to 4:30 p.m. Sunday, closed Thanksgiving, Christmas and New Year's Day. Free admission.

HASTINGS. Hastings Museum, 1330 N. Burlington, 68901. U.S. coins, medals, paper money, medieval and ancients. Open 9 a.m. to 5 p.m. Monday through Saturday, 1 p.m. to 5 p.m. Sunday. Closed Thanksgiving, Christmas and New Year's Day. $3 for adults; $1 ages 7-15.

OMAHA. Omaha Public Library, 215 S. 15th St., 68102. Ancients, medieval, foreign and U.S. coins, paper money and medals. Open 9 a.m. to 8:30 p.m. Monday through Friday, 9 a.m. to 5:30 p.m. Saturday, closed national holidays. Free.

Nevada

CARSON CITY. Nevada State Museum, 600 North Carson St., 89710. Exhibit of Carson City Mint mark coins and coin press. Open daily 8:30 a.m. to 4:30 p.m. Closed Thanksgiving, Christmas and New Year's Day. Admission 50¢ adults, children free.

New Hampshire

HANOVER. Hood Museum of Art, Dartmouth College, 03755. U.S. coins, paper money, medals, ancients and foreign coins. Open 9 a.m. to 5 p.m. Monday through Saturday; 2 p.m. to 5 p.m. Sunday. Numismatic collection shown by appointment only.

MANCHESTER. The Manchester Historic Association, 129 Amherst St., 03104. U.S. coins, paper money, medals and world medals. Open 9 a.m. to 4 p.m. Tuesday through Friday, 10 a.m. to 4 p.m. Saturday, closed national holidays. Free.

New Jersey

NEWARK. The Newark Museum, 49 Washington St., 07101. Extensive collection of coins, medals, tokens, paper money and numismatic literature. Open noon to 5 p.m. Tuesday through Sunday. Closed New Year's Day, July 4, Thanksgiving and Christmas. Free.

New York

BUFFALO. Buffalo and Erie County Historical Society, 25 Nottingham Court. Collections relate primarily to Buffalo, Erie County and Western New York. U.S. coins, paper money, medals, tokens and foreign paper money. Research by appointment.

NEW YORK. The American Numismatic Society, Broadway between 155th and 156th Sts., 10032. World's most comprehensive numismatic library and extensive numismatic collection in the United States, including over a million items; U.S. and foreign coins, medals, decorations, paper money, numismatic literature, medieval and ancients. "The World of Coins" art exhibition on the history of money. Open 9 a.m. to 4:30 p.m. Tuesday through Saturday and 1 p.m. to 4 p.m. Sunday. Closed national holidays. Free.

NEW YORK. The Jewish Museum, 92nd St. and Fifth Ave., 11028. Jewish/Israel coins, medals and ancients. Open noon to 5 p.m. Monday through Thursday, until 8 p.m. Tuesday evenings and 11 a.m. to 6 p.m. Sunday. Closed Jewish holidays. Admission charged.

POUGHKEEPSIE. The Elongated Coin Museum, 228 Vassar Road, 12603. 10,000 elongated coins with machines and data, still banks and numismatic literature. Open to collectors only, appointments two weeks in advance. Free.

North Carolina

CHARLOTTE. Mint Museum of Art, 2730 Randolph Road, 28207. Charlotte and Bechtler gold coins, Confederate, North Carolina and state bank notes and bonds. Open Wednesday through Saturday 10 a.m. to 5 p.m., Sunday 1 p.m. to 6 p.m. and Tuesday 10 a.m. to 10 p.m. Admission $2 adults, $1 senior citizens and students and childred 12 and under free.

RALEIGH. North Carolina Museum of History, 109 E. Jones St., 27611. Bechtler gold, ancient and mixed coins, military medals, paper money. Open to scholars only, 9 a.m. to 5 p.m. Tuesday through Saturday; 2 p.m. to 5 p.m. Sunday. Closed Christmas and New Year's Day. Free.

SHELBY. Cleveland County Historical Museum, Courtsquare, P.O. Box 1335, 28150. U.S. coins, paper money, medals, Civil War tokens and world medals. Open Monday through Friday 9 a.m. to 4 p.m. and Sunday 2 p.m. to 5 p.m. Closed holidays. Free.

Ohio

CLEVELAND. Cleveland Museum of Art, 11150 East Blvd., 44106. Ancients, modern coins, Renaissance medallions and the R. Henry Norweb British gold coin collection. Open 10 a.m. to 6 p.m. Tuesday, Thursday, Friday, 10 a.m. to 10 p.m. Wednesday, 9 a.m. to 5 p.m. Saturday and 1 p.m. to 6 p.m. Sunday. Closed New Year's Day, July 4, Thanksgiving, Christmas. Free.

CLEVELAND. Howard Dittrick Museum of Historical Medicine, 11000 Euclid Ave., 44106. Medical medals. Open 10 a.m. to 5 p.m. Monday through Friday and noon to 5 p.m. Saturday. Closed national holidays and Friday after Thanksgiving. Free.

DAYTON. Air Force Museum, Wright-Patterson Air Force Base, 45433. U.S. and world Air Force aircraft insignia, decorations, medals and commemorative coins. Open 9 a.m. to 5 p.m. weekdays, 10 a.m. to 6 p.m. weekends, closed Christmas. Free.

MARIETTA. Campus Maritus Museum, 45750. Coins, medals, paper money. Some items in storage available by appointment.

MILAN. Milan Historical Museum, 10 Edison Drive, 44846. U.S. coins, medals, tokens and paper money. Open 1 p.m. to 5 p.m. daily except Monday, closed Oct. 1 to April 1. Free.

OXFORD. Miami University Art Museum, Patterson Ave., 45056. Greek and Roman ancients in storage, available for research on request. Open 11 a.m. to 5 p.m. Tuesday through Sunday. Closed national and university holidays. Free.

PIQUA. Johnston Farm, 9845 N. Hardin Road, 45356. Indian peace medals. Open Memorial Day to Labor Day 9:30 a.m. to 5 p.m. Wednesday through Saturday, noon to 5 p.m. Sunday and holidays; open Saturdays and Sundays in September and October only; closed from November through March. Admission $3 for adults and free to children 12 and under.

WAPAKONETA. Neil Armstrong Museum, 45895. U.S. and world air and space medals. Open March through November 9:30 a.m. to 5 p.m. Monday through Saturday, noon to 5 p.m. Sunday and holidays. Admission $2 adults and children 6-12 $1. Group rates available.

Oregon

JACKSONVILLE. Jacksonville Museum, Southern Oregon Historical Society, P.O. Box 480, 206 N. 5th St., 97530. U.S. coins, foreign coins and paper money. Open 10 a.m. to 5 p.m. daily Memorial Day to Labor Day. Closed Mondays, Labor Day to Memorial Day. Free.

Pennsylvania

FRANKLIN CENTER. The Franklin Mint Museum, 19091. Modern foreign coins, medieval and ancients. Open 9:30 a.m. to 4:30 p.m. Tuesday through Saturday, 1 p.m. to 4:30 p.m. Sunday, closed Mondays and major holidays. Free.

PHILADELPHIA. Atwater Kent Museum, History Museum of Philadelphia, 15 S. 7th St., 19106. Collection of U.S. coins, medals, tokens and paper money. Exhibition galleries open to general public, storage collections can be seen by appointment with the curators in advance. Open 9:30 a.m. to 4:45 p.m. Tuesday through Satuday. Closed Sunday, Monday and city holidays. Free.

PHILADELPHIA. Philadelphia Civic Center, Civic Center Blvd. at 34th Street, 19104. Medals won by the Philadelphia Commercial Museum in national and international expositions and American Negro Commemorative Society medals.

PHILADELPHIA. Presbyterian Historical Society, 425 Lombard St., 19147. 6,000 communion tokens shown by appointment. Open Monday through Friday. Closed regular holidays. Free.

PITTSBURGH. Carnegie Museum of Natural History, 4400 Forbes Ave., 15213. U.S. coins, medals and ancients.

Rhode Island

PROVIDENCE. Museum of Art, R.I. School of Design, 224 Benefit St., 02903. Ancient Greek coins, U.S. and world medals. Open during the winter: Tuesday, Wednesday, Friday and Saturday 10:30 a.m. to 5 p.m., Sunday and holidays 2 p.m. to 5 p.m., Thursdays 1 p.m. to 7 p.m. Summer: Tuesday-Saturday 11 a.m. to 4 p.m. Adults $1, Children 5-18 25¢. Closed some holidays.

South Carolina

COLUMBIA. South Carolina Confederate Relic Room and Museum, World War Memorial Building, Sumter St. at Pendleton, 29201. Confederate bonds, U.S. coins, paper money, medals, foreign paper money and medals. Open 9 a.m. to 5 p.m. Monday through Friday, closed national and state holidays. Free.

South Dakota

PIERRE. Robinson Museum, Memorial Building, 500 E. Capitol Ave., 57501. South Dakota trade tokens, U.S. medals, foreign paper money and coins. Most open to scholars only. Open 8 a.m. to 5 p.m. Monday through Friday, 10 a.m. to 5 p.m. Saturday and 1 p.m. to 5 p.m. Sunday. Closed national holidays. Free.

Tennessee

HARROGATE. Abraham Lincoln Library and Museum, Lincoln Memorial University, 37752. Coins, medals, tokens, paper money and historical artifacts of the Lincoln Civil War Period. Open 9 a.m. to 4 p.m. Monday through Friday, 11 a.m. to 4 p.m. Saturday and 1 p.m. to 4 p.m. Sunday. Closed academic holidays. Research collection open for study by appointment only. Admission charge.

KNOXVILLE. Students' Museum, 516 Beaman, Chilhowee Park, 37914. U.S. coins and paper money, foreign paper money, ancients, slides and tapes on coinage history, story of money and silver dollars and a Mint errors exhibit. Open 9 a.m. to 5 p.m. Monday through Friday, 1 a.m. to 5 p.m. Saturday and 2 p.m. to 5 p.m. Sunday. Admission $1.75 adults, $1.25 children; group rates.

Texas

AUSTIN. Texas Memorial Museum, 2400 Trinity St., 78705. Swenson collection of coins and medallions. U.S. coins, paper money and medals, foreign paper money and medals, medieval and ancients. Open 9 a.m. to 5 p.m. Monday through Friday and 1 p.m. to 5 p.m. Saturday and Sunday

GARLAND. Garrett Electronics Treasures Found Museum, Garrett Electronics Plant, 2814 National Drive, 75041. U.S. coins and medals. Open Monday through Friday from 8:30 a.m. to 4:30 p.m.. Free.

NACOGDOCHES. Stone Fort Museum, Stephen F. Austin University, 75962. Confederate money, U.S. coins, paper money and medals, foreign paper money and medals. Numismatic material available for reseach by appointment only. Open 9 a.m. to 5 p.m. Monday through Saturday, 1 p.m. to 5 p.m. Sunday. Closed Christmas and New Year's Day. Free.

WACO. Strecker Museum, Baylor University, 76798. Large collection of German notgeld, Chinese coins previous to 1850, U.S. and foreign medals, thousands of notes and coins from many countries. All collections available for examination upon appointment.

Open 9 a.m. to 4 p.m. weekdays, 10 a.m. to 1 p.m. Saturdays; 2 p.m. to 5 p.m. Sundays and closed university holidays.

Vermont

BENNINGTON. Bennington Museum, Inc., West Main St., 05201. Coins and paper money of Vermont. Open 9 a.m. to 5 p.m. March 1-Nov. 30. Closed Thanksgiving Day. Admission charged.

Virginia

PETERSBURG. Farmers Bank Museum, 19 Bollingbrook St., 23803. Confederate money and documents. Open daily 9 a.m. to 5 p.m.

RICHMOND. Money Museum, Federal Reserve Bank of Richmond, 701 E. Byrd St., 23219. History of U.S. coins and paper money, money-related artifacts, primitive, ancients and precious metals. Open 9:30 a.m. to 3:30 p.m. Monday through Friday.

RICHMOND. Virginia Museum, Boulevard and Grove Ave., 23221. Ancient Greek and Roman coins. Open 11 a.m. to 5 p.m. Tuesday through Saturday, until 10 p.m. Thursday evenings, 1 p.m. to 5 p.m. Sunday, closed major holidays. No admission fee for members, senior citizens and children under 16. Non-members $2. Part of Greco-Roman collection on permanent view; remainder by appointment.

Washington

GOLDENDALE. Maryhill Museum of Art, 55 Maryhill Museum Drive, 98620. U.S. coins, ancients and U.S. and world medals. Open March 15-Nov. 15 daily 9 a.m. to 5 p.m.. Adults $3, senior citizens $2 and students 6-16 $1.50.

West Virginia

CHARLESTON. West Virginia State Museum, The Cultural Center, Capitol Complex, 25305. U.S. coins, paper money and medals, foreign coins, paper money and medals. Open 9 a.m. to 9 p.m. Monday through Friday and 1 p.m. to 9 p.m. Saturday and Sunday. Closed Christmas.

Wisconsin

MADISON. State Historical Society of Wisconsin, 816 State St., 53706. U.S. coins, paper money and medals. Open 8 a.m. to 5 p.m. Monday-Friday to scholars only. Closed Wisconsin state holidays. Free.

STURGEON BAY. Door County Historical Museum, 18-4th and Michigan, 54235. U.S. coins, paper money and medals. Open 10 a.m. to 5 p.m. daily from May 1-Oct. 30.

CANADA

Alberta

CALGARY. University of Calgary Nickle Arts Museum, 2500 University Dr. N.W., T2N 1N4. Ancients, medieval, foreign coins, world medals, U.S. paper money and Carl O. Nickle collection of North America numismatics. Open Sept. 1-May 31 Tuesday, Thursday and Friday 10 a.m. to 5 p.m. and Saturday and Sunday 1 p.m. to 5 p.m. Closed holidays.

British Columbia

KAMLOOPS. Kamloops Museum and Archives, 207 Seymour St., V2C 2E7. Foreign coins, medals, tokens and paper money. Open 11 a.m. to 5 p.m. Monday through Saturday, 1 p.m. to 5 p.m. Sunday. Free.

KELOWNA. Kelowna Museum and National Exhibit Centre, 470 Queensway Ave., V1Y 6S7. Foreign coins, paper money, medals and tokens. Open 10 a.m. to 5 p.m. Tuesday through Saturday. Free.

PRINCE RUPERT. Museum of Northern British Columbia, Box 669, V8J 3S1. Ancients, U.S. and foreign coins, medals and paper money. Open 10 a.m. to 5 p.m. Monday through Saturday during the winter, 9 a.m. to 9 p.m. Monday through Saturday and 9 a.m. to 5 p.m. Sunday during the summer. Closed Christmas, New Year's, Easter and Remembrance Day. Donations accepted at door.

New Brunswick

SAINT JOHN. New Brunswick Museum, 277 Douglas Ave., E2K 1E5. Coins, medals, tokens, paper money and numismatic literature. Only a small portion of exhibit on display at present. Open May 1 to August 31 daily 10 a.m. to 5 p.m., Sept. 1 to April 30 Tuesday to Sunday 10 a.m. to 5 p.m. Closed Christmas and Good Friday only. Admission $2 for adults, 50¢ for students and senior citizens, free to children under 6 and family $4.

Nova Scotia

HALIFAX. Public Archives of Nova Scotia, 6016 University Ave., B3H 1W4. Coins, tokens and paper money. Open 8:30 a.m. to 10 p.m.. Monday through Friday, 9 a.m. to 6 p.m. Saturday and 1 p.m. to 10 p.m. Sunday, closed national holidays. Free.

Ontario

OTTAWA. Bank of Canada Currency Museum. 245 Sparks St. K1A 0G9. National Currency Collection of Canada. U.S. coins and paper money, foreign coins and paper money, medieval, ancients and primitives. Open Tuesday through Saturday 10:30 a.m. to 5 p.m. and Sunday 1 p.m. to 5 p.m. Closed Monday and most statutory holidays except during the summer months.

OTTAWA. Canadian War Museum, 330 Sussex Drive, K1A 0M8. Canadian, U.S. and foreign military medals, orders, badges, insignia and scrip. Material on display and in reference collections. Research scholars may have access to reference materials subject to request to curator in chief. Open daily 10 am. to 5 p.m. Free.

OTTAWA. Public Archives of Canada, 395 Wellington St., K1A 0N3. National Medal Collection. 12,000 Canadian, British, French, U.S. and other medals. Open 8:30 a.m. to 4:30 p.m. Monday through Friday for viewing or research by appointment. Closed on statutory holidays. Free.

OTTAWA. Royal Canadian Mint, 320 Sussex Drive, K1N 8V5. Viewing of striking of gold and silver coins, audio and visual presentations on coin production and displays of coins, medals and other products of the RCM, with an emphasis on current issues. Open Monday through Friday 8:30 a.m. to 11 a.m. and 12:30 p.m. to 3 p.m. Admission if free, tours are guided and reservations are recommended. (613) 992-2348.

PEMBROKE. Champlain Trail Museum, 1032 Pembroke St. E., Box 985, K8A 1V5. U.S. coins and foreign paper money. Open 1 p.m. to 5 p.m. daily from April 11 to Nov. 20.

TORONTO. Royal Ontario Museum, 100 Queen's Park, M5S 2C6. Ancient Greek and Roman coins, foreign and Canadian coins and medals. Open 10 a.m. to 6 p.m. daily and until 8 p.m. Tuesday and Thursday. Canadian Decorative Arts, Sigmund Samuel Building open 10 a.m. to 5 p.m. daily, 1 p.m. to 5 p.m. Sunday, free admission. Closed Christmas and New Year's Day. Admission $3.50 adults, $2 senior citizens, students, children and family rate $7. Free admission after 4:30 p.m. Thursday and senior citizens free on Tuesday.

Quebec

MONTREAL. Bank of Montreal Museum, 129 Saint-Jacques St., H2Y 1L6. Bank of Montreal and other Canadian financial institutions paper money. Coins, medals, tokens, paper money, numismatic literature and other related items. Open 10 a.m. to 4 p.m. all banking days. Free.

MONTREAL. Musee du Seminaire de Quebec, 9 rue de l'Universite, C.P. 460, Hauteville G1R 4R7. Ancient, medieval and world coins, medals, tokens, paper money, and numismatic literature. Specializing in Canadian paper money, tokens and coins.

Open to public June through Oct. 11 a.m. to 6 p.m. October through June 11 a.m. to 5 p.m. Admission $2 adults, $1 students and senior citizens, $2.50 for families. Group rates available. Free admission on Saturday.

WORLD

This list was compiled through inquiries to World museums and from *Coin World* files.

Australia

HOBART. Tasmanian Museum and Art Gallery, Macquarie St. Tasmanian tokens and promissory notes, U.S. coins, paper money, ancients, medieval coins, world coins and medals. Open daily 10 a.m. to 5 p.m. Free.

SYDNEY. The Mint and Barracks Museum, Queens Square, Macquarie St., World coins and medals of all periods, Australian colonial era and early federation issues. Open daily 10 a.m. to 5 p.m., except Wednesday 12 a.m. to 5 p.m. Free.

Austria

ENNS. Enns Stadtmuseum, Hauptplatz 19, Modern and Roman coins. Open daily 2 p.m. to 4 p.m., Sunday 10 a.m. to 12 a.m. and 2 p.m. to 4 p.m.

GRAZ. Landesmuseum Joanneum, Schloss Eggenberg, A-8020. World coins, medals and paper money, medieval and ancient coins. Open daily 9 a.m. to 5 p.m., closed Dec. and Jan. Free.

INNSBRUCK. Tiroler Landesmuseum, Ferdinandeum, Museumstrasse 15, A-6020. Coins, medallions. Open May to Sept. Monday through Saturday 10 a.m. to 5 p.m., Thursday 7 p.m. to 9 p.m.

KLAGENFURT. Landesmuseum fur Karnten, Museumgasse 2, A-9021. Ancient and medieval coins.

VIENNA. Kunsthistorisches Museum, Burgring 5, A-1010. Contains numismatic collection. Open Tuesday through Friday 10 a.m. to 6 p.m., Saturday and Sunday 9 a.m. to 6 p.m.

WAIDHOFEN A. D. THAYA. Verein Heimatmuseum, Postfach 80, A-3830. World coins and medals, German notgeld from 1920-1925. Open Sunday 10 a.m. to 12 a.m.; also by appointment.

Belgium

BRUSSELS. Koninklike Bibliotheek Albert I, Keizerslaan 4, Penninskabinet. Special section displaying coins and books, orders and decorations, scales and weights. Open Monday through Wednesday 9 a.m. to 12 a.m. and 2 p.m. to 5 p.m. Free.

Bermuda

HAMILTON. Bermuda Monetary Authority, Numismatic Bureau Museum, 4th Floor, Government Administration Building, Parliament St., HM 12. Bermuda coins and paper money. Open Monday through Friday 9 a.m. to 5 p.m.

Denmark

COPENHAGEN. Copenhagen Museum, Vesterbrogade 59, DK-1620. History and life of Copenhagen for 800 years. Open Oct. through Apr. 1 p.m. to 4 p.m., closed Monday. Open May through Sept. 10 a.m. to 4 p.m. Free.

COPENHAGEN. National Museum, Frederiksholms Kanal 12, DK-1220. European coins and medals. Open June 16 to Sept. 15 daily, 10 a.m. to 4 p.m.; Sept. 16 to June 15, 11 a.m. to 3 p.m.; Sunday 12 a.m. to 4 p.m., closed Monday. Collections viewed by appointment only. Free.

Finland

HELSINKI. National Museum Kansallismuseo, Mannerheimintie 34, P.O. Box 913, 00101. Finnish, Swedish and Russian coins, bank notes and medals. Ancient and medieval coins, world coins, medals and paper money. Open May through Sept. daily 11 a.m. to 4 p.m.; Oct. through April 11 am. to 3 p.m.; Saturday and Sunday 11 a.m. to 4 p.m., Tuesday 6 p.m. to 9 p.m. Admission 5 FIM, children 2.50 FIM.

France

PARIS. Cabinet des Medailles, Bibliotheque Nationale, 58 Rue de Richelieu, F-75084. Coins, medals and French antiques. Open 1 p.m. to 5 p.m.. Admission 10 francs.

PARIS. Paris Mint Museum, 11, Quai de Conti, F-75270. Ancient and medieval coins, world coins, medals and paper money and a large collection of French medals and jetons.

STRASBOURG. Numismatic Cabinet, Bibliotheque Nationale et Universitaire, 5 rue Marechal Joffre, F-67000. Ancient and medieval coins specializing in coins from Alsace Lorraine. Open Tuesday 2 p.m. to 5:30 p.m.

Germany, East

BERLIN. Staatliche Museum of Berlin Hauptstadt, Munzkabinett, Bodestrasse 1-3, DDR-1020. Ancient and medieval coins, world coins, medals and paper money. Stamps, jetons, seals, shares and bonds.

Germany, West

AUGSBURG. Stadtische Kunstsammlungen Augsburg, Maximilianstr. 46, (Schaezler Palais), D-8900. Ancient and medieval coins, and coins and medals of Augsburg. Open Tuesday to Sunday 10 a.m. to 4 p.m., closed Monday.

BRAUNFELS. Furstliches Familien-Museum, Schloss, D-6333. Medieval, Roman and German coins from 1871-1918. Coins and dies of Solms dynasty. Open daily 8 a.m. to 5 p.m. April through Sept. and daily 9 a.m. to 4 p.m. Oct. through March. Admission DM 2.

COBURG/BAY. Furstenbau-Veste Coburg, D-8630. Ancients, medieval coins and world coins, medals and paper money.

COLOGNE. Kolnisches Stadtmuseum, Zeughausstrasse 1-3, D-5000. Coins of the Bishops of Cologne and city of Cologne.

FRANKFURT/MAIN. Deutsche Bundesbank, Money Museum, Central Bank of the Federal Republic of Germany, Postfach 100602, D-6000. Over 230,000 bank notes and 80,000 coins.

FRANKFURT/MAIN. Degussa Munzkabinett, Postfach 110533, D-6000. German coinages since 1871. Not open to public.

HAMBURG. Museum fur Hamburgische Geschichte, Munzkabinett, Holstenwall 24, D-2000. Modern world coins and coins from Hamburg.

KARLSRUHE. Badisches Landesmuseum, Schloss, D-7500. World coins, medals and paper money. Ancients and coins of South Germany. Open Tuesday to Sunday 10 a.m. to 5:30 p.m.. Free.

KASSEL. Staatliche Kunstsammlunger Kassel, Hessisches Landesmuseum, Bruder Grimm Platz 5, D-3500. Modern European medals, German paper money and coins from Hessen-Kassel.

LUBECK. Archiv der Hansestadt Lubeck, Muhlendamm 1-3, D-2400. Coins of Lubeck. Open Monday to Friday 8 a.m. to 4. p.m.

MAINZ. Landesmuseum Mainz, Grosse Bleiche 49-51, D-6500. Ancient, medieval and world coins. Open Tuesday to Friday 10 a.m. to 5 p.m., closed Monday.

MAINZ. Romanisch-Germanische Zentralmuseum, Forschungsinstitut fur Vor-u. Fruhgeschichte, Ernst-Ludwig-Platz 2, D-6500. Celtic and Roman republic coins. Open by appointment.

MUNICH. Staatliche Munzsammlung Munich, Residenzstrasse 1, D-8000. World coins, medals and paper money, Ancient classical world and numismatic publications. Office and library open Monday to Friday 8 a.m. to 4:30 p.m., exhibition open Tuesday to Sunday 10 a.m. to 5 p.m.

MUNSTER. Westfalisches Landesmuseum fur Kunst u. Kulturgeschichte, Domplatz 10, D-4400. World coins, medals and paper money. German paper money, coins and medals of the region of Westphalia. Open Tuesday to Sunday 10 a.m. to 6 p.m.

NUERNBERG. Germanic National Museum, Kartausergasse 1, D-8500. Coins and medals from German speaking countries. Open daily 9 a.m. to 5 p.m.

SIEGBURG. Finanzgeschichtliche Sammlung der Bundesfinanzakademie, Michaelsberg, D-5200. Numismatic custom duty tax items and marks. Open Monday to Friday. Free.

SPEYER. Historisches Museum der Pfalz, Grosse Pfaffengasse 7, D-6720. Ancient, medieval and modern material. Open daily 9 a.m. to 12 a.m. and 2 p.m. to 5 p.m. Admission DM 1.50, groups of 10 DM 1.00 and students 50 pf.

TRIER. Rheinisches Landesmuseum Trier, Ostallee 55, D-5500. Ancient and medieval coins of Trier. Open daily 10 a.m. to 4 p.m.

Greece

ATHENS. Athens Numismatic Museum, Tossitsa 1 Gr. 10682. Greek, Roman, Byzantine, medieval, modern coins and medals, Greek and Byzantine weights. Open summer 9 a.m. to 1:15 p.m. Tuesday through Saturday, Sundays 9 a.m. to 2 p.m. Winter 9 a.m. to 1:45 p.m. Tuesday through Saturday, Sunday 9 a.m. to 2 p.m. Closed Monday. Free.

Other coin collections in Greece can be found in museums in Thessalonika, Iraklion (Crete), Volos, Keffalenia, Rhodes and Ioannina.

Hungary

BUDAPEST. Hungarian National Museum. Muzeum korut 14-16, 1370 Bp. VIII. Ancient, medieval and modern coins and medals.

Ireland

DUBLIN. National Museum of Ireland, Kildare street. Irish coins and medals from medieval to modern. Open weekdays 10 a.m. to 5 p.m.; Sunday 2 p.m. to 5 p.m.; closed Mondays.

Israel

HAIFA. National Maritime Museum, 198 Allenby Rd., 44855. Large collection of coins and medals pertaining to the sea. Extensive collection of Hebrew and Mediterranean maritime history and archaeology. Open Sunday through Thursday 10 a.m. to 4 p.m.; closed Friday. Saturday and holidays 10 a.m. to 1 p.m. Adults IS3 and children 0.75 sheqel.

JERUSALEM. Israel Museum, Kiryat Ben-Gurion. Bronfman Biblical and Archaeological Museum, contains collection of ancient Jewish, Greek, Roman Provincial, Islamic and Crusader coins. Open Sunday, Monday, Wednesday and Thursday 10 a.m. to 5 p.m.; Tuesday 4 p.m. to 10 p.m. and Friday and Saturday 10 a.m. to 2 p.m.

Italy

BARI. Museo Archeologico, Palazzo dell'Ateneo, Piazza Umberto 1. Greek, Roman, Byzantine and modern coins. Open daily 8:30 a.m. to 1:30 p.m.; closed Sunday. Free.

NAPLES. Museo Archeologico Nazionale, Piazza Museo. Greek, Roman and modern coins. Open Tuesday through Sunday 9 a.m. to 4 p.m.; closed Monday. Admission 2,000 lira.

ROME. Museo Nazionale Romano delle Terme di Diocleziano (Terminal railway station), transferred from Instituto Italiano di Numismatica, Palazzo Barberini, Via Quattro Fontaine 13. Numismatic collection of King Victor Emanuel II, containing 100,000 numismatic items spanning coins from the fall of the Roman empire to modern times. The institute also directs numismatic research and study in Italy. It is advisable to write for an appointment.

ROME. Museo Numismatico dellla Zecca , Via Principe Umberto 4. Historic collection of Pontifical medals from 1417 and models in wax by Benedetto Pistrucci. Appointment preferred.

Luxemburg

LUXEMBURG. Musees de l'Etat, Marche-aux-Poissons, 2345. More than 60,000 numismatic items from Celtic to modern times. Open Tuesday through Friday 10 a.m. to 12 p.m. and 1 p.m. to 5 p.m.; Saturday 2 p.m. to 6 p.m.; Sunday 10 a.m. to 12 p.m. and 2 p.m. to 6 p.m. Closed Monday.

Malaysia

KUALA LUMPUR. National Museum of Malaysia, 50566. Malaysian and world coins and paper money.

Netherlands

HAARLEM. Teyler's Museum, Spaarne 16, 2001 CH. Dutch medals and coins, U.S. coins, paper money and medals. Ancient, medieval and world coins. Open Tuesday through Saturday 10 a.m. to 5 p.m., Sunday 1 p.m. to 5 p.m. Oct. through Feb. closes at 4 p.m. Adults 3 guilders; children 1.50 guilders.

LEIDEN. Rijksmuseum Het Koninklik Penningkabinet, Rapenburg 28, 2301 EA. Exhibition will open in 1988. Dutch coins, paper money, medals and tokens, with ancient and medieval coins, world coins, medals and paper money. Open Tuesday through Saturday 10 a.m. to 5 p.m.; Sunday 1 p.m. to 5 p.m.

UTRECHT. Museum 'sRijks Munt, Leidseweg 90, 3500 GK. Medieval Dutch coins and modern world coins. Open Monday through Friday 2 p.m. to 4 p.m.

Norway

OSLO. University of Oslo, Coin Cabinet, Historical Museum, Frederiksgate 2, 0164. Display of Norwegian ancient and foreign coins, medals, orders and decorations. Open May 15-Sept. 15 11 a.m. to 3 p.m., remainder of year 12 a.m. to 3 p.m. Closed Mondays and public holidays. Free.

Philippines

MANILA. Central Bank of Philippines, Money Museum, 2801. Philippine coins and paper money, modern world coins and medals. Open Tuesday through Sunday 9 a.m. to 4:30 p.m.

Poland

WARSAW. The Royal Castle, Plac Zamkowy 4, 00277. Polish coins and medals, medieval coins, modern world coins and paper money. Open daily 10 a.m. to 3 p.m.

WARSAW. Archaeological and Ethnographical Museum, Plac Walnosci, Nre. Zemreszkaty, 97. Coins and medals.

Portugal

LISBON. Portuguese Numismatic Museum, Casa da Moeda, Rua de D. Francisco Manuel de Melo 5, 1092. 5th century Portuguese and foreign coins and medals. Open by appointment only.

South Africa

JOHANNESBURG. Barclays Museum, Barclays National Bank Limited, 90 Market Street, 2001. Bank notes and coins of the early South African banks. Each year the museum hosts a different exhibition from various museums and private collections. Open Monday through Friday 9 a.m. to 4 p.m.; Saturday 9 a.m. to 12:30 p.m. Closed Sunday and holidays. Free.

Spain

MADRID. Royal Palace, Plaza de Oriente. Ancient and medieval coins and world medals.

MADRID. Madrid Mint, Fabrica Nacional de Moneda y Timbre, Jorge Juan 106, 28009. World coins from all periods; notes, medals, postage stamps, tools and machinery for manufacturing coins and medals.

MADRID. Museo del Ejercito, c/oMendez

Nunez, No. 1, 28014. Medals and decorations. Open daily 10 a.m. to 1:45 p.m. Closed Tuesday. Admission 50 pesetas.

MADRID. Lazaro Galdiano Museum, Calle Serrano 122, 28006. Medal collection. Open daily 10 a.m. to 2 p.m. Closed Monday.

SEGOVIA. Cathedral de Segovia museum. Coins minted from all Spanish periods, in copper, silver and gold. Open daily May to October 9:30 a.m. to 6:30 p.m.; October to April 9:30 to 1 p.m.

Sweden

GOTEBORG. Goteborg Historiska Museum, Norra Hamgatan 12, 41114. Coins and medals. Open Sept. through April, Tuesday through Saturday 12 a.m. to 4 p.m.; Sunday 11 a.m. to 5 p.m.; Wednesday also open 6 p.m. to 9 p.m. May through August, 11 a.m. to 4 p.m. daily, closed Monday. Children free, adults 5 krona.

MALMO. Malmo Museums, Malmohusvagen, Box 406, 20124. Ancient, medieval and Scandinavian coins. Open daily 12 a.m. to 4:30 p.m. Adults 50 krona; children under 15 free.

STOCKHOLM. Ostasiatiska Museet (Museum of Far Eastern Antiquities), Skeppsholmen, S-103 27. Chinese coins, spade and knife money. Coins are not on permanent display. Open daily 12 a.m. to 4 p.m; Tuesday until 9 p.m. Closed Monday. Adults 20 crowns, students 10 crowns and youths under 16 free.

STOCKHOLM. Kungl Myntkabinettet, (The Royal Coin Cabinet) Statens Museum for Mynt-, Medalj- och Penninghistoria, Storgatan 41, Box 5405, S-11484. Viking Age hoards 800-1100 A.D., history of banking and economy, Swedish coins, medals, tokens, shares and bank notes. Open Tuesday through Sunday 11 a.m. to 4 p.m. Free.

UPPSALA. Uppsala University coin cabinet. Swedish coins and medals, Viking age coins. Open Thursday 2 p.m.to 4 p.m. except summer.

Switzerland

GENEVA. Museum of Art and History, 2 rue Charles Galland, CH-1211. Ancient, medieval and world coins, and coins of Geneva. Open Tuesday through Sunday 10 a.m. to 5 p.m. Closed Monday.

LAUSANNE. Cabinet des Medailles du Canton de Vaud, Palais de Rumine, CH-1005. Ancient, medieval and world coins, medals and paper money. Open by appointment only.

LUCERNE. Historisches Museum Luzern, Pfistergasse 24, Postfach 164, CH-6000. Coins and medals of Lucerne, Ancient, medieval and modern world coins. Open Tuesday through Friday 10 a.m. to 12 a.m. and 2 p.m. to 5 p.m.; Saturday aand Sunday 10 a.m. to 5 p.m.

WINTERTHUR. Munzkabinett der Stadt Winterthur, Villa Buhler, Lindstrasse 8, CH-8401. Ancient Greek and Roman coins.

ZURICH. Swiss National Museum, Museumstrasse 2, CH-8023. Swiss coins and medals, world coins, medals and paper money. Open Tuesday through Sunday 10 a.m. to 12 a.m. and 2 p.m. to 5 p.m. Closed Monday.

United Kingdom

BELFAST. Ulster Museum, Botanic Gardens, BT9 5AB. 50,000 coins, tokens and medals from ancients to modern, plus Irish bank notes. Open Monday through Friday 10 a.m. to 5 p.m.; Saturday and Sunday 2 p.m. to 5 p.m. Free.

BIRMINGHAM. Birmingham Assay Office, P.O. Box 151, Newhall St., B3 1SB. Coins medals and tokens of Birmingham. Private museum with viewing by appointment only. Free.

BIRMINGHAM. City Museum and Art Gallery, Chamberlain Square, B3 3DH. Ancient and medieval coins. Products of Birmingham Mint. Open Monday through Saturday 10 a.m. to 5 p.m.; Sunday 2 p.m. to 5 p.m. Free.

BRISTOL. City of Bristol Museum and Art Gallery, Queens Road, B8 1RL. Roman, British and local Iron Age trade tokens. Open Monday through Saturday 10 a.m. to 5 p.m. Reserve collections by appointment only. Free.

CAMBRIDGE. Fitzwilliam Museum, Department of Coins and Medals, CB2 1RB. Collection comprises some 100,000 specimens, of Ancient, British Isles, European medieval and Indian coins. Open Monday through Friday 10 a.m. to 1 p.m. and 2 p.m. to 5 p.m. A collection of art medals are on permanent display in the main museum galleries: Tuesday through Saturday 10 a.m. to 5 p.m.; Sunday 2:15 p.m. to 5 p.m. Free.

EDINBURGH. Royal Museum of Scotland, Chambers Street, EH1 1JF. Classical, European and oriental items, and modern world coins. Open 10 a.m. to 5 p.m. Free.

LONDON. British Museum, Great Russell Street, WC1B 3DG. 500,000 coins and medals. Open Monday through Friday 10 a.m. to 12:30 p.m. and 2 p.m. to 4:30 p.m.; Saturday 10 a.m. to 12:30 p.m. Free.

OXFORD. Ashmolean Museum, Heberden Coin Room, Beaumont Street, OX1 2PH. Coins of all periods and areas. Open Tuesday through Saturday 10 a.m. to 4 p.m.; Sunday 2 p.m. to 4 p.m. Free.

SPALDING. Spalding Gentlemen's Society Museum, Broad Street, Lincs. Maples collection of 18th century tokens and English coins. Open by appointment only.

Organizations 20

American Numismatic Society

Broadway Between 155th and 156th Sts.
New York, N.Y. 10032

The American Numismatic Society was founded by a group of 12 New Yorkers on April 6, 1858. Its objective was "the collection and preservation of coins and medals, with an investigation into their history, and other subjects connected therewith." The group was incorporated in 1864.

Coins, medals and books were collected from the Society's early days. As the collections grew, it became necessary to find quarters to house them. A succession of rented rooms served as meeting-places and headquarters during the first 50 years.

Through contributions by interested officers and members, the Society was able to erect its own building in 1907. Since then, its collections and activities have grown progressively.

The ANS Museum houses one of the finest collections of numismatics in the United States. Located in uptown Manhattan, New York City, in the same building which houses its offices, collections and libraries, the museum includes coins of all periods from their inception to modern times, and medals and decorations.

Selections from the museum cabinets are on display in an exhibition.

The ANS Library is the most comprehensive numismatic library in the world, consisting of some 100,000 items. In addition to its excellent book collection, which includes virtually all of the standard references on numismatics, the library holds rare manuscripts, all of the major numismatic periodicals, a special collection of some 8,000 auction catalogs and six distinct topical pamphlet files.

In all, the ANS houses over a million numismatic items. Located on Broadway between 155th and 156th Streets, the exhibit halls are open from 9 to 5 Tuesday through Saturday, 1 to 4 Sunday, and are closed national holidays. No admission is charged.

The ANS has been active in publishing since its founding. Today it publishes the *Numismatic Notes and Monographs*, separately issued publications, each on a single topic. *The American Numismatic Society Museum Notes*, is the official journal of the Society which appears annually; *Numismatic Literature*, published twice a year, listing current numismatic publications with abstracts of their content; *Ancient Coins in North American Collections* and *Numismatic Studies*, a series accommodating works in a larger format.

The Society is governed and managed by a council of 15 members from which a president and two vice presidents are elected. The other officers are appointed by the council.

There are four classes of members: Fellows, Honorary Fellows, Associate Members, and Corresponding Members. The Fellows are limited in number to 200; persons or organizations who have rendered special service to the Society or to numismatics may be elected Honorary Fellows. Only Fellows and Honorary Fellows may vote at the meetings of the Society, and it is from their number the council is selected.

Persons or organizations not residing in the U.S. may be elected Corresponding Members. Associate membership, which is unlimited in number, is open to all with an interest in numismatics.

The annual dues for an Associate membership are $20. A "Publication Subscription" has been established for a range of publications for one annual fee.

A summer seminar in numismatics has been held by the Society since 1952. Grants-in-aid are offered to university graduate students in humanistic fields such as classics, archaeology, Oriental languages, history, economics, and art history. The aim of the seminar is to provide the students with an understanding of the contribution numismatics has to make in their own fields of study and to provide them with sufficient training in numismatic techniques to be of use to them in their future careers.

The ANS has offered, since 1958, Graduate Fellowships to qualified university students in the fields of the humanities or the social sciences. Applications are accepted annually from students who have completed the general examinations (or the equivalent) for the doctorate, who will be writing dissertations on topics in which the use of numismatics plays a significant part, and who will have attended one of the Society's summer seminars.

Other activities of the Society include a photographic service, specially equipped for the photography of numismatic objects; and two awards, the Archer M. Huntington Medal, awarded for outstanding scholarly contributions to numismatics, and the J. Sanford Saltus Medal, honoring sculptors who have achieved merit in the art of the medal.

For more information about the American Numismatic Society, write: Secretary of the Society, The American Numismatic Society, Broadway Between 155th and 156th Sts., New York, N.Y. 10032.

Officials, American Numismatic Society

President .... Harry W. Fowler
First Vice President . R. Henry Norweb Jr.
Second Vice President .. Roger A. Hornsby
Director and Secretary ..... Leslie A. Elam
Treasurer .... John D. Leggett Jr.
Assistant Treasurer .... Orin Joseph
Executive Committee .. Harry W. Bass Jr.
.... Harry W. Fowler
.... Roger A. Hornsby
.... John D. Leggett, Jr.
.... Baldwin Maull
.... R. Henry Norweb Jr.
.... Mrs. Marion G. Russell
Finance Committee .. Edward Glassmeyer
.... Alan B. Coleman
.... Harry W. Fowler
.... John D. Leggett Jr.
.... Baldwin Maull
.... R. Henry Norweb Jr.

Council
Term ending January 1992
.... Harry W. Bass Jr.
.... Glen W. Bowersock
.... Mrs. Marion G. Russell
Term ending January 1991
.... Harry W. Fowler
.... John H. Kroll
.... John D. Leggett Jr.
Term ending January 1990
.... Alan B. Coleman
.... Baldwin Maull
.... Speros Vyronis Jr.

Term ending January 1989
.... Roger A. Hornsby
.... R. Henry Norweb Jr.
.... John J. Slocum
Term ending January 1988
.... Edward Glassmeyer
.... Arthur A. Houghton
.... Eric P. Newman

Museum staff
Director .... Leslie A. Elam
Chief Curator .... William E. Metcalf
Roman, Byzantine
Curatorial staff ... Alan M. Stahl, Medieval
.... Nancy M. Waggoner, Greek
.... Michael L. Bates, Islamic
...... William L. Bischoff, Modern coins/
currency
..... Carmen F. Arnold-Biucchi, assistant
of ancient coins
.... Rose Chan Houston, associate of
Far Eastern
.... Margaret Thompson, chief
curator emeritus
Technician .... Tatyani I. Feynberg
Librarian .... Francis D. Campbell Jr.
Library Assistant .... Frank J. Tarsney
Editor .... Leslie A. Elam
Associate Editor .... Marie H. Martin
Assistant Editor of
Numismatic Literature .... Candace Carter
Photographer .... Frank Deak
Assistant Photographer ..... Charles Badal

Archer M. Huntington Medal award

The Archer M. Huntington Medal award is given by the American Numismatic Society for outstanding numismatic scholarship. It is the highest award the society bestows.

Winner	Year Awarded
Edward T. Newell	1918
Agnes Baldwin Brett	1919
Howland Wood	1920
Jean N. Svoronos	1921
Ernest Babelon	1922
George F. Hill	1923
Albert R. Frey	1924
George Macdonald	1925
Jose Toribio Medina	1926
Robert James Eidlitz	1927
Edouard von Zambaur	1928
Kurt Regling	1929
Baumann L. Belden	1930
Harrold E. Gillingham	1931
Adolph Dieudonne	1932
Wilhelm Kubitschek	1933
Adrien Blanchet	1934
E. Stanley G. Robinson	1935
John Allan	1936
Sydney P. Noe	1937
Harold Mattingly	1938
Sir Arthur J. Evans	1940
Albert Gallatin	1941
Alfred Bellinger	1943
J. Grafton Milne	1944
A.F. Pradeau	1945
Max Bernhart	1946
Richard Bertram Whitehead	1947
J.W.E. Pearce	1948
George C. Miles	1949
C.H.V. Sutherland	1950
Henri Seyrig	1952
Walter Havernick	1953
Charles T. Seltman	1954
John Walker	1955
Jocelyn M.C. Toynbee	1956
Arthur Suhle	1957
Robert I. Nesmith	1958
Oscar Ulrich-Bansa	1959
Humberto F. Burzio	1960
Margaret Thompson	1961
Philip Grierson	1962
Jean Mazard	1963
Michael Grant	1964
Andrew Alfoldi	1965
Georg Galster	1966
Willy Schwabacher	1967
George LeRider	1968
Emanuela Nohejlova-Pratova	1969
Anne S. Robertson	1970
Paul Balog	1971

Winner	Year Awarded
H. Enno van Gelder	1972
Christopher Blunt	1973
Jean LaFaurie	1974
Pierre Bastien	1975
G. Kenneth Jenkins	1976
R.A.G. Carson	1977
Eric P. Newman	1978
Felipe Mateu y Llopis	1979
Colin Kraay	1980
Otto Morkholm	1981
Michael Dolley	1982
Herbert Cahn	1983
Peter Berghaus	1984
Leo Mildenberg	1985
Paul Naster	1986

J. Sanford Saltus Medal award

The J. Sanford Saltus Medal award is given by ANS for distinguished achievement in the field of the art of the medal.

Winner	Year Awarded
James E. Fraser	1919
A.A. Weinman	1920
John Flanagan	1921
Victor D. Brenner	1922
Hermon A. MacNeil	1923
Paul Manship	1925
Laura G. Fraser	1926
Anthony de Francisci	1927
Edward W. Sawyer	1931
Lee Lawrie	1937
Chester Beach	1946
Henry Kreis	1948
C.P. Jennewein	1949
Gertrude K. Lathrop	1950
Albert Laessle	1951
Bruce Moore	1952
Walker Hancock	1953
Sidney Waugh	1954
Theodore Spicer-Simson	1955
Thomas G. Lo Medico	1956
Abram Belskie	1959
Bruno Mankowski	1960
Robert A. Weinman	1964
Albino Manca	1966
Donald DeLue	1967
Michael Lantz	1968
Stanley F. Martineau	1969
Joseph Kiselewski	1970
Granville W. Carter	1975
Karen Worth	1979
Agop Agopoff	1980
Guido Veroi	1983
Marcel Jovine	1984
Edward R. Grove	1985
Kauko Rasanen	1986

American Numismatic Association

818 N. Cascade Ave., Colorado Springs, Colo. 80903

Board of Governors

President . . . . Florence M. Schook
Vice President . . . . Stephen R. Taylor
Governors . . . . Grover C. Criswell
. . . . Bill Fivaz
. . . . David L. Ganz
. . . . Kenneth L. Hallenbeck
. . . . A.M. Kagin
. . . . Kurt R. Krueger
. . . . Bob Medlar
Executive
  Vice President . . . . Ruthann Brettell
General Counsel . . . . George D. Hatie
Treasurer . . . . Adna G. Wilde
Sergeant-At-Arms . . . . . . John J. Gabarron
Historian . . . . Carl W.A. Carlson
Legislative Counsel . . . . David L. Ganz
Public Relations . . . . Glenn B. Smedley
Director of Administration . Gary L. Gowen
Editor of *The Numismatist* . . . N. Neil Harris
ANACS Director . . . Richard S. Montgomery
Education Director . . . . Kenneth E. Bressett
Controller . . . . Robert D. Binz
Museum Curator . . . . Robert W. Hoge
Librarian . . . . Nancy W. Green
Director of
  Communications . . . Deborah Muehleisen

History of the ANA

George F. Heath, M.D., of Monroe, Mich., a physician of the "old school," when not involved in his practice of medicine, gained a knowledge of world history through the study of his collection of coins. The obscurity of his little town hampered his efforts in the gaining of additional knowledge of the hobby he loved so dearly, and in obtaining certain specimens for his cabinet, and made almost impossible his meeting with fellow numismatists. In 1888 his ingenuity was tested when he, alone, printed, published and distributed a four-page leaflet, *The Numismatist,* in which he listed his coin needs, advertised duplicates for sale, and discussed numismatic topics.

The little publication found many friends among the few hundred collectors who, like the doctor, were too isolated to take advantage of the numismatic societies in existence in large cities such as Boston, Montreal, New York, Philadelphia and Pittsburgh. These organizations were quite active; however, their sphere of influence was limited. As Heath's subscription list increased, it became evident that there was a growing need for a society similar to those in the cities, but one which would reach the more isolated, and serve the less advanced and the beginner: a national organization of numismatists.

The February 1891 issue of *The Numismatist* printed a question, "What is the matter with having an American Numismatic Association?" Wisely, Heath added, "There is nothing like the alliance of kindred pursuits to stimulate growth and interest." Aided by Charles T. Tatman, the youthful numismatic editor of a leading hobby magazine, *Plain Talk,* a campaign was begun to organize such an association. Numismatists from across the United States reacted favorably when they were urged to band together in order to derive greater benefits and pleasure from their avocation.

Founding

On Oct. 7-8, 1891, five men, Heath, William G. Jerrems, David Harlow, J.A. Heckelman, and John Brydon, holding 26 proxies, met in Chicago and with 61 charter members, founded the American Numismatic Association. Tatman, just entering Harvard law school, was unable to attend. Dr. Heath declined the presidency in favor of his good friend, Jerrems, a collector of ancient coins. He did, however, accept number one on the membership roll, a number significant of the honor bestowed upon him by his constituents.

Since that meeting in October 1891, more than 120,000 persons and corporate members have been listed on the ANA membership roster, and today the American Numismatic Association, a non-profit educational association, is the largest numismatic organization of its kind in the world.

The ANA was progressing smoothly when a national monetary crisis and threat of war caused interest in numismatics to recede at an alarming rate, and the association all but perished. Dr. Heath and his magazine were chiefly responsible for its reorganization in 1898. Shortly after the turn of the century, the doctor and his followers saw their efforts rewarded in a renewed interest in numismatics; an interest which has continued to grow since that time.

Heath originated the idea of a numismatic convention where members could make personal contacts with fellow numismatists, and exchange ideas and coins. These small-scale meetings, forerunners of the expansive modern conventions, were held annually from 1891 to 1895, in 1901, and in 1904. In 1907, with the aid of Dr. John M. Henderson, the convention was held in Columbus, Ohio, and was so successful that it was decided to hold annual meetings, henceforth. This procedure has been followed, with the exception of war years 1918 and 1945.

On June 16, 1908, the beloved Dr. Heath suddenly died. Farran Zerbe, then president, assumed the task of editing and publishing *The Numismatist,* and soon purchased the publication from Heath's heirs. In 1911, through the generosity of W.C.C. Wilson of Montreal, Canada, *The Numismatist* was purchased from Zerbe and presented to the ANA. The official organ has been owned and published monthly by the Association since that time.

Due to the scarcity of most of the volumes prior to 1920, many of the more worthwhile articles were reprinted in four books published in 1960. The first six volumes, 1888 to 1893, were combined into one book and reprinted a few years later. Only eight, or possibly nine, original sets of these first six volumes are in existence today and are, in themselves, collector's items. Three indexes have been published, the first in 1940; the second, a continuation, in 1959; and the third in 1980.

Federal charter

National prominence was attained by the Association when, on May 9, 1912, the association was granted a federal charter, signed by President Taft. This was accomplished through the untiring efforts of a group headed by Dr. Henderson. The legislative action was conducted by Reps. William A. Ashbrook of Ohio and Arthur W. Kopp of Wisconsin, both of whom were ANA members. An amendment to make the charter permanent and allow for a larger board of governors was introduced in 1962 by Rep. Wilbur Mills and Sen. John L. McClellan, both of Arkansas. This amendment passed the Congress and was signed by President Kennedy on April 10, 1962. S.W. Freeman and John Jay Pittman headed the ANA group which was instrumental in making possible the speedy legislative action on the amendment.

The ANA maintains the distinction of being one of the very few organizations in the United States operating under a federal charter. The 1912 charter opened the way for corporate memberships within the mother organization. Six clubs took immediate action

and became members and today the vast network of corporate members covers the globe with nearly 1,800 individual clubs and an estimated membership of more than a half million.

An ANA national home and headquarters building fund was established April 29, 1961, under the chairmanship of Charles M. Johnson. Sixteen cities in the central region of the United States made offers for location of the building site. Finally, upon nearing the fund goal, Colorado Springs was selected and ground breaking ceremonies were held Sept. 6, 1966. On Dec. 20, 1966, the building fund goal of $250,000 was reached, and $32,000 of the needed $40,000 furnishing fund was attained. A team of benefactors, patrons, numismatic clubs and 3,800 other contributors from all over the country made reaching fund goals possible. Debt free, the new home and headquarters of the American Numismatic Association was dedicated and officially opened in Colorado Springs June 10, 1967. The original headquarters building — with 16,000 square feet of space — was designed to accommodate a staff of 10 employees, plus a museum and library. By 1981, the number of ANA staff members had grown to more than 40, as a result of the association's growth.

Ground was broken May 7, 1981, for a 16,000-square-foot addition to the existing facility, which was completed in early 1982. In addition to providing needed workspace for personnel and additional space for the library, the new area provides expanded facilities for the ANA museum, which has been expanded to include seven galleries.

ANA library

One of the first services, established in the early years for the benefit of its members, was a numismatic library. This library remained small and unpretentious for years, but gained in size with the growth of the membership. Today, housed in the home and headquarters, members have use of the largest circulating numismatic library in the world. The library contains more than 10,000 hard-cover reference books and other library items which are loaned to members without charge, other than postage. In 1977 an entirely new sectionalized library catalog was published for members.

The association, through a fund established by Robert P. King in 1927, deposited in the Smithsonian Institution in Washington, D.C., a collection of coins and medals. This was known as the Moritz Wormser Memorial Loan Exhibit and supplemented until 1967 the Mint collection on display at the Institution. This, and other collections of coins, medals, tokens and paper money are housed in the association's own museum at the Colorado Springs headquarters. Many gifts have been donated by members to the ANA museum, representing collections consisting of coins, paper money and medallic art. More galleries have been added, including an Amos Press Theater.

Coin Week was introduced in 1924 by Julius Guttag of New York City. Now an annual event, hundreds of numismatists and many clubs are given the chance to promote and inform the public of their hobby.

In 1950 the Edward T. Newell Visual Educational Program was established. This illustrated program was introduced by George J. Bauer, the ANA's 17th president. The first group of projection slides was perfected by M. Vernon Sheldon and Glenn B. Smedley. Today, there are nearly 80 illustrated programs, complete with narrative material.

Numismatic displays have been outstanding attractions at ANA conventions since 1904. Thousands of numismatists, as well as curious non-collectors, have viewed these displays featuring famous collections and highly publicized rarities. Prizes for exhibits, inaugurated in the early 1940s, were individually sponsored. Later, the association initiated award ribbons. In recent years, the awards have expanded to include 15 or more categories of paper money, coins, medals, and other specialties. Competition for awards is spirited and the decisions made by the judges often hang on a single point. First-place winners in all classifications are presented with memorial award plaques, dedicated to distinguished numismatists. Second- and third-place awards are engraved medals. All exhibitors, competitive and non-competitive, receive specially designed exhibitor medals for their efforts in sharing their numismatic knowledge and enjoyment with others.

Awards and prizes

Numismatic literary awards were initiated in 1924 by a resolution passed at the 1923 Montreal convention. Articles published in *The Numismatist* are judged on their merits by an impartial committee. Robert P. King won the first donated award with his article about Lincoln medals. In 1925, it was resolved to present a suitably designed medal as the award, but this didn't materialize until 1945, during the presidency of V. Leon Belt. Until that time, due to costs of producing a medal, cash prizes were awarded. In 1949, the established award was renamed the "Heath

Literary Award" through a suggestion by John Jay Pittman. Silver and bronze medals, along with cash awards, were presented from 1945 through 1954, with honorable mention certificates commencing in 1947. Cash awards were discontinued in 1955, but were resumed in 1973.

Typically 10 to 15 awards are presented annually in three groups: one or two top silver medal awards, three or more bronze awards and, usually, five or more honorable mention citations. The competition for these awards has brought about a noticeable improvement in the quality of the published papers. Since their inception, more than 250 writers have received gold or bronze medals and/or cash awards for their superior efforts.

Through a suggestion by Jack W. Ogilvie, two membership awards were established during the 1947 convention. A gold medal is presented to 50-year members of the association, and a silver medal is given to members who have completed 25 consecutive years of membership. Nearly 70 members have received the gold medal and more than 1,800 members have received the silver medal. Included in these totals are clubs that have received gold or silver certificates for corporate milestones.

The Medal of Merit was first awarded in 1948 to members rendering outstanding service to the ANA and the science of numismatics. This silver medal, truly a medallic masterpiece, was designed and sculptured by Adam Pietz and Julius Widner. The association has bestowed this high award upon more than 100 dedicated numismatists. Presentations are made at the annual convention.

In 1950 the Farran Zerbe Award was instituted and first sponsored by Louis S. Werner. The award, in memory of Zerbe, a great scholar of numismatics, champion of good fellowship and, during his 50 years as a member, the association's most faithful and devoted friend, is presented annually to a member for distinguished services to the ANA. This is the highest honor awarded by the association and has been presented at the annual convention banquet to 36 recipients. The traditional plaque was replaced in 1984 with a two-inch 10-karat gold medallion.

The ANA Numismatic Hall of Fame was established Aug. 18, 1964, at the suggestion of Ralph Cleaver and Historian Jack W. Ogilvie. The Hall of Fame enshrines the names of famous numismatists. Elections were first held in 1969 and again in 1970 and prior to the 1972 convention. At the present time 52 famous numismatists' names are enshrined in the hall.

Education

The annual educational forums were formulated in 1946 during the Davenport, Iowa, conclave. Dr. J. Hewitt Judd and M. Vernon Sheldon, both future ANA presidents, were panelists on that first forum. The association moved closer to adequately fulfilling its credo as stated in the federal charter and constitution, "that the objectives of said corporation shall be to advance the knowledge of numismatics along educational, historical and scientific lines in all its various branches. ..."
In its effort to fulfill these objectives, the ANA calls upon several authorities in various areas of numismatics to speak at the annual educational forum. Since that first 1946 forum the educational forum has become increasingly important to the membership. Today it is a convention highlight, receiving extensive coverage in the national numismatic publications. Many of the most accomplished numismatists of the United States and other countries have shared their knowledge and experience with the membership as forum speakers. Forums have featured officials of the United States government, Mint Directors, officials of the Bureau of Engraving and Printing, coin designers and sculptors, numismatic authors, scholars, researchers and many other renowned numismatists in various specialty areas. The names of more than 100 people appear on the roll of past forum participants.

Through the efforts of Hazel Lindstrom and President Matt Rothert, a new official ANA movement came to light in 1965 with the establishment of the Young Numismatists Committee. Since its inception, the committee has worked hard to bring the junior movement into its own by sponsoring literary awards, service awards, exhibit awards and other beneficial achievement tributes to those who will, one day, carry on the hobby. In 1965 the ANA lowered the minimum membership age from 17 to 11 and the junior movement really sprang to life! The youth movement, championed by many adult members acting as advisers, now has developed a well-rounded program for the Young Numismatist at the annual convention. A few of the programs under way or in the planning stages are a Young Numismatist quarterly publication and a correspondence course. Trophies, coins, supplies, books and magazines can be requested by local clubs from the Committee for Junior Activities.

By board action in 1965, a code of ethics was established. The code of ethics, binding on each member, outlines principles of moral conduct that collectors and dealers are required to follow. Any breach of the code is considered cause for disciplinary action by the board.

Medals

During the 1966 Chicago convention, Aug. 16-20, at the Pick-Congress Hotel, only a stone's throw from the old hotel where the ANA was born Oct. 7, 1891, the American Numismatic Association celebrated its diamond anniversary. This gala event was commemorated by the issuance of bronze 3-inch medals struck by the United States Mint in Philadelphia through an act of Congress. Via a petition prepared and presented to Sen. John L. McClellan and Rep. Wilbur Mills of Arkansas, the proper bills were instituted and presented to both bodies of Congress. They passed April 5, 1966, and President Lyndon B. Johnson signed the bill into law April 16. The medal designs were executed by Chief Engraver Frank Gasparro of the United States Mint, with Mint Engraver Edgar Z. Steever assisting in the final design and execution of the reverse. Gasparro is well known for the reverse design of the Lincoln cent revised in 1959, the reverse of the Kennedy 50-cent piece, the Eisenhower dollar coin and the Anthony dollar.

The ANA has issued commemorative medals on many other occasions. In 1908 the practice of issuing medallic convention badges was initiated. Usually, the issues consisted of a nameplate or pin bar, a ribbon attachment and metal pendant combination. Significantly designed as symbolic tributes to the occasion with the wearer's name and place of residence inserted, these badges have provided instant introductions among members and visitors. Occasionally, since 1960, medals or sets of medals struck in bronze, silver and gold have been issued in addition to the badge. The majority of these medals have been identical to the badge pendants. Some have been designed by famous coin designers and medalists such as Victor D. Brenner, Frank Gasparro, Edward Grove, Alphonse Kolb, and J.M. Swanson. Special issues have included the George Heath Memorial Medallion in 1911, 50th anniversary in 1941, 75th anniversary in 1966, and the dedication of ANA home and headquarters in 1967. Some of the older issues and many of the more recent ones are available from the headquarters in Colorado Springs.

In 1966 the ANA, in conjunction with the Franklin Mint, brought into existence an award to pay tribute to talented sculptors, the unsung heroes in numismatics. The ANA

Numismatic Art Award for Excellence in Medallic Sculpture is presented annually at ANA conventions. The first recipient of the large gold medal award was Paul Vincze, the world renowned sculptor and medalist from London. In the years following, more than 13 other eminent sculptors have been recognized for their talents.

A District Representatives Committee was established in 1967, through which appointed ANA representatives served the United States, Canada and Mexico through 18 districts. Today, there are 55 districts with one or more representatives (depending on the size of the area involved) for each of the 50 states, Canada, Mexico and certain foreign countries. Representatives promote good will for ANA, assist in resolving complaints and misunderstandings, visit ANA members at club meetings and conventions, provide information regarding all ANA services and, generally, act as a liaison between the membership and the ANA board.

In 1969, the ANA initiated the first Summer Seminar, now an annual numismatic educational opportunity conducted at Colorado Springs and elsewhere. The program provides instruction on various numismatic subjects and offers tours, food and lodging at a very nominal cost to students. The first seminar attracted 20 numismatists from 13 states. This popular event is made possible by the cooperation of Colorado College, on whose campus the ANA home and headquarters is located.

The ANA announced in February 1970 an allrisk coin insurance plan. The low-cost plan offers the member a broad coverage of theft and fire insurance for his collection. Premium payments are in accordance with individual requirements according to how and where his collection is housed. The ANA announced a hospital money plan in November 1971 — another low-cost insurance plan. Also available to ANA members are term life insurance, catastrophe/major medical and personal accident insurance plans.

ANACS

One of the most important recent services of the ANA was the inauguration, on June 22, 1972, of the ANA Certification Service in Washington, D.C. This service was transferred in 1977 to the association's headquarters in Colorado Springs. The ANA brought into being the world's first service designed specifically to give an authoritative answer as to the authenticity of numismatic material submitted by anyone, from any place in the world. Numismatic material is photographed and, if genuine, a certificate is issued to verify same. This service is available to the general public; members are entitled to a fee discount.

A more controversial service was added March 1, 1979, when ANACS began grading coins for a fee and issuing ANACS certificates stating opinion as to grade. Since its inception, the grading service has generated controversy. Some collectors and dealers defended the service as an impartial answer to sometimes erroneous grading in the marketplace. Others claimed the ANACS graders were poorly trained, unskilled and inconsistent, and said the ANA grading system itself was flawed. However, many dealers and collectors insist that coins they trade in have ANACS grading certificates. Some dealers deal exclusively in ANACS-certified and -graded coins, and charge a premium above coins of similar type without the certificates.

On May 31, 1987, the ANA Board authorized for the first time ANACS grading of foreign and ancient coins, in addition to the authentication services already provided.

For information on ANACS, write: American Numismatic Association Certification Service, 818 N. Cascade Ave., Colorado Springs, Colo. 80903.

The ANA and its home and headquarters have other services available to the membership, such as free certificate awards for speakers and exhibitors at functions of member clubs, and ribbons for coin show awards; the latter services provided at approximate cost.

Many North American numismatists, amateur and professional, have held or now hold the prestige of an ANA membership number. Many people, in all walks of life, have enjoyed ANA's fraternal aspects, appreciated the multiple facets of its conventions, gained knowledge through its library, obtained desired numismatic items, profited by contacts made through the association, and spent many pleasant hours perusing *The Numismatist*. ANA's doors have opened to such a roster of famed people that it would be impossible to name all of them. Wealthy numismatic scholars and collectors, millionaire industrialists, government officials, famous numismatists, stars of the entertainment and music world, philanthropists and kings have graced its membership roll. Authors, painters, sculptors, composers, doctors, clergymen, people from the four corners of the world, rich and poor, young and old, through their interest and devotion to its cause, brought ANA thus far, and made it the largest numismatic organization on earth. Its span of life is short in the march of time, but filled with many accomplishments.

For more information, write: American Numismatic Association, 818 N. Cascade Ave., Colorado Springs, Colo. 80903.

Membership

The ANA will accept for membership all worthy persons who have an interest in the collecting and study of coins, paper money, tokens, medals or related items.

Membership applications must be approved in writing by two persons, at least one of whom is an ANA member.

Youths up to 17 years of age may apply for a junior membership.

A $5 application fee is charged for regular and club memberships, in addition to the yearly dues. However, this fee is waived for juniors under 17 years of age. Annual dues for members in the United States are $21 for individuals, $23 in all other countries. The club dues of $25 are charged, regardless of location.

Dues for the second calendar year are adjusted for new members for the months missed during the original membership year.

Persons 18 years of age or older are eligible for life membership. Life membership is $400, and may be paid on the installment plan within 12 months of application. A $10 fee will be charged to cover bookkeeping costs unless final payment is made in 90 days.

Junior membership is $11 annually and associate membership is $4. This includes child or spouse of a regular or life member. Life membership for a club is $1,250.

New members receive a book introducing them to numismatics and a dictionary of numismatic terms. An index to the ANA library is also available to new members.

The Numismatist is mailed free each month to each member except associates. Advertising in *The Numismatist* comes from members only, who agree to operate according to a code of ethics all members adhere to in course of business.

For information on membership, write to: American Numismatic Association, 818 N. Cascade Ave., Colorado Springs, Colo. 80903.

Visual education

The ANA collection of Visual Education material is available to members for use as educational presentations at club meetings or for schools and civic groups. The collection consists of a series of 2 x 2 slide sets and accompanying lecture notes which describe each slide. Clubs furnish their own projectors. The glass-enclosed slides are suitable for use in a carousel slide tray designed for a maximum of 80 slides.

Slides and films are shipped by United Parcel Service when a street address is provided, and by Parcel Post to a post office box number. Borrowers are requested to return sets via United Parcel Service whenever possible. Parcel Post shipments should be insured for $50—insurance is included in the UPS fee. When returning slide sets borrowers are asked to include payment to cover the ANA's costs for shipping and insurance. Sets must be returned promptly after the scheduled use dates to avoid possible disappointment to other scheduled users. Cancellations are occasionally unavoidable when scheduled sets are returned too late for reshipment.

When requesting slides, indicate club's name and ANA number, give exact date of meeting, include the name and number of the slide set desired and list several alternate selections. More popular slide sets are frequent-ly scheduled months in advance. The longer the notice given, the greater the opportunity of receiving slides for a specific meeting.

Address all correspondence to: ANA Visual Education Program, P.O. Box 2366, Colorado Springs, Colo. 80901. Return slides to: ANA Visual Education Program, 818 N. Cascade Ave., Colorado Springs, Colo. 80903.

Films

The Granite Lady

A 30-minute, 16mm, color, sound film on the history of the San Francisco Mint. The film was produced and distributed by the Bureau of the Mint.

Slide sets

SET #1: COINS OF COLONIAL AMERICA

Includes 61 color slides of the principal types of coins used in Colonial America. The series begins with the Sommer Island Shilling of 1616 and runs through the Spanish Milled dollar.

SET #2: TYPES OF COMMEMORATIVE HALF DOLLARS

Includes 48 color slides containing both obverse and reverse of each of the U.S. Commemorative half dollar coins.

SET #3: U.S. COPPER COIN TYPES

Includes 51 color photographs of types of half cents, large cents, 2-cent pieces and small cents through the current coinage.

SET #3-B: U.S. TYPES, 3-CENT PIECES THROUGH 20-CENT PIECES

Includes 54 color photographs of 3-cent nickel, 3-cent silver, half dimes, nickels, dimes, and 20-cent pieces. Includes current coinage as well as early types.

SET #4: U.S. TYPES, QUARTERS TO SILVER DOLLARS

Includes 67 color slides of quarters, half dollars and silver dollars including all types through the current coinage.

SET #7: FAMOUS WOMEN ON COINS AND MEDALS

Includes 34 photographic slides depicting famous women. The lecture notes give a short historical summary about each woman. An interesting set for non-collectors as well as advanced numismatists.

SET #8: ANCIENT GREEK COIN TYPES

Includes 59 color slides covering the period of 700 B.C. to 336 B.C. showing the development of coinage from its beginning to its peak of artistic achievement.

SET #9: ANCIENT GREEK COIN TYPES

This is a continuation of SET #8 and has 64 color slides covering the period from 336 B.C. to 57 A.D.

SET #10: CONFEDERATE STATES OF AMERICA CURRENCY

Includes 69 color slides illustrating the principal types of currency issued by the Confederacy. The notes are numbered according to Confederate Treasury Notes by Chase.

SET #11: CIRCLE OF FRIENDS OF THE MEDALLION & SOCIETY OF MEDALLISTS MEDALS

Includes 61 color slides illustrating some of the finest examples of medallic art. Twelve bronze medals are of the Circle of Friends of the Medallion and the balance are issues of the Society of Medallists through 1938.

SET #12: MEDALLIC ISSUES OF THE SOCIETY OF MEDALLISTS, 1939 to 1951

Includes 53 color photographs of the medals of this society. Most are bronze, circular in shape and approximately three inches in diameter. They cover a variety of subjects as the sculptors of this series are urged to create and interpret original designs.

SET #13: COINS OF THE PAGAN ROMAN EMPIRE

Includes 46 color slides providing basic information on the Roman Imperial coinage, 29 B.C. to early 4th century A.D.. The various denominations and types are illustrated.

SET #13-A: COINAGE OF CHRISTIAN IMPERIAL ROME

Includes 39 slides with lecture notes covering Roman coins from the early 4th to mid-15th centuries.

SET #14: TYPES OF POSTAGE AND FRACTIONAL CURRENCY

Includes 26 color slides of major types of fractional paper money of the U.S. from the first issue in 1862 through the fifth issue in 1876.

SET #15: UNITED STATES PAPER MONEY 1861-1923, ILLUSTRATED BY $5 NOTES

Includes 40 color slides of the beautiful large notes of the above period. Lecture notes describe each note and provide a short background summary of U.S. paper money.

SET #16: UNITED STATES PAPER MONEY 1861-1923, ILLUSTRATED BY $10 NOTES

Includes 39 color slides of the seven principal kinds of paper money issued during the period. Commentary is practically identical to that of SET #15 and either SET #15 or Set #16 may be used to illustrate the history of paper money of the period. Unless paper money specialists wish to see both $5 and $10 notes, either of these two sets will cover the subject.

SET #17: COINS WITH SPECIAL SIGNIFICANCE

Includes 44 slides representing mile posts in the history of money. Each coin has a story of its own and is of general interest to numismatists and non-collectors as well. U.S., foreign, ancient and colonial pieces are included. One of the most popular slide sets we have. Lecture notes are available in English and Spanish. English notes will be sent unless otherwise specified.

SET #19: STATE BANK NOTE ENGRAVINGS

Includes 34 color slides of highlights of engravings on bank notes, sometimes called broken bank notes or obsolete bank notes.

SET #20: MEDIEVAL COINAGES OF WESTERN EUROPE

Includes 47 color slides that trace, in a general way, the transition of Western European coinages from their source in the coins of the Roman Empire of the 4th and 5th centuries to the beginning of the modern style in the late 15th and early 16th centuries. Detailed lecture notes are included.

SET #21: REGULAR ISSUE ODD SHAPED COINS OF THE 20TH CENTURY

A short but interesting slide set of 19 color photographs of minor foreign coins. Three principal categories are illustrated (1) irregular shape without definite pattern, (2) angular with four or more sides, (3) scalloped edges varying in the number and arrangement of projections. Lecture notes include pronunciation aids.

SET #22: BRITISH CAMPAIGN (WAR) MEDALS

Includes 49 color slides illustrating awards given to British servicemen for participation in certain battles. "War Medals" are not awards for exceptional bravery such as the Victoria Cross. About two-thirds of the various campaign medals authorized for British and Empire servicemen since Waterloo are illustrated.

SET #23: COINS AND EARLY CHRISTIANITY

Includes 38 color slides of coins associated with the Biblical period and the rise of Christianity. Includes coins mentioned in the Bible, coins struck by persons who played important roles during this period and coins closely associated with this historical period in the Near East.

SET #24: KOREAN COINAGE CONVERSATION PIECES

Includes 31 color slides tracing the history of Korean coinage from 996 A.D. to the present. Also contains sketches of antiquated minting operations.

SET #25: TYPES OF REGULAR ISSUE U.S. GOLD COINS

Includes 52 color photographs of all regular issue gold types from 1795 through 1933.

SET #26: CROWN AND MINOR COMMEMORATIVE COINS OF THE 19th and 20th CENTURIES, WESTERN HEMISPHERE (PART I)

Includes 34 color slides of modern commemorative coins of Canada, Mexico, Costa Rica, Salvador, Panama, Bermuda, Cuba and the Dominican Republic. Detailed lecture notes include aids to pronunciation.

SET #27: CROWN AND MINOR COMMEMORATIVE COINS OF THE 19th and 20th CENTURIES, WESTERN HEMISPHERE (PART II)

Includes 35 color slides of the commemorative coins of South America. Countries included are Colombia, Argentina, Peru, Uruguay and Brazil.

SET #27-A: COMMEMORATIVE COINS OF BRAZIL (PART III)

Includes 42 slides of the commemorative coins of Brazil with commentary notes.

SET #28: ROMAN REPUBLICAN COINAGE

Includes 53 color slides covering the period from the 3rd century B.C. to the time of the first emperor. The various denominations and types are shown.

SET #29: COMMEMORATIVE COINS OF THE WEIMAR REPUBLIC, 1919-1933

Includes 26 color slides with lecture notes of these interesting pre-Hitler German Republic coins. Notes are available in either English or German. English notes will be sent unless otherwise specified.

SET #30: PRIMITIVE MONEY

SET #32: A HISTORY OF COLONIAL PAPER CURRENCY

Includes 51 color slides showing the paper currency and related monetary history of Colonial America.

SET #33: THE MILLED COINAGE OF ENGLAND

Includes 29 color slides of English coins issued from 1507 to 1676. The main purpose of this set is to illustrate the change from hammered to screw-press coins, often called "mill money." Examples of both types of coinage manufacture are shown.

SET #34: WORLD TRADE DOLLARS

The 40 slides in this set cover some 37 coins, both sides of a coin on each slide. Notes explain the reasons for the issuance of these interesting crown-size silver pieces.

SET #35: LOVE TOKENS

The 49 slides in this set show U.S. coins made into various types of "love tokens" by having the design on one side replaced with, usually, an engraved name, initials, and/or emblem or message. Brief lecture notes are included.

SET #36: HARD TIMES TOKENS (PART I)

Includes 27 color slides of the political and/or patriotic tokens issued during the 1834-1844 decade, usually called "Hard Times Tokens" or "Jackson Cents." Many of them relate to President Jackson's monetary policy and his refusal to re-charter the Second Bank of the United States.

SET #37: HARD TIMES TOKENS (PART II)

The 40 slides in this set present the "Merchants Cards" or "Store Cards" of the Hard Times Token series. Most of them show the name of the issuing firm, hence they were a form of advertising.

SET #38: LARGE SIZE NATIONAL BANK NOTES

Includes 67 color slides showing the three charter periods of National Bank notes (both sides) issued from 1863 to 1923. Denominations are from $1 to $100 and included are some rare notes, such as the second charter period $50 greenback with denomination spelled out, one of four known.

SET #39: LARGE SIZE SILVER CERTIFICATES

The old "saddle-blanket" certificates, issued from 1878 to 1923, are shown in this set of 66 color slides. These certificates were politically important, depicting many historical persons, and are beautifully engraved and printed.

SET #40: CROWNS OF THE WORLD, COUNTRIES A – I

Silver, crown-size coins have been a popular series with collectors for a long time, and this set of 59 color slides depicts examples (one side only) from 58 different countries from Afghanistan to Italy, issued during the period of 1780 to 1960. Most of the coins are from scarce to rare.

SET #41: CROWNS OF THE WORLD, COUNTRIES J – Z

A continuation of the coins shown in set #40, the 61 slides in this set cover countries from Jaipur to Zanzibar, from 1768 to 1963. With few exceptions, only one side of the coin for each country is shown.

SET #42: SHIPS AND BOATS ON MODERN COINS

Includes 45 color slides of modern coins of the world depicting various kinds of boats and ships used from ancient times to the present.

SET #43: MORGAN DOLLAR VARIETIES

Developed by Leroy C. Van Allen, this set of 34 slides includes many micro-photographs of various aspects of each variety. A feature for the Morgan dollar collector.

SET #44: THE HISTORY AND COLLECTING OF CHECKS

An 80-slide set developed by the Check Collectors Round Table to explain the historical background of checks and to explore some of the aspects of check collecting. This well done set will be of interest to collectors and non-collectors of all ages.

SET #45: HARD TIMES TOKENS, HISTORICAL BACKGROUND AND SYMBOLISM

Hard Times Tokens were both a political statement and a private attempt to reduce the shortage of small denomination coinage. This 45-slide set explores the political background of each of the pieces included. Helpful in understanding an economically confusing period in U.S. history.

SET #46: ART ON PAPER MONEY

Includes 34 slides depicting the artistry of paper money. Paintings that have been sources for the engraved vignettes found on many notes and the notes themselves are shown.

SET #47: AMERICAN GAME COUNTERS

Used in the nineteenth century much as poker chips are used today. These tokens are pictured in this set of 60 slides with brief lecture notes. Another example of the diversity possible for the collecting numismatist.

SET #48: MILITARY PAYMENT CERTIFICATES

A 41-slide set of military payment certificates. The scrip issued by the U.S. government for use by the armed forces stationed abroad from 1946 to 1973. This beautifully photographed set covers the entire 90 piece set of MPCs.

SET #50: A BICENTENNIAL PROGRAM: COINS AND CURRENCY OF EARLY AMERICA

Developed by the Ogden Coin Club with a grant from the Utah Bicentennial Commission, this set of 29 color slides shows examples of early coins and notes used in the United States. The historical perspective of this set makes it of special interest to beginning numismatists and to young people studying Colonial and Revolutionary America.

SET #51: COUNTERFEIT DETECTION: KEY CENTS AND NICKELS

The first of a proposed series of five slide programs on counterfeit detection which will cover some of the most often seen counterfeits. The set was developed by the Photo-Education Department of ANA from ANACS files and consists of 45 black and white slides of both genuine and counterfeit coins.

SET #52: COUNTERFEIT DETECTION: DIMES THROUGH SILVER DOLLARS

The second of the ANA Photo-Education series on counterfeits with 41 black and white slides from the files of ANACS.

SET #53: COUNTERFEIT DETECTION: GOLD DOLLARS AND QUARTER EAGLES

Includes 59 slides showing the diagnostics of both genuine and counterfeit specimens in these two U.S. coin series. The set was developed by ANACS from photographs in their files.

SET #54: COUNTERFEIT DETECTION: $3 AND HALF EAGLES

Containing 48 slides, this set is the fourth in the ANA Photo-Education series on counterfeit detection. Both genuine and counterfeit coins are shown.

SET #55: COUNTERFEIT DETECTION: EAGLES AND DOUBLE EAGLES

This set of 48 slides is the last in the series on counterfeit detection. Diagnostics of both genuine and counterfeit pieces are explained.

SET #56: STATE AND FEDERAL COPPERS OF MEXICO

ANA member C.C. Andrews has developed this historically fascinating catalog of some of the hard-to-find coins of early Mexico. The set consists of 43-color slides depicting Mexican state and federally-issued copper coins from the 1800s.

SET #57: THE OLD MINT OF SAN FRANCISCO: FROM THE BEGINNING THROUGH THE RESTORATION

An outstanding set of 80 color slides on the history of the second U.S. Mint in San Francisco from the California gold rush through the transformation of the Mint building into the present museum.

SET #58: LOVE TOKEN JEWELRY

Compiled by the Love Token Society, this set of 80 slides pictures some magnificent examples of love token jewelry. The lecture notes consist of a brief description of each piece. Collectors interested in this area of numismatics will enjoy these examples which could be considered the "state of the art."

SET #59: TREASURY NOTES OF THE CONFEDERATE STATES OF AMERICA

This set contains 71 slides and provides a chronological catalog of the treasury notes of the Confederate States of America. Included in the lecture notes are historical comments on events of the Civil War contemporary with the issuance of the notes.

SET #60: RUSSIAN COPPER COINAGE

Includes 25 slides showing Russian copper coins from 1533 through the Communist revolution. The extensive notes provide a clear historical perspective for these issues.

SET #61: FRENCH ASSIGNATS — FIAT MONEY OF THE REVOLUTION

The French Revolution is an economically interesting period which produced the numismatic items shown in this set. The 35 slides depict the notes and events from this turbulent time.

SET #62: A TRIBUTE TO PROMINENT BLACK AMERICANS

This set of 40 slides shows the medals minted by the Franklin Mint for the American Negro Commemorative Society. The men and women portrayed have made significant contributions to many aspects of our society.

SET #64: PRE-1947 PHILIPPINE COINS

The first winner of the M. Vernon Sheldon Award for the outstanding slide program submitted to ANA in 1983, this well written and photographed set will broaden understanding of a lesser known area of numismatics. The set contains 52 slides.

SET #65: NUMISMATIC FINE ART PHOTOGRAPHY

Using the beautiful photographs from *The Art of Coins and Their Photography,* by Gerald Hoberman, this set of 60 slides traces the art of coinage from ancient to modern. A good general set which shows the magnificence of coin designs.

SET #67: THE U.S. POSTAL NOTES OF 1883-1894

SET #69: DATING SYSTEMS OF COINS

SET #70: THE BASICS OF GRADING: OFFICIAL ANA GRADING STANDARDS

The first of a series of seven programs, this is an overview of grading which explains the critical wear points of each U.S. coin series, using the dime as an example to trace the wear for each grade designated in the ANA Grading Standards. The set contains 77 slides. The photography in this series is courtesy of Bill Fivaz.

SET #71: GRADING SMALL CENTS — FLYING EAGLE. 1856-58; INDIAN HEAD, 1859-1909; LINCOLN, 1909-DATE

This set of 66 slides gives a detailed explanation of the grading of U.S. small cents using the ANA Grading Standards.

SET #72: GRADING NICKEL FIVE CENTS — SHIELD, 1866-1883; LIBERTY HEAD, 1883-1912; BUFFALO, 1913-1938; JEFFERSON, 1938 TO DATE

Includes 86 slides explaining in detail the grading of U.S. copper-nickel coins according to the ANA Grading Standards.

SET #73: GRADING DIMES — BARBER, 1892-1916; MERCURY, 1916-1945

The ANA Grading Standards for these two types of U.S. dimes are shown using 48 color slides.

SET #74: GRADING QUARTERS — LIBERTY STANDING, VARIETY II, 1917-1930; WASHINGTON, 1932 TO DATE

The grading of two types of U.S. quarters is explained in this set of 45 slides.

SET #75: GRADING — LIBERTY SEATED QUARTERS, 1838-1891; LIBERTY SEATED HALF DOLLARS, 1839-1891; BARBER QUARTERS, 1892-1916; BARBER HALF DOLLARS, 1892-1915; WALKING LIBERTY HALF DOLLARS, 1916-1947

Grading of Liberty Seated quarters and half dollars; and Barber quarters and half dollars have been combined because of the similarities of designs. The set contains 79 color slides on these series.

SET #76: GRADING DOLLARS — MORGAN, 1878-1921; PEACE, 1921-1935

The last in the series on grading using ANA Grading Standards, this set of 52 slides shows wear details of these two popular U.S. dollar series.

SET #78: ANA SUMMER SEMINAR

Video tapes

TAPE #1: COLLECTING AND GRADING U.S. COINS

TAPE #2: COINS — COUNTERFEIT, GENUINE AND ALTERED

Prepared by a private firm with the guidance of the ANACS staff. The tapes are available in both VHS and BETA formats. Please specify which when ordering.

Seaby slide sets

Each of the following "SS" sets consists of 30 color slides of coins in famous collections in England and the United States. The coins are in choice Uncirculated condition and the photography is excellent. The sets were obtained from B.A. Seaby Ltd. of London, England.

SS #1: Greek Coins, Sixth Century B.C. to Alexander the Great.

SS #2: Roman Coins, the Twelve Caesars and Other Imperial Portraits.

SS #3: Hammered Gold English Coins, Edward III to Charles II.

SS #4: Milled Gold English Coins, Elizabeth I to Elizabeth II.

SS #5: English Silver Crowns, Edward VI to Elizabeth II.

SS #6: Scottish Gold Coins, Robert III to William III.

SS #7: English Pattern and Trial Pieces, 1813-1891 (12 patterns for coins of Edward VII are included).

SS #8: Coins of Bible Days, Fourth Century B.C. to Second Century A.D.

SS #9: Coins and Medals of the Renaissance.

SS #10: United States Gold Coins.

SS #11: United States Coins in Silver and Copper.

SS #12: United States Commemorative Coins in Gold and Silver.

SS #13: Byzantine Coins in Gold, Silver and Copper.

SS #14: Greek Coins, the Hellenistic Monarchies from Alexander the Great to Cleopatra VII.

SS #15: The Coinage of Republican Rome.

Reprints and numismatic material for sale
(ANA member prices)

If you are interested in 12 or more copies of a specific title, discounts are available.

ANACS Counterfeit Detection, a reprint from *The Numismatist* (postpaid).... 7.50

ANACS Counterfeit Detection Reports, Series I (post-paid) 105.00

ANACS Counterfeit Detection Reports, Series II (post-paid) 50.00

Special Offer: All three of the above... 99.00

ANACS Counterfeit Detection Reports, Series III (post-paid) member price . 29.95

ANACS Counterfeit Detection Reports, Series III (post-paid) non-member price 34.95

ANACS Visual Grading Reports (post-paid) member price 29.95

ANACS Visual Grading Reports (post-paid) non-member price 34.95

Basic Grading, Fahey 1.50

Coin Collecting, a Fascinating Hobby for Young and Old .... .50

Coinage of Iceland and Greenland ..... .50

Coinage of the Chinese Emigre Government, 1949-1957 .... 1.00

Coinage of the Slovak Republic, 1939-1944 .... .25

Coinology, Reed 4.50

Coins of the Nuestra Senora de Atocha, reprint from *The Numismatist* 2.95

Copper Coins of Austria-Hungary 1.00

Copper Coins of Denmark and Possessions 1.00

Copper Coins of Luxemburg.......... .50

Copper Coins of Norway .... .25

Copper Coins of the German Empire... .50

Dating of the Shekel 1.00

Financial History of Colonial Virginia. . 1.00

German Siege Pieces 1.00

Hispaniola Divided 1.00

Index to *The Numismatist*: Vol. 1-91 (postpaid)........................ 4.95

Index to *The Numismatist*: Vol. 52-71.. 1.00

Indian and Post Trader Tokens 1.00

Introduction to Numismatics (Includes dictionary of numismatic terms)..... 2.00

Library Catalogue of the American Numismatic Association, 1977, (postpaid)........................ 4.95

Supplement to the ANA Library Catalogue 1978-84 (postpaid) 3.95

Matte Proof Lincoln Cents, 1909-1917, Albrecht........................ 1.00

The Medallic Art of Baltimore Sculptors Hans Schuler and Hans C. Schuler... 1.50

Medals of China 1900 .... .75

Medieval Feudal French Coinage...... 1.00

Michigan Depression Scrip of 1930's... 1.00

Modern Chinese Copper Coins........ 1.00

National Bank Notes in Early Years ... 1.00

Previously Unknown Spanish Gold.... .50

Rubles of Peter the Great and His Successors 1.00

The Selling of the Stone Mountain Half
Dollar, Hyder/Colbert 1.50
A Study and Catalog of 19th-Century
Photographic Tokens, Gale/Gale 1.50
Theodore Roosevelt and Numismatics . 1.50
The Works of Victor David Brenner, A
Descriptive Listing, Smedley........ 2.50
Video Tape: "Collecting and Grading U.S.
Coins" (specify VHS or Beta) 79.95
Video Tape: "Coins: Genuine, Counterfeit
and Altered" (VHS or Beta)........ 59.95

Back Issues of The Numismatist

1920s and earlier, each.............. 7.50
1930s, each....................... 5.00
1940s, each....................... 3.00
1950s, each....................... 2.00
1960-1974, each 1.00
1975-1980 each 1.25
1981-1982, each 1.50
1983-1985, each 2.50
1986-, each....................... 3.00

The Numismatist on Microfiche

Volumes 1-100, 1888-1987 (1986-87 to be
published) 285.00
Volumes 1-20 each 5.00
Volumes 21-40 each 4.50
Volumes 41-60 each 4.00
Volumes 61-80 each 3.50
Volumes 81-100 each 3.00
Microfiche readers are available at special
prices to members.

Other Numismatic Literature

The following titles have been donated to
the ANA Library. Many of these publications
are being specially offered at 50 percent off
the regular price. No quantity discounts.

Orders less than $5 add $1 for postage. Orders more than $5 add $2 for postage. Overseas postage will be billed. Orders should be
sent to: Librarian, American Numismatic Association, 818 N. Cascade Ave., Colorado
Springs, Colo. 80903.

Adventures With Rare Coins, Bowers. 14.95
American Centennial Tokens and Medals,
1981, Slabaugh 3.00
Beskrifning Ofver J.F.H. Oldenburgs Samling
af Svenska, Oldenburg............ 12.35
Blue Books, (please write for
availability).................... 1.00
California Fractional Gold, (second edition),
Doering 30.00
A Catalog of Silver Coins of the World Since
1900, Garner.................... 2.50
Catalogue of European Paper Money Since
1900, (second edition), Pick 8.75
Catalogue of Unlisted Civil War Storecards
in the Collection of the American
Numismatic Society.............. 2.00

Coins of Ancient Lycia, 1976, Fellows,
(reprint) 10.00
Coins of the Republic of Mexico, 1823-1905,
and the Empire of Maximilian (hard
cover), 1976, Vogt 5.00
Coins of the Republic of Mexico, 1823-1905,
and the Empire of Maximilian (paper
cover), 1976, Vogt 2.50
Confederate and Southern States Bonds,
(second edition), Criswell......... 12.50
Copper Coins of India, Pts. I & II, (1971),
Valentine....................... 8.75
Current Coins of the World, (seventh
edition), Yeoman 2.75
A Descriptive History of National Bank
Notes 1863-1935, Dillisten........ 10.00
Guide Book of English Coins, (eighth
edition), Bressett.................. .75
Hard Time Token Plates, Low, (plates
only)........................... 5.00
High Profits from Rare Coin Investments,
(first edition, 1974), Bowers 2.00
High Profits from Rare Coin Investments,
(sixth edition, 1979), Bowers 2.50
History of Coins of Honduras 1.00
How to Grow Money, Sternfeld....... 2.50
The Lima Pieces of George II of England
(CCJ #156, 1954), Nesmith........ 1.00
Market Value Index of Circulated U.S. Coins,
(1963), Brown/Dunn .... .65
The Medals of Ecuador, Almanzar/
Seppa 1.25
Official Inaugural Medals of the Presidents of
the United States, (1971), Dusterberg 5.00
Pageant of World Commemorative Coins,
(1962), Becker................... 5.00
Paper Money of Bolivia, Seppa/
Almanzar....................... 1.25
Paper Money of Guatemala, 1834-1946,
Clark 1.50
Personal Tokens of Vecturists, (1975).. 1.00
The President's Medal 1789-1977, (1977),
MacNeil........................ 5.00
Price List of Paper Money in Sheets,
Muscalus .... .50
Red Books, 1965-1982 (please write for
availability)..................... 1.75
A Revised Check List and Valuation of
Military Tokens of the United States 1866-
1969, Book I, 1981, Curto.......... 5.00
Standard Catalogue of Canadian Coins,
Tokens and Paper Money, 1963-1968,
(Please write for availability) 1.50
A Tentative Check List of Spanish American
Bust-Type Coins, Ramsey.......... 1.25
United States Half Dimes: A Supplement
(CCJ #160), Breen 1.00
United States Large Size Paper Money,
(fourth edition), Donlon 1.00

United States Large Size Paper Money, (sixth edition), Donlon 2.50
U.S. Small Size Paper Money, (14th edition),

Hewitt/Donlon 1.75
Variety-Oddity Check List Record Book, (1965-66), Spadone 50

ANA presidents, 1891-1985

President	Elected	President	Elected
William G. Jerrems	1891	J. Douglas Ferguson	1941
George F. Heath	1892	Martin F. Kortjohn	1943
A.G. Heaton	1894	V. Leon Belt	1945
Joseph Hooper	1898	Loyd B. Gettys	1947
B.P. Wright	1901	M. Vernon Sheldon	1949
A.R. Frey	1904	Joseph Moss	1951
Farran Zerbe	1907	J. Hewitt Judd	1953
J.M. Henderson	1909	Leonel C. Panosh	1955
Judson Brenner	1911	O.H. Dodson	1957
Frank G. Duffield	1913	C.C. Shroyer	1961
H.O. Granberg	1915	P.K. Anderson	1963
Carl Wurtzbach	1917	Matt Rothert	1965
Waldo C. Moore	1919	Arthur Sipe	1967
Moritz Wormser	1921	Herbert M. Bergen	1969
Harry H. Yawger	1926	John J. Pittman	1971
Charles Markus	1927	Virginia Culver	1973
George J. Bauer	1930	Virgil Hancock	1975
Alden Scott Boyer	1932	Grover C. Criswell	1977
Nelson T. Thorson	1933	George D. Hatie	1979
T. James Clarke	1935	Adna G. Wilde	1981
J. Henri Ripstra	1937	Q. David Bowers	1983
L.W. Hoffecker	1939	Florence M. Schook	1985

ANA board chairmen
(Office discontinued in 1937)

Chairman	Term	Chairman	Term
B.P. Wright	1907	H.H. Yawger	1921-1925
Howland Wood	1908	Charles Markus	1926
William F. Dunham	1909	Harry W. Rapp	1927
H.O. Granberg	1910-1914	Farran Zerbe	1928
Judson Brenner	1915	Nelson Thorson	1929-1932
Carl Wurtzbach	1916	Harley L. Freeman	1933-34
Waldo Moore	1917-18	Henry Hunt	1935
Moritz Wormser	1919-20	T. James Clarke	1936

Editors of The Numismatist

The Numismatist is the official publication of the American Numismatic Association. It was first published in September, 1888.

Editor	Term	Editor	Term
George F. Heath	1888-1908	Stuart Mosher	1945-1954
Farran Zerbe	1909-1910	Elston G. Bradfield	1954-1966
Albert Frey	1911-1912	Glenn B. Smedley	1966-1967
Edgar H. Adams	1912-1915	Edward Rochette	1967-1972
Frank G. Duffield	1915-1942	Thomas Marshall	1972-1973
Lee F. Hewitt	1942-1943	Edward Rochette	1973-1974
Burton H. Saxton	1943-1944	N. Neil Harris	1974-

ANA convention sites

Location	Date Held
Chicago, Ill.	Oct. 7, 1891
Pittsburgh, Pa.	Oct. 1, 1892
Douglas Hall, Chicago, Ill. ..	Aug. 21, 1893
Detroit Museum of Art	
Detroit, Mich.	Aug. 23-24, 1894
Art Parlors of B. H. Collins	
Washington, D.C.	Sept. 19-20, 1895
Office of Dr. B. P. Wright	
Buffalo, N.Y.	Aug. 22, 1901
Congress Hall, World's Fair Grounds	
St. Louis, Mo.	Oct. 15, 1904
Neil House,	
Columbus, Ohio	Sept. 2-4, 1907
Hotel Stenton	
Philadelphia, Pa. .	Sept. 28-Oct. 2, 1908
St. Lawrence Hall Hotel	
Montreal, Canada	Aug. 9-14, 1909
American Numismatic Society Bldg.	
New York, N.Y.	Sept. 6-10, 1910
Art Institute	
Chicago, Ill.	Aug. 28-31, 1911
Hotel Rochester	
Rochester, N.Y.	Aug. 26-28, 1912
Detroit Museum of Art	
Detroit, Mich.	Aug. 23-27, 1913
Springfield Group Auditorium	
Springfield, Mass.	Aug. 22-26, 1914
Hotel Stewart	
San Francisco ...	Aug. 30-Sept. 1, 1915
Peabody Institute	
Baltimore, Md.	Sept. 23-27, 1916
Memorial Art Gallery	
Rochester, N.Y.	Aug. 25-29, 1917
Academy of Fine Arts	
Philadelphia, Pa.	Oct. 4-8, 1919
Art Institute	
Chicago, Ill.	Aug. 23-26, 1920
Boston Public Library	
Boston, Mass.	Aug. 20-25, 1921
American Fine Arts Society Bldg.	
New York, N.Y.	Aug. 26-31, 1922
Chateau de Ramezay	
Montreal, Quebec	Aug. 25-30, 1923
Hollenden Hotel	
Cleveland, Ohio	Aug. 23-28, 1924
Hotel Statler	
Detroit, Mich.	Aug. 21-27, 1925
Hotel Washington	
Washington, D.C.	Aug. 21-26, 1926
Supreme Court, State Library Bldg.	
Hartford, Conn.	Aug. 20-25, 1927
Hotel Seneca	
Rochester, N.Y.	Aug. 18-23, 1928
Congress Hotel	
Chicago, Ill.	Aug. 24-29, 1929

Location	Date Held
Hotel Statler	
Buffalo, N.Y.	Aug. 23-28, 1930
Netherland Plaza Hotel	
Cincinnati, Ohio .	Aug. 29-Sept. 3, 1931
Hotel Biltmore	
Los Angeles, Calif. ...	Aug. 20-26, 1932
Congress Hotel	
Chicago, Ill.	Aug. 26-31, 1933
Carter Hotel	
Cleveland, Ohio	Aug. 18-23, 1934
Carnegie Institute	
Pittsburgh, Pa.	Aug. 24-29, 1935
Nicollet Hotel	
Minneapolis, Minn. ..	Aug. 22-27, 1936
Hotel Washington	
Washington, D.C.	Aug. 21-26, 1937
Neil House	
Columbus, Ohio	Aug. 13-18, 1938
Hotel Pennsylvania	
New York, N.Y. .	Sept. 31-Oct. 5, 1939
Detroit-Leland Hotel	
Detroit, Mich.	Aug. 24-29, 1940
Benjamin Franklin Hotel	
Philadelphia, Pa.	Aug. 18-21, 1941
Netherland Plaza Hotel	
Cincinnati, Ohio	Aug. 24-26, 1942
LaSalle Hotel	
Chicago, Ill.	Sept. 11-13, 1943
LaSalle Hotel	
Chicago, Ill.	Aug. 27-28, 1944
Blackhawk Hotel	
Davenport, Iowa	Aug. 17-21, 1946
Statler Hotel	
Buffalo, N.Y.	Aug. 23-27, 1947
Copley-Plaza Hotel	
Boston, Mass.	Aug. 21-25, 1948
Palace Hotel	
San Francisco, Calif. ..	Aug. 23-27, 1949
Schroeder Hotel	
Milwaukee, Wis.	Aug. 25-29, 1950
Westward Ho Hotel	
Phoenix, Ariz.	Aug. 25-28, 1951
Hotel Statler	
New York, N.Y.	Aug. 16-20, 1952
Baker Hotel	
Dallas, Texas	Aug. 22-26, 1953
Carter Hotel	
Cleveland, Ohio	Aug. 17-21, 1954
Hotel Fontenelle	
Omaha, Neb.	Aug. 24-27, 1955
Congress Hotel	
Chicago, Ill.	Aug. 22-25, 1956
Sheraton Hotel	
Philadelphia, Pa.	Aug. 21-24, 1957
Statler-Hilton Hotel	
Los Angeles, Calif. ...	Aug. 13-16, 1958

Location	Date Held
Multnomah Hotel Portland, Ore.	Aug. 26-29, 1959
Statler-Hilton Hotel Boston, Mass.	Aug. 24-27, 1960
Atlanta-Biltmore Hotel Atlanta, Ga.	Aug. 16-19, 1961
Sheraton-Cadillac Hotel Detroit, Mich.	Aug. 15-18, 1962
Hilton Hotel Denver, Colo.	Aug. 7-10, 1963
Sheraton Hotel Cleveland, Ohio	Aug. 19-22, 1964
Shamrock-Hilton Hotel Houston, Texas	Aug. 25-28, 1965
Pick-Congress Hotel Chicago, Ill.	Aug. 16-20, 1966
Americana Hotel Miami Beach, Fla.	Aug. 8-12, 1967
El Cortez Hotel San Diego, Calif.	Aug. 20-25, 1968
Sheraton Hotel Philadelphia, Pa.	Aug. 12-16, 1969
Chase Park Plaza Hotel St. Louis, Mo.	Aug. 18-22, 1970
Statler-Hilton Hotel Washington, D.C.	Aug. 10-14, 1971
Jung Hotel New Orleans, La.	Aug. 15-19, 1972
Sheraton-Boston Hotel Boston, Mass.	Aug. 23-27, 1973
Americana Hotel Miami Beach, Fla.	Aug. 13-18, 1974
Marriott Hotel Los Angeles, Calif.	Aug. 19-24, 1975
Americana Hotel New York, N.Y.	Aug. 24-29, 1976
Atlanta Marriott Hotel Atlanta, Ga.	Aug. 23-28, 1977
Astro-World Hotels Houston, Texas	Aug. 22-27, 1978
Chase Park-Plaza Hotel St. Louis, Mo.	Aug. 14-19, 1979
Stouffer's Cincinnati Towers Cincinnati, Ohio	Aug. 19-24, 1980
Hilton Hotel New Orleans, La.	July 28-Aug. 2, 1981
Sheraton-Boston Hotel Boston, Mass.	Aug. 16-21, 1982
Town & Country Hotel San Diego, Calif.	Aug. 15-20, 1983
Westin Hotel/Cobo Hall Convention Center Detroit, Mich.	July 28-Aug. 1, 1984
Baltimore Convention Center Baltimore, Md.	Aug. 20-25, 1985
Milwaukee Exposition & Convention Center & Arena Milwaukee, Wis.	Aug. 6-10, 1986
Georgia World Congress Center Atlanta, Ga.	Aug. 26-30, 1987
Convention Center Cincinnati, Ohio	July 20-24, 1988
Pittsburgh, Pa.	Aug. 5-9, 1989
Seattle, Wash.	Aug. 1-5, 1990
Chicago, Ill.	Summer 1991

ANA Midwinter convention sites

Location	Date Held
Broadmoor Hotel Colorado Springs, Colo.	Feb. 15-18, 1978
Albuquerque Inn Albuquerque, N.M.	Feb. 15-17, 1980
Hilton Hawaiian Village Honolulu, Hawaii	Feb. 5-8, 1981
Broadmoor Hotel Colorado Springs, Colo.	Feb. 18-21, 1982
Marriott Hotel Tucson, Ariz	Feb. 24-27, 1983
Broadmoor Hotel Colorado Springs, Colo.	Feb. 22-26, 1984
Marriott Hotel, San Antonio, Texas	Feb. 21-24, 1985
Salt Palace Convention Center Salt Lake City, Utah	Feb. 20-22, 1986
Charlotte Convention Center Charlotte, N.C.	Feb. 27-March 1, 1987
Statehouse Convention Center Little Rock, Ark.	March 11-13, 1988
Honolulu, Hawaii	Feb. 1989

The Farran Zerbe Award

The Farran Zerbe Memorial Award, highest American Numismatic Association honor, was established by Louis S. Werner of New York, a close friend of Zerbe. Zerbe was at one time the owner and editor of *The Numismatist*; he was often referred to as the dean of American numismatics. Zerbe served two terms as president of the American Numismatic Association. He died Dec. 25, 1949, at the age of 78.

The recipient of the Zerbe award each year is selected by the awards committee and approved by the board of governors of the ANA as one considered to have rendered the association distinguished service and to be worthy of the highest honor it can bestow. The traditional plaque was replaced in 1984 by a two-inch, 10-karat gold medal.

Winner	Year Awarded	Winner	Year Awarded
M. Vernon Sheldon	1951	Charles M. Johnson	1970
June T. Pond	1952	Don Sherer	1971
Joseph Moss	1953	Abe Kosoff	1972
Lewis M. Reagan	1954	Matt Rothert	1973
J. Hewitt Judd	1955	Herbert M. Bergen	1974
Richard S. Yeoman	1956	Margo Russell	1975
Burton H. Saxton	1958	Maurice M. Gould (posthumous)	1976
Louis S. Werner	1959	Fred Bowman	1976
Glenn B. Smedley	1960	Chester L. Krause	1977
John F. Lhotka Jr.	1961	William Henderson	1978
Lee F. Hewitt	1962	John J. Gabarron	1979
Elston G. Bradfield	1963	John J. Pittman	1980
Jack W. Ogilvie	1964	Virgil Hancock	1981
Leonel C. Panosh	1965	George D. Hatie	1982
J. Douglas Ferguson	1966	Clyde Hubbard	1983
John S. Davenport	1967	Clifford Mishler	1984
Oscar H. Dodson	1968	Adna G. Wilde Jr.	1985
Eric P. Newman	1969	Charles H. Wolfe	1986

Members of ANA Hall of Fame

The ANA Hall of Fame is open to "persons whose contributions to the field of numismatics have been of the highest excellence and most outstanding." Nominations are accepted between October and December of the year preceding the year of award, and may be made by any ANA member except junior members.

Member	Inducted	Member	Inducted
Edgar H. Adams	1969	Howard Rounds Newcomb	1974
George J. Bauer	1969	William A. Philpott, Jr.	1974
Frank G. Duffield	1969	Dr. Benjamin P. Wright	1974
George F. Heath	1969	Frederick Boyd	1978
Edward T. Newell	1969	Victor Brenner	1978
Wayte Raymond	1969	Lee Hewitt	1978
David C. Wismer	1969	J. Ripstra	1978
Howland Wood	1969	David Bullowa	1978
Farran Zerbe	1969	Richard Yeoman	1978
George H. Blake	1970	Herbert Bergen	1982
Henry Chapman	1970	Abe Kosoff	1982
Sylvester S. Crosby	1970	Glenn B. Smedley	1982
Lewis M. Reagan	1970	Elston G. Bradfield	1982
Moritz Wormser	1970	J. Douglas Ferguson	1982
Olie P. Eklund	1972	Robert Wallace McLachlan	1982
Albert Frey	1972	Louis W. Werner	1982
Barclay P. Head	1972	Sheldon S. Carroll	1984
John M. Henderson	1972	William T.R. Marvin	1984
Lyman H. Low	1972	Lionel Panosh	1984
Waldo C. Moore	1972	Norman Schultz	1984
Stuart Mosher	1972	Eva B. Adams	1986
Burton H. Saxton	1972	S.W. Freeman	1986
Agnes Baldwin Brett	1974	Robert Friedberg	1986
Capt. John W. Haseltine	1974	Eric P. Newman	1986
Joseph Hooper	1974	Margo Russell	1986
B. Max Mehl	1974		

Heath Literary Awards

Heath Literary Awards were established in 1945 while V. Leon Belt was president of the American Numismatic Association. Each year, all papers published in *The Numismatist* are judged on their merits by an impartial committee. First, second and third place medals are presented with as many as five honorable mention awards possible. Winners of the silver medals since 1945:

Winner	Year Awarded	Winner	Year Awarded
P.H. Chase	1945	Thomas Becker	1967
James J. Curto	1946	Philip Chase	1968
Philip H. Chase	1947	Randolph Zander	1968
William H. Dillistin	1948	John D. Wright	1969
H.A. Seaby	1949	John S. Davenport	1969
Lt. Sheridan L. McGarry	1950	Ray Byrne	1970
Wm. A. Philpott, Jr.	1951	Miguel L. Munoz	1970
Stanley J. Schillinger	1952	Phares Sigler	1971
Richard T. Hoober	1953	Walter J. Zimmerman	1972
Col. Phares O. Sigler	1954	Ray Byrne	1973
Dr. John F. Lhotka	1955	David R. Cervin	1974
Loyd B. Gettys and E.M. Catich	1956	Thomas P. Rockwell	1975
Melvin and George Fuld	1957-1958	William G. Anderson	1976
Eric P. Newman	1959	Miguel Munoz	1977-1978
Helen Woodburn	1960	Eric P. Newman	1979
Philip Chase	1961	Peter Gaspar	1979
Ted Weissbuch	1961	David McBride	1980
James Risk	1962	Eric Newman	1980
David F. Spink	1962	John Isted	1980
Alan B. Shaw	1963	Tom DeLorey	1981
Ernest Weidhaas	1963	Thomas Schweich	1982
Eric P. Newman	1964	R.W. Julian	1983
George Fuld	1964	Carl W.A. Carlson	1983
John F. Lhotka Jr.	1965	David & Charlotte Gale	1984
Eric P. Newman	1965-1966	Henry Schab	1985
Miguel L. Munoz	1966	David & Charlotte Gale	1986

Wayte and Olga Raymond Literary Awards

The Wayte and Olga Raymond Literary award is for distinguished numismatic achievement in the field of United States numismatics.

	For work published in	Award presented in		For work published in	Award presented in
Gerome Walton	1977	1978	Ronald J. Guth	1982	1983
Adna G. Wilde Jr.	1978	1979	Eric P. Newman	1983	1984
Eric P. Newman	1978	1979	Glenn B. Smedley	1983	1984
David P. McBride	1979	1980	Henry Schab	1984	1985
Thomas K. DeLorey	1980	1981	David & Charlotte		
Thomas Schweich	1981	1982	Gale	1984	1985
Kirk Hillman	1981	1982			
Anthony Swiatek	1981	1982	William D. Hyder &		
Jeanne Madeline			R.W. Colbert	1985	1986
Weinmann	1981	1982	Thomas K. DeLorey	1985	1986

Winners of ANA Medal of Merit

The ANA Medal of Merit is one of the highest awards of the ANA, and is reserved for "those who have shown outstanding devotion to numismatics, the organization and its goals." The medals are given each year in ceremonies at the ANA Convention.

Medals of Merit are always accompanied by special citations which describe in detail the contributions made by the recipient to the American Numismatic Association.

The Grecian-styled medal, approximately two and one-eighths inches in diameter, bears a Greek warrior on the obverse, and on the reverse, a goddess-driven biga ascending a panel on which the recipient's name is engraved.

Winner	Year Awarded	Winner	Year Awarded
J. Douglas Ferguson	1947	John F. Lhotka	1959
Martin Kortjohn	1947	C.C. Shroyer	1959
Joseph Moss	1947	P.O. Sigler	1959
Max M. Schwartz	1947	Leo G. Terry	1960
Louis S. Werner	1948	Don Sherer	1960
Damon G. Douglas	1949	Matt Rothert	1960
C.H. Ryan	1949	George T. Fuld	1961
M. Vernon Sheldon	1949	William N. Worth	1961
J. Hewitt Judd	1949	Earl C. Schill	1961
Louis M. Reagan	1949	Arthur Sipe	1962
Julius Windner	1949	George M. Todd	1962
George H. Blake	1950	Dolly Maude Harris	1962
Floyd B. Newell	1950	John J. Pittman	1962
Lee F. Hewitt	1950	Robert G. McArthur	1962
Ted R. Hammer	1950	Sol Kaplan	1962
Oscar H. Dodson	1950	Melvin Fuld	1962
Burton H. Saxton	1950	S.W. Freeman	1963
T.O. Mabbott	1950	John W. Dunn	1964
Charles L. Ruby	1950	Richard T. Hoober	1964
Charles F. Nettleship	1950	Ralph C. Mitchell	1964
Lawrence Lee Howe	1950	Eric P. Newman	1964
Loyd B. Gettys	1951	William A. Philpott	1965
Vernon L. Brown	1951	Dan Brown	1965
V. Leon Belt	1952	Doris Martin	1966
Marcella L. Sheldon	1952	Michael M. Dolnick	1966
William Sheldon	1952	Julian Blanchard	1966
Richard Yeoman	1952	Chester A. Krause	1967
Stuart Mosher	1953	Al Overton	1967
Jack W. Ogilvie	1953	Margo Russell	1967
Glenn B. Smedley	1953	Lois Otis	1968
Marjorie L. Williams	1953	Charles R. Hoskins	1968
Ernst Kraus	1954	Harley Freeman	1968
Harold R. Klein	1954	Aubrey Bebee	1968
John S. Davenport	1955	Byrnadette Gabarron	1969
Edward Fogler	1955	Jake B. Sureck	1969
Leonel C. Panosh	1955	Albert F. Pradeau	1969
Michael A. Powills	1955	Henry Grunthal	1970
Earl C. Brown	1956	Maurice M. Gould	1970
James W. Curtis	1956	Ray Byrne	1971
John J. Gabarron	1956	Sheldon S. Carroll	1971
Elston G. Bradfield	1957	William C. Henderson	1971
August F. Hausske	1957	Vir Den Mayo	1971
D.Dee DeNise	1957	Edward C. Rochette	1972
James J. Curto	1958	Herbert M. Bergen	1972
P.K. Anderson	1958	Herbert W. Price	1972
Abe Kosoff	1958	Charles M. Johnson	1973
A.H. Leatherman	1958	Geneva Karlson	1973

Winner	Year Awarded	Winner	Year Awarded
Evie Kelley	1973	Virginia Culver	1981
Genevieve Herdegen	1974	Charles Wolfe	1981
Ellis Edlow	1974	Margaret Lloyd	1982
Joseph M. Segel	1974	Betty Higby	1982
Valentine Pasvolsky	1975	John Smies	1982
Pat Suthers, posthumously	1975	Ben Stack	1982
		Harvey Stack	1982
Clyde Hubbard, Florence Schook	1976	Norman Stack	1982
Robert E. Medlar	1977	Gene Hynds	1983
Rev. Arthur Braddan Coole	1977	Clifford Mishler	1983
Frank & Laurese Katen	1978	Austin M. Sheehen Jr.	1983
Ruthann Brettell	1978	Arthur M. Kagin	1983
Paul Whitnah	1978	David R. Cervin	1984
Kenneth Bressett	1978	Bill Fivaz	1984
Miguel Munoz	1979	Eva B. Adams	1984
Col. Robert Kriz	1979	Frank Annunzio	1985
James Miller	1979	Cheryl & Robert Maisch	1985
		Roy Pennell	1985
Eldridge Jones	1980	Harry X Boosel	1986
Henry Spangenberger	1980	Robert & Marjorie Hendershott	1986
N. Neil Harris	1980	John A. Muscalus	1986
Ralph Cleaver	1981		

Howland Wood Award winners

The Howland Wood Grand Award for "The Best in Show" is presented at the annual convention of the ANA. A proposal and resolution for the exhibit medal award program was introduced at the 1949 convention in San Francisco. It was continued at the 1950 Milwaukee gathering and established at the 1951 Phoenix convention.

Winner	Year Awarded	Winner	Year Awarded
Richard S. Yeoman	1951	Lelan G. Rogers	1969
Dr. J. Hewitt Judd	1952	Margaret Frantz	1970
William A. Philpott Jr.	1953	David R. Cervin	1971
New York Orders and Medals Society	1954	Lt. Col. Frank O'Sullivan	1972
Burton H. Saxton	1955	Ray Byrne	1973
R.F. Schermerhorn	1956	Emil Voigt	1974
Amon G. Carter Jr.	1957	Peter E. Brander	1975
August F. Hausske	1958	Dr. C. Radford Stearns	1976
C.L. Liss	1959	Maurice M. Burgett	1977
Mrs. James Nestor	1960	Stephen Taylor	1978 & 1979
R.E. Cox Jr.	1961	Jean Bullen	1980
Gaston Di Bello	1962	Jack Huggins	1981
Julius Turoff	1963	Dennis Loring	1982
Fred R. Marckhoff	1964	F.M. Rose	1983
Robert E. Medlar	1965	Nancy Wilson	1984
George L. Podlusky	1966	Robert F. Kriz	1985
Julio M. Ruiz	1967	Jean Bullen	1986
Opal H. Morris	1968		

ANA Numismatic Art Award for Excellence in Medallic Sculpture

The ANA Numismatic Art Award for Excellence in Medallic Sculpture, popularly known as the Outstanding Sculptor of the Year Award, was brought into existence in 1966 by the ANA, in conjunction with the Franklin Mint. The large gold medal award is presented annually to pay tribute to talented sculptors.

Winner	Year Awarded	Winner	Year Awarded
Paul Vincze	1966	Karen Worth	1977
Gilroy Roberts	1967	Miko Kaufman	1978
Frank Gasparro	1968	Donald De Lue	1979
Edward R. Grove	1969	Bruno Mankowski	1980
C. Paul Jennewein	1970	Joseph Kiselewski	1981
Ralph Menconi	1971	Adlai S. Hardin	1982
Elizabeth Jones	1972	Not Awarded	1983
Gertrude Lathrop	1973	Anthony Jones	1984
Abram Belskie	1974		
Robert Weinman	1975	Phillip Nathan	1985
Adolph Block	1976	Not Awarded	1986

Young Numismatist awards

Thirteen awards in connection with the Young Numismatist program are offered yearly. These awards are given by the Association, other organizations and individuals interested in encouraging the participation of young collectors in the hobby. The 13 awards are designated as follows:

(1) The Abe Kosoff Memorial Literary Award

(2) The Gould Memorial Literary Award

(3) The Ray Byrne Memorial Literary Award

(4) The Florence Schook Outstanding Young Numismatist Award

(5) The Outstanding Adult Leader or Advisor Award — anonymous

(6) The Charles H. Wolfe Class C (YN) Convention Exhibit Award

(7) The Gordon Z. Greene Memorial U.S. Exhibit Award

(8) The James L. Betton Foreign Exhibit Award

(9) The Kurt Krueger Paper Money Exhibit Award

(10) The Melissa Van Grover Israel or Judiac Exhibit Award

(11) The Arlie Slabaugh Medals and Tokens Exhibit Award

(12) The Charles E. Wolfe Medieval and Ancient Exhibit Award

(13) The Alan Herbert Error/Variety Exhibit Award.

Qualifications for all of these awards (except No. 5) are that contestants be junior members (ages 11 through 17) of the ANA at the time of their achievements, although they may have become adults when the awards are actually presented at the convention; their achievements must be originated and carried out on their own, and their entries received by Chairwoman Florence Shook by the published deadline.

In the case of written articles, there is no minimum or maximum limit or length. The manuscript must be typed or printed on 8.5" by 11" sheets, double spaced, and on only one side of the paper; and it must bear the author's name, ANA number, affiliations with other numismatic organizations, a short biographical sketch, and his or her black-and-white glossy photograph. In all cases, the decisions of the judges shall be final.

An article once submitted may be resubmitted for judging in a future year if the author has done further research on the subject matter and the article is revised substantially. However, should the author pass the eligible age of junior status, the article or manuscript cannot be further altered, edited, or otherwise changed for resubmission. An article or manuscript may only be submitted in one category.

A manuscript or article may be submitted by an officer or editor of a local, state or regional organization; but all rules herein must apply. In the case an article is submitted by other than the author, the written permission of the author for such submission must accompany it; and it will then be treated as if submitted by the author.

Rules and qualifications for the individual awards are as follows:

(1) As the name implies, this is a literary award to be presented to the young numismatist who writes the best essay or gives the best talk on a numismatic subject. The information may be from original research or may have been gathered from various sources, but credit must be given by the author for his source or sources. Original conclusions are encouraged, particularly when logically presented. Manuscripts will be judged for their content, general interest and literary excellence. The award will be a plaque.

(2) This is an educational award to be made to the junior author of the best article

submitted. Each entrant is expected to have conducted in-depth research of his area of interest, going beyond information previously published in standard numismatic reference works, and his article must demonstrate individual and specialized involvement with his topic. The article submitted may have been published or not and may have been submitted to a local, state or regional organization in competition or for publication. The award will be in the form of a plaque.

(3) Qualifications and rules for this award are the same as the preceding (2) except that the article must have been published in *The Numismatist, Coin World, Numismatic News* or any other accredited numismatic publication.

(4) This award is given to the Young Numismatist judged most deserving of it over the year. Selection of the recipient shall be on a similar basis as the ANA award to the Outstanding Club Representative on a cumulative point basis for consideration of nominees' numismatic service rendered. Nominations may be made by any ANA individual or club member.

Talks given before numismatic or educational groups, papers published (including locally), enthusiasm for numismatics and leadership in local numismatic circles will all be considered in the awarding of points. The Outstanding Young Numismatist Award form must be submitted by the young numismatist along with copies of documented evidence of achievement no later than the published date. Forms are available for nominating a candidate for this award and may be otained from Florence M. Schook, P.O. Box 2014, Livonia, Mich. 48154.

(5) This award shall be presented to the adult judged to have contributed most toward the encouragement of Young Numismatists. Nominations for this award may be made by individual or club members of the ANA or by educators. (In Michigan, for example, it is necessary that junior and senior high school clubs have adult faculty advisors; and for this reason it is felt that educators, properly identified, should be allowed to submit nominations).

The qualities to be considered in awarding points are: time, knowledge, educational contributions such as books, papers, etc., leadership in ethical and moral standards, ability to organize, attract new members to the hobby, etc. Monetary contributions shall not be considered a basis for this award. A form is available for nominating a candidate from Florence M. Schook.

(6) ANA junior members may enter exhibits in Class C at the ANA annual convention. This award will be made to the Young Numismatist whose exhibit in this class is judged best in accordance with exhibit rules; identical standards applying to adult exhibits will prevail. Young Numismatist exhibitors shall mount, prepare, and place their own exhibits. This is, in effect, the Young Numismatist best in show award.

(7) Qualifications and rules for the Gordon Z. Greene Memorial Award are the same as for the preceding (6) except that only exhibits of United States material will be considered in competition for it.

(8) Qualifications and rules for the James L. Betton Award are the same as for the ANA Convention Exhibit Award (6) except that only exhibits of foreign coinages will be considered in competition for it.

(9) Qualifications and rules for the Kurt Krueger Award are the same as for the ANA Convention Exhibit Award (6) except that only exhibits of U.S. or foreign paper money will be considered in competition for it.

(10) Qualifications and rules for the Melissa Van Grover Award are the same as for the ANA Convention Exhibit Award (6) except that only exhibits of Israel or Judaic Numismatic material will be considered in competition for it. In the event there is no qualifying exhibit, the award may be given to a deserving exhibit at the discretion of the judges.

(11) Qualifications and rules for the Arlie Slabaugh Award are the same as for the ANA Convention Exhibit Award (6) except that only exhibits of medals and/or tokens will be considered in competition for it.

(12) Qualifications and rules for the Charles H. Wolfe Exhibit Award are the same as for the ANA Convention Exhibit Award (6) except that only exhibits of medieval, ancient and related numismatic material will be considered in competition for it.

(13) Qualifications and rules for the Alan Herbert Award are the same as for the ANA Convention Exhibit Award (6) except that only exhibits of error, variety, etc., items will be considered in competition for it.

Those wishing to enter or submit an entry for any of the awards (Nos. 1, 2, 3, 4 and 5) should contact Young Numismatist Chairwoman Florence M. Schook, P.O. Box 2014, Livonia, Mich. 48154.

Those wishing to submit an entry for an exhibit award (Nos. 6, 7, 8, 9, 10, 11, 12 or 13) should write for exhibit rules and information to the Exhibit Chairman, American Numismatic Association, 818 N. Cascade Ave., Colorado Springs, Colo. 80903.

National Coin Week

National Coin Week has been sponsored by the American Numismatic Association since 1924. Its purpose is to bring numismatics to the attention of the general public and to win new coin collecting devotees.

National Coin Week aims to advance the cultural and artistic aspects of coin collecting, to advance the enjoyment of the hobby through proper education and to advance interest in coin collecting as a science. In 1974 it was acclaimed by Presidential proclamation.

Julius Guttag founded the annual effort in 1924 and served as the first chairman. Other National Coin Week chairmen include:

Chairman	Year
Julius Guttag	1924
Moritz Wormser	1925
H.H. Yawger	1926-1927
Ted Hammer	1939
David N. Bullowa	1940
Various regional chairmen	1941
Ted Hammer	1942
Lewis M. Reagan	1943-1944
Richard S. Yeoman	1945
Lillard W. Culver	1946
Harry Schumacher	1947
Charles Wormser	1948
Abe Kosoff	1949
Harry X Boosel	1950
James W. Curtis	1951
F. Steven Epps	1952
E. Ward Russell	1953
Don Sherer	1954
I.T. Kopicki	1955
Peter B. Payne	1956

Chairman	Year
Gene Nichols	1957
Leo Terry	1958
Wilma Dean Roethke	1959
E.I. (Jack) Rand	1960
Dolly-Maude Harris	1961-1962
Jack R. Koch	1963-1964
Lois R. Otis	1965-1966
Rick and Virginia Bronson	1967
Clark A. Yowell	1968
Edward C. Rochette	1969-1970
Lee Martin	1971
Edward C. Rochette	1972
John Watson	1973
Maurice M. Gould	1974-1975
F. Morton Reed	1975-1978
ANA Staff	1979-1980
Gary Lewis	1981
Les Winners	1982-1983
Nancy Green	1984-1987

National, regional coin associations

Following is a list of national and regional coin associations.

Active Token Collectors
Organization
7411 Edledale Lane
Omaha, Neb. 68112

American Medallic
Sculpture Association
431 Buena Vista Road
New City, N.Y. 10956

American Numismatic
Association
818 N. Cascade Ave.
Colorado Springs, Colo.
80903

American Numismatic
Society
Broadway at 155th St.
New York, N.Y. 10032

American Political
Items Collectors
Joseph D. Hayes
P.O. Box 340339
San Antonio, Texas 78234

American Tax Token
Society
Tim Davenport
Box 614
Corvallis, Ore. 97339

American Vecturist
Association
46 Fenwood Drive
Old Saybrook, Conn. 06475

Amusement Token
Collectors Association
328 Avenue F
Redondo Beach, Calif.
90277

Bank Token Society
John D. Mullen
P.O. Box 383
Newtonville, Mass. 02160

Blue Ridge
Numismatic Association
1501 Akins Drive
Chattanooga, Tenn. 37411

Bust Half Nut Club
P.O. Box 4875
Margate, Fla. 33063

Central States
Numismatic Society
Robert Douglas
P.O. Box 223
Hiawatha, Iowa 52233

Civil War Token Society
6733 Post Oak Lane
Montgomery, Ala. 36116

Colorado-Wyoming
Numismatic Association
519 W. Mountain Ave.
Fort Collins, Colo. 80521

Combined Organization of
Numismatic Error
Collectors of America
Ed Miller
Route 2, Box 6
Andover, S.D. 57422

Dedicated Wooden
Money Collectors
1028 Azalea Court
La Marque, Texas 77568

Early American
Coppers
Rod Burress
P.O. Box 15782
Cincinnati, Ohio 45215

The Elongated Collectors
Raymond Dillard
Box 161
Fenton, Mich. 48430

Essay Proof Society
Route 4, Colonial Drive
Katonah, N.Y. 10536

Franklin Half Dollar
Collectors Consortium
P.O. Box 6663
San Pedro, Calif. 90734

Great Eastern
Numismatic Association
490 Green Hill
Berwyn, Pa. 19312

Indiana-Kentucky-Ohio
Token & Medal Society
Dave Gossett
P.O. Box 192
Dayton, Ohio 45449

International Organization of
Wooden Money Collectors
N.R. Mack
P.O. Box 395
Goose Creek, S.C. 29445

Liberty Seated Collectors
Club
5718 King Arthur Drive
Kettering, Ohio 45429

Love Token Society
Art Gershman
P.O. Box 16421
Arlington, Va. 22215

Middle Atlantic
Numismatic Association
James K. Brandt
P.O. Box 787
Pearl River, N.Y. 10965

Midwest Numismatic
Association
9723 Marsh
Kansas City, Mo. 64134

New England
Numismatic Association
Eliott Goldberg
P.O. Box 99
W. Roxbury, Mass. 02132

Numismatic Bibliomania
Society
Linda Kolbe
P.O. Drawer 3100
Crestline, Calif. 92325

Old Timer Assay
Commission Society
3070 S. Franklin
Denver, Colo. 80210

Pacific Coast Numismatic
Society
610 Arlington Ave.
Berkeley, Calif. 94707

Pacific Northwest
Numismatic Association
20121 1st Ave. S.
Seattle, Wash. 98198

PAK Jefferson Full Step
Nickel Club
Susan Sisti
P.O. Box 1205
Montclair, N.J. 07042

Penn-Ohio Coin Clubs
612 White St.
Toledo, Ohio 43605

John Reich Collectors
Society
David J. Davis
P.O. Box 205
Ypsilanti, Mich. 48197

Society of Bearded
Numismatists
David Alexander
P.O. Box 970218
Miami, Fla. 33197

Society of Lincoln Cent
Collectors
Dr. Sol Taylor
P.O. Box 5465
N. Hollywood, Calif. 91616

Society of Philatelists
and Numismatists
1929 Millis St.
Montebello, Calif. 90640

Society of Ration
Token Collectors
Bob Johnson
P.O. Box J
Baltimore, Md. 21228

Society for U.S.
Commemorative Coins
912 Bob Wallace Ave.
Huntsville, Ala. 35801

Token and Medal Society
611 Oakwood Way
El Cajon, Calif. 92021

World's Fair Collectors
Society
P.O. Box 20806
Sarasota, Fla. 33583

Professional organizations

Industry Council for
Tangible Assets
25 E St. N.W.
8th Floor
Washington, D.C. 20002

International Association of
Professional Numismatists
Lowenstrasse 65
CH-8001900 Zurich,
Switzerland

International Numismatic
Trade Organization
Richard A. Nelson
19900 Ventura Blvd.
Suite 200
Woodland Hills, Calif. 91364

Numismatic Literary Guild
David T. Alexander
P.O. Box 970218
Miami, Fla. 33197

Professional Currency
Dealers Association
Kevin Foley
P.O. Box 589
Milwaukee, Wis. 53201

Professional Numismatists
Guild
Paul L. Koppenhaver
P.O. Box 430
Van Nuys, Calif. 91408

Syngraphic organizations

Bond & Share Society
Micheline Masse
P.O. Box 120, Station K
Montreal, Que., Canada
H1N 3K9

American Society of
Check Collectors
Route 2, Box 1
Iola, Wis. 54945

Currency Club of
Chester County, Pa.
420 Owen Road
West Chester, Pa. 19380

International Bank
Note Society
Milan Alusic
P.O. Box 1642
Racine, Wis. 53401

Latin American Paper
Money Society
3304 Milford Mill Road
Baltimore, Md. 21207

National Scrip
Collectors Association
Walter Caldwell
P.O. Box 29
Fayetteville, W.Va. 25840

Paper Money Collectors
of Michigan
1733 Victory-Holcomb
Road
Victor, N.Y. 14564

Society of Paper
Money Collectors
Bob Cochran
P.O. Box 1085
Florissant, Mo. 63031

Souvenir Card Collectors
Society
Dana Marr
P.O. Box 4155
Tulsa, Okla. 74159

World Paper
Currency Collectors
430 Mt. Shasta
Ridgecrest, Calif. 93555

Treasure hunting clubs

Black Diamond Treasure
Hunters Club
P.O. Box 1523
Kingston, Pa. 18704

Central Iowa Treasure
Hunters Club
Route 1
Cumming, Iowa 50061

Central Pennsylvania
Treasure Seekers
R.D. 6, Box 442
Newville, Pa. 17241

Colonial Relic Hunters
Association of America
Box 361
Boston, Mass. 02130

Federation of Metal
Detector & Archeological
Clubs
R.D. 2, Box 263
Frenchtown, N.J. 08825

First State Treasure
Hunters Club
3502 Caley Road
Newtown Square, Pa.
19073

Hawkeye State
Coinshooters
P.O. Box 251
Waverly, Iowa 50677

Keystone Searchers
Kim Krajnak
Box 143
Yukon, Pa. 15698

Massachusetts Treasure
Hunting Association
Paul White
P.O. Box 185
Fayville, Mass. 01745

Midwest Historical
Research Society
5311 N. Austin Ave.
Chicago, Ill. 60630

Mt. Diablo Metal
Detectors Club
Bob Westlund
P.O. Box 5492
Concord, Calif. 94524

New England Treasure
Finders Assoc.
P.O. Box 490
Agawam, Mass. 01001

New York Treasure
Hunters League
9203 Flatlands Ave.
Brooklyn, N.Y. 11236

Niagara Frontier Relic
Hunters Assoc.
P.O. Box 493
Buffalo, N.Y. 14215

Northwest Treasure
Hunters Club
E. 2917 18th Ave.
Spokane, Wash. 99203

Pilchuck Treasure
Hunting Club
3096 125th N.E.
Bellevue, Wash. 98005

Puget Sound Treasure
Hunters Club
P.O. Box 98206
Tacoma, Wash. 98499

Rubber City Treasure
Hunters Club
1225 S. Diamond St.
Ravenna, Ohio 44266

Stone Mountain
Treasure Hunters
P.O. Box 352
Stone Mountain, Ga. 30086

Treasure Coast
Coin Club
1023 Hispania Ave.
Ft. Pierce, Fla. 33482

Yankee Territory
Coinshooters
P.O. Box 447
Suffield, Conn. 06078

State numismatic associations

Alabama Numismatic
Society
Purnie Moore
P.O. Box 3601
West End Station
Birmingham, Ala. 35211

Arkansas Numismatic
Society
115 Donaghey Building
Little Rock, Ark. 72201

California Association of
Token Collectors
516 W. 99th St.
Los Angeles, Calif. 90044

California Exonumist
Society
Catharine Edgerton Lenker
P.O. Box 6599
San Diego, Calif. 92106

California State
Numismatic Association
Ethel Lenhert
P.O. Box 63
Upland, Calif. 91786

Northern California
Numismatic Association
P.O. Box 4104
Vallejo, Calif. 94590

Numismatic Association of
Southern California
Richard Lebold
P.O. Box 5173
Buena Park, Calif. 90622

Metropolitan Washington
Numismatic Association
Frank Katen
P.O. Box 4047
Silver Spring, Md. 20904

Washington Numismatic
Society
Ron Menichetti
P.O. Box 1848
Rockville, Md. 20853

Florida Token Society
11818 N.W. Highway 27
Ocala, Fla. 32675

Florida United
Numismatists
Polly Abbott
P.O. Box 4578
Clearwater, Fla. 33518

Georgia Numismatic
Association
Mike Griffith
P.O. Box 611
Lilburn, Ga. 30247

Georgia State Token-
Exonumia Association
1361 Oxford Road, Apt. 3
Atlanta, Ga. 30307

Hawaii State
Numismatic Association
M.F. Kendrick
P.O. Box 477
Honolulu, Hawaii 96809

Illinois Numismatic
Association
116 Cooper Drive
New Lenox, Ill. 60451

Club of Illinois
Numismatists
P.O. Box 171
Markham, Ill. 60426

Indiana State
Numismatic Association
P.O. Box 44337
Indianapolis, Ind. 46204

Iowa Numismatic
Association
Joann Peters
P.O. Box 41
Kanawha, Iowa 50447

Kansas Numismatic
Association
Alan Johnson
P.O. Box 5
Chanute, Kan. 66720

Kentucky State
Numismatic Association
1318 E. Breckinridge
Louisville, Ky. 40204

Louisiana Numismatic
Society
P.O. Box 1162
Gretna, La. 70053

Maine Numismatic
Association
P.O. Box 676
Bath, Maine 04530

Maryland State
Numismatic Association
Carl Shrader
P.O. Box 6533
Sparrows Point, Md. 21219

Maryland Token & Medal
Society
P.O. Box 3273
Baltimore, Md. 21228

Michigan State
Numismatic Society
Pamela Kocembo
P.O. Box 393
Wyandotte, Mich. 48192

Paper Money Collectors of
Michigan
1733 Victor-Holcomb Road
Victor, N.Y. 14564

Minnesota Organization
of Numismatists
Jerry Swanson
P.O. Box 565
Rochester, Minn. 55903

Mississippi Numismatic
Association
Brenda Bain
P.O. Box 2362
Laurel, Miss. 39440

Missouri Numismatic Society
P.O. Box 1085
Florissant, Mo. 63031

Nebraska Numismatic
Association
Elmer Nelson
P.O. Box 683
Sutherland, Neb. 69165

New Hampshire
Numismatic Association
James Rolston
P.O. Box 37
Greenland, N.H. 03840

New Jersey Exonumia
Society
Herbert Weiss
P.O. Box 363
Cranford, N.J. 07016

New Jersey
Numismatic Society
41 Bassett Ave.
Dover, N.J. 07801

Garden State Numismatic
Association
Sanford Ross
P.O. Box 3462
Toms River, N.J. 08756

New York State Wooden
Money Society
25 N. Wayne Ave.
West Haverstraw, N.Y.
10993

Empire State Numismatic
Association
8026 Trina Circle W.
Clay, N.Y. 13041

North Carolina
Numismatic Association
Russell E. Southworth
P.O. Box 20653
Greensboro, N.C. 27420

Oklahoma Numismatic
Association
Vincent Hill
P.O. Box 18753
Oklahoma City, Okla. 73154

Oregon Numismatic Society
4144 S.E. Clinton
Portland, Ore. 97202

Pennsylvania Association of
Numismatists
Eileen Kelly
P.O. Box 144
Pittsburgh, Pa. 15230

South Carolina
Numismatic Association
Doris B. Whitehouse
P.O. Box 12163
Columbia, S.C. 29211

South Dakota Coin &
Stamp Association
106 W. 5th
Pierre, S.D. 57501

Tennessee State
Numismatic Society
1501 Akins Drive
Chattanooga, Tenn. 37411

Texas Numismatic
Association
2901 Silverleaf Drive
Austin, Texas 78757

Utah Numismatic Society
P.O. Box 15054
Salt Lake City, Utah 84115

Virginia Numismatic
Association
Malvern L. Powell Jr.
P.O. Box353
Hampton, Va. 23669

Numismatists of Wisconsin
Hank Thoele
P.O. Box 12703
Green Bay, Wis. 54307

American Israel Numismatic Association
P.O. Box 25790, Tamarac, Fla. 33320

Organized in 1967, the American Israel Numismatic Association serves a specialty collecting interest: The coins, medals, tokens and bank notes of Israel and the Holy Land; numismatic Judaica, including the ancient coins of Israel; and all forms of later medals, tokens and scrip.

AINA publishes *The Shekel,* a journal of Judaic numismatics, participates in major coin conventions, issues an annual membership medal and others on important occasions, and sponsors annual study tours to Israel.

AINA membership dues are $10 per year; junior membership, $2.50. Life memberships are available for $150.

I.N.S. of Brooklyn
Nat Sobel
P.O. Box 518, Wall St. Station
New York, N.Y. 10268

I.N.S. of Broward
1721 White Hall Drive
Ft. Lauderdale, Fla. 33324

I.N.S. of Central Jersey
David Paszamant
P.O. Box 215
New Brunswick, N.J. 08903

I.N.S. of Cleveland
2579 N. Moreland, #D-4
Shaker Heights, Ohio 44120

I.N.S. of Colorado
Bill Rosenblum
P.O. Box 355
Evergreen, Colo. 80439

I.N.S. of Illinois
Harry Flower
P.O. Box 427
Skokie, Ill. 60076

Israel Coin Club of L.A.
Nate Bromberg
P.O. Box 1661
Whittier, Calif. 90609

I.N.S. of Los Angeles
432 S. Curson, #7E
Los Angeles, Calif. 90036

I.N.S. of Massachusetts
Herman Balkan
P.O. Box 116
Newton, Mass. 02195

I.N.S. of Michigan
Diane Colton
P.O. Box 942
Royal Oak, Mich. 48068

I.N.S. of New York
Moe Weinschel
P.O. Box 277
Rockaway Park, N.Y. 11694

I.N.S. of Phoenix
Samuel Abrams
P.O. Box 17332
Phoenix, Ariz. 85011

I.N.S. of San Fernando
Valley
Jerry Yahalom
P.O. Box 5022
Woodland Hills, Calif. 91365

I.N.S. of San Gabriel Valley
15540 E. Lambert Road
Whittier, Calif. 90604

I.N.S. of South Jersey
Eric Baelen
P.O. Box 3258
Cherry Hills, N.J. 08034

I.N.S. of Tampa
4762 46 St. N.
St. Petersburg, Fla. 33714

I.N.S. of Tidewater, Va.
Sidney Berg
P.O. Box 383
Norfolk, Va. 23501

I.N.S. of Toronto
Dr. Albert Rose
Faculty of Social Work
University of Toronto
Toronto, Ont., Canada
M5S 1A1

I.N.S. of Westchester
Michael Druck
P.O. Box 305
Wykagyl Station
New Rochelle, N.Y. 10804

American-based world numismatic organizations

American British
Numismatic Association
P.O. Box 652
Saugus, Calif. 91350

American Israel
Numismatic Association
Julius Turoff
P.O. Box 25790
Tamarac, Fla. 33320

American Society for
Portuguese Numismatics
3491 Clearview Ave.
Columbus, Ohio 43220

Armenian Numis. Society
8511 Beverly Park Place
Pico Rivera, Calif. 90660

Atlanta Society for the
Study of Money other than
American
4316 Hale Dr.
Lilburn, Ga. 30247

Azteca Numismatic Society
Betty Brander
P.O. Box 33035
Granada Hills, Calif. 91344

International Numismatic
Society
P.O. Box 66555
Washington, D.C. 20035

International Primitive
Money Society
John E. Lenker
P.O. Box 1510
Redlands, Calif. 92373

Lithuanian Numis. Assoc.
Robert Douchis
P.O. Box 612
Columbia, Md. 21045

Minnesota International
Numismatists
5315 Hodgson Road
St. Paul, Minn. 55126

Numismatics International
Ross Schreader
P.O. Box 670013
Dallas, Texas 75367

Oriental Numis. Society
William B. Warden Jr.
P.O. Box 356
New Hope, Pa. 18938

Original Globe Coin
Traders Club
3941 Pacific Blvd.
San Mateo, Calif. 94403

Philippine Collectors
Society
P.O. Box 267
Biloxi, Mich. 39533

Polish-American
Numismatic Association
Ed Muszynski
P.O. Box 1873
Chicago, Ill. 60690

Russian Numismatic Society
Samuel T. Clements
P.O. Box F-334
Akron, Ohio 44308

Societe Americaine Pour
l'Etude de la Numismatique
Francaise
204 Rose Lane S.W.
North Canton, Ohio 44720

Society for Ancient
Numismatics
Beate Rauch
P.O. Box 2138
Terminal Annex
Los Angeles, Calif. 90051

Society for
International Numismatics
E. Carolyn Nestrick
P.O. Box 943
Santa Monica, Calif. 90406

Society for
Medieval Numismatics
John Gabriel
P.O. Box 160
Bank Plaza Station
Merrick, N.Y. 11566

World Coin Club of
Missouri
1591 Eastham Drive
St. Louis, Mo. 63141

World Proof
Numis. Assoc.
Gail Gray
P.O. Box 4094
Pittsburgh, Pa. 15201

Numismatic Literary Guild

David T. Alexander, Executive Director
P.O. Box 970218, Miami, Fla. 33197

The Numismatic Literary Guild was founded in August 1969 during the 77th anniversary convention of the American Numismatic Association in San Diego, Calif.

Membership is open to publications numismatic full-time staff members of publication, researchers, museum workers, free-lance writers, editors, and publishers in the field of numismatics, as well as full-time numismatic staff members of publications. New members must be sponsored by one NLG member in good standing; dues are $10 per year.

The purposes of NLG are to encourage numismatic writing, provide a central forum for both full-time and part-time writers, and to share conviviality and fellowship at ANA conventions.

NLG recognizes excellence by a series of annual awards for writers and columnists, as well as offering the "Clemy" award and the Maurice M. Gould award for outstanding literary contributions to numismatics.

Members receive a regular newsletter, keeping them informed of the activities of fellow writers everywhere, and featuring original articles and observations of the members.

New NLG members accepted by the membership committee pay an initial fee of $25, besides the first year's dues.

Directors are: Col. Bill Murray, Ed Reiter, Tom DeLorey, Donn Pearlman and Anthony Swiatek.

Treasurer: Kay E. Lenker.

Newsletter Editor: Trey Foerster

Members of the Numismatic Literary Guild are:

Robert B. Aaron, David T. Alexander, Don Alpert, J. Pearson Andrew, Stanley Apfelbaum, Nelson Page Aspen, Dorothy C. Baber, Richard Bagg, Don Bailey, Richard Baker, Cem Cordircilar Barlok, Joseph Battaglia, J. Richard Becker, Aubrey Beebe, Harold S. Beecher Jr., Gary Beedon, Ralph W. Behringer,

R. C. Bell, Yasha L. Beresinger, Howard M. Berlin, James Betton III, Col. Joseph E. Boling, Pamela Bonk, Harry Boosel, Herman Boraker, Q. David Bowers, Walter Breen, Kenneth Bressett, Mary Brooks, Vernon L. Brown, William B. Bugert,

Gabriel Calbeto, Carl W.A. Carlson, Mike Carter, James E. Charlton, Ted F. Clark, Courtney L. Coffing, Jack Collins, Mary B. Comstock, William Corsa

William Craig III, Grover Criswell, D. Larry Crumbley, Elmer L. Curran, Norman M. Davis, Beth Deisher, Thomas K. DeLorey, Oscar H. Dodson, Dr. Harold Don Allen, Richard Doty, Frank Draskovic, Fred Drost, Michael J. Druck,

Robin Ellis, Eric Engstrom, George Ewing Jr., C. Belmont Faries, Steven Feller, Ronn Fern, Jack H. Fisher, William Fivaz, Harold T. Flartey, Harry Flower, Trey Foerster, Harry J. Forman, Marvin L. Fraley, Kent Froseth, Dr. George Fuld, Michael Fuljenz,

David Ganz, Soterios Gardiakos, Paul Garner, Jeff C. Garret, Frank Gasparro, George Gilbert, Cory Lee Gillilland, Miriam Gilmore, David D. Gladfelter, Nancy W. Green, Paul M. Green, Michael Greenspan, Barbara Jean Gregory, John Grellman, Lee Grossman, Henry Grunthal, Ronald Guth, Albert K. Hall, Virginia M. Hall, Kenneth L. Hallenbeck, James Halperin, Thomas V. Haney,

W. Larry Hanks, Kenneth Harbour, David Harper, N. Neil Harris, George D. Hatie, James N. Heine, Alan Herbert, Gene Hessler, Michael Hodder, D. Bernard Hoenig, Patrick Hogan, Ralph A. Holmes, Donald J. Hoppe, Charles R. Hoskins,

Cloyde P. Howard, Serge Huard, Clyde Hubbard, John G. Humphris, John L. Hunter, Barbara Hyde, Steve Ivy, James J. Jelinski, F. C. Jewett, Byron Johnson, James G. Johnson, Samuel W. Johnson, Jr., Robert W. Julian,

A. M. Kagin, Dr. Donald Kagin, Judith Frank Kaller, John Kamin, Geneva R. Karlson, Frank J. Katen, Laurese Katen, Keith N. Kelman, Sally Kirka, Alvin Kleeb, Myron Kliman, George F. Kolbe, Chester L. Krause, William Krieg, Col. Robert F. Kriz, Simcha Kuritzky, Robert Lacewell, Thomas Lacey, David W. Lange, Robert Larkin, Jimmie Lawrence,

Dr. Benito J. Legarda, Robert F. Lemke, Kay Edgerton Lenker, Robert D. Leonard, J.C. Levesque, George Lill III, Leonard Lindheim, Denis W. Loring, Dennis Lundheim, Russell MacKendrick, Sylvia Haffner Magnus, A. George Mallis, Fredric G. Mantei, Harrington E. Manville, Arnold Margolis, Yvon Marquis, Lee Martin, John W. McCloskey, Dudley L. McClure, William H. McDonald,

Robert E. Medlar, Ray Merena, James Miller, Cliff Mishler, Martin Morgenstern, Barbara Mueller, Thomas Mulvaney, Miguel L. Munoz, Paul H. Munson, Col. Bill Murray, John Mussell, Adrian F. Nader, William Nawrocki, Eric P. Newman,

Chuck O'Donnell, Dr. Walter A. Ostromecki, Gary L. Palmer, Donn Pearlman, J. Roy Pennell, Walter Perschke, Clifton Potter Jr., Edwin Quagliana, Ginger Rapsus, Beate Rauch,

Mort Reed, Ed Reiter, Jerry Remick, Harry Resigno, Joel Rettew, Helen B. Rhodes, Charles J. Ricard, Gilroy Roberts, M.R. Roberts, Edward Rochette, Jeff Rock, Delma K. Romines, Maurice Rosen, William Rosenblum, Richard Rosichan, Matt Rothert Sr., James F. Ruddy,

Russell Rulau, Margo Russell, Dean M. Ryder, Austin Ryer Jr., John J. Ryer, Paul Rynearson, Arno Safron, David E. Schenkman, Hans M.F. Schulman, Carlton F. Schwan, Fred Schwan, Richard Schwary, Ted Schwarz, Howard Seaver, Thomas H. Sebring, Dale Seppa, Neil Shafer, Austin M. Sheehan Jr., Arlyn Sieber, Donna Sims, Arlie Slabaugh, Glenn B. Smedley, Peter Craig Smith, J. Whitmell Smithwick, E. Victor Snell, William Snyder, Nathan Sobel, Ekrem Spahich,

Hank Spangenberger, William Spengler, Spink and Sons, Michael Standish, Leonard W. Stark, Leonard J. Sterling, Martha V. Stevenson, Thomas C. Stires, Barry Stuppler,

Rick Sundman, Charles Surasky, James O. Sweeney, Anthony Swiatek, Paul Taglione, Dr. Sol Taylor, Gerald Tebben, Michael Thorne, Edwin S. Trautman, Scott A. Travers, George K. Tyson, Barry Uman, Thomas Underwood, Joseph Uphoff,

Ora Vaketta, Leroy Van Allen, Robert Van Ryzin, Jean-Paul Vannier, Emil Voigt, Kurt A. Von Fischer, Mel Wacks, Dick Wagner, George W. Wait, Don Wallace, O.W. Wallis,

Philip Walton, M. Owen Warns, Alan R. Weinberg, Fred Weinberg, William Whetstone, Paul R. Whitnah, Raymond Whyborn, Robert Wilharm, Robert C. Willey, Dale L. Williams, Raymond H. Williamson,

Doug Winter, Dr. Lubomir Wojtiw, Robert L. Wolenik, John D. Wright, Jerry Yahalom, Richard S. Yeoman, Randolph Zander, Keith M. Zaner, Morton Jay Zerder.

Professional Numismatists Guild

Professional Numismatists Guild Inc. was founded in the mid-1950s by the late Abe Kosoff with 33 members represented. The group was incorporated in 1955.

PNG is a non-profit membership corporation which will accept those who qualify with seven basic membership qualifications:

• Applicant must be 21 years of age or over and have a minimum of 5 years as a full-time professional numismatist.

• Applicant must have a minimum of $100,000 in numismatic assets.

• Applicant must agree with the PNG's strict Code of Ethics.

• Applicant must be screened by the PNG's Board of Directors.

• Applicant's finances and character must be examined by an outside firm.

• Applicant must be accepted by ballot of the entire PNG membership.

• Applicant must agree to submit to legally binding arbitration to settle any dispute between a buyer and the PNG member-dealer.

Aims and purposes of PNG

"We seek the establishment and the maintenance of an harmonious atmosphere in which all who participate as amateur or professional numismatists will derive the pleasure and profit they seek, giving an equal measure of satisfaction in the process.

"First, we must make the organization available to any professional numismatists of good moral character who meet reasonable simple qualifications.

"We must recognize that, as simple as these requirements may be, some may not qualify and yet be worthy of collectors' confidence.

"We must insist that our members live up to our code of ethics, and that those who are found to be in violation be appropriately penalized.

"We must contribute leadership in the field of numismatic education by preparing papers, giving talks, supplying information and contributing to organizations which can assist in this endeavor.

"We must lend our talents to collector organizations in any manner possible.

"We must help provide authentication programs to create the confidence of the collector and to discourage the traffic in spurious coins.

"We must try to prevent the theft of coin collections and assist in the apprehension of any guilty persons. Let us continue to do these things and we will indeed create the atmosphere which will give all who participate, be it as a hobby or as a profession, the ultimate in satisfaction."

To obtain a membership application for PNG, write: Paul L. Koppenhaver, P.O. Box 430, Van Nuys, Calif. 91408.

PNG code of ethics

As a coin dealer, I recognize my obligations towards the public and towards fellow-members in my industry. It is my intention to be worthy of the confidence and respect of those with whom I come in contact in the numismatic trade. For this purpose I have pledged myself as follows:

A. In my relation with the public:

1. To furnish my clientele advice on numismatic matters to the best of my ability.

2. To sell at prices commensurate with a reasonable return of my investment and the then-prevailing market conditions.

3. To purchase coins from the public at reasonable prices, with due allowance for buyers' risks and prevailing market conditions.

4. To neither broadcast, publish nor advertise in any manner a representation or an implication with the intent to lead a false or incorrect conclusion with regard to my own goods, prices or services, or in regard to the goods, services, or prices of a competitor, or lay false claim to a policy, or continuing a practice of generally underselling any of my competitors.

5. To assist recognized government authorities in the prosecution of violators of the law in numismatic matters.

6. To refrain from knowingly dealing in stolen coins, medals or other numismatic material or publications, or offering counterfeits as genuine coins; and when knowingly selling altered coins as such, to furnish the buyer with an invoice showing in detail the nature of such coins sold.

B. In my relations with fellow-members of this Association:

1. To refrain from voluntary public expressions of adverse criticism of other members or their merchandise.

2. To recognize and respect my own contracts and undertakings and those of fellow-members.

3. To exchange freely credit information with fellow-members when requested.

4. To avoid false statements or representations in my relations with my competitors, and co-operate generally towards the betterment of our industry and the hobby in my relations with fellow-members.

PNG Founding President
Abe Kosoff 1954-1955

PNG Past Presidents	Elected
Sol Kaplan	1955
Arthur Cohn	1960
Max Kaplan	1961
Tom Wass	1962
Arthur Kagin	1963
Abe Kosoff	1964
Leo Young	1965
Dan Brown	1967
David Shapiro	1969
Jess Peters	1971
Douglas Weaver	1973
Robert R. Johnson	1975
Q. David Bowers	1977
Joe Flynn	1979
Gary Sturtridge	1981
Ed Milas	1983

PNG Board of Directors
President . . . . Leon E. Hendrickson
Vice president . . . . Harvey G. Stack
Treasurer . . . . Ronald J. Gillio
Secretary . . . . Edwin Leventhal
Directors . Julian M. Leidman, Michael A. Pesha, Ira M. Goldberg, Harlan White
Immediate Past President . . . . Ed Milas
Executive Director . . Paul L. Koppenhaver
Legal Counsel . . . . David L. Ganz

Members of PNG

Aamlid, Jan Olav
Oslo Mynthandel AS
Kongens Gate 31
0101 Oslo 1, Norway

Abbott, John T.
Abbott's-Coinex Corp.
1393 S. Woodward Ave.
Birmingham, Mich. 48011

Adams, Al C. Jr.
Al. C. Adams Rare Coins
6633-C Roswell Road
Atlanta, Ga. 30328

Adkins, Gary
Allied Coin Investments Inc.
1302 E. 66th St.
Richfield, Minn. 55423

Akers, David W.
Paramount International Coin Corp.
3785 N.W. 82nd Ave.
Suite 315
Miami, Fla. 33166

Akers, Wayne
P.O. Box 790
Plymouth, Fla. 32768

Alster, Michael Lee
Manfra, Tordella & Brookes
59 W. 49th St.
New York, N.Y. 10112

Anastasio, Charles O.
Charles Coin Co. Inc.
209 Cooper Ave.
Upper Montclair, N.J. 07043

Apte, Donald
Virginia Coin Investments
444 Maple Ave. E.
Vienna, Va. 22180

Aron, Michael H.
Michael Aron Rare Coins
P.O. Box 33166
Granada Hills, Calif. 91344

Bauer, Ruth W.
Forman Ent. Ltd.
P.O. Box 5756
Philadelphia, Pa. 19120

Bebee, Aubrey E.
Bebee's Inc.
P.O. Box 4290
Omaha, Neb. 68104

Benedetti, Philip E.
P.O. Box 2007
Westport, Conn. 06880

Berg, David A.
P.O. Box 381
Wexford, Pa. 15090

Berk, Harlan J.
Harlan J. Berk Ltd.
2417 W. Jefferson St.
Joliet, Ill. 60435

Bernberg, Jeffrey F.
Rare Coin Co. of America Inc.
31 N. Clark St.
Chicago, Ill. 60602

Beymer, Jack H.
Jack Beymer Coins & Stamps
367 Coddingtown Center
Santa Rosa, Calif. 95401

Bland, David Jr.
David Bland Jr.
Galleries Inc.
300 Highland Mall Blvd.
Suite 200
Austin, Texas 78752

Blumert, Burton S.
Camino Coin Company
P.O. Box 4292
851 Burlway Road
P.O. Box 4292
Burlingame, Calif. 94010

Bowers, Q. David
Bowers and Merena
Galleries Inc.
P.O. Box 1224
Wolfeboro, N.H. 03894

Brigandi, Donald E.
Donald E. Brigandi Co. Inc.
60 W. 44th St.
New York, N.Y. 10036

Bronson, Jan M.
P.O. Box 3802
Beverly Hills, Calif. 90212

Brownlee, Mike G.
Dallas Federal Savings Bldg.
8333 Douglas
Suite 1400
Dallas, Texas 75225

Bryan, Roger P.
Bryan Ltd. Inc.
P.O. Drawer D
Gainesville, Fla. 32602

Bullowa, Mrs. C.E.
Coinhunter
1616 Walnut St.
Philadelphia, Pa. 19103

Cammack, Jay Addison
Camco, Dollarama Clubs
P.O. Box 236
Portales, N.M. 88130

Causey, Bill
American Gold
& Silver Corp.
9463 Central Ave.
Montclair, Calif. 91763

Cayon Fernandez, Juan
Ramon
Juan R. Cayon
P.O. Box 4117
Madrid, Spain

Christensen, William W.B.
Henry Christensen Inc.
P.O. Box 1732
Madison, N.J. 07940

Cohen, Jerry
Jerry Cohen Corp.
9465 Wilshire Blvd.
Suite 519
Beverly Hills, Calif. 90210

Collins, Louis H.
Louis H. Collins Inc.
311 Market St.
Dallas, Texas 75202

Corbin, H.G. "Bill"
Tyler Stamp & Coin Co.
400-A West Rusk St.
Tyler, Texas 75701

Cross, William K.
Charlton International Inc.
299 Queen St. W.
Toronto, Ontario
Canada M5V 1Z9

Dannreuther, John West
868 Mt. Moriah
Suite 202
Memphis, Tenn. 38117

Demerer, Larry
National Coin Investments
Inc.
9665 Wilshire Blvd.
Suite 220
Beverly Hills, Calif. 90212

Denly, Thomas M.
Denly's Coins of Boston
P.O. Box 1010
Boston, Mass. 02205

Derman, Alberto J.
Cooke & Co.
Av. Corrientes 368
(1043) Buenos Aires
Argentina

Derzon, David
David Derzon Co. Inc.
Greater Milwaukee
Bank Building.
7635 W. Bluemound Road
Suite 218
Milwaukee, Wis. 53213

De Vore, Don P.
2048 Willowick Circle
Columbus, Ohio 43229
Office: Numismatic
Investment Consultant Ent.
5918 Sharon Woods Blvd.
Suite 170-180
Columbus, Ohio 43229

Dragoni, Augusto
The Numismatic Studio
P.O. Box 5136
Largo, Fla. 33540

Dugas, Donald Edward
Liberty House Rare Coins
P.O. Box 353
Highlands, N.J. 07732

Edwards, Gene B.
SJRC Ltd.
R.D. 2
Yellow Springs Road
Chester Springs, Pa. 19425

Eyer, Steve
Steve Eyer Inc.
P.O. Box 123
Mt. Zion, Ill. 62549

Jess Peters Inc.
P.O. Box 123
Decatur, Ill. 62525

Fairfield, James W.
Fairfield Rare Coins
3909 E. State Blvd.
Fort Wayne, Ind. 46805

Feldman, Mark R.
Mark R. Feldman Inc.
P.O. Box 185
Beverly Hills, Calif. 90213

Fillers, Gary
Classic Coins
109 E. 7th St.
Chattanooga, Tenn. 37402

Fisher, Donald I.
Currency Unlimited
Decatur Coin & Auction
P.O. Box 481
727 W. Pershing Road
Decatur, Ill. 62525

Flynn, Joe
Joe Flynn Rare Coins and
Bullion Inc.
P.O. Box 3140
Kansas City, Kan. 66103

Follett, Mike
Mike Follett Rare Coin Co.
Inc.
13101 Preston Road
Suite 400
Dallas, Texas 75240

Forgue, Dennis J.
Oakbrook Numismatic
Enterprises Ltd.
Auction Galleries of
Oakbrook Ltd.
P.O. Box 7310
Westchester, Ill. 60153

Forman, Harry J.
Forman Enterprises Ltd.
P.O. Box 5756
Philadelphia, Pa. 19120

Friedberg, Arthur L.
The Coin & Currency
Institute Inc.
P.O. Box 1057
Clifton, N.J. 07014

Garrett, Jeff C.
Mid American Rare Coin
Galleries
Mid American Rare Coin
Auctions
1707 Nicholasville Road
Lexington, Ky. 40503

Gillio, Dennis M.
Ronald J. Gillio Inc.
1013 State St.
Santa Barbara, Calif. 93101

Gillio, Ronald J.
Ronald J. Gillio Inc.
1013 State St.
Santa Barbara, Calif. 93101

Goldberg, Ira M.
Superior Stamp & Coin Co.
Inc.
9748 W. Olympic Blvd.
Beverly Hills, Calif. 90212

Goldberg, Lawrence S.
Superior Stamp & Coin Co.
Inc.
9748 W. Olympic Blvd.
Beverly Hills, Calif. 90212

Goldberg, Mark E.
Superior Stamp & Coin Co.
Inc.
9748 W. Olympic Blvd.
Beverly Hills, Calif. 90212

Goldman, Kenneth
Kenneth Goldman Inc.
P.O. Box 1477
Boston, Mass. 02104

Gordon, Stephen M.
Numismatics Ltd.
9665 Wilshire Blvd.
Suite 600
Beverly Hills, Calif. 90212

Gorny, Dieter
Giessener Munzhandlung
Dieter Gorny GmbH
Maximiliansplatz 16
8000 Munchen 2
West Germany

Gouveia, S. A. "Tony"
Nashua Coin & Stamp Co.
168 Main St.
Nashua, N.H. 03060

Graham, Michael A.
"1841" Corporation
P.O. Box 997
Sisters, Ore. 97759

Greenberg, Frank
Delaware Valley Coin &
Stamp Co. Inc.
Stoney Creek Center
455 Baltimore Pike
Springfield, Pa. 19064

Griffin, John I.
3180 E. Indian School Road
Phoenix, Ariz. 85016

Grosz, Paul H.
Allied Coin Investments
Inc.
1302 E. 66th St.
Richfield, Minn. 55423

Hanks, Larry
Hanks & Associates Inc.
415 N. Mesa
El Paso, Texas 79901

Hanson, Jon G.
P.O. Box 5499
Beverly Hills, Calif. 90210

Harwell, Robert L. II
Harwell and Company
2 Concourse Parkway
Suite 155
Atlanta, Ga. 30328

Hendrickson, David J.
Silver Towne Coin
P.O. Box 424
Winchester, Ind. 47394

Hendrickson, Leon E.
Silver Towne Coin
P.O. Box 424
Winchester, Ind. 47394

Henry, Gene L.
Rare Coin Galleries of
Seattle Inc.
1416 3rd Ave.
Seattle, Wash. 98101

Highfill, John Wayne
Oklahoma Federated Gold
& Numismatics Inc.
3778 S. Elm Place
Broken Arrow, Okla. 74011

Hinderling, Wade
Wade Hinderling Rare
Coins
P.O. Box 140
Bayside, N.Y. 11361

Hipps, Ed
Ed Hipps Gallery
Caruth Plaza, No. 143
9100 N. Central Expressway
Dallas, Texas 75231

Hirschhorn, Steve
M & S Hirschhorn Inc.
Silver Dollar Collectors
Club Ltd.
238 N. Indiana Ave.
Vista, Calif. 92083

Hull, Everett W.
Fort Worth Coin Co. Inc.
2822 W. 7th St.
Fort Worth, Texas 76107

Humbert, Max J.
Paramount International
Coin Corp.
P.O. Box F-3713
Freeport, Grand Bahama
Bahamas

Humphreys, George B.
George B. Humphreys Inc.
500 Main St.
P.O. Box 3686
Daytona Beach, Fla. 32018

Irwin, Louis M.
Shaker Coin & Stamp Shop
Inc.
2101 Richmond Road
Beachwood, Ohio 44122

Iskowitz, Ronald D.
Renrob
4 Cornwall Drive
East Brunswick, N.J. 08816

Jelinski, James J.
Essex Numismatics Inc.
8 Cannon Road
Wilton, Conn. 06897

Johnson, Robert R.
Robert R. Johnson Inc.
353 Geary St.
San Francisco, Calif. 94102

Jones, Harry E.
P.O. Box 30369
Cleveland, Ohio 44130

Kagin, Arthur M.
Kagin's Inc.
910 Insurance Exchange
Building
Des Moines, Iowa 50309

Kagin, Paul
Paul Kagin Ltd.
P.O. Box 15
Des Moines, Iowa 50301

Kliman, Myron M.
Numismatic Enterprises
P.O. Box 365
South Laguna, Calif. 92677

Knight, Lyn F.
Lyn Knight Rare Coins
P.O. Box 22650
Kansas City, Mo. 64113

Koppenhaver, Paul L.
The Coin Haven
P.O. Box 430
Van Nuys, Calif. 91408

Korosec, Robert C.
Bob's Coins In West Allis
8307 W. Becher St.
West Allis, Wis. 53219

Kovacs, Frank L. III
P.O. Box 3113
San Mateo, Calif. 94403

Krasowski, Witold E.
Kraso Coins
2349 W. 95th St.
Chicago, Ill. 60643

Kreisberg, Abner
The Coin Gallery
344 N. Beverly Drive
Beverly Hills, Calif. 90210

Krueger, Kurt R.
Kurt R. Krueger
160 N. Washington St.
Iola, Wis. 54945

Kuehnert, Joseph
P.O. Box 99814
Pacific Station
San Diego, Calif. 92109

Kutcher, Bruce
Bruce Kutcher Inc.
P.O. Box 922
Boston, Mass. 02103

LaPointe, Adrien J.
Ambassador Coins &
Stamps Inc.
4 Front St.
Worcester, Mass. 01608

Lecce, Robert B.
Robert B. Lecce,
Numismatist
P.O. Box 50
Lawrence, N.Y. 11559

Lee, Larry L.
Coins and Such
P.O. Box 3787
Panama City, Fla. 32401

Leidman, Julian M.
8433 Georgia Ave.
Silver Spring, Md. 20910

Leister, Arthur C.
Commercial Coin Co.
P.O. Box 607
Camp Hill, Pa. 17011

Leventhal, Edwin
J. J. Teaparty Inc.
51 Bromfield St.
Boston, Mass. 01208

Levin, Albert
Albert Levin, Numismatist
P.O. Box 1403
Racine, Wis. 53403

Levin, Benjamin
516 W. Taft Ave.
Bridgeport, Conn. 06604

Liddell, D.G.
Spink & Son Ltd.
5,6 & 7 King St.
St. James's
London, S.W. 1, England

Lobel, Richard
Coincraft
P.O. Box 112
45 Great Russell St.
London, WC1B 3LU
England

Loecher, Roger P.
L & L Coins Inc.
L & L Building
5500 W. 44th Ave.
Denver, Colo. 80212

Lopresto, Samuel L.
Zaidman & Lopresto Rare
Coins & Jewelry Inc.
112 E. Broadway
Long Beach, Calif. 90802

Love, John B.
Record Coin Shop
P.O. Box 698
Cut Bank, Mont. 59427

Lowe, Vernon W.
Lowe's Rare Coins
Waikiki Shopping Plaza
2250 Kalakaua Ave.
3rd Floor, #305
Honolulu, Hawaii 96815

Lubbock, Richard M.
Lubbock & Son Ltd.
315 Regent St.
London, W1R 7YB
England

Maben, John F. Jr.
Certified Numismatic
Investments Inc.
P.O. Box 2123
Cherry Hill, N.J. 08034

Markoff, Steve
A-Mark Precious Metals
9696 Wilshire Blvd.
Beverly Hills, Calif. 90212

Martin, Richard E.
San Diego Coin Exchange
3812 Grim Ave.
San Diego, Calif. 92104

Medcalf, Gordon
Island Coin Exchange Inc.
658 Front St., No. 178
Lahaina, Hawaii 96761

Medlar, Robert E.
Medlar's Inc.
40 N.W. Loop 410
Suite 338
San Antonio, Texas 78216

Mercer, Daryl L.
Tebo Coin Co.
Alternative Capital
Preservation Inc.
2863 28th St.
P.O. Box 4900
Boulder, Colo. 80306

Merena, Raymond N.
Bowers and Merena
Galleries Inc.
P.O. Box 1224
Wolfeboro, N.H. 03894

Milas, Edward
Rare Coin Company of
America Inc.
31 N. Clark St.
Chicago, Ill. 60602

Mileham, Joseph R.
B & J Coin Shop
3123 S. Dirksen Parkway
Springfield, Ill. 62703

Miller, Jay C.
Numismatic Professionals
Inc.
33 Boston Post Road W.
Suite 320
P.O. Box 645
Marlborough, Mass. 01752

Miller, Wayne
Miller-Contursi Inc.
P.O. Box 8510
Newport Beach, Calif. 92658

Moreno, Louie Jr.
Western Numismatics Ltd.
Inc.
19063 E. Colima Road
Rowland Heights, Calif.
91748

Munzner, Richard T.
Laurel City Coins
462 Main St.
P.O. Box 383
Winsted, Conn. 06098

Murray, William
Dynamic Coin Investments
802 Silas-Deane Highway
Wethersfield, Conn. 06109

Nelson, Richard A.
The Money Co.
19900 Ventura Blvd.
Suite 200
Woodland Hills, Calif.
91364

Noble, Edgar F.
Noble Coins
180 Linden St.
Wellesley, Mass. 02181

Noe, Thomas W.
Numismatic Investments of
Ohio
5577 Monroe St.
The Promenade Shops
Sylvania, Ohio 43560

Nugget, Paul
National Coin Investments
Inc.
265 Sunrise Highway
Suite 56
Rockville Centre, N.Y.
11570

Oakes, Dean
Dean Oakes, Numismatist
229 S. Dubuque St.
P.O. Box 1456
Iowa City, Iowa 52240

Oswald, Vernon H.
Ossie's Coin Shop
1007 Hamilton St.
Allentown, Pa. 18101

Parker, Leon B.
A & F Coin & Stamp
Exchange Inc.
3180 E. Indian School Road
Phoenix, Ariz. 85016

Patrick, Jesse
The Patrick Mint
P.O. Box 3486
Santa Rosa, Calif. 95402
Larkfield Coins
686 Larkfield Center
Santa Rosa, Calif. 95401

Payette, James A.
New Hampshire
Numismatics
P.O. Box 300
Bethlehem, N.H. 03574

Person, Joseph F.
Joe Person & Co.
Bank of Florida Building
Suite 2
1101 Pasadena Ave. S.
P.O. Box 66616
St. Petersburg, Fla. 33736

Pesha, Michael A.
Gold Dust Coin
3115 S. Halsted St.
Chicago, Ill. 60608

Pienta, Peter R.
Crystal Coin Inc.
349 Main St.
Wakefield, Mass. 01880

Polito, Robert V.
Steinmetz Coins & Currency
Inc.
843 Park City Center
Lancaster, Pa. 17601

Pollock, Randall L.
Numismatic Resources Inc.
P.O. Box 64
Lawrence, N.Y. 11559

Ponterio, Richard H.
Ponterio & Associates Inc.
3823 Park Blvd.
P.O. Box 33588
San Diego, Calif. 92103

Pullen, Norman W.
Norman W. Pullen Inc.
Key Bank Building
One Marginal Way
P.O. Box 10600
Portland, Maine 04104

Pullen, William C. Jr.
2325 Ulmerton Road
Suite 6
Clearwater, Fla. 33520

Rettew, Joel D.
Rare Coin Galleries Inc.
201 N. Indian Ave.
Palm Springs, Calif. 92262

Rhue, Robert J.
Robert Rhue Numismatic
Investments
P.O. Box 4465
Englewood, Colo. 80155

Richardson, M.M. Jr.
Georgia Silver & Gold
4073 La Vista Road
Suite 399
Tucker, Ga. 30084

Robins, Douglas
Douglas Robins Inc.

Rose, Joseph H.
Harmer, Rooke
Numismatics Ltd.
3 E. 57th St.
New York, N.Y. 10022

Rose, Robert C.
Renrob Coins Inc.
4 Cornwall Drive
East Brunswick, N.J. 08816

Rosing, Arnold
P.O. Box 556
San Mateo, Calif. 94401

Rowe, John N. III
Southwest Numismatic
Corp.
6301 Gaston Ave., Suite 650
Dallas, Texas 75214

Rubenstein, M. H.
Edison Coin Company
P.O. Box 59
Deer Park, N.Y. 11729

Schulman, Hans M. F.
Apartado 416
Alicante, Spain

Schwary, Richard Joseph
California Numismatic
Investments Inc.
1712 S. Pacific Coast
Highway
Redondo Beach, Calif.
90277

Seaby, Peter J.
B. A. Seaby Ltd.
8 Cavendish Square
London, W1M OAJ
England

Shapiro, Edwin R.
P.O. Box 807
Teaneck, N.J. 07666

Simek, James A.
Numisgraphic Enterprises
Auction Galleries of
Oakbrook Ltd.
2121 Mannheim Road
Suite 400
Westchester, Ill. 60153

Smies, John J.
P.O. Box 371
Courtland, Kan. 66939

Smith, Arthur J.
Sidney W. Smith & Sons
Inc.
2510 Biscayne Blvd.
Miami, Fla. 33137

Smith, James V.
James V. Smith Galleries
Suite 100 Norwest
55 E. 5th St.
St. Paul, Minn. 55101

Spanier, Kurt
P.O. Box 37
Las Rozas (Madrid) Spain

Spence, Larry Gerald
Larry Spence Rare Coins
2913 San Gabriel
Austin, Texas 78705

Stack, Harvey G.
Stack's
123 W. 57th St.
New York, N.Y. 10019

Stack, Lawrence R.
Stack's
123 W. 57th St.
New York, N.Y. 10019

Stack, Norman
Stack's
123 W. 57th St.
New York, N.Y. 10019

Steinberg, Robert L.
Steinberg's
P.O. Box 1565
Boca Raton, Fla. 33432

Steinmetz, Dennis E.
Steinmetz Coin & Currency
Inc.
843 Park City Center
Lancaster, Pa. 17601

Stephens, Karl C.
Karl Stephens Inc.
Quality Rare Coins
P.O. Box 458
Temple City, Calif. 91780

Stone, Jack M.
Hub Stamp & Coin Co.
14A Beacon St.
Boston, Mass. 02108

Strauss, Edwin B.
Strauss Coins & Stamps Inc.
F-310 Woodfield Mall
Schaumburg, Ill. 60195

Stuppler, Barry S.
Gold & Silver Emporium
Inc.
16764 Ventura Blvd.
Encino, Calif. 91436

Sturtridge, Gary
The House of Stuart Ltd.
P.O. Box C
Tonganoxie, Kan. 66086

Tallarico, Thomas V.
Tallarico Rare Coins Inc.
20 Maple St.
Springfield, Mass. 01103

Tavenner, Dean W.
Dean Tavenner
427 Main St.
Deer Lodge, Mont. 59722

Terranova, Anthony
Anthony Terranova Inc.
P.O. Box 985
F.D.R. Station
New York, N.Y. 10150

Tordella, Jean R.
Manfra, Tordella & Brookes
Inc.
59 W. 49th St.
New York, N.Y. 10112

Ungar, Sam
Sam Ungar Rare Coins
P.O. Box 8928
Virginia Beach, Va. 23450

Vaganis, Charles S.
C.S.V. Numismatic
Investments Inc.
P.O. Box 615,
Beverly, Mass. 01915

Van Grover, Jacob Jay
J.J. Van Grover Ltd.
7 E. 35th St.
New York, N.Y. 10016

Varner, Mal
Alhambra Coin Center Inc.
254 E. Main St.
Alhambra, Calif. 91801

Vigdor, Luis
Manfra Tordella &
Brookes Inc.
59 W. 49th St.
New York, N.Y. 10112

Vogt, Dr. George W.
Colonial Coins Inc.
909 Travis
Houston, Texas 77002

Waddell, Edward J. Jr.
Edward J. Waddell Ltd.
7910 Woodmont Ave.
Suite 1104
Bethesda, Md. 20814

Ward, John F.
John Ward Coins
P.O. Box 1194
1000 E. Palestine Ave.
Palestine, Texas 75801

Weber, Frederick G.
Rt. 2, Oak Hill Road
Emmaus, Pa. 18049

Weinberg, Fred C.
Fred Weinberg & Co. Inc.
16311 Ventura Blvd.
Suite 550
Safrabank Building
Encino, Calif. 91436

Werner, Frederic S.
F. S. Werner
P.O. Box 97
Bellmore, N.Y. 11710

Westfall, Robert E.
Colonial Coins Inc.
15600 Drummet Blvd.
Suite 150
Houston, Texas 77032

White, Harlan
Old Coin Shop
2425 El Cajon Blvd.
San Diego, Calif. 92104

Whitlow, Larry
Larry Whitlow Ltd.
100 Tower Drive
Suite 217
Burr Ridge, Ill. 60521

Wilkerson, Arthur W.
Modern Coin Inc.
212 E. Grace St.
Richmond, Va. 23219

Wilkison, John
Wilkison & Son Inc.
P.O. Box 50762
Nashville, Tenn. 37205

Willis, Donald W.
Mike Follett Rare
Coin Co. Inc.
13101 Preston Road
Suite 400
Dallas, Tex. 75240

Winterstein, Christian
Swiss Bank Corporation
CH-4002, Basel
Aeschenvorstadt 1
Switzerland

Wise, Claude R. II
Wise's Rare Coin Inc.
1430 Walnut St.
P.O. Box 328
Lebanon, Pa. 17042

With, Dennis C.
Legacy Investments/
Collectors Coin Exchange
Cinderella City Blue Mall
701 W. Hampden Ave.
Englewood, Colo. 80154

Wolfe, Charles H.
P.O. Box 222
Lakeside, Ohio 43440

Wrubel, Gorden J.
Rare Coin Investments Inc.
P.O. Box 12506
Overland Park, Kan. 66212

Wyatt, Charles E.
P.O. Box 178623
San Diego, Calif. 92117

Young, Gary L.
P.O. Box 9
Manton, Calif. 96059

Youngerman, William J.
William Youngerman Inc.
95 S. Federal Highway
P.O. Box 177
Boca Raton, Fla. 33432

Zurawski, Stanley M. Jr.
Nevada Coin Mart Inc.
750 E. Sahara Ave.
Las Vegas, Nev. 89104

Zurawski, Stanley M. Sr.
Nevada Coin Mart Inc.
750 E. Sahara Ave.
Las Vegas, Nev. 89104

Trade organizations
Canadian Association of Numismatic Dealers

The Canadian Association of Numismatic Dealers is an association for numismatic professionals who adhere to a code of ethics. It provides a collector indemnity fund. The association lobbies for passage of legislation favorable to numismatics and provides educational activities. Speakers are available to discuss numismatics.

For membership a person must be age 21 and have a minimum of three years profes-

sional experience. Annual meetings are at various locations. There were 52 members as of spring 1987. The mailing address is P.O. Box 37, Station A, Toronto, Canada M5W 1A2.

The 1987 officers were Sandy Campbell, president; Phil Pratt, vice president; Michael Findley, secretary; and Jeffrey Hoare, treasurer.

Industry Council for Tangible Assets

The Industry Council for Tangible Assets is a trade association representing the interests of dealers in tangible assets, including bullion and coins. The members are interested in upholding ethical standards in the industry and working to create a favorable regulatory climate in the states and federal government for manufacture, distribution and sale of tangible assets.

Members must uphold a code of ethics and be dealers. The dues range from $250-$25,000 depending on the size of the compa-

ny. The headquarter's address is 25 E St. N.W., 8th Floor, Washington, D.C. 20002. There were 620 members in 1987.

Formed in 1983, ICTA conducts annual meetings and has a monthly newsletter

The 1987 officers are Bruce Kaplan, chairmen; Henry Beckler, treasurer; Stan Medlar, secretary; Howard Segermark, president; Cindy J. Arenberg, director of public affairs; Marcus Y. Kettles, director of membership; William Olson, counsel; and Lauri Turner, director of state legislative affairs.

World coin organizations

ARGENTINA
Circulo Numismatico
De Rosario
Laprida 1145
Rosario, Argentina

AUSTRALIA
Adelaide Coin Club
Box 329 G.P.O.
Adelaide 5001
South Australia

Australian Numis. Society
Brisbane Branch
The Secretary
P.O. Box 78
Fortitude Valley,
Queensland
4006 Australia

Australian Numis. Society
The Secretary
P.O. R4, Royal Exchange
Sydney, N.S.W.
2000 Australia

Bathurst Stamp & Coin
Club
The Secretary
P.O. Box 63
Bathurst, N.S.W.
2795 Australia

Bendigo & District Coin
Club
The Secretary
P.O. Box 589
Bendigo, Victoria
3550 Australia

Broken Hill Stamp & Coin
Club
The Secretary
P.O. Box 852
Broken Hill, N.S.W.
2880 Australia

Cairns Coin Club
Bradfords Coins and Stamps
Shop 5, 51 Sheridan St.,
Cairns, N.Q., 4870 Australia

Canberra Coin Club
P.O. Box 1063
Woden, A.C.T.
2606 Australia

Capricorn Coin Club
The Secretary
433 Homer Street
Earlwood, N.S.W.
2206 Australia

Central Gold Coast Stamp
& Coin Club
P.O. Box 86
Miami, Queensland
4220 Australia

Crookwell Stamp & Coin
Club
The Secretary
Grabben Gullen, via
Crookwell, N.S.W.
2625 Australia

Griffith Stamp & Coin Club
Post Office
Griffith, N.S.W.
2680 Australia

Gympie & District Coin
Club
P.O. Box 111
Gympie, Queensland
4570 Australia

International Bank Note
Society
Sydney Chapter
c/o Spink & Son (Australia
Pty. Ltd.)
53 Martin Place
Sydney, N.S.W.
2000 Australia

Mackay & District Coin
Club
The Secretary
27 Hoey Street
Mackay, Queensland
4740 Australia

Maitland & District
Coin Club
P.O. Box 185
East Maitland, N.S.W.
2323 Australia

Melbourne Numis. Society
The Secretary
Box 312
Box Hill, Victoria
3128 Australia

Metropolitan Coin Club
of Sydney
P.O. Box 137
Strathfield, N.S.W
2135 Australia

Morwell Numis. Society
The Secretary
P.O. Box 432
Moe, Victoria
3825 Australia

Newcastle Numis. Society
The Secretary
P.O. Box 5237D
Newcastle West, N.S.W.
2302 Australia

Numismatic Association
of Victoria
Box 615D
G.P.O. Melbourne, Victoria
3001 Australia

Numismatic Society
of South Australia
Box 80B, G.P.O.
Adelaide, 5001
South Australia

Orana Numis. Society
P.O. Box 1456
Dubbo, N.S.W.
2830 Australia

Orange & District Coin
& Stamp Club
P.O. Box 324
Orange, N.S.W,
2800 Australia

Perth Numis. Society
G.P.O. Box 259
Fremantle 6160 Australia

Queensland Numis. Society
P.O. Box 399
North Quay, Queensland
4000 Australia

Rockhampton Coin Club
P.O. Box 490
Rockhampton, Queensland
4700 Australia

Tamworth and District
Coin Club
P.O. Box 123
West Tamworth, N.S.W
2340 Australia

Tasmanian Numis. Society
G.P.O. Box 884J
Hobart, Tasmania
7001 Australia

Wollongong Coin Club
The Secretary
P.O. Box 118
Thirroul, N.S.W.
2515 Australia

AUSTRIA
Grazer Num. Vereinigung
Stainzerhofgasse 1,
Graz 1, Austria

Oesterreichische Num.
Gesellschaft
Burgring 5
A-1010 Vienna, Austria

Vorarlberger Coin Friends
Frz. Michel Felderstrasse 4,
A-6850 Dornbirn, Austria

BELGIUM
Alliance Numismatique
Europeene
Maurice Colaert,
20 Rue de L'Anemone,
B-1180 Brussels
Belgium

Cercle d' Etudes
Numismatiques
Boulevard de l'Empereur 4,
B-1000 Brussels
Belgium

BRAZIL
Brazilian Numis. Society
Caixa Postal 3660
Sao Paulo, Brazil

BULGARIA
Bulgarian Numismatic
Society
P.O. Box 1122
Sofia, Bulgaria

CHINA, P.R.C
Chinese Numis. Society
c/o China Mint Co
Jia-1, Xin an Nan Li,
You An Men Nie,
Beijing, People's Republic of
China

COLOMBIA
Numismaticos Colombianos
Dr. Hernando Albornoz
Plata, Sec.,
Apartado Aereo 5630
Bogota, D.E., Colombia

CUBA
Federation of Numismatists
of Cuba
Apartado No. 736
La Habana, Cuba

Cuban Numis. Assoc.
456 Aguiar St.
Havana, Cuba

CYPRUS
Cyprus Numismatic Society
27A Makarios Avenue
Larnaca, Cyprus

CZECHOSLOVAKIA
Numismaticka Spolecnost
Ceskoslovenska
Brezinova 5
Prague 8, CSSR

DENMARK
Aabybro Montklub
Peter Madsen
Mortensgade 25
DK-9440 Aabybro,
Denmark

Amagerlands Numismatiske
Association
Skottegaardssden
Saltvaerksvej 65
Kastrup, Denmark

Dansk Montsamler Union
Erik Storgaard
Hestehavvej 4
DK-5492 Vissenbjerg,
Denmark

European Token Society
Jorgen Thingvad
Lapmejsevej 9
DK-6500 Vojens, Denmark

Fyns Numismatiske
Forening
Jorgen Larsen
Staugstedlund 71
DK-5600 Faborg, Denmark

Holstebro Og Omegns
Montklub
K. E. Halgaard
Nygade 11
DK-7570 Vemb, Denmark

Montklubben for
Udenlandsk Mont
Norrevold 19
Krudttarnsvej 117
Copenhagen, Denmark

ENGLAND
Bampton & District
Numis. Society
Barry Allan
76 Meadow Close
Farmoor, Oxford
OX2 9NZ England

Banbury & District
Numis. Society
A. Bedford
12 Grosvenor Road
Banbury, Oxford
OX16 8HN England

Barrow Numis. Society
H. Walker
18 Brighton St.
Barrow-in-Furness
Lancashire, England

Bath & Bristol
Numis. Society
M.C.J. Manning
c/ 75 North Street
Berdminster, Bristol
BS3 1ES England

Bedford Numis. Society
G.W. Dawson
51 Northampton Road
Lavendon, Bucks
MK46 4EY England

Bexley Coin Club
A.J. Gilbert
76 Merlin Road
Welling, Kent
DA16 2JR England

Birmingham Numis. Society
Philip J. Leighton
17 Roughley Dr.
Four Oakes,
Sutton Coldfield
West Midlands
B75 6PW England

Bradford & District
Numis. Society
A.J. Ferguson
58 Spennithane Avenue
Leeds LS16 6JA
England

Brighton & Hove Coin Club
L.R. Keen
74 Hangleton Road
Hove, East Sussex
BN3 7GF England

British Cheque
Collectors Society
John Purser
71 Mile Lane, Cheylesmore
Coventry, W. Midlands
CO3 4GB England

British Numis. Association
David Fletcher
P.O. Box 82
Coventry CV5 6RS
England

British Numis. Society
W. Slayter
63 West Way
Edgeware, Middlesex
HA8 9LA England

British Society for Young
Numismatists
A.N. Wilkinson
7 Carnoustie Dr.
Eaglescliffe
Stockton-on-Tees,
Cleveland, England

Buckinghamshire
Numis. Society
J.A. Wilson
21 Finmere Crescent
Aylesbury, Bucks
HP27 7DQ England

Cambridgeshire
Numis. Society
M.A. Marsh
Northgate
63 St. Neots Rd.
Hardwick, Cambridgeshire
CB3 7QH England

Cheltenham Numis. Society
B.M. Greenaway
Lordswood
The Butts
Lydiard Millicent, Swindon
Wilts SN5 9LR, England

Cleveland Coin Club
L. Whitehouse
85 Hambledon Road
Middlesborough, Cleveland
England

Crawley Coin Club
M.F. Dixon
78 St. Marys Drive
Crawley, West Sussex
RH10 6NW England

Crewe & District Coin &
Medal Society
Brian Edge
48 Woodside Ave.
Crewe, Cheshire, England

Darlington & District
Numis. Society
Mrs. P. Laycock
48 Langholm Crescent
Darlington, Durham
DL1 5DX England

Derbyshire Numis. Society
E.W. Danson
63 Ferrers Way
Darley Abbey, Derby
DE3 2BB England

Devon & Exeter
Numis. Society
Norman Shiel
4 St. Leonards Road
Exeter, Devon
EX2 4LA England

Dewsbury & District
Coin Club
D. Firby
13 Glendale Estate
Morley, Leeds,
W. Yorkshire
LS27 9HL England

Durham Numis. Society
J.J.A. Morris
High Farm, Elwick,
Hartlepool, Cleveland
TS27 3HD England

Edward VIII Coin
Collectors Club
D.J. Shepherd
18 Wide Lane, Swaything,
Southampton, Hampshire
SO2 2HH England

Enfield & District
Numis. Society
R.B. Burnett
14 Gerrards Close
Southgate, London
N14 4RH England

Essex Numis. Society
R.I. Thomas
The Mowles
Courtlands, London Rd.
Billericay, Essex
CM7 7LU England

Harrow & Northwest
Middlesex Numis. Society
G.H. Hickman
49 Grafton Rd.
Harrow, Middlesex
HA1 4QS England

Havering Numis. Society
F. Bonner
80 Painesbrook Way
Harold Hill, Romford,
Essex RM3 9JS England

Hayes & District Coin Club
C.D. Haselden
83 Parkfield Crescent,
Biuslip, Middlesex
HA4 ORD England

Horncastle & District
Coin Club
W.A. Mant
6 Linden Drive
Burgh-Le-Marsh
Skegness, Lincs.
PE24 5BP England

Hull & District
Num. Society
G. Percival
86A Victoria Ave.
Hull, England

International Bank Note
Society
S.K. Gupta
11 Middle Row
Kensington, London
W10 5AT England

Ipswich Numis. Society
S.E. Sewell
103 Penzance Road
Ipswich, Suffolk
1PS 7LEl England

Kent & Medway Towns
Num. Society
E.H. Redfern
Perrydene,
Pear Tree Lounge
Shorne, Gravesend, Kent
DA12 3JS England

Kingston Numis. Society
R.N. Clarkson
62 Cheshire Gardens
Chessington, Surrey
KT9 2PS England

Lancashire & Cheshire
Numis. Society
Dr. M. Robinson
c/o Friends Meeting House
6 Mount St.
Manchester 2, England

Leicester & District
Num. Society
E.H. Papworth
98 Leire St.
Leicester, England

Lincolnshire Numis. Society
D. Goodey
13 Hunsley Cres.
Grimsby, South Humber-
side
DN32 8PU England

London Numismatic Club
S.J. Mansfield
P.E.B.M. Rueff
2 Kings Bench Walk
Temple, London
EC4 7DY England

Loughborough Coin &
Search Society
G.C. Fowler
155 Parklands Dr.
Loughborough, Leicester-
shire, England

Merseyside Num. Society
W.H.R. Cook
c/o E.C. Southworth
Merseyside County Museum
William Brown St.
Liverpool LS 8EN England

Mid Northamptonshire
Coin & Medal Society
F.H. Harris
7 Dene Close
Kettering, Northampton
NN16 9HH England

Morecambe & Lancaster
Numis. Society
K.F. Brook
55 Yorkshire St.
Morecambe, Lancs, England

Newbury Coin & Medal
Club
J.W. Child
97 Enborne Road
Newbury, Berkshire
RG14 6AR England

Norfolk & Norwich
Numis. Society
A.W. Gidney
10 Rocelin Close
Norwich, Norfolk
NR3 4DQ England

Northhampton Numis.
Society
P. Waddell
69 Marlon Road
Towcester, Northampton
NN12 7QR England

Numismatic Society of
Nottinghamshire
Grenville Chamberlain
32 Park St.
Beeston, Nottingham
NG9 1DF England

Orders & Medals Research
Society
N.G. Gooding
123 Turnpike Link
Croydon, Surrey CR0 5NU
England

Oriental Numis. Society
K.N. Wiggins
9 Cold Harbour Close
Cronsborough, East Sussex
TN6 1EU England

Ormskirk & West
Lancashire
Numis. Society
D.M. Regan
62 Thirlmere Drive
Ainsdale, Southport,
Merseyside
PR8 3TY England

Paignton & District
Coin Club
D.B. Cox
22 Shirburn Rd.
Torquay, Devon
TQ1 3JL England

Peterborough & District
Numis. Society
R. Heford
105 Welland Rd.
Peterborough, Cambs
PE1 3SJ, England

Plymouth Coin & Medal
Club
James Cavanaugh
27 Sutherland Rd.
Plymouth, Devon
PL5 2EG England

Preston & District
Numis. Society
William G. Kay
1 Reigate
Great Knowley, Chorley
Lancs PR6 8UJ England

Reading Coin Club
Secretary
c/o The Numismery
1898 Oxford Rd.
Reading, Berkshire
RG1 7UZ England

Rochford Hundred
Numis. Society
J. Bispham
103 Ferry Road
Hullbridge, Essex, England

Romsey Numis. Society
R. Chuter
5 Peverells Wood Ave.
Chandlers Ford, Hamps.
SO5 2AX England

Royal Numismatic Society
J.E. Cribb
Dept. of Coins & Medals
British Museum
London WC1B 3DG,
England

Rye Coin Club
C.W. Banks
9 Conqueror Rd.
St. Leonards on Sea
East Sussex TN38 8DD
England

St. Albans & Hertfordshire
Numis. Society
Gerald G. Sommerville
19 The Lawns, Mount
Pleasant
St. Albans, Herts.
AL3 4TB England

St. Helens Coin &
Medals Society
W.S. Pennington
53 Hold Lane
Rainhill, Merseyside
L35 8NA, England

Scunthorpe & District
Numis. Society
E.S. Smith
11 Morley St.
Gainsborough, Lincs.

DN21 2NF England

Sheffield & District
Numis. Society
A.J. Miller
22 Spooner Road, Sheffield
S10 5BN England

Southampton & District
Numis. Society
H.J.M. Good
7 Wood Rd.
Ashurst, Nr. Southampton
SO4 2BD England

Swindon & District
Numis. Society
Princess Hotel
Beatrice Street, Swindon,
Wilts, England

The North Devon
Numis. Society
F. Metherell
16 Fort Street
Barnstaple
Devon EX32 8BJ, England

Thurrock Numis. Society
R.H. Clark
152 Hamlet Court Road
Westcliff-on-Sea
Essex SSO 7LL England

Torbay & District
Numis. Society
D.B.W. Cox
22 Shirbyron Road
Torquay, Devon
TQ12 4DN England

Tyneside Numis. Society
J.H. Corbitt
11 Ashfield Grove
Whitley Bay, Tyne & Wear
NE26 1QT England

Uxbridge Coin Club
C.E. Watkins
35 Sherborne Way
Croxley Green
Rickmansworth, Harts.
WO3 3PE England

Wessex Numis. Society
D.W. Sadler
Oakdene, 30 Oak Ave.
Christchurch, Dorset
BH23 2QE England

Wickford Numis. Society
J. Bispham
103 Ferry Rd.
Hullbridge, Essex, England

Wiltshire Numis. Society
M.J. Butt
1 Court Orchard, Bratton
Westbury, Wilts.
BA13 4RY England

Worksop & District
Numis. Society
W.E. Gray
12 Hamilton Park Rd.
Cusworth, Doncaster
South Yorkshire
DN5 8TX England

Worthing & District
Numis. Society
J.A. Warner
6 Wallace Ave.
Worthing, West Sussex,
BN11 5RA England

Yorkshire Numis.
Society
Cyril Peel
162 Acreshall Ave.
Pudsey, West Yorkshire
LS28 9EQ England

York Numis. Society
W. Moore
66 Sutherland St.
York, North Yorkshire
YO2 1NQ England

FINLAND
Helsinki Numismatic
Association
Erik Johanson
Louhentie 1B5
02130 Tapiola 3, Finland

FRANCE
Association Numismatique
Armoricaine
M.E. Grall, Sec.
32 Avenue de Brequigny
F-35100 Rennes, France

Cercle Numismatique
Clermontois
Maurice Muszynski
Apt. 132
ILM Lavoisier
Rue de Nohanent
F-6300 Clermont-Ferrano
France

Club Francaise de la
Medaille
11 Quai de Conti
Paris F-75006
France

Groupe Numismatique de
Provence
Harry Lips
24 Bd Chancel "Le Gallia"
F-06600 Antibes
France

Societe Numismatique
de Paris
Bernard Favier
4 av. des Marronniers
F-94350 Villiers sur Marne
France

GREECE
Hellenic Numis. Society
P.O. Box 736
Athens, Greece

HAITI
Societe Numismatique
d'Haiti
Post Office Box 63
Port-au-Prince, Haiti

HONG KONG
Hong Kong Numismatic
Society
Cheng Po-hung
G.P.O. Box 8977
Hong Kong

HUNGARY
Hungarian Numismatic
Society
Csepreghy u.4 II. 15
H-1085 Budapest, Hungary

ICELAND
Icelandic Numis. Society
P.O. Box 5024
Reykjavik, Iceland

INDIA
Gujrat Coin and Stamp
Collectors Society
Ghanshyam V. Thacker
Vokla-Falia
Bhuj-Kutch (Gujrat), India

Numismatic Society of
India
Prof. A.K. Narain, Secy.
P. O. Hindu University
Varanasi 5, India

INDONESIA
Indonesian Numis. Society
H. Natasuwarna
J.l. Syryalaya Tengah
7 Buah Batu
Bandung, Indonesia

IRAQ
Iraqi Club for
Stamps and Coins
P.O. Box 2294
Alwiya, Iraq

Iraqi Philatelic Society
P.O. Box 344
Baghdad, Iraq

IRELAND, NORTHERN
Northern Branch of
Numismatic Society
of Ireland
S.G. Rowe, Hon. Secy.
"Langdale,"
Kensington Ave.
Banbridge, Co. Down
N. Ireland

Numismatic Correspond-
ents
of Ireland
Munster, Portora
Enniskillen
N. Ireland

IRELAND, REPUBLIC
Numismatic Society
of Ireland
Francis Heaney
St. Heliers
Stillorgan Park
Blackrock, Co. Dublin
Irish Republic

Royal Dublin Society
Ballsbridge
Dublin
Irish Republic

ISRAEL
Haifa Numismatic Society
Mike Fox
38 Pinsker Street
Neve Shaanan
Haifa 31060 Israel

Israel Numismatic Society
Dr. E. Klimowsky
43 Yehuda Halevi St.
Tel Aviv, Israel

ITALY
Associazione Filatelica
Numismatica Modenese
Casella Postal 224
I-41100 Modenese, Italy

Associazione Medaglistica
Esaltazioni
Storiche (A.M.E.S.)
Via Poggi D'oro 35
I-00179 Rome, Italy

Assonummus
Via Santa Maria
Fulcorina 17
I-20123 Milano, Italy

Circolo Filatelica Numis.
Piazza Cavour-4
I-47037 Rimini, Italy

Circolo Filatelico Numis.
"G. Piani" Imola
Galleria Risorgimento 1
I-40026 Imola, Italy

Circolo Filatelico Numis.
Mantovano
Casella Postale 229
I-46100 Mantova, Italy

Circolo Filatelico Numis.
Reggiano
Casella Postale 102
I-42100 Reggio Emilia, Italy

Circolo Numismatico
"Alfa Cure"
Via Firenzuola 7/9R
I-50133 Firenze, Italy

KOREA
Korea Coin Club
United States Forces
Stephen W. Gaunt
Yongsan District
Seventh Region, USA CIDC
APO San Francisco 96301

MALAYSIA
Malaysian Numis. Society
Secretary
P.O. Box 2367
Kuala Lumpur
01-02 Malaysia

MEXICO
Sociedad Numismatica
de Mexico
Gloria Camarena Torres
Eugenia No. 13-301
Apartado Postal 60-589
Mexico 18, D.F., Mexico

Sociedad Numismatica de
Monterrey, A.C.
P.O. Box 422
Monterrey, N.L.-Mexico

Sociedad Numismatica de
Morelos A.C.
Calle 8 No. 4 Condominio
Bugambilias
Cuernavaca, Morelos,
Mexico

MOROCCO
American Coin and Stamp
Club of Morocco
USNCS
P.O. Box 303
FPO New York 09544

NEW ZEALAND
Auckland Coin Club
Box 1440, G.P.O.
Auckland 1, New Zealand

Numismatic Society
of Auckland
Box 818
Auckland C.1, New Zealand

Royal Numismatic Society
of New Zealand
G.P.O. Box 2023
Wellington, New Zealand

Tauranga Numis. Society
P.O. Box 202
Tauranga, New Zealand

Wellington Coin Club
P.O. Box 3705
Wellington, New Zealand

NORWAY
Norsk Numismatisk
Forening
Box 180
Oslo, Norway

PANAMA
Crossroads Coin Club
(Club Cruce de Camino)
P.O. Box 1833
Balboa, Rep. of Panama

PERU
Sociedad Numismatica
del Peru
P.O. Box 4345
Lima 1, Peru

PHILIPPINES
Bank Note Society
of the Philippines
P.O. Box 1960 MCC
Makati, Philippines

Philippine Numismatic
and Antiquarian Society
P.O. Box 1955
Manila, Philippines

POLAND
Polskie Towarzystwo
Archeologiczne
Polish Arch. Society
Numismatic Section
ul. Jezuicka 6
00281 Warsaw, Poland

PORTUGAL
Associacao Recreativa
Aurora de Liberdade
Numismatic Section
Matosinhos, Leca
Portugal

Clube Numismatico
de Portugal
Nestor Vital
Casa do Minho
Lisbon, Portugal

PUERTO RICO
Sociedad Numismatica
de Puerto Rico
P.O. Box 178
San Juan, Puerto Rico
00902

SCOTLAND
Aberdeen Coin Club
N. Thomson
54 Richmondhill Place
Aberdeen AB2 4EP
Scotland

Glasgow & West of Scotland
Numismatic Society
N.G. Brodie
Cruachan, Dullatur
Glasgow G68 OAW
Scotland

Mid-Lanark Coin Circle
J.W. Wright
Milton View, Waygateshaw
Carluke ML8 5PX
Scotland

SINGAPORE
Singapore Numismatic
Association
GPO 2594
Singapore 2, Republic of
Singapore

SOUTH AFRICA
Johannesburg Numismatic
Society
75A Troye St.
Johannesburg, South Africa

Natal Numismatic Society
7 Hansworth-on-the-Hill
169 Jan Smuts Highway
Westridge
Durban, South Africa

South African Numismatic
Society
P.O. Box 1689
Cape Town 8000
South Africa

Transvaal Numismatic
Society
P.O. Box 2594
Pretoria, Transvaal
South Africa

SPAIN
Associacion Numismatica
Espanola
Gran Via de les Cortes
Catalanes 627,
Barcelona 10, Spain

SWEDEN
Svenska Numismatiska
Foreningen
Ostermalmsgatan 81
S-114 50 Stockholm,
Sweden

SWITZERLAND
Numimatischer Verein Bern
Postfach 1995
S-3001 Bern, Switzerland

THAILAND
Thai Numismatic Society
P.O. Box 189
Bangkok, Thailand

VENEZUELA
Associacion Venezolana
de Numismaticos
Apartado Los Ruices
170165
Caracas, Venezuela

WALES
South Wales & Mon-
mouthshire Numis. Society
A.G. Cox
9 Maynard Court
Fairwater Road
Cardiff, South Glamorgan
CF5 2LS Wales

WEST GERMANY
Augsburger Munzfreunde
Ernst Stempfle
Am Zehntstadel 18
D-8900 Augsburg
W. Germany

Bayerische Numismatische
Gesellschaft e.V.
Residenzstr. 1
D-8000 Munich,
W. Germany

Bremer Numis. Gesellschaft
K. H. Buhse
Blumenkamp 6
D-2820 Bremen-St. Magnus
W. Germany

Bremerhavener
Munzfreunde
Heinrich Walker
Max-Eyth-Platz 2
D-2850 Bremerhaven-Mitte
W. Germany

Eifeler Munzfreunde
Otto Kersting
1M Wiesengrundig 19
D-5332 Schleiden
W. Germany

Frankfurter Numismatische
Gesellschaft
Frau Dr. Gisela Forschner
Historisches Museum,
Munzkabinett
Saalgasse 19
D-6000 Frankfurt/Main
W. Germany

Giessener Numismatische
Gesellschaft e.V.
Dr. H.D. Kahl
Otto Behagel Str. 10
D-6300 Giessen
W. Germany

Heidelberg Coin & Stamp
Club
Harley G. Miller
im Kreuz 18
D-6927 Wollenberg
W. Germany

Munzfreunde Fulda
Gunther Auth
Bachstrasse 22
D-6418 Hunfeld
W. Germany

Numismatische Gesellschaft
Mainz
Dr. Rudolph Walther
Nikolaus Beckerstrasse 8
D-6500 Mainz,
W. Germany

Numismatische Gesellschaft
Speyer E.V.
Helfried Ehrend
Laharstrasse 17
D-6720 Speyer,
W. Germany

Oberhausener
Munzfreunde
Hans-Gunter Beck
Laubstrasse 39
D-4200 Oberhausen 11
W. Germany

Wuppertaler Munz-
freunde
Horst Kimpel
Reichstrasse 12
D-5600 Wuppertal 2
W. Germany

Wurttembergischer
Verein fur
Munzkunde e.V.
Dr. Ulrich Klein
Wurttemburg Landes-
museum
Schillerplatz 6
D-7000 Stuttgart 1
W. Germany

ZIMBABWE
Zimbabwe Numis. Society
Glyn Tunley
P.O. Box 2356
Salisbury 705701,
Zimbabwe

Canadian Numismatic Association

The Canadian Numismatic Association was established in 1950 and incorporated in 1963. Application for membership in the CNA may be made by any reputable person upon payment to: Executive Secretary, P.O. Box 226, Barrie, Ont., Canada L4M 4T2.

Cost for regular membership (21 years and older) is $20, for a junior membership (under 21) $10, for a family membership (husband, wife and children under 21 years of age) $30, for a corporate (clubs, societies, libraries and other non-profit organizations) $20 and life membership $350. Applications by persons under 21 years of age must be sponsored by a parent or guardian.

The CNA publishes *The Canadian Numismatic Journal* monthly, distributed free to members.

Officers of CNA

Executive Committee:

President .... Stan Clute
Immediate Past President .. Geoffrey G. Bell
First Vice-President ....Al Bliman
Second Vice-President...... Louis H. Lewry
Directors: .... Bernard G. Kline
.... Tim Henderson
.... Barry Uman
.... Yvon Marquis
.... Paul Johnson
.... Don R. Robb
.... Nick Gerbinski
.... Dennis Naphin
.... Garry Braunwarth
.... Ralph R. Burry
.... J. Richard Becker
.... George Beach
.... Charles D. Moore

Appointed Officers:
Executive Secretary .... Kenneth B. Prophet
Editor .... Robert C. Willey
Advertising Manager ... Kenneth B. Prophet
Librarian .... Carol Gregory

Honorary President
Sheldon S. Carroll

Honorary Past President
L.J.P. Brunet (1950-1953)*
J. Douglas Ferguson (1953-1981)*

Past Presidents
Sheldon S. Carroll (1950-1953)
L. J. P. Brunet (1953-1955)*
G. R. L. Potter (1955-1956)*
Vincent G. Greene (1956-1959)
C. C. Tannahill (1959-1961)
Dr. John S. Wilkinson (1961-1963)
Edwin Echenberg (1963-1965)
A. Mitchell MacDonald (1965-1967)*
E. Victor Snell (1967-1969)
John Jay Pittman (1969-1971)
Norman W. Williams (1971-1973)
Mrs. Louise Graham (1973-1975)*
A. L. Munro (1975-1977)
James E. Charlton (1977-1979)
Jack Veffer (1979-1981)
John Regitko (1981-1983)
Geoffrey G. Bell (1983-1985)
*Deceased

Conventions 1954 to 1989

Location	Date/Host Club
Toronto, Ontario	Aug. 23-34, 1954
King Edward Hotel....	Toronto Coin Club
Ottawa, Ontario	Sept. 7-8, 1955
Chateau Laurier	C.N.A. Ottawa Chapter No. 1
London, Ontario	Sept. 21-22, 1956
Hotel London	London Numis. Society
Hamilton, Ontario	Aug. 30-31, 1957
Wentworth Arms	Hamilton Coin Club
Ottawa, Ontario	Sept. 4-6, 1958
Chateau Laurier	C.N.A. Ottawa Chapter No. 1
Regina, Saskatchewan	Sept. 2-4, 1959
The Saskatchewan Hotel	Regina Coin Club
Sherbrooke, Quebec	Aug. 18-20, 1960
Hotel Sherbrooke	Sherbrooke Coin Club
Hamilton, Ontario	Aug. 31, Sept. 1-2, 1961
Sheraton-Connaught Hotel	Hamilton Coin Club
Detroit, Mich.	Aug. 15-18, 1962
Sheraton Cadillac	American & Canadian Numismatic Assoc.
Vancouver, B.C.	Aug. 15-17, 1963
Hotel Vancouver............	Vancouver Numismatic Society
Halifax, Nova Scotia	Aug. 27-29, 1964
Nova Scotian..........	Halifax Coin Club

Location	Date/Host Club
Montreal, Quebec	Aug. 12-14, 1965
Sheraton Mount Royal........	Montreal Numismatic Society
Winnipeg, Manitoba	Aug. 25-27, 1966
New Marlborough....	Manitoba Coin Club
Ottawa, Ontario	Aug. 31, Sept. 1-2, 1967
Chateau Laurier	Ottawa Coin Club & Capital City Coin Club
Calgary, Alberta	July 15-17, 1968
Palliser Hotel........	Calgary Coin Assoc.
Toronto, Ontario	Aug. 28-30, 1969
Royal York	Toronto Coin Club
Halifax, Nova Scotia	Aug. 5-8, 1970
Nova Scotian..........	Halifax Coin Club
Vancouver, B.C.	Aug. 26-28, 1971
Hotel Vancouver............	Vancouver Numismatic Society
Toronto, Ontario	Aug. 2-5, 1972
Holiday Inn	Canadian Numis. Assoc. & Canadian Paper Money Society
Saskatoon, Saskatchewan	July 19-21, 1973
Sheraton-Cavalier...	Saskatoon Coin Club
Hamilton, Ontario	Aug. 21-24, 1974
Royal Connaught	Hamilton Coin Club
Calgary, Alberta	July 11-15, 1975
Palliser Hotel.....	Calgary Numis. Society
Ottawa, Ontario	July 7-10, 1976
Chateau Laurier..........	City of Ottawa Coin Club

Location	Date/Host Club
Vancouver, B.C.	Aug. 1-7, 1977
Holiday Inn ... Vancouver Numis. Society	
London, Ontario	July 27-30, 1978
Holiday Inn ..... London Numis. Society	
Edmonton, Alberta	July 19-21, 1979
Chateau Locombe...Edmonton Coin Club	
Montreal, Quebec	July 23-27, 1980
Mount Royal Hotel.... Assoc. des Numis-	
mates et Philatelistes de Boucherville, Inc.	
Winnipeg, Manitoba	July 15-18, 1981
Holiday Inn Downtown .... Manitoba	
	Coin Club
Toronto, Ontario	July 23-26, 1982
Royal York Hotel ..... Toronto Coin Club	
Moncton, New Brunswick	July 20-23, 1983
Keddy's Brunswick Hotel ...... Moncton	
	Coin Club

Location	Date/Host Club
Hamilton, Ontario	July 18-22, 1984
Royal Connaught Hotel .... Canadian	
	Numismatic Assoc.
Regina, Saskatchewan	July 17-21, 1985
Regina Inn .... Regina Coin Club	
Toronto, Ontario	July 24-26, 1986
Westbury Hotel.... North York Coin Club	
Calgary, Alberta	July 16-18, 1987
Westin Hotel .... Calgary Numismatic	
	Society
Charlottetown, P.E.I.	July 1988
Prince Edward Island Numismatic Assoc.	
Quebec City, Quebec	July 1989
La Societe Numismatique de Quebec	

Canadian coin associations

Alberni Valley Coin Club
P.O. Box 71
Port Alberni
British Columbia V9Y 7M6

Assoc. des Collectionneirs de
Monnaies des Laurentides
1349 Chemin Lac Conneux
St. Hippolyte, Quebec

Association des
Numismates et Philatelistes
de Boucherville
C.P. 111
Boucherville, Quebec J4B 5E6

Assoc. des Numismates
Francophones du Canada
P.O. Box 1000
Daveluyvill, Quebec
G0Z 1C0

Assoc. des Numismatistes
de St. Hyacinthe Inc.
C.P. 81
St. Hyacinthe, Que. J2S 7B2

Association Numismatique
et Philatelique de
Chateauguay
Michel Laplante
108 rue St. Denis
Chateauguay, Que. J6K 2C2

Atlantic Provinces
Numismatic Association
R.R. 1
College Bridge
New Brunswick E0A 1L0

Brantford Numis. Society
P.O. Box 351
Brantford, Ontario N3T 5S1

British Columbia
Numismatic Association
P.O. Box 4311
Vancouver, B.C. V6B 3Z7

Calgary Numismatic Society
P.O. Box 633
Calgary, Alberta T2P 2J3

Cambridge Coin Club
37 Grand Ave.
Cambridge, Ontario

Canadian Association
of Numismatic Dealers
P.O. Box 37, Station A
Toronto, Ont. M5W 1A2

Canadian Association
of Token Collectors
10 Wesanford Place
Hamilton, Ont. L8P 1N6

Canadian Association of
Wooden Money Collectors
P.O. Box 48, Station M
Calgary, Alberta T2P 2G9

Canadian Cents Club
L.H. Lewry
1161 3rd Ave. N.W.
Moose Jaw, Saskatchewan
S6H 3V1

Canadian Numis. Assoc.
Kenneth Prophet
P.O. Box 226
Barrie, Ont. L4M 4T2

Canadian Numismatic
Research Society
Ronald Greene
P.O. Box 1351
Victoria, B.C. V8W 2W7

Canadian Paper Money
Society
Box 465
West Hill, Ontario M1E 2P0

Cape Breton Coin Club
P.O. Box 12
Sydney, Nova Scotia
B1N 3B1

City of Ottawa Coin Club
P.O. Box 2180, Station D
Ottawa, Ontario K1P 5W4

Le Club de Numismates Du
Bas St-Laurent
C.P. 1475
Rimouski, Quebec
G5L 8M3

Club Philatelique N-D-V
5855 Pierre de Coubertin
Montreal, Quebec

Collingwood Coin & Stamp
Club
P.O. Box 565
Collingwood, Ont. L9Y 4B2

Edmonton Coin Club
P.O. Box 4111
Edmonton, Alberta T6E 4S8

Fort McMurray Coin &
Stamp Club
Box 5860
Fort McMurray, Alberta
T9H 4V9

Fraser Valley Coin Club
P.O. Box 13
Abbotsford, B.C. V2S 4N7

Fredericton Numismatic
Society
P.O. Box 445
Fredericton, N.B. E3B 4Z9

Gananoque Coin & Stamp
Club
Gananoque Secondary
School
Gananoque, Ontario

Halifax Coin Club
Nova Scotia Museum
1747 Summer St.
Halifax, N.S. B3H 3A6

Hamilton Coin Club
P.O. Box 9271
Stoney Creek, Ont. L8G 3X9

Huronia Numismatic Assoc.
P.O. Box 243
Barrie, Ontario L4M 4T2

Israel Numismatic Society
of Montreal
1388 Elizabeth St.
Chomedey, Laval, Quebec
H7W 2J8

I.N.S. of Toronto
Dr. Albert Rose
Faculty of Social Work
University of Toronto
Toronto, Ontario M5S 1A1

Ingersoll Coin Club
823 Van St.
London, Ontario N5Z 1M8

Kamloops Numismatic
Society
P.O. Box 585
Kamloops, B.C. V2C 5L7

Kent Coin Club
P.O. Box 95
Chatham, Ont. N7M 5K1

Lahr Base Coin Club
Box 2014
CFPO 5000
Belleville, Ont. K0K 3R0

Lake Superior Coin Club
P.O. Box 874
Thunder Bay, Ont. P7C 4X7

Lakeshore Coin Club
P.O. Box 1137
Pointe Claire, Quebec
H9S 4H9

Lethbridge Numismatic
Society
142 Ojibway Road
Lethbridge, Alberta T1K 5L1

London Numismatic Society
P.O. Box 6221, Station D
London, Ontario N5W 5S1

Manitoba Coin Club
P.O. Box 321
Winnipeg, Manitoba
R3C 2H6

McKay Clements Coin Club
P.O. Box 249
Haileybury, Ont. P0J 1K0

Medicine Hat Coin & Stamp
Club
P.O. Box 1353
Medicine Hat, Alberta
T1A 7N1

Miramichi Coin Club
P.O. Box 107
Newcastle, N.B. E1V 3M2

Mississauga Coin Club
Senior Citizens Centre
1389 Cawthra Road
Mississauga, Ont. L5G 4L1

Moncton Coin Club
P.O. Box 54
Moncton, N.B. E1C 8R9

Montreal Numismatic
Society
MacDonald Stewart
Foundation
1195 Sherbrooke St. W.
Montreal, Quebec H3A 1H9

Newmarket Numismatic
Society
Box 142
Newmarket, Ont. L3Y 4W3

Niagara Falls Coin Club
P.O. Box 932
Niagra Falls, Ont. L2E 6V8

Nickel Belt Coin Club
P.O. Box 593
Sudbury, Ontario P3E 4P8

Nipissing Coin Club
P.O. Box 1825
Hornell Heights, Ontario
P0H 1P0

North Shore Numismatic
Society
P.O. Box 86315
N. Vancouver, B.C.
V7L 4K6

North York Coin Club
P.O. Box 294
Station A
Willowdale, Ont. M2N 5P0

Ontario Numis. Assoc.
P.O. Box 33
Waterloo, Ontario N2J 3Z6

Orillia Champlain Coin
Club
100 James St.
Orillia, Ontario L3V 1L5

Oshawa & District Coin
Club
Box 212
Oshawa, Ontario L1H 7L1

Pembroke Centennial Coin
Club
10 White St.
Petawawa, Ont. K8H 1Z6

Peterborough Numismatic
Association
P.O. Box 1870
Peterborough, Ont. K9J 7X7

Port Colborne Coin Club
Bethel Community Centre
Chippawa Road
Port Colborne, Ontario
K0K 1S0

Prince Edward Island
Numismatic Association
P.O. 2921
Charlottetown, P.E.I.
C1A 8C5

Prince George Numismatic
Society
Northland Coin & Stamp
201-1253 5th Ave.
Prince George, B.C.

Regina Coin Club
Box 174
Regina, Sask. S4P 2Z6

Richmond Hill Coin Club
10441 Young St.
Richmond Hill, Ontario
L4C 3L2

St. Catharines Coin Club
P.O. Box 1492
St. Catharines, Ontario
L2R 7J9

St. John Coin Collector's
Club
P.O. Box 4
Dominion Park
St. John, N.B. E2M 4Y9

Sarnia Coin Club
P.O. Box 62
Sarnia, Ont. N7T 2H8

Saskatoon Coin Club
Box 7514
Saskatoon, Sask. S7K 4L4

Scarborough Coin Club
P.O. 465
West Hill, Ont. M2E 2P0
La Societe Numismatique
de Quebec
C.P. 281
Sillery, Quebec G1T 2R1
Stoney Creek Coin & Stamp
Club
199 Green Road
Stoney Creek, Ontario
L8E 2A4
Stratford Coin Club
P.O. Box 262
Stratford, Ont. N5A 6T1
Summerside Coin & Stamp
Club
Freeland, R.R. #2
Ellerslide, P.E.I. C0B 1J0
Thistletown Coin Club
P.O. Box 1143, Station B
Weston, Ont. M9L 2R8
Thompson Coin Club
Thompson Public Library
Thompson, Manitoba
R8N OA2

Timmins Coin Club
475 Randall Drive
Timmins, Ont. P4N 7S1
Toronto Coin Club
P.O. Box 865
Adelaide St.
Toronto, Ont. M5C 2K1
Truro Coin Club
60 Lawnwood Drive
Truro, Nova Scotia
University Coin Club
Glen Kunzman
Box 8
University Centre Building
University of Manitoba
Winnipeg, Man. R3T 2N2
Vancouver Numismatic
Society
P.O. Box 67737
Station O
Vancouver, B.C. V5W 3V2
Victoria Numis. Society
P.O. Box 1601
Victoria, B.C. V8W 2X7

Victoria-Simco Numismatic
Association
R.R. 2
Cannington, Ont. L0E 1E0
Waterloo Coin Society
P.O. Box 41
Waterloo, Ont. N2J 3Z6
Welland Coin Club
Indian Head Lodge Hall
75 Southworth St. N.
Welland, Ont. L3B 1Y3
Windsor Coin Club
1165 Lincoln Road
Winsdor, Ont. N8Y 2H6
Woodstock Coin Club
69 Tobin Place
Woodstock, Ont. N4S 8N4
Yellowhead Stamp & Coin
Collectors Society
Box 820
Hinton, Alberta T0E 1B0

Sociedad Numismatica de Mexico

The Mexican Numismatic Society, founded Sept. 11, 1952, serves individuals in Mexico and abroad, as well as eight associated organizations in Mexico.

Members receive a quarterly illustrated bulletin which provides cultural, educational and scientific information to members, the local press and hobby publications.

Annual dues for active members, in United States dollars, include $20 for adults; $2.50 for juniors; $5 for corresponding members in Mexico and other countries. Membership information is available from Sociedad Numismatica de Mexico, Apartado Postal 60-589, Mexico 18, D.F. Mexico.

Officers of SNM
President .... Enrique Torres de Alba
Vice President .... Duane D. Douglas

Secretary .... Adolfo Loredo Hill
Treasurer .... Eduardo Malagon Kamel
Delegates:
Promotion ... Gustavo Del Angel Mubarak
Publication .... Mariano A. Montero
Public Relations .... Clyde Hubbard
Commissioner .... Gabriel Gomez Saborio
Administrator ... Lourdes Gonzalez Castro

Past Presidents
.... Jose Tamborrel Jr.
.... Miguel L. Munoz
.... Charles Hale
. Jose Luis Herrera Somellera
..... Rogello Charteris Reyes
..... Javier Lopez de Lerena
. Anna Maria Cross de Torres
Editor .... Javier Lopez de Lerena

International Association of Professional Numismatists

The object of the IAPN is, according to its charter, "the coordination of all efforts and ideas of the development of the numismatic trade, the encouragement of scientific research and the propagation of numismatics, and the creation of lasting and friendly relations among professional numismatists throughout the world.

"The members of the Association guarantee the authenticity of all coins and medals which they sell."

The IAPN was founded in Geneva, Switzerland, on May 12, 1951. The registered office of the Association is in Switzerland.

To be eligible to join the IAPN, a candidate must:

1. Have been established as a professional numismatist as his or her principal activity for at least four years, and to have carried on a numismatic business honorably for at least the same period.

2. Have given proof of his or her numismatic knowledge by submitting his or her commercial publications, catalogues, price lists, books, articles, or the text of lectures.

3. Be proposed to the Association by three members:

For information on the IAPN, write Jean-Paul Divo, Secretary, I.A.P.N., Lowenstrasse 65, CH-8001 Zurich, Switzerland.

IAPN Executive Committee

President	Robert Schulman
First Vice President ..	Michel Kampmann
Second Vice President ..	Richard Margolis
Secretary	Jean-Paul Divo
Treasurer ...	Wilfried Albrecht assisted by
....	Robert Schulman
Committee	Jan Olav Aamlid
....	Wilfried Albrecht
....	Giulio Bernardi
....	Francisca Bernheimer
....	Emile Bourgey
....	Lawrence Brown
....	Ferran Calico
....	William Christensen
....	Alberto De Falco
....	Jean-Paul Divo
....	Silvia Hurter
....	Michel Kampmann
....	Richard Margolis
....	Edward Milas
....	Peter Schulten
....	Hans Voegtli

IAPN General Assemblies

Location	Date
Florence	May-June 1952
Paris	July 1953
Oxford	June 1954
Munich	May 1955
Amsterdam	May 1956
Barcelona	June 1957
Vienna	May 1958
Copenhagen	May 1959
Lausanne	June 1960
Rome	Sept. 1961
Igls (Austria)	May 1962
Monte Carlo	May-June 1963
London	May 1964
Paris	June 1965
New York	May 1966
Stockholm	May 1967
Naples	May 1968
Palma	May 1969
Scheveningen	May 1970
Estoril	May 1971
Athens	May 1972
Washington	Sept. 1973
Brussels	June 1974
Edinburgh	May 1975
Corsica	June 1976
Wiesbaden	May 1977
Malta	May 1978
Interlaken	Sept. 1979
Los Angeles	June 1980
Marbella	June 1981
Salzburg	May 1982
Singapore	May 1983
Greek Islands	June 1984
Oslo	May 1985
Kent	Sept. 1986
Haifa & Jerusalem	June 1987

Members of IAPN

Following is a list of members of the International Association of Professional Numismatists. The date of admission to membership is given at the end of each entry.

AUSTRALIA

Spink & Son (Australia) Pty.
A.P.A. Chambers
53 Martin Place
Sydney, NSW 2000, 1978

AUSTRIA

Herinek, G.
Josefstadterstrasse 27,
A-1082, Wien VIII, 1958

Munzhandlung Lanz
(Prof. Dipl. Ing. Hermann
Lanz, Dr. Hubert Lanz, Ernst
H. Lanz)

Hauptplatz 14
(Postfach 677)
A-8011, Graz, 1951

BELGIUM

Elsen, Jean
Avenue de Tervuren 65, Bte 1,
B-1040 Bruxelles, 1980

Franceschi, B. and Fils
10, rue Croix de Fer,
B-1000 Bruxelles, 1958

Magain, Pierre
Rue de Lennery 52
B-6430 Walcourt, 1981

DENMARK

Gert Hornung Monthandel
Vimmelskaftet 47
DK-1161 Copenhagen K, 1977

EGYPT

Bajocchi, Pietro
45 Abdel Khalek Sarwat St.
Cairo, 1957

ENGLAND

Baldwin A. H. & Sons, Ltd.
(P.D. Mitchell, A.H.E.
Baldwin, B. Curtis)
11 Adelphi Terrace,
GB-London WC2N 6BJ, 1969

Lubbocks
(R.M. Lubbock)
315 Regent Street
GB-London W1R 7YB, 1973

Seaby B.A., Ltd.
(L. Brown, G.L. Mantin,
S. Mitchell)
Audley House
8 Cavendish Square,
GB-London, W1M OAJ, 1951

Spink & Son, Ltd.
(D. Liddell, P. Finn, A. de
Clermont, M. Rasmusson, D.
Saville)
5/7 King Street, St. James's
GB-London SW1 Y 6QS, 1951

Vecchi, V.C. & Sons
(P.E. Vecchi)
Church House, 23 Great
Smith St.
GB-London SW1 P 3BL, 1976

FRANCE

Antika 1 (Marcel Pesce)
33, rue Sainte-Helene,
F-69002 Lyon 1985

Barre, Gerard
8, Grande Rue,
Adresse postale: B.P. 18,
F-35401 Saint-Malo Cedex,
1983

Bonvallet, Jacques
64, rue de Richelieu
F-75002 Paris, 1975

Bourgey, Emile
7 rue Drouot,
F-75009 Paris, 1951

Burgan, Claude
(C. Burgan, P. Crinon)
68, rue de Richelieu
F-75002 Paris, 1978

Maison Platt S.A.
(Michel et Colette Kampmann)
49, rue de Richelieu,
F-75001 Paris, 1951

Numismatique et Change de
Paris (Annette Guyonnet-
Vinchon)
3, rue de la Bourse
F-75002 Paris, 1978

Page, Etienne
16 rue Milton,
F-75009 Paris, 1951

Poinsignon Numismatique
(A. Poinsignon)
4, rue des Francs Bourgeois
F-67000 Strasbourg, 1986

Silberstein, Claude
39 rue Vivienne,
F-75002 Paris, 1974

Vannier, Jean-Paul
6, rue des Remparts
F-33000 Bordeaux, 1977

Vinchon, Jean & Cie.
(Jean Vinchon, Francoise
Berthelot-Vinchon)
77, rue de Richelieu,
F-75002 Paris, 1951

Weil, Alain
54, rue de Richelieu
F-75001 Paris, 1979

GERMANY

Frankfurter Munzhandlung
(R. G. Wolf)
Freiherr-vom-Stein Str. 9,
D-6000 Frankfurt 1, 1951

Galerie fur Numismatik
(A. Ringberg GmbH)
Achenbachstrasse 3,
D-4000 Dusseldorf 1, 1978

Giessener Munzhandlung
(Dieter Gorny GmbH)
Maximiliansplatz 16
D-8000 Munchen 2, 1974

Grabow, Ludwig
(Frl. H. Grabow)
Lietzenburger Strasse 64,
D-1000 Berlin 15, 1957

Hirsch, Gerhard, Nachfolger
Munzhandlung
(Dr. Francisca Bernheimer)
Promenadeplatz 10/II,
D-8000 Munchen 2, 1953

Kricheldorf, H.H. Nachf.
(Volker Kricheldorf)
Gunterstalstrasse 16
D-7800 Freiburg 1, 1957

Kunker, Fritz Rudolf,
Munzhandlung
Guntenbergstrasse 23,
D-4500 Osnabruck, 1983

Kurpfalzische Munzhandlung,
(H. Gehrig, F. Rupertus)
Augusta-Anlage 52
D-6800 Mannheim 1, 1977

Numismatik Lanz
(Dr. Hubert Lanz)
Maximiliansplatz 10
D-8000 Munchen 2, 1978

Menzel, Niels
Beckerstrasse 6-A
D-1000 Berlin 41, 1980

Munz Zentrum, Albrecht &
Hoffmann GmbH.
(Wilfried Albrecht)
Rubenstrasse 42,
D-5000 Koln 1, 1972

Peus Nachf., Dr. Busso
(Dieter Raab)
Bornwiesenweg 34,
D-6000 Frankfurt, 1967

Munzhandlung Ritter
(E. & J. Ritter)
Bastionstrasse 31
Postfach 200 629
D-4000 Dusseldorf 1, 1981

Schramm, H.J.
Lindenallee 21-A
D-5000 Koln 51, 1977

Schulten & Co. GmbH
(P.N. Schulten)
Klingelputz 16
D-5000 Koln 1, 1979

Tietjen & Co.
Spitalerstrasse 30
D-2000 Hamburg 1, 1983

GREECE

Sepheriades, E.
Havriou 5, Athens (125), 1953

IRELAND

Coins & Medals (Regd.)
(Emil Szauer)
10 Cathedral St.
Dublin 1, 1976

ISRAEL

Eidelstein and Holland
(Adolfo Eidelstein)
61 Herzl St., Haifa, 1985

Qedar, Shraga
P.O. Box 520, 91004
Jerusalem,
1983

ITALY

Bernardi, Giulio
Via Roma 3, P.O. Box 560
I-34121 Trieste, 1969

Crippa, Carlo
Via degli Omenoni 2
(Angolo Piazza Belgioioso),
I-20121 Milano, 1966

De Falco, G.
Corso Umberto 24
I-80138 Napoli, 1951

Fallani
(Drs. Giorgio e Carlo-Maria)
Via del Babuino 58a,
I-00187 Roma, 1951

Giannantoni, Renato
Via Farini 31,
I-40124 Bologna, 1966

Marchesi, Gino e Figlio
Viale Pietramellara 35
(Scala A)
I-40121 Bologna, 1970

Muschietti, Walter
Galleria Astra,
P.O. Box 125,
I-33100 Udine, 1960

Ratto, Mario
Via A. Manzoni 14
(Palazzo Trivulzio)
I-20121 Milano, 1951

Raviola, Rag. Mario
Corso Vittorio Emanuele 73
I-10128 Torino, 1962

Rinaldi, O. & Figlio
Via Cappello 23
(Casa di Giulietta),
I-37100 Verona, 1951

Santamaria, P. & P., S. & S
Piazza di Spagna 35,
I-00187 Roma, 1951

Simonetti, Luigi
Piazza della Stazione 1,
I-50123 Firenze, 1962

Toderi, Dr. Giuseppe
Via Agostino Bertani 14
I-50137 Firenze, 1975

Varesi, Clelio
Via Frank 32
I-27100 Pavia, 1985

JAPAN

Taisei Stamps & Coins
(Masamichi Oka, president)
Ohno Bldg., 1-19-8 Kyobashi
Chuo-ku, Tokyo, 1973

LUXEMBOURG

Centre Mercure Lux Numis
(Romain Probst)
41-43 ave. de la Gare
L-1611 Luxembourg-Gare,
1979

MONACO

Gadoury, Victor
38, Boulevard des Moulins
Monte Carlo, 1981

NETHERLANDS

Schulman B.V., Jacques
(Jacques, Leny, Robert and
Laurens Schulman)
Keizersgracht 448,
NL-1016 GD Amsterdam,
1951

Van Der Dussen B.V., A.G.
Hondstraat 5
NL-6211 HW Maastricht, 1969

Westerhof, J.B.
Hoogend 18,
NL-8601 AE Sneek, 1985

NORWAY

Oslo Mynthandel AS
(Jan Olav Aamlid)
Kongens gate 31
N-0101 Oslo 1, 1980

PORTUGAL

Uniao de Bancos
Portugueses
(Dept. Numismatica)
Rue de Sa da Bandeira 53,
Porto, 1957

SINGAPORE

Taisei Stamps and Coins,
(S) Pte. Ltd., (B.H. Lim)
177 River Valley Road
Liang Court Complex,
No. 01-32/33 0617 Singapore,
1985

SOUTH AFRICA

Kaplan & Son (Pty.) Ltd.
(Michael Kaplan)
P.O. Box 132, Germiston 1400,
Transvaal, 1976

SPAIN

Calico, X. & F.
(Ferran Jr. and Xavier Jr.
Calico)
Plaza del Angel 2,
E-08002 Barcelona 2, 1951

SWEDEN

B. Ahlstrom Mynthandel A.B.,
(Bjarne Ahlstrom)
Kungsgatan 28,
P.O. Box 7662
S-103 94 Stockholm 7, 1969

Ulf Nordlinds Mynthandel
A.B., (Hans Hirsch, Ulf
Nordlind)
Nybrogatan 36,
P.O. Box 5132
S-102 43 Stockholm, 1977

SWITZERLAND

Bank Leu AG, Numismatik
(S. Hurter, U. Friedlander, Dr.
A.S. Walker, Dr. L.
Mildenberg, H. Stotz)
Im Gassen 20,
CH-8001 Zurich, 1951

Credit Suisse
Schweizerische Kreditanstalt
Numismatik
(Max Hiltbrand, Miklos Dobal,
Italo Vecchi)
Bundesplatz 2/Marktplatz 49,
CH-3001 Bern, 1976

Galerie Des Monnaies S.A.
6, rue Adhemar-Fabri
P.O. Box 294
CH-1211 Geneva 1, 1975

Hess, AD. AG
(J. Tones)
Haldenstrasse 5,
CH-6000 Luzern, 1951

Monetarium,
Schweizerische Kreditanstalt,
(Dr. G. Giacosa, J.R. Juon, B.
Silk, K. Zimmermann)
Bahnhofstrasse 89, 4.Stock,
CH-8021 Zurich, 1980

Munzen und Medaillen AG
(Prof. H. Cahn, P. Strauss,
Dr. H. Voegtli, Dr. B. Schulte)
Malzgasse 25,
CH-4002 Basel, 1951

Schweizerischer, Bankverein
(Ch. Winterstein, P.
Hiltbrunner, L. Neumann)
Aeschenvorstadt 1
CH-4002 Basel, 1976

Spink & Son Numismatics
Ltd. (J.P. Divo, Sonja Wild)
Lowenstrasse 65
CH-8001 Zurich, 1979

Sternberg, Frank
Schanzengasse 10,
(Bahnhof Stadelhofen)
CH-8001 Zurich, 1957

Stuker, Heiner
Feilengasse 5,
CH-8034 Zurich, 1968

UNITED STATES

Bebee's Inc. (A.E. Bebee)
4514 North 30th St.
Omaha, Neb. 68111, 1955

Berk, Harlan J. Ltd.
2417 W. Jefferson St.,
Joliet, Ill. 60435, 1986

Bullowa, C.E.
(Mrs. Earl E. Moore)
Coinhunter
1616 Walnut Street
Philadelphia, Pa. 19103, 1951

Henry Christensen, Inc.
(William B. Christensen)
P.O. Box 1732
Madison, N.J. 07940, 1956

Coin and Currency Institute
Inc. (Arthur and Ira Friedberg)
223 Main Ave.
Passaic, N.J. 07055, 1951

Coin Galleries
(James Risk, Bob Archer)
123 West 57 St.,
New York, N.Y. 10019, 1978

Cordry, Scott E.
4655 Cass St., Suite 310
P.O. Box 9828,
San Diego, Calif. 92109, 1979

Donner, William, Inc.
(William & Thomas Donner)
P.O. Box 4409
Grand Central Station,
New York, N.Y. 10017, 1968

Elmen, James F.
World-Wide Coins of
California
P.O. Box 3684
Santa Rosa, Calif. 95402, 1986

Ford, John J., Jr.
P.O. Box 706
Rockville Centre,
N.Y. 11571, 1972

Froseth, K.M. Inc.
P.O. Box 23116
Minneapolis, Minn. 55423,
1986

Gillio, Ronald J. Inc.
(Ronald and Dennis Gillio)
Goldmunzen International
1013 State St.,
Santa Barbara, Calif. 93101,
1985

Katen, Frank and Laurese
13311 New Hampshire Ave.
P.O. Box 4047, Colesville,
Silver Spring, Md. 20904, 1951

King, James D.
41 Highview Terrace
Hawthorne, N.J. 07506, 1982

Kreisberg Corporation
344 N. Beverly Dr.
Beverly Hills, Calif. 90210
1954

Malter, Joel L. & Co. Inc.
(Joel and Michael Malter)
16661 Ventura Blvd.,
Suite 518, P.O. Box 777,
Encino, Calif. 91316, 1970

Manfra, Tordella & Brookes,
Inc. (Luis Vigdor, Gina
Tordella, Gerald Bauman)
59 West 49th St.
30 Rockefeller Plaza,
New York, N.Y. 10112, 1983

Margolis, Richard
P.O. Box 2054,
Teaneck, N.J. 07666, 1966

Merkin, Lester
515 Madison Ave., Suite 926
New York, N.Y. 10022, 1961

Numismatic Fine Arts Inc.
(Bruce P. McNall, Steve L.
Rubinger, David Sear)
10100 Santa Monica Blvd.,
6th Floor,
Los Angeles, Calif. 90067, 1978

Rare Coin Co. of America, Inc.
(E. Milas, J. Bernberg)
31 North Clark St.
Chicago, Ill. 60602, 1966

Ross, John G.
12 West Madison St.,
Chicago, Ill. 60602, 1960

Stack's (Harvey, Norman and
Lawrence Stack)
123 West 57th St.
New York, N.Y. 10019, 1960

Steinberg, Robert L. &
William F.
P.O. Box 1565
Boca Raton, Fla. 33432, 1956

Stephens Inc., Karl
P.O. Box 458
Temple City, Calif. 91780,
1981

Subak Co., Carl
(Carl and Jon Subak)
22 West Monroe St.,
Room 1506
Chicago, Ill. 60603, 1977

Superior Stamp & Coin Co.
(Lawrence S., Ira M. and
Mark E. Goldberg)
9478 West Olympic Blvd.
Beverly Hills, Calif. 90212,
1973

Wyatt, Charles E. Inc.
P.O. Box 178623
San Diego, Calif. 92117, 1985

World coin dealer organizations

Canadian Assoc. of Numismatic Dealers
P.O. Box 3145, Station D,
Willowdale, Ontario M2R 3G5 Canada

British Numismatic Trade Association
of the United Kingdom, The Secretary
3c Earlsdon St., Coventry CV5 6EP England

Syndicat National des Experts Numismates
et Numismatique Professionnels
38 rue de Richelieu, F-75001 Paris, France

Verband der Deutsche Munzenhandler e.V.
Anders Ringberg
Achenbachstrasse 3
D-4000 Dusseldorf 1, W. Germany

Verband der Deutschen Munzenhandler e.V.
Mittelweg 54,
D-6000 Frankfurt 1, W. Germany

Verband der Munzhandler im APHV
Klettenberggurtel 60,
D-5000 Koln-Klettenberg, W. Germany

Japan Coin Dealers Association
3-9-9 Kyobashi, Chuo-ku, Tokyo 104, Japan

Verband Schweizerischer Munzenhandler
Erwin Dietrich
Postfach 73 84, CH-8023 Zurich, Switzerland

Organizing a coin club

Organizing a coin club, although not the easiest thing in the world to do, really is not as difficult as it sounds. Actually, the most difficult part of organizing such a club is making the initial move. This move is only difficult in the sense that it requires a leader known for his or her quality of pushing through the idea.

First, the collector thinking of forming such a club should give considerable thought to the matter before making this initial move. If he or she has friends who collect coins, currency or medals, or are in any way interested in the field of numismatics, he or she should contact these friends and determine how they feel about the matter of organizing.

Maybe these friends know of other collectors and they, too, should be contacted, either in person, or if this is not possible, then by telephone or by mail. The next step would be to call a meeting of these people, setting the meeting date for such time as would allow the majority to be present.

Time and place

It is up to the person making the initial move to determine and arrange the meeting place. This can either be at home, at the office, the public library, church social room, bank, city hall, or any of a number of places which usually invite and encourage the use of meeting facilities by the public.

After locating a meeting place, the leader should set the time and date and so notify all interested parties. He or she should also act as temporary chairman at this meeting until activities have progressed to a point where the appointment of a permanent chairman becomes advisable and the members know each other well enough.

Up until now our future coin club has been planned and has moved along without the use of newspaper, or radio and television announcements. These media serve to alert the general public to what is going on around it. And dotted throughout the public are hundreds of others just like our leader and his little band of organizers.

Of the hundreds, there are many who have just been waiting for someone to make the initial move toward organizing a coin club, and there are probably just as many who, although they are collectors, are not interested at this time in becoming a part of such an organization.

If the first meeting can be arranged by the leader without the use of the three public information media, it would be well to do so. The first general meeting should be pre-planned and some sort of a program set up so that the first public meeting can move along smoothly. Nothing can be more irritating than attending a meeting where it appears that all present are unaware of what is happening or should be happening.

Maybe several meetings of the general group are in order before the public meeting is called, but no officers other than a temporary chairman should be named. This matter should be left to the public meeting, and, even then, not at the first public meeting. In fact, this is a part of the organization that should remain open until everyone becomes better acquainted and has had an opportunity to watch and study other members, so that when the first election is held, members will have a pretty good idea of who is best suited to guide the new club through its roughest period, the first year.

At the general meetings (not public) some thought should be given to the questions that will be presented when the public meeting is held, such as the purposes of a coin club and how it will benefit the average collector by arranging trading sessions, auctions, purchasing key or semi-key coins from members at discount prices, and, last but not least, presenting programs designed to increase the numismatic knowledge of not only the club member, but the general public as well, thereby placing the collector in a more understandable position in the eye of the non-collector.

Public meetings

When all of these things have been worked out, it is time to call the first public meeting. This is accomplished to greater advantage by using all three means of public contact, including radio, television and newspaper. Understanding that the average collector is not familiar with the workings of these three services, the following announcement outline may be followed, with changes being made where necessary to fit the situation, in making the first public announcement of intention to organize a coin club.

This form is acceptable to all three news services, and is designed so that in the event your announcement reaches them at an unusually busy time, then the news editor will find it a simple matter to edit the article to fit the space or time available.

News copy should always be typewritten if possible. Handwritten copy presents a problem to the news editor and copy editor, and could result in your story being filed in the "round file," meaning the wastebasket. Following is the proper form to use in calling the public meeting:

A meeting of all area coin collectors and persons interested in other numismatic activities has been called for Friday, Feb. 5, at 7:30 p.m., in the law library of the Good County Courthouse, according to an announcement made today by John Doe of 435 First Street, City.

Doe said the formation of a coin club in the Good County area has been under consideration for some time, and during recent weeks several smaller meetings have been made to prepare for this, the first public meeting.

"There are some 1,900 coin clubs around the country," Doe pointed out in his announcement, "and coin collecting (numismatics) during the past few years has grown." He added that estimates place the number of active collectors at "several million."

The Feb. 5 meeting will be devoted to giving area collectors a chance to meet their fellow collectors, and to outlining the purposes of the new club, should its formation become a reality.

Doe said that purposes of a coin club include holding auctions, holding swap-trade sessions, and arranging for programs with numismatic interest for the beginner, as well as the advanced numismatist.

He urges the attendance of all area collectors, and placed special emphasis on his welcome to the beginning collector.

The preceding announcement should be typed and delivered in person by someone who attended the general meetings. This person should deliver a copy to each of the three news services, radio, television and newspaper, and he or she should be prepared and qualified to answer any questions that the editor or copy editor may ask. He or she should also ask for opinions and advice on the preparation of future news items for broadcast or publication.

Power of the press

It is extremely important that the initial contact with the news reporting people be handled with tact and diplomacy. Do not approach any newspaper or other news medium with the idea that you are there to help them, because they are there to help you, and if the public relations person who is representing your group approaches in a demanding way, he or she is likely to put the new organization in an awkward position, as far as future publicity is concerned. Nothing can be so important to a coin club as good publicity.

Publicity can, one way or another, make or break the club. See that it is handled correctly from the beginning.

When making the initial announcement to the public of the intention to form a coin club, make it far enough in advance to allow potential members time to arrange for their attendance. In addition to the original announcement, spot periodic announcements should also be arranged. These can be made more interesting to the general public by including short paragraphs about scarce or semi-scarce coins, such as the 1950-D Jefferson 5-cent piece. This type of information whets the public's appetite, and may result in adding new members to the hobby.

The saying, "A good picture says more than a thousand words," also holds true in numismatics, and most collectors would be surprised at the willingness of the press to cooperate along this line. A good idea here is to arrange with the newspaper photographer ahead of time, setting a time convenient to him or her, not yourself, for taking a picture. Make the picture interesting by having on hand a supply of numismatic items for possible use as props by the person taking the picture.

A picture of a collector is not newsworthy enough to draw attention, but if this collector is holding or displaying a Lincoln cent, that to the public means nothing, but to a collector represents $20 or $30, then you have an eye-catching photograph, and, again, it may serve as a means of "whetting" the public's appetite.

Invite a reporter to the organizational meeting. It is surprising the appeal an article about numismatics has when it is written by a non-collector. The non-collecting reporter is filled with awe at the fantastic prices being paid today for numismatic items, and the report to the public is another enticement to the beginner or near-beginner.

Go all out to make this reporter your "friend," and keep your relationship that way, because when you lose the publicity, your club will begin slipping. This reporter can also advise your group of the proper method for putting announcements in the newspapers of neighboring towns, where there are additional collectors who may drive to your city to enjoy the fellowship and opportunities offered by association with other collectors.

But all possible assistance should be given the reporter in making sure numismatic terms are properly used since it would be easy for a non-collecting reporter to say things that would be absurd to a collector.

Elections

At the organizational (general) meeting, the first order of business should be electing temporary officers to serve until the club is well organized. Other members should be given committee assignments.

Organize activity for the next meeting, and appoint someone as publicity chairman. The publicity chairman should keep newspapers and radio (and TV if possible) advised of club activity. He or she should contact these news sources immediately after the first meeting, giving names of officers and all other information to attract additional members.

Also, at the first or organizational meeting, a bylaws committee should be appointed to prepare a constitution and a set of bylaws.

This committee will prepare a sample set of rules and present them at the next meeting for approval of members; changes and additions should be made before the constitution and bylaws are approved.

Next, we come to the order of business during meetings. This is usually decided by the president, but can be set aside by majority votes of members present. A good procedure for conducting meetings is as follows:

Call to order by the president or next ranking officer; reading of the minutes of last meeting by the secretary; reading of correspondence by secretary or other person named for this post; reports of officers; reports of board of directors; reports of standing committees; reports of special committees; elections to membership; unfinished business; new business; announcements; presentation of program; adjournment.

In making announcements of intentions to organize a coin club in your community remember that newspapers can do the most good. It isn't necessary for one to be an accomplished writer to have an article placed in a newspaper. Most newspapers will write the article for you, provided you take all necessary information to the newspaper office. Do not phone information unless it is impossible to appear at the newspaper in person.

Newspapers, radio stations, and television stations are constantly on the search for news, and the fact that a coin club is being organized certainly is a news item of importance.

One last request . . . if you are successful in organizing a new club, please let us know at *Coin World,* and when you decide where the organizational meeting will be held, let us have plenty of information in time to reach readers before the meeting is held.

We keep our *Coin World* club files as up-to-date as possible but cooperation from every club — new and old — is vital. Letters may be addressed to: Club Center, Coin World, P.O. Box 150, Sidney, Ohio. 45365.

Exhibits

If one starts with a poor selection of numismatic material, he or she will have a poor selection when the display is completed, despite the sophistication of color, lights, and plastic. On the other hand, if two displays are of equal material, the more attractively arranged exhibit could easily win the judge's nod.

Prior to considering the display, one should bear in mind a central theme, if any, and where the display will be exhibited.

If your display will be in a case at a club meeting, one arrangement may be called for. In a bank lobby or a store show window, something else may be necessary. One must consider security, lighting, distance from the viewing public to the exhibit and even height of the display if it will have an audience of children.

If one is entering a display competitively, especially away from his or her home club, each exhibitor deserves a copy of the grading standards and categories that will be accepted for judging. Some clubs will take off as much as 30 out of 100 points if an exhibit is not in a case of a certain size. Homemade cases, currency displays, revolving globes, etc., can lose so much under such rules that a contestant has no chance of winning unless he or she does conform to the local display rules.

There seems to be a tendency that the larger the occasion, the larger the exhibit must be. Too often this means showing all of one's coins or medals, when a single phase of a display could be more effective. A person with a large collection can do more with a small exhibit than trying to spread a whole collection over the wall, and trying to win on quantity.

Win on quality.

"Numismatic information" conveyed by the display rates high on a judge's point list. What is numismatic information? To some, the coin on display is the exhibit, and what more information would one need?

This could be a collector's line of thinking, but it will probably not satisfy the judges. Typed information on a sheet about the designer of the coin, the Act of Congress which authorized the coin, the economic conditions which brought about its issuance, metallic content, acceptance by the public, and if no longer in use, acts and conditions which brought its demise, could all be called numismatic information.

Pictures of the designer, other medals or coins attributed to the designer and pictures of the original model on the coin could be used to effectively catch the viewer's eye.

A word of caution on display of "off-metal" coins and counterfeits. While a display containing these items may be educational, there is a good chance they could be confiscated by the government off the display table. It is against the law for an American to hold any counterfeit coin of any nation.

The Treasury Department has ruled that off-metal coins, such as a cent on a dime planchet, are illegal for collectors to hold. If a collector is to display these items, it would be best to obtain Treasury or Secret Service clearance prior to doing so and display the authorization with the "coin."

Perhaps primitive money, items used as barter material, would be a good beginning on what to display. The specialist in this field often tends to put all his or her primitive material in one case, leaving out pictures, uses of the material, and descriptions.

It might be better to show Indian Wampum, for instance, and pictures of Indians wearing it, trading it, how they made it, how it was made into long strings, how it is displayed in museums today.

The same could be done for ivory. Elephant tusks and whale teeth have been used for money, and just a display of pictures of obtaining the ivory and its uses in barter would make an attractive, informative display.

First the Book　　　　**21**

First the book

An oft-repeated adage by longtime numismatists is "First the book and then the coin." We at *Coin World* believe that to be an important philosophy that every collector, especially the beginner, should adopt.

Books are an open door to knowledge, and knowledge is power. Knowledge is also history, art, politics and science — subjects which numismatics has to offer in large quantities. Knowledge is never dull, and is invaluable in the hobby.

Books, when used properly, arm the potential buyer with the knowledge to buy numismatic material intelligently, and the seller to sell wisely. Investors will find advice from market analysts to consider when investing in the market.

The editors of this almanac believe every collector and investor should have his own library, whether it is just a few books or a multi-volume library that gives its owner hours of enjoyment. A good numismatic library is essential for full enjoyment of the hobby, and we have found that most collectors will turn from their collections to their library as their thirst for knowledge grows.

Where does one buy numismatic books? A good, economical place to start is category 181 of *Coin World* classified advertisements, "coin books." Dealers advertising in this section offer the latest in numismatic books, as well as the useful volumes published earlier, often at competitive prices. Purchasing numismatic books through advertisements introduces buyers to numismatic book specialists. They often conduct mail-bid sales and auctions of out-of-print books, many of which bring high prices, but also others which are within the budgets of most collectors.

Other sources of books include local coin dealers, newsstands and book stores. Both businesses should be able to order books not in their stocks from wholesalers or directly from the publisher. Coin dealers often bring books with them to coin shows and conventions. Larger conventions often have dealers who deal exclusively in numismatic books.

Major libraries have selections of numismatic books. Librarians are always willing to consider requests and recommendations about books they might want to buy for the library. Collectors should consider a visit to the local library, armed with a list of books they would like to see on its shelves. Some coin clubs purchase and deposit books in their local library to serve the general public.

Many small coin clubs have libraries, usually maintained by an officer, and the books are available for members to borrow.

Membership in the American Numismatic Association offers two special advantages: The world's largest free, circulating numismatic library, and a numismatic book club that offers newly published books at substantial discounts from the retail price. The ANA library has 35,000 circulating volumes, most available only for a few dollars each to cover postage and insurance both ways.

Volumes available in the ANA library cover all aspects of U.S. and world numismatics: coins, paper money, tokens, medals, orders and decorations, and stocks and bonds. In addition to books, the library has one of the finest selections of auction catalogs in the world plus a wide range of numismatic periodicals, including more than 26 years of *Coin World* on microfilm.

ANA members may borrow all materials from the library, except for rare books and catalogs. Items can be ordered by telephone or through the mail by author, title or call number (listed in the library catalog); auction catalogs should be requested by name of the auctioneer and date of the sale. Periodicals can be ordered by title and issue date or volume and issue number. Material is loaned for six weeks, and may be renewed for a second six weeks if there are no other requests for the material. Requests to borrow must be accompanied by the borrower's ANA membership number.

When borrowing by mail, members pay postage and insurance both ways. Insurance fees are based on value of the items borrowed; if the material is shipped back inadequately insured and is lost, the borrower is expected to make up the difference. The average cost of shipping most ANA library material is less than $2.

The following books are recommended by *Coin World* staff members because these are the books they turn to most often when researching, answering a letter from a reader, or writing an article for publication. *Coin World* has a working reference library. The lists are not meant to be complete, and in fact many good, useful specialized books do not appear on these lists. For a complete listing and scope of numismatic literature, the ANA Library catalog of 768 pages has no equal; a 1985 supplement is 113 pages long.

Books listed here should be available in the United States, although many in the sections concerning world material and ancients are published in other countries. Some of the books are out of print, though available through some numismatic book dealers. Other older volumes have been reprinted in modern editions. For the ordinary collector, these inexpensive reprints are recommended over the expensive original editions, some centuries old and collector's items themselves.

An introduction to books in these listings should inspire readers to explore the entire numismatic publishing field for more scope. These just touch the surface.

U.S. coins
General works

Annual Report of the Director of the Mint. United States Mint, Department of the Treasury, issued annually. An invaluable source for numismatists with mintage figures, photographs of new coins and medals, reports about new coinage programs, reports

about technology changes at the Mint, charts about gold and silver deposits to Mint and more. May be ordered from the United States Mint, Treasury Department, Washington, D.C. 20220.

Coin Collecting Made Easy: Basic Knowledge for the Coin Collector and Investor. Staff of *Coin World.* Amos Press Inc., Sidney, Ohio, 1981, with 1982 second printing, 1986 third printing and 1987 fourth printing. This softcover work offers information for the beginning collector and investor, both youths and adults.

Coin World Almanac. Staff of *Coin World.* Amos Press Inc., Sidney, Ohio. Four earlier editions dated 1976, 1977, 1978 and 1984.

The Catalogue & Encyclopedia of U.S. Coins. Taxay, Don. Scott Publishing Co., New York, 1976. Includes patterns, rarity ratings for many pieces, pedigrees of rarer coins and all regular issues, commemoratives, Colonials, state issues and pioneer gold.

A Guide Book of United States Coins. Yeoman, R.S. Western Publishing Co., Racine, Wis., annually since 1947. The basic catalog listing of U.S. Colonial, state, Mint and commemorative coins, plus pioneer gold; the "Red Book."

A Handbook of United States Coins. Yeoman, R.S. Western Publishing Co., Racine, Wis., annually. Formerly hard-cover, now softcover, this guide is for the beginning collector of U.S. coins; the "Blue Book."

The History of United States Coinage as Illustrated by the Garrett Collection. Bowers, Q. David. Bowers and Ruddy Galleries Inc., Los Angeles, Calif., 1979. Covers the history of U.S. coins and collecting, with numerous letters and other documents quoted extensively.

The Macmillan Encyclopedic Dictionary of Numismatics. Doty, Richard G. Macmillan Publishing Co., New York, 1982. Illustrated dictionary, plus bibliography.

Numismatic Art in America. Vermeule, Cornelius. Belknap Press of Harvard University Press, Cambridge, Mass., 1971. Examines the aesthetics of U.S. coinage, and traces development of engraving skills of U.S. engravers.

Official American Numismatic Association Grading Standards for United States Coins. ANA and Western Publishing Co. Racine, Wis., 1987. Black-and-white photos of all regular issues in most conditions from Mint State 70 to About Good 3, plus section about commems. (Earlier editions have line illustrations.)

U.S. Mint and Coinage. Taxay, Don. Durst Numismatic Publications, New York, 1983 (reprint of 1966 book). Early history of U.S. Mint and minting processes in detail, plus history from mid-19th century to current coinage.

Special series

California Pioneer Fractional Gold. Breen, Walter, and Gillio, Ronald J. Pacific Coast Auctions Galleries Inc., Santa Barbara, Calif. 1983. Catalog listing of varieties of California fractional gold, including black and white photos of most coins.

The Early Coins of America. Crosby, Sylvester S. Quarterman Publications Inc., New York, 1983 (facsimile reprint of 1875 book). Covers all Colonial, Confederation and state issues, with extracts from authorizing legislation, plus plates.

Encyclopedia of United States and Colonial Proof Coins 1722-1977. Breen, Walter. FCI Press Inc., Albertson, N.Y., 1977. Historical information and pedigrees about U.S. Proofs, with sections covering branch Mint Proofs and fantasy and restrike pieces.

The Encyclopedia of United States Silver & Gold Commemorative Coins. Breen, Walter, and Swiatek, Anthony. Arco Publishing Inc., New York, 1981. Historical and investment information about all U.S. commemorative coinage through 1954.

Private Gold Coins and Patterns of the United States. Kagin, Donald H. Arco Publishing Inc., 1981, History and catalog of pioneer gold, excluding fractional parts of a dollar.

United States Pattern, Experimental and Trial Pieces Judd, J. Hewitt, and Kosoff, A. Western Publishing Co. Inc., 1982. Covers all non-issued U.S. coin designs in catalog form, with illustrations, pedigrees, rarity ratings and recut prices.

U.S. copper coins

American Half Cents. Cohen, Roger S. Wigglesworth & Ghatt Co., Arlington, Va., 1982. Catalog listing of all known half cent varieties, with photos accompanying listings.

America's Copper Coinage 1783-1857. American Numismatic Society, 1985. Features articles about state and federal copper coinage through the demise of the large cent. Reprints of papers presented at the ANS's 1984 Coinage of the Americas Conference.

Encyclopedia of United States Half Cents 1793-1857. Breen, Walter. American Institute of Numismatic Research, South Gate, Calif., 1984. Historical information and pedigrees, plus catalog listing of all known half cent varieties, with photos accompanying the listings.

The Fugio Cents. Kessler, Alan. Colony Coin Co., Newtonville, Mass., 1976. A catalog listing of varieties of the United States' first coinage, with historical information.

Penny Whimsy. Sheldon, William H. Quarterman Publications Inc., Lawrence, Mass., 1983 (reprint of 1958 edition, 1976 copyright). Catalog listing of known varieties of large cents from 1793 to 1814, with plates in back.

The Two-Cent Piece and Varieties. Kliman, Myron M. Sanford J. Durst Numismatic Publications, New York, 1983. Catalog listing of known varieties, with no photos.

United States Copper Cents 1816-1857. Newcomb, Howard R. Quarterman Publications Inc., Lawrence, Mass., 1981 (facsimile reprint of 1944 book). Catalog listing of known varieties of later large cents, with plates in back.

United States Copper Coins — An Action Guide for the Collector and Investor. Bowers, Q. David. Bowers and Merena Inc., Wolfeboro, N.H., 1984. Covers half cents, large cents, small cents and 2-cent pieces with historical information and investment advice.

U.S. silver dollars

The Comprehensive Catalogue and Encyclopedia of U.S. Morgan and Peace Silver Dollars. Van Allen, Leroy C., and Mallis, A. George. Arco Publishing Co., New York, 1976. Historical information and catalog listing of all known varieties.

The Fantastic 1804 Dollar. Bressett, Kenneth E., and Newman, Eric. P. Whitman Publishing Co., Racine, Wis., 1962. A wonderful numismatic mystery is solved in this in-depth study of the 1804 dollar, one of the United States' greatest rarities.

The Morgan and Peace Dollar Textbook. Miller, Wayne. Adam Smith Publishing Co., Metairie, La., 1982.

The United States Early Silver Dollars from 1794 to 1803. Bolender, M.H. Krause Publications, Iola, Wis., 1980 (revised reprint of 1950 book). Catalog listing of dollar varieties, with plates in back.

The United States Trade Dollar. Willem, John M. Sanford J. Durst Numismatic Publications, New York, 1983 (reprint of 1959 edition). Historical treatment of the Trade dollar, with mintages by month, varieties and rarity levels.

U.S. silver half dollars

Early Half Dollar Varieties. Overton, Al C. Colorado Springs, Colo., 1970. Catalog listing of all known varieties, with photos accompanying listings.

The Walking Liberty Half Dollar. Swiatek, Anthony. Sanford J. Durst Numismatic Publications, New York, 1983. Catalog listing, with emphasis on distinguishing between strong strikes and weak strikes.

U.S. silver quarter dollars

The Early Quarter Dollars of the United States. Browning, A.W. Sanford J. Durst Numismatic Publications, New York, 1977 (reprint of 1925 book). Catalog listing of known varieties, with plates at back.

Standing Liberty Quarters. Cline, J.H. Cline's Rare Coins, Palm Harbor, Fla., 1986. Historical information, including correspondence between designer and Treasury officials, plus catalog listing and investment advice.

U.S. silver dimes

Encyclopedia of United States Liberty Seated Dimes. Ahwash, Kamal M. Kamal Press, 1977. Catalog listings of known varieties, with over-sized photos accompanying listings.

Early United States Dimes: 1796-1837. Davis, David J.; Logan, Russell J.; Lovejoy, Allen F.; McCloskey, John W.; Subjack, William L. John Reich Collectors Society, 1984. Catalog of known varieties for Draped Bust and Capped Bust dimes, with over-sized photos accompanying listings.

U.S. silver half dimes

The United States Half Dimes. Valentine, Daniel W. Quarterman Publications Inc., Lawrence, Mass., 1975 (reprint of 1931 book). Valentine catalog listing, plus updated information by other individuals.

U.S. gold coins

United States Gold Coins, an Illustrated History. Bowers, Q. David. Bowers & Ruddy Galleries, Los Angeles, 1982. The history of U.S. gold coins.

U.S. Gold Dollars through *U.S. Double Eagles.* Akers, David W. Paramount Publications, Englewood, Ohio, 1975-1982. A series of six books covering gold dollars, quarter eagles, $3 and $4 gold pieces, half eagles, eagles, and double eagles; basically it records auction appearances by denomination, date and Mint mark.

United States Gold Patterns. Akers, David W. Paramount International Coin Corp., Engle-wood, Ohio, 1975. Subtitled "A photographic study of the gold patterns struck at the United States Mint from 1836 to 1907."

U.S. exonumia

The Atwood-Coffee Catalogue of United States and Canadian Transportation Tokens. Coffee Jr., John M., and Ford, Harold V. The American Vecturist Association, Boston, 1983. The book catalogs mass transportation tokens and similar items, based on earlier Atwood system and catalog. Other volumes catalog minor die varieties and record the history of the transportation token.

Early American Tokens, Hard Times Tokens, U.S. Merchant Tokens 1845-1860, United States Trade Tokens 1866-1889, Tokens of the Gay Nineties 1890-1900. Rulau, Russell. Krause Publication, Iola, Wis., 1981-1983. Five volumes in a planned series listing of all U.S. merchant tokens (except Civil War pieces) and related pieces in a soft-cover catalog format.

Medals of the United States Mint — The First Century 1792-1892. Julian, Robert W. Token and Medal Society Inc., 1977. Massive historical work covering all medallic works produced by the Mint during its first 100 years.

Medals of the United States Mint Issued for Sale. Department of the Treasury, 1972. Lists medals struck by the Mint of which it sells duplicates; does not list the many medals it struck and does not sell.

Patriotic Civil War Tokens. Fuld, George, and Fuld, Melvin. Civil War Token Society, 1982 (released 1984). Catalog lists all Civil War patriotic tokens, with historical information and chapters on related topics.

So-Called Dollars. Hibler, Harold E., and Kappen, Charles V. The Coin and Currency Institute, New York, 1963. Covers commemorative and exposition medals of near-dollar size in catalog format, listing metal varieties and historical information.

U.S. Civil War Store Cards. Fuld, George, and Fuld, Melvin. Quarterman Publications, Lawrence, Mass., 1975. Catalogs all Civil War store cards by city and state, with historical information.

Video Arcade, Pinball, Slot Machine, and Other Amusement Tokens of North America. Alpert, Stephen A., and Smith, Kenneth E. Amusement Token Collectors Association, Redondo Beach, Calif., 1984. It catalogs all known amusement tokens by state, province and miscellaneous categories.

Counterfeit detection

Counterfeit Detection. Staff of the American Numismatic Association Certification Service. American Numismatic Association, Colorado Springs, Colo., two volumes, 1983 and 1987. Reprints ANACS's columns appearing in *The Numismatist,* discussing and illustrating counterfeits and genuine specimens of dozens of U.S. coins, plus information about collectible varieties and ANACS procedures.

Counterfeits of U.S. States Coins. Spanbauer, Larry. Service Litho-Print Inc., Oshkosh, Wis., 1975. Illustrates many Colonial, private Mint and modern counterfeits and replicas.

Detecting Counterfeit Coins, Book 1. Devine, "Lonesome" John. Heigh Ho Printing Co., Newbury Park, Calif., 1975. Illustrates and describes many counterfeit U.S. minor and silver coins.

Detecting Counterfeit Gold Coins, Book 2. Devine, "Lonesome" John. Heigh Ho Printing Co., Newbury Park, Calif., 1977. Illustrates and describes many counterfeit gold coins.

Grading

The Accugrade System. Hager, Alan. Silver Dollars Unlimited Inc., Bedford, N.Y., 1984, Accugrade Inc., Greenwich, Conn. 1986. A three-volume guide to grading Uncirculated, Proof and prooflike Morgan, Peace and Eisenhower dollars.

Grading Coins: A Collection of Readings. Edited by Bagg, Richard, and Jelinski, James J. Essex Publications, Portsmouth, N.H., 1977. Collection of articles about grading from *The Numismatist, Whitman Numismatic Journal* and *Numismatic Scrapbook Magazine* from 1892 to 1976. Takes a historical approach.

A Guide to the Grading of United States Coins. Brown, Martin R. and Dunn, John W. General Distributors Inc., Denison, Texas, 1980. Uses line illustrations for U.S. coins in all denominations from half cent to double eagle in all grades.

NCI Grading Guide. Halperin, James L. Ivy Press, 1986, Dallas, Texas. Written by a principle grader of the Numismatic Certification Institute. Provides a step-by-step approach to the grading of Uncirculated and Proof coins. Does not cover circulated grades.

New Photograde. Ruddy, James F. Bowers and Ruddy Galleries Inc., Los Angeles, Calif., 1972. Photographic guide to the grading of U.S. coins in all denominations from half cent to double eagle.

Official American Numismatic Association Grading Standards for United States Coins. Bressett, Kenneth, and Kosoff, A. Whitman Numismatic Products, Western Publishing, Racine, Wis., 1987. Official ANA guide to grading U.S. coins; third edition (1987) uses black-and-white photographs; first two editions use line illustrations. Includes non-illustrated guide to grading U.S. commemorative coins.

Errors

The Classification and Value of Errors on the Lincoln Cent. Cohen, Jean. Bonita Springs, Fla., 1969. Out of print. Illustrates through line drawings minor errors on Lincoln cents, and lists their (outdated) values.

The Design Cud. Marvin, Paul, and Margolis, Arnold. Heigh Ho Printing Co., Newbury Park, Calif., 1979. In-depth explanation and photographs of how major die breaks, cuds, occur.

The Encyclopedia of Doubled Dies, Vol. 1 and 2. Wexler, John A. Robert C. Wilharm News Printing Co. Inc., Fort Worth, Texas, 1978 and 1981. Illustrates and describes doubled dies on U.S. coins, and how they occur.

How Error Coins are Made at the U.S. Mints. Margolis, Arnold. Heigh Ho Printing Co., Newbury Park, Calif., 1981. Describes and illustrates how coins are minted and how error coins occur.

Modern Mint Mistakes. Steiner, Phillip, and Zimpfer, Michael. Whispering Pines Printing, Indiana, 1975-1976. Provides general information and a price guide to error coins.

Official Price Guide to Mint Errors and Varieties. Herbert, Alan. House of Collectibles Inc., Orlando, Fla., 1981. Offers a general, overall look at error coins.

The RPM Book. Wexler, John A., and Miller, Tom. Lonesome John Publishing Co., Newbury Park, Calif., 1983. Describes and illustrates repunched and over Mint marks, with price information.

U.S. paper money

U.S. government issues

Bureau of Engraving and Printing — The First Hundred Years 1862-1962. Sanford J. Durst Numismatic Publications, New York, 1978 (reprint of 1962 book published by the Treasury Department). Government history tracing history of BEP and government-issued paper money, postage stamps and revenue items.

The Comprehensive Catalog of U.S. Paper Money. Hessler, Gene. BNR Press, Port Clinton, Ohio, 1983. Catalog listings of government issues, with historical information.

The Encyclopedia of United States Fractional & Postal Currency. Friedberg, Milton. Numismatic and Antiquarian Service Corporation of America, Long Island, N.Y., 1978. Historical information and catalog of federal fractional notes of Civil War and Reconstruction.

Military Payment Certificates. Schwan, Fred. BNR Press, Port Clinton, Ohio, 1981. Covers notes issued for use by U.S. military personnel stationed overseas from 1946 to 1973.

Paper Money of the United States. Friedberg, Robert. Krause Publications, Iola, Wis., 1986. Catalog listings, with numbering system that is used hobby-wide.

Standard Catalog of National Bank Notes. Hickman, John, and Oakes, Dean. Krause Publications, Iola, Wis., 1982. Lists 117,007 different national bank notes in catalog fashion, plus historical information.

Standard Handbook of Modern United States Paper Money. O'Donnell, Chuck. Krause Publications, Iola, Wis., 1982. For collectors of small-sized notes, with complete listings of all blocks and star blocks issued, varieties and quantities produced.

Non-federal issues

America's Currency 1789-1866. American Numismatic Society, New York City, 1985. Examines paper money in the United States as issued by private issuers and local and state governments. Reprints papers presented at the 1985 Coinage of the Americas Conference.

Confederate and Southern States Currency. Criswell, Grover C. Criswell's Publications, Florida, 1976. Covers all CSA issues, plus states issues of the Civil War.

The Early Paper Money of America. Newman, Eric P. Western Publishing Co., Racine, Wis., 1976. Covers all paper money issued by the Continental Congress, 13 original Colonies.

Society of Paper Money Collectors Wismer update series. The SPMC has published a series of catalogs of obsolete notes by state and territory. Books available from the SPMC (see numismatic organizations chapter) include Rhode Island, Florida, Mississippi, Texas, Iowa, Minnesota, Alabama, Maine, Indiana, New Jersey, Vermont, Arkansas, Pennsylvania and a volume covering the Indian Territory, Oklahoma and Kansas.

Ancients
Ancient Greece

Greek Coins & Their Values. Sear, David R. Seaby Publications Ltd., London, England, 1978. Two volumes; Europe, and Asia and Africa in catalog form.

An Outline of Ancient Greek Coins. Klawans, Zander H. Western Publishing Co. Inc., Racine, Wis. (1982 reprint by Sanford J. Durst, New York, N.Y.). Identified and explains Greek coinage in general form.

Historia Numorum. Head, Barclay V. Oxford, England, 1911 (1983 reprint of 1911 work by Sanford J. Durst, New York, N.Y.). Comprehensive catalog of ancient Greek city-state coinage.

Greek Coins. Seltman, Charles, Spink & Son, London, 1977. A history of metallic currency and coinage down to the fall of the Hellenistic kingdoms.

Greek Coin Types and Their Identification. Plant, Richard. Seaby, London, 1979. Line drawings help to identify Greek coins.

Dictionary of Greek Coin Inscriptions. Icard, Severin, Sanford Durst, New York, 1979. This is a comprehensive reference for translating Greek coin inscriptions.

Ancient Greek & Roman Coins: A Handbook. Hill, Sir George F. Argonaut, Chicago, 1964.

Greek Imperial Coins and Their Values. Sear, David R. Seaby Publications Ltd., London, England, 1982. General catalog of the subject; illustrated.

Roman Republic

The Coinage of the Roman Republic. Sydenham, Edward A. Spink & Son, Ltd., London, England. 1952 (1982 reprint of 1952 work by Sanford, J. Durst, New York, N.Y.). Catalog with historical entries on the field in general.

Descripcion General de las Monedas de la Republica Romana (General Description of the Money of the Roman Republic). Cohen, Por H. Chez M. Curt, London & Paris, 1857 (1976 reprint of 1857 work by Juan R. Cayon, Madrid, Spain). Catalog with historical entries on the field in general.

Roman Republic Coinage. Crawford, Michael H. Cambridge University Press, London, 1974. Two volumes. A comprehensive catalog of Roman Republican coins.

Roman Silver Coins. Seaby, H.A. Seaby, London. Four volumes. A catalog of Roman silver coins.

Roman Empire

Roman Coins and Their Values. Sear, David R. Seaby Publications Ltd., London, England, 1981. Catalog form of the field in general.

Roman Imperial Coins. Klawans, Zander H. Western Publishing Co. Inc., Racine, Wis., 1977 (1982 reprint of 1977 work by Sanford J. Durst, New York, N.Y.). Identifies and explains Imperial Roman coins in general form.

The Roman Imperial Coinage. Mattingly, Harold, edited by Edward A. Sydenham, Spink & Son. Ltd., London, England, 1968 (1968 reprint of the 1884 work). Catalog form, eight volumes, contents: 1. Augustus to Vitellius, 2. Vespasian to Hadrian, 3. Antoninus Pius to Commodus, 4. Pertinax to Geta & Macrinus to Pupienus & Gordian III to Urania Antoninus, 5. Valerian I to Florian, Probus to Amandus, 6. Diocletian's reform to death of Maximinus, 7. Constantine & Licinius, 8. Valentinian I to Theodosius I.

Reading and Dating Roman Imperial Coins. Klawans, Zander H. Sanford Durst, New York, 1982. Simple guide for identifying and attributing Roman coins.

Judaea

Handy Guide to Jewish Coins. Rogers, Edgar, Spink & Son Ltd., London, England, 1914 (1982 reprint of 1914 work by Sanford J. Durst, New York, N.Y.). Catalog form on the field in general.

Sylloge Nummorum Graecorum, (Sylloge of Greek Money). American Numismatic Society, New York, N.Y. 1981. Part six Palestine-South Arabia volume only. Comprehensive catalog form of the field from the ANS collection.

Moneys of the Bible: An Illustrated Digest of the Coinage of Biblical Times with Scriptural References. Yeoman, R.S. Whitman, Racine, Wis., 1961.

Ancient Jewish Coinage. Meshorer Ya'akov, Amphora Books, N.Y., 1982. Two volumes in catalog form covering 1) Persian period-Hasmonaeons, and 2) Herod the Great-Bar Cochba.

Catalog of Judaea Capta Coinage. Brin, Howard B. Minnesota, 1986. Complete listing of Judaea Capta coins; illustrated.

The Coinage of the Bar Kokhba War. Mildenberg, Leo. Verlag Sauerlander. Frankfurt am Main, West Germany, 1984. Examines coinage of Jews in Judaea about A.D. 132-135.

Other ancient empires

An Introduction to the Coinage of Parthia. Sellwood, David, Spink & Son Ltd., London, England, 1971. Catalog form of the field in general.

Chinese Currency. Schjoth, Fr. Andrew Publ. Co., London, England, 1929 (1976 reprint of 1929 work by W & J Mackay Ltd., Chatham, England). Catalog format with line drawings.

Coins in China's History. Coole, Arthur Braddan, Inter-Collegiate Press, 1965. Comprehensive, historical overview of Chinese numismatics including a time line relating events in China with events in the Western world.

Imperial Persian Coinage. Hill, George F. Obol International, Oak Park, Ill., 1968. Catalog form of the field of the Persian Empire.

Sasandische Numismatik, (Sassanian Numismatics). Gobl, Robert, Klinkhardt & Biermann, Braunschweig, West Germany, 1968. Catalog form of the field of Sassanian coinage.

Medieval
General Medieval works

The Coinage of the European Continent. Hazlitt, W. Carew, Swan Sonnenschein & Co., London, England, 1893 (1974 reprint of the 1893 work by Ares Publ. Enc., Chicago, Ill.). General text with data on the subject.

Medieval European Coinage with a Catalogue of the Coins in the Fitzwilliam Museum. Grierson, Philip, and Blackburn, Mark. Cambridge University Press, England, 1986. First in a series of books about medieval coinage.

Reading Medieval European Coins. Walker, Ralph S. Attic Books Ltd., New York, N.Y. 1979. Basic book on how to decipher inscriptions on medieval coins.

The Dated European Coinage Prior to 1501. Frey, Albert R. American Journal of Numismatics, New York, N.Y., 1915 (1978 reprint of the 1915 work by Sanford J. Durst, New York, N.Y.). Catalog of all Christian dated coins before 1501.

Die Ritter von Schulthess-Rechberg'sche Munz-u. Medaillen-Sammlung (The Knights of Schulthess-Rechberg, Money and Medals). Erbstein, Julius and Albert. Quarterman, Boston, 1974 (reprint of 1869 edition). Invaluable in identifying coins not cataloged elsewhere.

Beschreibung der Bekanntesten Kupfermunzen (Description of Copper Money). Neumann, Josef. Johnson Reprint Corp., New

York, 1965 (reprint of 1858 edition). Seven volumes. Very useful reference for identifying copper coins of Europe.

Austria

The Coinage of Medieval Austria, 1156-1521. Szego, Alfred, A. Szego Publ., West Sayville, N.Y. 1970. A basic outline on the subject.

Corpus Nummorum: Moser/Tursky, Die Munzen Kaiser Rudolfs II aus der Munzstatte Hall in Tirol 1602-1612. Lanz, Dr. Herbert. Numismatik, Munich, West Germany, 1987. Comprehensive syllogue about the subject; illustrated.

Byzantine

Byzantine Coins and their Values. Sear, David R. Seaby Publishing Ltd., London, England, 1974. General catalog on the subject, illustrated.

Byzantine Coins. Grierson, Philip, University of California Press, Berkeley & Los Angeles, Calif., 1982. Text with charts and tables on the subject, very detailed.

Imperial Byzantine Coins in the British Museum. Wroth, Warwick. Argonaut Inc., Chicago, Ill., 1966. Detailed catalog format with photographic plates and charts.

Moneta Imperii Byzantini. Hahn, Wolfgang. Vienna, Austria, 1981. Three-volume illustrated set covering subject from 491-720. Volume I: Anastasius I to Justinian I; Volume II: Justin II to Phocas; Volume III: Heraclius to Leo II.

England

England Hammered Coinage. North, J.J. Spink & Son Ltd., London, England, 1960. Two volumes in catalog form, illustrated.

Coins of England and the United Kingdom. Seaby, Peter. Seaby Publications, London, England, 1984. Catalog of ancient, medieval and modern coins of the realm. A new edition is printed annually.

France

Carolingian Coinage of France. Morrison, Karl F. Karl F. Morrison & Henry Grunthal, New York, N.Y., 1967. Maps, notes and monograms; part of the ANS series.

The Barbaric Tremissis in Spain & Southern France. American Numismatic Society, New York, N.Y. 1964. Notes and monograms; part of the ANS series.

Catalogue General Illustre et a Prix Marques en Francs or de Monnaies Francaises Provinciales (General Illustrated Catalog of the Money of France and the Provinces). Boudeau, E. Nouvelle ed., Maastricht,

Netherlands, 1970. Catalog format with illustrations and maps, text in French language.

Germany

Germanic Coinages, Charlemagne Through Wilhelm II. Craig, William D. Wm. D. Craig, Mountain View, Calif., 1954. General work with illustrations on the subject.

Altdeutschland 768-1806 (Old Germany). Ernst Battenberg, Munich, West Germany, ca. 1975 (1982 reprint of 1975 work by Sanford Durst, New York, N.Y.). Catalog format of general work in German language.

The Coinage of South Germany in the Thirteen Century. Metcalf, David M. Spink & Son Ltd., London England, 1961. Catalog format on the subject.

Islamic countries

Oriental Coins and Their Values, The World of Islam. Mitchiner, Michael, Hawkins Publications, London, England, 1977. Catalog form with photographs and some historical facts.

A Catalogue of the Muhammadan Coins in the British Museum. Walker, John, British Museum, London, England, 1956. Two volumes: 1) Arab-Sassanian coins, 2) Arab-Byzantine & post-reform Umaiyad coins.

Oriental Coins and Their Values, the Ancient & Classical World 600 B.C.-A.D. 650. Mitchiner, Michael. Hawkins Publications, London, 1978. Contains much information on ancient coins from this area not found elsewhere.

Italy

The Venetian Tornesello: A Medieval Colonial Coinage. Stahl, Alan. American Numismatic Society, New York, 1985.

Modern
General works

World Coin Catalogue, Twentieth Century. Schon, Gunter. Simon and Schuster, New York, 1982. Catalog form with listings by country, hard-cover.

A Catalog of Modern World Coins, 1850-1964. Yeoman, Richard S. The Coin and Currency Institute, Fort Lee, N.J. 13th edition. Catalog form.

Current Coins of the World. Yeoman, Richard S. Whitman Publ. Co., Racine, Wis. seventh edition. Catalog form.

Standard Price Guide to World Crowns & Talers, 1484-1968. Draskovic, Frank & Rubenfeld, Stuart. Krause Publ., Iola, Wis. 1984. Catalog form.

Standard Catalog of World Coins. Krause, Chester L. & Mishler, Clifford. Krause Publ., Iola, Wis., 1987. Catalog form.

Gold Coins of the World. Friedberg, Robert, Coin and Currency Institute Inc., New York, N.Y., 1980. Catalog format.

The Beauty & Lore of Coins, Currency & Medals. Clain-Stefanelli, E. & V. Riverwood Publ., Croton-on-Hudson, N.Y., 1974.

The Art of Coins & Their Photography. Hoberman, Gerald. Spink & Son Ltd., London, 1981.

Numismatic Bilbliography. Clain-Stefanelli, Elvira Eliza. Battenberg, Munich, West Germany, 1985. A comprehensive listing by subject of numismatic books.

Dictionary of Numismatic Names with Addenda. Frey, Albert R. Spink's, London, 1973. A comprehensive dictionary of numismatic terms, which includes a glossary of equivalent terms in English, French, German, Italian and Swedish.

Coins of the World. Carson, R.A.G. Harper & Brothers, New York, 1962. A brief numismatic history of virtually every country which has issued coins from ancient times to modern.

Biographical Dictionary of Medallists. Forrer, L. A.H. Baldwin & Sons, London. 8 volumes. A comprehensive encyclopedia listing coin and medal engravers and their works from ancient times to modern.

Africa, general works

The Silver Dollars of Africa. Davenport, John S. Whitman Publ. Co., Racine, Wis., 1959. Catalog format with photographs.

Australia

Renniks Australian Coin and Banknote Guide. Skinner, Dion H. Skinner & Warnes, Salisbury Heights, South Australia, 1976. Catalog form with illustrations, later editions exist.

Coins & Tokens of Tasmania. McNeice, Roger V. Platypus Publ., Hobart, Australia, 1969. Text with some photographs.

Coinage and Currency in New South Wales, 1788-1829. Mira, W.J.D. Wentwork Press, New South Wales, Australia, 1981. Text and almanac form with some photographs.

Austria

Osterreichische Munzpragungen von 1657-1969 (Austrian Money from 1657-1969). Herinek, Ludwig. Herinek, Munzhandlung, Vienna, 1970. Two volumes. Catalog with illustrations of Austrian coins.

Bolivia

The Coins of Bolivia. Seppa, Dale. Almanzar's, San Antonio, Texas, 1970.

Canada

The Charlton Standard Catalogue of Canadian Coins. Charlton, James. The Charlton Press, Toronto, Canada, 1987. Catalog form with prices.

Standard Grading Guide to Canadian Decimal Coins. Charlton, James E. & Willey, Robert C. Whitman Publ. Co., Racine Wis., 1965. Line drawing guide to grading Canadian coins.

Striking Impressions: The Royal Canadian Mint and Canadian Coinage. Haxby, James A. Royal Canadian Mint, Ottawa, 1984. A history of the Royal Canadian Mint and its coinage.

Coins of Canada. Haxby, J.A. and Wiley, R.C. Unitrade Press, Toronto, Ontario, Canada, 1983. Catalog form with prices.

China

The Currencies of China. Kann, Eduard. Kelly & Walsh Ltd., Shanghai, China, 1926 (1978 reprint of 1926 work by Sanford J. Durst, New York, N.Y.). Discussion of the currencies and their effects.

Colombia

Coins of Colombia. Seppa, Dale, and Almanzar, Alcedo. Almanzar's Coins of the World, San Antonio, Texas, 1973.

Cuba

The Coinage of Cuba, 1870 to date. Lismore, Thomas. Roy Renderer, Miami, Fla., 1966.

Czechoslovakia

Czechoslovak Coins. Davis, Dolores H. Numismatics International, Dallas, Texas, 1972. Catalog form with some illustrations.

Dominican Republic

Monedas Dominicanas, (Dominican Money). Gomez, Miguel E. Sociedad Dominicana de Biblofilos, Santo Domingo, Dominican Republic, 1979. Text in Spanish.

El Salvador

The Coins and Paper Money of El Salvador. Almanzar, Alcedo F. & Stickney. Brian R.

Ethiopia

Ethiopia, Treasure House of Africa. Kohl, Melvin J. The Society for International Numismatics, Santa Monica, Calif., 1969. Text with photographs.

Finland

Suomi, Rahat Ja Setelit (Finland, Coins and Bank Notes 1811-1981). von Schantz, C. Holmasto Coins & Medals Co. Helsinki, Finland,

1982. Catalog form in Finnish and English language.

France

Monnaies Francaises. Gadoury, Victor, Franz W. Wesel Druckerie und Verlag, Baden, West Germany, 1977. Catalog form, text in French.

Repertoire de la Numismatique Francaise Contemporaine, 1793 a nos jours (Numismatics of Contemporary France from 1793). De Mey, Jean & Poindessault, Bernard, Imprimerie Cultura, Brussels, Belgium, 1976. Catalog form, text in French.

Les Monnaies Royales Francaises de Hugues Capet a Louis XVI (French Royal Money from Hugh Capet to Louis XVI). Ciani, Louis, Paris, 1926. (Reprinted by A.G. Van der Dussen in Maastricht, Netherlands.) Comprehensive catalog of early-modern French coins.

Catalogue General Illustre des Editions de la Monnaie de Paris (General Illustrated Catalog of Issues of the Paris Mint). Monnaie de Paris, Paris, Four volumes. Illustrated catalog of the medals of the French Mint.

The Talers or Ecus of Alsace-Lorraine. Davenport, John S. American Numismatic Association.

Germany

Germanic Coinage (Charlemagne through Wilhelm II). Craig, William D. Mountain View, 1954. Invaluable reference for identifying and dating rulers of German city-states.

German Talers 1500-1600. Davenport, John S. Schulten, P.N., Frankfurt, 1979. Illustrated catalog of taler-size silver coins from 1500-1600.

German Secular Talers, 1600-1700. Davenport, John S. Schulten, P.N., Frankfurt, 1976. Illustrated catalog of talers from 1600-1700.

German Church and City Talers, 1600-1700. Davenport, John S. Galesburg, 1975. Illustrated catalog of talers, 1600-1700.

German Talers, 1700-1800. Davenport, John S. Spink & Son, London, 1979. Illustrated catalog of talers issued from 1700-1800.

Silver Gulden, 1559-1763. Davenport, John S. Schulten, P.N., Frankfurt, 1982. An illustrated catalog of gulden, a denomination of silver coin smaller than the taler.

Great Britain

Standard Catalogue of British Coins: England. Seaby, Peter. Seaby Publications, London, England, 1987 edition. Catalog with illustrations, published annually.

Sylloge of Coins of the British Isles. Various authors, British Academy & Carlberg Foundation, London, England, 1970. Comprehensive catalog in 23 volumes. Contains 1. Fitzwilliam Museum, Cambridge Part, 2. Hunterian & Coats collections, Univ. of Glasgow, Part I, 3. Coins of the Coritani, 4. Royal collection of coins & medals, Nat. Museum, Copenhagen, Part I 5. Grosvenor Museum, Chester Part I, 6. Nat. Museum of Antiquities of Scotland, Edinburgh, Part I, 7. The Royal Danish Collection, Copenhagen, Part II, 8. The Hiberian-Norse coins in the British Museum, 9. Ashmolean Museum, Oxford, Part 1, 10. Ulster Museum, Belfast, 11. Reading University, 12. Ashmolean Museum, Oxford, Part II 13-15. The Royal Danish Collection Copenhagen, Part III, 16. Mrs. Emery May Norweb, Part I, 17. Ancient British, Anglo-Saxon & Norman coins in Midlands Museums, 18. The Royal Danish Collection, Copenhagen, Part IV, 19. Ancient British coins and coins of the Bristol & Gloucestershire Mints, 20. n/a, 21. n/a, 22. The Royal Danish Collection, Copenhagen Part V, 23. Ashmolean Museum, Oxford, Part III.

Standard Catalogue of British Coins: Coins of Scotland, Ireland and the Islands. Seaby, Peter, and Purvey, P. Frank. Seaby, London, 1987. Basic price catalog of coins of Scotland, Ireland and the islands of Jersey, Guernsey, Man and Lundy.

English Coins. Brooke, George C. Methuen, London, 1966. History of the coinage of Great Britain.

British Tokens and Their Values. Seaby, Peter, Bussell, Monica Seaby, London, 1984. Priced catalog of British tokens, 17th through 19th century.

Coins of England and the United Kingdom. Seaby, London, England, 1985.

Guatemala

Historia Numismatica de Guatemala (Numismatic History of Guatemala). Prober, Kurt. Bank of Guatemala, 1973. Text and catalog in Spanish language.

Haiti

Coins of Haiti, 1803-1970. Arroyo, Carmen. Almanzar's Coins of the World, San Antonio, Texas 1970.

Hungary

Munzkatalog Ungarn von 1000 bis Heute (Catalog of Hungarian Coins from 1000 Forward). Huszar, Lajos. Battenberg, Munich, West Germany, 1979. Catalog form with illustrations, in German language.

India

Coins. Gupta, Parmeshwari Lal. Natl. Book Trust, New Delhi, India, 1969. Catalog form, text in English.

Studies in Indian Coins. Sircar, D.C. Motilal Banarsidas, Delhi, India, 1968. Catalog form, text in Indian language.

Iran

Modern Coinage of Iran, 1876-1974. Clarke, Robert L. & Mohabat-Ayin, A. Numismatics International, Dallas, Texas, 1974. Catalog form with some illustrations.

Israel

The History of Modern Israel's Money, 1917-1970. Haffner, Sylvia. Philip J. Matthew, Tarzana, Calif., 1970.

Israel's Money & Medals, 1948-1973. Kagan, A.H. Valley Stream, N.Y., 1974. Later editions may exist.

AINA Guide Book of Israel Coins & Medals. Schuman, Edward. American Israel Numismatic Assn, Tamarac, Fla., 1980.

Israel Coins and Medals. Shoham, David. Ben Zvi Printing Enterprises Ltd., Jerusalem, Israel, 1982.

Israel's 20-year Catalog of Coins and Currency. Bertram, Fred & Weber, Robert. Louis Denberg Foundation Inc., N.Y., 1968.

Numismatics of the Holocaust, The Shekel. American Israel Numismatic Assn., Tamarac, Fla., Sept.-Oct., 1982 and March-April, 1983, combined reprint.

Italy

Super Collezionista di Monete Decimali Italiane, (*Comprehensive Manual of Collecting the Decimal Money of Italy*). Cesare Bobba, Torino, Italy, 1977. Catalog form with text in Italian. Later editions exist.

Jamaica

The Coinage of Jamaica. Byrne, Ray & Remick, Jerome H.

Japan

Japanese Coin Catalogue 1985. Oka, M. An illustrated, 1985 catalog in the Japanese language of coins and paper money.

Modern Japanese Coinage. Cummings, Michael L. Far East Journal, Tokyo, Japan, 1978. Catalog form with illustrations, later editions may exist.

Japanese Coinage. Jacobs, Norman & Vermeule, Cornelius C. Numismatic Revue, New York, N.Y. 1972. Text and illustrated catalog.

Lithuania

Senoves Lietuviu Pinigai (*Ancient Lithuanian Currencies*). Karys, Jonas K. Immaculata Press, Putnam, Conn. 1959. Identifies and explains coinage, text in English and Lithuanian.

Mexico

A Guidebook of Mexican Coins, 1822 to Date, fourth edition. Buttrey, T.V. & Hubbard, Clyde. Krause Publications, Iola, Wis. 1986. Catalog with prices.

Coins of Mexico. Grove, Frank W. Quarterman Publ. Inc., Lawrence, Mass., 1981. Catalog format.

Standard Catalogue of Mexican Coins, Paper Money, Stock, Bonds and Medals. Bruce, Colin R. II. Krause Publ., Racine, Wis., 1981. Catalog form with text of history, illustrated.

Numismatic History of Mexico. Pradeau, Alberto Francisco, Durst, Sanford J. New York. 1978 (reprint of 1938 edition). A numismatic history of Mexico.

Coins of Mexico, 1905-1971. Utberg, Neil S. Colonial Publ. Co., Houston, Texas, 1971.

Morocco

Mondeas de Marruecos, (*Moroccan Coins, 1879-1971*). Sanchez-Giron, J.M. publ. by author, Ceuta, Spain, 1972. Catalog format, in Spanish and English languages.

Mozambique

Catalogo das Moedas de Mocambique (*Catalog of Money of Mozambique*). Azevedo, Vasco, Livraria Fernando Machado, Porto, 1969. Catalog with each coin photographed, text in Portuguese.

Netherlands

Nederlandse Munten van 1795-1961 (*Dutch Money from 1795-1961*). Schulman, Jacques, Jacques Schulman N.V., Amsterdam, Netherlands, 1962. Catalog form, well illustrated. Text in Dutch language.

Norway

Norges Mynter, (*Coinage of Norway*). Ahlstrom, Bjarne, Brekke, Bernhard F. & Hemmingsson, Bengt, Numismatiska Bokforlaget AB, Stockholm, Sweden, 1976. Catalog form in Swedish and English language.

Oriental, general works

The Standard Guide to South Asian Coins & Paper Money Since 1556 AD. Bruce, Colin R. II, Deyell, John S. Rhodes, Nicholas, & Spengler, William F. Krause Publ., Iola, Wis., 1981. General catalog of non-Japanese & non-Chinese oriental coins.

Numismata Orientalia Illustrata, (*Oriental Numismatics Illustrated*). Album, Stephen. Attic Books Ltd., New York, N.Y., 1977. Catalog form with some charts.

Panama
Coins & Currency of Panama. Grigore, Julius Jr. Krause Publ., Iola, Wis., 1972. Illustrated text in English language.

Paraguay
The Coins of Paraguay. Seppa, Dale & Almanzar, Alcedo, Almanzar's Coins of the World, San Antonio, Texas, 1971.

Poland
Hanbuch der Polnischen Numismatik (Handbook of Polish Numismatics). Gumowski, Marian, Akademische Druck-U, Graz, Austria, 1960. Identifies and explains coinage in German language.

Rhodesia-Zimbabwe
Keogh On Coins of Rhodesia-Zimbabwe. Keogh, John, Keogh Coins, Durban North, South Africa, 1980. Catalog form.

Russia
A Guidebook of Russian Coins, 1725-1982. Harris, Robert P. Mevius Numisbooks Int. B.V., Vriezenveen, Netherlands, 1983. Catalog form with many illustrations.

Scandinavia, general works
Sieg Montkatalog 1978 (Sieg's Catalog of Money). Sieg, Frovin. Ulbjerg gl. Skole, Skals, Denmark, 1977. Catalog form in Danish language with English summary. Covers all of Scandinavia, revised annually.

South Africa
The Coins of South Africa. Kaplan, Alec. Alec Kaplan & Son Pty. Ltd., Germiston, South Africa, 1984. Catalog form.

Coins of South Africa. Jacobs, Ken Publ. by author. Boksburg North, South Africa, 1983. Catalog form of type coins, in full color.

Spain
Las Monedas Espanolas Desde D. Pelaya 718 a Juan Carlos I 1980, (The Money of Spain from D. Pelayo in 718 to Juan Carlos I 1980). Castan, Carlos & Cayon, Juan R. Artegraf, IGSA, Madrid, Spain, 1979. Catalog form with illustrations, text in Spanish.

Sweden
Sveriges Mynt 1521-1977 (Coinage of Sweden). Ahlstrom, Bjarne. Almer, Yngve & Hemmingsson, Bengt, Numismatiska Bokforlaget AB, Stockholm, 1976. Catalog form in Swedish and English language.

Switzerland
Die Munzen der Schweiz (The Money of Switzerland). Divo, Jean-Paul & Tobler, Edwin. Bank Leu, Zurich, Switzerland, 1974. Catalog form in German language. Possible later editions exist.

Uruguay
The Coins of Uruguay, 1840-1971. Seppa, Dale & Almanzar, Alcedo F. Almanzar's Coins of the World, San Antonio, Texas, 1971.

Coinage of the Americas
America's Foreign Coins; An Illustrated Standard Catalogue with Valuations of Foreign Coins with Legal Tender Status in the U.S., 1793-1857. Schilke, O.G. Coin & Currency Institute, N.Y., 1964. (Reprint of 1964 edition.)

Coinage of the Americas. Buttrey, Theodore V. Jr. American Numismatic Society, New York, N.Y. 1973. Discussions of coinage of both continents.

The Coins of Central America, Silver & Copper, 1824-1940. Raymond, Wayte. New York, 1941.

The Coins of South America, Silver & Copper, Raymond, Wayte. New York, 1942.

The Coins of the West Indies, Silver & Copper, Including the Cut & Counterstamped Pieces. Raymond, Wayte. New York, 1942.

Copper Coins of Central & South America. Eklund, O.P. from *The Numismatist*, Colorado Springs, Colo., 1962.

The Gold Coins of North & South America, An Illustrated Catalogue of All the Types with an Indication of Their Retail Value. Raymond, Wayte. New York, 1937.

Gold Coins of the Americas with Values. Harris, Robert P. Anco, Florence, Ala., 1971. Catalog form with some illustrations.

The Julius Guttag Collection of Latin American Coins. Adams, Edgar H. Quarterman Publ., Lawrence, Mass., 1974.

Sammlung Uberseeischer Munzen und Medaillen, (Oversees Money and Medals). Weyl, Adolph, J.A. Stargardt, Berlin, Germany, 1878 (1970 reprint of 1878 work by Organization of International Numismatists, Sepulveda, Calif.). Catalog form with some line drawings and text in German language.

The Silver Dollars of North & South America; An Illustrated Catalogue of All the Types & an Indication of Their Retail Value. Raymond, Wayte. New York, 1964.

The Silver & Minor Coins of North & South America Exclusive of the United States, Raymond, Wayte. New York, N.Y.

Spanish American Gold Coins; Being a Detailed List of the Gold Coins Struck by the Spanish Kings in America at the Mints of Mexico, Guadalxara, Lima, Potosi, Bogota,

Popayan, Guatemala, Santiago. Raymond, Wayte. New York, 1936.

Odd & curious

Odd and Curious Money: Descriptions and Values. Opitz, Charles J. First Impressions Printing, Ocala, Fla., 1986. Encyclopedic listing of odd and curious moneys.

A Survey of Primitive Money. Quiggin, A. Higston. Methuen & Co. Ltd., Strand, Great Britain, 1963 (Reprint of the 1963 edition by Sanford J. Durst, New York, N.Y.). Text with line drawings and photographs.

Primitive Money in its Ethnological, Historical and Economic Aspects. Einzig, Paul. Eyre & Spottswood, London, England, 1948 (1982 reprint of the 1948 edition by Sanford J. Durst, New York, N.Y.). Text with photographs.

Odd and Curious. Reed, Mort. Fisher Printing Co., 1963 (1980 reprint of the 1963 edition by Sanford J. Durst, New York, N.Y.). Text and line drawings.

Paper money
General works

A Collector's Guide to Paper Money. Beresiner, Yasha. Stein & Day Publ., New York, N.Y., 1977. Text with some photographs.

Banknotes & Banking in The Isle of Man, 1788-1970. Quarmby, Ernest. Spink & Son Ltd., London, England, 1971. Text with photographs.

The Charlton Standard Catalogue of Canadian Paper Money. Charlton Press, Toronto, 1980. Priced and illustrated guide to Canadian paper money.

English Paper Money. Duggleby, Vincent. Stanley Gibbons Publ. Ltd., London, England, 1980. Catalog form.

Scottish Banknotes. Douglas, James. Stanley Gibbons Publ. Ltd., London, England, 1975. Catalog form, later editions may exist.

Standard Catalog of World Paper Money. Pick, Albert, Krause Publ., Iola, Wis. 1986. Catalog form in two volumes: 1. general issues, 2. specialized issues.

World War II Military Currency. Schwan, C. Frederick & Boling, Joseph E. BNR Press, Portage, Ohio, 1978. Catalog form.

Notgeld

Das Deutsche Notgeld, (The German Notgeld). Keller, Arnold, Battenberg, Verlag, Munich, West Germany, 1976. Catalog in German language in 11 volumes: 1. 1914, 2. Germany, Austria, Hungary 1914-1918, 3.

large paper money 1918-1921, 4. small paper money 1916-1922, etc.

Das Lagergeld der Konzentrations—und DR—Lager, 1933-1945, (The Money of the Concentration Camps and Displaced Persons Camps, 1933-1945). Oick, Albert, and Siemsen, Carl. Battenberg, Verlag, Munich, West Germany, 1976. Catalog in German language.

Investing

Past performance of coins as an investment is not necessarily an indication of the future. It is important to remember that the future is unknown.

There are hundreds of books on investing in rare coins. The following titles are provided as a sampling of those published within recent years. They do not reflect the personal recommendations of any *Coin World* staff member or an endorsement by the publication. The listing is alphabetical and in no way reflects importance or selectivity.

Opinions and advice contained in these and other investment books are those of the authors.

The Big Silver Melt. Merton, Henry A.; Macmillan Publishing Co. Inc., New York. 1983.

The Coin Collector's Survival Manual. Travers, Scott A. Arco Publishing Inc., New York City, 1987.

Donald Kagin's Personal Guide to Rare Coin Investments. Kagin, Donald; Kagin's Investment Corp., Des Moines, Iowa. 1984.

Heads You Win, Tails You Win. Prichard, Jeffrey J.; Reston Publishing Company Inc., Reston, Va. 1983.

High Profits From Rare Coin Investment. Bowers, Q. David; Bowers and Merena Galleries Inc., Wolfeboro, N.H. 1983 (Ninth edition.)

Investing in Rare Coins. Steinmetz, Dennis; Steinmetz Coins and Currency, Lancaster, Pa. 1981.

The Investor's Guide to United States Coins. Berman, Neil S., and Schulman, Hans M.F. Coin & Currency Institute Inc., New York City, 1986.

Investor's Yearbook - 1984. Owen, Al; Newsletter Digest, Huntsville, Ala. 1984.

A Mercenary's Guide to the Rare Coin Market. Hall, David. 1987.

Survive and Win in the Inflationary '80s. Ruff, Howard J.; Warner Books, New York. 1982.

Rare Coin Investment Strategy. Travers,

Scott A. Prentice Hall Press, New York City, 1986.
The World of Coins and Coin Collecting. Ganz, David L.; Charles Scribner's Sons, New York. 1980.

Common book references

Most definitive reference catalogs assign numbers to the coins, bank notes or whatever listed in them, as a convenience to the collectors of that series. This also allows advertisers of this material to list a particular item for sale with only the briefest description of the piece, where otherwise several paragraphs might be necessary to describe the type or variety.

To help the beginning collector identify a reference he might not be familiar with, we include here a listing of the references most likely to be encountered in an advertisement or an auction catalog. The title of the book is given first, followed by the name of the author and the style in which one might find a catalog listing.

Colonial and state coins

The Early Coins of America. Sylvester S. Crosby. Crosby 2-A, C-2A.
The Coins of New Jersey. Edward Maris. Maris 1-A, M 1-A.
The State Coinage of Connecticut. Henry C. Miller. Miller 2-B, M 2-B.
The Silver Coinage of Massachusetts. Sydney P. Noe. Noe 2-A, N 2-A.
The Copper Coins of Massachusetts. Hillyer Ryder. Ryder 2.
The Colonial Coins of Vermont. Hillyer Ryder. Ryder 2.

Copper coins

The Fugio Cents. Alan Kessler.
Walter Breen's Encyclopedia of United States Half Cents 1793-1857. Walter Breen. Breen 3c, Breen 9.
American Half Cents: The "Little Half Sisters". Roger S. Cohen Jr. Cohen 1-A, C-1.
United States Half Cents. Ebenezer Gilbert. Gilbert 1, G-1.
Penny Whimsy. William H. Sheldon. Sheldon 101, S-101.
United States Copper Cents: 1816-1857. Howard R. Newcomb. Newcomb 1, N-1.

Silver coins

The United States Half Dimes. Daniel W. Valentine. Valentine 1a, V-1a.
Early United States Dimes: 1796-1837. David J. Davis, Russell J. Logan, Allen F. Lovejoy, John W. McCloskey, William L. Subjack. Variety 13.
Encyclopedia of United States Liberty Seated

Dimes. Kamal M. Ahwash. Ahwash 1.
The Early Quarter Dollars of the United States. A.W. Browning. Browning 1, B-1.
Half Dollar Die Varieties. M.L. Beistle. Beistle 1.
Early Half Dollar Varieties: 1794-1836. Al C. Overton. Overton 110, O-110.
The United States Early Silver Dollars from 1794 to 1803. M.H. Bolender. Bolender B-14a.
The Comprehensive Catalogue and Encyclopedia of U.S. Morgan and Peace Silver Dollars. Leroy C. Van Allen and A. George Mallis. Van Allen-Mallis 1, VAM-1.

Special U.S. series

California Pioneer Fractional Gold. Walter Breen and Ronald J. Gillio. Breen-Gillio 753.
Private Gold Coins and Patterns of the United States. Donald H. Kagin. Kagin 20, Kagin 20a.
United States Pattern, Experimental and Trial Pieces. J. Hewitt Judd and A. Kosoff. Judd 1294, J-1294.

Exonumia

Hard Times Tokens. Lyman H. Low. Low 151.
Patriotic Civil War Tokens. George and Melvin Fuld. Fuld 120/256.
U.S. Civil War Store Cards. George and Melvin Fuld. Fuld NY10H.
So-Called Dollars. Harold E. Hibler and Charls V. Kappen. Hibler and Kappen 11a, HK-11a.
The Atwood-Coffee Catalogue of United States and Canadian Transportation Tokens. John M. Coffee Jr. Denver 260.
Medals of the United States Mint: The First Century, 1792-1892. By R.. Julian. Julian IP-1, J-IP-1.

Paper money

Paper Money of the United States. Robert Friedberg. Friedberg 18, F-18.
The Encyclopedia of United States Fractional & Postal Currency. Milton Friedberg. Milton 3R25.2c.
Standard Catalog of World Paper Money. Albert Pick. Pick 101.

World coins

Coins of the World. William D. Craig. Craig 13, C-13.
Standard Price Guide to World Crowns & Talers. Frank Draskovic and Stuart Rubenfeld. Davenport 143, Dav-143.
A Catalog of Modern World Coins: 1850-1950. R.S. Yeoman. Yeoman 1, Y-1.
Current Coins of the World. R.S. Yeoman. Yeoman 1, Y-1.

Numismatic Terms 22

Numismatic terms

Those basic numismatic terms likely to cause the most difficulty for both the novice and the advanced collector are included in this guide. Experts in the science of numismatics differ in their interpretation of a number of terms, and reference to a standard dictionary often fails to settle disputes. Terms relating to error coins and notes are more comprehensively defined in Chapter 13; grading definitions can be found in Chapter 14.

The definitions here are based in part on the American Numismatic Association's *The Dictionary of Numismatic Terms.*

— A —

Accolated, conjoined, jugate: Design with two heads facing the same direction and overlapping.

Accumulation: Coins, tokens, etc., unsorted, unclassified, and unattributed; not a collection.

Adjustment: Filing down the face of an overweight planchet. Such filing marks often survive the coining process. This is common on 18th century coins.

Aes grave: Cast bronze issue of the Roman republic; literally "heavy bronze."

Aes rude: Large cast rectangular bronze coin, one of the earliest Roman coins.

Alloy: Mixture of more than one metal.

Altered: A coin or other numismatic item that has been deliberately changed, usually to make it resemble a rare or more valuable piece.

American Arts Gold Medallions: A series of 1-ounce and half-ounce gold bullion medals issued by the U.S. Mint from 1980-84. Medals depict great American artists, writers and actors.

American Eagle: Bullion coins released by the U.S. Mint beginning in October 1986. Five coins are available: a 1-ounce, .999 fine silver coin with $1 face value; a 1-ounce, .9167 fine gold coin with $50 face value; a half-ounce, .9167 fine gold coin with $25 face value; a quarter-ounce, .9167 fine gold coin with $10 face value; and a tenth-ounce, .9167 fine gold coin with $5 face value. Coins are sold at prices based on current metal prices plus a markup.

Ancient coin: Generally any coin issued before A.D. 500.

Anneal: To soften dies, planchets or metal by heat treatment.

Ant nose: Primitive copper money of China ca. 600 B.C.

As: (Plural: asses) Bronze or orichalcum coins of the Roman republic.

Assay: Analytic test or trial to ascertain the fineness, weight and consistency of precious or other metal in coin or bullion. An assay piece is one that has been assayed.

Attribution: The identification of a numismatic item by characteristics such as issuing authority, date or period, Mint, denomination, metal in which struck, and by a standard reference.

Auction: Method of selling by which items are presented for sale to the highest bidder.

Authentication: Authoritative determination of the genuineness of a numismatic item.

— B —

Back: The paper money side opposite the "face"; analogous to the reverse of a coin.

Bag marks: See contact marks.

Bank note: A promissory note issued by a bank in useful denominations, payable to bearer and intended to circulate as money.

Should not be used as a generic term for all forms of paper money.

Base metal: Non-precious metal; e.g., copper.

Bas-relief: Sculpture style featuring slight differences between the raised design and the field and in which no part of the design is undercut; used to execute models for coins and medals.

Bicentennial coins: The special quarter dollar, half dollar and dollar struck from mid-1975 to the end of 1976 in honor of the 200th anniversary of American Independence. Coins feature the dual date 1776-1976 and special reverses emblematic of the celebration. Issued in copper-nickel clad versions for circulation. Special 40 percent silver clad versions were sold to collectors.

Bid-buy sale: A combination form of fixed-price list and mail-bid sale. Rules may vary from dealer to dealer. However, customers usually may either buy a lot outright at the fixed price or place a bid (higher or lower). It permits buyers to purchase a lot at less than fixed price (in some cases), or by paying more, ensures a greater chance of obtaining the lot.

Bid sheet: A form used by a buyer in an auction or mail-bid sale, on which the buyer lists the item being bid on by the number it is assigned and the price he is willing to pay.

Billon: A low-grade alloy used for some minor coin issues consisting usually of a mixture of silver and copper, and sometimes coated with a silver wash.

Bison: Species considered typically North American, used on coinage and paper money of the United States; bison is a better term than buffalo, which is a more general term referring to a number of related but different species outside North America.

Bit: A popular term for the Spanish-American 1-real piece (also Danish West Indies and other neighboring islands) which formerly circulated in the United States. More often used in the plural, as two bits (25 cents) or four bits (50 cents). A bit is 12½ cents.

Blank: (See **planchet**.)

Block: In paper money collecting, a series of related notes indicated by the same prefix and suffix letters in the serial number. When the suffix letter changes, a new block is created. The suffix currently changes when the serial number reaches 99 920 000.

"Blue Book": Nickname given to *Handbook of United States Coins,* an annual price guide for collectors. The book has a blue cover, hence the nickname. Gives wholesale prices, or what dealers might pay for U.S. coins.

Brass: Coinage metal alloy containing chiefly copper and zinc.

Britannia: Gold bullion coin and its fractionals to be issued by Great Britain beginning in 1987; also, the allegorical figure representing Britain.

Broadstrike: Coin struck outside a restraining collar.

Broken bank note: Paper money of a defunct bank or a bank which has failed (broken), but often applied to any obsolete bank note.

Bronze: Coinage metal alloy containing chiefly copper and tin.

Brown Back: A Brown Back note is a Second Charter, First Issue national bank note. Has brown ink on the back.

Buffalo: (See **bison**.)

Buffalo nickel: More properly: Indian Head 5-cent piece.

Bullion: Uncoined precious metal in the form of bars, plates, ingots, and other items.

Bullion coin: A precious metal coin traded at the current bullion price.

Buyer's fee: Winning bidders in a public auction in the United States are usually charged a buyer's fee based on a certain percentage of the winning bid. Most U.S. auction houses charge a 10 percent buyer's fee; a buyer placing a $110 hammer bid on a coin would pay an additional $11 buyer's fee, or $121.

— C —

Cabinet friction: Slight surface wear on a coin, token or medal caused by friction between it and the tray or envelope in which it is contained.

Check number: On modern paper money, used as a cross reference for the plate number — which appears on the margin of a currency sheet and which is trimmed from the note before it enters circulation — to identify the printing plate from which the note came. On the obverse, the check number is a letter and number combination appearing in lower right corner; on the reverse, it is a number only appearing at the lower right. Often incorrectly called the plate number.

Chop mark (shroff mark): A small punched impression applied by Chinese (chop) or Indian (shroff) banks or change offices to attest to the full weight and metallic content of a coin.

Civil War tokens: Privately-issued emergency coin-like tokens, the approximate size of current U.S. cents, which circulated during the Civil War because of a scarcity of small change. Two major types were issued: patriotic tokens, with patriotic themes; and store cards, advertising pieces often carrying the issuer's name, address and type of business or services.

Clad: Composite coinage metal strip composed of a core, usually of a base metal such as copper, and surface layers of more valuable metal, silver (or sometimes copper-nickel). Cladding is a cost-saving measure, making coins cheaper to produce while maintaining a desired appearance.

Clip: Sometimes used to denote an incomplete planchet coin; in earlier days, clipping was a process of shaving edges of coins to remove small amounts of metal for illegal gain (which gave rise to lettered or reeded edges).

Coin: Usually a piece of metal, marked with a device, issued by a governing authority and intended to be used as money.

Coin note: See Treasury note.

Collar: A retaining ring die within which the coin dies operate; the collar forms the edge design of the piece such as reeding or lettering.

Colonial: Refers to coins or paper money issued by the Colonial governments of the 13 British Colonies that became the United States. See "state coinages."

Commemorative: A piece issued to mark, honor or observe an anniversary, other event, place or person, or to preserve its memory.

Compound-interest Treasury note: A type of U.S. paper money authorized in 1863 and 1864; they brought 6 percent interest, and were to be redeemed three years after issue.

Condition census: Term introduced by Dr. William H. Sheldon to denote the finest specimen and average condition of next five finest known of a given variety of large cents. Catalogers are gradually extending the use of the term to other series.

Conjoined: (See: accolated.)

Continental currency: Paper money issued by the authority of the Continental Congress during the Revolutionary War.

Contact marks: Minor abrasions on an otherwise Uncirculated coin, caused by handling in Mint-sewn bags and contact with other surfaces. Sometimes called bag marks.

Continental dollar: A dollar-sized pattern struck in 1776 as a proposed coinage.

COPE, COPE PAK: Acronyms used at Bureau of Engraving and Printing for Currency Overprinting and Processing Equipment and Currency Overprinting and Processing Equipment, Packaging. Machines used to apply overprinting of seals, serial numbers and Federal Reserve index numbers to 16-note half sheets of paper money; then the COPE

cuts the half sheets into single notes, bundles them into 100-note packages with a paper band, and into larger plastic-wrapped packages.

Copper-nickel: Coinage alloy composed of copper and nickel in varying amounts.

Copy: A reproduction or imitation of an original.

Coronet: Style of Liberty Head used on U.S. copper and gold coins for much of the 19th century. Liberty wears a coronet (most depicting the world LIBERTY).

Counterfeit: An object made to imitate a genuine numismatic piece with intent to deceive or defraud, irrespective of whether the intended fraud is primarily monetary or numismatic.

Crown: A general term embracing most silver coins from about 20 to 30 grams in weight and from about 33 to 42 millimeters in size. The term has become applicable also to most nickel-alloy coins of the same range of size and weight. Coins of 43 or more millimeters in diameter are said to be multiple crowns.

Cud: A form of die break that leaves a shapeless lump of metal on part of a coin.

Cupro-nickel: Copper-nickel; term often employed by the government.

Currency: Applies to both coins and paper money. Many use the word currency for paper money only. Currency is legal tender.

Current: Coins and paper money in circulation.

- D -

Date Back: A Date Back note is a Second Charter, Second Issue national bank note. Refers to the dates 1902-1908 found on the back.

Denarius: (Plural: denarii) Roman silver coin, later debased, roughly equal to a Greek drachm. Initiated in 268 B.C, it equaled 16 asses; 25 denarii equals 1 gold aureus.

Denomination: The face value of a coin or paper note; the amount of money it is worth.

Denticles: Ornamental device used on rims of coins, often resembling teeth, hence the name; also "beading."

Device: The principal element, such as a portrait, shield or heraldic emblem, of the design on the obverse and reverse of a coin, token or medal.

Devil's Face note: On some of Bank of Canada notes, First Issue of 1954, Queen Elizabeth II's hair has a coincidental combination of shading and light that looks like a "devil's" face. Shading was quickly changed under public pressure to remove the "face."

Demand note: Demand notes, authorized in 1861, were the first paper money issued by the United States federal government for circulation. Nicknamed the "greenback" because of the green ink used on the reverse.

Die: A hardened metal punch, the face of which carries an intaglio or incuse mirror-image to be impressed on one side of a planchet.

Die scratch: Raised line on the surface of a coin, caused by a scratch in the coinage die.

Disme: Spelling of the word "dime" on U.S. 1792 pattern pieces and name given the 10-cent coin authorized in the Mint Act of April 2, 1792. Probably pronounced like "steam" or "time." The 's' is silent.

Double eagle: A gold $20 coin of the United States.

Doubled die: A die which has a multiple image created during the die-making process. Coins struck from a doubled die show a doubled image. There are many different causes of doubled dies, and many doubled die coins. Sometimes mistakenly called double die.

Doubloon: Popular slang name given to Spanish gold 8-escudo pieces of the Conquistador era, often associated with pirate treasure; also, a medal in special circumstances — Mardi Gras doubloon.

Drachm: (Pronounced "dram") An ancient Greek silver coin, plural drachms. Drachma (pronounced "DRAHK-muh") is the modern Greek denomination, plural drachmas.

Ducat: (Pronounced "DUCK-et") Medieval gold coin; also any of a number of modern issues of the Dutch Mint. Modern slang has spread its use to mean "ticket."

- E -

Eagle: A gold $10 coin of the United States.

Educational notes: The Series 1896 $1, $2 and $5 silver certificates are called Educational notes because of the allegorical and educational themes of the vignettes. Replaced in 1899 with a new series.

Edge: Often termed the third side of a coin, it is the surface perpendicular to the obverse and reverse. Not to be confused with rim. Edges can be plain, lettered or milled (reeded or with some other repetitious device). Edges became particularly important with the advent of machine-struck coinage.

Electrotype: A copy or reproduction of a coin, token or medal made by the electroplating process.

Electrum: Naturally-occurring alloy of gold and silver used for early coins of the Mediterranean region.

Elongated coin: An oval medalet produced by a roller die using a coin, token or medal as a planchet — usually a cent.

Encased postage stamp: A postage stamp unofficially encased in a metal, plastic or cardboard frame and intended to be used as small change.

Error: A coin, token, medal or paper money item evidencing a mistake made in its manufacture.

Essai; essay: In paper money, a print made to test a design; analogous to a trial strike in coinage. (See also: **proof**)

Exergue: (Pronounced "EX-surge") Area on a coin generally below the main design area, often site of date.

Exonumia: A broad category of non-money, non-legal-tender numismatic items, including tokens, medals and badges. An exonumist is a specialist in exonumia.

Experimental pieces: Struck from any convenient dies to test a new metal, new alloy or new denomination; those testing a new shape; those testing a standard metal for a new denomination; and those representing changes in planchets for the purposes of combating counterfeiting.

- F -

Face: The front of a currency note, generally the side with signatures; analogous to the obverse of a coin.

Face value: Refers to the value of a piece of currency; the denomination multiple that appears on the note or coin.

Fantasy: An object having the physical characteristics of a coin, issued by an agency other than a governing authority yet purporting to be issued by a real or imaginary governing authority as a coin.

Federal Reserve Bank note: A form of U.S. paper money authorized by the Federal Reserve Acts of Dec. 23, 1913, and April 23, 1918, and by the Act of March 9, 1933. The obligation to pay was by the individual issuing bank, not the federal government or other Federal Reserve Banks. The 1933 notes were an emergency issue to alleviate a shortage of paper money. Not to be confused with Federal Reserve notes.

Federal Reserve note: A form of U.S. paper money authorized by the Federal Reserve Act of February 1913. The obligation to pay is on the United States government and not the issuing banks. This is the only form of paper money currently being printed in the United States.

Fiat money: "Unbacked" currency, that which cannot be converted into coin or specie of equal value.

Field: The flat part of a surface of a coin

surrounding and between the head, legend or other designs.

Fineness: Represents the purity of precious metal, either in monetary or bullion form. Most forms of precious metal require an additional metal to provide a durable alloy. Often stated in terms of purity per 1,000 parts: A .925 fine silver coin has 92.5 percent silver and 7.5 percent other metal.

Fixed-price list: A price list or catalog of coins, exonumia, paper money or other numismatic items offered at set prices.

Flan: Planchet.

Flow lines: Microscopic striations in a coin's surface caused by the movement of metal under striking pressures.

Follis: A Roman and Byzantine coin denomination; plural is folli.

Fractional: Referring to bullion coin, those of less than 1 ounce.

Fractional currency: Usually refers to the United States paper money issued from 1862 to 1876 in denominations from 3 to 50 cents.

Frost: Effect caused by striking coin with sandblasted dies, often used in reference to Proof coins.

- G -

German silver: An alloy of copper, nickel and zinc but no silver. Also called American silver, Feuchtwanger's composition, nickel silver.

Gold certificate: A form of U.S. paper money once redeemable in gold coin. Temporarily made illegal for most to hold between 1933 and 1964.

Goldine: A gold-colored finish often used for medals or tokens.

- H -

Half dime, half disme: A silver 5-cent coin of the United States. The Mint Act of April 2, 1792, authorizes "half dismes."

Hairlines: Fine scratches in the surface of the coin. Not to be confused with die scratches.

Half eagle: A gold $5 coin of the United States.

Hard Times token: An unofficial large cent-sized copper token struck in a wide variety of types during 1833-1843, serving as de facto currency, and bearing a politically inspired legend; or issued with advertising as a store card.

Helvetia: Gold bullion coins issued by Switzerland; also, the allegorical figure representing Switzerland. From the name given to the area by the Romans.

Hoard: Usually a deposit of coins, secreted at some time in the past, discovered accidentally.

Hobo nickel: An Indian Head 5-cent coin with Indian bust engraved to resemble "hobo" or other individual. Engraving may also alter the bison on the reverse.

Hub: A right-reading, positive punch used to impress wrong-reading working dies.

- I -

Inaugural medal: A medal issued by the official inaugural committee commemorating the inauguration of a U.S. president.

Incuse: The opposite of bas-relief; design is recessed rather than raised. Used when referring to coins, medals, tokens and other metallic items.

Indian Head: The preferred name for the 5-cent coin often called "Buffalo nickel." Indian Head cents, gold dollars, gold $3 coins, $5 half eagles, $10 eagles and $20 double eagles exist.

Indian peace medal: A medal issued by a government agency to an Indian in an attempt to earn goodwill. The U.S. government issued Indian peace medals from the administration of George Washington through the administration of Andrew Johnson.

Intrinsic: As applied to value, the net metallic value as distinguished from face and numismatic value.

Intaglio: A method of printing using engraved plates. Paper is forced into the ink-filled lines of the plate, leaving a raised line of ink on the paper. All U.S. paper money is printed by the intaglio method.

Irradiated dime: Collectible made by exposing Roosevelt dimes to cesium or other radioactive substance and then placing in a special package; harmless, as any "acquired radioactivity" has dissipated by the time it reaches collectors' hands.

- J -

Jugate: Accolated, conjoined.

- K -

Krugerrand: A gold bullion coin of South Africa. It is composed of .9167 fine gold. Exists in 1-ounce, half-ounce, quarter-ounce and tenth-ounce sizes.

- L -

Lamination: Coinage defect consisting of a portion of the metal separating from the rest due to impurities or internal stresses; common with clad or plated coinage.

Large cent: Refers to the U.S. cents of 1793 to 1857, with diameters between 26-29 millimeters, depending on the year it was struck.

Large date: A variety of coin on which the date is physically larger than other varieties of the same year.

Legal tender: Currency explicitly determined by a government to be acceptable in the discharge of debts.

Legend: The inscription on a numismatic item.

Lepton: Denomination of various values and weights used throughout the ancient Greek world and in modern Greece, generally a small copper or bronze coin.

Lettered edge: An incused or raised inscription on the edge of a coin.

Libertad: A silver bullion coin of Mexico, containing 1 ounce of .999 fine gold.

Lignadenarist: A collector of wooden nickels and similar items.

Love token: A coin which has been altered by smoothing one or both surfaces and engraving initials, scenes, messages, etc., thereon.

Luster: Surface quality of a coin, result of light reflected from the microscopic flow lines.

- M -

Mail-bid sale: Similar to an auction, but all bids and transactions are completed through the mail or by telephone; no bidding is conducted "in person."

Maple Leaf: A gold bullion coin of Canada. It is composed of .9999 fine gold. Produced in four sizes: 1-ounce with a $50 face value; half-ounce, $25; quarter-ounce, $10; and tenth-ounce, $5. Plural, Maple Leafs.

Maria Theresia taler: An Austrian silver trade coin dated 1780, but struck repeatedly since then with the one date.

Matte Proof: Especially U.S. gold coins of 1908-1916, coins produced from dies entirely sandblasted with no mirror surfaces. (See **frost**)

Maverick: An unidentifiable specimen, generally referring to a token.

Medal: Usually a piece of metal, marked with a design or inscription, made to honor a person, place or event; not intended to pass as money.

Medalet: Depending on sources, a small medal no larger than 1 inch in diameter or a medal 35 millimeters in diameter or less.

Medallion: A large Roman presentation piece of the fifth century. Sometimes used for a large medal, usually 3 or more inches in diameter.

Medieval coin: A coin struck from about A.D. 500 to 1500.

"Mercury": The unofficial nickname given to the Winged Liberty Head dime of 1916-45. The designer never intended the coin to depict Mercury, a male Greek god with wings on his ankles. The bust on the dime is an allegorical female Liberty Head figure with a winged cap. Also, some coins have been plated outside the Mint with mercury to give them a "Prooflike" appearance; mercury metal is highly toxic and these coins should be destroyed.

Microprinting: Extremely small lettering difficult to discern with the naked eye, used as an anti-counterfeiting device on paper money.

Milling; milled coin: Milling refers to the devices on the edge of a coin; a milled coin is one struck by machine. They are related due to the rise of the importance of the collar with machine-produced coinage.

Minor coin: A silver coin of less than crown weight, or any coin struck in base metal.

Mint luster: The sheen or bloom on the surface of an Uncirculated numismatic object resulting from the centrifugal flow of metal caused by striking with dies. Mint luster or bloom is somewhat frosty in appearance as opposed to the mirror-like smoothness of the field of a Proof.

Mint mark: A letter or other symbol, sometimes of a privy nature, indicating the Mint of origin.

Mint set: Common term for an Uncirculated Mint set, an official set containing one of each coin struck during a given year.

Mirror: Highly reflective surface or field of a coin; usually mirror field with frosted relief.

Model: A clay or plaster three-dimensional design for a coin or medal.

Modern coin: A coin struck after about A.D. 1500.

Money: A medium of exchange.

Mule: A coin, token or medal whose obverse die is not matched with its official or regular reverse die.

- N -

National bank note: Paper money issued in United States by national banks from 1863 through 1929 and secured by government bonds or other collateral. Also called national currency.

National Coin Week: An annual observance sponsored by American Numismatic Association to acquaint the public with the hobby and science of numismatics.

National gold bank note: National bank notes payable in gold coin by some California banks and one Boston bank pursuant to authorization by Act of July 12, 1870.

Nickel: A silver-white metal widely used for coinage, usually alloyed with copper. Do not use for the copper-nickel 5-cent coin. In the mid-19th century, copper-nickel cents universally accepted scale of rari-

ok": Nickname given to *A Guide
United States Coins,* an annually
price guide. The cover is red, hence
me. Gives retail prices, or what
ght charge for U.S. coins.

edge: The result of a minting pro-
creates vertical serrations on the
oin.

Raised. In coinage and medallic
ic items, a relief design is raised
surface of the field. Sometimes
-relief. Opposite of incuse and inta-

: A copy of the original, a facsimile.
uction.

e: A numismatic item produced
inal dies at a later date; in the case
usually not with a view to meeting
requirements but to fill a demand
nismatic rarity.

se: The side opposite to that on
he head or principal figure is im-
The side opposite from the obverse.
r money this is called the back.

Raised border around the circumfer-
a coin, not to be confused with the

- S -

ce: Not common, but not as uncom-
rare.

: Paper currency usually of denomi-
less than $1 issued as substitutes for
cy to private persons or organizations.
s issued by coal mines and sutlers also
ed scrip.

pophily: The study and science of col-
financial documents, including stock
cates, shares, government and private
, and checks. A student of scripophily is
ophilist.

l: A device placed on paper money in-
ng authority of issue. Modern Federal
ve notes have two seals — a green De-
ent of Treasury seal and a black Fed

gniorage: The profits resulting from the
ence between the cost to make a coin
ts face value, or its worth as money and
tender. Most coins cost less to make
their face value; when it becomes too
nsive to make a certain coin, size, weight
composition are often changed.

rial number: Number used chiefly on pa-
money and sometimes on limited-issue
als to indicate order of production.

eries: Related coinage of the same de-
ination, design and type, including mod-

ifications, or varieties, of design. The Lincoln/Wheat Ears cents of 1909 to 1958 represent a complete series.

Sestertius: An ancient Roman coin; plural, sestertii.

Shekel, sheqel: Shekel is a silver coin of ancient Judea of various weights; sheqel is modern Israeli denomination, plural "sheqal-im."

Silver certificate: Authorized by the Acts of Feb. 28, 1878, and Aug. 4, 1886. Were redeemable in silver coin, and in early to mid-1960s, silver bullion. No longer produced, but all specimens remain legal tender although the notes can no longer be redeemed in silver.

Slug: A term applied to the $50 gold coin issued by various private Mints in California from 1851 to 1855 occurring in both round and octagonal shapes, or to tokens manufactured expressly for use in certain coin-operated machines.

Small date: A variety of coin on which the date is physically smaller than other varieties of the same year. Similar varieties include medium date and large date.

So-called dollar: A silver dollar-sized medal commemorating a special event. Cataloged in *So-Called Dollars* (see Chapter 20, books).

Souvenir Mint sets: An issue of the U.S. Mint, containing the coinage of one Mint. It is generally sold only at the Mint represented by the coins.

Special Mint sets (SMS): Coins produced under special conditions by the United States Mint at San Francisco during the years 1965, 1966 and 1967. Coins have no Mint marks.

Specie: In the form of coin, especially precious metal coin; paper money redeemable in coin. From Latin meaning "in kind"; see also **fiat money.**

Star notes: Mainly intended as replacements for notes that were damaged or produced with errors or mistakes at the Bureau of Engraving and Printing. On modern Federal Reserve notes, a solid star appears at the end of the serial number; on earlier notes, the star appears at the beginning of the number. Until the 1980s, star notes were also used to represent the 100 millionth note since the serial numbering machinery has only eight digits.

State coinages or notes: Refers to coins issued by one of four state governments (Connecticut, Massachusetts, New Jersey and Vermont) between the Declaration of Independence and the ratification of the U.S. Constitution when the states' rights to issue and 3-cent coins were also nicknamed "nickel," like the 5-cent coin.

Numismatics: The science, study or collecting of coins, tokens, medals, orders and decorations, paper money and similar objects.

Numismatist: A person knowledgeable in numismatics, with greater knowledge than a collector.

- O -

Obol: Greek denomination equal to one-sixth drachma.

Obsolete bank note: Note of an American bank of issue prior to 1865; a more accurate term than "broken" bank note, since many note-issuing banks converted into national banks or liquidated without failing.

Obverse: The side of a numismatic item which bears the principal design or device, often as prescribed by the issuing authority. In paper money, this is called the face.

Offset: Printing method in which a metallic plate places an ink impression on an elastic blanket and is then transferred to the paper. Also, a term sometimes used to describe a blanket impression paper money error.

OPA token: A cardboard fiber token issued in the United States by the Office of Price Administration in 1944 during World War II. They were used to make change for meat and processed food coupons (to keep track of ration points awarded each family during periods of rationing). They were issued in red and blue versions. Both sides of the OPA token depicts a numeral 1 flanked by two small initials.

Overdate: The date made by a Mint engraver superimposing one or more numbers over the date on a previously dated die.

- P -

Pattern: Coin-like pieces designed to test proposed coin designs, mottoes or denominations proposed for adoption as a regular issue, struck in the metal to be issued for circulation and which were not adopted, at least in year of pattern issue. Do not use as a generic term describing experimental pieces and trial pieces.

Pieces of eight: Popular term for silver Spanish 8-real pieces; often associated with pirate treasure.

Piefort: A piece struck on a planchet twice or more the normal thickness. The French spelling used in Europe is piedfort.

Pioneer gold: Gold coins, often privately produced, struck in areas of the United States to meet the needs of a coin shortage, generally in traditional U.S. denominations. The U.S. Assay Office coins of California — offi-

cial coinage str
of the San Fran
series. Also kno
torial gold.

Planchet: The
rial on which th
medal are impres
flan. In paper m
embedded in the
terfeiting device.

Plaster: See **mod**
Plasticene: Synt
PNC: Abbrevi
ismatic combinatic
tion of a coin, me
ismatic item inserte
postmarked on a sp
release of a new p
ismatic item (or nu
through a window in

Postage note: Th
note series.

Postal note: Foreru
ey order, issued by th

Prestige Proof set:
commemorating regu
commemorative coins
first in 1983 with 198
lar; also offered in 198
pic dollar) and 1986 (w
half dollar and 1986-S

Privy mark: Small d
often commemorative
Mint mark in placemer
of Mint of origin.

Proof: A coin struck
planchets on special pr
highest quality strike po
collectors. For paper mor
test the plate, analogous t
coinage.

Prooflike: An Uncircu
received special minting t
ror surface for the benefit
minor imperfections due t
cess permissible.

Proof set: A set of one
current denomination issue
Mint for a specific year. S
set."

- Q -

Quarter eagle: A gold $
United States.

- R -

Rare: A comparative term
degree of scarcity. Often mod
ly, e.g., very rare or extremel
fied by the use of figures, e.

There is n
ty.

"Red B
Book of
published
the nickr
dealers m

Reedec
cess whic
edge of a

Relief:
numisma
above t
called ba
glio.

Replic
A repro

Restr
from o
of a co
moneta
for a nu

Reve
which
pressed
On pap

Rim
ence o
edge.

Sca
mon a

Scr
natio
curre
Toke
are ca

Scr
lectin
certi
bond
a scr

Se
dica
Rese
part
seal

S
diff
and
lega
tha
exp
and

pe
me

no

coins were suspended. Among paper money, refers to notes issued between Declaration of Independence and Civil War by state governments. See "Colonials."

Stater: Greek coin equal to two drachms or didrachm, or 12 obols.

Stella: A gold $4 pattern never issued for circulation. Also struck in other metals.

Sterling silver: Silver that is .925 fine; in Israel, .935 fine silver. From the British standard "pound sterling."

Store card: A token bearing a business name and/or address, and often intended as a local or ad-hoc medium of exchange as well as an advertisement for the issuer.

- T -

Token: Usually a piece of durable material appropriately marked and unofficially issued for monetary, advertising, services or other purposes.

Trade dollar: A silver dollar coin produced for overseas markets. The United States issued a Trade dollar between 1873-85 for use in the Orient. Great Britain also issued a trade dollar. Also used incorrectly to refer to Canadian trade tokens of $1 nominal value.

Treasury note: Sometimes called a coin note. Issued under the Act of July 14, 1890. Redeemable in silver and gold coins.

Tree coinage: Silver coins issued by the Massachusetts Colony in three forms: Willow Tree, Oak Tree and Pine Tree. Issued between 1652-82 although all but one are dated 1652.

Trends: A market value guide based on averages derived from auction results, dealer advertisements, price lists and other sources. Represents a guide, not firm buying or selling prices.

Tribute penny: A silver denarius of the Roman emperor Tiberius.

Trime: Unofficial nickname given to the silver 3-cent coin. Formed by combining "tri" and the last two letters of "dime."

Type set: A collection composed of one of each coin of a given series or period.

- U -

Uncut sheet: Refers to the 32-note (or 32-subject) sheets of Federal Reserve notes being sold by the Bureau of Engraving and Printing. The 16-note and four-note sheets being sold are cut partial sheets, although they are often referred to as uncut sheets. Earlier sheets of U.S. paper money came with different numbers of notes.

Uncirculated set: Set of coins issued by the U.S. Mint, consisting of one of each coin issued for circulated. Also called Uncirculated

Mint set, or unofficially, a Mint set.

Uniface: Having a design on one side only.

Unique: Extant in only one known specimen. Very often misused, as in "semi-unique."

United States note: A specific type of note first authorized in 1862 and called legal tender notes; name officially changed to United States notes in July 1873. By law, $346,681,016 in United States notes must be kept in circulation. The term United States note is not a generic term for all forms of U.S. paper money.

U.S. Gold: Marketing name for American Arts Gold Medallions.

- V -

Vectures: Transportation tokens.

Vecturist: A collector of tokens pertaining to all types of transportation.

Vignette: A pictorial element of a bank note design that shades off gradually into the surrounding unprinted paper or background rather than having sharp outlines or a frame.

- W -

Want list: A list given by a collector to a dealer listing items the collector needs for a collection. The dealer keeps the want list and attempts to purchase items listed on it for the collector.

Watermark: Design formed by differing thickness of paper during production; often used as security device in paper money.

Whizzing: The severe polishing of a coin in an attempt to improve its appearance and salability to the uninformed. A form of alteration regarded as misleading by the numismatic community, and which actually lowers the value of the coin.

Widow's mite: An ancient Jewish lepton denomination coin of the time of Christ.

Wooden nickels: Originally, substitute for coins first used in the 1931-35 depression, having originated in Tenino, Wash. Issued in round or rectangular form and in many denominations. Currently used for advertising and souvenir purposes.

Wire rim: Slight flange on coins or medals caused by heavy striking pressure, often characteristic on Proof coins. The metal is squeezed up the side of the die faces by the collar die. Sometimes incorrectly called wire edge.

- Y -

Year set: A set of coins for any given year, generally containing one specimen of each coin from each Mint issued for circulation, and packaged privately, not by the government.

Index

Numbers in *italics* refer to Chapter 1, "Review of Numismatics 1984-1987"

Numbers in *italics* refer to Chapter 1, "Review of Numismatics 1984-1987"

Numbers in *italics* refer to Chapter 1, "Review of Numismatics 1984-1987"

Numbers in *italics* refer to Chapter 1, "Review of Numismatics 1984-1987"

Numbers in *italics* refer to Chapter 1, "Review of Numismatics 1984-1987"

Numbers in *italics* refer to Chapter 1, "Review of Numismatics 1984-1987"

—D—

Numbers in *italics* refer to Chapter 1, "Review of Numismatics 1984-1987"

Numbers in *italics* refer to Chapter 1, "Review of Numismatics 1984-1987"

Index

Numbers in *italics* refer to Chapter 1, "Review of Numismatics 1984-1987"

Franklin, Benjamin.......... 190, 211, 268

Franklin Mint...........*4, 9,* 182-183, 186, 371, 372, 402, 625, 643
(See also **General Numismatics Corp.**)

Fraser, James Earle........ 204, 295, 296, 298, 311, 602

Fraser, Laura G...................... 212

Fraudulent advertising................. *26*

Freedom of Information Act....... 105-109

French Antilles (See **France**)
(See also **Martinique; Guadeloupe; French Guiana**)

French colonies (See **France**)

French Equatorial Africa.............. 395

French Guiana........................ 417
Chronology...................... 374

French Oceania (See **French Polynesia**

French Polynesia.................... 417
Chronology...................... 401

French West Africa (See **West African States**)

Frere, Francis B. "Barry"............... *7*

Fulton, Robert...................... 268

Futures contract, regulated............. 59

—G—

Gabon............................. 416
Chronology...................... 395

Gainesville, Ga...................... 292

Gallatin, Albert.............. 187, 213, 268

Gambia........................ 417, 445
Chronology...................... 395

Ganz, David L. *9, 11, 17, 26*

Gardner, John Smith............. 310, 314

Garfield, James A. 188, 195, 207, 229, 268

Garrett family collection.............. 575

Garrett, John Work................ *3, 575*

Gasparro, Frank......*23,* 183-184, 196-197, 203, 212-214, 310, 312, 313, 316, 643

Gault, John..................... 254, 605

Gaver, Esther LaSure.................. *28*

General Agreement on Tariffs and Trade....................... 55, 498

General Numismatics Corp. 182

General Services Administration ... *7,* 35-37, 49, 62, 572

Germany.......... 385, 386, 388, 389, 390, 391, 394, 400, 444, 447
German Togo..................... 394
German New Guinea............... 400

Germany, East................... 417, 446
Chronology...................... 385

Germany, West.......... *3,* 222, 402, 417, 420, 444, 445, 446
Chronology...................... 385

Ghana..................... 394, 417, 445
Chronology...................... 395

Gibraltar.......................... 417
Chronology...................... 391

Gillilland, Cory............... *13, 21,* 622

Giori (See **DeLaRue Giori**)

Girl Scouts USA...................... *2*

Gjurovich, Rudolph.................... *9*

Glass-Steagall Act............... 234, 235

Gobrecht, Christian..... 178, 310, 311, 312, 313, 314, 315

Gold
General......*4,* 46, 47, 50, 52, 57, 447-467
Coins...................... 68, 70, 132
(See also individual denominations)
Bullion coins
American Eagle (See **Coins, U.S.**)
Britannia (See **United Kingdom**)
Krugerrand (See **South Africa**)
Maple Leaf (See **Coins, Canadian**)
Nugget (See **Australia**)
Prices..............*4, 11,* 109, 450-452, 456, 467, 502, 503

Gold Bullion Coin Act...... *23,* 56, 104, 111

Gold bullion coins (U.S.) (See **Coins, U.S.**)

Gold certificates (See **Paper Money, U.S.**)

Gold clauses........................ 47

Gold Coast (See **Ghana**)

Gold Institute........................ *28*

Gold ownership........... 78, 450, 453-456

Gold regulations (1934)............ 77, 450

Gold Reserve Act of 1934..... 53, 77-78, 450

Gold standard......... *15, 16,* 448-450, 470

Government Financial Operations, Bureau of..................... 68, 155

Government marketing of commemorative coins (See **Marketing of commemorative coins, government**)

Government Printing Office...... 37, 38-39

Numbers in *italics* refer to Chapter 1, "Review of Numismatics 1984-1987"

Numbers in *italics* refer to Chapter 1, "Review of Numismatics 1984-1987"

Numbers in *italics* refer to Chapter 1, "Review of Numismatics 1984-1987"

Numbers in *italics* refer to Chapter 1, "Review of Numismatics 1984-1987"

Numbers in *italics* refer to Chapter 1, "Review of Numismatics 1984-1987"

Numbers in *italics* refer to Chapter 1, "Review of Numismatics 1984-1987"

Numbers in *italics* refer to Chapter 1, "Review of Numismatics 1984-1987"

Numbers in *italics* refer to Chapter 1, "Review of Numismatics 1984-1987"

Numbers in *italics* refer to Chapter 1, "Review of Numismatics 1984-1987"

Numbers in *italics* refer to Chapter 1, "Review of Numismatics 1984-1987"

Numbers in *italics* refer to Chapter 1, "Review of Numismatics 1984-1987"

Index

Numbers in italics refer to Chapter 1, "Review of Numismatics 1984-1987"

South Africa (Continued)
Gold production 448, 451
Krugerrand . . 388, 395, 495, 496, 497, 499
Paper money 444
South America 372-375, 706
South Arabia (See Yemen)
South Dakota (See Bullion pieces, state)
Southeast Asia 396-398
Souvenir cards, BEP 223-227
Soviet Union *7*
Space shuttle "Challenger" *18*
Spain 52, 283, 284, 446, 706
Chronology 381-382
Colonial era coins 376, 381, 383,
395, 396, 402, 409
Coins 368, 378, 380, 393, 400, 445
Coins based on Spanish coins 375, 388
Paper money 443
Special drawing right certificates 223
Specific gravity 609-611
Spider press 228
Spink & Son *7*
Spinner, Francis Elias 274, 278, 279, 281
Sri Lanka (Ceylon) 397, 418, 445
Stack, Benjamin *8, 9*
Stack's Rare Coins . . *1, 2, 5, 6, 9, 16*, 575, 576
Stahl, Dr. Alan M. *8, 20, 21*
Stamps, postage & revenue 181
"Standard Catalog of World Coins" *6*
Stanton, Edwin McMasters 274
Star notes (See Paper Money, U.S.) 222
Stalin, Joseph 315
Stark, Rep. Fortney H. *4*
Starr, Floyd T. *5*
Statue of Liberty, rededication *24*
Statue of Liberty coins (See Coins, U.S.)
Statue of Liberty coins, France 380
Statue of Liberty/Ellis Island
Foundation *17, 18, 21, 23*
Steever, Edgar Z. 213, 298, 314
Steinbeck, John *7*
Stella (See Coins, U.S.)
Stephens, Alexander Hamilton 274
Stewart, Capt. Charles 189
Stickney, Matthew Adams 573
Stone, Harlan 229

Stone Mountain 295
Storage and preservation 605-608
Strategic & Critical Material Stockpile
(See Silver)
Stuart, Gilbert 310, 311, 312
Stuyvesant, Petrus 274
Sudan 393, 418, 445, 446
Sumner, Charles 274
Sumter, Gen. Thomas 274
Superior Galleries *6, 10, 16, 18, 24*,
203, 520, 577
Supreme Court, U.S. *4, 5*, 229
Suriname 374, 415, 418
Sutter's Mill 164
Swaziland 395, 418, 445
Sweden 388, 419, 445, 446, 706
Chronology 389-390
Switzerland *3, 9*, 222, 384, 444,
445, 446, 706
Helvetia 388, 713
Symbols 309-310
Syria 392, 393, 394, 415, 419

—T—

Taft, William Howard 188, 195, 209, 229
Tampa, Fla. *2, 17, 18*
Taney, Roger Brooke 229
Tatman, Charles T. 640
Taiwan 399, 415, 417, 445, 446
Tanzania 384, 385, 394, 395, 419, 445
Tax Equity and Fiscal Responsibility
Act 57
Taylor, Kenneth 190
Taylor, Zachary 188, 189, 195, 229, 274
Teletrade *17-18*
Ten-cent note (See Paper money, U.S.)
Ten-dollar note (See Paper money, U.S.)
Ten thousand-dollar note (See Paper
money, U.S.)
Texas bullion pieces (See Bullion
pieces, state)
Thailand 419, 446
Chronology 397
Coins 407, 415, 446
Thomas, Danny *11*, 190
Thomas, Gen. George Henry 274

Numbers in *italics* refer to Chapter 1, "Review of Numismatics 1984-1987"

Numbers in *italics* refer to Chapter 1, "Review of Numismatics 1984-1987"

United States Claims Court (See **Claims Court, U.S.**) 12

United States Code *14,* 87, 43-54, 68, 81-87, 74, 155

United States Coin Reserve *14*

United States Constitution *15*

United States Constitution Council of the Thirteen Original States Inc. *28*

Customs Service, U.S. (See **Custom Service, U.S.**)

United States Gold & Silver Investments Inc. 11

United States Government Bonds 248, 253, 257

United States Government Securities 223, 240

United States Mint
  "Annual Report of the Director of the Mint" *5, 15,* 37, 160, 696
  Facilities, current 160
    Customer Service Center 160
  Denver Mint
    History 161-164
    Officers/Officials 49, 63, 64, 159, 160, 165, 172, 176
    Operations *10, 17, 24,* 162, 303
  Fort Knox Gold Bullion Depository 166-167, 450
  Philadelphia Mint
    History 53, 160-161
    Officers/Officials 49, 64, 160, 174
    Operations 7, 65, 164, 165, 168, 172, 292, 304
  San Francisco Assay Office
    History 164-166, 304
    Officers/Officials 49, 63, 175
    Operations *4, 5, 20, 24, 25,* 159, 165, 170, 172
  San Francisco Old Mint 166
  West Point Bullion Depository
    History 168
    Officers/Officials 64, 160
    Operations *15, 18, 23, 27,* 159, 168, 304
  New Orleans 171-173, 174-175, 304
  Former Assay Offices
    Boise 173
    Deadwood 173
    Helena 173
    New York 49, 63, 173, 189
    St. Louis 173
    Salt Lake City 173
    Seattle 173

United States Mint (Continued)
  Former Mints
    Charlotte . . . 168-169, 176, 170, 171, 303
    Dahlonega 169-170, 177, 303
    Carson City 35, 109, 110, 170-171, 176, 303, 572
  History *5,* 154, 159
  Offices/Officials *2, 3, 3, 7, 10, 20, 26,* 43, 49, 50, 65, 159, 163, 173-174, 160-177, 157, 160, 215
  Operations *2, 3, 4, 5, 8, 11, 15,* 37, 159, 160, 187, 197-199
  Products for sale . . *6, 7, 10, 11, 16,* 186-190
  Regulations 43, 61-67

United States notes (See **Paper money, U.S.**)

"United States of America" as a legend . . . 45

United States Postal Service *2, 12, 26*

United States Savings Bonds (See **Savings bonds**)

United States Secret Service 68, 70, 77, 154, 190

United States Supreme Court *4*

Upper Volta (See **Burkino Faso**)

"U.S. Gold" (See also **American Arts Gold Medallions; J. Aron & Co.**) *11*

Urrutia, Napoleon Gomez *15*

Uruguay 375, 419, 445, 706

—V—

Vanuatu 401, 419

Van Buren, Martin 188, 194, 229, 275

Vance, Zebulon 275

Vatican *4,* 419, 445

Vectures *11,* 602

Venezuela *5,* 375, 415, 419

Verani, Patricia Lewis 298

Vermont coinage 283

Veroi, Guido *2*

Verret Enterprises Inc. *14*

Videotape recordings *15*

Vietnam 398, 399, 419

Vietnam veterans medal *20,* 190

Vinson, Fred 229

Virgin Islands, U.S. 376, 710

Voight (Voigt), Henry 177, 310, 314

Voyageur (See **Coins, Canada**)

Numbers in *italics* refer to Chapter 1, "Review of Numismatics 1984-1987"